The Mississippi Flows Into The Tiber

The Mississippi Flows Into The Tiber

A Guide to Notable American Converts to the Catholic Church

John Beaumont

Fidelity Press
South Bend, Indiana
2014

The Mississippi Flows Into The Tiber:
A Guide to Notable American Converts to the Catholic Church

Cover by Michael Murphy Design, Inc.

ISBN: 978-0-929891-13-2
Printed in the United States of America

Fidelity Press and the author
wish to acknowledge
the generous aid from
the Stella Maris Fund
towards the publication of
The Mississippi Flows Into the Tiber.

The Convert

After one moment when I bowed my head
And the whole world turned over and came upright,
And I came out where the old road shone white.
I walked the ways and heard what all men said,
Forests of tongues, like autumn leaves unshed,
Being not unlovable but strange and light;
Old riddles and new creeds, not in despite
But softly, as men smile about the dead

The sages have a hundred maps to give
That trace their crawling cosmos like a tree,
They rattle reason out through many a sieve
That stores the sand and lets the gold go free:
And all these things are less than dust to me
Because my name is Lazarus and I live.

G. K. Chesterton

Contents

The Mississippi Flows Into The Tiber

Foreword

At least forty years ago while making a silent retreat in New England I came across a dilapidated book that certainly dated to the beginning of the last century if not a decade or two earlier. It was a book that had some similarities to the one you are about to read. It simply listed well known American converts to Catholicism together with a small amount of data on their lives. I thought many times about that book and even searched for it in later visits to the same retreat house, but I could not find it. I presume it went into the fireplace (or the trash can), or was "borrowed" by a retreatant and never returned.

I never forgot it and often said to myself that something should be done to publish an up to date version with much more detail, which would include not only names and dates of the convert, but also provide, if possible, a little "apologia" for the conversions written by the convert himself. Even an account by some knowledgeable third party might be useful. And so we would have something of the person's story. This would be of great value to anyone considering making the move to Rome.

Of course, the converts would be men and women who in one way or another would be for the most part persons of a certain renown. This of course does not mean they are greater in God's eyes, but that their stories might be more influential in moving others to examine the case for the Catholic Faith in a country that is rapidly becoming dechristianized. We live in a much more secularized society than was the case when the book to which I referred above was written. Today Christianity is no longer the default position and great is the hostility towards it in the media, the political forum, and many other influential sectors of society. In addition, the poison of relativism has come to the fore, as was stressed so often by Pope Benedict XVI. Even within the Christian camp itself, there has been the corroding influence of liberalism and subjectivism. There has also been, in part a consequence of this, a rapid decline in numbers of Protestant denominations, leaving behind only Evangelical free standing congregations. These latter bodies worship with enthusiasm, but they are without valid Sacraments and with no authority other than the Bible itself, on the interpretation of which even their governing bodies cannot agree.

And what of the Catholic Church in all of this? Well, her holiness stems not from her individual members (we are all sinners). She is the source of holiness because her head is Christ and she dispenses the means of holiness through the Sacraments which he instituted. Our Lord promised to be with her always and guide her into all truth. And then there is the rock, Peter and the successors of Peter. All of this still offers great opportunities for the conversion of many Evangelicals and fallen away Protestants to the Church that Christ founded and left to be guided by the power of the Holy Spirit and governed by the Vicar of Christ and his Bishops who descend directly from the Apostles.

I mentioned earlier a dream that I had. The dream was related to the need to evangelize and promote the Catholic truth. Well, my dream has now come true. John Beaumont who writes from the other side of the Pond in England has put together an encyclopedic work on American converts, their biography, and in many cases their reason for conversion, that goes from A to Z.

The means to achieve the New Evangelization launched by Blessed John Paul II are contained in the book. Some are based on historical points (remember what that great convert, Blessed John Henry Newman, said: "To be deep in history is to cease to be a Protestant"). But, the book also deals with several philosophical issues, which underpin all true conversions. It thereby offers the means to forestall the onslaught of the "New Atheism" and to answer the unbridled, and yet naïve, philosophy of materialism. It sets out, mainly in the words of those who have been through the fire of argument and debate, and have discovered the way to Christ.

As St. Peter himself put it, "Master to whom shall we go? You have the words of eternal life. We believe and are convinced that you are the holy One of God."

There are currently many books by or about converts and even more in the way of collections of their stories, but only here will you find the essential data you are looking for in one book. Also, the beauty of this book is that with time it can be updated as more notable men and women convert and other converts who were not known about at the time will in due time be inserted in the book, together with their short general biography and, perhaps what is the crucial matter, an account of their conversion story.

Remember this book is about worthy of notice American converts alone. The author has written a related volume, *Roads to Rome* (2010) on converts from Britain and Ireland. This is still available, and will be followed by an extended edition. However, within the ambit of the present book, which covers both the United States and Canada, there is much variety in the different stories and these give much food for thought and provide the reader with ammunition for the fight for Catholic truth.

As you may know I am a priest and how delighted I was to see several persons listed with whom I played a small part in their conversion. But all Catholics are called to bring converts to our Holy Church. In this context the users of this book will find useful my afterword, which gives practical advice in fostering and promoting conversions. So, you too may be fishers of men as the great new project launched by Blessed John Paul II of the New Evangelization has continued into this new millennium down through the centuries ahead.

Then let us pray, "All may be one."

Fr. C. John McCloskey III

Feast of All Saints
1st November 2013

Preface

"For you were as sheep going astray; but you are now converted to the Shepherd and Bishop of your souls" (St. Peter)

Like its predecessor, *Roads to Rome*, this book would not have been written but for the encouragement of the late Fr. Stanley Jaki, OSB (1924-2009). It was he who encouraged me to write on the topic of converts to the Catholic Church. His main reason for doing so was his belief that the Church was neglecting this issue and this was at a serious cost.

Fr. Jaki's initial idea was for a simple register of the names of people who had "gone over to Rome," rather on the lines of that compiled in Great Britain by W. Gordon Gorman under the title *Converts to Rome* and in the United States by D. J. Scannell-O'Neill in his book *Distinguished Converts to Rome in America.*

Books on converts have taken various forms. They range from simple lists, as in the two cases above, through detailed autobiographical works by individuals, collections of several convert stories put together, to sophisticated analyses of the mental process of conversion. I began by compiling four short booklets. Three of these concentrated on Great Britain and Ireland in the 20th century, 19th century, and 18th and earlier centuries respectively, with very short accounts of individual notable converts. I then put together a similar booklet on notable converts from Judaism. The preparation of these was accompanied by a request to readers to suggest further names.

The feedback that resulted, and the further research that followed on, certainly contributed greatly to the enlargement of the list of candidates for inclusion, plus the information available about them. It also led to an appreciation on my part of the potential value of accounts of converts from the perspective of apologetics and the defense of the Catholic faith. Converts had in many cases gone to great trouble in arriving at their decisions to become Catholic and powerful arguments, not always in a form accessible to readers today (many of the accounts were out of print), were often presented. Certainly, to return for a moment to the views put to me by Fr,. Jaki, the subject of apologetics was one that was neglected for a quite lengthy period of time after the Second Vatican Council. This was perhaps due, at least in part, to the fact that subjectivist and relativist accounts of the faith were in vogue at that time. Things have changed and in recent years, perhaps due in part to attacks on religion in general, and

Christianity in particular, leveled by the "New Atheists", attempts have been made to put forward apologias that are much better grounded, both philosophically and historically. Certainly, Benedict XVI's papacy was marked by his endeavors to scotch the joint hydra of subjectivism and relativism. For whatever reason there has certainly been a return recently to more objective and well referenced arguments as to why an individual should become a Christian and, in particular, a Catholic.

On the basis of this the present writer put together a much more detailed and extensive account of notable converts from Britain and Ireland from the Reformation to the present day in the aforesaid *Roads to Rome*, published in 2010. The present book is an attempt to do an equivalent text for North American converts, meaning the United States and Canada.

So what are the criteria for inclusion in this book, bearing in mind the above statement and also the fact that the book is meant to be a definitive reference text? Well, this all depends, it is submitted, on what is understood by the term "notable" in this context. To begin with, it is obvious that certain individuals would have to be included, irrespective of whether or not they have contributed to a defense of the Catholic faith by writing about their reasons for their conversion. These are those who are clearly notable in every sense. No book on American converts to the Catholic Church could be written without the inclusion, for example, of Saint Elizabeth Seton or Orestes Brownson. Of course, very famous converts have in any case frequently written about their reasons for converting, although some have not done so in detail.

Most converts are not famous, though they may be quite well known, usually because of their role on the public stage as politicians, writers, artists, and such. These also have a reasonable claim for inclusion, whether or not they have gone into print about what brought them into the Church. Again, however, in many cases stimulating accounts of their Romeward path are available, if only in obscure sources very often. These should be brought into the light and this book is hopefully a vehicle for that.

In addition, there are certain other categories. If apologetics, or the defense of the faith, is an important factor, and it is submitted that it is, then whether one is well known or not would seem to be irrelevant. What is important is the quality of the arguments for converting that are being put forward. This has resulted in my having to make a judgment in each case and this has been done, though with some trepidation and in several cases only after consulting respected colleagues. Many are the reasons put forward for a person becoming a Catholic and different things appeal to different persons. The Catholic faith has a wealth of riches and therefore motivating factors can come in many different forms. As that great convert

G. K. Chesterton stated, “The Church is a house with a hundred gates; and no two men enter at exactly the same angle.” In addition, although the Catholic faith consists of a definitive set of doctrines, and truth does not change, different factors appeal at different times. If the Church is to go forward, these factors need to be tapped into. They may come from many directions, but basically they stem from philosophy (reasoned argument) or historical factors. It is submitted by the present writer that arguments from reason, say for the existence of God, put forward by many philosophers are very compelling. Take for instance the words of Fr. Benedict Ashley, OP:

> The universe in continual process of motion and other changes cannot exist and continue in change unless there is an unchanging First Cause, that is intelligent, free, and thus personal, God, otherwise science and all rational thought would be impossible.

Another modern thinker, Professor Charles Rice, puts the essential point vigorously and with more than a touch of humor:

> The fact is, it is unreasonable – even stupid – not to believe in God, the eternal Being who always existed and had no beginning. To deny this we must say instead that there was a time when there was absolutely nothing. And we therefore must say that something can come from nothing. Actress Julie Andrews, in the motion picture, *The Sound of Music*, had it right: “Nothing comes from nothing. Nothing ever could.” If there was ever a time when there was nothing, there could never be anything. If we think hard about this, it will blow our minds. And change our lives.

But some come to the faith after an examination of the historical evidence. This also provides us with strong grounds for belief. The person who claims that the Gospels are a set of lies and that Christ did not perform his miracles, including the Resurrection, should surely acknowledge that if this is the case then Christianity is the most brilliant hoax ever. The Catholic writer Dennis Sewell, in discussing some words of Supreme Court Justice Antonin Scalia, explains this line of thought:

> To deny Christ’s Resurrection implies that "everything from the Easter morning to the Ascension had to be made up by the groveling enthusiasts as part of their plan to get themselves martyred." No meeting along the road to Emmaus, no Doubting Thomas, no fishing trip to Tiberias. If Christ’s followers were indeed fabricators of evidence, why would they make up these stories, in all their puzzling complexity and, let’s face it, intimacy of scale?

In other words, it is much easier to accept that Christ rose from the dead than that a complicated and unlikely conspiracy was put together by his disciples.

Then there is the incomparable impact on history of Christ himself and his unparalleled character and personality that surely leads on to something more. Fr. Jaki takes this phenomenon and sets it in a particular historical example:

> No greater impact has been made on countless humans through an impact originally made on so few. The measure of that impact found an incomparable expression in a remark which Talleyrand, a priest turned diplomat, addressed to Larevalliere-Lepeaux, a member of the Directorate, who thought up a religion, called "Theophilanthropia." On finding that he gained no adherents to it, he complained to Talleyrand, who then gave him the best conceivable advice: "If you want to make converts perform miracles. Cure the sick, revive the dead, allow yourself to be crucified and rise on the third day."

When it comes to the Church itself, history is very clear on another point. This is that the Catholic Church is the only Church existing today which goes back to the time of Christ. How strange it is that so many miss the obviousness of this point. And then there is the simple fact of the endurance of the Church, and in circumstances that make this very fact utterly astonishing. The French-American writer Julien Green drew inspiration from such reasoning and brings this out so clearly:

> It is not the saints that one has to talk about if one is to prove the sanctity of the Church. It's bad priests and popes. A Church governed by saints continues on, that's normal and human. But a Church that can be governed by villains and imbeciles, and still continue, that is neither normal nor human.

This may seem a negative way to establish a positive conclusion. If this is so, we must remember to take account also of the positive witness of the galaxy of great saints nurtured under the aegis of the Church. This factor operating a particular historical period made a firm impression on one of the greatest of all converts, Blessed John Henry Newman:

> The outburst of Saints in 1500-1600 after the monstrous corruption seems to me one of the great arguments for Christianity. It is the third marvellous phenomenon in its history; the conversion of the Roman Empire, the reaction under Hildebrand, the resurrection under Ignatius Loyola, Teresa of Avila, Vincent de Sales and a host of others. Think of the contrast between Alexander VI and Pius V, think of the Cardinals of the beginning, and then those of the end of the 16th century.

However, it must be remembered that not all of us are led to change our fundamental philosophy of life because of strictly logical reasoning or the strength of historical witness. In any case, it is God's ineffable grace that is crucial in all cases and this is extended to all who come to him with a genuine heart and in good faith. Conversion is also not always about Catholic dogma and doctrines. Many converts emphasize more the attractions of Catholic practices, art, and culture, and also the feature of beauty. In addition, as human beings we are all moved by humble and courageous actions performed in conditions of adversity. We see in such cases examples worthy to be followed. The case of the British scientist Frank Sherwood Taylor is in point here:

> I was fortunate enough to fall in quite separately with two Catholics of personal qualities which throw some light on what Christianity in action could be – and this, in my belief, is an essential in almost every conversion. If a man or woman goes about the world being charitable, humble yet inflexible in the faith, and radiating sanctity to those who have eyes to see it, the people who meet them will find their difficulties disappearing and will tumble one after another into the laver of regeneration. I suspect that one Living Christian is worth a shop full of hortatory treatises or an army of eloquent preachers.

All of these later things are, it is submitted, also relevant to the process of choice of who to include in a book of this kind. Several persons given space in this book come to be there because of actions that move the heart.

The choice of who to include, even with the above criteria having been adopted, is not always easy. There are several marginal cases and decisions have been made after much thought and discussion. A line has to be drawn at some point and this can give rise to difficult decisions. On a lighter note, however, it may be said that the choice of persons now deceased is much easier than that of those still with us. After all, the dead are unable to complain (at least in my present hearing) at being excluded! Decisions about the living may be more difficult, since the important factor of the passage of time in making judgments on such matters may not apply in their case. The living may also be much more voluble potentially in stating their opinions. What I would say is that I have tried to be objective in my choices and have taken advice from many who may well have more knowledge on this question than myself, a mere Englishman not as familiar as he should be in relation to the American scene.

Although the arguments for the Catholic faith don't change fundamentally, it is the case that in different eras certain issues are seen as more significant and important and others less so. This explains why a book of this kind, aiming at arguments for the defense of the faith at the present time, will sometimes involve relatively lengthy quotations from the writings of persons alive and working today, whose arguments may sometimes have a persuasive effect greater than those of an earlier era. This is not to say that previous generations cannot provide forceful accounts for conversion, examples of such being available on almost every page. Another relevant factor is that historically the contribution of some persons has been somewhat neglected, notable examples being those of Justine Bayard Ward, David Goldstein, Edward Lee Greene, James Kent Stone ("Fr. Fidelis") and Horatio Robinson Storer. I have tried to redress the balance here.

Some of the persons dealt with in this book have associations with more than one country. I have tended to adopt an intuitive approach to whether they should be classified as "American". One important factor I see to be their final nationality. Where a person has, say, been born in Europe, but spent the greater part of their lives in America, I have included them, even where they have not formally become United States (or, of course, Canadian) citizens. Naturalization is taken as evidence of how they wanted to be seen, unless there is evidence to the contrary. Even with these principles there are still marginal cases, but this is inevitable.

I should add at once that the list of entries is in no way seen as complete and irreformable. It is hoped that this volume will at some stage give way to a second edition. The process of conversion to the Church will go on and this will mean more potential entrants. In addition, it would be a foolhardy person who would claim to have noted all the potential notable entrants from the past. I would ask, then, for the assistance of readers who may well know of candidates, both living and dead, who should be included and I am supplying an e-mail address for this purpose. This is john.beaumont7@virgin.net. In this context, it is worth noting that a second edition of the earlier book will appear shortly in a much more extensive version, thanks in an important sense to responses from readers.

I would venture to make a few "technical" points. Each entry refers first of all to the main activity of the person in question. It then gives a date and place of birth, conversion and death, where these are known. This is followed by a factual biographical account of the person, including, of course, some consideration of the circumstances of and reasons for their conversion where these are known. It should be said that where the person is very well known, the biographical facts do not go into great detail. In fact, more detail is often given in cases where the subject is less well known, as the reader is likely to be less familiar with him or her and therefore in need of such. In each entry reference is then given to any writing by them and about them. The order of this last section is that I deal firstly with writing which is either exclusively written by the entrant, or where they have contributed in a major way (say, in the case of an interview). These references are done in chronological order. The references to writings about them by third parties are also done in date order, except that general works, e.g., encyclopedias, standard reference books, and accounts of multiple converts, are given at the end of the entry, as are unpublished materials. Sometimes the reading list has to be selective, because of the extent of such references. In such cases preference is given to those writings that are most closely linked with the aims of this book as set out above.

There are many quotations, some pretty extensive. In many ways these are the most important parts of the book. They give, where available, accounts of the direct reasons for conversion. In addition, where a person writes powerfully about what might be termed indirect apologetics, e.g., a compelling account of a particular Catholic doctrine or a very effective rebuttal of an attack on the Catholic position, I try to include this. The reason is, as with the other quotations, that it makes the reader more able to defend his or her faith in Christ and the Church.

Not all of the entries relate necessarily to what might be termed "good" people. Some may have fallen away from the faith after espousing it. Some may have had difficulties in certain areas. For instance, not a few of them went through several "marital" relationships, whether or not these were recognized by the Church. One entrant (Dutch Schultz) is referred to as a mobster and certainly he murdered a number of people. Some may criticize the choice of such a person, which ironically is just what Catholics did in the case in question, where the person converted on his deathbed after a wicked life, was baptized, died shortly afterwards, was buried in a Catholic cemetery, and thereby perhaps (we don't know, of course, whether the actions were genuine) did what is sometimes referred to as "stealing heaven". However, there as elsewhere, the Church had good grounds for the actions of the priest in question. These were set out by another priest, and it is valuable for us to read this account and know how to approach such issues.

I have defined "convert" to include "revert", a term often used to refer to those originally raised Catholic, who then, for whatever reason, fell away from the faith, but later returned into full communion with the Church. They have therefore made a similar step to those traditionally thought of as converts and their grounds for doing so are equally worthy of consideration.

An expression of gratitude is merited to all those who have committed their convert stories to print over the years. A special expression of thanks must go, in the context of America, to the redoubtable Georgina Pell Curtis (1859-1922) for her sterling efforts to bring to public attention a large number of converts in her two books, *Some Roads to Rome in America* (1909) and *Beyond the Road to Rome* (1914). These are both sadly now long out of print, but the present work, which has included several of the entries therein, will help to bring some of their contents back into the public domain.

I am particularly grateful to Fr. McCloskey for agreeing to write the foreword to this book, but also for his very valuable afterword. This, it is submitted, fits perfectly into the overall scheme of the book in that it gives valuable advice on how the reader may use the arguments for the faith contained in the text in the vital apostolate of evangelization.

Finally, it is to be hoped that readers will not consider this book to be elitist in the sense that it only contains "notable" converts. The present writer is all too well aware that there is no difference in merit between converts. All depend upon the grace of God for the privilege they have been granted. It is hoped that no apology is needed and that there is nothing more to be said on this matter.

Every endeavor has been made to make the text and references as up to date as possible. Any errors and omissions are entirely due to my own negligence.

I hope the reader will gain as much pleasure in reading this book as the present writer has done in putting together the materials.

John Beaumont
Apperley Bridge
West Yorkshire
England

Feast of All Souls
2nd November 2013

Preface

Acknowledgements

It is a pleasure to take this opportunity to thank those who have assisted me in the preparation of this book. They are many and it is impossible to single out everybody individually, but I would like to give an especial thanks to the following. Michael Dolan is the librarian of the excellent Talbot Library in Preston, England and his kindness and efficiency in answering all the many queries I have put to him is most appreciated. I am also indebted to his staff, most notably John Shaw and Margaret Pannikar. Fiona Mercey has been unstinting in the help she has given me in suggesting tracking down candidates for entry in the book, and I am in awe of her ability to draw out the most obscure matters from the internet (so much so that I have nominated her as a veritable Autolycus, or rather Autolyca (see Shakespeare's *The Winter's Tale* for this "snapper up of unconsidered trifles")). This is so even though her abilities are such as to bring to light important issues. My good friend John Walsh has contributed in a major way and I have valued our discussions about many aspects of the book. My friends Jerry Bruen and Bill Dowling have been very quick to make enquiries on my behalf and report back their findings. David Wemhoff has kindly shared something of his own research in related matters. William Higgins has kindly helped with names I might otherwise have missed, especially relating to convert bishops. Dale Ahlquist has also encouraged and assisted me. I must also mention one person who has helped in many ways, but who has asked to remain anonymous. My debt there is a great one.

Another friend, Anthony Cornwell, is primarily an expert on the Catholic history of my own country, Britain, but his commitment to rigorous standards in scholarship has always been an example to me and he has helped me once again. In addition, I have benefited greatly from the resources of the libraries of the University of Leeds, the Lancashire County Library Service, and that of West Yorkshire. I am grateful for the help given by the staff of these organizations.

Abbreviations

References in the text of this book to "*ANB*" are to the *American National Biography Online* (an earlier print version of this was published in 1999 with a supplement published in 2002).

References to "*DCB*" are to the *Dictionary of Canadian Biography Online* (a print version of this is available).

References "*DNB*" are to the *Oxford Dictionary of National Biography*, online edition (the latest version of an earlier print version was published in 2004).

References to "Catholic Encyclopedia" are to what is referred to today as the *Old Catholic Encyclopedia* or *Original Catholic Encyclopedia* published between 1907 and 1914.

In relation to individual entries, "b" refers to date of birth, "c" to date of conversion in the sense of reception into the Church, and "d" to date of death.

The Mississippi Flows Into The Tiber

The Mississippi Flows Into The Tiber

Abrams, Creighton Williams Jr. ("Abe") – general; b. 15 September 1914, Springfield, Massachusetts; d. 4 September 1974, Washington, D.C.; father a rail mechanic and farmer; brought up a Methodist; graduated from the United States Military Academy at West Point in 1936; armor officer in World War II; one of the great combat officers of the war; twice decorated with the Distinguished Service Cross; served on the Army General Staff 1945-1946; various Cold War assignments in Europe; served in Korea 1953-1954; transferred to the Pentagon as deputy Chief of Staff for Operations 1962–1963; promoted to General in 1964 and appointed Vice Chief of Staff of the Army; commanded military operations in the Vietnam War 1968-1972; presided over the withdrawal from Vietnam; converted to the Catholic faith during the Vietnam War; Chief of Staff of the United States Army 1972-1974; was the first Army Chief of Staff to die in office; three times on the cover of *Time Magazine*; his wife, Julia Bertha (1915-2003) dedicated to humanitarian causes; his three sons became Army general officers; his three daughters all married Army officers; buried in Arlington National Cemetery; see Will Lang Jr., *Colonel Abe* (1945); Lewis Sorley, *Thunderbolt: General Creighton Abrams and the Army of His Time* (1992); Lewis Sorley, *A Better War: The Unexamined Victories and Final Tragedy of America's Last Years in Vietnam* (1999); *arlingtoncemetery.net* ("He was noted for his concern for soldiers, his emphasis on combat readiness, and his insistence on personal integrity"); *ANB.*

Adams, Don (born Donald James Yarmy) - actor, comedian and director; b. 13 April 1923, Manhattan, New York City; c. 1960 (revert); d. 25 September 2005, Los Angeles, California; his brother was Dick Yarmy (1932-1992), an actor; he was raised in the religion of his mother, Consuelo, a Catholic, who had him baptized as an infant, while his brother was raised in the Judaism of his father; by the age of sixteen he had no particular religious beliefs (he did believe in God in a vague, indefinable way and he subscribed to the Ten Commandments and the Golden Rule, but he neither understood nor embraced the dogma of a particular faith); he enlisted in the United States Marine Corps in 1941; he was the only survivor of his platoon at the Battle of Guadalcanal, since he was invalided out to New Zealand after contracting blackwater fever; after discharge from the marines he had various jobs before working as a stage and night club comic; his best known role was as Maxwell Stuart (agent 86) in the television situation comedy *Get Smart* (1965-1975) (he won three consecutive Emmy awards for this); he provided the voices for several successful animated television series and follow up films; he found it difficult to avoid typecasting; host of *Don Adams' Screen Test* (1975-1976), a syndicated game show; married Adelaide Efantis Adams, a divorced night club singer, in 1947 when both were outside the Church, but divorced 1958 (four daughters of the marriage); in 1960 married Dorothy Bracken Adams in the Catholic Church (two children of the marriage), but divorced in 1976; married Judy Luciano in 1977 (one daughter of the marriage), but divorced in 1990; buried in the Hollywood Forever Cemetery, Hollywood; see Polly Terry, "God Knows Why I Am a Catholic and a Jew..." *TV Radio Mirror*, May 1966 ("'I doubted, I questioned, I challenged,' Don says. 'I felt that Catholicism was the religion that offered what I sought, but I couldn't accept it blindly. After a year and a half of instruction, I was climbing the walls.' A Jesuit priest was his mentor. 'I wanted clear-cut answers to questions. The answer, 'Because it's God's will,' was never enough for me. If you grow up with a complete, unquestioning faith - as my wife did - it's easy. But when you wait until you are nearly twenty years old and then approach religion intellectually, it's very difficult. Very, very difficult.

'I remember that the priest finally said to me, "You wouldn't like to have a religion that makes things easy for you." Now I know that both faith and intellect are components of religious belief'"); *ANB*.

Adams, Elizabeth Laura – author; b. 9 February 1909, Santa Barbara, California; c. 1929; d. 1982; from an African American family; mother a devout Methodist; father a freemason; as a child detested church attendance – except for the music; was taken by Catholic friends on Good Friday to the historic Santa Barbara Mission and was converted by the experience; her father refused to allow her to become a Catholic; studied music and dramatic art in California; suffered much racial prejudice;

influenced in her conversion by the life of Rose Hawthorne Lathrop (see below), the work of Father Damien De Veuster, and accounts of the miracles at Lourdes; she prepared to join a convent, but had to look after her mother; started writing poetry and then wrote a very successful spiritual autobiography, *Dark Symphony*; several poems and articles for the journals *Torch* and *Westward*; member of the Third Order of St. Francis; see *Dark Symphony* (1942); "Finding Christ," in John A. O'Brien (ed), *The Road to Damascus, Vol. II* (1950) ("Then came the Good Friday when friends drove us in their car to religious service at the historic Santa Barbara Mission. We entered the Mission, and I, an eleven-year-old colored girl, looked about with wonder like that of Alice in Wonderland. Members of the congregation were prayerfully kneeling. I noticed that those nearest me were not distracted by my impolite staring. Some were reading small books with black covers; others fingered strings of beads. I did not know, at that time, that the small books were prayer books and the beads rosaries. I beheld the altars. I listened to the voices of the priests. I heard the words 'Ave Maria' – not knowing the meaning was Hail Mary. This was a new world. While sitting there I thought to myself: 'If this is church – why have I disliked it so much?'

And so conversion came to me quickly and quietly. I experienced no emotional reaction other than the desire to attend service at the Santa Barbara Mission forever").

Adler, Mortimer Jerome – philosopher and educator; b. 28 December 1902, New York City; c. December 1999; d. 28 June 2001, San Mateo, California; son of non-observant Jewish parents; father immigrant jewellery salesman born in Bavaria and brought up in an Orthodox Jewish home; in pre-adolescence taken by mother and maternal grandmother to a Reform synagogue, but no effect on him; dropped out of school at fifteen and worked as secretary and copy boy at the *New York Sun*; inspired by the autobiography of John Stuart Mill, which introduced him to Plato, and he studied philosophy at Columbia University (first in his class, but the university refused to grant him a degree because he could not pass a required swimming test!); in college years ceased to have anything to do with the Jewish religion and became a pagan; taught a great classics program at Columbia from 1920s; promoted study of the great books of Western civilization and the idea that philosophy should be integrated with science, literature, and religion; later Professor Emeritus 1930-1952 at the University of Chicago (started The Great Books Foundation and the Basic Program of Liberal Education for Adults (both with Robert Maynard Hutchins (1899-1977), the President of the University));

advocate of the Socratic method in teaching; founded the Institute for Philosophical Research, and Aspen Institute; co-founder, with Max Weismann, of The Center for the Study of The Great Ideas (developed *The Great Ideas* seminars and lectures); on the board of the Ford Foundation and chairman of the board of editors of the *Encyclopedia Britannica*, changing its format in the fifteenth edition; started the Paideia Project (a plan for major reform of public school education); spent his life in promoting liberal education and making philosophy's greatest texts accessible to everyone; influenced by Aquinas and became a Thomist philosopher, but did not become a Christian until late in life ("Simply being able to understand Thomist theology was what Aquinas calls dead faith. It was not enough to carry one into a Christian religious life"); first an Episcopalian (baptized 21 April 1984), before converting to the Catholic Church; moved from being intellectually convinced of the existence of God to loving the God that he knew; huge number of publications; married to Helen Leavenworth Boyton in 1927 (two sons of the marriage); divorced in 1961; married Caroline Sage Pring, an Episcopalian, in 1963 (two sons); see (selective list) *How to Read a Book: The Art of Getting a Liberal Education* (1940); *The Difference of Man and the Difference it Makes* (1967); *Philosopher at Large: An Intellectual Autobiography* (1977) (memoirs); *How to Think About God: A Guide for the 20th-Century Pagan* (1980) ("I am now prepared to state the propositions that constitute a cosmological argument for God's existence. Only four propositions are needed as premises. They are as follows: 1. The existence of an effect requiring the concurrent existence and action of an efficient cause implies the existence and action of that cause. The causal principle, thus stated, is self-evidently true... 2. The cosmos as a whole exists. Here we have the existential assertion that is indispensable as a premise in any existential inference. While it does not have the same certitude possessed by my assertion of my own existence, or your assertion of yours, it can certainly be affirmed beyond a reasonable doubt. 3. The existence of the cosmos as a whole is radically contingent, which is to say that, while not needing an efficient cause of its coming to be, since it is everlasting, it nevertheless does need an efficient cause of its continuing existence, to preserve it in being and prevent it from being replaced by nothingness… 4. *If* the cosmos needs an efficient cause of its continuing existence to prevent its annihilation, *then* that cause must be a supernatural being, supernatural in its action, and one the existence of which is uncaused, in other words, the supreme being, or God. We have understood that no natural cause can be an exnihilating cause, and that no natural cause is uncaused in its existence or action. In the light of this understanding we are in a position to *affirm* the truth of this hypothetical proposition – this *if-then* premise. Since *natural* and supernatural represent an exhaustive set of alternatives, the cause being sought must be supernatural if it cannot be natural

Two of the four premises – the first and last – appear to be true with certitude. The second is true beyond a reasonable doubt. If the one remaining premise – the third – is also true beyond a reasonable doubt, we can conclude, beyond a reasonable doubt, that God exists and acts to sustain the cosmos in existence); *The Angels and Us* (1982); *Ten Philosophical Mistakes* (1985); *Intellect: Mind Over Matter* (1990); *Truth in Religion: The Plurality of Religions and the Unity of Truth* (1990); (ed), *Great Books of the Western World*, 2nd Edition (60 vols.) (1990); (ed), *A Syntopicon: An Index to The Great Ideas*, 2nd Edition (2 vols.) (1990); *A Second Look in the Rearview Mirror: Further Autobiographical Reflections of a Philosopher At Large* (1992) (memoirs) ("In March of 1984, after a trip to Mexico in February, I fell ill...During this long stay in hospital, I suffered a mild depression, and often...I would, unaccountably, fall into tears. Father Howell, the Rector of Saint Chrysostom's Church, also visited me, and once when, at my bedside, he prayed for my recovery, I choked up and wept. The only prayer that I knew word for word, was the *Pater Noster.* On that day and in the days after it, I found myself repeating the Lord's Prayer, again and again, and meaning every word of it. Quite suddenly, when I was awake one night, a light dawned on me, and I realized what had happened without my recognizing it clearly when first it happened. I had been seriously praying to God. But had I not said at the end of *How to Think About God*, that no one who understood the God of the philosophers as well as I thought I did, would worship that God or pray to him. Only if, by the gift of grace, one made the leap of faith across the chasm to the God of religious Jews and Christians, would one engage in worship and prayer, believing in a morally good, loving, just, and merciful God. Here after many years of affirming God's existence and trying to give adequate reasons for that affirmation, I found myself believing in God and praying to Him"); *The Four Dimensions of Philosophy: Metaphysical-Moral-Objective-Categorical* (1993); *Adler's Philosophical Dictionary* (1995); Ralph McInerny, "In Memoriam: Mortimer J. Adler," *Crisis Magazine*, November 2001 ("Adler was regularly asked how he could know so much about Catholic theology without accepting it as true. He gave what he called a Thomistic answer. He had not been given the grace of faith. But that, one might say, is a Calvinist rather than Thomist reply. The grace of faith is not offered to a select few and withheld from the rest. It is offered to all, but each must accept it himself. Eventually, Adler became a Christian. Finally, he became the Roman Catholic he had been training to be all his life. That a number of prominent notices of Adler's death failed to mention this central event in his life is a distressing sign of how peripheral religion has become for many in our time"); Deal W. Hudson, "The Great Philosopher Who Became Catholic," *Inside Catholic*, 29 June 2009; Dorothy Vining, "Mortimer J. Adler, Catholic," *musingsat85.com*, 2 January 2009; Benedict Ashley, *Friar's Folly, Vol. 1: Atheism Bumps Into Reality: A Conversion Story, 1915-1952* (2010) ("I first heard Mortimer Adler lecture in my freshman year. He asked the odd question, 'Have There Been Any New Ideas in the Last Five Hundred Years?' This lecture was one of the most important incidents of my life. I was imbued, as almost all young Americans of intellectual pretensions were in those days, with the Myth of Progress in thought as well as in machines. Surely the newest in thought was the truest, just as the newest detergent is 'improved'! Adler laughed at this myth and claimed that he had found only three really illuminating new ideas in the last five hundred years...What struck me was not whether these were the only good new ideas, but that old, old ideas may still be valuable, though today often obscured by intellectual fads and unexamined prejudices. That opened wide to me the treasures of tradition without closing to me the door to future search for wisdom...Adler and Hutchins convinced me that modernity at least is not the final word"); *ANB* ("Adler's emphasis on the classics as the basis for a sound education, as well as his belief in universal truth, put him squarely at odds with the American philosopher John Dewey (1859-1952), who espoused a pragmatic belief that truth is relative and is determined by its usefulness at a given moment in history. Moreover, Dewey preached an educational philosophy of flexibility and experimentation in both subject matter and teaching method, an approach known as progressive education that was now - thanks to Dewey's influence at the Teachers College of Columbia University - in the ascendancy in America's schools. Adler...believed that Dewey's philosophy was wishy-washy and that his style of education not only produced sloppy thinking but ultimately was dangerous because it led to social breakdown. Adler's ideas on education met with both commendation and criticism: his supporters included many Catholic educators who admired his respect for Thomism; critics accused him of being a reactionary").

Ahlquist, Dale – writer and Catholic apologist; c. 28 December 1997 (feast of the Holy Family: his wife came back to the Church at the same time); paternal grandfather a missionary doctor in North East India; both parents devout Baptists; brought up with a great love for the Scriptures; graduate of Carleton College (BA) in Northfield, Minnesota, and Hamline University (MA) in St. Paul, Minnesota; became dissatisfied with the churches he was attending, finding something missing there; also very troubled by the deep divisions within Christianity; started reading G. K. Chesterton (whom he knew had influenced C. S. Lewis), specifically *The Everlasting Man, on his honeymoon in Rome and was heavily influenced by him in becoming a Catholic;* president and co-founder of the American Chesterton Society; creator and host of the EWTN series *G. K. Chesterton: The Apostle of Common Sense*; publisher of *Gilbert Magazine*, devoted to Chesterton's work; has given hundreds of lectures on Chesterton; married with six children; see (selective list) *EWTN Audio Library, The Journey Home* (12 March 1999) ("First of all [Chesterton] talked about the historical Church. I think so many Protestants somehow think that Christianity began sometime in the 1500s. His was a defense of the historical Church and what happened in the early Church and throughout the medieval times; how there was a more solid society in the medieval times when there was one faith. And I think I have to say this too. I was always troubled by the divisons within Christianity. That was always something that bothered me very much; that there were too many churches. I knew that there should be only one church. I just didn't think it would be the Catholic Church…

One of the things Chesterton said about his own conversion was it's all the things that you initially object to the Church, object to for your reasons for joining the Church, those are eventually the reasons why you become a Catholic. And interestingly enough, something stuck that I had read about Chesterton, that there had been a cause introduced for his sainthood; and some of the Catholic Chestertonians were saying, 'Well, this is bad, because this is going to turn people off towards Chesterton. And I was sitting there thinking, as someone who thought that the cult of the saints was completely backward, 'That makes sense. Chesterton's a saint. Yes, that makes perfect sense to me.' It seems now that if Chesterton is not a saint for the twentieth century then there isn't one. And suddenly the whole idea of sainthood made sense when it never had before. Because I saw someone not only of heroic virtue, but someone gifted to express the Christian faith and I understood what the cult of the saints meant. There's certainly a

Chesterton cult, of a group devoted to his thinking. That made sense. It had never done so before…

His historical view got more and more of my time initially, but it was his defense of the faith and every aspect of it, from the Eucharist to confession; certainly confession was one of the main things that hit on me. Faith based on the sacrament of confession is one based on truth; because that's what confession is, telling the truth…

For me the thing that finally convinced me that becoming a Catholic is what I've got to do was having an argument with a friend of mine about Chesterton. And interestingly enough this person was only arguing about Chesterton's economic ideas, and he was saying to me, 'Dale, you don't really understand Chesterton.' And of course I had read far more Chesterton than he had and I should have been insulted by what he said. But instead something hit me, saying 'You know, I really haven't embraced all of Chesterton yet. And I haven't embraced him until I've followed him all the way to Rome.' And it was driving home from that conversation when I made a decision that I've got to go all the way to Rome, I've got to join the Catholic Church"); *G. K. Chesterton: The Apostle of Common Sense* (2003); *Common Sense 101: Lessons from G. K. Chesterton* (2006); Carl E. Olson, "Seeing With the Eyes of G. K. Chesterton," *Ignatiusinsight.com*, July 2006 (interview) ("I never would have thought about becoming Catholic if I had not read Chesterton. He comes from such a different angle, a wider angle, too! Nothing like classic apologetics, which is sort of one question at a time. Chesterton gets you to see the big picture, and the more you read him, you find that you start thinking like a Catholic and stop thinking like a Protestant. And yes, I am only one of many whom Chesterton has escorted into the Catholic Church. I've started a list. There are a lot of people on it"); "The Outline of Sanity," *Distributist Review*, 29 August 2010; "Dorothy Day and Distributism," *Distributist Review*, 29 November 2010; "The Basis of Civilization," *Distributist Review*, 28 February 2011; "The Trouble With Catholic Social Teaching," *Distributist Review*, 19 April 2011; "Immigration," *Distributist Review*, 11 May 2011; "The Triumphs and Failures of Feminism," *Distributist Review*, 5 June 2011; "G. K. Chesterton's Distributism," *Distributist Review*, 11 August 2011; "Christmas and Contraception," *Distributist Review*, 3 January 2012; "Upon This Rock That Doesn't Roll," *The Coming Home Network International*, *Conversion Stories*, chnetwork.org, 31 October 2012 ("People get a good laugh out of the fact that I read *The Everlasting Man* on my honeymoon. What makes it even funnier is that my bride was reading *Les Miserables*. And crying her eyes out. In contrast to her experience, my sensation upon reading my book was the same as that described by Dorothy L. Sayers the first time she read Chesterton: she said it was like a strong wind rushing into the building and blowing out all the windows. It was utterly fresh, and it knocked me over. I knew I had encountered a writer like no other. His words resounded with a splendor of confidence and truth from the opening sentence: 'There are two ways of getting home; and one of them is to stay there.' In the book, which is a condensed history of the world, Chesterton demonstrates that Christ is the center of history, the center of the human story. He brings together history, literature, mythology, science and religion, and swats the skeptics who scoff at the Christian claims. 'The most ignorant of humanity know by the very look of earth that they have forgotten heaven.' Chesterton gave me a completely new perspective of the coming of Christ: a baby, outcast and homeless. 'The hands that had made the sun and the stars were too small to reach the huge heads of the cattle.' He awed me with his description of the crucifixion, when the darkness descended, and 'God had been forsaken of God.' And then the resurrection, which was the first morning of a new world, when 'God walked again in the garden'...

I found myself longing for the ancient, historical faith. I had to admit, reluctantly, that Baptists were a relatively recent phenomenon in the history of Christianity. What, I had to ask, was going on during that huge period of time before the Reformation? None of that had ever been explained to me. It had only been explained away. I started to dig into that history, reading the early Church Fathers, and books on the history of the Church. I also read the Catechism, and Chesterton's most Catholic books: *The Thing, The Catholic Church and Conversion, The Well and the Shallows.*

Chesterton describes the three stages a convert goes through. The first is deciding to be fair to the Catholic Church. But there is no being fair to it. You are either for it or against it. When you stop being against it, you find yourself being drawn towards it. Then comes the second step, the fun one. It is learning about the Catholic Church, which is like exploring an exotic country full of strange new animals and flowers that you had never imagined existed. It is fun because there is no commitment, and you can run away anytime you want. Which is what the third step is: running away. You do everything you can to avoid becoming Catholic. You know it is the right Church, and you will not admit it, because admitting it means changing your life forever. Your head is convinced, but your heart is still trying to talk you out of it.

One by one, I had dealt with each of my Baptist objections to Catholicism. Any good Baptist is raised with a subtle and sometimes not-so-subtle anti-Catholicism. The Baptist way could almost be described as a point-by-point reaction against and rejection of Catholicism. We rejected the Pope, the priest, the Eucharist, celibacy, saints, confession, crucifixes, and so on. We identified ourselves by the name of a sacrament we also rejected. Though we insisted on 'believer's baptism' and full immersion, we also insisted that it had absolutely no effect on a person whatsoever. It was merely a symbol. The Bible was our final authority in all matters, and we were quite convinced that the Catholic Church deliberately kept its members from reading the Bible in order to keep them ignorant and malleable - which is quite a trick, especially if you can do it for two thousand years.

There is a major hole in the logic of those Christians who protest against the Catholic Church: you cannot use the authority of Scripture to attack the authority of the Church when it was the Authority of the Church that gave Scripture its authority. The hierarchy, the sacraments, the major doctrines of the Catholic Church were all well in place before the Biblical Canon was in place. Centuries in place. And of course it was the Church that authorized the Biblical Canon. Chesterton says he can understand someone looking at a Catholic procession, at the candles and the incense and the priests and the robes and the cross and the scrolls, and saying 'It's all bosh.' But what he cannot understand is anyone saying, 'It's all bosh - except for the scrolls. We're going to keep the scrolls. In fact, we're even going to use the scrolls against the rest.'

I also learned that the Catholic Church, in spite of its reputation among Baptists, is intensely scriptural. Ironically, at any Catholic Mass you will hear far more scripture than at any Baptist service. And it was also my observation that every Protestant sect at some point simply disregards certain Scriptures that are not convenient to its own teachings. Someday I'll make a list...

There is not enough space here to deal with all of my objections to Catholic doctrine and how each was resolved, but I must mention one. The first hurdle and the final hurdle for me was Mary. I'm sure it is the same for most Baptist converts to the Catholic Church. Mary represents all the things we object to in one package. She is the pagan remnant in the Catholic faith, goddess worship, idolatry, bigger than Christ in all those prayers and art and music devoted to her, appealing to the ignorant who do not read their Bibles, and so on.

My objections to the Catholic view of Mary were deeply ingrained. The first thing that helped me overcome them was reading something that Cardinal Leo Suenens once said when speaking to a group of Protestants. He said, 'I'm going to say to you what the angel said to Joseph in a dream: "Don't be afraid of Mary."'

I was indeed afraid of Mary. Do not be afraid of Mary. This is the first step. And it was like the three steps of conversion. I had to start by deciding not to fear Mary but to be fair to her. Then it was a matter of discovering her. Then…running away from her.

The next thing that helped me with Mary was something I read when I went on a retreat to a Trappist monastery in Iowa. (Imagine! Here's a guy who thinks he's running away from the Catholic Church, and he goes on a retreat to a monastery! Though I have never been too bright, I have still always managed to outsmart myself.) In that place of silence and solitude I read how the monks there model themselves on Mary because Mary is the model Christian. She obeyed God's call, she carried Christ within her, and she then revealed him to the whole world. She stayed close to him, she experienced the suffering of his death, the glory of his resurrection, and the coming of the Holy Spirit. We are to imitate her. What she did literally, we must do in every other way. Who can argue with that beautiful image? It is an image worth meditating on every day, which is what devotion is, and why so many have meditated on and been devoted to Mary. They have also fulfilled her prophecy in Scripture by rising up and calling her Blessed. Next I grappled with the paradoxical but theologically accurate description of her as 'The Mother of God.'

After a few more intermediate steps, I went to another monastery on a retreat. (I was obviously retreating in the direction of the Church.) The priest there looked me in the eye and asked, 'Why haven't you converted yet?' I mumbled something about Mary. He did not loosen his gaze, but asked, 'Do you believe that her soul magnifies the Lord?' The literal Baptist had never considered that verse literally before. 'My soul makes God bigger.' I had run out of excuses.

It became clear that every other Christian sect was exactly that - a sect, a section, something less than the whole. I discovered, as Chesterton had discovered, that 'the Catholic Church is not only right, but right where everything else is wrong'"); *The Complete Thinker: The Marvelous Mind of G. K. Chesterton* (2012); *G. K. Chesterton: The Apostle of Common Sense (two DVDs).*

Akin, James ("Jimmy") – Catholic apologist; b. 1965, Corpus Christi, Texas; c. 22 August 1992; grew up in Arkansas and was taken to a local Church of Christ until age five or six, but after that raised only nominally Christian; started reading the Bible at thirteen or fourteen; next joined the New Age movement, but broke with that; had a profound conversion to Christ at the age of twenty; eventually settled on the Presbyterian Church in America (PCA); planning on becoming a Protestant pastor or seminary professor, he started an intensive study of the Bible; however, the more he immersed himself in Scripture, the more he found to support the Catholic faith (Catholicism was rooted in Scripture); then had difficulties with the doctrines of *sola fide* and *sola scriptura*; also began to discover the sacramental principle throughout the Bible; finally came to appreciate the Petrine primacy; in June 1992 his wife Renée, a cradle Catholic who had left the Church but later returned to it, was diagnosed as having cancer and died 26 August 1992; he was received into the Catholic Church four days before his wife died; after his conversion active in Catholic apologetics; see (selective list) "Is the Soul Inherited or Created?" *This Rock*, June 1993; "A Tiptoe Through Tulip," *This Rock*, September 1993; "A Triumph and a Tragedy," in Patrick Madrid (ed), *Surprised by Truth* (1994), p.57 ("Since becoming a Christian I had read theology intensively, but I started making discoveries in the Bible which troubled me. For example, the shocking 'Catholicity' of certain verses leaped out at me. I was bothered by Christ's statements about the apostles having the power to bind and loose (Matt. 16:18 and 18:18) and about their having the power to forgive sins (John 20:21-23). I didn't know what to make of these passages, so I simply put them aside, planning to deal with them later. Eventually, when the time came to deal with them, I had to conclude that Jesus had meant exactly what he had said: His ministers really do have the power to forgive and retain sins. I had to admit to myself that the Catholics were right about the sacrament of confession, and Presbyterianism was simply out of synch with Scripture on this point...

I also began to have problems with the two fundamental doctrines of Protestantism: *sola fide*, the claim that we are saved by faith alone, and *sola scriptura*, the claim that Christians are to use only the Bible in matters of doctrine and practice.

The first began to be problematic for me because I started noticing certain passages in Scripture which contradicted the doctrine. In Romans 2:7, for example, the Apostle Paul tells his readers that God will give the reward of eternal life to those who 'seek after glory, honor, and immortality by perseverance in good works.' In Galatians 6:6-10, Paul tells his readers that those who 'sow to the Spirit' by 'doing good to all' will from the Spirit reap a harvest of eternal life. It was especially noteworthy that I was finding these verses in Romans and Galatians, the very epistles on which Protestants claim to base the doctrine of justification by faith alone...

The Protestant doctrine of *sola scriptura* also began to trouble me as I wondered how it is that we can know for certain which books belong in the Bible. Certain books of the New Testament, such as the synoptic gospels, we can show to be reliable historical accounts of Jesus' life, but there were a number of New Testament books (e.g.,

Hebrews, James, 2 Peter, 2 and 3 John, Jude, and Revelation) whose authorship and canonical status were debated in the early Church. Eventually the Church decided in their favor and included them in the canon of inspired books, but I saw that I, a person two thousand years removed from their writing, had no possibility of proving these works were genuinely apostolic. I simply had to take the Catholic Church's word on it.

This meant that for one very foundational doctrine - the doctrine of what Scripture is - I had to trust the Church since there was no way to show from within Scripture itself exactly what the books of the Bible should be, But I realized that by looking to the Church as an authentic and reliable witness to the canon, I was violating the principle of *sola scriptura*. The 'Bible only' theory turned out to be self-refuting, since it cannot tell us which books belong in it and which don't!

What was more, my studies in Church history showed that the canon of the Bible was not finally settled until about three hundred years after the last apostle died. If I was going to claim that the Church had done its job and picked exactly the right books for the Bible, this meant that the Church had made an infallible decision three hundred years after the apostolic age, a realization which made it believable that the Church could make even later infallible decisions, and that the Church could make such decisions even today"); *Mass Confusion: The Do's and Don'ts of Catholic Worship* (1999); *EWTN Audio Library, The Journey Home* (21 July 2000) ("The more I read the more things I found in Scripture that really matched up with the Catholic faith. And the turning point probably came one day in August of 1991 when I was reading a Catholic book and there was an extended quotation from Matthew 16, which is the 'You are Peter' passage, and as I read this passage I typically to this point said what many Evangelicals say, that Peter is not the rock, but that the rock on which the Church is built is Peter's faith, the revelation of the fact that Jesus is the Messiah. And I had assumed in this passage that Jesus was diminishing Peter, saying 'You're not important, Peter. The real important thing is who I am as Christ.'

Well, as I read this passage on this day I noticed certain structural features in the text that required me to say that Peter *is* the rock. And as soon as I saw them it was locked in place. I realized he had to be and so I did an about face on the interpretation of that passage just in a moment, and said that this is it, it is crystal clear, it has to be Peter.

What I noticed was that in this passage Jesus makes three statements to Peter. The first statement he makes begins 'Blessed are you, Simon Bar-Jona.' The second statement is 'You are Peter.' It begins that way. And the third statement begins 'I give you the keys to the kingdom.' Now, what I noticed is that the first statement, 'Blessed are you, Simon Bar-Jona,' is clearly a blessing. The third statement, 'I give you the keys' is also clearly a blessing. And so if you are going to interpret 'You are Peter' in its immediate context, then we're going to have to say that 'You are Peter' is also a blessing.

It would be inconsistent to bless him and then to put him down. It would be like saying 'Blessed are you, Simon Bar-Jona; you are really insignificant; here are the keys to the kingdom!' you know, it just wouldn't scan. AndsoIjusthadtoconcludethatwhat the linguists were saying was right.

Now, sometimes you know, Protestants will say, 'Well, there's a different word in Greek here. He is saying you are *petros* and on this *petra* I will build my Church. And that's true. But, what they will sometimes argue is *petros* means small stone whereas *petra* means large rock, and so he's contrasting Peter with the rock. Well, if he'd said that six or seven hundred years earlier it would have carried that meaning. In some early Greek poetry they did have that meaning, but as D. A. Carson, who is one of the deans of Protestant exegesis, admits, by the first century the term had lost that meaning. They were synonyms. And so you really can't drive a wedge between them in that way.

So, I realized that because it's in a context of blessings, the middle statement, 'you are Peter,' also has to be a blessing. And so he's not running Peter down and contrasting him with the rock.

I also noticed that each one of these three statements has a continuation which explains it. So, for the statement 'Blessed are you, Simon Bar-Jona' the continuation is 'For flesh and blood has not revealed this to you, but my Father who is in heaven.' That explains why he's blessed; because the Father has revealed it to him. Similarly, in the third statement, 'I give you the keys,' the continuation and explanation is 'Whatever you bind on earth will be bound in heaven, and whatever you loose on earth be loosed in heaven.' That explains part of what it means to have the keys. So in the same way with the middle statement, 'You are Peter.' The continuation of that, 'And on this rock I will build my Church, and the gates of hell will not prevail against it,' that explains what it means to be Peter. To be Peter means to be the rock on which the Church is built.

And so I had to conclude, 'Wow, if Catholics were right about that, they could be right about other things.' And so I had to conduct a survey over the course of the year of all the different areas of systematic theology, looking at them for the first time really with an open mind to the Catholic position. When I did, the verses came back down off the shelf and I said 'I have to become a Catholic'"); *The Salvation Controversy* (2001); "Debating 101," *This Rock*, July-August 2002; *Mass Appeal: The ABCs of Worship* (2003); "Eternal Gamble," *This Rock*, March 2003; *EWTN Audio Library, The Journey Home* (3 November 2003); *The Fathers Know Best* (2010); *Mass Revision: How the Liturgy is Changing and What It Means for You* (2011); *Mass Appeal: The ABCs of Worship* (2012); *jimmyakin.com.*

Algase, Gertrude (pronounced "Algaze") – literary agent; b. 1906; c. 1942 (received by Mgr. Fulton Sheen); d. 2 August 1962, New York; brought up in a Jewish family; very aggressive and effective literary agent in New York; her clients included President Kennedy and many other public figures (e.g., the historians Charles and Mary Beard and the journalist Arthur Krock); widowed just before her conversion; in 1942 she signed Mgr. Fulton Sheen to a contract; converted to the Catholic faith under the direction of Mgr. Sheen; in 1943 she became Cardinal Spellman's literary agent, earning for him over a million dollars in royalties, all of which went into various charitable and educational organizations; Spellman's staff admired her "physical appearance and brassy ways" and nicknamed her "Mortal Sin"; known locally for her charitable events, being the founder of the Alfred E. Smith Memorial Dinner, which raised a quarter of a million dollars a year for a diocesan hospital; also known for the New York Foundling Hospital Christmas Party; in 1955 she quarreled with Sheen about her share of television and radio payments, but settled out of court.

Allen, Frances Margaret ("Fanny") – nun, b. 13 November 1784, Sunderland, Vermont; c. 1807; d. 10 September 1819, Montreal, Canada; her father was Ethan Allen (1738-1789), the patriot, Revolutionary War general, pioneer of the state of Vermont, and skeptic in religion; her mother was Ethan Allen's second wife, Frances Montressor; after Ethan Allen's death her mother married Dr. Jabez Perriman, who was also hostile to religion; as she grew up she enquired and found out about the Catholic religion; in 1805 she requested her parents to allow her to go to Montreal to learn French, but intending to become more familiar with Catholic belief and practice by going to a convent school there; her parents consented subject to her being baptized by Rev. Daniel Barber (see below), an Anglican minister and later a convert to the Catholic faith himself (she strongly objected, but consented to please her parents); in 1807 she became a pupil of the Sisters of the Congregation of Notre Dame, at Montreal; she became filled with the Real Presence of Christ in the tabernacle; later she rejected her Protestantism; she was instructed and baptized (her earlier baptism having been held invalid); at her first communion she felt within her a vocation to the religious life; her parents at once withdrew her from the convent and tried to distract her by giving her every social and worldly pleasure and even trying to persuade her to become an Episcopalian instead; this did not distract her from the desire of a religious life, though she agreed to wait a year before taking any action; she then returned to Montreal; in 1808 she entered the Hôtel-Dieu, the convent of the Religious Hospitallers of St. Joseph, making her religious profession in 1811; she was the first woman of New England birth to become a nun; she spent the rest of her life working as a nurse in the hospital's apothecary; died early from complications from a lung disease; buried under the chapel at the Hotel-Dieu; the Fanny Allen Hospital in Colchester, Vermont, built in 1879 and run by her order, was named in her honor; see Louis De Goesbriand, *Catholic Memoirs of Vermont and New Hampshire* (1886); William Byrne, *History of the Catholic Church in the New England States* (1899); *Catholic Encyclopedia* ("One day, a Sister requested her to place some flowers on the altar, recommending her also to make an act of adoration of the Real Presence of Jesus Christ in the tabernacle. When the young woman attempted to step into the sanctuary she found herself unable to do so. After three futile attempts, she was filled with conviction of the Real Presence, and fell upon her knees in humble adoration").

Alliluyeva, Svetlana Iosifovna (born Svetlana Stalina; later Lana Peters) – writer and lecturer; b. 28 February 1926, Moscow; c. 13 December 1982 (received at Cambridge, England); d. 22 November 2011, Richland Center, Wisconsin; youngest child and only daughter of Joseph Stalin, the Soviet leader, and Nadezhda Alliluyeva, Stalin's second wife; her mother died in 1932 (probably suicide); brought up mainly by nannies; became fluent in German, French and English; studied history and political thought at Moscow University; married at the age of seventeen Grigori Morozov, a fellow student (one son, Iosif (1945-2008)); divorced in 1947; married in 1949 Yuri Zhdanov (1919-2006), an associate of her father (one daughter, Yekaterina in 1950); marriage dissolved; baptized into the Russian Orthodox Church in 1962; very close relationship with Brajesh Singh (d. 1966), an Indian Communist; after Singh's death she was allowed in 1967 to visit India to return his ashes to his family; while there she defected, was granted political asylum and began a new life in the United States; on arrival there she denounced the Soviet government and her father; she became an American citizen; lectured and wrote at Princeton; married in 1970 William Wesley

Peters (1912-1991), an architect (one daughter, Olga); divorced 1973; after her father died in 1973 she worked in Moscow as a lecturer and translator; her children in the Soviet Union disowned her; she tried out various religions, before turning to the Greek Orthodox Church; moved to England in 1982, where she became a Catholic, then to the Soviet Union in 1984; she returned to the United States in 1986; her conversion was influenced in part by the writings of Raissa Maritain; see *Twenty Letters to a Friend* (1967) (memoir); *Only One Year* (1969) (memoir); *Faraway Music* (1984) (autobiographical).

Anderson, Henry James – scientist and educator; b. 6 February 1799, New York City; c. 1849; d. 19 October 1875, Lahore, India; graduated at Columbia College in 1818; studied medicine at the Columbia University College of Physicians and Surgeons, New York; in 1825 appointed Professor of Mathematics and Astronomy at Columbia College (Emeritus Professor from 1866); geologist on the United States Dead Sea Exploration in 1848; head of the Supreme Council of the St. Vincent de Paul Society in New York; Knight Commander of the Order of St. Gregory the Great; organizer and president of the Catholic Union; married to Fanny Da Ponte, daughter of Lorenzo Da Ponte (1749-1838), the opera librettist; many contributions to scientific journals and two geological reports on the Dead Sea Exploration; died suddenly of disease; buried in a vault under the Church of the Madonna, Fort Lee, New Jersey; see *Geological Reconnaissance of Part of the Holy Land* (1848 & 1849); *Catholic Encyclopedia* ("His requiem was sung in St. Patrick's Cathedral, and Cardinal McCloskey, in the sermon, said: 'I remember to have heard from the lips of a distinguished Oxford scholar that he had never met a man of greater learning tempered with such humility'").

Anderson, Robert Gordon – writer; b. 18 April 1881, Somerville, New Jersey; c. Spring 1950; d. 25 September 1950, New York; his ancestors were mostly early settlers and founded townships; his paternal grandfather came to the United States from Scotland in the middle of the nineteenth century, adding Anderson to his name; his Gordon associations in Britain included the fourth Earl of Aberdeen (1784-1860), Prime Minister in a coalition government 1852-1854, and the sixth Earl, who served as Lord Lieutenant of Ireland and Governor General of Canada; studied at New York University; worked for an encyclopedia, wrote advertising copy, and was a newspaper reporter in New York City; after working on a Montana ranch he managed a bookstore in New York; later represented publishers, acting as a sales manager and literary advisor, and as a ghost writer; started his own career as a serious writer at the age of thirty-seven; he published twenty works, comprising essays, biographies, novels, books for juveniles, poetry, and travel; married Marion Blake in 1911; always interested in French civilization, he spent the Summer of 1920 in France and formed a great love for the country and for Paris in particular; visited there often with his wife and three children; wrote two major works on the Cathedral of Notre Dame, *Biography of a Cathedral* and *The City and the Cathedral*, in both of which he exhibited a great interest in Catholicism, which eventually led to his reception into the Catholic Church; see *Not Taps But Reveille (In Memoriam Lieutenant W. L. M.)* (1918); *The Little Chap* (1919); *Leader of Men (Theodore Roosevelt)* (1920); *Seven O'Clock Stories* (1922); *Half-Past Seven Stories* (1922); *The Isle of Seven Moons* (1922); *Eight O'Clock Stories* (1923); *For Love of a Sinner* (1924); *Over the Hill Stories* (1925); *Those Quarrelsome Bonapartes (A Novel)* (1927); *An American Family Abroad* (1931); *The Tavern Rogue* (1934); *Villon (A Lyric Drama of François Villon)* (1937); *Biography of a Cathedral* (1944); *The City and the Cathedral* (1948); Matthew Hoehn, OSB (ed), *Catholic Authors* (1952) ("He felt that he came to know almost every stone of the city [of Paris], every historic landmark, and every old church. The fruit of this knowledge is apparent in his two major works. He also got to know something more important, for antiquarianism in his case was not something dead, but the key to the vivid and vigorous life of Catholicism. The Cathedral of Notre Dame with him was a passion, for he never tired of walking her aisles and aerial galleries, nor in meditating in the light of her rose windows, nor of attending her Masses and processions, thus unconsciously becoming saturated with Catholicism. At first he wrote of the Cathedral as man's greatest artistic achievement, peopled throughout the ages with colorful characters. But gradually something more molded his first conception: the Cathedral was Christ, and the heart of the whole matter was the Host on the altar. In writing about the Cathedral, he found that he was writing himself into the Church. Probably it was sometime before he was himself aware of what was happening, as it was some time before he brought himself to take what he saw later was for long an inevitable step...

These last two books by Mr. Anderson become...a tender and vibrant interpretation, not only of Paris and of its Cathedral, but of medieval culture and of Christian civilization. They constitute a remarkable crown to a very varied career").

Antoninus, Brother - see under Everson, William.

Arkes, Hadley P. – political scientist; b. 7 July 1940; c. 24 April 2010 ("A year later, I still leave the Church, at the close of Mass, in a curiously buoyant state, with the sense that I must look like Charles Ryder at the end of *Brideshead Revisited,* after he has absorbed deep, serial disappointments ('You're looking unusually cheerful today [Ryder]')"); born and raised a Jew; awarded a B.A. degree at the University of Illinois; PhD from the University of Chicago (was a student of Leo Strauss there); taught at Amherst College, Massachusetts from 1966; was the William Nelson Cromwell Professor of Jurisprudence there; in 1987 appointed Edward N. Ney Professor of Jurisprudence and American Institutions at Amherst; argued that moral principles are true and necessary across cultures; opponent of moral relativism and proponent of natural law jurisprudence ("The person who asks, 'Can I reach judgments in the law without appealing to natural law?' is rather like the man who asks, 'Can I order coffee without using syntax?'"); argues that it is necessary to move "beyond the Constitution," to the principles that stood antecedent to the text, if we are to understand the text and apply the Constitution to the cases that arise every day in our law; a leader in the pro-life movement; one of the chief architects of the Born Alive Infant Protection Act; frequent contributor to and member of the editorial board of *First Things* journal; see (selective list) *The Philosopher in the City* (1981); *First Things: An Inquiry Into the First Principles of Morals and Justice* (1986); *On Natural Rights: Speaking Prose All Our Lives* (1992); *A Jurisprudence of Natural Rights: How an Earlier Generation of Judges Did It* (1992); *Beyond the Constitution* (1992); *The Return of George Sutherland: Restoring a Jurisprudence of Natural Rights* (1997); *The Mission of the Military and the Question of "The Regime"* (1997); *Natural Rights and the Right to Choose* (2002); *Constitutional Illusions and Anchoring Truths* (2010); "Finalmente: Coming Into the Church," *The Catholic Thing*, 26 April 2010 ("It was last October, the Red Mass, said on that first Sunday in October just before the opening of the Supreme Court on the first Monday. My wife Judy and I were at the service at St. Matthew's in Washington, and we were on the way to the Hilton on Sixteenth Street for the lunch following the Mass. Suddenly, and happily, we were joined on the walk by Fr. Arne Panula, whom I'd met years ago at the Opus Dei house in New York. He had moved over to direct the chapel and programs at the Catholic Information Center at Fifteenth and K. In a bantering way, Fr. Arne confronted me: 'You, the most notable figure at the threshold, never quite crossing it.' (Never actually coming into the Church.) 'What's holding you back?' I dipped into the repertoire of Bert Lahr from the *Wizard of Oz*: 'C-c-c courage! It's what puts the 'ape' in 'apricot'; it's what I haven't got.'

That move deftly got me out of the challenge posed here in an affectionate way. But only for a moment. One month later I dropped in to a noon Mass at the CIC and Fr. Arne, in the homily, remarked that 'the one thread that connected these two readings today is c-c-c-c courage.' That was the hook that finally worked. We had lunch, we mapped out a series of five or six sessions of instruction, for the decision was finally made. And just yesterday (as I write this), on April 24, I came into the Church in Fr. Arne's chapel...

To my astonishment, friends were willing to fly in from Boston and Cleveland and places even more exotic for this occasion...To me they had come to represent the 'body of the Church': every one of them marked a moment, or even a chapter in the story, for they each revealed to me, in their own character, what it meant to lead a Catholic life. Each in his own way, taught me something of the teachings of this Church, and each showed me the welcoming face of the Church.

It began with Dan Robinson, when we were on the faculty together at Amherst. I was beginning to think in a probing way about the issue of abortion, and Dan showed me that the Church's position really depended on a combination of empirical evidence (embryology), woven with moral reasoning. It was natural law reasoning. As Aquinas said, the divine law we know through revelation, but the natural law we know through that reason that was natural for human beings. The Church's moral position here did not depend on faith or belief. One didn't have to be Catholic to understand it. And that was precisely the teaching of the Church.

As I began to write myself on abortion and marriage and the issues of the day, I was filling out a natural law perspective, and drawing to myself a constituency certain that I was a Catholic writer. Joe Reilly, in Boston, was the first one to tell me years ago that I was becoming a notable 'apologist' for Catholic teaching...

One friend, who converted at Oxford, told me that the resonating line for him came from our friend Dermot Quinn. Dermot said that you can believe everything the Church tells you and not be a good Catholic. The question is, 'Do you believe in the Church as a truth-telling institution?' And I thought: I do, I really do. When the Church stands *contra mundum*, against the currents of relativism in the world, my inclination is to think that the Church has it right.

As Fr. Jim Burtchaell used to say, the Church draws on vast experience and lifts a mirror to put in one's face: it shows you what you are going to look like if you proceed along this path. The Church has become the main enclave to preserve the sobriety of moral reasoning, natural law reasoning, when the currents of relativism have inundated and corroded the academy and other institutions.

I've come to this matter then through the Church. But the Church cannot be understood apart from the one who planted the Mustard Seed from which it grew and took its shape and character. Nor can it be detached from the Spirit that managed to preserve the discipline of its moral teachings even through times of trouble and disarray.

There is more to the story, of course, than I can relate in this space; it will have to come later. But to take a line from Richard Neuhaus, it may be a story about, 'How I became the Catholic I was'"); "Coming into the Church – A Year Later," *The Catholic Thing*, 26 April 2011; Robert George, "The Operation of Divine Grace on Hadley Arkes" *mirrorofjustice.blogs.com*, 26 April 2010 ("In remarks after [Hadley Arkes' reception into the Church], he explained that his faith in Christ had come through the Church. The Church's moral witness, especially on the sanctity of human life and on marriage and sexual morality - a witness that has in our time made the Church a 'sign of contradiction' to the most powerful and influential elements of the elite sector of contemporary western culture - persuaded him that the Church is, despite the failings of so many of its members and leaders, fundamentally 'a truth-teaching institution.' In teachings that many find to be impediments, Hadley found decisive evidence that the Church is, indeed, what she claims to be"); Marcia Segelstein, "Courage and conversion: An Interview With Hadley Arkes," *Touchstone*, March/April 2011 (reprinted in *Crisis*, 16 August 2012) ("MS: You talk about the Church standing *"contra mundum,"* and there's certainly a lot to stand against these days. Why do you believe society has strayed so far from traditional Judeo-Christian values? HA: The drift away is not something so remarkable or unthinkable. After all, isn't there a constant drumbeat of complaints by God in the Old Testament about his people drifting away? In the normal laxity of ordinary persons, it's always easier to fall away from the things that are good and rightful. Remember Mark Twain's line in *Pudd'nhead Wilson's New Calendar* [from *Following the Equator*] that we have a moral sense and an immoral sense. The moral sense tells us what is good and how to avoid it, and the immoral sense tells us what is bad and how to enjoy it.

It's no wonder that human beings, faced with a collision between their interests and things that are rightful to do and that demand sacrifice have strong temptations to prefer their own interests. The unfolding logic of modernity is the notion that all passions should be gratified, that all inclinations should be pursued, that all desires

stand on the same plane. 'All men are created equal' has come to mean in its vulgar notion that we cannot discriminate between the finer desires and the coarser desires, between the more selfish desires and the more generous desires.
MS: How do we change course?
HA: My friend Daniel Robinson would say that what has rescued things in the past is conversion. And if you find conversions in persons, you can find conversions affecting many people, and at a certain point running through the whole country, running through the culture. Richard Neuhaus's line was, 'We can still turn this around.' And I think the possibility of turning it around is always lurking there. I guess that's why so many people I know, Catholics and others who are involved in the so-called culture wars, haven't given up. It reminds me of Michael Novak's joke about the pessimist and the optimist. The pessimist says, 'Oh, things could never get any worse,' And the optimist says, 'Oh, yes they can!'

What may be truly remarkable in the overall sweep of human history, and of our daily experience, is how many examples we see of ordinary people preferring the interests of others to their own. Parents, for example, who are holding things together in order to sustain their children. In my own case I can see the effects on discrete students. You know particular persons who tell you that their own lives were changed. You see this before you and you know it must be possible. I know I sound like the cockeyed optimist in *South Pacific*. There's no question there's been a tendency toward the vulgar, and yet you keep seeing these signs of regeneration, of people turning their lives around, thinking anew.
MS: How has moral relativism come to be so predominant?
HA: I think the erosion of natural law and the tendency toward moral relativism go back to ancient times with ancient skeptics making the argument for relativism. You can see the arguments surfacing in Plato's *Protagoras*. In the Anglo-American law, it was getting accelerated from the early part of the twentieth century. It was bound up with historicism and the notion taking hold in Germany that we could know things only within their historical context, i.e., that certain things will be made clear only as history unfolds.

My late professor, Leo Strauss of the University of Chicago, wrote his critical book, *Natural Right and History,* in 1953. That was mid-century and he was already standing against the currents of relativism. Already they were deeply at work. Here was a country established on the Declaration of Independence - on truths grounded in nature, objective moral truths, self-evident truths - and yet falling into the wave of relativism. Strauss spoke about the effect of German philosophy on America - and here I'm paraphrasing - that it would not be the first time that a country defeated on the battlefield imposed on the victor the yoke of its own thought. Here we defeated the Germans, and yet German philosophy in its worst forms was taking hold in this country.

In the course I teach at Amherst that became the basis for the book *First Things,* I tell my students the biblical story of God instructing Elijah to journey to Damascus. Ultimately it is Elisha who fulfills this directive, traveling there to tell Hazael that 'the Lord has shown me that you are to be king over Syria,' and that the current king, Ben-Hadad, 'shall certainly die.' One commentator thought that this story, dating to the sixth century B.C., was a sign of how early the Jews were committed to monotheism. I ask the students what the connection is with moral relativism.

The answer is that a God who could tell a prophet to cross the lines of one jurisdiction to cashier a leader in another place was obviously not one of those local gods known to antiquity. This was evidently a God with universal jurisdiction. After all, I ask, did the same God who authored a universal law of physics author separate morals for Zanzibar and Jersey City? And what were the Ten Commandments? Were they municipal regulations, meant only to govern the immediate environs of Mt. Sinai?

Then I ask how many of them were raised in households that could be called Christian or Jewish or even Islamic. Almost all the hands go up. And yet, how is it that most students arrive at college with the assumptions of moral relativism, of cultural relativism? My question to them is, why do they think that the doctrines of cultural relativism have a firmer hold on them - or have been more deeply absorbed by them - than the logic of that monotheism in which they've been raised?

MS: Why do you think that is?

HA: I know there's been a falling away. If you take a look at the writings of the revolutionary period, particularly the sermons of the period, you find people who are utterly clear on the doctrines of natural rights and natural law. You don't need revelation in order to understand it. There was a time in this country when preachers, pastors, and ordinary people were remarkably clear on those things and could impart them. It may have something to do with the fact that these people weren't burdened with a college education!

In class I use the example of Plato's *Meno,* where you start feeding questions to the slave boy and pretty soon he's working out geometry. The message is that the logic of these moral understandings is locked away in our souls. It's there when people are treated badly and they take offense. They'll say, "I don't like it and it's wrong." So, I tell my students, so much of all this is getting fed the right questions that allow them to draw out the understandings that are already locked away within them. MS: So the moral understandings are there, but they're not acknowledged? HA: Some of my colleagues who object to natural law and, of course, to religion, will say that God is dead and everything is permitted. Yet they'll still talk about the man in the gutter who's broken his own life, and they'll want to help him. They'll say that there's a sanctity to him. This from people who are atheists.

An example I use in my book [*Natural Rights and the Right to Choose*] came from doing a piece on the Holocaust Museum and coming across a vat filled with shoes of the victims. What came flashing back at that moment were those lines of Justice McLean in the *Dred Scott* decision when he said, in essence, 'You may think that the black man is chattel but he's a creature made in the impress of his Maker. He is amenable to the laws of God and man and he is destined to an endless existence.' That is, he has a soul that will not decompose when his material existence comes to an end. The Nazis thought that the shoes were the durables. It was the shoes they wanted to keep.

People of the most liberal sympathies cannot give you the same account that McLean was able to give - the wrong of slavery or the wrong of genocide - because McLean would say it's because these creatures are made in the image of Someone higher. Those colleagues of mine who say that God is dead will say there's something sacrosanct about the alcoholic in the gutter. But they can't explain what's redeeming about him or why there's something about him that deserves their efforts to reach out and help. And they can't quite explain that.

The point is that their language, their reflexes, their dispositions on these things all spring from this religious understanding. You might say that religious capital is at work in our culture. But we've reached the point where people are no longer much aware of its origins and the source from which it was drawn.

Many liberals will express as much concern over dead Iraqi soldiers as American soldiers. They care about these strangers. So what is their problem with the lives of unborn children in the womb? They're as human as those strangers in Iraq of whom they know nothing. They are strangers for them here in their own country. They are nothing other than human beings. Their human standing doesn't depend on their height or weight, so what is it that's deflecting their judgment here?"); Francis J. Beckwith, Robert P. George and Susan McWilliams, *A Second Look at First Things: A Case for Conservative Politics: The Hadley Arkes Festschrift* (2013).

Armstrong, Dave – Catholic apologist; b. 1958, Detroit, Michigan; c. 8 February 1991 (received by Fr. John Hardon, SJ); raised as a United Methodist in Detroit; after the church closed in 1968 he rarely attended church;

got involved with several forms of occultism; after experiencing severe depression in 1977, he watched Franco Zeffirelli's film *Jesus of Nazareth*, and marveled at the character of Christ; began to comprehend the heart of the gospel for the first time; started to read the Bible seriously; had the experience of getting "saved"; educated at Wayne State University, Detroit (BA 1982); throughout the 1980s he attended Lutheran, Assembly of God, and non-denominational churches with strong connections to the "Jesus Movement"; developed into a typical Evangelical; became a missionary on college campuses for four years; got involved in the Pro-Life movement and later Operation Rescue, and in both these was impressed by the contribution of Catholics; influenced by Catholic apologetics books, and in particular *The Spirit of Catholicism* by Karl Adam ("a nearly perfect book about Catholicism as a worldview and a way of life") and the writings of Thomas Merton (see below), Christopher Dawson and Joan Andrews; realized that contraception was utterly anti-biblical and accepted the moral distinction between contraception and natural family planning; came to greatly respect Catholicism's "sense of community, devotion, and contemplation"; reading Newman's *Essay on the Development of Christian Doctrine* brought a true understanding of Tradition; also influenced by Newman's *Apologia* and Tom Howard's *Evangelical Is Not Enough*; after his conversion he concentrated on writing apologetic works, mostly aimed at Protestants; many books and articles; married to his wife Judy in 1984 (four children of the marriage); see (selective list) "Confessions of a 1980s Jesus Freak," in Patrick Madrid (ed), *Surprised by Truth* (1994), p.241 ("This book [*Essay on the Development of Doctrine*] demolished the whole schema of Church history which I had constructed. Up to that point I assumed (without any evidence to support the notion) that early Christianity was 'Protestant' and that Catholicism was a later corruption. I thought the corruption reached its zenith in the late Middle Ages rather than the time of Constantine in the fourth century, which is the more common view of Evangelicals.

Martin Luther, so I reckoned, had discovered in '*sola scriptura*' the means to scrape the accumulated Catholic barnacles off of the original lean and clean Christian 'ship.' Newman, in contrast, exploded the notion of a barnacle-free ship. Ships always got barnacles. The real question was whether the ship would arrive at its destination. Tradition, for Newman, was like a rudder and steering wheel, and was absolutely necessary for guidance and direction. Newman brilliantly demonstrated the characteristics of true developments, as opposed to corruptions, within the visible and historically continuous Church instituted by Christ. I found myself unable and unwilling to refute his reasoning, and a crucial piece of the puzzle had been put into place - Tradition was now plausible and self-evident to me.

Thus began what some call a 'paradigm shift.' While reading the *Essay* I experienced a peculiar, intense, and inexpressibly mystical feeling of reverence for the idea of a Church 'one, holy, catholic and apostolic.' Catholicism was now thinkable and I was suddenly cast into an intense crisis. I now believed in the visible Church and suspected that it was infallible as well. Once I accepted Catholic ecclesiology, the theology followed as a matter of course, and I accepted it without difficulty (even the Marian doctrines)…

I knew that if I was to reject Protestantism, then I had to examine its historical roots: the so-called Protestant Reformation. I had read about Martin Luther, and considered him one of my biggest heroes. I accepted the standard Protestant textbook myth of Martin Luther as the bold, righteous rebel who stood against the darkness of 'Romanist tyranny, superstitious ritualism, and unbiblical traditions of men' that had been added on to the original, 'pure' Christianity described in the book of Acts. But when I studied a large portion of the six-volume biography of Luther, by the German Jesuit Hartmann Grisar, my opinion of Luther was turned upside down. Grisar convinced me that the foundational tenets of the Protestant Revolution were altogether tenuous. I had always rejected Luther's notions of absolute predestination and the total depravity of mankind. Now I realized that if man had a free will, he did not have to be merely declared righteous in a judicial, abstract sense, but could actively participate in his redemption and actually be made righteous by God. This, in a nutshell, is the classic debate over justification.

I learned many highly disturbing facts about Luther; for example, his radically subjective existential methodology, his disdain for reason and historical precedent, and his dictatorial intolerance of opposing viewpoints, including those of his fellow Protestants. These and other discoveries were stunning, and convinced me beyond doubt that he was not really a 'reformer' of the 'pure,' pre-Nicene Church, but rather, a revolutionary who created a novel theology in many, though not all, respects. The myth was annihilated. I was unconvinced of the standard Protestant concept of the invisible, 'rediscovered' church. In the end, my innate love of history played a crucial part in my forsaking Protestantism, which tends to give very little attention to history, as indeed is necessary in order to retain any degree of plausibility over against Catholicism"); see (selective list) *A Biblical Defense of Catholicism*

(1996); *Bible Conversations: Catholic-Protestant Dialogues on the Bible, Tradition, and Salvation* (2002); *Development of Catholic Doctrine: Evolution, Revolution, or an Organic Process* (2002); *Family Matters: Catholic Theology of the Family* (2002); *Mere Christian Apologetics* (2002); *More Biblical Evidence for Catholicism* (2002); *Pensées on Catholic Traditionalism* (2002); *Top Ten Questions Catholics are Asked* (2002); *Protestantism: Critical Reflections of an Ecumenical Catholic* (2003); *Twin Scourges: Thoughts on Anti-Catholicism and Theological Liberalism* (2003); *The Catholic Verses: 95 Biblical Passages That Confound Protestants* (2004); *Orthodoxy and Catholicism: A Comparison* (2004); "On Sinners in the Church," *This Rock*, April 2004; *The New Catholic Bible* (2005) (with Paul Thigpen); *The Church Fathers Were Catholic: Patristic Evidences for Catholicism* (2007); *The One-Minute Apologist: Essential Catholic Replies to Over Sixty Common Protestant Claims* (2007); *Martin Luther: Catholic Critical Analysis and Praise* (2008); *Bible Proofs for Catholic Truths* (2009); *501 Biblical Arguments Against Sola Scriptura: Is the Bible the Only Infallible Authority?* (2009); (ed), *The Wisdom of Mr. Chesterton* (2009); *Biblical Catholic Answers for John Calvin* (2010); *Biblical Catholic Salvation: "Faith Working Through Love"* (2010); *"The Catholic Mary": Quite Contrary to the Bible?* (2010); *Science and Christianity: Close Partners or Mortal Enemies?* (2010); *Biblical Catholic Eucharistic Theology* (2011); *100 Biblical Arguments Against Sola Scriptura* (2012); *The Quotable Newman: A Definitive Guide to his Central Thoughts and Ideas* (2012); *A Biblical Critique of Calvinism* (2012); *Catholic Converts and Conversion* (2013) (includes an account of his own conversion).

Arrington, Alfred W. (sometimes wrote under the pseudonym of Charles Summerfield) – author and judge; b. 17 September 1810, Iredell County, North Carolina; d. 31 December 1867, Chicago; his father and grandfather were Methodist ministers (father also a Congressman for North Carolina); mother's family Scottish and originally Catholic; much bible reading in his early education; Methodist minister from the age of eighteen before losing his faith and ceasing his ministry in 1834; admitted to the bar in Missouri in 1835 and practiced law for twelve years; member of the Arkansas legislature; elected a judge in Texas 1850-1855; later well respected lawyer in Chicago; all this time he wrote about American life and history (especially on outlaws); later on wrote poetry dealing with spiritual and religious subjects; married to Leora (three children of the marriage); returned to the Christian faith on his deathbed and was received into the Catholic Church; see *The Desperadoes of the South-West* (1847); *Duelists and Duelling in the South-West* (1847); *The Rangers and Regulators of the Tanaha* (1856) (novel); *Poems* (1869); *ANB*.

Ascoli, Max – political philosopher and editor; b. 25 June 1898, Ferrara, Italy; c. 1970 (received by Fr. James Lloyd, CSP in the church of St. Paul the Apostle, New York City; d. 1 January 1978, New York City; Jewish background; LLD at the University of Ferrara in 1920; PhD in Philosophy at the University of Rome in 1928; active opponent of Fascism; came to the United States in 1931 and took up a post at the New School for Social Research in New York City; wrote several books and articles on politics and political philosophy; became an American citizen in 1939; married Marion Rosenwald in 1940 (one child of the marriage); first president of the Mazzini Society, an Italian-American group founded to oppose fascism, 1940-1943; in 1949 he founded the *Reporter*, a liberal political magazine; he was its editor for its entire nineteen years of publication, when it received many awards for excellence; the journal opposed both Fascism and Communism; ceased publication in 1968; bad eyesight and recurrent health problems; late in life converted to the Catholic Church (Fr. James Lloyd: "He came twice a week for his "lesson" arriving in a long, black chauffeur-driven limo. He was very tall, leaned unsteadily on a cane, and assessed me up and down with his one good eye in a kind of Long John Silver style. He sat opposite me in my little office and lectured me with a rich and deep grasp of Catholic history and theology. Throughout his superb presentations he inserted the phrase 'I love Chriiiiiiist,' said with unmistakable sincerity through his heavy Italian accent. Recognizing that he knew more Catholic theology than I would ever know, I shortened his 'lessons' and baptized him"); see *Intelligence in Politics* (1936); (ed), *Political and Economic Democracy* (1937); *Fascism for Whom?* (1938) (with Arthur Feiler); (ed), *The Fall of Mussolini: His Own Story by Benito Mussolini* (1948); *The Power of Freedom* (1949); (ed), *The Reporter Reader* (1956); (ed), *Our Times: The Best from the Reporter* (1960); Martin K. Doudna, *Concerned about the Planet: The Reporter Magazine and American Liberalism 1949-1968* (1977); his papers are in Boston University Library; *ANB* ("Though ethnically a Jew, Ascoli held beliefs that could best be described as Catholic, and in 1970 he received the Catholic rite of baptism").

Ashley, Benedict Mary, OP (born Winston Norman Ashley) – Dominican friar and theologian; b. 3 May 1915, Neodesha, Kansas; c. 10 April 1938 (Palm Sunday; St. Thomas the Apostle Church,

Chicago; his father, Arthur, was received shortly before his death in 1947; his mother, Bertha, was received in 1948; his brother Richard (1909-1980) was baptized shortly before his death); d. 23 February 2013, Chicago; parents were non-practicing Protestants who sent their children to Methodist and Presbyterian Sunday schools, but did not have him baptized; spent his childhood in Blackwell, Oklahoma; by the time of high school his constant reading had made him a humanistic atheist ("my atheism, as I suspect is the case with most declared atheists, was actually a kind of Spinozan pantheism in which God and Nature were simply aspects of one reality"), believing that evolution explained it all; won a scholarship to the University of Chicago, where he studied under Mortimer Adler (see above, in particular Ashley's account of Adler's effect on him) and Robert Maynard Hutchins (1899-1977), former Dean of the Yale Law School; joined their "Great Books of the Western World" course; became a Marxist and joined the Trotskyite Socialist Workers Party; wrote much poetry at this time; attended political meetings and agitational activities; awarded Masters Degree in Comparative Literature in 1937; graduate assistant to Adler; conversion influenced by his study of St. Thomas Aquinas under Adler; also influenced by Herbert Schwartz (see below) ("Faith is an objective and certain truth grounded formally on the Word of God who cannot deceive or be deceived and attested by signs accessible to human reason. The sufficient sign, for me, was and is, the moral miracle of the Catholic Church, the public fact that, in spite of all the frailties and scandals of its members from top to bottom, including myself, it is one, catholic, apostolic, and holy in a way no merely human institution is or can be"); received instructions from the Dominicans ("As I look back on the time of my instructions, I realize more clearly than ever that a sign accessible to natural human knowledge had already been given to me that was sufficient to demand from me a supernatural act of faith in the Word of God precisely as the Word of God…[T]his sign is the Catholic Church as I had come to know it in its miraculous existence today, in its apostolicity, catholicity, unity, and holiness in our confused, despairing, and sinful world. What had been lacking on my part was the submission of the will which grace had now given me, wholly undeserving as I was then and am now. I marvel now, looking back, how simple it all was!"); entered the Dominican Order in 1940; doctorate in Political Science at the University of Notre Dame in 1941; ordained to the priesthood 4 June 1948; post-doctoral masters in Sacred Theology, University of St. Thomas Aquinas, Rome; taught at the Aquinas Institute,

River Forest, Illinois 1957-1969; Professor of Moral Theology, Institute of Religion and Human Development, Texas Medical Center, Houston, Texas 1969-1972; Professor of Moral Theology, Aquinas Institute of Theology, Dubuque, Iowa (1969–1981) and St. Louis (1981-1988); Professor of Theology at the Pontifical John Paul II Institute for Studies in Marriage and Family, Washington, D.C. 1988-1992; Center for Health Care Ethics, St. Louis University 1997-2003; consultant in moral theology for the Committee on Doctrine and Pastoral Practice of the U.S. Conference of Catholic Bishops for several years; from 2003 worked as a consultant for the Institute of Psychological Sciences, Washington DC; many visiting fellowships and honors; a major influence on theology and ethics; developed a "poetic empiricism" which seeks to place abstract argument in the context of our concrete experiences as a way of freeing these arguments from prejudice; founded the River Forest School of natural philosophy; at the age of ninety-five he published a three volume autobiography under the title *Friar's Folly* (published in 2013 under the name of *Barefoot Journeying: The Autobiography of a Begging Friar*, but referred to below under its original title) ("In this book I have, with considerable embarrassment and only with the urging of my religious superior decided to relate the story of my own conversion to the Catholic faith as a concrete example of how poetry and science can support each other"); buried in All Saints Cemetery, River Forest, Illinois; see (selective list) *Vision and Revision: Autobiographical Notes* (1976) ("My growing curiosity about the Catholic Church had its roots in my love of beauty, my intellectual fascination with the dialectics of belief, and above all in my Marxist concern for commitment to action and to social change. It began soon after I came to college and met Catholics (there were few in Blackwell, a town that was Ku Klux Klan dominated in the 20's). Several times I attended Mass with friends, and found the liturgy, even in its South-Side Irish mode, everything that Protestant worship lacked. But I regarded the Catholic Church as a socially reactionary institution, with strongly fascist tendencies. Nevertheless I read a good deal of Catholic history and theology, and sympathized with it as an un-American minority religion, persecuted by the Protestant capitalist establishment. When the study of Aquinas showed me that in Catholicism there was an intellectually profound view of reality, I realized that here was the best competition for Marxism. In fact I gradually was convinced by my own reflections that Aquinas had provided a better case for theism, than Marx or Darwin had provided against it. During a long week in Billings Hospital recovering from an appendectomy, with time to read Dante and to think, I began to try to pray. I had no idea, however, of joining the Church that had blessed the armies of Mussolini.

I will not here relate the stages of my conversion, except to say that intellectually the following position shaped itself in my mind: (1) if Catholicism could accept the social revolutionary ideas of Marxism, leaving aside what now seemed to me Marx's inadequate metaphysics; (2) then I would still have to make a great step of *faith*, a step which would have to transcend reason but yet must be wholly compatible with it; (3) this step would seem to require some kind of sign or event (probably the conversion of the Catholic Church to the Marxist revolution) which in fact Catholicism with its reactionary stance toward the modern world could never present; (4) hence I had no obligation to be a Catholic.

At this point in my life I did not think more about it. In spite of various struggles, my life was exciting and full. I had begun to work for a PhD in political science, I had many good friends and a growing position in the Trotskyite movement, I was full of ideas for my poetry and writing every day.

Then quietly, suddenly and in solitude I was confronted with a new question: What if Christianity is God's truth? What is demanded on your part to be able to honestly reject or accept it? Is it not necessary that you at least ask the Catholic Church to speak its message to you, while you listen and can discover if you can or cannot believe? It came to me as the confrontation with Jesus Himself, the image of the Crucified Man, but in terms of listening to the message of the Roman Catholic Church, that fascist, but very old, very vital, very wise, and very beautiful organization. I saw that I must place myself as a listener. Through a close friend, a Catholic who had become a Trotskyite without being willing to let go his religion, I asked if there was some way I could 'take instructions.' He put me in touch with a Dominican priest and I began 'taking instructions' from another Dominican at their house of studies in River Forest, a Chicago suburb, where I was soon to be spending much of my life.

This was a quiet, peaceful and calm time, like opening of a beautiful vista. I simply found that I believed, in the midst of many intellectual problems and of profound disagreement with many social and political aspects of the Church, but with a fundamental conversion of my whole self and my whole way of life. From the vague bohemianism of the college student subject to an external discipline by my Marxist comrades, I now found myself committed every day to prayer, an examination of conscience, and an effort to keep the commandments of God, understood by me in a rigorist sense. Every day I got up with delight to attend 7:00 Mass at

St. Thomas the Apostle parish, a simple reversal of my communist life which had meant rising at 10 or 11 and staying up to daybreak every night"); *Thy Kingdom Come! An Overview of Catholic Social Doctrine* (1976); *Theologies of the Body: Humanist and Christian* (1985); *The Dominicans* (1991); *Spiritual Direction in the Dominican Tradition* (1995); *Thomas Aquinas: The Gifts of the Spirit* (1995); *Justice in the Church: Gender and Participation* (1996); *Living the Truth in Love: A Biblical Introduction to Moral Theology* (1996); *Choosing a Worldview and Value System: An Ecumenical Apologetics* (2000); *Ethics of Health Care: An Introductory Textbook* (2002) (with Kevin D. O'Rourke, OP); *The Arts of Learning and Communication: A Handbook of the Liberal Arts* (2005); *The Ashley Reader: Redeeming Reason* (2006); *Health Care Ethics: A Theological Analysis* (5th edition, 2006) (with Jean deBlois, CSJ and Kevin D. O'Rourke, OP); *The Way Toward Wisdom: An Interdisciplinary and Contextual Approach to Metaphysics* (2006); *Meditation on the Luminous Mysteries* (2009); *Friar's Folly, Vol. 1: Atheism Bumps Into Reality: A Conversion Story, 1915-1952* (2010) ((1) "I became intellectually convinced of God's existence through what I was reading in St. Thomas' *Summa Theologiae* about his famous Five Ways of proving God's existence… Similar arguments also led to the conviction that the human soul must survive bodily death. Thomistic philosophy proposes a proof that the material cosmos is not self-explanatory but manifests that it is the effect of a non-material First Cause, which is intelligent, and creatively free. It also leads to the conclusion that the human ability not only to perform animal activities as a body but also to think abstractly and hence to be free and 'creative' manifests that its soul is non-material. This spiritual cause transcends its bodily organs and hence is not liable to bodily death. Unlike the First Cause, however, the human soul although spiritual and immortal is created and is a caused cause dependent on the First Cause for its existence and entire activity…

What I saw was that although modern scientific explanations may be very true, they are never complete. Science can only explain events by the action of some changing entity, but such changing entities exist and act only because they are being actualized by some other changing entity. Such a chain of material causation cannot be circular nor can it be infinite but must have a first cause, since without a first cause an infinite chain of agents and recipients would be merely potential and unable to produce the final observed effect. The First Cause cannot itself be changing and material, since if it were such it would again require another cause to actualize it. Thus the causes of our changing material world always presuppose the existence and action of some unchanging and non-material cause or perhaps causes. I had (and, today I have even more), an acute sense of the vivid reality of this tangible, colorful, noisily musical world and hence of its utter changing temporality, so real, yet so unnecessary. Unfortunately today Christian writers largely depend on the 'Design Argument' to refute atheism. This is a combination of Aquinas' Fourth and Fifth Ways which are valid, but which Aquinas points out are less evident than the First Way and presuppose it. Moreover they defend it not on the basis of simple and evident facts of experience but on advanced modern hypotheses that are open to dispute. Instead the First Way depends only on the fact of motion which if denied destroys the whole of natural science!

Aquinas also notes that there are only two serious arguments for atheism: that the world is self-explanatory and that a good God could not permit the evils of this world. The first of these arguments today takes the form of saying that science can give such good explanations of the world, that the old recourse to gods or a God is unnecessary. But...the kind of explanations that science gives, although true and useful, stop at causes which are still only caused causes, and thus in no way contradict Aquinas' proofs. The only way to escape these proofs is that taken by Hume, namely to deny causality all together and this dead-ends first in positivism and finally in absolute skepticism. Kant thought he found the way out of this dead-end by considering the principle of causality to be a feature of our human thinking projected on the data of the senses, but this is just a more subtle form of skepticism. As for Kant's claim that the classic proofs beg the question because they suppose the definition of God as the most being possible, which is what we are trying to prove, this is a confusion between a merely nominal definition of God and a real one. While the proofs make use of a nominal definition of 'God' this does not occur in the premises of the argument but in the conclusion to identify the First Cause that has been demonstrated to be what we ordinarily mean by the term 'God.'

The other argument against God's existence from the evil in the world depends on the analogy taken from human experience that a good person does no evil and seeks to prevent it when possible. Thus if there were an all-powerful God, He would neither cause nor permit evil to occur. But this overlooks the fact that good persons do in fact sometimes permit evil to occur that they could prevent, namely, when they permit an evil to occasion a greater good. This happens in two cases: First, in the case of merely physical evils, because in the material order the existence of one good thing is usually contrary to the existence of other good things, good persons can sacrifice the existence of a lesser good to a greater good. Thus we can weed a garden yet weeds are vitally beautiful in their own way. Second, in the case of spiritual or moral goods, there is no such contrariety of one good to another, but because of human freedom, a good parent or good teacher can permit a student to make a mistake in order to learn to do better. As a teacher I have felt uncomfortable about that, yet knew it was best for the student, and hence for me too. Thus there is no contradiction in an absolutely good God causing physical evils or permitting (not causing) spiritual evil, i.e. sin, for a greater good. Of course we do not always know what this greater good is to be, as we do not know how a great drama will play out, but our ignorance is no contradiction to the wisdom and goodness of God who is a greater dramatist than Shakespeare. Would we like to be players in a game without excitement?..." (2) "[M]y life, just, it seemed, getting under way, was somehow nothing but wind, in Aristotelian terms 'All accidents and no substance.' Then everything changed. I was born again and life finally and really began. In 1942, sitting in church in the presence of Jesus in the Tabernacle to thank him for my conversion, I decided to record the crucial event as I then remembered it.

'While preparing for the fourth anniversary of my conversion, in order to put it down before memory and gratitude grow weaker, the greatest grace I ever received from the Precious Blood through the intercession of the Blessed Virgin, I want to write as well as I can exactly what I remember without adding or interpreting. It happened in the afternoon - I imagine close to 3 o'clock or maybe a little afterwards. I was alone in the apartment which I shared with my two friends. I believe I was reading or sorting papers and my mind was wandering over a number of topics. I think I was in a good mood as I had been most of that rather self-satisfied year. As my mind wandered on it came quite accidentally it seemed to a topic about which I had thought little recently, namely the Catholic Church. I had come to the conclusion which I had frequently expressed some months before that while the system of Catholicism was self-consistent it could neither be proved nor disproved on natural grounds, that the only convincing evidence for it would be historical and those [data] in fact on which it depended were involved in endless probabilities, and that God would not expect anyone to stand or fall on such uncertainties. Therefore the Catholic Faith must be illusory. Because I believed in God I sometimes prayed even asking for light but without any moral movement of the will. I knew that theoretically one should prepare oneself morally for Faith but I seemed content enough with my life in spite of certain strong revulsions and problems which I had suffered the year previously. All the features of struggle, however, were in abeyance and had not been occupying me much. I had been writing poems nightly during this period and they show my emotional occupations to have been largely with desiring some mystical participation in the Revolution, considerably pondering over the paradoxes between the grand undertaking at which the Revolution aimed and its rather miserable beginnings, and a general tendency to find emotional uplift in the sort of poetry written when very tired which plays on the mystery of the present. As I remember the sequence of ideas which passed through my mind at this moment it was somewhat as follows. Here you have thought how logical Catholicism is for a long time, but that there never could be anything which would make one sure of it and since it is all of [a] piece it either is to be all held as perfectly certain or not at all. But if it were true and knowable what could make me certain of it? A miracle. Yes, if one experienced a miracle personally one could be certain, at least if it were also something internal, that is a miracle in one's own being. Do you expect a vision or some great external experience especially for you? Then I was overwhelmed (I must say overwhelmed because as I recall it was here my emotions were aroused) with the thought "What right have you to expect any such thing? God who is perfect and infinitely above man, above you, is not in anyway obligated to reveal supernatural truths to you. If the Catholic Church is true He may in justice and power never allow you to know it." When I thought this I was overcome not with fear, as I remember, but with a very intense feeling of humiliation and nothingness. Now during this time I had in my imagination in the ordinary way a distinct impression of the Sacred Wound in the side of Our Blessed Lord. When this came to my mind I cannot remember whether before, during, or after these thoughts, since, like imaginations do, it remained in conscience more or less independent of my real thinking. I believe, however, that it was this imagination which perhaps set me off on my train of thoughts. Perhaps it was something in my reading or day dreaming which led to it. I had previously felt some strong attraction to the idea of Jesus having been thrust through the heart and knew something of its theological significance. The image was very vivid and the contrast of the white flesh and wound impressed me. In any case the presence of this image seemed to me as it were the motive or the center of the deep humiliation which I felt. Intellectually I felt completely abased or subjected by the thought of my helplessness. Emotionally I clung as it were to the wound. Whether I felt sorrow for having caused it was not clear to me, but it made me feel deeply contrite and abased. As soon as I made the judgment, "You can do nothing for yourself, but God can help you if He will. You are foolish to expect a miracle," possessed by this feeling I resolved to do whatever He wanted me to do, and it was plain to me that it would be honest and sensible to begin instructions and see if the Church itself could solve my difficulties, I must give her the chance to convince me. While saying this to myself I remember I still sat where I was on the low divan and that my emotions brought tears to my eyes. It seemed to me as if something amazing was happening to me and I was doing nothing but submit. Then the thought occurred to me, "Perhaps here while you rejected a demand for a miracle God has given you a vision." I immediately analyzed the mental impression I had to see if it was something extraordinary, but it was certain the image was only entirely in the imagination and in itself no wise different than ordinary rather vivid stray pictures often had in day dreaming. I remember resolving as it were with a sort of effort never to allow myself to be fooled into believing something miraculous had occurred. I got up and walked around the apartment thinking very fast, I realized that if I delayed I might let my resolution to take instructions slip, so I resolved to go and meet my Catholic friend [Leo] and ask him to arrange for them [the instructions] immediately. I was very clearheaded and the blowing snow about me as I walked to see him was impressed vividly on my memory. I kept saying, "Remember this is a great moment in your life"...On my way I kept saying, "How shall I tell him [Leo]? I mustn't say, `I have made up mind to' [take instructions] or `I have decided'; because that might offend God by pride. I must say, `Something has made me decide to.' I began to take instructions and although my decision had not been to believe all the Church taught, nevertheless I did and without any real difficulties'"...'

Later as I studied apologetics I came to see that the 'miracle' which Vatican I taught is accessible to all at all times is the One, Holy, Catholic, and Apostolic Church which, as I have recounted, I had well encountered by that time, in sharp contrast to Secularist and Marxist atheism, as well as my earlier Pantheism and Idealism." (3) "'The 'New Atheism' of Richard Dawkins, Daniel C. Dennett, Sam Harris, Christopher Hitchens and Victor J. Stenger, among others, confirms St. Thomas Aquinas' view that atheism, whenever it historically erupts, always presents two fundamental objections to God's existence: (1) that the universe is self-explanatory and (2) that it is filled with too many evils to have a good Creator. The first of these is the more fundamental, since the second presupposes that there is some reason to think God exists; while the first implies that theism is simply unintelligible. Yet a careful reading of these currently popular authors shows that it is this argument from evil that concretely *motivates* most atheists' absolute convictions. But why are they so blind to the classical arguments for God's existence?...

Reason, under the hard-headed guidance of Mortimer Adler [see above] and, still better, of St. Thomas Aquinas had convinced me abstractly of God's existence. And the grace of God had led me to open my mind to His further instruction. I had committed myself to him in baptism, solemn religious vows, and priestly ordination. Yet I know that my journey to union with Him had only begun. Now these many years later as I read the works of the so-called New Atheists their best arguments shatter on the rock of reality as I have experienced it. Why can't they open their minds to see: (1) the universe in continual process of motion and other changes cannot exist and continue in change unless there is an unchanging First Cause, that is intelligent, free, and thus personal, God, otherwise science and all rational thought would be impossible; (2) Am I not bound in conscience to inquire without prejudice whether God has given me signs of a trustworthy guide (and that cannot be atheism) to living in this world of which I am a part and whose condition I share and which I see is wonderful but has somehow got very mixed up? As a Christian, a Dominican, and a Catholic priest I give many thanks!"); *Friar's Folly, Vol. II: Completing Vatican II: On Science, Education, and Health, 1952-1981* (2010) (letter about the Faith written to his brother Richard during the latter's last illness: "Dear Dick, I am writing you because I feel very helpless at this time which must be very hard for you with your illness not going so well. I hope that you will not be exasperated by what I am trying to say, because I certainly do not want to add to your burdens. Yet I feel that I cannot just let you face the crisis of possible death without talking with you about what it means to both of us. Up to now I haven't said much, because I know you don't like unnecessary fuss.

I have admired the courageous way you have faced this, as Helen also did, and I hope that I will be able to do so when I have to. You have always seemed to me to be a strong person, and I always marveled how you and Helen [Dick's wife] met all your troubles in life with little complaint and much hard work. Yet I sincerely wish that at this time you could also draw some strength from a faith in a future life. You said once that you do believe in God, and so I suppose that you have some religion of your own which you don't talk about, although lately you have probably had to think even more about it. I know that you have always been turned off by 'religious' people whom you have found to be so often dishonest and untrustworthy. That very fact shows me that you have a high ideal of what religion ought to do for people (and which it often does not do, I admit), namely, make them honest and trustworthy in their dealings with others. But I want to explain to you, as honestly as I can what my own convictions are about life and death.

1. God created the world. Although science has shown that everything has come to be through evolution, there still must be a God who is the cause of evolution itself. He is a wise God and a loving God to have made this world.

2. The evil in the world, which we experience every day of our lives - the wars, the corruption, the injustices, the sicknesses, were not caused by God but by human wickedness and stupidity. God gave us free will, so that we could do either good or evil, but we have done evil and made the world a pretty miserable place. Why then hasn't the good God put an end to all this? God is like a good father who allows His children to bear the consequences of their own actions, so that we can learn from our mistakes and grow up.

3. Yet God has not just abandoned us. He is going to give us a future life beyond death, after our time of trial is over, in which He will see that the wicked are punished and the good rewarded for every least good they have done. This future life is something we cannot imagine, but in it we will be reunited with those we have loved in this life and we will at last understand all the things that puzzled us here. That this hope for a future life is not just an illusion is clear from the fact that many of the best and wisest through the ages have been convinced of it and science has never disproved it. We human beings are more than animals, because, unlike the animals, we have an intelligence and free will which make us want to live after death, and God would not have given us this inborn desire just to frustrate it.

4. In order that we might keep our hope alive in a dark world, God through the ages has sent great religious leaders who founded the different religions of the world which have kept the human race from sinking into barbarism. All of these great religions contain some truth and they have led men of every country to a better life, but only in Jesus, His Son, has God clearly manifested Himself to us. Jesus showed by His life of courage, of truthfulness, of concern and sacrifice for every human being and by his death of sacrifice, that God is in fact love, mercy, and forgiveness, as well as a God of justice. 'God so loved the world that he gave his only Son, that whoever believes in him may not die but may have eternal life' (John 3:16).

5. We know that the Biblical account of Jesus' life and teaching is not a myth, because He founded

a Church which for two thousand years has been guided by the Spirit of Jesus in preserving His memory and witnessing to its conviction that He rose from death and is still alive today with God. This Christian Church has often failed in many ways, and being made up of human beings has shown all the human weaknesses. It has been divided by internal squabbles and it has compromised with the world's evils. Nevertheless, in spite of these human failures, this Church, which is centered in the Catholic Church, has been able to outlast every human empire and survive every internal division. Today it continues all over the world (it includes one-fifth of the human race) to tell the story of Jesus to show what God is really like.

6. Jesus did *not* teach that only membersofHisChurchorganization will be saved or that the rest of the world will be damned. Rather He showed that God in His mercy will save all those who put their trust in God, as they know Him, and do the best they can in their life. The purpose of the Church is not to condemn those who are not members of the Church, but to offer comfort, hope, and strength to all who are sorry for whatever harm they may have done in their life, and who want to have a greater hope and confidence in a future life. The 'Gospel' means 'Good News' for us, not condemnation.

You see then, Dick that why I am writing you is just to let you know that my prayer for you is that you will find hope in God at this hard time in your life, and that you will be convinced that death is not the end for us. God is a loving God who never rejects anyone who puts his trust in Him. He is a God who is wise and knows how to bring out all things right in the end. I believe that what is important is not whether you are a Catholic (although it was a great joy to me that Dad and Mother became Catholics), but that in this time of sickness, you will find confidence in God (however you understand Him) to make up to you for whatever you have had to suffer in this life and to repair whatever harm you may have done in your life and which you regret (we all have failed in many ways). Prayer to God helps us to find Him and to realize that He really is there. For me the best prayer in the world is the Lord's Prayer which I learned as a child.

This is what I have often wanted to say to you, but perhaps you have already been thinking it yourself. Anyway this will let you know that I love you, even if I seldom say so, and that is why I have wanted to share with you my confidence that God will take care of you, even at this time when the future is so cloudy. I look forward to be with you and Helen and Dad and Mother when this life has turned into eternal life...Love, Wint"); *Friar's Folly, Vol. III: Keeping Vigil: The Spirituality of Aging, 1981-2010* (2010) ("The real enemy of the Church in our times is the secular humanism of the Enlightenment and…this arose as a punishment from God for the religious wars of the Reformation period"); *Meditations on the Mysteries of Light in the Rosary* (2010); *How Science Enriches Theology* (2012) (with John Deely); Richard A. Peddicord, OP (ed), *In Medio Ecclesiae; Essays in Honor of Benedict M. Ashley, OP* (2007); Benjamin Recchie, "Cloth Bound: How the Great Books Seminar Turned a Radical Poet Into a Philosopher and Priest," *The Core* (the publication of the alumni office of the University of Chicago) (also at *ordopraedicatorum.org*).

Astor, Mary (born Lucile Vasconcellos Langhanke) – actress; b. 3 May 1906, Quincy, Illinois; c. 1941; d. 25 September 1987, Woodland Hills, California; only child of her parents who were both teachers; her father Otto Langhanke was born in Berlin and came to the United States in 1891; her mother Helen de Vasconcellos was born in Illinois of Portuguese and Irish extraction; she was home-schooled, took drama lessons and appeared in amateur stage productions; family moved to Hollywood and she eventually signed a six month contract with Paramount Pictures; in minor silent movies until starring with John Barrymore in *Beau Brummel* (1924); her affairs were run by her parents until she broke free at the age of twenty-six; moved to Warner Bros and then on to Fox Film Corporation, and later MGM; in 1928 she married the director Kenneth Hawks; he was killed in an air plane crash in 1930, she suffered delayed shock over his death and had a nervous breakdown; in 1931 she married her doctor Franklin Thorpe; continued success in the sound era, notably in *Red Dust* (1932) with Clark Gable and Jean Harlow; there were allegations that she had affairs with many celebrities related in her diary, but she proclaimed most entries were forged; her husband divorced her in 1935; married Manuel del Campo ("Mike") (1913-1969), Mexican film editor, in 1936 (divorced in 1941); after the birth of her child in 1941, she took instruction in the Catholic faith and was received into the Church; returned to theater and many appearances on radio and in film during this period; best known role was as Brigid O'Shaughnessy in *The Maltese Falcon* (1941) with Humphrey Bogart; won an Oscar for Best Supporting Actress for *The Great Lie* (1941); other notable films were *Dodsworth* (1936), *The Hurricane* (1937), *The Prisoner of Zenda* (1937), *Brigham Young* (1940), *Meet Me in St. Louis* (1944), *Little Women* (1949), *Return to Peyton Place* (1961), *Hush...Hush, Sweet Charlotte* (1964); married Thomas Wheelock in 1945 (divorced 1955); developed a lengthy and major problem with alcohol; later joined Alcoholics Anonymous;

she attributed her recovery from alcoholism to Fr. Peter Ciklic, a Catholic priest and also a practicing psychologist, who encouraged her to write about her experiences as part of her therapy; acted regularly on television; appeared in 109 films in 45 years; buried in Holy Cross Cemetery, Culver City, California; see (memoirs, both of which were best sellers); *My Story: An Autobiography* (1959) ("Christ's miracles I could accept without any difficulty; I felt that if God had made the world and everything in it He could most certainly do anything He wanted with it. Nature's miracles were occurring all the time right under our noses – the fusing of two cells, and their growth into a human being – what greater miracle than this! But all these remained isolated facts for me. I could not see them as part of the pattern that led to something infinitely greater.

I was reading a biography of St. Thérèse one morning. I didn't care for it very much; it was a bit sticky and sentimental, so I was not reading with much concentration. I don't remember what the context was, but I read the words, 'Jesus Christ was God,' and something seemed suddenly to flash in my mind. I had heard this and read it many times before, but now I felt the illumination of understanding. The light seemed an actual physical brilliance that I had to close my eyes against. Things that had had no real meaning before assumed meaning. The Incarnation, the Resurrection, the Sacrifice of the Mass. I slipped to my knees and prayed"); *A Life on Film* (1971) ("There are five stages in the life of an actor: Who's Mary Astor? Get me Mary Astor. Get me a Mary Astor type. Get me a young Mary Astor. Who's Mary Astor?"); (novels) *The Incredible Charley Carewe* (1960); *The Image of Kate* (1962); *The O'Conners* (1964); *Goodbye, Darling, Be Happy* (1965); *A Place Called Saturday* (1968); *ANB*.

Atwater, Lee (born Harvey Leroy Atwater) – political consultant and strategist; b. 27 February 1951, Atlanta, Georgia; c. 1990; d. 29 March 1991 (Good Friday), Washington, D.C.; father an insurance adjustor; brought up in Aiken, South Carolina in a Methodist family; played guitar in a rock band as a teenager (as an adult released an album with B. B. King and other performers); educated at Newberry College, South Carolina, a private Lutheran college; governor of the South Carolina Student Legislature; gained MA degree in Communications from the University of South Carolina in 1977; married Sally Dunbar in 1978 (three children of the marriage); rose in the South Carolina Republican Party; managed a hard edged campaign in the 1980 Congressional elections against a Democratic nominee Tom Turnipseed; after this he went to Washington and became an aide in the Reagan administration; deputy director and political director for President Reagan's re-election campaigh in 1984; became aligned with Vice-President George H. W. Bush who chose him to manage his 1988 presidential campaign; he ran a very aggressive and successful media campaign against the Democratic nominee Michael Dukakis; after the election he was named chairman of the Republican National Committee; organized a public relations campaign against Bill Clinton, whom he viewed as a serious threat in the next election; in 1990 he contracted a very aggressive form of brain cancer and spent the rest of his life in a wheelchair; at this time he said he had converted to the Catholic faith; influenced by Fr. John Hardon, SJ; he wrote to individuals to whom he had been opposed during his political career, notably Michael Dukakis, expressing his repentance; buried at Greenlawn Cemetery, Columbia, South Carolina; see Lee Atwater and T. Brewster, "Lee Atwater's Last Campaign," *Life* magazine, February 1991, p. 67; John Joseph Brady, *Bad Boy: The Life and Politics of Lee Atwater* (1997); "The Conversion of Lee Atwater: An interview with John A. Hardon, SJ," *Culture Wars*, November 2009, p.14 (interview conducted in 1991 by James G. Bruen for *Fidelity* magazine, the predecessor to *Culture Wars*) ("Fidelity: Father Hardon, what can you tell us about Lee Atwater's conversion? Fr. Hardon: Let me talk for a few minutes on how I became involved in Lee Atwater's life and his conversion. Let me then briefly describe how I became involved in the last year of Lee Atwater's life and the glorious conversion.

There was a good friend of mine here in Washington by the name of Gary Maloney. I had Gary in class at the Notre Dame Institute. They came to know each other, and Gary was working with the Republican Party. One day Gary called me up. He asked if I could come to Washington the next day. I asked him what the emergency was. He said Lee Atwater, the head of the Republican Party, has had some seizures, blackouts, and he might go out any moment.

Gary told me he talked to Atwater, and asked him, Lee, are you afraid to die? He said, I sure am. And I suppose you're afraid, Gary told Lee, of what's going to happen to you after you die. Yes, I'm scared. So then Gary told Lee: Tell you what, there's only one way you can be sure that when you die you'll be safe in the next world. You need a Catholic priest to absolve you of all your sins. Lee said, Where do I get a Catholic priest, because I'm not a Catholic. I'll get one, said Gary. So he called me up from the Republican offices and asked if I could come in the next day. And, he said, if you can make it, the Republican Party will take care of your transportation. We'll have the tickets waiting for you.

So, whatever adjustment I had to make, I took an early flight from Metro airport in Detroit to National, and Gary Maloney was waiting for me. He took me right over to the Atwater residence. F: What happened next? Fr. H: Lee was in bed, fully conscious. Part of his body was paralyzed, but in great pain. So I introduced myself and then began the shortest instruction in the faith that I have ever given. It was, I would say, almost two full days; give or take, more than five hours each day. I found out that Lee had been of some Southern Protestant background. He thought he was baptized but it wasn't all that clear. So after we talked I asked him questions. There was no question: Lee wanted to believe everything that the Catholic Church teaches.

So the second day, in the evening, I was taken to Georgetown. I talked to the rector. I told him what I was going to do, to make sure that I was covered by Jesuit permissions. Whatever you have to do for Lee, why go ahead. So I got some water for baptismal water, brought the Blessed Sacrament, and also the oils. I gave him conditional baptism because he may have been, but I'm not sure he was baptized validly.

Then, well, every minute that I was in Lee's room, there was someone from the Republican Party. So Lee was never left alone with me. So when time to hear confession arrived, I said, 'Look, you've got to leave.' They weren't ready to leave. I said, 'Look, I'm going to hear his confession. Strictly private.' So they left. I heard his confession and explained that if the baptism was valid - that is if he had never been baptized validly before - then the baptism had done it. I questioned Lee, and there was no doubt: he was sure that if he was now validly baptized that his sins are removed, and that if he was not validly baptized, then I would of course hear his confession. I told Lee, 'Lee, in the event that you have been validly baptized [before], you have got some repairing to do.' So I spent all the time that was necessary.

And I brought the pyx with me with the Blessed Sacrament, and held up the host and said, 'Lee, do you believe this is Jesus Christ, son of Mary, in the flesh?' And he looked at me and said, 'Do you believe it?' 'I sure do.' 'So do I.' Then I gave him his first communion, anointed him, and explained that if the first baptism as a child was valid, then of course confession and anointing – anointing will remove even the punishment due to sin. So, then, the third day… F: Several times before Mr. Atwater's death, the newspapers referred to his accepting Christ. They used words that led the reader to think that he had an evangelical Protestant conversion. Was that involved? Fr. H: No. It wasn't. F: It wasn't two steps? Fr. H: No. F: The newspapers also said that after he accepted Christ, he went through a period of making telephone calls to people either apologizing for what he did in the past or reconciling himself to people he'd made enemies with. Did you have any knowledge about that?

Fr. H: No. I did not touch that part of his life. But I would say this: It would be totally in character from what I understand Lee had been before and what I knew of Lee Atwater…

F: Were you familiar with Lee Atwater's public *personae* before you met him? The big tent theory, the hardball politician, that type of thing?

Fr. H: I had heard there was a Lee Atwater, but not much else. But during the year, I heard a lot. He became a totally different person.

Each time that I came to Washington, Lee just put out his hands, and I could embrace him. And if you know much about Lee Atwater, he was not the naturally affable type. He was a tough hombre. But Lee talked a good deal, and Lee changed my life in the sense that I saw a marvel, a work of grace.

F: Did Mr. Atwater develop a prayer life?

Fr. H: The first time that we met at his residence when I received him into the Church, he told me that a Catholic nurse had been on duty in the hospital where he was taken after his first seizures. She said, Mr. Atwater, this is a Miraculous Medal. He knew nothing about miraculous medals. Would you mind if I pin it on you? He said, sure. And he told me: 'Father, I will never take this medal off my clothing until I die.' I'm not sure he was buried with the medal; I know he would have wanted to be buried with the medal…

I enrolled Lee Atwater in the Confraternity [of the Miraculous Medal]. And I can say honestly, for the year from when I received him into the Church until our last visit before he died, Lee told me more than once, 'Father, every conscious moment, I am praying.'

At the first stage, he was hospitalized in Washington, then he was sent up to New York for brain surgery. They removed whatever malignancy there was on his brain. He told me when he got back to Washington that the surgery lasted about four hours and for whatever reason, they either gave him no anesthetic or just minimal anesthesia; they couldn't because of the brain. Couldn't do it. So they asked him if he wanted to have the surgery in effect without anesthesia. He said, 'Father, I never thought a human being could suffer that much, but I prayed every moment of those four hours'…

F: What condition was Mr. Atwater in during your later visits?

Fr. H: He needed all the strength that he could get – he couldn't do much talking – just to hear. He could hear, and you knew that he was listening. Talk about Our Lord and the God of mercy. Lee told me in the early stages when there was still some prospect of his recovery, if I recover, he said, I'm getting out of politics; I'll spend the rest of my life working for others. His great concern was to be of service to others. In our conversations uniformly we never talked politics, never. It was always about God and His mercy, His goodness, His mysterious providence.

I can say that when I came to know Lee Atwater, he was as resigned as any person that I've dealt with in forty-four years of priesthood to accepting God's providence in his life...

He was as cold as a piece of steel in our conversation, and he asked very explicit questions. I did go through the Creed, the authenticity of Christ's teaching, the historicity of the gospels. It wasn't just whether you accept Christ as your savior"); *ANB*.

Avery, Martha Gallison Moore (born Martha Moore) – writer and Catholic campaigner; b. 6 April 1851, Steuben, Maine; c. 1 May 1904 (her daughter Katherine converted in 1900 and later became a nun, Sr. St. Mary Martha, CND); d. 8 August 1929; one of a family of nine children; her mother died when she was thirteen and she went to live with her grandfather, Samuel Moore, who was a member of the Maine Senate (a "Jeffersonian Democrat") and a leading Mason; joined the Unitarian Church; in 1880 married another member of that church, Millard Avery (d. 1890) (one child of the marriage), and moved to Boston; she became interested in Marxian Socialism and in 1891 joined the Socialist Labor Party of Boston, and worked in Socialist politics for several years; in 1896 she founded the Karl Marx Class (later renamed the Boston School of Political Economy), and taught classes on the works of Marx to students and radical trade unionists; she became acquainted with David Goldstein (see below); she stayed with socialist friends whose daughters had been educated in a convent school and was impressed by the daughters' deportment; she sent her own daughter to a Catholic convent school in Canada; the daughter converted a few months later and sent her mother much literature on the Catholic faith; finally she converted; she and David Goldstein both became disenchanted with the irreligious and immoral implications of a socialist society; they withdrew from the new American Socialist Party and became very active anti-socialists, jointly publishing a book, *Socialism: The Nation of Fatherless Children* (attacked socialism for its affront to marriage and the family, arguing that socialism would inevitably lead to every child being an orphan under the control of the state); became increasingly interested in Catholicism; continued to work for social reform, but now based on the Church's teaching, in particular Pope Leo XIII's encyclical *Rerum Novarum*; supported trade unions and collective bargaining; president of the Common Cause Society, a

Catholic labor organization, from 1922 until her death; strongly opposed women's suffrage, arguing that it served to destroy family coherence; in 1916, with David Goldstein, she founded the Catholic Truth Guild, which became the largest lay apostolate in the United States, and for which she worked tirelessly until her death, speaking to thousands of people and distributing many books and pamphlets ("If the rank and file of Catholics knew their religion they could convert all thinking people"); the inscription on her gravestone reads, "Martha Moore Avery, Convert from Marx to Christ"; see *Woman: Her Quality, Her Environment, Her Possibility* (1901); *Socialism: The Nation of Fatherless Children* (1903; new edition 1909) (with David Goldstein) ("How often is the statement made, by those new converts whose ardor outstrips their knowledge, that socialism is identical with Christianity. In 'green' socialist papers and in 'literature for beginners,' one may frequently read the statement that 'the ethics of Christianity and socialism are identical,' when an investigation will conclusively prove that the ethic of socialism is as directly opposite to the ethics of Christianity as the positive is from the negative pole of human activity"); *The Longest Way Home to Rome* (1910) (unpublished autobiography); *Bolshevism: Its Cure* (1919) (with David Goldstein); *Campaigning for Christ* (1924) (with David Goldstein); D. Owen Carrigan, "Martha Moore Avery: The Career of a Crusader," PhD dissertation, University of Maine, Orono (1966); Owen Carrigan, "A Forgotten Yankee Marxist," *New England Quarterly*, March 1969, p.23; D. Owen Carrigan, "Martha Moore Avery: Crusader for Social Justice," *Catholic Historical Review*, April 1968, p.17 ("Mrs. Avery charged that the socialists' advocacy of economic equality for women was an example of their opposition to the traditional concept of the home in a Christian society. She maintained that equality for women would remove all distinction between the sexes. She argued that this would ultimately destroy the dignity of the wife and radically alter the traditional family relationship. She also stressed the importance of private property as a bulwark to the home and society. She charged that the socialists' desire to abolish private property was another example of how their program would undermine the family and ultimately the state…

Devotion to the Church also motivated much of Mrs. Avery's defense of the traditional role of women in society and her fight against the feminist movement. She maintained that the basic issue in the whole question of women's rights was: 'Shall the family maintain its place as the unit of civil society, or shall the state establish the individual as its unit without regard to sex.' She maintained that there was a natural order in society whereby the home and social concerns were the preserve of women, while commerce and politics were the male spheres. If society tampered with this arrangement chaos would result. The demand for equal rights she characterized as a 'rebellious attempt to undo God's plan...'

These beliefs led Mrs. Avery to carry on a vociferous campaign against woman suffrage. She was also motivated in part by a conviction that the socialists played a major role in the genesis of the woman suffrage movement. According to her the socialists hoped that if women were given the vote they could be influenced to use it in support of socialist causes, especially the collective ownership of capital. Mrs. Avery was convinced that private property was the foundation of the monogamous family and if the state nationalized all property the traditional Christian family would break up...

Mrs. Avery's concept of Catholic education was completely orthodox. She maintained that the secular universities were not qualified to protect and transmit traditional American values because 'their philosophy is not quite sure of anything.' For her the Catholic college, with its fixed philosophy, authority, and discipline, was the only real bulwark of American values...

Of the many interests that Mrs. Avery pursued as a Catholic a desire to spread the teachings of the Church in as direct and effective a manner as possible ultimately took precedence over all else...

The intent behind the Guild was twofold. Mrs. Avery wanted to spread the teachings of the Catholic Church far and wide. She hoped in this way not only to bring converts into the Church but to create a more favorable public opinion as well. At the same time she hoped that the adoption of these teachings, particularly the Church's principles of social justice, would hasten the coming of social reform, for which she and other Catholics like John Ryan and Peter Dietz had been striving for some time"); Debra Campbell, "'I Can't Imagine Our Lady on an Outdoor Platform': Women in the Catholic Street Propaganda Movement," *U.S. Catholic Historian*, Spring/Summer 1983, p.103; Eleonore Villarrubia, "David Goldstein and Martha Moore Avery: From Socialists to 'Campaigners for Christ,'" *catholicism.org*, 8 June 2011; Patrick Allitt, *Catholic Converts: British and American Intellectuals Turn to Rome* (1997), pp.144-147 ("Starting in 1917, Goldstein and Avery also collaborated in the Catholic Truth Guild, driving a modified Ford Model T painted in the papal colors, yellow and white, preaching prolabor Catholicism on street corners in working-class districts and speaking against suffrage for women as a latently socialist assault on the family"); her papers (and the personal papers of her daughter) are in the Martha Moore Avery and Family Collection, Beaton Institute, College of Cape Breton, Sydney, Nova Scotia; *ANB*.

Baker, Francis Asbury, CSP – priest; b. 30 March 1820, Baltimore, Maryland; c. April 1853 (received by Fr. Augustine Francis Hewit (see below) in the chapel of the orphan asylum of the Sisters of Charity, Baltimore); d. 4 April 1865; son of Dr. Samuel Baker, a Baltimore doctor and professor of medicine; his parents, who died when he was young, were Methodists, but their surviving children joined the Episcopal Church; graduated from Princeton University in 1839; ordained Episcopalian minister in 1846; engaging personality, very devout, and gifted preacher; ardent admirer of the Tractarians and great reader of Pusey and Newman; friend of Dwight Edward Lyman (see below), who was at that time also an Episcopal minister; during one of their discussions, he made the following statement to Lyman: "The Church that is good enough for Manning is good enough for me"; when Manning converted, Lyman reminded him of this statement; his conversion caused a sensation in Baltimore; entered the Redemptorist Order; ordained to the priesthood on 21 September 1856 in the cathedral of Baltimore; gave many missions with his four companions, Fathers Deshon, Hecker, Hewit and Walworth (see below and, in particular, the entry for Fr. Hecker); one of the original Paulist fathers; established a tradition of rubrical exactitude and ceremonial splendor in the liturgy; died suddenly from typhoid pneumonia contracted in ministering to the sick; an excellent missioner and an eloquent preacher; buried at Old St. Patrick's Cathedral, New York; see *The Reason and Method of Doing Penance - The Miracle of Pardon - The Power of the Holy Ghost, as Exemplified in Good Christians* (1867) (sermons); Rev. A. F. Hewit, *Sermons of the Rev. Francis A. Baker. With a Memoir of His Life* (1866); Clarence Alphonsus Walworth, *The Oxford Movement in the U.S.* (1895); Katherine Burton, *In No Strange Land: Some American Catholic Converts* (1942), p.77; *Catholic Encyclopedia* ("He brought to his work the zeal of an apostle, a matured and persuasive eloquence, and the attraction of a character at once magnetic and saintly. Nor are these the words of mere eulogy. The recollections of the generation which listened to him, the judgment of competent critics, the numerous conversions, the abiding impressions he effected, the evidences which his printed sermons display of oratorical gifts - all entitle Father Baker to a high place among Catholic preachers").

Baker, Gladys Leslie (married name Patrick) – journalist; b. 1910, Jacksonville, Florida; c. 1 April 1950 (received by Mgr. Fulton Sheen); d. 1991; born into a wealthy family; received a classical education from tutors and at private schools; starred in a film at the age of seventeen, but turned down a Hollywood contract and took up journalism; started on *The Jacksonville Journal*; had a career in international journalism, interviewing many celebrities; moved to the *Birmingham News-Age-Herald*, where she was made their special New York correspondent; later became foreign correspondent for the North American Newspaper Alliance; ordered back home in 1941 because of the War; married Roy Leonard Patrick, director on the boards of the Federal Reserve Bank and the Boston and Maine Railroad; in 1946 she became suddenly and mysteriously ill with what was diagnosed as an incurable hypo-proteinemia and was given five years to live; since childhood she had sensed that 'the Real World held eternal values,' but now began a more earnest search for truth; her autobiography, *I Had to Know*, describes this quest and ends with a description of her instruction in Catholicism by Mgr. Fulton Sheen; see *I Had to Know* (1951); *The Finger of God is Here (History of the Apparitions of Fatima)* (1961); Matthew Hoehn, OSB (ed), *Catholic Authors* (1952).

Baldwin, Marshall Whithed – historian and educator; b. 1903, New Haven, Connecticut; c. 29 November 1930 (his mother, Gracia, was received on 4 June 1931; his father was received on 15 April 1934); d. 1975; son of Charles Sears Baldwin (1867-1935), Professor of English Literature at Yale University; brought up in a devout Anglo-Catholic family; brother a High Anglican clergyman; educated at Columbia University and the Graduate School at Princeton University, where he received his PhD in History; influenced by contact with Professor Dino Bigongiari, a great Dante scholar, and by the historian Professor Carlton J. H. Hayes (see below); conversion also influenced by travel in 1929 in Belgium, Germany and France where he was "impressed by the all-pervasiveness of the Church and the geographical and national limitations of Anglicanism"; member of the History Departments at Yale, Rutgers, Notre Dame and New York University; co-president of the American Catholic Historical Association in 1941; see *Raymond III of Tripoli and the Fall of Jerusalem (1140-1187)* (1936); *The Medieval Papacy in Action* (1940); C. J. H. Hayes and M. W. Baldwin, *History of Europe, Vol. 1, To 1648* (1949); *The Medieval Church* (1953); "Our Pilgrimage to Rome," in John A. O'Brien, *The Road to Damascus, Vol. IV: Roads to Rome* (1955), p.81 ("I had always been interested in the Church's history, but like most Anglicans I thought of it as my Church, at least until the sixteenth century. As my historical studies progressed, I found myself following with greater attention the post-Reformation story. Most important, I was increasingly troubled by the English break with Rome.

The thesis to which I had always subscribed, that the Anglican Church had preserved the essentials of Catholicism and therefore remained a branch of the Catholic Church now seemed questionable. I was dismayed to discover that intelligent Protestants could readily grasp the full Catholic position, but were unable to understand the High Anglican view. As a Methodist minister once remarked to me many years later, 'If I wanted to be a Catholic, I certainly wouldn't stop with Henry VIII'"); "The Latin States Under Baldwin III and Amalric I, 1143-1174," in Marshall W. Baldwin (ed), *A History of the Crusades, Vol. I, The First Hundred Years* (1969-1989), p.528; "The Decline and Fall of Jerusalem, 1174-1189" in Marshall W. Baldwin (ed), *A History of the Crusades, Vol. I, The First Hundred Years* (1969-1989), p.590.

Bandelier, Adolph Francis Alphonse – archaeologist and historian; b. 6 August 1840, Bern, Switzerland; c. 1881; d. 18 March 1914, Mexico; his father, a jurist and banker, moved to Brazil, then on to the United States, where his wife and son joined him in Illinois; educated at home; married Josephine Huegy (d. 1892) in 1861 (no children of the marriage); studied the history and native populations of Spanish America and became the leading authority in his field; much research in Mexico, where he became a Catholic; employed on several expeditions (great fieldworker); in 1893 he married Fanny Ritter, who helped him greatly in his work; close friend of Fr. Anton Docher (1852-1928), "The Padre of Isleta," Franciscan missionary and defender of the Indians; also of Charles Fletcher Lummis (1859-1928), the journalist and Indian activist; lectured at Columbia University; contributed many articles to the *Catholic Encyclopedia*; fine watercolorist; buried in Mexico, but his remains were returned to Santa Fe in 1977; see *History of the Colonization and Missions of Sonora, Chihuahua, New Mexico, and Arizona to the Year 1700* (1886); *The Delight Makers* (1890) (novel); *The Gilded Man (El Dorado) and other Pictures of the Spanish Occupancy of America* (1893); *Aboriginal Myths and Traditions Concerning the Island of Titicaca, Bolivia.* (1904); *The Islands of Titicaca and Koati* (1910); Edgar A. Goad, *A Study of the Life of Adolph Francis Alphonse Bandelier, with an Appraisal of His Contributions to American Anthropology and Related Sciences* (PhD dissertation, University of

Southern California, 1939); *ANB*.

Barber, Daniel – lay Catholic; b. 2 October 1756, Simsbury, Connecticut; c. 1819, (received in Washington; his wife, Chloe, *née* Case (d. 1825) converted in 1818, plus several of her relatives; his son, Virgil Horace (see below), and his wife, Jerusha (see below) converted in 1817; their other children also converted; there were twenty-two converts in all among the Barber family and relatives; of these, thirteen entered the religious life of the Church); d. 1834, the house of the Society of Jesus, Saint Inigoes, Maryland; his family were originally Calvinists who fled from England in 1635 and settled in Massachusetts; his father and mother were Congregational Dissenters of strict Puritanic rule; he was brought up under that rule and remained in it for twenty-seven years; then became an Episcopalian; served as a soldier in the continental army; in 1785 he was ordained a minister in the Episcopalian Church; after a long period of ministry he began to doubt his own Anglican orders; in 1807, at the instance of her parents, he baptized Frances ("Fanny") Allen (see above), who subsequently became a convert and a nun (a subsequent visit by him to her convent greatly impressed him); in 1818 he gave up his place as minister of the Episcopalian parish of Claremont; see *Catholic Worship and Piety Explained and Recommended in Sundry Letters to a Very Dear Friend and Others* (1821); *History of My Own Times* (1827); Louis De Goesbriand, *Catholic Memoirs of Vermont and New Hampshire* (1886); Br. James Mary, MICM, "The Barber Family," *catholicism.org*, 1 August 2005; *Catholic Encyclopedia* (under the entry for "The Barber Family") ("He exercised the duties of the ministry for thirty years in Claremont, New Hampshire without doubt concerning the soundness of his ordination, when one day the chance reading of a Catholic book opened up for him the whole issue of the validity of Anglican orders, by impugning Parker's consecration. This doubt was further increased by a visit for conference to the famous Bishop Cheverus, then a priest in Boston, and the inability of his Episcopalian associates to offer any satisfactory refutation of the arguments advanced by the Catholic priest. Father Cheverus [who later, as Bishop Cheverus ordained Virgil Barber to the priesthood] also gave him a number of Catholic books, which he and the other members of his family read eagerly...

[His son] Virgil returned to Claremont from New York, taking with him Father Charles French, a Dominican [and fellow convert] who was officiating there at St. Peter's church. The priest remained a week in Daniel Barber's house preaching and saying Mass, with the result that he had seven converts, including Mrs. Daniel Barber and her children, Mrs. Noah Tyler, who was Daniel Barber's sister, and her eldest daughter Rosetta. Mrs. Tyler was the mother of William Tyler, first Bishop of Hartford, Connecticut [see below]. Her husband and six other children were subsequently converted, and four of the daughters became Sisters of Charity").

Barber, Jerusha (*née* Booth) (name in religion Sr. Mary Augustine) – nun; b. 20 July 1789, New Town, Connecticut; c. 1816 (received in New York with her husband and their five children); d. 1 January 1860, Mobile, Alabama; wife of Virgil Horace Barber (see below); after their conversion both she and her husband determined to enter religious life, he the Society of Jesus, and she the Visitation Order (for further details see the entry for Virgil Barber below); she was admitted into the Visitation convent in 1817; her novitiate was very difficult on account of her affection for her husband and the burden to this poor community of her children;.served in several convents of the Order; all of her children entered the religious life; see Louis De Goesbriand, *Catholic Memoirs of Vermont and New Hampshire* (1886); *Catholic Encyclopedia* (under the entry for "The Barber Family") ("She had the happiness of seeing all her children embrace a religious life. Mary, the eldest, entered the Ursuline convent, Mt. Benedict, near Charlestown, Massachusetts, as Sister Mary Benedicta, 15 August 1826, and died in the convent of the order in Quebec, 9 May 1844. Abigail, Susan, and Josephine also became Ursulines. The first died in Quebec, 8 December 1879, and Susan in the convent at Three Rivers, Canada, 24 January 1837. Samuel, the son, graduated at Georgetown College in 1831 and immediately entered the Society of Jesus. After his novitiate he was sent to Rome, where he was ordained. He returned to Georgetown in 1840, and died, aged fifty years, at St. Thomas's Manor, Maryland, 23 February 1864").

Barber, Virgil Horace, SJ – priest and educator; b. 9 May 1782, Simsbury, Connecticut; c. 1816 (received in New York with his wife Jerusha (see above) and their five children Mary (1810-1844), Abigail (1811-1879), Susan (1813-1837), Samuel (1814-1864), and Josephine (b. 1816)); d. 27 March 1847, Georgetown, D.C.; son of Daniel Barber (see above); educated at Dartmouth College; became an Episcopalian minister at Fairfield, near New York; conversion especially influenced by Benedict J. Fenwick, SJ, vicar-general of the Catholic diocese and by Milner's *End of Controversy*; resigned his ministry and was received into the Catholic Church; both he and his wife determined to enter the religious life, he the Society of Jesus, and she the Visitation Order;

he and his son Samuel went to the college of the Jesuit Fathers at Georgetown, D.C.; his wife and the three oldest girls were received into the Visitation convent; the youngest child, Josephine, then ten months old, was taken care of by the mother of Fr. Benedict Fenwick, later the second Bishop of Boston, who had received them into the Church; nearly three years after their separation, 23 February 1820, he and his wife met in the chapel of Georgetown convent and made their vows in religion (their five children were present); all of their children entered the religious life (for further details see the entry for Jerusha Barber above); ordained to the priesthood on 3 December 1822; he was sent to Clarement where he built a church and established the first Catholic boys' school in New England; spent some time on the mission to the Penobscot Indian tribes of Maine and Vermont; he was then recalled as an instructor to Georgetown, where he spent the rest of his life; see Louis De Goesbriand (ed), *Catholic Memoirs of Vermont and New Hampshire* (1886); Hudson Mitchell, "Virgil Horace Barber," *Woodstock Letters* (1950), p.297; Br. James Mary, MICM, "The Barber Family," *catholicism.org*, 1 August 2005 ("It was at this point in Virgil's life that we see Divine Providence manifested preeminently through the prayers of Saint Francis Xavier. He recalls his introduction to the Apostle of the Indies: 'I had in my house a good Catholic Irish servant girl whom I often noticed using a certain prayer book. I was then a Protestant minister, but I was *sincere*. A happy curiosity which was undoubtedly an effect of Divine grace made me open and examine the little book which proved to be a Novena to Saint Francis Xavier. I was very much impressed with the brief life of the Saint which was contained therein, and thought I must try to get a complete life of that wonderful missionary. I acted upon this idea, and after carefully reading that life so remarkable, I had to say to myself: 'Behold a man who lived at the very time of the Reformation, one therefore who was so close to our own time that his existence cannot be myth.' This life being so remarkable must have excited the attention of the learned as soon as it came out in print, and was scattered everywhere. No one has contradicted it, and this would surely have been done, had the history of Saint Francis Xavier been untrue. It has, moreover, all the marks of authenticity and veracity which can be desired. How could a religion that formed such men be a mere human institution?'

Although Virgil was admittedly 'sincere' as a Protestant, he knew his sincerity was only a predisposition and not a means of salvation. Saint Francis Xavier had encountered many 'sincere' Buddhist and Hindu. But without abandoning their error and converting to the one true Faith, salvation could not be theirs" [fittingly it was on the feast of St. Francis Xavier in 1822 that Virgil Barber was ordained to the priesthood]); *Catholic Encyclopedia* (under the entry for "The Barber Family"); *ANB*.

Barnes, Binnie (born Gertrude Maude Barnes) – actress; b. 25 May 1903, Islington, London, England; c. 1940; d. 27 July 1998, Beverly Hills, California; Jewish father and Italian mother; raised Jewish; worked at first in several jobs ("as a milkmaid, an asylum nurse, a chorus girl, a dance hostess, and a cabaret partner" (*ANB*)); then went into vaudeville and later in cabaret and revue; West End debut in 1928; film career from 1923 to 1973, first in England, then (from 1934) in Hollywood; most famous film was *The Private Life of Henry VIII* (1933), starring Charles Laughton, where she played Catherine Howard; mainly in historical dramas; converted on her marriage to football star and film producer Mike Frankovich (1908-1992) (three adopted children in a marriage that lasted until his death); became an American citizen; two of her three children became film producers; much work for charities; buried in Forest Lawn Memorial Park Cemetery, Glendale, Los Angeles; see *ANB*.

Bayley, James Roosevelt – bishop; b. 23 August 1814, Rye, Westchester County, New York; c. 28 April 1842 (received in the room of St. Ignatius Loyola in Rome by Father Esmond, SJ); d. 3 October 1877, Newark, New Jersey; his family came from Dutch and English non-Catholic ancestors; his grandfather was Dr. Richard Bayley, Professor of Anatomy in Columbia College, New York; his aunt was St. Elizabeth Ann Seton (see below), foundress of the Sisters of Charity in the United States; distant cousin of Theodore Roosevelt and Franklin D. Roosevelt; educated at Amherst College; entered Trinity College, Hartford, Connecticut to prepare for the Episcopalian ministry; graduated in 1835 and received orders; influenced by Fr. John McCloskey, who would later become Archbishop of New York and the first American cardinal, and became increasingly drawn to Catholicism; resigned his ministry in 1841 and went to Rome where he was baptized and received into the Catholic Church; entered the seminary of St. Sulpice in Paris, but completed his studies at St. John's College, Fordham; ordained to the priesthood in New York on 2 March 1844; professor and later acting president of the seminary at Fordham; for several years private secretary to Bishop John J. Hughes of New York; first Bishop of Newark 1853-1872; developed the diocese greatly, aiming to get every Catholic child in the state in a Catholic school; founder of Seton Hall University; founded the North American College in Rome; in 1872 became eighth Archbishop of

Baltimore; buried beside his aunt, St. Elizabeth Ann Seton, at the National Shrine of her, Emmitsburg, Frederick County, Maryland; see *A Brief Sketch of the Early History of the Catholic Church on the Island of New York* (1853); *Memoirs of Simon Gabriel Bruté, First Bishop of Vincennes* (1855); Flynn, *The Catholic Church in New Jersey* (1860); M. H. Yeager, *Life of James Roosevelt Bayley, First Bishop of Newark and Eighth Archbishop of Baltimore 1814-1877* (1947); *Catholic Encyclopedia* ("He was a noble model of a Christian bishop. He seemed animated with the spirit of St. Francis de Sales, full of zeal in the episcopal office and of kindness and charity to all mankind"); *ANB*.

Beach, Charles Fisk, Jr. – lawyer; b. 4 February 1854, Paris, Kentucky; c. between 1903 and 1908 (received in the Church of the Carmelites, rue de Vaugirard, Paris); d. 1934; son of the Rev. Charles Fisk (1827-1908), a Presbyterian clergyman, and Harriette Adelia Lockwood Beach; brought up in Calvinism "of the strictest and extremist sort"; educated at Columbia University and the University of Paris; called to the bar in New York in 1881 and practiced law there until 1895; always had the germ of Catholicism in his mind during this time; worked as an American consul 1896-1900; then settled in Paris; influenced in his conversion by Fr. Gordon of the London Oratory, a confrere of Newman in Oxford; came to see the "religious anarchy" of Protestantism as compared with the certitude of Catholicism; his conversion was confirmed by reading Newman's *Development of Christian Doctrine* and *Apologia Pro Vita Sua*, and also by Cardinal Gibbons *Faith of Our Fathers*; author of several legal textbooks and many articles; see *A Practical Treatise on The Law of Receivers* (1887); *Manual of The Law of Wills* (1888); *Modern Law of Railways* (1890); *A Treatise on The Law of Private Corporations* (1891); *Commentaries on Modern Equity Jurisprudence* (1892); *A Treatise on The Law of Contributory Negligence* (1892); *Commentaries on The Law of Public Corporations* (1893); *Modern Equity Practice* (1894); *Commentaries on The Law of Injunctions* (1895); *Commentaries on The Law of Insurance* (1895); *Treatise on The Modern Law of Contracts* (1896); essay in Georgina Pell Curtis (ed), *Some Roads to Rome in America* (1909), p.15 ("Protestantism had never appealed to me either intellectually or spiritually, and when I came to consider it as a religious system as critically as I could, that which most impressed me with it in its ensemble was that it is in its essence religious anarchy. I saw that the Protestantism of Luther and Calvin had, with us, quickly become the Protestantism of the English Puritans and the English State Church; that that soon developed into the newer

Protestantism of Wesley and the Baptists; and that that of Wesley and the Baptists soon grew into that of Brigham Young and of Alexander Campbell and of scores of other nondescript sects, and in my own time had further degenerated into that of Dowie and of Mrs. Eddy, and of the Higher Life and of what not, ad infinitum and ad nauseam. A system of religion in which I myself seem to have as good a right as Luther or Wesley, or any Puritan or Mrs. Eddy, to start a sect and to promote a schism, seemed to me no 'system' at all. All this multiplication of sects and schisms impressed me as the logical and inevitable outcome of the cardinal Protestant doctrine of private interpretation. If there is no final and authoritative interpretation of the Holy Scriptures, if each may and must interpret for himself, if one man's gloss is as good as another man's gloss, and if there is no one to decide finally, no source of authority which is infallible and supreme and ultimate and of divine sanction, then it seemed to me that there is absolutely nothing in Christianity. It is something for noisy and designing scamps, male or female, to exploit for their own gain and to the ruin of their dupes. Religious anarchy never seemed to me any better than civil anarchy…

Protestantism thus appeared to me to be a system of confusion that no wise and just God could create or sanction. I could not understand how a God infinitely wise and just could authorize a system upon which was to depend the eternal salvation of the human race which nobody could understand and about which none agree.

There are several hundred local Protestant sects scattered here and there over the earth, all claiming to teach the truth, all of equal rank, all pretending to derive their doctrine from the same book, many of them putting up claims to exclusive prerogative, no two of which teach the same system, many of which teach the most contrary doctrines, some of which promulgate what most men agree is nonsense, and all of which have but a local and generally but an ephemeral existence. The distinctive doctrine of each little sect, that particular ism which constitutes its raison d'etre, is stoutly denied and held for heresy by most or all of the rest. Each sect conclusively and to its own satisfaction 'proves' its doctrine from the Scriptures. Thus the pro and the con of every conceivable religious tenet is asserted by one sect or another and claimed to be 'proved' by holy writ. There being no one to decide, it results that for these people taken in the mass and as a whole, the Bible means nothing, proves nothing, teaches nothing, and produces nothing but confusion and anarchy. That is precisely the net result of the sum total of Protestant doctrine. Some of these sects keep the same name for a century or two; most of them do not even do that, but all are constantly changing. Within my lifetime most of the leading sects in America have modified one or other of their tenets some of them radically. Some sects in the same time have about died out and many new ones have been born. Upon the Protestant theory this must go on for all the future; and just as the Methodism of to-day is very little kin to the Methodism of John Wesley's time, and as the Presbyterianism of the twentieth century has almost nothing in common with the Presbyterianism of Jonathan Edwards, so the sects of the next century will inevitably develop new phases of belief and teach new doctrines and proclaim new dogmas as essential to salvation. Where is it to end? And considering that one's soul's salvation depends upon it, what shall one do to make a wise choice among the sects?...

The sixteenth century struck me as far too late for the discovery of ultimate religious verity. If the proposition is that until then the Christian system had been wrong, if it then called for repudiation, and if only then real divine light was finally vouchsafed to a few schismatics in Germany and England, I could not resist the conclusion that the whole Christian system is unworthy of serious consideration; because who shall say that some centuries hence, or for the matter of that the day after to-morrow, a new 'Reformation' may not break out, and new light - new gospel truth essential to salvation - be discovered, superseding all previous issues - like railroad time-tables, or the catalogues of the department stores or the telephone books. So it seemed to me more and more as I thought of it.

In contradistinction to all this confusion I saw the certitude of Catholicism; I saw historically a real Church, not a kaleidoscopic jumble of sects organized and reorganized by schismatics from time to time, but the Church of God coming down to us from the Apostles and from Christ himself, continuing in ordinary generation the work begun on earth by the divine Saviour. I was much impressed, as I considered its history, by the community of Catholicism, its direct derivation from the Head of the Church, its historic oneness from the beginning; and I then was in a frame of mind to accept its claim to divine authority to govern and to interpret. That seemed to me reasonable and rational, and to be what a wise God would naturally have ordained for His church on earth, if He ordained anything. Anything else leaves all men in doubt, and in practice inevitably lets many men go wrong. All of Protestantism cannot possibly be true, much of Protestantism is certainly untrue and no human mind can decide what of Protestantism is true. There is therefore no safety in it. Who shall decide how far one sect is right and the others wrong? All make the same pretence to truth with equal fervor, while gravely putting out claims the most diametrically opposite.

The mind rejecting that system turns necessarily to the only thing that is left, namely to Catholicism. If anything in Christianity is true, Catholicism is that thing. It is rational and reasonable and what serious men would expect of a wise God. It works order in religion, and works along lines that in other spheres commend themselves to sane men. The Catholic system is what we have in the home and in the State; it provides an authority from which there is no appeal. It gives us certitude. It does about divine law precisely what the State does and must do for civil law, that is it sets our doubts at rest by ultimate and final decision. If there is no power under heaven given among men of divine sanction so to decide, then the Bible means nothing and is no safe guide and Christianity is a dream. Lawyers know that statutes, even the most carefully drawn, must he interpreted by courts of last resort before they can safely advise their clients as to their true and ultimate force and effect. Everybody knows that what a statute really means is what the Supreme Court finally says it means - not what wrangling attorneys argue and claim it means. That is the position and pretension of the Catholic Church as to her authority to interpret the divine statutes. No other religious organization makes or can make any such claim. Historically it is Catholicism or nothing. No truth was ever any truer than that. Unless, then, God has thus provided on earth a sure interpreter of His law and of His will, a final arbiter to speak a language that we can all understand, and to which we all must bow, divine law as attempted to be set forth in the Holy Scriptures is an inscrutable mystery; no man knows what it is, or what to believe and can only stake his soul's salvation upon the best guess he can make. Under the Protestant scheme one man guesses Mormonism, another guesses High Church or Low Church Episcopacy, another guesses Alexander Campbellism, another guesses Mrs. Eddy-ism, and so on all through the long list of the sects. Some surely guess wrong.

It seemed to me that the authority of the historic Church, her divine sanction as against this chaos of conflicting isms is the only ark of safety. Reasoning of this sort, enforcing itself upon my understanding for a series of years, finally made me a Catholic from conviction. Then the grace of God I trust did the rest").

Becker, Thomas Albert Andrew – bishop; b. 20 December 1832, Pittsburgh, Pennsylvania; d. 29 July 1899, Washington, Georgia; parents were German Protestant; studied at the Allegheny Institute, the Western University of Pennsylvania, and the University of Virginia; he was received into the Catholic Church in early manhood (persuaded to convert by Bishop John McGill while in Virginia); went to Rome in 1854 to study theology at the College of Propaganda; ordained to the priesthood there on 18 July 1859; returned to the United States, where after a mission in West Virginia. he became a professor at Mount St. Mary's College, Emmitsburg; then secretary to Archbishop Spalding; in 1868 appointed first Bishop of the new diocese of Wilmington, Delaware, for which he was consecrated in the same year; transferred to the see of Savannah, Georgia, in 1886 as its sixth bishop; very accomplished bishop who was also a fine linguist; oversaw a large increase in priests and the number of churches in his diocese, and did much for schools; wrote for many reviews and journals, notably a series of articles in the *American Catholic Quarterly Review* on the idea of a true university; promoted the cause of temperance; see *Catholic Encyclopedia*.

Beckwith, Francis J. ("Frank") – philosopher and lecturer; b. 1960, New York City; c. 28 April 2007 (revert; his wife Frankie, a Presbyterian, was received into the Church on 18 August 2007); brought up in the Catholic Church; at age thirteen he had a real interest in the person of Christ; gravitated to Evangelical Christianity and joined that church at the age of fourteen; educated at the University of Nevada, Las Vegas (graduated BA in Philosophy); later studied at Simon Greenleaf School of Law, Anaheim (MA in Apologetics), Fordham University (MA and PhD in Philosophy) and Washington University School of Law, St. Louis (Master of Juridical Studies); taught at Whittier College (1996–1997) and Trinity International University (1997–2002); in 2005 became president-elect of the Evangelical Theological Society (resigned when he became a Catholic); he and his wife then attended both Episcopalian and Baptist churches; closely associated with the Discovery Institute and its campaigns on behalf of intelligent design; claims not to be an advocate of intelligent design, but rather to be interested in the legal and cultural issues raised by it; has defended the constitutional permissibility of the teaching of intelligent design in public schools; appointed Associate Director of the J. M. Dawson Institute of Church-State Studies and Associate Professor of Church-State Studies at Baylor University; won a tenure battle at Baylor over the fact that he was a former fellow of the Discovery Institute; influenced in his conversion to the Catholic Church by the writings of Pope John Paul II and Pope Benedict XVI; also influenced by the evidence in the early Church for belief in the Real Presence, and how Catholic the Church Fathers were; deeply pro-life since the mid-1980s; see (selective list) *David Hume's Argument Against Miracles: A Critical Analysis* (1989); *Politically Correct Death:*

Answering the Arguments for Abortion Rights (1993); (ed), *Are You Politically Correct?: Debating America's Cultural Standards* (1993) (with Michael E. Bauman); *See the Gods Fall: Four Rivals to Christianity* (1997) (with Stephen E. Parrish); (ed), *Affirmative Action: Social Justice or Reverse Discrimination?* (1997) (with Todd E. Jones); *Relativism: Feet Firmly Planted in Mid-Air* (1998) (with Gregory Kouki); (ed), *The Abortion Controversy 25 Years After Roe v Wade: A Reader* (1998) (with Louis Pojman); *Do the Right Thing: Readings in Applied Ethics and Social Philosophy* (2002); *Law, Darwinism, and Public Education: The Establishment Clause and the Challenge of Intelligent Design* (2003); (ed), *To Everyone An Answer: A Case for the Christian Worldview* (2004) (with William Lane Craig and J. P. Moreland); *Defending Life: A Moral and Legal Case Against Abortion Choice* (2007); *Return to Rome: Confessions of an Evangelical* Catholic (2009) (Letter written on 6 March 2007 to his sixteen-year-old nephew, Dean Beckwith: "Jesus of Nazareth is the smartest and wisest man who ever lived. No one can compare with his insights, his deft combination of love, tenderness, tough-mindedness, and mercy. His life and his ideas reshaped the ancient world and changed the trajectory of history itself. You are one of his followers. What an amazing privilege.

Either Jesus was who he said he was – the Son of God – or he was a liar, or he was a lunatic (as C. S. Lewis once put it). These are the only options. Yet, the picture of Jesus that we receive is one of a psychologically balanced individual who had incredible wisdom concerning our duties to others and our relationship to God. He was willing to die, which means he believed himself to be who he said he was…A liar may do many things, but he does not march to his death for what he knows to be false. Thus, Jesus was either a lunatic – he sincerely believed himself to be the Son of God even though he was not – or he was Lord – he sincerely believed himself to be the Son of God because he was the Son of God. As the Cambridge scholar C. S. Lewis has pointed out, many people believe that Jesus was a great moral teacher. But if he was, it is unlikely that he was a lunatic. Great moral teachers are typically balanced, mature people possessing intestinal fortitude and personal integrity. Do you think the picture of Jesus we get from history and the New Testament is that of a lunatic, a David Koresh or Osama Bin Laden, bent on a single idea that is self-defeating? It does not seem that way to me. It seems to me that Jesus was neither a liar nor a lunatic. But that means that he was Lord. Those are the only options. I know that you confess Jesus as Lord. But it's always good to remind ourselves about Jesus and why he stands out in history and why we measure history by his birth.

There are certain core-facts about Jesus's that virtually all scholars agree on: (1) Jesus died by crucifixion; (2) His tomb was found empty three days later; (3) His followers (the apostles and other disciples) believed that they had had experiences with Christ after his death; (4) His followers were willing to suffer death for their belief that they had met the risen Christ. These facts, which are not even disputed by most unbelieving scholars, are difficult to account for apart from Jesus actually rising from the dead. Although it is common for those who doubt the resurrection to say that the early Church made up the story, this theory fails to account for the Church itself (not to mention having no evidence in its favor). That is, Jesus's resurrection makes sense as the cause of the early Church, a body of believers who personally knew Jesus and would have recanted their belief if they knew that the resurrection was a fabrication. But not one of Jesus's early disciples who believed that they had met Jesus after the resurrection ever recanted. In fact, many of them (including 11 of the 12 apostles) suffered horrible torture and death for their beliefs, something that does not make sense if they had made up the whole thing. Granted, people die for false beliefs. But rarely if ever does anyone die for a belief they know is false. These are some of the earliest witnesses that form the cloud that surrounds us.

Under the leadership of St. Peter and St. Paul, the Church grew from a small band of believers to an international phenomenon that through its message slowly but eventually dismantled the spiritual infrastructure of the greatest empire the world had ever known, the Roman Empire. As the Church moved through history, it began to reflect on its own theology and produce some of the clearest creeds ever penned, such as the Apostles' Creed and the Nicene Creed. But that is not all. The Church's finest minds were willing to wrestle with and respond to the non-Christian challenges of their day, to follow St. Paul's instruction to take 'every thought captive to the obedience of Christ' (2 Cor. 10:5). Throughout Church history, and even to this present day, gifted Christians became well versed in the philosophy, literature, sciences, and arts of their day. For they believed, as we all should believe, that all truth is God's truth, that the Christian world view illuminates our understanding of the world and the order and nature of things. The enormity of Christian influence in the shaping of Western civilization boggles the mind. Ideas about human nature, economics, the sciences, the arts, ethics, architecture, music, mathematics, and politics flourished under the direction of Christian intellectuals and leaders. According to...Professor Rodney

Stark (in his book *For the Glory of God* (2002)), without Christianity's understanding of God and nature, much of what we take for granted today – including our legal system, our understanding of truth, and the success of the sciences – would have never come to be.

You, indeed we, stand on the shoulders of predecessors whose beliefs about God, man, and nature – derived explicitly from their Christian faith – furnished the cultural infrastructure that gave rise to the knowledge, wealth, and liberties that make it possible for us today to freely worship God and to study his world.

The Lord has given you many gifts. Use them wisely. But do not ever forget that you now stand with that great cloud of witnesses"); *EWTN Audio Library, The Journey Home* (29 April 2007) ("I was actually invited to speak at a conference at Boston College on John Paul II's work in applied ethics and I was the token Protestant Evangelical. And my friends, Laura and Jorge Garcia [on the former see below], who are both philosophers in the faculty, were directing this conference. They invited me to attend and deliver a paper. And so I delivered a paper dealing with the problem of what I call anti-credal Protestantism, that is what's wrong with a Protestantism that denies the authority of what are called the ancient Catholic creeds. After I gave my talk, in fact interspliced with my own comments, and comments by John Paul II, there was a question in the audience by Laura Garcia. She raised her hand in front of four hundred people: 'Why aren't you Catholic?' And I really gave a lame answer…She wanted me to explain how I could accept the authority of these creeds and at the same time reject the magisterium when it responded on the Counter-Reformation. A really good question, one for which I had never had an answer. And so I gave her an answer I thought was pretty convincing. It made me think though, 'How can I really answer her question in a way that keeps me Protestant; at the same time shows great respect and deference for these early creeds?'"; *EWTN Audio Library, The Journey Home* (14 September 2009); *Politics for Christians: Statecraft as Soulcraft* (2010); "Reformation Day and Schism," *The Catholic Thing*, 29 October 2010; "Transubstantiation: From Stumbling Block to Cornerstone," *The Catholic Thing*, 21 January 2011 ("The Catholic doctrine of the Eucharist is a real stumbling block to some Protestants who are seriously considering Catholicism. It was for me too, until I explored the subject, historically and scripturally…

Catholicism holds that bread and wine literally become the body and blood of Christ when they are consecrated by the priest celebrating the Mass. Oftentimes non-Catholics get hung up on the term *transubstantiation*, the name for the philosophical theory that the Church maintains best accounts for the change at consecration. The Church's explanation of transubstantiation was influenced by Aristotle's distinction between substance and accident...

There are several reasons why it would be a mistake to dismiss transubstantiation simply because of the influence of Aristotle on its formulation. First, Eastern Churches in communion with the Catholic Church rarely employ this Aristotelian language, and yet the Church considers their celebration of the Eucharist perfectly valid. Second, the Catholic Church maintains that the divine liturgies celebrated in the Eastern churches not in communion with Rome (commonly called "Eastern Orthodoxy") are perfectly valid as well, even though the Eastern Orthodox rarely employ the term transubstantiation. Third, the belief that the bread and wine are literally transformed into Christ's body and blood pre-dates Aristotle's influence on the Church's theology by over 1000 years. For it was not until the thirteenth century and the ascendancy of St. Thomas Aquinas' thought, that Aristotle's categories were employed by the Church in its account of the Eucharist. In fact, when the Fourth Lateran Council (1215) employed the language of substantial change, St. Thomas had not even been born!

It was that third point that I found so compelling and convinced me that the Catholic view of the Eucharist was correct. It did not take long for me to see that Eucharistic realism (as I like to call it) had been uncontroversially embraced deep in Christian history. This is why Protestant historian, J. N. D. Kelly, writes: 'Eucharistic teaching, it should be understood at the outset, was in general unquestioningly realist, i.e., the consecrated bread and wine were taken to be, and were treated and designated as, the Savior's body and blood.' I found it in many of the works of the Early Church Fathers, including St. Ignatius of Antioch (AD 110), St. Justin Martyr (AD 151), St. Cyprian of Carthage (AD 251), First Council of Nicaea (AD 325), St. Cyril of Jerusalem (AD 350), and St. Augustine of Hippo (AD 411). These are, of course, not the only Early Church writings, that address the nature of the Eucharist. But they are representative.

This should, however, not surprise us, given what the Bible says about the Lord's Supper. When Jesus celebrated the Last Supper with his disciples (Mt. 26:17-30; Mk. 14:12-25; Lk. 22:7-23), which we commemorate at Holy Communion, he referred to it as a Passover meal. He called the bread and wine his body and blood. In several places, Jesus is called the Lamb of God (John 1:29-36; I Peter 1:19; Rev. 5:12). Remember, when the lamb is killed for Passover, the meal participants ingest the lamb. Consequently, St. Paul's severe warnings about partaking in Holy Communion unworthily only make sense in light of Eucharistic realism (I Cor. 10:14-22; I Cor. 11:17-34). He writes: 'The cup of blessing which we bless, is it not a participation in the blood of Christ? The bread which we break, is it not a participation in the body of Christ?...Whoever, therefore, eats and drinks the cup of the Lord in an unworthy manner will be guilty of profaning the body and blood of the Lord' (I Cor. 10:16; 11:27).

In light of all these passages and the fact that Jesus called himself the bread of life (John 6: 41-51) and that he said that his followers must "eat the flesh of the Son of Man and drink his blood" (John 6:53), the Eucharistic realism of the Early Church, the Eastern Churches (both in and out of communion with Rome), and the pre-Reformation medieval Church (fifth to sixteenth centuries) seems almost unremarkable. So, what first appeared to be a stumbling block was transformed into a cornerstone"); "In the Time of My Confession," *The Catholic Thing*, 4 February 2011; "Apostolic Succession," *The Catholic Thing*, 4 March 2011 ("What amazed me was how uncontroversial apostolic succession was in the Early Church, as Protestant historian, J. N. D. Kelly points out in his book *Early Christian Doctrines*. I expected to find factions of Christians, including respected Church Fathers, who resisted episcopal ecclesiology. There aren't any. In fact, a leading argument in the early Church against heretics was their lack of episcopal lineage and continuity and thus their absence of communion with the visible and universal Church. In his famous apologetic treatise, *Against Heresies* (AD 182-188), St. Irenaeus (c. AD 140-202) makes that very point in several places. Tertullian (AD c. 160-220) offers the same sort of apologetic as well"); "Come Let Us Reason," *The Catholic Thing*, 1 April 2011; "Reason, Coinversion and Plausibility," *The Catholic Thing*, 15 April 2011; "Reformation Day and What Led Me Back to Catholicism," *The Catholic Thing*, 28 October 2011; "The New Anti-Catholicism: Occupy the Vatican," *The Catholic Thing*, 3 February 2012; "Catechesis, Conversion, and the Reason for the Hope within You," *The Catholic Thing*, 30 March 2012; "Then I Confessed, I Could Do No Other," *The Catholic Thing*, 27 April 2012; "In Defense of First Philosophy," *The Catholic Thing*, 22 June 2012; "Purgatory: An Objection Answered," *The Catholic Thing*, 26 October 2012; "Benedict, Dawkins, and the Fullness of Reason," *The Catholic Thing*, 15 February 2013; *francisbeckwith.com*.

Bentley, Elizabeth Terrill – spy; b. 1 January 1908, New Milford, Connecticut; c. 5 November 1948 (at her baptism on that occasion Louis Budenz (see below) and his wife, Margaret, acted as godparents); d. 3 December 1963, New Haven, Connecticut; brought up as an Episcopalian; graduated from Vassar College in 1930 with a degree in English, Italian, and French; attended graduate school at Columbia University; in 1933 won a fellowship to the University of Florence; briefly flirted with Fascism but converted to Communism; back at Columbia she joined the Communist Party of the United States in 1935; in 1938 she obtained a post at the Italian Library of Information in New York City (Italy's propaganda bureau in the United States) and began spying on the fascists; played a major role in Soviet intelligence 1938-1945 under the code name Umnitsa, or "clever girl"; in 1944 became depressed and had a drink problem; relationship with the Soviets deteriorated and her then controller recommended her liquidation; after Louis Budenz (see below), who knew she was a spy, defected, she was imperiled from both sides; in 1945 she defected from the Communist Party and Soviet intelligence and became an informer for the United States; she exposed two networks of spies, ultimately implicating about 150 people in spying for the Soviet Union, including 37 federal employees; the secrecy around her defection was breached by the Soviet spy Kim Philby and Moscow immediately shut down all contact with the people she implicated, making evidence difficult to obtain; the suspects invoked the Fifth Amendment right not to testify or maintained their innocence; she testified at grand jury hearings, trials and Congressional committees; she was dubbed by the tabloid press as the "Blond Spy Queen"; her behavior was erratic; after her defection she worked as a secretary and teacher; her conversion to the Catholic faith was as a direct result of meetings with Mgr. Fulton Sheen; she was also impressed by the life of St. Francis of Assisi; she lectured to Catholic groups on the Communist threat; some sources claim that in a moment of disillusionment she left the Church; buried in New Milford, Connecticut; her evidence was definitively and publicly verified when the Venona Project transcripts of decrypted wartime cables sent between Soviet intelligence agents and Moscow, and some Soviet intelligence archives, were made available; see *Out of Bondage* (1951) (autobiography); Kathryn S. Olmsted, *Red Spy Queen: A Biography of Elizabeth Bentley* (2002); Lauren Kessler, *Clever Girl: Elizabeth Bentley, the Spy Who Ushered in the McCarthy Era* (2003).

Berenson, Bernard (born Bernhard Valvrojenski) – art historian and connoisseur; b. 26 June 1865, Butrremanz (now in Lithuania); c. February 1891, Monte Oliveto Maggiore Benedictine monastery (received by the abbot, Dom Gaetano di Negro); d. 6

October 1959, Settignano, Italy; born to a Jewish family; emigrated to Boston Massachusetts in 1875, when the family name was changed to Berenson; educated at Harvard University (a brilliant student); married to Mary Costelloe, *née* Pearsall-Smith (1864-1945), a notable art historian, after her first husband died; substantial collector of paintings; great authority on the Renaissance; advisor to many important American art collectors; fearless attributor, though have been subsequent criticisms of some of his work; many publications on art history; dislike of modern art; beautiful residence in Settignano near Florence, called "I Tatti"; see *Venetian Painters of the Renaissance* (1894); *Lorenzo Lotto: An Essay in Constructive Art* (1895); *Florentine Painters of the Renaissance* (1896); *Central Italian Painters of the Renaissance* (1897); *The Sense of Quality: Study and Criticism of Italian Art* (three series, 1901, 1902 and 1906); *The Drawings of the Florentine Painters* (1903); *North Italian Painters of the Renaissance* (1907); *A Sienese Painter of the Franciscan Legend* (1910); *Venetian Painting in America: The Fifteenth Century* (1916); *Essays in the Study of Sienese Painting* (1918); *Three Essays in Method* (1926); *Studies in Medieval Painting* (1930); *Aesthetics and History in the Visual Arts* (1948); *Sketch for a Self-Portrait* (1949) (autobiography); *Alberto Sani: An Artist Out of his Time* (1950); *Italian Pictures of the Renaissance* (1952); *Rumor and Reflection* (1952); *Caravaggio, His Incongruity and His Fame* (1953); *Seeing and Knowing* (1953); *The Arch of Constantine or The Decline of Form* (1954); *Decline and Recovery in the Figure Arts* (1954); *Piero della Francesca or The Ineloquent in Art* (1954); *Essays in Appreciation* (1958); *One Year's Reading for Fun* (1960); *The Passionate Sightseer* (1960); *Rudiments of Connoisseurship: Study and Criticism of Italian Art* (1962); *Sunset and Twilight* (1963); *Homeless Paintings of the Renaissance* (1969); Hanna Kiel (ed), *The Bernard Berenson Treasury* (1964) ((1) Letter to Mary Costelloe, 1 February 1891, Perugia: "The people in the church were all of the lowest class. I felt so at one with them and that alone made me happy, but the Mass itself has such an effect on me. It occurs to me that I am talking of the Mass as if that too were only an impression. I suppose it is in a way, but how much more I feel the bodily presence of God in such a way that prayer at the moment becomes the most naturally personal of all things…I had seen much before in Catholicism that attracted me irresistibly, but not that…

I wanted so much to…thank God that he had led me to him so much just by those beautiful pictures. Without them I should have been nowhere…How I used to loathe myself for being one of those whom I knew, as Dante describes,

Heaven rejects and Hell disdains… How glad I am to take sides, to give up the fancied freedom…I am so sick of constantly questioning my own pulse, and of making believe that I can comprehend the Universe…I was not an out and out pessimist, but my intense love for nature and art somehow only made me hate people more. Today I felt so at one with everybody, and I am sure I always will now with all people. I know one can't be a Catholic and feel otherwise…" (2) Letter to Mary Costelloe, 8 February 1891, Perugia: "Religion means too much to me from the inside, henceforth to despise any person's strivings, no matter how mistaken. Oh, I have been so narrow, and what is more absurd bigotted…What I needed so much was religion. I hope I have made the beginning, and with God's help the rest will come. To myself scarcely anything is so significant as the ease with which I can use the name of God. It is quite wonderful. Now it is so natural to pray, to kneel down, to cross myself, and to use many of the symbols, as if I had done so all my life. What a difference it is making to me. With this new light Italy itself seems so infinitely more beautiful…" (3) Diary, 8 December 1951, I Tatti: "We can speak of a European civilization but scarcely of a European culture. If culture is the mental and above all spiritual atmosphere in which we live and breathe, which penetrates our thought and feeling and conditions our reactions and actions; then that culture is above all Christian. I tried to convince a very liberal Jewess that what I meant did not refer to theology or dogma, did not necessitate our acceptance of its rites even. Nor did it matter that this culture owes so much to Judaism, as much to Hellenism, and somewhat to Rome. Nowadays one cannot go back and be a Greek, a Jew or an ancient Roman. One cannot get away from Christian ways of feeling no matter how much Judaism went to make it. This feeling is no longer Jewish because it is also Greek and Roman. Nor can we get away from the Christian calendar, its holidays, its saints' days, nor Christian nomenclature, Christian references, Christian phrases in our speech"); A. K. McComb, *The Selected Letters of Bernard Berenson* (1965); Elisabetta Mariano, *Forty Years With Berenson* (19660; Kenneth Clark, *Another Part of the Wood* (1974); Ernest Samuels, *Bernard Berenson: The Making of a Connoisseur* (1979); Meryle Secreste, *Being Bernard Berenson: A Biography* (1980); Ernest Samuels, *Bernard Berenson: The Making of a Legend* (1987); Mary Ann Calo, *Bernard Berenson and the Twentieth Century* (1994); William Weaver, *A Legacy of Excellence: The Story of Villa I Tatti* (1997); Richard Davenport-Hines, *Letters from Oxford: Hugh Trevor-Roper to Bernard Berenson* (2006); Patrick Allitt, *Catholic Converts:*

British and American Intellectuals Turn to Rome (1997), pp.220-221 ("Outside Italy he found it hard to sustain his faith. 'In Italy,' he wrote…, 'it is easy to feel Catholic, just as in England it is so inevitable to feel antagonistic to it. Elsewhere it is repelling. Yet in Italy it is as much at home as the sun and sky.' After reading Leopold von Ranke's history of the papacy he lost his reverence for the hierarchy and from then on attended church only when he was in Italy. There was, he came to believe, an intrinsically Catholic quality to Italy itself which faded as he traveled to England or America. His was the quirkiest and most aesthetically driven Catholic conversion, unable to withstand the chilly Protestant wind of Northern Europe or North America").

Bissell, William Henry - politician; b. 25 April 1811, near Hartwick, Otsego County, New York; c. 1854; d. 18 March 1860, Illinois Executive Mansion, Springfield, Illinois; studied at Jefferson Medical College of Philadelphia (MD in 1834); practiced medicine; in 1840 he married Emily Susan James (d. 1844) (two daughters of the marriage); elected for the Democratic Party to the Illinois legislature in 1840; he was admitted to the Illinois bar in 1841 and practiced law; served as a colonel in the Mexican War; elected in 1848 to the House of Representatives (served three successive terms); held anti-slavery convictions and disliked his southern colleagues; argument with Jefferson Davis nearly led to a duel; in 1851 he married Elisabeth Kintzing Kane, a Catholic; became seriously ill in 1854 and converted secretly to the Catholic faith; stricken with paralysis and walked with crutches; did not seek re-election, but stood as a Republican for the Governorship of Illinois in 1856 and was elected (served until his death); he was the first Catholic governor of Illinois, the first Republican governor of Illinois and the first Illinois governor to die in office; buried in Oak Ridge Cemetery, Springfield, Illinois; see Robert P. Howard, *Mostly Good and Competent Men: Illinois Governors, 1818-1988* (1988); *ANB*.

Bitzer, Billy (born Johan Gottlieb Wilhelm Bitzer) (known as "Billy" or "G.W.") - cinematographer; b. 21 April 1874, Roxbury, Boston, Massachusetts; d. 29 April 1944, Hollywood, California; parents were German immigrants (father a blacksmith); his younger brother was John C. Bitzer, the photographer; raised as a Lutheran; trained as a silversmith, then worked as an electrician in New York City; took on the role of photographer and began filming newsreels and short fiction movies; by his footage of the Spanish-American war he became the first photographer to film war in motion picture; teamed up with the director D. W. Griffith (1875-1948) for fifteen years to become the best-known director-cameraman pair in American film history; their most celebrated collaborations were on *The Birth of a Nation* (1915) and *Intolerance* (1916); noted for his diffused softened lighting, use of perspective and lighting, the fade out, and iris shots; he was the first cinematographer to shoot a film using entirely artificial lighting; the partnership eventually collapsed; worked as a union organizer, founding the International Photographers of the Motion Picture Industry (later known as the International Alliance of Theatrical Stage Employees) in 1926; worked as a film historian; converted to the Catholic faith in middle age; married to Ethel Boddy (one son of the marriage); buried in Cedar Grove Cemetery in Flushing, New York; in 2003 the International Cinematographers Guild named him one of the ten most influential cinematographers in history; see *Billy Bitzer: His Story* (1973) (autobiography); Karl Brown, *Adventures with D.W. Griffith* (1973); his papers are housed in the D. W. Griffith Archives, Museum of Modern Art, New York City*; ANB*.

Black, Conrad Moffat (Baron Black of Crossharbour, PC, OC, KCSG) - publisher, investor, columnist, and historian; b. 25 August 1944, Montreal, Quebec, Canada; c. 18 June 1986 (received by Cardinal Carter of Toronto; his elder son was received at the same time); born to a wealthy family originally from Winnipeg, Manitoba; his father, George Montegu Black, Jr. (1911-1976) was president of Canadian Breweries Ltd; his mother was Jean Elizabeth, *née* Riley, whose grandfather founded the Great-West Life Assurance Co.; brought up nominally Protestant ("My family was divided between atheism and agnosticism, and I followed rather unthinkingly and inactively in those paths into my twenties"); studied at Carleton University, Ottawa, Canada (BA in History and Political Science, 1965); attended Osgoode Hall Law School, Toronto, but failed his first year exams; completed a law degree at Université Laval, Quebec City, in 1970; MA in History from McGill University, Montreal in 1973 (thesis on Maurice Duplessis (1890-1959), premier of Quebec); became involved in a number of businesses, mainly publishing newspapers; controlled Hollinger International Inc. and through affiliates published major newspapers (e.g., *The Daily Telegraph*, *Chicago Sun Times*, *National Post* (Canada), *Jerusalem Post*), plus hundreds of local papers in North America; regular columnist for the *National Post*; contributor to several papers and magazines (e.g., *The American Spectator*, *National Review Online*, *The Huffington Post*, *Catholic Herald*); also author of two memoirs and historian (author of three biographies); by his early thirties he "no longer had any confidence in the non-existence of

God" and slowly approached Rome; his conversion to the Catholic faith was influenced by the writings of many Catholic thinkers, notably St. Augustine, St. Thomas Aquinas, Cardinal Newman, Jacques Maritain, G. K. Chesterton, Evelyn Waugh, Malcolm Muggeridge, and Edith Sitwell; came to accept the possibility of miracles and therefore of the Resurrection of Christ; Officer of the Order of Canada (OC) in 1990; became a British citizen in 1999; given a life peerage in Britain in 2001; renounced his Canadian citizenship in 2001; in 2005 subject of a high profile prosecution in the United States; charged with seventeen counts of misconduct and of defrauding his company of $60 million; convicted in 2007 of three counts of fraud and one count of obstruction of justice; sentenced to six and a half years' imprisonment; granted bail in July 2010 following a unanimous judgment of the United States Supreme Court narrowing the scope of the honest services fraud statute; in October 2010 the United States Court of Appeals for the Seventh Circuit overturned two of the three remaining mail fraud counts; in June 2011 he was re-sentenced on the one remaining count of mail fraud and on the one count of obstruction of justice to a prison term of 42 months (the 29 months he had already served were included in this sentence) and a fine of $125,000; returned to prison in 2011 to serve the remaining term of thirteen months; released from prison on 4 May 2012; granted a one-year temporary resident permit to re-enter Canada upon his release from prison (valid until May 2013); married in 1978 to Joanna Hishon (two sons and a daughter); divorced in 1992; married the English journalist, Barbara Amiel (b. 1940), later in 1992; see *Duplessis* (1977); *A Life in Progress* (1993) ("I had never been seriously encouraged to consider Protestantism otherwise than as a congregationalist gesture by those who found agnosticism imprudent or unsustainable. This has usually been my experience of practicing high-church Protestants. Most have been best defined as Christians who aren't papist, with almost as much doubt as faith, as much goodwill as eternal truth, and often, as much fear of atheism, popery and the rabbinical persuasion as intellectual sectarian attachment.

Caught between a limited need for spirituality and fear of surrendering too much authority to an autonomous or even internationally directed episcopate, orthodox Protestantism is generally too heavily conditionalized to be more than congregational national churches. 'Sailing', as Newman wrote 150 years ago, and despite the sincerity of many intelligent adherents, 'through the channel of no meaning between the Scylla and Charybdis of yes and no…They can not go on forever standing on one leg, or sitting without a chair, or walking with their feet tied, or like Tityrus's stags, grazing in the air.'

Not forever, perhaps, but for at least another century and a half from when Newman wrote"); *Franklin Delano Roosevelt: Champion of Freedom* (2005); *Richard Nixon: A Life in Full* (2007); "How I woke up from spiritual slumber and inched at snail's pace to Rome," *Catholic Herald*, 11 September 2009 (longer account of his conversion than the National Post article below; later published in *Canadian Converts: The Path to Rome* (see below) ("I read a good deal of the most admired arguments in support of God's existence, especially Aquinas and Newman…Newman's most picaresque argument, valuable for its almost impish wit, was the quotation of Napoleon, near the end at St. Helena, from the not entirely reliable Lacordaire, at the end of Newman's tour de force, *A Grammar of Assent*. Napoleon was introduced as 'the great man who so influenced the destinies of the nations of Europe at the start of this century.' Lacordaire wrote that Napoleon had mused: someone who 'died a miscreant's death 1800 years ago, whose likeness is displayed in the principal squares of great cities, at rural crossways, in palaces and in hovels; before the newborn and the failing vision of those about to die; effortlessly achieved what Alexander and Caesar and I did not begin to accomplish. Can he be less than divine, one to whom our eyes turn, as to a father and a God?'"); "Why I Became a Catholic," *National Post*, 29 September 2009 ("The spiritual edifice of the Church functions obliviously to market share, and there is a common strain of intelligent and hopeful faith, regardless of fashion, age, or economics. Whether in packed and mighty cathedrals, like St Peter's or St Patrick's (New York), a simple wooden building like the Indian church in Sept-Îles, Quebec, in primitive religious structures in Cameroon, at fashionable resorts like Biarritz, St-Jean-Cap-Ferrat, Portofino, or even Palm Beach ('The Lord is my shepherd, even in Palm Beach,' as a guest homilist proclaimed some years ago), or in the improvised chapel in my prison as I write, there is a discernible, but almost inexpressible denominator that unites communicants. I am still impressed by the purposeful spring in the step of people approaching a Catholic Church as the hour of a service peals.

It may be that I was startled to discover this because I was so accustomed from my early years to think of Protestantism, except for the evangelicals, as conditional and tentative, protesting, after all, against the worldliness of Rome. When I first went to Rome, in 1963, I had just read a description of John Updike's, in the *New Yorker*, of his first visit to St Peter's, in which he was so astounded by the grandeur of the basilica, by its size, solidity, magnificence, architectural genius and collections of high art, that he felt compelled to add his name to thousands of others written in the graffiti in the wall of the curved stairway to the cupola, 44 storeys above the ground (in a building constructed continuously between the 15th and 18th centuries). I dimly and roughly remembered Byron's words: 'Worthiest of God, the holy and the true... Majesty, power, glory, strength and beauty, all are aisled in this eternal ark of worship undefiled.'

It was hard not to see what he meant. The sense of indulgent receptivity of this incomparable building was somehow emphasized by its ostentatious affordability of indifference to those who would come as skeptics or antagonists. My visits to Lourdes and Fatima in the ensuing couple of years revealed concepts of mass faith in the miraculous, scientifically attested to, that were also amazing to a former spiritually slumbering Protestant, and difficult to ignore or discount.

By the time I left Quebec in 1974 and returned to Toronto, I was satisfied that there were spiritual forces in the world, and that it was possible, occasionally and unpredictably, to gain something enlightening and even inspiriting from them. I had lost faith in the non-existence of God, and had begun to pray at the end of each day, developing my own groping formulations of worship.

I read a good deal of the most admired arguments in support of God's existence, especially Aquinas and Newman. When Gerald Emmett Carter became the Archbishop of Toronto in 1979, I quickly became an acquaintance, then a friend, and eventually an intimate...

From the early Seventies to the mid-Eighties, I approached Rome at a snail's pace. Having concluded that God existed, I could not seriously entertain the thought of not trying to be in contact with Him. And since I believed in general and prayed to and worshipped Him, it was not long before I wished to do so in some framework, to benefit from accumulated wisdom and traditions and from a community of faith.

It was not especially challenging, given my light Protestant upbringing, to stay in the Christian tradition. From all accounts, Christ appeared to be a divinely inspired person, in traditional parlance, a divine. There was no reason to doubt that he told St. Peter to found a church. I had never much doubted that, whatever its 'inanities, fatuities, and compromises' (a quote from Cardinal Léger), the Catholic Church was the premier Christian church.

As a nominal Anglican, I had always had some problems with Henry VIII as a religious leader. The Anglicans, moreover, have never really decided whether they are Protestant or Catholic, only that they 'don't Pope,' though even that wavers from time to time. Luther, though formidable and righteous, was less appealing to me than both the worldly Romans, tinged with rascality though they were, and the leading papist zealots of the Counter-Reformation.

The serious followers of Calvin, Dr Knox and Wesley were, to me, too puritanical, but also too barricaded into ethnic and cultural fastnesses, too much the antithesis of universalism and of the often flawed, yet grand, Roman effort to reconcile the spiritual and the material without corrupting the first and squandering the second. Fanatics are very tiresome, and usually enjoy the fate of Haman in the book of Esther; of Savonarola, Robespierre, Trotsky, Goebbels, and Guevara.

Islam was out of the question; too anti-western, too identified with the 13th-century decline and contemporary belligerency of the Arabs; and the Koran is alarmingly violent, even compared to the Old Testament. Judaism, though close theologically, is more tribal and philosophical than spiritual. And it was the spiritual bait that I sought, that converted me from atheism, that I premeditatedly swallowed, and that prompted me to agitate the line and be reeled in by the Fisher of Souls. I thought it more likely that the 80% of the early Jews who became Christians, starting with Christ, had correctly identified the Messiah than that the proverbially 'stiff-necked' rump of continuing Jewry are right still, ostensibly, to be waiting for Him.

It need hardly be said that the Jews are the chosen people of the Old Testament, that they have made a huge contribution to civilization, and that they have been horribly persecuted. But being Jewish today, apart from the orthodox, is more of an exclusive society, and a tradition of oppression and survival, than an accessible faith. The Eastern religions, to the very slight degree that I have studied them, are philosophical guides to living, not frameworks for the existence and purpose of man. In terms of real religious affiliation for me, it was Rome or nothing.

In the spring of 1986, Cardinal Carter asked me my religious beliefs. I recited my plodding baby steps on the ladder: There were spiritual aspects to life that were not mere superstition, and that constituted or at least evidenced God; that Christ was divinely inspired, had told St. Peter to found a Church, and that the legitimate continuator of that Church was Roman Catholicism. I desired to be in communion with God, and accepted that the surest means of doing so, though not sure, and not the only one, was as a communicant in the Roman Catholic Church. I believed that miracles occurred, though I couldn't attest to particular ones, that given the wonders of creation and of the infinite, and the imperfections of man, we all properly belonged, frequently, on our knees before an effigy of the Creator or his professed and acclaimed son, and that sincere and concentrated worship could be enlightening. I also, like Chesterton and countless millions of others, wished some method of being 'rid of my sins,' as I agree with Newman that 'our conscience is God speaking within us.'

The cardinal replied that I was 'at the door,' but that the one point I had to embrace if I wished to enter, and without which, all Christianity, he boldly asserted, 'is a fraud and a trumpery,' was the Resurrection of Christ. If I believed that, I was eligible; if I did not, I wasn't. What he was asking was not unreasonable, and I reflected on it for a few minutes and concluded that since, as defined, I believed in God and in miracles, I could at least suppress doubt sufficiently to meet his criterion. I considered it a little longer to be sure that I wasn't allowingmomentum,contemplative fatigue, or my great regard for him to push me over the finish line.

After a silence of perhaps five minutes, I said that I thought I could clear that hurdle. He asked me if I wished to be received. I did, and was, in the chapel in his home a few days later, on June 18, 1986. I have taken the sacraments at least once a week since, and have confessed when I feel sinful. This is not an overly frequent sensation, but when it occurs, I can again agree with Cardinal Newman that our consciences are 'powerful, peremptory, unargumentative, irrational, minatory and definitive.' The strain of trying to ignore or restrain an aroused conscience can be intolerable. Confession and repentance, if sincere, are easier, more successful, and more creditable.

Though there are many moments of skepticism as matters arise, and the dark nights of the soul that seem to assail almost everyone visit me too, I have never had anything remotely resembling a lapse, nor a sense of forsakenness, even when I was unjustly indicted, convicted, and imprisoned, in a country I formerly much admired"); "Catholicism, and the Oceans, Will Survive," *National Review Online*, 16 December 2010; "Rome After All!" in *Canadian Converts: The Path to Rome* (2009); *A Matter of Principle* (2011); Greg Watts (ed), *Catholic Lives* (2001); Tom Bower, *Conrad and Lady Black: Dancing on the Edge* (2006); Tom Bower, *Outrageous Fortune: The Rise and Ruin of Conrad and Lady Black* (2006); Steven Skurka, *Tilted: The Trial of Conrad Black* (2008; second edition 2012).

Black Elk (Heȟáka Sápa) (later known as Nicholas Black Elk) ("Nick") – Lakota Sioux medicine man; b. 1 December 1863, Little Powder River, Wyoming; c. 6 December 1904 (his first wife, Katie War Bonnet (d. 1903) became a Catholic earlier and all three of her children were baptized Catholic); d. 19 August 1950, Manderson, South Dakota; son of Black Elk, a Lakota medicine man, and Mary Leggins Down (also called White Cow Sees); claimed to have had a great vision at the age of nine in which he met the spirit that guided the universe; seen by his family as a clairvoyant; chosen to be the savior of the Sioux nation; took part in the Battle of the Little Big Horn against the U.S. Cavalry in 1876; became a famous medicine man or holy man of the Oglala Lakota Sioux; second cousin of the great war chief Crazy Horse (1840-1877); travelled to England in 1887 with the Wild West Show of Buffalo Bill (see under William Cody, below); part of a command performance for Queen Victoria and in the crowd at her Golden Jubilee; part of the Ghost Dance movement in 1890 and was injured in the Wounded Knee Massacre where his people were defeated and forced to live on a reservation; married his first wife Katie War Bonnet in 1892 (three children of the marriage); after his wife's death he too was baptized, taking the name Nicholas Black Elk; his Christian conversion was caused in part by a confrontation with a local Jesuit priest, Fr. Lindebner, who interrupted his Lakota ritual at the bedside of a sick child; out of this collision of cultures came a relationship that he could understand as providential; he then questioned the Pine Ridge Jesuits constantly about the story of Christ and the Church; he embraced Christianity as the full revelation of the Wakan Tanka (Lakota for God) he had begun to know as an Oglala holy man; he had a long and productive career as a Catholic catechist on the Pine Ridge reservation (responsible for some four hundred conversions); in 1906 he married Anna Brings White, also known as Brings White Horses) (d. 1941), a widow with two daughters; they had three more children; in 1930 he told his story to the poet and historian John Neihardt, and in 1947 he gave further details to Joseph Epes Brown, but both of these deal primarily with his early life only; see John G. Neihardt, *Black Elk Speaks: Being the Life Story of a Holy Man of the Oglala Sioux* (1932); John G. Neidhart, *When the Tree Flowered: An Authentic Tale of the Old Sioux World* (1951); *The Sacred Pipe: Black Elk's Account of the Seven Rites of the Oglala Sioux* (1997) (as told to Joseph Epes Brown); Raymond J. DeMallie, (ed), *The Sixth Grandfather: Black Elk's Teachings Given to John G. Neihardt* (1984) (tells the story of Black Elk the Catholic) ("Black Elk was healing a sick person when a priest entered, grabbed Black Elk's sacred things, threw them out, and then grabbed Black Elk by the neck and screamed 'Satan, get out!' The priest prayed over the boy, then invited Black Elk to the Holy Rosary Mission. Black Elk began to believe the priest's powers were stronger than his, and a couple weeks later, he became a Catholic"); Michael F. Steltenkamp, *Black Elk: Holy Man of the Oglala* (1993); Hilda Neihardt, *Black Elk and Flaming Rainbow* (1995); Christopher T. Dodson, "Black Elk: Native American and

Catholic," *New Oxford Review*, April 1995 ("Black Elk did not consider his conversion a betrayal of his Lakota heritage or his vision. He viewed it as part of his search for Wakan Tanka. He repeatedly spoke of how the Lakota ways were 'connected' to Catholicism, and how the spiritual experiences of the Lakota prepared them for Christ…

Scholars and commentators have often taken an 'either/or' approach to Native American spirituality and Christianity. Some scholars, apparently contrary to the evidence, have concluded that Black Elk's conversion was either a rejection of his 'Indianess,' insincere, or misguided. Vine Deloria Jr., in the popular *God is Red*, states that in Native American religion 'there is no demand for a personal relationship with a personal savior.' Nevertheless, most Lakota, like Black Elk, became Christians. Moreover, they, like Black Elk, viewed their conversion as consistent with the essentials of Lakota spirituality - that one could search for and rely upon Wakan Tanka in the everyday course of events…

Many Native Americans attempt to return to the 'ways of the grandfathers' without examining why their grandfathers became Christians. But advocates of a 'return' might find themselves embracing what their forebears chose to relinquish, modify, or regard as nonessential and, therefore, run the risk of replicating moviedom's tendency toward romantic portrayals. Ironically, the Black Elk portrayed by Neihardt and Brown stands with the 'revitalists' as an unreal grandfather.

Catholics who rely on Black Elk and the archetypal images and symbols in *Black Elk Speaks* and *The Sacred Pipe* for new directions in worship and liturgy could make a similar mistake. While Black Elk did not reject all Lakota practices, he found their essence present, or even deeper, in the practices of the Catholic Church - indeed, a pre-Vatican II Catholic Church. Many 'green' Catholics may not relish the idea that to 'be like Black Elk' means to evangelize and pray the Rosary"); Clyde Holler, *Black Elk's Religion: The Sun Dance and Lakota Catholicism* (1995); Clyde Holler (ed), *Black Elk Reader* (2000); Damian Costello, *Black Elk: Colonialism and Lakota Catholicism* (2005) (a demonstration of how essential the Catholic faith was to Black Elk, permeating every aspect of his life; also shows how the Lakota people embraced Catholicism both as in continuity with their past traditions, as well as using their Catholic Christian faith as a means of resisting colonialism); Michael F. Steltenkamp, *Nicholas Black Elk: Medicine Man, Missionary, Mystic* (2009); Brother André Marie, "Black Elk, Catholic Catechist, Speaks," *catholicism.org*, 20 May 2011; *ANB*.

Blenk, James Hubert Herbert, SM – archbishop; b. 28 July 1856, Edenkoben, Bavaria, Germany; c. 1869; d. 20 April 1917, New Orleans, Louisiana; raised in a Protestant family; youngest of seventeen children and also a twin; in 1866 the family emigrated to the United States and settled in New Orleans; his parents died some weeks later and he was brought up in a Catholic family, converting to the Catholic faith at the age of twelve; entered Jefferson College, Convent, Louisiana; in 1878 he joined the Society of Mary (the Marist Fathers); did his probationary studies in France, then further studies at the Catholic University of Ireland in Dublin; ordained to the priesthood on 16 August 1885; served at Jefferson College (president 1891-1897); in 1896 he made a visitation to all the houses of the Marist Fathers in Europe; appointed Bishop of Puerto Rico in 1899; promoted to be the seventh Archbishop of New Orleans in 1906; much work on schools and education for all ethnic groups; set up many Catholic organizations; struggled to improve the standing of the Catholic Church in his diocese, but much opposition, e.g., to his appeals for a major seminary for New Orleans and restoration of St. Louis Cathedral; he continued the practice of segregated parishes for African-Americans, believing that through these "racial feelings and natural differences can be best adjusted"; see Sr. Mary Bernardine Hill, "The Influence of James Hubert Blenk on Catholic Education in the Archdiocese of New Orleans, 1885-1917" (MA thesis, Louisiana State University, 1964); Michael Doorley, "Irish Catholics and French Creoles: Ethnic Struggles Within the Catholic Church in New Orleans, 1835-1920," *Catholic Hiustorical Review*, January 2001, p.34.

Bombeck, Erma Louise (*née* Fiste) – writer and humorist; b. 21 February 1927, Bellbrook, Ohio; c. 1949; d. 22 April 1996, San Francisco, California; brought up in Dayton, Ohio, in a working class family; good student who read widely, particularly on popular humor writing; part-time work in journalism; enrolled at Ohio University at Athens, but left after one year; in 1945 she enrolled in the University of Dayton, a Catholic college, where the relaxed, supportive atmosphere moved her to convert to the Catholic faith (formerly a member of the United Brethren Church); in 1949 she married William Lawrence Bombeck ("Bill"), a Catholic war veteran and teacher (three children of the marriage, one of whom was adopted); after graduating with a degree in English she worked full-time for the *Dayton Journal-Herald*; became a full-time housewife, but wrote humorous articles for a number of papers; her articles were soon syndicated nationwide and she became a very popular humorist on the topic of family life; wrote over 4,000 newspaper columns between 1965 and 1996; gave lectures; also broadcasts on radio; many television appearances (notably on ABC's *Good Morning America*); "When I stand before God at the end of my life, I would hope that I would not have a single bit of talent left, and could say, 'I used everything you gave me'"; very high annual earnings; actively supported the Equal Rights Amendment; much ill health; her remains are interred in Woodland Cemetery, Dayton, Ohio; see *At Wit's End* (1967); *Just Wait Until You Have Children of Your Own* (1971) (with Bill Keane); *I Lost Everything in the Post-Natal Depression* (1974); *The Grass is Always Greener Over the Septic Tank* (1976); *If Life is a Bowl of Cherries, What Am I Doing in the Pits?* (1978); *Aunt Erma's Cope Book* (1979); *Motherhood: The Second Oldest Profession* (1983); *Family - The Ties that Bind.. and Gag!* (1987); *I Want to Grow Hair, I Want to Grow Up, I Want to Go to Boise: Children Surviving Cancer* (1989); *When You Look Like Your Passport Photo, It's Time to Go Home* (1991); *A Marriage Made in Heaven... or Too Tired for an Affair* (1993); *All I Know about Animal Behavior I learned in Loehmann's Dressing Room* (1995); *Forever Erma: Best Loved Writing from America's Favorite Humorist* (1996); Lynn Hutner Colwell, *Erma Bombeck: Writer and Humorist* (1992); Susan Edwards, *Erma Bombeck: A Life in Humor* (1997); Edward T. James, Janet Wilson James, Paul S. Boyer, *Notable American Women: A Biographical Dictionary*, Vol. V (2004) ("As a humorous chronicler of family life, Bombeck endeared herself to legions of American women who identified with the good-natured figure she cut in her columns, but also shared her concerns that militant feminism disrespected domesticity…

In what is probably her most famous column, called 'If I Had My Life to Live Over,' made all the more poignant to readers aware of her health problems, Bombeck compiled a list of life's simplest pleasures, like eating popcorn in the 'good' living room or sitting on the lawn without worrying about grass stains").

Bork, Robert Heron – judge and law professor b. 1 March 1927, Pittsburgh, Pennsylvania; c. 21 July 2003 (received at the chapel of the Catholic Information Center, Washington, D.C.); d. 19 December 2012, Arlington, Virginia; only child of parents' marriage; brought up in the Presbyterian Church; educated at the University of Chicago; passed the bar exams in Illinois in 1953; served in the United States Marine Corps; began as a lawyer in private practice in 1954; Professor at Yale Law School 1962-1975 and 1977-1981; married to Claire Davidson 1962-1980 (three children of the marriage); in 1982 he married Mary Ellen

Pohl, earlier a Sacred Heart nun, but still actively Catholic; advocate of "originalism", the theory that constitutional adjudication is to be guided by the framers' original understanding of the United States Constitution (i.e., the court's task is to adjudicate, not "legislate") ("The truth is that the judge who looks outside the Constitution always looks inside himself and nowhere else"); Solicitor-General in the United States Department of Justice 1973-1977; Acting Attorney-General 1973; Circuit Judge for the United States Court of Appeals for the District of Columbia Circuit 1982-1988; nominated to the Supreme Court by President Reagan in 1987; at the confirmation hearings he was attacked by liberal politicians for his opposition to unbridled "civil liberties," and, most notably, to the decision on abortion in *Roe v Wade*; the Senate rejected his confirmation; at that time he was an atheist; resigned his appellate-court judgeship in 1988; very influential on antitrust law; senior fellow at the American Enterprise Institute for Public Policy Research, a conservative think tank; fellow at the Hudson Institute; Tad and Dianne Taube Distinguished Visiting Fellow at the Hoover Institution; Visiting Professor at the University of Richmond; Professor at Ave Maria School of Law, Naples, Florida; senior legal advisor to Republican Mitt Romney's presidential campaign in 2012; conversion influenced by his second wife's example, by the Opus Dei priest, Fr. C. John McCloskey, and by Mgr. Ronald Knox's *The Belief of Catholics*; see *The Tempting of America* (1990) (about the nomination issue and his judicial philosophy); *Slouching Towards Gomorrah: Modern Liberalism and American Decline* (1996) ("The truth is that, despite the statistics on churchgoing, etc., the United States is a very secular nation that, for the most part, does not take religion seriously. Not only may the statistics overstate the religious reality - people may be telling pollsters what they think makes a good impression - but statistics say nothing of the quality or depth of American religious belief. It is increasingly clear that very few people who claim a religion could truthfully say that it informs their attitudes and significantly affects their behavior.

The practices and beliefs of the Catholic laity offer a good test case because the Catholic Church's teachings on contraception, abortion, divorce and remarriage, and the infallibility of the pope on matters of faith and morals, are unusually clear. Yet it is also clear that many of the laity display the Tocqueville syndrome and 'keep their minds floating at random between liberty and obedience'... Conformity to the spirit of the times appears to characterize the clergy as well as the laity...

The obtrusive fact is that the

churches that make the highest demands on their members, that focus on salvation, community, and morality, that stand against the direction of the secular culture, are the churches that have gained in membership...

If religion is being altered internally by the forces of feminism and left-wing ideology, it is simultaneously being marginalized in our public life by the hostility of the intellectual class. The two most significant manifestations of that hostility are the federal judiciary's wholly unwarranted expansion of the First Amendment's prohibition of the establishment of religion and the national press's ignoring of religion as a topic of any importance"); "Thomas More for Our Season," *First Things*, June/July 1999 ("The culture war of the early sixteenth century was fought over the breaking apart of Christianity, its loss of central authority, and the consequent fragmentation of European civilization. Our war rages about the collapse of traditional virtues across all of the West and the rise of moral indifference and cheerful nihilism. Many parallels between the two eras could be drawn, but a crucial similarity lies in the central role played by law in each. Though More was a profoundly religious man, it should not be forgotten that he was also a preeminent lawyer and judge. The law, quite as much as Catholicism, is crucial to an understanding of the man and the martyr. Law and its institutions were, of course, major forces of cohesion in More's age, and are perhaps the primary symbols in ours of stability and continuity as well as justice. When moral consensus fades, as it did in More's time and does in ours, we turn to law; when law falters, as it must when morality is no longer widely shared, society and culture teeter on the brink of chaos.

That is another way of saying that law cannot be divorced from morality - and, there is reason to think, morality, at least in the long run, cannot be divorced from religion. Law and religion are alike, therefore, as reinforcements of social order. It is a subject for speculation at least, whether either can long remain healthy and self-confident without the other. Each imposes obligations, but each is subject to the therapeutic heresy, softening those obligations to accommodate individual desires. It is a sign of our distemper that Thomas More is today so often regarded as a hero of civil disobedience, a man who refused to obey law with which he was in profound moral disagreement. That is a considerable distortion of the truth, and it was not More's understanding of his motives. For him, in a very real sense, law *was* morality. It is equally true that for More morality was superior to law and was the standard by which law must be judged. If that seems a paradox, I do not think it truly is one"); *Coercing Virtue* (2003); Tim Drake, "Judge Bork Converts to the Catholic Faith," *National Catholic Register*, 20 July 2003 ("TD: What sparked your interest in the Catholic Church? RB: After I wrote *Slouching Toward Gomorrah* the priest at St. Anne's Catholic Church in Washington, D.C., Mgr. William Awalt, told me that my views on matters seemed to be very close to those of the Catholic views, which was true. Not being religious, the fact that our views corresponded wasn't enough to bring me into the Church, so it took me a while before I was ready to enter.

I had a number of conversations with Fr. C. John McCloskey III. He gave me some readings and he would drop by on his way home and we would talk for an hour to an hour and a half in my office. The one I liked best was Ronald Knox's *The Belief of Catholics*. I've taught classes, but I didn't feel like being taught a class. I wasn't eager to be a student. Our time together was informative and highly informal. TD: Were there any misconceptions that you had to overcome? RB: When I was between 15 and 16, I was taught that the Catholic Church was highly authoritarian and that the priests had strict control over your thoughts and ideas. By the time I came to convert I had been around the world a while, so I no longer had those ideas. I knew too many Catholics to believe that. TD: Does it seem to make a difference converting at age 76 rather than when you were younger? RB: I don't know that it has any effect...There is an advantage in waiting until you're 76 to be baptized, because you're forgiven all of your prior sins. Plus, at that age you're not likely to commit any really interesting or serious sins. TD: Was there anything in particular that pulled you toward the Church? RB: I found the evidence of the existence of God highly persuasive, as well as the arguments from design both at the macro level of the universe and the micro level of the cell.

I found the evidence of design overwhelming, and also the number of witnesses to the Resurrection compelling. The Resurrection is established as a solid historical fact.

Plus, there was the fact that the Church is the Church that Christ established, and while it's always in trouble, despite its modern troubles it has stayed more orthodox than almost any church I know of. The mainline Protestant churches are having much more difficulty"); (ed), *A Country I Do Not Recognize: The Legal Assault on American Values* (2005); Edward G. Lengel, "Robert Bork, the Cultural War, and the Catholic Church," *freerepublic.com*, 20 February 2007 ("Instigated by liberal elites who manipulated - and were manipulated by - the so-called 'youth movement' of the 1960s, this cultural decadence has become evident in ways that are now all too familiar. Bork spells them out, describing the deterioration of art and music; the popularization of pornography; the collapse of the family and consequent social disintegration; the radicalization of academia, law, and politics; legislation for divorce on demand, abortion, assisted suicide, and euthanasia; racial politics; and the decline of religion under multiple assaults from feminism and political correctness. The revolution has been both deliberate and successful, and has transformed our society into something no one could have imagined fifty years earlier.

Yet *Slouching Towards Gomorrah* is not just a tale of gloom and doom. Deep as the moral rot has penetrated into the vitals of society, Bork sees a faint hope for an eventual cure - in religion. 'We may be witnessing a religious revival, another awakening,' he writes. Evangelical Protestants and orthodox Jews are gaining strength as never before, and struggling to hold the ramparts against the decadent tide. All of their efforts are destined for naught, however, unless they are joined by one institution, the most important of all: the Catholic Church. It is 'a crucial question for the culture whether the Roman Church can be restored to its former strength and orthodoxy,' Bork observes"); *A Time to Speak: Selected Writings and Arguments* (2008); Austin Ruse, "The Whole World and the Soul of Robert Bork," *The Catholic Thing*, 24 September 2008 ("Bork has referred to judges as Olympians, and not as a compliment. By that he means those judges around the world who have decided that they, and not elected representatives, should rule. Bork has a different, more limited view of the role of a judge. Even so, being a member of the Supreme Court is Olympian, a chance at a kind of secular immortality given to very few. Bork did not get this; he got something else instead.

Five years ago, Robert Bork was baptized into the Catholic faith. Accompanied by his saintly wife Mary Ellen, in a chapel bursting with friends, Bork nearly ran the table of sacraments. He got five that day: baptism, confirmation, first confession, first Communion, and his marriage was regularized according to the Church. All that was missing were last rites and priestly ordination.

At the time of his Senate hearings, according to Bork himself, he was an atheist. And here is what I wonder. Would Bork have journeyed to Rome had he served on the Supreme Court? While Mary Ellen's example and influence would have remained present either way, other influences certainly would have been brought to bear, namely, power, and our tendency to attach ourselves to it. The rich young man went away because he was too attached to his things. How much more alluring is power? How heady is it to be in the very thick of the most important questions of our time; questions that affect hundreds of millions of lives and that reverberate through time even unto a kind of immortality? Wouldn't the danger of hubris and the Olympian nature of the Supreme Court make such interior considerations difficult, if not even impossible? There is another puzzling question. With Bork on the court, *Roe* might have been overturned in 1992. But on the court Bork might not have found God and the Church. I don't even know how to think about that except in light of the shepherd who left the ninety-nine sheep to find the single lost one. The Church teaches that a single soul is worth more than the whole universe. Figure that one out, Christopher Hitchens.

A more pleasant thought: Is it possible that Robert Bork lost the whole world - the court and all that meant - but gained his soul?").

Bouchard, James Chrysostom, SJ (also known as Watomika ("Swift Foot")) - priest; b. 1823, Muskagola, near Leavenworth, Kansas; c. 1846; d. 1889, San Francisco, California; son of Kistalwa, chief of the Lenni Lenape, or Delaware Indians, and his French wife, Monotowa (White Fawn); his mother had been captured and raised by the Commanche; his father died at the hands of the Sioux in 1834; taken away by a Protestant missionary; he became a Presbyterian and studied for the ministry in Ohio; influenced in his conversion to the Catholic faith by Fr. Arnold Damen, SJ (1815-1890), Chicago's Jesuit apostle; after his conversion he began studies in Missouri for the Jesuit Order; ordained to the priesthood in 1855 (the first Native-American priest in the United States); served as a missionary to miners in San Francisco; won hundreds of converts to the faith through his work in California, Nevada, Oregon, and other western territories. lectured on his experience; he died in 1889, on his death a newspaper in New York referred to him as "the Father Damen of the West"; see John Bernard McGloin, *Eloquent Indian: The Life of James Bouchard, Californian Jesuit* (1950); Jay Miller, "The Early Years of Watomika (James Bouchard): Delaware and Jesuit," *American Indian Quarterly*, Spring 1989, p.165; *New Catholic Encyclopedia*.

Bowie, James ("Jim") – pioneer; b. 10 April 1796, Tennessee (probably, but there are disputes on his birthplace); c. 28 April 1828 (received in San Antonio, Texas); d. 6 March 1836, The Alamo, San Antonio; ninth of ten children of his parents; raised in Louisiana; answered the plea for volunteers to fight the British in the War of 1812 by joining the Louisiana militia (with his elder brother Rezin (see below)), but arrived too late to participate in the fighting; joined the Long Expedition, an attempt to liberate Texas from Spanish rule; he and his brother developed several estates; they took part in the slave trade, using the money earned in further land speculation; used forged documents in several land sales; bought several plantations; in 1827 he was involved in a fight after attending a duel between two other men, during which, after being shot and stabbed, he killed the local sheriff with a large and unusual knife, and was seriously injured himself; this became known as the Sandbar Fight and confirmed his reputation as a superb knife fighter; the "Bowie knife" (possibly designed by Rezin) became very popular; in 1828 he moved to Texas, then a part of the Mexican federation; the Mexican Constitution proscribed religions other than Catholicism and gave preference to Mexican citizens in receiving land; he then became a Catholic; he took an oath of allegiance to Mexico and joined the Texas Rangers; became a Mexican citizen in 1830 and embarked on land speculation; in 1831 he married Maria Ursula de Veramendi, the daughter of his business partner who was vice governor of the province (two children of the marriage); his reputation grew after his expedition to find the lost San Saba silver mine, during which his small party repelled an attack by a large Indian raiding party; his wife, children, and all of his wife's family died in a cholera epidemic; he took part as a colonel in the volunteer militia in the Texas revolution against the Mexicans in 1835 and 1836, where he added to his reputation as a fine commander; he offered to lead volunteers to defend the Alamo; commanded the volunteer forces until an illness left him bed-ridden; he died with the rest of the Alamo defenders; his body was placed with the others on the funeral pyre; the remaining ashes from the pyre were interred at the Cathedral of San Fernando, San Antonio; thought of as one of the legendary characters of the American frontier; see Walter W. Bowie, *The Bowies and Their Kindred: A Genealogical and Biographical History* (1899); Evelyn Brogan, *Jas. Bowie: A Hero of the Alamo* (1922); Doris Shannon Garst, *James Bowie and His Famous Knife* (1957); Virgil Baugh, *Rendezvous at the Alamo: Highlights in the Lives of Bowie, Crockett, and Travis* (1970); Jean Flynn, *Jim Bowie: A Texas Legend* (1980); Clifford Hopewell, *James Bowie Texas Fighting Man: A Biography* (1994); William C. Davis, *Three Roads to the Alamo: The Lives and Fortunes of David Crockett, James Bowie, and William Barret Travis* (1998); *ANB*.

Bowie, Rezin Pleasant – land speculator and inventor; b. 8 September 1793, near Gallatin, Tennessee; c. 1814; d. 17 January 1841, New Orleans, Louisiana; one of ten children (and himself a twin) of the family; a younger brother was James ("Jim") Bowie (see above); after becoming a Catholic he married Margaret Nevil in the Catholic Church in 1814 (three daughters of the marriage); he and James enlisted in the Louisiana militia, answering the plea for volunteers to fight the British in The War of 1812, but arrived too late to take part in the fighting; worked with his brother to develop several large estates; raised money by slave-trading; he served in the Louisiana legislature three times; after the Sandbar Fight (see above under the entry for James Bowie) the "Bowie knife" (which he may well have designed) became very popular; he also took part in the search for the San Saba mine (see under James Bowie); in 1832 he began to suffer from poor eyesight; spent his last years on a plantation in Louisiana; originally buried in the San Gabriel Catholic Church Cemetery, but in the 1850s his body was disinterred and reburied at St. Joseph Catholic Cemetery, Coffee Street, Port Gibson, Mississippi; see Walter W. Bowie, *The Bowies and Their Kindred: A Genealogical and Biographical History* (1899); Clifford Hopewell, *James Bowie Texas Fighting Man: A Biography* (1994)

Bozell, (Leo) Brent Jr. – conservative activist and writer; b. 15 January 1926, Omaha, Nebraska; c. 1947; d. 15 April 1997, Bethesda, Maryland; his father was Leo Brent Bozell Sr. (1886-1946), co-founder of the public relations and advertising agency *Bozell Worldwide*; served in the U.S. Merchant Marine in the Pacific in World War II; educated at Yale University; best friend at Yale of William F. Buckley Jr (1926-2008) the conservative author and commentator; both were excellent debaters at Yale; married Patricia Lee Buckley (1927-2008), writer, editor, co-founder of the Catholic journal, *Triumph*, and William's sister; worked for a San Francisco law firm; became a speechwriter and legislative assistant for Senator Joseph McCarthy; worked on the *National Review* founded by Buckley in 1955; unsuccessfully ran for the Maryland House of Delegates in 1958; speechwriter for Senator Barry Goldwater; left the *National Review* in 1963 after a dispute with Buckley over Catholic principles in relation to the conservative movement; in 1964 unsuccessfully ran for the U.S. House of Representatives from Maryland; in 1965 moved his family to Spain; co-founder of the Catholic magazine *Triumph*; now attacked conservatism as "an inadequate substitute for Christian politics" and opposed both democratic capitalism and Communism; became increasingly devoted to Catholicism and promoted this in *Triumph*; supporter of Franco's Spain; also founded the Society of the Christian Commonwealth out of which came many of the staff of and donors to Christendom College; strongly defended Pope Paul VI's encyclical on birth control, *Humanae Vitae*, but disagreed with Paul VI's decisions on the liturgy; a founding member of Catholics United for the Faith; in 1970 he and his wife led the first "Operation Rescue" mission to try by direct action to stop abortion (he was clubbed, arrested, and given a suspended sentence); closed down *Triumph* in 1975; gave much help to Hispanic immigrants and did much prison visiting; father of ten children, including L. Brent Bozell III (b. 1955), also a conservative activist and founder and president of Media Research Center, and Michael Bozell, a Benedictine monk at Solesmes Abbey; in his later years suffered from bipolar disorder and endured great physical pain without complaint, offering it all to Christ; see *McCarthy and His Enemies* (1954) (with William F. Buckley, Jr.); *The Warren Revolution: Reflections on the Consensus Society* (1966); *Mustard Seeds: A Conservative Becomes a Catholic* (1986) ("There is no greater paradox in the cosmos than the apparent contradiction of our helplessness ('without me, you can do nothing') alongside God's 'helplessness.' Oh, I know, God is all-powerful, and so on; but he cannot undo what he has done, and what he once did was to make men free. This means that he 'needs' us in order to get us to Heaven as his lovers, and in order to do his will in the world. All we have to do in order to frustrate those wishes - to render God 'helpless' - is to say No. But God is not helpless, really, because he has mercy - himself. And what mercy does is convert, change our hearts. Which God never stops trying to do until we are dead. This means continued suffering for him, which is what Christ is all about"); Warren H. Carroll, "In Memoriam: L. Brent Bozell," *The Society of Catholic Social Scientists* (1997) ("Brent Bozell...had to the highest degree the convert's special awareness of how truly different it is to be a Catholic. It was an important part of the reason why he laid so much stress on the necessity of Catholicizing America rather than Americanizing Catholicism. While the true Church does and should bring out the best in the character of a nation as in that of an individual, this can only be accomplished fully in a nation when the true Church is publicly recognized and Christ is proclaimed its heart and its king. Brent Bozell believed in, and advocated, the confessional state - a nation publicly committed to the Catholic Faith - at a time when it was disappearing from the earth"); Linda Bridges and John R. Coyne, Jr., *Strictly Right: William F. Buckley, Jr. and the American Conservative Movement* (2007); Deal Hudson, *Onward Christian Soldiers* (2008).

Brady, Thomas Allan – historian and educator; b. 1902, Richmond, Missouri; c. 1947; d. 1964; mother a Presbyterian and father a Campbellite; grew up with virtually no contact with Catholics; educated at the State University of Columbia and the University of Missouri, majoring in History; became secularized and lost his religious faith, but continued to read and study religion; studied Law at Harvard University, later switching to History; influenced by Robert H. Lord, the Harvard history scholar and devout Catholic; received his PhD in Ancient History in 1934; married in 1934 Mary E. Leslie, a Catholic, with whom he had eight children; awarded a Guggenheim Fellowship in 1936, enabling him to spend a year doing historical research in Europe; taught history at the University of Missouri; member of many historical associations; see *The Reception of the Egyptian Cults by the Greeks (330-30 B.C.)* (1935); *Repertory of Statuary and Figured Monuments Relating to the Cult of the Egyptian Gods* (1938); "By God's Grace," in John A. O'Brien, *The Road to Damascus, Vol. IV: Roads to Rome* (1955), p.32 ("As an historian, I have learned the hard way that we cannot rule out, by fiat, all causation except that which belongs to the natural order. During all this time...my study and research had been in the History of Religion – specifically the spread of the cult of the pagan Egyptian Gods among the Greeks and Romans. My studies for eighteen years when I entered the Church, had centered on the period of time when Christ walked on the earth and founded His Church.

I knew an historian who entered the Church several years before I did. One year I met him at the meeting of the American Historical Association and we talked about his conversion. I said to him that presumably he now knew the answer to a problem that bothered me, namely 'What does the historian make of the conversion of St. Paul? Did it happen or not?' He pushed me off by saying the solution was not within our province since we aren't, as historians, trained to deal with it. I said then and say now that we cannot avoid the issue. Either God spoke to Saul on the Damascus road or He didn't. If He did, then it is an historical fact and one of tremendous importance").

Brégy, Katherine Marie Cornelia – writer; b. 1882, Philadelphia, Pennsylvania; c. 27 May 1904 ("I should like to record...that this is the only step of my entire life about which I have never had any subsequent misgiving. I have never, in moments of the most searching introspection, questioned its wisdom. I could have said that fair spring day with Sydney Carton (and quite as truthfully): 'It is a far, far better thing that I do than I have ever done - It is a far, far better rest that I go to than I have ever known'"); d. 1967; French and Irish Catholic ancestors, but parents Protestant; brought up in a "dignified, moderately "high" Episcopalianism"; attracted early by Catholicism and refused to be confirmed in the Protestant Episcopal Church; her conversion to

Catholicism was greatly influenced by Newman's writings and later by the life of Fr. Isaac Hecker (see below); parents objected to her becoming a Catholic, but consented later; educated at the University of Pennsylvania; wrote much poetry and prose (much of it literary criticism) for British and American journals; elected president of the Catholic Poetry Society of America in 1939; assisted in the revival of the poetry of Gerard Manley Hopkins; unmarried; see "The Poetry of Francis Thompson," *Catholic World*, August 1905; *The Poet's Chantry* (1912) (essays); essay in Georgina Pell Curtis, *Beyond the Road to Rome* (1914), p.58 ("Theoretically, at least, the Church idea was not new to me. Then somehow - I cannot say whether it was through constantly passing a hospital of the Sisters of Charity, or through dipping into the Memoirs of Mme. Navarro, or through accidentally hearing a description of the office of Tenebrae, - I woke up to the fact that this Church idea was still a vital force in the world. I was just a school-girl at the time: I had never been through a convent or spoken to a priest in my life. But the immensity of the thought did certainly arrest me. That simple linking of past and present was so vivid, so majestic, so incredibly thrilling! I did not talk much about the subject (never being able to talk of deep things without a certainty of sympathy in the listeners), but I began to read. First it was every scrap of Catholic news in the daily papers, the magazines, the encyclopedias, - prolific sources, if dubious! Then, like a thief in the night, I stole off to a little Catholic bookshop, where I happened very fortunately upon the Baltimore Catechism and Father di Bruno's *Catholic Belief.* I was more interested in these than (even!) in the Shakespearian dramas in which I had immersed myself for months before. Considering my age, I think I was abnormally interested! I suspect I gave my first romantic love to that venerable, tangible, mystical thing known as Catholicism. I had been accustomed to a very 'respectable' religion: here I found sanctity and the seven deadly sins. I had been used to the compromises of Anglicanism: here I found one 'speaking with authority, and not as the scribes.'

It was a great joy, this secret of mine: then, presently, I perceived that it was going to be a great pain. The pearl had its price, and I was not to be alone in paying for it…I drew the traditional storm upon my head. It was quite electrical for a while. The family pastor, a pious but impractical man, called upon me and talked vaguely about the 'Forged Decretals.' Other well-meaning hands brought me books in which all the vile accusations of nineteen hundred years were gatheredtogetheragainstthe 'Scarlet Woman'. Well, I had read my New Testament rather attentively, and the charges sounded familiar. The

Christ of Galilee and Jerusalem had been called seducer and liar and worldling and blasphemer, I seemed to remember; St. Peter was charged with tyranny and St. Paul had to defend himself against preaching that the end justified the means. These precedents comforted me: but the real historic scandals of the Church did hurt me bitterly. I had to pray against these. I had to remember the apostles once again - and the pitiful earthen vessel which bore the Treasure age after age. It was a lesson I needed to learn: that everything had happened before and might happen again; and still Mother Church would travel on, clothed with the sanctity of God and the frailty of man - infallible yet nowise impeccable – 'doing the King's work all the dim day long.' To apprehend this early in the religious life saved me, I think, from that sorry disease of 'taking scandal' which so often afflicts the newly received.

It was during those troubled days that I first began to read Cardinal Newman - perhaps the strongest literary influence of my life. His keenness of thought, his lucidity of form, his snow-white elevation of soul enchanted me. I literally sat at the great Oratorian's feet for a year and a half, and while reading the *Apologia* I was as conscious of his personality as of any actual living friend. He made faith an intellectual rather than an emotional thing to me. He taught me conclusively that Catholicism was the true Church of the Past; and I stood quite ready to burn my bridges on the strength of 'development' and Patristic testimonies...

Some five years after becoming a Catholic, I paid my first visit to the Old World I had long so passionately loved. This again was very much like going home, and my citizenship in the Church Catholic proved in a new sense a citizenship of the World. More poignantly than ever was I aware of my kinship with the past. I felt it, kneeling at the tomb of Peter or gathering poppies along the Appian Way. I felt it in the high seriousness of Oberammergau, in the beautiful, tragic triviality of Versailles, in the chateau-fort of my school time hero, Godfrey de Bouillon. In the mysterious gloom of Notre Dame de Paris it enveloped me - nor was it far away in the noble, outraged shrines of old Westminster...

It is by breaking loose from harbor chains that the ship finds herself: and I take it that by travel, mental or physical, the character is most truly defined. I do not think I came back from those months in Europe a worse Catholic or a better one; but there was indubitably some new quality in my religion and in my whole mental and spiritual viewpoint. For one thing, the ancestral note had been accentuated - I was less a convert than ever before. I had absorbed something of that curious toleration of the Romance nations, and something of their hunger after beauty. Beyond all this, a sense of the largeness and fullness of life possessed me. One phase of this was an exhilarating, almost intoxicating delight in the enormous heritage of culture which is, as it were, the birthright of every child of historic Christendom. To find Catholicity, then, means more even than to find religion: we may save the soul (if we can) and the mind, too, by her immemorial wisdom! It is a heartening thing to feel that we reap not only where the martyrs have sown in blood but where the doctors have sown in brain - where Dante and Chaucer and the Troubadours have sung - where the Tuscans and Umbrians, the Spanish and Flemish have wrought their rainbow canvases - even where, century after century, the French have talked so exquisitely. It is an inspiration, surely, to remember that the great universities of Europe were as authentically our own as the great cathedrals; that under normal conditions Catholicity stands committed not to ignorance, not even to mediocrity, but to culture of the entire spirit. Obviously, we are dealing now with a side issue: it is not for the sake of Catholic culture that our sacrificial missionaries sleep upon desert sands. But none the less, it is a part of the divine spaciousness of Catholicity - a part of that large inclusiveness which is implied in the Communion of Saints. It has indelibly colored the Catholic ideal of life. It has given that mature yet youthful graciousness which Walter Pater (who possessed, I think, a very delicate insight into Catholic thought) found in St. Catherine of Siena, when he declared that she had achieved her 'undying place in the House Beautiful, not by her rectitude of soul only, but by its fairness'

Now this, I take it, is the very keynote of the higher spirituality: not *rectitude* of soul only, but fairness: the tables of the Law indeed for a foundation, but above these all the soaring grace and intricacy of the Gothic cathedral. I recall once hearing a very suggestive and long-felt distinction - it came from one of the most typical monks of recent times - to the effect that the Dominican ideal placed Truth as the highest Love, while the Franciscan placed Love as the highest Truth. He was, of course, reconciling the claims of emotion and intellect. But to many a modern soul (as to many an ancient) Beauty becomes, I think, the synthesis of this Truth and this Love; and the beauty of holiness becomes the last word in religion. It is the leaven which permeates the whole mass of Christian life - the key to that wisdom which 'stretches from end to end mightily and orders all things sweetly.'

In this sense, Beauty is not merely a sensuous thing; although certainly the sensuous side - the delight of color and music and form and movement - is not to be despised.

Nor is it wholly an intellectual thing, nor absolutely a moral thing. It is an all-embracing sense of the harmony of life, reaching up to God as the primal Artist, the first and final source of 'whatsoever things are lovely.' I do not hesitate to affirm that my own religion has become increasingly a worship of Beauty - and that Beauty seems to me the most satisfying synonym for God Himself"); "Aspects of Recent Drama in English," *Catholic World*, April 1918; "Joyce Kilmer, Poet and Patriot," *The Outlook*, 23 July 1919, p.467; *Poets and Pilgrims: From Geoffrey Chaucer to Paul Claudel* (1925); *Bridges with Other Verse in Varying Moods* (1930); *From Dante to Jeanne d'Arc: Adventures in Medieval Life and Letters* (1933); *Ladders and Bridges: A Book of Verse* (1936); "Of Poets and Poetry," *Catholic World*, February 1939; *Queen of Paradox* (1950) (novel about Mary Queen of Scots); *The Story of Saint Francis de Sales: Patron of Catholic Writers* (1958); "Gerard Hopkins, An Epitaph and an Appreciation," in Gerald Roberts, *Gerard Manley Hopkins: The Critical Heritage* (1987) (originally appeared in *Catholic World*, January 1909); Patrick Allitt, *Catholic Converts: British and American Intellectuals Turn to Rome* (1997), pp.141-142 ("She channeled her emotional energy into the Church itself and wrote about her approach to conversion in the language of romantic love. As a teenager, 'my secret visits to singularly unattractive Catholic bookshops and above all my shyly wistful prayers before the tabernacle in nearby Catholic churches, began to take on the romance of a clandestine if supernatural love affair'...

What [Elizabeth] Kite [see below] had attempted for American history, Brégy attempted for English and American literature, arguing that its explicitly Protestant character was really no more than a thin covering over sturdy Catholic timbers and that all the really inspiring elements of post-Reformation literature could be traced to the old faith. Brégy maintained that Pilgrim's Progress, though undeniably the work of a Protestant, owed what strengths it had to Bunyan's familiarity with the great Catholic tradition... Even so, she emphasized, the Reformation had impoverished the tradition of Christian allegory, so that 'one turns back with a sigh to the wholesome, unstudied sanity of pre-Reformation standards'").

Brewster, Anne Hampton (used "Enna Duval" as a pseudonym at first) – writer, foreign correspondent and teacher; b. 29 October 1818, Philadelphia, Pennsylvania; c. 1848; d. April 1892, Siena, Italy; second child of Francis Enoch Brewster and Maria Hampton; brought up in a middle-class Protestant family; her older brother Benjamin Harris Brewster (1816-1888), served as Attorney-General of the United States 1881-

1885; educated mainly at home by her mother who encouraged her intellectual pursuits; her father abandoned the family in 1834 to live with his mistress and their two sons; began her writing with poetry, then moved on to short fiction; editor at *Graham's American Monthly Magazine* 1850-1851; many financial disputes with her brother over family property; traveled to Switzerland and Italy, then settled in New Jersey in 1858; her novels and short stories often featured heroines who must choose between marriage and celibacy (a common theme was that "marriage brings happiness only if one marries for love, not financial security"); her conversion to the Catholic faith made her independent of her family; in 1868 she moved to Rome where she became one of the earliest female foreign newspaper correspondents from the United States; became a popular journalist over nineteen years; she was a member of Arcadia, the poetical academy in Rome, and hosted a highly celebrated weekly salon, in which she entertained sculptors, painters, musicians, and writers; moved to Siena in 1889; she had a prolific writing career, publishing three novels, seven pieces of nonfiction, fifty-two short stories, and four poems, along with her many newspaper articles; unmarried; see *Spirit Sculpture* (1849) (novella concerning religious conversion, partly autobiographical); *Compensation; or, Always a Future* (1860); *Saint Martin's Summer* (1866); Estelle Fisher, *A Gentle Journalist Abroad: The Papers of Anne Hampton Brewster in the Library Company of Philadelphia* (1947); Denise M. Larrabee, *Anne Hampton Brewster: Nineteenth-Century Author and "Social Outlaw"* (1992) ("Anne converted to Catholicism when she was thirty years old. Her romantic nature found Catholic ritual, its iconographic beauty, and the timeless historical tradition of the Roman Church irresistible"); Anne Hampton Brewster Papers, Library Company of Philadelphia; *ANB* ("In her journal of [1848] Brewster maintains that 'stern, strict duty' is necessary for one's own well-being. Catholicism had a prescribed role for Brewster, which she defines in her first book *Spirit Sculpture...*, a moderately successful novella concerning religious conversion: '...our [women's] duty lies in a silent performance of the virtues of self-denial, self-control, and the willing performance of the most disagreeable home duties, that we may thereby show the influence of the blessed faith we profess'").

"Bricktop" – see under Smith, Ada Beatrice Queen Victoria Louise Virginia.

Brisbane, Abbott Hall ("Abbott" a family name, not an ecclesiastical title) – author, soldier, engineer and professor; b. 4 December 1804, Charleston, South Carolina; c. early

1830s (received with his wife); d. 28 September 1861; son of John S. Brisbane; accepted by the U.S. Military Academy, West Point, in 1821 (graduated in 1825); he was the earliest student at West Point who afterwards became a Catholic; in 1829 he married Adeline E. White (1807-1872), daughter of the painter John Blake White (1781-1859); their only son died in infancy; heartbroken at the loss, he and his wife both converted to the Catholic faith, partly as a result of the comfort they received from Bishop John England, but also because of his admiration of the Irish Catholics who served with him in the Seminole War; by 1836 he was colonel of the South Carolina Volunteers; served in Florida in the Seminole Wars and promoted to Brigadier General; worked as a supervising engineer; professor at The Citadel, The Military College of South Carolina 1848-1853; he was very devout and wrote a celebrated Catholic inspirational novel, *Ralphton*; retired to his slave-holding plantation outside of Charleston; after his death Adeline moved into the Ursuline convent in Columbia in 1870; diocesan records indicate that she took vows with the Ursulines, becoming Sr. Mary Borgia; see *Ralphton: The Young Carolinian of 1776, A Romance on the Philosophy of Politics* (1848) (modeled the character Fr. Duane on Fr. John Carroll, SJ, who became the first bishop of the United States in 1789); Mary Catharine Brisbane Hickox, *Abbott Hall Brisbane 1804-1861* (n.d.); Willard Thorp, *Catholic Novelists in Defense of Their Faith, 1829-1865* (1978); Stella Uttley, "Abbott Hall Brisbane," *Catholic Life*, June 2010, p.60.

Brooks, (Mary) Louise – actress and dancer; b. 14 November 1906, Cherryvale, Kansas; c. 1953; d. 8 August 1985, Rochester, New York; daughter of a lawyer; began her career as a dancer; from 1925 appeared in several films; first noticed in her role as a vamp in Howard Hawks' *A Girl in Every Port* (1928); worked in Germany with the film maker G. W. Pabst, notably as Lulu in *Pandora's Box* (1929), then in *Diary of a Lost Girl* (1929); became famous for her visual image and eroticism; in the United States she was outspoken about Hollywood and got into contractual difficulties, and her career declined; ran a dance studio 1940-1943; relied on generosity of family and friends; rediscovered in the 1950s and began a new career as a writer; married twice, first to Edward Sutherland (1926-1928), director, then to Deering Davis 1933-1938; involved in many relationships, notably with George Preston Marshall (1896-1969), the businessman; buried in Holy Sepulchre Cemetery, Rochester, New York; see *Lulu in Hollywood* (1982; expanded edition, 2000) (memoir); Richard Leacock, *Lulu in Berlin* (1974); Kenneth Tynan, "The Girl in the Black Helmet -

Louise Brooks," *New Yorker*, 11 June 1979 (reprinted in Tynan's *Show People* (1979); Barry Paris, *Louise Brooks* (1989); Peter Cowie, *Louise Brooks: Lulu Forever* (2006); Jan Wahl, *Dear Stinkpot: Letters From Louise Brooks* (2010); Tom Graves, *My Afternoon With Louise Brooks* (2011); *ANB* ("With her famous bobbed black hair, spit curls curving across white cheeks, sultry eyes, and penetrating gaze, Brooks created a screen persona of beauty, sensuality, and eros").

Broun, Heywood Campbell – journalist; b. 7 December 1888, Brooklyn, New York; c. 23 May 1939 (received by Mgr. Fulton Sheen); d. 18 December 1939, New York City; brought up an Episcopalian, but developed into a freethinker; attended Harvard University 1906-1910, but left without a degree; married to Ruth Hale (1887-1934), the freelance writer and feminist; joined the *New York Morning Telegraph* as a sportswriter; during World War I; covered the war as correspondent in France for the *New York Tribune*, where he worked from 1912-1921; in 1921 joined the *New York World*, where he launched a daily column, "It Seems To Me", which he took with him to the *New York World-Telegram* and the *New York Post*; in 1927 he and his wife protested the executions of Sacco and Vanzetti; in 1930 unsuccessfully ran for Congress as a Socialist; in 1933 co-founder of The Newspaper Guild; member of the famed Algonquin Wits, who met at the Round Table in the Algonquin Hotel on Forty-fourth Street 1919-1929; often described as "looking like an unmade bed"; close friend of the Marx Brothers and of Dorothy Parker; wrote books and articles on sports, theater, unemployment and social justice; second wife was Constantina Maria Incoronata Fruscella Dooley ("Connie"), an actress and a Catholic; he was agnostic until seven months before his death when he converted to Catholicism after discussions with Mgr. Fulton Sheen; funeral at St. Patrick's Cathedral, New York, attended by three thousand mourners (eulogy delivered by Mgr. Sheen); buried in the Cemetery of the Gate of Heaven in Hawthorne, New York; see *It Seems to Me* (1935); *Collected Edition* (1941); Fulton J. Sheen, *Treasure in Clay* (1982), pp.260-261; Thomas C. Reeves, *America's Bishop: The Life and Times of Fulton J. Sheen* (2001) ("The day after the election of Pius XII, Broun approached Fr. Edward Dowling, a priest-journalist friend, and asked him if it was possible for a social and political progressive to be Catholic. Dowling replied, 'Don't you realize that you're a little naïve, Heywood? You like to call yourself a radical, but the doctrines of the Church to which I belong imply so many deep changes in human relationship that when they are accomplished – and they will be – your own notions will be nothing more than an outmoded pink liberalism...

A month after his conversion, Sheen asked Broun for his reactions, and remembered him mentioning three. 'The first was great peace of soul and a feeling of being home at last; the second, a realization that much liberalism was extremely illiberal. Some of his friends, he said, who were loudest in shouting for freedom were also loudest in protesting against him because he acted freely.' Broun said, 'I discovered that freedom for them meant thinking as they did.' A third reaction also involved his former leftist colleagues. 'It has dawned upon me that the basis of unity in radicalism is not love, but hate. Many radicals love their cause much less than they hate those who oppose it.' Fr. Dowling's general observation had proven true: 'As regards radicalism, I have also discovered that no social philosophy is quite as revolutionary as that of the Church'"); Lorene Hanley Duquin, *A Century of Catholic Converts* (2003), p.108 ("While Broun was always susceptible to melancholy, thoughts of death began to plague him and he suffered mild bouts of depression. In 1939, Msgr. Fulton Sheen was having lunch with a magazine editor [Fulton Oursler (see below)] and Heywood Broun happened to walk by. 'Did you ever try to make a convert of Heywood?' the editor asked. When Sheen said no, the editor urged him to try. A short time later Sheen called Broun and told him that he wanted to meet with him. 'About what?' Broun asked. 'Your soul,' Sheen replied. 'When?' Broun asked. 'Three o'clock Saturday at the Navarro Hotel on Fifty-ninth Street,' Sheen said.

When they met, Heywood Broun admitted that he was interested in the Catholic Church for three reasons: "I am convinced that the only moral authority left in the world is the Holy Father; second, I made a visit to Our Lady of Guadalupe in Mexico and was deeply impressed by the devotion to the Mother of Christ. Finally, and most important, I do not want to die in my sins'"); *ANB*.

Brown, Beatrice Bradshaw (*pseud.* Michael Kent) – writer; b. New York City; c. February 1934; her father, Harold Haven Brown (d. 1932), was an artist, educator, lecturer and writer; her mother, Florence Bradshaw, was also an artist; she had a devotion to Joan of Arc from early childhood; educated at the University of Chicago; for several years she also studied music intensively; traveled in Italy and France; wrote two children's books, the first in collaboration with her sister, Barbara; continued to write for various periodicals and in 1934 had a story, *Debt of Honor*, published in a Catholic periodical (her writing always had a Catholic flavor); she had an innate Catholicism and began to attend Mass regularly and was soon received into the Church; wrote from now on about Catholic themes, mainly in periodicals, but also wrote *The Bond of Peace*, "a plea for a crusade of sacrifice to repair the divisions caused in the modern world by the Protestant revolt," and a novel, *The Mass of Brother Michel* (illustrated by herself); see *A Paris Pair, Their Day's Doings* (1923); *A Doll's Day* (1931); *The Mass of Brother Michel* (1942); *The Armitage Case* (1943); *A Bond of Peace* (1945); *Hail, Victor, Hail!* (1946); Matthew Hoehn, OSB (ed), *Catholic Authors* (1952) ("In 1933, on the advice of a friend, she submitted a story to *The Catholic World.* This story, *Debt of Honor*, was accepted by Father Gillis and published in January, 1934. It was subsequently listed in the O'Brien Best Short Stories Anthology for that year. This story pointedly illustrates the strong Catholic flavor that had always characterized her writings, long before she received any formal instruction in the faith. She does not like to be labeled a convert. 'Conversion means a turning, but in my case there was no turning, but rather a discovery. Had I ever succeeded in being a Protestant, that would have been a conversion, or turning, from what I really was to something I could never be...All the stories I wrote, even in school days, were essentially Catholic'")

Brownback, Samuel Dale ("Sam") – politician; b. 12 September 1956, Garnett, Kansas; c. 2002 (received in Washington D.C.); brought up as a Methodist; educated at Kansas State University; received his JD from University of Kansas 1982; married to Mary Brownback, *née* Stauffer (five children of the marriage); worked as an attorney in Manhattan, Kansas; Kansas Secretary of Agriculture 1986-1990 and 1990-1993; worked in Washington in the Office of the U.S. Trade Representative 1990-1991; member of the Republican Party; member of House of Representatives 1995-1996; Senator from Kansas 1996-2011; joined a nondenominational evangelical church, Topeka Bible Church; influenced in his conversion to the Catholic faith by Fr. C. John McCloskey III of Opus Dei ("I felt a deep calling to make that move and spent roughly four years really studying, reading, thinking about it, praying about it before deciding to join. I was very happy in the Evangelical church I was in. I had no problems with the Evangelical church at all. It's just I felt a deep spiritual calling to do it and have been delighted to join the Catholic Church. The readings that I've done since then by Catholic writers – I've really enjoyed the depth and the beauty of the expression. It's been very helpful to my faith journey"); interested in the writings of the Desert Fathers; unsuccessful candidate for the

Republican nomination in the 2008 presidential election, withdrawing before the primaries; 46th Governor of Kansas from 2011; signed three anti-abortion bills in 2011 ("I see it as the lead moral issue of our day, just like slavery was the lead moral issue 150 years ago"; when asked his opinion of repealing *Roe v Wade*, he said "It would be a glorious day for human liberty and freedom"); attempted to block Planned Parenthood of Kansas and Mid-Missouri from receiving family planning funds from the state; he has stated that he opposes homosexuality on the grounds he believes it to be immoral, as a violation of both Catholic doctrine and natural law; he opposes both same-sex marriage and same-sex civil unions; he supports adult stem cell research and the use of cord blood stem cells instead of embryonic stem cells; criticized for supporting President Obama's nomination of pro-choice Kathleen Sebelius as Secretary of Health and Human Services; in 2013 signed a bill into law, reaffirming the state's current ban on abortion at 20 weeks (without exceptions for rape or serious fetal anomalies), blocking tax breaks for abortion providers, expanding "conscience protections" for anti-choice groups and writing into state law that life begins "at fertilization."

Brownson, Henry Francis – editor, publisher and soldier; b. 7 August 1835, Canton, Massachusetts; c. 18 November 1844 (received with his brother William; his father, mother, and the rest of the family were received a month earlier); d. 19 December 1913, Detroit, Michigan; son of Orestes Brownson (see below) and Sally Healy Brownson; most of his religious education came from his mother and was Episcopalian; attended the University of Notre Dame; joined the Jesuit novitiate, then studied philosophy at Georgetown and theology in Paris; returned to the United States and studied Law; admitted to the New York Bar in 1856; served in the Union Army during the Civil War, reaching the rank of Major; published in his father's review and republished all his father's works; in 1868 he married Josephine "Fifine" Van Dyke (seven children of the marriage); one of the leaders of the American Catholic Congress of Baltimore in 1889; see *The History of Waterbury* (1858); (ed), *The Works of Orestes Brownson*, 20 Vols. (1882-1887); *Life of Orestes A. Brownson*, 3 Vols. (1898-1900); *The Religion of Ancient Craft Masonry* (1890); *Faith and Science* (1895); *The Proof of Miracles* (1898); *Orestes A. Brownson's Early, Middle and Latter Life*, 3 Vols. (1898-1900); essay in Georgina Pell Curtis (ed), *Some Roads to Rome in America* (1909), p.28 ("One day, in the summer of 1844, I was reading the sixteenth chapter of St. Matthew's Gospel, and when I came to the 18th verse, I asked my mother, 'What church was it that Christ built on the rock, which the gates of hell should not prevail against?' She answered, 'That was the Catholic Church.' 'Then,' I said, 'that must be the true church?' 'It was,' she replied, 'at first; but it became very corrupt, and in the sixteenth century holy men believed they were commissioned to reform it.' 'Then,' I said, 'the gates of hell did prevail against it.'

My mind kept on revolving this thought, that the Catholic Church was the church which Christ founded; and by the time that I came to read in St. Matthew's last chapter, 'Behold! I am with you all days, even to the consummation of the world,' I was fully convinced that the Catholic Church was the true church, that Christ was in that Church and in no other...

Once satisfied that Christ founded the Catholic Church, and abides with it through all time, and that He sent the Holy Ghost to teach it all truth, I have always believed what that Church teaches, and have never been inclined to prefer my own views to the teachings of the Spirit of Truth"); his papers are at the University of Notre Dame; *ANB*.

Brownson, Orestes Augustus – educator and philosopher; b. 16 September 1803, Stockbridge, Vermont; c. 19 October 1844 (received with his wife Sally and some of his family by Coadjutor Bishop of Boston, John B. Fitzpatrick; his sons Henry and Channing were received a month later; his son Orestes Jr. was received at the end of the year); d. 17 April 1876 (Easter Sunday), Detroit, Michigan; from a farming family; his father Sylvester Brownson died early; given up for adoption at the age of six; raised in Calvinist Congregationalism; little formal schooling, but much reading; in 1822 baptized into the Presbyterian Church, but withdrew from it in 1824; became a Universalist preacher, but later the pastor of a Unitarian community; then on the fringes of the Transcendentalist movement; in 1836 set up his own church which he called The Society for Christian Union and Progress; during this period published much on religious issues; friend of Emerson and Thoreau; friend and correspondent of Isaac Hecker (see below); influenced by the Oxford Movement; final impetus to become a Catholic came from Bishop Fenwick of Boston (see the two extracts below); after his conversion to the Catholic faith he wrote aggressively with the purpose of converting America to Catholicism; became politically conservative, though later liberal on some issues; during the Civil War he supported the union and emancipation; ran *Brownson's Quarterly Review* from 1844 to 1864 as a Catholic journal; argued that the Church was supreme over the state; incurred the displeasure of many bishops by getting into arguments with them; Newman offered him a post in the university he was about to head in Dublin, Ireland; married to Sally Healy (eight children of the marriage); buried first in Detroit, but afterwards in the crypt of the Basilica of the Sacred Heart at the University of Notre Dame; see (selective list) *The Convert; or, Leaves from My* Experience (1857); *The Works of Orestes A. Brownson*, 20 Vols. (1882-1887) (collected and arranged by Henry F. Brownson); Henry F. Brownson, *Orestes A. Brownson's Early, Middle and Later Life*, 3 Vols. (1898-1900); Daniel Sargent, *Four Independents: Studies of Charles Péguy, Paul Claudel, Gerard Manley Hopkins, Orestes Augustus Brownson* (1935); Arthur M. Schlesinger, Jr., *Orestes Brownson: A Pilgrim's Progress* (1939) ("Eight years before [his conversion] Brownson had proclaimed the *Church of the Future*. This church, he declared in *New Views*, would arise inevitably out of the perfectibility of man; and it would unite the partial truths of the existing churches by reconciling Catholicism and Protestantism, the spirit and the flesh. He now realized that he had misunderstood man, who was essentially imperfect, and misinterpreted Catholicism, which actually unified spirit and flesh. Grace alone could cause the perfection of man and the establishment of the true church. Brownson had sought the *Church of the Future* through weary years of distress and disappointment. Then he looked around him, and discovered it to be the great church of the past"); Katherine Burton, *In No Strange Land: Some American Catholic Converts* (1942), p.43 ("Brownson himself had read deeply the writings of the Oxford men. He too was close to the Church now; he had outgrown all the various Protestant sects, harsh or kindly, that had held him at various times. He had gone beyond the social philosophy of Cousin and his own dream of building a 'church of the future,' a universal church that would replace and yet embrace all the warring sects; he was past the belief that social reform could come about without moral reform. He had studied much and sought long, and now, near the end of his seeking, he was seeing the true church of the future and of the present and the past too, the Catholic Church…

He had lost all his objections to the papacy. The only thing that still troubled him was that he could not give up hope for the salvation of his friends outside the Church and yet he could not feel sure of it either. He went to Bishop Fenwick of Boston with his difficulties, and the Bishop suggested that since he knew God was just it might be well to leave his Protestant friends in His hands.

'But there is one other thing; if I could only find some excuse for the Protestant Reformation, I am sure I would feel better' and he looked appealingly at the Bishop. But Bishop Fenwick, as he shook hands in farewell, said only, 'Come and see me again and if you do find some excuse for the Reformation don't fail to let me know about it.'

Brownson told Isaac Hecker [see below] about the interview. 'And the Bishop said not one unkind word about Protestantism, but neither did I win from him any concessions at all. I liked that. Had he been less uncompromising, I fear I would have distrusted his sincerity.'

In two weeks he was back with the Bishop again, asking to be prepared for admission into the Church. In October 1844 he was received...

To George Ripley [see the entry below for Sophia Ripley] he opened his heart, for him he could trust. 'It was that suddenly I saw that the Church is the body of which Christ is the spirit. I saw that the Catholic is the only Church.'

'But hasn't it failed too?' asked Ripley. 'Not unless we choose to give the lie to its Founder. You must reject Christ too, I am afraid, if you reject His Church. I have tried in every possible way to escape this conclusion but I cannot. And besides I see the Catholic Church has ever been the friend of the humble and the poor and friendless, and that should convince even you'"); Theodore Maynard, *Orestes Brownson, Yankee, Radical, Catholic* (1943) ("In the April [1844] number [of *Brownson's Quarterly Review*] he had had an article that had shown the direction he was taking. This postulated the necessity of a church as the only means of social reform. Man could not raise himself; and just as Archimedes said he could lift the world if he were provided with a fulcrum, so the dynamic law must be applied to moral conditions. He concluded: 'Either there is already existing the Divine Institution, the Church of God, or there are no means of reform.' At that time, however, he was not prepared to say that the Catholic Church was the divine institution he had in mind; he was still trying to cling to his own notion of the Catholic Church as made up of scattered fragments.

Between April and July the whole thing had broken down. In the July issue Brownson told his readers bluntly: 'The church in communion with the See of Rome is the one holy catholic apostolic church, or the one holy catholic apostolic church does not exist. We have tried every possible way to escape this conclusion, but escape it we cannot. We must accept it or go back to the no-church doctrine. Our logic allows us no alternative between Catholicism and Come-outerism. We are thoroughly convinced in mind, heart, and soul, that Christ did institute a visible church; that he founded it upon a rock; that the gates of hell have not prevailed, and cannot prevail, against it; and that it is the duty of all of us to submit to it, as the representative of the Son of God on earth'...

Brownson called on Bishop Fenwick, a Marylander and a Jesuit, for the first time during Holy Week, a bad time to call, because the Bishop was busy. The conversation did not touch the question of Brownson's admission to the Church but was carried on 'in a lively and half-sporting strain.' The visitor thought Fenwick a very pleasant man but of no remarkable ability. At least none had manifested itself during those twenty minutes. However, he saw him again in May, and then came to the point. The Bishop said he had been reading the *Review* and had observed that Brownson was approaching the Catholic position, but asked, 'What can be your objections to the Pope?'

'I do not object to the Pope,' Brownson told him. 'Some time ago I was foolish enough to say that the problem of the age is Catholicism without papacy; but I no longer entertain that notion. The Church without the Pope would be to me no church at all.'

'Why then, are you not a Catholic?'

Brownson explained that he would be one except for wanting to discover some ground for becoming a Catholic without at the same time declaring Protestants all wrong and that they could not he saved. To which the Bishop answered, 'God is just, and you may leave your Protestant friends in His hands. If they break the order He has established, that is no good reason for you to remain where you are and to neglect to make sure of yourself.' Subsequent visits were made and books were lent; then Fenwick turned Brownson over to his young coadjutor, Bishop Fitzpatrick...By now Brownson had reached the conclusion that, though to become a Catholic was an unpleasant step, 'To be eternally damned would, after all, be a great deal unpleasanter'"); Alvin S. Ryan (ed), *The Brownson Reader* (1955); R. W. B. Lewis, *The American Adam: Innocence, Tragedy, and Tradition in the Nineteenth Century* (1955); Theodore Maynard, *Great Catholics in American History* (1957), p.117 ("Whether Orestes Brownson was the greatest and most luminous mind produced by American Catholicism, as many believe, he surely was one of the most rugged and forceful of personalities, as also of an unpredictable eccentricity that colors, if not always charms, all that he did and said. Without pretending to be a Brownsonian - for such people are often too earnest and solemn in their admiration for his philosophy - I am Brownsonian at least in the sense that I delight in this forthright, booming, table-thumping man"); John A. O'Brien, *Giants of the Faith* (1960), p.245; Americo D. Lapati, *Orestes A. Brownson* (1965); Allen Guttman, "From Brownson to Eliot: The Conservative Theory of Church and State," *American Quarterly* (1965), p.484; Hugh Marshall, *Orestes Brownson and the American Republic* (1971); Leonard Gilhooley, *Contradiction and Dilemma: Orestes Brownson and the American Idea* (1972); Thomas Richard Ryan, *Orestes Brownson: A Definitive Biography* (1976); Richard M. Leliaert, "The Religious

Significance of Democracy in the Thought of Orestes A. Brownson," *Review of Politics* (1976), p.3; Joseph F. Gower and Richard M. Leliaert, *The Brownson-Hecker Correspondence* (1979); Leonard Gilhooley (ed), *No Divided Allegiance: Essays in Brownson's Thought* (1980); Patrick W. Carey, "American Catholic Romanticism, 1830-1888," *Catholic Historical Review* (1988), p.590; Mark S. Burrows, "The Catholic Revision of an American Myth: The Eschatology of Orestes Brownson as an Apology of American Catholicism," *Catholic Historical Review* (1990), p.18; Gregory S. Butler, *In Search of the American Spirit: The Political Thought of Orestes Brownson* (1992); Jenny Franchot, *Roads to Rome: The Antebellum Protestant Encounter with Catholicism* (1994), Ch. 17, "Orestes Brownson: The Return to Conspiracy"; Robert A. Herrera, *Orestes Brownson: Sign of Contradiction* (1999); Peter Augustine Lawler, "Orestes Brownson and the Truth About America," *First Things*, December 2002; Richard J. Dougherty, "Orestes Brownson on Catholicism and Republicanism," *Modern Age*, Fall 2003; Patrick W. Carey, *Orestes A Brownson: American Religious Weathervane* (2004); John P. Reidy, "Nineteenth-Century American Apologist," *This Rock*, February 2010; David Jerome Callon, "Converting Catholicism: Orestes A. Brownson, Anna H. Dorsey, and Irish America," unpublished PhD dissertation, Washington University in St. Louis, 2008; Charles P. Connor, *Classic Catholic Converts* (2001), p.63; *Catholic Encyclopedia*; *orestesbrownson.com* (Orestes Brownson Society); *ANB* ("A few key issues prepared Brownson for his conversion in 1844. For one, he dissented from other Democratic intellectuals who espoused radical individualism and anti-statism. Not adhering to the maxim *vox populi, vox dei*, he stressed the organic unity of society and located its collective soul in the state, which, he believed, must be more than the sum of its individuals. He soon concluded that Catholicism underscored such an ideal in a way that Protestantism could not. Also, the election of 1840 had left him bitterly disillusioned. The defeat of the Democratic incumbent, Martin Van Buren, in the famous 'log cabin and hard cider' presidential campaign, led him to distrust the political wisdom of the masses. He saw how easily people were humbugged by slogans, symbols, and songs.

Brownson sought a principle of order amid the disintegration of the modern world. He saw that Protestantism legitimized individualism and thus promoted capitalism. To this extent, he believed that Transcendentalism signified the logical culmination of the Reformation, a purely spiritual and individualistic religion with no corporate structure and no organic relationship to the larger society...

The doctrine of the Incarnation became critical for Brownson's linking of religion and social reform. Christ's mediating activity, he insisted, could not take place apart from the universal, institutional Church. He broke from his earlier liberal faith in progress and placed no hope in unaided humanity to effect its own salvation. Without the corporate life and discipline of the Church, such effort would invariably succumb to anarchic individualism and its destructive tendencies, he said. Only the Catholic Church could supply the need, he believed, because Protestantism could not repair what it had created").

Brubeck, David Warren ("Dave") – jazz pianist; b. 6 December 1920, Concord, California; c. 1980 (Our Lady of Fatima parish, Wilton, Connecticut); d. 5 December 2012, Norwalk, Connecticut; parents nominally Christian, but he was not baptized as a child; his father was a cattle rancher; his mother, Elizabeth (*née* Ivey), a music teacher, studied piano in England under Myra Hess; he and his three brothers all took music lessons from his mother; began to study veterinary science at the College of the Pacific, but transferred to the music department (graduated in 1942); drafted into the army and served overseas in Patton's Third Army; after the war he attended Mills College, Oakland, California, and studied under Darius Milhaud, the French composer; helped to establish *Fantasy Records*, Berkeley, California; founded the Dave Brubeck Quartet in 1951; they combined classical and jazz techniques, became very popular, and recorded several albums; toured Europe and Asia in 1958; the quartet experimented with unusual time signatures; his recording, *Time Out* (1959) became the first instrumental jazz album to become a gold record; he and his wife Iola developed a jazz musical, *The Real Ambassadors*; used local music he encountered on travels; he disbanded the quartet at the end of 1967 in order to have time to compose longer works; composer of orchestral music; wrote *Light in the Wilderness* (1968), an oratorio on the teachings of Christ, and *The Gates of Justice* (1969), a cantata containing Biblical texts; *Truth Is Fallen* (1971) was dedicated to the memory of the 1970 Kent State University and Jackson State shootings during Vietnam War protests, and draws upon the biblical words of Isaiah and Jeremiah; *La Fiesta de la Posada* (1975) was inspired by the Mexican Christmas tradition of community celebration and music; he believed that what he saw in World War II contradicted the Ten Commandments; from this developed a spiritual awakening and his conversion to the Catholic faith; shortly after that he completed *The Mass to Hope*; his family was shocked by his conversion;

in 1996 he received the Grammy Lifetime Achievement Award; founded the Brubeck Institute at the University of the Pacific in 2000; in 2006 he was awarded the University of Notre Dame's Laetare Medal; issued many records and composed several jazz standards; best remembered piece, *Take Five*, was written by his musical partner in the quartet, the alto-saxophonist Paul Desmond; see Fred M. Hall and Gene Lees, *It's About Time: The Dave Brubeck Story* (1996); Mark Lombard, "Dave Brubeck: Making a Joyful Noise Unto the Lord," *St. Anthony Messenger*, October 2009 ("He has adamantly asserted for years that he is not a convert, saying to be a convert you needed to be something first. He continues to define himself as being 'nothing' before being welcomed into the Church"); Lorene Hanley Duquin, *A Century of Catholic Converts* (2003), p.185; Hedrick Smith, "Rediscovering Dave Brubeck," *pbs.org*.

Brumley, Mark – Catholic apologist; b. St. Louis, Missouri; c. 1980; parents were theists, but not churchgoers, and he was raised in this belief; in high school in the 1970s he became a Christian, but a very anti-Catholic fundamentalist; in late 1970s he became a more mainstream Evangelical Protestant; greatly influenced in his conversion to the Catholic faith by Louis Bouyer's book *The Spirit and Forms of Protestantism*, and by the works of C. S. Lewis, G. K. Chesterton, and Frank Sheed; concluded that the Catholic Church was the fullness of Christian truth; holder of a Masters degree in Theology from the University of Dallas; former staff apologist for *Catholic Answers*; author of many articles in Catholic periodicals; president of Ignatius Press; see "The Witnesses: Masters of Misquotation," *This Rock*, April 1990; "Mary's Assumption: Irrelevant and Irreverent?" *Catholic Dossier*, May-June 1996; *EWTN Audio Library, The Journey Home* (20 November 1998) ("I came to see that the Church had to have some concrete, historical embodiment; that it wasn't this invisible, nebulous thing out there. And really I have to accredit C. S. Lewis for helping me to see that. It's ironic that this Anglican, who never became a Catholic, has been so influential in bringing so many people to the Catholic Church. I didn't immediately come on to that idea that the Catholic Church was the Church, but I began to look into the history of the Church going back to the Reformation; even before the Reformation, looking into the Church Fathers; and I began to be open to certain doctrines that were taught by the Catholic Church. But I was open to them in spite of the fact that they were taught by the Catholic Church, not because they had been taught by the Church.

What it was in my own journey that opened my heart to the Catholic Church was really studying scripture and Church history, and asking myself, 'Where do I belong?' Jesus is the reason why I'm a Catholic. People ask, 'Why did you become a Catholic?' Ultimately it was Jesus, fidelity to Jesus, wanting to do his will. Where is your truth? Where is your Church? Trying to answer these questions.

And really studying and finding that in the pages of the New Testament we see a Church which is united in its faith. It's a concrete, visible institution. It's not an invisible, nebulous reality out there, but a concrete, visible institution. If the Church in Corinth had had an address, you could write it down and send them a letter. It was that concrete, one faith, one in a liturgical life, although I wouldn't have used the word 'liturgical'. But we see baptism, we see confirmation, we see the Holy Eucharist. These were all shared. You know, Paul could go to Corinth and they had the Eucharist. Or Paul could go to Galatia and they had the Eucharist. It was the same Church. It wasn't like in our church, where we only had two sacraments. And then down there in Philippi it's three sacraments; and then you go back to Jerusalem and it's back to two. No, they had a common sacramental, and they had a common authority structure. The apostles were a universal authority in the Church, recognized everywhere.

Paul, as you read his Pastoral Epistles (1 and 2 Tmothy and Titus), what does he do? He establishes pastors and invests them with a share of his authority. And I came to the conclusion this is what the Church in the New Testament looks like. And that left me with some options. The options were either that Church no longer exists. It once existed at the time of the New Testament, but has disappeared. And if that's true, then Jesus was a liar, because Jesus said the gates of hell would not prevail against his Church. So, I couldn't believe that.

Or that New Testament Church existed throughout history and existed today. And when I looked at Evangelicalism and the various denominations – these are good men and women of God, trying to follow Christ and Scripture – what we see is constant disagreement. Even when people get along they still disagree on some very important issues. How many sacraments are there? What is a sacrament? Did Christ establish sacrifices or ordinances? How are we saved? Are we saved by faith alone? And what's the nature of the salvation that you receive?

All sorts of questions about Church government. Is it Congregationalism? A Presbyterian structure? An Episcopal structure? I find good Christian men and women who were all committed to the Scripture. It wasn't a matter of, well, some followed the Bible, some didn't. They all tried to follow the Bible. They studied the Scripture, and yet they came to conflicting conclusions on these very important issues. So, I had to conclude not that there was something wrong with the Bible, but that these very good men and women were trying to use the Bible in a way God never intended. And so I was forced to conclude that the priniciple was in Protestantism in general that looked to the Scriptures, but without any kind of authority that could say that this is the authentic message. That this was not compatible fundamentally with what we see on the pages of the New Testament.

And that really left me with two options. It was either the Roman Catholic Church or it was Eastern Orthodoxy. And partly for cultural reasons orthodoxy doesn't mean anything to me, but also because it seemed to me that Eastern Orthodoxy, although there is much to respect there, and Catholics recognize the validity of the Orthodox sacraments and the great common heritage we have with the Eastern Church, it nevertheless was fundamentally what I called Congregationalism with cope and mitre. There was no principle of unity, as we have in the Catholic Church, that could unite the various patriarchs. There was no Peter, there was no Petrine ministry. And once I accepted that, it was pretty much a done deal that the Catholic Church was Christ's Church. So, I sort of backed my way into the Church…

The Church teaches that the Catholic Church was established by Christ. So that it's not like Christ established a Church and then over time it gradually evolved into the Catholic Church. No, there is a concrete historical continuity between the apostles that Jesus established and the men that those apostles appointed as bishops and their successors on down through today. It's a continuity of authority. It's a continuity of faith, because they teach the same faith. The faith of the apostles is the faith of the Church today; has been throughout history. It's a continuity in ritual, the seven sacraments of the Church on the pages of the New Testament throughout the history of the Church down to the present day. The authority of the Bishop of Rome and the successor of St. Peter – Matthew 16:18-19, where Jesus gives Peter the authority to be the foundation of the Church; gives him the keys of the kingdom of heaven; makes him in effect his apostolic Prime Minister for the kingdom of heaven. All of that is on the pages of the New Testament. We see that that is the Church, the true Church.

Now, we want to be clear, and this is the point that the Second Vatican Council really wanted to stress: that when we think of the Catholic Church as the Church Christ founded, that doesn't mean that non-Catholic Christians aren't Christians, that they don't have any kind of fellowship with Jesus; that they don't have any of the gifts that Christ bequeathed the Church.

What it does mean is that in history, if you want to see where the Church that Christ founded exists concretely, it exists in the Catholic Church. Other churches, more or less what we call churches, or, as the Second Vatican Council says, 'ecclesial communities', will have this element or that element of what Christ gave his Church. But only in the Catholic Church do you find the fullness of Christianity, the fullness of what Christ bequeathed to his Church. So, yes, the Catholic Church is the true Church in that sense without meaning to demean or take anything away from those elements of Christianity that exist outside the visible structure of the Church"); "Let My People Go: The Catholic Church and Slavery," *This Rock* July/August 1999; "Why Only Catholicism Can Make Protestantism Work: Louis Bouyer on the Reformation," *Catholic Dossier*, September-October 2001, p.30; *EWTN Audio Library, The Journey Home* (4 August 2003) ("I encountered the Church of Vatican II, but the people who were doing really the kind of aggressive, energetic evangelization apologetics were Sheed and Chesterton and folks like that. There was not this burgeoning explosion of Catholic apologetics at the time, and so I had to find my way into the Church through folks like that"); *How Not to Share Our Faith: The Seven Deadly Sins of Apologetics* (2006); *A Study Guide for Joseph Ratzinger's Jesus of Nazareth: From the Baptism in the Jordan to the Transfiguration* (2008) (with Matthew Levering, Laura Dittus, and Tom Harmon); "Aquinas Proves Atheists are Closer to God than They Think," *This Rock*, March 2009 ("It may seem obvious to say that a Christian or even a generic theist is someone who says, 'God exists,' and an atheist is someone who says, 'God does not exist.' However, the traditional Christian (even the mere theist) wants to say more things about God, things that affect the use of the word *exist* as applied to God. Here is where Thomas [Aquinas] comes in. When he says, 'God exists,' he doesn't mean by *exist* exactly the same thing that he means when he says, 'Rome exists' or 'Jupiter exists' or even, 'I exist.'

There are, says Thomas, things that *receive* their existence, that are *dependent* for their existence. I exist because my parents existed; I received my existence from them. That mountain exists because the earth exists and certain geological principles exist that go into the formation of mountains. And so on.

Not everything, argues Thomas, can be a *receiver* of existence. Something (or Someone) must exist in its (his) own right, and not because of something else. Otherwise, there would be no existence to be passed on by the all various receivers of existence we encounter in the world around us. That something which (or Someone who) exists in its (his) own right and not as dependent on another is God. He, says Thomas, simply is, with the fullness of all that the word 'is' can contain. This is why God is called 'the Supreme Being.' Lesser beings are dependent for their existence on others. Not so God.

I have just summarized one of Thomas's arguments for God's existence. Whatever you make of it, my point here is to focus on the *kind* of existence that Thomas says God has, not on Thomas's argument for God's existence. God's kind of existence is uncaused and independent. That is why Thomas can say that God 'is to be thought of as existing outside the realm of existents' (*Commentary on Aristotle's Peri Hermeneias*, 1.14). That does not mean it is right to say, 'There is no God.' If we use the word *existent* to refer to beings that get their existence or are dependent for it on another or others, then it is right to say that God is 'outside the realm of existents.' Indeed, God, in this view, would be the *cause of existence*, the reason there is something rather than nothing. Yes, there is a perfectly good sense in which we must speak of God as 'existing,' but, as Thomas would quickly add, God's existence is radically different from the existence of everything else"); "Was Jesus Married?" *This Rock*, May 2009; *A Study Guide for Jesus of Nazareth: Holy Week* From the Entry into Jerusalem to the Resurrection (2011) (with Curtis Mitch); executive producer of several documentaries, e.g., *The Story of the Nativity*, *Lost Gospels or False Gospels*, and *Did Jesus Really Rise from the Dead?*

Budenz, Louis Francis – activist and writer; b. 17 July 1891, Indianapolis, Indiana; c. 10 October 1945 (a revert; received by Mgr. Fulton Sheen at St. Patrick's Cathedral, New York; on the same occasion his second wife, Margaret (1908-2002), also became a Catholic and their three daughters were baptized, one of whom later became a nun); d. 27 April 1972, Newport, Rhode Island; fourth-generation descendant of German-Irish immigrants; both of his parents were devout Catholics; brought up in the Catholic faith and was an altar boy; educated by the Jesuits at St. Xavier University in Cincinnati and St. Mary's College in Kansas; admitted to the Indiana State Bar in 1912; left the Church in 1916 to marry a divorced woman; the marriage did not last; later married Margaret Rogers, a social worker and atheist, and their children were brought up with no religious beliefs; arrested many times as a labor organizer; in 1935 he became a member of the Communist Party and later of its National Committee; from 1935 to 1945 he worked for the party's newspaper, the *Daily Worker*, and later editor of it; also editor of another Communist daily, the *Midwest Daily Record*; president of the Freedom of the Press Company, a Communist publishing house; debated in print and verbally with Mgr. Sheen, a persistent critic of

Communism; in 1945 he renounced Communism and returned to the Catholic Church after instruction by Mgr. Sheen; his statement to the press said, "Communism and Catholicism are irreconcilable. Communism, I have found, aims to establish a tyranny over the human spirit; it is in unending conflict with religion and true freedom"; after his conversion his marriage was validated; he became an anti-Communist advocate; testified as an expert witness at various trials of Communists and before many of the Senate and House committees that were formed to investigate Communists; he confessed that he had spied on behalf of the Soviet Union; teaching posts at University of Notre Dame and Fordham University; wrote many articles for Catholic journals and books against Communism; see *This Is My Story* (1947) ("To be a Catholic is to be of the Communion of Saints, and to be of God's centuries"); *Rome Moskou Rome* (1948); *Men without Faces: The Communist Conspiracy in the U.S.A.* (1950); *The Cry Is Peace* (1952); *The Techniques of Communism* (1954); What Every Citizen Can Do for the Good of His Country: Attack Communism! (1963); The Bolshevik Invasion of the West: Account of the Great Political War for a Soviet America (1966); Fulton J. Sheen, Communism Answers the Questions of a Communist (1937); Walter Romig, The Book of Catholic Authors (1960); Margaret Budenz, *Our Sunday Visitor* (1979); Fulton J. Sheen, Treasure in Clay (1982), pp.171-172 ("I told him I was not interested in discussing Communism; I wanted to talk about his soul. Six or seven years passed. Then he wrote and asked to see me again, and returned to the Faith. Only recently did I learn from Mrs. Budenz that he would not allow any radio in the house to be turned on to me while I spoke - so much did he detest me. Later she asked him why he chose to contact me since he bore such animosity. His answer was: 'He told me that he was interested in my soul'"); Charles P. Connor, Classic Catholic Converts (2001); Lorene Hanley Duquin, *A Century of Catholic Converts* (2003), p.129 ("His first attack on Mgr. Fulton Sheen, a persistent critic of Communism, appeared in the December 1936 issue of the *Daily Worker.* He challenged Sheen to prove his statements. Within a short time, Budenz received a manuscript from Sheen entitled *Communism Answers a Communist.*

The manuscript was well-researched. 'If Communism is the friend of the downtrodden, why do so many oppressive laws and regulations exist in the Soviet Union?' Sheen wrote, and cited pages of examples. 'The more I read about Communism, the more I am convinced that its greatest propagandists know practically nothing factual about it,' Sheen concluded. 'They talk of Russia either in general terms or in stereotyped language of its propaganda. That is why I believe many Communists are in good faith, and here I include you, Mr. Budenz.'

Budenz intended to reply but came down with the flu. When he returned to the office, there was a letter from Sheen saying his manuscript had been published as a pamphlet by Paulist Press and suggesting that they should meet in person.

Fulton Sheen listened as Budenz launched into a defense of Communism. 'He was not disposed to contradict me, in our face-to-face discussion,' Budenz recalled. 'That would only have aroused my personal pride and incited me to further argument. What he did, instead, took me totally by surprise.' He simply bent forward and said, 'Let us now talk of the Blessed Virgin.'

Budenz could not describe what went on in his soul at those words. 'Immediately, I was conscious of the senselessness and sinfulness of my life as I then lived it. The peace that flows from Mary, And which had been mine in the early days, flashed back to me with an overwhelming vividness...The drabness of life without Divinity, the slaughter which science will wreak on mankind without Divine Law, pressed in on my consciousness.'

When they parted, they agreed to meet again, but it was almost nine years before it happened. Budenz continued to rise in the Communist Party...His encounter with Fulton Sheen haunted him, however"); Kevin Schmeising, "Margaret Budenz – From Communism to Catholicism," *InsideCatholic.com*, 2011 ("Margaret had little religious background and decided during her adolescent years that she did not believe in God. She remembered setting foot in a Catholic Church only once in her life before she and Louis began attending church when she was in her mid-30s: When she was growing up in Pittsburgh, she accompanied her Catholic friend to a novena service at the girl's parish...

'God's grace! What a mystery!,' Archbishop Sheen began his foreword to Margaret's autobiography...A mystery, indeed. Remember the parish novena Margaret attended as a child? The preacher that evening was a relatively unknown but unusually gifted young priest from the Diocese of Peoria whose name meant nothing to her at that point. He was Fulton Sheen"; Steve Rosswurm, *The FBI and the Catholic Church, 1935-1962* (2009); John Beaumont, "Louis Budenz: Communist Radical, Catholic Convert," *Saint Austin Review*, November/December 2012, p.26; *ANB*.

Budziszewski, Jay (pronounced Boojee-shefski) - philosopher; b. 1952 Milwaukee, Wisconsin; c. 11 April 2004 (Easter Sunday; received with his wife Sandra); raised in a devoutly Baptist family; serious Christian through his teenage years; moved to Florida at age of thirteen; abandoned his faith completely when he went off to college ("first faith in Christ, then belief in God, then belief in a real right and wrong"); also denied free will at that time; studied political science at the University of Chicago; at that time politically far to the left; after two years he left the university "to learn a trade and join the proletariat"; worked as a welder for a while; went back to studies at the University of South Florida in Tampa (BA); MA at the University of Florida in Gainesville and PhD at Yale University (1981); appointed to a post at the University of Texas at Austin in 1981 (later made Professor of Government); even when an atheist, influenced by Catholic friends and writers (Augustine, Aquinas and especially Dante); came back to the Christian faith but as an Episcopalian, wanting one foot in Catholic tradition; conversion to the Catholic Church influenced by the nourishment gained from Catholic writers and the charism of Pope John Paul II; also became awed by the figure of the Blessed Virgin; also influenced by the "melt-down" going on in the Anglican communion; specializes in political philosophy, ethics, and religion; teaching courses on the American Founding and the natural law tradition; much research and writing, primarily advocating natural law theory (in this context much on the problem of moral self-deception: what happens when human beings tell themselves that they don't know what they really do); has also written on the general issues of tolerance and virtue ethics, and specific moral and political issues, e.g., abortion, marriage, sexuality, capital punishment, and the role of judges; all his work is influenced by St. Thomas Aquinas; also much work on apologetics; see (selective list) *The Resurrection of Nature: Political Theory and the Human Character* (1986); *The Nearest Coast of Darkness: A Vindication of the Politics of Virtues* (1988); *True Tolerance: Liberalism and the Necessity of Judgment* (1992); *Written on the Heart: The Case for Natural Law* (1997); *The Revenge of Conscience: Politics and the Fall of Man* (1999); "But What Do I Say," *catholiceducation.org*, 2000; *What We Can't Not Know: A Guide* (2003; 2nd edition 2010); *How to Stay Christian in College* (2004); *Ask Me Anything: Provocative Answers for College Students* (2004); "Objections, Obstacles, Acceptance: An Interview With J. Budziszewski," *ignatiusinsight. com, 2005 ("I ought to explain that during those wilderness years, I was a practical atheist. I was never a theoretical atheist; I wasn't quite fool enough to think that I could prove that there isn't a God. What I thought was that there wasn't any God who could make a difference.*

Similarly, I was a practical nihilist. I wasn't quite fool enough to think that I could prove that there isn't a real difference between good and evil. What I thought was that the difference couldn't make a difference. You see, I denied free will. I reasoned that if the mind is enchained, then we can't have any confidence that any of our reasoning about good and evil has validity. For practical purposes, they would have to be viewed as human constructs.

Of course, the hole in that line of thought is large enough to drive a truck through. If I couldn't have any confidence in my reasoning about good and evil, why should I have any confidence in my reasoning about having no basis for confidence? Why should nihilism make any more sense than morality? I papered that problem over with clever talk about taking an ironic view of reality.

But I was going to tell you the Catholic influences that worked on me during my wilderness years. I read St. Augustine, St. Thomas Aquinas, and especially Dante Alighieri. When I read Dante's imaginative description of the center of Hell - the Lake of Cocytus, where the damned are imprisoned in ice, unable to move a muscle to the right or to the left - I thought that he was describing me. I couldn't move either. I'd thrown out all possible motives for movement.

Naturally I taught my students Thomas Aquinas, but I found it difficult to do so. The problem was that his arguments presented such a strong appearance of truth. For the very beauty of this appearance, I had to exercise strong discipline not to weep. One of my students in those days asked permission to put a personal question. 'I've been listening carefully,' he said, 'and I figure that you're either an atheist or a Roman Catholic. Which one is it?'

...What actually led me back was a growing intuition that my condition was objectively evil. I didn't believe in objective evil, so that seemed to make no sense. But the intuition became so strong that I could no longer ignore it. It wasn't a 'feeling.' I was forced to regard it as a perception of truth.

At this point I suppose intellect does come in, because I was familiar with Augustine's argument about evil. Evil is deficiency in good; there is no such thing as an evil 'substance,' an evil-in-itself. So if my condition really was evil, there had to be some good of which my condition was the ruination. And if there really were both good and evil, then I had been so wrong, for so long, so profoundly, that it seemed that almost anything might be true – even the faith that I had abandoned.

So I began studying all those Christian things I had forgotten. There was no distinct moment in time at which I could have said, 'I believe, but a moment ago I didn't.' One day, though, I realized that without having noticed it, I had been believing for some time.

But if the Christian revelation about Jesus Christ is true, then it makes no sense to do anything else except to follow him...

The first push [that prompted the move on from Anglicanism] was the discovery that Anglicanism was dying and all but dead. When my wife and I resumed Christian worship, we assumed that the reason the congregation recited the Nicene Creed together was that they all believed it. After years of self-imposed exile, this was indescribably wonderful. The 'cloud of witnesses' of which St. Paul speaks was almost palpable; we felt that you could reach out and touch those millions of Christians from bygone generations.

Then came the day when the college chaplain, who happened to be giving the homily that day, announced to the congregation that he 'was no longer able' to believe in the Resurrection. I wanted to ask, 'What happened to your vows?' and 'How dare you continue to call yourself a priest?' But I merely asked, 'I see you every week, reciting the Nicene Creed like the rest of us. If you don't believe it, how can you?'

He responded, 'I do it as an act of solidarity with the community.' In other words, it meant nothing at all. I came to realize that this was true for a great many Episcopal priests. The principle of doctrinal education in our parish was 'anything goes' - that is, anything but historic Christian doctrine. If you stood up for Holy Scripture and Apostolic Tradition you would quickly find yourself on the outs.

The question we faced was whether it would be more pleasing to God to get out of the Episcopal communion altogether, or stay behind as a 'faithful remnant.' ...[T]he ongoing collapse of the Episcopal enterprise forced us to ask deeper questions about the nature of the Church. Our ecclesiology was very nearly Catholic, long before we actually joined the Catholic Church. This fact made our picture of ourselves as part of a 'faithful remnant' inside the Anglican communion harder and harder to believe in. After all, if what the Catholic Church teaches about her nature and authority is true, then how can you justify not becoming part of her?...

Not all converts come into the fold in the same way. For some people on the way into the Catholic Church, the ecclesiastical objection is the last one to be overcome. First they become convinced about doctrine A, doctrine B, and doctrine C, and then at last they becoming convinced that the Church has authority to teach about these matters. For me it was the other way around. First I became convinced that the Church has authority to teach. That didn't mean that my various difficulties about doctrine A, doctrine B, and doctrine C disappeared, but it converted my 'objections' into 'obstacles.'

After several years of wrestling, becoming convinced on one point after another, I finally found myself able to say with respect to the remaining issues, 'I am ready to obey.' That turned out to be crucial. As Augustine said, we believe in order to know. There are some things you have to understand before you can accept them - but there are others you have to accept before you can understand them...

[W]e decided that if the Episcopal church ever came to incorporate the prevalent abominations into its canons, that would be our signal to get out. The signal we were waiting for came unmistakably during the summer of 2003. It was bad enough that the Episcopal general convention ordained as bishop a man who had abandoned his wife and children in order to live in sin with another man. That might have been viewed as an aberration. Much worse was the fact that the general convention authorized drawing up rites for the blessing of same-sex unions. That converted the aberration into a rule.

But the signal turned out to have been unnecessary, because we had already crossed our Rubicon. That summer, we visited an Episcopal church in another town. No sooner had we entered than we encountered a 'tract table' offering visitors free pro-abortion bumper stickers bearing the Episcopal shield. That was the last straw. We knew that we could never consider ourselves members of the Episcopal Church again"); *Evangelicals in the Public Square: Four Formative Voices* (2006); *Natural Law for Lawyers* (2006); "Natural Law as Fact, as Theory, and as Sign of Contradiction," *The Catholic Social Science Review*, 2007, p.11; *Ask Me Anything 2: More Provocative Answers for College Students* (2008); "Natural Law Revealed," *First Things*, December 2008; *The Line Through the Heart: Natural Law as Fact, Theory, and Sign of Contradiction* (2009); *EWTN Audio Library, The Journey Home* (22 June 2009) ("One of the things that I'm interested in now in my studies of the natural law is how it is that we can know something at one level and yet at another level tell ourselves that we don't know it. How we can pretend to ourselves that we don't know things that we really do. And in order to justify my slide into atheism, and into more than atheism (I stopped believing eventually not only in God but in the very difference between good and evil). In order to justify that I had to tell myself all sorts of stories that on a deeper level I knew were not true. I knew deep down still that there was a God. I knew deep down at some level that there was a real difference between good and evil, between right and wrong, but I had to keep telling myself that I knew no such thing, and that everything was really very difficult shades of grey, and that I was doing the best that I can, and who really knew about any of this"); *On the Meaning of Sex* (2012); "So-Called Gay Marriage: A Dialogue," *Crisis*, 9 January 2013; "Escape From Nihilism," *Leadership University* (n.d.) (reprinted in *catholiceducation.org*); Francis J. Beckwith, "Doing What Comes

Naturally and Not Knowing It: A Reflection on J. Budziszewski's Work," *The Catholic Social Science Review*, 2007, p.33.

"Buffalo Bill" – see under Cody, William Frederick.

Bull, George Joseph - physician and surgeon; eye specialist; b. Hamilton, Ontario, Canada; c. 25 July 1892; parents were Irish Protestants, active members of the Low Church party in the Church of England; brought up in the Church of England, educated at McGill University, Montreal (MD, CM. 1869); left Canada to practice medicine in the United States; moved to New York in 1883 to specialize in the study of diseases of the eye; left the Church of England and joined the Society for Ethical Culture; in 1886 went to Paris to study at the Sorbonne (MD in 1889) and worked there as an ophthalmic surgeon; became a Catholic as a result of reading the New Testament on the question of Christ and the Church; also influenced by Newman; married in 1898 Susan Montague Caldwell, daughter of Howard Hayne Caldwell (1831-1860), the poet (himself a convert to Catholicism); contributor to ophthalmological magazines in several countries; founder and President of the St. Genevieve's Club, Paris, for English speaking Catholics; see *Lunettes et Pince-Nez* (1889); *How I Became a Catholic* (1908) (reprinted in Georgina Pell Curtis, *Some Roads to Rome in America* (1909, p.37) ("I made a more or less complete study of the New Testament, and discovered several important truths...I had been familiar from my youth with the doctrine of the Unitarians, for whom Jesus Christ is only a man; later I had been influenced by the writings of the freethinkers, who pretend that the New Testament is but a collection of legends brought together in the interest of priestcraft. But as I advanced in my studies every page of the New Testament tore away the veil from before my eyes; I recognized the history as true. It is told in such a way as to leave no doubt as to the veracity of the story; one knows instinctively that eye-witnesses are speaking. The life of the Apostles transported me with admiration; their zeal, their devotion, the firmness which they manifested in their teachings showed the Holy Spirit acting in them. In comparison with such men, all that I had admired in the pretended reformers seemed unworthy of attention...

It was obvious to me from the Bible that Jesus of Nazareth was God. This fundamental truth fixed itself in my mind with a force that admitted of no resistance; the prejudices due to Unitarians and freethinkers disappeared forever. I observed how from the crowd which followed Him, Jesus had chosen and ordained His twelve Apostles to found a society, a Church...

I remarked then that the society

founded by Jesus Christ was established to last forever. I observed the care given by the Master in the instruction of the first pastors of His church; how He took them apart to explain His doctrine saying: - 'It is given unto you to know the Mysteries of the kingdom of Heaven (St. Matthew xiii, 11). He exacted from His disciples a most perfect faith, even in circumstances where that faith seemed to be most in opposition to reason. In his sixth chapter, St. John records how after He had accomplished the miracle of the multiplication of the bread, Christ announced a nourishment still more marvellous: - 'I am the living bread which came down from heaven; if any man eat of this bread he shall live forever, and the bread that I will give is my flesh which I will give for the life of the world.' At these words they disputed among themselves and left Him; The Gospel says expressly: - 'From that time many of his disciples went back and walked no more with Him' (St. John, vi, 66). In order to keep them, human wisdom would have stopped and disguised the truth; but the Divine Master did not seek to keep those who would not believe.

I do not know exactly if at the time when I read this chapter I fully understood its meaning; but today, instructed on the doctrine of the Eucharist, I make this observation: the hearers of the words of Jesus Christ made no mistake as to their real sense. By these words, 'the bread that I will give is My flesh' (St. John vi, 51), they perfectly understood that the Savior did not speak figuratively, but literally. It was that which they refused to believe: 'How, said they, 'can this man give us His flesh to eat?' (St. John vi, 52). Far from correcting them in this, our Lord employed expressions (St. John vi, 53-58) still more clear and more energetic, that there might remain no doubt as to the true sense of His words.

To be a member of the Church of Christ it was then necessary to believe all that Christ taught. No one had ever told me this; my Protestant instructors, on the contrary, boasted of the breadth of their views on doctrinal questions....

If we admit the divinity of Jesus Christ, I said to myself, we must naturally accept His teachings; one is the logical consequence of the other.

From a practical point of view the insistence of the Divine Master on the unity of His Church seemed to me of absolute necessity. Without that, how could this Church, according to the promise which He made to the Apostles, last until the end of the world?...

I began to see that the Church founded by Jesus Christ must exist in our own days and bear through all the centuries the mark of a veritable unity; not a factitious or relative unity but an absolute one, as real as that which exists between God the Father and God the Son.

Never in my youth had this thought been suggested to me. I had learned that Jesus Christ had come to redeem the world by His death; that He had given certain doctrines which each one might interpret as it pleased him; I had some vague idea of an apostolic succession in the Church of England; but never had I been shown Jesus Christ accomplishing the work of which He speaks in the chapter quoted (St. John, xvii, 4) that is to say, founding His Church.

The Church then was a divine institution and must last forever; such was the second capital truth which was borne in upon me. But where, after so many centuries, was this church to be found? One in its belief, so little like that which I knew, the Church of England - which allows its ministers to hold different and contradictory doctrines and whose members make a boast of the elasticity of their belief.

Proceeding with the reading of the New Testament I saw that Jesus after His resurrection completed the instruction of His Apostles, promising them His Spirit to confirm them in their faith. He charged them to teach all nations: - 'Go ye therefore, and teach all nations, baptizing them in the name of the Father and of the Son and of the Holy Ghost; teaching them to observe all things whatsoever I have commanded you : and, lo, I am with you always, even unto the end of the world' (St. Matthew xxviii, 19, 20).

The Acts of the Apostles and the Epistles showed me a Church remaining united, in spite of innumerable difficulties; and again the thought came to my mind: - Where is that Church to-day ?

Never did it occur to me to look for it among the Anglicans, the Methodists or the Presbyterians, still less among the Unitarians. Could it be the Catholic Church, I said to myself - the Church of Rome?...

The Bible had shown me Jesus Christ founding a society, a body, of which all the members must be in communion and in perfect unity of faith. This society was to have continued through all ages even to the end of the world. I had seen Jesus Christ choosing one of His Apostles to be the head of His Church, and now I found in the Church, the history of which I was studying, the marks indicated by the Bible. I beheld this Church teaching, always, in all countries, with the authority which had been conferred upon her by Jesus Christ Himself; the bishops and priests exercising their ministry as the Apostles had done before them, and always above them all the Pope, recognized by them as the head of the Church. The writings of the Fathers of the Church and the decisions of the councils were a proof of this; in spite of heresies and attacks of all sorts the Church had always maintained the supremacy of the Pope, successor of St. Peter: the rock, the safeguard of unity. And then came back to mind the words of Jesus Christ to him of the Apostles, whom He established head of the early Church: 'And I say also unto thee, that thou art Peter, and upon this rock I will build my Church; and the gates of hell shall not prevail against it. And I will give unto thee the keys of the kingdom of heaven: and whatsoever thou shalt bind on earth shall be bound in heaven: and whatsoever thou shalt loose on earth shall be loosed in heaven' (St. Matthew xvi, i8, 19)").

Bunting, Josiah - military officer and educator; b. 1939, Torrington, Connecticut; c. 2010 (received by Fr. C. John McCloskey III, a major influenceonhisconversion);brought up in a conventional Protestant family, attending a Congregational Church; entered the U.S. Marine Corp; went on to Virginia Military Institute (graduated as an English major); Rhodes Scholarship to Oxford University (MA); entered the United States Army in 1966, reaching the rank of major in 1972 (finally a general); served in Vietnam and taught at West Point; left West Point in 1972, expressing criticism of army policy in Vietnam; active in education as president of a college and headmaster of a school; superintendent of the Virginia Military Institute 1995-2003; appointed in 2004 chairman of the National Civic Literacy Board of the Intercollegiate Studies Institute; taught history at Columbia University; appointed in 2007 president of ISI's Lehrman American Studies Center; president of The Harry Frank Guggenheim Foundation in New York City; finally converted to the Catholic faith after many years' thought; married with four children; his half-brother Dick Ebersol, creator and former producer of *Saturday Night Live*; see (non-fiction) *Small Units in the Control of Civil Disorder* (1967); *Ulysses S. Grant* (2004); (fiction) *The Lionheads* (1972); *The Advent of Frederick Giles* (1974); *An Education for Our Time* (1998); *All Loves Excelling* (2001); "I Know This is Where I Should Be," *National Catholic Register*, 28 April 2011 ("In college in the United States, and at the University of Oxford, and in significant ways through my reading of the poet Gerard Manley Hopkins and his early spiritual mentor, Cardinal John Henry Newman, I began to recognize what I might call a spiritual hunger for something which the church of which I remained a nominal member was unable to assuage. I began also, through Newman, but also through much reading (not very purposive or well-organized), to be drawn to the very early Church (Paul in particular), to the Church Fathers, to the sacrifices of its first Christians, and to what I was coming to believe was the Christian communion that had sustained their creeds, their faith, their consciousness of Christ's glory.

This must be the holy Catholic Church. Its creeds were dogma - immanent, unchanging, beyond cavil - and I embraced them with an overwhelming consciousness that I was called to embrace them. I had to").

Buren, William Holme Van – surgeon; b. 5 April 1819, Philadelphia, Pennsylvania; c. 1845; d. 25 March 1883, New York; his ancestors emigrated to New York from Beuren, near Amsterdam; educated at Yale University and did his medical training at the University of Pennsylvania and in Paris; in 1845 appointed as prosector to the medical department of the University of New York; Professor of Anatomy 1852-1865; Professor of Surgery in the Bellevue Hospital Medical College from 1868 until his death; President Lincoln offered to make him surgeon general at the time of the war, and on his refusal consulted him with regard to the appointment; consulting surgeon to many of the prominent New York City hospitals; president of the Pathological Society; vice-president of the New York Academy of Medicine; corresponding member of the Société de Chirurgie of Paris; after his conversion always professed his Catholic faith; contributed many articles to medical journals; see *Contributions to Practical Surgery* (1865); *A Practical Treatise on the Surgical Diseases of the Genito-Urinary Organs* (1878) (with Edward L. Keyes); *Diseases of the Rectum and Anus* (1881); *Lectures on the Principles of Surgery* (1884); *Catholic Encyclopedia.*

Burnett, Peter Hardeman (original surname Burnet) – politician and judge; b. 15 November 1807, Nashville, Tennessee; c. June 1846, Oregon City (received with his family); d. 17 May 1895, San Francisco, California; father a farmer and carpenter; raised in modest circumstances; brought up as a traditional southern Protestant; elementary education only in Missouri; returned to Tennessee and married Harriet W. Rogers in 1828 (three children of the marriage); went into business, owning a general store; studied law and admitted to the bar in 1839, but financial problems; in 1840 joined the Church of the Disciples, or Campbellites, founded by Alexander Campbell (1788-1866), who had seceded from the Baptists; in 1843 he went with his family to Oregon and did farming and mining ("After my arrival…I attended High Mass as a mere spectator, on Christmas, at midnight. I had never witnessed anything like it before, and the profound solemnity of the services – the intense, yet calm fervor of the worshippers – the great and marked differences between the two forms of worship – and the instantaneous reflection, that this was the Church claiming to be the only true Church, did make the deepest impression upon my mind for the moment. In all my religious experience, I had never felt an impulse so profound, so touching"); member of Oregon legislature 1844-1848; confidence in Protestantism became less and he undertook a systematic investigation of the true religion; this led to his acceptance of the Catholic claims and his conversion; in 1848 went to California; elected a member of the Legislative Assembly; Independent Democratic in politics; in 1849 appointed judge of the superior tribunal; worked on the framing of the State Constitution; in the same year chosen Chief Justice and then elected the first American Governor of California; resigned the governorship in 1851; in 1857 appointed as a justice of the Supreme Court of California; co-founder and President of the Pacific Bank 1863-1880; buried in the Santa Clara Mission Cemetery at Santa Clara, California; see *The True Church: The Path Which Led a Protestant Lawyer to the Catholic Church* (1860) (published in 1909 in an edited and abridged version by Fr. James Sullivan, SJ; full version republished in 2010) ("The great Dr. Johnson said: 'A man who is converted from Protestantism to Popery may be sincere; he parts with nothing; he is only superadding to what he already had. But a convert from Popery to Protestantism gives up so much of what he has held as sacred as any thing that he retains; there is so much *laceration of mind* in such a conversion, that it can hardly be sincere and lasting.' There certainly is a great deal of truth, though not the whole truth, in this reflection. The convert from the Catholic Church seems conscious that he is embracing an inferior and lower grade of faith, and adopting a colder and more suspicious estimate of human veracity, He cuts himself loose from the holy ties that bound him to the suffering martyr-Church of old, He severs all connection with the apostles, except that *hidden* one, which is supposed to be buried in the darkness and silence of the dim distant ages of the past. He leaves the sweet communion of saints, which combines the children of the true faith everywhere, in every age, in one holy brotherhood. What are the heroic martyrs and saints of old to him? They are now become 'mystics and visionaries.' What to him is now the great and universal Church of the mighty past? 'The Man of Sin.' Who were the clergy of the Old Church - that Church which won the world to Christianity? To him they are now become impostors, who betrayed the faith of Christ. And the laity, who were they? Simple dupes. In short, to him what is the Christian past? A blurred and blotted page for evil, and a practical blank for good. It is a melancholy view of Christianity - a humiliating estimate of human veracity - a mighty accusation against humanity itself. No wonder it produces so much *'laceration of mind.'*

But it is not so with the convert to the Catholic Faith. He is conscious that he has embraced a higher grade of faith, has been brought into closer and holier communion with the unseen world, and has adopted a more just and charitable estimate of human veracity. He has taken a step towards the Celestial City, from the low murky valleys of discord, where the fogs of error do love to dwell, He shakes hands with the brethren of every kindred, name, and tongue. He worships with the people of every nation. He joins his prayers with those who speak the varied languages of earth. On every shore, in every land, beneath every sky, and in every city, he meets his brethren of the universal Church. He is at home everywhere, and bows down with the millions who have worshipped, and still worship, at the same altar, and hold the same faith.

But not only so. He looks back over the pages of past history, and ascends by a plain, visible, and unbroken chain to the apostolic day. He has no chasms to leap, no deserts to cross. At every step in this progress he finds the same Old Church - the same faith - the same worship still pre-eminent in the Christian world. He sees the rise and fall of empires and sects; but the same Old Church always pre-eminent. The records of the past are with him. He has the sanction of antiquity. Time tells for him a glorious story. He meets with myriads of brethren all along the slumbering ages. The old martyrs and saints are his brethren. He claims companionship with them. Their memories are beloved by him. And Blandina, the poor slave, but noblest of martyrs, was his sister. And old Ignatius, and Polycarp, and Justin, and Irenaeus, are also his brethren. And she, the humblest of the humble - the purest of the pure - the stainless Virgin Mother of his Lord, whom all generations call 'blessed,' is revered by him as the noblest of creatures. And the old apostles - the noble and the true - the holy and the just - the despised and persecuted - they, too, are his brethren. In short, the saints and martyrs of the olden time, held the same faith, worshipped at the same altar, and used the same form of worship that he does. He venerates and loves their memory, admires their virtues, calls them brethren, and asks their prayers in heaven. He has no accusations to bring against them - no crimes to lay to their charge.

Besides all this, his faith is sustained by a logical power, and a Scriptural proof, that cannot he fairly met and confuted. It is sustained by every plain and luminous principle upon which society and government are founded. His reason, his common sense, the best feelings of his nature. the holiest impulses of his heart, all satisfy him beyond a doubt, that he is in the right.

It is not at all surprising, then, that it is so difficult to convert a Catholic to Protestantism, even when in the vigor of life; and so difficult, that it never has been done, at the hour of death. For there is no known instance where a Catholic changed his faith upon a dying bed; while thousands of Protestants have done so. If a Catholic can live a faithful member of his Church, he can always die in it. In that awful hour - that honest hour – 'When all the blandishments of life are gone./ 'When tired dissimulation drops her mask,/ And real and apparent are the same'; when eternity, with all its mighty consequences, rolls up its endless proportions before the dying vision – Ah! then, no Catholic asks to change his faith! Oh! give me the last sacraments of the Church! Let me die in her holy communion! Let me be buried in consecrated ground! Let my brethren pray for me!

But there is still another most weighty consideration with him. He examines carefully the doctrines of his Church. From the first to the last article of faith, they are as consistent with each other as truth itself could be. There is no discrepancy - no contradiction. The whole theory, in all its parts, is perfectly consistent with itself. He finds few, if any, to deny this entire consistency of parts with the whole. He knows that every part of a true system must be consistent with each, and with all. No one truth jars with another. There can be no enmity, no discord, in a true system. But he knows it is exceedingly difficult to find this consistency and harmony in a theory of pure error; and still more difficult to find it in a mixed theory of truth and error. And he cannot understand how the alleged additions to the faith could have been made, and so *nicely fitted to the true system, as to be perfectly consistent with it.* He finds it conceded that his Church has the fundamental truths of Christianity, and that her faith is consistent throughout; and he cannot see how this consistency could be found between the alleged added errors and the old truths; and he is forced to conclude, that a theory so consistent in all its parts and admitted to contain many truths, must be true in every particular.

I will close this work in the words of that distinguished French writer, La Bruyère: 'If my religion be false, it is, I must own, the most artful snare that could possibly be devised. It is impossible to avoid falling into it and being caught. What majesty, what magnificence, in its mysteries! What coherency, what connection, in all its doctrines! What sound reasons! What candor! What innocence of morals! What an invincible and overwhelming body of evidence is given successively, and for three whole centuries, by millions of the most learned and most considerate persons then in the world, and whom the conviction of one and the same truth supported in exile, in fetters, at the approach of death, and under the most cruel torments'"); *The American Theory of Government, Considered with Reference to the Present Crisis* (1861); *Recollections and Opinions of an Old Pioneer* (1860); *Reasons Why We Should Believe in God, Love God and Obey God* (1884); William E. Franklin, "The

Religious Ardor of Peter Hardeman Burnett, California's first American Governor," *California Historical Society Quarterly*, June 1966, p.125; *Catholic Encyclopedia*; his papers are at the California State Archives, Sacramento, California; *ANB*.

Burnham, James – political and social commentator; b. 22 November 1905, Chicago, Illinois; c. 1987 (revert on his deathbed); d. 28 July 1987, Kent, Connecticut; his father, Claude George Burnham (d. 1928), was a poor English immigrant and later prosperous railroad executive in the Midwest; his father was a Protestant, but his mother was a devout Catholic; brought up as a Catholic in a cultivated family, educated at Princeton University where he majored in English and graduated at the top of his class; strongly influenced as a student by St. Thomas Aquinas and T. S. Eliot; post-graduate student in English and Medieval Philosophy at Balliol College, Oxford (taught by J. R. R. Tolkien and by Fr. Martin D'Arcy, SJ); shed any religious commitment while at Oxford, but continued to read widely; in 1929 he became Professor of Philosophy at New York University; radical activist in the 1930s, influenced by the depression and the writings of Trotsky; one of the organizers of the American Workers Party in 1933; supported merger with the Communist League of America in 1934 to form the U.S. Workers Party; became a Trotskyist (and corresponded with Trotsky) for a short time and formed the Socialist Workers Party (SWP) in 1937; the Nazi-Soviet Non-agression Pact of 1939 was the immediate cause of his split with Trotsky; in 1940 resigned and helped to form the Workers Party, but resigned from that shortly afterwards, having rejected Marxism; long association with the *Partisan Review*, the main intellectual journal of the anti-Stalinist left; published his best known and most influential work, *The Managerial Revolution*, an analysis of the development of economics and society in 1941 (the book influenced George Orwell's book *1984*); worked for the Office of Strategic Services (OSS) during World War II (worked on political and psychological warfare); argued for a democratic world order, led in the beginning by the United States, as a stage in the building of a world government; in 1949 he joined the Office of Policy Coordination, a branch of the CIA; during the Cold War he worked on strategies to undermine Soviet power, calling for a propaganda offensive; refused to condemn Senator Joseph McCarthy and wrote some articles in defense of him; saw the Catholic Church as "probably the strongest present anti-communist force" and noted the strength of Catholic labor unions; later turned to writing from a conservative perspective; in 1955 he helped William F. Buckley to found the *National Review*; wrote many contributions for the journal, mainly on foreign policy issues; in his later work he chronicles Western political decline and lists liberal fallacies; under-rated political and social commentator; in 1978 he suffered a stroke, which prevented him from writing; in 1983 awarded the Presidential Medal of Freedom; returned to the Catholic Church shortly before his death; buried in Kent, Connecticut; great influence on Samuel Francis (see below); see *The Managerial Revolution: What is Happening in the World* (1941); *The Machiavellians: Defenders of Freedom* (1943); *The Struggle for the World* (1947); *The Coming Defeat of Communism* (1949); *How Does a Country Go Communist* (1951); *The Case Against Adlai Stevenson* (1952); *Containment or Liberation: An Inquiry into the Aims of United States Foreign Policy* (1953); *The Web of Subversion: Underground Networks* (1954); *Congress and the American Tradition* (1959); *Bear and Dragon: What is the Relation Between Moscow and Peking* (1960); *Suicide of the West: An Essay on the Meaning and Destiny of Liberalism* (1964); *The War We Are In: The Last Decade and the Next* (1967); John P. Diggins, *Up From Communism* (1975); Samuel Francis, *Power and History: The Political Thought of James Burnham* (1984); Kevin J. Smant, *How Great the Triumph: James Burnham, Anticommunism, and the Conservative Movement* (1992); Samuel Francis, *James Burnham: Thinkers of Our Time* (1999); Daniel Kelly, *James Burnham and the Struggle for the World: A Life* (2002); Roger Kimball, "The Power of James Burnham," *New Criterion*, September 2002 ("Today, Burnham is best known - to the extent that he is known at all - as an anti-Communist crusader. He was that. But he did not confine his criticism to Communism. On the contrary, he understood that the impulse to totalitarian surrender comes in many guises. The 'managerial revolution' that he warned about was a revolution that aimed to repel freedom for the sake of bureaucratic efficiency and control. That revolution has not - not yet - succeeded in the monolithic fashion that Burnham envisioned. He did not, as his subtitle promised, so much tell us 'What Is Happening in the World' as what might happen should certain tendencies be left unchecked. But who can gaze upon the ever-increasing routinization of life and regulation of individual liberty in our society without acknowledging the pertinence of Burnham's gloomy analysis?...

Written at the moment when Hitler's army seemed poised to overrun Europe, [*The Managerial Revolution*] is a grim exercise in dystopian prognostication. It is not, I think, one of Burnham's better books. As he himself later admitted, it is full of 'remnants of Marxism,' above all the depressing aroma of economic determinism and praise for the superiority of central planning. But *The Managerial*

Revolution certainly is a bold, an impressive book. Its vision of the rise of an oligarchy of experts and alignment of world powers into three competing super-states made a deep impression on many readers...

The Machiavellians is ostensibly an exposition of, and homage to, some modern followers of Machiavelli. Its larger purpose is to distinguish between the sentimental and the realistic in politics. Dante (in *De Monarchia*), Rousseau, and the architects of the French Revolution are prime examples of the former: they represent 'politics as wish': noble, optimistic, ultimately futile (indeed, ultimately 'reactionary and vicious' in Burnham's judgment).

Machiavelli and his heirs belong to the latter camp. They saw things as they were and faced up to unpleasant facts about human nature. Because they saw humanity as it was - in its imperfection, its treachery, its unceasing desire for power - they were the true friends of liberty. They did not exchange real freedoms for pleasant-sounding but empty idealities. They understood that all political freedom is imperfect freedom, won through struggle, preserved with difficulty, constantly subject to assault and diminution...

Burnham's political thought is often described as 'hard-boiled.' *The Machiavellians* is the cauldron in which the promised firmness is achieved. 'All societies,' he writes, 'including societies called democratic, are ruled by a minority.' Although the minority, the ruling 'élite,' naturally seeks to legitimize its power in the eyes of society, in the end 'the primary object of every élite, or ruling class, is to maintain its own power and privilege,' an aim that is sought largely on 'force and fraud.' Burnham had high hopes for 'an objective science of politics'; at the same time he believed that 'logical or rational analysis plays a relatively minor part in political and social change.' The true friends of freedom budget heavily for the imperfection of humanity and acknowledge the relative impotence of reason in political affairs. Above all, they understand that the possession of power is inseparable from its intelligent exercise.

In terms of the evolution of Burnham's thought, *The Machiavellians* is perhaps most important not for its exposition of power politics but for its implicit recognition of the value of freedom, 'that minimum of moral dignity which alone can justify the strange accident of man's existence.' As the 1940s and the Second World War unfolded, Burnham came more and more to understand that the preservation of freedom was primarily a salvage operation. And as the war hurried to its end, he looked on aghast as the West timidly made concession after concession to the Stalinist tyranny. In 1944, Burnham wrote a paper on postwar Soviet ambitions for the Office of Strategic Services. In 1947, an expanded version of this document appeared as *The Struggle for the World.* It is with this book, I believe, that Burnham comes into his own, for it is here that he first clearly articulates the opposition between the West as a precious heritage to be defended and Communism as a murderous tyranny to be defeated.

Was Burnham's opposition 'oversimplified,' as many critics charged? Doubtless it was. But it was also right in essentials and was, moreover, a salutary corrective to the naïve - and therefore deluded - advice of good-hearted liberals. Burnham understood with searing clarity two fundamental facts. First, that Communism was an expansionist ideology bent on world domination. And, second, that its triumph would entail the destruction of every liberty, intellectual as well as political, that we in the West held sacred and yet (perilously) took for granted - above all 'the absolute value of the single human person.' Communism, Burnham saw, was opportunism elevated to a position of absolute power. Unchecked, no human good, not even the commitment to truth, can withstand its assault. Anyone who has leafed through Marxist-inspired writings will remember attacks on 'mechanical logic.' But this, Burnham notes, is at bottom an attack on 'the rules of objective inference and proof, the rules that permit us to test for truth and falsity.' The alternative, what is called 'dialectical logic,' is simply a device that declares 'whatever serves the interest of communist power is true'"); Daniel Kelly, *James Burnham and the Struggle for the World* (2002); William Main, "Altrusitic Imperialism," *Culture Wars*, January 2003, p.40.

Burton, Katherine (*née* Kurz) – writer; b. 1884, Cleveland, Ohio; c. 8 September 1930; d. 22 September 1969, New York City; brought up in a German Lutheran family that rarely practiced its religion; little interest in religion as a child; graduated from Western Reserve University in 1906 and entered the teaching profession; became agnostic; joined the Episcopalian Church from social motives; in 1910 married Harry Payne Burton, a journalist and ex-Episcopalian minister, who committed suicide in 1952; three children of the marriage; her conversion was influenced greatly by Selden Peabody Delany (see below), the former Anglo-Catholic clergyman at her church, who converted before her; also influenced by Newman, in particular by his *Difficulties of Anglicans*; she wrote mainly religious biography, but also poetry and short stories; also campaigner for family rights; she was the first major Catholic woman journalist in the United States; close friend of Dorothy Day (see below); wrote a column, "Woman to Woman", from 1933 to 1969 in *Sign*, the magazine published by the Passionist Fathers (the first women's column in the history of American Catholic journalism); she advocated marriage and motherhood as the greatest possible vocation, but also that work in no way demeaned women; advocate of natural family planning; initially pacifist, but revised her views during World War II because of the threat from totalitarianism; see *Sorrow Built a Bridge: A Daughter of Hawthorne* (1937) (biography of Rose Hawthorne Lathrop); *Paradise Planters: The Story of Brook Farm* (1939); *His Dear Persuasion: The Life of Elizabeth Ann Seton* (1940); *In No Strange Land: Some American Catholic Converts* (1942) (From the introduction: "In one way or another, each of the converts mentioned here was attracted to the Catholic Church by the consideration of its continuity. Sarah Peter found that continuity when she saw the catacombs; Sophia Ripley found it when she read Dante. Some of the Episcopalians, attracted by the ritual of their denomination, remained where they were so long as they believed it had continuity. When their eyes were opened, they no longer dallied there. Others found evidence of the Catholic Church's continuity in various places, but this one great fact had to come home to them first, no matter what the argument or what beauty or pain or joy first drew them. The altar light gleaming in a shadowy church is but a symbol pointing to a Faith, not the Faith itself"); *Celestial Homespun: The Life of Isaac Thomas Hecker* (1943); *Mother Butler of Marymount* (1944); *No Shadow of Turning: The Life of James Kent Stone – Father Fidelis of the Cross* (1944); *According to the Pattern: The Story of Dr. Agnes McLaren and the Society of Catholic Medical Missionaries* (1946); *Difficult Star: The Life of Pauline Jaricot* (1947); *The Next Thing: Autobiography and Reminiscences* (1949); "The Outstretched Arms," in John A. O'Brien (ed), *The Road to Damascus, Vol. II* (1950) ("One day I decided to brush up my Greek. I thought of going back to the essays of Plato or to the *Iliad*, which we had read in college; but Dr. Delany suggested that instead I get a New Testament in Greek. Much of it was already familiar to me in English, and one phrase would give a whole paragraph's meaning and thus renew my vocabulary

After some months I found I could translate with a good bit of ease, and then I became aware of differences here and there between the Greek and English Bible with which I helped myself over hard passages. Some words did not seem to have the same meaning in translation as in the Greek; some things seemed actually left out altogether. For instance, in Luke the Authorized Version read, 'Hail, thou that art highly favored,' and the Greek looked definitely like "Hail, full of grace.' In Corinthians, I found a disturbing place which read in the Authorized, 'Whosoever shall eat this bread and drink this cup'; my Greek Testament plainly said, 'Eat this bread or drink this cup.'

When I mentioned these things to Dr. Delany, he laughed. 'You have a Protestant Bible,' he said. 'Get the Douay'...

The Roman Catholics who had talked of their faith with me had one beginning and one end to every argument: the everlastingness of their Church. It was the first Church established by Our Lord, and there was no other and would be no other...

I came across an historical article on benediction. The account stated that it was the invention of a Jesuit some three hundred years before. At St. Mary's we had benediction, yet three hundred years ago was obviously not far enough back for the primitive Church to have had anything to do with it...

I came across the story of Athanasius, the ancient bishop who had held out for a single word, who had let himself be driven into exile from his see for the sake of that word, which he knew, with all his mind and his heart and his spirit, must be retained if the faith were not to suffer. Small as this last fact might seem as a reason to trouble a modern like myself, it was one which affected me most and which eventually brought me to the door of the rectory of a Catholic church"); *The Great Mantle* (1951) (biography of Pope Pius X); *Brother André of Mount Royal* (1956); *Children's Shepherd: The Story of John Christopher Drumgoole* (1956); *The Golden Door: The Life of Katharine Drexel* (1957); *Witness of the Light: The Life of Pope Pius XII* (1958); *Make the Way Known* (1959); *The Dream Lives Forever: The Story of St. Patrick's Cathedral* (1960); Rebecca L. Kroeger, "Katherine Burton," in Mary R. Reichardt, *Catholic Women Writers: A Bio-Bibliographical Sourcebook* (2001); Patrick Allitt, *Catholic Converts: British and American Intellectuals Turn to Rome* (1997), pp.152-154 ("She bridled when a prominent priest, Father Leonard Feeney, spoke patronizingly about nuns, calling them 'dear little women.' To the contrary, said Burton, 'they are fearless women, intelligent women, happy women, hardworking women, and they have many other qualities, but I have never yet met one whom I would characterize as a "dear little woman."' The picture she drew of nuns and sisters, in her columns and books, was of decisive, capable, hard-headed women, never women of unthinking docility"); Lorene Hanley Duquin, *A Century of Catholic Converts* (2003), p.83.

Bush, John Ellis ("Jeb") – politician; b. 11 February 1953, Midland, Texas; c. 1995; second son of former President George H. W. Bush and Barbara Bush; younger brother of former President George W. Bush; brought up as an Episcopalian; educated at the University of Texas at Austin, graduating with a BA in Latin

American Studies in 1973; married to Columba Garnica Gallo (b. 17 August 1953) (three children of the marriage); worked for the international division of Texas Commerce Bank; moved to Florida and worked in several businesses; several civic and charitable activities; member of the Knights of Columbus; member of the Republican Party; 43rd Governor of Florida 1999-2007; in 2009 he said that what primarily attracted him to the faith were the "sacraments of the Catholic Church, the timeless nature of the message of the Catholic Church, and the fact that the Catholic Church believes in and acts on absolute truth as its foundational principles and doesn't move with modern times as my former religion did."

Cabaud, Judith (married name Judith Anthony) – writer and teacher; b. 1941, Brooklyn, New York; brought up in Brooklyn; parents were offspring of Jewish immigrants from Russia and Poland in the 1900s; majority of pupils at school were Jewish; family's religion was a matter of social conformity; inspired by the beauty of nature and of music; then took up literature, science and French; after the death of her father and grandparents, the last vestiges of Jewish tradition died; spent 1960-1961 at the Sorbonne studying *Civilisation Française*; greatly influenced in her conversion by Pascal's *Pensées*; wrote a well received book on the famous Jewish convert, Rabbi Zolli; married a Frenchman and lives in France (nine children of the marriage, one being a priest); see *Eugenio Zolli: Prophet of a New World* (2000); *When Time Becomes Space* (1979) (a spiritual autobiography); Wlodzimierz Redzioch, "The Christian Rabbi," *Inside the Vatican*, June-July 2002, p.44 (an interview with Cabaud about her book on Rabbi Zolli) ("While trying to improve my French, I would go to Catholic churches to listen to sermons, as I would go to the theater to hear good texts. One day, something very strange struck me: I had the feeling that there was a link between the Passover meal and the Catholic Mass. Something warm and familiar came flowing out of that beautiful liturgy, especially from all those marks of adoration shown by the priest and the assembly - kneeling, praying with the same fear of offending God as the Jewish people who hardly dare to utter His Name. I learned that the Catholic Church had been saying this for the past 2,000 years.

Then, by the grace of God, I realized that Jesus Christ is God, that the Old and the New Testaments were one and the same religion, Christianity being the continuation of ancient Judaism, and Christ being the Messiah announced by the prophets of old"); "Where Time Becomes Space," in in Roy H. Schoeman, *Honey from the Rock* (2007) ("[Pascal] told me what we are; our true state of being, our human condition. Man is not the center of things but is in the middle of things – that is, uncertain, 'floating' in a universe whose limits escape us. And yet, man could be considered as great because of his consciousness of things. Here my pseudoscientific ideas were shaken. It gave me a keen awareness of my own shortsightedness. Then, my reflection came to a standstill before what I considered as a wall: 'Man is only a subject full of error, natural and ineffaceable without grace.' In grace lay the entire mystery...

Pascal summed up the Jewish religion better than any Rabbi I had ever known. The prophecies of the Old Testament were the stumbling blocks of modern Judaism. For the first time in my life, in spite of my Hebrew school education, I found out that we were awaiting the Messiah, a Savior to redeem our fallen humanity...But who was this Messiah? Everything turns on the Person of Jesus Christ 'that both Testaments regard, the Old Testament in its expectation, the New in its model, as their center.' Now, at least, I understood why and for what we were a Chosen People...

Everything looked the same, yet everything was different. Nothing appeared changed, and yet everything was – because I knew that God existed and Jesus Christ was God. Everything was singing His presence to my ears. I thought, 'If He exists, then everything exists because of Him; everything exists in Him and He in everything'...

I was eager to know what happens at Mass for, having seen it, I was intrigued and wanted to know its meaning. I read through the missal completely and was amazed. The Mass had nothing of a sociological character; rather, it represented the reality of sacrifice, still occurring in the present as a continuation of its occurrence in the past.

Everything was logical now, because if Christ is God, there can never be too many signs of adoration, too many genuflections, and so the Mass was full of them.

At the time of Christ, sincere believers expected the Messiah to be a liberator from Roman occupation, a sovereign, a king who with his army would reorganize the Promised Land. The Jews too were waiting for a 'somebody'. And who was this Jesus who didn't have a cradle to His name? All His life He was a professional 'nobody.' How could a Son of God be so poor? There they were, confusing the Messiah with a material goal. The prophets had warned them beforehand, but to no avail").

Campbell, Thomas Bowyer – writer and lecturer; b. 1886 or 1887, Virginia; c. August 1931 (received at the Paulist Fathers' church of Santa Susanna, Rome); d. 1976; forebears were all Protestants; from an early age he loved the Episcopalian liturgy; at the start of his college career he reverted to liberalism; graduated from William and Mary

College in 1908; in his last year at college a fellow student brought him back to Episcopalianism ("He told me of the doctrine of Apostolic Succession, and I caught my first notion of sacramentalism") and he went in 1910 to train for the Episcopal ministry; after ordination he went to China as a missionary; entered the novitiate of the Cowley Fathers back in America, but eventually left; spent several years in one Anglo-Catholic parish after another; co-founder of the Confraternity of Unity to work for the "return of the schismatic Anglican Communion to the center of Catholic authority and unity"; faced great hostility from the High Church party; wrote many pro-Roman articles; wrote *Black Sadie*, a successful novel about colored people; traveled to England in 1928 and promoted the work of the Confraternity; the pronouncements of the Lambeth Conference in 1930 killed off any confidence he had in the Anglican communion and he was received into the Catholic Church; took up a post teaching History at the University of Notre Dame and became a Professor of History; worked there for sixteen years; Dean of the College of Arts and Letters 1935-1936; taught at St. Bede, Illinois from 1949; see *Black Sadie* (1928); *Old Miss* (1929); *Far Trouble* (1931); *White Nigger* (1932); *Towards the Chair of Peter: The Story of One Anglican Venture* (1951); *Catholicauthors.com.*

Carroll, Warren Hasty – historian and author; b. 24 March 1932, Maine; c. 7 December 1968; d. 17 July 2011, Manassas, Virginia; not baptized as a child; father an agnostic; mother believed in God, but refused to join a church, since they were "always fighting and criticizing one another": believed in God, but knew nothing about Christ; loved the C. S. Lewis interplanetary books, but did not appreciate the Christian undertones; became what he described as a "pagan deist with a strong desire for the truth"; received an MA and PhD in History from Columbia University; between 1955 and 1961 served two years with the U.S. Army Signal Corps, worked for the Central Intelligence Agency (serving in the anti-communism division as a Communist propaganda analyst); worked as an assistant command historian for the Second Air Force, Strategic Air Command; attended law school 1962-1964; member of the California Senate staff 1967-1970; worked at this time for a devout Catholic, John G. Schwartz, a state senator, who served as a role model; worked as a staff member for the U.S. Congress 1970-1972; converted to the Catholic faith under the influence of the pious example of his cradle Catholic wife Anne Westhoff, author of *Christ the King, Lord of History* and *Christ in the Americas*; after his conversion he worked for the Catholic journal *Triumph*, becoming its education director and in charge of its catechetical section, the Christian Commonwealth Institute; coordinated weekend lecture series throughout the country and oversaw *Triumph's* Summer program in El Escorial, Spain; wrote many books on history, including a five volume history of Christendom, written from a Catholic perspective, with the papacy as its unifying thread; concerned at the effect of the cultural revolution on Catholic education, he founded Christendom College, Front Royal, Virginia, the Catholic liberal arts college, in 1977 to provide a truly Catholic education faithful to the Church's magisterium; first President of the college until 1985, as well as the Chairman of the History Department until he retired in 2002); returned to give many public lectures at the college; first recipient of the Pius XI award for history given by the Society of Catholic Social Scientists; his teaching was famous for several memorable phrases, e.g., "History can be summed up in five words: Truth exists. The Incarnation happened," "You can never bribe a pope," and "One man can make a difference"; suffered several strokes from 1997 onwards; buried in the grounds of Christendom College; see (selective list) *1917, Red Banners, White Mantle* (1981); *Our Lady of Guadalupe and the Conquest of Darkness* (1983); *The Founding of Christendom* (1985); *The Guillotine and the Cross* (1986); *The Building of Christendom* (1987); *70 Years of the Communist Revolution* (1989); *Isabel of Spain: The Catholic Queen* (1991); "The Historical Truth about Christopher Columbus," *Fidelity*, April 1992, p.24; *The Glory of Christendom* (1993); *The Rise and Fall of the Communist Revolution* (1995); "Banning the Supernatural: Why Historians Must Not Rule Out the Action of God in History," (1996) *The Catholic Social Science Review* ("Scholarly history as written today and for the past forty years, has banned everything supernatural as though it were an intellectual plague. The very possibility of action by God in history has become academically taboo. This prohibition applies not only to miracles and apparitions, but even to the power of prayer. So universal is this ban, so chilling its effect even on the minds of historians who personally believe in the supernatural, that its imposition has gone virtually unchallenged the past forty years. Indeed, in all honesty I must say that since I began writing scholarly Catholic history thirteen years ago I have found no other contemporary historian who writes in defiance of this ban.

This situation cannot be allowed to continue. For our Christian and Catholic faith is preeminently a historical faith. We believe that God, the Creator and Sustainer of the universe, entered history, incarnate as the man Jesus Christ, at a particular time and place. No other religion has ever claimed that. In G. K. Chesterton's words:

'Right in the middle of all these things stands up an enormous exception...nothing less than the loud assertion that this mysterious maker of the world has visited his world in person. It declares that really and even recently, or right in the middle of historic times, there did walk into the world this original invisible being, about whom the thinkers make theories and the mythologists hand down myths; the Man Who Made the World. That such a higher personality exists behind all things had indeed always been implied by all the best thinkers, as well as by all the most beautiful legends. But nothing of this sort had been implied in any of them. It is simply false to say that the other sages and heroes had claimed to be that mysterious master and maker of whom the world had dreamed and disputed. Not one of them had ever claimed to be anything of the sort. Not one of their sects or schools had ever claimed that they had claimed to be anything of the sort. The most that any religious prophet had said was that he was the true servant of such a being. The most that any visionary had ever said was that men might catch glimpses of the glory of that spiritual being; or much more often of lesser spiritual beings. The most that any primitive myth had ever suggested was that the Creator was present at the Creation. But that the Creator was present at scenes a little subsequent to the supper parties of Horace, and talked with tax collectors and government officials in the detailed daily life of the Roman Empire, and that this fact continued to be firmly asserted by the whole of that great civilization for more than a thousand years - that is something utterly unlike anything else... It makes nothing but dust and nonsense of comparative religion.'

If that is our faith, we should never allow ourselves to be persuaded or pressured to consent to any field of study - especially history - being declared off limits to it. Rather we should say, with Dom Prosper Gueranger: 'History ought to be Christian, if it is to be true: for Christianity is the truth complete; and every historical system which disregards the supernatural order in its explanation and evaluation of the fliers, is a false system which explains nothing, and which leaves the annals of humanity in chaos and a permanent contradiction with all the ideas that reason forms on the destinies of our race here below.'

From the first Catholic historian, Eusebius of Caesarea, through St. Augustine's magisterial *City of God*, to Caesar Baronius, the first modern Catholic historian, and Bossuet's *Discours sur l'histoire universelle*, and on down to the middle of this twentieth century with the works of Belloc, Chesterton, and William Thomas Walsh, strong and indeed mighty voices were always heard telling history from the Catholic viewpoint, which puts God and His Son and the Church He founded at the center of history. But the last great avowedly Catholic historian, Christopher Dawson, was much more cautious, seeking academic acceptance as he was for his presentation of Christian culture; and since Dawson, even Catholic historians have generally accepted, without even a protest, the academic ban on the supernatural, which consequently now reigns supreme...

[T]he arbitrary a priori assumption that apparitions and miracles and the Incarnation itself could not have happened, that historical events never transcend the natural order, is not a critical standard. It is a flagrant bias that ought to he firmly rejected. Jettisoning this prejudice is a reasonable and fair position to demand even from non-Christian historians. For the Christian historian it is nothing less than a duty. In the hard-hitting but just words of Dom Gueranger: 'The Christian has not only a duty to believe, but also a duty to confess what he believes. This double obligation, founded in the doctrine of the Apostle [Paul] (Rom. 10,10), is the more binding in ages of naturalism, and the Christian historian ought to understand that it is not enough for him to declare his belief, in passages here and there in his book, if its Christian character then immediately disappears'"); *The Last Crusade* (1996) (a history of the Spanish Civil War); *The Cleaving of Christendom* (2000); *The Revolution Against Christendom* (2006) (with Anne Carroll); *The Crisis of Christendom* (2013) (with Anne Carroll); Michael N. Kelsey, *Christendom's Triumph: The Profile of Warren H. Carroll* (2003); Lorene Hanley Duquin, *A Century of Catholic Converts* (2003), p.170 ("When Dr. Carroll's search for truth led him to examine Christianity, he turned back to C. S. Lewis. After reading *Mere Christianity*, *Miracles*, and *The Problem of Pain*, he became convinced of the divinity of Jesus Christ: 'Lewis does not let you evade the fundamental question: Who was this Man? He shows you why you must answer that He is God Himself.'

This new understanding of faith altered the course of Carroll's life. 'I had never been a Christian until I was finally convinced that Jesus Christ is God. Now I knew I must put Jesus at the center of my life, because His Godhead is truth'

The Catholic faith is always at the center of his work. 'It is the pivot around which true history revolves,' he explains, 'and the one standard by which the importance of every historical event and figure should be judged'").

Carson, "Kit" (born Christopher Houston Carson) – frontiersman, army officer and Indian agent; b. 24 December 1809, Madison County, Kentucky; c. 1842; d. 23 May 1868, Fort Lyon, Colorado; father, whose ancestors were Scottish/Irish, was a farmer who fought in the Revolutionary War; eleventh child of fifteen in the family, by two wives; family moved to a rural area near Franklin, Missouri, when he was one year old; known as "Kit" from an early age; father killed by a falling tree in 1817, reducing the family to great poverty; he had to leave school and work on the family farm; he never learned to read or write, other than signing his name; apprenticed to a saddlemaker, but left; signed on with a large merchant caravan traveling to Santa Fe and looked after the livestock; learned the skills of a trapper; worked in several states trapping and trading and first saw combat with Indians; went through a form of marriage to an Arapaho woman, who died, then to a Cheyenne woman, but she went back to her tribe; in 1842 he received instruction in the Catholic faith from Padre Antonio José Martinez (1793-1867) and was received into the Catholic Church; in 1843 he married his third wife, Josepha Jaramillo (1829-1868), aged fourteen (they had eight children); from 1842 to 1846 he was the guide on the three famous expeditions of John C. Frémont (1813-1890), becoming a hero in the public image; took part in the Mexican American War and in the First Navajo Indian campaign; he concluded various peace treaties with the Indians; in the American Civil War he joined the New Mexico volunteer infantry and fought for the Union, but then occupied with further Indian troubles in the Second Navajo campaign and the Southern Plains Campaign; awarded the brevet rank of Brigadier General and then General; then took up ranching; supported additional government assistance for the Indians; buried in Taos, New Mexico, next to Josepha; see Charles Burdett, *Life of Kit Carson: The Great Western Hunter and Guide* (1870); J. S. C. Abbott, *Life of Kit Carson* (1873); Edwin Legrand Sabin, *Kit Carson Days (1809-1868)* (1914); Harvey Louis Carter, *Dear Old Kit: The Historical Christopher Carson* (1968); Carter Guild and Thelma S. Guild, *Kit Carson, a Pattern for Heroes* (1984); David Roberts, *A Newer World: Kit Carson, John C. Fremont and the Claiming of the American West* (2001); Marc Simmons, *Kit Carson and His Three Wives* (2003); *ANB.*

Cary, Diana Serra ("Baby Peggy") (born Peggy-Jean Montgomery) – child star; b. 26 October 1918, Merced, California; c. 1948 (hger father converted later); her father Jack Montgomery was a stuntman in the movies; at the age of nineteen months she visited Century Studios on Sunset Boulevard and was hired to appear in a series of short films with Century's canine star, Brownie the Wonder Dog; between 1921 and 1924 she made about 150 short comedy films; in 1922 she received 1.2 million fan letters; in 1923 she began working with Universal Studios and appeared in full-length dramatic films; she became a major star, made personal appearances around the country, and endorsed various products; her contract with Universal was worth $1,500,000 a year by 1923 (she was dubbed "the million dollar baby"); her career was controlled by her father; because of her father's wild spending and his corrupt business partners the fortune was quickly gone; she suffered much illness; her film career ended in 1925, when her father fell out with her producer and cancelled her contract; she continued to perform successfully in vaudeville 1925-1929; after the stock market crash her career declined; in the 1930s she found herself poor and working as an extra; at the age of seventeen she tried to escape the film industry by running away from home; married Gordon Ayres, the actor, in 1938, but they divorced in 1948; she married Bob Cary in 1954 (one son of the marriage); she adopted the name Diana Serra Cary (the Serra in honor of Fr. Junipero Serra); later had successful careers as a publisher, historian, and author on Hollywood subjects; she has worked for reforms in child performer protection laws; in 2012 a campaign to get her a star on the Hollywood Walk of Fame was begun; see *What Ever Happened to Baby Peggy: The Autobiography of Hollywood's Pioneer Child Star* (1996); *The Hollywood Posse: The Story of a Gallant Band of Horsemen Who Made Movie History* (1996); *Hollywood's Children: An Inside Account of the Child Star Era* (1997); *Jackie Coogan: The World's Boy King: A Biography of Hollywood's Legendary Child Star* (2003); *astarforbabypeggy.com* ("1948 found Peggy Montgomery Ayres living off a small stipend and working switchboards. Feeling smothered by the town and industry, she turned to religion, finding comfort in the Catholic church. She converted and soon found an opportunity to run the Serra Mission Gift Shop in Santa Barbara, CA…a few hours away from Los Angeles. On the advice of a Father at the mission, Peggy told no one of her movie past and eventually adopted the name Diana Serra Cary. The name she still uses today…

Just weeks before his death her father asked to convert to Catholicism saying, "Peggy believes in this religion and I want to be in the right pen." In her autobiography, Diana remarked his death seemed to free her from the last bits of control he held over her").

Catherine de Ricci of the Sacred Heart of Christ, Mother – see under Smith, Lucy Eaton.

Chambers, B. Stuart – priest; b. 24 September 1869, Lexington, Kentucky; c. 18 March 1894; d. 15 February 1918, New York City; member of an old Kentucky family; attracted by the writings of Herbert Spencer and became an agnostic; went to New York as a young man and worked in publishing; accepted Christianity and became an Episcopalian; influenced in his subsequent conversion to the Catholic Church by studying the Mass and the Blessed Sacrament; made his classical studies at St. Francis Xavier College, New York; in 1896 he entered the American College in Rome to study for the priesthood; ordained on 25 July 1902 in Rome; completed degree of doctor of divinity in Rome before returning to New York; later contracted pneumonia and died; see essay in Georgina Pell Curtis (ed), *Some Roads to Rome in America* (1909), p.75 ("I went to Mass with [a Catholic friend] once or twice on Sunday - to Solemn High Mass. It was about as interesting as a Chinese puzzle and quite as understandable. I determined, mainly from motives of curiosity, to find out what it was all about. And I did - thank God, I did - I found out what the Holy Sacrifice of the Mass meant, the idea of it all; the Blessed Sacrament with Christ really, objectively present on the Altar. Here was love indeed! Love only the heart of a God could conceive, only the omnipotence of a God effect. Here was God not as an abstract idea but a concrete reality; God Incarnate, Divine and Human, and never more divine than when most human. God living and dying not only at Jerusalem nineteen hundred years ago but here, *hic et nunc*, every day and every hour of every day; here really present on the Altar for me, as though no one existed in the wide world for Him but me. Here was the Friend of Friends I could always and everywhere, *semper ubique*, count upon, and to the end, the only one. Here at last was the vital force to sustain when all else should fail; here the Eternal Spring to make a desert earth blossom like the rose!

The Blessed Sacrament, the idea of it, thus electrified my whole being and took possession of it. How wonderful, how sublime - and how preposterous to my Protestant tendencyofthinkingitallawaybythe light (?) of a sophisticated reason…

The whole question was too important to doubt about one way or the other. It was either true or it was false. I wished it to be true, such was the attitude of my will; a most important condition, by-the-way, as in the mysteries of faith the assent of the intellect to what is true is predetermined by the consent of the will to what is good. 'But is it true?' I asked. Nobody seemed to be sure but Rome. She alone gave a clear, definite and positive answer. And finally I believed Her, for She spoke as no one else ever speaks in religious matters, as one teaching with authority.

If Christ be the Redeemer of men, I thought, and if He founded a Church at all (rather than churches, which is absurd) to represent Him, to apply to all men, collectively and individually, the fruits of His Redemption, that Church should surely know her own mind in a matter so spiritually vital as the Real Presence of Christ in the

Blessed Sacrament. It did not take me long to find that only Rome knew what she was talking about on this subject, so dear to my heart; nor was she less sure and explicit about anything else I wanted to know concerning God and my own soul"); essay in Georgina Pell Curtis, *Beyond the Road to Rome* (1914), p.83.

Chapman, Mgr. Michael Andrew – priest; brought up in the Episcopalian Church by his mother, who was the daughter of a Baptist minister and who was never "extreme," but content with a vague Anglicanism; spent his choirboy days in a moderately High Episcopalian atmosphere; as an adolescent he was an Anglo-Catholic; always attracted by Catholic practices ("My mother's distress upon finding a rosary in my pocket in my teens seemed unreasonable, as it did also to her good pastor, who told her not to worry unless she found worse things in my pocket!"); began to reject the Episcopalian position and converted to the Catholic faith (received by Fr. Paul of Graymoor); said that if Canon Moyes' book *Bishop Barlow and Anglican Orders* had appeared while he was not yet a Catholic, it would have made him one; his conversion was also influenced by Mgr. Robert Hugh Benson and by G. K. Chesterton ("Chesterton, both before and after his conversion, was an idol"); later ordained to the Catholic priesthood; author of thirteen books; associate editor of *Our Sunday Visitor*; in 1948 he retired to Mercy Hospital, Elwood, Indiana, where he was chaplain; see *The Mass of the Cross* (1925); *The Faith of the Gospel: Brief Sermons for the Sundays of the Year* (1926); *The Epistle of Christ: Short Sermons for the Sundays of the Year* (1927); *Peregrinus Gasolinus: Wandering Notes on the Liturgy* (1928); *The Prayer of Faith: Brief Sermon Outlines for the Sundays of the Year, On the Orations or Collects of the Mass* (1928); *Sundays of the Saints: Sermon Outlines for the Feast Days Which May Occur on Sundays* (1928); *Garland of Saints for Children* (1929); *Judas, A Study of Possibilities; Jude, A Study of the Contrasts* (1929); *The Heart of the Fathers: Brief Sermons on the Sunday Gospels* (1931); *Peregrinus Goes Abroad* (1931); *The Liturgical Directions of Saint Charles Borromeo* (1934); "A Miracle of the Holy Ghost," in John A. O'Brien (ed), *The Road to Damascus, Volume III: The Way to Emmaus* (1953) ("Once convinced of the truth of the Catholic Faith in its entirety, there was only one thing to do - submit to the only human agency to which God has given the deposit of faith and authority to teach and practice it.

What I failed to realize was that my personal acceptance of Catholic doctrine was as definitely an exercise of 'private judgment' as any Protestant interpretation could he.

The 'glorious comprehensiveness' of Anglicanism, which prides itself on its freedom to tolerate mutually exclusive 'schools of thought' in one ecclesiastical household, gave me the 'freedom' to believe the whole Catholic Faith, including papal supremacy and infallibility, but left my neighbor equally free to reject it *in toto.* I was impressed by Kinsman's conclusion that a Church which tolerated everything could officially teach nothing...

The fact is that my submission to the Catholic Church brought only one change in my personal position, theological and devotional, and that was that the authority of the Catholic and Roman Church took the place of my individual and personal attitude and thinking on religion as a whole. I now accepted, for example, the supremacy and infallibility of the Pope, not as a conclusion of my own, based on the limited study and thinking I had been able to do about the matter, but as a pronouncement of the Catholic Church. It was 'of faith', not because I believed it, but because the Catholic Church declared it so to be.

Starting with a vague aesthetic interest in Catholic art, as enshrined principally in the liturgy, I had come, step by step, to accept all that lay back of liturgy. I say 'all', and there perhaps I have hit upon the crux of the whole matter. Not only had my acceptance of Catholic belief sprung from that beginning, but I had come to see that it must be all or nothing at all, that the Catholic religion was a perfect summation: remove any one tenet, and the whole perfect structure must be irretrievably impaired")

Chervin, Ronda de Sola – philosopher and writer; b. 1937, New York; c. 4 January 1959 (received in the Church of the Holy Name, New York; her twin sister, Carla, then her mother, and finally her husband, Martin (d. 1993) were received later); her maternal grandparents were atheist Communist Jews in Russia who fled to the United States; grandfather's side of the family were Sephardic Jews from South America and he married a Protestant; both her parents were atheists, but from Jewish backgrounds (never brought up as Jews), and were Communists until becoming informers for the FBI; she was brought up as a total atheist; she did not know of her Jewish background for several years; studied philosophy at college, but was disappointed at the skeptical approach taken by the teachers, its subjectivist attitude to truth, and its relativism in ethics; shortly afterwards influenced by Dietrich and Alice Von Hildebrand and transferred to Fordham University, where she obtained a PhD; subsequently professor of Philosophy and Theology at Loyola Marymount University, the seminary of the Archdiocese of Los Angeles, and the Franciscan University of Steubenville; taught philosophy at the Lenoir-Rhyne

College in Hickory, North Carolina; professor of Philosophy at St. John's Seminary Theologate, Camarillo, California; author of many Catholic books; conversion influenced by Chesterton, Newman, and C. S. Lewis; suffered a series of great personal losses, including the death of her mother, father, husband, and godparents, the suicide of her own son, and the loss of a breast to cancer; became a member of a new religious order, The Handmaids of Nazareth, but that did not work out; became a Dedicated Widow of the Holy Eucharist; see *Prayer and Your Everyday Life* (1980); *Spirit and Your Everyday Life* (1980); *Bringing the Mother with You* (1982); "The Truth Shall Set You Free," in *The Ingrafting: The Conversion Stories of Ten Hebrew-Catholics* (1987) ("Von Hildebrand, who was my professor in theory of knowledge, showed that when the skeptic claims 'there is no truth,' he is at least making a truth-claim for that very statement. That there is no truth is supposed to be really true and not just his own opinion. Hence, the statement is self-contradictory, since if it is true, there is one truth; and if it is false, there is also a truth…

According to [Von Hildebrand's ethical] philosophy, the fact that people in different cultures may have different moral ideas does not change the fact that there are some basic moral truths which are either universal or should be so. Every society values justice. Every man knows the difference between kindness and malice; between fidelity and betrayal. Every man has an idea of a moral 'ought' which transcends his own immediate desires. Even the man who claims that morality has no absolute validity – because he holds that ethics can be reduced to conditioning – in his own daily life will respond with moral indignation to the breach of those rights which he personally holds to be inalienable"); "In Search of the Savior," in Robert Baram (ed), *Spiritual Journeys* (revised edition, 1988), p.50 ("That summer after my first semester at Fordham found me in a new state of mind. I could see that there was a truth worth seeking; and I knew that moral values were real and objective, not merely conditioned and subjective. I vaguely thought that materialism could not be correct if there were such non-physical things as truth and moral norms which were higher than society…

More converts from atheism first come to believe in God and then to decide whether or not the Person Jesus was God. For me the process was reversed. In the Person of Christ depicted in the Bible, I sensed for the first time what the divine is. I came to see what [my philosophy professor] Dr. Baldwin V. Schwarz meant in marveling at the *uninventibility* of Christ. To claim that later Christians just made up the figure of Christ as a ruse to start a new religion, as some skeptics claim, was unthinkable: they would have had to be holy themselves to invent such a personality, and if they were holy they would not have lied...

I continued to study Catholic philosophy, but my greatest interest was in reading books of apologetics. Writers such as C. S. Lewis, Chesterton and Newman were able to show in an intellectual manner why it was rational to accept what is beyond reason: the mysteries of Christianity. For example, C. S. Lewis in *Mere Christianity* shows that it is impossible to conceive of Jesus as a mere man, or even the best of men, because a man who claims to be divine is either mad or really authentic. The books of Newman, especially his *Apologia* and his *Development of Christian Doctrine*, show why the need for unity of religious truth depends upon one Church guided in matters of doctrine by the Holy Spirit. My own way of explaining this comes out of years of studying philosophy. Christ comes with a message of love. In order to spend our time loving, we cannot be expending all our energies in theological debate. Faith in dogma gives us a source of truths we can be certain of so that we can go ahead and worship and love instead of bickering or setting up rival sects"); *Love of Wisdom: An Introduction to Christian Philosophy* (1988) (with Eugene Kevane); *Living in Love: About Christian Ethics* (1989); *Signs of Love: How Jesus Loves Us Through the Sacraments* (1989); *Great Saints Great Friends* (1990) (with Mary O'Neill); *Treasury of Women Saints* (1991); *Prayers of the Women Mystics* (1992); *Spiritual Friendship: Darkness and Light* (1992); *En Route to Eternity: The Story of My Life* (1994); *Bread From Heaven: Stories of Jews Who Found the Messiah* (1994); *Tell Me Why: Answering Tough Questions about the Faith* (1994) (with Joseph Pollard); *The Kiss from the Cross: Saints for Every Kind of Suffering* (1994); *A Mother's Treasury of Prayers: Prayers and Blessings for Your Children, Your Husband, Your Home, and for Every Occasion* (1995); *The Book of Catholic Customs and Traditions* (1995); *A Widow's Walk: Encouragement, Comfort, and Wisdom from the Widow-Saints* (1998); *Seeking Christ in the Crosses and Joys of Aging* (2000); *Help in Time of Need: Encouragement, Practical Advice, and Prayers* (2002); *Taming the Lion Within: Hungry For Heaven* (2002); *Becoming a Handmaid of the Lord: From the Journals of Ronda De Sola Chervin* (2003); *Feminine, Free, and Faithful* (2003); *5 Steps from Anger to Peace* (2003); *Freed to Love: Healing for Catholic Women* (2003); *Holding Hands with God: Catholic Women Share Their Stories of Courage and Hope* (2003); *Quotable Saints* (2003); *Ties That Bind: The Story of a Marriage* (2003); *Voyage to Insight* (2003) (with Lois August Janis); *EWTN Audio Library, The*

Journey Home (22 August 2005) ("I like to say when I'm teaching a philosophy class and I get to the subject of beauty, well if it's totally subjective, wouldn't you have everyone suing the highway department because they actually have the gall to say 'Here's a special scenic spot. Get off the road and look at it.' How could there be scenic spots that everyone would agree are beautiful and not resent being pulled off the road because of someone's subjective idea of beauty"); "I Have Called You By Name; You Are Mine!" in Roy H. Schoeman, *Honey from the Rock* (2007) ("I saw Chartres Cathedral in France. I looked at the amazing shape of that church with the beautiful stained glass windows, and I started to cry. The line for Keats: 'Beauty is truth, truth is beauty,' came to mind, and I asked myself, 'How could this be so beautiful if there is no truth to it, just medieval ignorance?'...

...I studied books like C. S. Lewis' *Mere Christianity.* The chapter in which Lewis shows that it is no good fence-sitting by deciding Jesus was just a wonderful man or a prophet was an intellectual turning point. When a man claims to be divine, he is either really God, insane, or a liar. Since no one thinks Jesus was insane or a liar, He must have been divine"); *Before the Altar* (2008); *Walk with Me, Jesus: A Widow's Journey* (2008); *What the Saints Said about Heaven: 101 Holy Insights on Everlasting Life* (2011); *Last Call: Fourteen Men Who Dared to Answer* (2012); *The Way of Love: The Battle for Inner Transformation* (2013).

Churchill, Harriet Brewer – Catholic laywoman; b. 7 January 1855, Boston, Massachusetts; father of Pilgrim descent, some of his ancestors having come in the Mayflower; mother's ancestors fought in the War of Independence; father agnostic ("admirer of Voltaire (whose works filled whole shelves in our library), of Buckle, Parker, Darwin, Huxley and the rest"); given little religious instruction ("I was taught to tell the truth, and not to steal, etc., more as a matter of social polity than because lies and thieving were sins against the law of God"); educated in private schools in Massachusetts and Switzerland; while in Europe spent several weeks in Rome; conversion to the Catholic Church mainly influenced by her belief in the papacy and authority; in his will probated in 1892 her father gave a part of his estate in trust for her use during her life with the express understanding that neither of the trustees (her two brothers) nor she "shall expend any part of such income for the use or benefit of the Roman Catholic Church, its priests or clergy, charities, nuns, saints, or rites, its ceremonies or exhibitions, its images or masses, its lectures or preaching, its cemeteries or processions, or in aid or encouragement or support of anything connected with or pertaining to that church or sect"; see essay in Georgina Pell Curtis (ed), *Some Roads to Rome in America* (1909), p.85 ("[T]he peculiar tenets of the Puritans for which my forefathers braved the perils of the wilderness are dead and buried like themselves: while the Papacy which saw them come has seen them go - into oblivion, while the Holy Father from the banks of the Tiber still rules a Church greater in numbers and more perfect in organization than at any time in the history of the world.

I often think I should like to add to Lord Macaulay's famous passage and to say that when the New Zealander himself shall have passed away and his land be but a desert; when the inevitable catastrophe shall have occurred and this old earth drifts a derelict in space, then and not till then will the Church militant have failed to exist. Then and not till then will the Sacraments cease to be administered and the Pope be no more...

I remember on one rare occasion my stepmother read aloud to me the famous chapter of St. Paul on charity, and I recall wondering at the time, why she should attach any importance to it unless she believed that the Bible was an inspired work and the Word of God. Her idea seemed to be that it was 'a beautiful chapter.' But no more so than something from Marcus Aurelius. I said that 'if that was all there was to it there were other things more interesting.

It was a little later than this that I astonished my family one day by remarking that 'I could not understand, if a person wished to lead a really good life, why it was not a good idea to go to confession as Catholics did.' The idea was evolved out of my own brain and represented my childish idea of the fitness of things...

Before returning home [from Europe] I spent several weeks in Rome, and hours and hours were passed in the churches in presence of the Blessed Sacrament. Here began, as Bishop Spalding declared, my conversion. Not that I was aware of it, or cared much for any religion...

After I had been at home about a year circumstances took me to New York where I for the first time came in contact with the workings of the Catholic Church. I saw the doctrines of the Church applied alike to rich and poor, gentle and simple, learned and unlearned. I witnessed the atmosphere of devotion, the unanimity of worship, the daily succession of Masses, the coming and going of one congregation after another, the devout genuflections, and all this in the most commercial and latter day city in the world.

I was much impressed; and then a Protestant friend lent me a copy of The *Imitation of Christ* of which I had never heard. A book written presumably by one of those idle and dissolute monks we read so much of in Protestant books.

Then I read Newman, and now that

I have spoken of the great Cardinal, who is there who does not know that in the matter of a conversion, his is a name to conjure with?

Although I had never been strictly speaking a Protestant, I felt that I could not openly denounce the opinions under the influence of which I had been educated until I had heard what a Unitarian minister should have to say for that particular sect. I called on the Rev. James Freeman Clarke. I remember one day his offering to pray with me. But I never could divest myself of the idea that all he said was merely the sum of his own reflections and opinions and being such was no more worthy of credence than the sum of my own. I felt that he had no more authority for anything he chose to put forward than that 'he, James Freeman Clarke, thought so' and I think I can with truth say that just on this hinge turned the door through which I entered the Church...

The Unitarians in New England were founded by William Ellery Channing, who having decided that the Scriptures did not teach the doctrine of the Trinity established a sect on that opinion. They prided themselves at that time on their progressiveness and they progressed so well that the first members having denied that the Son was God, their children denied that the Creator is our Father. A most logical conclusion, but quite a pagan one.

The Rev. James Freeman Clarke having failed to convince me in any way I applied to the Reverend Phillips Brooks. The conclusion of his advice was that if there were any church on earth which seemed to me to have been founded by Christ it was my duty to join it.

A little later the Rev. Father Edward Holker Welch, SJ, of Boston College, gave me conditional baptism. The root of my conversion was my belief in the Papacy, the principle of authority; and I think to-day as I thought then that an honest study of its history is enough to convince the world of its claims. Its very existence carried along and protected through the ages is a perpetual miracle").

Clarke, Hansen H. – politician; b. 2 March 1957, Detroit, Michigan; his father, Mozaffar Ali Hashim, was a Muslim immigrant from Bangladesh; his mother, Thelma Clarke, African-American, grew up in the African Methodist Episcopal Church in Detroit; his father died when he was eight years old; educated at Cornell University (degree in Fine Arts); Law degree from the Georgetown University Law Center in 1987; member of the Democratic Party; worked as chief of staff to U.S. Representative John Conyers; member of the Michigan House of Representatives in 1991-1992 and 1999-2002; served in the Michigan Senate 2003-2011; member of U.S. House of Representatives from Michigan from 2011; first U.S. Congressman of Bangladeshi descent; married to Choi Palmer-Cohen, born in

South Korea and adopted by a Catholic mother and Jewish father.

Cody, William Frederick ("Buffalo Bill") – soldier and showman; b. 26 February 1846, near Leclaire, Iowa Territory; c. 9 January 1917 (deathbed convert; received by Fr. Christopher Walsh of the Denver Cathedral of the Immaculate Conception); d. 10 January 1917, Denver, Colorado; parents were Canadian and originally Quakers and against slavery; family moved in 1847 to Canada where they had a farm; he lived there until they moved to Leavenworth, Kansas Territory, in 1853; worked as a rider for the Pony Express; enlisted as a soldier in the 7th Kansas Cavalry in 1863 and served in the Civil War; employed as a scout for the United States Army 1868-1872 (scouted for Indians and hunted and killed bison to supply the Army); earned his nickname after the Civil War when, under a contract to supply Kansas Pacific Railroad workers with buffalo meat, he killed 4,280 American bison in eight months (1867-1868); received the Medal of Honor in 1872 for service to the United States Army as a scout; founded one of the original Wild West shows and toured with it for many years throughout the United States and Europe, becoming famous world-wide; later extended to cover other horse-culture groups; other performers included "Wild Bill" Hickok (1837-1876), Annie Oakley (1860-1926), and Sitting Bull (c.1831-1890); when the show was in London he met Cardinal Manning; in 1890 he met Pope Leo XIII; involved in the damming of the Shoshone River in Wyoming (the name of the dam and reservoir was later changed by an act of Congress to the Buffalo Bill Dam); also founded the town of Cody, the seat of Park County in northwestern Wyoming; his wife and family were always Catholic; the priest who received him into the Church, Fr. Walsh, originally from Ireland, gained such a reputation as a crack shot that the pair became friends and fellow hunters; they seldom discussed religion as he described himself as an agnostic, yet in his last illness he sent for Fr. Walsh; he told the priest that he had never belonged to any religion, but that he had always believed in God; he said he knew he had only a short time to live and he wished to die in the Catholic Church; Fr. Walsh asked the appropriate questions, then administered the sacrament of baptism; his grave lies atop Lookout Mountain in Golden, Colorado; see *The Life of Hon. William F. Cody, known as Buffalo Bill, the Famous Hunter, Scout and Guide. An Autobiography* (1879); *Buffalo Bill's Own Story of His Life and Deeds* (1917); Don Russell, *The Lives and Legends of Buffalo Bill* (1960); Joy S. Kasson, *Buffalo Bill's Wild West: Celebrity, Memory and Popular History* (2001); Louis S. Warren, *Buffalo Bill's America:*

William Cody and the Wild West Show (2005); Michelle Anne Delaney. *Buffalo Bill's Wild West Warriors: A Photographic History* (2007); Buffalo Bill Historical Center, Cody, Wyoming; ANB.

Coleman, Caryl - ecclesiologist, church glass manufacturer and decorator; b. 1847; c. 1868 (received by Fr. George Deshon (see below); d. 1930, New Rochelle, New York; son of John Hull Coleman and Charlotte Augusta Coleman, his father's forebears were Quakers from Marlborough, Wiltshire, England; his mother's forebears were part Catholic part Anglican from Sussex, England; his parents both became Unitarians, but ultimately became indifferent to most elements of religion; brought up with no religion, but had a passionate love for history and archaeology; educated at Bellevue Medical College, New York, and Canisius College, Buffalo, New York; much travel in Europe studying Ecclesiology; commercial life in church glass and decorating; pleaded for a revival of the handcraftsmanship advocated by William Morris; numerous articles relating mostly to the decorative arts, symbolism, iconography and archaeology; contributor to *The Dictionary of Architecture* and to the *Catholic Encyclopedia*; married Nonna Agnes Black in 1881; brother of Charles Caryl Coleman (1840-1928), the painter; see *Symbolism in Religious Art* (1899); *A Mark of Honor* (1903); *The Sacred Ciphers* (1903); *A Day with Mary* (1908); essay in Georgina Pell Curtis, *Some Roads to Rome in America* (1909), p.95 ("I knew very little, or nothing concerning the life of Christ, or about the Christian faith, the history of its planting and propagation. To remove this gross ignorance, and with the intention of getting a general idea of the subject, I read the New Testament through, always regarding it, however, as a collection of historical documents of doubtful authenticity, yet of sufficient authority as to the ordinary facts therein narrated. At the same time I supplemented this reading by studying the *Ecclesiastical History* of Eusebius (A.D. 325), and *The First Apology* of Justin Martyr (A.D. 139) . When I had finished this investigation, Jesus of Nazareth had become a living reality to me - as much so as Plato - and henceforth I looked upon him as an historical character, if nothing more. This was a great step, as I had hitherto been inclined to believe Him a mythical being... [T]he more I studied the life and works of Christ, the greater grew my admiration for His character. Almost immediately I saw that if it were stripped of its supernatural qualities, it would be meaningless and contradictory. An early Christian writer truthfully said 'that when the intellect has been enlightened by truth, our Lord comes to take up His abode in our hearts' (St. Gregory the Great,

A.D. 540-604). So it was not surprising that this newly acquired knowledge acted as a goad to spur me on to further study. At once I took up all the Christian writers of the first three hundred years, together with a few of the post-Nicene authors. I read them carefully through, in order that I might clearly understand what the followers of the Apostles and the promoters of the Faith, thought and taught concerning their Master. I then made a comparison and an analysis of the historical testimony concerning the public life of Jesus and that of Alexander the Great, only to find, as all will who make a similar investigation, that for every documentary, monumental, and traditional witness to the life and deeds of the Grecian hero, there were a greater number, and more trustworthy ones, for those of Jesus of Nazareth. In addition, in the case of Jesus, I found two classes of witnesses peculiar to Him, and of the greatest value, viz., the Jewish Prophets, who foretold His life; and the Christian martyrs: thousands of men and women and even children, the noblest of the human race, who, at the time of the planting of the Faith, willingly and gladly laid down their lives as a testimony of the truth of the Gospel narrative. So overwhelming was the evidence in favor of the truth of the life, words and work of Jesus Christ, as recorded in Holy Writ, that I was compelled, willingly or unwillingly, to either doubt all history, all human testimony, or to believe in Him and His divine mission to mankind...The moment my historical research led me to believe in the historic Christ, I entered into the fulness of faith...

This Word made flesh further promised this organization of men, that the gates of hell shall not prevail against it, that the Holy Spirit would abide with it and guide it into all truth, and that He, Himself, would never abandon it, for He said, 'I am with you all days, even to the consummation of the world'...

Where was I to find the living, speaking voice of God and His Christ?...Had the words of Christ failed and His promises proved worthless? No. For when I cast my eyes upon Christendom, I saw that there was one body that claimed these prerogatives, to the exclusion of all others; and moreover, plainly bore the marks that substantiate the claim. The marks were:

I. Apostolicity: *The persevering in the doctrine of the Apostles...*

II. Authority : *For how shall they preach unless they be sent...*

III. Unity: *For there shall be one fold and one shepherd...*

IV. Visibility : *A city seated on a mountain cannot be hid...*

V. Indefectibility : *His kingdom shall have no end...*

VI. Sanctity: *Christ also so loved the Church, and delivered Himself up for it; that He might sanctify it, cleansing it by the laver of water in the word of life, that He might present it to Himself a glorious Church...*

VII. Catholicity: *The Gospel of the Kingdom shall he preached in the whole world for a testimony to all nations...*

It was plain to my eyes, and it is easy to be seen by all, that the one Church claiming to be the only Church of Christ, and at the same time bearing all these Marks of Authenticity, to the exclusion of all other organizations, was the Holy Roman Catholic Church... Moreover, it was just as plain to me, and to be seen by all who look, that all other Christian organizations 'mutually refuted and condemned each other' (St. Ephrem), for among them there are as many faiths as wills, and that each one was the offspring of some disobedient Catholic, and in most cases bore his name. 'Before Valentinus there were no Valentinians; nor Marcionites before Marcion' (St. Irenaeus), nor Arians before Arius, nor Manicheism before Manes, nor Pelagians before Pelagius; and coming down nearer to our own time: before Luther there were no Lutherans, nor Calvinists before Calvin. All of these so called Christian Churches at the best were nothing more than branches torn off the parent tree...These facts, together with the fact, that the Apostles preached, not themselves, but Christ Jesus the Lord, and that not a single sect or church is called after any one of them, made it more and more evident to me that 'they ceased to be Christians, who, having lost the name of Christ, assumed human and extraneous titles' (Lactantius, A.D. 320). I saw then how true were the words of the great Saint Cyprian, written in the third century, 'The spouse of Christ cannot become adulterate; she is undefiled and chaste; she owns but *one house*; with spotless purity, she guards the sanctity of *one chamber*. She keeps us for God; she appoints unto the kingdom the sons she has borne. Whosoever, having separated from the Church, is joined to an adulteress, he is cut off from the promises of Christ. Neither shall he come unto the reward of Christ who leaves the Church of Christ. He is an alien, he is an outcast, he is an enemy. He can no longer have God for a Father, who has not the Church for a mother.'

The more I studied the history of private judgment, the source of heresy and schism, the plainer I saw that the Church of Christ, 'begotten from one faith, and brought forth by means of the Holy Ghost' (St. Cyprian), must of necessity be endowed with a continuity of authority and doctrine, or it could not be of God"); essay in Georgina Pell Curtis, *Beyond the Road to Rome* (1914), p.90.

Coleman, Emily Holmes – poet and novelist; b. 1899, Oakland, California; c. 1944; d. 13 June 1974, Tivoli, New York; graduated from Wellesley College in 1920; married Lloyd Ring Coleman, a psychologist, in 1921; went to live in Paris in 1926; society editor of the *Paris Tribune* (the European edition of the *Chicago Tribune*); was part of the group of writers who contributed to *Transition* magazine, edited by two of her fellow *Tribune* staff members, Eugene Jolas and Elliot Paul; had several poems, stories and articles published in *Transition* and in the *New Review*; wrote one novel, *The Shutter of Snow*, based on her own experience in childbirth and her subsequent stay in a mental hospital while suffering from postpartum psychosis after the birth of her son John; spent one year in St. Tropez as secretary to Emma Goldman (1869-1940), the anarchist philosopher, while Goldman was writing her autobiography, *Living My Life* (1931); by late 1932 she was spending most of her time in Italy; a second novel, *The Tygon*, plus numerous poems, essays, stories, and plays, remain unpublished; kept a lifelong diary in which she reflected on her life quest and raised spiritual issues, which led her eventually to the Catholic Church; corresponded with and later was a personal friend of Jacques and Raissa Maritain; after her conversion all of her writing was focused on the Catholic faith; friend of Dorothy Day (see below); her marriage (1940-1944) to Jake Scarborough was disavowed after her conversion; lived in a number of Catholic communities; had many literary friends; one particular group of friends in England, sometimes referred to as the "Hayford Hall Circle" (named after Peggy Guggenheim's estate) were writers Djuna Barnes, John Holms, and Edwin Muir, as well as Peggy Guggenheim herself, Beatrix Wright, Antonia White, and others; also a friend of Hugh Kingsmill, Robert Liddell, Kathleen Raine, Dylan Thomas, Mary Wesley, and Malcolm Williamson; her later years were spent in Italy, writing mainly poetry; returned to the United States before her death and was cared for by nuns at The Farm, Tivoli, New York; see *The Shutter of Snow* (1930); Minna Besser Geddes, "Emily Coleman," *Dictionary of Literary Biography* (1980); The Emily Holmes Coleman Papers, University of Delaware.

Conley, James Douglas – bishop; b. 19 March 1955, Kansas City, Missouri; c. 6 December 1975 (his parents, Carl (d. 2006) and Betty (b. 1923), converted in 1991); of Wea Native American descent through his paternal grandmother's family; brought up as a Presbyterian; educated at the University of Kansas on its Integrated Humanities Program, the well-known classical great books program; an influence on his conversion to the Catholic faith during his junior year was Professor John Senior (see below) his teacher and mentor, who became his godfather; graduated BA in English Literature in 1977; traveled through Europe and considered a monastic vocation at the Abbey of Notre Dame de Fontgombault in France; returned to the United States in 1978; studied for the priesthood at St. Pius X Seminary, Erlanger, Kentucky and later at Mount St. Mary's Seminary in Emmitsburg, Maryland (Master's degree in Divinity in 1985); ordained to the priesthood 18 May 1985; licenciate in moral theology from the Alphonsian Academy of the Pontifical Lateran University; served in Rome as an official of the Congregation for Bishops 1996-2006; consecrated in 2008 as Auxiliary Bishop of the Diocese of Denver, Colorado, and Titular Bishop of Cissa; in 2009 he wrote a personal letter to Rev. John Jenkins, CSC., president of the University of Notre Dame, to express his opposition to the University's decision to have President Obama deliver its commencement speech and receive an honorary degree; insisted that healthcare reform needs to include explicit, ironclad conscience protections for medical professionals and institutions so that they cannot be forced to violate their moral convictions.

Connelly, Venerable Cornelia Augusta, SHCJ (*née* Peacock) – nun, foundress of a religious order and educational reformer; b. 15 January 1809, 1 Filbert Street, Philadelphia, Pennsylvania; c. December 1835 (received at the Cathedral in New Orleans; her husband was received subsequently in Rome); d. 18 April 1879, the convent at Mayfield, Sussex, England; youngest of six surviving children of an affluent Philadelphia family; her father had emigrated from Yorkshire, England; both parents died early; lived with her older sister and her sister's husband, who were both strict Episcopalians; brought up a Presbyterian but baptized in the Episcopalian church in 1831; a beautiful young woman with many suitors; in 1831 she married Pierce Connelly (1803-1883), an Episcopalian clergyman, against her family's wishes; they moved to Natchez, Mississippi where he had a parish; the marriage produced five children, her fourth child, Mary, dying shortly after birth; on 27 March 1836 her husband became a Catholic (attracted very much by a fascination with ornamentation and ritual), he also petitioned to be considered for ordination, which canon law allowed if both partners willingly agreed to live separate and chaste lives; for two years they lived in Rome, her husband mingling with the wealthy and famous, but no nearer ordination; she began reading theology and Church history, being especially impressed by St. Ignatius Loyola; on returning home, having lost money in a financial recession, her husband taught at a Jesuit college in Louisiana, while she taught music part-time at a school run by the Sacred Heart Sisters, experiencing at first hand the life of religious sisters and Catholic education; she also continued her spiritual reading and acquired a spiritual director; during this time her two-year-old son, John Henry, died of severe burns in her arms after forty-three hours when his dog accidentally pushed him into a vat of boiling sugar; from this anguish her lifelong devotion to the Blessed Virgin Mary as Mother of Sorrows was born; she and her husband took a mutual private vow of celibacy in October 1840 after his final decision to seek ordination (he was finally ordained in July 1846 and became private chaplain to Lord Shrewsbury), in 1841 she decided to pursue her vocation as a nun; in 1844 their vow was made canonically binding when they signed a deed of perpetual separation before Vatican witnesses in Rome; she was accepted as a postulant by Rome's Sacred Heart nuns, but decided she had no call to enter the order; encouraged by Nicholas Wiseman, Cardinal Fransoni, Lord Shrewsbury, and Pope Gregory XVI, she agreed to found a new religious congregation in England rather than America, the aim being to start an educational congregation suitable for middle-class English converts wanting to become nuns; in August 1846 she moved to England; the two younger children, who had lived with her until then, were now placed in boarding schools at the insistence of her husband; in October she, together with three other women, opened the first convent of the Holy Child Jesus, in the industrial town of Derby; the sisters opened a day school and a boarding school; she wrote a Rule for the order as she was asked to do; from Maryvale, Newman sent her a convert friend of his, Emily Bowles (1818-1904); in December 1847 she made her vows and was installed by Cardinal Wiseman as the Superior-General of the Society of the Holy Child Jesus, the first new native congregation of women to be founded in England since the Reformation; its work was in the field of education; her husband returned to England, tried to take a hand in running the convent, and then removed the three children to Italy; in 1849 he renounced his priesthood and sued to have his conjugal rights restored; much publicity in the press; the Court of Arches ordered her to leave the convent and return to him; she won her appeal to the Judicial Committee of the Privy Council; he then resumed his position in the Episcopal Church, and for thirty years wrote anti-Catholic articles, many against his wife; she won closer control of her convents against priests and bishops; she was recognized as an outstanding educator; by the time of her death the order had expanded throughout England, onto the Continent, and across the United States; only in 1893 was the original Rule finally approved; of her children, Adeline finally returned to the practice of the Catholic faith; declared Venerable in 1992; buried in the chapel of the convent at Mayfield,

Sussex; see M. C. Gompertz, *The Life of Cornelia Connelly, 1809-1879, Foundress of the Society of the Holy Child Jesus* (1922); Katherine Burton, *In No Strange Land: Some American Catholic Converts* (1942), p.57 "What Mother Connolly did during these years was to reform the education of Catholic girls in England. Her students were taught the usual basic subjects but she believed in a liberal rather than a specialized curriculum for girls; besides the usual school subjects, she provided lectures on philosophy, geology, art, architecture, and even heraldry and some of Mother Connolly's graduates could read the Gospel of St. John in the original Greek.

Her chief contention was that Catholic girls must be taught to take their place in society and to be a part of the world they lived in. At first her ideas and innovations hindered the growth of the School but later they became so highly regarded that they became a part of the educational system of other schools.

She believed in trusting children and in giving them a certain amount of freedom, and she saw the value of attractive clothes. At one time the school uniform was a silver gray trimmed with velvet"); Juliana Wadham, *The Case of Cornelia Connelly* (1957) ("[Cornelia's] own former attitude to the Faith would have done justice to Maria Edgeworth: 'I am proud to say that, against my prejudices and in spite of the horrors which I have always nurtured for the Catholic faith, I am ready at once to submit to whatever my loved husband believes to he the path of duty.' But the path of duty is never easy and, in spite of her convictions, she confessed to Ady [her daughter Adeline]: 'How Our Savior should have allowed His Church to remain in the hands of the Devil 1,500 years and be spread in the miraculous manner it was, while under diabolical influence and that too from the time of his Ascension until the days of Martin Luther, a degraded priest, who allowed bigamy and was notoriously unmoral, I don't pretend to explain. You must remember, dearest Ady, I once thought *all* Catholic priests instruments of the Devil, if not the Devil himself, and believed all Hume's falsehoods about monastic ignorance and superstition, etc., and entertained a thousand other prejudices. We have seen Miss Read's *Six Months in a Convent*, *De Ricci's Secrets*, etc., etc., etc., and sundry periodicals, so you see we cannot be much in the dark respecting all that can be urged against Catholicism'...

[F]or the first time, Cornelia took the initiative from Pierce. She would not wait for Rome to be received into the Church. Her determination is curious, considering how superficial her introduction to Catholicism has appeared...If Catholicism is the right faith then there is no point in remaining outside it; no point in remaining cut off from the sacraments and the means of grace"); Mother Marie Thérèse, *Cornelia Connelly: A Study in Fidelity* (1963); Caritas McCarthy, *The Spirituality of Cornelia Connelly; In God, for God, with God* (1986); Radegunde Flaxman, *A Woman Styled Bold: Life of Cornelia Connelly, 1809-1879* (1991); Elizabeth Mary Strub, *Yes, Lord, Always Yes: A Life of Cornelia Connelly, 1809-1879* (2003); Catie McElwee, *A Generous Love: The Life of Cornelia Connelly* (2009); *DNB*; *ANB.*

Cooper, Gary (born Frank James Cooper) – film actor; b. 7 May 1901, Helena, Montana; c. 1958; d. 13 May 1961, Los Angeles, California; son of Charles Henry Cooper (1865-1956), an English farmer from Bedfordshire who later became a lawyer and judge; family moved to Los Angeles in 1924; found work as an actor in 1925, mainly as an extra in cowboy films; hired on a long-term contract by Paramount Pictures; changed his name to Gary in 1925; appeared in over one hundred films, including *The Virginian* (1929) (made him a major star); *Mr. Deeds Goes to Town* (1936); *Meet John Doe* (1942); *Sergeant York* (1942) (first academy award for best actor); *For Whom the Bell Tolls* (1943); *High Noon* (1953) (second academy award for best actor); *Vera Cruz* (1954); *Man of the West* (1958); turned down the role of Rhett Butler in *Gone With the Wind*; known for his quiet style of acting; received five nominations for best actor; joined the anti-Communist Motion Picture Alliance for the Preservation of American Ideals in 1944; in 1947 testified as a "friendly witness" before the House Committee on Un-American Activities; great friend of Ernest Hemingway; married Veronica "Rocky" Balfe (1913-2000), a New York Catholic socialite, in 1933 (they had one child, Maria Cooper Janis); slowly drawn towards the Catholic faith in 1950s; after his marriage but before his conversion he had relationships with several co-stars, including Marlene Dietrich, Grace Kelly and Patricia Neal (see below); forced Patricia Neal to have an abortion in 1950; committed supporter of the Republican Party; originally buried in Holy Cross Cemetery, Culver City, California, but in 1974 the body was relocated to Sacred Heart Cemetery, Southampton, New York; see George Carpozi, Jr., *The Gary Cooper Story* (1970); Rene Jordan, *Gary Cooper* (1974); Hector Arce, *Gary Cooper: An Intimate Biography* (1979); Stuart M. Kaminsky, *Coop: The Life and Legend of Gary Cooper* (1980); Larry Swindell, *The Last Hero: A Biography of Gary Cooper* (1980); Jeffrey Meyer, Gary Cooper: American Hero (1998); Maria Cooper Janis, *Gary Cooper Off Camera: A Daughter Remembers* (1999); *ANB.*

Copway, George (known in Ojibwa as Kahgegagahbowh, meaning "He Who Stands Forever") - North American Indian writer and lecturer; b. 1818, near present-day Trenton, Ontario, Canada; c. 17 January 1869; d. several days later in January 1869; son of John Copway, an Ojibwa chief and medicine man, and his Ojibwa wife; both parents converted to Methodism in 1827; attended a mission school run by Methodists, then at sixteen went as a Methodist mission worker to the Lake Superior Ojibwa, later becoming a minister; his work included translating the *Gospel of Luke* and the *Acts of the Apostles* into Ojibwa; married in 1840 Elizabeth Howell, the daughter of an English settler (of their several children only two lived to adulthood); eventually returned to Canada to continue with his missionary work; his informal handling of money led to him being accused of embezzlement and imprisoned; expelled by the Upper Canadian Methodists; on his release he went to the United States and wrote an autobiography and gave a series of public lectures on North American Indians; his book was very successful; later publishing initiatives failed, he sank further into poverty, and abandoned his wife and infant daughter; he ended up at the Catholic Indian mission at the Lake of Two Mountains, west of Montreal and to the resident Sulpician missionary, Abbé Jean André Cuoq, he described himself as a "pagan" and announced that he had come to study and embrace Catholicism; he was baptized by the Sulpicians as "Joseph-Antoine"; several days later he suddenly died on the night before his first communion as a member of the Catholic Church; see *The Life, History, and Travels, of Kah-ge-ga-gah-bowh (George Copway). A Young Indian Chief of the Ojebwa Nation, a Convert to the Christian Faith, and a Missionary to his People for Twelve Years* (1847); *The Life, Letters and Speeches of Kah-ge-ga-gah-bowh, or George Copway, Chief of the Ojibway Nation* (1850); *Organization of a New Indian Territory, East of the Missouri River* (1850); *Traditional History and Characteristic Sketches of the Ojibway Nation* (1850); *Running Sketches of Men and Places* (1851); *Indian Life and Indian History* (1858); A. LaVonne Brown Ruoff, "George Copway: Nineteenth-Century American Indian Autobiographer," *Auto-Biography* (1987); Donald B. Smith, "The Life of George Copway or Kah-ge-ga-gah-bowh (1818-1869) - and a Review of His Writings," *Journal of Canadian Studies* (1988*); DCB*; *ANB.*

Cori, Gerty Theresa (*née* Radnitz) – biochemist; b. 15 August 1896, Prague; d. 26 October 1957, St. Louis, Missouri; born into a Jewish family; father a chemist; mother a friend of Franz Kafka; admitted to the medical school of the German

Charles-Ferdinand University in Prague in 1914; awarded Doctorate in Medicine in 1920; met her husband, Carl Ferdinand Cori (1896-1984), a fellow student; they emigrated to the United States in 1922 to do medical research; they became naturalized citizens of the United States in 1928; they collaborated in their work; as a woman she found it difficult to obtain positions; they worked in Buffalo, St. Louis, and Washington; she received the Nobel Prize in Physiology or Medicine in 1947 with her husband and Bernardo Houssay for the discovery of the mechanism by which glycogen - a derivative of glucose - is broken down in muscle tissue into lactic acid and then resynthesized in the body and stored as a source of energy (known as the Cori cycle); they also identified the important catalyzing compound, the Cori ester; she was the third woman – and the first American woman – to win a Nobel Prize in science; board member of the National Science Foundation; elected to the National Academy of Sciences; diagnozed as suffering from myelosclerosis, a fatal disease of the bone marrow, but worked on for ten years; one child of the marriage, Tom, who married the daughter of the conservative activist Phyllis Schlafly (b. 1924); see Olga S. Opfel, *The Lady Laureates: Women Who Have Won the Nobel Prize* (1978); Sharon Bertsch McGrayne, *Nobel Prize Women: in Science: Their Lives, Struggles and Momentous Discoveries* (2001); *ANB*.

Cort, John C. – writer, editor, and activist; b. 1913, Woodmere, Long Island, New York; c. June 1935; d. August 2006; youngest of five brothers in a wealthy family; his father was the son of a frontier missionary of the Reformed Church in Iowa; his mother's family were Quakers; family became Episcopalians, although his father was more of a deist who believed the ancient teachings of Christianity were outmoded by the advance of science and enlightenment; studied French History and Literature at Harvard University; influenced at Harvard by his tutor, Paul Doolin (later to become a Catholic) on Plato and Socrates ("What Plato did for me...was simply to take the old Christian words and the old Christian concepts, dust off the accumulations of a thousand dull sermons, the association of a thousand pious platitudes, and all the bigotry, hypocrisy, and general dry rot of two thousand years, and leave them shining with the intellectual glamour of ancient Greece"), Alfred North Whitehead, C. H. McIlwain ("He taught political theory. He was one of the few men at Harvard who knew and respected Thomas Aquinas. He was quick to point out that the chain of theories that produced our modern notions of democracy, popular sovereignty, civil rights, and representative government runs back through Cardinal Bellarmine, Suarez, and Saint Thomas, and to the New and Old Testaments"), Louis Mercier ("He was a Catholic, the real thing..., a man not only of intelligence and faith, but of works; a good man and a happy man. I looked at Professor Mercier and I thought to myself, if a man like that can be a Catholic, then there can't be very much the matter with Catholicism"), and Irving Babbitt ("Babbitt's favorite target was romanticism...[He] refused to admit that virtue was either a passion or a feeling – voluptuous, ravishing, burning, or otherwise...He insisted on the distinction between soul and body; between the law of the spirit and the law of the flesh; between the law for thing and the law for man"); graduated in 1935 and was received into the Catholic Church in the same year; in 1936 he was moved by a speech by Dorothy Day (see below) in Boston, and it changed his life; he moved to New York and worked for the *Catholic Worker* for a few years; helped to found the Association of Catholic Trade Unionists and for several years he edited their paper, *Labor Leader* (promoted the papal social encyclicals and wrote many articles and reviews); on the editorial staff of *Commonweal* magazine 1943-1959; assistant director of the Peace Corps; founding editor of *Religious Socialism* magazine; wrote for many other journals, including *Catholic Digest*, *National Catholic Reporter*, and *New Oxford Review*; opposed the Vietnam War; reputation as a conservative personally, but a radical politically and socially; father of ten children with his wife Helen Cort (*née* Haye); see "A Bizarre Conversion," in Dan O'Neill (ed), *The New Catholics: Contemporary Converts Tell Their Story* (1987), p.1 ("Somewhere about this point he [he is writing about himself] opens the Bible and reads all four Gospels. There are inconsistencies, but nothing that cannot be accepted as the understandable disagreement of honest witnesses or the understandable failure of honest memories. There are many consistencies and agreements, notably, that a poor Jew named Jesus lived in Palestine and that this man had extraordinary powers of speaking and healing.

These powers attracted a sizable following, especially among the poor. He claimed to have a special and unique relationship to God, and this claim, together with His denunciations of corruption in high places, brought down upon Him the wrath of the Jewish and Roman power structures. He was therefore crucified. And the central and most basic point of agreement among the witnesses: several days after His crucifixion He rose from the dead in a form that seems to have been alternately tangible and intangible.

The internal evidence has credibility. The evangelists write like conscientious reporters. The detail is realistic and much of it is unflattering to the founders of the Christian community, such as the denials of Peter and passages highlighting the mental and spiritual obtuseness of the Apostles. The zeal and missionary success of the early Christians, revealed in the Epistles and Acts of the Apostles, give further evidence of the strength of their conviction that Christ rose from the dead and remains alive.

While he is thinking about all this, our Harvard undergraduate is going to Christ Church on the Cambridge Common and singing in the choir, for pay, for the nice middle and upper-middle-class Christians among whom he was born and raised, He begins to listen a little more attentively to the sermons of the rector and various visiting preachers of the liberal Episcopal persuasion He gets the impression that these preachers do not take very seriously the teachings of the creed that all of us recite together during the service. The folks in the pews, in effect, are encouraged to pick and choose those teachings that suit their fancy. The young man thinks that this does not make much sense, that a proper church ought to have some teaching authority that commands respect and is recognized as having the right and power to teach *with* authority, and is not afraid to use that authority. Perhaps he is even too conscious of that kind of need. And while he is thinking along these lines he is taking a course entitled the Intellectual History of the Middle Ages.

Although there was no course offered by the philosophy department in the thought of Thomas Aquinas, or any medieval philosopher, the history department was not quite so prejudiced. There was this course taught by Charles Taylor…, a tall, lean, hawk-nosed man who looked like a medieval knight himself.

Taylor introduced us first to Augustine, and Augustine introduced us to his own concerns about predestination and free will, based largely on his reading of Saint Paul's Epistle to the Romans. We discussed these subjects in class and I proceeded to contract an intellectual headache that lasted for about a week. It revolved around the question: if God knew from the beginning of time (recognizing that with God there is no time) that Johnny Jones was going to shoot his dear old mother on the night of 21 November 1933, how could it be maintained that Johnny was free not to shoot his dear old mother? Or: if certain people are predestined by God to be saved and others to be damned, must we not, as Calvin did, deny free will? And doesn't that make God basically unfair and irrational?

Of course, if we read Saint Paul carefully it becomes evident that my headache sprang from a misunderstanding of what concerned him, for he was not so much dealing with the salvation or damnation of individual Jews, but rather with their predestination as a people fated, in the main, to reject Christ as the Messiah.

At any rate I was worried about some legitimate questions. In this mood I went to Widener Library and consulted the *Catholic Encyclopedia.* Just why or how I came to do this I do not recall. I read two articles by J. Pohle, Jesuit professor of dogmatic theology at Breslau University. One was on grace and the other on predestination. I have a very vivid memory of the experience, including just where I was sitting, facing west at one of the tables in the big reading room near the windows that looked out toward Memorial Church. When I came to Pohle's statement that the Church teaches that all are given sufficient grace to be saved and that 'grace is condemned to unfruitfulness only in the event of the free resistance of the will,' I stopped reading the article on grace. That was enough for me. My sense of fairness was satisfied.

In the article on predestination Pohle distinguished between the Calvinist view and the Catholic view by way of two Latin phrases that I found peculiarly clarifying as well as reassuring. He wrote that Calvin believed in *praedestinatio ante praevisa merita* (predestination before foreseen merits), a teaching that effectively negates free will, whereas the Catholic Church holds to *praedestinatio post praevisa merita* (after foreseen merits). Pohle quoted Saint Ambrose: 'He did not predestine before he foreknew, but for those whose merits he foresaw he predestined the reward.'

As I read I conceived a pleasantly anthropomorphic image of God as a man sitting in a balloon suspended over the River of Life. Because, however, He is not a man, or woman, but God and because with God there is no time, no past or future, but everything is present, He sees and knows simultaneously everything that has happened, is happening, or will happen on the river. He knows the speed and direction of all currents, the location of all rocks. He knows the size and capabilities of all boats that proceed down the rapids of the river and, most important, He knows precisely how the free will, intellect, nerves, and muscles of the men and women who guide those boats will react to the rocks and whirlpools of the river as well to the assistance (grace) that He Himself gives them. Then, knowing all that, He predestines how they will come out, whether they are wrecked along the way, get stuck on a sandbar, or arrive safely at the mouth of the river and float serenely into the Sea of Paradise.

My headache was gone. I walked out of Widener Library into the Yard, not with a sense of being born again but with a profound sense of gratitude to the Catholic Church for having produced a book like the *Catholic Encyclopedia* and a writer like J. Pohle and two Latin phrases that could preserve my faith in the fact of my own freedom on the one hand and the basic intelligence and decency of God on the other. Out of that gratitude I went to Saint Paul's Church and asked to see a priest…

I have been happy in the Roman Catholic, Christian faith – very happy. My only regret is that some of my fellow Catholics – lay and cleric – seem to be losing their faith in the magisterium of the Church and in those ancient truths of the gospel that the magisterium upholds. I keep telling them, 'I've been where you are heading and, believe me, you wouldn't like it'"); *Christian Socialism: An Informal History* (1988); *Dreadful Conversions: The Making of a Catholic Socialist* (2003); his papers are housed at the American Catholic History Research Center and University Archives at Catholic University.

Crawford, F. Marion (born Francis Marion Crawford) – novelist, journalist, historian and playwright; b. 2 August 1854, Bagna di Lucca, Italy; c. 1880 (his wife converted later; one of his sisters, Mary ("Mimoli") Crawford Fraser (also known as Mrs. Hugh Fraser, see below) was also received into the Church; his half-sister, Margaret Terry Chanler ("Daisy") (1862-1952), also converted: see her essays in Georgina Pell Curtis, *Some Roads to Rome in America* (1909), p.83, and in Georgina Pell Curtis, *Beyond the Road to Rome* (1914), p.85); d. 9 April 1909 (Good Friday), Villa Crawford, Sant' Agnello di Sorrento, Italy; son of the distinguished American sculptor, Thomas Crawford (1814-1857), a Protestant who settled in Rome; his mother Louisa Cutler Ward was a sister of Mrs. Julia Ward Howe (1819-1910), social activist, poet, and author of *The Battle Hymn of the Republic*; spent most of his youth in Rome; educated at Cambridge University, University of Heidelberg, and University of Rome; in 1879 went to India where he studied Sanskrit and edited *The Indian Herald*; studied Sanskrit at Harvard University 1881-1882; in 1882 he met Isabella Stewart Gardner (1840-1924), the philanthropist and art collector, who became a life-long friend; turned to writing after being advised against a professional singing career; became one of the best known and prolific novelists in England and America (his work far outsold such as Henry James); Italy was his great love and he returned there in 1883; in 1884 he married Elizabeth Berdan ("Bessie"), daughter of Hiram Berdan (1824-1893), the Civil War Union General (four children of the marriage); in 1885 he took up residence at the Villa Renzi, which became known as Villa Crawford, at Sant' Agnello di Sorrento on the Bay of Naples, which he had bought and remodeled for himself; in a writing career of twenty-seven years he was the author of some forty-four novels and one play; also history, biography and descriptive books on Italy; several of his novels were filmed; wrote several short stories in the horror genre; wrote numerous articles for major periodicals; the *Saracinesca Trilogy* (*Saracinesca*, *Sant Ilario*, *Don Orsino*) is often thought of as his best work; buried in the cemetery at Sant' Agnello di Sorrento; after his death his villa was donated by his daughters, Lady Eleanor Rocca-Crawford and Mother Clare Marion-Crawford, to the Salesian Sisters (Mother Clare, a nun, lived there); the sisters operate the villa today as a high school for girls; the F. Marion Crawford Society was founded in 1975; see (selective list) (fiction) *Mr. Isaacs* (1882); *Dr. Claudius* (1883); *A Roman Singer* (1884); *Zoroaster* (1885); *A Tale of a Lonely Parish* (1886); *Saracinesca* (1887); *Marzio's Crucifix* (1887); *Paul Patoff* (1887); *Greifenstein* (1889); *Sant' Ilario* (1889); *A Cigarette Maker's Romance* (1890); *The Witch of Prague* (1891); *Don Orsino* (1892); *Pietro Ghisleri* (1893); *The Ralstons* (1895); *Corleone* (1897); *Via Crucis* (1899); *In the Palace of the King* (1900); *Marietta, A Maid of Venice* (1901); *The Heart of Rome* (1903); *Whosoever Shall Offend* (1904); *Soprano, A Portrait* (1905); *Fair Margaret* (1905); *The Primadonna* (1907); *The Diva's Ruby* (1908); (play) *Francesca da Rimini* (1902); (non-fiction) *The Novel: What It Is* (1893); *Constantinople* (1895); *Ave, Roma Immortalis: Studies From the Chronicles of Rome* (2 Vols.) (1898); *Rulers of the South* (1900) (renamed *Southern Italy and Sicily and The Rulers of the South* (1905)); *The Life of Pope Leo XIII* (1904); *Gleanings From Venetian History* (1905) (re-issued as *Venice; the Place and the People* (1909)); Walter Lecky, *Down at Caxton's* (1895), p.21 ("To those who know Italy and Mr. Crawford's wonderful drawing of it, there could be but one opinion, that the faith of the novelist was the same as that of his characters. No Protestant novelist, no matter how many years he had lived in Italy, could have drawn the portraits that play in the Saracenesca pages"); Vittoria Colonna, Duchess of Sermoneta, *Things Past* (1929); Maud Howe Elliott, *My Cousin, F. Marion Crawford* (1934) ("When we contrast the service in the cold, little Protestant church on the Via Nazionale with the splendid pageantry of the Roman Church, its traditions, its pomp and circumstances, its glamor and glow, his change of faith seems quite natural...

The circumstances of his conversion to Catholicism are unknown. The fact was inevitable, given his temperament and early environment. His Catholicism was of the broadest variety. He was no bigot, and while to him the road to Rome led on to ultimate beatitude, he was tolerant of those who strove to attain to perfection by another path...

Norman Douglas, writing of Crawford, speaks of him as 'a

rabid Catholic' and as 'more Catholic than the Pope.' *Per contra* George Brett, his intimate friend, says: 'He told me it was a great thing to have peace of mind. After considering all the philosophies in the field it was a great thing to give up your own opinion and take that of the Church. The Church that, for hundreds of years, has had the best minds in its keeping knew better than you, its judgment was much better than yours. He had thought about this for a long time, he was a great student of the philosophies of the world, and this study leads eventually to chaos, he said, and so he deliberately came to the conclusion that, in order to have peace of mind, one must abide by the Church"); Louise Hall Tharp, *Three Saints and a Sinner* (1956); John Pilkington Jr., *Francis Marion Crawford* (1964) ("The circumstances of his conversion are not known, but very probably it was a gradual process begun in Italy and completed in India. Although Crawford had been reared in the Episcopalian faith of his mother, he had lived much of his life among surroundings pervaded by a Catholic atmosphere; but, had he avowed any sentiments toward Catholicism while in Rome, his mother would certainly have strenuously opposed them. In India, however, he was at liberty to follow his own inclinations without parental interference; and, under the guidance of a priest in Allahabad, he was converted. Later Crawford described himself as 'a staunch adherent to the faith and a conscientiousobserverofprescribed duties.' Crawford's conversion had important consequences for his subsequent career. By giving, him a more sympathetic understanding of the religious customs of the Italian people, it enabled him to use religious material effectively in his novels"); John Charles Moran, *An F. Marion Crawford Companion* (1981); Gordon Poole (ed), *The Magnificent Crawford. Writer by Trade: Acts of the International Conference Held in Sant' Agnello on 7-8-9 May 1988* (1990); Fr. Richard Whinder, "Francis Marion Crawford: A Forgotten Catholic Novelist," *Catholic Life*, June 2004, p.26 ("Crawford saw the 'convenience' of the Catholic faith: it made it possible for a society, as well as an individual, to follow Jesus Christ. Crawford was a practical, active man: he was also a romantic and an idealist. It was these twin attractions which drew him to the Catholic Church"); Ralph McInerny, *Some Catholic Writers* (2007); Gordon Poole (ed), *A Hundred Years Later: New Light on Francis Marion Crawford* (2011); Jane Hanna Pease, *Romance Novels, Romantic Novelist. Francis Marion Crawford* (2011) ("He was never tempted to leave the only church whose 'Credo in unum Deum' united all believers past and present, regardless of their place in society"); F. Marion Crawford Memorial Society, Nashville,

Tennessee; *Catholic Encyclopedia*; *ANB* ("In 1893 Crawford published a defense of his work in *The Novel: What It Is*. In it he declared that the novel was an intellectual luxury, a commodity, whose purpose is not to instruct but to entertain. In opposition to William Dean Howell's *Criticism and Fiction* (1891), Crawford argued that the novel must show men and women as they could or should be, not as they are in real life. Realism in fiction produced vulgar, if not dirty, pictures of boring, ordinary life. Crawford wanted his novel to be, in his phrase, a 'pocket theatre' that one could read for amusement. Thus he became the spokesman for the literature of entertainment in the genteel tradition").

Crocker, Harry W. III – writer and book editor; brought up as an Episcopalian; moved to a position of skepticism and secularism; BA degree in English and American Literature from University of California at San Diego; Masters degree from University of Southern California's School of International Relations in London; influenced by a number of Catholic writers, e.g., Chesterton, Newman, Waugh, and Greene; book editor at Regnery Publishing, Washington DC; has also worked as a journalist and speechwriter for the governor of California; see (selective list) *Robert E. Lee on Leadership: Executive Lessons in Character, Courage, and Vision* (2000); *Triumph: The Power and Glory of the Catholic Church – A 2,000 Year History* (2001); *The Old Limey* (2001) (novel); *EWTN Audio Library, The Journey Home* (16 September 2002) ("Newman was very powerful reading, especially for someone from my background, because Newman wrote a book called the *Apologia Pro Vita Sua*, which is the nineteenth century version of St. Augustine's *Confessions*, and it's just as powerful. He talks about his whole life and his whole belief as an Anglican and how inevitably he was driven, against every desire of his own, to become a Catholic, because it was obviously true, and there was really no alternative. To be an authentic Christian was to be a Catholic. And, to take the quote from Newman – "To be deep in history is to cease to be a Protestant" – a little bit further, later in the same passage it says, 'And Protestants have always known it to be so, for why else would they base their religion on the Bible.'

So that was a telling point. I'd already learned earlier on that Protestantism lacked an anchor; and I know that for many Protestants the anchor is the Bible. But that couldn't be an anchor. You could go to a Presbyterian church and another Presbyterian church down the street, and they would interpret a passage differently. You looked in the phone book and you saw that there were dozens, if not hundreds, just in your own neighborhood, of Protestant denominations, all of whom had their own differences of opinion on this, that and the other. So, that couldn't be an anchor.

And, moreover, the more you get deep in the history, you know, the Bible, the New Testament at least, wasn't around for the early Christians. How did Paul make his conversions? How did the Apostles make their conversions? They weren't handing out the New Testament as we have it today.

The key thing for me, as I figured out, was apostolic succession. And the verbal tradition was the tradition of the Church"); "What's So Great About Catholicism?" *Crisis*, November 2002 ("What's so great about Catholicism? Here are ten things - in countdown order - to which one could easily add hundreds of others.

10. Hope: Classical paganism, as we know, always ended in despair - a noble despair sometimes, but despair nevertheless. Eastern religions don't offer much in the way of hope, as they are tied to doctrines of fate, cycles of history, and a nirvana of extinction. Reformation Protestantism is pretty despairing, too, with Calvin's belief that it would have been better for most people if they had never been born, predestined as they are for damnation. Secularism and materialism are no better, as wealthy secular societies tend to have the highest rates of suicide.

But in the Catholic Church, there is hope. Salvation is open to every man willing to take it. And though Jesus warned His apostles that following His way meant enduring inevitable persecution and hatred, He also gave them this promise: The gates of hell would not prevail against the Church. Even outsiders recognize this. Who ever heard of a deathbed conversion to Methodism? Hope comes from the Real Thing.

9. The Inquisition: The Inquisition? Yes, let's not be shy. The Inquisition is every Catholic-basher's favorite tool of abuse - though it is one that is very much not in the basher's favor. There were several Inquisitions. The first in order of importance in Catholic history was the Inquisition against the Albigensians - a heresy that encouraged suicide, euthanasia, abortion, sodomy, fornication, and other modern ideas that were distasteful to the medieval mind. The struggle against the Albigensians erupted into war - and a war that could not be carefully trammeled within crusading boundaries. So Pope Gregory IX entrusted the final excision of the Albigensian heresy to the scalpel of the Inquisition rather than the sword of the Crusader.

Did this Inquisition of the 113th century strike fear into the people of western Europe? No. Its scope was limited; its trials and punishments more lenient to the accused than were those of its secular counterparts. Inquisitional punishment was often no more than the sort of penance - charity, pilgrimage, mortification - that one might be given by a priest in a confessional. If one were fortunate enough to live in England, northern France, Belgium, the Netherlands, Scandinavia, or, with the exception of Aragon, even, at this time, Spain, the risk that one might be called before an inquisitional trial was virtually zero. The focus of the Inquisition was in the Albigensian districts of southern France; in Germany, where some of the worst abuses occurred; and in those parts of chaotic Italy rife with anticlerical heresy. In all cases, inquisitional courts sat only where Church and state agreed that peace and security were threatened. Nevertheless, the courts were abused. The Church could not modify an ironclad rule of life as true in the 13th century as it is today: Every recourse to law and the courts is a calamity. But the Church then, and people today, seemed to assume it is better than vigilantes and war. There's no accounting for some tastes.

More famous, certainly, is the Spanish Inquisition. The Spanish Inquisition was a state-run affair, where the Church's role was to act as a brake of responsibility, fairness, and justice on the royal court's ferreting out of quislings (who were defined, after centuries of war against the Muslims, as those who were not sincere and orthodox Catholics). Recent scholarship, which has actually examined the meticulous records kept by the Spanish Inquisition, has proven - to take the title of a BBC documentary on the subject - *The Myth of the Spanish Inquisition.* We now know, beyond all doubt, that the Monty Python sketch of inquisitors holding an old lady in 'the comfy chair' while they tickle her with feather dusters is closer to the truth than images of people impaled within iron maidens. (One of the standard works of scholarship is Henry Kamen's *The Spanish Inquisition: A Historical Revision*, Yale University Press). In the course of an average year, the number of executions ordered by the Spanish Inquisition - which covered not only Spain but its vast overseas empire - was less than the number of people put to death annually by the state of Texas. And this at a time when heresy was universally considered a capital crime in Europe. The myth of the Spanish Inquisition comes from forged documents, propagandizing Protestant polemicists, and anti-Spanish Catholics, who were numerous. The fact is, far from being the bloodthirsty tribunals of myth, the courts of the Spanish Inquisition were probably the fairest, most lenient, and most progressive in Europe.

8. The Crusades: All right, I recognize that this is another problem area for some milquetoast Catholics, but let's be blunt: Do we believe in reclaiming the world for Christ and His Church, or don't we? Medieval knights took that responsibility seriously, wore the cross on their capes and tunics,

and prayed and understood an incarnational faith that acted in the world. It was these knights' defensive war - and the defensive war of the Church and its allies up through the 18th century, for a millennium of Western history - that repelled Islamic aggression and kept western Europe free. For that we should be ashamed? No: It is one of the glories that was Christendom that in the Middle Ages the pope could wave his field marshal's baton and knights from as far away as Norway - not to mention England, France, and Germany - would come to serve. Men were Catholics first in those days.

Today, because of Islamic terror groups, the West is again strapping on its armor. We shouldn't be ashamed of our predecessors who were compelled to do the same.

7. The Swiss Guards and the French Foreign Legion: Though only one of these institutions is under the direct supervision of the Vatican, both qualify as Catholic institutions that should warm the very cockles of our hearts...

6. Art: Certainly the famous literary Catholics of the English-speaking world - John Henry Cardinal Newman, Hilaire Belloc, G. K. Chesterton, Graham Greene, Evelyn Waugh, Siegfried Sassoon (who converted later in life), and Thomas Merton - have all played an enormous part in my own conversion and continuing appreciation of the faith. Even Catholics of an unorthodox stripe (like Greene) have had a powerfully orthodox influence on me.

Writing, of course, is far from the only artistic testimony to the faith. Catholicism has always surrounded itself with beauty, regarding it as the splendor of truth. In the words of the German priest, professor, and theologian Karl Adam, 'Art is native to Catholicism, since reverence for the body and for nature is native to it.' The Puritan influence is foreign to Catholicism - just as the idea that smashing altars, defacing Madonnas, and breaking stained glass as a religious act is foreign, and indeed heretical, to Catholics. The Catholic Church leaves such Talibanism to the Protestants and iconoclastic heresies. The Catholic Church, instead, offers a celebration of beauty; and beauty, in our world of pierced faces, body tattoos, gangsta rap, and concrete tower blocks, is something we could use much more of.

5. Freedom: Yes, the good old reactionary, repressive Catholic Church has been the most ardent defender of freedom in the history of the world - though it almost never gets credit for it. We live in an age of determinist ideologies - with the fate of nations and individuals supposedly determined by race, economics, history, psychology, genetics, or even - insofar as Protestants have any common doctrinal beliefs - predestination. The Catholic Church stands alone in radical defense of man's free will.

When the media, Protestants, and

dissenters tell practicing Catholics that the impulse to sexual activity is overwhelmingly powerful and can't be controlled or renounced, Catholics alone say, 'No, man is free. All Christians are called to chastity, and what they are called to do, they can do, and some can freely take on celibacy as a sacrifice to better serve God and His Church'...

Think of the Enlightenment, the French Revolution, the *Kulturkampf* of Bismarck, and later intellectual and political currents, including fascism, communism, and the liberalism of our own time, all of which saw - or see - the state as the essential thing, centralization of state authority as the central task, and state direction as the essential instrument of reform. And what was the roadblock to these 'reformers'? The Catholic Church. It was the Church that asserted the independence of 'subsidiary institutions.' It was the Church that defended the rights of the family against the state. It was the Church that protested, in the words of Pope Pius XI, against the 'pagan worship of the state.'

4. The Saints: The Catholic is never alone. God is always near. The Catholic remembers Mary. He remembers her saying yes to the Incarnation. He remembers those who have gone before him: the vast parade of saints whose personalities and attributes are so various, so free, and yet so devoted to the singular path that leads to holiness and union with God...

And what saints there are. 'St. Michael the Archangel, defend us in battle'; the beloved St. Francis, 'Lord, make me a channel of Your peace'; the 'Dumb Ox' of logic and reason, St. Thomas Aquinas; St. Ignatius Loyola, who showed what miracles of conversion the Pope's marines could achieve when they were all devoted and orthodox (let us hope that they will be again); and on and on in endless panorama. All this belongs to the priceless Catholic heritage. Catholicism does not circumscribe and narrow the truth and practice of religion as all heresies do but celebrates the fullness of humanity and God's creation.

The saints show us the way. Catholics do not presume that they are saved through faith alone - as do Protestants. Salvation, of course, comes through God's grace. But as part of our free acceptance of that grace, we are called to become holy: to work, to act, to participate in that constant drama where we struggle to live the life of a saint - to live, that is, the life of Christ. None of us is the elect, predestined to salvation, with the remainder (the majority) predestinedly condemned to hell, as Calvin taught. The Catholic believes he is called to acts of corporal and spiritual mercy and that these help him, by God's grace, to achieve expiation of sin. Our models and aides in our never-ending effort to achieve sanctity are Jesus, the apostles, and all the saints.

3. Unity: When we affirm the

Nicene Creed, we affirm our belief in the 'one, holy, Catholic, and apostolic Church.' The Creed does not say 'many, reformed, anti-Catholic, Bible-based churches.' Nor does it say, 'several nation-based, autocephalous, and selectively conciliar churches.' The Church is called to be *one* - one body of Christ, one bride of Christ.

Over the course of 2,000 years, its unity has denied the law of entropy. That it has avoided the most common of temptations - to embrace nationalism or solipsism as the essence of belief - always and everywhere affirming the catholicity of the Church, is proof of its authentic teaching. It is indeed a glory of the Church that it encompasses all men and can use the talents of all nations...

Objective truth knows no borders. Surely when Paul preached 'one Lord, one faith, one baptism,' he did not envisage, and would not approve of, the 20,000 or more varieties of Protestant experience. The story of the early Church is the story of the Catholic attempt to maintain Christian unity in accordance with the truth against a sea of heresies - a sea that, as a working out of the Reformation, has now in the popular mind washed away the very idea of heresy. The Reformation marks the entrance of relativism into Christian life, and relativism denies unity. More important, it denies objective truth, and therefore relativism itself can't be true, however attractive it might be to those who, in the words of St. Irenaeus writing in the second century, are 'heretics and evil-thinkers, faction makers, swelled-headed, self-pleasing.' Our unity as the *one, holy, Catholic, and apostolic church* is one of the proofs of the verity of the Catholic faith...

2. The Sacraments: The sacraments and the visible Church are another proof and nurturer of the faith. I am among the least mystical of men, but I will gladly stump up and affirm the efficacy of the sacraments, sincerely and prayerfully entered into. With Pascal I would affirm that one actually learns the Catholic faith by doing - which is why deracinated, prissy, critical *philosophes* standing outside will never 'get it.' The faith of the Catholic is a great drama unfolding before God, and we are the players in it. There is the awesome reality of the Eucharist, God made flesh at every Mass, and our responsibility before Him and in receiving Him. There is the visible *alter Christus* of the priesthood. Even those sacraments that many Catholics find painful - such as penance - are powerful reminders of the reality of God and of the necessity of both our faith and our good works...

It is extremely odd to me that Protestants should take pride in reducing the transmission of God's grace from the seven sacraments held by the apostolic Catholic Church and Orthodox churches to two. When Protestants say that the celibate priesthood and religious life show a lack of respect for marriage, it's worth reminding them that to Catholics marriage is a sacrament, an institution of divine grace - something rather more elevated than it is for Protestants. And for Catholics, holy orders is a sacrament, making our priesthood rather more important than a Protestant ministry. For Catholics, religion is not all in the mind. It is tangible, present, and living. In short, it is real.

1. Truth: Nothing else would matter about Catholicism if it weren't true. But it is our firm belief as Catholics that it is true. And, indeed, I believe that the historical case for the Catholic Church is virtually irrefutable, as irrefutable as it was to Cardinal Newman. And there is something else. We know that the Church affirms that its members and servants are all subject to original sin. But while men might falter, the teaching of the Church does not. That has been our rock, tested through the tempests of centuries and undiminished through time.

Innumerable secular and other forces are against us. Even within our own midst we have been painfully reminded of the work that needs to be done to cleanse and purify our Church. Evil stalks the world. But then, it always has. And the Church has survived, and in the heat of persecution, it has grown in numbers and strength. Let us remember that fact. And let us always keep in mind the immortal words of Auberon Waugh: 'There are countless horrible things happening all over the country, and horrible people prospering, but we must never allow them to disturb our equanimity or deflect us from our sacred duty to sabotage and annoy them whenever possible.' Amen to that. Keep the faith and remember that our ultimate destination is heaven."); "Monasteries and Madrassas: Five Myths About Christianity, Islam, and the Middle Ages," *Crisis*, July-August 2006 ("Myth One: Medieval Christendom was barbarous, while Islam was refined. Here's a simple test: Have you ever heard and enjoyed Gregorian chant? If you're lucky, you've done more than that; you've actually heard the work of medieval composers performed on period instruments. Both the music and the instruments are recognizably our own. It bridges naturally to what most people generically call 'classical music.' (Our system of musical notation dates from the Middle Ages, coming from the monasteries, and most especially from the eleventh-century Benedictine monk Guido D'Arezzo.) Mohammed, on the other hand, like his Talibanic followers, prohibited music. Thanks to Danish cartoonists, we're all pretty familiar with Islamic attitudes about drawing or painting a likeness of Allah or his Prophet. As for science, mathematics, and technology, the Muslims were quite good at preserving and adopting the Classical heritage of the Christians (and the achievements of the Zoroastrian Persians and Hindus) whom they conquered. They were rather less good at going beyond it, which is one very large reason why the West made progress and Islam did not. The other big reason is that while Western medieval churchmen taught natural law and that God had created a rational and orderly universe, Islamic theologians countered that nothing - certainly not reason - could limit the power of Allah; he was beyond all such constraints; and Muslim leaders were contemptuous of the West.

Myth Two: Medieval women were oppressed. While we're on the subject of the fairer sex, let's dispense with the feminist idea that the Catholic Middle Ages were an era of oppression against women. That's rather hard to square, on the face of it, with medieval devotion to the Virgin Mary; the medieval invention of courtly, romantic love; the practice of chivalry; and the existence of queens and princesses. In every case, we have men making pledges of loyalty, fidelity, honor, and protection to women - women, it might be noted, with power and favor, whether it be royal, romantic, or divine.

The New Testament has a rather higher estimation of women than does the Koran. Jesus consistently treats women with respect. Christians, from the beginning, did as well. The idea of woman as a 'sex object' is profoundly un-Christian in a way that it is not unpagan or un-Islamic. Christianity has no temple prostitutes or harems, no slave girls or houris. The New Testament never recommends scourging women, nor does it compare women to a field to be plowed (as the Koran does). In Islamic law, divorce is a matter of three words ('I divorce you'); women are property, and women have essentially two purposes (you can guess what these are).

Myth Three: Medieval culture was crude and ignorant. Chaucer brings us face to face with medieval culture, and far from being crude and ignorant, we regard it as being a still-bright feature of our literary heritage. If medieval castles and cathedrals, art, crafts, and music aren't enough; if *Beowulf*, the *Song of Roland*, the *Poem of the Cid*, and the *Morte D'Arthur* don't speak to you; if Boethius, Boccaccio, Dante, Petrarch, and Machiavelli are as nothing; if you have no respect for St. Anselm, St. Francis, and St. Thomas Aquinas, to select a mere handful of the literary riches of the period, there's really not much more to say.

Myth Four: Medieval politics were despotic. Similarly, medieval politics were neither crude and ignorant, nor totalitarian and despotic. Far from it; the Middle Ages - from the start - practiced separation (and conflict) between church and state. It was the Reformation, the desire of the state to absorb the Church, that combined church and state with the creation of state churches. Medieval politics supported a wide dispersion of power, which is what feudalism was, and why England's nobles - led by the Catholic Archbishop of Canterbury, Stephen Langton - were able to hold King John accountable with the Magna Carta. Medieval man believed in the great hierarchy of society, where every man and woman had rights and responsibilities and was individually responsible before God. Medieval man was never threatened by totalitarianism. A totalitarian state was not even possible until the Reformation abolished the Church as a check on state power.

Myth Five: The Middle Ages were uniquely violent. The Middle Ages were certainly violent enough, but they had no Hitler, Stalin, or Mao. The Middle Ages did have its inquisitors, but the various myths surrounding the inquisitions are nowadays pretty well debunked, and anyone who wants to can know from the relevant historical scholarship that the inquisitional courts of the Middle Ages did not strike fear into the people of Western Europe. Their scope was limited, their trials and punishments more lenient than those of their secular counterparts. Inquisitional punishment was often no more than penance, and throughout much of Europe, the inquisition never appeared at all. It was not a major feature of the Middle Ages. From its 13th century imposition against the Albigensians through the Spanish Inquisition - the most 'notorious' inquisition, which operated under a royal rather than a papal charter - the history of inquisitional courts runs over the course of roughly 600 years, expiring in early 19th-century Spain. In the 350 years of the Spanish Inquisition, for which meticulously kept records have been preserved, the grand total of those sentenced to death is perhaps 4,000.

When it comes to body counts, the thousand years of the Middle Ages can't come close to the hecatombs of the enlightened 20th century. If the wars of the Age of Faith are to be regarded as a scandal that discredits Christianity, what are we to surmise from the state-authorized genocides, mass murders, and class eliminations of the pagan national socialists and the atheistic communists, who managed in the course of 70 years, less than one man's lifetime, to kill incomparably more people - by a factor of untold tens upon tens upon tens of millions - than were killed in the entirety of the Middle Ages?"); "Lepanto, 1571: The Battle That Saved Europe," *Crisis*, December 2006; *The Politically Incorrect Guide to the Civil War* (2008); *The Politically Incorrect Guide to the British Empire* (2011).

Currie, David B. - theologian; b. 1954; c. 1993 (his wife and his six children at that time were received at the same time); raised in a devout Christian family; father a fundamentalist minister; both parents taught at Moody Bible Institute; received a degree from

Trinity International University and studied in the Masters of Divinity program; became a Protestant minister; eventually began to see the many divisions in Protestantism and the real truth of what the Catholic Church taught ("It has been said that few people disagree with what the Church actually teaches, while there are multitudes who disagree with what they mistakenly think she teaches. I fit into the second category, finding offensive many teachings that I thought were Catholic"); the key issues behind his conversion were the question of authority and *sola scriptura*; after his conversion to the Catholic faith he became a research associate of the St. Paul Center for Biblical Theology in Steubenville, Ohio; married to Colleen Currie (eight children of the marriage); see *Born Fundamentalist, Born Again Catholic* (1996); *EWTN Audio Library, The Journey Home* (5 December 1997) ("It was like a bolt of lightning one day. I realized there wasn't enough information in the Old Testament to be a good Jew in the Old Testament. I realized there had to be a tradition that was passed down from this priest to the next generation of priests that was never written down in Scripture. That there had to be this oral tradition. Well, I knew where that was leading and I didn't like it...

I started to realize that *sola scriptura* is never taught in the New Testament. And it's a logical problem, because it's like the person who says, 'All generalizations are false.' Well, that in itself is a generalization, and I realized that if I was saying I could only trust what was in the Bible, but that statement wasn't in the Bible, then I was in trouble. And that was what made me realize I could not be a Protestant anymore...

I started to study the Eucharist and *sola scriptura* is the doctrine that drove me out of the Protestant church. The Eucharist is what made me fall in love with the Catholic Church, and when I saw how clearly it was taught in Scripture, I look back and I'm still amazed that I never saw the Eucharist...

The irony...is that so many [Protestant] churches are trying to be like the early Church. They want to re-create the New Testament Church, and the irony is that the New Testament Church didn't have this Bible. All they had was the Apostles' teaching. They had the tradition and not the written word, and yet when people go back and try to re-create that Church, they do it on the basis of what they see in a book those people did not have"); *Rapture: The End-Times Error That Leaves the Bible Behind* (2003); "Are the Gospels Anti-Semitic," *This Rock*, February 2004; *EWTN Audio Library, The Journey Home* (1 August 2011) ("What was pulling me away from where I was was the whole issue of authority. Because I was raised *sola scriptura*. The only authority I needed was what was written in the

Bible and yet…as I started studying I realized that that doctrine, that belief, was never taught in Scripture. So that was what was pulling me away from where I had been, because how can you accept as an authority something that doesn't claim to be an authority?"); "Born Fundamentalist, Born Again Catholic," *chnetwork.org*, 26 September 2011 ("[M]y Church history class was taught by a devout Presbyterian. I came away from the course with the distinct impression that the Protestant Reformation was very complex. There were important political forces at play that overshadowed any theological disagreements.

This fracturing of Christianity had continued right down into our own day. I had seen congregations split over 'theological issues.' But when all the facts came to light, a different story usually emerged. There were political disagreements in these congregations that were at least as important as the theological. There would be two strong-willed men, or two groups of men, that simply chose to split a congregation rather than submit to any authority. Theology was many times the public justification, but certainly not the entire reason.

I also discovered that when Protestants study early Church history, they rarely read the primary sources at length. We read a great many comments about what the early Church Fathers believed. But any actual writings by the Fathers were read in snippets.

I later found what I thought might be a large part of the reason why. When I read the Fathers on my own, I came to the distinct impression that they were thoroughly sacramental and thoroughly obedient to a hierarchy already existent within the Church. In other words, they were not Protestants, evangelicals, or fundamentalists. The early Fathers had been thoroughly Catholic.

I found the theological terrain within evangelicalism in crisis. During college, I had majored in philosophy. I had come to the point where I no longer considered myself a fundamentalist. The rigidity of its theology and the lack of charity were exhibited most clearly in its doctrine of 'separation.' But overall, I had just come to disagree with too much that fundamentalists held important.

In seminary, however, I found that evangelicalism was 'all over the map.' There were disagreements about everything even within the seminary itself. Some of the matters of disagreement were perhaps understandable: predestination, premillennialism, the ordinances of the church. But other issues seemed to be basic enough that there should have been some semblance of consistency. There was not.

The most disturbing disagreements centered on the many Bible passages that had no plausible 'Protestant' explanation. I had tucked some of them in the back of my mind before seminary. I was sure I would discover the answers to these passages. But rather than finding them answered, I found myself with a longer and longer list as I progressed through my training.

I was surrounded by the brightest and best that evangelicalism had to offer. My professors came from many different Protestant traditions. But none of them had a satisfying interpretation of these passages - even though these verses were in the one Book that they all agreed contained all they needed for salvation.

We all reach certain critical decision points in our Christian pilgrimage. God gives us a choice: to follow or not to follow. These crisis points are never easy. They always involve sacrifice and suffering. And they are always an occasion of grace.

At the rather late age of forty, I knew that I had approached one of these crisis points. I had been studying Scripture all my life. By this time, I had spent the previous months studying Catholic teaching in relation to Scripture. I had desperately attempted to find a reason not to become Catholic.

I had spent months trying to justify to myself what I had always believed: the Protestant interpretation of John 6. Jesus had said, 'I am the living bread which came down from heaven; if any one eats of this bread, he will live forever; and the *bread which I will give for the life of the world is my flesh*' (v. 51, emphasis added).

After studying this text from a Catholic perspective, I knew in my head that the Church was right. John 6 clearly taught that the Body of Christ was the sustenance that I needed for eternity. Zechariah had predicted it. Jesus had instituted it. And only one Church in town taught this truth as Jesus stated it: the Catholic parish five blocks from my house").

Curtis, Alfred Allan Paul – bishop; b. 4 July 1831, Pocomoke, near Rehobeth, Somerset County, Maryland; c. 10 May 1872, Oxford (received by John Henry Newman); d. 11 July 1908, St. Agnes Hospital, Baltimore; one of six children; his parents were Episcopalians, though he was baptized by a Methodist minister; as a young boy he mastered Latin and Greek and learned entire Shakespeare plays by heart; his father died early and he worked as an assistant teacher to provide for the family; studied for the Episcopal ministry and was ordained in 1859; gradually became more Catholic in his beliefs and practices; resigned his ministry in 1871; went to England and to Oxford, where he visited several leading Anglicans to seek assurance; their responses did not satisfy him and he consulted Newman and was received by him into the Catholic Church; "If the Roman Catholic Church is not truth, then there is no God," he wrote to a friend; his family were unable to understand his conversion; in 1872 he returned to Baltimore and entered St. Mary's

Seminary; ordained a Catholic priest by Archbishop James Roosevelt Bayley on 19 December 1874; served as Archbishop Bayley's private secretary; fine preacher and spiritual director; consecrated as second Bishop of Wilmington, Delaware in 1886 and served until 1896; greatly built up the diocese, in particular bringing in the Josephite Fathers to serve African American Catholics, and erected a cloistered convent for the sisters of the Visitation; resigned due to poor health; Auxiliary Bishop of Baltimore 1897-1908; close friend of John Banister Tabb (see below); buried at Visitation Monastery in Wilmington; see Anon, *The Life and Characteristics of Right Reverend Alfred A. Curtis, D.D.* (1913); Dom Antoine Marie, OSB, "Spiritual Newsletter," Abbey of Saint-Joseph de Clairval, Flavigny-sur-Ozerain, France, 1 November 2006 ("In 1871, an event took place that marked a decisive turn in Pastor Curtis' life. His superior, the Episcopalian bishop of Maryland, published a pastoral letter on the Holy Eucharist, in which he stated that if Christ is present in this sacrament, it is not in order to be adored, but only to become food for our souls. He was therefore forbidding his flock from worshiping this sacrament as the Person of Christ. Curtis, shocked, reacted strongly and resigned from his pastoral duties. His 8 November 1871 letter to his bishop contains this beautiful profession of faith: 'If it is not the truth that the very Human and Divine Christ is Himself first offered, for the living and the dead in the Holy Eucharist, and there put according to His whole Living Person into my very hands, to be then and there adored and endowed with all I am, and all I possess perpetually - there is no truth for me, at least no truth I greatly care to know...All my teaching grows out of, and depends upon the fact, that the Lord is actually one with and present in the Eucharist, under the form of Bread and Wine as He was of old present in the stable, one with and under the form of Babyhood'...A few days later, he further explained his thoughts: 'I cannot at all see how Christ can be received as Christ without adoration. To say that He is present but is not to be adored is to me only a certain way of saying that He is not veritably present at all'...

In 1908, Bishop Curtis developed stomach cancer. No longer able to eat, he was soon at the point of death. On 3 July, the first Friday of the month, he celebrated his last Mass with the fervor one can imagine of a man who had said several years earlier: 'We ought to be able to say after each Mass, This is the best Mass I have ever said. I have offered more to God, more for souls *this* day than I have ever done before; more love and more zeal for the conversion of souls. I have sacrificed to Him more of my own will.' On Saturday 11 July, after much suffering, the servant of God fell asleep in the Lord, 'like a child who finds the longed-for rest on the bosom of its mother,' according to the testimony of one witness").

Darling, Flora Adams – author; b. 25 July 1840, Lancaster, New Hampshire; d. 6 January 1910, New York City; educated at Lancaster Academy; in 1860 she married Colonel Edward Irving Darling, a southerner (he was twenty-two years older than her) (one son of the marriage, who became a composer (d. 1894)); her husband was wounded twice fighting for the Confederates in the Civil War and died shortly afterwards; arrested on her way back to the north under a flag of truce and later sued the government successfully for false imprisonment and the theft of her possessions; settled in Washington D.C.; contracted malaria, impairing both her hearing and sight; wrote several books; also wrote romantic short stories and poetry; one of the founders in 1890 of the Daughters of the American Revolution (DAR) (a society whose members were women who descended collaterally from participants of the revolutionary war); the members agreed that the DAR's official publication would be entitled *Adams Magazine*, edited by her nephew; she served as vice-president in charge of organization; after disagreements with the board she resigned in 1891 and founded a new organization, the Daughters of the Revolution, based on lineal descent; in 1892 she started the Daughters of the United States of the War of 1812 and was named president-general; converted to the Catholic Church from Episcopalianism; see *Mrs. Darling's Letters, Or Memories of the Civil War* (1883) (a pro-southern book); *Mrs. Darling's Letters, or Memoirs of the Civil War* (1884); *A Social Diplomat* (1889); *A Winning, Wayward Woman* (1889); *Was It a Just Verdict?* (1890) (all these three were autobiographical); *Senator Athens, C.S.A.* (1889); *A Winning, Wayward Woman: Chapters in the Heart-history of Amélie Warden* (1889); *The Bourbon Lily* (1890); *A Social Diplomat* (1891); *The Senator's Daughter* (1892); *From Two Points of View* (1892); *Helen Wadsworth* (1899); *A War Episode, Or History of the Darling Claim vs. the United States* (1900); *The Founding and Organization of the Daughters of the American Revolution and Daughters of the Revolution* (1901); *1607-1907: Memories of Virginia: A Souvenir of Founding Days* (1907); her papers are at the library of the College of William and Mary; *ANB*.

Daugherty, (Hugh) Duffy – football coach and player; b. 8 September 1915, Emeigh, Pennsylvania; c. 1964; d. 25 September 1987, Santa Barbara, California; his grandparents were immigrants from Scotland; brought up as a Presbyterian in Barnesboro, Pennsylvania; played college football as a guard for Syracuse University (captain of the team in his senior year in 1939); joined the U.S. Army before the United States entered World War II, and served throughout the war, being promoted from private to major and earning the Bronze Star; in 1946 became assistant coach to Clarence L. "Biggie" Munn (1908-1975) at Syracuse University; from 1947 to 1953 he was assistant coach to Munn at Michigan State University when they won the AP national championships in 1952; the lines coached by him in these years became known as "Duffy's Toughies"; in December 1953 he became Michigan State's head football coach; his team won the 1956 Rose Bowl; his 1965 and 1966 teams won national championships; he retired after the 1972 season; inducted into the College Football Hall of Fame in 1984; many other awards; see papers located in the Michigan State University Archives and Historical Collections; *ANB*.

Day, Dorothy – social activist and writer; Servant of God; b. 8 November 1897, Brooklyn, New York; c. 28 December 1927 (received at Our Lady Help of Christians, Staten Island); d. 29 November 1980, Maryhouse, New York City; father a newspaperman; brought up in San Francisco and Chicago ("In my family the name of God was never mentioned. Mother and Father never went to church, none of us children had been baptized, and to speak of the soul was to speak immodestly, uncovering what might better remain hidden"); baptized an Episcopalian at the age of twelve; wrote the following in one of her high school books: "Life would be utterly unbearable if we thought we were going nowhere, that we had nothing to look forward to. The greatest gift life can offer would be a faith in God and a hereafter. Why don't we have it? Perhaps, like all gifts, it must be struggled for. 'God, I believe' (or rather, 'I must believe or despair'), 'Help Thou my unbelief. Take away my heart of stone and give me a heart of flesh'"; in 1914 attended as a student the University of Illinois but left after two years; went to live in New York; in 1916 worked for the socialist journals, *The Liberator*, *The Masses* and *The Call*; passionate about the sufferings of the poor; also worked for women's suffrage; became part of a hard drinking Greenwich Village group; despite her Communism, started attending St. Joseph's Catholic church in Brooklyn; saw the Catholic Church as the church of the poor and also a body which helped her deal with the psychological problems caused by an abortion that she had during a love affair with a journalist, Lionel Moise; short lived marriage to Barkeley Toby; lived with the anarchist, Forster Batterham for three years; she had their daughter, Tamar Therese (1926-2008), baptized in 1927, which ended their relationship as Batterham was completely opposed to all forms of religion ("Dorothy Day has said that the birth of her daughter was so joyous it convinced her of the existence of God" (Barbara Grizzuti Harrison, see below)); in December 1932 she met Peter Maurin (1877-1949), a Christian Brother, and they established the Catholic Worker movement, its aim being to "live in accordance with the justice and charity of Jesus Christ"; followed the path of voluntary poverty as the supernatural way to save others' souls; influenced by the Catholic social doctrine of Pope Leo XIII's encyclical *Rerum Novarum* (1891) and Pope Pius XI's *Quadregesimo Anno* (1931); also influenced by Nicholas Berdyaev and Jacques Maritain and, in particular, by Emmanuel Mournier's belief that the capitalistic system had created a distortion of Christianity and his espousal of a Christian personalism and communitarianism; attacked Capitalism, but also completely repudiated Communism; advocate of distributism as much more "worthy of the human person" than capitalism; the retreats given by Fr. John Hugo and Fr. Onesimus Lacouture gave her the inner strength to live her life of poverty by teaching her Christian "detachment" and "how to die to ourselves, to live in Christ"; wrote for Catholic publications *Commonweal* and *America*; opposed the sexual liberation movement of the 1960s on the grounds of her own experience of a similar movement in the 1920s; given the *Pacem in Terris* award in 1971; awarded the *Laetare* Medal by the University of Notre Dame in 1972; on 18 March 2000 Pope John Paul II granted permission to open her cause for sainthood; buried in the Cemetery of the Resurrection, Staten Island; see (selective list) *The Eleventh Virgin* (1924) (autobiographical novel); *From Union Square to Rome* (1938) (earlier account of her conversion) ("There was a Catholic girl in the bed next to me in the ward. She was a young Italian, not more than twenty-two, and she had just had her third child. She had a very serious and very obscure heart condition which led every physician who examined her to declare that she should not have children, that death was certain if she did. But she had had three, and, day by day, doctors gathered around her bed to examine her and exclaim over the novelty of her heart disease and expostulate with her for bringing children into the world. Several times they stood there giving her information on birth control and she listened with her eyes cast down, not answering them. They assumed she was stupid and repeated in the simplest phrases their directions, speaking in phrases as they spoke to foreigners who cannot understand English. Then when they looked on her chart and saw she was a Catholic they expressed their impatience and went away.

'I just don't pay any attention,' she told me. 'God will take care of me. I know I have to be careful. We live on the first floor and I never walk up and down stairs, and my mother-in-law helps me all the time, so I'm all right'...

That bitterness felt by so many in the radical labor movement towards what they call 'organized religion' was mixed with the knowledge of the divinity of the Catholic Church. It was ever in my mind that human frailties and the sins and ignorances of those in high places throughout history only proved that the Church *must* be divine to have persisted through the centuries. I would not blame the Church for what I felt were the mistakes of churchmen. I could only always console myself with Christ's words that the greatest enemies would be those of the 'household.' I felt, too, that there were going to be many obstacles put in my path, and that this in a strange way was one of them...

I had become convinced that I would become a Catholic, and yet I felt I was betraying the class to which I belonged, you my brother, the workers, the poor of the world, the class which Christ most loved and spent His life with....

Finally with precipitation, with doubts on my part at my own unseemly haste, I made the resolution to bring an end to my hesitation and be baptized. It was in December, 1927, a most miserable day, and the trip was long from the city down to Tottenvile, Staten Island. All the way on the ferry through the foggy bay I felt grimly that I was being too precipitate. I had no sense of peace, no joy, no conviction even that what I was doing was right. It was just something that I had to do, a task to be gotten through. I doubted myself when I allowed myself to think. I hated myself for being weak and vacillating. A most consuming restlessness was upon me so that I walked around and around the deck of the ferry, almost groaning in anguish of spirit. Perhaps the devil was on the boat.

Sister Aloysia was there waiting for me, to be my godmother. I do not know whether I had any other godparent. Father Hyland, gently, with reserve, with matter-of-factness, heard my confession and baptized me. I was a Catholic at last though at that moment I never felt less the joy and peace and consolation which I know from my own later experiences religion can bring.

A year later my confirmation was indeed joyful and Pentecost never passes without a renewed sense of happiness and thanksgiving. It was only then that the feeling of uncertainty finally left me, never again to return, praise God!"); *House of Hospitality* (1939); *On Pilgrimage* (1948) (diaries); "From Communism to Christ," in John A. O'Brien (ed), *The Road to Damascus, Vol. II* (1950) ("I became convinced, little by little, of the necessity for religion and for God in my everyday life. I know now that the Catholic Church is the church of the poor, no matter what you say about the wealth of her priests and bishops. I met few Catholics before my conversion, but daily I saw people coming from Mass.

Never did I set foot in a Catholic church but that I saw people there at home with Him, First Fridays, novenas, and missions brought the masses thronging in and out of the Catholic churches. They were of all nationalities, of all classes, but most of all they were the poor. The very attacks made against the Church proved her Divinity to me. Nothing but a Divine institution could have survived the betrayal of Judas, the denial of Peter, the sins of many of those who professed her Faith and who were supposed to minister to her poor.

Christ is God or He is the world's greatest liar and impostor. How can Communists who claim to revere Him as a working class leader fail to see this? And if Christ established His Church on earth with Peter as its rock, that faulty one who denied him three times, who fled from him when he was in trouble, then I, too, wanted a share in that tender, compassionate love that is so great. Christ can forgive all sins and yearn over us no matter how far we fall…

It was ever in my mind that the human frailties, sins, and ignorance of those in high places throughout history only proved that the Church *must* be divine to have persisted through the centuries. I would not blame the Church for what I felt were the mistakes of churchmen. I could only always console myself with Christ's words that the greatest enemies would be those of the 'household'"); *Confession* (1952) ("When you go to confession on a Saturday night, you go into a warm, dimly lit vastness, with the smell of wax and incense in the air, the smell of burning candles, and if it is a hot summer night there is the sound of a great electric fan, and the noise of the streets coming in to emphasize the stillness. There is another sound too, besides that of the quiet movements of the people from pew to confession to altar rail; there is the sliding of the shutters of the little window between you and the priest in his 'box.'

Some confessionals are large and roomy – plenty of space for the knees, and breathing space in the thick darkness that seems to pulse with your own heart. In some poor churches, many of the ledges are narrow and worn, so your knees almost slip off the kneeling bench, and your feet protrude outside the curtain which shields you from the others who are waiting. Some churches have netting, or screens, between you and priest and you can see the outline of his face inclined toward you, quiet, impersonal, patient. Some have a piece of material covering the screen, so you can see nothing.. Some priests leave their lights on in their boxes so they can read their breviaries between confessions. The light does not bother you if that piece of material is there so you cannot see or be seen, but if it is only a grating so that he can see your face, it is embarrassing and you do not go back to that priest again.

Going to confession is hard – hard when you have sins to confess, hard when you haven't, and you rack your brain for even the beginnings of sins against charity, chastity, sins of detraction, sloth or gluttony. You do not want to make too much of your constant imperfections and venial sins, but you want to drag them out to the light of day as the first step in getting rid of them. The just man falls seven times daily.

'Bless me, Father, for I have sinned,' is the way you begin. 'I made my last confession a week ago, and since then…'

Properly, one should say the Confiteor, but the priest has no time for that, what with the long lines of penitents on a Saturday night, so you are supposed to say it outside the confessional as you kneel in a pew, or as you stand in line with others.

'I have sinned. These are my sins.' That is all you are supposed to tell; not the sins of others, or your own virtues, but only your ugly, gray, drab, monotonous sins"); *The Long Loneliness* (1952) (autobiography) ("I had heard many say that they wanted to worship God in their own way and did not need a church in which to praise Him, nor a body of people with whom to associate themselves. But I did not agree to this. My very experience as a radical, my whole make-up, led me to want to associate myself with others, with the masses, in loving and praising God. Without even looking into the claims of the Catholic Church, I was willing to admit that for me she was the one true Church. She had come down through the centuries since the time of Peter, and far from being dead, she claimed and held the allegiance of the masses of people in all the cities where I had lived. They poured in and out of her doors on Sundays and holy days, for novenas and missions. What if they were compelled to come in by the law of the Church, which said they were guilty of mortal sin if they did not go to Mass every Sunday? They obeyed that law. They were given a chance to show their preference. They accepted the Church. It may have been an unthinking, unquestioning faith, and yet the chance certainly came, again and again, 'Do I prefer the Church to my own will,' even if it was only the small matter of sitting at home on a Sunday morning with the papers? And the choice was the Church…

I studied my catechism; I learned to say the Rosary; I went to Mass in the chapel by the sea; I walked the beach and I prayed; I read the *Imitation of Christ*, and St. Augustine, and the New Testament. Dostoevski, Huysmans (what different men!) had given me desire and background. Huysmans had made me at home in the Church…

I loved the Church for Christ made visible. Not for itself, because it was so often a scandal to me. Romano Guardini said the Church is the Cross on which Christ was crucified; one could not separate Christ from His Cross, and one must live in a state of permanent dissatisfaction with the Church.

The scandal of businesslike priests, of collective wealth, the lack of a sense of responsibility for the poor, the worker, the Negro, the Mexican, the Filipino, and even the oppression of these, and the consenting to the oppression of them by our industrialist-capitalist order – these made me feel often that priests were more like Cain than Abel, 'Am I my brother's keeper?' they seemed to say in respect to the social order. There was plenty of charity but too little justice. And yet the priests were the dispensers of the sacraments, bringing Christ to men, all enabling us to put on Christ and to achieve more nearly in the world a sense of peace and unity. 'The worst enemies would be those of our own household,' Christ had warned us. We could not root out the tares without rooting out the wheat also. With all the knowledge I have gained these twenty-one years I have been a Catholic, I could write many a story of priests who were poor, chaste and obedient, who gave their lives daily for their fellows, but I am writing of how I felt at the time of my baptism"); *Loaves and Fishes* (1963) (account of the Catholic Worker movement); *Thérèse: A Life of Thérèse of Lisieux* (1979); Dwight M. MacDonald, "Dorothy Day," in Melville Harcourt (ed), *Thirteen for Christ* (1963), p.231; David J. O'Brien, "The Pilgrimage of Dorothy Day," *Commonweal,* 19 Dec. 1980; William D. Miller, *Dorothy Day: A Biography* (1982); Mel Piehl, *Breaking Bread: The Catholic Worker and the Origin of Catholic Radicalism in America* (1982); Nancy Roberts, *Dorothy Day and the Catholic Worker* (1984); Conrad Pepler, OP, *Dorothy Day and the Catholic Worker Movement* (1986); Robert Coles, *Dorothy Day: A Radical Devotion* (1987); William D. Miller (ed), *All is Grace: The Spirituality of Dorothy Day* (1987); James Terence Fisher, *The Catholic Counterculture in America, 1933-1962* (1989); Jim Forest, *Love is the Measure: Biography of Dorothy Day* (1994); Brigid O'Shea Merriman, *Searching for Christ: The Spirituality of Dorothy Day (1897-1980)* (2001); Patrick Jordan (ed), *Dorothy Day: Writings from Commonweal* (2002); David E. Scott (ed), *Praying in the Presence of Our Lord: With Dorothy Day* (2002); Elaine Murray Stone, *Dorothy Day: Champion of the Poor* (2003); Deborah Kent, *Dorothy Day: Friend to the Forgotten* (2004); Elaine Murray Stone, *Dorothy Day: Champion of the Poor* (2004); Robert Ellsberg, *Dorothy Day: Selected Writings* (2005); Mark and Louise Zwick, *The Catholic Worker Movement: Intellectual and Spiritual Origins* (2005) (brilliant analysis of Day);

Rosemary Fielding, "A New Day," *Culture Wars*, December 2006, p.38 (review of the Zwick book); Rosalie G. Riegle (ed), *Dorothy Day: Portraits by Those who Knew Her* (2006); Fr. Ashley Beck, *Dorothy Day: Devoted Daughter of the Church* (2008); Robert Ellsberg (ed), *The Duty of Delight: The Diaries of Dorothy Day* (2008); Robert Ellsberg (ed), *All the Way to Heaven: The Selected Letters of Dorothy Day* (2010); Dale Ahlquist, "Dorothy Day and Distributism," *Distributist Review*, 29 November 2010; Jim Forest, *All Is Grace: A Biography of Dorothy Day* (2011); Stephen Beale, "The Dorothy Day Few of Us Know," *Crisis*, 19 March 2013 ("She lamented the encroachment of the state and the perils of the welfare system. She once compared abortion to genocide and the U.S. government to Nazi Germany. She cheered on income tax resisters, dismissed the benefits of the minimum wage, and worried about the decline of freedom in an increasingly bureaucratic society.

But this was no Sarah Palin or Michelle Bachmann. It was Dorothy Day, the heroine of the Catholic left who walked a picket line with Cesar Chavez, was a civil rights advocate and anti-nuclear weapons activist, and made no secret of her contempt for capitalism, consumerism, and corporations.

But Day's status as a Leftist icon...has always chafed against certain inconvenient facts. Day's advocacy of distributism – a third way between socialism and capitalism advocated by such Catholic conservative stalwarts as G. K. Chesterton and Hilaire Belloc – has always made her an uncomfortable fit for the Left...But just how far out of step she was with the Left remains largely unknown.

[S]he expressed grave misgivings about the New Deal in her columns for the Catholic Worker newspaper...

Day became an ardent pro-lifer... She urged her readers to follow the entirety of the Church's teaching on abortion, birth control, and divorce in a column published in the early 1970s – when the modern feminist movement was in full swing"); Charles P. Connor, *Classic Catholic Converts* (2001), p.157; Lorene Hanley Duquin, *A Century of Catholic Converts* (2003), p.78; her papers are housed at Marquette University; *ANB* ("Day was attracted to Maurin because he embodied the ideal of voluntary poverty that she identified with Catholicism, which offered solace from the bourgeois radicalism of her unhappy early adulthood. In this respect she resembled other disaffected rebels from bohemia, but in the depth of her commitment to her new faith she was unrivaled. Out of her own beliefs and the inspiration of Maurin she shaped a new Catholic ethos, rejecting both capitalism and communism in the name of a community in which all women and men were spiritually linked as members of the Mystical Body of Christ...

While other prominent Catholic women clamored for revisions in the Church's teachings regarding sexuality and birth control, Day worked intensively on her spiritual journals and defended the Church against its critics on the left and right").

Delany, Selden Peabody – priest and author; b. 24 June c. 1874, Fond du Lac, Wisconsin; c. 24 June 1930 (received at the church of Our Lady of Lourdes, New York City, by Mgr. Joseph McMahon); d. 5 July 1935, Highland Mills, New York; born into a Presbyterian family; educated at Harvard University, where he became a High Church Episcopalian; ordained to the Episcopal ministry in 1899; dean of the Episcopal Cathedral in Milwaukee, Wisconsin 1907-1915; curate at the Church of St. Mary the Virgin, New York City 1915-1929; the chief obstacle to his conversion was the primacy of the papacy (he was wont to say that he believed in Catholicism without the Pope); influenced by Vernon Johnson's *One Lord, One Faith*; two hundred Episcopalians followed him into the Catholic Church; he regretted delaying so long; after his conversion he studied for the priesthood at the Beda College in Rome; ordained to the priesthood 17 March 1934; chaplain at Thevenet Hall, Highland Mills, New York; much illness in later life; buried in the nuns' cemetery at Highland Mills; see *Why Rome?* (1930) ("After a varied experience of thirty years in the ministry of the Protestant Episcopal Church, I am forced to the conclusion that Catholicism without the pope, so far as I am concerned, has been weighed in the balances and found wanting.

But why not Catholicism with the pope? Why this extraordinary antipathy to the most ancient and venerable of all institutions in the modern world? Any schoolboy could tell us that Catholicism without the pope is a contradiction in terms. It is like speaking of Catholicism without confession or Catholicism without the Mass. The only body of Christians in the world today that officially calls itself Catholic is that very considerable section of Christendom that is living under the papal obedience. The Churches of the East call themselves Orthodox; to them a Catholic is one that is subject to the jurisdiction of the pope. If any national group in the Anglican communion began to officially call itself Catholic, it would result in a schism in that group. In ordinary modern speech everywhere a Catholic is a Roman Catholic. Anglicans who claim to be Catholic are reduced to the necessity of calling themselves Anglo-Catholics, if they wish to be understood; even then, it requires much explanation…

The Roman Catholic position is simple by comparison, and it can be stated cogently even by the unlearned. One morning a rough-looking young fellow spoke to me at the church door and asked what was the difference between our church and the Roman Catholic. I answered that we did not accept the claims of the pope to supreme jurisdiction over the whole Church. He then wanted to know how we interpreted Christ's words to Peter: 'On this rock I will build my Church, and the gates of hell shall not prevail against it.' I was amazed at such an apt retort from a man who was apparently uneducated. I replied that many of the Fathers of the early Church interpreted the rock as referring to Peter's confession, 'Thou art the Christ, the Son of the living God.' He shook his head as he added, 'But Christ said, Thou art Peter, and Peter means rock.' As I left him I wondered how many Anglicans of his station could explain so concisely their ecclesiastical position.

Every human organization, whether political, industrial, commercial, financial, or social, has its administrative head. Why should not the Church Militant here on earth likewise have an administrative head? The Church of England has her primate; the Protestant Episcopal Church has found it necessary to elect a presiding bishop; why should not the Catholic Church have a pope? If our Lord had founded his Church without making provision for such an administrative head, he would have founded a Church that was ill-adapted to succeed in a world where so much depends upon organization. . . .

Dr. Foakes Jackson makes the interesting suggestion that when the Acts of the Apostles records that the sick used to be brought into the streets that 'even the shadow of Peter passing by' might overshadow them, it is a figure of his subsequent influence on the Christian world, the history of which for countless generations was dominated everywhere by 'the shadow of Peter passing by.' Jackson goes on to say that while the personality, writings, and achievements of Paul have wrought much, he has not captured the imagination of mankind as fully as the mighty shadow of his great colleague. 'Of the religion of Christ it may be said that its outward manifestations in the world are its Church and its theology; and that the one is connected with the name of Peter, the other with that of Paul. But, if only the few in any age have understood Christian doctrine, the Church has been evident to all, and, judged by this test Peter is of even greater importance than Paul himself.'

Anglican controversialists make a great deal of the fact that there is no evidence that Peter was ever in Rome or that he was the first bishop of the Roman Church. Of course, no argument can be built upon lack of evidence. The belief that Peter was in Rome, and was the first bishop of the Church there, is grounded upon the constant tradition in the early Church, which was never questioned, that these things were so…

It is undeniable that our Lord conferred upon Peter a distinctive gift, the power of the keys. In dealing with this fundamental fact, the question at issue is as follows: In committing to the Prince of the Apostles the power of the keys, did the Founder of the Church intend to bestow upon Peter not merely a primacy of distinction and honor, or even of responsibility to the whole Church, but in addition a magisterium, a magistracy over the new messianic kingdom? Two arguments are brought forward by Anglo-Catholic controversialists against the claim that the pope possesses by divine right a magisterium, or the supreme power ofjurisdictionoverthewholeChurch.

The first argument is that nothing is heard of Peter exercising such a power during the latter part of his apostleship and, furthermore, that we hear of no provision for its continuance in his successors. The argument from silence has never appealed to me as convincing. It is quite possible that no occasion arose for the exercise of this power of the keys until the middle of the third century. But it is also possible that our records are defective. The same argument from silence, based on the lack of evidence, can be used against the belief that the diocesan episcopate inherited, by divine right, all the powers of the apostolic college. Naturally, during the years of persecution, there was little time or opportunity for writing, and what was written may easily have been destroyed. Therefore the lack of evidence is no argument against the episcopate or papacy. Two significant facts stand out: our Lord gave the power of the keys to Peter, which he exercised frequently in the early part of his apostolate; and from the middle of the third century on the bishops of Rome claimed to exercise that power by right of succession from Peter. What more could we ask for: a power conferred by divine authority and the subsequent exercise of that power by the popes without its being contested by the rest of the Church?

But is it so certain that there is no evidence of the supremacy of Peter in the missionary development of the early Church? The churches founded by Paul were jealously watched over by Paul himself, and he apparently did not recognize any authority as being capable of putting a check on his own. That is characteristic of his character and method. But the churches founded by him did not always admit this principle. They welcomed other missionaries. The Corinthian community had welcomed Apollos, and there was a division among them; some were of Paul, and some were of Apollos. Still others claimed to be of Christ, and it looks very much as if the authority they invoked was that of Cephas, who had never been in Corinth. It is interesting to note the order in which Paul lists these authorities, naming

Christ last, a progression certainly intentional: 'Now this I say, that everyone of you saith, I am of Paul; and I of Apollos; and I of Cephas; and I of Christ' (1 Cor. 1:12). From this it appears that Peter is known to the Corinthians as an authority in the Church - and an authority who ranks above Paul and Apollos. The only higher authority than that of Peter is the authority of Christ.

In writing to the Corinthians, Paul insists that all of these leaders - whether himself, Apollos, or Cephas - are but servants of the servants of God and that all, apostles and the faithful, are Christ's as Christ is God's. He never contests the privilege accorded to Peter as having been the first to whom the risen Lord showed himself (cf. 1 Cor. 15:5). He puts Peter ahead of the other apostles, even the brethren of the Lord, when he says, 'Have we no right to lead about a wife that is a believer, as well as other apostles, and as the brethren of the Lord, and Cephas?' (1 Cor. 9:5). He utters no word of criticism against the authority that some of the Corinthians recognized in Peter.

The second argument against the claim to supremacy is that the general consent of the Church has always been lacking. In particular, it is alleged that the papal claims were never recognized in the East. A great deal is made of a quotation from the history of the Church by Duchesne, a Roman Catholic historian, vol. II, pp. 659–661. In this passage the historian is explaining how the authority of the emperor insinuated itself into Catholicism. He says that the Christian religion in the fourth century became the religion of the emperor not only in the sense that it was professed by him but in the sense that it was directed by him. And this evolution was brought about because 'the papacy as the West knew it later on was yet to be born.' In other words, there was not, in the Church of the fourth century, 'an authority central, recognized, and effective.' Of course it is obvious that the papacy, as it later developed, did not yet exist in the fourth century. It had not sufficient power and prestige to assert itself effectively against the imperial power. But no one who is familiar with the facts of history can deny that there existed in the Catholicism of the time of Theodosius a Church that was a norm of authority, recognized and consulted by all. The Roman Church was the Church in communion with which it was necessary to be if one were to belong to the *Ecclesia*. It was the only Church in the world that pretended to have a care for all the churches. It was a Church that believed it had a right to welcome the bishops whom Eastern councils had deposed, pronounce on their causes, and send them back to their dioceses vindicated and strengthened. It was the Church to which the Orientals appealed as in the time of St. Basil to determine for them the orthodoxy of doctrines or persons.

This normal development of the Apostolic See as the center of unity was interfered with in the East by the policy of Constantine toward the end of his reign and the subsequent policies of the emperors Constance II and Valens. As a result there was imposed on Catholicism a Caesaro-papism, against which the Catholicism of St. Athanasius and St. Hilary was a magnificent protest. This Caesaro-papism was itself the product of Arianism in its efforts to revise the Nicene Creed. The East returned to the faith of Nicaea in the time of Theodosius but never wholly threw off the shackles of temporal domination, which even to the present day has been the chief defect of Greek Catholicism. Western Catholicism, on the other hand, strengthened the ties that bound it to Rome. St. Ambrose of Milan helped greatly in this process by his doctrine of the independence and supremacy of the Christian ministry. Greek Catholicism and Western Catholicism tended more and more to oppose each other as two mentalities and two distinct methods of government. The Roman Church sensed the danger of this disunity and bent all her energies to forward the cause of unity through the primacy of the Apostolic See. Unity and primacy were two values that she knew belonged to the past of Catholicism…

Undoubtedly it is true that from the time of Constantine to the seventh ecumenical council (323–787) the Greek Church was often in schism from the Church of the West…For 203 out of the 464 years of this period the Eastern bishops were in schism from the Apostolic See. The grounds for these schisms will hardly bear examination. One schism was in defense of Arianism, another arose over the condemnation of Chrysostom, another was the schism of Acacia, another was in regard to Monothelitism, and another was on the worship of images. In all these instances the Apostolic See was defending the orthodox faith!

It is argued by Anglo-Catholics that the general councils never consented to recognize any primacy in the bishop of Rome except the same kind of primacy that they claimed for the bishop of Constantinople. The twenty-eighth canon of Chalcedon enunciated this principle of equality between Constantinople and Rome, but Pope Leo the Great protested vigorously against this canon. The emperor Marcian intervened and compelled Anatolius, the bishop of Constantinople, who inspired this canon, to make amends to the bishop of Rome and obey the laws of the Church. Thereupon Anatolius wrote to Pope Leo that he had nothing to do with the passing of the canon but that some of his clergy had drawn it up and the bishops had voted for it. He added that the confirmation of all the acts of the Council was of course reserved to the Pope. These are his words: *Cum et sic gestorum vis omnis et confirmatio auctoritate vestrae beatitudinis fuerit reservata.* ('Since the whole validity and confirmation of the acts of the Council will be reserved to the authority of Your Holiness.') This does not look like a 'presidency of honor'...

It has often been said that the growth of the papacy in the early centuries, and later in the Middle Ages, was entirely due to its connection with the empire and the importance of the city of Rome as a center of world rule. But this is an argument that can be used equally well in favor of the papacy. May we not say that it was by the divine ordinance that the papacy was established in the city of Rome rather than in Constantinople or Jerusalem or Alexandria or Antioch, where it would later on be deprived of its power? Shall we call it simply a piece of good luck, or shall we ascribe it to the providence of God?

The alternative to believing that the papacy is a part of the divine constitution of the Church is to believe that it has been foisted on the Church by the machinations of evil men and the fortuitous turn of historical events. If we accept the latter alternative, then we are forced to the conclusion that the greater part of the Catholic Church has fallen into error. This involves too much, for it means that the Holy Spirit has not been guiding the Church into all truth and that our Lord was mistaken when he promised that the gates of hell should not prevail against his Church"; *Married Saints* (1935); *Rome From Within* (1935); Katherine Burton, *In No Strange Land: Some American Catholic Converts* (1942), p.235 ("He came at last to consider the one important question - that of Anglican orders and their validity. After reading and after prayer, he decided that his conclusion was that of the papal contention in the famous Encyclical on Anglican Orders; that at the Reformation the Anglican Church had intentionally departed from the historical Catholic concept of the ministry. Father Woodlock's little volume - *Constantinople, Canterbury, and Rome* gave his heart the consolation he needed, for the Jesuit said that even though the church he had served for so long had not the Real Presence, that though the Sacrament he had adored so long was only a wafer of flour and water, yet the devotion, the love, the prayers and fastings, the desire to make God's house more beautiful and the ceremonies more seemly all these things must surely have brought an outpouring of grace on those who administered them and those to whom they were administered"); Katherine Burton, "The Outstretched Arms," in John A. O'Brien (ed), *The Road to Damascus, Vol. II* (1950); *New Catholic Encyclopedia.*

Deshon, George M. CSP – priest; b. 30 January 1823, New London, Connecticut; c. 1851; d. 30 December

1903, New York; graduated with high honors in 1843 from the United States Military Academy at West Point (classmate and roommate of General U.S. Grant); afterwards taught mathematics and ethics at the Academy; promoted to the rank of captain, but in 1851 suddenly resigned his commission, was received into the Catholic Church and entered the Redemptorist Order; ordained to the priesthood in 1855; gave many missions with his four companions Fathers Baker, Hecker, Hewit, and Walworth (see above and below respectively and, in particular, the entry for Fr. Hecker); one of the original Paulist fathers; remained in the New York house of the Society for the rest of this life, being novice-master for several years; later assistant superior and in charge generally of the temporal interests of the community; considerable business ability; also superintended the building of the church of St. Paul the Apostle, using his skill and knowledge as an engineer, acquired at West Point; continued to spend much time on the missions where his sermons and practical instructions were valued; elected third Superior General of the Paulist Institute in 1897; see *Guide for Catholic Young Women, Especially for those who earn their own living* (1863); *Parochial Sermons* (1901); Katherine Burton, *In No Strange Land: Some American Catholic Converts* (1942), p.77 ("Father Deshon, the practical member and former army man, who was the architect of the new church and had been accused by some of making it look like a fort, outlived them all. He was a gentle, kindly man, but he did occasionally act with almost military precision if a wrong needed righting"); *Catholic Encyclopedia* ("Though his life-work was so largely practical, he was noted for his interior spirituality, his favorite saints being the hermits and cenobites of the desert, and his spare time was always devoted to recollection and spiritual reading, in which he had evidently been occupied on the last night of his life, before retiring").

Dillard, Annie (born Melanie Ann Doak) – author; b. 30 April 1945, Pittsburgh, Pennsylvania; c. 1990 ("When I went to the third world countries, I always went into Catholic churches"); oldest of three daughters; brought up as a Presbyterian; as an adolescent she stopped attending church but later returned to religious belief; studied Literature and Creative Writing at Hollins College, Roanoke, Virginia (MA in English in 1968); married her writing teacher, the poet R. H. W. Dillard (b. 1937) (divorced in 1975); attended an Episcopalian church in college; has published works of poetry, essays, prose, and literary criticism, as well as two novels and one memoir; won the 1974 Pulitzer Prize for General Nonfiction for *Pilgrim at Tinker Creek*, an account of the natural world near her home in Roanoke, Virginia; taught for many years in the English Department of Wesleyan University in Middletown, Connecticut; converted to the Catholic faith from Episcopalianism ("What I like about the Catholics is that they have this sort of mussed-up human way. You go to the Episcopal church, and people are pretty much all alike. You go to a Catholic church, and there are people of all different colors and ages, and babies squalling. You're taking a stand with these people. You're saying: 'Here I am. One of the people who love God.' They're really universal, really catholic"); married three times; see (memoir) *An American Childhood* (1987); (poetry) *Tickets for a Prayer Wheel* (1974); *Mornings Like This* (1995); (non-fiction narrative) *Pilgrim at Tinker Creek* (1974); *Holy the Firm* (1977); *Living by Fiction* (1982); *Teaching a Stone to Talk* (1982); *Encounters With Chinese Writers* (1984); *The Writing Life* (1989); *For the Time Being* (1999); (fiction) *The Living* 1992); *The Maytrees* (2007); Linda L. Smith, *Annie Dillard* (1991); Sandra Humble Johnson, *The Space Between: Literary Epiphany in the Work of Annie Dillard* (1992); Nancy C. Parrish. *Lee Smith, Annie Dillard, and the Hollins Group: A Genesis of Writers* (1998); John C. Waldmeir, *Cathedrals of Bone* (2009), Ch. 3: "Preserving the Body: Annie Dillard and Tradition"; *anniedillard.com.*

DiMucci, Dion Francis ("Dion") – singer-songwriter; b. 18 July 1939, The Bronx, New York; c. late 1990s (revert; received at Mount Carmel Church, The Bronx); born to an Italian-American family; his father was a vaudeville entertainer; formed a group, Dion and the Belmonts; first success in 1958; took part in the Winter Dance Party Tour with Buddy Holly, Richie Valens, The Big Bopper (J. P. Richardson), and others; the others decided to fly from Clear Lake, Iowa to the next venue, instead of traveling on the tour bus; he declined as it was too much money; the plane crashed and all on board were killed ("The next day, I stood in the lobby of the hotel in Moorhead, Minnesota. There was a television on the wall, announcing that the plane carrying Buddy, Ritchie and the Big Bopper had gone down in the storm. There were no survivors. From that moment on, I knew God had a plan for me"); several hit records with the group; he had a problem with heroin addiction; began a solo career in 1960; in 1961 *Runaround Sue* reached No. 1 in the U.S. charts; in 1962 *The Wanderer* reached No. 2; married to Susan Butterfield since 1963 (three daughters of the marriage); had several other records in the top ten and also successful in Britain; several successful albums; became a major star; the first rock and roll singer signed to Columbia Records; further problems with drug addiction in the middle and late 1960s; moved into blues and briefly reunited with the Belmonts; declining fortunes, but still featured with Bob Dylan as the only two American artists featured on the album cover of The Beatles' *Sgt. Pepper's Lonely Hearts Club Band* in 1967; on 1 April 1968 he experienced what he described as a strong religious experience ("I became aware of God's power before I became aware of his reality"); his recording of *Abraham, Martin and John* in 1968 revived his career; became a born again Christian and recorded many contemporary Christian and Gospel songs between 1979 and 1987 (compiled in *The Best of the Gospel Years* (1997)); returned to rock music, notably the album *Yo Frankie* (1989); and came back to the Catholic faith in the late 1990s, returning to Mount Carmel Church in The Bronx; still many live performances; works in prison ministry and helps men going through addiction recovery; see *The Wanderer: Dion's Story* (1988) (with Davin Seay); *EWTN Audio Library, The Journey Home* (18 June 1999) ("I think the primary central issue was authority. What is truth and who defines it…I started finding out that there are different teachings on baptism, on the Lord's Supper, on the Eucharist, on salvation. I mean essential issues. So then you start realizing that there's 35,000 denominations out there that are all saying, 'I have the Holy Spirit and if it's not in the book we don't teach it.' But everyone teaches something different and there's a new church opening up every week, you know, in some shopping center. You just take the book and open up the church; and what is truth and defining it becomes increasingly difficult to feel, you know, any kind of solid foundation.

It was in this sense that something was incomplete, something was missing. Now I know it was the beauty of truth, the fullness of the Church, two thousand years of family history, rich tradition, you know, the early Fathers, the beautiful Church I belong to now. But I didn't know it then. And it seemed to me that each individual believer had to acquire enough knowledge on his own to choose or find a church that was going to lead him to eternal life. It's like I pick the church of *my* choice, what I think that church is. What about the Church that Jesus started? You know, entering that Church on his terms, not on my terms…

I was surfing the channels and I'd come across this show. Sitting in my chair one night…was a converted Episcopal priest, John Haas, telling you that when he was an Episcopal priest he went on a pilgrimage to France…and he was talking to a Dominican priest and he was saying that there are a lot of disputes and controversies in my church, ordaining women, on and on and on. And the priest said, 'Well, who is the authority in your church?' and he said, 'Well, the faith and practice of the early undivided Church'...And the little Dominican priest says to him, 'No, who is the living authority in your church?' And John Haas said there was none. There was no-one to settle disputes and controversies. And he said that put him on the journey, and eventually he found out that there was a Church that did settle disputes and controversies.

Now, that sat me up in my chair and I was going 'Whoa, what's going on here? And I started looking at some of the teachings that I just had accepted and a lot of the things I heard outside of the church. So, I started to re-examine Matthew 16:17-19 where Jesus gives the keys of the kingdom to Peter, passes on the Davidic kingdom in the light of Isaiah 22:22, and says to him 'What you bind on earth will be bound in heaven. What you loose on earth will be loosed in heaven.' And the Catholic Church actually has the authority to bind you to its teaching. Growing up, I thought it was a tyrant. I didn't know it was a servant, a custodian, a humble keeper of the deposit of faith that Jesus gave it. And this is it. You either accept it – they have no right to change it and they haven't changed it. It's been the same for two thousand years. Periodically they define a doctrine, at times when there's controversies or a need...

When I understood the teaching authority in the Church, or of the Church in the magisterium, centered around the see of Peter; when I understood and accepted this doctrine, then I could trust the Church on everything else. And after that it was like somebody pulled the curtain open, and it was like another conversion for me. It was like when I first met Jesus. It was like I met Jesus and was trying to find his Church you know. Then all of a sudden the family was there, the rich tradition, the communion of saints...

I went back to my church, the church I left, the church of my youth, and I went to confession to Fr. Frank. And I walked in and I said, 'Fr. Frank, I've been anti-Catholic.' Because everything I learned was – I thought I knew about the Catholic Church, but I learned all of this outside the Church. I think there's a lot of people out there that dislike or are against the Catholic Church who don't even know what it teaches, but they hate what they don't understand – and I said, 'I feel like I've been persecuting the body of Christ.' And he said, 'Dion, welcome home!'"); "The Spiritual Journey of the Wanderer Who Came Home," *Semper Fidelis*, 20 June 2005 ("I started regularly attending a Protestant church where there was much exuberance and volume in the worship and teachings. Having a mild Catholic upbringing and not knowing exactly what I was leaving, I drifted away from the Church. The last eighteen years, going through different denominations, there was always something missing and incomplete. Now, I know it's the

Eucharist, the fullness of the Faith, the communion of saints, the beauty of Truth. I was missing 2,000 years of family history and rich tradition.

It seemed to me that each individual believer has to acquire enough knowledge on his own in order to know which church can bring him to eternal life. Instead of accepting the Church on God's terms, I'd have to choose a church of my liking, a church that agreed with me. In those years, I did come to love God's Word and met some wonderful pastors. But with a new church opening every week with a little different doctrine, it became increasingly difficult and confusing to know what the truth really was.

In late 1997, I came upon a television program called 'The Journey Home' on the *Eternal Word Television Network.* John Haas, a former Protestant clergyman, was Marcus Grodi's guest. He was talking about the question of authority in the Church. As a protestant, his final authority was 'the Faith and practice of the early, undivided Church.' However, there was a problem. He saw there was no living voice of authority to really settle and resolve disputes or controversies in the church he was in.

This started my inquiry into some of the teachings I'd accepted and believed from a Protestant standpoint without serious study. When I looked, I found that St. Paul called the Church the 'pillar and foundation of truth' (1 Tim. 3:15) and said to hold to the traditions passed on, 'either by word of mouth or by letter' (2 Thess. 2:15). I saw how the early Church recognized the bishop of Rome as the earthly head.

I discovered that the Church is guided by the Holy Spirit to make decisions without error. This promise by Jesus - this infallible divine guidance - gave us the Bible.

I discovered that Jesus is present in the Eucharist. Not symbolically present. Not kind of present. He is really there, under the appearance of bread and wine. Ignatius, Bishop of Antioch in the first century, wrote about the truth of the Real Presence in the Lord's Supper. And he sat at the feet of St. John who penned John 6:25-69.

Little by little, God helped break through my defiance and ignorance. My misconceptions about the Church were falling away fast. All the questions I had as a Protestant were being answered, as I finally felt those deep parts of me satisfied"); *EWTN Audio Library, The Journey Home* (1 May 2006); "The Wanderer," *The Coming Home Network International*, *Conversion Stories*, chnetwork.org, 12 January 2011; *Dion: The Wanderer Talks Truth* (2011) (with Mike Aquilina) ("'Imagine' has become an anthem for internationalism – one-world government - and a favorite hymn for those who are 'spiritual but not religious.'

'Imagine there's no heaven - it's easy if you try - no hell below us, above us only sky. Imagine all the people living for today.'

John [Lennon] was a beautiful man, but this song represents a huge failure of imagination. In 1971 we didn't need to imagine atheistic internationalism. Communism was living and active, in at least two forms. and it wasn't producing peace. The Eastern Bloc, was a repressive, unhappy place. China was sustaining its self-holocaust into Chairman Mao's senility. What made it possible for so many leaders to issue the orders for atrocities over the course of a half-century and more? They feared neither heaven nor hell. Imagine that.

A few years ago *Rolling Stone* magazine polled a select group of recording-industry professionals, critics, and artists, and they ranked 'Imagine' the third-greatest song of all time.

In the video for the song John plays a white grand piano in a white room. His wife, Yoko Ono, walks around the room, throwing open the curtains on all the windows, one by one. When I saw the video, I wanted to shout: *No! She should be closing the curtains! The song isn't enlightening anything. It's a deepening darkness*"); Rory Fitzgerald, "The rock star who met Christ on a jog," *Catholic Herald*, 30 March 2012.

Dodd, Bella (*née* Maria Assunta Isabella Visono) – professor of political science and lawyer; b. October 1904, Picerno, Basilicata, southeast of Naples, Italy; c. 7 April 1952 (revert; received by Bishop Fulton Sheen at St. Patrick's Cathedral, New York); d. 29 April 1969, New York City; youngest in a family of ten children; the rest of the family had moved to the United States when her mother had to return to Italy to deal with problems relating to her farm there; born during that trip and spent her first five years there with foster parents before going to the United States; brought up in the Catholic faith but then rejected it; in 1916 a trolley car accident necessitated the amputation of her left foot; educated at Hunter College, New York ("Since we had no common basis of belief, we drifted into laissez-faire thinking, with agnosticism for our religion and pragmatism for our philosophy...We had no real goals because we had no sound view of man's nature and destiny. We had feelings and emotions, but no standards by which to chart the future"); did graduate work in political science at Columbia University; in 1930 she received the Doctor of Jurisprudence degree from New York University; married in 1930 John Dodd (divorced in 1943); admitted to the New York bar in 1931; taught political science at Hunter College 1935-1944; active in several labor organizations and a leader in the Communist Party of America (CPUSA) in the 1930s and 1940s; became disillusioned by her experience in Communism (especially the purges of members and attacks on herself) and broke with the party (was formally expelled); converted to the Catholic Church, influenced in her reading by St. Augustine and St. Thomas Aquinas, but most notably by the witness of Mgr. Fulton Sheen; later a vocal anti-communist; in 1953 she testified before the U.S. Senate about widespread Party infiltration of labor unions and other institutions; she asserted that the Communist Party's structure "was in reality a device to control the 'common man'"; lectured at St. John's University, Brooklyn and practiced law; between 1952 and 1957 she was subpoenaed and testified several times before the Internal Security Subcommittee of the U.S. Senate, which investigated communist activities of teachers; in 1955 she formed the law firm Dodd, Cardiello, and Blair, which represented the interests of the disadvantaged; twice (1965 and 1966) failed in attempts to be elected to the New York State Supreme Court as a conservative; in 1968, again as a conservative, she made an unsuccessful bid for a New York State congressional seat; see *School of Darkness: The Record of a Life and of a Conflict between Two Faiths* (1954) ("I have had many occasions to see that this cataloging of people as either 'right' or 'left' has led to more confusion in American life than perhaps any other false concept. It sounds so simple and so right. By using this schematic device one puts the communists on the left and then one regards them as advanced liberals - after which it is easy to regard them as the enzyme necessary for progress.

Communists usurp the position of the left, but when one examines them in the light of what they really stand for, one sees them as the rankest kind of reactionaries and communism as the most reactionary backward leap in the long history of social movements. It is one which seeks to obliterate in one revolutionary wave two thousand years of man's progress...

There had been many things I had not really understood. I had regarded the Communist Party as a poor man's party, and thought the presence of certain men of wealth within it accidental. I now saw this was no accident. I regarded the Party as a monolithic organization with the leadership in the National Committee and the National Board. Now I saw this was only a facade placed there by the movement to create the illusion of the poor man's party; it was in reality a device to control the 'common man' they so raucously championed...

Now I realized that, with the best motives and a desire to serve the working people of my country, I, and thousands like me, had been led to a betrayal of these very people. I now saw that I had been poised on the side of those who sought the destruction of my own country...

What now became clear to me was the collusion of these two forces: the Communists with their timetable for world control, and certain mercenary forces in the free world bent on making profit from blood. But I was alone with these thoughts and had no opportunity to talk over my conclusions with friends...

Early in the fall of 1950 I went to Washington...I ran into an old friend, Christopher McGrath, the congressional representative of the Twenty-seventh District, the old East Bronx area of my childhood... When I last saw him he had taken me to lunch and given me some advice. He asked me if I wanted FBI protection, and I must have shivered noticeably. Though I was afraid, I was reluctant to live that kind of life. He did not press the issue. Instead, he said: 'I know you are facing danger, but if you won't have that protection, I can only pray for your safety.' He looked at me for a moment as if he wanted to say something else. Then he asked: 'Bella, would you like to see a priest?' Startled by the question, I was amazed at the intensity with which I answered, 'Yes, I would.' 'Perhaps we can reach Monsignor Sheen at Catholic University,' he said...[A]n appointment was made for me late that evening at the Monsignor's home. I was silent as we drove to Chevy Chase. All the canards against the Catholic Church which I had heard and tolerated, which even by my silence I had approved, were threatening the tiny flame of longing for faith within me. I thought of many things on that ride, of the word 'fascist,' used over and over by the communist press in describing the role of the Church in the Spanish Civil War. I also thought of the word 'Inquisition' so skillfully used on all occasions. Other terms came to me - reactionary, totalitarian, dogmatic, old-fashioned. For years they had been used to engender fear and hatred in people like me. A thousand fears assailed me. Would he insist that I talk to the FBI? Would he insist that I testify? Would he make me write articles? Would he see me at all? And then before my mind's eye flashed the cover of a communist pamphlet on which was a communist extending a hand to a Catholic worker. The pamphlet was a reprint of a speech by the French Communist leader Thorez and it flattered the workers by not attacking their religion. It skillfully undermined the hierarchy in the pattern of the usual communist attempt to drive a wedge between the Catholic and his priest. By what right, I thought, was I seeking the help of someone I had helped revile, even if only by my silence? How dared I come to a representative of that hierarchy? The screeching of the brakes brought me back to reality. We had arrived, and my friend was wishing me luck as I got out of the car. I rang the doorbell and was ushered into a small room. While I waited, the struggle within me began again. Had there been an easy exit I would have run out, but in the midst of my turmoil Monsignor Fulton Sheen walked into the room, his silver cross gleaming, a warm smile in his eyes. He held out his hand as he crossed the room. 'Doctor, I'm glad you've come,' he said. His voice and his eyes had a welcome which I had not expected, and it caught me unaware. I started to thank him for letting me come but I realized that the words which came did not make sense. I began to cry, and heard my own voice repeating over and over and with agony, 'They say I am against the Negro.' That accusation in the Party resolution had made me suffer more than all the other vilification and I, who had for years been regarded as a hard Communist, wept as I felt the sting anew.

Monsignor Sheen put his hand on my shoulder to comfort me. 'Don't worry,' he said. 'This thing will pass,' and he led me gently to a little chapel. We both knelt before a statue of Our Lady. I don't remember praying, but I do remember that the battle within me ceased, my tears were dried, and I was conscious of stillness and peace. When we left the chapel Monsignor Sheen gave me a rosary. 'I will be going to New York next winter,' he said. 'Come to me and I'll give you instructions in the Faith.' On my way to the airport I thought how much he understood. He knew that a nominal Christian with a memory of the Cross can easily be twisted to the purposes of evil by men who masquerade as saviors. I thought how communist leaders achieve their greatest strength and cleverest snare when they use the will to goodness of their members. They stir the emotions with phrases which are only a blurred picture of eternal truths. In my rejection of the wisdom and truth which the Church has preserved, and which she has used to establish the harmony and order set forth by Christ, I had set myself adrift on an uncharted sea with no compass. I and others like me grasped with relief the fake certitude offered by the materialists and accepted this program which had been made even more attractive because they appealed for 'sacrifice for our brothers.' Meaningless and empty I learned are such phrases as 'the brotherhood of man' unless they have the solid foundation of belief in God's Fatherhood. When I left Monsignor Sheen I was filled with a sense of peace and also with an inner excitement which stayed with me for many days…I had my hand in the pocket of my blue wool coat and it was closed over a string of beads with a cross at the end. All the way to New York I held tightly to the rosary Monsignor Sheen had given me…Now and then I stepped into a church to sit there and rest, for only there was the churning inside of me eased for a while and only then fear left me…

And so I began to receive instructions in the Faith. Something strange was apparent to me in my behavior - I who had generally been skeptical and argumentative now found that I asked few questions. I did not want to waste one precious moment. Week after week I listened to the patient telling of the story of God's love for man, and of man's longing for God. I listened to the keen logic and reasoning that have lighted the darkness and overcome the confused doubts of others of my group who had lost the art of reasoned thinking and in its place had put assertive casuistry. I saw how history and fact and logic were inherent in the foundations of the Christian faith. I listened to the Bishop explaining the words of Jesus Christ, the founding of His Church, the Mystical Body. I felt close now to all who received Communion in all the churches of the world. And I felt the true equality which exists between people of different races and nations when they kneel together at the altar rail - equal before God. And I came to love this Church which made us one"); "I Found Sanctuary," in John A. O'Brien, *The Road to Damascus, Vol. IV: Roads to Rome* (1955), p.70 ("It seems peculiar that a philosophy which believes in nothing except that which one can see or feel and which has enthroned itself as a Messianic ideal dedicated solely to the purely animal well-being of man, should have captivated so many young people…

We were the sex-saturated generation who did not have the power to love and who understood love only in its twisted manifestations. I lived through twenty staccato years in this kind of atmosphere. My personal life was meaningless and chaotic, and my spiritual life was void. So blind was I that the murder of 5,000,000 farmers (called kulaks) in Soviet Russia in the name of a classless society and a planned economy aroused only a small twinge of conscience. And the word 'liquidation' meant not the murder of those who did not agree with the leaders of world Communism but the purification of the party.

Little by little the sparks of conscience caught fire. I began to realize and to feel uneasy at the contradictions between what the Communists preached and what they did...I no longer saw Communism as an unadulterated doctrine of social betterment. I began to see it as a dominant, aggressive force which contained many evil features of the existing materialist society and added new ones. Individual life and liberty were expendable in the interest of the class.

I began to question the answers Communists were giving to the problems besetting the world. Repeatedly I asked myself, 'What is man's goal?' I questioned whether it was merely his physical development and whether his goal would be reached when man is well fed, well clothed and well housed. Who of us has not seen the neurotic misery of people who have all the material security which they need? Who of us is not aware of the fact that the excellent physical specimens called Nazis were a cruel and dehumanized people? I found myself repeating to myself, 'Man does not live by bread alone'...

I remember Christmas Eve of 1949. I was in New York alone. My past life had made any real relationships with members of my family very difficult. I was invited to spend the evening at the home of Jim and Clotilda McClure... Like many Negro people they were deeply spiritual, and I found peace in their company. Jim said grace before our simple meal, and we talked about Christmas and its meaning and forgot the ugly events of the past few years.

When I left their company, I got on a Madison Avenue bus. Without knowing what I was doing, I went down to Thirty-fourth Street, though I lived in the opposite direction. At a quarter before midnight, I found myself in the Church of St. Francis of Assisi on Thirty-first Street - beads of perspiration on my forehead.

The church was crowded. People stood so close to each other in the aisles that they could hardly move. Their faces were etched in the soft light, faces tired and warm. They knelt in reverence and in thanksgiving. Here were the masses I had sought, the people I wanted to love. Here was the brotherhood of men, cemented by their love of God. I prayed, 'God help me! God help me!' I walked for hours that night – oblivious of the merry-makers. And I knew I was on the right road"); Fulton J. Sheen, *Treasure in Clay* (1982) ("She was testifying one day before the Un-American Activities Committee in Washington, and Senator McGrath of Rhode Island asked her to pay me a visit. 'What has he to give me?' Senator McGrath answered: 'He teaches communism at the Catholic University, that is to say, he knows the philosophy of Marx and Lenin.' The senator then asked her if she was afraid to visit me. She accepted the challenge and telephoned me that she was on the way.

We met in a small outer room at my residence and exchanged generalities, after which I observed: 'Dr. Dodd, you look unhappy.' She said: 'Why do you say that?' I said: 'Oh, I suppose in some way, we priests are like doctors who can diagnose a patient by looking at him.' When the conversation came to a dead end, I suggested that she come into the chapel and say a prayer. While we knelt, silently, she began to cry. She was touched by grace. Later on, I instructed her and received her into the Church"); "Present at the Demolition," (an interview with Dr. Alice von Hildebrand), *Latin Mass Magazine*, Summer 2001 ("I can only tell you what I know. It is a matter of public record, for instance, that Bella Dodd, the ex-Communist who reconverted to the Church, openly spoke of the Communist Party's deliberate infiltration of agents into the seminaries. She told my husband and me that when she was an active party member, she had dealt with no fewer than four cardinals within the Vatican 'who were working for us'") (In the early 2000s Dr. von Hildebrand confirmed that Dodd had said: "I, myself, put some 1,200 men in Catholic seminaries." Dr. von Hildebrand said that Dodd had originally desisted from talking about the seminary infiltration at the request of Fulton Sheen. She also provided an affidavit from Paul and Johnine Leininger, a couple who witnessed Dodd making the public statements. The Leiningers confirmed that there were others who could also verify that Dodd made the statements about seminary infiltration); Eleonore Villarubia, "Bella Dodd – From Communist to Catholic," *catholicism.org*, 31 August 2010 ("Perhaps most frightening of all was her testimony that during her time in the Party, 'more than eleven hundred men had been put into the priesthood to destroy the Church from within,' the idea here being that these men would be ordained to the priesthood and progress to positions of influence and authority as monsignors and even bishops. She stated that 'right now they are in the highest places in the Church' where they were working to weaken the Church's effectiveness against Communism. These changes, she declared, would be so drastic that 'you will not recognize the Catholic Church'"); her papers are in the records of the New York City Teachers Union at the Kheel Center for Labor-Management Documentation and Archives at Cornell University; *ANB.*

Dodson, Edward Ottway – biologist; b. 1916, Fargo, North Dakota; c. 1938; d. 2002; Protestant parents; raised in the Congregational Church; awarded a PhD by University of California at Berkeley; lectureship in Zoology at UCLA, Associate Professor of Biology at University of Notre Dame 1947-1957; at University of Ottawa until retiring in 1981; see "The End of a Pilgrimage," in John A. O'Brien (ed), *The Road to Damascus, Vol. II* (1950) (this essay is not included in all editions of this book) ("If I were to pick any one fault which, more than any other, seems to pervade and vitiate Protestantism as a whole, I should say that it is one-sidedness. Each church seems to be a distinct unit because it emphasizes disproportionately some one aspect of Christianity at the expense of many other equally important aspects. This is signalized by the very names of many sects: they are Baptists, Congregationalists, Presbyterians, Episcopalians, or Seventh-Day Adventists...

As I read the current literature of Protestantism, I found unmistakably that the leaders of present-day Protestantism were still pleading the justification of the Reformation. It seemed to me that after four hundred years they would assume the justification an accomplished fact, unless they themselves were in doubt as to whether the events which led to the formation of their respective churches were actually justified. Furthermore, it became clear that the things of which they were proudest and to which they clung with the greatest tenacity were things which might be called their Catholic heritage, although they did not often. acknowledge the source openly: they referred to such things as a return to Primitive Christianity, the New Testament practices, or the heroism of the Martyrs. Such things are the sacraments, especially baptism and Holy Communion, though various churches recognize some others; the idea of ordination through the authority of Christ as represented through apostolic successors; some of the very old prayers, hymns, and ejaculations, such as 'In the name of the Father, and of the Son, and of the Holy Ghost,' the Gloria in Excelsis, and the creeds, especially the Apostles' Creed...

[The] characteristic of nationalism, or of limited group appeal of some other sort, I found to be a rather general characteristic of Protestantism. The various Lutheran sects are fundamentally German or Scandinavian. The Presbyterian Church is Scotch. The Church of the Nazarene and the Salvation Army appeal almost exclusively to the economically downtrodden. The Unitarian Church draws its members principally from intellectuals who for the most part substitute ethical culture for religion. But none seems to have universal appeal for all peoples and all classes...

I found that the Catholic Church actually is catholic. It is catholic in point of time, because its corporate existence has been uninterrupted since its founding by Christ. It is catholic in doctrine because it has always taught the same orthodox doctrine in all places. It is catholic in teaching because it has always taught the whole faith and has not yielded to the tendency of Protestant churches to develop pet doctrines at the expense of others. It is catholic in appeal because in all nations people of all classes kneel at its altar, and social considerations do not determine which Catholic church in a given community one shall attend: for white and black, merchant and laborer, rich and poor all kneel at the same altar, side by side.

The Catholic Church cannot be considered as a social luxury. For every Catholic it is the first among his necessities. The tremendous number of priests and nuns who give their lives - not simply their professional services - to the Church must certainly be a cogent indication, to anyone who will consider it, of how vital and important a factor the Church must be to Catholics"); *A Textbook of Evolution* (1952); "Mendel and the Rediscovery of His Work," *Scientific Monthly*, October 1955; *Evolution: Process and Product* (1976); *The Phenomenon of Man*

Revisited: A Biological Viewpoint on Teilhard de Chardin (1984); *Teilhard and Mendel: Contrasts and Parallels* (1984); *Creation or Evolution: Correspondence on the Current Controversy* (1990) (with George Franklin Howe); "Toldot Adam: A Little-Known Chapter in the History of Darwinism," *Perspectives on Science and Christian Faith*, March 2000, p.47.

Doherty, Catherine De Hueck, CM (*née* Ekaterina Fyodorovna Kolyschkine) – social activist and foundress of the Madonna House apostolate; Servant of God; b. 15 August 1896, Nizhny Novgorod (now Gorki), Russia; c. 27 November 1919; d. 14 December 1985, Combermere, Ontario, Canada; her parents belonged to the minor nobility and were devout members of the Russian Orthodox Church; her parent's care for the poor affected her (her mother taught her to "see the face of the Christ in the poor"); at the age of about six she went with her family to Alexandria, Egypt, where her father had been posted by the government; for several years she attended a Catholic school there conducted by the Sisters of Sion (this influenced her later conversion to the Catholic Church); at the age of twelve she wanted to convert to Catholicism, but her father refused; the family returned to St. Petersburg in 1910 and she attended the Prince Obolensky Academy; married at the age of fifteen in 1912 to her first cousin Boris De Hueck (1889-1947); during World War I she worked as a Red Cross nurse at the front (decorated for bravery under fire); returned to St. Petersburg, but then she and Boris had to flee to Finland as refugees in order to escape the Russian Revolution, nearly starving to death; they then made their way to Scotland, then England; discovered the Sisters of Sion had a convent in London, visited them and was eventually received into the Church; one of her influences was Vladimir Soloviev (1853-1900); by then penniless they emigrated to Canada; gave birth to their only child, George, in 1921; because of great poverty, and the poor health of her husband, she did many menial jobs during this period; her marriage fell apart; she became a successful lecturer and prosperous, but felt a more spiritual call; drawn to one particular passage in the New Testament: "Arise - go...sell all you possess...take up your cross and follow Me"; after discussions with the Church authorities she sold all her possessions and provided for her son; then in the early 1930s she began a lay apostolate among the poor in Toronto, calling it Friendship House, the spirituality was based on that of St. Francis of Assisi; fought against the rising Communism by publicizing the social teaching of the Church; given support by Dorothy Day (see above); there was much opposition to her interracial approach and Friendship House was forced to close in 1936; she went to Europe and investigated the Catholic Action movement; returned to the United States and revived Friendship House in New York City among the poor in Harlem; supported by Cardinal Hayes and Cardinal Spellman; gradually founded more Friendship Houses in North America; in 1942 her first marriage was annulled and she married Edward J. ("Eddie") Doherty (1890-1975) (see below), a famous newspaper reporter and author, who had written an account of her apostolate; disagreements arose between herself and the staff of Friendship House, which could not be resolved, and she stepped down as Director General; she and her husband moved to Combermere, Ontario, in 1947; she began to serve those in need in the area and began a training center for the Catholic lay apostolate; in 1951, she and her husband made an act of consecration to Jesus through Mary, according to St. Louis de Montfort; Mary, Mother of the Church, became guide to their lives and to their apostolate; in 1954, those living in Combermere voted to embrace a permanent vocation with promises of poverty, chastity and obedience, and the community of Madonna House (named in honor of the Blessed Virgin Mary) was established; in 1955 she and her husband took a promise of chastity and lived celibate lives thereafter; this apostolate of Madonna House has since spread throughout the world; author of many books and articles; recipient of many awards; the cause for her canonization was officially opened in 2000; she was named a Servant of God; the essence of her spirituality (known as "the Madonna House way of life") is "The Little Mandate," which she believed she received from Christ and took as her guide in life and which reads: "Arise - go! Sell all you possess. Give it directly, personally to the poor. Take up My cross (their cross) and follow Me, going to the poor, being poor, being one with them, one with Me. Little - be always little! Be simple, poor, childlike. Preach the Gospel with your life - *without compromise!* Listen to the Spirit. He will lead you.. Do little things exceedingly well for love of Me. Love...love...love, never counting the cost Go into the marketplace and stay with Me. Pray, fast. Pray always, fast. Be hidden. Be a light to your neighbor's feet. Go without fear into the depth of men's hearts. I shall be with you. Pray always. *I will be your rest*"; a key emphasis in her spirituality is "the duty of the moment" expressed as follows: "The duty of the moment is what you should be doing at any given time, in whatever place God has put you. You may not have Christ in a homeless person at your door, but you may have a little child. If you have a child, your duty of the moment may be to change a dirty diaper. So you do it. But you don't just change that diaper, you change it to the best of your ability, with great love for both God and that child...There are all kinds of good Catholic things you can do, but whatever they are, you have to realize that there is always the duty of the moment to be done. And it must be done, because the duty of the moment is the duty of God"; she also introduced to the West from her Russian past the idea of the *poustinia* (Russian for "desert"), a small sparsely furnished cabin or room where a person goes to pray and fast alone in the presence of God for twenty-four hours; she looked for an alternative to the depersonalizing effects of modern technology; she reacted to modern individualism by calling for *sobornost* (Russian for "a spiritual community of many jointly living people"); friend of Thomas Merton (see below); see (selective list) *Friendship House* (1947); *Poustinia: Christian Spirituality of the East for Western Man* (1975); *The Gospel Without Compromise* (1976); *Not Without Parallels: Stories of Yesterday, Today, and Eternity* (1977); *Fragments of My Life* (1979) (autobiographical); David Meconi, SJ (ed), *Catherine De Hueck Doherty: Essential Writings* (2009); Robert A. Wild, *Journey to the Lonely Christ: The "Little Mandate" of Catherine De Hueck Doherty* (1987); Emile Briere, *Katia, A Personal Vision of Catherine De Hueck Doherty* (1988); Robert A. Wild, *Love, Love, Love: The "Little Mandate" of Catherine De Hueck Doherty* (1989); Robert A. Wild, *Journey in the Risen Christ: The "Little Mandate" of Catherine De Hueck Doherty* (1992); Lorene Hanley Duquin, *They Called Her the Baroness: The Life of Catherine De Hueck Doherty* (1995); Robert A. Wild (ed), *Comrades Stumbling Along: The Friendship of Catherine de Hueck Doherty and Dorothy Day as Revealed through Their Letters* (2009); Robert A. Wild (ed), *Compassionate Fire: The Letters of Thomas Merton and Catherine De Hueck Doherty* (2009); Lorene Hanley Duquin, *A Century of Catholic Converts* (2003), p.47; *madonnahouse.org*; *ANB.*

Doherty, Edward J. ("Eddie") – journalist, author and priest; b. 30 October 1890, Chicago, Illinois; c. 1939 (revert); d. 4 May 1975, Combermere, Ontario, Canada; oldest of ten children in an Irish-American Catholic family; father a police officer; as a child he wanted to become a priest; entered a Servite monastery in Wisconsin at the age of thirteen; returned to Chicago within two years; started as a newspaper copy boy; gradually made a name as a police beat reporter; married Marie Ryan in 1914 (one son of the marriage), but she died in the flu epidemic of 1918; he was badly affected by this and left the Catholic Church; married his second wife, Mildred Frisby, writer under the pseudonym Mildred Spain (d. 1939), secretly in

1919 (one son of the marriage); he became a famous reporter working mainly in Chicago and then New York; headlined as "America's Star Reporter"; wrote for many newspapers, including *Chicago Tribune, Chicago American, New York News, New York American,* and *Chicago Sun* (later *Sun-Times*); wrote over a thousand articles for *Liberty Magazine*, then edited by Fulton Oursler (see below); his second wife also wrote for newspapers, but tragically she died in a freak accident while out walking; he found peace in his grief by returning to the Catholic Church; in 1940 he met Catherine De Hueck at her Friendship House mission while doing a story on Harlem; they married in 1943; nominated for an Oscar for his screenplay for the film *The Sullivans*; differences with the staff at Friendship House led to Catherine and him moving to Combermere, Ontario, Canada, and serving those in need in the area, and eventually starting Madonna House, a new apostolate, in 1954; in 1969 he obtained permission to transfer from the Latin Rite to the Byzantine Rite Melkite Greek Catholic Church (which allows married men to become priests); on 15 August 1969 he was ordained to the Catholic priesthood at the age of seventy-eight by Archbishop Joseph Raya; see *Tumbleweed* (1948, second edition 1988) (memoirs); *Gall and Honey: The Story of a Newspaperman* (second edition, 1989); *A Cricket in My Heart: An Autobiography* (1990); *Wisdom's Fool: A Biography of St. Louis de Montfort* (1992); *Getting to Know God* (1998); *Matt Talbot* (second edition, 2001); *Splendor of Sorrow: The Seven Sorrows of the Mother of God* (2010); Walter Romig, The Book of Catholic Authors (1945) (reprinted in catholicauthors.com) ("I had met lots of Russians in Finland. They lay in burned tanks alongside the roads. They lay buried in the snow. They filled the woods. Russian soldiers frozen months before. But this Russian woman had nothing frozen about her. She burned with the love of God. So great was the flame of that love that it warmed and quickened all who came close to her. This was the Baroness Catherine de Hueck, founder of Friendship House, a social settlement in 135th street, between Fifth and Lenox avenues - a social settlement different than any I had ever stumbled upon in all my hoodlum years.

Friendship House worked for and with the Negroes. It dispensed charity of all kinds, without asking questions, without hesitation. It fought for interracial justice. It fostered study clubs, credit unions, co-operative associations, and other advanced ideas of self-help for the Negro poor. And it disseminated Catholicity in a thousand ways.

I became enamored with the place, with the young people who worked under the direction of the Baroness, and with their mode of life. And, eventually, of course,

I fell in love with the foundress. These young men and women were college graduates, mostly, with the right to put letters after their names, if they wished. They had left good jobs to enter Friendship House. They received no salaries. They were given second-hand clothes to wear. They ate at a common table, and there were times when there was nothing but stale bread and warmed-over tea on that table. Yet they were the happiest group in New York. They loved 'holy poverty' - I had never heard that phrase used until I visited Friendship House - and they loved to talk about God. Imagine that! A little band of saints in 'the wickedest city in the world!'

I went to school to the Baroness and to her 'children'; and for the first time in fifty years began to get some little insight into the warmth, the beauty, the majesty, the color, the infinite glory of the Catholic Church"); Mary Bazzett, *The Life of Eddie Doherty: Co-Founder of Madonna House Apostolate* (1998).

Dorsey, Anna Hanson (*née* McKenney) – novelist; b. 12 December 1815, Georgetown, District of Columbia; c. 1840 (received with her husband); d. 25 December 1896, Washington, D.C.; descended from prominent Maryland colonists on both sides of her family; educated entirely at home; converted under the influence of the Oxford movement; wrote many light and highly melodramatic Catholic novels, many on historical themes and for young adults; always much involved in governmental affairs and moral and religious questions; awarded the *Laetare* medal, University of Notre Dame; married Lorenzo Dorsey (d. 1861) in 1837; mother of a son and four daughters; her son was killed while fighting in the Union Army during the Civil War; her youngest daughter, Ella Loraine, became as popular a Catholic writer as her mother; see *The Orient Pearl* (1848); *Flowers of Love and Memory* (1849); *Guy, The Leper* (1850); *The Sister of Charity* (1850); *Tears on the Diadem: or, the Crown and the Cloister, a Tale of the White and Red Roses* (1850); *Woodreve Manor, or Six Months in Town: A Tale of American Life* (1852); *Conscience; Or The Trials of May Brooke. An American Catholic Tale* (1856); *"They're Coming, Grandad!" A Tale of East Tennessee* (1865); *Coaina. The Rose of the Algonquins* (1866); *The Student of Blenheim Forest (or The Trials of a Convert)* (1867); *The Flemmings or Truth Triumphs* (1869); *Mona the Vestal* (1869); *Nora Brady's Vow* (1869); *Tangled Paths* (1879); *Ada's Trust* (1887); *Adrift* (1887); *Beth's Promise* (1887); *The Heiress of Carrgmona* (1887); *The House at Glenara* (1887); *Palms* (1887); *Warp and Woof* (1887); *The Fate of the Dane, and Other Stories* (1888); *Zoe's Daughter* (1888); *Tomboy* (1891); *The Two Ways* (1891); David Jerome Callon, "Converting Catholicism: Orestes

A. Brownson, Anna H. Dorsey, and Irish America (2008), unpublished PhD dissertation, Washington University in St. Louis; Patrick Allitt, *Catholic Converts: British and American Intellectuals Turn to Rome* (1997), pp.131-132; *Catholic Encyclopedia*; *ANB* ("Her works are religious in tone and are primarily concerned with the Catholic Church. *The Student of Blenheim Forest* (1847), for example, is an account of the alienation of Louis, a Catholic, from his anti-Catholic father, Colonial Clavering, who is an important Virginian. Mrs. Clavering, Louis's mother, secretly baptizes Louis. The book has a pro-Catholic tone. In addition to presenting the history of Catholicism in Maryland, the novel contains explanations of various Catholic traditions such as confession, the adoration of the Virgin Mary, High Mass, priestly vestments, the Benediction, and convents. In the preface to the second edition of *The Student of Blenheim Forest*, Dorsey explained that the work 'does not pretend to be a complete system of instruction in Catholic dogmas, although several of the doctrines and practices of the Church are explained in a manner quite simple enough to be understood by all. [My] object has been to illustrate some of the difficulties which those who become converts to the True Faith are frequently destined to encounter from the persecutions of the world'").

Douthat, Ross Gregory – author and columnist; b. 28 November 1979, San Francisco, California; c. 1997 (received with his father and mother); his father, Charles Douthat, a partner in a law firm; mother, Patricia Wright, a writer; baptized Episcopalian; grew up in New Haven, Connecticut; attended Evangelical and Pentecostal churches as an adolescent; his mother, originally Episcopalian, searched around for religion and the whole family finally became Catholics; his conversion was influenced by reading C. S. Lewis, G. K. Chesterton and Fr. Richard John Neuhaus; educated at Harvard University (graduated in 2002; had a major involvement in the student newspapers); politically conservative; was senior editor at *The Atlantic Monthly* 2002-2009; an online and youngest ever op-ed political columnist for *The New York Times* from 2009 (succeeding William Kristol); contributor to several other papers and magazines, notably *National Review* and *The Wall Street Journal*; strongly anti-abortion; in 2007 married Abigail Tucker, writer and journalist; see (selective list) *Privilege: Harvard and the Education of the Ruling Class* (2005); *Grand New Party: How Republicans Can Win the Working Class and Save the American Dream* (2008) (with Reihan Salam); "The Catholic Church Is Finished," *The Atlantic*, July-August 2010 ("This was the year when the cover-up of priestly sex abuse, a long-simmering crisis for Catholicism, became something much, much bigger. It was Watergate. It was Waterloo. It was another Reformation. The pope had to apologize. No, the pope had to resign. No, the pope had to be arrested. The Church could be saved only if every bishop stepped down. No, the Church could be saved only if a Third Vatican Council was convened. No, the Church could be saved only if it became as liberal as the Episcopal Church, and quickly. No, nothing could save the Church: it was too corrupt, too compromised, too medieval, too anachronistic. And now, at last, it was finished.

A little historical perspective suggests otherwise. The Church has been horrifyingly corrupt in previous eras and still survived. It's been led by ecclesiastics who make Bernard Law's hands look clean, and still survived. It's faced fiercer enemies than Richard Dawkins (think Nero, or Attila, or Voltaire) and still survived. Time after time, G. K. Chesterton wrote, 'the Faith has to all appearance gone to the dogs.' Each time, 'it was the dog that died.'

But if the Church isn't finished, period, it can still be finished for certain people, in certain contexts, in certain times. And so it is in this case: for millions in Europe and America, Catholicism is probably permanently associated with sexual scandal, rather than the gospel of Jesus Christ. And as in many previous dark chapters in the Church's history, the leaders entrusted with that gospel have nobody to blame but themselves"); "Choose Your Own Jesus," *The New York Times*, 27 May 2010 ("Here's a striking passage - an aside, really - from Adam Gopnik's *New Yorker* essay on the continuing (and continuing, and continuing) quest for the historical Jesus: 'James Tabor, a professor of religious studies, in his 2006 book *The Jesus Dynasty*, takes surprisingly seriously the old Jewish idea that Jesus was known as the illegitimate son of a Roman soldier named Pantera - *as well attested a tradition as any* [emphasis mine - RD], occurring in Jewish texts of the second century, in which a Jesus ben Pantera makes several appearances, and the name is merely descriptive, not derogatory.'

The whole problem with two centuries worth of historical Jesus scholarship is summed up in those seven words: 'As well attested a tradition as any.' Because obviously if you don't mind a little supernaturalism with your history, a story about Jesus being a Roman soldier's bastard that dates from the second century - and late in the second century, at that - is dramatically *less* 'well attested' than the well-known tradition (perhaps you've heard of it) that Jesus was born of a virgin married to Joseph the carpenter, which dates from the 70s or 80s A.D. at the latest, when the Gospels of Luke and Matthew were composed. Bracket the question of miracles, and there's really no comparison: Giving the Roman soldier story equal weight with the accounts in Matthew and Luke is like saying that a tale about Abraham Lincoln that first surfaced in the 1970s has just as much credibility as a story that dates to the 1890s (and is associated with eyewitnesses to Lincoln's life).

Now of course what Gopnik means by 'well attested' is 'well attested and non-miraculous,' which is fair enough so far as it goes. But this no-miracles criterion is why the historical Jesus project is such a spectacular dead end - because what would ordinarily be the most historically-credible sources for the life and times of Jesus Christ are absolutely soaked in supernaturalism, and if you throw them out you're left with essentially idle speculations about Jesus ben Pantera and other phantoms that have no real historical grounding whatsoever.

Think about it this way: If the letters of Saint Paul (the earliest surviving Christian texts, by general consensus) and the synoptic gospels (the second-earliest) didn't make such extraordinary claims about Jesus's resurrection, his divinity, and so forth, no credible historian would waste much time parsing second-century apocrypha for clues about the 'real' Jesus. They'd thank their lucky stars that the first-century Christians were such talented narrative writers, and spend most of their time trying to reconcile the discrepancies and resolve the contradictions in Matthew, Mark and Luke, while arguing amongst themselves about how much historical weight to give to the events and sayings recorded in John's gospel. The gospel of Thomas would attract some modest attention; the later 'lost gospels,' very little, save as evidence of how intra-Christian debates developed long after Jesus's death. For the most part, the argument over how the Nazarene lived and died would revolve around competing interpretations of the existing Christian canon, and the rough accuracy of the synoptic narrative would be accepted by the vast majority of scholars.

In the event, the synoptic gospels and Saint Paul's epistles do make absolutely extraordinary claims, and so modern scholars have every right to read them with a skeptical eye, and question their factual reliability. But if you downgrade the earliest Christian documents or try to bracket them entirely, the documentary evidence that's left is *so* intensely unreliable (dated, fragmentary, obviously mythological, etc.) that scholars can scavenge through it to build whatever Jesus they prefer - and then say, with Gopnik, that their interpretation of the life of Christ is 'as well attested' as any other. Was Jesus a wandering sage? Maybe so. A failed revolutionary? Sure, why not. A lunatic who fancied himself divine? Perhaps. An apocalyptic prophet? There's an app for that...

But this isn't history: It's 'choose your own Jesus,' and it's become an enormous waste of time. Again, there's nothing wrong with saying that the supernaturalism of the Christian canon makes it an unreliable guide to who Jesus really was. But if we're honest with ourselves, then we need to acknowledge what this means: Not the beginning of a fruitful quest for the Jesus of history, but the end of it"); *Bad Religion: How We Became a Nation of Heretics* (2012); Mark Oppenheimer, "Ross Douthat's Fantasy World," *Mother Jones*, January-February 2010 ("After all the church hopping, Douthat was happy when the family finally settled on Catholicism. 'I was seventeen, a socially awkward teenager, and I was relieved to join a church where no one asked you to pray spontaneously,' he told me. His reading had prepared him well: 'You start reading C. S. Lewis, then you're reading G. K. Chesterton, then you're a Catholic. I knew a lot of people who did that in their twenties - I just did it earlier, and with a different incentive structure.'

A certain kind of cerebral Christian will recognize the young Douthat's reading list, especially the prominence of English apologetic writers like Lewis, the mid-twentieth-century Anglican who penned *The Chronicles of Narnia*, and Chesterton, an English Catholic who, prior to his death in 1936, promoted an agrarian, anti-modern agenda and is now beloved by fantasy writers like Neil Gaiman. Douthat was also a huge fan of J. R. R. Tolkien, another anti-modern conservative Catholic").

Dubin, Al (born Alexander Dubinsky) - lyricist; b. 10 June 1891, Zurich, Switzerland; c. 1924; d. 11 February 1945, New York City; from a Russian Jewish family which emigrated from Switzerland to Philadelphia in 1896; father a medical doctor, mother a chemistry teacher; grew up in Philadelphia; parents against him pursuing a career in music; by the age of fourteen he was missing school in order to see Broadway shows and vaudeville; enrolled in medical school, but was expelled in 1911; little song writing success before World War I in which he served; much success after the war; in 1921 he married Helene McCloy, a devout Catholic (two daughters of the marriage); converted to the Catholic Church after the constant urgings of his wife, but still at times considered himself to be Jewish; songwriter and lyricist for various companies; wrote the lyrics for several Broadway shows and many famous films; many collaborations with the composer Harry Warren; he loved the poems of Robert Service, Poe, Shelley and Byron; gave up the practice of the faith; serious alcohol problems and extra-marital relationships; divorced in 1941; entered another marriage, which only lasted two months; died from barbiturate poisoning; buried in Holy Cross Cemetery, Culver City, California; inducted into the Songwriters Hall of Fame in 1970; see (Broadway) *Charlot Review* (1925); *White Lights* (1927); *Streets of Paris* (1939); *Keep off the Grass* (1940); *Star and Garter* (1942); (films) *Gold Diggers of Broadway* (1929); *42nd Street* (1933); *Footlight Parade* (1933); *Gold Diggers of 1933* (1933); *Gold Diggers of 1935* (1936); *Gold Diggers of 1937* (1936); *Gold Diggers in Paris* (1938); (notable songs) *42nd Street*; *Shanghai Lil*; *I Only Have Eyes for You*; *Shuffle off to Buffalo*; *You're Getting to Be a Habit with Me*; *Lullaby of Broadway*; *The Anniversary Waltz*; *September in the Rain*; *We're in the Money*; *Tiptoe Through the Tulips*; *Painting the Clouds with Sunshine*; *I'll String Along with You*; Patricia Dubin McGuire, *Lullaby of Broadway: A Biography of Al Dubin* (1985); *ANB*.

Dulles, Cardinal Avery Robert, SJ – Cardinal priest and theologian; b. 24 August 1918, Auburn, New York; c. November 1940, St. Paul's, Harvard; d. 12 December 2008, Fordham University, New York; son of John Foster Dulles, later U.S. Secretary of State (as was his great-grandfather and great-uncle); brought up a Presbyterian in a family strongly involved in that faith; educated at Harvard University in History and Philosophy (by then an agnostic, who was a materialist and saw morality as merely a social convention); the years from 1936 to 1940 at Harvard were the years of his conversion; after graduation entered Harvard Law School in 1940; served in the navy in World War II; entered the Society of Jesus in 1946; ordained to the priesthood in 1956; doctorate in sacred theology from the Gregorian University in 1960; Professor Emeritus at the Catholic University of America; visiting professor at several universities; president of the Catholic Theological Society of America; Laurence J. McGinley Professor of Religion and Society at Fordham 1988-2008; created a Cardinal on 21 February 2001 (dispensed from Episcopal ordination owing to his advanced age); many awards and honorary doctorates; author of twenty-two books and over seven hundred articles on theological topics; buried in the Jesuit cemetery in Auriesville, New York; see *Testimonial to Grace* (1944) (republished in 1996 with appendix) (account of his conversion) ((1) "The words of Our Lord, as recorded in the Gospels, rang with undeniable truth, but never more so, to my mind, than when He insisted, as He repeatedly did, on the knowledge and love of God as the only things that mattered. Suffering and persecution, He reiterated, were positive blessings when endured for His sake. Religion was the pearl of great price, the water which alone could wholly quench our thirst;

and He was the way, the truth and the life. Far more clearly than any man He taught that blessedness, not pleasure, should be the object of our lives. This was the doctrine for which I had been searching, and I accepted it with joy.

Who was this Teacher, or better this Lover, Who could not be restrained from giving until the last drop of blood had left His martyred body? Who was He, that He bade us so insistently to follow Him, begged to refresh us with His doctrine and to make us partakers of His joy? Was He, as He claimed, God and the Son of God?

After acquainting myself a little with the Gospels, I could have no patience with those modern writers and speakers who were incessantly trying to water down His 'hard' doctrine, and to represent Christ Himself as a mild, tolerant and ever gentle moralist. I was impressed by His unsparing rage against the Pharisees and by His use of physical violence to cleanse the Temple from the moneychangers. I saw that He was a man Whom one could hate tremendously, as most of His contemporaries did hate Him, for what they took to be His bad manners and extravagant ideas. The thought occurred to me that most of those who attempted to make Christ seem so moderate and 'respectable' would have hated and feared Him had they known Him as He was.

Christ, as He appeared in the Scriptures, was not primarily a moralist. For conduct as such He cared relatively little; love and faith He cherished above measure. His teaching took the form, not of dry aphorisms like those of Confucius or Poor Richard, but of parables charged with the poetry of life. These parables were so direct that the most unlettered could grasp their message. At the same time they were so rich in doctrine and symbolism that the most learned could not exhaust their subtle moral implications, their wealth of dogma and their deep prophetic meaning. The moralists never seemed to rise above the obvious. Christ never paused to state the obvious. He told of things no man had seen.

Nor was He merely a philosopher, another Socrates or Plotinus. They, after long inductive processes, came to tentative conclusions about the nature of God, the immortality of the soul, and the good life. Christ, Who seemed a stranger to discursive thought, spoke readily and with finality about these matters. He could use keen logic, and often did so to confute the Scribes and Pharisees, but His knowledge of spiritual matters was direct and immediate. His doctrine, higher than that of the philosophers, did not have the same source.

But could not Christ be classed as a religious fanatic, like Mohammed for example? To compare Him with the frenzied Arab epileptic was outright blasphemy. His judgment, unlike that of the fanatics, was always calm and clear, and His perception of His environment complete and penetrating. His doctrine, moreover, was thoroughly consistent with itself and with the facts of nature. When the philosophers later made it their study they found that the Christian faith enabled them to see clearly what Plato and Aristotle had hesitantly inferred. Once Christ had lived, Western philosophy could never be the same again. Mohammed had had no comparable influence on Arabic philosophy.

Was it possible, then, that Christ was more than a man? I investigated the arguments for His divinity, and found them no less cogent for being conventional. First, there was an embarrassing frequency of miracles in all the accounts of Christ. If He had performed any of them, He might well have performed all, He was neither a charlatan nor a fool, yet He repeatedly claimed miraculous powers, and, if the accounts had any normal degree of veracity, demonstrated that power again and again. The doctrine of the Gospels was sublime, and was indubitably a faithful account of Christ's teaching. To whom else could one accredit it? But was the view tenable that the miracles were something superadded by ignorant and credulous disciples? In Lionel Curtis' *City of God* I had read an able presentation of that thesis, but I found it unacceptable. Christ's doctrine was inseparably wedded to His miracles. Time and again He had illustrated His doctrine by His miracles and invoked His miracles as proof of His doctrine. One had to take both or neither, If, then, the Gospel accounts of Christ's doctrine were authentic - as I could not but concede - the miracles also must be accepted. Mr. Curtis, I felt, was not meeting the facts squarely. He was tailoring them to fit the frame of his own narrow rationalism.

One miracle which stood up to every test was the Resurrection. Any attempt to dismiss it as a hallucination was useless. That thousands of persons should have suffered a hallucination extending over a period of forty days was harder to account for than the Resurrection itself. Was it, then, a clever trick of Christ or His disciples? Nothing could have been more unlike Christ than to masquerade as a walking corpse in order to deceive His followers. And nothing could have been more unlike the disciples, who had weakly denied Christ in His Passion, than to go out and die for a myth of their own coinage.

The most persuasive proof of all for me was the way in which this risen Christ acted. What literary artist could have thought up such conversations as Christ held when He said Mass for the pilgrims at Emmaus ('Did not our hearts burn within us as He spoke?'), when He convinced the doubting Thomas, and when He commissioned Saint Peter to feed His sheep? In all these incidents one senses unmistakably the personality of Christ. The very detail is evidence of a sane and honest witness. It is even recorded that He ate broiled fish and honeycomb. If an accomplished novelist could not have invented all this, how could a group of lying or demented fishermen have done so?

Further testimony of the divinity of Christ was contained in the Prophecies. It seemed at least a peculiar coincidence that this righteous, wise, and powerful Person, Whose works and teachings themselves suggested that He was more than a man, should have been born, not a Greek or a Roman, but a Jew - a member of that race which had cherished from time immemorial the promise of a Messias. Still more remarkable did it appear that Jesus was conceived in the manner predicted of the Redeemer, born in the prescribed village, and that He suffered in every detail the afflictions and death foretold of the Messias.

The wicked Herod, the holy Simeon, and a handful of others were alone in recognizing the applicability of the Prophecies. The priests and Pharisees utterly misconstrued them, and so likewise did the disciples when they took scandal at His death. Yet the Scriptures were strangely accurate. How eloquently the dolorous Passion had been depicted in the Psalms: 'All they that see Me laugh Me to scorn…They pierced My hands and My feet: they have numbered all My bones. They look and stare upon Me. They part My garments among them, and upon My vesture they cast lots.' The Psalms were filled with similar predictions, and likewise the Book of Jeremias, but none had foreseen so accurately as Isaias, and in such marvelous detail, the birth, life, and death of Our Lord. His writings abounded in startling prognostications: 'Behold a virgin shall conceive,' 'All ye that pass by the way attend and see,' 'There is no beauty in Him nor comeliness.' Was it not possible that in these and other texts, unsurpassed in literary merit, the Holy Ghost had revealed to the ancient seers the life of Him upon Whom they set their hopes? Indeed it seemed likely that Christ was the promised Savior of Whom they had written.

If the Messianic commission of Christ was attested by the Prophecies, the same could equally well be said of the Figures, in which Christ was foreshadowed not in thought only, but in deed. I was deeply impressed by the mysterious symbolism which penetrated the actions of Noe, Isaac, Moses, Jonas, Melchisedech, and the other precursors of Christ. Most apt of all the Figures, to my mind, was the Joseph episode. The most beloved of Jacob's sons, he arouses the jealousy of his brothers. They equivalently put him to death and entomb him in a pit. He rises from the pit and goes before them into a far country. A famine occurs, and the family of Joseph are forced, with the humility of the Prodigal Son, to beg sustenance from him whom they had thought to kill and who now reigns in a land of abundance. On discovering his identity, his brothers fear for their lives. He forgives them, however, and bestows upon them far more than they had dared to ask. Written many centuries before Christ's birth, the story of Joseph was a perfect parable of His death and resurrection.

Indeed, I observed, the entire Old Testament could be read as an allegory of the New. Every sacrifice offered up by the priests and patriarchs under the Old Law was an inadequate effort to accomplish in advance the Paschal sacrifice of Christ, the Lamb of God, Every aspiration to reach the Promised Land was a mystical striving to force the gates of heaven, which were to be opened by Christ. The works and sufferings of the ancient Prophets could not be properly interpreted except in terms of the coming of Him to whom their hearts incessantly went forth, 'the desire of the everlasting hills.'

The Messianic character of Christ's mission appeared not only in these adumbrations of His coming, but equally in the events which filled His life as He walked on earth. His personal eminence as a teacher and as a virtuous man paled to insignificance beside the vicarious role which He played as Victim and Redeemer. He was the second Adam, the progenitor of grace, and was destined, through the fruit of the Tree of the Cross, to repair the damage wrought by the first Adam in partaking of the fruit of the forbidden Tree.

Every incident in the life of Christ was intimately linked with His redemptive mission. Each of His miracles, I perceived, illustrated in a particular way His relation to the entire human species in the order of grace. When He changed the water into wine at Cana, for example, He was not merely performing a courteous service to relieve His host's embarrassment. The wine which He gave to the marriage guests was symbolic of His own Advent when the sources of prophetic wisdom seemed to have run dry. More precisely, that exquisite wine could be interpreted as signifying the Precious Blood which He was to shed for mankind on the altar of the Cross. Again, when Our Lord satisfied the hunger of the five thousand on the mountain, He mystically anticipated the immolation of His Body on Calvary, explicitly declaring at the time, 'The bread that I will give is My flesh.' Similarly, when, after the Resurrection, He brought in the miraculous draft of fishes, He was not merely giving evidence of His divine power or ministering to the material needs of His disciples: He was demonstrating to Peter how great a multitude of souls He would later draw into the Church. The event must be understood in terms of the words, 'Behold, I will make you fishers of men.' The extraordinary strength of the net, which causes the Evangelist to remark that it did not break, is an indication of the indivisibility of the Church.

In the whole of Christ's earthly sojourn, I perceived, there is not one occurrence, however trivial in appearance, which does not take on momentous proportions in terms of His capacity as Messias. Each event tends to confirm and to clarify His cosmic mission. Nothing is left to chance: a dramatic necessity presides over all. In one way or another every circumstance serves to establish more positively Christ's supernatural role as an acceptable oblation for man's sin,

Even his enemies assist Our Lord to become the protagonist of this colossal drama of reparation. The anguish and contumely which they rudely heap upon Him are the predestined lot of one who is to be offered up to the Father as an immaculate victim. The callous indifference of the enrollees who had congregated at Bethlehem excluded Our Lady from the hospitality of the inn, and brought upon Our Lord the humble circumstances of His Birth. The jealousy of Herod made Him an exile from the first moment of His childhood. The hypocrisy of the Pharisees compelled Him to live His public life as an outcast and a wanderer. The avarice of Judas, the worldliness of Pontius Pilate, and the savage inconstancy of the populace prepared His mournful Passion and staged the ignominy of His triumph. The irony of the events is unparalleled: the unconscious adoration of Pilate in crowning Christ's head with thorns and in pinning the royal inscription on the Cross; the raucous crying of the Jews, 'We will have no king but Caesar...His blood be upon us and upon our children.' How terribly history was to fulfill that optative when Jerusalem was sacked and the Temple destroyed! How beautifully history would fufill it yet again when that same blood descended on Christ's kinsmen to redeem them!

Here was a drama more perfect than if it had been humanly planned. Yet the actors were real men, unconscious of their roles. What better proof could there be than this of Christ's supernatural destiny as the Messias of the Jews and the Redeemer of mankind?

Probable indeed it was that Christ was the Divine Being Whom He claimed to be. But probability was not enough. Christ asked us to consent to give up everything and follow Him, and this one could not rationally do on the basis of mere probability. It was necessary to put away every doubt and to commit oneself without reservation. Christ constantly insisted on this act of unqualified faith as an essential step. Even the love of which He spoke was a love founded on faith. Merely sentimental affection was insufficient. That which would be so amply rewarded was not the act of giving a cup of water to the least of men: it was doing so for Christ's sake.

Before I could make this final

act of faith, a full year and a half were to elapse after I had accepted the divinity of Christ as probable. Saint Matthew had not taken five minutes to make a total surrender! Trained as I was in the habits of skepticism, the act of faith was for me a terrible stumbling block. In a sense it seemed to be the surrender of that which I valued more than anything else: intellectual honesty. To make a subjective certainty out of an objective probability was a sacrifice of reason itself. Yet, paradoxically, it was a reasonable sacrifice: for how else could one consent to follow Christ with that singleness of devotion which He, as God, could rightfully exact?

That I did eventually make this act of faith is attributable solely to the grace of God. I could never have done so by my own power. The grace which I received was a tremendous and unmerited privilege, but I sincerely believe that it is one which God, in His faithfulness, will deny to none who earnestly seeks Him in prayer. I found Him to be exactly as Our Lord had described Him - a Father Who would not give a stone in place of bread, or anything but the Holy Ghost to those who asked for It. 'Knock, and it shall be opened unto you'..." (2) ("[Christ] had said that He would not leave us orphans. He had promised to remain in our midst. 'Behold,' He had said, 'I am with you all days, even to the consummation of the world.' Between Him and me two thousand years had run their course. What could bridge that gulf? A Church, if there was one, in which Christ continued visibly His ministry on earth.

Christ had founded such a Church. The Gospel was explicit. Because of your faith, He had said to Saint Peter, I will build My Church on you, and it shall never fail. I commission you to feed My sheep in My absence. For a lifetime only? No, surely for all posterity. To the Apostles He had said, I charge you with teaching all nations, baptizing them in the name of the Father, of the Son, and of the Holy Ghost. I will send the Holy Ghost to guide you, so that your teaching may be infallible. The sins which you forgive on earth will be forgiven in heaven. Continue to enact the sacrifice of My Body and Blood: he who eats My Body and drinks My Blood will be saved.

Christ, then, had not omitted to supply this fundamental need of human nature. When He left us, He appointed representatives to answer men's questions concerning faith and morals and to carry on His sanctifying work on earth, forgiving sins, administering the cleansing waters of Baptism, and distributing the Body which He had immolated for us on the Cross. With His deep understanding of mankind, He had inaugurated visible rites and had chosen to confer invisible graces by means of them. It was thoroughly characteristic of Our Lord to require us to do small physical acts evidencing a little faith and a little humility, and then to recompense them with enormous spiritual rewards. It was part of the logic of the Incarnation that He should give Himself to us in Holy Communion, not only by spiritual indwelling in the soul, but sensibly under the appearances of the bread and wine. With ineffable joy I read that He had actually done so: that the Word had been made flesh not only for Peter and James and John, but for all posterity. One could still adore God visibly in the Eucharist. One could still be united physically to His Sacred Person - both human and divine - more closely (in a sense) than was Our Lady when she had carried the Infant Jesus in her womb...

From my most rudimentary notions of the Church, as I have outlined them here, it will be noted that I originally conceived of it as a visible and organic institution. The Protestant theory which reduced the Church to the status of a merely invisible society, consisting of the community of the elect, had no place in my thought. Such a society would not have answered the fundamental needs of which I have spoken and for which, I knew, Christ had made provision. The Church in which I was interested had certain organic functions, namely, to safeguard the integrity of the faith, to spread the Gospel to all nations, to enunciate the moral law, and to administer the sacraments. None of the Protestant denominations even claimed to exercise all of these functions. They had reduced the number of the sacraments from seven to two, or none. They denied the efficacy of the sacraments, describing them as mere 'signs' of election. None of these various sects, moreover, made any serious pretense to teach with finality the content of Christian dogma or of the moral law, For some of them faith was a word without content; others denied that faith was necessary at all. For many of these reformers Christ had, it seemed, suffered in vain the excruciating torments of his death. No debt of original sin, apparently, was thereby cancelled; no healing graces were thereby conferred.

If there existed any power on earth which could authoritatively declare what the Christian should believe and how he should act, and which could validly administer the sacraments which Christ had instituted, there was no doubt in my mind that it was none of the Protestant sects. There was but one serious contender for the position, and that was the Catholic Church presided over by the Bishop of Rome.

Before admitting the claims of the Catholic Church, I exercised what I now regard as an excess of caution. I examined its credentials with all the diligence of which I was capable. I gave particular attention to the 'notes' of the Church - those qualities which an institution fulfilling the Gospel promises must inevitably have: unicity ('that they may be one'), sanctity ('by this shall all men know that you are my disciples'), catholicity ('teaching all nations'), and apostolicity, which meant in effect historical identity with the original Church. All these qualities appeared to be present in the Roman Catholic communion as in no other.

I then asked myself whether the Catholic Church had exhibited infallibility ('He will teach you all things'). In order to answer this question I immersed myself in the intricacies of ecclesiastical history and delved into the complexities of medieval theology. I studied the decrees of numerous Councils from that of Nicaea to that of the Vatican, comparing them with modern Catholic catechisms. If I could find one inconsistency of dogma, one article of faith which the Church had been compelled to suppress or to retract, or one binding doctrine which was absurd in the light of reason or of natural science, I was resolved to conclude that there existed on earth no visible institution endowed with the powers which Christ had ostensibly vested in the Apostles. I read the most scathing diatribes of Luther and of Calvin: I found them eloquent but intemperate. Luther was illogical and Calvin inhuman. I studied the controversies surrounding Galileo in the Seventeenth Century, and satisfied myself that the Church had in no respect committed herself to geocentrism. I studied the controversies surrounding Darwin in the Nineteenth Century, and was astonished to discover that, even in the time of Saint Thomas Aquinas, the Church had declared it possible that the human body had been fashioned not instantaneously but by a series of creative acts.

The more I examined, the more I was impressed with the consistency and sublimity of Catholic doctrine. Through dark ages and enlightened, through ages of fervor and ages of corruption, under saintly popes and ordinary popes, the treasure of the faith had been preserved intact. Neither the sordid political issues at stake nor the worldly cynicism of meddling statesmen had been able to detract from the majestic decrees of the Council of Trent. Not even the greed and depravity of wicked pontiffs (of whom, be it known, I found but few) had been capable of impairing the integrity of Catholic doctrine. In peril often, the deposit of the faith remained untarnished and entire...

Surely it was a divine protection which had saved the Church through all these centuries from the human failings of princes and prelates alike. Like the boat in which Christ slept, the Church was tossed by tempests, but was always safe. When one asked for an explanation, there could be but one reply: 'Wist ye not that I was with you?'

Finally, I asked myself whether the Church had the appearances of being indefectible ('the gates of hell shall not prevail against it'). For nearly two thousand years, I noted, the voice of Holy Church had rung above the clamor of the nations. No fear of worldly opposition had silenced her, nor any desire to win applause seduced her. With uncompromising logic she continued to set forth the full content of the charter of her liberties. The temporalities of the Church were taken away, her jurisdiction over spiritual matters abridged, and her claims of indirect political power repudiated by jealous secular rulers. In many lands she had been divested of her teaching authority and her ecclesiastical immunities were insolently violated. The great powers of Europe, finding her yoke too harsh, had many of them lapsed into heresy. Yet not one claim did she retract. With patience and confidence amid calamities the successors of Peter continued to admonish a deaf, unreasoning world.

Yet that voice still spoke and by many was heeded. Empires had decayed, kingdoms had been overthrown, philosophies outmoded, and heresies forgotten. The strident voices of dictators rang round the globe. The air was filled with the din of wars and rumors of wars. Yet whither turned the eyes of honest men, dismayed by the spectacle of famine, slaughter, and appalling ruin? To whom did their ears, pierced by the anguished cries of the innocent, strain yet to listen? To the pale occupant of Peter's chair in the beleaguered Vatican.

Thither I turned also, to hear his voice, not with the passing interest of the world, but with that faith which, proving all things, holds fast to that which is good"); "Coming Home," in John A. O'Brien (ed), *The Road to Damascus, Vol. II* (1950) ("From history courses in the Middle Ages and the Renaissance, I learned that there were other outlooks on life than that of twentieth-century materialism. In the past, great numbers of men had attempted to order their actions to the service of Christ, seeking not so much the pleasures of this life as the blessedness of eternity. In the Middle Ages the predominance of this ideal had produced a culture of great richness and beauty. When, in the Renaissance, men focused their interest more on the things of this world, disorder and decay crept into Western civilization. Italian art lost its aura of mystery and budded into gross sensuality. Poetry forsook its lofty themes and became a vehicle for private emotion. Rulers grew cynical about right and wrong and waged wars for sordid gain. The world was launched on a series of struggles that could not be settled on principle, but only repressed by force...

I found it impossible to understand the Renaissance thinkers without delving into medieval philosophy, and to understand anything of this I was forced to go back to Plato and Aristotle...Thanks to the Greek philosophers, I was able to reverse my pre-collegiate position on nearly every fundamental question. I knew now that reality was more than a mere aggregation of material particles, that life was instinct with progress and could not be fully explained in terms of mere chemical formulae; that man, whatever his origin might be, was bound to pursue the good which his reason could discern; and that God, far from being a vague abstraction, was the highest reality, necessary and eternal.

At a certain point, however, both Plato and Aristotle left me unsatisfied...The Greeks...had correctly reasoned to the existence of a Prime Mover to account for motion in the world; but they had left unsolved the problem of being. The Christian philosophers showed that in like manner the existence of finite beings must be explained in terms of the activity of Infinite Being. Thus the Christian doctrine of Creation was more philosophical than Greek necessitarianism...

In studying the history of Christ, I felt increasingly attracted to Him as a Person. Who, so marvellously as He, had united grandeur with simplicity, firmness with tact, insistence with compassion? Who had ever spoken with comparable assurance of the things of God or manifested a like power over the created order?

The Gospels were sufficient evidence of their own substantial accuracy, for no human imagination could have invented this Person whose every word and act was a revelation of the deep things of God. And if the Gospels had but the accuracy of ordinary human documents, nothing was more obvious than that this Christ had worked miracles, risen from the dead, claimed to be the Son of God, and demanded our complete faith and trust. How could I give Him less? He was a teacher without rival, but far more than a teacher. He was also a model in whom shone forth all meekness and majesty, a spotless victim slain for our sins, a victor who could lead us to eternal life. Every reason for loving any creature was, I sensed, even more cogently a reason for loving Him - our Creator and Preserver, our Teacher and Model, our Physician and Deliverer, most beautiful, most wise, most strong. And He was our Lover, who had loved us even to death, that we might have life in closest union with Him, on earth through grace, through glory in the life to come...

Looking upon Christ as the source of true life, I desired with all my heart to approach Him more closely. He must, I knew, have established some bridge by which we could come to Him across the gap of two millennia to hear His authentic teaching and receive His ministrations. It would argue a contradiction in God if He had revealed the truth through Christ and then suffered that Revelation to be mutilated. It would violate the logic of the incarnation for Christ to have left no visible sacraments to serve as channels of His grace. And in fact, as the Gospels themselves clearly testified, Christ had instituted a Church to keep

His doctrine incorrupt and to carry on His work of sanctifying souls. To the Apostles He had given a share in His own infallibility, so that to despise their words was to despise the words of Christ. He had endowed them with power to baptize, to forgive sins, and to celebrate the mysteries of His Body and Blood. Thus He enabled us not only to approach Him with our minds but to unite our very being to His by the partaking of His Body. To reason, this might seem a 'hard saying,' but love, believing all things, was impatient to receive Christ's Sacrament of Love.

Gradually I turned more and more to Catholicism. I began to become aware that the Catholic Church was not a fossil of the Middle Ages, but a very living force in the world today As I read the works of living Catholics – men like Maritain, Martindale, Knox, Watkin, Lunn, and others – I discovered that they had clear and convincing answers to the objections to faith supposedly founded on modern science. I became familiar with the Papal Encyclicals and found that they prescribed masterly remedies for the economic, political, and ideological diseases of our day. I heard a few sermons of Monsignor Sheen, and recognized that his oratorical powers were rooted in a wisdom and a charity not of this world.

I became conscious, too, that there were large numbers of persons about me – if not among my friends at Harvard, at least in Cambridge – who adhered to Catholicism out of something more than inheritance and routine. One weekday morning before daylight I chanced to pass St. Paul's Church. From the door of the lower church there streamed a crowd of men of every station in life who were attending the annual mission. It was obvious that only a vital faith could have drawn them there at that hour against every natural inclination"); *Apologetics and the Biblical Christ* (1963) ("I have discussed two basic methods of using the New Testament to establish the credibility of the Christian faith. One way, which I call the historicist apologetic, seeks to get behind the interpretation of the primitive Church and to show that the facts themselves, objectively considered, admit of no other interpretation than that which Christian dogma proclaims. This approach, in my view, is inadequate for two reasons. In the first place, the external facts, including even the words and works of Jesus, do not prove the truth of the Christian message in such a way that a coldly scientific investigator would feel obliged to assent. Secondly, we do not have any way of getting at the facts except through the testimony of the Church herself. That testimony, which is found chiefly in the Gospels, falls far short of what a scientific historian would consider optimum source material for the events in question.

The other method, which I have advocated as primary, is to treat the New Testament writings as religious testimony - a testimony embracing both factual memories and spiritual insights. The attributes of the testimony are such that the prudent man in search of religious truth can find it satisfying. The intrinsic sublimity of the message, its coherence, and its adaptation to man's religious needs make it eminently worthy of consideration as a revelation from God. The novelty of the message, and the conviction, unanimity, constancy, and spiritual power with which it was heralded, give us every reason to conclude that the apostles were the bearers of revelation. As men most intimately involved in the spiritual events of which they speak, they have an excellent claim to our trust.

The conviction that the Christian message is from God is not something we are forced to accept on blind faith. Our faith is a leap, but not a leap into the dark, It has a solid rational basis, and part of that basis is provided by the New Testament. But the New Testament is not simply the expression of an ancient faith. We read it today with full consciousness that the religion born with the apostles still retains its vitality. The witness of the primitive Church is enhanced by the witness of the Church today. The arguments from history thus ultimately rejoin the arguments based on the living reality of the Church: its marvelous propagation, its stability through the centuries, and its undying fruitfulness in all good works. In the last analysis, as Fr. Levie has observed, there are not many signs of credibility, but only one: the whole Christ in His Church. In apologetics these two together, Christ and His Church, should be viewed as a single sign, just as in dogmatic theology they are seen to be two facets of a single mystery"); *A Revelation and the Quest for Unity* (1968); *Models of the Church* (1974); *Models of Revelation* (1983); *The Catholicity of the Church* (1985); *The Craft of Theology: From Symbol to System* (1992); "Historians and the Reality of Christ," *First Things*, December 1992; *The Assurance of Things Hoped For: A Theology of Christian Faith* (1994); "The Challenge of the Catechism," *First Things*, January 1995; *The Priestly Office: A Theological Reflection* (1997); "The Way We Worship," *First Things*, March 1998; *The Splendor of Faith: The Theological Vision of Pope John Paul II* (1999); *The New World of Faith* (2000); "Can Philosophy Be Christian?" *First Things*, April 2000; "Religious Freedom: Innovation and Development," *First Things*, December 2001; *John Henry Newman* (2002); "The Population of Hell," *First Things*, May 2003; "True and False Reform," *First Things*, August/September 2003; *EWTN Audio Library, The Journey Home* (12 January 2004); *A History of Apologetics* (2005); "Mere Apologetics," *First Things*, June/July 2005; "The Covenant With

Israel," *First Things*, November 2005; "From Ratzinger to Benedict," *First Things*, February 2006; "The Orthodox Imperative," *First Things*, August/September 2006; *Magisterium: Teacher and Guardian of the Faith* (2007); "God and Evolution," *First Things*, October 2007; "Saving Ecumenism From Itself," *First Things,* December 2007; *Church and Society* (2008); "Who Can Be Saved?" *First Things*, February 2008; "The Freedom of Theology," *First Things*, May 2008; Robert Royal, "Avery Dulles's Long Road to Rome," *Crisis Magazine*, July-August 2001; Thomas G. Guarino, "Why Avery Dulles Matters," *First Things*, May 2009; Patrick W. Carey, *Avery Cardinal Dulles, SJ: A Model Theologian, 1918-2008* (2010); George William Rutler, *Cloud of Witnesses: Dead People I Knew When They Were Alive* (2010); Lorene Hanley Duquin, A Century of Catholic Converts (2003), p.117; *averydulles.com* (full bibliography).

Dunaway, (Dorothy) Faye – actress; b. 14 January 1941, Bascom, Florida; c. 27 December 1996; born on a farm; father was John MacDowell Dunaway, Jr., a career non-commissioned officer in the United States Army; her mother a housewife; attended the University of Florida, Florida State University, and Boston University; converted to the Catholic faith when in Boston; graduated from the University of Florida in theater; joined the American National Theater and Academy in 1962; appeared on Broadway in 1962 as the daughter of Sir Thomas More in *A Man for All Seasons*; starred opposite Warren Beatty in *Bonnie and Clyde* in 1967 and gained an Oscar nomination; also starred opposite Steve McQueen in *The Thomas Crown Affair* in 1968; starred in several major films in the 1970s, including *Chinatown* (1974), *Three Days of the Condor* (1975), and *Network* (1976) (won the Academy Award for Best Actress in the latter); continued to appear in film and television roles; married twice (1974-1979 to Peter Wolfe, the rock singer; 1984-1987 to Terry O'Neill, a British photographer); one adopted child; see *Looking for Gatsby: My Life* (1995) (with Betsy Sharkey).

Durant, W. Clark - educator, lawyer, and politician; b. 13 May 1949, Detroit, Michigan; c. 2006; educated at Tulane University, New Orleans, Louisiana (graduated in 1971 with an Economics major); reservist in the U.S. Army; JD from Notre Dame Law School in 1976; admitted to the Michigan bar in 1976; spent six years defending low income people in criminal and civil matters; worked as assistant to the president at Hillsdale College, Michigan, then as Vice-President in 1972-1973; appointed in 1983 by the Secretary of Transportation as the bankruptcy trustee for the Ann Arbor Railroad and turned the railroad into a profitable private-sector enterprise; in 1984 nominated by President Reagan to the board of the Legal Services Corporation (served as chair 1984-1988); represented Michigan on the 1984 Republican National Committee Platform Committee where he helped draft the party platform on which President Reagan ran and won re-election; served as one of four national co-chairs of Jack Kemp's presidential campaign; in 1990 ran in the Republican primary for the U.S. Senate, but lost to Bill Schuette; in 1991 a co-founder of the Cornerstone Schools (Michigan) with Adam Cardinal Maida, setting up low cost, high performing independent and charter schools in Detroit as alternatives to the public system (Chairman of the Board 1991-2003 and CEO 2003-2009); elected to the State Board of Education in Michigan in 1994 (president until resigning in 1999); member of several education boards and organizations in Michigan; director of an investment firm 1997-2001; married with four children; Republican Party candidate for the U.S. Senate in 2012; converted to the Catholic faith from Episcopalianism.

Dutton, Ira Barnes ("Brother Joseph") – lay brother; b. 27 April 1843, Stowe, Lamoille County, Vermont; c. 27 April 1883 (immediately afterwards changed his name to Joseph, in honor of the saint he had grown to love; his mother, with whom he lost touch for a few years, became a Catholic in 1885); d. 26 March 1931, Honolulu, Hawaii; spent his youth in Janesville, Wisconsin; brought up as an Episcopalian; captain in the Union Army during the Civil War; when he was engaged in many battles; after the war ended, he volunteered to find the dead, scattered on various battlefields; then he brought them to a common burial site which eventually became a national cemetery; after the war, the pressures of a failed business and his broken marriage caused him to drink heavily; eventually on 4 July 1876, he realized that he needed God's help and made and kept a vow never to touch a drop of whisky again; he sought atonement for his sins and became a Catholic; determined to spend the rest of his life in penance for past wrongs; later he entered the Trappist Monastery of Our Lady of Gethsemane in Kentucky, but found that monasticism was not his true vocation and so, with the blessing of the abbot, he left the monastery; he wanted a life of action rather than one of contemplation; in 1886 he learned that Father Damien (now Saint Damien) at the Molokai leper colony needed help with the lepers; gave away all his possessions and volunteered to help; worked with Father Damien for two years and eight months before Father Damien died; after that he continued the work; he served there for more than forty years and never contracted leprosy; when commenting on his life he said the graph of his life represented "forty-five years down and forty-five years up"; met Robert Louis Stevenson, who visited the colony and later wrote defending Father Damien against attacks on him by a Protestant clergyman; eventually nuns came headed by St. Marianne Cope (1838-1918); buried next to Father Damien in St. Philomena Catholic Church Cemetery, Kalaupapa, Kalawao County, Molokai, Hawaii; see Charles Dutton, *Samaritans of Molokai* (1932); Katherine Burton, *In No Strange Land: Some American Catholic Converts* (1942), p.125 ("[O]n 4 July 1876, he made his own declaration of independence: he would drink no more from that day on. And he kept his word…Aghast, one of his friends reported that Ira was reading a Catholic catechism!

No doubt he found the catechism among the books left in his room by his landlady, Mrs. Sullivan, who kept the hotel where he lived in Memphis, and who used to put literature of a pious kind in all her lodgers' rooms. At all events, Ira Dutton was received into the Catholic Church in 1883, in the fortieth year of his life. He paid up all his bills before he entered, and immediately after he changed his name to Joseph in honor of the Saint whom he had grown to love.

His whole life was changed now. 'I had determined' he wrote later, 'to spend the remainder of my life in penance for past wrongs, to find some work where I could be helpful and do my best for all'"); Howard E. Crouch, *Two Josephs on Molokai: Damien and Dutton* (1998); Howard E. Crouch, *Brother Dutton of Molokai* (2000); John Tayman, *The Colony* (2006); Rev. George W. Rutler, "Glorious Janitor: The Life of Brother Joseph," *Crisis*, 14 November 2012.

Duval, Enna – see under Brewster, Anne Hampton.

Dwight, Thomas – anatomist; b. 1843, Boston, Massachusetts; c. 1856 (received with his mother); d. 8 September 1911, Nahant, Massachusetts; son of Thomas Dwight and Mary Collins Warren; graduated from Harvard Medical School in 1867; appointed in 1872 instructor in comparative anatomy at Harvard; appointed Parkman Professor of Anatomy in 1883; many articles in scientific journals; international reputation as an anatomist; critic of Darwinism; married to Sarah C. Isiagi (eight children of the marriage); see *Frozen Sections of a Child* (1872); *A Clinical Atlas of Variations of the Bones of the Hands and Feet* (1907); *Thoughts of a Catholic Anatomist* (1911) (work of apologetics) ("Religion, from the verb *religio* is, according to St. Augustine, the link that binds man to God. This strikes one at first as rhetorical rather than exact, but it will bear examination. The more one thinks of it the more satisfactory it becomes. This implies first the existence of God with all His infinite attributes. It implies further that man is conscious of having immortality and freewill; that in some way and to some extent he has been brought into relation with God's plans, and that he acknowledges God's right to his worship and obedience. Now the acceptance of these truths from a purely natural standpoint constitutes what may be called natural religion, but the embracing of revealed mysteries comes by faith, springing from a supernatural gift of God. ..

So much for what religion is; let us now consider more particularly what religion teaches that concerns science. We believe in God, infinite, absolutely perfect in His wisdom, His mercy and His justice. We know therefore that when He made man it was for an end worthy of Himself, far transcending human understanding. The catechism tells us that it was to love and serve Him in this life and to be happy with him forever in the next. Let us think for a moment what this implies. Who makes this offer? God Himself. This happiness, then, is altogether supernatural. Heaven is not what so many seem to think it: a kind of glorified picnic with pleasing music and the society of old friends. If it may be said without offence this seems to be the idea of eternal blessedness among non-Catholics. The great defect in this view, apart from its materialistic nature, is that of omission. Nothing is said of God; and yet the beatific vision of God imparting knowledge and love is alone the essential happiness of heaven. Everything there is supernatural. The risen body has new powers which presumably we never dreamed of. 'Eye hath not seen, ear hath not heard, nor hath it entered into the heart of man what joys God has prepared for those that love Him but far above all, as Catholic theologians tell us, this knowledge and love of God bring about a union with Him by which the soul without losing its identity glows in the immensity of God as a coal glows in the fire. And of this there shall be no end. For this destiny God created man. So much we know now, but Infinity being unfathomable, the very highest intelligences can never reach to the depths of God's reasons for doing it. They may continually see new and more stupendous reasons of goodness and wisdom for the act, but to the deepest depth they can never come.

Needless to argue that man thus made, absolutely dependent on God, is not his own master, but God's servant. He has been endowed with reason and the terrible responsibility of free-will. Moreover, he is immortal. Never shall the time come when he shall cease to be. He shall outlive time itself in the, to us, incomprehensible present of eternity. He is here on earth on trial. So far as we know, the earth and all physical creation exists that this trial may take place. At least we know that this trial involving the eternity of one single soul is of infinitely greater importance than all non-rational creation...What is now insisted upon is this: that God having appointed this probation for man, the disposition of the universe, the structure of nebulae and suns and systems of senseless matter, though expressed in terms implying age, size, weight, distance, speed beyond imagination, is of absolutely secondary importance.

The Catholic Church teaches that the first man was created in a condition distinctly higher than our present one. His reason held his lower nature in full subjection and death, as we now know it, was not to close his life, but, having stood the test, he was to enter into heaven without separation of soul and body. Now all this is *of faith.* That is to say that Catholics are bound to believe it. It is the reverse of my intention to minimize what to outsiders may seem the burdens laid upon us. When Adam fell death was in store as a punishment for him and his race, for him because he fully deserved it, for his race because the supernatural condition of the first man was no right, but a gratuitous gift to which the descendants have no claim. Moreover, the consequences of that sin left man's descendants with a less clear vision of the higher things and with lower tendencies and passions no longer held in subjection. All this too is *of faith.*

We further believe that God in His mercy has given man a revelation, has redeemed him, and has established the Church, unerring in faith and morals, to be his guide...How great is the need of the Church is shown by the religious condition throughout the world, by all the forms of paganism, by the confusion of the various sects of so-called Christianity, and by absolute atheism. If things are as they are when there is a Church, what would they be had we been left to ourselves?

Here then is the Catholic view: Man, God's creature, not a little higher than the beast, but a little lower than the angels, now fallen from his higher estate is (or should be) in fear and trembling working out his salvation, aspiring to an eternity of endless glory with God, supported on his way by revelation and guided by the Church...

[T]he crucial point is this, that if we believe in God our religion must be supernatural throughout. This life and this world are but episodes in a tremendous and supernatural drama. The eternal future of every individual man is at stake, of man, who contemptible as he may appear to himself and his neighbors, is of enough importance to draw the Son of God from heaven to redeem him by death. The future of the angels has been decided; but those of them who stood and those who fell are permitted to take an active part in man's struggle. The solar system, nay the universe, is to pass away to give place to 'a new Heaven and a new earth.' These are things that we believe; let us not make the mistake of being ashamed to acknowledge them. In fact they are the only things that matter. And finally all the end results are as much above our conception in our present state as mathematics would be were there, not only a fourth, but an indefinitely larger number of dimensions in space. Truly this seems fantastic and extraordinary. The supernatural is indeed overwhelming! Yet all this follows logically from accepting the existence of God") *Catholic Encyclopedia.*

Eccleston, Samuel, PSS – bishop; b. 27 June 1801, Chestertown, Maryland; c. 1818 (his mother converted on her second marriage); d. 22 April 1851, Georgetown, Washington D.C.; his grandfather, John Eccleston, was from Preston in north west England, and came to the United States in the middle of the 18th century; his father was an Episcopalian; after his death his mother married a Catholic who brought to him Catholic influences; he was sent to St. Mary's College, Baltimore, where he was converted; in 1819 he entered St. Mary's Seminary; ordained to the priesthood 24 April 1825; entered the Society of Saint-Sulpice, more commonly known as the Sulpicians, and was sent to continue his studies at the Grand Seminary of Saint-Sulpice in Issy-les-Moulineaux, France; visited England and Ireland; returned to Baltimore in 1827, eventually becoming president of St. Mary's College; in 1834 he was consecrated coadjutor bishop with the right of succession for Baltimore; in 1834 he succeeded to the metropolitan see, being the fifth Archbishop of Baltimore; the youngest cleric to become Archbishop of Baltimore in the history of the archdiocese; he was the first convert in the American Catholic hierarchy; in office until his death; built many churches including the cathedral (towards which he contributed largely of his own means); brought in several religious orders, notably in 1841 the Redemptorists from Austria (to provide for German Catholics), in 1846 the Brothers of the Christian Schools (to establish a school), and the Brothers of St. Patrick (to take charge of a manual labor school); see Columba E. Halsey, "The Life of Samuel Eccleston, Fifth Archbishop of Baltimore, 1801-1851," *Records of the American Catholic Historical Society of Philadelphia* (1965), p.69; *Catholic Encyclopedia*; *ANB* ("Eccleston proved sympathetic and responsive to the needs of the increasing number of immigrants who were transforming the Church over which he presided. He marched in their parades and presided at the inaugurations of organizations designed to meet their spiritual, material, and psychic needs. He helped create the institutions providing such basic services as education, health care, and poor relief and recruited the personnel needed to conduct them efficiently. Under him the parochial school system of the archdiocese was established, as were such enterprises of the immigrant church as mutual-aid societies, pious associations, parish missions, and a militant press. Eccleston persuaded the Redemptorist order to make Baltimore its headquarters and entrusted the German parishes of the archdiocese to them. These represented the beginnings of the national, as distinct from territorial, parishes in the oldest see").

Eden, Dawn (full name Dawn Eden Goldstein) – author and journalist; b. 3 September 1968; c. 2006; born into a Reform Jewish family, older sister a rabbi; her parents divorced when she was young and she was raised by her mother, but became agnostic; suffered sexual abuse when young; from 1985 she wrote on rock music and history; became a "committed Christian" and left the field of rock journalism; worked as a copy editor at the *New York Post* 2002-2005; forced to leave the *Post* after she made edits to a story about in vitro fertilization, thereby revealing her pro-life sympathies; in 2005 she became associate news editor of the newly launched national edition of the *New York Daily News*; later became deputy news editor for the paper's new weekly regional editions, edited some regular features; her conversion to the Catholic faith was influenced by G. K. Chesterton; she has appeared on many platforms to discuss her book *The Thrill of the Chaste*, addressing society's misconception of sex as a consumer item instead of as a marital act with deep meaning; with the help of books like Bishop Fulton J. Sheen's *Three to Get Married*, she realized that chastity is more than mere abstinence, but is about learning to love fully and appropriately; successfully treated for thyroid cancer in 2008; in 2010 she received an MA in Theology from the Dominican House of Studies on the theology of the body; see *The Thrill of the Chaste: Finding Fulfillment While Keeping Your Clothes On* (2006); *My Peace I Give You: Healing Sexual Wounds with the Help of the Saints* (2012); *EWTN Audio Library, The Journey Home* (12 November 2012) ("I had no idea that Chesterton was this great convert to the Catholic faith from Anglicanism, who himself had gone through a dark night of near atheism. I'd no idea that he was the man whom C. S. Lewis credits with converting him from atheism, and so I picked up this book [*The Man Who Was Thursday*] and started reading it and…I started to get an impression of Christianity, because I realized as I was reading it that there was this whole sub-text of the journey towards Christ, seeking his face. And I realized that according to Chesterton, Christian faith was a rebellion. Chesterton in the book has this character who considers himself a poet of anarchy and he contrasts this with a poet who is a poet of law and order. And I myself thought that in order to be creative as an individual I had to be against whatever Christians were for. But Chesterton presented the true rebel as the one who is rebelling for truth, for beauty, for law and order, against a world that has gone into darkness. And that intrigued me, particularly one line that Christ has in the voice of the poet of law and order. He is arguing with the anarchist poet about what constitutes true poetry and he says the most poetical thing in the world is not being sick. And I read that and I was very touched by that, because I longed for that kind of poetry, the poetry of not being sick. It awoke this longing in me to have my life ordered from the top down. And so I couldn't really believe that there were other Christians like Chesterton. I still thought that Christians were this amorphous, conformist, moral majority mass. And I still thought that the only way I could be individual and have my own identity, which I desperately wanted, was to be not Christian. But I was curious enough to read more Chesterton and over the course of four years I was reading a lot of Chesterton…").

Elder, Susan Blanchard – writer; 19 April 1835, Fort Jessup, Sabine Parish, Louisiana; c. 1855; d. 3 November 1923, Cincinnati, Ohio; daughter of Albert Gallatin Blanchard (1808-1891), an officer in the U.S. and later the Confederate army; her mother Susan Thompson died when she was a child; brought up by relatives; educated in a Catholic convent school; at the age of sixteen began writing for the press under the name of "Hermine"; in 1855 she married Charles D. Elder (1822-1890), the brother of William H. Elder, Catholic archbishop of Cincinnati (one child of the marriage, Mary Eleonora (b. 1868)); always devoted to the southern cause; moved to Selma, Alabama during the Civil War and turned their home into a Confederate hospital; wrote the war song *The Confederate Flag*; moved to New Orleans and taught mathematics and natural science in schools; wrote about the family, the Church and the south; after the death of her husband lived with her daughter Mrs. E. D. Seghers in Cincinnati; see *James the Second* (1874); *Savonarola* (1875); *Ellen Fitzgerald, A Southern Tale* (1876); *The Leos of the Papacy* (1879); *Character Glimpses of the Most Reverend William Henry Elder, D.D.* (1911); *Elder Flowers* (1912) (poetry); *The Life of Abbé Adrien Rouquette* (1913); *A Mosaic in Blue and Gray* (1914); Mary Lee Cooke, *Southern Women, Southern Voices: Civil War Songs by Southern Women* (2007); *ANB*.

Eliot, Ray ("Mr. Illini") (born Raymond Eliot Nusspickel) – football coach; b. 13 June 1905, Brighton, Massachusetts; c. 1929; d. 24 February 1980, Urbana, Illinois; educated at University of Illinois at Urbana-Champaign (played as a guard on the football team); head football coach Illinois College 1933-1936 (also head baseball coach there 1933-1937); head football coach University of Illinois at Urbana-Champaign 1942-1959; his teams won three Big Ten Conferences (1946, 1951, and 1953) and two Rose Bowls (1947 and 1952); later associate athletic director and interim athletic director for the university to which he gave great loyal service; president of American Football Coaches Association 1955; see Doug Cartland, *Ray Eliot: The Spirit and Legend of Mr. Illini* (1995).

Ellet, Elizabeth Fries (*née* Lummis) - writer, historian and poet; b. October 1812 or 1818, Sodus Point, New York; d. 3 June 1877, New York City; father was William Nixon Lummis (1775-1833), a prominent doctor; her mother was Sarah Maxwell (1780-1849), daughter of John Maxwell, the American Revolutionary War captain; educated under the direction of an English Quaker; Episcopalian for most of her life; began by publishing poetry and translations of European literature; married William Henry Ellet (1806-1859), chemistry professor (no children of the marriage); moved to South Carolina where her husband taught; moved back to New York to be again part of literary society; became involved in a public scandal involving Edgar Allan Poe and Frances Sargent Osgood, concerning money and flirtatious letters; wrote a series of travel books; her most original contribution was to be the first person to give an account of the American Revolutionary War based on the lives of women (wrote of the women as giving "nurture in the domestic sanctuary of that love of civil liberty which afterwards kindled into a flame and shed light on the world"); wrote many articles on a wide range of subjects; much charitable work; became a Catholic late in life; buried beside her husband at Green-Wood Cemetery, Brooklyn; see *Poems, Translated and Original* (1835); *The Characters of Schiller* (1839); *Rambles about the Country* (1840); *Scenes in the Life of Joanna of Sicily* (1840) (novel); *The Women of the American Revolution*, 3 Vols. (1848-1850); *Evenings at Woodlawn* (1849); *Family Pictures from the Bible* (1849); *Domestic History of the American Revolution* (1850); *Novelettes of the Musicians* (1851); *Watching Spirits: Pioneer Women of the West* (1852); *Summer Rambles in the West* (1853); *The Practical Housekeeper* (1857); *Women Artists in All Ages and Countries* (1859); *The Queens of American Society* (1867); *Court Circles of the Republic*

(1869); *ANB* ("Ellet's historical scholarship remains valuable for its exemplification of the efforts of a generation of American women intellectuals to participate in civic life while sharply distinguishing women's roles from men's, a set of ideals that became known as 'Republican motherhood'... Ellet argued that the republic accorded women all the power they needed in indirect and private forms appropriate to their nature").

Elmsley, John - naval officer, businessman and philanthropist; b. 19 May 1801, Elmsley House, York, Toronto, Upper Canada; c. 1833; d. 8 May 1863, Toronto; ancestors from Scotland, but moved to England, then Canada; father was John Elmsley (1762-1805), born in England, but Chief Justice of Upper Canada and afterwards of Lower Canada, and President of the Executive Council; brought up as an Anglican; after his father's death his mother, Mary, *née* Hallowell, sent him to England; he entered the Royal Navy there and became a Lieutenant, but left in 1824; returned to Canada and became a gentleman farmer on his property at York; great wealth and influence; became a member of the Executive Council in 1830 and a member of the Legislative Council in 1831; involved in banking and various other businesses, including trading by sea; in 1831 he married Charlotte Sherwood, a Catholic, daughter of Levius Peters Sherwood (1777-1850), a judge; before his conversion he was "a staunch Protestant" and an active and zealous Anglican, so his conversion to the Catholic Church caused a great stir; his conversion was very much influenced by the issue of the Real Presence; at the time of his conversion the fortunes of the Catholic Church at York were at a low ebb; he became one of the bishop's principal advisers; active for the Crown against the 1837 rebellion, when he commanded a boat; from about 1852 he acted as bishop's secretary; gave immense financial support to the Catholic Church and Catholic education and causes, e.g., the effects of the Irish famine; father of seven sons and three daughters; his body buried in St. Michael's Cathedral, Toronto; his heart deposited in the west wall of St Basil's Church, Toronto; see Rev. Brother Alfred Dooner, FSC, LLD, "The Honorable John Elmsley: Legislative and Executive Councillor of Upper Canada (1801-1863)," *Canadian Catholic Historical Association* (1936-1937), p.47 ("His sudden and unexpected conversion was brought about by the reading of a Catholic pamphlet entitled, *Bishop of Strasburg's Observations on the Sixth Chapter of St. John's Gospel*, which most likely he had picked up on a visit to London in 1830. The pamphlet was a London publication and was unknown in this country until circulated by John Elmsley himself. It is a strong argument in favour of the Catholic doctrine of transubstantiation and the real presence of the body and blood of Christ in the Blessed Eucharist, doctrines which the Church of England denied. Apparently a comparative study of the teachings of the Church of England and of the Catholic Church on the Real Presence must have interested Elmsley for some time, for when writing Archdeacon Strachan regarding the pamphlet of the Bishop of Strasburg, he says, 'I have perused, I believe, every work to be found in the catalogue on this subject (the Blessed Eucharist) before I fell in with this.' He evidently had been inquiring for some time and looking for the truth. Having been once convinced of the truth of the Catholic teaching, he moved rapidly towards Mother Church. In the summer of 1833, he wrote to Bishop Macdonell, the Catholic Bishop of Kingston who was in York at the time...This letter ran as follows: 'It is now with the most hearty joy and satisfaction that I acquaint your Lordship of my intention of returning to the bosom of the Catholic Church from which my forefathers went forth in an evil hour and I take this opportunity of begging your Lordship to receive me, a strayed sheep, into the one fold of the one Shepherd, Christ Jesus...

I beg of your Lordship to maintain secrecy with respect to this, my purpose,. because my old mother, who, in the common course of nature cannot long remain in this world, would be most terribly shocked to learn that I had embraced a religion against which she has ever entertained the most violent prejudices.'

...Elmsley had five thousand copies of the *Bishop of Strasburg's Observations on the Sixth Chapter of St. John's Gospel* printed at his own expense and distributed and broadcast throughout the Province of Upper Canada"); *DCB*.

Emery, Susan Lyman – author; b. 1846, Dorchester, Boston, Massachusetts; c. 1874 (received in Boston); d. 1923; from a Yankee family and conservative Protestant background; parents were both Episcopalians and she was brought up according to this; grew more and more "High Church" and held strongly to the Three Branch Theory; began editing a religious journal; started to have great religious doubts and appealed to the Blessed Virgin Mary for help; after becoming a Catholic she made a secret vow of virginity, and afterwards dressed always in black; faced great hostility from her family; did much editorial work; her own poems, stories, and non-fiction were published in many journals; see *The Inner Life of the Soul: Short Spiritual Messages for the Liturgical Year* (1903); Catholic Stronghold (1910); essay in Georgina Pell Curtis, *Some Roads to Rome in America* (1909), p.155 ("The roads that lead souls into the Catholic Church are many and various. Rome rhymes with home, and indeed all roads lead there...

There was, in our house, a volume of sermons by the great Irish Dominican, Father Thomas Burke, belonging to one of those Irish maidens who have done so much towards spreading the Faith in New England. I opened the book. Whether the day was the exact feast of the Epiphany, or whether it was in the Octave or season, I do not now recall; but, in that time of illumination of the Gentiles, I looked down upon the page, and distinctly before me lay the words that I had read and heard unnumbered times before, (I tell it as I recall it after many years are fled), Our Divine Lord's own words spoken to His chosen and great Apostle: 'Thou art Peter; and upon this rock I will build My Church, and the gates of hell shall not prevail against it. And I will give to thee the keys of the kingdom of heaven. And whatsoever thou shalt bind upon earth, it shall he bound also in heaven: and whatsoever thou shalt loose on earth, it shall he loosed also in heaven.'

As I say, I had read and heard these words unnumbered times already, in my own quiet room, and at family prayers, and in church. I had never once realized, however, that the promise to St. Peter in St. Matthew's Gospel, xvi, 18, 19, was far and away in importance beyond that given to all the Apostles in St. John's Gospel, xx, 22, 23: 'Receive ye the Holy Ghost. Whose sins you shall forgive, they are forgiven them; and whose sins you shall retain, they are retained.' To-day, however, I saw printed on the same page of Father Burke's sermon containing the promise to Peter, these words from St. Ambrose: 'Show me Peter, and I will show you the Church.'

And then my cry for help to the Blessed Virgin was manifestly answered; for then I knew, and then I willed God's will. As clearly as I see now before me the page on which I write - as absolutely as I know that two and two make four - I saw and I knew that the Church of which the Pope, the successor of Peter, was the visible head, was the one true Church of God; I saw that therein Peter had the supreme prerogative; and that where he was, my place was. No fear came over me, either to make me take the step, or not to take it, into that Church that loomed magnificently now before my gaze. I saw the truth, and the truth had made me free").

Emmet, Thomas Addis -surgeon and gynecologist; b. 29 May 1828, Charlottesville, Virginia; c. 1864; d. 1 March 1919, New York City; of Irish extraction; father a professor of natural history at the University of Virginia and nominally Episcopalian; grandmother, a Puritan, gave him a knowledge of the Bible; several founders of the republic were friends of his father, e.g., Thomas Jefferson, James Madison and James Monroe, and he was greatly influenced by accounts of them; studied at Jefferson Medical College (MD in 1850); in 1854 he married Catherine Rebecca Duncan, a Catholic (six children of the marriage); joined and worked closely with the pioneer gynecologist James Marion Sims (1813-1883) at the newly founded Woman's Hospital of New York 1855-1861; surgeon in chief there 1861-1872 and visiting surgeon until he retired in 1900; his main work was repair of vesico-vaginal fistulae, an abnormal passage between the bladder and the vagina; also devised equipment and procedures for the repair of several other gynecological disorders; also expert on early American history (put together a large collection of original documents); he converted to Catholicism and associated himself with the cause of Ireland, arguing for Irish "Home Rule"; president of the Irish National Federation of America 1892-1901; received the *Laetare* Medal of the University of Notre Dame (1899); see *Vesico Vaginal Fistula* (1868); *The Principles and Practice of Gynecology* (1879); *Ireland under English Rule; or, A Plea for the Plaintiff* , 2 Vols. (1903; 2nd edition 1909); *Incidents in My Life: Professional, Literary, Social, with Services in the Cause of Ireland* (1911) ("I am naturally of a religious turn of mind, but beyond the existence of a sincere belief in God the Creator, my faith had been at a standstill since I was a child...After reaching manhood, I read everything I could obtain having any bearing on the subject, and weighed without prejudice the belief of the different Christian bodies yet I could reach but one logical conclusion, and this was accomplished, notwithstanding all the unfavorable impressions from prejudice I had received in early life. I was forced to accept the belief that if there was any foundation whatever for Christianity, the authority could only rest with the teaching of the Catholic Church, as the representative on earth of our Lord Jesus. The Catholic Church had its origin from the days of the Apostles, if Christianity ever had any existence, and it has remained unchanged except in discipline and development of doctrine. Nothing that our Lord ever taught, or that was ever taught with authority in His name by His disciples and their successors, could ever need to be changed or reformed. This being the truth I was forced to believe, whatever may be said or claimed to the contrary. The Catholic Church is certainly the only Christian body having the power to enforce its authority and the only one daring to do so as the representative of God, in matters of faith, and to exact obedience without question. It cannot be supposed that our Lord failed in His promise to be with a representative power on earth, "until the end of time," nor that His influence could ever lead to false teaching, needing at any time to be reformed. If this were possible there can exist no logical proof, nor a possibility even, for the existence of Christianity. This hypothesis would be unanswerable were it possible to divest human judgment of the inherited blind and ignorant prejudice which exists on the subject. Of course this argument may be denied and with many this will be considered sufficient to disprove the accuracy of my statement, but it cannot be logically disproved, if divested of sophistry and false premises. Errors in discipline may well occur in relation to God's human agency on earth, but the same delegated power would necessarily provide for the correction of these in due time by those in authority, as we know has been going on all the time from the beginning.

If, under the circumstances, I could think a reformation had been at any time necessary, I would embrace the Jewish faith. Our Lord was a professed Jew until His death, when Christianity had its beginning with the first teaching of the Apostles, with St. Peter as the Rock, the Foundation of the Church, and the first Pope, and all who were with him were inspired for their work, and commissioned to transmit their power by Apostolic Succession. By the so-called reformers there has been given a human interpretation to the essential mysteries of the Church, and it seems incredible to one not in sympathy that any individual could read the Bible and be so blind as not to see that their teaching is not in accord with that of our Saviour, nor with that of His successors. As regards Transubstantiation in particular, something beyond the scope of human judgment to understand, we can but accept it literally as our Lord gave it; for, notwithstanding the populace complained it was a hard saying, it is the only instance where He refused to give any other explanation. Yet this has been so far reformed that only the second or accidental clause has been accepted nominally, where an act of simple remembrance has been substituted for a mystery of the faith. It is an illogical feature of the so-called reformers that an act should be performed in remembrance or commemoration of Transubstantiation, the mystic essence of our Lord's Supper, and at the same time deny the essential! Without Transubstantiation, the so-called Act of Remembrance becomes one without purpose, if judged in accord with our Lord's teaching.

God in His infinite power has allowed, as with the so-called Reformation, these great sloughs to be cast off from the body of the Church, from time to time, possibly to teach man the weakness of human faith, and the Church has always been the stronger afterwards.

History repeats itself, but the teaching is soon forgotten. The Arians were once numerous and formed a large portion of those who claimed to have been part of the Catholic Church. Yet, as the foundation of their belief rested no longer on a rock, they, as with other schismatics, were gradually brought back, and to-day there does not exist a vestige of their former power or influence.

Has not disintegration already begun in the hundreds of Protestant sects, who have each for themselves interpreted what constituted Christianity, and I may add, Quo warranto? Does not their widely different interpretation of itself show an absence of power and authority? The position would be untenable to claim that all, or even one possesses the truth. Which one among them has the authority to decide?

I can give the experience of an old man and state that when I was a boy there were very few Protestants who did not at least outwardly conform by regular attendance at some church, while the great majority of both men and women were sincere and conscientious in living up to what they believed. To-day the large majority of those who are nominally Protestants, in contradistinction to the teachings of the Catholic Church, are totally indifferent to all religious belief. Others render the service in the most perfunctory manner, as if the faith was not in them, and all are ignorant that the Catholic Church claims to hold the proof that the 'Reformation' was brought about more through human interests, than from supposed need or desire for spiritual change.

It is natural that I should wish all held in common with me the faith of the Catholic Church, but I have lived so much of my life with Protestants, so many of whom were bettered by their faith, that for the weal of the country I would rather see the indifferent ones all conscientious Protestants, living up to their belief, than to drift aimlessly through life as a derelict vessel at sea, with no master spirit to guide it. Without a strong religious faith no man is safe, nor can he resist temptation, and in time he must fall - consequently: every man to-day has his price, but has not yet been tempted. As a rule, the most ignorant Catholic has been taught the principles of the faith, and while many fall, from the weakness of human nature, the fall is entirely through the fault of the individual. The Catholic Church furnishes a perfect safeguard against mortal sin, and just in proportion as her precepts are made use of, which is something those outside of its fold cannot comprehend. But the mass of Protestants have no belief in common, and use the term Protestant as if it were an indication of their faith, while to one who is not a Protestant, it is indicative of nothing more than blind and ignorant hatred or opposition to the Catholic Church, and grounded on charges which have time and again been shown to be erroneous, and on proof which proves satisfactory to every one who seeks for the truth. To me, as a Catholic, it is no surprise that the world is so corrupt to-day, but a surprise it is that it is not worse. It shows that the grace of God is still with them from the teaching of the Catholic Church, and some day it will be the means by which their descendants, one and all, will leave the divergent course which others prepared in accord with their personal interests and surroundings, over three hundred years ago, and which are not tangible to-day. This influence will eventually bring all back to the Catholic Church, the only one of which we have any proof that it was God's work, under the New Dispensation.

Let the reader, if possible, divest the so-called Reformation of all personality and treat it as an abstract question, so that I may present the matter from another standpoint. From this point my first proposition will be that it is not possible for God to do wrong by false teaching, and that every act of His must be absolutely perfect and incapable of after defect, a proposition which should be unquestioned by any one claiming to be a Christian, or a believer in God alone. Among the Hindoos and other Eastern people, there are many profound and learned men in the law, as an abstract science. These men believe in the Almighty God, but, of course, have no belief in Christianity, yet from their legal training they could decide a question in connection with Christianity, strictly on the evidence. Let us imagine that "the Reformers," who claimed a necessity for a reformation in the Catholic Church, for there existed no other, before taking matters into their own hands, had presented their case and cause of complaint to a court formed of these Eastern men - what would have been the result? If it had been in the power of the 'Reformers' to show by their brief that Christianity was the work of God and that, if at the beginning, or at any after period, the slightest defect existed to be amended, it would have been held that the case could have no standing in court, on the plea that with any defect Christianity could never have existed as God's work. On the other hand, if it had been God's work, there could never have been a need at any time for 'reforming' something which must always remain unchanged in its perfection to the end of time.

From my study of the teaching and acts of the so-called 'Reformers,' it was made evident that each was for himself with certainly no Christian charity or love for each other. Had these men reached any approach to the same conclusions and taught the same doctrine, their position would have been different. The disciples of Luther and those of Calvin certainly can meet on no common ground, but one based on ignorant prejudice and groundless hatred against the Catholic Church. When we appreciate the extent to which the pendulum representing present public opinion has swung in the opposite direction from the teaching of these men, and when we consider the countless number who have lost all faith in Christianity through their course, and sum up with a thought as to the bloodshed and suffering which has resulted in religious strife from their uncharitable teaching in the past three hundred years or more, we cannot believe that they were inspired, nor had any authority for their work beyond their own will and profit. When we go behind the teaching of these men there remains but one question to be solved: Whom did our Saviour promise to be with in spirit to the end of the world, and against whom should the gates of hell not prevail? From the unprejudiced investigator but one answer can be given, that it was to the Catholic Church, for no other body has ever dared claim, as the Catholic Church has, from the beginning to the present time, to have been vested directly by our Lord with the power to teach, as His representative on earth.

When the Holy Father defines a matter of faith, as the representative of our Lord, he must be accepted as infallible, or Christianity could not exist, and yet as a human being he is as liable as another to sin, unless he be protected from temptation by the grace of God.

So far I found it comparatively easy to study the subject from an historical standpoint, and draw the deductions I have given, as I had no desire but to reach the truth, based on logical conclusions"); *ANB* ("[*Ireland under English Rule*] was dedicated to 'the Sons and Daughters of Ireland scattered over the earth in quest of a home denied them in their native land'").

Evans, Cora Louise Yorgason – Catholic laywoman; Servant of God; b. 9 July 1904, Midvale, Utah; c. 30 March 1935 (received in Ogden, Utah, by Mgr. William E. Vaughan; her husband, Mack, was received three months later; many family and friends were also received); d. 30 March 1957, Boulder Creek, near Monterey, California; at the age of three she had her first mystical experience, an apparition of the Blessed Virgin Mary; brought up a Mormon; married at the Mormon temple at Salt Lake City in 1924 (three children of the marriage); became disillusioned with Mormonism, in particular the doctrine that placed man-made gods above the God of Abraham; searched for ten years for the truth, culminating in her conversion to the Catholic faith; studied almost every religion and read the Bible, but she ignored the study of the Catholic faith, because of the deep prejudice and fear instilled in her from early childhood; on 9 December 1934, while recovering from illness, she happened to listen on the radio to Mgr. (later Bishop) Duane Hunt (see below); he spoke of Mary as the Mother of God (the humanity of Christ) and about the Virgin Birth; she was appalled that a religion could honor "a mere woman" and consulted a local Catholic priest, Fr. William E. Vaughan; her husband, also a Mormon, insisted on the Mormon elders being given equal time with her; after speaking with the Catholic priest she challenged the elders and they withdrew; they were both viewed as outcasts by their Mormon friends; she reported visions of Jesus and the saints and a mission from Jesus to promote devotion to the Mystical Humanity of Christ; moved to California in 1941; see *The Refugee From Heaven* (1970); *The Selected Writings of Cora Evans* (2012).

Everson, William (also known as Brother Antoninus, and the "Beat Friar") – poet; b. 10 September 1912, Sacramento, California; c. 1948; d. 3 June 1994, Santa Cruz, California; second of three children; both his parents, a mismatched couple, were printers and also Christian Scientists; raised on a farm outside Selma, California; his father was an immigrant from Norway whose wife was twenty years younger; attended Fresno State College, but dropped out and worked on building roads; returned to Fresno State, but then made the crucial literary discovery of his life, the poetry of Robinson Jeffers (1887-1962) ("suddenly the whole inner world began to tremble"); dropped out of college again and became a poet, supporting himself with laboring jobs; became an important member of the San Francisco Renaissance in poetry in the 1940s; married his high school girlfriend and bought a farm; registered as an anarchist and pacifist during World War II; was sent to Oregon to a work camp for conscientious objectors with several other poets, artists and actors; during his three year incarceration his wife left him for another man; his conversion to the Catholic faith was influenced by reading St. Augustine's *Confessions* and by several mystical experiences; he became involved with the Catholic Worker Movement in Oakland, California; joined the Dominican Order as a lay brother in 1951, taking the name Brother Antoninus; important in the Beat Movement in the 1950s; he became involved with a young woman who came to him for counseling and left the Dominicans in 1969 in order to marry her; contracted Parkinson's Disease in 1977; lived for many years in a cabin known as "Kingfisher Flat" on the Calfiornia coast just north of Santa Cruz; a distinguished letterpress printer; poet in residence at Kresge College at the University of California, Santa Cruz during the 1970s and early 1980s (also taught hand-set printing there); founded the Lime Kiln Press through which he printed fine art editions of his poetry and that of other poets; deeply influenced in his later years by Carl Jung; married three times; his papers are kept at the William Andrews Clark Memorial Library at UCLA and The Bancroft Library at UC Berkeley; see *Robinson Jeffers: Fragments of an Older Fury* (1968); *Birth of a Poet* (1982); *The Excesses of God: Robinson Jeffers as a Religious Figure* (1988); Allan Campo and Bill Hotchkiss, *The Collected Poems of William Everson (Brother Antoninus), Vol. 1: Residual Years, 1934-1948* (1997); Allan Campo and Bill Hotchkiss, *The Collected Poems of William Everson (Brother Antoninus), Vol. 2: The Veritable Years, 1949-1966* (1998); Allan Campo and Bill Hotchkiss, *The Collected Poems of William Everson (Brother Antoninus), Vol. 3: The Integral Years, 1966-1994* (2000); Lee Bartlett, *William Everson: The Life of Brother Antoninus* (1988); Albert Gelpi, *Dark God of Eros: A William Everson Reader* (2003); Dana Gioia, "Brother Beat," *Crisis*, April 2003 ("At a midnight Mass on Christmas Eve, 1948, Everson underwent a mystical experience, and the following July he was baptized at St. Augustine's Church in Oakland. He soon began working for Dorothy Day's Catholic Worker movement on Oakland's Skid Row, which provided food and lodging for the homeless. In his private devotions Everson continued to have mystical encounters. 'I was seized with a feeling so intense as to exceed anything I had previously experienced,' he recorded in a notebook. 'It was a feeling of extreme anguish and joy, of transcendent spirituality and of great, thrilling physical character... From the tabernacle had issued to me something like an intense invisible ray, a dark ray, like a ray of light seen in the mind only.'

In 1951 Everson joined the Dominican order as a lay brother (a member of the community with no intention of becoming a priest and, therefore, under no obligation to take the vows of poverty, obedience, and chastity). Given the name Brother Antoninus, the poet entered St. Albert's, a monastery in Oakland. In addition to washing dishes and cleaning the sacristy, he set up his letterpress in the basement. Soon he started working on an elaborate folio edition of the new Latin Psalter recently authorized by Pius XII, a book which would eventually be recognized as one of the central masterpieces of American hand-press printing.

Everson's conversion unleashed a torrent of poetic creation. Many critics rate the three major collections published under the name of Brother Antoninus as his finest poetic works - *The Crooked Lines of God* (1959), *The Hazards of Holiness* (1962), and *The Rose of Solitude* (1967), which were later collected in *The Veritable Years: 1949-1966* (1978). In this feverishly visionary poetry, Everson abandons his earlier style to create an expansive lyrical mode. The poems often sprawl reflecting the ebb and tide of the author's religious exhilaration, ecstasy, and despair. As poet William Stafford observed, this work offers 'a shock and a delight to break free into the heart's unmanaged impulses.'

As Brother Antoninus, Everson became one of the key figures of the San Francisco Renaissance - the 'Beat Friar' featured in *Time* magazine dressed in Dominican monastic robes dramatically intoning his work to huge audiences. What does Catholic Beat poetry sound like? Here are a few lines from 'The Making of the Cross,' a rhapsodic poem that imagines how the wood and iron that crucified Jesus came to be at Golgotha: Just as in life the good things of the earth/Are patiently assembled: some from here, some from there;/ Wine from the hill and wheat from the valley;/Rain that comes blue-bellied out of the sopping sea;/Snow that keeps its drift on the gooseberry ridge,/Will melt with May, go down, take the egg of the salmon,/Serve the traffic of otters and fishes,/Be ditched to orchards.../So too are gathered up the possibles of evil...

...Everson examined the nature of poetic creation. His critical methods may seem unconventional when compared with contemporary academic criticism, but they are firmly based in Catholic contemplative literature.

'Suffice it to say,' he explained in *Birth of a Poet* (1982), a little-known but major critical work, 'that when I left the monastery for academe the method that I brought with me was meditative rather than discursive. For I had learned how concepts seemingly exhausted by endless repetition could suddenly, under the probe of intuition, blossom into life.'

Everson's literary legacy is unique - with enduring achievements in poetry, criticism, and printing. Out of his large body of verse, he left a small group of powerfully original religious poems. His criticism continues to be provocative in its combination of literary insight and spiritual depth. No California writer has more profoundly articulated what it means to be a Western author. His printing stands in the first rank of American private press work. But beyond these varied accomplishments, he represents an important part of the American Catholic literary tradition - a legacy still too little known, even by Catholics").

Ewing, Thomas – jurist and statesman; b. 28 December 1789, West Liberty, Virginia (now West Virginia); c. September 1871 (received by his lifelong friend, Archbishop Purcell of Cincinnati); d. 26 October 1871, Lancaster, Ohio; born into a privileged family descended from Scottish Presbyterian ancestors; brought up outside of any religion; his father, an officer in the Continental Army after the Revolution, settled in pioneering country in Ohio; taught to read by his elder sister, Sarah, and managed to obtain a reasonable elementary education; in 1890 he left home and worked in the Kanawha salt establishments, pursuing his studies at night by the light of the furnace fires; eventually earned enough to enter Ohio University at Athens; graduated with a degree of AB in 1815; studied Law at Lancaster, Ohio and was admitted to the bar in 1816; gained a high reputation as a lawyer, both within the state and nationally; in 1829 he adopted and raised William Tecumseh Sherman (1820-1891), the subsequent famous General of the United States Army, then a boy of nine years, whose father had just died (in 1850 Sherman married Eleanor, the daughter of his benefactor) in 1831 he entered public life as a member from Ohio of the United States Senate; supported Whig measures; upheld the protective tariff system and argued for the abolition of slavery; when his term expired in 1837 he went back to the practice of law; in March 1841 he was appointed Secretary of the Treasury, but resigned from the cabinet in September 1841; in 1849 he was appointed secretary of the then recently created Department of the Interior; he urged the construction of a railroad to the Pacific; appointed senator from Ohio again, but afterwards went back to his legal practice; member of the famous Peace Conference in 1860 and tried to avert the secession of the Southern States; supporter of President Lincoln during the Civil War; conservative in his opinions, he opposed the radical measures of Reconstruction at the close of the War; in October 1869 he was taken ill while arguing a case before the Supreme Court of the United States and was baptized in the court room; converted very late in life, though always attracted by the Catholic Church through the influence of his Catholic wife, Maria; his sons, Hugh (1826-1905), Thomas, Jr. (1829-1896), and Charles (1835-1883), all became generals in the Civil War and were lawyers (Charles, who was appointed the Indian Commissioner, was also a great worker for the Catholic Indian Missions); the daughter, Eleanor (1824-1888), wife of William Tecumseh Sherman, devoted herself to the relief of suffering and of want, and to the advancement of the Church (through Fr. P. J. De Smet, SJ (1801-1873), the missionary among the Indians, an old friend of the Shermans); she also took a special interest in the cause of the Catholic Indians; see Ellen Ewing Sherman (ed), *Memorial of Thomas Ewing, of Ohio* (1873); *Catholic Encyclopedia* ("Descended of Scottish Presbyterian stock, Ewing, after a lifelong attraction to the Catholic Church, entered it in his latter years. Reared outside the fold of any religious body, he married, 7 January, 1820, Maria Wills Boyle, daughter of Hugh Boyle, an Irish Catholic. He was deeply influenced by the living faith and pious example of his wife during their long married life, and all his children were reared in the Faith"); *ANB*.

Fagerberg, David W. – from a strong Norwegian Lutheran family; educated at Augsburg College (BA); Luther Northwestern Seminary (MDiv); St. John's University, Collegeville (MA); Yale Divinity School (STM); Yale University (MA, MPhil, PhD); appointed Professor of Religion at Concordia College; later Associate Professor of Liturgy and Senior Advisor, Notre Dame Center for Liturgy, University of Notre Dame; also Associate Professor St. Paul Center for Biblical Theology; the influence of liturgical theology and of G. K. Chesterton drew him into the Catholic Church; specialist areas liturgical theology, sacramental theology, liturgiology, Eastern Orthodoxy, linguistic philosophy, scholasticism, and G. K. Chesterton; articles in many journals; see *What is Liturgical Theology: A Study in Methodology* (1992); *The Size of Chesterton's Catholicism* (1998) ("By way of autobiographical confession I admit that Chesterton was the single most influential person upon my own journey home to the Catholic Church…

Chesterton said that there are a thousand doors into Catholicism. On the surface it would not appear that I have entered by a door in any way similar to his. If he did not come to Catholicism from Luther and Laud and pietism, I did. (Perhaps I am his monstrous double; maybe that is why I am charmed by him.) He has been influential because the route to Rome he charted was a passageway from the partial to the replete. 'The Church drew me out of Anglicanism, as the very idea of Our Lady drew me long before out of ordinary Protestantism, by being herself, that is, by being beautiful. I was converted by the positive attractions of the things I had not yet got, and not by negative disparagements of such things as I had managed to get already.' Chesterton records a personal trek in which he does not surrender any truth he has learned along the way; he does not regret his past. Neither have I reneged on my tradition. I have brought along all good things into the Crystal Palace, without regret and without disparagement, on Chesterton's word that, due to its size, Catholicism can hold everything good in my tradition and still have room for things which my tradition could not fit. I was drawn by the positive attractions of things I had not yet got…

Chesterton's conviction [is] that in its practical relation to the soul the Church is a living teacher, not a dead one. It is the reason he gives for accepting the religion and not merely the truths of the religion. 'I do it because the thing has not merely told this truth or that truth, but has revealed itself as a truth-telling thing'…One's relationship with a Church which is a living teacher is quite different than one's relationship with a Church which is a lifeless catalogue of truths about which one is already convinced. Not until such a relationship is in place, does one trust the teacher regarding other matters, even those about which one does nor yet see the point...

Throughout this work I have presented Chesterton as too doctrinal to be appreciated by the secular relativist, and too charmed by the world to be understood by the doctrinaire cynic of secular life. He presents a stable, developing Catholicism which survives because it is alive and can grow alongside a firm, rooted Catholicism which survives because it does not move with the moods. When I was a child, my father planted a tree in the backyard and I had what seemed then the very clever idea of pounding a hoard into that tree each year as it grew taller so that when it was fully grown there would he a ladder to the top. My arboreal miscalculation, of course, is that trees don't grow out of the ground; they grow from the top. If a board is nailed three feet above the ground, it will remain three feet above the ground, yet the tree will continue to grow taller because it grows out the tips of the branches. Now, on the one hand, there are some who seem to think that doctrine can be modified like a step can be moved. But this is not true: neither the Nicene doctrine at the three-foot mark, nor the Tridentine board at fifteen feet, nor the most recent step taken by Vatican II, can be moved at our discretion. Chesterton would deter us from reinventing the Church every generation (in our image, no less) because the tree will never grow if its roots are disturbed by being replanted in every age's new ideology"); "Would Chesterton be a Convert in 2000?" *Priests and People*, January 2000, p.18; *Theologia Prima: What is Liturgical Theology* (2003); *Mary in the Liturgy* (2012); *Liturgical Asceticism* (2013).

Farmer, Frances Elena – actress; b. 19 September 1913, Seattle, Washington; c. 1968; d. 1 August 1970, Indianapolis, Indiana; father a prominent lawyer; at school she won a writing contest with an essay entitled "God Dies," influenced by her reading of Nietzsche; at this time she was an agnostic; studied Drama at the University of Washington; offered a seven year contract by Paramount Pictures in 1935; moved to Hollywood and was successful (notably in *Come and Get It* (1936)); rebelled against the studio's control; to enhance her reputation as a serious actress she moved to the New York theatre and was again successful; switched between films and theatre; reputation damaged by alcoholism and temperament and Paramount cancelled her contract in 1942; arrested and imprisoned over a driving incident, but transferred to a psychiatric hospital; diagnosed with paranoid schizophrenia and given insulin shock therapy; released, but committed again, when she received electro-convulsive shock treatment;

released in 1944 as completely cured; arrested for vagrancy and committed to hospital where she spent five years (her posthumous autobiography claimed she had suffered much brutal abuse); after her dearth claims of lobotomy were made, but probably untrue; worked anonymously in various jobs for several years; returned to the stage in 1957 and later appeared on television; hosted her own TV program; further erratic behaviour during this period; married three times, each followed by divorce; avoided contact with children for many years due to her guilt over her abortions; became attached to five little daughters of a friend and the affection of one of them caused her to feel that the evil surrounding her was being washed away; she felt that God had come into her life and that she "would have to find a disciplined avenue of faith and worship"; soon afterwards she found herself sitting in a Catholic church; she asked for instruction in the faith and was received into the Catholic Church; interred at Oaklawn Memorial Gardens Cemetery, Fishers, Indiana; she was the subject of two films, several magazine articles and numerous songs; in 1993 the rock group Nirvana recorded the single *Frances Farmer Will Have Her Revenge on Seattle* written by lead singer Kurt Cobain; see *Will There Really Be a Morning* (1972) (posthumous autobiography); William Arnold, *Shadowland: Search for Frances Farmer* (1978); Edith Farmer Elliot, *Look Back in Love* (1979) (written by her sister); Peter Shelley, *Francis Farmer: The Life and Films of a Troubled Star* (2010).

Farmer, Francis Xavier, SJ (original name Wilmoth Alexander Farmer) – priest; b. 16 October 1877, Conyers, Rockdale County, Georgia; c. 6 May 1915, Savannah Cathedral; d. 30 October 1970, Los Gatos, Santa Clara County, California; spent most of his boyhood in Covington, Kentucky; his family had been Methodists for generations; his father had no religion, but his mother was a devout Methodist; educated at Emory College, near Covington, a Methodist institution; studied for the Methodist ministry at Vanderbilt University, Nashville, Tennessee; then in preparation for the foreign missionary field, he studied at the Missionary Training Institute of the Christian and Missionary Alliance at Nyack, New York; in 1901 he sailed for China and worked there as a missionary; learned the Chinese language and took on their customs by adopting their dress, shaving his head, eating native food, etc.; in 1904 he married another American missionary, (Martha) Ada Beeson (1871-1911); they set up two missions together; their son died after two days of life; his wife later became ill and died also; he returned to the United States and wrote a memoir of his wife; then he returned to China; did much reading in theology and began to accept the Catholic position; final influence in his conversion came from Newman's *Apologia Pro Vita Sua* and *The Development of Christian Doctrine*; he consulted the Catholic chaplaincy in Shanghai; he went home on leave of absence to consider his position; at Honolulu he was given by a Belgian priest Fr. Conway's *Question Box,* which answered the Protestant objections against Rome; after converting he joined the Society of Jesus; ordained to the priesthood for the French province of the Jesuits; returned to China where he labored from 1926 to 1949 in Shanghai at the church of the Sacred Heart (and for a time in Japan); at Loyola University 1949-1966; see *Ada Beeson Farmer: A Missionary Heroine of Kuang Si, South China* (1912); *My Conversion* (1931); "A Long Journey," in John A. O'Brien (ed), *The Road to Damascus, Volume III: The Way to Emmaus* (1953) ("I began to read anew the history of the Christian Church…Now one of the first things to strike me with a new view was the very ugly aspect of the Protestant Reformation. In the light of plain historical facts, I saw, as never before, all the glaring inconsistency of Martin Luther and the rest. For the very principles which they claimed to be divinely called to maintain and defend they continually denied in word and deed; and if Catholic sovereigns used strong measures against heretics, Luther did not fail to employ the same arm of force against Catholics and would have gone further if he could, but the Catholic party was too strong. If anyone thinks that Luther, Calvin, and Henry VIII were lenient and merciful, let him read the facts of history, and if he thinks they were paragons of virtue, let him consider their moral side.

I speak with reverence when I say that it seems as if the Omnipotent God was surely in difficult straits to find suitable instruments to effect his work if He was obliged to use an apostate monk who had broken his vows of religion and who permitted Philip of Hesse to have two wives at the same time for no other reason than pure sensuality; or a 'much married' king whose lust, divorces, and murders recall the execrable house of the Herods; or a cold-blooded Calvin who watched from a half-opened window the dying agony of Michael Servetus, whom he himself had condemned to be burned at the stake because he denied the dogma of the Trinity.

Up to this point I had read only Protestant books, and now, for the first time, I opened a book written by a Catholic, a Catholic to whom I owe more gratitude than I shall ever be able to express. I refer to John Henry Newman, and the book is his famous *Apologia.* I read, then re-read it with the keenest interest, and it tended to augment my thirst to know the truth. In the public library in Shanghai

I found several other works of Newman's, such as *Lectures on the Present Position of Catholics in England*, *Essays*, and *Sermons…*

I read [*The Development of Christian Doctrine*] with greatest avidity. My previous study of sacred and profane history had prepared me fully to appreciate the thesis which Newman so ably defends in this book, viz., that the Roman Catholic Church of to-day is none other than that of all past centuries and that her teaching and discipline have ever been the same.

His proofs were so true and logical that the evidence was overwhelming. I could not withstand it. After all, there was indeed, and there had always been 'One Holy Catholic Apostolic Church', and that Church was Rome. I, too, saw so clearly that the Gnostics, Arians, Montanists, Donatists, and all the other heretical sects were in their day and time what schismatics - Anglicans, Methodists, Presbyterians, Baptists - are today in their relation to the one true Church, viz., heretics.

Now, while I have been describing the intellectual influence which was brought to bear upon my mind, I have said nothing about the struggle of my heart; it often happens that one's intellect is convinced long before the heart is willing to yield assent. All this light which had come to me plunged my heart and soul into the greatest anguish; for I saw so clearly that if Rome was what she claimed to be, there was nothing left for me to do but either to become a Roman Catholic or to turn my back upon the light. But how could I dare turn against the light?...

I knew the Holy Scriptures very well, and I saw from that standpoint, in reference to such important questions as Baptism, the Holy Eucharist, the promise of infallibility made by Christ to St. Peter, the power to absolve from sin, that the Catholic Church had the best of the argument and that Protestant exegetes had warped and twisted the Scriptures to prove theories utterly foreign to primitive Christianity. And if they treated the inspired Word of God thus, it is not surprising to find that they garbled, misquoted, and rejected wholesale the Fathers of the Church. This so called 'reform' had resulted in an absolute denial of some of the most common doctrines of the Christian faith! Indeed, with their preconceived theories and system of eclecticism, those would-be reformers had set up a church which Christ and the Apostles had never known.

More clearly than ever was it borne in upon my mind that the Christian religion, being a divine revelation, and not in a system of human philosophy, was bound to have but one meaning, and in order to preserve that message incorrupt, some official authority was adsolutely necessary. If God had confided the preservation of the Faith to numerous discordant sects, it was a fact too evident to deny that no one could any longer know the content and import of the original revelation made by Christ...

When I reached San Francisco, I bought a rosary and a Catholic copy of *The Imitation of Christ*. I had known this little book in former years, as it was one of the first which John Wesley had published for the use of the Methodists, though, of course, without the fourth book, which treats of the Real Presence and Holy Communion"); Katherine Burton, *In No Strange Land: Some American Catholic Converts* (1942), p.215 ("In the course of reading the books he had brought with him from the United States, he came across a baffling statement: never in the course of his later life could Martin Luther be brought to deny the Real Presence in the Blessed Sacrament As he read that, he suddenly thought: what if the Roman view is the right one?

For a Methodist missionary this was a truly terrifying thought and he tried to put it from him. But as he read more he found himself dissenting frequently from the Methodist statements he read, and he began to see with surprise and dismay that the Protestant Reformation had certain ugly aspects and glaring inconsistencies. He felt compromised, unhappy, and his preaching to his Chinese Christians became more and more difficult for him. Besides they often asked him why there was this puzzling division in Christian life, these wrangling sects. And he saw that interchurch movements, meant to give Protestantism cohesion, always collapsed. Over and over, one thought went drumming through his head: they could not all be true or authoritative. Perhaps the hated old citadel did hold the divine deposit of the Christian faith. To him the Church of Rome had been a cult, a superstition, a Gargantuan moral system almost pagan in principle. But the years of difficult mission work had given him a riper, soberer appraisal of doctrinal problems.

Finally he sent to England for two volumes by John Henry Newman, the *Apologia* and *The Development of Christian Doctrine* and when he had finished reading them, he knew that the evidence he had hoped to push from him was overwhelming. He knew he himself was nothing more than a heretic. He now saw, finally and irrevocably, that there had been only one Christian Church - the Church of Rome").

Farmer, William Reuben ("Bill") – bible scholar; b. 1 February 1921, Needles, California; c. 1990; d. 30 December 2000, Dallas, Texas; studied at Cambridge University with C. H. Dodd while completing a degree in Philosophy of Religion and Christian Ethics; did doctoral work at Union Theological Seminary; was an ordained Methodist minister; began writing on the social history of pre-70 Judaism and thereafter entered the field of synoptic studies; from 1965 to 1989 worked closely with Albert

C. Outler; in 1982 he co-founded with Dom Bernard Orchard the Institute for Gospel Studies; his later publications focused on the problem of Christian origins; was a Guggenheim Fellow and a Fellow of the International Institute for Gospel Studies; Visiting Fellow at Fitzwilliam College, Cambridge, in 1995; Emeritus Professor of New Testament at Perkins School of Theology, Southern Methodist University, and research scholar at the University of Dallas; in 1964 he challenged the two-source hypothesis, that Mark was the earliest Gospel and that the later Gospels, Matthew and Luke, made use of Mark and a hypothetical source called Q; his own theory, the Two-Gospel Hypothesis (formerly known in a more elementary form as the Griesbach Hypothesis), was that Matthew was written first, that Luke used Matthew in preparing his Gospel, and that Mark conflated the two; he also claimed that the politics of Bismark's *Kulturkampf* or "culture war" against the power of the pope led to the German authorities' favoring university scholars who supported Marcan priority; this was because, unlike Matthew, Mark does not contain the famous passage in which Jesus declares Peter to be the rock of the Church to whom is granted the keys of the kingdom (Matt. 16:18-19), and this passage was (and still is) used by Catholics as the basis for the primacy of Peter and his successors, the popes, as the supreme pastors of the Church; his spiritual pilgrimage eventually led him to become a Catholic; wrote many books and articles on New Testament issues; strong commitment to social justice throughout his life; married with four children; see *The Synoptic Problem: A Critical Analysis* (1964; expanded edition 1976); (ed), *Synopticon: The Verbal Agreement Between the Greek Texts of Matthew, Mark, and Luke Contextually Exhibited* (1969); *The Last Twelve Verses of Mark* (1974); *Jesus and the Gospel: Tradition, Scripture, and the Canon* (1982); *The Formation of the New Testament Canon: An Ecumenical Approach* (1983) (with Denis Farkasfalvy); *New Synoptic Studies: The Cambridge Gospel Conference and Beyond* (1983); "The Gospels as the Lips of Jesus," *Fellowship of Catholic Scholars Quarterly*, December 1989, p.13 ("Marcan primacy became a German dogma. It is literally taught to children without question. How did this happen? In. 1870, the Marcan Hypothesis was only a popular wissenschaftliche hypothese. But certainly by 1914, probably by 1890, and possibly as early as 1880 this popular Protestant hypothesis was converted into a dogma. Why? I suggest that belief in Marean primacy and the existence of 'Q' became dogmatic counterparts to the dogmas of Petrine Primacy and Papal supremacy. These dogmas (i.e., Marcan primacy and the existence of 'Q') cut the theological (i.e., scriptural) ground from underneath the Vatican Council decrees"); "Bismarck and the Four Gospels, 1870-1914," in F. Van Segbroeck, C. M. Tuckett, G. Van Belle, J. Verheyden (ed), *The Four Gospels (Festschrift Frans Neirynck)* (1992); *The Gospel of Jesus: The Pastoral Relevance of the Synoptic Problem* (1994); "The Historical Perimeters for Understanding the Aims of Jesus," in W. R. Farmer (ed), *Crisis in Christology: Essays in Quest of Resolution* (1995); (ed), *The International Bible Commentary: A Catholic and Ecumenical Commentary for the Twenty-First Century* (1998); *The Present State of the Synoptic Problem* (1998); *Anti-Judaism and the Gospels* (1999); "Robert Funk and the Jesus Seminar," *Crisis*, March 2000 ("The Church canonized only four Gospels. However, Robert Funk, the leader of the Jesus Seminar, wants to add the Gospel of Thomas and the Sayings Gospel Q to our canon. This poses the question: Why did the Church canonize four Gospels and no more? The answer is that Matthew, Mark, Luke, and John are the only Gospels that tell the story of 'the flesh and blood martyrdom of the Son of God.'

The Church rejected all Gospels that failed to tell this story. The Gospel of Peter says that while Jesus hung on the cross, He felt no pain. If Jesus felt no pain, His death was not a flesh-and-blood martyrdom. If he did not experience the pain we would have felt, His death could not have been redemptive. Similarly, the Gospel of Thomas is only a collection of Jesus' sayings. There is no flesh-and-blood martyrdom - no redemptive death of Jesus. The same can be said of the scholarly collection of sayings the Seminar calls 'Q'.

Despite all its faults, I find the Church to be essentially trustworthy. Robert Funk and other prominent members of the Jesus Seminar, such as the Catholic scholar Dominic Crossan, not without reason are constrained to draw our attention to the shortcomings of the Church when compared with the vision of Jesus. However, instead of being what they claim to be, historians, Robert Funk and his colleagues in the Jesus Seminar have collectively turned their backs on sound historiography.

Their first major failure has been their inability to properly construe the importance of certain data preserved in the letters of Paul for understanding Jesus and His role in Christian origins. The second major failure is they don't offer a credible account of Jesus' relationship to Judaism...

[On the first question] the heart of the issue is this: The Jesus Seminar suggests that Paul's version of the Last Supper sprouted in a soil of pagan Gentile tradition in Asia Minor or Greece. But historical scholarship suggests that the tradition of the Last

Supper Paul received and handed on to his churches was handed on to him by the same church he once persecuted and whose faith he had tried to destroy...

The faith Paul preached was closely related to the tradition he received, specifically, the tradition that 'Christ died for our sins, according to the scriptures' (1 Corinthians 15:3), which he handed on to his churches, along with other traditions that were decisive for the Church, including what Jesus did on the night he was betrayed.

In the tradition concerning the Lord's Supper handed on by Paul, Jesus identified His body with the broken bread, representing His death as a death for others (1 Corinthians 11:24). This offering of one's life for others is in accord with Isaiah 53, which is included in the Scriptures referred to in 1 Corinthians 15:3: 'Christ died for our sins in accordance with the scriptures.' The point is the tradition concerning the Lord's Supper that Paul handed on is doctrinally bound to the tradition that Christ died for our sins (1 Corinthians 15:3).

Through the interrelationship of these traditions, Paul, in giving counsel concerning pastoral problems in the Church at Corinth, is drawing on a larger body of authoritative tradition, namely, that formulated by, or under the influence of, Peter, John, and other apostles.

The faith Paul brought with him when he came to Jerusalem and spent 15 days with Peter must have been a faith Paul and Peter shared. However, this is not to say that he received it directly from Peter, certainly not during his 15 day stay, since it was a faith he had already been preaching during the preceding three years.

It is not surprising that this faith was embodied in the tradition Paul passed on to the Corinthians. Paul gives expression to this faith in the words of 1 Corinthians 15:3: 'For I delivered to you as of first importance what I also received, that Christ died for our sins in accordance with the scriptures.' It is clear that Paul embraced this faith and made it central in his preaching. For example, he addresses the churches of Galatia with these words: 'Grace to you and peace from God the Father and our Lord Jesus Christ, who gave himself for our sins' (Galatians 1:4).

This leads to the second charge against the members of the Jesus Seminar - namely, their failure as historians to credibly reconstruct the historical Jesus at the point of His relationship to Judaism and especially to the Jewish scriptures. There is a historical disconnection, if not a disruption...

What Jesus did [on the night he was betrayed] functioned as a prophetic, symbolic act in the tradition of Isaiah. It was also a parabolic act in which what Jesus was saying and doing was to be compared to what Isaiah had said that the wounded Servant would accomplish. Only when this connection was made would the full impact of the text of Isaiah grasp the minds of his heretofore disbelieving hearers. At that point, all who had ears to hear would have had their minds turned by what Jesus was communicating to them. For all who had eyes to see and ears to hear, this was an exhilarating moment, calling for a repentance for unbelief that was pregnant with hope:

Because *he poured out his soul to death*, and was numbered with the transgressors; *He bore the sins of many*, and made intercession for the transgressors [emphasis added].

Of course, until Jesus had actually (not just symbolically) freely given himself over into the hands of the transgressors, had been buried, and had been raised up and vindicated, most of Jesus' disciples would only continue to falter, as we are told Peter did. But the seeds for belief in Jesus' messianic vindication and exaltation were sown in the hearts of His disciples that night. Thus, after they had sung a hymn and had walked out into the night, there was still a song abiding in their hearts, and they followed Jesus to see what the Lord would do. The incredible words of Isaiah concerning the Servant would, as the word of God, hover over the chaos of God's new creation as the Spirit had hovered over the chaos of God's first creation.

What then keeps the Jesus Seminar from recognizing that the Jesus who spoke the parables is the same Jesus who died for the sins of others, a Jesus who freely accepted His death as a voluntary giving of himself for others? The answer is *they acknowledge no such connection*. They misconstrue the data that make this connection possible and give them short shrift. The failure of the Jesus Seminar to properly construe the importance of historical data that are decisive for understanding Jesus, preserved in the letters of Paul, is far reaching. The short shrift members of the Jesus Seminar have given to 1 Corinthians 11:23-26 and all related data from Paul's letters is representative of the myopic approach they take to much of the historical data concerning Jesus. Convergence between the second to fourth century Gnostic Gospel of Thomas and the hypothetical Q is a case in point. For them such convergence is given more weight, in general, than they have given to this case of convergence between our earliest historical witness, Paul, and the Gospels of Matthew and Mark"); "The Case for the Two-Gospel Hypothesis," in David Alan Black and David R. Beck (ed), *Rethinking the Synoptic Problem* (2001); E. P. Sanders (ed), *Jesus, the Gospels, and the Church: Essays in Honor of William R. Farmer* (1987); John Beaumont, "Kulturkampf and the Gospel," *Culture Wars*, December 1996, p.16.

Farrow, Douglas B. – theologian; c. 12 March 2005 (received by Bishop Anthony Mancini); raised in a Protestant home (which had for some time been Baptist) of mixed English and Scottish stock; trained for the ministry in evangelical institutions before going to Regent College, Vancouver; later became an Anglican; did graduate studies at King's College, London (awarded PhD); influenced by Cullman, Barth, and N. T. Wright; taught back at Regent College 1992-1994, lecturer in theology at King's College 1994-1998; appointed to a post at McGill University in 1997 (now Associate Professor in Christian Thought there); did much work on the doctrine of the Ascension; became strongly opposed to liberal developments in Anglicanism such as same-sex blessings and same-sex "marriage"; influenced in his conversion to the Catholic faith by the counsel of Fr. Richard Neuhaus (see below), by R. R. Reno (see below) and by the example of his wife's family; the crucial question for him was the Petrine ministry; married to Anna (*née* Whelan); see (selective list) *The Word of Truth and Disputes About Words* (1987); *Ascension and Ecclesia: On the Significance of the Doctrine of the Ascension for Ecclesiology and Christian Cosmology* (1999); (ed), *Recognizing Religion in a Secular Society: Essays in Pluralism, Religion and Public Policy* (2004); (co-ed) *Divorcing Marriage: Unveiling the Dangers in Canada's New Social Experiment* (2004) (with Daniel Cere); "Anglicanism Runs Aground," *First Things*, January 2005; *Nation of Bastards: Essays on the End of Marriage* (2007); *A Matter of Conscience* (2009) (with John Haas, Maria Kraw and Francois Pouliot); "Are You Catholic?" in *Canadian Converts: The Path to Rome* (2009) ("In Blair's Britain what Guy Fawkes had witnessed only in his dreams, before he leapt from the gallows, was actually taking place: the slow-motion destruction of Westminster and everything it once stood for. That Tony Blair, in recent days and for his own reasons, also became a Catholic, I think of as a grand irony (Fawkes was himself a convert, of course)...

The Anglican communion was in visible decline in Britain and North America...The presenting symptom of the disease that was paralyzing it was the same that had appeared when the Church of England came into existence: a dispute over the sacrament of marriage. King Henry had resolved the dispute about his own marriage by taking authority over the sacrament itself, or rather by taking authority over the church whose sacrament it was. In Canada the government of Jean Chrétien, though all but paralyzed by its shrinking number of seats in the House – ironically, it was a prominent opponent of same-sex marriage who propped up his government at the eleventh hour just long enough for it to pass Bill C-38, but that's another story - was completing the task Henry had begun. A Catholic prime minister and his Jewish Minister of Justice, with the blessing of the Supreme Court of Canada, were making marriage a mere creature of the State. And Anglicans, who better than anyone else ought to have understood what was happening, were a decade or more behind the curve and convulsing themselves over same-sex blessings...

But what, then, of Orthodoxy? Might I, ought I, consider looking for a home among the Orthodox?...I recalled being, much more recently, in an elevator at the Warwick in Houston with a couple of converts to Antiochian Orthodoxy, who were sharing in a seminar. There was also a Catholic or two in the elevator, and the brief conversation went something like this: Said one of the Orthodox to one of the Catholics: 'It is true, is it not, that Rome recognizes Orthodox sacraments as valid?' 'Yes,' came the reply. 'And it is also true, is it not, that among the Orthodox there are serious doubts about Rome?' The reply was again in the affirmative, though this time a little warier. The conclusion that followed from these premises came as quickly as the floor on which the Catholics would gratefully retreat to their rooms: 'All things considered, then, wouldn't it be safer to be Orthodox?'

What prevented me from considering Orthodoxy more closely, its sacramental validity notwithstanding, was the same thing that would have prevented me from reverting to congregationalism even had it not lacked sacramental validity. I mean the question of the Petrine ministry, which now impressed itself upon me as a very real and unavoidable problem.

I had taken to heart John Paul II's encyclical *Ut unum sint*, which revealed the burden that in a certain sense defined his pontificate. I had begun examining the ecclesiology of the two Vatican councils. I was convinced that Anglicanism was unconvincing, both historically and theologically, and that Orthodoxy, while profoundly compelling, could not by itself sustain the catholic unity for which the church, in the spirit of Christ's own 'high priestly' prayer, longed. I did not believe that the credal marks of the church were merely eschatological aspirations, as certain evangelical Protestants seemed to think; or that they had yet to be achieved by the march of progress, as many liberal Protestants fancied. I did believe that I myself was responsible to act consistently with the prayer of Jesus and so to take up the challenge of *Ut unum sint*, and I saw no other way to do that, in my own circumstances, than to become a Catholic.

Unless, of course, Catholicism were itself the problem. If it were, then the problem lay either in the way the Petrine office had been conceived and exercised or in the very claim to such an office. But if in the claim itself, then the great majority of Christians, past and present - including many non-Catholics - had been hoodwinked. Not to put too fine a point on it, the great gap theory was right after all. Indeed, Jack Chick was right after all, and Ian Paisley too. You can't claim to be the vicar of Christ, if you're not the vicar of Christ, without being an antichrist. Peter, yes or no? That was the question, and it was a question for every non-Catholic, myself included. Paisley, by the way, I had once heard in a pub (on another subject) and he was not unimpressive. But even putting for Paisley the humblest of Protestants - who would certainly not describe the pope as antichrist - this was no contest. It was not even a reasonable question. That popes can and have behaved like antichrists is difficult to dispute. The view that popes *are* antichrists, if held by a properly informed person, is schismatic sectarianism of the gravest sort.

Suppose, however, that the problem lay not in the claim itself but in the way the office was exercised...Was it not possible that the Petrine mandate, 'feed my sheep, take care of my lambs,' had not only been neglected from time to time but misunderstood and misapplied? And, if so, what then? One still ought to recognize the shepherd and seek the unity of the sheepfold. But could one do so, with integrity, as a sheep not quite shorn of its Protestant wool, or ought one to remain outside the fold, looking in, until convinced that the shepherd knew his business?

If all this sounds to my fellow Catholics impossibly hubristic, perhaps it was. Or perhaps it was simply my own experience of the uncertainty of the 'separated brethren": the uncertainty that arises whenever they remember, on the one hand, that they *are* separated and that they don't want to be; and, on the other, that their separation, whether they be Orthodox or Protestant, was not entirely their own fault or their own doing, as the Catholic Church has acknowledged.

I acknowledged the existence of a Petrine ministry and its most obvious implications respecting the nature and development of the church, the relation of scripture and tradition, the proper goal of ecumenism, etc. I understood that it had implications for how scripture was to be read and how theology ought to be done; that all these things were to be governed by a communion that was not merely notional but real, and not merely occasional but institutional. I recognized that a magisterium existed and must be heeded. But I had a problem. I still had reservations about certain things taught by the magisterium. Were I already a Catholic that problem - which is common enough! - would present itself differently. Were I not a theologian the solution might be to plead ignorance or incompetence and leave the solution to others. But I was a theologian who wished to become a Catholic and I feared that I would be asked to confess what I could not (even allowing for a degree of ignorance) in good conscience confess. For in the rite of reception the candidate says: 'I believe and profess all that the holy Catholic Church believes, teaches, and proclaims to be revealed by God'...

[I was put] in mind of Augustine's claim that 'there is nothing more wholesome in the Catholic Church than using authority before argument.' Augustine was thinking like this: Because we are made in the image of the living God, who has and is the fellowship of the Father and the Son in the Holy Spirit, *love* precedes knowledge, *faith* precedes reason, and *authority* precedes argument. (Substitute the word 'enables' for the word 'precedes,' if you like, and that will help you get the picture.) When I was a Protestant I had no difficulty with that, so long as the authority in question was mediated by the scriptures and by preaching; *as* a Protestant, of course, I resisted the notion that it was mediated by any formal magisterium. To be Catholic, however, is to accept, as I now do, not only that authority precedes argument, but that the church possesses this authority: in its prophets and saints and martyrs, yes, hence in the *sensus fidelium*; in its scriptures and creeds and liturgies, certainly, and even (though less certainly) in its great theological traditions; but *also* in its living magisterium, in the college of the apostles and their successors, united round Peter and his successors.

Catholics do not think that it is possible to do without a magisterium, or that there is any reason or justification to try, since God has provided one. Nor do they think, as Barth perhaps thought, that the gift of a magisterium is somehow like the gift of prophecy; that it shows itself here and then there, speaking with this voice, then that - as if it were no more than an 'echo' bouncing around in the ecclesial crater formed and reformed by the repeated impact of the word of God. Good Catholics, like good Protestants, know that the word of God is living and active, 'sharper than any two-edged sword,' but also that the Church's reception of the word of God is a process of growth, guided by a faculty of judgment invested in the apostolic college with Peter at its head. They believe that, when Jesus said to Peter that he was giving to him the keys to the kingdom, he meant it; and that the survival of the papacy and of the Catholic Church through thick and thin...is a work of God and not merely the work of man"); *Ascension Theology* (2011); "The Dignifying Family," *First Things*, November 2011; "Thirteen Theses on Marriage," *First Things*, October 2012.

Farrow, John Villiers – film director, producer, and screenwriter; b. 10 February 1904, Sydney, New South Wales, Australia; d. 27 January 1963, Beverley Hills, California; his mother died when he was three; passed the exams to get into the Australian Naval College at age twelve, but instead joined the merchant service as a cadet; much travel through the Pacific; started writing while a sailor; in 1927 he began working in Hollywood as a technical adviser on ship-related movies; soon became an established screenwriter in Hollywood, though also worked in England; moved to working as a film director; notorious playboy in his youth; married first to Felice Lewin; converted to the Catholic faith; he obtained an annulment of his first marriage; in 1936 he married Maureen O'Sullivan (1911-1998), the actress, best known for playing Jane in the Tarzan series of films (seven children of the marriage, four daughters and three sons); awarded Knight Grand Cross of the Order of the Holy Sepulchre by Pope Pius XI in 1937; in November 1939 he enlisted in the Canadian navy; for a time was loaned to the Royal Navy; reached rank of Commander in the Canadian navy, but was invalided out in 1942; returned to film directing; Oscar nomination for Best Director for *Wake Island* (1942); became a naturalized American citizen in 1947; made several films with Alan Ladd; won the Oscar for Best Writing/Best Screenplay for *Around the World in Eighty Days* (1957); tried to make a film of the life of Jesus Christ and was offered by Samuel Bronston the position of director of *King of Kings*, but was replaced by Nicholas Ray; all four of his daughters worked in the film industry, three as actresses, notably Mia Farrow (full name Maria de Lourdes Villiers Farrow) (b. 1945); buried in the Holy Cross Cemetery, Culver City, California; see (books) *The Bad Ones* (1930) (novel); *Laughter Ends* (1933) (novel); *Damien the Leper* (1937); *The Royal Canadian Navy 1908-1940* (1940); *Pageant of the Popes* (1943); *Seven Poems in Pattern* (1955); *Story of Sir Thomas More* (1956); John Villiers Farrow Papers at the American Catholic History Research Center and University Archives, Catholic University of America, Washington D.C.

Ferrara, Jennifer Mehl – part-time writer and speaker; c. 14 June 1998 (received by Fr. C. John McCloskey III in a chapel of the Aquinas Institute, Princeton University); father and several family members Lutheran ministers, though her father held Catholicism in high esteem; her mother grew up in the Catholic Church and became a Lutheran when she married; brought up on the campus of a Lutheran seminary where her father taught homiletics and literature courses; studied at the University of Virginia Religious Studies Department; attended Princeton Theological Seminary and the Lutheran Theological Seminary in Philadelphia; began as a feminist liberal, but influenced by John Neuhaus (see below), then still a Lutheran, to see herself as an evangelical catholic; ordained as a Lutheran minister in which capacity she served for eleven years; married to Steve Ferrara, from a devout Italian Catholic family (three children of the marriage); conversion to the Catholic faith was influenced by Robert Wilken (see below); see "Becoming Catholic: Making It Hard," *First Things*, January 1999 ("In its section on music, the *Catechism of the Catholic Church* quotes St. Augustine: 'How I wept, deeply moved by your hymns, songs, and the voices that echoed through your Church! What emotion I experienced in them! Those sounds flowed into my ears, distilling the truth in my heart. A feeling of devotion surged within me, and tears streamed down my face - tears that did me good.' As a former Lutheran pastor who is now Roman Catholic, I am sorry to say Augustine's wonderful words do not describe my experience with worship in the Church. Though at times I have been on the verge of tears, that was due to feelings of despair and not devotion. Far from drawing me into the Church, the manner in which the Mass is celebrated in most parishes constituted, in the end, the greatest stumbling block to my conversion…

The answer finally came after I resolved to speak to a visiting priest at the church where I attend daily Mass. I told him I was a Lutheran pastor who wanted to become Roman Catholic but couldn't find a place to worship. Did he know of a traditional parish without guitar music? He looked at me as if I resided on another planet. 'Can I ask you something?' he asked. 'Why do you want to become Catholic?' He asked the question in a tone that suggested, Why would you want to do a thing like that? I mumbled something about the problems in the ELCA and my belief that the Catholic Church is the fullest, most rightly ordered manifestation of the Church on earth. 'Oh,' he replied. 'In that case you want to go to Holy Rosary. It's an Italian parish with a beautiful sanctuary and traditional music and liturgy.'

I have attended Holy Rosary ever since. There are no guitars or missalettes. The organist and choir are first rate; the organist even plays Bach and the choir often sings in Latin. More importantly, the parishioners have an attitude of quiet piety and profound reverence for the liturgy that is quite moving. They observe the muscular prayers of kneeling, genuflecting, and crossing themselves. The monsignor never begins Mass with 'good morning,' offers no explanations, does the Canon with great dignity and reverence. Unlike other parishes I have attended, Holy Rosary offers a seemingly endless variety of distinctively Catholic devotions - prayer hours, rosaries, novenas, Fatima devotions, Divine Mercy Masses, and nocturnal adorations. I feel I have entered a world with endless layers of meaning with the mystery of Christ in the Eucharist at its center. Here at last the Truth has become manifest. Maybe I am not part of a Protestant–type church family, but I am part of something far bigger and more important - the community that traces its history back to the apostles and their living testimony of the Risen Christ. On Corpus Christi Sunday, I was received into full communion with that cloud of witnesses.

Holy Rosary's sexton, who left his neighboring parish when the guitars were moved to the front of the sanctuary, tells me some people travel up to an hour to attend a traditional Mass at Holy Rosary. Though I admire their devotion, I still must ask - should it really be that hard?"); "Real Churches Don't Kill Babies," in Timothy Drake (ed), *There We Stood, Here We Stand* (2001), p.70; "Ordaining Women: Two Views," *First Things*, April 2003 (with Sarah Hinkley Wilson); "Real Churches Don't Kill Babies," in Jennifer Ferrara and Patricia Sodano Ireland (ed), *The Catholic Mystique: Women Converts Tell Their Story* (2004), p.17 (slightly expanded version of the article above under the same title, above) ("'Real churches don't kill babies.' My trek to Rome began in the spring of 1996, the day I read this line by former Lutheran Pastor Leonard Klein [see below]. This was his critique of the decision of the Church Council of the Evangelical Lutheran Church in America (ELCA) to reject its own health care provider's carefully worked out restrictions on payment for abortions. Instead, the Church Council decided to cover the cost of any and all abortions procured by ELCA employees and their dependents. As I read Klein's editorial on the topic, I began to hyperventilate; I knew my life as a Lutheran pastor was never going to be the same...

As a pastor. I had come face-to-face with the terrible reality of abortion, Several of my parishioners opted to have abortions. Though I told these women abortion is murder, I sounded as if I were offering an opinion. I failed to explain that abortion is 'really a rejection of Christ.' I failed to tell them such action would put their very souls at stake. I failed to be the voice of a Church and Tradition that regard abortion as the murder of God's most innocent creatures. However, I also recognized that to take a firm stand on abortion was extremely difficult in a church that offers no authoritative stance on a single matter having to do with sexual ethics or the sanctity of human life...

By this time, another friend whom I deeply respect, the patristics scholar Robert Wilken [see below], had left the Lutheran ministry in order to become Roman Catholic. In a letter he wrote to me about his experiences as a new Catholic, he said the difficulty with the Reformation was that it conceived of the Church's continuity with the past and its unity in terms of an idea (justification by grace through faith). By contrast,

Catholicism thinks first of the concrete life of the Church - the life of a community with tangible links stretching back over the centuries. This observation made a profound impression upon me...

I was now questioning...the foundations of Lutheranism's separate existence as a church. Was it possible that Lutheranism was misconceived from its inception? Was the ELCA's funding of abortions a symptom of a more serious disease? A fellow pastor convert, Jeffrey Finch, puts it this way: 'The reformation had introduced two cancerous doctrines (*sola fide* and *sola scriptura*), which eventually metastasized and destroyed the very foundation of the faith as a whole, especially its accession to private judgment over the teaching authority of the Church.' Shared societal standards had masked the problem for five hundred years, but those original critics of Luther's theology who had warned of its tendencies toward antinomianism (lawlessness) had turned out to be right. I was becoming increasingly convinced Christians cannot do without a Magisterium that interprets Scripture in the light of the great Tradition of the Church...

History demonstrates that an insistence upon Scripture alone, no matter how much authority we grant it, inevitably leads to schism. If the teachings of Scripture are as self-evident as Luther argued, why do we have so many different Protestant groups all claiming their interpretation of Scripture is the right one? I could not believe the purest form of the Church was to be found in a remnant of a remnant of a remnant...

As I seriously contemplated becoming Roman Catholic, I began, on the advice of Robert Wilken 'to try to think with the Church.' Out of deference and obedience to the Magisterium, I finally concluded the Church knows better than I on [the issue of women's ordination]. I do not intend to trivialize the issue when I say this or imply there is no room for the workings of individual conscience in the Catholic Church. However, for Catholics, to have faith is to be obedient to the faith, that is, to a body of teachings and doctrines that define one's faith. I cannot pick and choose areas where I recognize the authority of the Church - to be able to do so would make the Roman Catholic Church no different from mainline Protestant communities which elevate individual conscience over even commonsense understandings of God's law. In other words, I cannot decide I like the Church's position on abortion but reject it in the case of women's ordination.

Over time, I have come to see the all-male priesthood as essential to the faith of the Church, not only to her eucharistic theology, but to the Catholic understanding of creation and the inherent differences between men and women and their respective roles in life. In other words, what is at stake in ordaining women is not the Gospel, as I had previously believed, but a truly Christian scriptural and doctrinal anthropology. I certainly continue to believe women and men are of equal dignity and worth and that women can do many of the jobs traditionally filled by men. However, I also believe God-ordained differences between men and women make the ordination of women as Catholic priests an impossibility. At the heart of the diversity between men and women lie the differences between motherhood and fatherhood. To state what has ceased to be obvious in a society governed in large measure by the principle of androgyny, women cannot be fathers. This means they cannot be priests because priests are not simply father figures - they are our spiritual fathers. Consecrated women are our spiritual mothers. We do not elevate the status of women by convincing them that what they need to be is men.

Those who insist otherwise reject all that is noble and holy about being wives and mothers (biological and spiritual) and, thereby, deny the importance of the feminine (Mother Church) in the whole economy of salvation. Christ, the embodiment of the Father's love, pours Himself out into the bridal Church. The male priest is an icon of Christ and acts '*in persona Christi*' at the altar and in the confessional. The woman Mary, representing all women, is an icon of the Church. These symbols, which tell us much about what it means to he male and female, are not interchangeable. Female priests would destroy not only this symbolism but the entire Catholic understanding of how God works through His creation to bring about our salvation.

I did not fully see this by the summer of 1997, but the women's ordination issue no longer posed a barrier to my conversion. I had arrived at the doorstep of *Lumen Gentium* (no. 14): 'Whosoever, therefore, knowing that the Catholic Church was made necessary by God through Jesus Christ, would refuse to enter or to remain in her could not be saved.' Even if I was willing to take a chance with my own soul, I had my children to consider, and that concentrates the mind...")

Feser, Edward Charles – philosopher and writer; c. end of 2001 (revert); brought up Catholic but lost the faith at age thirteen or fourteen; was atheist in the 1990s, influenced by Kierkegaard, Nietzsche, and Walter Kaufmann; educated at University of California State University at Fullerton (degree in Philosophy and Religious Studies); PhD in Philosophy from University of California at Santa Barbara; Associate Professor of Philosophy at Pasadena City College in Pasadena, California; previously Visiting Assistant Professor at Loyola Marymount University in Los Angeles and a Visiting Scholar at the Social

Philosophy and Policy Center at Bowling Green State University in Bowling Green, Ohio; author of several books and many articles; specialist in the philosophy of mind, moral and political philosophy, and the philosophy of religion; takes a strongly Aristotelian-Thomistic position; "I also write on politics, from a conservative point of view; and on religion, from a traditional Roman Catholic perspective"; married with six children; see (selective list) *Russell, Hayek, and the Mind-body Problem* (1999); *On Nozick* (2003); (ed), *The Cambridge Companion to Hayek* (2006); *Philosophy of Mind* (2006); *Locke* (2007); *The Last Superstition: A Refutation of the New Atheism* (2008) ("Let us elaborate on the nature of faith and its relationship to reason, argument, and evidence…The arguments we've been examining, if successful, show that pure reason can reveal to us that there is a God, that we have immortal souls, and that there is a natural moral law. These claims are, of course, elements in the teaching of the main monotheistic religions. But those religions also go beyond these elements, and claim access to further knowledge about God, the destiny of the human soul, and the content of our moral duties, which derive from a revelation from God. Does belief in such a revelation go beyond reason? Is this where faith comes in? The answer…is no… or at least, not necessarily. For the claim that a divine revelation has occurred is something for which the monotheistic religions typically claim there is evidence, and that evidence takes the form of a miracle, a suspension of the natural order that cannot be explained in any way other than divine intervention in the normal course of events. Christianity, for example, not only claims that Jesus Christ was God Incarnate and that what He taught therefore has divine authority; it also claims that He was resurrected from the dead, and that this incomparable miracle authenticates His teaching. Indeed, Christianity lays everything on this line. As St. Paul famously put it, 'if Christ has not been raised, then our preaching is in vain and your faith is in vain.' If the story of Jesus's resurrection is true, then you must become a Christian; if it is false, then Christianity itself is false, and should be rejected.

But the mainstream Christian tradition has also always claimed that the resurrection of Jesus Christ is a historical event the reality of which can be established through rational argument. Indeed, the philosophical arguments we've been examining so far play a role in the case for Jesus's resurrection. For that case can only be properly understood once it has already been established that there is a God and that human beings have immortal souls. Given that God exists and that He sustains the world and the causal laws governing it in being at every moment, we know that there is a power capable of producing a miracle, that is, a suspension of those causal laws Given that human beings have immortal souls, we know that the death of a person's body is not necessarily the annihilation of the person himself; for if some power were able to bring the matter of the person's body together again with his soul, the person would then come back to life. To establish the existence of God and the immortality of the soul through philosophical arguments is therefore to establish the realistic possibility of the sort of miracle on which Christianity rests its claim to a divine revelation.

The case for the resurrection of Christ doesn't exist in a vacuum, then; it presupposes this philosophical background. For without that background in place, the historical evidence for Christ's resurrection might seem inconclusive at best, since any miracle will obviously seem less likely *a priori* if you don't already know that there is a God who might produce one. But when interpreted *in light of* that background, as it should be, the evidence for Christ's resurrection can be seen to be overwhelming. That, at any rate, is what the mainstream Christian theological tradition has always claimed. And if it is overwhelming, then there are by the same token conclusive rational grounds for believing that what Christ taught was true, in which case the key doctrines of Christianity are rationally justified. The overall chain of argument, then, goes something like this: Pure reason proves through philosophical arguments that there is a God and that we have immortal souls. This by itself entails that a miracle like a resurrection from the dead is possible. Now the historical evidence that Jesus Christ was in fact resurrected from the dead is overwhelming when interpreted in light of that background knowledge. Hence pure reason also shows that Jesus really was raised from the dead. But Jesus claimed to be divine, and claimed that the authority of His teachings would be confirmed by His being resurrected. So the fact that He was resurrected provides divine authentication of His claims. Hence reason shows that He really was divine. But He was also obviously distinct from the Father to whom He prayed and the Holy Spirit whom He sent. Since this entails the doctrine of the Trinity, reason shows that doctrine must be true as well. And so forth. At every step, evidence and rational argumentation - not 'blind faith' or a 'will to believe' – are taken to justify our acceptance of certain teachings. Of course some of those teachings are taken on the basis of authority, but the point is that the trustworthiness of that authority is something that, it is claimed, can be established by reason. We can know that such-and-such a teaching was true because Christ taught it; we can know He is an authority to he trusted because His miraculous resurrection puts a divine seal of approval on what He said, including His claim to be divine, and a divine being cannot be in error; we can know that He really was resurrected because of such-and-such historical evidence together with our background knowledge that God exists and that the soul is immortal; we can know that God exists and that the soul is immortal because of such-and-such philosophical proofs; and so on. Every link in the chain is supported by argument.

Please keep in mind that I am not actually *giving* any of the arguments for the resurrection of Christ or for Christianity just now. So don't say, 'Oh how silly, I can spot a thousand holes in that case!' I *wasn't trying to make* the case; that would take a book of its own. All 1 am interested in doing here is sketching out the general strategy that Christian theology has traditionally used in justifying its doctrinal claims, and the point of doing so is to understand where faith fits into the picture. For notice that at no point in the strategy just described has it been mentioned. So how *does* it come into play? This way. Suppose you know through purely rational arguments that there is a God, that He raised Jesus Christ from the dead, and therefore that Christ really is divine, as He claimed to be, so that anything He taught must be true; in other words, suppose that the general strategy just sketched can be successfully fleshed out. Then it follows that *if you are rational* you will believe anything Christ taught; indeed, *if you are rational* you will believe it even if it is something that you could not possibly have come to know in any other way, and even if it is something highly counterintuitive and difficult to understand. For reason will have told you that Christ is infallible and therefore cannot be wrong in anything He teaches. In short, reason tells you to have *faith* in what Christ teaches, because He is divine. And that is at bottom what faith is from the point of view of traditional Christian theology: belief in what God has revealed because if God has revealed it it cannot be in error; but where the claim that He revealed it is itself something that is known on the basis of reason. Faith doesn't conflict with reason, then; it is founded on reason and completes reason.

Now of course Christianity does not teach that every believer must be able to make some fancy philosophical case for the existence of God, the resurrection of Christ, and all the rest. Most people probably could not even understand the arguments. Their belief is based on what they have been taught by some authority - the Church, or theologians or philosophers, say - and in that sense it is based on faith rather than reason. But that is just an elliptical way of saying that it is not *directly* based on rational arguments, even though it *is indirectly* based on them. For on the traditional Christian understanding of things, the authorities in question, or some of them anyway, must have and do have the arguments needed. We find an exact parallel in science. The man in the street who believes that $E = mc^2$ probably couldn't give you an interesting defense of his belief if his life depended on it. He believes it because his high school physics teacher told him about it, say, or because he heard it mentioned on an episode of *Star Trek*. Of course, a writer for *Star Trek* probably couldn't give a much better defense either - he was just citing some general background scientific knowledge in the same way the original man in the street was - and even the high school physics teacher wouldn't do so well defending it against a smart enough skeptic who knew the physics literature. You'd have to go to a university physics department, say, if you're going to find someone who can give a really solid explanation and defense, and even then some of those people are going to be more articulate and better informed than others. Most people who believe that $E = mc^2$, and who believe almost any other widely known and generally accepted scientific proposition, do so on the basis of faith in exactly the sense in question here. They believe it, in other words, on the authority of those from whom they learned it. Everyone acknowledges that this is perfectly legitimate; indeed, there is no way we could know much of interest at all if we weren't able to appeal to various authorities. But if this is legitimate in other aspects of life, there is nothing per se wrong with it in religion"); *Aquinas* (2009); "The Meaning of the Passion," *edwardfeser.com*, 2 April 2010 ("The bloody violence of the death of Jesus Christ - the skin torn by scourging, the nails driven through hands and feet, the thorns pushed into scalp and forehead, the spear thrust into the side - naturally impresses upon our minds His fleshly humanity. But it is in contemplating the Passion, perhaps more than in any other context, that we must fixate our minds precisely upon Christ's divinity, lest we miss the event's significance entirely. Modern people think they understand it well - a miscarriage of justice on the part of a corrupt political system, an affront to freedom of conscience, an expression of reactionary hostility to novel ideas comparable to the execution of Socrates. Thus is Christ transformed, absurdly, into something like an early martyr for Liberalism. (This gets the death of Socrates completely wrong too, of course. The popular understanding of both events reflects a Whiggish narcissism: 'He was a great man; ergo he *must* have been anticipating us moderns in some way.' But that is another subject.)

In fact the significance of the Passion has nothing to do with such comparative trivialities. 'We preach

Christ crucified,' wrote St. Paul; 'to the Jews a stumbling block, and to the Greeks foolishness.' The Jews and Greeks of old were (here as in so many other ways) closer to the truth than the moderns. For whatever else the crucifixion of Jesus Christ was, it was, first and foremost, the supreme blasphemy. It was Pure Act, *esse ipsum subsistens*, That Than Which No Greater Can Be Conceived, the 'I Am Who Am' of Exodus, our First Cause and Last End - spat upon, beaten, and nailed to a cross. All other meanings - political, socioeconomic, legal, moral - fade into insignificance in light of this most incomprehensible of sins. Unlike us moderns, always trying to wedge moral and religious truth into our narrow, this-worldly horizon, the ancient Jews and Greeks knew this, and rebelled at the thought. How could it be? How could Being Itself be put to death? How could the Most High allow Himself to be brought so low? A metaphysical impossibility! An inconceivable sacrilege! And yet it happened.

The 'death of God' of Nietzsche's 'madman' parable was not the crucifixion. Nor, of course, was it a literal killing of any sort. But the moral (if not the metaphysical) magnitude of deicide was not lost on him: 'How shall we comfort ourselves, the murderers of all murderers? What was holiest and mightiest of all that the world has yet owned has bled to death under our knives: who will wipe this blood off us? What water is there for us to clean ourselves? What festivals of atonement, what sacred games shall we have to invent? Is not the greatness of this deed too great for us? Must we ourselves not become gods simply to appear worthy of it?'

No silly talk here of 'Flying Spaghetti Monsters' and the like; Nietzsche, unlike so many of his successors, still had a sense of the noble, indeed of the Holy. (The New Atheist is none other than Nietzsche's Last Man in rationalist drag.) And what he said of the modern, metaphorical 'death of God' is true of the real thing: We are each of us guilty of it. We are each of us the worst of murderers. We have, each of us, slain our Maker and sought to make ourselves gods in His place. And we cannot possibly atone.

For the crucifixion, in its sublime gruesome blasphemousness, lays bare the true meaning of sin. It is *Non serviam*, 'My will, not thine, be done!' pushed through consistently. To rationalize evil, we must obliterate the Good. To justify lawlessness, we must put to death the Lawgiver. And yet there can be no 'rationalization' of any action in the absence of Good. There can be no 'justification' without Law. In the crucifixion we see the sheer, satanic *madness* of sin.

And we cannot possibly atone. Yet we are not without hope. For the Supreme Lawgiver against Whom we offend is also Infinite Mercy. The God Who can lay down

His life can raise Himself up again. And He lays it down willingly, for those He calls His 'friends' - for us, His very killers! Even as we commit the greatest of crimes against Him, His thoughts are - astoundingly - with us: 'Father, forgive them, for they know not what they do.' Having put Him on a cross, we can but humbly kneel before it - in sorrow, in thanks, in worship"); "The Meaning of the Resurrection," *edwardfeser.com*, 4 April 2010 ("As with Christ's Passion, people are always trying to attach to His Resurrection various counterfeit meanings. But it is, in this case, harder to do it with a straight face. Were you present at the crucifixion, you would have seen what on the surface required no supernatural explanation - a man nailed to a cross, as so many had been before by the Romans. Were you present at Christ's tomb on that first Easter Sunday, you would have seen a corpse returned to life. 'Keep hope alive!' 'Jesus is still with us in our hearts!' 'You can't keep a good man down!' and all the other banalities liberal pastors will waste their congregations' time with today rather fail to convey this central fact about the Resurrection. It was a divine suspension of the natural order, a miracle, or it was nothing. 'If Christ is not raised,' St. Paul tells the Christian, 'your faith is worthless.' And by 'raised' he meant *raised* - reanimated, brought back from the dead - not eaten by wild dogs but remembered fondly, or whatever it is the John Dominic Crossans of the world want to put in place of what Christianity has always claimed. The Christian faith has, historically, laid everything on that line: Accept the Resurrection, and you must accept what Jesus Christ taught; reject it, and you must reject Him too as a fraud.

Thus, while the Resurrection is an affront to naturalism, it is not primarily that. The most formidable pagan critics of Christianity already knew that naturalism is false. Indeed, almost all serious philosophers historically have known that; it was part of the common ground most of them took for granted in their disputes over less fundamental matters. (The atomists are an obvious exception, though their naturalism was less crude and less dogmatic than that of their modern successors.) In particular, the existence of God and the immortality of the soul were known by Neo-Platonists and others to be demonstrable through philosophical arguments; and such demonstrations ought in any event to form the *preamble* to an apologetic for the Resurrection, rather than its sequel (or so I would argue).

No, the Resurrection is primarily an affront to the *religious* rivals of Christianity. It is the point where the tedium of 'dialogue' finally ends and the serious business of conversion begins. The Man Who said 'I am the Way and the Truth and the Life; no one comes to the Father except through Me' was either raised from the dead or He was not. If He was, then His startling claims received thereby a divine seal of approval, and the only rational response of the non-Christian can be to request baptism. If He was not so raised, then His words reveal Him to have been a megalomaniacal lunatic. An interesting lunatic, maybe; a lunatic whose historical, cultural, religious, and moral impact has vastly - one might say miraculously - outweighed that of any sane man. But a lunatic all the same, and appropriately treated as such. There really is no third option. (Even C. S. Lewis's 'liar' alternative isn't all that plausible - what sane first-century Jew would think claiming personal divinity a good way to raise a following? And the 'guru' Jesus pushed by Crossan and his ilk is manifestly sheer unhistorical fantasy).

The Resurrected Christ will not be dialogued with. He will be worshipped, and obeyed, or He will simply be rejected as one would reject the ravings of a Jim Jones or David Koresh. Politely rejected, perhaps, at least this side of the grave; we can concede to the dialoguers their good manners. But rejected, and in no uncertain terms. 'Let your Yes be Yes and your No, No.' Unless you are prepared to call Him your Risen Lord, seek no religious meaning in His life and teachings. Nor in His death; for the Passion is what it is only in light of the Resurrection. If we who did not know Him in the flesh worship at the foot of His cross, it is because we have worshipped first at His empty tomb"); "Ten Years On," *edwardfeser.com*, 11 September 2011 ("I was raised a Catholic, but by the time I was a teenager I had been suckered by the standard arguments to the effect that Catholicism is 'unbiblical' etc. And by my early twenties the standard atheist arguments turned me away from religion altogether.

I was the original New Atheist, and went through the usual stages. Stage 1, the Angry Young Atheist, reading everything I could get my hands on critical of religion and endlessly and condescendingly arguing with my religious friends. Call it the 'Everything I Need to Know I Learned from Prometheus Books' stage. Though I was also a big Nietzsche and Walter Kaufmann fan, which I liked to think gave me a little more depth.

Then I reached Stage 2, what we might call the Keith Parsons Stage: I 'knew' that religion wasn't even worth arguing about any more because the arguments for it were 'obviously' so bad. Time was better devoted to More Serious Things. *Sola Scientia*! Well, and naturalistic philosophy, of course. What a stupid a***ole I was.

So, arguing with these people is like arguing with my younger self. Only I find that they are even more stupid and ill-informed than I was. Scary!

So Ed, in short, why is it Catholicism and not Islam or Orthodoxy or Mormonism or some Protestant denomination? Well, it's hard to give a *short* answer to that question, but if I had to try to give one I would say that there is no way that a divine revelation could be effective unless it is conveyed through an ongoing institution, and one with an executive having power to settle disputes. And that means a Church, and a Pope. But again, that's only the short answer. Ed, I seem to recall you mentioning in *The Last Superstition* that, even while an atheist, you nevertheless thought that (e.g.) Daniel Dennett was rather a blowhard. Yes, I always thought Dennett in particular was a blowhard, and that had to do not just with the things he's said about religion but also with his work in philosophy of mind, where he has also always had a tendency to attack straw men, condescend toward critics of materialism, substitute rhetoric for argument, and so forth. That doesn't mean that his work is never interesting and important. Sometimes it is both. But the weaknesses of his (quite awful) stuff on religion had precursors in his earlier, more technical philosophical work... [E]ven when I was an atheist I thought there was a kind of depth to at least certain kinds of religion that most New Atheist types don't want to acknowledge. That's why I said above that I thought my fondness for writers like Nietzsche and Walter Kaufmann - who always emphasized that religion was a serious thing, even though they rejected it - made my own atheism more serious. The Kaufmann-style atheist says 'I can't believe this stuff for a minute, but I can see that the life of a really devout believer has a kind of admirable gravitas.' New Atheist types typically don't have the decency or humanity even to allow that much. They're vulgar ideologues, who insist on seeing nothing in religion but stupidity and evil. And I don't think I was ever quite that bad, even though I could certainly be condescending. ('Yes, I can respect that, but I am beyond that sort of thing' - that was more my attitude'")); "The Road From Atheism," *edwardfeser.com*, 17 July 2012 ("Speaking for myself, anyway, I can say this much. When I was an undergrad I came across the saying that learning a little philosophy leads you away from God, but learning a lot of philosophy leads you back. As a young man who had learned a little philosophy, I scoffed. But in later years and at least in my own case, I would come to see that it's true").

Fidelis of the Cross, Father – see under Stone, James Kent.

Fleming, Thomas J. – political writer; b. 27 April 1945; educated at the University of North Carolina at Chapel Hill (awarded PhD in Classics); taught Latin at a private school in South Carolina; paleo-conservative; was founding member and board member of the League of the South, but resigned later; founding editor of *Southern Partisan* magazine in 1979; president of the Rockford Institute; editor of *Chronicles: A Magazine of American Culture* from 1985; see (selective list) "Old Rights and New Right," in Robert W. Whitaker (ed), *The New Right Papers* (1982); *The Conservative Movement* (1988) (with Paul Gottfried); *West Point: Blue and Grey* (1988); *The Politics of Human Nature* (1993); *Montenegro: The Divided Land* (2002); *The Morality of Everyday Life: Rediscovering an Ancient Alternative to the Liberal Tradition* (2003); *Socialism* (2007); "Ignatius II," *chronicles.org*, 19 May 2008 ("The Epistle to the Romans is in many ways the most significant contribution made by St. Ignatius to the formation of the early Christian Church…I would like to sketch a little of what I think we can agree on. The Church begins as a brotherhood of Jesus' disciples. Before returning to the Father, he informed the disciples (Matthew 28) of their mission: 'Then the eleven disciples went away into Galilee, into a mountain where Jesus had appointed them. And when they saw him, they worshipped him: but some doubted. And Jesus came and spake unto them, saying, 'All power is given unto me in heaven and in earth. Go ye therefore, and teach all nations, baptizing them in the name of the Father, and of the Son, and of the Holy Ghost: Teaching them to observe all things whatsoever I have commanded you: and, lo, I am with you always, even unto the end of the world.' This positive commandment excludes any unitarian or sub-trinitarian preaching.

Even though the Lord had appeared to nominate Peter as the chief of the apostles, the rock on which the Church - that is, the gathering of the faithful - would be built, Jerusalem, in the early days, was the center of the Church. Peter, meanwhile, had gone off preaching the Word in places like Antioch. When dissension arose between, on the one hand, Paul and Barnabas who were converting the gentiles, and certain Pharisees who had converted but insisted that the gentile converts had to be circumcised and live as Jews, the case was referred to the apostles and presbyters (seniors, elders) in Jerusalem: 'And the apostles and elders came together for to consider of this matter' (Acts 15:5). When the Church, presided over by James, decided (after a convincing speech by Peter) that Paul and Barnabas were in the right, a letter was sent out to various congregations of gentile Christians, declaring the decision in the name of the Holy Ghost and the apostles, elders, and brothers in Jerusalem. This decision, which was the express will of the apostles and senior members, was to apply to the entire Church, which is a unity and not a collection of fragments.

We have learned from Clement and Ignatius that the office of bishop, probably evolving rapidly, conferred important authority that should not be contradicted, even when the bishop in question was a young man. Ignatius teaches us to be humble and respectful in our dealings with the bishop, who is both our bulwark against heresy (a word that refers, literally, to those who prefer to make their own choice, to have things their way) and the embodiment of apostolic authority that derives ultimately from Christ.

As yet there is no clear-cut hierarchy beyond the bishop's church, though it is clear from Acts that the apostles in Jerusalem were appealed to. We are headed toward but have not yet reached the point at which each major church, typically in a city, was presided over by a bishop, and the chief city in a region, often capital of a Roman province, was home to a metropolitan or archbishop, who had authority to elect and to some extent oversee the other bishops in the district. As time went on certain churches, which had received and preserved the authentic teachings of the apostles, were designated as apostolic, and when theological disputes broke out, the unwritten tradition of the apostolic churches was appealed to.

Alexandria would have authority over all Egypt, while Rome was home to the only ancient metropolitanate in most of Italy and Sicily. Five of these churches came to be regarded as dominant: Rome, Alexandria, Antioch, and Jerusalem, after it had wrested the title from Caesarea, and last of all Constantinople, after it was founded by Constantine as 'New Rome.' Their bishops, the patriarchs, would exercise authority over the metropolitan archbishops in their region. Although Christianity was preached in many languages and dialects, the Church's primary language, in those early years, was Greek even in Rome, though Latin emerged later as the language of the Western Empire (Italy, Gaul, Spain, North Africa).

...What did Ignatius think of Rome's status. To determine that, let us look at his salutations to other churches. The Ephesian church is 'worthy of all felicitation' and 'blessed with greatness'; the Magnesians are not distinguished in the salutation, while the Trallians are 'beloved in God' and the Smyrnaeans' Church has 'obtained mercy in every gift and is filled with faith and love,' and the Philadelphians are similarly praised. Rome, too, has 'obtained mercy' but is also 'the church beloved and enlightened by the will of Him who has willed all things, which are, according to the love of Jesus Christ, our God, which also has the presidency in the country of the land of the Romans, worthy of God, worthy of honor, worthy of blessing, worthy of praise, worthy of success, worthy in its holiness, and preeminent in love' and the Roman Christians are themselves 'filled with the grace of God' and 'filtered clear from every foreign stain.'

This is a powerful salutation. Now, for all we know, a Roman bishop might have addressed Antioch in such terms, but there is no evidence. The least we can say is that the Roman Church is distinguished above all the other Churches to whom his surviving letters refer, and, after Titus' conquest of Jerusalem, Rome and perhaps a few other apostolic Churches would seem to have succeeded to the dignity of that first apostolic Church…

The Eastern position, from fairly early on and down to fairly late, was unequivocal in acknowledging the primacy of the Roman bishop, and even today most Orthodox bishops and theologians I know concede that if the Church were reunited, the heir of Peter would preside over the meetings of the patriarchs - indeed, in some Eastern ecclesiastical disputes in recent years, appeals have been made to the Pope. But all such discussion is premature, since in the age we are examining, it is not at all clear that the concept of a metropolitan, much less a patriarchal church has emerged"); "Clueless Catholics," *chronicles.org*, 20 February 2009 ("Obviously, the pre-Christian world included large numbers of morally serious people who believed in god or gods but did not entirely condemn either abortion or infanticide. The argument, then, that all seriously moral people would oppose abortion cannot be true. It is a little like saying anyone remotely interested in science would agree with Newton or Einstein. Obviously, something happened to change the discourse: the Incarnation. A self-described Catholic is supposed to know these things.

Now, there is an element of truth in the argument, which is that just as we do not wish to be killed unjustly, we should not kill unjustly. But what if abortion is not unjust? What if we regard it as, in some cases, a necessity or at least a preferable option? After all, just because we do not wish to be executed does not mean that we necessarily oppose the death penalty. We might even say that were we to commit a cold-blooded murder, we should deserve killing. Thus, if we think life is not worth living without an IQ above 75 or without a reasonably healthy body or without loving parents, we might say that abortion in such cases is reasonable and just and might even, honestly or not, say that we would apply the same criteria to ourselves.

It is also true that most of the arguments used to defend abortion are irrational arguments from analogy, implying that an unborn child is an alien space monster implanted in the womb or merely the seed from which a tree might grow. Like virtually everything said by the Left, the arguments are childish and irrational. But the fact remains that natural reason did not teach the Greeks and Romans that it is wrong to kill an unborn or newborn child, though some thought abortion shameful. There was no prohibition on abortion in Roman law, except where the father was not consulted. In that case, she was guilty of depriving him and his ancestors of an heir. This is, at least, a more wholesome approach than our current abortion law, though it rests not on reason but on family loyalty.

From the beginning Christian women did not kill their babies. This is one of the things we can learn from the early Apostolic Fathers. Christians did not practice either infanticide or sodomy. For both prohibitions, there is ample justification in natural law, as that phrase was understood by Aristotle, Cicero, and St. Thomas. We were not made sexual beings to violate each others' anuses or to enjoy ourselves while disposing of the fruits of our coition. Mothers, in this tradition, do not have a universal obligation to prevent abortion but a specific obligation not just not to kill their children but to nurture and cherish them. This is not like some corollary deduced from a basic logic axiom: It is a specific duty that arises both from the nature that God created and from God's love for us.

The real question is not whether abortion is consistent with reason but rather, whether it is right to lie in a good cause...Many pro-life arguments I have studied come down to well-intentioned lying, by which I understand not only a conscious and deliberate lie but the reckless disregard for truth engaged in by pseudo-intellectuals who pretend to learning and authority they do not possess.

The most basic error is to cover Christian truth with the tinsel trappings of Enlightenment universalism that makes everyone owe everyone else the same duties.

Thus, we hear sweeping claims, expressed in a Kantian idiom, that it is everyone's duty to prevent a non-Christian female from killing her child, whether she lives in China or Peru. Their arguments frequently rely on misused or misunderstood Scriptural citations, which, if refuted, might unsettle the convictions of a poor Fundamentalist. Among the worst are the utilitarian arguments that tell us we may be losing countless Beethovens and Shakespeares, to say nothing of millions of taxpayers who will pay my Social Security. But what if it turns out that in economic terms, abortion is a net gain, in preventing the birth of millions of welfare-dependent blacks and Mexicans? Would that make abortion a civic duty? Live by bad arguments, die by bad arguments. The cumulative effect of much of the professional pro-life ideology is to distort and deflect the question, away from the really important thing, which is how to convert nonbelievers, who will then be far less likely to kill their babies, toward comparatively trivial legislative policies and judicial agendas.

If everyone is rational enough to understand that abortion is wrong, why is it that so few defenders of the unborn are capable either of entering into a rational discourse or studying history?; "Beatitudes, not Platitudes," *chronicles.org*, 1 April 2009 ("'And seeing the multitudes, he went up into a mountain: and when he was set, his disciples came unto him: And he opened his mouth, and taught them, saying, □Blessed are the poor in spirit: for theirs is the kingdom of heaven. Blessed are they that mourn: for they shall be comforted. Blessed are the meek: for they shall inherit the earth. Blessed are they which do hunger and thirst after righteousness: for they shall be filled. Blessed are the merciful: for they shall obtain mercy. Blessed are the pure in heart: for they shall see God. Blessed are the peacemakers: for they shall be called the children of God. Blessed are they which are persecuted for righteousness' sake: for theirs is the kingdom of heaven□' (Matthew 5: 1-10).

It is difficult to convey the effect these now familiar paradoxes must have had upon Jesus' listeners. The conventional wisdom (not just of Jews but of Greeks and Romans) is turned on its head. Success is what mattered in the ancient world. Good fortune, wealth, and power were signs of divine favor. Jews, in looking back at their own history, would have admired the exploits of Joshuah, Gideon, and Samson, men who would not have been out of place in the American West. King David and his son Solomon were among their greatest heroes. David was a man of war who smote his enemies and built a powerful (albeit tiny) kingdom; Solomon was proverbial for his wealth as well as for his power.

For more recent heroes, Jews could turn for inspiration to the Maccabees, who had led a bloody insurrection that liberated their people from the Macedonian kingdom of Syria ruled by Antiochus Epiphanes. The successors to the Macedonians were the Romans, who had been ruling over the Jews, largely through proxies like the Herods, for years. In expecting a messiah or savior, the common belief was that he would come as a fighting prince, another David or Judas Maccabeus, with sword in hand to drive the Romans into the sea. Yet here is this prophet or (some might say) messiah, early in his career, calmly beginning an address to the multitude proclaiming the blessedness of 'the poor in spirit' or simply, as in the parallel passage in Luke, 'the poor.'

What do these words mean, really, 'blessed' and 'poor in spirit.' Blessed, for example, can mean several things in English. When we bless someone, we speak well of him. While poor can mean either lacking in wealth or in a poor condition or quality, as in 'the actor turned in a poor performance.' The original text is clearer. The Greek word makarios means happy, in the sense of having good fortune. The simpler word makar is typically used in early Greek to refer to the gods as opposed to mere mortals, and makarios thus retains a strong whiff of divine favor. In the plural (as Jesus uses it here), makarios refers to the rich and well-educated. Ptochoi (the poor), by contrast, are at the end of the socio-economic spectrum; they are the beggars that crouch and cringe, fearfully, in the presence of their superiors. A slightly educated listener might have thought of Odysseus, the noble Greek warrior who disguised himself as a beggar and had to endure insults and abuse in his own house - a story that eerily anticipates Jesus' own arrival in earthly form: the son of God who is born to a poor family, a man 'despised and rejected and acquainted with grief.'

Matthew's phrase 'poor in spirit' is even stronger than Luke's. Odysseus may have been without resources and beggarly in appearance, but, as a proud and violent Greek aristocrat, he was anything but poor in spirit. Jesus was telling his people that the greatest happiness one can have is to have the spirit of the cringing beggar. What a strange statement, then, to make that the abject and miserable, those who mourn the loss of a loved one, are the ones who have experienced divine good favor. Most of us have read or heard this sermon so many times we take it for granted as either hyperbole - He could not have meant these things literally, could he - or as a set of Sunday school clichés that we recite without any intention of living up to. But then they would not be the Beatitudes, but only the platitudes.

In Mathew's story, nothing has prepared us for this shocking message. We know only of Jesus' miraculous conception and birth, his precocious wisdom, his baptism by John the Baptist, and his temptation by Satan, who had promised him material comfort and power if he would only challenge his father, as Satan had done, and follow the fallen angel. Emerging victorious over the Enemy, Christ attracts a large following, not only from his home-area of Galilee but also from Jerusalem and Judea and even from the Decapolis, ten Hellenic cities that enjoyed important municipal privileges within the empire. These cities enjoyed Greek culture, which even the Semitic inhabitants (whether Jews or Syrians) had absorbed. The mention of these Decapolitans in the audience is the first indication that Jesus is not necessarily preaching only to Jews or to men and women of exclusively Jewish cultural traditions. What would these Greeks or Jews who had a Greek education think of the Sermon, with its disturbing inversion of values? Those who had read some Homer - and the *Iliad* and *Odyssey* were obligatory reading in any course of education - would think of the noble heroes who populate the epics, especially of Achilles, whom some believed to lead a life of eternal happiness in the Isles of the Blessed. These were men of violence and wrath, who took nothing from nobody, as the saying goes. The only lower-class character in the *Iliad*, the ugly rabble-rouser, is rebuked and beaten by Odysseus.

Early Greek poets had never tired of celebrating men of wealth and power or of complaining about their own failures and poverty. Traditional Greek culture taught that shame (aidos) and honor had to be respected. A sense of shame included having a regard for social conventions and being respectful to parents, elders, and social superiors, while honor (the Greek world literally implies price or value) was the respect to which you were entitled, by your family, social status, and personal qualities. When the great Achilles quarreled with Agamemnon and left the Trojan War, it was not so much that he missed the woman of whom he had been deprived as it was the honor he was losing. It would be little use telling Achilles (or most Greeks) to ignore public opinion, because they would interpret such a remark to be an indication of a base character.

If they had dabbled in philosophy, the Decapolitans might have been less shocked and connect Jesus' preaching with the diatribes of Cynic and Stoic philosophers who derided the pursuit of wealth and power as vanity and distraction, but in that case they might also suspect that Jesus was one more hypocritical guru, of the type that satirists routinely ridiculed. Wealth is nothing, say the philosophers? Then why are they always asking for handouts and taking fees for teaching - rather than practicing - the virtues of self-restraint, chastity, and humility?

In this sermon, Christ fulfills the highest traditions of the Jewish prophets and Greek moral philosophers. The implications might take us ordinary folks a lifetime to figure out to any degree. With these bold paradoxes he turned conventional wisdom on its head and forced his followers to acknowledge the humanity of people they may well have loathed - Samaritans, Syrians, Greeks, Romans. It has nothing in common with either Capitalism or Socialism, but offers us a truth that is also the way to life, both to a better life on earth and to eternal life"); "Religio Philologi: The Epistle of James," *chronicles.org*, 19 May 2009 ("The Christian faith is rooted in a sublime set of mysteries that inspire the human reason that can never quite comprehend them, rather as the circle can never be quite squared. Some of these mysteries concern the origins of all that is most important to us: How and why is there something rather than nothing, or, rather, how did God make something out of nothing? How did life come from non-life and human consciousness - the soul - out of the non-conscious? Some vain scientists think they have answers to these questions, but they are no more satisfying than the ancient image of the elephant standing on the back of the turtle floating in a basin of water.

Another set of mysteries appears to defy the principle of non-contradiction: How can Christ be both fully human and 'very God'? How can the elements of communion be both bread and wine and yet the body and blood of Christ? How can we be saved alone by the faith that is given by grace and yet be told that faith without works is dead?

It is only by subordinating our reason to Tradition that we can begin to understand some part of these mysteries. But this same subordination is required of the aspiring scholar or scientist, who, if he were to try to begin his studies by questioning step one, would never make it to step two. I would not presume to offer any original ideas here, and if I do deviate into originality, I hope someone will take me to task. The correct term for an original thinker is heretic, and the common fault of well-intentioned heretics - and such people exist - is that they take one side of a mysterious truth and develop it to the exclusion or prejudice of the other. This was the mistake of Arians and Docetists, Nestorians and Monotheists, and it is the fault of those who would elevate human free will to the exclusion of grace or grace to the exclusion of works"); "Athens and Jerusalem II: A Religion for Sissies?" *chronicles.org*, 24 October 2009 ("If humility is the *skandalon* of Neopagans, they typically base their more pragmatic case against Christianity on its supposed opposition to what pagan cultures regarded as the legitimate use of violence: personal self-defense, defensive war, and the execution of murderers, rapists, traitors, and other serious malefactors. They are entirely wrong, as they are about most things. The text most frequently cited is Matthew 5:38: 'Ye have heard that it hath been said, An eye for an eye, and a tooth for a tooth: But I say unto you, That ye resist not evil: but whosoever shall smite thee on thy right cheek, turn to him the other also. And if any man will sue thee at the law, and take away thy coat, let him have thy cloak also. And whosoever shall compel thee to go a mile, go with him twain. Give to him that asketh thee, and from him that would borrow of thee turn not thou away. Ye have heard that it hath been said, Thou shalt love thy neighbor, and hate thine enemy. But I say unto you, Love your enemies, bless them that curse you, do good to them that hate you, and pray for them which despitefully use you, and persecute you; That ye may be the children of your Father which is in heaven: for he maketh his sun to rise on the evil and on the good, and sendeth rain on the just and on the unjust. For if ye love them which love you, what reward have ye? do not even the publicans the same? And if ye salute your brethren only, what do ye more than others? do not even the publicans so? Be ye therefore perfect, even as your Father which is in heaven is perfect.

If the first recorded sin was Eve's and Adam's disobedience in the Garden, the second was Cain's murder of his brother. In the Pentateuch, revenge...was the only law on homicide. Now, that indulgence is being taken away (or at least turned over to the rulers of the commonwealth) and, along with it, even the desire to get even and the natural inclination to hate one's enemy. Some pacifists, Christians among them, have construed this passage to imply an express condemnation of all forms of violence and all use of force whether in self-defense or national defense or criminal justice, but neither the context of the passage nor the wider context of the Scriptures and tradition would bear out this interpretation.

Jesus is primarily addressing his followers, the brethren he had assembled from the towns of Galilee. Like most Mediterranean peoples, the Jews were a fractious and litigious lot. In Greek, the enemy He refers to is an *echthros*, that is, a personal enemy, and not the foreign enemy who rides in to slay, rape, and pillage. A personal enemy is someone with whom you are having a dispute over a property line, an inheritance, or insults that may have been exchanged when the two parties were in their cups. Anyone who has lived in a small town, suburban neighborhood, or coop apartment building knows that man is not just wolf to man but also weasel and jackal, ready to start a lifelong quarrel over a loose dog, an unpainted fence, or a noisy party. What a waste of time and energy this can be, especially among the brothers who are told to love each other.

Modern Christian pacifism is less a product of the Scriptures and Tradition than it is of the Enlightenment. From the beginning, some eccentric early Christians (*e.g.*, Tertullian) rejected legitimacy of the Roman Empire and, consequently, all forms of imperial service, including soldiering and serving in the bureaucracy, but they were for the most part extreme rigorists who withdrew from the Christian main stream. Early apologists, such as the author of the *Epistle to Diognetus* and Aristides the Athenian only distinguish Christians for their moral purity. Otherwise, 'Christians are not distinguished from the rest of mankind by country, speech, or custom,' and, although they are treated as aliens, they shoulder the burdens of citizenship.

St. Augustine, who argues strenuously against particular applications of the death penalty, did not repudiate the right of the ruler to inflict it. Christian pacifism, he insists, is a slander used to discredit Christians as loyal Roman citizens. In his letter to an imperial commissioner whose queries helped to prompt the writing of the *City of God*, Augustine argued that the admonitions to turn the other cheek and not repay evil with evil have to do with the Christian's mental disposition and not with the need to correct, with charity, an erring son, a criminal, or an invader. As a provincial administrator and yet a Christian, Macedonius had asked Augustine to justify his pleas for clemency. The bishop began his response by conceding that the state has been given the power to correct wickedness: 'Surely, it is not without purpose that we have the institution of the power of kings, the death penalty of the judge, the barbed hooks of the executioner, the weapons of the soldier, the right of punishment of the overlord, even the severity of the good father...While these are feared, the wicked are kept within bounds and the good live more peacefully among the wicked.'

This is obviously a gloss on the text of St. Paul's *Epistle to the Romans*, where Paul defends the sovereign power over life and death (Rom 13:1-4): 'Let every soul be subject unto the higher powers. For there is no power but of God: the powers that be are ordained of God. Whosoever therefore resisteth the power, resisteth the ordinance of God: and they that resist shall receive to themselves damnation. For rulers are not a terror to good works, but to the evil. Wilt thou then not be afraid of the power? Do that which is good, and thou shalt have praise of the same: For he is the minister of God to thee for good. But if thou do that which is evil, be afraid; for he beareth not the sword in vain: for he is the minister of God, a revenger to execute wrath upon him that doeth evil. In appealing to the Roman officer's mercy, Augustine goes on to say that while the Old Law did preach harsh justice, the New Testament urges us to pardon offenders either that we may be pardoned or as a means of commending gentleness. After surveying a number of arguments (not all of them convincing) for mercy, Augustine concludes that there is good both in the magistrate's severity and in the bishop's plea for mercy. 'Do not be displeased at being petitioned by the good, because the good are not displeased that you are feared by the wicked.'

In calling for mercy in specific instances, Augustine has simply repeated Christ's admonition to be merciful; he did not repudiate the death penalty itself or call for an unqualified defense of life for life's sake, unlike the modern theologians who, in attempting to weave a seamless garment of life, are really swaddling unborn babies in the uniform of the death-row convict. If all human life is equally precious, then none can be very valuable. In most cases, perhaps, the proponents of a seamless garment have simply failed to understand the consequences of their reasoning. But in using the same language to defend the innocent unborn and the condemned murderer, they are equating innocence with guilt.

If the ruler is justified in executing domestic criminals, how much more is he justified in defending his people against a foreign enemy? John the Baptist, after all, did not tell the soldiers to lay down their weapons and desert but was content with instructing them to 'do violence to no man, neither accuse any falsely; and be content with your wages' (Luke 3:14). The barbs were aimed at soldiers who augmented their incomes by collaborating in the extortions of tax-collectors.

When a Christian engages in homicide, either as executioner or soldier, it is the ruler and not he who is morally responsible for the killing. The soldier is merely the instrument of a ruler whose power comes from God, as Christ informs Pilate during the interrogation. In *Romans* 13 (cited above), St. Paul sums up the Christian position succinctly, 'Not in vain does he [the ruler] hold the sword.'

Vengeance belongs to God, who then delegates that power to the ruler. Christians, then, must foreswear the right to vengeance, though in exchange the ruler must protect the innocent from violence. The ruler must not only punish but defend his kingdom or empire against invaders. His subjects or citizens, correspondingly, have a duty to pay their taxes, obey the laws, and defend their country. This reasoning depends on an important premise, that a commonwealth - whether city republic or kingdom or empire - is a legitimate human institution that requires the power to defend itself. In the high Christian Age, Thomas Aquinas would make it clear that Christians owe a primary moral duty to their family and a civic duty to their commonwealth.

From the beginning, the adherents to the main current of Christianity acknowledged the duty to obey the laws and commands of the rulers. Christ did not resist Pilate, because Pilate, however badly, represented the sovereign authority of the Roman Emperor who did the Lord's will on earth. Aha, says the pagan, this is pacifism. No, not at all, since Christians also obeyed the command to defend the empire. Jews were absolved from military service, because Sabbath observance conflicted with the duties of a soldier. Christians, as they came to be distinguished from Jews, were not absolved. Some radicals - and who knows how many of them were either Jewish or Judaizing Christians - misconstrued Christ's teachings to be an exemption from all civic duties. The Apostolic writer known as the Disciple did not: '[Christians] obey the prescribed laws, and at the same time surpass the laws by their lives'"); "Athens and Jerusalem IV: Medieval Christian Wimps," *chronicles.org*, 17 November 2009 ("Like, for example, Charles Martel and his grandson Charlemagne, Otto the Great and Barbarossa, Henry II of England and his son Richard Coeur de Leon, or, going to the East, Belisarius and Heraclius, Leo the Great and Basil the Bulgar-Slayer, or the Christian Medieval rulers of Serbia - Stephan Dusan and Prince Lazar - and Hungary and Rumania - Janos Hunyadi and Vlad Drakul, whose enormities against the Muslims made his name a byword for vampirism.

If there were any merit in the case being made by the Anti-Christians who describe themselves as members of the so-called 'Alternative-Right,' it would collapse on the historical reality of the Medieval Christian fighting men who combined the toughness of the Texas Rangers with the violence of Icelandic revengers and, in many cases, with the piety of the saints. Take the case of Fulke Nerra, the count of Anjou, whose atrocious violence in maintaining and extending his territory are matched only by a religious fervor that sent him more than once on pilgrimage to the Holy Land.

Medieval history is an endless catalogue of violence, in causes good and bad, which might be interpreted as a residuum of Germanic paganism. So, to test the hypothesis of Medieval Wimpery, let us look only at a few people who have been honored with the title of 'saint': Saint Henry, Saint Joan, and Saint Louis. The first is a German emperor, who enforced his claims throughout the Empire, especially in Burgundy, the second a peasant girl who led the French liberation war against the English, the third a French king who defended his crown's authority in France and the faith on Crusade in the Middle East.

The Neo-Pagans might make two retorts that these tough guys were only superficially Christian and that their courage is a legacy from their Germanic pagan ancestors. There are two fatal flaws in this line of "reasoning." The first is the simple fact that it is all based on a single book, Russell's dissertation on the Germanization of Christianity [James C. Russell's *The Germanization of Medieval Christianity: A Sociohistorical Approach to Religious Transformation*], a piece of sociological speculation they have wildly misconstrued (if, indeed, they have actually read the book). The second is the martial valor and military successes of warriors who had little, sometimes no Germanic blood").

Floyd, John – politician and soldier; b. 24 April 1783, Floyds Station, Virginia; d. 17 August 1837, Sweet Springs. Monroe County, Virginia; from a prominent family in the Virginia political and social establishment; his father, Colonel John Floyd, was a pioneer who was killed by the Indians twelve days before his son's birth; a grandfather and great grandfather had been governors of Virginia;

suffered much illness as a young man, which influenced his decision to become a doctor; in 1804 he married Letitia Preston Floyd (see below) (twelve children of the marriage); qualified as a doctor at the University of Pennsylvania in 1806; entered the regular army in 1812; member of the Virginia House of Delegates 1814-1815; in 1816 elected as a Democratic-Republican to the United States House of Representatives and served 1817-1829; tirelessly pushed for the occupation of the Oregon area, both during and after his service in Congress; Governor of Virginia 1830-1834; during his governorship the state was economically prosperous; he initially supported emancipation for the state, but finally went with the majority against it; he was the last governor of Virginia to serve under its pre-Revolutionary War constitution and the first to serve under the post-Revolutionary War constitution; in 1832 he received votes (the eleven electoral votes of South Carolina) for the Presidency of the United States, running in the Nullifier Party, which was succeeded by the Democaatic Party; after leaving office as Governor of Virginia he became a Catholic (some say on his deathbed, but no records have ever been found); his wife and many of his children became Catholics (see under the entries for Letitia Preston Floyd, below, and Letitia Ford Lewis, below); his son John Buchanan Floyd (1803-1863) was Governor of Virginia 1849-1852, and Secretary of War under President Buchanan; another son, George Rogers Clark Floyd (1810-1895) was Secretary of Wisconsin Territory and later a member of the West Virginia Legislature; buried in the Lewis Family Cemetery, on the hill behind the remains of the historic Lynnside Manor, Sweet Springs; see Charles H. Ambler, *The Life and Diary of John Floyd Governor of Virginia, an Apostle of Secession, and the Father of the Oregon Country* (1918).

Floyd, Letitia Preston – author and educator; b. 29 September 1779, Smithfield, Montgomery County, Virginia; c. June 1852; d. 12 December 1852, Burkes Garden, Tazewell County, Virginia; from a prosperous Virginia family; her father Colonel William Preston (1729-1783) was surveyor of much of central and western Virginia and a figure of great influence in the South; her brother Francis Preston (1765-1836) represented Virginia in the House of Representatives 1793-1797; another brother, James Patton Preston (1774-1843), served as Governor of Virginia 1816-1819; brought up at Smithfield Plantation in the anti-slavery and populist Appalachian Mountains, not in the slave holding and aristocratic Tidewater, Virginia; surrounded by books purchased from London by her father; in 1804 she married John Floyd (see above), who later became Governor of Virginia; she became interested in the Catholic faith as a result of hearing the sermons of Fr. Shriver and Fr. O'Brien in Richmond with her eldest daughter, Letitia Floyd Lewis (see below) who then converted, followed by her other two daughters, her husband, and three of her sons; finally, and mainly under the influence of Bishop Richard Whelan of Richmond, she herself was received into the Church; great Catholic benefactor; also her three daughters, Letitia, Lavalette (d. 1887), and Nicketti (1819-1908) all built chapels on their estates, which became the centers of Catholic activity in the area; buried next to her husband in the Lewis family cemetery, Sweet Springs; see *Memoirs* (1843) (mainly reminiscences of eighteenth century pioneers of West Virginia and Kentucky); Harry E. Winter, OMI, "Letitia Preston Floyd – Pioneer Catholic Feminist," *lynnside.com* ("It was during [John Floyd's] governorship that their children started becoming Catholic, and therein lies a mystery. What led the family to become Catholic in a time when Catholicism was a very suspect religion?

Two people were certainly involved. The first was the very personable pastor of St. Peter's Church, Richmond, Father Timothy O'Brien. Gov. Floyd maintained a pew at St. Peter's during his term of office. The three daughters began to convert at this time, during their teens; three of the four sons eventually became Catholic. Undoubtedly, the sermons they heard from their pew helped. In fact, on 27 May 1832, their father recorded in his journal, 'went to the chapel to hear Mr. O'Brien, who is a man of talents and a respectable orator.'

The second person involved was Bishop Richard Whelan, second bishop of Richmond and first bishop of Wheeling. His views on slavery, and that of Gov. Floyd's, were remarkably similar: they wanted to stamp it out. Gov. Floyd wrote in his journal on 26 December 1831: 'I shall not rest until slavery is abolished in Virginia.' (The Nat Turner slave rebellion, which Floyd had to subdue, must have been a tragic time for the whole family). Slavery affected Bishop Whelan no less seriously. One of the main reasons why he left Richmond altogether for Wheeling was his hatred of and opposition to slavery.

So two clergymen undoubtedly influenced the Floyd family. But it is quite certain that the teenage girls could never have joined the Catholic Church without the permission of their mother...

Four of the letters from Bishop Whelan to her are available in the archives of the Diocese of Richmond; the one of May 8, 1845 is especially revealing. Bishop Whelan had lost patience with her, and used every argument to help her make up her mind. 'I feel sure that your intelligent and well informed mind will scarce allow you to admit any resting place between Catholicity and infidelity. I feel equally sure that Christianity carries with it too many evidences of truth to allow you to stake your everlasting hopes upon its rejection.' He wanted her to consider the influence of her example. He felt that many had attempted before God to excuse or lessen their own neglect by her example. He concluded these and other arguments by warning her 'it is now, my dear friend, the 11th hour for you, and you still have it in your power to repair much of the past,... by acknowledging before men that Savior whom you wish to acknowledge you before his Father in heaven.' He wrote that it would be a great consolation to him on his approaching visit to receive her and two others he named into the Catholic faith. Mrs. Floyd put off the final decision for seven more years, not being received into the Church by Bishop Whelan until June, 1852. She died on 12 December of the same year...

It is perhaps to her credit that she allowed her children to join as they approached their late teens, but took much more time for her intellect to accept the reasonableness of the Latin language and other externals of Catholicism at that time").

Ford, Henry II ("HF2"; "Hank the Deuce") – business executive; b. 4 September 1917, Detroit, Michigan; c. 1940 (received by Mgr. Fulton Sheen); d. 29 September 1987, Henry Ford Hospital, Detroit; son of Edsel Ford (1893-1943), president of the Ford Motor Company 1919-1943; grandson of Henry Ford (1863-1947), founder of the Ford Motor Company; eldest of four children; brought up a Methodist; educated at Yale University; he was received into the Church on the day he married Anne McDonnell (1920-1996); served in the navy in World War II, which was why he was unable to take over the presidency of the family business then; left the navy in 1943 and soon joined the management of the company; aggressive management style, but because of his own inexperience he brought in senior executives from other companies and hired ten young up-and-comers, known as the "Whiz Kids"; he re-established the company; president of the company 1945-1960; Chairman and Chief Executive Officer 1960-1979; in 1964 he and his wife divorced; he married twice more; ceased practicing the Catholic faith; awarded Presidential Medal of Freedom in 1969; see Charles E. Sorenson, with Samuel T. Williamson, *My Forty Years with Ford* (1956); Walter Hayes, *Henry: A Life of Henry Ford II* (1990); Thomas C. Reeves, *America's Bishop: The Life and Times of Fulton J. Sheen* (2001).

Foster, John Gray – soldier; b. 27 May 1823, Whitefield, Coos County, New Hampshire; c. 4 November 1861 (received in New York); d. 2 September 1874, Nashua, Hillsborough County, New Hampshire; descendant of a long line of Scottish-English ancestors; graduated at the United

States Military Academy at West Point in 1846 (fourth in his class of fifty-nine cadets); served as a lieutenant in the Engineer Corps during the Mexican War, when he was wounded at the Battle of Molino del Rey (won two brevet promotions for bravery); Assistant Professor of Engineering at West Point 1855-1857; at the start of the Civil War he was in command at Fort Moultrie, Charleston harbor; successful in transferring the garrison under his command into Fort Sumter; conspicuous in the defense of the fort; in October 1861 he was commissioned a brigadier-general of volunteers and assisted Burnside's North Carolina expedition (his conversion to the Catholic faith occurred at this time); conspicuous in action at the battles of Roanoke Island and New Bern; during 1862-1863 he was Commander of the Department of North Carolina with the rank of Major-General; he was next assigned the combined Departments of Virginia and North Carolina and then that of Ohio; assisted Sherman in the reduction of Charleston; distinguished himself in the capture of Savannah; during 1865-1866 he was in command of the Department of Florida; remained in the army after the war and was involved in military and underwater surveying; wrote on engineering topics, including the main text on underwater demolition; buried in Nashua Cemetery; see *Catholic Encyclopedia.*

Fountain, Clayton Anthony – murderer and monk; b. 12 September 1955, Fort Benning, Georgia; c. 19 April 1992 (Easter Sunday); d. 12 July 2004, Springfield, Missouri; born to a Baptist military family; dysfunctional childhood; served in the U.S. Marine Corps; in 1974, when stationed in the Philippines, he was convicted of murdering his staff sergeant; sentenced to life imprisonment in the U.S. Disciplinary Barracks at Fort Leavenworth, Kansas; in 1977 he was transferred to the "highest security facility in the country" in Marion, Illinois; between 1979 and 1983 he murdered three prisoners and one correctional officer; he also "established a legendary record of misconduct, unique even within Marion history;" he was labeled "the most dangerous person in the entire U.S. federal prison system"; was housed in a "Special Housing Unit" (SHU), an underground steel and concrete containment cell next to the criminally insane wing of the U.S. Medical Center for Federal Prisoners in Springfield, Missouri; he spent over twenty years in virtual isolation; during this time he converted to the Catholic faith; in 1989 a woman wrote to him, saying "they can lock you in a special cell, but they can't keep you from encountering God - only you can do that. Because I know from personal experience that God is still in the business of miracles"; he started studying to become a Catholic and received baptism, holy communion, and confirmation in 1992 ("Not long after my placement in the SHU I underwent a five year 'trial-by-fire purification' process in which God worked to purge me of the inner 'poisons' (that is, hatred, rage, bias, bitterness, revenge, vengeance, violence, and so forth) that I had foolishly permitted to control much of my life so that I not only failed to make responsible choices and decisions for my life, but also ended up in prison"); after his conversion he spoke of his cell as "no longer my burial place but an emptied tomb, for I had become a prisoner for Christ;" his spiritual director, a Cistercian Trappist monk, Father Robert, of Assumption Abbey, in Ava, Missouri, urged him to consider his cell a hermitage (it was eventually blessed as a monastic hermitage with the permission of the monastery); in 1996 he earned a BA with top honors from the College Program for the Incarcerated offered by Ohio University in Athens; in 2001 he enrolled at Catholic Distance University for the MA program in religious studies, which he pursued with straight A's, and hoped would lead to a Doctor of Theology program; Fr. W. Paul Jones became his unintended spiritual director, intellectual companion in his studies in philosophy and theology, and eventually friend; followed a fairly detailed daily regime of prayer, study, exercise, and work; he began to feel a call to the priesthood; he requested "a more formal tie to the monastery" as a Family Brother (a man who, after a prolonged relationship with the Abbey and its members, is acknowledged as having a particular spiritual bond with the Abbey, the way this bond is expressed being particular to each case); in his request he stated, "All I have to offer is to be a witness: that if you will have me, by far the least worthy of any who ever dared to ask, may my grave be a living declaration that no person is beyond the forgiving and reconciling mercy of God in Jesus Christ"; his request was accepted on 16 June 2004, but he died of a heart attack in his sleep on 12 July; on 18 July the community voted unanimously to accept him as a Family Brother posthumously; buried (as he had asked) next to his abusive father, because "God had helped him to be reconciled"; see Fr. Mark, *assumptionabbey.org*, September 2004 ("His life resembles in many ways the most dramatic stories of the early Desert Fathers. One is reminded, too, of the story of St Bernard. Returning to Clairvaux after a trip, Bernard came across a murderer being led by the authorities to his execution. Bernard spoke to the captain: 'Give him to me, and I will put him to death myself,' referring, of course, to the death to sin and conversion to Christ in the Cistercian monastic way of life"); W. Paul Jones, *A Different Kind of Cell: The Story of a Murderer Who Became a Monk*

(2011); W. Paul Jones, "Clayton A. Fountain: The Murderer Who Became a Monk," *huffingtonpost.com,* 14 January 2012.

Fowler, Gene (born Eugene Devlan) – journalist, screen writer, biographer and novelist; b. 8 March 1890, Denver, Colorado; c. June 1950 (his younger son Will and his wife and three children were received three years earlier); d. 2 July 1960; his family originally came from Ireland; his mother married a Protestant Irish boy; his parents divorced shortly before his birth; when his mother remarried he took his stepfather's name; brought up as a Protestant in a Catholic area of Denver; studied for a year in the University of Colorado; at first a printer, then a journalist in Denver; moved to New York where he worked on several papers during the legendary inter-war years; friend and contemporary of Damon Runyon; moved to Los Angeles, where he prepared scripts for the major cinema companies; married (1916) to Agnes Hubbard, with whom he had three children; his eldest son was Gene Fowler, Jr, (1917-1998), a notable Hollywood film editor and film and television director; wrote several screenplays including *The Mighty Barnum* (1934), *The Call of the Wild* (1935), *White Fang* (1936) and *Billy the Kid* (1941); buried in Holy Cross Cemetery, Culver City, Los Angeles; see *Father Goose: The Story of Mack Sennett* (1934); *Goodnight Sweet Prince: The Life and Times of John Barrymore* (1944); *A Solo in Tom-Toms* (1946) (autobiography); *Schnozzola: The Story of Jimmy Durante* (1951); "A Belated Wayfarer, " in John A. O'Brien, *The Road to Damascus, Vol. IV: Roads to Rome* (1955), p.92 ("It is a natural enough question, when someone outside the Church asks a man of my temperament, 'Why did you become a Catholic?' To that question I would ask in return: 'Where else can an old man go?' It is a Church that for almost two thousand years has been a refuge for sinners and for the poor. And I have been both sinful and poor during a life of incautious impulses, careless mischiefs, bad investments in business and in pleasures. And even today I have to make frequent visits to the Church when the horned fellow catches me napping. He never sleeps, you know...

The knowledge that no Catholic can be an orphan because we have the Blessed Mother Mary, the Rosary, the Mass, the Confessional, the Holy Eucharist – all suddenly bestowed graces and blessings and escapes from woe make it most difficult for the new-comer not to shout from the house-top...

Look here now, old man, wherever you may be...you will find the Confessional nearby, into which you go each time with feelings of trepidation, but emerge therefrom with a deep sense of peace and forgiveness. Why become a Catholic? Where else can a man go in this world?"); Will Fowler, *The Young Man From Denver: A Candid and Affectionate Biography of Gene Fowler* (1962); Matthew Hoehn, OSB (ed), *Catholic Authors* (1952).

Fox-Genovese, Elizabeth Ann ("Betsey") – historian; b. 28 May 1941, Boston, Massachusetts; c. 9 December 1995 (her husband Eugene D. Genovese (see below) returned to the Catholic Church in December 1996); d. 2 January 2007, Atlanta, Georgia; her father, Edward Whiting Fox, a professor of the history of modern Europe; brought up in a family that was not religious (father atheist, mother agnostic), but treated the Decalogue with utmost seriousness and her mother introduced her to the Bible; also "my father especially never doubted the truth of Dostoevsky's troubling question: If God is dead, is not everything permitted?"; her mother's heritage was Jewish; educated at the Institut d'Etudes Politique De Paris and then at Bryn Mawr College (BA in French and History); MA and PhD in History from Harvard University; fascinated by medieval history, in which she was encouraged by her father (who also spoke of Christ as the unique model of total self-consciousness and loving self-sacrifice, and of the redemptive power of suffering); saw herself as a cultural Christian, but did not attend church; imbibed Marxist materialist philosophy, and utilitarianism, though with misgivings as she yearned for a spiritual home; taught at several universities; specialist in History, but moved on to the study of women in the American south before the Civil War; Eleonore Raoul Professor of the Humanities at Emory University, Atlanta, where she was the founding director of the Institute for Women's Studies; collaborated with her husband (married in 1969) on lectures, articles, and books; gradually found troubling both moral subjectivism and relativism ("It seemed difficult to imagine a world in which each followed his or her personal moral compass, if only because the morality of some was bound, sooner or later, to clash with the morality of others. And without some semblance of a common standard, those clashes were more than likely to end in one or another form of violence"); her study of abortion led her to "an ever greater apppreciation for the claims of life, which were so often buried beneath impassioned defenses of a woman's right to self-determination, especially her right to sexual freedom"; slowly her reaction against modernity and post-modernism led her to the Catholic Church; among other influences were St. Teresa, St. Thérèse, Flannery O'Connor and Georges Bernanos; also moved from radical feminism to the conservative women's movement; had lifelong poor health, culminating in multiple sclerosis, bravely borne ("I found myself praying - at my little altar - Dear

Lord, let my pain and suffering be of some use to some one"); see *The Origins of Physiocracy: Economic Revolution and Social Order in Eighteenth-century France* (1976); *Fruits of Merchant Capital: Slavery and Bourgeois Property in the Rise and Expansion of Capitalism* (1983) (with Eugene D. Genovese); *Black and White Women of the Old South* (1988); *Feminism Without Illusions: A Critique of Individualism* (1991); *"Feminism Is Not the Story of My Life": How Today's Feminist Elite Has Lost Touch with the Real Concerns of Women* (1996) (a criticism of feminism for failing to take into account the ordinary lives of everyday women for whom motherhood was not seen as a burden but as a gift); "Caught in the Web of Grace," *Crisis*, November 1997 ("Perhaps the reality and the essence of my conversion - and any conversion - may best be captured by analogy to the real presence in the Eucharist. For in the Eucharist we come to understand that the greatest of all mysteries is the ultimate reality, and that groping toward faith consists in the continuing struggle to grasp the most ineffable and elusive as the most real. This quest unites my conversion to those of countless others and, by minimizing its uniquely personal cast, acknowledges it as less the work of the creature than the grace of the Creator. 'I am the good shepherd; I know my own and my own know me, as the Father knows me and I know the Father; and I lay down my life for the sheep. And I have other sheep that are not of this fold; I must bring them also, and they will heed my voice. So there shall be one flock, one shepherd'"); *Reconstructuring History* (1999) (with Elisabeth Lasch-Quinn); "A Conversion Story," *First Things*, April 2000 (reprinted under the title of "Only the Beginning of the Adventure," in Donna Steichen (ed), *Chosen: How Christ Sent Twenty-Three Surprising Converts to Replant His Vineyard* (2009)) ("As if barring my path to church membership stood the figure of Jesus Christ. The churches I most respected all required that prospective members affirm their personal faith in Christ as Lord and Savior. I did not question the legitimacy of the requirement, but nothing in my previous life seemed to have prepared me to meet it. To the best of my knowledge, I had no personal experience of religious faith and no real grasp of its nature...To this day, I cannot point to a single moment of conversion, no blinding light that opened my eyes, no arrow that pierced my heart. Almost imperceptibly, the balance between doubt and faith shifted, and, on one ordinary day, it came to me that I had decided to enter the Catholic Church.

In deciding to enter the Church, I had decided that I believed in Christ Jesus and accepted him as my Lord and Savior, but even as my love for and commitment to the Church deepened, I remained unsure of precisely what my faith meant or from whence it derived. Fr. [Richard] Lopez [who instructed her in the faith] reassured me that faith and faithfulness were, above all, matters of the will rather than the emotions, which, he insisted, remain inherently suspect.

Today I see more clearly than I could at the time that much of my initial hesitation and diffidence derived from my unconscious persistence in materialist habits of thought. Like any good rationalist, I kept looking for unambiguous explanations for my turn to faith, and, although the possible candidates abounded, none clearly stood out as *the* reason. It took two or three years for me to begin to understand that the decisive action had not been mine but God's. In principle, we all know that faith is a gift or grace, not a personal accomplishment. But if my case is as common as I suspect it is, we find that knowledge surprisingly difficult to believe and make fully ours. Thus, with the best of intentions, we try to earn that which lies beyond the reach of even our most heroic efforts and which exceeds any merit we can conceive.

An important part of what opened me to Catholicism - and to the peerless gift of faith in Christ Jesus - was my growing horror at the pride of too many in the secular academy…

Sad as it may seem, my experience with radical, upscale feminism only reinforced my growing mistrust of individual pride. The defense of abortion especially troubled me because of my inability to agree that any one of us should decide who has the right to live. But my engagement with faith drew me into more general reflection about the importance of charity and service in the life of the Christian. Initially, I had shied away from the idea of the imitation of Christ and even from the entreaty in the Universal Prayer to 'make me holy.' Such aspirations struck me as the ultimate presumption: who was I to pretend to holiness, much less the imitation of our Savior? Gradually, those fears began to dissipate, and I found myself meditating upon the Gospels' teaching on service, above all, that 'the Son of Man did not come to be served, but to serve and to offer his life as a ransom for all.' Having been received in the Church on the day after the feast of the Immaculate Conception, I also pondered the Holy Mother's response to the Annunciation: 'Let it be done unto me according to Thy Word.'

The injunctions to charity and service unmistakably applied to all Christians, but it was difficult to deny that, since the moment of the Virgin Mary's response to the Angel Gabriel, they applied in a special way to women. Her example, as Hans Urs von Balthasar has reminded us, offers the exemplary embodiment of faith. 'Faith is the surrender of the entire person: because Mary from the start surrendered everything, her memory was the unsullied tablet on which the Father, through the Spirit, could write His entire Word.' It is incontestable that, throughout most of history, women have suffered injustices and abuse that cry out for redress. It is no less incontestable that the path to justice and dignity for women - the recognition of their equal standing with men as human persons - cannot lead through the repudiation of the most basic tenets of our faith. No amount of past oppression can justify women's oppression of the most vulnerable among us - or even our repudiation of our own specific vocation as women...

In our time, it is countercultural indeed to see the loss or effacement of self as an admirable goal. Our culture's obsession with identity and the rights of the individual seems to suggest precisely the reverse. You will nonetheless recall the First Beatitude: 'Blessed are the poor in spirit, for theirs is the kingdom of Heaven' (Matthew 5:3). For years the passage, when I thought of it, puzzled me. In what way was poverty of spirit to be seen as desirable, especially in a Christian? And what, precisely, did poverty of spirit mean? I had left the question, together with others that I hoped some day to understand, in the back of my mind until I happened upon Erasmo Leiva–Merikakis' eye-opening explanation in his *Fire of Mercy, Heart of the Word: Meditations on the Gospel According to St. Matthew* (1996). Pointing out that this is not merely the first of the Beatitudes, but the only one in the present tense, Leiva–Merikakis explains that the poor in spirit are those who literally 'beg for their life's very breath' - those who depend upon God the way we all depend upon air to breathe. Poverty of spirit is the grace of those who have emptied themselves of everything but the desire for God's presence, 'who offer God a continual sacrifice from the altar of their spirit, and the sacrifice in question is the very substance of their being.' And those who achieve poverty of spirit have their reward in the present as well as the future, for to live in poverty of spirit is indeed to live with God.

A decisive moment in my journey in faith came when, one day, seemingly out of nowhere, the thought pierced me that Jesus had died for my sins. And, immediately on its heels, came the devastating recognition that I am not worth his sacrifice. Only gradually have I come truly to understand that the determination of worth belongs not to me but to him. God's love for us forever exceeds our control and challenges our understanding. Like faith, it is His gift, and our task is to do our best to receive it. The knowledge, even when partial and imperfect, that He loves us also opens us to new responsibilities and obligations. For if He loves us all, He also loves each of us. And recognition of that love imposes on us the obligation to love one another, asking no other reason than God's injunction to do so. As fallen human creatures, we are nonetheless likely to continue to search for human reasons that justify our loving service to those in whom we find little or no obvious redeeming value. And the best human reason may be found in the faith that God has freely given us: our nonjudgmental love of the other remains the condition of God's love for us. For, knowing how little we merit His love, our best opening to the faith that He does lies not in the hope of being better than others, but in the security that His love encompasses even the least deserving among us"); *Women and the Future of the Family* (2000); *The Mind of the Master Class: History and Faith in the Southern Slaveholders' Worldview* (2005) (with Eugene D. Genovese); *Marriage: The Dream that Refuses to Die* (2008); *Slavery in White and Black: Class and Race in the Southern Slaveholders' New World Order* (2008) (with Eugene D. Genovese); Robert L. Paquette, "Elizabeth Fox-Genovese, 1941-2007," *New Criterion*, February 2007; Eugene D. Genovese, *Miss Betsey: A Memoir of Marriage* (2008) ("An acute student of Marx and Marxism, she found the American Left intellectually shoddy and, worse, devoid of moral and ethical criteria. She and I agreed on the intellectual shoddiness and discussed the moral problem many times, always returning to Dostoyevsky's haunting statement: 'If God does not exist, then all is lawful.' The more Betsey studied, the more convinced she became that the Left had no moral grounding. But without belief in God, she could not respond, in good conscience, to the sense of community our churchgoing friends had.

I knew that Betsey was searching for more than earthly community. We used to joke that we may have been the only American Marxists who believed in original sin and human depravity. It was no joke, but neither was it necessarily accurate. We did believe in the essentials of original sin, as we understood them, but could not square it with our materialism. I am reminded of the outburst of a fellow Marxist and atheist, a superior historian from a Jewish family. We were having a cup of coffee with several Marxist graduate students, who seemed confused by our professed belief in original sin. After a while, they turned to our colleague and asked if he agreed with us. He scowled: 'I don't know anything about Christian theology or original sin or anything else they are talking about. But this I do know: People are rotten.' I should add that although I may have agreed with him on the rottenness of people - I plead the Fifth - Betsey did not. She was not yet close to conversion, but she had an intuitive grasp of the Resurrection and redemption.

In 1994, at age fifty-three, Betsey announced her conversion. I was not taken by surprise since I always knew she had a marked spiritual side. Contrary to the nonsense spewed across the academic rumor mill, her decision had nothing to do with politics. I asked what church she was planning to enter, assuming that it would be the Presbyterian...Then too, Betsey's father's family had Calvinist roots. Betsey answered, intending no disrespect for the Presbyterian Church or any other: 'You have lived with me for about a quarter of a century, and you take me for an evangelical Protestant?'

She explained that she was inquiring about instruction to enter the Catholic Church. I was relieved. Although not prepared to re-enter the Church, I had started to think about it and did return in 1995. Betsey later confessed - only a bit tongue-in-cheek - that she had another reason for her choice: "I knew that sooner or later you would return to the Catholic Church and thought we should worship together."

When Betsey entered the Church, she had no illusion that her quest for salvation would be easy. To the contrary, she understood faith as hard work. She much admired Saint Thomas Aquinas, but identified not with his 'I know so that I can believe,' but with Saint Augustine's 'I believe so that I can know.' A year or two after she entered the Church, she wrote in her notebook: 'I cannot put what I believe into words other than "I believe in God the Father...His only son, our Lord... the Holy Spirit, the Holy Catholic Church, the communion of saints, the forgiveness of sins..." And those I do believe in, but putting substance on them is gradual. The Gospel helps, Mass helps, prayer helps. That I can even write this tells me I trust my belief. But I know also that I want it stronger'...

Abortion had always made Betsey queasy. For years she remained sufficiently attached to the feminist movement to persuade herself to support 'free choice' during the first trimester and with such limitations as parental consent and absolute denial of partial-birth abortion. She supported such 'compromise' largely because she considered it the best politically available alternative to an incipient civil war. She gagged on abortion for a simple reason: She knew, as everyone knows, that an abortion kills a baby. Betsey responded with incredulity to the argument that the baby a woman carries in her womb is not a baby at all or, alternatively, that although it is a baby, her mother has a moral and constitutional right to kill her. And Betsey resented the denigration of women implicit in the 'pro-choice' campaign. Years later, in the private journal she kept after she entered the Church, she wrote: 'Paradox: intent of abortion has been to free women, but it has imprisoned them. *Anima Christi*: soul and body are one, not two. Abortion devalues and debases woman's bodies - strips them of their character as Temples of the

Holy Spirit. Abortion has not heightened respect for woman's bodies, but only confirmed their status as objects to be used.'

A related matter went down hard with her. We hear all the time that retarded and deformed children should never have been born - that their lives should have been snuffed out by parents and doctors sensitive to the 'quality of life.' Betsey did not take well to people who claimed the privilege of judging who deserved to live and who ought to be put to death. Again, as a Jew aware of the underlying ideology of the Holocaust, she had no tolerance for people who claimed the right to dispose of human life in accordance with whatever sick creed they were espousing.

Over the years, she met a number of retarded and autistic children. None struck her as floating miserably in a life without pleasure. Betsey saw for herself that, however painful their daily experiences, they awoke every morning secure in the knowledge that their parents loved them, considering them gifts of God.

The radical feminists' assertion that a woman has absolute property in her own body provoked mirth from those who, like Betsey, knew that the modern Left had arisen to oppose the bourgeois theory of absolute property in anything. Betsey steadily hardened her line against abortion while she maintained unsparing compassion for the unmarried young or poor pregnant women who felt trapped. She spent years as a volunteer in community groups that cared for pregnant teenagers, poor mothers and their children, and battered wives...

Betsey read and wrote for her favorite religious journals. And she kept up with books on the current Church. She favored the 'traditionalist' wing of the Church, although not as dogmatically as I. In particular, she refused to support my proposal to restore the Inquisition and the *auto-da-fé*. Betsey entered the Church in the same spirit as I returned to it, prepared to submit to the authority of its hierarchy. The Catholic Church is an elective monarchy, not a republic, much less a democracy. An honest Christian who cannot accept submission to the hierarchy is at liberty to join the Baptist Church or some other worthy Christian church. He is not at liberty to try to wreck our Church by pretending that it is or should be a 'participatory democracy.' In any case, Betsey's faith grew stronger year by year, and I have no doubt that she prayed as Jesus taught us: 'Thy will be done'").

Francis, Dale – journalist, editor and freelance writer; b. 1917, Newark, Ohio; c. 15 June 1945; brought up in a Christian household; became a Baptist at the age of seventeen; after high school got a job as a newspaper reporter; educated at Ohio Northern University and Bluffton College, a Mennonite school; became a Methodist minister, but continued in journalism; served in the army in World War II; one influence on his conversion was that of William Edwin Orchard; founded the *North Carolina Catholic* in 1947; read for a PhD degree at the University of Notre Dame and in 1949 was appointed director of the University Press; editor of *Our Sunday Visitor*, the national Catholic newspaper; see "Into the Light," in John A. O'Brien (ed), *The Road to Damascus, Vol. II* (1950) ("There came for me now two years of unrest and indecision. When I finally made my decision it seemed as simple as ABC. My thinking went something like this. Either there was a God or there was not a God. One of the two was right. Now, the unity of nature made it ridiculous for me to suppose there was no God. If the stars in the heaven ran with such precision that men could calculate their positions years in advance, then there must be a Mind greater than the minds of the men who made the calculations. There was a God. I was certain of that.

Well, after that I faced another problem. God was either a personal God or not a personal God. There was a chance that he had supplied the wisdom for the universe and left things there. But this was not true if God came to earth. This was not true if Jesus Christ was more than man, if He was God. I reserved my decision on the matter of a personal God for the decision on the divinity of Christ.

I was certain of one thing. Christ wasn't just a good man. He said He was God. If He wasn't God and said that He was, then He was an impostor and a liar. He couldn't be merely a good man, because good men don't lie. So He had to be God, or just a deceitful man. I decided I'd believe He was God if I could believe in the resurrection. There was the proof. I reserved another decision.

Now, did Christ really rise from the dead? That could just be a fanciful story, I reasoned. So I started making deductions. I tried to figure it out the way I might have had I been covering it as a newspaperman.

Christ said He was God, and His apostles apparently believed Him. Well, if they were really convinced, they should have stuck to Him when He was threatened with crucifixion. But, even though they'd seen His miracles, they bolted in the crisis. Only one even stayed around at all. Peter denied Him three times. While He lived, and they could reasonably hope that with His power He could free Himself, they were afraid. Then He was killed.

That should have been the end of the story. But it wasn't. A short time later His Apostles were openly proclaiming their devotion to Christ. Frightened Peter was no longer afraid. He even suffered death gladly.

Something had happened. The men who were frightened while Christ lived should have become more frightened with His death. Instead they were now willing to dare all things. Something had happened in the meantime, and that must have been the resurrection of Christ. It had to be something that big to make the difference. So I came to believe in the resurrection of Christ - and, with it, in His divinity - and, with that, in a personal God.

So I believed that Jesus was more than man. Truth was on the earth while He was here. Now, God, being infinitely wise, certainly knew that truth had to be maintained. I'd played that game where a sentence is whispered from one person to another and ends up by being entirely different from the way it started. Since I was aware of the way man exaggerates things, I know, of course, that God knows this too.

So I was sure that God would somehow protect the truth, see to it that it was maintained inviolate on earth. He would do it, it seemed to me, in one of two ways. Either through guidance by the Holy Ghost or through the Bible. I quickly made my decision on this. I'd seen the Bible interpreted too many different ways: there was no unity there, and there would have to be unity in God's guidance. It had to be through the Holy Ghost.

But how? One of two ways - either personally or through a Church. Now, I knew some people who claimed that the Holy Ghost guided them personally, but all of them were being led in different directions. That couldn't be. Besides, there had to be continuity, and that wouldn't be possible if guidance came only from humans. God's guidance must be continuous, it must stretch back to Christ. So it had to be through a Church.

All right, was it the Catholic Church or one of the Protestant churches? It couldn't be, as some of my Protestant friends said, all churches. They believed too many conflicting things. The truth couldn't contradict itself. I read much and I studied much. I found the teachings of the Catholic Church to be unchanged in fundamentals over the centuries. There was unity, there was continuity. No Protestant church could offer me the same.

I wasn't ready to submit yet, though. I wanted to make more certain. I came to the Holy Eucharist. I found Christ saying that we had to eat of His Body. Figuratively speaking, I thought hopefully. No, He said it again to the people who asked Him if He really meant what He said. The Bible told me that after that there were some who walked with Him no longer. So I ran into another incontestable fact. Christ either meant exactly what He said about eating of His body or He meant it figuratively. If he meant it as a figure of speech, then He was responsible for turning some people away from following Him. After all, He had only to tell them he was speaking figuratively. But He didn't. So, if He meant it figuratively, He was guilty of turning people away from God. But that couldn't be, since He was God. So I had to face it. He must have meant exactly what He said. It overwhelmed me, but there was no way out of it").

Francis, Samuel Todd ("Sam") – political columnist; b. 29 April 1947, Chattanooga, Hamilton County, Tennessee; c. 2005 (received on his deathbed by Fr. Paul Scalia); d. 15 February 2005, Cheverly, Prince George's County, Maryland; very bright student; educated at Johns Hopkins University (graduated BA in 1969), then at University of North Carolina at Chapel Hill (PhD in Modern History in 1979); policy analyst at the National Heritage Foundation in Washington DC 1977-1981 (became an expert on Communism and international terror); legislative assistant for national security affairs to Senator John P. East 1981-1986; on the editorial staff of *The Washington Times* 1986-1995 (he alleged he was removed from this post because of neo-conservative pressure); won national prizes for his editorials; syndicated columnist; his intellectual hero was James Burnham (see above); of paleo-conservative views; he was attacked by the neo-conservatives; allegations of racism were made against him; his response was that there are natural differences between the races, but that he did not believe that one race was better than another; also he wrote an essay criticizing the Southern Baptist Convention for passing a resolution repudiating slavery; his response was that this was a radical split from their own church traditions and that if they dismissed the New Testament passages about slaves obeying their masters as irrelevant, then they might as well join the Bolsheviks; his column continued only in the *Pittsburgh Tribune-Review*, but was dropped in 2004 after allegations that he was guilty of white supremacism; his defenders said this was merely political incorrectness; wrote for several other magazines, notably *Chronicles*; unmarried; died of a sudden aneurism in his aorta; buried at the Forest Hills Cemetery in Chattanooga, Tennessee; see *Power and History: The Political Thought of James Burnham* (1984); *The Soviet Strategy of Terror* (1985); "Sex and Consequences," *The Washington Times*, 2 February 1993 ("The lesson of 4,000 years of social history is that sexual behavior, consensual or not, has consequences for others, that it often affects (and hurts) others in ways society needs to control, and that unregulated sex renders social bonds, especially in the family but also beyond it, impossible. We can regulate it through law or through socially enforced moral custom or both, but we have to do it somehow. History knows of no human society that has not regulated sexual behavior and forbidden some kinds of it, nor is there any reason known to social science to suppose that a society that fails to do so is possible. A 'society' that makes no distinction between sex within marriage and sex outside it, that does not distinguish morally and socially between continence and debauchery, normality and perversion, love and lust, is not really a society but merely the chaos of a perpetual orgy. It is an invitation to just such an orgy that the proponents of normalized and unrestricted homosexuality invite America"); *Beautiful Losers: Essays on the Failure of American Conservatism* (1993); *Revolution From the Middle* (1997); *James Burnham: Thinkers of Our Time* (1999); *America Extinguished: Mass Immigration and the Disintegration of American Culture* (2002); *Ethnopolitics: Immigration, Race, and the American Political Future* (2003); *Shots Fired: Sam Francis on America's Culture War* (2006) ((1) "Guilt Trip Over Crusades: One anniversary that's not on this year's calendar is the 900th observance of the capture of Jerusalem by Christian crusaders on July 15, 1099. As a matter of fact, it's an anniversary that's probably never been on any year's calendar, since virtually everyone forgot about it sometime around the year 1600. But some never forget, and they're getting ready to do what 20th century man is supposed to do, at least in the West: apologize for it.

The London *Sunday Telegraph* reported last month that a movement is afoot among the Christian churches to apologize for the Crusades. The Crusades, you will recall, were a kind of medieval equivalent of making the world safe for democracy - in this case, Christianity - and a good many Europeans took themselves off to the Middle East to carve into confetti anyone who wasn't as Christian as they were. In the process, a good many Europeans got their behinds kicked by the locals. Eventually the Crusades failed, and most people went home.

But as with most historical episodes (the Crusades went on for a couple of hundred years), there were good things and bad things about them. The good things included a more or less authentic desire to enlighten the world with what the European Christians of the time deeply believed was religious truth. The bad things included pillaging, conquering, and massacring a lot of folks who never harmed the Crusaders. Nevertheless, whatever the good or the bad, only idiots would consider apologizing for them today.

But idiots, of course, is exactly what we're dealing with, and I for one would prefer the Crusaders. The *Telegraph* reports that on 15 July this year a delegation of idiots from Europe and the United States calling themselves the 'Reconciliation Walk' plans to go to Jerusalem and apologize to Muslim and Jewish leaders for the Crusades.

They will wear T-shirts saying 'I apologize' in Arabic and distribute apologetic messages to Muslims on the streets. About a thousand such apologizers have already worn out their welcomes in the area by getting an early start on the guilt trip. Yet the *Telegraph* also reports that the Christian churches in Europe and the United States are preparing a public expression of repentance for the Crusades.

There are several reasons these people are idiots, not the least of which is that the historical memory of the Crusades has almost entirely vanished today. Assuming the Crusades were wrong, no one feels the wrong any more, nor can anyone seriously claim that all the wrong was on the Christian European side. Apologizing for the Crusades is like looking up a kid you stole candy from when you were in kindergarten and telling him you're sorry. He not only doesn't remember the theft; he doesn't even remember you.

Some church leaders are arguing that there should be no apology from Christians until Muslims also show remorse for the killing they carried out themselves. The problem with that is that it's moral equivalence. If Christians knocked off a few Muslims in the siege of Jerusalem, that's no worse than the killing the Muslims themselves committed. The problem with moral equivalence is that it assumes both sides are wrong and does nothing to place ethical blame where it ought to lie. From church leaders we have a right to expect more than this.

Yet right or wrong, the fact that modern Westerners can't even defend the Crusades as a manifestation of Western man and his civilization tells us a good deal about what's wrong with Western man today. Western man no longer believes in himself or the civilization his ancestors created, crusaded for, and died for. In place of believing in it and defending it, our religious and political leaders are ashamed of it and want to apologize for it - even for those parts no one remembers.

The Crusades certainly involved some inglorious and unheroic deeds, not all of them committed against Muslims. Christians themselves were often the victims, as in the sack of Constantinople in 1204. But if the Crusades were not entirely right, a healthy civilization can still recognize them as a necessary part in the adventure of our own people in history. The importance of the Crusades is that they were one of the first expressions of the process of heroic dynamism and expansion that distinguishes our civilization from most others.

The same mentality that drove medieval warriors to wage war for the cross in the Holy Land also drove Columbus to the New World and Americans to the Moon. Without that spirit, the West - and America - will shrivel and die and would never have existed at all. That, of course, is exactly what the idiot party wants, and it's exactly why they deserve a good kick in the behind from the Crusaders still kicking around."

(2) "Media elite Versus Christian

Heritage: Easter, the most important religious holiday in the Christian calendar, passed almost without comment in the nation's press this year, but the *Washington Post* did carry a story somewhat related to it. The story had to do with the comic strip *B.C.* and its creator, artist Johnny Hart, who is a born-again Christian. But what the story really told us was perhaps more than it intended about the establishment media's view on open religious expression.

Mr. Hart in recent years has gotten into the habit of importing explicit - often very explicit - Christian messages in his strip, which is cast in prehistoric times and is a thinly masked commentary on modern life. The problem is that many newspaper editors, including some at the *Post*, don't much care for that sort of thing. Some of them simply refuse to publish those *B.C.* strips that thump a religious drum. Sometimes the *Post* kills individual *B.C.* strips if they are deemed to be too religious. And of course, the media that do all the killing have a bucketful of reasons why they're all for freedom of the press.

Yet the media lords aren't the only ones who have problems with *B.C.* The *Post's* 'Style' section piece on Mr. Hart and his strip interviewed Abraham Foxman, president of the Anti-Defamation League of B'nai B'rith. He is sort of the national censorship czar when it comes to publications that might offend Jewish sensitivities. Mr. Hart's strip is one such publication.

While rather graciously acknowledging that Mr. Hart has a right to express his religious convictions and saying he 'does not believe in stifling free speech,' Mr. Foxman 'confesses to uncertainty' about *B.C.* and declares that the strip's frequent Christian messages are 'particularly insidious.' 'It is a very clear exclusionary message if you are not of that faith,' he pronounces.

Mr. Foxman does not represent all Jewish opinion, and the *Post* story also cites law professor Daniel Polsby, whom it identifies as Jewish, who 'thinks Hart is a hero of free speech.' Moreover, Mr. Hart's critics say the issue is not his Christianity per se, but religion per se. Leonard Downie, the *Post's* executive editor, has killed several of Mr. Hart's cartoons because, he says, 'We don't promote individual religions anywhere in the paper. We let people discuss religion as an issue, but we don't advocate a particular religion.'

Well now, that's swell, isn't it? 'We' - the *Post*, the other papers, the Anti-Defamation League, and everybody else apparently except the millions of American newspaper readers who actually do advocate particular religions - decide what gets promoted and what doesn't. Religion, for them, is in the same category - maybe even in a somewhat more taboo category - as outright obscenity and explicit racial epithets. Advocating a specific religious position is forbidden -

except, of course, the intensely religious position of secularism.

Mr. Hart does indeed seem to harbor ideas and beliefs that I, for one, consider rather nutty, both from religious as well as scientific perspectives. He believes the world was created only 4,000 years ago and doesn't believe in the cavemen who populate his own cartoon strip. But he has as much right to these beliefs and to draw cartoons expressing his faith as anyone who believes something else.

What the elite media deny is not that right in the abstract but any concrete opportunity for Mr. Hart to exercise it. It's fine to thump your chest about how committed you are to freedom of expression. But when you insinuate that someone is 'anti-Semitic' and effectively deny him a place in your newspaper explicitly because of his religious beliefs, your 'commitment to free expression' is meaningless.

Mr. Hart's importance does not lie in the truthfulness of his beliefs or even in the clever ways he expresses them. Rather, it lies in the fact that simply by expressing them he helps expose the Big Lies of 'tolerance,' 'diversity,' and 'freedom' that the media chieftains are always yapping about. There is tolerance, diversity, and freedom for those views of which the elite media approve. For those views they don't like and don't want to publish - and explicit Christian commitments are among them - the media send a very clear exclusionary message"); *Essential Writings on Race,* (2007); Joseph Sobran, "Samuel Francis R.I.P," *The Wanderer*, 24 February 2005 ("He was an uncompromising Southern paleo-conservative, with an abiding contempt for Lincoln and the liberal tradition…

I never heard him say anything about religion; my impression is that he had no particular faith, though I never asked; on the other hand, I never heard him say anything anti-religious.

I'm only guessing, but my sense is that Sam regarded Christianity, and Catholicism in particular, with a puzzled respect. He had many devout Catholic friends, including Pat Buchanan, and it can hardly have failed to impress him that his idol Burnham, an apostate of great intelligence, had returned to the Church on his deathbed.

Sam was an enigma. You never knew what was going on inside him, since he discussed political problems rather than ultimate questions. I was never even sure how well informed he was about Christianity; I still have no idea whether he had a religious upbringing in Tennessee.

Given his pessimistic temperament, Sam wasn't given to inspiring affirmation. His outlook was bleak. The news was always bad, and I sometimes wondered what, if anything, he would regard as good news…Burnham had taught him how deluding political labels and professed principles can be in the realm of power.

And yet, when a seemingly unbelieving man surrounds himself with Catholic friends, you can safely assume that he's attracted to the faith. Whether or not he believes, he wishes he did.

Some years ago my pastor remarked on how inappropriate it is that eulogies are now delivered at Catholic funerals, celebrating the virtues, rather than remembering the sins, of the deceased. It was a resonant comment. This is an age that combines spiritual laxity with a false optimism, as if it were natural, if not automatic, for the dead to go immediately to Heaven. Why bother praying for their souls if salvation is their birthright - or shall we say their deathright?

As his readers know, Sam Francis rejected false optimism in any form. If there is one Christian doctrine he would have believed without much argument, it is the doctrine of original sin"); Patrick J. Buchanan, "Sam Francis: Obdurate for Truth," *WMD Commentary*, 7 March 2005 ("In 1994, Sam merrily ridiculed Baptist churchmen who had issued an apology for slavery. As the preachers had never owned slaves and there was no Bible command against slavery, Sam asked, what exactly were the preachers apologizing for?...

What he cherished was the civilization and culture that had nurtured him. He loved Southern and American literature, history and heroes, and few men of his time were so widely read. Sam was convinced Western culture and civilization could not survive the dispossession or death of the European peoples who gave them birth. He opposed the mass immigration of non-Western peoples, cultures and creeds, and regarded as the 'Stupid Party' a GOP that truckled to corporate contributors and refused to defend our borders");

Fraser, Mary Crawford (usually known as Mrs. Hugh Fraser) – writer; b. 8 April 1851, Italy; c. 1884, Rome; d. 1922; father was the distinguished American sculptor Thomas Crawford (1814-1857), a Protestant who settled in Rome; her mother was Louisa Cutler Ward; her brother was the novelist Francis Marion Crawford (see above); her aunt was Mrs. Julia Ward Howe (1819-1910), social activist, poet, and author of *The Battle Hymn of the Republic*; brought up mainly in Italy, but also in England and New Jersey; in 1874 she married the British diplomat Hugh Fraser (1837-1894); accompanied her husband to posts in Peking, Vienna, Rome, Santiago and Tokyo; converted to the Catholic faith over the opposition of her mother; her husband was head of the British legation in Japan, but died suddenly; wrote various memoirs and historical novels under her married name; see (selective list) *Palladia* (1896); *The Looms of Time* (1898); *The Customs of the Country: Tales of New Japan* (1899); *A Diplomatist's Wife in Japan: Letters From Home* *to Home* (1900); *The Slaking of the Sword: Tales of the Far East* (1904); *The Stolen Emperor* (1904); *Further Reminiscences of a Diplomatist's Wife* (1912); *Italian Yesterdays* (1914); *More Italian Yesterdays* (1915); *Storied Italy* (1915).

Frazier, Terry L. – Catholic apologist; from a broken home, which was nominally Christian (liberal Presbyterianism); took refuge in books; brought up in the liberal ethos of the 60s and 70s; one Advent he discovered the Bible and the figure of Christ and put aside his pagan outlook; joined a Presbyterian church, but soon moved towards Fundamentalism ("I had concluded that liberal Protestantism was less driven by a thirst for objective truth than by subjective emotional compulsions; became a Baptist; concerned at the many different interpretations of bible texts by Protestant bodies; influenced by the graphic Eucharistic language in chapter six of St. John's Gospel; lost faith in Fundamentalism's ability to interpret Scripture objectively and discovered the early Church Fathers; began to appreciate the powerful evidence for the petrine primacy; started questioning Catholic priests and attending Mass and finally converted to the Catholic faith; see "The Call of the Minaret," *This Rock*, April 1992; "Assumptions About Mary," *This Rock*, May-June 1992; "No Bones About Dem Bones," *This Rock*, June 1993; "The Antichrist at the Manger," *This Rock*, December 1993; "Into the Crimson Light," in Patrick Madrid (ed), *Surprised by Truth* (1994), p.181 ("In the library one day I ran across a book of ancient Christian literature. I was ecstatic. I had been wanting to see early Christian writings to help me gain the ancient Christian perspective from which to study the Word of God. I began studying the epistles of St. Ignatius, a convert of the Apostle John and second Bishop of Antioch. In the year AD 110, Roman soldiers were leading Ignatius to Rome where the lions awaited him. Along the way, he wrote several letters to churches along his route, encouraging them in the faith. These letters were regarded so highly by the early Christian community for their witness to the apostolic Faith that they were even held by many to be part of the New Testament, frequently being bound with the apostolic writings.

Writing to the church at Smyrna, a major Christian center in Asia Minor, Ignatius condemned heretics who denied that Christ had an actual physical body, likely referring to Docetism. (This was a form of the Gnostic heresy. The Apostle John may have had these same people in mind when he penned 1 John 1:1-4.) To refute them, Ignatius wrote, 'They [the heretics] even absent themselves from the Eucharist and the public prayers [cf. Acts 2:42], because they will not admit that the Eucharist is the flesh of our Savior Jesus Christ which suffered for our sins and which the Father in his goodness afterwards raised up again' (7:1).

I believe I nearly suffered cardiac arrest. This was the bishop of Antioch, the city where Jesus' followers were first called Christians (Acts 11:26) and a major center of Christianity. This was a man who had heard the Good News from the lips of the Apostle John himself, the very Apostle who had written that graphic Eucharistic passage in his Gospel (Jn. 6:48-58). Writing merely ten or fifteen years after the death of St. John, Ignatius refers to the 'real presence' of Christ in the Eucharist as though it were common knowledge throughout the Church! Indeed, if Christ weren't really present in the Eucharist Ignatius' whole apologetic argument would have come to naught…

Protestants often ask me why I became a Catholic. I reply that Scripture states the Church is the mystical Body of Christ and Christ is its head (Eph. 1:22-23; Col. 1:18). One can't have a personal relationship with the Head as Lord and Savior in its fullness if one doesn't embrace the Body as well. One can't decapitate Jesus from the Body and expect to have a 'personal' relationship with just the severed head. That isn't what Jesus intended for us (cf. Jn. 17:20-23). In the Acts of the Apostles we read about an organized Christian community lead by the Holy Spirit, a visible Church which St. Paul could call 'the pillar and foundation of truth' (1 Tim. 3:15), not merely a bunch of individualists running around with Gideon Bibles and 'Just Me and Jesus' attitudes. As a Fundamentalist I couldn't claim to belong to a visible Church which is 'the pillar and foundation of truth.' As a Catholic I now can"); "The Rosary Dissected," *This Rock*, September 1994; *Holy Relics* (1997); A Second Look at the Second Coming (1999) (with A. J. Bernstein).

Fremantle, Anne Marie (*née* Jackson) – writer, editor and translator; b. 15 June 1910, Tresserve, near Aix-les-Bains, Savoie, France; c. 11 July 1943, St. Matthew's Church, Washington D.C.; d. 26 December 2002, London; member of a prominent English family and grew up in an atmosphere of social, artistic and political awareness; daughter of Rt. Hon. Frederick Huth Jackson, the youngest Director of the Bank of England ever appointed; her mother, Annabel Grant Duff, an author, was a High Anglican; she inherited her maternal grandfather's flaming red hair; brought up in the High Church, but always attracted by the Catholic Church; became interested in Islam, but a French priest argued her out of this ("Instead of only reading the best bits of the Koran, the curé made me read it all, the endless trifling legal points, the personal spites, the pseudo-divine permissions to lust or to murder"); educated at Lady Margaret Hall College, Oxford University (MA in History; and won a blue for swimming); then studied at the London School of Economics; in 1930 she married Hon. Christopher Fremantle (d. 1978), artist and son of Lord Cottesloe; they had three sons; her husband was a life-long follower and teacher of the philosophy of Gurdjieff and Ouspensky; lived in England working as a journalist for several papers and magazines; ran as a Labour Party candidate for Parliament in 1935; traveled all over the United States in the mid-1930's to lecture on British life for the English-Speaking Union; broadcaster for the BBC and volunteer ambulance driver at start of World War II; then settled in the United States in 1942; worked in the Indian section of British Embassy, Washington; believed the Catholic Church to be the one true Church from 1923, but deliberately stayed out of it until finally converting ("My own reasons for 'verting' – that I am an historical and a linguistic snob, preferring a faith that goes clear back nearly two thousand years to one which stems from around 1500, and to sing the liturgy…in an unchanging language, rather than in a language subject to the vagaries of slang and fashion"); in leaving Britain during the war, and then converting to Catholicism, she was condemned by many of her family, friends and colleagues; became an American citizen in 1947; supported Dorothy Day (see above) at the *Catholic Worker*; assistant editor of *Commonweal*; taught at Fordham University 1948-1961 and at New York University 1971-1979; writer of biography, anthology of the Fathers, literary criticism, and poetry; author of thirty books and many articles; translator of many works from French and German; see *Poems, 1921-1931* (1931); *George Eliot* (1933); *Sicily* (1935); *James and Joan* (1948) (novel); *Desert Calling: The Life of Charles de Foucauld* (1950); "All This, and Heaven Too," in John A. O'Brien, *The Road to Damascus, Vol. IV: Roads to Rome* (1955), p.198 ("The Church of Rome to [my mother] meant intolerance and cruelty, Savonarola, Galileo, Servetus. She fed me Voltaire, as did my French teacher, a passionate anti-clerical. But Voltaire didn't worry me, or Rousseau either. I loved reading them, but countered mother with Blake: 'Mock on, mock on, Voltaire, Rousseau,/ Mock on, 'tis all in vain./ You throw the dust against the wind/ And the wind blows it back again'… Then, above all, I found – what I had never consciously bothered about – Truth. The great, slow, inevitable march of the eternal verities: God within reach of our reason, the possibility of That beyond which we can imagine nothing higher and the certainty that He has not left Himself without witness – these were crammed into the crowded six months of my instruction. They also became part of the daily bread for which I now pray and that is given me each day. Each moment must mean a movement towards Him or a movement away, and because of that choice, each movement is infinitely precious. I learned to burn what I had adored: birth control, euthanasia, cremation – three absolute tenets of my mother's that we were brought up to think were 'musts' for all right-thinking people.

They had become suspect to me even before I knew I wanted to become a Catholic. And I came to see them for what they are, hideous, glaring examples of the '*Non serviam*' – 'I will not serve' – of Satan and of Adam and Eve. I will not accept the total consequences of marriage, that is really what birth-control advocates are saying. I will not wait, say euthanasia advocates, to be given death, as Eve would not wait for the apple to be given her but took it. I will not let my body serve the soil, giving back to earth what I took from her in being born, that is what I say if I insist on cremation…

History, above all, held me. I had read history at Oxford and, as far as English history went, I saw the Reformation as the most horrendous dislocation of faith and charity, the end of Christian collective life in England, the beginning of centuries of civil strife ending in materialism and the blight that was called the Industrial Revolution. It was not Belloc or Dawson who convinced me. At Oxford we read only the Protestant apologists, but they themselves, J. R. Green, Bishop Stubbs, Gardiner, Lecky and the rest of them only pointed up the rightness of Thomas à Becket and Thomas More, the infamy of Thomas Cromwell and Thomas Cranmer. No one can read history and not conclude with Newman that in time the Church's position is unique and has been and will be world without end.

The absolute gratuity of God's gifts daily overwhelmed me. 'All this and Heaven too,' I found myself saying. Nothing else that ever happens or could happen is of comparable importance to the daily celebration of the sublime sacrifice of the Mass. The horrifying humility of God 'given for us and condescending' grows more truly awful with the years"); *The Papal Encyclicals in Their Historical Context* (1956); *The Age of Belief: The Medieval Philosophers* (1957); *This Little Band of Prophets: The Story of the Gentle Fabians* (1960); *The Protestant Mystics* (1964); "The Papacy and Social Reform," in Christopher Hollis (ed), *The Papacy* (1965); *Pilgrimage to People* (1968); *Three Cornered Heart* (1970) (memoir written in the third person) ("From Augustine Anne learned…that 'in the beginning was the Word: behold Him whom Mary worshiped. And the Word was made flesh: Behold Him whom Martha served.' She learned that 'He who made me without myself cannot save me without myself,' and that man's salvation *caused* God's wondrous incarnation; that since man has denied and betrayed his Creator, only that Creator (not, repeat not, His Son, but *Himself*) could repair the primal fault Love loving Itself *is* the Trinity: the Love that loves is the Father, the Love beloved is the Son, the Love by which Love loves is the Holy Ghost"); *Age of Faith* (1971); *Saints Alive!* (1978); Matthew Hoehn OSB (ed), *Catholic Authors* (1952); Walter Romig, *Book of Catholic Authors* (1952).

Fry, James C. – soldier; b. 1897, Sandpoint, Idaho; brought up in a devout Christian family; educated at the United States Military Academy at West Point; his wife Marjorie was a cradle Catholic; served in Texas, Hawaii, Georgia, France and the Philippines (where he was immediate assistant to Lieutenant-Colonel Dwight D. Eisenhower); later religious views influenced by travels in Catholic Europe and in the Middle East; at the start of World War II he was an assistant military attaché in Turkey; in 1942 military observer with the British Eighth Army in the Western Desert when Field-Marshal Rommel drove the British back to El Alamein; in 1944 in command of the 350th Infantry Regiment, 88th Division, during the fierce fighting in Italy; wounded four times and awarded the Distinguished Service Cross and Silver Star for valor; after World War II served on the General Staff in Washington, then sent to Austria as a brigadier-general; commanded the Second Infantry Division in Korea; received many other military awards; see "I Found Christ's Church," in John A. O'Brien, *The Road to Damascus, Vol. IV: Roads to Rome* (1955), p.43 ("All of my travels have had some influence upon my eventual decision. But my first trip to Europe in 1931 probably had as much effect as any other. The fine old cathedrals of Europe attracted me and we spent many hours visiting them. One cannot walk through churches that were started almost a thousand years ago without realizing the profound influence that Catholicism had on the people that constructed those magnificent edifices. I cannot see how anyone can reflect upon the history of those centuries without inevitably reaching the conclusion that such a religion must have been inspired by God, and have had the continuous influence of Jesus Christ, as passed on through His disciples throughout the years. People were kneeling before these shrines centuries before the founders of all the Protestant sects were born...

But the pinnacle of these experiences was reached when I attended midnight mass at Jerusalem on Christmas. It was an emotion-stirring event which was magnified when I stopped to reflect that history definitely proved that on a nearby hill Christ had been crucified. Soul-searching thought brought me to the conclusion that elementary logic could only lead one to deduce that God must have intended that one Church would exist and would teach throughout the centuries the religion Christ taught His disciples. Except for the Jewish Faith and certain oriental beliefs only one Church could claim to have been in existence for those two thousand years.

Eventually the years were to take me to Rome, where positive elements of evidence are available, pointing toward the Catholic Church as the Church originated by Christ. On 6 June 1945, my regiment was passing through Rome, and in the middle of the night I stood in the shadows of the Colosseum. The city was shrouded in total blackout. And the moon silhouetted the amphitheatre where Christians had been persecuted 1,200 years before a British king had elected to sponsor the Church of England in order that he might marry for a second time").

Gallitzin, Demetrius Augustine ("The Apostle of the Alleghenies") - prince and priest; Servant of God; b. 22 December 1770, The Hague, Holland; c. 1788 (received with his sister Mimi; his mother had come back to the Catholic Church in 1786; other members of the family in Europe also converted, e.g., the young Prince Alexander Gallitzin, in 1814 at the age of fifteen, his aunt, and the latter's daughter, the Princess Elizabeth Gallitzin, who also entered the Community of the Sacred Heart in Paris); d. 6 May 1840, Loretto, Pennsylvania; born into one of the oldest and wealthiest royal Russian families; his father was Prince Demetrius Alexejewitsch Gallitzin (d. 1803), the Russian ambassador to Holland (previously ambassador to France), nominally Russian Orthodox; his mother was a German countess Amalia von Schmettau (1748-1806), whose religious education was neglected even though her mother was Catholic; both parents were close friends of Voltaire, Diderot and other rationalists, and espoused the Enlightenment creed; he was baptized into the Orthodox Church, but not brought up in it; as a young child he was cradled in the arms of Catherine the Great as a sign of special favor to his father; in 1772 his mother separated from her husband; in 1786 she came back to the Catholic Church and remained a fervent Catholic until her death; he was educated in the best schools; he became a Catholic at the age of seventeen (influenced by his mother and her intellectual Catholic friends); in 1792 his mother sent him to America to broaden his education (Europe being in the throes of the French Revolution); he assumed the name Augustine Smith in order to conceal his royal background; in 1792 he entered the Sulpician seminary in Baltimore, Maryland, intent on being a missionary priest; on 18 March 1795 he was ordained (the first to receive in the limits of the original thirteen of the United States all the orders from tonsure to priesthood); in 1799 he founded a small Catholic community at Loretto, Pennsylvania, in the Allegheny Mountains; in 1802 he became a naturalized citizen of the United States; for forty years he ran a mission within a radius of one hundred miles from Loretto; he encouraged Catholic immigrants to come there and out of his considerable fortune he purchased much land and financed many buildings; he was disinherited by the Russian government in 1808; in 1816 his name became well known nationally when he responded to an attack on the Catholic faith by a Presbyterian minister, Rev. Mr. Johnson, by publishing *Defense of Catholic Principles*; he published several similar works of apologetics; he was nominated for the episcopacy, but declined to be considered; had an authoritarian style of running things; died a poor man; from a dozen Catholics when he went there, Loretto had 10,000 at the time of his death; he was buried, according to his request, midway between his residence and the church, St. Michael's (they were about thirty feet apart); in 1847 his remains were transferred to a vault in a field nearer the town, which is now capped by a bronze statue of the prince-priest; his cause for canonization is ongoing; see *Defense of Catholic Principles* (1816) ("For God's sake, dear sir, if you value the glory of God, and the salvation of your soul, give up protesting against the Catholic Church; in it alone you will find salvation. As sure as God lives, it is the true church of Christ. May the day of judgment be for me the day of God's eternal vengeance, if the Roman Catholic Church is not the only one true and immaculate spouse of Christ. May my soul be doomed to suffer for you to all eternity, all those torments, which you would deserve by following all the pretended superstitions of the church of Rome...

The question then before us is concerning theological toleration, viz. whether Almighty God can approve of so many different religious systems, which we find established upon earth; whether all these different religious systems can be considered as so many different ways to heaven. If so, we ought to be in favor of universal toleration...

The Catholic Church teaches, that Jesus Christ established but one church for the salvation of man, and that out of that one church salvation is not to be had"); *An Appeal to the Protestant Public* (1819); *A Letter to a Protestant Friend on the Holy Scriptures* (1820); *Six Letters of Advice* (1834); Thomas Heyden, *A Memoir on the Life and Character of Rev. Prince Demetrius A. de Gallitzin* (1869); Sarah M. Brownson, *Life of Demetrius Augustine Gallitzin, Prince and Priest* (1872); Robert Gorman, *Catholic Apologetical Literature in the United States, 1784-1858*

(1939); Grace Murphy, *Gallitzin's Letters: A Collection of Polemical Works of the Very Reverend Prince Demetrius Augustine Gallitzin, 1770-1840* (1940); Daniel Sargent, *Mitri, Or The Story of Prince Demetrius Augustine Gallitzin, 1770-1840* (1945); Stasys Maziliauskas, *Pioneer Prince in USA: An Historical Account of Prince Demetrius Augustine Gallitzin and His Eminent Relatives* (1982); Margaret Bunson and Matthew Bunson, *Apostle of the Alleghenies, Reverend Demetrius Augustine Gallitzin* (2001); Anon, "Father Gallitzin and the Cliptown Exorcism," *catholicism.org*, 21 May 2008; Brother André Marie, "Father Demetrius Gallitzin: The Princely Apostle of Western Pennsylvania," *catholicism.org*, 23 May 2008 ("The hand that rocked the cradle ruled the world of our future American apostle. Raised a Catholic until age nine, when a freethinking tutor soured her on religion, Amalia passed through a number of strange enthusiasms on her way back to the Faith of her baptism. From being a disciple of Diderot and Voltaire (the former of whom was a frequent household guest in the Gallitzin home), she began to follow an eccentric Dutch antiquarian named Hemsterhuis, after whose tutelage she came under the salutary influence of a formidable German educator in the person of the very Catholic Baron Franz von Fuerstenberg. The Baron, who did much to improve education in Westphalia after the suppression of the Jesuits, had in his circle of collaborators many priests who helped ensure the Catholicity of his energetic undertakings. After a providential illness, Amalia was brought back to the Faith. She would not be - could not be - mediocre in its practice. Princess Amalia wanted to be another Saint Monica, and her son, of course, was to be another Saint Augustine, even if she had to drag him to that pinnacle of greatness kicking and screaming. Lacking Monica's demure nature, the princess was a strong personality, charming, brilliant, beautiful, and - how say it? - *excessive* in everything she did. One gets the impression that the princess brought to every venture, including child-rearing, the decisiveness of one squeezing the last bit of toothpaste out of the tube, though she looked good doing it. She was a bright light who often eclipsed all around her, including her son, whom she found disappointingly 'empty' well into his teens and beyond"); *Catholic Encyclopedia* ("Father Gallitzin's reputation for sanctity, the fame of his talents, and the account of his labours had spread far and wide; and it was his deep humility as well as his love for his community that prevented his advancement to the honours of the Church. He accepted the office of Vicar-General for Western Pennsylvania, conferred on him by Bishop Conwell of Philadelphia, in 1827, because he felt that in that office he could promote the interests of the Church; but he strongly resisted the proposals to nominate him for the position of first Bishop of Cincinnati and first Bishop of Detroit"); *ANB* ("Gallitzin gained national attention in 1816 when he published a *Defense of Catholic Principles* in response to a Pennsylvania Protestant minister's attack on "popery." This pamphlet, the first widely distributed American Catholic apologetical tract, went through many editions, and Catholics throughout the country referred to it to clarify their beliefs, religious practices, and customs and to demonstrate the compatibility of Catholic and American principles").

Garacontié, Daniel (also Garakonthie, Garaconthie, Sagochiendagehté) – American Indian leader; fl. 1654 ; c. July 1670 (received in the cathedral of Quebec); d. 1677, Onondaga; member of the Onandaga Iroquois tribe; early life unknown ; first appeared in 1654 in Montreal at the head of an Iroquois League delegation; he exchanged prisoners, bringing to an end ten years of war with the French and negotiating a thirty year peace; he welcomed the French Jesuit missionaries, thereby incurring the enmity of the Mohawks; confirmed his alliance with the French by accepting Christian baptism which was performed by the bishop, Francois de Montmorency de Laval; also negotiated the Covenant Chain Treaties with the English Crown and colonies; he opposed the superstitions and dances of the tribes; see *ANB* ("At last, in July 1670 Garacontié carried his alliance with the French to the point of accepting Christian baptism, 'renouncing polygamy, the vanity of dreams, and all kinds of sins'").

Garcia, Laura L. – philosopher; c. Fall 1981 ("I embraced as my teacher, my mother, and my home what I had once viewed as my mortal enemy"); raised in the Pacific Northwest by parents who were devoutly Christian; her father was a minister in non-denominational Bible churches within the Calvinist tradition; believed in God from her earliest years, and developed a deep commitment to Evangelical Protestantism, but began to be concerned by her religious communion's lack of interest in deeper theological and philosophical questions, e.g., the doctrine of predestination, the problem of evil, and the authority of the Bible; at high school came across Francis Schaeffer's *The God Who Is There* and Arthur Holmes' *Christianity and Philosophy*, and became more optimistic at the possibility of combining faith with philosophical inquiry; also great admirer of Alvin Plantinga; graduated from Westmont College, Santa Barbara, California (interdenominational liberal arts college) with honors in Philosophy (1977); came to believe that "the relationship between faith and reason from the Reformed perspective gave too little credit to reason, even reason marred by the effects of sin"; in 1977 went to the University of Notre Dame to do graduate work in the Philosophy of Religion (awarded MA and PhD in Philosophy (1983)); came to doubt the doctrine of justification by faith alone and the view that Scripture alone is our authority in matters of faith; this caused a deep personal crisis; she turned first to the Episcopal Church ("hoping that I could accommodate my new convictions without leaving the familiar and comfortable umbrella of Protestantism"); read Chesterton, Newman, Merton (see below), Aquinas and the early Church Fathers; influenced greatly by meetings with Ralph McInerny of the Philosophy Department, his arguments and his deep faith; converted to the Catholic faith while still in graduate school; has taught at Calvin College, University of Notre Dame, University of St. Thomas (St. Paul, Minnesota), Catholic University of America, Georgetown University, Rutgers University, New Jersey, and Boston College; specialist in Philosophical Theology and Metaphysics; her work has concentrated on philosophical questions about the nature and attributes of God, the relationship between faith and reason, and the prospects for natural theology; also on the basis of human dignity and its moral implications for bioethics and the dignity of women and children; founding member of both Women Affirming Life and University Faculty for Life (1989); articles in several leading journals; married to Jorge Garcia (four children of the marriage); see "Can There Be a Self-Explanatory Being?" *The Southern Journal of Philosophy* (1986); "Philosophy and Faith," in Thomas V. Morris (ed), *God and the Philosophers: The Reconciliation of Faith and Reason* (1994) ("The Catholic Church retains great confidence in the ability of Christ to redeem the world; and not just to replace it with the kingdom of God. The Catholic view that grace perfects nature means that even the fallen world shows the glory of God and that fallen human beings can produce goodness and truth and beauty that are genuine, albeit imperfect or incomplete. That some truths, even about the moral law and about God, can be known independently of revelation, and that truth and beauty are good in themselves - these are fundamental claims that have always seemed right to me and that are most strongly articulated and defended within Catholicism…

One wants to give arguments or evidences that will make a move [to the Catholic Church] look as intellectually respectable as possible, whereas the real causes of one's conversion are often more personal and diffuse, and in the end outside oneself altogether, assuming that faith is a gift..

One difficulty with telling

the story of one's own religious pilgrimage is that described by G. K. Chesterton in recounting the story of his conversion (from Protestantism to Catholicism): 'I happen to have a strong feeling that this method makes the business look much smaller than it really is. Numbers of much better men have been converted to much worse religions.' What one would like to say about one's religion, I think, is that one believes it because it is true, and, of course, there are always many ways of arriving at the same truth. A second major obstacle to telling the reasons for one's conversion has been well described by John Cardinal Newman, also a convert to Catholicism. It is that the deliberations leading to such a decision are so numerous and varied that it is almost impossible to choose one or two considerations as the reason(s) for converting, as though the whole matter could he put into a neat syllogism. Consequently, what follows is much more a narrative than an argument, though I think it will seem a familiar story to many who have followed the path to Rome…

On the intellectual side, I would say that two major considerations led me toward the Catholic view. The first was that I began to have doubts about the Reformation doctrine of justification by faith alone. Another Evangelical friend in the graduate program persuaded me over time that the Scriptures did not support this view, and that many Scriptures suggested just the opposite (the Letter of James, for example). I will not attempt to reconstruct those arguments here. Suffice it to say that I became more and more attracted to the view that God saves us by grace alone, where grace is to be understood as a genuine divine force in our lives that seeks to transform us into the likeness of Jesus Christ, to make us fit for heaven. Faith is a necessary condition for salvation, on this view, but it must be a living faith, informed by grace and leading to a certain kind of life. On such a view, it is possible to reject God's grace, not just by refusing to come to faith but refusing to accept and obey His laws. At the time, I saw this change in my thinking as significant but not particularly as a step in the direction of Rome.

The next major shift in my views focused on the second pillar of the Reformation: the view that Scripture alone is our authority in matters of faith, and that the claims made by tradition or Catholic teaching are strictly optional for believers. One vexing problem was that it was difficult to find in Scripture a clear justification for the view that only Scripture can be the guide of our faith. But I was even more influenced by the recognition that the canon of Scripture could not itself have been decided by appealing to Scripture, so was forced to acknowledge the authority of the Catholic Church in at least that one instance. I also began to wonder how the basic creeds of the church, setting out the orthodox doctrine on the Incarnation or the Trinity, could be defended as settled or permanent without some appeal to the Holy Spirit's guidance in these important matters.

This problem became more obvious to me during a year I spent teaching at Calvin College, since one of the papers everyone was discussing that year was written by a theologian defending social trinitarianism, the view that there are three divine beings who have in common the property of being divine, and who know and will all the same things. My reaction to this view was that, although it solved various thorny theological problems and could be made (with not too much effort) consistent with the Scriptures, it simply was not acceptable because Christendom would view it as heretical. (In fact, such a view was explicitly condemned by the Fourth Lateran Council in 1215; it had been suggested by a certain Joachim in opposition to his teacher, Peter Lombard.). If the Scriptures alone are to be our guide, then it seems incumbent on each person confronted with a new theological opinion to learn enough Greek, Hebrew, biblical studies, and history of the Near East to decide what the Scriptures do in fact teach. And it began to seem implausible to me that God would have left the essential doctrines of the faith so inaccessible to the average layperson and so open to revision. So, on this point as well, I began to lean in the direction of the Catholic view that the apostles (and their successors) have been entrusted with the care and guidance of the Church in matters of faith and morals, and that Peter holds a kind of primacy in this mission"); "Edith Stein - Convert, Nun, Martyr," *Crisis*, June 1997; "Christians and the Joy of Sex," *National Catholic Bioethics Quarterly*, Summer 2003; "The Importance of Parental Choice," *Logos*, Summer 2003; "Ethics on the Wing," *Fellowship of Catholic Scholars Quarterly*, Fall 2003; "Preserving Persons," in Christopher Tollafsen (ed), *The Contribution of John Paul II to Bioethics* (2004); "Modal Arguments for God," in Kelly James Clark (ed), *Readings in the Philosophy of Religion* (2005); "Worth Dying For," in Jerry Walls and Gregory Bassham (ed), *Philosophy and Narnia* (2005); "Liberating Motherhood," *Crisis*, 12 February 2011.

Gasson, Thomas Ignatius - priest and educator; b. 23 September 1859, Sevenoaks, Kent, England; d. 27 February 1930; from a family part of the landed gentry with a Huguenot background; raised as a member of the Church of England; emigrated to the United States in 1872; influenced by two Catholic women, Catherine Doyle and Anne McGarvey, he was received into the Catholic Church; joined the

Society of Jesus in 1875; ordained to the priesthood on 26 July 1891 in Innsbruck; returned to the United States in 1892; did mainly teaching; appointed Professor of Ethics and Political Economics at Boston College, Massachusetts; president of the college 1907-1914 when he developed it into a leading academic institution; Dean of the Graduate School at Georgetown University in Washington, D.C. 1914-1923; assisted in the reorganization of the Jesuits in Montreal, Quebec; buried in the cemetery of the College of the Holy Cross, Worcester, Massachusetts; see *ANB*.

Genovese, Eugene, Dominick ("Gene") – historian; b. 19 May 1930, Brooklyn, New York; c. December 1996 (revert; his wife, Elizabeth Fox-Genovese (see above) converted in December 1995); d. 26 September 2012, Atlanta, Georgia; brought up in an ethnic Italian family; as a youth he was active in the Communist Party of America until expelled in 1950 (for "having zigged when I was supposed to zag"); remained a Marxist and Socialist; educated at Brooklyn College (BA) and Columbia University (MA and PhD in History); two early marriages ended in divorce; professor at Rutgers University 1963-1967 (he made controversial statements applauding the Viet Cong victory in South Vietnam) and the University of Rochester 1969-1986 (chairman of Department of History 1986); taught part-time at several other universities; editor of *Studies on the Left* and *Marxist Perspectives* (founded the latter); first Marxist president of the Organization of American Historians; several studies on slavery in the American South, employing a Marxist perspective; in the 1990s he rejected the Left and Marxism and explored the history of conservatism in the South; moved to the right and adopted traditionalist conservatism; at all times a critic of liberalism; collaborated with his wife (married in 1969) on lectures, articles, and books; he and his wife helped to found The Historical Society to resist the encroachment of ideology in historical studies; his ashes were buried with his wife; see *The Political Economy of Slavery* (1965); *The World the Slaveholders Made* (1969); *In Red and Black: Marxian Explorations in Southern and Afro-American History* (1971); *Roll, Jordan, Roll: The World the Slaves Made* (1974); *From Rebellion to Revolution: Afro-American Slave Revolts in the Making of the Modern World* (1979); *Fruits of Merchant Capital: Slavery and Bourgeois Property in the Rise and Expansion of Capitalism* (1983) (with Elizabeth Fox-Genovese); *The Slaveholders' Dilemma: Freedom and Progress in Southern Conservative Thought, 1820-1860* (1992); *The Southern Tradition: The Achievement and Limitations of an American Conservatism* (1992); "The Question," *Dissent*,

Summer 1994, p.371 ("For many years I have lived in dread of having to answer The Question. Curiously, no one has asked it...

The Question: 'What did you know, and when did you know it?' For at the age of fifteen I became a Communist, and, although expelled from the party in 1950 at age twenty, I remained a supporter of the international movement and of the Soviet Union until there was nothing left to support. Now, as everyone knows, in a noble effort to liberate the human race from violence and oppression we broke all records for mass slaughter, piling up tens of millions of corpses in less than three-quarters of a century. When the Asian figures are properly calculated, the aggregate to our credit may reach the seemingly incredible numbers widely claimed. Those who are big on multiculturalism might note that the great majority of our victims were nonwhite.

Never having been much good at math, I shy away from quibbles over statistics. Still, all quibbles aside, we have a disquieting number of corpses to account for.

Those of us who have preached the need to break eggs in order to make omelets might note the political complexion of some of the eggs. About twenty years ago, picking up on some passages in Roy Medvedev's *Let History Judge*, I wondered if Comrade Stalin had not killed more communists than were killed by all the bourgeois, imperialist, Fascist, and Nazi regimes put together. 'It can't be true,' said I. 'Has Comrade Medvedev taken up serious drinking?' So I sat down to do some rough arithmetic. (You do not have to be good at math to do that much arithmetic.) Alas, Comrade Medvedev had not taken up serious drinking.

Reflecting here on moral responsibility, I have referred to 'we.' For it has never occurred to me that the moral responsibility falls much less heavily on those of us on the American left than it fell on Comrade Stalin and those who replicated his feats in one country after another. And I am afraid that some of that moral responsibility falls on the 'democratic socialists,' 'radical democrats,' and other left wingers who endlessly denounced Stalinism but could usually be counted on to support – 'critically,' of course - the essentials of our political line on world and national affairs.

Especially amusing has been the spectacle of those who pronounced themselves anti-Stalinists and denounced the socialist countries at every turn and yet even today applaud each new revolution, although any damned fool has to know that most of them will end in the same place. For that matter, how could we have survived politically were it not for the countless liberals who, to one extent or another, supported us, apparently under the comforting delusion that we were social reformers in rather too much of a hurry - a delusion we ourselves never suffered from"); "The Riposte," *Dissent*, Summer 1994, p.386 ("Yes, I know the history of atrocities committed by Christians, but where outside the Christian West did concepts of personal freedom and of limits to state authority arise and flourish"); *The Southern Front: History and Politics in the Cultural War* (1995); *A Consuming Fire: The Fall of the Confederacy in the Mind of the White Christian South* (1998); "The Dulcet Tones of Christian Disputation in the Democratic Up-Country," *Southern Cultures*, Winter 2002, p.56; *The Mind of the Master Class: History and Faith in the Southern Slaveholders' Worldview* (2005) (with Elizabeth Fox-Genovese); *Miss Betsey: A Memoir of Marriage* (2008) (A memoir of his wife) ("In 1975, the national Unitarian Church honored me with an award for my book *Roll, Jordan Roll: The World the Slaves Made*. Shortly thereafter the Unitarians in Rochester, where we lived, invited me to speak at their Sunday service on the religion of the slaves. I agreed…Having been brought up on Catholic Masses, nothing prepared me for what followed: a large room that resembled a high-school gymnasium; a pleasant woman pastor who opened the proceedings with dignity but without mention of God; a series of announcements from the floor on the scheduled picketing of local businesses for racism or something and requests for signatures on petitions against injustice, oppression, and persons' unpersonhood to persons. I thought I was at a political meeting, and I was.

In my talk, I spoke respectfully of religion but identified myself as an atheist who found the evidence of black spirituality in slavery a surprise. The congregation received my presentation warmly, for which I was grateful. But afterwards at a coffee circle, kind people invited me to join their church. I reminded them that I was an atheist. They assured me that their church welcomed atheists and that most of the congregants did not believe in God. Apparently with the intention of putting me at ease, someone asked how anyone could believe in God in view of the constant horrors across the world. Would He have permitted the recent terrible earthquake in Nicaragua, in the aftermath of which the great Roberto Clemente lost his life in an attempt to bring relief to its victims? 'Would a good God permit such evil?'

I gasped. How could well-educated and intelligent people talk such rubbish? Stunned and momentarily forgetting my atheism, I responded with an impassioned defense of Christian theology. I may not have believed in God, but I considered their objections an insult to my intelligence. I interpreted their remarks as meaning that God, to be worthy of worship, had to do whatever they wanted Him to - that God had to follow the dictates of their various consciences. I reminded my Unitarian hosts of the words of Genesis 23:50: 'The thing proceedeth from the Lord. We cannot speak unto you bad and good.' I returned home shell-shocked. A 'church' of unbelievers!

I attended a Catholic Mass for the first time in about fifty years — except for an occasional wedding or funeral. The changes since Vatican II brought me up short, but, to my surprise, it was as if I had never left"); *Slavery in White and Black: Class and Race in the Southern Slaveholders' New World Order* (2008) (with Elizabeth Fox-Genovese); *Fatal Self-Deception: Slave Holding Paternalism in the Old South* (2011); Jay Nordlinger, "Up From Leftism: A Visit With the Historian Eugene D. Genovese," *The National Review*, 14 November 2011; Robert P. George, "Eugene Genovese: Truth-Teller," *Public Discourse*, 2 October 2012 (and reprinted in *catholiceducation.org*); Leo Ribuffo, "Eugene D. Genovese (1930-2012)," *Jacobin.com*, 3 October 2012 ("I liked to tease Gene that he had always hated liberalism more than he loved socialism; liberalism (in the twentieth century American sense) was intellectually too messy for him as well as insufficiently disciplined in its means and ends. Sometimes Gene conceded that I might have a point. A few years ago he half joked that he would tell me the single most important reason for his shift 'if you promise not to laugh.' Gene said that he had concluded that liberals in their optimism were 'wrong about human nature.' I didn't laugh. Neither did I offer the futile response that he might have moved a shorter distance on the spectrum to become a Niebuhrian social democrat. I have no doubt that Gene considered this quip part of a serious explanation of his transition.

Although honored by conservative organizations and claimed especially by traditionalists after his return to the Roman Catholic Church, Gene in his last years is better categorized as a 'man of the Right' rather than as a conservative (to recall a distinction Whittaker Chambers made to William F. Buckley, Jr.). Even this distinction does not fully capture the continuing idiosyncrasies of his worldview. A fierce defender of Israel, Gene nonetheless voted for Pat Buchanan at least once because he distrusted Republican neocon dreams of creating a worldwide capitalist utopia. Despite his return to Catholicism, Gene talked often and nostalgically about the Communist Party of his youth as well as about the ex-Communists and Popular Fronters who energized New York City Democratic reform politics during the early 1960s. It is almost as if he considered Communism a necessary stage in both his own life and the life of the country").

Gillars, Mildred Elizabeth (*née* Sisk) ("Axis Sally") - radio propagandist; b. 29 November 1900, Portland, Maine; c. 1960; d. 25 June 1988, Columbus, Ohio; her abusive father abandoned her on her seventh birthday and never returned; her parents divorced and shortly afterwards her mother married Robert Bruce Gillars, a dentist; appeared in theater when young; studied dramatic arts at Wesleyan University, Ohio, from 1918, but left in 1922 without graduating; attempted a career as an actress in New York, but little success and much poverty in the economic downturn; in 1929 she moved to North Africa, then on to Europe, eventually settling in Berlin in 1935; several years of poverty; in 1940 she obtained work with German State Radio, taking part in chat shows and announcing records; in 1941 chose to stay in Germany after her fiancé, Paul Karlson, a naturalized German citizen, said that he would never marry her if she returned to the United States (he was later killed on the Eastern Front); the program director (and her lover), Max Otto Koischwitz (1902-1944), a naturalized American citizen, cast her in new shows; she broadcast Nazi propaganda to American servicemen, became an immediate star, and was highly paid; she referred to herself as "Midge at the Mike"; the GIs referred to her as Berlin Bitch, Berlin Babe, Olga, and Sally, but most commonly as "Axis Sally"; her last broadcast was on 6 May 1945, two days before the German surrender; after the war she hid in Berlin, but was discovered in 1946; in 1948 she was flown to the United States and indicted for treason on ten counts, but only eight were proceeded with at the trial in 1949; the defense argued that her broadcasts stated unpopular opinions but did not amount to treasonable conduct; it was also contended that she was under the influence of Koischwitz, and that many announcements attributed to her were done by another woman broadcasting from Rome; convicted of treason for one broadcast on the eve of the Normandy invasion; sentenced to ten to thirty years' imprisonment and fined $10,000; served her sentence at the Federal Reformatory for Women in Alderson, West Virginia; proved a model prisoner and became a Catholic while in the reformatory; paroled on 10 July 1961; went to live at Our Lady of Bethlehem Convent, Columbus, Ohio, spent the rest of her working days teaching French, German and music at St. Joseph Academy, Columbus; in retirement she lived a secluded life; in 1973 she returned to Wesleyan University and completed her degree; buried in Saint Joseph Cemetery, Lockbourne, Franklin County, Ohio (unmarked grave); see Nathaniel Weyl, *Treason: The Story of Disloyalty and Betrayal in American History* (1950); Richard Lamparski, *Whatever Became* *of...?* (1968); Jules Archer, *Treason in America: Disloyalty vs. Dissent* (1971); John C. Edwards, *Berlin Calling: American Broadcasters in Service to the Third Reich* (1991); M. Williams Fuller, *Axis Sally* (2004); Richard Lucas, *Axis Sally: The American Voice of Nazi Germany* (2010); *ANB* ("German radio, she explained later, gave her 'the outlet for the dramatic expression I had always sought.' Unlike other Americans who broadcast for Nazi Germany out of ideological conviction, Gillars appears to have drifted into treason because of her love for Koischwitz as well as her desire for the fame and fortune she had craved much of her life. The Nazis offered her a 'chance to be somebody,' as William Shirer observed in 1943 of other American radio traitors. It offered her a career").

Gilmour, Richard – bishop; b. 28 September 1824, Glasgow, Scotland; c. 1844; d. 13 April 1891; his parents were Reformed Presbyterians; in 1829 the family moved to Nova Scotia and then settled near Latrobe, Pennsylvania; a friendship with a priest, Rev. Francis Rafferty, led him to convert to Catholicism; in 1846 he entered Mount St. Mary's Seminary, Emmitsburg, Maryland; ordained priest 30 August 1852; worked as a parish priest and briefly as a professor at Mount St. Mary's Seminary of the West, Cincinnati, Ohio (1868-1869); in 1872 appointed the second Bishop of Cleveland by Pope Pius IX.

Gingrich, Newton Leroy ("Newt") (born Newton Leroy McPherson) – politician, political consultant and author; b. 17 June 1943, Harrisburg, Pennsylvania; c. 29 March 2009 (St. Joseph's, Capitol Hill, Washington D.C.); adopted by his mother's second husband Robert Gingrich (1925-1996), an army officer; brought up as a Lutheran; graduated in History from Emory University, Atlanta in 1965; PhD in Modern European History from Tulane University, New Orleans in 1971; became a Southern Baptist in graduate school; taught History and Geography at West Georgia College in the 1970s; represented Georgia in Congress 1979-1999; served as House Minority Whip 1989-1995; co-author of *Contract With America* in 1994; a major factor in the Republican victory in the congressional election in 1994; 58th Speaker of the U.S. House of Representatives 1995-1999; political consultant from 1999; candidate for the Republican Party presidential nomination in 2012; married three times, the first two marriages ending in divorce; claimed that his conversion to the Catholic faith (that of his third wife, Callista Bisek (b. 1966)) was a decade long journey ("When you have 2,000 years of intellectual depth surrounding you, it's comforting"); influenced also by Pope Benedict XVI; see *The Government's Role in Solving*

Societal Problems (1982); *Window of Opportunity* (1985); *Contract With America* (1994); *Restoring the Dream* (1995); *To Renew America* (1996); *Lessons Learned the Hard Way* (1998); *Saving Lives and Saving Money* (2003); *Winning the Future* (2005); *Rediscovering God in America* (2006); *The Art of Transformation* (2006) (with Nancy Desmond); *A Contract With the Earth* (2007) (with Terry L. Maple); *Real Change: From the World That Fails to the World That Works* (2008); *5 Principles for a Successful Life: From Our Family to Yours* (2009) (with Jackie Gingrich Cushman); *To Save America: Stopping Obama's Secular-Socialist Machine* (2010) (with Joe DeSantis); *A Nation Like No Other: Why American Exceptionalism Matters* (2011); "Why I Became a Catholic," *National Catholic Register*, 26 April 2011 ("It is more truthful to say that over the course of several years, I gradually became Catholic and then decided one day to accept the faith I had already come to embrace... Worshipping with believers across the world opened my eyes to the diversity and richness of the Catholic Church.

Over the course of a decade, the depth of faith and history contained in the life of the Catholic Church were increasingly apparent to me, and the centrality of the Eucharist in the Catholic Mass became more and more clear").

Gipp, George ("The Gipper") - college football player; b. 18 February 1895, Laurium, Michigan; c. December 1920 (deathbed conversion); d. 14 December 1920, South Bend, Indiana; from a family of moderate means; his parents were devout (and very anti-Catholic) Baptists; undisciplined in high school, but excelled at all sports; entered the University of Notre Dame in 1916 on a baseball scholarship, but he was recruited by Knut Rockne (see below) for the football team, although he had never played football before; he played in many positions, most notably halfback, quarterback, and punter; he led the team in rushing and passing in each of his last three seasons (1918, 1919 and 1920); he led the 1919 and 1920 teams to two undefeated seasons (outscoring opponents 560 to 27); once drop-kicked a record 62-yard field goal to win a game; never allowed a completed pass as a defensive back; several of his records still stand at Notre Dame; referred to by Knut Rockne as "the perfect performer who comes once in a generation"; led a somewhat dissolute personal life; two weeks before his death he was elected as Notre Dame's first All-American and second consensus All-American; died of a streptococcal infection days after leading Notre Dame to a win over Northwestern University; on his hospital bed he is said to have delivered the celebrated "win just one for the Gipper" line (apparently to Knut Rockne); converted to the Catholic faith nine hours before his death (his family claimed the conversion story was faked, or that he "converted" when he was delirious with fever); buried in Lakeview Cemetery, Calumet, Michigan; he was voted into the College Football Hall of Fame in 1951; the phrase "Win one for the Gipper" was later used as a political slogan by Ronald Reagan who had played George Gipp in the film *Knut Rockne, All-American* (1940) and was often referred to as the "The Gipper"; in 2007 his body was exhumed for DNA testing to determine if he had fathered a child out of wedlock with an 18-year-old high school student; the tests showed that Gipp was not the father of the child; see James A. Peterson, *Gipp of Notre Dame* (1959); James A. Cox, "Was the Gipper Really for Real? You Can Bet He Was," *Smithsonian*, December 1985, p.130; George Gekas, *The Life and Times of George Gipp* (1987); Murray Sperber, *Shake Down the Thunder: The Creation of Notre Dame Football* (1993); Emil Klosinski, *Gipp at Notre Dame - The Untold Story* (2003); Todd Tucker, *Notre Dame Vs. The Klan: How the Fighting Irish Defeated the Ku Klux Klan* (2004), pp.80-83 ("The Gipps' anger grew to the point that Vice-President Matthew Walsh was tasked with conducting a formal investigation. In his official report, Walsh stated that George Gipp expressed several times during his years at Notre Dame that he might like to become a Catholic. Walsh wrote that several times after becoming ill, Gipp brought it up 'without the matter having been suggested to him.' Walsh's report did admit that Gipp was delirious when he was baptized"); Patrick Chelland, *One For The Gipper -George Gipp, Knute Rockne and Notre Dame* (3rd edition, 2008); Jack Cavanaugh, *The Gipper: George Gipp, Knute Rockne, and the Dramatic Rise of Notre Dame Football* (2010); *ANB*.

Goldstein, David – author and Catholic campaigner; b. 27 July 1870, Spitalfields, London, England; c. 21 May 1905 (received at Immaculate Conception Church, Boston); d. 30 June 1958; father a cigar maker; brought up in a poor Dutch Jewish family who brought him to the United States in 1871; received his only formal education in two public schools in New York; worked from the age of eleven as a cigarmaker; family moved to Boston; joined the Socialist Labour party; became acquainted with another Socialist, Martha Moore Avery (1851-1929) (see above); both had growing consciousness that happiness in society depended primarily on the stability of the family and that economic reform is secondary to the moral reform of society; wrote with her a criticism of the doctrines of Socialism and Bolshevism as being both immoral and anti-religious; doubted whether it was possible to be a Socialist and value the traditional family system; began to see the role played by the Catholic Church in defending the family; later wrote influenced by Pope Leo XIII's encyclical, *Rerum Novarum*, which warned of the dangers of Socialism while saying that a remedy must be found for those wrongs that the working classes suffer; his conversion was also influenced by Sr. Augustine of the Mother of God, the Carmelite Prioress at Roxbury, Boston; following his conversion he continued to work for five years in a cigar factory and studied Catholic doctrine in his spare time; then pursued a nationwide apostolate (set up by Cardinal O'Connell of Boston) of bringing knowledge of Catholic doctrine and life to the general public, and especially to the Jews; this apostolate was initially called the Catholic Truth Guild and later renamed the Catholic Campaigners for Christ (he was known as "the lay apostle to the man in the street"); worked on this all over the country until 1941; much of this work was with Martha Moore Avery (though her poor health kept her in Boston); wrote a column on the principles of the Catholic faith for ten years in *The Pilot*, the newspaper of the Boston archdiocese; named a Knight of St. Gregory by Pope Pius XII in April 1955; see *Socialism: The Nation of Fatherless Children* (second edition, 1911) (with Martha Moore Avery); *Bolshevism: Its Cure* (1919) (with Martha Moore Avery); *Campaigning for Christ* (1924) (with Martha Moore Avery); "From Socialism to the Church – Why I Am a Catholic," in Rosalie Marie Levy, *Why Jews Become Catholics* (1924), p.12 ("[Sister Augustine] had impressed upon me the necessity of going to fundamental principles and to original sources. From this instruction, I could see that an examination of the doctrines of the hundreds of sects, all claiming to be Christian, would lead only to confusion, without having a root knowledge of the Christian Church. Just as I realized that the discussion of the Talmud might be interminable though not enlightening, as one can get no nearer to the Mosaic Law save by study of the Law itself.

On walking through the Jewish quarter of Boston one evening on my way home from work, I chanced to look into a store window of a Protestant Mission. My eyes lighted upon a pamphlet – 'Israel's Messiah' - just the subject I wanted to know something about. Fortune favored me, for, although the only copy was in the window yet the attendant insisted upon giving it to me.

The pamphlet told, in simple and eloquent language, the story of our Lord. It brought out the fact that both Joseph and Mary were of the house of David, from which it was foretold the Messiah would come. It told of the strictness with which the Jews kept, protected and cherished their genealogical tables; that all the people of Israel 'were reckoned by genealogies.' Thus it was that the Jews were able to trace the ten tribes - to know who was a true son of the house of Levi, from whom their priests were selected, and the records would show who was a true son of the house of David, in which the Messiah was to be born. The pamphlet made clear that at the time of the birth of the Christ Child no one had ever disputed that both Mary and Joseph belonged to the house of David - nor was it disputed during the life of our Lord Himself that He was a son of the house of David. But, since all the records were destroyed by Titus when Jerusalem was destroyed, how desolate must be the hearts of those Jews who still look for the coming of their Messiah! From reading this pamphlet, I turned to the prophecies in the Bible. The more I read, the more I believed in the Messiahship of the Child of Bethlehem.

Especially was I impressed with the prophecy of Daniel, in which he foretold the exact time when the vision and the prophecy would be fulfilled; when the Saint of Saints would be anointed; when the Messiah would be here, in accordance with God's promise, for in the fullness of that time Christ our Lord was born"); *Campaigners for Christ Handbook* (third edition, 1934 under thew title *Campaigning for Christ*); *Autobiography of a Campaigner for Christ* (1936) (full-length autobiography); *Jewish Panorama* (1940); *Letters of a Hebrew-Catholic to Mr. Isaacs* (1943); *Suicide Bent: Sangerizing Mankind* (1945); *What Say You?* (1945); "The Flowering of Judaism," in John A. O'Brien (ed), *The Road to Damascus, Vol. II: Where I Found Christ* (1950), p.175 ("I found the religion divinely set forth in the Old Testament expressed through a visible, authoritative spiritual society, as a religion of God's making must be. This I found entirely lacking in present-day Jewry, it being devoid of theological exactitude to the extent of even failing to be in agreement as to what constitutes a Jew. I found the Orthodox group alone adhering, in principle and in hope, to belief in such things of basic import as a priesthood, sacrifices, and an expected personal Messiah. On the other hand, I found that Reform Judaism repudiates these Orthodox principles as well as belief in miracles; it also rejects the idea that the Books of the Old Testament are the word of God in the traditional sense of the term. In time I came to the realization that Reform Judaism…is as far out of line with the Judaism of the Old Testament as is Unitarianism with New Testament Christianity. In fact, Reform Judaism is not Judaism at all, save in name…

I found that all rabbis, Orthodox and Reform, are in agreement that an end had come in the first century of the Christian Era to the Aaronic priesthood, to the Temple, and to those Mosaic sacrifices which traditional Jews hold to be the highest expression of the love of God. This is so important to the understanding of present-day Judaism that it were best to let Jews themselves tell of it. The *Jewish Encyclopedia*, quoting authorities, says: 'Judaism saw in the sanctuary the manifestation of God's presence among His people, and in the priest the vehicle of divine grace, the mediator through whose ministry the sins of the community, as of the individual, could be atoned for... [that] through the Temple Israel is cleansed of its sins, that the chief purpose of altar and priesthood is to make atonement for, and effect the forgiveness of sin, as stated again and again in Talmud and Midrash.'

The *Encyclopedia of Jewish Knowledge* says: 'The fall of the Temple and the disappearance of the high priesthood occurred at the same time. That form of intercession, ground for possible belief in human symbols of divine authority, vanished. Nothing remained but the sublime faith in the invisible omnipresent Creator.'

The same thing is reported in *Mid-Channel*, by Ludwig Lewisohn, professor of English literature, Brandeis University, Waltham, Massachusetts. He writes: 'With the destruction of the Temple the sacrificial cult of Jews was destroyed. For among the people there was but one temple and one altar, hence the Jewish people were suddenly laicized. Priests and sacrifices and tangible mysteries were no more.' In *The Brandeis Avukal Volume* (1936), Rabbi Louis Epstein, of Brookline, Massachusetts, writes: 'In the course of time the priest and sacrificial cult gave away to rabbinical orders.' But rabbis are not priests, as Joseph Leftwich, former editor of the *Jewish Telegraph Agency*, says in *What Will Happen to the Jews?*, without being questioned by any Jewish reviewer of his book. 'The Rabbi is not a priest. The priesthood passed with the Temple. Even the rabbinical diploma, unlike the Christian ordination, confers no sacred power and is not a licence. It is simply a testimonial of ability of the holder to act as a Rabbi if he wished to be elected by some congregation.'

Rabbi Epstein, quoted above, goes on further to let us know that no one speaks with authority in Jewry, saying: 'When a dispute of the interpretation of the law arises, there is no authoritative body to give final decision. Authority is contained in a dead-letter book, not in any living individual or organized body.'

Surely, I concluded, a 'laicized' ruled Judaism, a Judaism with 'a dead-letter book' as its only authority, is not Old Testament Judaism. I found further evidence that it is devoid of a priesthood, sacrifices, and Temple, vital to Old Testament Judaism, in the fact that the Orthodox Jews, the intensely religious division of Jewry, prayed daily for the reinstitution of the Aaronic priesthood, with their sacrifices, and for the coming of a personal Messiah. This impressed me as pathetic, for - as I discovered to my amazement – there is no genealogical evidence whatsoever to prove the existence of a family of Aaron from which an Aaronic priesthood could possibly be reinstituted and there are no genealogical records whatsoever to prove the existence of a family of David, in which a Messiah could possibly be born. Thus Orthodox Jews remain like 'An infant crying in the night; An infant crying for light; And with no language but a cry'

It was this religious catastrophe that prompted me to conclude that present-day Judaism is not, and cannot possibly become, the Judaism of my Israelitish fathers of old. It was the claim of the Catholic Church that Christianity is the fulfilment, the perfection, of Old Testament Judaism that gave me the key to understanding that the end of the Aaronic priesthood, the Levitical sacrifices, and the Temple was providential and not accidental; that it was a blessing, and not the calamity that orthodox Jewry believes it to be. This finally led me to the baptismal font of the Catholic Church with love of the faith of my fathers of old in my heart. God had not abandoned His chosen people! The promised Messiah had come. Jesus is His name!.. I 'found Him of whom Moses in the Law, and the prophets, did write, Jesus,' as did Philip, one of the Twelve Jews who became Apostles.

I found that Jesus was born in the family of David of the tribe of Judah, as Moses and Ezekiel said He would be born. I found that God promised a sign that something unusual would take place. 'A virgin shall conceive and bear a son, and his name shall be called Emmanuel'; that signifies 'God with us,' that is, with the children of Israel, as was Jesus who was born of the Virgin Mary.

I found that Jesus was born in the time foretold by Daniel nearly five centuries before Mary, the Lily of Israel, brought him forth in the city of David. I found Jesus to be the fulfillment of the prophecies of Isaiah, whom the Jews classify as 'the greatest of the prophets.' Isaiah said about seven centuries before the Christian Era that 'God Himself will come and save you,' the children of Israel; that he 'shall be called Wonderful, Counsellor, God the Mighty, the Father of the world to come, the Prince of Peace'; who was to 'sit upon the throne of David…for ever'; and that he would be adored by kings.

I found that Jesus was conspired against; betrayed; sold for thirty pieces of silver; led like a sheep to slaughter; suffered His hands and feet to be pierced; and withal rose from the dead as foretold by Isaiah, by Zechariah, and David.

I found Jesus to be the 'Prophet' of whom Moses told the children of Israel: 'The Lord thy God will raise up…like unto me,' to whom Israel should give ear. This likeness to Moses was seen in Jesus being meek, yet courageous; a mediator, lawgiver, and deliverer; and still more, in that He, 'God with us,' was the Prophet of prophets.

I found that during the days of Jesus in Palestine, and the days when the Apostles, inspired by the Holy Spirit, preached things Christian, that Mary, Joseph, John the Baptist, the Apostles, and thousands of other Jews were convinced that the hope of Israel had been fulfilled in Jesus the Messiah, who instituted the 'new covenant' foretold by Jeremiah. I was strongly convinced that nearly all of the Jews of those days would most likely have cried out to Jesus, as did a multitude of them during His triumphal ride through Jerusalem: 'Hosanna to the Son of David. Blessed is He who comes in the name of the Lord,' were it not for official Jewry, which was subservient to the political power in Rome. The high priests, whose office was hereditary and tenable for life, were appointed and deposed by the Romans at their pleasure. The Herodian priests, including Caiaphas and Annas, and the members of the Sanhedrin were the enemies of the people as well as of Jesus. This is recorded in the *Talmud*; in *Jesus of Nazareth*, by Professor Joseph Klausner of the Hebrew University, Jerusalem; in *The Nazarene*, by Sholem Asch, and in other Jewish writings.

Surely, I reasoned, God our All-Merciful Heavenly Father did not leave His children without a safeguard against the changing whims and fancies of men. After an end had come to the guidance He gave to the Jews through their priesthood, He gave them a religion which binds man to Him. Surely God did not leave man without the consolation of the sacrificial means of paying homage to Him and atoning for their sins! If Christianity is Judaism full-blossomed, as its foremost proponents claim it to be, I concluded that this should be evidenced in the existence of a spiritual society superior to the one that guided the Jews in pre-Christian times. Then must this spiritual society have a priesthood and sacrificial worship of a higher order than was enjoyed by the children of Israel. This I found in the Christ-established Catholic Church, with its Christ-instituted priesthood according to the Order of Melchisedec. I found the Church to be as superior to the Temple as Jesus is to Moses. I found this to center in the superiority of Christian to Jewish principles; in the Church being universal – Catholic – whereas the Temple was for an exclusive people, the children of Israel; and in having altars all over the world, whereas the Mosaic law permitted but one Altar, in a central sanctuary, the Temple. This temple containing the Holy of Holies was destroyed by the soldiers of Titus in the year 70 A.D, thus fulfilling the prophecy of Daniel, and the prediction of Jesus that 'not a stone upon a stone' would be left to the Temple.

I found that Jews held, as did the Council of Trent, that 'priesthood and sacrifice are indissolubly united.' Hence the end of Israel's priesthood meant that an end had come to offering the sacrifices called for in the Book of Leviticus. Thus Jews could no longer make atonement for their sins…as Jehovah commanded Moses…

I found that the last remnant of the Judaism of my forebears had disappeared with the destruction of the Temple by the soldiers of Titus, which was the one and only place in which communal sacrifices could be offered in honor of the One True God and to atone for sin"); *My Boston Pilot Column* (1956); Theodore H. Dorsey, *From a Far Country: The Conversion Story of a Campaigner for Christ* (1939); Debra Campbell, "David Goldstein and the Lay Catholic Street Apostolate," PhD dissertation submitted to Boston University (1982); Debra Campbell, "A Catholic Salvation Army: David Goldstein, Pioneer Lay Evangelist," *Church History* (1983), p.322; Debra Campbell, "David Goldstein and the Rise of the Catholic Campaigners for Christ," *Catholic Historical Review*, January 1986, p.35 ("Goldstein's decision to be baptized in the Catholic Church was primarily the result of his own personal search for moral absolutes, the same quest which had prompted his break with the Socialist Party. Many years after his conversion Goldstein recalled: 'It was the Catholic attitude towards the family, in striking contrast to the Socialist attitude I was opposing, that caused me to look at things Catholic inquiringly and sympathetically. It was then that I found that the basic principles of the Church re the origins of man, the Trinity, etc., to be in harmony with the principles I had learned as a non-Catholic'"); Eleonore Villarrubia, "David Goldstein and Martha Moore Avery; From Socialists to 'Campaigners for Christ,'" *catholicism.org*, 8 June 2011; Patrick Allitt, *Catholic Converts: British and American Intellectuals Turn to Rome* (1997), pp.145-147 ("Starting in 1917, Goldstein and Avery also collaborated in the Catholic Truth Guild, driving a modified Ford Model T painted in the papal colors, yellow and white, preaching prolabor Catholicism on street corners in working-class districts and speaking against suffrage for women as a latently socialist assault on the family"); "From Socialism to the Church," in Roy H. Schoeman, *Honey From the Rock* (2007) (reprint of essay in Rosalie Marie Levy, *Why Jews Become Catholics* (see above)); the David Goldstein Papers are located in Boston College Special Collections, Chestnut Hill, Massachusetts; *ANB*.

Gordon, Caroline Ferguson – author, literary critic and teacher; b. 6 October 1895, Merimont Farm, near Trenton, Kentucky;

c. 24 November 1947; d. 11 April 1981, Chiapas, Mexico; brought up mainly privately in the Old South traditions; her family were Deists; attended her father's school for boys in Montgomery County, Tennessee; educated at Bethany College, West Virginia; worked for the Chattanooga Reporter newspaper; in 1925 met and married Allen Tate (see below) (one child of the marriage); much traveling; friend of many well-known writers, including T. S. Eliot, William Faulkner, F. Scott Fitzgerald, Ford Madox Ford (a special influence, for whom she acted as a secretary), Ernest Hemingway (see below), Flannery O'Connor, and Robert Penn Warren; at first torn between modern and southern life; always interested in classicism; published ten novels 1931-1972; during the war years she embarked on a search for a system of order to replace the dark side of life; divorced in 1945, followed by a 1946 remarriage and an ultimate divorce in 1959, though they continued to correspond and remained friends; influenced in her conversion by Jacques Maritain; after her conversion wrote novels with an overtly Christian and Catholic themes; aware of the problem for the Catholic writer of the great gap in vision between the writer of faith and his secular reading audience ("Ours is the first age in which a man would call himself educated and know no theology"); in her final work she merges classicism and Catholicism; taught at several universities; she chose for her tombstone a line from Maritain: "It is for Adam to interpret the voices that Eve hears"; see *Penhally* (1931); *Aleck Maury: Sportsman* (1934) (her most famous and popular work); *None Shall Look Back* (1937); *The Garden of Adonis* (1937); *Green Centuries* (1941); *The Women on the Porch* (1944) ("Gordon here strips away man's unsatisfactory pursuits at achieving happiness until all that is left is the sanctity of Christian faith" (Robert H. Brinkmeyer))"; *The Forest of the South* (1945); *The House of Fiction: An Anthology of the Short Story* (1950) (with Allen Tate); *The Strange Children* (1951); *The Malefactors* (1956); *A Good Soldier: A Key to the Novels of Ford Madox Ford* (1957); *How to Read a Novel* (1957); *Old Red and Other Stories* (1963); *The Glory of Hera* (1972); *Collected Stories* (1981); Robert E. Golden and Mary C. Sullivan, *Flannery O'Connor and Caroline Gordon: A Reference Guide* (1977); Thomas H. Landess (ed), *The Short Fiction of Caroline Gordon* (1977); Rose Ann C. Fraistat, *Caroline Gordon as Novelist and Woman of Letters* (1984); Sally Wood (ed), *The Southern Mandarins: Letters of Caroline Gordon to Sally Wood, 1924-1937* (1984); Robert H. Brinkmeyer, Jr., *Three Catholic Writers of the Modern South* (1985) ("In 1947 Caroline Gordon joined the Catholic Church. Apparently the horrors of World War II, which prompted her to consider more seriously the flawed nature of humanity and the existence of the divine, influenced her decision. Finding faith, Gordon said…, meant discovering the key to life's puzzle…She went on to say that discovering faith 'revolutionized my life,' and that 'it is, to me, a little as if I had all my life been engaged in the writing of a novel and only recently had discovered that the plot is entirely different from what I thought it was!' As a Catholic, Gordon now had a vital tradition and faith by which to structure her life and art. Before her conversion, Gordon admitted in a letter to a Trappist monk, art had been her only religion. 'I was nearly fifty years old,' she wrote, 'before I discovered that art is the handmaid of the Church.' Her art now, she believed, had greater depth and was truer to reality, since her imagination was now fired with the Church's vision of the world and creation"); John M. Dunaway (ed), *Exiles and Fugitives: The Letters of Jacques and Raïssa Maritain, Allen Tate and Caroline Gordon* (1993); her papers are in the Firestone Library, Princeton; *ANB*.

Gray, Nellie Jane – pro-life activist; b. 24 June 1924, Big Spring, Texas; d. 10 or 11 August 2012, Washington, D.C.; she was not a Catholic as a child, but said that she "had elements of the Catholic faith in my life"; as a young woman, she met a priest who brought to light what the Catholic Church was about, and he tutored her until she was received into the church; enlisted into the army in 1944; served as a corporal in the Women's Army Corps (WAC) during World War II; later studied at Georgetown University (first degree in Business and masters degree in Economics); worked for the federal government for twenty-eight years in the Departments of State and Labor; during this time studied in the Georgetown University Law School in the evening; then practiced law; after the Supreme Court ruling *Roe v Wade* in 1973 decriminalizing abortion she retired from professional life; became a pro-life activist; founded the annual March For Life on 22 January 1974; after the first march she established the March for Life Education and Defense Fund to sustain it; she went on to lead the largest pro-life gathering in the United States and built it into the longest-running, most successful annual event in the pro-life movement; she was referred to by Sean Cardinal O'Malley, Archbishop of Boston, as "the Joan of Arc of the Gospel of Life"; her body was discovered at her home on 13 August 2012; unmarried; see Fr. Frank Pavone, "What Motivated Nellie Gray?" *priestsforlife.org*, 2012 ("Nellie did not like the term 'unborn.' She said that it wasn't clear enough as to whether it referred to the baby before or after abortion. It was too negative. So she began using the term 'preborn' to refer to the child in the womb. And she referred to herself as 'One Note Nellie,' sounding the note of 'no exceptions, no compromise.' No government, no human authority, can authorize even a single abortion.

This is why Nellie could not tolerate any of the 'exception clauses' in pro-life legislation. She understood the need to save as many lives as possible in any situation. But she held that as soon as the government says that life is to be protected 'except in this case and except in that,' those exceptions were an unjustified attempt to authorize killing. Such attempts, moreover, did not 'legalize' abortion, according to Nellie. They simply 'decriminalized' it").

Green, Anne – writer and translator; b. 1891, Savannah, Georgia; c. July 1947 (her father and her brother were received in 1915); d. 1979, Paris; while she was a child her parents moved to Le Havre, France, and finally settled in Paris; participated as an ambulance driver in World War I; she wrote several novels (her first, *The Selbys*, was a best-seller) and volumes of short stories; sister of Julien Green (see below); translated some of her brother's works into English and works by other authors, e.g., Charles Peguy and Francoise Sagan; see *The Selbys* (1930); *Reader, I Married Him* (1931); *Marietta* (1932); *A Marriage of Convenience* (1933); *Fools Rush In* (1934); *That Fellow Perceval* (1935); *16 Rue Cortambert* (1937); *The Delamer Curse* (1940); *Just before Dawn* (1943); *With Much Love* (1948); *La Porte des Songes* (1969).

Green Julien (born Julian Hartridge Green) – writer; b. 6 September 1900, Paris; c. 29 April 1916 (received in the crypt of the Chapelle des Soeurs Blanches (Chapelle Notre-Dame du Saint-Sacrament, rue Cortambert, Paris); his sister Eleanor (1880-1965) became a Catholic some years earlier; his father was received some months earlier; his sister Anne (see above) was received in 1947; another sister Mary (1883-1926) also converted); d. 13 August 1998, Paris; youngest of eight children of American parents who were Protestants; his father, Edward Moon Green (1853-1927), was a businessman and secretary of the American Chamber of Commerce in Paris; his mother, Mary Adelaide Hartridge (d. 1914), was from a distinguished southern family (daughter of a Savannah judge); brought up in an over-protected manner by her and as an Episcopalian; this led to a "sense of exile on the geographical, linguistic, cultural and spiritual levels"; became a Catholic after his mother's death; his conversion was greatly influenced by reading Cardinal Gibbons', *The Faith of Our Fathers*, by his godmother Agnes Power-Farley, an Irish Catholic, and by his mother who become much more open to Catholicism; his conversion was followed by a period of intense religious fervor; in 1917 volunteered as an ambulance man in the American Field Service (enlistment canceled on his true age being discovered); joined an ambulance unit of the American Red Cross and then joined the French Army, serving until 1919; educated at the University of Virginia 1919-1922; became increasingly aware of homosexual tendencies, which intensified the conflict between flesh and spirit already present and led to his severing his links with the Catholic Church; he suffered a loss of faith 1919-1924; returned to France and began a successful career as a novelist; period of unbelief 1924-1934; his name was changed to Julien by his French publisher in the late 1920s; became a life-long friend of Jacques and Raïssa Maritain; after becoming interested in Buddhism 1934-1939, he re-converted to Catholicism in April 1939 (main influence was Jacques Maritain; their discussion on the works of Plato and Aristotle forced him to question his admiration of Buddhism); also influenced by the writings of Fr. Louis Bouyer; tendency at times towards Jansenism; lived in the United States 1940-1945; worked in New York at the United States Office of War Information; for nearly a year and five times a week he broadcast to France as part of the Voice of America; returned to France after World War II and settled there permanently; most of his books were on faith and religion; wrote several novels, but his main works were his journals, published in many volumes, in which he reviewed his literary and religious life and the literary and cultural life of Paris; also wrote plays, articles, essays, short stories, biography and translations; always thought of himself as a "Sudiste", a supporter of the Southern States of the United States; adopted an austere style; wrote almost exclusively in French, but also in English (he was bilingual); he translated some of his books into English, doing some of them with his sister Anne; his writings are relatively unknown in Britain and Ireland; in 1970 the Académie francaise awarded him its grand prize for literature; in 1971 he became the first non-French national to be elected to the Académie française, but he resigned in 1996, stating that he was "exclusively American"; this caused some controversy and the Académie pointed out that it was not possible to resign from this body as membership is a lifelong honor; met Robert de Saint-Jean (1901-1987) in 1920 and became his companion; later legally adopted the homosexual novelist and playwright Ėric Jourdan (b. 1938); never became a French citizen; sometimes used as pen names Théophile Delaporte and David Irland; buried in a chapel designed for him in St. Egid Church, Klagenfurt, Austria; see (selective list) *Pamphlet Contre les Catholiques de France* (1924) ("It is not the saints that it is necessary to talk about if one wants to prove the sanctity of the Church. It's bad priests and bad popes. One sees debauched religious, priests without doctrine, ridiculous popes. You find that ignoble, but I find that, on the contrary, marvelous and adorable. Alexander VI edifies me more than Gregory the Great, for a Church governed by saints and continuing on, that's normal and human, but a Church that can be governed by villains and imbeciles, and still continue, that is neither normal nor human"); Mont-Cinère (1926); *Adrienne Mésurat* (1927, *The Closed Garden*); *Léviathan* (1929, *The Dark Journey*); *L'autre sommeil* (1930); *Le Visionnaire* (1934, *The Dreamer*); *Minuit* (1936, *Midnight*); *Memories of Happy Days* (1942) (only major work written in English); *Moïra* (1951) (his masterpiece); *Sud* (1953, *South*) (play); *L'Ennemi* (1954, *The Enemy*) (play); *Chaque homme dans sa nuit* (1960, *Each in His Own Darkness*); *Partir avant le jour* (1963, *The Green Paradise*); *Mille chemins ouverts* (1964, *The War at Sixteen*); *Terre lointaine* (1966, *Love in America*); *La Nuit des fantômes* (1976) (a children's book); *Demain n'existe pas* (1979) (play); *Frère François* (1983, *God's Fool: The Life and Times of Francis of Assisi*); *Journal,* 17 Vols.(1938-1996)*; auto*biography in English: *The Green Paradise: 1900-1916* (1992); *The War at Sixteen: Autobiography: 1916-1919* (1993); *Love in America: Autobiography: 1919-1922* (1994); *Restless Youth: Autobiography: 1922-29* (1996); M. Eigeldinger, *Julien Green ou la tentation de l'irréel* (1947); S. Stokes, *Green and the Thorn of Puritanism* (1955); J. Semolue, *Green ou l'obsession du mal* (1964); R. de Saint-Jean, *Julien Green par luimême* (1967); M. G. Rose, *Julien Green: Gallic-American Novelist* (1971); G. S. Burne, *Julien Green* (1972); N. Kostis, *The Exorcism of Sex and Death in Julien Green's Novels* (1973); J.-P.J. Piriou, *Sexualité, religion et art chez Julien Green* (1976); J.M. Dunaway, *The Metamorphoses of the Self in the Works of Julien Green* (1978); J.-P-J. Piriou, *Une grande amitié* (1979); Anthony Newbury, *Julien Green: Religion and Sensuality* (1986); Kathryn Wildgren, *Julien Green: The Great Themes* (1993); Flavia Vernescu, *Clivage et integration du moi chez Julien Green* (1994); Michael O'Dwyer, *Julien Green: A Critical Study* (1997) (excellent review of Green's life and work) ("Green describes his rediscovery of the joy of being called by a personal God to a life of repentance and hope. He contrasts this experience with his impression of Buddhism which he sees as being a form of rational mysticism where man is abandoned to himself and where the call from a personal God is lacking"); Michael O'Dwyer & Michèle Raclot, *Le journal de*

Julien Green: miroir d'une âme, miroir d'un siècle (2005); Myriam Kissel, *Le cheminement de l'écriture: l'espace dans l'œuvre de J. Green* (2005); Fr. Christopher Smith, "Julien Green, Liturgical Reform and Our Spiritual Combat," *chantcafe.com*, 11 March 2011 ("Green remained, despite his perpetual spiritual and moral anguish, a convinced Catholic. Having read Pascal, he imbibed some of the rigorism of Jansenism which probably exacerbated a sensitive conscience. But he was always aware of the reality of the body and soul composite that is man, and realized the futility of dualist temptations to pretend that one can have purity of soul without purity of the body. He also knew that the 'thorn in his flesh' was something which would be put to rest and healed only in the resurrected body in heaven, and that the supernatural life of the sacraments in the Church alone could get him there.

Green also realized that tremendous paradox of life in the Church, that its holiness is proved, not by its saints, but by its perseverance amidst sin. As he wrote in an ironically titled work, *Pamphlet Against the Catholics*, 'It is not the saints that one has to talk about if one is to prove the sanctity of the Church. It's bad priests and popes. A Church governed by saints continues on, that's normal and human. But a Church that can be governed by villains and imbeciles, and still continue, that is neither normal nor human.' Green's intensely lived struggles, lived openly through his literature, and his devout frequentation of the sacraments, caused Jacques Maritain to declare that he was a mystic. For Green, the true mystic, the true man, was St Francis, 'God's fool' as he entitled a book dedicated to the saint. That encounter with Christ, which was the true reality which allowed man to transcend the struggle between flesh and spirit, came through the humanity of Christ which gave man access to Divinity via the sacraments.

Green's profoundly sacramental humanism, if we can call it that, conditioned his reaction to the way the sacraments came to be celebrated after the Second Vatican Council. One would expect that this master of the French language and celebrant of sacramental realism would have welcomed the liturgical reform. When he first heard French used for the Psalms at Tenebrae on Good Friday in 1956, he wrote, 'Psalms mooed as if by cows in French...How can Catholics not revolt against such ugliness? One bitterly misses the Latin of former times.' As the reforms progressed and the liturgy took on what to him were more Protestant characteristics, he and his sister Mary, also a convert, suffered intensely. He once wrote to her, 'Why did we even convert?'

Green's biographer Anthony Newbury suggests that, for Green, the 'solitude of the individual with his conscience as unique authority' that was Protestantism was simply untenable. Green needed a Church with 'real authority' so he felt he actually had a place other than the tortured one of his own conscience. If Newbury is right, it indicates why Green suffered the apparent Protestantization of the liturgy as a real crisis of faith. But the Frenchman clung to his faith until his death in 1998, and continued to explore in his later novels the crass sexualization of a world in which conscience has been emptied of its ties to the sacraments and to true religion.

Green's reaction to the liturgical reform is very instructive. He did not reject the post-conciliar liturgy because he was a decadent aesthete or a nostalgic stick-in-the-mud. He rejected the deformation of the liturgy because he foresaw its disastrous consequences in the moral realm. One of the byproducts of vernacular liturgy in the post-Vatican II Church has been a didacticism which borders on pedantry. At its best, the didactic liturgy becomes a vehicle for teaching which, while orthodox, preaches moral rectitude in conformity with the ethical teachings of the Church, but comes across as little more than moralizing and preaching at people. At its worst, it strips the real authority of the Church in the moral sphere of any imaginative ability to inspire people to live a life worthy of the Mystery to which the liturgy and faith call them.

The dramatic situation in which we find ourselves today finds orthodox Catholics calling out for clear teaching on sexual morality and life issues to challenge the hedonism of our day. But if the faith is reduced merely to the observance of a moral code, and liturgy to explaining how to observe it, that faith will not be able to dialogue with anyone except those who are already convinced and opens itself up to Pharisaism. (This is incidentally a point that Pope Benedict makes in his new book). A Julian Green could be inspired to struggle against his passions and cling to Christ, not because of moralizing from the pulpit, but by entering into those beautiful Prayers over the People from the Lenten liturgies of the Roman Mass, which gave him hope that he could, by prayer, fasting and works of mercy, create a space in his heart where God could take Him up into Himself, where Love would find him.

The restoration of the sacred in the liturgy is a must. Clear teaching on the moral life is a must. But if the way of the disciple is not to be highjacked by self-righteousness, that moral teaching must be expressed not by the lips of us sinners, but in the beauty and the transcendence of the sacred liturgy.

I have known many young men and women like Julian Green in my parishes. They come from a world which hates everything the Church stands for in the culture wars. They come because they think the Catholic Church will give them something more. That desire does not keep them from falling into sin, or being tempted. But they come. They want a real place where they can live besides the dreary world and their own weak consciences. A banal liturgy, clerical officiousness, and a poorly formulated moral teaching cloaked in crusader talk will extinguish the pale flame of faith that has been lit in them. But if we trust in the power of Christ acting through the sacraments, through a liturgy celebrated according to the real authority of the true religion and in all of its transcendent beauty, that flame will burst into a fire which will consume them with zeal.

His whole life, Julian Green struggled to master himself and convert to Christ in whom he found authentic love. He was not always successful in his quest, but he held fast to a faith which is real and true because it is not from mortal flesh and human spirit. He was able to do so because of his experience of the true religion, the power of the sacraments, and heavenly liturgy. His works are difficult reads, because they expose the deep fault lines of the spiritual combat. They are as uncomfortable as the Lenten penances which train us for that war against princes and principalities. But for all of that, they are also profoundly Catholic, not because they show the saint in the apotheosis of glory, but because they show what sinful humanity is capable of when assumed by the LORD of glory").

Greene, Edward Lee – botanist; b. 20 August 1843, Hopkinton, Rhode Island; c. 5 February 1885; d. 10 November 1915, Washington D.C.; attracted to plants even as a young child; raised in a Baptist household, but received no religious instruction (said that at the age of thirteen he had never heard of Good Friday or Easter and that even Christmas had no religious significance for him); moved to Wisconsin in 1859 and studied botany at Alma College; private in the Union army 1862-1865 (collected botanical specimens as he marched through Tennessee, Kentucky and Alabama!); returned to the college and earned his Bachelor of Philosophy in 1866; became a botany teacher; was a Methodist at this time; later became an Episcopalian and a candidate for the Episcopal ministry (ordained in 1873); ministered in the Southwest while continuing to collect plants; while ministering in Yreka, California, he discovered the first specimens of *Phlox hirsula*, a small flowering plant found only in that area; moved away from Episcopalianism towards Catholicism, eventually being locked out of his church in 1883, converting shortly afterwards; greatly influenced in his conversion by Fr. Francis Xavier Weninger's book, *Protestantism and Infidelity* (1864); began lecturing at the

University of California, Berkeley, and became the first Professor of Botany there 1885-1895; involved in a controversy over his advocacy of reform of botanical nomenclature; he was widely regarded as a proponent of fixed species, though he did not oppose in print the concept of organic evolution; also he did not formally reject evolution, but had a tendency towards the fixity of species; taught at Catholic University, Washington D.C. 1895-1904; associate in botany at the Smithsonian Institute 1904-1915; moved to studying botanical history and wrote a seminal work on that subject; worked at the University of Notre Dame before returning to Washington; he published 565 original papers, named over 4,400 species of plants, and collected a library of over 4,000 books; his library and collections are at the University of Notre Dame; unmarried; buried in Holy Cross Cemetery, Notre Dame, Indiana; see *Landmarks of Botanical History: Part 1. Prior to 1562 A.D.* (1909) (revised edition by Frank N. Egerton, 1983, containing an introduction, "Greene: The Man," by Robert P. McIntosh); essay in Georgina Pell Curtis (ed), *Some Roads to Rome in America* (1909), p.187 ("("Father Weninger's book, with its blunt uncompromising title, was the book I needed at the time it came to me. More than that; something less than a score of different volumes of Catholic argument that I have read between that day and this have left in no instance so deep an impression on my mind in favor of the Catholic religion as did that; and I am persuaded that such result was not due to its having been the first book of Catholic controversy that I had read.

The title in itself declares the argument, I should say quite unmistakably. He who denies so much as one article of the Catholic faith has started on a course, the end of which is total disbelief; not that this individual will necessarily reach that extreme; but that is logically the ending of the course, and others more logical will arrive at it"); *Landmarks of Botanical History: Part 2* (original rough draft published posthumously in 1936; revised edition by Frank N. Egerton, 1983); Margaret Brent Downing, "Edward Lee Greene: Altiora Petivimus," *Catholic World*, 1917, p.13 (Greene's description of a perfect day: "He attended an early mass, and after breakfast retired to an upper chamber to write out some notes which he had been collecting for days. This engaged him until long past noon. He prepared his meal and then, feeling a little fatigued, sat at his piano and for two hours played Beethoven and Grieg until he was as refreshed as if from an icy bath. He then read an hour or so something light and entertaining, then something heavy and edifying – his well thumbed Greek testament and his favorite edition of the Psalms…He returned to the Church in time for Benediction. Supper and another attack on his writing followed. At ten, he found his task completed and prepared for rest. 'And throughout the day,' he exclaimed fervently, 'not a human being came to my door, and to and from the Church, I met no one with whom I had to exchange a syllable'"); Angie Kumlien Main, "Life and Letters of Edward Lee Greene, "*Transactions of the Wisconsin Academy of Sciences, Arts and Letters* (1929), p.147; J. Barber, "Edward Lee Greene," *Catholic World*, 1945, p.444; Eugene Jercinovic, "Ninety Years After Greene," *newmexicoflores.com*; *ANB*.

Gregory, Wilton Daniel - archbishop; b. 7 December 1947, Chicago, Illinois; c. 1959; one of three children (two sisters); his parents divorced when he was quite young; entered a seminary in 1961; ordained to the priesthood in 1973; continued his studies in Rome (doctorate in liturgical studies 1980); returned to pastoral work in the United States; in 1983 he was appointed auxiliary bishop of Chicago; appointed seventh Bishop of Belleville in 1993; President of the United States Conference of Catholic Bishops 2001-2004 (the first African American ever to head an episcopal conference); vigorous in his handling of the sexual abuse crisis; named the seventh Archbishop of Atlanta in 2004; had surgery for cancer in 2007; written extensively with numerous articles on the liturgy; bi-weekly column, "What I Have Seen and Heard" in *Georgia Bulletin*.

Griffin, John Howard – author, journalist and photographer; b. 16 June 1920, Dallas, Texas; c. 1952 (his second wife was also a convert); d. 9 September 1980, Fort Worth, Texas; second oldest in a family of four children; father of Irish descent, but from a family that had been Southern Baptist for several generations; mother a devout Episcopalian and classical music teacher; brought up as an Episcopalian; taught to see black people as racially inferior; disappointed with his schooling, he applied for and obtained a scholarship to the Lycée Descartes in Tours, France, and went there at age fifteen; then studied medicine at the University of Poitiers in Tours; when World War II started he worked in the resistance movement, helping Jewish children escape from the Nazis; joined the United States Air Force in 1941 and served in the South Pacific, spending 1943-1944 on Nuni, one of the Solomon Islands, marrying an islander; suffered brain damage in an artillery attack and lost much of his sight; the latter forced him to give up the study of medicine; returned to France in 1946 to study music; lived at the Benedictine Abbey of Solemnes, famous for its liturgical tradition; he became immersed there in Catholic culture, liturgy and music; became totally blind; returned to the United States and attended a school for the blind, where he was encouraged to become a writer; also taught piano, marrying one of his students; referred to his conversion having been "crystallized" long before he was finally received into the Catholic Church; also became a Third Order Carmelite; diagnosed with diabetes and contracted a spinal virus that paralysed him, but that later disappeared; in 1957 he regained his sight and became an accomplished photographic artist; worked for school desegregation; in 1959 he darkened his skin and lived as a black man, travelling through Louisiana, Mississippi, Alabama and Georgia; wrote of his experience of discrimination in the monthly magazine *Sepia* in 1960; his account in book form, *Black Like Me*, became a best-seller; forced to flee from Texas to Mexico because of death threats from white racists; friend of Thomas Merton (see below), whom he met in 1962 and on whom he wrote much in his later years; received the *Pacem in Terris* award; several of his books have been published posthumously (see below); see *The Devil Rides Outside* (1952) (autobiographical novel about a young man living in a Benedictine monastery, the writing of which finally convinced him that he had no alternative but to convert); *Nuni* (1956) (another autobiographical novel); *Land of the High Sky* (1959); *Black Like Me* (1961); *The Church and the Black Man* (1969); *A Hidden Wholeness: The Visual World of Thomas Merton* (1970); *Twelve Photographic Portraits* (1973); *Jacques Maritain: Homage in Words and Pictures* (1974); *A Time to Be Human* (1977); *The Hermitage Journals: A Diary Kept While Working on the Biography of Thomas Merton* (1981); *Follow the Ecstasy: Thomas Merton's Hermitage Years, 1965-1968* (1983); *Pilgrimage* (1985); *Encounters With the Other* (1997); *Street of the Seven Angels* (2003) (another novel); *Scattered Shadows: A Memoir of Blindness and Vision* (2004); *Available Light: Exile in Mexico* (2008); *Friendship and Second Innocence: Two Souls in Conversation* (2008) (with Tom McKillop); Brad Daniel (ed), *The John Howard Griffin Reader* (1968); Jeff H. Campbell, *John Howard Griffin* (1970); Beverly Stanford Frank, "John Howard Griffin: The Unshed Tear" (master's thesis, University of Texas, 1989); Robert Bonazzi, *Man in the Mirror: John Howard Griffin and The Story of Black Like Me* (1997); Lorene Hanley Duquin, *A Century of Catholic Converts* (2003), p.154; *ANB*.

Grodi, Marcus – television presenter and Catholic apologist; b. 2 March 1952, Toledo, Ohio; c. 20 December 1992 (received at St. Peter's Church, Steubenville, Ohio, with his wife Marilyn); brought up in a nominally Evangelical

Protestant family; rebelled as a teenager; graduated from the Case Institute of Technology, and worked in plastics engineering; at the age of twenty experienced a radical re-conversion to Christ; decided he was being called to be a minister; studied at Gordon-Conwell Theological Seminary in Boston, graduating with a Master of Divinity degree in 1982; ordained to the Protestant ministry (Presbyterian denomination); found wide variations in doctrinal teaching and in administrative and liturgical matters within Protestantism ("doctrinal confusion and procedural chaos"); his wife pointed out the inconsistency of their staunch pro-life convictions and the pro-abortion stance of their Presbyterian denomination ("How can you be a minister in a denomination that sanctions the killing of unborn babies?"); decided to leave the ministry until his situation was resolved and enrolled on a graduate program in molecular biology at Case Western Reserve University in Cleveland; conversion influenced by hearing a talk by Scott Hahn (a fellow student at Gordon Conwell Theological Seminary in the 1980s) and an audio tape of his conversion story; also influenced by Karl Keating's *Catholicism and Fundamentalism* ("It was clear to me now that the two central dogmas of the Protestant Reformation, *sola scriptura* (Scripture alone) and *sola fide* (justification by faith alone), were on very shaky biblical ground, and therefore so was I"); also influenced by the Church Fathers on Church history before the Reformation, by Fr. Stanley Jaki's *The Keys of the Kingdom* and *On This Rock* on the primacy of Peter, and by John Henry Newman's *Essay on the Development of Christian Doctrine* on the gradual development of papal authority; director of *The Coming Home International Network*; host of "The Journey Home" on *Eternal Word Television Network*; see "What is Truth," in Patrick Madrid (ed), *Surprised by Truth* (1994), p.33 ("I knew I could no longer remain a Protestant. It had become clear that the Protestant answer to Church renewal was, of all things, unscriptural. Jesus had prayed for unity amongst his followers, and Paul and John both challenged their followers to hold fast to the truth they had received, not letting opinions divide them. As Protestants we had become infatuated by our freedom, placing personal opinion over the teaching authority of the Church. We believed that the guidance of the Holy Spirit is enough to lead any sincere seeker to the true meaning of Scripture.

The Catholic response to this view is that it is the mission of the Church to teach with infallible certitude. The apostles and their successors were promised by Christ, 'He who listens to you listens to me. And he who rejects you rejects me and rejects the one who sent me' (Luke 10:16). The early Church believed this too. A very compelling passage leaped out at me one day while I was studying Church history:

'The Apostles received the gospel for us from the Lord Jesus Christ; and Jesus Christ was sent from God. Christ, therefore, is from God, and the Apostles are from Christ. Both of these orderly arrangements, then, are by God's will. Receiving their instructions and being full of confidence on account of the Resurrection of our Lord Jesus Christ, and confirmed in faith by the Word of God, they went forth in the complete assurance of the Holy Spirit, preaching the Good News that the kingdom of God is coming. Through countryside and city they preached; and they appointed their earliest converts, testing them by the spirit, to be the bishops and deacons of future believers. Nor was this a novelty: for bishops and deacons had been written about a long time earlier. Indeed, Scripture somewhere says: 'I will set up their bishops in righteousness and their deacons in faith' (Clement of Rome, *Epistle to the Corinthians* 42:1-5 [ca. AD 80]).

Another patristic quote that helped breach the wall of my Protestant presuppositions was this one from Irenaeus, bishop of Lyons: 'When, therefore, we have such proofs, it is not necessary to seek among others the truth which is easily obtained from the Church. For the apostles, like a rich man in a bank, deposited with her most copiously everything which pertains to the truth; and everyone whosoever wishes draws from her the drink of life. For she is the entrance to life, while all the rest are thieves and robbers. That is why it is surely necessary to avoid them, while cherishing with the utmost diligence the things pertaining to the Church, and to lay hold of the tradition of truth. What then? If there should be a dispute over some kind of question, ought we not have recourse to the most ancient churches in which the apostles were familiar, and draw from them what is clear and certain in regard to that question? What if the apostles had not in fact left writings to us? Would it not be necessary to follow the order of tradition, which was handed down to those to whom they entrusted the Churches?' (*Against Heresies* 3,4,1 [ca. AD. 180]).

I studied the causes of the Reformation. The Roman Catholic Church of that day was desperately in need of renewal but Martin Luther and the other Reformers chose the wrong, the *unbiblical*, method of dealing with the problems they saw in the Church. The correct route was and still is...: Don't leave the Church; don't break the unity of faith. Work for a genuine reform based on God's plan, not man's, achieving it through prayer, penance, and good example.

I could no longer remain a Protestant. To do so meant I must deny Christ's promises to guide and protect his Church and to send the Holy Spirit to lead it into all truth (cf. Matt. 16:18-19, 18:18,

28:20; John 14:16, 25,16:13)...

Eventually I realized that the single most important issue was authority. All of this wrangling of how to interpret Scripture gets one nowhere if there is no way to know with infallible certitude that one's interpretation is the right one. The teaching authority of the Church in the magisterium centered around the seat of Peter. If I could accept this doctrine. I knew I could trust the Church on everything else.

I read Fr- Stanley Jaki's *The Keys of the Kingdom* and *Upon This Rock*, and the Documents of Vatican II and earlier councils, especially Trent. I carefully studied Scripture and the writings of Calvin, Luther, and the other Reformers to test the Catholic arguments. Time after time I found that the Protestant arguments against the primacy of Peter simply weren't biblical or historical. It became clear that the Catholic position was the biblical one.

The Holy Spirit delivered a literal *coup de grace* to my remaining anti-Catholic biases when I read John Henry Newman's landmark book, *An Essay on the Development of Christian Doctrine*. In fact, my objections evaporated when I read 12 pages in the middle of the book in which Newman explains the gradual development of papal authority. 'It is a less difficulty that the papal supremacy was not formally acknowledged in the second century, than that there was no formal acknowledgment on the part of the Church of the doctrine of the Holy Trinity till the fourth. No doctrine is defined till violated'...

I think it's important that I mention in closing one more of John Henry Newman's insights that made a crucial difference in the process of my conversion to the Catholic Church. He wrote that 'To be deep in history is to cease to be a Protestant.' This one line summarizes a key reason why I abandoned Protestantism, bypassed the Orthodox Church, and became a Catholic"); (ed), *Journeys Home* (1997) (revised edition 2011) (containes a later version of "What is Truth," in Patrick Madrid (ed), *Surprised by Truth* (1994) (see above); also reproduced at *The Coming Home Network International*, *Conversion Stories*, chnetwork.org, 13 January 2011); "The New Wave of Converts: A Vision of the Future from the USA," in Dwight Longenecker (ed), *The Path to Rome: Modern Journeys to the Catholic Church* (1999) ("But then through the witness of other Protestant clergy and laity who had discovered the truth of the Catholic Church, I came to understand that there is a reliable Tradition. There is a teaching authority that one can trust - one that was established by Christ Himself in his hand-picked Apostles and guided by the Holy Spirit, and that this ancient authority continued down through the ages and existed in a living, dynamic way today in the Catholic Church. These fellow clergy converts brought Scripture passages to my attention that I had never 'seen' before. I don't know why; I didn't skip over them intentionally. But when they pointed them out and helped me see their implications I was stunned. One such text was 1 Timothy 3:15. Scott Hahn [see below], who was an old friend from seminary days and who had already converted to the Catholic Church one day asked me, 'What is the pillar and bulwark of truth?' My Protestant knee-jerk response was 'The Bible, of course!'

'But what does the Bible say?' asked Scott, turning to the text and asking me to read. I had never 'seen' this verse, though I had taught and preached from I Timothy many times. There in front of me was Paul writing:

'I am writing these instructions to you so that...you may know how one ought to behave in the household of God, which is the church of the living God, the pillar and bulwark of the truth.' The Church is the pillar and bulwark of the truth, not just the Scriptures. All I could do was stare silently at this verse, for I had no comeback. Which Church today can claim to be this pillar and bulwark of truth? My Presbyterian denomination? My local Presbyterian church? The 'invisible church' that we Protestants claimed was the 'true church?' If another church could be that pillar and bulwark where was it and how could we hear its defense and support of the truth?

Another verse was II Thessalonians 2:15. It was there all along but I didn't 'see' it until another clergy convert pointed it out: 'So then, brethren, stand firm and hold to the traditions which you were taught by us, either by word of mouth or by letter.' The authoritative truth to which we were to hold fast was passed down both in written and oral form. But which church tradition claims to have faithfully preserved this oral tradition throughout the ages so that Christians today can be sure they are believing what is true? Only the Catholic Church makes such a claim. Again I was silenced...

But maybe the biggest thing that opened my heart to the truth of the Catholic Faith was not all the apologetic arguments convincing me of the trustworthiness of the Catholic truth, but the realization that the Catholic Church, with all her saints and sinners, was exactly what Christ had promised. The majority of complaints against the Catholic Church over the centuries have been aimed at the decisions and actions of bad popes, or immoral clergy, or ignorant laity, or corrupt Catholic nobility, and the correct answer to this is, 'But, of course! The Church is made up of wheat and tares, from the bottom to the top, we are all sinners in need of grace! This is no reason to leave and form a new church, for any church made up of human beings is made up of sinners.' And who am I to point to any bad pope, bishop, priest, religious or layman? It is enough to know that I am a member of the Church to realize fully that the Church is but a family of sinners who, in looking at the troubles of others, can only recite 'but for the grace of God there go I'"); *The Rapture Trap: A Catholic Response to "End Times" Fever* (2001) (with Paul Thigpen); Marilyn C. Grodi, "I Never Wanted to Be a Minister's Wife Anyway," in Marcus Grodi (ed), *Journeys Home* (1997) (revised edition 2011).

Gurney, Marion Frances (name in religion Mother Marianne of Jesus) – nun and foundress of a religious order; b. 6 July 1869, New York City; c. 31 October 1897 (received at St. Francis Xavier Church, 16th Street, New York City); d. 9 February 1957; one of her ancestors was Elizabeth Fry, the English prison reformer; family had no particular religious leanings; family moved to California when she was a small child; as she grew up she became interested in the Anglican Church; graduated from Wellesley College, Massachusetts, where she had become an Anglican in 1883 or 1884; became for a time a novice in an Anglican convent; she came back to New York City to live and became greatly interested in the settlement work of the Episcopal Church, especially the work among the children; as a High Anglican she was disappointed when the bishop in her diocese forbade reservation in his churches; she turned to the Catholic Church and converted; she opened a Catholic settlement house, St. Rose's, on East 69th in a crowded neighborhood nearly all traditionally Catholic (mainly immigrants), but fallen away from regular religious observance and attendance at church; she stayed for five years and got it well established; in 1902 she formed a Confraternity of Christian Doctrine training catechists to teach the children there; later she established a small house and women who became associated with her went about their Christian doctrine work there and in the parishes; inspired by Fr. Francis McCarthy, SJ, she finally founded in 1908 the Society of the Sisters of Our Lady of Christian Doctrine, taking herself the name of Mother Marianne of Jesus, moving into a house (given the name Madonna House) at 173 Cherry Street, Cherry Hill, a tough section of the city; the purpose of the order was the teaching of Christian doctrine and the promoting of its practice by suitable social activities; over the years the house and its activities expanded greatly; very devoted to Our Lady of Walsingham; see Katherine Burton, *In No Strange Land: Some American Catholic Converts* (1942), p.201 ("One afternoon an Irish maid in the family took Marion for a walk and she took the child into a church with her. Marion was very little impressed. There was an unintelligible gabbling going on alternately between the man up in front and the people about her and it was certainly not English. But suddenly her boredom left her at the sight of a boy lighting many candles and the man who had been gabbling came out again, this time in a gleaming white cloak, and held out over the people something white in a case of glass framed in glittering gold. With the instinct of childhood, which sometimes brings undulled perceptions to holy things, the child felt the Presence there.

She walked home, the spell still on her, and next day went to work to make her own playroom look as much as possible like the scene she had witnessed. She put in a corner the dolls and toys. She brought in masses of bright California flowers and put them around the room. She begged some candles from the cook and put them on her little nursery table, and then sat down in her chair to try to recapture that wonderful feeling she had when the gold and glass had flashed across her fascinated gaze. She sat for a long time but the feeling she had experienced in the church the day before would not come back to her…

…She came to New York one day for supplies for her settlement children, and dropped into her own very liturgical church to say a few prayers to ease her worry. Inside in the front of the church was glowing the familiar red light and she began to genuflect as was her invariable custom. But try as she would she could not make the familiar gesture, even though her will tried to force her to do it.

Bewildered, unhappy, feeling she had no spiritual home at all, she decided to go to talk to an old friend of hers, once an Anglican, but now a Catholic convert and a priest. She took a cab to his rectory, the nearby one of Saint Francis Xavier. Before calling on him she went into his church to pray, and this time she found she had no trouble whatever in genuflecting before the altar. When later in the rectory of the church she told her story to Father van Rensselaer, he smiled at her encouragingly. 'But it is not at all mysterious. Of course you belong here. Come right in'"); Margaret M. McGuinness, *Neighbors and Missionaries: A History of the Sisters of Our Lady of Christian Doctrine* (2012).

Hahn, Kimberley (*née* Kirk) – author and Catholic apologist; b. 24 December 1957, Cincinnati, Ohio; c. Easter 1990 (received at Joliet, Illinois); brought up in a strongly Presbyterian family (her father and an uncle were ministers); early love for the Scriptures; educated at Grove City College, Pennsylvania; obtained a Masters degree in Theology from Gordon-Conwell Theological Seminary, Boston; first doubt about her Protestantism was her and her husband's conviction that contraception was contrary to God's law ("I remember having a tremendous respect for a Church that was willing to take a stand that was obviously very, very unpopular. So I had respect for the

Catholic Church on moral issues but no desire at all to be a part of it"); married Scott Hahn (see below) in 1979 (six children of the marriage); became concerned at her husband's adoption of Catholic principles; found particularly difficult the question of the Virgin Mary; found a tranquility sufficient to have her third child baptized as a Catholic and began to study the sacraments, justification and to accept transubstantiation; see *My Conversion Story: Kimberley Hahn* (1991) ("Back in Joliet, we had a man named Mark Miravalle who came and visited as a professor giving a lecture. Scott said, 'He's going to talk on Mary, and I thought you'd like to come to the lecture.' I wasn't sure that I wanted to, but I thought it would be helpful to hear someone else. I want to share just a few of those thoughts because it really was a turning point for me. The first thing he pointed out is that Catholics don't believe she is a goddess. She's just a creature, but a creature who was specially made. It was the only time that a son made the mother first. What a beautiful thought. In the Magnificat where Mary says, 'I rejoice in God my Savior?' I used to think, 'That proves she sinned because otherwise how could she say she had a Savior.' But the point is, when she was saved, she was saved from conception on. She was saved completely. One of my friends when he stood up to give a testimony in high school said, 'God saved me from drugs, alcohol and wild sex.' I thought, I know this guy; he didn't do this stuff. It does make a pretty interesting entry into his telling his testimony.' He said, 'God saved me from all of that stuff before I got into that stuff.' Well, that's what He did with Mary. He saved her before she got into any of that stuff.

She wasn't called Queen of Heaven because she was married to God and equal to God. She was Queen of Heaven because she's Queen Mother of Heaven and if Jesus is the King of kings and Lord of lords and she's really his mother, then she is the Queen Mother, just like Bathsheba was the queen mother honored by Solomon. And Mary never wants you to just stop and focus on her, but Mary's whole mission is to bear Jesus to us…

I signed up for the RCIA class and in the class I asked the question, 'Isn't it idolatrous to have all of these statues and paintings and pictures, you know, people bowing down and worshipping them?' The priest so lovingly said, 'Kimberly, do you have a family photo wall? You know, you got your parents, your husband, your children?' I said, 'Oh, yeah, sure.' And he said, 'Isn't that rather idolatrous?' 'Well, no.' He said, 'What's the difference?' And I said, 'Well, they just represent people I love.' And he said, 'Right. These represent our Blessed Mother. These represent our older brothers and sisters who have gone before us, and we love them.' He said further, 'If you look in the Old Testament,' (because my concern was with the Ten Commandments - the one which says 'Don't make a graven image:')' He said, 'Remember that not only did the Lord say that, but when he commanded them to make the tabernacle, what did he say that had to go over the Ark of the Covenant?' 'Well,' I said, 'The two angels, the two Cherubs.' He said, 'Is that a graven image?' Apparently not. Okay, that helped…

I was concerned about whether or not the Hail Mary was just being repetitious until I read a little book by a nun and she said, 'Now, don't think that you're such a big hotshot adult. You're a little child and how many times does a child come up to you and say, "Mommy, I love you?"' It can happen ten times in an hour. My daughter would say, 'Mommy, I love you, I just love you, I love you.' I never looked at her and said, 'Honey, that's just vain repetition.' What we're doing in the rosary is saying, 'Mommy, I love you, pray for me. Mommy, I love you, pray for me. Mommy, I love you, pray for me.' And isn't it appropriate for us to do?"); *Rome Sweet Home: Our Journey to Catholicism* (1993) (with Scott Hahn); *Life-Giving Love* (2002); Lorene Hanley Duquin, *A Century of Catholic Converts* (2003), p.196 ("Catholics were the ones who had Jesus physically present in churches and saw themselves as living tabernacles after receiving the Eucharist. And because Jesus is the Eucharist, keeping him in the center allows all of the rich doctrines of the Church to emanate from him, just as the beautiful gold rays stream forth from the Host in the monstrance").

Hahn, Scott W. – author, theologian and Catholic apologist; b. 28 October 1957, Pittsburgh, Pennsylvania; c. 29 March 1986 (Easter Vigil, Milwaukee, Wisconsin; received by the then Mgr. Bruskewitz, later Bishop of Lincoln, Nebraska); brought up in a family that was not very religious; had a conversion experience in high school; soaked himself in the Bible and studied Luther and Calvin; became a convinced Protestant and anti-Catholic; Bachelor of Arts degree from Grove City College, Pennsylvania in 1979; married Kimberley Hahn (see above) in 1979 (six children of the marriage); Master of Divinity degree from Gordon-Conwell Theological Seminary, Boston, in 1982; ordained to the Presbyterian ministry in 1982; first influence on his conversion to the Catholic faith was his and his wife's conviction that contraception was contrary to God's law; the main factor was his covenant theology; another influence came from the early Church Fathers; a further one was Opus Dei; Ph.D. in Biblical Theology from Marquette University in 1995; Professor of Theology and Scripture at the Franciscan University of Steubenville from 1990; founder and director of the St. Paul Center for Biblical Theology; in 2005 appointed to the Pope Benedict XVI Chair of Biblical Theology and Liturgical Proclamation at St. Vincent Seminary in Latrobe, Pennsylvania; many books and talks on Scripture and the Catholic faith; great influence in the conversion of many other Protestants; several writers have criticized his novel ideas on the feminine role and/or identity of the Holy Spirit, and doubts have been expressed about his views on some other theological issues (the Trinity, the Millennium, *Prima Scriptura*, and some aspects of Justification); see (selective list) *The Scott Hahn Conversion Story* (1991) ("I began to read through the book [*Birth Control and the Marriage Covenant* by John Kippley] with great interest because in my own personal study, going through the Bible several times, I had come upon this strong conviction that if you want to know God, you have to understand the covenant, because the covenant was the central idea in all of Scripture. So when I picked up this book I was interested to see the word 'covenant' in the title…

His arguments made a lot of sense. From the Bible, from the covenant, he showed that the marital act is not just a physical act; it's a spiritual act that God has designed by which the marital covenant is renewed. And in all covenants you have an opportunity to renew the covenant, and the act of covenant renewal is an act or a moment of grace. When you renew a covenant, God releases grace, and grace is life, grace is power, grace is God's own love. Kippley shows how in a marital covenant, God has designed the marital act to show the life-giving power of love. That in the marital covenant the two become one, and God has designed it so that when the two become one, they become so one that nine months later you might just have to give it a name. And that child who is conceived, embodies the oneness that God has made the two through the marital act. This is all the way that God has designed the marital covenant. God said, 'Let us make man in our image and likeness,' and God, who is three in one, made man, male and female, and said, 'Be fruitful and multiply.' The two shall become one and when the two become one, the one they become is a third child, and then they become three in one. It just began to make a lot of sense, and he went through other arguments as well. By the time I finished the book, I was convinced.

It bothered me just a little that the Roman Catholic Church was the only denomination, the only Church tradition on earth that upheld this age-old Christian teaching rooted in Scripture, because in 1930 the Anglican Church broke from this tradition and began to allow contraception, and shortly thereafter every single mainline denomination on earth practically caved in to the mounting pressure of the sexual revolution. By the 1960's and 70's, my own denomination, the Presbyterian Church in the United States of America, not only endorsed contraception, but abortion on demand and federal funding for abortion, and that appalled me. And I began to wonder if there wasn't a connection between giving in a little here and then all of a sudden watching the floodgates open later…

In the Protestant world the idea of covenant is understood practically as synonymous with or interchangeable with contract. When you have a covenant with God, it's the same as having a contract. You give God your sin; He gives you Christ, and everything is a faith-deal for salvation.

But the more I studied, the more I came to see that for the ancient Hebrews, and in Sacred Scripture, a covenant differs from a contract about as much as marriage differs from prostitution. In a contract you exchange property, whereas in a covenant you exchange persons. In a contract you say, 'This is yours and that is mine,' but Scripture shows how in a covenant you say, 'I am yours and you are mine.' Even when God makes a covenant with us, He says, 'I will be your God and you will be my people.' After studying Hebrew, I discovered that 'Am, the Hebrew word for people, literally means, kinsman, family. I will be your God and father; you will be my family, my sons and my daughters, my household. So covenants form kinship bonds which makes family with God...

I discovered that for Luther and for practically all of Bible Christianity and Protestantism, God is a judge, and the covenant is a courtroom scene whereby all of us are guilty criminals. But since Christ took our punishment, we get his righteousness, and he gets our sins, so we get off scot-free; we're justified. For Luther, in other words, salvation is a legal exchange, but for Paul in Romans, for Paul in Galatians, salvation is that, but it's much more than that. It isn't just a legal exchange because the covenant doesn't point to a Roman courtroom so much as to a Hebrew family room. God is not just simply a judge; God is a father, and his judgments are fatherly. Christ is not just somebody who represents an innocent victim who takes our rap, our penalty; He is the firstborn among many brethren. He is our oldest brother in the family, and he sees us as runaways, as prodigals, as rebels who are cut off from the life of God's family. And by the new covenant Christ doesn't just exchange in a legal sense; Christ gives us His own sonship so that we really become children of God…

I came to the conclusion that *sola fide* is wrong. First, because the Bible never says it anywhere. Second, because Luther inserted the word 'alone' in his German translation, there in *Romans* 3, although he knew perfectly well that the word 'alone' was not in the

Greek. Nowhere did the Holy Spirit ever inspire the writers of Scripture to say we're saved by faith alone. Paul teaches we're saved by faith, but in Galatians he says we're saved by faith working in love. And that's the way it is in a family isn't it? A father doesn't say to his kids, 'Hey, kids, since you're in my family and all the other kids who are your friends aren't, you don't have to work, you don't have to obey, you don't have to sacrifice because, hey, you're saved. You're going to get the inheritance no matter what you do.' That's not the way it works.

So I changed my mind and I grew very concerned. One of my most brilliant professors, a man named Dr. John Gerstner, had once said that if we're wrong on *sola fide*, I'd be on my knees outside the Vatican in Rome tomorrow morning doing penance. Now we laughed, what rhetoric, you know. But he got the point across; this is the article from which all of the other doctrines flow. And if we're wrong there, we're going to have some homework to get done to figure out where else we might have gone wrong.

I was delving into John chapter 6. I don't know how many of you've ever studied the Gospel of John. In many ways it's the richest Gospel of all. But John chapter 6 is my favorite chapter in the fourth Gospel. There I discovered something that I think I read before, but I never noticed. Listen to it. 'Jesus said to them, "Truly, truly I say to you, unless you eat the flesh of the Son of Man and drink His blood you have no life in you. He who eats my flesh and drinks my blood has eternal life and I will raise him up at the last day, for my flesh is food indeed and my blood is drink indeed. He who eats my flesh and drinks my blood abides in me and I in him."' I read that; I reread that; I looked at it from ten different angles. I bought all these books about it, commentaries on John. I couldn't understand how to make sense out of it.

I had been trained to interpret that in a figurative sense; Jesus is using a symbol. Flesh and blood really is just a symbol of His body and blood. But the more I studied, the more I realized that that interpretation makes no sense at all. Why? Because as soon as all the Jews hear what Jesus says, they depart. Up until this point, thousands were following him, and then all of a sudden the multitudes just simply are shocked that He says, 'My flesh is food indeed, my blood is drink indeed' and they all depart. Thousands of disciples leave Him. If Jesus had intended that language to only be figurative, He would have been morally obligated as a teacher to say, 'Stop, I only mean it figuratively.' But He doesn't do that; instead, what does he do?

My research showed me that he turns to the twelve, and he says to them, what? 'We better hire a public relations (P.R.) agent; I really blew it guys.' No! He says, 'Are you going to leave me too?' He doesn't say, 'Do you understand

I only meant it as a symbol?' No! He says that the truth is what sets us free, I have taught the truth. What are you going to do about it?

Peter stands up and speaks out; he says, 'To whom shall we go? You alone have the words of eternal life and we've come to believe.' Peter's statement, 'To whom shall we go?' implies that, 'You know, Jesus, we don't understand what you mean either, but do you have another Rabbi on the scene you can recommend? You know, to whom shall we go? It's too late for us; we believe whatever you say even if we don't understand it fully, and if you say we have to eat your flesh and drink your blood, then somehow you'll give us the grace we need to accept your words at face value.' He didn't mean it figuratively.

As I began to study this, I began to realize it's one thing to convince Presbyterians that being born again means being baptized, but how in the world could I possibly convince them that we actually have to eat His flesh and drink His blood? I focused then a little bit more on the Lord's supper and communion. I discovered that Jesus had never used the word 'covenant' in His public ministry. He saved the one time for when He instituted the Eucharist and he said, 'This cup is the blood of the new covenant.' If covenant means family, what is it that makes us family? Sharing flesh and blood. So if Christ forms a new covenant, that is a new family, what is He going to have to provide us with? New flesh and new blood. I began to see why in the early Church for over 700 years, nobody any place disputed the meaning of Jesus' words. All of the early Church fathers without exception took Jesus' words at face value and believed and taught the real presence of Christ in the Eucharist. I was scared; I didn't know who to turn to.

Then all of a sudden an episode occurred one night in a seminar I wasn't ready for. An ex-Catholic graduate student named John raised his hand. He had just finished a presentation for the seminar on the Council of Trent. The Council of Trent, you'll recall, was the Church's official response to Martin Luther and the Reformation.

In about an hour and a half he had presented the Council of Trent in the most favorable light. He had shown how many of their arguments were in fact based on the Bible. Then he turned the tables on me. The students were supposed to ask him a question or two. He said, 'Can I first ask you a question, Professor Hahn? You know how Luther really had two slogans, not just *sola fide*, but the second slogan he used to revolt against Rome was *sola Scriptura*, the Bible alone. My question is, "Where does the Bible teach that?"'

I looked at him with a blank stare. I could feel sweat coming to my forehead. I used to take pride in asking my professors the most stumping questions, but I never heard this one before. And so I heard myself say words that I had sworn I'd never speak; I said, 'John, what a dumb question.' He was not intimidated. He look at me and said, 'Give me a dumb answer.' I said, 'All right, I'll try.' I just began to wing it. I said, 'Well, Timothy 3:16 is the key: "All Scripture is inspired of God and profitable for correction, for training and righteousness, for reproof that the man of God may be completely equipped for every good work...."' He said, 'Wait a second, that only says that Scripture is inspired and profitable; it doesn't say ONLY Scripture is inspired or even better, only Scripture's profitable for those things. We need other things like prayer,' and then he said, 'What about 2 Thessalonians 2:15?' I said, 'What's that again?' He said, 'Well, there Paul tells the Thessalonians that they have to hold fast, they have to cling to the traditions that Paul has taught them either in writing or by word of mouth.' Whoa! I wasn't ready. I said, 'Well, let's move on with the questions and answers; I'll deal with this next week. Let's go on.'

I don't think they realized the panic I was in. When I drove home that night, I was just staring up to the heavens asking God, why have I never heard that question? Why have I never found an answer? The next day I began calling up theologians around the country, former professors. I'd ask them, 'Where does the Bible teach *sola Scriptura*? Where does the Bible teach us that the Bible is our only authority?' One man actually said to me, 'What a dumb question coming from you.' I said, 'Give me a dumb answer then.' I was catching on. One professor whom I greatly respect, an Oxford theologian, said to me, 'Scott, you don't expect to find the Bible proving *sola Scriptura* because it isn't something the Bible demonstrates. It is our assumption; it is our presupposition when we approach the Bible.' That struck me as odd; I said, 'But professor, that seems strange because what we are saying then is that we should only believe what the Bible teaches, but the Bible doesn't teach us to only believe what the Bible teaches. Our assumption isn't taught by the Bible.' I said, 'That feels like we're cutting off the branch that we're sitting on.' Then he said, 'Well what other options do we have?' Good point, all right.

Another friend, a theologian, called me and said, 'Scott, what is this I'm hearing that you're considering the Catholic faith?' 'Well, no, Art, I'm not really considering the Catholic faith.' Then I decided to pose him a question. I said, 'Art, what for you is the pillar and foundation of truth?' And he said, 'Scott, for all of us Scripture is the pillar and foundation of truth.' I said, 'Then why, Art, does the Bible say in 1 Timothy 3:15 that the pillar and foundation of truth is the church, the household of faith?' There was a silence and he said, 'Well, Scott, I think you're setting me up with that question then.' And I said, 'Art, I feel like I'm being set up with lots of problems.' He said, 'Well, which church, Scott? There are lots of them.' I said, 'Art, how many churches are even applying for the job of being the pillar and foundation of truth? I mean, if you talk about a church saying, "We're the pillar and foundation of truth; look to us and you will hear Christ speak and teach"? How many applicants for the job are there? I only know of one. I only know that the Roman Catholic Church teaches that it was founded by Christ; it's been around for 2000 years and it's making some outlandish claims that seem awfully similar to 1 Timothy 3:15'"); *Rome Sweet Home: Our Journey to Catholicism* (1993) (with Kimberley Hahn); *A Father Who Keeps His Promises: God's Covenant Love in Scripture* (1998); *The Lamb's Supper: The Mass as Heaven on Earth* (1999); *Hail Holy Queen: The Mother of God in the Word of God* (2001); *Understanding Our Father: Biblical Reflections on the Lord's Prayer* (2002); *First Comes Love: Finding Your Family in the Church and the Trinity* (2002); *Scripture Matters: Essays on Reading the Bible from the Heart of the Church* (2003); *Lord, Have Mercy: The Healing Power of Confession* (2003); *Living the Mysteries: A Guide for Unfinished Christians* (2003) (with Mike Aquilina); *Swear to God: The Promise and Power of the Sacraments* (2004); *Understanding the Scriptures: A Complete Course on Bible Study* (2005); *Letter and Spirit* (2006); *Ordinary Work, Extraordinary Grace: My Spiritual Journey in Opus Dei* (2006); *Reasons to Believe: How to Understand, Explain, and Defend the Catholic Faith* (2007); *Answering the New Atheism: Dismantling Dawkins' Case Against God* (2008) (with Benjamin Wiker); *Kinship by Covenant: A Canonical Approach to the Fulfillment of God's Saving Promises* (2009); *God's Covenant with You: The Bible Tells a Story* (2009) (with Stratford Caldecott); *Signs of Life: 40 Catholic Customs and Their Biblical Roots* (2009); *Spirit and Life: Essays on Interpreting the Bible in Ordinary Time* (2009); *Covenant and Communion: The Biblical Theology of Pope Benedict XVI* (2009); *Hope for Hard Times* (2010); *Many Are Called: Rediscovering the Glory of the Priesthood* (2010); *Study Guide for the Lamb's Supper* (2010); *Politicizing the Bible: The Roots of Historical Criticism and the Secularization of Scripture, 1300-1700* (2012) (with Benjamin Wiker); Lorene Hanley Duquin, *A Century of Catholic Converts* (2003), p.196; *scotthahn.com.*

Hardee, William Joseph ("Old Reliable") – soldier; b. 12 October 1815, Savannah, Georgia; d. 6 November 1873, Wytheville, Virginia; graduated from the United States Military Academy at West Point in 1838 (twenty sixth in a class of forty five); served in the Second Dragoons in the Second Seminole War in Florida; in 1840 sent to the French military training school at St. Maur for professional study and attached to the French cavalry department; on return was stationed in the West and promoted to be Captain of Dragoons in 1844; conspicuous service during the Mexican War (won two brevet promotions); was captured and exchanged in 1846; after the death of his wife in 1853, he returned to West Point as a tactics instructor; in 1855 he wrote a manual of tactics for the army, which was used extensively by both sides in the Civil War; served as commandant of cadets 1856-1860; resigned his U. S. Army commission in 1861 after his home state of Georgia seceded from the Union; joined the Confederate States Army and was given the rank of Colonel; served throughout the war and attained the rank of Lieutenant-General and Corps Commander; wounded in the arm at the Battle of Shiloh in 1862; married Mary Foreman Lewis, an Alabama plantation owner in 1864; opposed Sherman's March to the Sea and fiercely defended Savannah against Sherman's much larger army; when the siege of Savannah began, he slipped away at night achieving a masterful escape of his greatly outnumbered force; fought his last battle at Bentonville, North Carolina, in 1865, where his only son, Willie, aged sixteen, was mortally wounded in a cavalry charge; surrendered to Sherman at Durham Station; after the war he retired to live on his wife's plantation; buried in Old Live Oak Cemetery, Selma, Alabama; see *United States Rifle and Light Infantry Tactics for the Exercise and Manoeuvres of Troops When Acting as Light Infantry or Riflemen* (known as "Hardee's Tactics") (1855); *The Irish in America* (1868); William Douglas Pickett, *Sketch of the Military Career of William J. Hardee, Lieutenant-General C.S.A.* (1910); Nathaniel Cheairs Hughes Jr., *General William J. Hardee: Old Reliable* (1992); *Catholic Encyclopedia*; *ANB*.

Harland, Henry – novelist and journal editor; b. 1 March 1861, Brooklyn, New York (his claim to have been born in St. Petersburg, Russia, is probably false); c. 1898 (received with his wife); d. 20 December 1905, San Remo, Italy; son of Thomas Harland (1830-1900), of Norwich, Connecticut, a journalist, and Irene Jones Harland (1839-1925); the only one of three children to survive childhood; attended the College of the City of New York (left without taking a degree); studied briefly at Harvard Divinity School 1881–1882; then spent a year in Italy, mainly in the most fashionable artistic and cultural centers of Rome; he returned to the United States a Catholic at heart; then worked 1883-1886 as a clerk during the day in the Surrogate's Court of New York, writing his first (very successful) novel, *As It Was Written*, between 2am and breakfast time ("fortified by wet towels and black coffee"); his first ten novels were written under the name Sidney Luska, but he later dismissed all of these works; in 1884 he married Aline Herminie (later Herminé) Merriam, a beautiful girl, half American and half French ("charming, gifted and cosmopolitan") (no children of the marriage); they went to Paris in 1887, but settled in London and became part of the literary set; he wrote several beautifully crafted short stories during this period; founding editor of the literary quarterly, *The Yellow Book*, in 1894 (the black and white work was done by Aubrey Beardsley); he and Beardsley found fame through this; in it they published the works of such as Max Beerbohm, "Baron Corvo" (Frederick Rolfe), Edmond Gosse, Henry James, and Lord Frederick Leighton, along with their own; the publication ceased in 1897 because of his failing health from tuberculosis; something of a fantasist, but not malicious; conversion to the Catholic faith probably influenced in part by his wife; may also have been influenced by the illness and conversion of Aubrey Beardsley, whose sincerity in his own conversion impressed him; his novel *The Cardinal's Snuffbox*, written after his reception into the Catholic Church, was a best-seller, but some consider *The Lady Paramount* his masterpiece; he had little money at his death; buried in San Remo cemetery on the day of his death; re-buried at Yantic cemetery, Norwich, Connecticut; see *As It Was Written: A Jewish Musician's Story* (1885); *Mrs. Peixada* (1886); *The Yoke of the Thorah* (1887) (these three works were written about Jewish life in New York and grew out of a friendship with a young Jew); *The Light Sovereign* (1889) (a play); *A Latin-Quarter Courtship and Other Stories* (1889); *Grandison Mather* (1889) (auto-biographical novel with a portrait of his wife); *Two Women or One?* (1890); *Mea Culpa: A Woman's Last Word* (1891); *Mademoiselle Miss and Other Stories* (1893); *Grey Roses* (1895); *Comedies and Errors* (1898) (the last three items are collections of short stories); *The Cardinal's Snuff Box* (1900); *The Lady Paramount* (1902); *My Friend Prospero* (1903); *The Royal End* (1909) (unfinished at his death; his wife finished it, following his notes); K. L. Mix, *A Study in Yellow: the Yellow Book and its Contributors* (1960); Margaret M. Maison and Brocard Sewell, "The Mission of Gaiety: Henry Harland: 1861-1905," *The Month*, May 1961, p.302 ("One fruit of his conversion was the best-selling novel *The Cardinal's Snuffbox*, which describes how a young Englishman in Italy comes to the Catholic faith, helped by a Cardinal, 'a heavenly old man,' and a gloriously beautiful young Duchess.

This light-hearted romantic story, full of wit and gaiety and sunny happy scenes of Italian life, was a new type of conversion novel and caught the public's fancy at a time when interest in Catholicism was becoming fashionable and the French and Italian cultures were exciting Anglo-Saxon admiration. The book was enormously popular both in England and America, and the New York *Catholic World* reported that it had been the cause of several conversions.

It is particularly pleasant today to enjoy the books which reflect Harland's belief that 'the world is always romantic if you have the three gifts needful to make it so – faith, the sense of beauty and the sense of humor'"); Henry Maas, J. L. Duncan, and W. G. Good (ed), *The Letters of Aubrey Beardsley* (1970); J. G. Nelson, *A View From the Bodley Head* (1971); Karl Beckson, *Henry Harland: His Life and Work* (1978) ("Some time in 1898 the Harlands were both received into the Roman Catholic Church, thus following many associated with the Aesthetic Movement, such as Lionel Johnson, Ernest Dowson, John Gray, and Aubrey Beardsley, who sought certainty in faith and beauty in ritual. At the end of the nineteenth century, when, for many, art itself had become a religion, it was only a further step for religion to become the supreme art. Harland, according to Aline, had early in his life been attracted to Catholicism. After he had settled in London, his stories were often set in Rome frequently with churchmen as characters; and his progressive pre-occupation with royalty in his tales also suggests a growing conservatism. Writing of their conversion, Aline states: 'One had not rather try even to narrate the facts which preceded this fortunate event, except to say that Henry Harland had, in spirit, been of the True Faith for many years. He was what is called an "intellectually convinced Catholic." He had the metaphysical mind. Their [i.e., the Harlands'] instruction by Father Charnley, S.J., did not draw out points of argument or of difficulty on Henry Harland's side, because, evidently, he was already enlightened and convinced regarding the dogma of Holy Mother Church'"); Stanley Weintraub, *The London Yankees* (1979); *Catholic Encyclopedia* ("In 1898 appeared *The Cardinal's Snuff Box*, a delightfully buoyant novel of Italian life. It is so pervaded with the beauty of the Catholic Faith (as are all of Harland's writings from this on) that it has made converts… Despite ill health, Harland, always whimsically joyous, was, still more than Beardsley, a 'boy who never grew up.' At thirty his physician gave him two years to live, but he prolonged them to fourteen most fruitful ones"); *DNB*; *ANB*.

Harney, John Milton, OP – priest, doctor and poet; b. 9 March 1789, near Georgetown, Delaware; d. 15

January 1825, Somerset, Kentucky; second son of Major Thomas Harney, who was an officer in the Revolutionary War; older brother of William Selby Harney (see below); when he was two the family moved to Tennessee and later to Louisiana; studied medicine and settled at Bardstown, Kentucky; in 1814 he married Eliza, daughter of Judge John Rowan, the statesman; his wife died in childbirth in 1818; he abandoned his practice and sought solace in England; he accepted an appointment in the navy and spent several years in South America; on his return to America he edited a paper, the *Savannah Georgian*; he overexerted himself at a fire, which resulted in a violent fever and a breaking of his health; he returned to Bardstown and became a Catholic; joined the Dominican Order, which was then beginning its mission in Kentucky, author of a number of poems printed in various magazines and others published after his death; first of the Kentucky poets to gain a wide reputation; see *Crystallina; a Fairy Tale, in Six Cantos* (1816); *The Fever Dream* (n.d.); *Echo and the Lover* (1837.

Harney, William Selby – soldier; b. 27 August 1800, near Hasboro, Tennessee; d. 9 May 1889, St. Louis, Missouri; his father, Major Thomas Harney, was an officer in the Revolutionary War; younger brother of John Milton Harney (see above); appointed to the United States Army in 1818; fought in the Black Hawk and Florida Indian Wars, and in the Mexican conflict; promoted to brigadier-general; in 1855 had command in the far West during the Sioux troubles; while there he became the friend and admirer of the famous missionary, Fr. J. B. DeSmet, SJ, who greatly helped him in making peace; when the Civil War broke out he was in charge of the Department of the West at St. Louis, and was captured and held prisoner for a short time by the Confederates; brevet promoted as Major-General for long and faithful services after his retirement in 1863; see U. L. Reavis, *The Life and Military Service of Gen. W. S. Harney* (1887); George Rollie Adams, "General William Selby Harney: Frontier Soldier, 1880-1898" (PhD dissertation, University of Arizona, 1983); Richmond L. Clow, "William S. Harney," in Paul Hutton (ed), *Soldiers West: Biographies from the Military Frontier* (1987); *Catholic Encyclopedia*; *ANB*.

Harriman, Pamela Beryl (*née* Digby) (also known as Pamela Churchill Harriman) – socialite, political activist and diplomat; b. 20 March 1920, Farnborough, Hampshire, England; d. 5 February 1997, Paris, France; daughter of Edward Kenelm Digby, eleventh Baron Digby, and Constance, daughter of Henry Campbell Bruce, second Baron Aberdare; educated privately; married Randolph Churchill (1911-1968), son of Sir

Winston Churchill, in 1939 (one child of the marriage, Winston); had many affairs with wealthy and well-known men, notably Averell Harriman (1891-1986), then U.S. envoy to England; divorced in 1945 (after her conversion to Catholicism she obtained an annulment of the marriage); married to the Broadway producer, Leland Hayward (1902-1971) from 1960 until his death; married to Averell Harriman, by now a businessman and Democratic Party politician, until his death; became a United States citizen in 1971; great fund raiser for the Democratic Party; supported Bill Clinton for the presidency in 1992; he rewarded her by appointing her United States Ambassador to France 1993-1997; buried at Arden, the Harriman estate near New York; see Christopher Ogden, *Life of the Party:the Biography of Pamela Digby Churchill Hayward Harriman* (1994); Sally Bedell Smith, *Reflected Glory: The Life of Pamela Churchill Harriman* (1996); *ANB* ("Extraordinarily able to adapt herself to changing circumstances, Harriman was courtesan, adviser, wife, political fundraiser, and, finally, successful diplomat").

Harris, Joel Chandler - folklorist, novelist, poet and journalist; b. 1848, Eatonton, Georgia; c. 20 June 1908; d. 3 July 1908, Atlanta, Georgia; from a poor family with little education; his mother, Mary Ann Harris, was unmarried and his father's identity was unknown, he having abandoned the family shortly after the birth; mother an avid reader, who gave her son a love of language; limited education himself; in 1862 a plantation owner, Joseph Addison Turner, hired him as a printer's devil for his newspaper, *The Countryman*, which had a large circulation in the South; he set type and wrote pieces for the paper; devoured the many books in Turner's library; spent many hours in the slave quarters absorbing the stories and language; worked next on various Louisiana and Georgia papers; on the staff of the *Atlanta Constitution* 1876-1908, finally as associate editor; although himself a white man, best known for his stories (185 in total) from the African-American oral tradition, narrated by "Uncle Remus", a wise old negro, for children of all ages; they featured Bre'r Rabbit, the hero, Bre'r Fox, the villain, and other animals; they were translated into more than forty languages; also founded *The Uncle Remus's Home Magazine* in 1906 to further "the obliteration of prejudice against the blacks, the demand for a square deal, and the uplifting of both races so that they can look justice in the face without blushing"; also a fine novelist, notably on the race problem; wrote his journalism under the name of Joe Harris, where he promoted the New South, emphasizing regional and racial reconciliation during and after the Reconstruction era; his eldest child, Julian LaRose Harris, won a Pulitzer Prize with his wife, Julia Harris, in part for their fight against the Ku Klux Klan; see (the children's books) *Uncle Remus, His Songs and Sayings* (1880); *Nights with Uncle Remus* (1883); *Uncle Remus and His Friends* (1892); *Little Mr. Thimblefinger and his Queer Country* (1894); *Mr. Rabbit at Home* (1895); *The Tar Baby and Other Rhymes of Uncle Remus* (1904); *Told by Uncle Remus: New Stories of the Old Plantation* (1905); *Uncle Remus and Brer Rabbit* (1907); *Uncle Remus and the Little Boy* (1910); *Uncle Remus Returns* (1918); *Seven Tales of Uncle Remus* (1948); (novels) *Mingo and Other Sketches in Black and White* (1884); *Free Joe and Other Georgian Sketches* (1887); *Daddy Jake, The Runaway: And Short Stories Told After Dark* (1889); *Balam and His Master and Other Sketches and Stories* (1891); *Sister Jane: Her Friends and Acquaintances* (1896); *The Story of Aaron* (1896); *Aaron in the Wildwoods* (1897); *The Chronicle of Aunt Minervy Ann* (1899); *Gabriel Tolliver* 1902); Julia Collier Harris, Harris's daughter, *The Life and Letters of Joel Chandler Harris* (1918); Robert Lemuel Wiggins, *The Life of Joel Chandler Harris, from Obscurity in Boyhood to Fame in Early Manhood* (1918); Julia Collier Harris, *Joel Chandler Harris: Editor and Essayist* (1931); Alvin P. Harlow, *Joel Chandler Harris: Plantation Storyteller* (1941); Stella Brewer Brookes, *Joel Chandler Harris: Folklorist* (1950); Paul M. Cousins, *Joel Chandler Harris: A Biography* (1968); R. Bruce Bickley, Jr., *Joel Chandler Harris: A Biography and Critical Study* (1987); Bryan A. Giemza, "Joel Chandler Harris, Catholic," *Logos: A Journal of Catholic Thought and Culture*, Summer 2011, p.86; most of his papers are at the Joel Chandler Harris Memorial Collection at Emory University, Atlanta; *Catholic Encyclopedia* ("His favorite reading - the Bible, Newman, Faber, à Kempis, and Sheehan - his mental honesty, and the example of his wife, a cultured Canadian Catholic..., to whom he credited his mental growth and the best that was in him, had long convinced him of Catholic truth. But a sensitive modesty that shunned notoriety and crowds, and confined him to the society of his family, restrained him from seeking baptism till 20 June 1908, a few weeks before his death. He died with the sole regret that he had so long deferred his entrance into the Catholic Church"); *ANB.*

Harris, Miriam Coles – novelist; b. 7 July 1834, Dosoris, Long Island Sound; c. 1890s; d. 23 January 1925, Pau, France; raised as an Episcopalian; educated at a boarding school; her first work was a novel, *Rutledge*, a gothic romance, written anonymously, in which she adopted a skeptical and unconventional approach; used a similar format on several occasions and sold well among ordinary readers; in 1864 she married a lawyer Sidney Smith Harris (d. 1892) (two children of the marriage); after her husband's death she moved to Europe where she lived until her death; see *Rutledge* (1860); *The Sutherlands* (1862); *Louie's Last Term at St. Mary's* (1864); *A Rosary for Lent, Devotional Readings* (1867); *Frank Warrington* (1872); St. Philip's (1865); *Roundhearts and Other Stories* (1867); *Richard Vandermarck* (1871) ("'What is it to be a Catholic?' inquired Benny, gazing at his tutor's face with wonder. 'To be a Catholic, is to be in a safe prison; to have been a Catholic, is to be alone on a sea big and black with billows, Benny'"); *Marguerite's Journal* (1875); *A Perfect Adonis* (1880); *Happy-Go-Lucky* (1881); *Missy* (1882); *Dear Feast of Lent* (1883); *Phoebe* (1884); *An Utter Failure* (1891); *A Chit of Sixteen and Other Stories* (1892); *A Corner of Spain* (1898); *Tents of Wickedness* (1907); *ANB.*

Harris, William Laurel – artist and writer; b. 18 February 1870, Brooklyn, New York; d. 24 September 1924, Lake George, New York; orphaned at four and brought up by his grandmother in Vermont; studied with T. W. Dewing (1851-1938), the painter, at the School of the Museum of Fine Arts, Boston; in 1888 he studied art at the Académie Julian in Paris with, among others, Paul Gauguin (1848-1903); his major work was to continue the work of John LaFarge (1835-1910) in decorating the church of St. Paul the Apostle, the Paulist Fathers' massive church in New York, under Fr. George Deshon (see above); worked and lived with the Paulists 1898-1913, when he was dismissed after a personal dispute (some of his work was later destroyed after a ruinous cleaning); decorated many other churches and chapels; co-founded with Katherine Dreier (1877-1952) the Art Center in New York City, an "arts and trades" school; taught painters and wrote for several magazines articles on furnishing, church decoration, plus book reviews; buried in Windsor, Vermont; see *John White Alexander: His Influence on American Art and Industry* (1915); John Talbot Smith and Joseph F. Mooney, *The Catholic Church in New York: A History of the New York Diocese*, Vol. II (1905; republished 2008)) ("[A] noted artist and decorator of the time, William Laurel Harris, not only became a Catholic, but set himself, in the ancient spirit, the task of reviving Christian art, and working at the decoration of the Paulist church as the old painters of the Middle Ages worked at the adornment of their grand cathedrals").

Harrison, Barbara Grizzuti – journalist and writer; b. 14 September 1934, Jamaica, Queens, New York City; c. 1970s (revert); d. 24 April 2002, Manhattan, New York (in a hospice); her family was originally from southern Italy; unsettled childhood, including abuse by her father; at the age of nine she (plus her mother) were converted by a Jehovah's Witness missionary; fell in love with her English teacher at school, Arnold Horowitz; they had a platonic relationship, remaining friends and corresponding until he died in the late 1960s; worked at the Watchtower Bible and Tract Society in Brooklyn Heights, but renounced that faith in 1956; lived a bohemian life in Greenwich village, associating with several jazz musicians; married for eight years to a relief worker and living abroad (had two children); returned to New York in 1968 and became involved with the women's movement; wrote for feminist publications; came to national attention when she wrote a history of the Jehovah's witness movement and her involvement with it; by now agnostic, but then influenced by the medieval female mystics and by the Catholic Worker Movement (interviewed Dorothy Day (see above)), she returned to the Catholic Church (the last chapter of the book deals with her conversion to the Catholic faith); wrote books and many articles on travel; see *Unlearning the Lie: Sexism in School* (1969); *Visions of Glory: A History and a Memory of Jehovah's Witnesses* (1978) ("In the end, whether or not one is a Christian has almost nothing to do with persuasive intellectual argument: it has to do with whether one has experienced God; it has to do with the grace of God – a mystery. It has little to do with how 'good' a person is...

When I compare the Church with the Witnesses, I think: The Witnesses explained everything, and explained everything legalistically. The Church does not attempt to explain everything: triumphant, militant, glorious, it is humble enough to get on its august knees and say 'We do not know'; 'We have committed grave errors'...

Mostly when I compare the Witnesses with the Church, I think: To be a Witness meant not to give, but to give up; whereas the Church says that not to use one's talents to join one's efforts to God is 'a serious wrongdoing.' The Church says that to be godly is to be fully human, and to be fully human is to be godly"); *Off Center* (1980) (essays and interviews); *Foreign Bodies* (1984) (novel); *Italian Days* (1989); *The Islands of Italy: Sicily, Sardinia, and the Aeolian Islands* (1991); *The Astonishing World* (1992) (more essays and interviews); *An Accidental Autobiography* (1996).

Harrison, Francis Burton – statesman; b. 18 December 1873, New York City; c. 1950; d. 21 November 1957, Flemington, New Jersey; father was Burton Harrison, a lawyer and private secretary to Jefferson Davis; his mother, Constance, a novelist; descended from some of the founding fathers; graduated from Yale University in 1895 and from the New York

Law School in 1897; served in the United States army in the Spanish-American War; married and divorced six times; member of Congress for the Democrats 1903-1905 and 1907-1913; Governor-General of the Philippines 1913-1921; increased the transfer of authority to the Filipinos; lived in Scotland until recalled to the Philippines in 1934; served as principal advisor to Manuel L. Quezon, first President of the Commonwealth of the Philippines, at different times before, during and after World War II; made an honorary Filipino citizen; served as an advisor to the first four Presidents of the Philippine Republic; retired to Spain for six years, then moved to New Jersey; became a Catholic late in life; buried in the Manila North Cemetery, La Loma, Manila, Philippines; see *Aris Sonis Focisque: Being a Memoir of an American Family* (1910); *The Corner-Stone of Philippine Independence* (1922); *Indo-China, A Sportsman's Opportunity* (1933) (with Archibald Cary Harrison); *Origins of the Philippine Republic* (1974); his papers are part of the Harrison Family Collection at the Library of Congress; the University of Virginia, Charlottesville, has a copy of his unpublished memoirs; *ANB*.

Hart, Mother Dolores, OSB (born Dolores Hicks) – nun and former actress; b. 20 October 1938, Chicago, Illinois; c. 1948; an only child of parents who married very young, separated when she was three, and ultimately divorced; lived first few years in Beverly Hills, when her parents were both contracted to a film studio, then lived with her grandparents in Chicago; precocious child who converted at her own request to the Catholic faith at the age of ten; returned to Los Angeles to live with her mother; studied at Marymount College; engaged to Los Angeles businessman Don Robinson (d. 2011) before she entered the convent (he never married, but visited her every year at Christmas and Easter, and helped the convent); made ten films in five years; made her film debut with Elvis Presley in *Loving You* (1957); played opposite Presley again in *King Creole* (1958); made her debut on Broadway in 1959 in *The Pleasure of His Company*; later played opposite such actors as Montgomery Clift and Robert Wagner; starred in the film *Francis of Assisi* (1961), where prophetically she played a nun; in 1960 and 1961 she met Pope John XXIII in Rome and he was influential in her vocation; broke off her engagement and entered the Benedictine Abbey of Regina Laudis in Bethlehem, Connecticut, in 1963; she took her final vows in 1970; in 2001 she became the prioress of the monastery; she has raised awareness for peripheral idiopathic neuropathy disorder, from which she herself also suffers; testified at a congressional hearing on the need for research into the disease; formed a friendship with Patricia Neal; (see below), who supported the monastery; a documentary film about her life, *God Is the Bigger Elvis* was a nominee for the 2012 Academy Award for Best Documentary (Short Subject).

Hart, Frederick Elliott ("Rick") – sculptor; b. 7 June 1943, Atlanta, Georgia; d. 13 August 1999, Baltimore, Maryland; father, Frederick William Hart, a journalist; mother, Joanna, *née* Elliott, a failed actress; baptized into the Presbyterian Church; his mother died from scarlet fever when he was three; lived with an aunt and his maternal grandmother in South Carolina; became a juvenile delinquent and was expelled from school; scored highly on a college admission test and gained a place at the University of South Carolina; the lone white student on a civil rights protests, he was arrested and then expelled from the university; moved to Washington and got a job as a clerk at the Washington National Cathedral; persuaded the master carver to take him as an apprentice; entered and won the competition to find a sculptor to adorn the Cathedral's west façade; gained international reputation for his *The Creation* sculptures at the Cathedral, commissioned in 1974 and dedicated between 1978 and 1984; these include three tympana *Ex Nihilo (Out of Nothing)*, *Creation of Day* and *Creation of Night*, and three trumeau figures, *St. Peter*, *St. Paul*, and *Adam*; met Lindy Lain in 1977 and they married in 1978 in a civil ceremony later blessed by a Catholic ceremony in 1980; in 1979 he created a processional cross for Pope John Paul II's historic Mass on the National Mall in Washington, D.C.; created the bronze statue, *The Three Soldiers*, at the Vietnam Veterans Memorial in Washington, D.C., dedicated in 1984; he invented and patented a technique for casting sculptures in acrylic resin, which he described as "sculpting with light"; the result resembled Lalique glass; many of the smaller pieces were nudes using his wife as a model; these acrylic castings sold for large sums of money; commissioned to create the *James Earl Carter Presidential Statue* in bronze installed at the Georgia State House, Atlanta; created three sculptures for the United States Senate in Washington; in 1997 he presented a unique casting of *The Cross of the Millennium* to Pope John Paul II who referred to it as "a profound theological statement for our day"; he opposed modernism and post-modernism and found his work ignored by the critics; he believed in a more traditional definition of the artist's moral responsibility and promoted the realistic representation of the human form; worked in new mediums, but worked in the classical tradition; he and like-minded colleagues called themselves Centerists; died two days after being diagnosed with lung cancer; awarded the National Medal of Arts in 2004; see J. Carter Brown and Tom Wolfe, *Frederick Hart: Sculptor* (1995); Jeffrey Rubin, "Sacred Art: A Rebirth?" *Sursum Corda*, 1996 ("Hart has always worked outside the modern art mainstream. In the '60s, when other sculptors were welding junk-metal abstractions, he served apprenticeships with the likes of Felix de Weldon, sculptor of the famous Iwo Jima Memorial. But it was the National Cathedral commission that drew him deeper into the tradition of Western religious art - and ultimately to the Faith. As he studied the works of his great precursors in cathedral sculpture, and the theology they expressed, he found himself on the road to belief.

Three years later he became a Roman Catholic. Why not an Episcopalian? (The National Cathedral is Episcopal.) 'When you get into any Christian doctrine, once you do more than scrape the surface, you get back into the Roman Catholic Church.' He was soon appointed to the Sacred Arts Commission for the Archdiocese of Washington, and in 1979 created the processional cross for Pope John Paul II's historic Mass on the Mall in Washington, D.C.

Hart has used his celebrity to inveigh against the corrupt moral and aesthetic standards that guide most modern art, and to propound his alternative vision for a 'great rebirth of art.' That rebirth must begin, Hart says, by rediscovering and renewing the 'discarded axioms' and forgotten standards of past art - such as that 'ancient trinity of truth, beauty and goodness' and the idea of art as 'service to something it holds in greater esteem than itself.' And it must go along with an overall renewal of the moral and spiritual foundations of Western civilization itself.

As for Christian art in particular, Hart believes contemporary artists make a fundamental mistake by trying to express traditional Christianity in modernist styles. 'I think they're to a large extent mutually exclusive; and to try to do that is an impossible task.'

At best the results, as seen in many contemporary churches, are 'weak,' like an 'old lady in mini-skirts.' The reason? 'Modernism is fundamentally antagonistic towards any kind of tradition or any kind of faith with a capital F'"); Tom Wolfe, "The Lives They Lived: Frederick Hart, b. 1943; The Artist the Art World Couldn't See," *The New York Times Magazine*, 2 January 2000 ("The hot-blooded boy's passion, as Hart developed his vision of the Creation, could not be consummated by Woman alone [he married Lindy Lain Hart who posed for his rendition of the Creation]. He fell in love with God. For Hart, the process began with his at first purely pragmatic research into the biblical story of the Creation in the Book of Genesis. He had been baptized in the Presbyterian Church, and he was working for the Episcopal Church at the Washington National Cathedral. But by the 1970's, neither of these proper, old-line, in-town Protestant faiths offered the strong wine a boy who was in love with God was looking for. He became a Roman Catholic and began to regard his talent as a charisma, a gift from God. He dedicated his work to the idealization of possibilities God offered man...

The art magazines opened Hart's eyes until they were bleary with bafflement. Classical statues were 'pictures in the air.' They used a devious means - skill - to fool the eye into believing that bronze or stone had turned into human flesh. Therefore, they were artificial, false, meretricious. By 1982, no ambitious artist was going to display skill, even if he had it. The great sculptors of the time did things like have unionized elves put arrangements of rocks and bricks flat on the ground, objects they, the artists, hadn't laid a finger on (Carl Andre), or prop up slabs of Cor-Ten steel straight from the foundry, edgewise (Richard Serra); or they took G.E. fluorescent light tubes straight out of the box from the hardware store and arranged them this way and that (Dan Flavin); or they welded I-beams and scraps of metal together (Anthony Caro). This expressed the material's true nature, its 'gravity' (no stone pictures floating in the air), its 'objectness.'

This was greatness in sculpture. As Tom Stoppard put it in his play *Artist Descending a Staircase*, 'Imagination without skill gives us contemporary art.'

Hart lurched from bafflement to shock, then to outrage. He would force the art world to see what great sculpture looked like"); Tom Wolfe, "Frederick Hart: Life and Passion," *Sculpture Review*, Spring 2000; Frederick Turner and Michael Novak, *Frederick Hart: Changing Tides* (2005); Donald Kuspit and Frederick Turner, *Frederick Hart, The Complete Works* (2007); Donald Kuspit, *Frederick Hart* (2007).

Hasley, Lucile Charlotte – writer; b. 1909, South Bend, Indiana; c. 1930 (in 1931 her mother returned to the Catholic fold after forty-seven years); father a Presbyterian deacon; mother a lapsed Catholic; brought up as a Presbyterian; educated at the University of Wisconsin, reading for an arts degree; married to Louis Leonard Hasley (1906-1986), writer, poet, essayist, editor, critic and Professor of English at the University of Notre Dame 1931-1973; writer of short stories, articles and personal essays for several Catholic magazines; friend of the writer Caryll Houselander (1901-1954); see "House of Light," in John A. O'Brien (ed), *The Road to Damascus, Vol. II* (1950) ("The priest happened to take me into the Log Chapel at Notre Dame. He was giving me the tourist's tour – pointing out the burial place of the first priest ordained in the United States, the Indian murals on the walls, the ancient altars – when I (only half listening to him) suddenly burst out with what was really on my mind. It was that old time-honored Protestant question: 'If Catholics really believe that God is really and truly present on their altars, why don't they *crawl* into church on their hands and knees?'

And suddenly I knew, with a shock, that what I was really thinking was: 'Why aren't *we* on our hands and knees, right this minute, instead of standing here like tourists?'

It is impossible for me to explain this sudden right-about-turn. All I know is that the Blessed Sacrament, all these past nineteen years, has been the strongest point in my faith"); *Reproachfully Yours (A Catholic Convert's View)* (1951) ("I accepted with complete faith the Church as the true Church. Its historical pedigree left me speechless"); *The Mouse Hunter: Essays and Short Stories* (1954); *Saints and Snapdragons* (1958); *Play It Cool, Sister* (1959); *Mind If I Differ?: A Catholic-Unitarian Dialogue* (1964) (with Betty Mills); "Lucile Hasley," *CatholicAuthors.com*; Matthew Hoehn, OSB (ed), *Catholic Authors: Contemporary Biographical Sketches* (1952).

Hassard, John Rose Greene – editor and historian; b. 4 September 1836, New York; c. 1851 or 1852; d. 18 April 1888, New York; parents were Episcopalians; graduated at St. John's College, New York; intending to study for the priesthood he entered the diocesan seminary; had to withdraw because of ill health; spent most of his working life as a journalist; first editor of the *Catholic World Magazine*; assistant editor of the *Chicago Republican* and the *American Cyclopedia*; literary and musical critic for the *New York Tribune* (promoted the work of Richard Wagner); wrote two biographies and a general history of the United States; see *Life of the Most Reverend John Hughes* (1866); *The Ring of the Nibelungs: A Description of its First Performance in August 1876* (1877); *History of the United States of America* (1878); *Life of Pope Pius IX* (1878); *Pickwickian Pilgrimage* (1881); *An Abridged History of the United States for the Use of Schools* (1889); *Catholic Encyclopedia*.

Hastings, Serranus Clinton - politician and lawyer; b. 22 November 1814, near Watertown, Jefferson County, New York; d. 8 February 1893, San Francisco, California; brought up as a Baptist; attended Gouverneur Academy, New York, for six years; studied law in Indiana and called to the bar; settled in Iowa and practiced law there; married Azalea Brodt (eight children of the marriage); elected a Democrat member of Congress for Iowa in 1846; appointed chief justice of the Iowa Supreme Court in 1848; joined the gold rush and opened up a law office and a loan company; chosen by the legislature as California's first chief justice of the Supreme Court; attorney-general of California 1852-1854; returned to his law practice and that, together with a full-time career in banking and land acquisition, made him a multimillionaire by the 1870s; his wife died suddenly in 1876 on a European tour; in his grief he founded in 1878 Hastings College of Law, the law department of the University of California (disagreements with the rest of the board meant that he withdrew later); he was later converted to Catholicism by the Dominican Archbishop of San Francisco, Joseph Allemany; in 1885 he married Lillian Knust, a much younger woman (divorced in 1890, but were reconciled and remarried shortly before his death); buried at St. Helena Public Cemetery in St. Helena, California; see *ANB.*

Haver, June (born Beverley June Stovenour) – film actress; b. 10 June 1926, Rock Island, Illinois; c. 1942; d. 4 July 2005, Brentwood, California; father a musician and mother an actress; brought up Presbyterian; when her mother remarried she adopted the name of her stepfather Bert Haver; child and teenage performer as a singer; after high school moved to Hollywood in 1942; signed by 20th Century Fox in 1943; groomed as a glamor girl to be the next Betty Grable; several starring roles, notably in fourteen musicals; best known for *The Dolly Sisters* (1945) and *Look for the Silver Lining* (1949); of a sunny disposition; in 1947 married a musician James Zito, but divorced a year later; engaged to Dr. John L. Duzik, but he died suddenly in 1949; turned to the Church to forget her unhappiness; in 1950 she went on a pilgrimage to Rome and Jerusalem to find peace of mind and obtained an audience with the Pope; in February 1953 she announced her intention to become a nun and entered Xavier Convent of the Sisters of Charity (St. Mary's Academy, Leavenwirth, Kansas) as a novice; left the convent in September 1953, giving "poor health" as a reason; returned to Hollywood; married the actor Fred MacMurray (1908-1991) in 1954; after her marriage she acted very rarely; she and MacMurray adopted two twin daughters, Katie Marie and Laurie Ann; buried with her husband at Holy Cross Cemetery, Culver City, California; see "Film Star to Become a Nun," *Catholic Herald*, 13 February 1953, p.1 ("'June's mother and I were divorced in 1936. It made quite an impression on her and it influenced her in finding a religion where divorce was not permitted,' her father, Mr. Stevenour, told reporters"); "'Noble Effort' to Become Sister of Charity," *Catholic Herald*, 16 October 1953, p.5 ("Praise for 'the noble effort' film star June Haver made to become a Sister of Charity was given by her superior, Mother M. Ancilla, after Miss Haver returned recently to her mother's home in Santa Monica, California.

'It is unfortunate that the incident has stirred up so much publicity,' said Mother Ancilla. 'It is nothing for Miss Haver to be ashamed of. It has happened to others before her. The physical strain was just too much. She made a noble effort and it is wonderful that she tried so hard, but the life was too hard for her. That's all there is to it.'

Miss Haver abandoned her star career last February to enter Xavier Convent, Kansas. She received the habit in August, but a month later found the strain too much.

Miss Haver is still hoping to become a nun. but a statement issued on her behalf added: 'It all depends on my health and God's will'").

Hawks, Mgr. Edward F. – priest; b. 1878, Crickhowell, Brecknockshire, Wales; c. 20 February 1908; d. 1955; studied at London University; went to Canada to study for the Anglican ministry at Lennoxville University, Quebec; ordained to the Anglican ministry; from 1903 taught at the Anglican seminary at Nashotah, Wisconsin; was a High Church Episcopalian; member of a group, the Companions of the Holy Savior (CSSS), which accepted celibacy as the ideal state for ministers of Christ, making celibacy a matter of divine precept rather than discipline; also an insistence on the use of auricular confession and a devotion to the rubrics of the Book of Common Prayer; the Pope was given a "primacy of honor"; began to see that the differences of opinion with the high Church was tearing it apart; the "Open Pulpit" decision of the Episcopal Church in 1907 was the final factor leading to his conversion; also he decided that he could be sure that he was a priest only if the Church said so, and she did not; he went to the house of the Paulist fathers in New York and was received into the Church; one of several hundred Episcopalians (clergy, sisters, and lay people) who were received into the Catholic Church in the year of crisis, 1908; entered St. Charles Seminary, Overbrook, Philadelphia, and was ordained to the priesthood on 27 May 1911; chaplain to the Canadian Expeditionary Force during World War I; internationally known writer and lecturer; regular contributor to many Catholic journals; an outstanding authority on non-Catholic efforts towards unity, both among themselves and in relation to the Church; rector of St. Joan of Arc's Church, Philadelphia, 1919-1955 (he established the parish); founder of the Catholic Evidence Guild, an organization designed to attract converts and lapsed Catholics; in 1936 he became a Domestic Prelate to the Pope; supporter of the Nationalist cause in the Spanish Civil War (toured Spain 1936-1938 for the United States Catholic hierarchy as an independent observer of conditions); later appointed a Knight Commander of the Order of Isabella the Catholic; see *William McGarvey and the Open Pulpit:*

An Intimate History of a Celibate Movement in the Episcopal Church, and of Its Collapse, 1870-1908 (1935); *A Pedigree of Protestantism* (1936); *History of the Parish of St. Joan of Arc, Harrowgate, Philadelphia* (1937); "In Newman's Footsteps," in John A. O'Brien (ed), *The Road to Damascus, Volume III: The Way to Emmaus* (1953) ("No doubt there were many secondary and confirmatory causes for my conversion, but I think that the fundamental reason was the fact that I had become, in a small way, part of a critical movement from which it was impossible to disengage myself in any logical manner. Modernism had demonstrated the crumbling of all those theories upon which Protestantism had hitherto maintained its life: the supremacy and inerrancy of Holy Scripture, the authority of national churches governed by a temporal power, and the emotional appeal of religion based upon personal experience. The church in which I was brought up seemed plainly to be falling apart...

The searchings of heart aroused by the continual discussions of the religious situation drove some of us to examine the history of two crucial periods. The first was the latter part of the seventeenth century, when those known as the Caroline divines wrote the most solid theological defenses of the Church of England. We had always supposed that these men were strongly 'Catholic', although not 'Roman Catholic'. It was a great disappointment to discover that they were the most consistent of the Protestants. One and all they defended the divine right of kings and the duty of 'passive obedience' to any order issued by the Crown. Moreover, they were all strongly antipapal, and specifically rejected Transubstantiation, although admitting a belief in some sort of Real Presence. Their idea of the Eucharistic Sacrifice was the symbolical offering of Bread and Wine. None of them repudiated the name Protestant, and most of them recommended that European travelers should take their Communions in Lutheran or Calvinistic churches.

The other period that interested us was the fifth century, especially the time of the Third and Fourth General Councils. It seemed clear to us that the See of Rome in exerting its authority in accordance with the needs of that age was acting as it does in the present day. These growing convictions concerning the Protestantism of Anglicanism and the papalism of the Early Church were turning our faces towards Rome...

The final stage in our conversion was due to the action of the General Convention in 1907, when the bishops of the Episcopal Church, almost unanimously, permitted the preaching of ministers of any denominations in Anglican pulpits. This seemed to us to be a denial of dogmatic principles.

The preaching of the Gospel is the expression of Divine Revelation. To make preaching depend on the ingenuity and personal opinions of every sort of minister showed an indifference to truth...

Catholics often ask how converts feel after their change of religion. Are they satisfied? Are they happy? Do they experience any lingering doubts as to the wisdom of the step they have taken? These questions miss the mark because those who have the Faith find it impossible to think of themselves as anything but Catholic. They are part of the life of the Catholic Church. Their happinessdependsuponthemselves, as does their attitude toward any difficulties that may arise. A Catholic cannot accept a part of the Faith. Those who have lingering doubts are not really converted.

The human side of the Church is probably much more evident to a convert than to one who has been a Catholic from childhood. What difference does this make? In Protestantism there is a constant attempt to segregate the saints from the sinners and regard the church as a select body of holy people. In the Catholic Church the reproach cast at Our Lord that he was a friend of the ungodly is always remembered.

We Catholics possess that gift of faith which fears no peril. We are not in danger so much of losing the Faith as of failing to utilize the graces that it offers. For myself it seems impossible that I should be anything else but a Catholic, and I pray that I may always be of this mind. Life in the Church cannot be compared with life outside it because the Church is unique. The latter life is a matter of opinion, shot through with doubt and uncertainty; the former is a matter of certitude, replete with inner security and peace"); essay in Georgina Pell Curtis, *Beyond the Road to Rome* (1914), p.240 ("For years before I became a Catholic I had come to regard the so-called Reformation and all its results as deplorable. But I did not perceive that the 'Catholic Party' that held this view, was something quite apart from the normal life of Anglicanism - that it was itself a parasite sapping the strength of the Church to which it nominally adhered. What sympathy indeed could High Churchmen of the new school of 1833 have with Acts of Supremacy and Uniformity; with the total destruction of Catholic altars and all their furnishings; with the fanatical hatred of even the word 'Mass'; with the martyrdom of the Marian and the Seminarist priests; with the savage attempt to suppress Nonconformists who refused to have their religion doled out by Act of Parliament or Royal warrant; with 'Popish Plots' and occasional Conformity Scandals; with the religious policy of the Houses of Orange and Guelph? And yet are not these the real things in Post-Reformation English Church History? I deplored all this, but could not see the true significance of it. I understand now why converts, against their better judgment, sometimes become irritating and even uncharitable when speaking of their Anglican days. It is due to their disillusionment with Anglicanism. When they leave it, they see the Church of England as everyone outside it has always seen it. I know this is so in my own case. When I was in it, I could not see the Anglican wood for the trees. The system had no definite shape in my mind. Consequently it was possible to ignore its separated existence and to think of it as only a province of the Universal Church. It was a purely mental fiction, this idea that Anglicanism was a part of anything. Once a Catholic, one quickly comes to the realization of the identity and unique individuality of the Church of England. For the first time I clearly heard her voice, recognized her policy and discovered her foundations"); Harry Hawks, "Atrocities in Spain," *Catholic Herald*, 21 September 1962, p.2.

Hayes, Carlton Joseph Huntley – historian; b. 16 May 1882, Afton, New York; c. 1904; d. 3 September 1964, Afton, New York; son of a medical doctor; born into a Baptist family; later attracted to Catholic liturgical life; educated at Columbia University (PhD in 1909); appointed lecturer at Columbia in European History in 1907; full professor 1919; several times head of the Columbia History Department; co-founder of American Catholic Historical Association; a founding member in 1924 of *Commonweal*, the Catholic magazine; co-founder in 1927 of the National Conference of Jews and Christians; saw America as the Western frontier of Europe; one of the founders of the academic discipline of international relations; sceptical of evolutionary ideas in historical study and of the theory of progress; against materialism and nationalism; linked his study of the past with contemporary political issues; attacked Nazi racial theory; active interventionist in World War II and served in the U.S. army; U.S. Ambassador to Spain 1942-1945; played important role in preventing General Franco from siding with the axis forces during the war; in 1945 first Catholic President of the American Historical Association; retired in 1950; many awards and honorary degrees; married to a very devout Catholic, whose influence resulted in a more powerful contribution of Catholicism to his writings; buried in Glenwood Cemetery, Afton, New York; see *Sources Relating to Germanic Invasions* (1909); *British Social Politics* (1913); *A Political and Social History of Modern Europe* (1916); *Brief History of the Great War* (1920); *Essays on Nationalism* (1926); *Modern History* (1928); *Ancient and Medieval History* (1929); *France, A Nation of Patriots* (1930); *The Historical Evolution of Modern Nationalism* (1931); *A Political and Cultural History of Modern Europe*

(1932-1936; revised edition 1939); *A Generation of Materialism, 1871-1900* (1941); *Wartime Mission in Spain* (1945); *The United States and Spain: An Interpretation* (1951); *Modern Europe to 1870* (1953; revised edition 1958); *Contemporary Europe Since 1870* (1953; revised edition 1958); *Nationalism: A Religion* (1960); Arthur J. Hughes, "Carlton J. H. Hayes: Teacher and Historian" (PhD dissertation, Columbia University, 1970); Carter Jefferson, "Carlton J. H. Hayes," in Hans A. Schmitt (ed), *Historians of Modern Europe* (1971), p. 15; Patrick Allitt, "Carlton Hayes and His Critics," *U.S. Catholic Historian*, Summer 1997; John Joseph Shanley, "The Story of Carlton Hayes," *The University Bookman*, Winter 2010; Patrick Allitt, *Catholic Converts: British and American Intellectuals Turn to Rome* (1997) *passim* ("Hayes's conversion to Catholicism came in two stages. He was strongly attracted to Catholic ritual and romantic medievalism as a teenager and joined the church in 1904 when he was twenty-two. But it was not until his 1920 marriage to Evelyn Carroll, a graduate student at Columbia Teacher's College and herself a born Catholic, that Catholicism became a salient issue in his work. 'Marriage to a born Catholic,' says his biographer, 'seems to have intensified his interest in his adopted religion and it certainly stepped up his public avowal of his faith'

[H]is idea that the zealous nationalism of modern Europe could be traced to the breakdown of Catholic *inter*nationalism in the Reformation era...

[H]e maintained that the Declaration of Independence and the principles embodied in the Constitution had their antecedents in the Catholic natural law tradition...

In...1939 Hayes drew an extended parallel between Communism and Nazism as enemies of the Judeo-Christian tradition and called on all religious and civilized Americans to arm themselves for the fight"); Charles P. Connor, *Classic Catholic Converts* (2001), p.198 ("He discussed the strong Catholicism that had existed on the Continent prior to the Reformation and concluded that its breakdown resulted in the development of strong nationalistic fervor in many countries"); *ANB* ("Of great importance to Hayes's outlook and life's work was his conversion to Roman Catholicism in 1904. His association with the church expressed and deepened his preference for the universal over discrete groups, whether Protestant denominations or national entities. Influenced heavily by Pope Leo XIII's encyclical *Rerum Novarum* (1891), Hayes became a critic of unfettered capitalism and, at least for a while, virtually a socialist, albeit one who looked more to medieval guild society for inspiration than to utilitarian and secular outgrowths of the Enlightenment, a distinction that left him somewhat out of step with many fellow reformers…

He linked the growth of nationalism - from 'blessing' to 'curse' - primarily to the effects of industrialization and the decline of religious faith; indeed, he saw exclusivistic nationalism as a new form of religion. He drew a distinction between 'original,' or 'liberal,' nationalism, which he viewed as primarily cultural and liberal, and 'derived,' or 'integral,' nationalism, which he described as exclusive, bellicose, and intolerant").

Hayward, Susan (born Edythe Marrenner) – actress; b. 30 June 1917, Brooklyn, New York; c. 30 June 1966 (received by Fr. Daniel McGuire at SS. Peter and Paul's Catholic Church, Larimar Avenue, East Liberty, Pittsburgh); d. 14 March 1975, Hollywood, California; started her career as a photographer's model in New York; went to Hollywood in 1937, aiming to secure the role of Scarlett O'Hara in *Gone with the Wind*; secured a film contract and played several supporting roles; eventually established herself as one of Hollywood's leading ladies; appeared in over sixty films; five academy Award nominations; won the Academy Award for best actress in 1958 for her role in *I Want to Live!*; married in an Episcopalian church to Jess Barker, an actor, in 1944 (two children of the marriage); divorced in 1954; survived a suicide attempt after the divorce; married (Floyd) Eaton Chalkley (d. 1966), a Catholic, in 1957; she met the priest who received her while she was in China and promised him that if she ever converted to the Catholic faith that she would ask him to receive her; diagnosed with brain cancer in the early 1970s; buried beside Eaton Chalkley at Our Lady of Perpetual Help Catholic Church in Carrollton, Georgia; see Eduardo Moreno, *The Films of Susan Hayward* (1979); Christopher P. Andersen, *A Star Is a Star, Is a Star, Is a Star! The Lives and Loves of Susan Hayward* (1980); Beverly Linet, *Susan Hayward: Portrait of a Survivor* (1980); Robert LaGuardia and Gene Arceri, *Red: The Tempestuous Life of Susan Hayward* (1985); Kim R. Holston, *Susan Hayward: Her Films and Life* (2002); Gene Arceri, *Brooklyn's Scarlett Susan Hayward: Fire in the Wind* (2010); *ANB*.

Hecker, Isaac Thomas, CSP – priest, missionary, author and founder of the Paulist Fathers; Servant of God; b. 18 December 1819, Lower New York; c. 1 August 1844 (received by Bishop McCloskey in New York; his brother George became a Catholic soon afterwards and supported financially the Paulists); d. 22 December 1888, New York; youngest of three children of parents who were bakers and came from Prussia; father had no religious faith; mother originally Lutheran, but became a devout Methodist; had to begin work in the bakery at age eleven; had no proper education, but was studious and thoughtful and read much philosophy and theology; in his teens was a street speaker on political and social topics; anxious to improve the social condition of working people; friend and correspondent of Orestes Brownson (see above), the famous philosopher and social reformer, and was a member of the Brook Farm Movement for six months; had mystical and religious temperament and was appalled by the teaching of Luther and Calvin; became convinced that the Catholic faith was the true faith; drawn to the ideal of religious life in community and to the apostolic priesthood; entered the Redemptorist order in Belgium in 1845 ("I want to bring other people to see the light of the Faith. And I want to work for the conversion of America"); ordained to the priesthood by Bishop Wiseman in 1849 in London; returned to New York in 1851 as one of a group of Redemptorist missionaries; continuous and hard labor with his four companions, Fathers Baker, Deshon, Hewit and Walworth (see above and below) among the rapidly increasing population of Catholic immigrants; won reputation as a powerful speaker on doctrinal and historical aspects of the Catholic faith; went to Rome to request that a Redemptorist novitiate be opened in the United States for English speakers, but was expelled from the order for coming to Rome without sufficient authorization; Pope Pius IX dispensed him and his companions from their vows and encouraged them to found a new missionary order in the United States under the hierarchy; the Missionary Society of St. Paul the Apostle (the "Paulists") in the State of New York was founded by him in 1858; he was elected superior and continued in that post until his death; the aim of the order was to evangelize both believers and non-believers in order to convert America to the Catholic faith; the order was the first strictly American congregation in the United States; he continued his work as a lecturer and promoted an apostolate of the press among Catholics in America; also promoted Catholic literary activities; he created *The Catholic World*, a monthly magazine, in 1865; in 1866 he founded the Catholic Publication Society (now the Paulist Press); in 1870 he established *The Young Catholic*, a magazine for young boys and girls; in 1869-1870 he attended the First Vatican Council as a theologian for Bishop James Gibbons of North Carolina; struggled against leukemia during the last years of his life; his name was mentioned at the time of the controversy over "Americanism", but the American hierarchy all but unanimously gave spontaneous testimony that he had never countenanced any deviation from, or minimizing of, Catholic doctrines; cause for sainthood formally opened on 25 January

2008; he was declared a Servant of God; see *Questions of the Soul* (1857); *Aspirations of Nature* (1857) (both of these works had for their main object the presentation and teaching of the Church to non-Catholics); *The Catholic Church in the United States* (1879); *Catholics and Protestants Agreeing on the School Question* (1881); *The Church and the Age* (1887); Rev. Walter Elliott, *Life of Isaac Thomas Hecker* (1891); Barry, "Father Hecker, Founder of the Paulists," *Dublin Review*, July 1892; Henry Dwight Sedgwick, *Father Hecker* (1901); Vincent F. Holden, *The Early Years of Isaac Thomas Hecker, 1819-1844* (1939); Katherine Burton, *In No Strange Land: Some American Catholic Converts* (1942), p.77; Katherine Burton, *Celestial Homespun: The Life of Isaac Thomas Hecker* (1943); Joseph McSorley, *Father Hecker and His Friends* (1952); Theodore Maynard, *Great Catholics in American History* (1957), p.181; Vincent F. Holden, *Yankee Paul: Isaac Thomas Hecker* (1958); John A. O'Brien, *Giants of the Faith* (1960), p.301; Hilda Graef, *Mystics of Our Times* (1962), p.65; Joseph McSorley, *Father Hecker and His Friends* (1972); Joseph F. Gower and Richard M. Leliaert, *The Brownson-Hecker Correspondence* (1979); John Farina, *An American Experience of God* (1981); John Farina, *Hecker Studies: Essays on the Thought of Isaac Hecker* (1983); William Portier, *Isaac Hecker and the First Vatican Council* (1985); John Farina (ed), *Isaac Hecker: The Diary: Romantic Religion in Ante-Bellum America* (1988); David J. O'Brien, *Isaac Hecker: An American Catholic* (1992); Jenny Franchot, *Roads to Rome: The Antebellum Protestant Encounter with Catholicism* (1994), Ch. 16, "Isaac Hecker: The Form of the Missionary Body"; Charles P. Connor, *Classic Catholic Converts* (2001), p.63; *Catholic Encyclopedia* ("Father Hecker's work has been likened to Cardinal Newman's, by the cardinal himself – 'I have ever felt,' Newman wrote to Father Hewit on the occasion of Father Hecker's death, 'that there was a sort of unity in our lives, that we had both begun a work of the same kind, he in America and I in England.' In spite of some obvious differences in the character of the two men and of their work, the comparison is justifiable. Newman, better than anyone else, it has been said, made Catholic dogmas and practices acceptable to the English mind, which had long been estranged from Catholicity on the pretence that the Church was a foreign institution. Hecker, a man of and from the people, strove unceasingly to recommend the Catholic Faith to the democratic American people, who had been reared in hostility to the Church on the pretence that she was foreign and anti-democratic. He was an ardent American, in love with American institutions, but he was likewise absolutely and uncompromisingly Catholic. He won the respect and confidence of his non-Catholic countrymen to a surprising extent, while at the same time eliciting repeated letters of approval from the highest authorities of the Church at Rome"); *ANB*.

Hemingway, Ernest Miller – author and journalist; b. 21 July 1899, Oak Park, Chicago, Illinois; c. 1927 (formalized at the time of his marriage to Pauline, but arrived at intellectually and emotionally before then and may actually have been received in 1919); d. 2 July 1961, Ketchum, Idaho; father a doctor, mother a musician; five siblings; baptized, confirmed, and raised in the Congregational Church; much outdoor activity (hunting and fishing) as a boy; editor and contributor to his school newspaper; after high school he went to work as a journalist; in 1918 he went to be a Red Cross ambulance driver in Italy; suffered serious wounds to his legs in mortar fire; returned to the United States in 1919 and worked as a journalist; married Hadley Richardson in 1921; he was hired as a foreign correspondent for the *Toronto Star* and they went to live in Paris; fell away from the religious liberalism of his youthful Protestantism; he met many writers (e.g., Gertrude Stein, James Joyce, F. Scott Fitzgereld, John Dos Passos, Ford Madox Ford, and Ezra Pound) and influential painters (e.g., Pablo Picasso, Joan Miro); wrote novels (including his first major work, *The Sun Also Rises* at this time) and short stories, with some non-fiction; his marriage to Hadley was dissolved by the Church and he married Pauline Pfeifer (from a wealthy Catholic Arkansas family) in May 1927 (the marriage took place at the Catholic church of Saint-Honore d'Eylau in Paris); he formally converted to the Catholic faith before their marriage, but had considered himself Catholic from 1918 onward; left Paris in 1928 and moved back to the United States, settling in Key West, Florida; *A Farewell to Arms* was published in 1929; his father committed suicide; in 1929 he went to Spain to research *Death in the Afternoon*, his major work on bullfighting; much hunting, fishing and drinking, plus a safari in Africa; reported on the Spanish Civil War for the North American Newspaper Alliance; he began to question his religion at this time, eventually leaving the Church (though friends indicated that he had "funny ties" to Catholicism for the rest of his life); longstanding devotion to the specifically Catholic pilgrimage of Santiago de Compostela; his wife sided with the pro-Catholic regime of General Franco, whereas he mostly supported the Republican government, for all his criticisms of it; wrote *To Have and Have Not* at this time; lived for some time in Cuba and did much sailing; divorced from Pauline in 1940 and married the journalist and writer,

Martha Gellhorn; she inspired him to write his most famous novel, *For Whom the Bell Tolls*, which was based on the Spanish Civil War; as a correspondent he was with the American forces in Europe during and after the D-Day landings; present at the liberation of Paris and covered the Battle of the Bulge; in 1946 he married Mary Welsh, *Time* magazine correspondent; much illness after the war and depression at the death of his literary friends; in 1953 he won the Pulitzer Prize for Fiction for *The Old Man and the Sea*; in 1954 seriously injured in two successive plane crashes; awarded the Nobel Prize for Literature in 1954 (the citation referred to "his mastery of the art of narrative... and for the influence that he has exerted on contemporary style"); main themes of his writing were nature, women and death, dealt with in a spare and tight style; spent much time in Cuba, but moved to Ketchum, Idaho, in 1959; further illness and severe depression (for which he had electroconvulsive therapy, which was unsuccessful); committed suicide by deliberately shooting himself with his favorite shotgun (though initially the story told to the press was that the death had been accidental); the local Catholic priest (who believed the death was accidental) officiated at the funeral, which consisted only of graveside prayers; later both his sister Ursula and his brother Leicester committed suicide; buried in Ketchum cemetery; see *The Sun Also Rises* (1926); *A Farewell to Arms* (1929); *For Whom the Bell Tolls* (1940); *The Old Man and the Sea* (1952); *A Moveable Feast* (1964); *Ernest Hemingway, Selected Letters* (1981); *The Garden of Eden* (1986); *The Complete Short Stories of Ernest Hemingway* (1987); *True at First Light* (1999); Marcelline Hemingway Sanford, *At the Hemingways* (1961); Leicester Hemingway, *My Brother, Ernest Hemingway* (1962); A. E. Hotchner, *Papa Hemingway* (1966); Carlos Baker, *Ernest Hemingway: A Life Story* (1969); Gregory Hemingway, *Papa* (1976); Mary Welsh Hemingway, *How It Was* (1976); Michael Reynolds, *Hemingway's First War: The Making of* A Farewell to Arms (1976); Lloyd R. Arnold, *Hemingway: High on the Wild* (1977); Scott Donaldson, *By Force of Will: The Life and Art of Ernest Hemingway* (1977); Michael Reynolds, *Hemingway's Reading* (1981); Arnold Samuelson, *With Hemingway* (1984); Jeffrey Meyers, *Hemingway: A Biography* (1985); Michael Reynolds, *The Young Hemingway* (1986); H. R. Stoneback, "From the rue Saint-Jacques to the Pass of Roland to the Unfinished Church at the Edge of the Cliff," *Hemingway Review*, Fall 1986, p.2; Kenneth S. Lynn, *Hemingway* (1987); Michael Reynolds, *Hemingway: The Paris Years* (1989); H. R. Stoneback, "'Lovers' Sonnets Turn'd to Holy Psalms': The Soul's Song of Providence, the Scandal of

Suffering, and Love in *A Farewell to Arms*," *Hemingway Review*, Fall 1989, p.33; *Hemingway: An Annotated Chronology* (1991); H. R. Stoneback, "In the Nominal Country of the Bogus: Hemingway's Catholicism and the Biographies," in Frank Scafella (ed), *Hemingway: Essays of Reassessment* (1991), p.105 ("It is difficult at best, perhaps an effort doomed from the outset, for commentators to come to terms with Hemingway's Catholicism…

Hemingway insisted that writers should possess priestly 'probity and honesty'; yet that probity and honesty need not be manifest in social actions so much as it is incarnate in the work of art. For even if Hemingway were consistently devout, an untroubled, once-married, exemplary Catholic - even if he were a priest - he would not want to be known as the leader of a 'Catholic literary renaissance.'

One course for biographers to follow in these matters is suggested by casual memoirists like Arnold Samuelson, who, for example, notes briefly and without comment that in the midst of a Cuban fishing trip in 1934, Hemingway went ashore and attended Mass... Lloyd Arnold, on the other hand, follows the course of sympathetic engagement without inquisition. Of Hemingway in the last two decades of his life, Arnold says: 'I did not know Papa as a man without God'... And whatever fault some may find with A. E. Hotchner's *Papa Hemingway*, it is far more useful and effective on Hemingway's Catholicism in his later years than most of the other biographies.

For example, Hotchner notes that Hemingway went into the cathedral at Burgos to kneel and pray on his way to Madrid in 1954. Afterward, he said that he wished he were 'a better Catholic.' Hotchner also notes, briefly and without comment, that Hemingway subscribed to *The Southern Jesuit*, that he 'contributed the cost of a badly needed' roof for the Catholic church in Hailey, Idaho, in 1958, and, surprisingly enough, that he gave a public address to the young people of that parish, telling them, among other things, that it was 'very bad luck to work on Sunday.' Moreover, Hotchner notes that Hemingway talked sympathetically with Gary Cooper about Cooper's conversion to Catholicism in 1958, and that when Hemingway placed an ad in the newspaper in 1959 asking a Spanish pickpocket to return his billfold, he cared most about getting back the 'image of St. Christopher in it'…

I would go so far as to say that Hotchner's concluding paragraph might serve as a model for any biographer dealing with religious matters. In Rome at the time of Hemingway's funeral in Idaho, Hotchner went into Santa Maria Sopra Minerva, 'his church, not mine,' says Hotchner, 'because I wanted to say good-bye to him in his own place.' Hotchner offers a good-luck prayer, thinking,

'I figured he knew how much I loved him, so there was no point in mentioning that,' then lights a candle for Hemingway before he leaves...Hotchner, then, reports and respects the facts, refrains from calling Hemingway's Catholicism into question. Such is not the case with other Hemingway biographers.

The heart of the problem seems to me to be the facile assumption made by most Hemingway biographers that Hemingway was a 'nominal' Catholic. This is flatly inaccurate, far worse, the careless employment of the term strikes me as arrogant. In *Hemingway: A Biography*, Jeffrey Meyers compounds the enormity when, with vast presumption, he labels Hemingway a 'bogus' Catholic...

In spite of Hemingway's eighteen years of close engagement with the Congregational church, as choir member, for example, and as youth fellowship speaker and officer, and in spite of some four decades during which Hemingway as Catholic attended Mass and confession, prayed with great intensity in various phases, named one son after a pope, displayed great pride in Patrick's confirmation mastery of the catechism, gave money and support to the Church – in spite of all this, Meyers is capable of writing this utterly inaccurate and oddly detached pronouncement: 'He had superficial connections with various Christian sects'...

Hemingway's disillusionment with the Protestantism of his youth leads not away from religion but rather in the direction of the sacramental vision of the ritual-centered Catholic Church...

If Meyers is the self-appointed Grand Inquisitor, pursuing and testing the Marranos and Moriscos and Hemingways who try to sneak into the church, and Lynn is the do-it-yourself self-help psychobiographer who is oh-so-disappointed that Hemingway's involvement with the church-as-group-therapy didn't quite work out, then Carlos Baker is the careful, cautious, suburban curate who doesn't want to offend anybody by talking too much or too specifically about the church, the Creed, the fundamentals of the faith, or the religious identity of his most famous parishioner...

I would prefer to say that a specifically Catholic tension informs his books and his life...

Following Baker's lead of offering dates and schemata for phases of Hemingway's religious sensibility, and fully aware of the dangers inherent in such an act, I propose the following revised outline: 1908-1917 Period of more-or-less 'cheerful Protestant Christianity.' 1917-1925 Period of bitter rejection of Protestantism and discovery of Catholicism, an awakening to an aesthetic sense centered on ritual and ceremony (as in the world of toreo and the church), and deepening engagement with the sacramental sense of experience and the incarnational patterns of the Catholic church.

1925-1937 Period of rather intense Catholicity, formalized at the time of the marriage to Pauline but intellectually and emotionally arrived at pre-Pauline.
1937-1947 Period of confusion, aridity, or 'dark night of the soul,' a cycle of 'spiritual dryness' that has, for Hemingway aesthetic, moral, and religious consequences; his Catholic marriage ends, betrayal breeds betrayal, his work falters, the self parodic mythic persona emerges; the role of the Catholic church in Fascist Spain profoundly troubles him, but he does not reject the church, knows better than to mix politics and religion.
1947-1960 Period of resurgent belief, coinciding, at first, with Hemingway playing Dante to Adriana Ivancich's Beatrice; partial recovery of creative powers; longing for purgation, for the 'grace of a happy death'; Colonel Cantwell, for example, asks himself if he is going 'to run as a Christian' (*Across the River and Into the Trees*); best answer given in *The Old Man and the Sea*, where Santiago incarnates Hemingway's lifelong pilgrimage, a quest that issues not in some so-called religion of man or 'sentimental humanism' but in a profoundly Catholic sense of expiation and redemption; gives Nobel Prize medal, symbol of life's work, to Virgin Mary.
1960-1961 Period of despair, which Hemingway had earlier noted was the sin against the Holy Ghost, a sin he had not committed - it is not known that electroshock causes despair; it is known that it does not cure it...

In all of my conversations with Mary [Welsh Hemingway], I was keenly aware of her Christian Science upbringing and her non-Catholic, nonbeliever status. (I was also aware of Hemingway's contempt for Christian Science, which, as he said, was neither Christian nor scientific.) It became very clear, however, that Mary had made a real effort to see that the texture of her daily life with Hemingway was Catholic: eating fish on Fridays, observing Lent, singing Christmas carols and fixing the creche under the tree, celebrating Ernest's saint's day, having prayers and masses said for friends and family, observing Catholic feasts and holy days, driving miles out of the way on journeys to visit and revisit churches and cathedrals, and attending religious processions. Much of this is a matter of record in *How It Was*, but a much clearer sense of the Catholic composition of Hemingway's sensibility, even in his last years, emerged from my conversations with Mary, and the picture sharpened gradually over the years...

Whatever conclusions we draw about Hemingway's Catholicism in the last decades of his life, it is clear that, as Mary Hemingway saw the matter, he was not a 'sentimental humanist,' neither a 'nominal' nor a 'bogus' Catholic, but something wholly other.

There are many other crucial touchstones that clarify Hemingway's Catholicism, none of which has been addressed by any of the biographers. I will simply list here a few of these items, based on conversations, correspondence, and other unpublished material…

Allen Tate told me in the 1960s that he had gone to Mass with Hemingway in Paris in the 1920s, that Hemingway was 'very Catholic,' that his attitude toward sport was 'rooted in a religious sensibility.' Toby Bruce, Hemingway's longtime friend and associate, thought Hemingway was a 'good Catholic.'

Hemingway's fishing logbooks have notations of the times he goes ashore and attends Mass. (Do 'bogus' and 'nominal' Catholics, having a wonderful time boating marlin out in the stream, always come ashore for Mass and to do their 'Easter duty'?.

The well-known sportsman George Leonard Herter asserts that Hemingway was 'a strong Catholic [whose] religion came mainly from the Apparitions of the Virgin Mary.'

In his unpublished memoir, the philosopher Ralph Withington Church recalls his conversations with Hemingway about the 'problem of redemption' and Malebranche's 'theory of grace.'

Hemingway's unpublished letters are filled with references to religion, with clarifications of his Catholicism, especially the letters to various priests, certain letters to Pauline, and the late letters to Adriana Ivancich and Robert Brown. The Adriana Ivancich letters have a consistently Catholic texture, with references to prayer, priests, having masses said, quotations of St. Teresa of Avila, allusions to Dante, pilgrimages, the Middle Ages, saints and martyrs, the cathedrals of Chartres and San Marco, and the basic stance that people who don't understand their code cannot understand how one can be a serious artist and like to drink and have fun in the sun and go to church. The letters to Robert Brown provide the most precise, succinct summation anywhere of Hemingway's later sense of himself as Catholic. He employs the language of the Church, speaks exactly of states of sin and grace, distinguishes between blasphemy and heresy (and does so using technical language worthy of a student of theology, e.g., bestemnia for blasphemy). These letters, when they have been noted at all by biographers, have received only the most superficial gloss…

And so I wave farewell to the biographers, turning from them, and turning somewhat wearily, as one would turn to wave good-bye to Hemingway, if the road were time and he at the end of the road. I have tried here to clear the frontier, to get across the border and revoke that passport, that husband-and-wife passport which declares that Hemingway's Catholicism was a convenience which lasted as long as his marriage to Pauline, and to rescind that invalid visa for the country of the nominal bogus. Hemingway was a Catholic, most of his life, and we will have to accept and to understand that. It is not, finally, our business to judge what kind of Catholic he was. What matters most is that it is everywhere in his work, which is fundamentally religious and profoundly Catholic from the earliest good work to the last. Many live in it and never feel it, but it is there, and once we have the biographical record clarified, it is in the fiction that we must undertake the pilgrimage with Hemingway. The route is clearly marked, if we know how to read old maps"); H. R. Stoneback, "'Mais, Je Reste Catholique': Communion, Betrayal, and Aridity in 'Wine of Wyoming,'" in Susan F. Beegel, *Hemingway's Neglected Short Fiction: Current Perspectives* (1992), p.209; H. R. Stoneback, "'The Priest Did Not Answer': Hemingway, the Church, the Party, and *For Whom the Bell Tolls*," in Rena Sanderson (ed), *Blowing the Bridge: Essays on Hemingway and For Whom the Bell Tolls* (1992), p.99; James Mellow, *Hemingway: A Life without Consequences* (1992); Michael Reynolds, *Hemingway: The American Homecoming* (1992); Matthew Bruccoli, *Fitzgerald and Hemingway: A Dangerous Friendship* (1994); Michael Reynolds, *The Young Hemingway* (1998); Michael Reynolds, *Hemingway: The Final Years* (1999); H. R. Stoneback, "Pilgrimage Variations: Hemingway's Sacred Landscapes," *Religion & Literature*, Summer-Autumn 2003, p.49 ("Pilgrimage, the notion and motion of spiritualized travel, is at the center of Hemingway's religious vision and his work from his earliest stories to the final, unfinished and posthumously published novels and memoirs...

Beginning with his wounding and near-death experience on an Italian battlefield in 1918, and continuing with increasing intensity through the early and mid-1920s, Hemingway's personal religious pilgrimage takes him through a rejection of Puritanism, and far beyond the social-gospel brand of Protestantism, into an ever-deepening discovery of Catholicism. This personal faith-journey is manifest, in his life and his work, by profound engagement with the aesthetic and historical and spiritual sensibility centered in ritual and ceremony (e.g., most obviously, as in the world of Toreo, or the bullfight; and, less obviously, in the vision of life-as-pilgrimage). Hemingway's rootedness in the sacramental sense of experience, in the incarnational paradigms of Catholic Christianity, grows ever deeper. Before his twenty-eighth birthday (in 1927), he has accepted the tradition, the authority, and the discipline of Rome and formalized his conversion. Far from being a 'nominal' or 'bogus' Catholic as some biographers would have it, Hemingway is a devout practicing

Catholic for much of his life. He believed that 'the only way he could run his life decently was to accept the discipline of the Church,' and he could not imagine taking any other religion seriously (Baker, *Life Story*, 333).

What matters for students of Hemingway's writing, and what matters most for me, is that his fiction…is rooted in his religious sensibility, and the work is most deeply accessible through an understanding of his Catholic vision. Prose, Hemingway famously said, is architecture, not interior decoration. The spirituality, or if the reader prefers, the faith, the religion, the Catholicism of Hemingway's prose is architecture not mere interior decoration. And the foundational mode of that architecture is pilgrimage"); H. R. Stoneback, *Reading Hemingway's The Sun Also Rises* (2007); H. R. Stoneback, *Hemingway's Paris: Our Paris?* (2010); Brian Kelly, "With the Pope's Visit to Cuba in the News, I am Reminded of Enigmatic Ernest Hemingway," *Catholicism.org*, 28 March 2012 ("He was devoted in some hesitant way to Our Lady, but he loved his vices more. Poor soul. To have come so close to the Faith (as he did) only to spurn grace, turn away too many times, and end up in fatal despair a suicide.

His famous boat he named after Our Lady of the Pilar whose shrine he had visited in Spain. What I did not know until today was that he had made a promise, like Captain Santiago in *The Old Man and the Sea*, to make a pilgrimage to the Catholic shrine of La Virgen de la Caridad del Cobre (Our Lady of Charity) in Cuba if he would "catch this fish."

After winning the Nobel Prize for literature in 1954, Hemingway went to the shrine to thank Our Lady, and he left his Prize medallion there as a gift to her"); Matthew Nickel, *Hemingway's Dark Night: Catholic Influences and Intertextualities in the Work of Ernest Hemingway* (2013); *Hemingway Review*; *ANB*.

Henderson, Isaac Austin – novelist, playwright and newspaper publisher; b. 1850, Brooklyn, New York; c. 1896; d. March 1909, Rome; his ancestors were from Scotland and Ireland; his father co-owned the *New York Evening Post*; educated at Williams College, Williamstown, Massachusetts (graduated BA, MA, and Doctor of Civil Law); became assistant publisher of the *Evening Post* in 1875 and publisher in 1877; sold his interest in 1881 and went to Europe, living in London and Rome; did much charitable work for the poor in the Trastevere quarter of Rome; see *The Prelate* (1886); *Agatha Page* (1888) (dramatized twice, as *The Silent Battle* in 1892 , then as *Agatha* later in that year); *The Mummy and the Humming Bird* (1901) (play); *Catholic Encyclopedia*.

Hewit, Augustine Francis, CSP (name before entering the Paulist community was Nathaniel Augustine Hewit) – priest; b. 27 November 1820, Fairfield, Connecticut; c. 25 March 1846 (Holy Saturday; received at Charleston, South Carolina); d. 3 July 1897, New York City; son of Rev. Nathaniel Hewit, a Congregationalist minister, whose ancestors were of old New England stock and who was himself an outstanding preacher of his day; his grandfather, James Hillhouse, had been for years a United States senator from Connecticut; brought up in the Calvinistic creed of his parents; graduated from Amherst College in 1839; became a Congregationalist minister in 1842; he continued to read and became convinced that episcopacy was of divine origin, so he entered the Episcopal Church; studied for the Episcopal ministry in Baltimore; read Newman and the Tractarians; received the Anglican order of deacon in 1844, but with the express condition that he might interpret the Thirty-nine Articles in the sense of *Tract 90*; Newman's conversion in 1845 unsettled his belief in the validity of the claims of Anglicanism and he was received into the Catholic Church; studied Catholic theology privately under direction; ordained priest on 25 March 1847; became acquainted with St. John Nepomucen Neumann, C.SS.R; entered the Redemptorist Order in 1849; gave many missions with his four companions Fathers Baker, Deshon, Hecker, and Walworth (see above and below and, in particular, the entry for Fr. Hecker); one of the original Paulist fathers; drafted the first constitution and laws of the new institute; he was always the ablest scholar of the group; became in his later days even more of a teacher than a preacher; he wrote many articles for *The Catholic World* and was its editor from the time of Isaac Hecker's death (1888) until his own death; also on the death of Fr. Hecker, he was almost unanimously chosen the second Superior General of the Society and held this office until his death; he moved the Society seminary onto the grounds of the new Catholic University in Washington, D.C.; for seven years he lectured on Church history at Catholic University; buried in St. Paul the Apostle Church, Manhattan, New York; see *A Few Thoughts concerning the Theories of High-Churchmen and Tractarians* (1846) (his apologia for joining the Catholic Church); *Life of the Venerable Servant of God, Monseigneur Dumoulin Borie, Bishop Elect of Acanthus and Martyr* (1859); *Sermons of the Rev. Francis A. Baker. With a Memoir of His Life* (1866); *Problems of the Age; with Studies in St. Augustine on Kindred Topics* (1868); *Light in Darkness* (1871); *The King's Highway; or, The Catholic Church the Way of Salvation as Revealed in the Holy Scriptures* (1874); "How

I Became a Catholic," *Catholic World*, October 1887, p.32; *How I became a Catholic, Stories of Conversions* (1892); *Problems of the Age* (1893); *The Teaching of St. John the Apostle to the Churches of Asia and the World* (1895); Clarence Alphonsus Walworth, *The Oxford Movement in the U.S.* (1895); O'Keefe, "Very Rev. Augustine F. Hewit," *American Catholic Quarterly Review*, July 1903; Katherine Burton, *In No Strange Land: Some American Catholic Converts* (1942), p.77; *Catholic Encyclopedia* ("He was a deep student of philosophy, theology, patristic literature, church history, and Scripture, and taught all of these branches to the first novices of the institute. He was also a prolific writer and for twenty years was one of the foremost Catholic apologists in the United States. In this field he was chiefly noted for his loyalties to the magisterium of the Church and his agreement with the opinions of the most approved theologians. He wrote nothing that could be styled original; he simply aimed to explain and popularize the teaching of the doctors and saints of Holy Church"); Joseph McSorley's *Father Hecker and His Friends* (1972); *ANB* ("For Hewit the continuity, infallibility, and development of the primitive church could be found in no other denomination, and he saw his own movement toward Catholicism as the logically consistent consequence of his studies of the Oxford school").

Hitchcock, Helen Hull – writer and editor; c. 1984; brought up in Kansas with a strong Christian formation in a devout Protestant family, mainly attending Methodist churches, but also Congregational and Baptist ones; also very interested in Judaism and in Episcopalianism and its ritual; educated at the University of Kansas (majored in Art History); stopped going to church while at college; became an insurance underwriter in Kansas and then San Francisco; sometimes went to Mass with a Catholic woman co-worker ("I do not know if 'cradle Catholics' really understand that their piety and fidelity is and had always been an important witness to believers and unbelievers alike"); enrolled on a philosophy course and found Thomistic philosophy "exhilarating, both intellectually and spiritually"; drawn to the sacramental; moved to New York and was confirmed in the Episcopal Church; met and soon after (in 1966) married James E. Hitchcock, Catholic historian (later Professor of History at St. Louis University); they assisted in each other's churches as well as their own; disappointed by the liturgical changes in the Catholic Church ("The radical changes in the Roman Catholic liturgy, which were intended to make the faith more immediate and personal to believers, was having the unexpected effect of destroying the idea of the sacred…I found the 'new liturgy' often almost unbearably ugly"), but more by the capitulation to liberalism by the Episcopal Church (eliminating the Book of Common Prayer, ordaining women, and accepting abortion); eventually converted to the Catholic Church; frequent contributor to Catholic periodicals; co-organizer in 1984 of Women for Faith and Family, which circulated the Affirmation for Catholic Women, a statement of fidelity to and unity with Church teaching; editor of its quarterly journal, *Voices*; also editor of the *Adoremus Bulletin*, a monthly publication of *Adoremus - Society for the Renewal of the Sacred Liturgy*, of which she was a co-founder; speaker on Catholic issues; see "With God's Help," in Robert Baram (ed), *Spiritual Journeys* (revised edition, 1988), p.127 ("The Supreme Court decision of 1973, which overturned by fiat a universal moral assumption of two millennia, opened a chasm in Western culture so vast and deep and so cataclysmic in its after-shocks that it can be safely said that no individual, no human institution was unaffected by it.

The Catholic Church, by immediate and vigorous action, gave evidence of its authentic role as a 'sign of contradiction' in – and witness to – the world. The Episcopal Church, at its next General Convention barely three years later, not only capitulated to the *Zeitgeist* in the matter of abortion, but, while they were at it, also scrapped the traditional book of Common Prayer which had been substantially unchanged since 1549, and unilaterally departed from Catholic (and Anglican) tradition by approving the ordination of women, including avowed lesbians, to the priesthood...

It became strikingly clear to me that the teaching authority of the Catholic Church alone could consistently affirm and maintain Christian Truth. My increasing knowledge of the effects of feminist ideology made me realize the importance of the role of Mary in salvation history. That such a pope as John Paul II could be given to Christianity in this age of chaos and cultural upheavals seemed to me a clear sign that the Holy Spirit truly was with this Church - this *Roman* Catholic Church. If this scandalized my Anglo-Catholic-Protestant-Evangelical soul, how much greater is the 'scandal of particularity' of the incarnation of God as Jesus of Nazareth?...

Far from denying my own religious heritage, I have come back to that Faith which saints believed of old. I am a Catholic - because it is within the Catholic Church that I can affirm the Christian Truth which I was taught as a child, and have believed, by the Grace of God, all of my life. I am a Catholic - because it is here that the Faith of my fathers is living still. Here I stand. I can do no other"); "Why Fidelity to the Church," *This Rock*, May 1990; (ed), *The Politics of Prayer: Feminist*

Language and the Worship of God (1992); *EWTN Audio Library, The Journey Home* (22 May 2006).

Hochschild, Joshua P. – philosopher; b. 1972; c. 2004; studied philosophy at Yale University (BA 1994); graduate work in medieval philosophy at the University of Notre Dame (PhD on Cajetan 2001; adult convert to evangelical Christianity; taught at Wheaton College, Illinois, 2001-2005, where the statement of faith reflects evangelical Protestant theology; he was dismissed from Wheaton when he became a Catholic (he never challenged the right of the college to exclude Catholics); Assistant Professor in the Department of Philosophy, Mount St. Mary's University, Emmitsburg, Maryland; later Dean of the College of Liberal Arts there; main interest medieval logic and metaphysics; publications on a variety of areas of philosophy in several journals; Assistant Director of the McInerny Center for Thomistic Studies, Washington; one influence on his conversion was his coming to believe that evangelical Protestantism was vaguely defined and had a weak scholarly tradition, which increased his appreciation of Catholicism's self-assurance and intellectual history; his distaste for the "evangelical suspicion of philosophy" also a possible contributing factor; see *Ethics Without God: The Divine in Contemporary Moral and Political Thought* (2008); *Virtue's End: God in the Moral Philosophy of Aristotle and Aquinas* (2008); *The Semantics of Analogy: Rereading Cajetan's De Nominum Analogia* (2010); Daniel Golden, "A Test of Faith," *The Wall Street Journal*, 7 January 2006.

Hoffman, Ross John Swartz – historian; b. 1902, Harrisburg, Pennsylvania; c. 1931; d. 1979; brought up in a Protestant family of German descent; educated at University of Pennsylvania (MA in 1926, PhD in 1932); had been agnostic (as an undergraduate he had rejected Christianity as he sensed that intelligent modern man did not regard it "as anything more than a pious fable tied up with some rather commendable morality"; he become a Socialist, but his research in history and his travel to Europe influenced his conversion to the Catholic Church ("The Church was the mother of the new learning, the founder of the great universities, the inspiration of the great new architecture, the patron of towns and guilds, the defender of popular liberty, the very citadel and source of European culture and unity, fabulously rich in the capacity for galvanizing new life in a thousand directions"); also influenced by a loving marriage to a Catholic, Hannah McCruden, by a thorough reading of Scripture and by the writings of Hilaire Belloc and G. K. Chesterton; worked at New York University 1926-1938, then Professor of European History at

Fordham University 1938-1967 (Professor Emeritus there until his death); the main theme of his work is the psychological and spiritual interpretation of history; president of the American Catholic Historical Association in 1938; later in his career wrote much on Edmund Burke (saw him as a model for connecting the eighteenth century world to ours); secured teaching jobs for the Austrian "liberal monarchist" Erik von Kuehnelt-Leddihn and the émigré Hungarian historian John Lukacs; close relationship and lengthy correspondence with Russell Kirk (see below); see *Great Britain and the German Trade Rivalry, 1875-1914* (1934); *Restoration* (1934) (a study in the philosophy of history written to explain his conversion); *The Will to Freedom* (1936); *Tradition and Progress, and Other Historical Essays in Culture, Religion, and Politics* (1938); "Catholicism and Historismus," *The Catholic Historical Review*, January 1939, p.401; *The Organic State: An Historical View of Contemporary Politics* (1939); *The Great Republic: A Historical View of the International Community and the Organization of Peace* (1942); *Durable Peace: A Study in American National Policy* (1944); (ed), *Burke's Politics: Selected Writings and Speeches of Edmund Burke on Reform, Revolution, and War* (1948) (with Paul Levack); "The Verdict of History," in John A. O'Brien (ed), *The Road to Damascus* (1949) ("I felt very sure that the eye with which to recognize a revelation could not be in the eye of the intellect alone, since that would make of God a secret to which only the learned could be privy…It seemed to me… that the chief test of the truth of revelation must lie in its successful recognition by men of simplicity and humility, and in the nature of its transforming influence upon their lives. And yet another conviction was this: I was very sure I could not love God without apprehending His Personality in the Incarnation. Without that He could be only an abstraction, difficult to grasp as a genuine reality; and, moreover, the keystone of the whole arch of Christianity was not there if Christ were nothing more than a philosopher. I had come to see clearly what, it seems to me, so many persons fail to grasp, namely, that *Catholicism is an organic whole springing from the germinal seed of the Incarnation.* So that my last question was just the old question and the most deeply important one that has ever been asked: 'What think ye of Christ?'

I acted upon my decision by seeking help from one who was wonderfully equipped to give it. He set me a simple exercise. 'Divest yourself,' he advised, 'as completely as possible of all previous ideas of Christ that you have ever entertained. Take the Gospels as historical documents throwing light upon a strange and unknown personality and approach them as a rationally-minded man hearing for the first time of Christ. See then what you think of Him afresh. Your mind has reached a measure of maturity, you have seen something of men and speculated upon their nature. You have encountered various philosophies and, through reason and experience, learned to assess them. Your experience has a certain validity. Now check the personality and the philosophy of this Man with the experience you have had in the world of men and ideas.'

I followed the general direction of these suggestions and took up the Gospels anew with quite the same attitude I would take toward any other historical documents. I sought to study a man and not a God, for I was deliberately proceeding upon the theory that no man had ever been or ever could be God. Let there be no mistake about this: the idea of the Incarnation was purposely excluded from the exercise. It proved a very interesting and quite surprising inquiry, for although I believe that in the past 1 had read, at intervals and in broken sections, every word of all four documents, I had never before attempted to draw a full-length portrait of Christ. Not the least part of my surprise now was the discovery that I had never really known much about Christ. I had known somewhat vaguely the Christ of the Sermon on the Mount, the preceptor of humility, brotherly love, and self-effacement. I had known the meek Christ, but I had not known the *terribly* meek Christ, nor the angry Christ of authority and violent words. Here, I saw, was no mere benevolent philosopher urging the gentler virtues, but an imperious and demanding figure who taught 'as one having authority and not as the scribes.'

But the greatest amazement was finding myself becoming a partisan of His enemies. For the first time in my life I began to have some understanding of the mad rage which this presumptuous and irritating Person must have aroused. I began to wonder what we would think of a man who, after violating one of our most precious institutions (as He broke the Jewish Sabbath), coolly remarked that he was superior to it. I thought we should have rather a serious case against Him as an outrager of our laws. My reaction to Jesus at Nazareth when He entered the synagogue, read from the Scriptures, and announced their fulfilment that day, was exactly the same. I murmured with the people who heard Him, 'Is not this the son of Joseph?' And when He rebuked them I was strongly tempted to join with those that 'rose up and thrust Him out of the city.'

Again and again I was scandalized by His acts and words. When He presumed to forgive sins I said with the scribes and Pharisees, 'Who is this who speaketh blasphemies? Who can forgive sins but God alone?' He exhibited a most arrogant and offending egotism: 'Behold a greater than Jonas is here…behold a greater than Solomon is here.' I also discovered in this preacher of the Sermon on the Mount a quivering and terrible anger which found expression in such words as 'hypocrites, whited sepulchres,' and 'generation of vipers,' and in such awful threats as the one for the city which should not receive His disciples: 'It shall be more tolerable for the land of Sodom and Gomorrah in the day of judgment than for that city.' This man's tongue could sting like a whiplash laid upon an open wound. And I found in Him, too, a demand, for personal allegiance reaching the very limits of effrontery. His disciples are to keep His commandments and not be scandalized by Him. 'He that loveth father or mother more than me is not worthy of me' - so does He ask that loyalty to Himself be the first of all loyalties, making bold to promise His disciples that if they would take up the cross and follow Him they should have a crown of life. What kind of man was this who could ask for Himself all that men could conceivably owe to God? 'All things are delivered unto me by my father…I and my father are one… He that hath seen me has seen the father…I am the way, the truth and the life' - what preposterous sayings are these from a mere man! I understood for the first time the passion of the high priest when he rent his robes and said, 'What need we any further witnesses? You have heard the blasphemy.' I was both puzzled and scandalized by His vaunted sinlessness: His most violent words of denunciation was reserved for hypocrites, and yet He could ask, 'Which of ye convinceth me of sin?' Such words from one who is no more than human are downright revolting. The more I speculated upon the character and personality of the man Jesus the more offended I became, the more monstrous His imposture appeared. His fellow countrymen 'wondered and said: How came this man by this wisdom and miracles? Is not this the carpenter's son?... Whence therefore hath he all these things? And they were scandalized in His regard.' And so was I.

It seemed to me, indeed, that if this Man were just a man, like any other man, it would be charitable to write Him down as a lunatic; else the Pharisees were right and He met a deserved end. But as mere man He was not credible at all, for He was a defiance of the common nature of man. No man putting forward the preposterous claims He made for Himself could have also inspired that perfect love which we find His disciples paying to Him, for He scandalized even them on several occasions. Nor is it even imaginable that any man could unite so perfectly in himself the qualities of meekness and terrible anger, and although with knowledge of his own stainless perfection could yet weep with compassion for all men. How indeed could it have been that this imperious egotist lived and taught a timeless philosophy of life, yet surrendered willingly His own perfect life in the passion and ignominy of the cross? His absolute sincerity stands proved on Calvary, yet He declared Himself to be God! A man who would set out to be God (as blasphemous an imposture as can be imagined) must, it seemed to me, end in moral ruin. But Calvary was surely not that. It became very plain to me that Jesus was not to be explained in terms of humanity alone, not even humanity touched with lunacy. The latter theory is unworthy of discussion. The Sermon on the Mount and the parable teachings are sanity and we all know it. The mind of Christ had a flashing rapierlike gift for going to the heart of things in swift simplicity. The theory that he was insane cannot survive a thoughtful reading of the Gospels.

I could not conceive of more than four possible interpretations of Christ. He was (1) a philosopher and prophet, only human but sane; or (2) He was a lunatic; or (3) His character as we know it in the Gospels is wholly or largely fictitious; or (4) He was the Incarnate Son, true man and true God. Now the first two theories failed to solve the riddle of this strange personality. As a mere man I found it impossible to believe in His real existence, and when I subjected Him to the lunacy test I found Him superlatively sane. But what of the theory that the whole Gospel story is fiction or just a legend grown up around some man of forceful personality, some impressive Eastern prophet?

With the exception of a few writers who have never been taken seriously, no historical student questions the historicity of Jesus; many, however, have striven laboriously to show the Man of the Gospels as one very much obscured by decorative legend. Was this not the most probable explanation of Christ? The East has always been prolific in cults and prophets, and the Roman Empire swarmed with them in early Christian times; so that it seemed rather plausible that the Christ we know from apostolic writings was the creature of fertile religious imagination or even conscious fraud. This is the theory of most persons who find themselves unable to give credence to the doctrines of the Incarnation and Redemption.

Now I was no expert in the so-called higher criticism, but I was not so innocent of a knowledge of antiquity and the history of the New Testament as to be unable to see the weakness of the legend theory. Indeed, I am now disposed to think that this is the weakest of all the theories. It cannot be squared with the ascertainable facts of early Church history. I know the early days of the Church are commonly regarded as having a rather dim historical visibility, but actually that is not the truth at all. I began to see that this visibility was not so low if one was able to grasp the nature of the Church and to estimate rationally the value of tradition as historical evidence. Even the documentary evidence is much more formidable than most persons appear to realize, the New Testament alone containing four sketches of the life of Christ, a history of the early Apostolic Church and twenty-one letters from the hands of Paul, Peter, James, John, and Jude. I am not aware that any other phase of first-century history is so copiously documented.

But the great question was how far this New Testament portrait of Christ departed from a likeness of the Man as He actually was. There seemed no conceivable way of resolving that problem save by speculation, but all such speculation has been governed too much by personal philosophy. Now I tackled the problem in this fashion: I considered the nature of the Catholic Church and her history, contrasting what she taught in one age with what she taught in another. That is to say, I sought to discover deviations in doctrine from one age to another in order to determine whether, in the clear light of unimpeachable historical record, it was in the nature of the Church to make departures from the original deposit of alleged revelation.

I went back to the Council of Trent, from there to Constance, from there to Innocent III and the Fourth Lateran, then back to Nicaea, and from Nicaea to the apostolic documents. Instead of discovering doctrinal deviations and improvisations I found that one of the most conspicuous characteristics of the Church was a constant, purposeful conservation of doctrine, a careful guardianship of the whole treasure of revelation. The Church, of course, grew in function, in definition, in assimilation, but it did not innovate any teaching foreign to, or inconsistent with, the faith of apostolic times. The history of the Church from the age in which the New Testament books were written down to the present day revealed a constant and unchanging nature, and it was in that nature to maintain with jealous care a certain body of doctrine, Now if the New Testament portrait of Christ disfigures and obscures the original Man, the nature of the Church during the first few decades after Calvary and Pentecost must have been in striking contrast with the nature of the Church at the time, say, that Paul wrote his earliest epistles and Mark composed his gospel. This amounts to saying that those who knew Jesus personally - that is, in the flesh - made a legendary figure of Him, while all the generations that came afterward disfigured the concept of His personality not at all. The more I thought about this, the more absurd it appeared. From what I could learn of Peter, Paul, and the other Apostles it seemed quite unbelievable that they were perpetrators of a great fraud. If they sincerely believed in what they taught to the world (and their sincerity is proved by their martyrdom), surely they must have regarded their knowledge of Him as the most precious of all knowledge and therefore not to be tampered with. Moreover, they were mostly simple men, close to reality, and such men are not so easily deceived by things they see, touch, and experience. The more I strove to build up, through historical imagination, a picture of apostolic times the more firmly I became convinced of the honesty and trustworthiness of the first witnesses.

So there was left only one possible explanation of the riddle of Christ: He was what He claimed to be - the Incarnation of God, the Divine Word made flesh. When I added His divinity to His humanity the pieces of the puzzle fell into shape. I could find no escape from the conclusion and I felt that I must either banish it all from my mind as an insoluble enigma or accept this only possible solution. But that solution no longer warred with my philosophic outlook upon the universe! It no longer violated my experience of myself and of my fellow men. Moreover, I found myself coming under the imperious spell of this mighty and towering Personality, found myself capable of loving Him. God granted me the gift of faith, and I confessed with Peter: 'Thou art the Christ, the son of the living God.' He no longer seemed a remote figure out of the East two thousand years ago, but a timeless life as young and fresh today as ever. I had no sudden conversion. Faith came very slowly, and it was not easy to feel the reality of it after so many years of negation. As the new point of view was gradually gained I had alternating moments of lively conviction and sluggish doubt. But grace was not wanting and when I knew that I had found my Father, I also knew my Mother, the Mother of us all, and she designed to adopt me as her own"); *Man and His History: World History and Western Civilization* (1958); *The Spirit of Politics and the Future of Freedom* (1951); *Medieval History* (1955); *Edmund Burke, New York Agent* (1955); *The Marquis: A Study of Lord Rockingham*, 1730-1782 (1973) (Rockingham was Burke's patron); John P. McCarthy, "Ross J. S. Hoffman: Conservative Spokesman in a Utopian Period – The War and Post-War Years," *The Intercollegiate Review*, Spring 1993, p.42; Jeffrey O. Nelson, Hoffman, Ross J. S.," *First Principles*, 8 April 2011 (*firstprinciplesjournal.com*) ("As Hoffman saw it, the post-World War I world was characterized by 'doubt, despair, bewilderment and anarchy.' In such a climate, there was for the church a particular obligation to profess the truth of 'the Faith' to the present age. Hoffman accepted his own charge, and as much as any American Catholic of his time shaped the thinking of his coreligionists (if not always his secular adversaries). Hoffman's approach was historical. He confidently sought to demonstrate how in the wake of the Great War the Catholic Church was in a unique position to offer a compelling alternative to what he believed was the total failure of nineteenth-century liberalism. Catholicism alone was 'totally exonerated from all responsibility and involvement' in the breakdown of European civilization, 'for the faith had been sent in exile and the frontiers closed around it.'

Hoffman was to America what G. K. Chesterton, Hilaire Belloc, and Christopher Dawson were to England: an assured, reasoned, even lyrical voice for restoration. What he hoped to restore was a modern form of medieval Christendom, which he viewed as a 'fresh world' full of 'vigor' and 'health' and 'hard thinking.' He regarded the orthodox Catholic as 'almost the last rationalist left in the world today.' In economics and politics Hoffman rejected both individualist capitalism and collectivist socialism, instead gravitating toward the 'distributism' developed by Belloc and Chesterton, which centered questions of political economy around the family, seeking to secure its independence and dignity from both a growing central state and an avaricious capitalist class through a wide distribution of property and ownership...

It is generally understood that the protagonist in Evelyn Waugh's novel *Scott-King's Modern Europe* (1947) is roughly based on Hoffman, with whom Waugh traveled in Spain, and with whom he shared an uneasiness about the modern world"); Walter Romig, *The Book of Catholic Authors* (1945); Patrick Allitt, *Catholic Converts: British and American Intellectuals Turn to Rome* (1997), *passim.*

Hooper, Walter McGehee – writer; b. 27 March 1931, Reidsville, North Carolina; c. 1988; brought up as Anglican; studied at University of North Carolina at Chapel Hill; lecturer in English Literature at University of Kentucky; greatly influenced by the writings of C. S. Lewis; companion and secretary of Lewis in 1963; ordained to the Anglican ministry in Oxford; Anglican chaplain of Wadham College, Oxford, then of Jesus College, Oxford; literary advisor to Lewis's estate and editor of many of his writings; converted to the Catholic faith partly over the issue of women's ordination; see *C. S. Lewis: A Biography* (revised edition 2002) (with Roger Lancelyn Green); *C. S. Lewis: A Companion and Guide* (1996); *EWTN Audio Library, The Journey Home* (21 July 2003; repeated 20 June 2005) ("At that time in the sixties people were still speaking with more of a single voice in the Anglican Church than they do today. Now, within a few years of that I realized it was a a matter of many voices, and what I simply can't understand is how something one could regard, say the belief that Christ rose from the dead, as true, and others say it's not true. I simply cannot think that way. Like Lewis, I believe in objective truth. But what converted Lewis, through Tolkien's help, in 1931 was believing in the real *things* of resurrection, crucifixion, incarnation, real things. Not our thoughts about them, but real things. What happened to the real things? It seemed to me that they were being bargained away.

And then when the Church of England set up its General Synod, you simply had people voting on truth…So, the ordination of women, this issue was before the Church, as it was for so many years, I began to feel that the Church was losing sight of Christ. Where was truth in all of this? And I really didn't want to spend the rest of my life… simply debating what I thought was essentially a political issue. Not what the truth was, but what people voted for, what the world wanted. But, the Archbishop of Canterbury said in 1992, 'How can we hold up our heads if we disappoint the world?' And I thought we are doing things for people who don't even believe in Christ. I don't say that he saw it that way, but anyway I was losing sight of Christ. And I thought, 'Who is in charge?'… And so my eyes began to turn to the only one who I thought was the legitimate authority, the Pope…

Many of the priests I met in Italy simply didn't understand the Anglican system and they said 'But how can all these ordinary people be talking about something that is so divisive, the ordination of women? Why doesn't the Archbishop of Canterbury tell them what the truth is?' And I realized, of course, that the Catholic Church just doesn't have this problem. You have authority, not everybody his own Pope.

And so in the end I thought what a wonderful witness. You have one tremendous witness for Christ. And then I began to see. Of course! Of course! Christ would not leave this world without a single advisor to settle all of these matters. And I think how odd it would be if Christ said 'I love you. I die for you, and now I'm going to leave you without any particular witness for the next two thousand years.' I just don't think it could happen. But then I realized I was in a church which didn't teach that…

You see I believe not least in Purgatory, I believe in prayers for the faith, and I believe in praying for the dead. But I realized I could be called down at any moment by a fellow Anglican or by one of the Anglican bishops who would call me heretical. So, in one way, I thought, 'Well, it's wonderful to be in the Church where those things are not just merely permitted, but they are the standard fare of the Catholic.

Anyway, it was beginning to be clear to me that I knew what I ought to do. But then came the question which I'm sure would be true of many Protestants like myself. How do you do it if you love all your fellow Anglicans, or Baptists, or Presbyterians? How do you do it?

And I thought, if the Church I'm in does not teach the true faith, and I know one that does, how do I help my fellow Anglicans by remaining in the Church which I don't think is ever going to bring them to total satisfaction and lead them to the truth? How do I do it? Well, I know they want me to stay. But then finally came true what seemed to me to be the biggest question I had to face in myself. 'Walter Hooper,' I said, I've been trying to save the Anglican Church for forty years. Now, I've run out of steam. I want the Catholic Church to save me.' So, in one way I turned over the authority that I just barely held for authority which looked after me"); foreword to Ian Ker, *Mere Catholicism* (2006) ("I converted from Anglicanism to the Catholic Church in 1988 mainly because, quite simply, I believed the claims of the Catholic Church to be true. What led me to believe those claims were – besides [C. S. Lewis'] *Mere Christianity* – such unashamedly Catholic books as Cardinal Newman's *Apologia Pro Vita Sua* (1864), and *An Essay on the Development of Christian Doctrine* (1845). I was particularly affected by the suggestion in Cardinal Newman's *Essay on the Development of Christian Doctrine* (II, iii, 5) that if St. Athanasius or St. Ambrose came suddenly to life 'it cannot be doubted what communion he would take to be his own.' And were those saints to travel northwards to Oxford 'the holy brothers would turn from many a high aisle and solemn cloister which they found there, and ask the way to some small chapel where Mass was said in the populous alley or forlorn suburb' I was more than happy to give up Anglican high aisles and solemn cloisters for the small chapel where Mass was said"); Joseph Pearce, *Literary Converts* (1999) *passim*; Judith Wolfe and Brendan N. Wolfe, *C. S. Lewis and the Church: Essays in Honor of Walter Hooper* (2011); Jonathan Luxmoore, "You Couldn't Be Lazy Around C. S. Lewis," *Catholic Herald*, 5 October 2012, p.7.

Hope, Bob (born Leslie Townes Hope) – comedian and actor; b. 29 May 1903, Eltham, London, England; c. 1996 (received by Mgr. Thomas Kiefer); d. 27 July 2003, Toluca Lake, California; his father William Hope was a stonemason; his mother, Avis, was a light opera singer from Wales; his parents were Presbyterian; fifth of seven sons; the family moved to Cleveland, Ohio, in 1908; he became a U.S. citizen in 1920; from the age of twelve he worked on a local boardwalk, including comedy, dancing and busking; in 1918 admitted to a reform school (to which he donated much money as an adult); made his first films in New York; joined Paramount Pictures in 1938; became a major star appearing in many Hollywood films, on radio and in live concerts; best known for the "Road" movies with Bing Crosby (1903-1977) and Dorothy Lamour (1914-1996); many television specials (long associated with NBC); many wartime performances entertaining the troops, including World War II, Korea, Vietnam, and the Persian Gulf (a 1997 Act of Congress named him an "Honorary Veteran"); in 1934 he married Dolores Defina (1909-2011), a professional singer under the name Dolores Reade and a devout Catholic (they adopted four children); his many extra-marital relationships were an open secret in Hollywood; presented with the United States Congressional Gold Medal in 1962, given the Presidential Medal of Freedom in 1969; in 1998 made a Knight Commander of St. Gregory for the charitable and philanthropic works of his wife and himself; received many other awards; for decades he resisted baptism and Church membership, though he often attended Mass both with and without his wife, and offered financial support to Church endeavors; influences on his conversion were Fr. Benedict Groeschel, Cardinal Cooke, and Fr. George Rutler, but it was mainly due to his wife who prayed for many years for his conversion (to a woman who asked her "Is Mr. Hope going to become Catholic soon?" she replied, "Keep those rosaries coming, sweetheart"); Cardinal Roger Mahoney: "Over the years I would invite him to join the church, but he would respond in his typical humor, 'My wife, Dolores, does enough praying to take care of both of us.' But eventually her prayers prevailed and he was baptized into the Catholic Church and was strengthened these past years through the regular reception of holy Communion"; on his one hundredth birthday he remarked, "I'm so old, they've canceled my blood type"; buried in the Bob Hope Memorial Garden at San Fernando Mission Cemetery in Los Angeles, where his mother is also buried; see I *Never Left Home* (1944); *Have Tux, Will Travel* (1954) (with Pete Martin); Joe Morella, Edward Z. Epstein, and Eleanor Clark, *The Amazing Careers of Bob Hope: From Gags to Riches* (1973); Charles Thompson, *Bob Hope: Portrait of a Superstar* (1981); Pamela Trescott, *Bob Hope: A Comic Life* (1987); Arthur Marx, *The Secret Life of Bob Hope: An Unauthorized Biography* (1993); Lawrence J. Quirk, *Bob Hope: The Road Well-Traveled* (1998); William Robert Faith, *Bob Hope: A Life in Comedy* (2003); Donald W. McCaffrey, *The Road to Comedy: The Films of Bob Hope* (2005); *ANB*.

Horner, William Edmonds – doctor, teacher and author; b. 3 June 1793, Warrenton, Fauquier County, Virginia; c. 1839; d. 13 March 1853, Philadelphia, Pennsylvania; his grandfather emigrated from England prior to the Revolutionary War; slender and frail child; brought up as an Episcopalian; at the outbreak of the war of 1812 between the United States and the British he was a medical student and applied for a commission as surgeon's mate in the hospital department of the army; he worked with "a quiet perseverance and enduring patience"; he returned to his studies in Philadelphia and earned his medical degree in 1814; he then returned to his military assignment and was in charge of a hospital until the end of the war in 1815; in 1816 appointed dissector at the University of Pennsylvania; dean of the Medical School of Pennsylvania 1822-1852; in 1924 he discovered a muscle in the eye that is named for him (the Musculus Hornerii); in 1826 he published the first pathology textbook printed in America; appointed to the chair of Anatomy in 1831; he was so impressed with the work of Catholic priests and nuns during the 1832 cholera epidemic in Philadelphia that after years of prayer and investigation he became a Catholic himself; numerous contributions to medical periodicals; married Elizabeth Welsh (ten children of the marriage); see *Lessons in Practical Anatomy, for the Use of Dissectors* (1823); *Treatise on Special and General Anatomy* (1826); *Treatise on Pathological Anatomy* (1829); *Special Anatomy and Histology* (1843); J. Walsh and C. H. Goudiss, "Notes on the Life of William Edmonds Horner," *Records of the American Catholic Historical Society* (1903), pp.275 and 423; William Shainline Middleton, "William Edmonds Horner (1793-1853)," *Annals of Medical History* (1923), p.33; David Y. Cooper, "William Edmonds Horner (1793-1853), America's First Clinical Investigator," *Transactions & Studies of the College of Physicians of Philadelphia*, ser. 5, 8 (1986), p.183; James Breig, "Doctor Became Catholic After Watching Church Workers Fight Cholera," *Catholic Life*, June 2012, p.56 (reprinted from the *Catholic Review* of the Archdiocese of Baltimore, 2012) ("In his autobiography, Dr. Samuel D. Gross, another Philadelphia doctor, told how Horner was impressed by the extraordinary efforts of Catholic clergy and nuns to serve the victims. 'When other ministers fled in dismay from the dread pestilence,' Gross wrote, 'there was the Catholic (priest) bending down to catch the last whispered word of penitence from the dying, and when nurses were not to be procured these noble women (the nuns) stepped forward to offer their services without fee or reward; they tended the sick and soothed the dying agony; they looked to heaven for their reward. Here then were people really practicing what they preached, really willing, nay anxious, to brave death in doing duty.'

According to Gross, Horner's natural curiosity 'was excited to know more of the faith which produced such works. He studied their tenets. His enquiries were not those of the excited enthusiast, ready to believe all things, but the calm investigations of the wise and learned man, who sought for a rock on which to plant himself to withstand the storms of life and to rest his hopes of salvation in the world to come'"); *ANB*.

Horszowski, Mieczyslaw (pronounced myeh-chih-swahf hor-shofdf-skee) ("Miecio") – pianist; b. 23 June 1892, Lvov (Lviv) (then Poland, now Ukraine); d. 22 May 1993, Philadelphia, Pennsylvania; his family was of Jewish origin; taught by his mother, a pupil of Karol Mikuli (1819-1897), pianist, composer and conductor (himself a pupil of Chopin); played at age three; at the age of seven he became a pupil in Vienna of Theodor Leschetizky (1830-1915), pianist and composer, who had studied with Beethoven's pupil, Carl Czerny (1791-1857), pianist and composer; early convert to the Catholic Church and a devout one; he toured Europe and the Americas as a child prodigy; played for Pope St. Pius X and Pope Pius XII at the Vatican; small in height with rather small hands; known for his natural performances and tonal quality; turned away from music in 1911 to study literature, philosophy, and art history in Paris; returned to the concert stage in 1913; settled in Milan after World War I until moving to the United States during World War II; became an American citizen in 1948; had a very diverse and extensive repertoire; performed on three occasions at the White House; made several recordings and did much teaching; in 1981 at the age of 89 he married Bice Costa, an Italian pianist; gave his final performance in October 1991 (he had the longest known career in the history of the performing arts); gave his final lesson the week before his death; friend of many composers and performers; see Darrell Rosenbluth, "Horszowski Plays Beethoven," *arbiterrecords.com* (1999) ("'How much do you practice each day, Mr. Horszowski?' 'Well, I get up at 6 a.m. and dress and go to the church at 7 a.m. Then I take the breakfast at Dewey's - low salt, you see - then I read the newspaper. Time to teach my lessons. Then I go to Rindelaub's for the lunch, excellent cookies... then another few lessons. Then I take the walk in the park. When I go home, I grill a little hamburger for dinner and watch the news. By then it's late. I go to bed. I guess I do not practice very much'").

Howard, Thomas – writer and scholar; b. 1935; c. 6 April 1985 (Easter Vigil; "I don't use the word 'conversion' myself in referring to my having become Catholic. I prefer to say that I was 'received into the Ancient Church'"; his wife, Lovelace, *née Oden, a former Episcopalian, was received* in 1995); brought up in a family of six children; son of David M. Howard, author (editor of a Protestant religious weekly journal) and missionary; brother of Elisabeth Elliot, author and missionary; brought up in a strong Evangelical family ("It was fundamentalism that taught me to take the Scriptures seriously"); studied at Wheaton College, Illinois; then had a yearning for beauty; taught English in England where he became an Episcopalian in 1962 (mainly for aesthetic reasons); returned to teach in the United States and joined an Anglo-Catholic parish; cited the influence on his conversion to the Catholic faith of Newman (especially on the development of Christian doctrine), Ronald Knox, G. K. Chesterton, Romano Guardini, the then Cardinal Ratzinger, Karl Adam, Louis Bouyer, Dietrich von Hildebrand, St. Augustine and the early Church Fathers; Emeritus Professor of English, St. John's Seminary, Boston, Massachusetts; visiting lecturer in many institutions; author of many books; his articles have appeared in such periodicals as *Christianity Today*, *New Oxford Review*, and *New York Times Magazine*; see (selected list) *Christ the Tiger* (1967); *The Liturgy Explained* (1981); "Lead Kindly Light," *Communio*, Winter 1981; *Evangelical Is Not Enough* (1984); *Christianity: The True Humanism* (1985) (with J. I. Packer); Interview: "Why Did Thomas Howard Become a Roman Catholic?," *Christianity Today*, 15 May 1985, p.49; *C. S. Lewis: Man of Letters* (1987); "Lead Kindly Light," in Dan O'Neill, *The New Catholics: Contemporary Converts Tell Their Stories* (1987), p.90 (this is a re-publication of the article first published in *Communio*, Winter 1981, written when he was still an Episcopalian) ("My free-church friends and colleagues have the simplest solution of all: the Church - the entire Church - went off the rails about AD 95, and so Church history is a farce. Only the faithful (read 'evangelical') remnant matters. My difficulty with this line of thought has been settled forever by Saint Augustine's argument against the Donatists: no matter how mucked up the Church is, you can't start anything new. It is the only church we have, and Christ calls it His Spouse and sanctifies it with His Holy Spirit, not with the right living of its members. I am aware that this raises the awesome question of Apostolic Succession. The only comment I might venture here is that the notion of there being any such succession apart from the *physical laying on of apostolic hands* is unknown either to the New Testament or the Early Church. You couldn't just hive off and start something *else*...

The fundamental question, of course, is whether the Roman claim is true. There are only two possible answers to that. If I say no, then I have Augustine and Bede and Gregory and Aquinas and Erasmus and Thomas More and Ignatius and Bellarmine and Bossuet and Suarez and Newman and Chesterton and Knox against me for starters, and that makes me nervous. But infinitely more serene than that, I have the colossal *securus judicat orbis terrarum* looking passionlessly at me. 'The calm judgment of the whole world' is against me. The Roman Church has, as it were, nothing to prove. Everyone else has to do the sleeve plucking and arm pawing to validate their cases.

I know the clamorous rejoinders to everything I have said so far. Libraries have been written pro and con. I would interpose the following books between my own remarks here and any agitated letters to the editor: J. H. Newman, *An Essay on the Development of Christian Doctrine*; Ronald Knox, *A Spiritual Aeneid*; Louis Bouyer, *The Spirit and Forms of Frotestantism*; Henri de Lubac, *Catholicism*; Dom Bede Griffiths, *The Golden String*; and the Baltimore Cathechism. Demolish them before you demolish me.

Second, there is the intractable question of authority. Here again we all know the whole discussion before we start. The items that stick in my imagination on this point are these: Christ's words giving authority to His Apostles, and especially His words to Peter, come first, of course. He did not say that the Church would be built on Peter's confession, and it takes jiggery-pokery to make the text say that. He even named Peter Cephas, a stone. Furthermore, Christ founded one Church: He did not ascend leaving behind a book that anyone could take up and run off with (although as an evangelical, I will defend against all comers the authority of the Bible). That Church was built on the foundation of the Apostles, and in the apostolic Church it was the bishops in council who defined doctrine and anathematized heresy. All the heresiarchs believed in the inspiration of the Bible, but it took the Church to say, 'This is orthodox' or 'That is heterodox.' The notion of *Sola Scriptura* is a new-fangled and disastrous one: we have only to look at the jumble of Protestant sects to see this and the stranglehold that the riddle of 'verbal inerrancy' has on every evangelical seminary and theologian. They never talk of anything else at all.

On this point of authority, as an Anglican I am despondent over the bleak fact that there is no magisterium in my church....[M]ost Anglican clergy and theologians will either chuckle in an avuncular way or argue quite earnestly that 'the glory of Anglicanism' is its very lack of definition, or better, its comprehensiveness. It does not worry them at all that two neighboring parish churches, both claiming to be Anglican, will have irreconcilable views on such matters as the priesthood, the Eucharist, the Apostolic Succession, the nature of the sacrament itself, and let's face it, on the church itself. The nice old Anglican phenomenon is here, cranking along after 450 years, to silence any anxious protestings on the part of any fevered layman that this sort of thing is at the very least nonsense, and at the worst cynicism. If this is a quality that we must call 'Anglican,' then I am appalled at being an Anglo-Saxon. It makes it sound synonymous with 'cretinous' or 'woolly-minded.'

Third, there is the sheer question of antiquity and catholicity. I know the Anglican case is that we did not begin with Henry, and that the extreme Anglican case is that we and not Rome represent the true Church of the Fathers. So be it. But something started in the sixteenth century in the scuffle, and it wasn't Rome…If Anglicanism can claim catholicity in the sense of being widespread geographically, that claim is snowed under by the sheer magnitude of the comparable Roman data.

Fourth, there is a factor that I can only call splendor. I do not refer to ceremonial dazzle. The Anglicans are generally better than the Romans on this front, with the exception of what goes on in the basilica in Rome itself. I mean the sheer splendor of the Roman Catholic vision. It is immense. It is full of glory. It is unsupportably bright. But not only this: it is present, in the Mass…[T]he thing I am speaking of seems, somehow, to show itself in that sense of the ineffable sublimity and sheer plenitude that animates not only such phenomena as the liturgical music of Palestrina, Victoria, and Mozart, but also the serene sense in which Roman Catholic philosophy may claim that the Catholic faith, rightly understood, is *absolutely satisfying* to the human intellect…

This brings me to my last point, and Romano Guardini would embody what I would like to say here. There is something about what one finds in Catholic spirituality that is - what is the word I want? - ripe. It believes in the Incarnation, and in the limitations of our mortal flesh. It is wise. It talks of day-to-day matters with an authority that is both high and charitable…The Eucharist is the great paradigm of this. It is very difficult for me to chase down, even for my own satisfaction, just what this quality is. If one reads Guardini's *The Lord*, one will see what I mean. Perhaps I ought to phrase this last point as a question, then: if the Roman Church has nourished that sort of thing (*and* the writings of the Lady Julian and Richard Rolle and Bernard of Clairvaux and Saint John of the Cross and Saint Teresa of Avila and ten thousand others whose work towers above the terrible flea-market junk filling religious bookstores these days), then I must ask myself whether that source is worth finding. Nearly all mere *arguments* - about Petrine claims, about Loreto, about indulgences and the Immaculate Conception and the Perpetual Virginity and infallibility and the Infant of Prague and bingo and the Mafia and horrible Mexican cults and Borgia popes and Torquemada and the Duke of Alba - die away in the light of this question of spirituality. Not that doctrinal questions do not matter. But one pauses before some such syllogism as this: 'If the Church that makes *those* claims has nourished *this* spirituality, then what is one to make of' it?' Of course there are riddles and horrors. Anything as old and enormous as the Roman Church is bound to be a horror show. But then one remembers how Christ insists on calling His poor Church, who paints herself up like the Whore of Babylon sometimes - how He insists on calling her his spotless Bride"); "From Evangelicalism to Rome," in Robert Baram (ed), Spiritual Journeys (revised edition, 1988), p.152; *Evangelical Is Not Enough: Worship of God Liturgy and Sacrament* (1988); *Chance or the Dance: A Critique of Modern Secularism* (1989); *The Novels of Charles Williams* (1991); "Letter to my Brother: A Convert Defends Catholicism," *Crisis*, December 1991, p.23 ("Rome's opulence, her political machinations down through the centuries, her tyrannies and hauteur and self-assertiveness, not to mention the Dionysian romp in the Vatican in the Renaissance, what with Borgia popes and catamites and so forth: all of that is bad - very bad. The Catholic Church knows that. Dante, of course, had half of the popes head down in fiery pits in hell. Chaucer, contemporary with the Lollard Wyclif, but himself a loyal Catholic, is merciless - scathing even - in his portraiture of filthy and cynical clergy. St. Thomas More and Erasmus, contemporary with Luther and Calvin, were at least as vitriolic in their condemnation of Roman evils as were the Reformers…[But] Israel was not less Israel when she was being wicked…The Church is in the same position in its identity as people of God. We have Judas Iscariot, as it were, and Ananias and Sapphira, and other unsavory types amongst us, but we have no warrant to set up shop outside the camp, so to speak…Evangelicals, in their just horror at rampant evils in Catholic history,…unwittingly place themselves somewhat with the Donatists of the fourth century, who wanted to hive off because of certain evils which they felt were widespread in the Church. Augustine and others held the view that you can't go that far. You can't set up shop independently of the lineage of bishops…As far as the ancient, orthodox Church was concerned, nobody could split off…The problems of the Roman Catholic Church (sin, worldliness, ignorance) are, precisely, the problems of the Church. St. Paul never got out of Corinth before he had all of the above problems. Multiply that small company of Christians by 2000 years and hundreds of millions, and you have what the Catholic Church has to cope with. Furthermore, remember that the poor Catholics aren't the only ones who have to cope. Anyone who has ever tried to start himself a church has run slap into it all, with a vengeance…Worldliness, second-generation apathy, ossification, infidelity, loss of vision, loss of zeal, loss of discipline, jiggery-pokery, heresy - it's all there"); *Lead, Kindly Light: My Journey to Rome* (1994) ("First, the antiquity of the Church confronts me. As an Anglican I wanted to see myself as obedient to this ancient Church. But why were we not in obedience, or communion, with that Church as it has understood itself, apparently, for nearly two thousand years? Something had introduced a fissure between us in Canterbury and the Apostolic See in Rome, and the mixture of Henry VIII's sins and highhandedness with Reformation doctrines, to my mind, did not constitute a footing from which one should launch a new church. Whatever could be said about Anglicanism's still having the apostolic succession, we were manifestly out of communion with the See which had constituted the touchstone of Catholic identity for all Christians for more than a millennium before the sixteenth century(andstilldidforninehundred million of my fellow-Christians.

As a Fundamentalist I had discovered while I was in college that it is possible to dismiss the entire Church as having gone off the rails by about AD 95. That is, we, with our open Bibles, knew better than did old Ignatius or Clement, who had been taught by the very apostles themselves, just what the Church is and what it should look like. Never mind that our worship services would have been unrecognizable to them, or that our governance would have been equally unrecognizable: we were right, and the fathers were wrong (about bishops, and about the Eucharist). That settled the matter.

The trouble here, for me, was what these wrong-headed men wrote – about God, about our Lord Jesus Christ, about his Church, about the Christian's walk and warfare – was so titanic, and so rich and so luminous, that their error seemed infinitely truer and more glorious than my truth. I gradually felt that it was I, not they, who was under surveillance. The 'glorious company of the apostles, the noble army of martyrs, and the holy Church throughout all the world' (to quote the ancient hymn, the 'Te Deum') judge *me*, not I them. Ignatius, Polycarp, Clement, Justin, Irenaeus, Cyprian, Cyril, Basil, the Gregorys, Augustine, Ambrose, Hilary, Benedict – it is under the gaze of this senate that I find myself standing. Alas. How tawdry, how otiose, how flimsy, how embarrassing seem the arguments that I had been prepared so gaily to put forward against the crushing radiance of these men's confessions.

The Church is here, in all of its antiquity, judging me. Second, the Church in its authority confronts me. That strange authority to bind and loose which our Lord bestowed on his disciples, recorded in Matthew 16 and 18, has not evaporated from the Church – or so the Church has believed from the beginning. If one will read the story of those decades which followed Pentecost, and especially that followed upon the death of the apostles, one will discover that the unction to teach and to preside in the Church that passed from the Lord to the apostles, and from the apostles to the bishops, was understood to be an apostolic unction. I, for example, could not start up out of the bullrushes and say, 'Hi, everybody! The Lord has led me to be a bishop! I'm starting me a church over here.'

The whole Christian community – bishop, presbyters, deacons, and laity – would have looked gravely at me and gone on about their business…

[T]he Church down through the centuries has understood herself to be the appointed vessel for God's working, in the ordinary run of things. Her authority is not her own. She arrogates nothing to herself. Her bishops are the merest custodians, the merest passers-on, we might say, of the Deposit of Faith. As a Roman Catholic now, I am acutely conscious of this. When someone objects to me, 'But who does the Catholic Church think she is, taking this high and mighty line?' (about abortion, say, or about sexual morality, or about who may or may not come to the Lord's Table), the answer is, 'She doesn't think she is anyone in particular, if you mean that she has set herself up among the wares in the flea market as somehow the best. She has her given task to do – to pass on the teaching given by the apostles – and she has no warrant to change that. She is not taking her cues from the Nielsen ratings, nor from a poll, nor even from a sociological survey as to what people feel comfortable with nowadays. *She* didn't start the Church and it's not her Church.'

The Church is here, in all of its authority, judging me.

Third, the Church in its unity confronts me. This was a most difficult and daunting matter. But one thing was becoming inexorably clear: my erstwhile and happy idea of the Church's unity as being nothing more than the worldwide clutter that we (especially we Fundamentalists) have under our general umbrella was not what the ancient Church had understood by this word 'unity'…

Once again I found myself driven back to the understanding of things at work in the ancient Church. Whatever varieties of expression there may have been – in Alexandria as over against Lyons, or in Antioch as over against Rome – when it came to the Faith itself, and also to order and discipline and piety in the Church, no one was left groping or mulling over the choices in the flea market. Where we (non-Catholics) were pleased to live with a muddle, and even with stark contradictions (Luther vs. Zwingli, for example, on the Lord's Supper), the Church of antiquity was united. No one needed to remain in doubt forever as to what the Church might be, or where it might be found...

There was one Church: the Church was one. And this was a discernible, visible, embodied unity, not a loose aggregate of moderately like-minded believers with their various task forces all across the globe. The bishop of Antioch was not analogous to the General Secretary of the World Evangelical Fellowship, nor to the head of the National Association of Evangelicals...He could speak with the full authority of the Church behind him, whereas these latter gentlemen can only speak for their own organizations...

The Church is here, in its unity, judging me"); *If Your Mind Wanders At Mass* (1995); *EWTN Audio Library, The Journey Home* (5 September 1997); *On Being Catholic* (1997) ("The eternal... attires itself in the routine, the inauspicious, the anonymous. It does this because it reserves itself (it is so holy) for the pure eye of faith...The eye of faith alone can pierce the surface and see Reality. That is why Catholics genuflect when they come to church. They know that this is a holy place, and to be found on one's knee is a very good posture in such precincts. It says, ceremonially, not verbally, 'I am a creature, and thou art my Creator. I am thy child and thou art my Father. I am a subject and thou art my Sovereign. And alas, I am a sinner, and thou art holy'...A Catholic has difficulty in grasping what it is that non-Catholics espouse that precludes this act. Surely we are not mere minds? Surely all of us bring physical gesture to bear on all situations (a wave, a nod, a kiss). Why is the physical excluded here? Surely to exclude it here and here alone is to imply a gnostic (disembodied), not a Christian (incarnational) state of affairs?"); *Splendor in the Ordinary: Your Home as a Holy Place* (2000); *EWTN Audio Library, The Journey Home* (5 February 2001) ("I then read the early Fathers. These are men I'd never heard of. There was a bishop called Ignatius of Antioch. There was a bishop called Polycarp in Smyrna. There was a bishop called Clement. These men had been taught by the Apostles. I mean this was square one! Ignatius had John for his teacher, St. John the Apostle; and in his letters here is the Eucharistic liturgy and here is the Episcopate.

And the rest is history you might say. That was the camel's nose in the tent you might say, and from there on it was an inevitable straight line...right through to the Catholic Church. And I might say to those who think, 'But isn't there an awful lot of clutter that you have to beat your way through, shrubbery? – I would say there is a sense in which there is a remorseless simplicity, because the question comes down to one question, what is the Church?...

I think it's true and fair to say that for very many believers the formula is 'Jesus, the Bible, and me' – which is not altogether a bad formula, let's face it. It just doesn't happen to be what Jesus left and it's not what the Apostles understood to be the enterprise that they were engaged in. If you wanted to become a Christian in those early decades, it was very much a question of coming and submitting yourself to the teaching authority of the Apostles, or the local bishop, who was appointed by the Apostles, and so on.

And here's this titanic, living entity moving down through history and I think the people who feel, well, essentially it's Jesus, the Bible, and me, and Church is really somewhat marginal, they need to have another look at the thing…

I often thought, as I was teaching at a very good Evangelical college, it used to occur to me again and again, you know, if the Apostles were to pop up briefly out of their coffins and come visit us on this campus, they wouldn't know what was going on. They wouldn't know what this enterprise was. They would say, 'Where is your bishop; where is the Eucharist; and where is the authority of the Church? Our apostolic spokesman, St. Paul, says the Church is the pillar and ground of the truth. How do you all relate to that?'"); *Dove Descending: A Journey Into T. S. Eliot's "Four Quartets"* (2006); *Narnia and Beyond: A Guide to the Fiction of C. S. Lewis* (2006) (with Peter Kreeft); *A Treasury of Thomas Howard* (2007); *EWTN Audio Library, The Journey Home* (10 September 2007); Vivian W. Dudro (ed), *The Night Is Far Spent.*

Hudson, Deal Wyatt - political activist; b. 20 November 1949, Denver, Colorado; c. 1984 (his wife was also a convert from the Baptists); raised as a Presbyterian; educated at the University of Texas-Austin (studied Philosophy); became a Southern Baptist while at the university; attended Princeton Theological Seminary; graduate school in Theology and Literature at Emory University; taught philosophy at Mercer University, Atlanta 1980–89 and at Fordham University 1989–1995; led into the Catholic Church by the thought of St. Thomas Aquinas, St. Augustine and Jacques Maritain; in 1995 he becamepublisheroftheconservative Catholic magazine, *Crisis*; director of Catholic Outreach for George W. Bush's presidential campaign in 2000 and 2004; in 2004 accusations of sexual misconduct led to his severing his relationship with the Bush White House and from his post at Fordham; prominent Catholic supporter of John McCain's presidential campaign; president of Catholic Advocate; has written, edited, or contributed to several books, and also for certain newspapers and journals; married to Theresa Carver Hudson (two children of the marriage); see (selected list) (ed), *Understanding Maritain* (1987) (with Matthew J. Mancini); (ed), *The Future of Thomism: The Maritain Sequence* (1992) (with Dennis William Moran); (ed), *Sigrid Undset: On Saints and Sinners* (1994); *Happiness and the Limits of Satisfaction* (1995); An *American Conversion: One Man's Discovery of Beauty and Truth in Times of Crisis* (2003) ("The Catholic Church stands for a conception of reality very different from that preached by the fundamentalist version of Protestantism. Reality in the Catholic tradition is objective in a way that the recent generations have rejected, and desperately need to reclaim.

My father was raised as a natural Aristotelian, although he never read a word of philosophy...[H] e understood, as did those of his generation, that values belong to the world outside the mind, that the mind discovers them through the course of experience and reflection. The meaning of life is not something a person invents. It is 'out there' and has to be wrested or received from the world as it is. Nature, in other words, precedes our choices and our understanding. Catholics of an older generation called this the natural law.

The last few generations have been raised as natural Nietzscheans, again without having read the so-called father of existentialism. Values are created by each individual. There is no single meaning to life that comprises all human lives; in fact, the very suggestion lacks authenticity. Each person does not discover but creates the world that he or she decides to live in. Imitation is not flattery but evinces a lack of personal choice regarding one's values, as if the choice of values itself was more important than the truth of them.

Highly sophisticated versions of the infatuation with subjectivity followed the sixties. Nietzsche was morphed into something called postmodernism, which basically announced the end of all objectivity, or what is called the logocentric view of the world. Logos, of course, is the Greek word for form or word and is used in the prologue to the Gospel of John to describe the second person of the Trinity, who became incarnate in Jesus Christ: 'In the beginning was the Word...and the Word became flesh and dwelt among us.'

If the world is not logocentric, then the Catholic Church is wrong. All Christians who accept the truth of the Scriptures believe that God created the world through the Word, and the Word's imprint and form is found everywhere in creation. 'Through him all things were made.' The world, the 'out there' of our experience, is not an utterly alien thing - mysterious, yes, but mysterious in a way that can gradually reveal its depths and allow us to see into it. Mystery does not mean that something is unknowable; it means that knowing it requires time and patience, and that all that can be known will never be known, except to God"); *Onward, Christian Soldiers: The Growing Political Power of Catholics and Evangelicals in the United States* (2008).

Hughes, John Jay–priest; b. 14 May 1928, Manhattan, New York City; c. Easter 1960; his father, William Dudley Foulke Hughes (1898-1964), an Episcopal clergyman, was headmaster of the Cathedral Choir School and Precentor at the Cathedral of St. John the Divine in New York City; through his mother, Marguerite Montgomery Jay he is a direct descendant of John Jay, one of the Founding Fathers and first Chief Justice of the United States; his father's family, originally from Wales, had contributed many Presbyteriam ministers, and later Episcopalian clergymen; his mother died when he was six; "from age twelve I knew that I wanted to be a priest"; close relationship with his father's second wife, Frances ("Bina") (1903-1997); educated at Harvard University (BA in 1948); studied Anglican theology at the House of the Sacred Mission, Kelham, near Newark-on-Trent, England 1948-1950; completed his studies at the General Theological Seminary of the Episcopal Church in New York City; his spirituality was most deeply influenced by Jean-Baptiste Chautard's *The Soul of All Apostolic Work*; up till now Anglo-Catholic ("My personal faith in 1950, and for a decade thereafter, could be called 'Catholicism without the pope'"); had long-standing concerns about whether to convert to Rome; eventually ordained into the Episcopal ministry in 1953; thought of a monastic vocation, but settled into parish work; his later reception into the Catholic Church led to an estrangement from his father; entered the Canisianum in Innsbruck to study for the Catholic priesthood, but eventually left; finally accepted by Bishop Höffner for the diocese of Munster; his research into Anglican Orders resulted in two books and a plea by him to be conidtionally ordained to the priesthood ("The orders of the Episcopalian bishops who had ordained me deacon and priest respectively were not identical with the orders condemned by Pope Leo XIII in 1896; these prelates could trace their consecration, through others, to Old Catholic and other prelates recognized by Rome as true bishops"); this was eventually accepted and on 28 January 1968 he became the first Anglican priest to be conditionally ordained to the Catholic priesthood; later teaching posts at the Catholic University of Louvain and at St. Louis University; joined the St. Louis archdiocese, teaching at St. Louis University and working as personal theologian of Archbishop John L. May; see *Absolutely Null and Utterly Void: An Account of the Papal Condemnation of Anglican*

Orders (1968); *Stewards of the Lord: A Reappraisal of Anglican Orders* (1970); *Man For Others: Reflections on Christian Priesthood* (1970); *Praying in Silence: An Introduction to Centering Prayer* (1982); *A Pocket Catechism for Kids* (1983); *Sea Psalms* (1988); *Pontiffs: Popes Who Shaped History* (1994); "Hope: When a Loved One Dies in Sin," *Crisis*, March 2007 (reprinted in *Crisis*, 6 April 2012; *Stories Jesus Told: Modern Meditations on the Parables* (1999); *No Ordinary Fool: A Testimony to Grace* (2008) (autobiography) ("A conversation with two English Catholics…initiated the change…I told them that I considered myself a Catholic already. What made it impossible for me to join their Church, I explained, were the papal claims to primacy (the pope as universal bishop, with all other bishops papal functionaries rather than chief shepherds of their local churches) and to infallibility.

Every Roman Catholic church I entered, I told these new friends, displayed in its tract rack numerous publications arguing that non-Catholic Christians were floundering in uncertainty advancing mutually conflicting claims that left people confused about what to believe. Catholics, this popular apologetic contended, possessed in Rome an infallible voice that gave the answer to every question…

'But that's not what we believe at all,' my friends responded…What then, I asked, did Catholics believe?

The answer I received was unlike any explanation of papal infallibility I had ever encountered. The pope, they assured me, was certainly no oracle He possessed, according to the definition of the First Vatican Council in 1870, not so much a personal infallibility as the infallibility of the Church. Even this he exercised only under narrowly defined, and correspondingly rare, circumstances…

The best theologians agreed that infallibility was essentially negative - not inspiration but protection from error. Papal definitions were nor necessarily the last word. Indeed, given the limitations of human language there could never be, strictly speaking, a 'last word' in matters of faith, apart from Jesus himself as Word of God - the Father's personal communication to us. The truths of faith would always require restatement as language and patterns of thought changed, and insight deepened. In a given case, it might have been better for a pope to have said nothing, or to have expressed himself differently. But on the rare occasions when he articulated the Church's faith as its official and supreme teacher, at least he would not be wrong…

My study of Church history had persuaded me that my Anglican forebears in the sixteenth century had stumbled into schism. There was no need to assign blame, and there was clearly plenty to go around. But having recognized that I was the heir of that schism, it was incumbent upon me to do something about it.

I found myself confronted, as an Anglican priest, by the question put to Jesus by his critics: 'By what authority do you do these things?' (Mark 11:28). I had no answer. I realized that I could not, in conscience, remain in the Anglican Church. Once my doubts and misunderstandings about Catholic teaching had been completely removed, I had to act on my convictions, however difficult that might he.

Completely removed? No, that is an overstatement. To the end I had nothing more than moral certainty...Another convert, the late Monsignor Ronald Knox, wrote once: 'In the end the convert is faced with just one question. The Church says: "Look into my eyes. Do you trust me?" All else is irrelevant'").

Huizenga, Leroy Andrew – theologian; b. Minot, North Dakota; c. 23 April 2011 (Easter Vigil); baptized Catholic, but raised Lutheran; studied at Jamestown College, North Dakota (BA in Religion 1996); Master of Divinity from Princeton Theological Seminary 2001; PhD in New Testament from Duke University 2006; Assistant Professor of New Testament at Wheaton College, Illinois 2006-2011; became a Catholic; Chair of the Department of Theology and Director of the Christian Leadership Center at the University of Mary, Bismarck, North Dakota; several articles for learned journals, notably *First Things*; married to Kari (two children of the marriage); see *The Akeda in Matthew* (2006); *The New Isaac: Tradition and Intertextuality in the Gospel of Matthew* (2009); *Reading the Bible Intertextually* (2009) (with Richard B. Hays and Stefan Alkier); "A Modest Proposal," *First Things, On The Square*, 26 September 2011 ("A major reason I became Catholic concerned the Church's profound theology of the Eucharist, which I (as a New Testament scholar) found squared well with the biblical witness, once certain modern lenses fell like scales from my eyes. Paul speaks of our real participation in the body and blood of Christ as that which unites the Church (1 Corinthians 10:16-17) and soon thereafter remarks that some of the Corinthians have fallen infirm and dropped over dead because of their eating and drinking unworthily (11:27-32). One doesn't die from mishandling symbols; one dies from mishandling that in which God is found, as readers familiar with Uzzah's demise in 2 Samuel 6 and viewers of *Raiders of the Lost Ark* know.

In Luke 24:30-31 the risen Jesus vanishes from the two disciples' sight precisely after Jesus 'took the bread and blessed and broke it and gave it to them' to signal that Christ is to be found thereafter in the Eucharist. John 6 presents a view of the Eucharist as high as any, bringing to mind the famous description of St. John's disciple, St. Ignatius, of the Eucharist as the 'medicine of immortality.' Having done the exegetical work, I must confess with true charity I don't understand how some can strain out the gnat of transubstantiation in John 6 (or some other high view, such as the Lutheran) having swallowed the camel of the Incarnation just a few chapters prior. Indeed, we Catholics believe so strongly in both the Incarnation and transubstantiation that we engage in the real 'Worship of the Eucharist' (*Catechism of the Catholic Church*, 1378) as if it's God, because we believe it is.

Or at least we're supposed to. As a new Catholic, I'm beginning to wonder if the way we receive the Eucharist at Mass has served to undercut our particularly Catholic understanding of the Eucharist. *Lex orandi lex credendi*, after all. Liturgy teaches. A Pew survey of religious knowledge taken last year discovered that 45 percent of Catholics 'do not know that their church teaches that the bread and wine used in Communion do not merely symbolize but actually become the body and blood of Christ.' (Of course, regular mass-goers seem better informed.) And of course the liturgy does more than just teach, as if religion were merely a matter of propositional doctrine; liturgy ought also inspire deep reverence for the Eucharist, because, again, we believe it's God"); *The New Isaac: Tradition and Intertextuality in the Gospel of Matthew*(2012);"The White House's Contraceptive Kulturkampf," *First Things, On The Square*, 17 May 2012 ("We must…explain why Christians historically have held contraception to be an intrinsic evil. Otherwise, we'll be regarded at best as irrational eccentrics the state merely tolerates. In the long run, those simply tolerated tend not to fare well. It is not important, I think, that we actually convince people that Catholics are right on contraception, as amply demonstrated by the support for Catholic rights shown by many Protestants who accept contraception. I do think it is important that people see that we have substantive and well-thought-out reasons for why Catholics reject contraception (as did all major Christian bodies until 1930). We need to show that what is now the Catholic position isn't simply the fruit of a papal diktat but rather that our position is beautiful, issuing forth from the most profound reflection on Nature and the human person, that our position is a matter of reason and not only revelation, that it's not really a matter of a mere 'religious exemption' at all.

We ought to show how our thinking flows from our reasoned and realist conviction that grace completes nature, while the modern biotechnological nightmare we're facing is a secularized version of the old voluntarist and nominalist idea that grace destroys it. Modern wills use technology to shape their bodies apart from any concern for our natures as embodied men and women. We might make the point that contraception isn't healthcare because pregnancy isn't a disease, even though our Gnostic culture considers children a cancer. We ought to argue that *Humanae Vitae* has proven prophetic. In the face of the West's demographic decline, we ought to ask progressives what the ultimate ideal future towards which they're progressing actually *is* - a sterile secular simulacrum of Eden bereft of the messiness of children?"); "God With Us, Every Day," *First Things, On The Square*, 27 December 2012; "Ban Contraception," *First Things, On The Square*, 7 February 2013 ("In *Humanae Vitae*, Pope Paul VI dealt not so much with issues of particularly Catholic morality but with the profound issues of the human person and human culture, arguing - indeed, prophesying, as it turns out - that contraception would lead to a 'general lowering of morality' and the treatment of women as 'mere instruments of selfish enjoyment.' He warned, too, of 'the danger of this power passing into the hands of those public authorities who care little for the precepts of the moral law' who 'may even impose their use on everyone.' When dealing with sexuality, we are not merely in the realm of religion but the realm of reason. These are not matters of religious scruples, but matters of public concern concerning the common good. Thus, when Michael Gerson writes, 'It is a valid public health goal to promote the broad availability of contraception' so long as it doesn't trample fundamental rights, the faithful Catholic must object. For the widespread availability of contraception involves risks to women and consequences for society even beyond those envisioned by the prophetic Pope Paul VI.

Research results have found the Pill to be carcinogenic, which may help explain the dramatic rise of breast cancer rates since the Pill's introduction. There are also real ecological concerns, as European studies have found high levels of synthetic hormones (used in contraceptives) in fish, leading to their sterility. Edward Green, senior research scientist at the Harvard School of Public Health, defended Pope Benedict's claim that saturating the African continent with condoms wasn't helping in the fight against AIDS. And whereas Malthusian demographers once fired apocalyptic fears of a population bomb, many are now concerned with the social and economic upheaval involved in the demographic decline that most modernized nations face").

Hume, Paul Chandler – music critic and radio broadcaster; b. 13 December 1915, Chicago, Illinois; d. 27 November 2001, Baltimore, Maryland; brought up in a Presbyterian family ("I was a Presbyterian because my mother had been an Episcopalian and my father a Congregationalist. When they married they agreed to compromise and join the Presbyterian Church because it seemed a good middle-of-the-road solution"); he studied the piano for seven years and the organ for four years, and had seven years of voice training; educated at the University of Chicago (majored in English, but also studied music history and theory); conversion influenced by Herbert Schwartz (see below); conscientious objector during World War II; music editor for the *Washington Post* 1946-1982; host of a long-running classical music program on WGMS Radio, Washington D.C.; guest commentator for intermission broadcasts from the New York Metropolitan Opera; Professor of Music, Georgetown University 1950-1977; Visiting Professor of Music, Yale University 1975-1983; received a Peabody Award in 1977 for his outstanding achievement in music criticism; in 1979 awarded the prestigious University of Pennsylvania Glee Club Award of Merit; married in 1949 to the writer on medical history, Ruth Fox, 1922-1980 (four children of the marriage); he wrote with her two volumes on the life of the Polish pianist and statesman Jan Paderewski, and a book on John McCormack; he was perhaps best known for his critical review of a vocal concert given in 1950 by Margaret Truman, the daughter of the then President, Harry S. Truman, who wrote him a vitriolic letter in response (they later became friends); see *Catholic Church Music* (1956); "Double Take," in John A. O'Brien (ed), *The Road to Damascus, Vol. V: Where Dwellest Thou* (1956) ("I was by no means a skeptic, like great-uncle David Hume. I believed very definitely that God had designed a human intellect capable of comprehending knowledge. As far as belief in absolute truth went, I was right in there with St. Thomas and the Council of Trent. The confusion resulting from good old free interpretation and individual judgment had long since reached the *reductio ad absurdum* point. It boiled down to something very simple and literal, as it has to so many converts: somebody was right and somebody was wrong. But if there was such a thing as belief being 'right' or 'wrong' then there must be an authority to define what is and what is not"); *The Lion of Poland* (1962) (with Ruth Hume); *King of Song: The Story of John McCormack* (1964) (with Ruth Hume); *Puccini: The Man and His Music* (1977) (with William Weaver); *Verdi: The Man and His Music* (1977); the Paul Hume papers are kept at the University of Georgetown.

Hunt, Duane Garrison – bishop, scholar, editor, author, administrator, and radio speaker;

b. 19 September 1884, Reynolds, Nebraska; c. January 1913 (received at St. Thomas the Apostle Church, Chicago); d. 31 March 1960, Salt Lake City, Utah; parents devout Methodists; educated at Cornell College, Iowa; taught in the public schools of Iowa, then entered the University of Iowa Law School in 1911 (forced to withdraw because of poor eyesight); entered graduate school at the University of Chicago in the field of public speaking; after his conversion he taught in the speech department at the University of Utah 1913-1916 he studied for the priesthood under the Sulpician Fathers at St. Patrick's Seminary, Menlo Park, California; ordained to the priesthood for the diocese of Salt Lake City in June 1920; chancellor, vicar-general, rector of the cathedral, and diocesan administrator; appointed Papal Chamberlain in 1924; he was the weekly speaker on NBC's radio program, "Catholic Hour", 1927-1949; made a domestic prelate in 1930; consecrated bishop of Salt Lake City 28 October 1937 and served in that post until his death; the first convert from Methodism to become a Catholic bishop in the United States; fine apologist for the faith; one delightful story: As he waited at the Cedar City train station to be taken to a parish Confirmation, he enjoyed a chat with some residents of the southern Utah town. The topic turned, as it often does in Utah, to religion. When the bishop said he was Catholic, one woman shook her head and exclaimed, "All these new religions springing up all over the place!"; buried in Mount Calvary Catholic Cemetery, Salt Lake City; see *The People, the Clergy and the Church* (1928); "Not For Mental Cowards," in Severin and Stephen Lamping, OFM (ed), *Through Hundred Gates* (1939) (similar to, though briefer than, the next article) ("To my great surprise, I found that the accusations against the Church could not be proved. I mention one illustration, as typical of others. A friend gave me a pamphlet in which the author tried to prove that St. Peter was never in Rome. He asserted most confidently, in the light of his argument, that the primary claims of the Catholic Church were false. I read the pamphlet, and then read some Catholic literature on the same subject. I found that the Catholic Church could support her claim by a mass of evidence, from the best of non-Catholic historians. The result was, of course, that I had more respect for the Catholic Church after the incident than I had before. It was precisely the same with every subject I looked into, whether it was criticism of the confessional, of indulgences, of the Knights of Columbus, or Catholic education, or of anything else concerning the Catholic religion"); "Through the Church to God," in John A. O'Brien (ed), *The Road to Damascus, Vol. II* (1950) (reprinted in *This Rock*, October 1993) ("I reviewed once more the whole process of my thinking. Starting all over again, I set down the premises which were undebatable. As though it was yesterday, I recall sketching my analysis: I believe in God; I need to be taught the truths which He wishes me to believe; since Christ is God and came on earth to teach me this truth, it is to Him I must look. But how does Christ teach me? There could be, I answered, only three ways: (1) By direct and personal revelation; (2) Through a written record (the Sacred Scripture); (3) Through the agency of men, that is, through an organization commissioned by Him for that purpose.

Did Christ, I asked, teach me by direct revelation? Not that I was aware. Furthermore, if, in spite of this insensitiveness on my part, He really had chosen this means, then He must teach all men in the same way. Honesty of intention and the sincere desire to hear His voice would be the only prerequisites. But how, then, could the fact be explained away that so many men of obvious and unquestionable good will held so many and such contradictory beliefs? With a gesture of finality, I discarded the first possibility.

Did he teach me through the Bible? Here was old ground, well-trodden, thoroughly mulled over. But how was I to know that it was the Bible, the inspired record of God's dealings with men? Perhaps it contained much spurious matter; perhaps its canon was uncertain - books left out which should have been retained, books incorporated which should be rejected. Again, how could I know the real meaning of the many disputed passages? There were, I reminded myself, over two hundred religious groups all claiming the Bible as their font and origin, all asserting their particular interpretations as correct. My common sense repeated, what I already knew, that Christ must have appointed some agent to compose the Sacred Scripture and to interpret its meaning for all men.

Why should I gag, then, at considering calmly and dispassionately the possibility of the third answer, even if it led directly to the Catholic Church? Who else could this appointed teacher be? What could she be but infallible? My right to certitude was as great as that of the fortunate few who heard the Master speak, who saw Him pass along the way. And if He was in truth divine, and if He had appointed His agents to teach and govern and sanctify in His name, He could not help but make them share His infallibility. I needed no biblical texts to bolster my assurance that His Church was founded upon a rock; it could not be otherwise. Her infallibility was as inevitable and as inescapable as His own. It was His own.

Perhaps this is the correct point in my narrative to indicate explicitly how I reacted to the stock argument against the Catholic Church. As my decision became apparent, it was unavoidable that I should be asked for explanations. Why was I attracted to the Church? Did I not know that she had ingloriously failed? How could I get around the facts of history? No doubt the reader is thoroughly informed about the oft-repeated premise that the Catholic Church had been untrue to her divine calling and had failed sometime during early centuries or Middle Ages. (There is no agreement among the critics about when the failure occurred.) The Church fell into evil ways, the argument continues; her ministers became selfish, dishonorable, and corrupt, even a few of the popes falling into public sins. According to the argument, the Church departed from the original Gospel of Christ and introduced spurious doctrines of faith. Therefore, the argument concludes, the Church lost the grace of God and the authority to speak as His agent. A reformation was necessary. The old Church had to be abandoned; a new organization (or organizations?) was needed to lead Christianity back to its pristine purity.

Over and over again I had heard and read this argument. As it failed to hold me back, my friends asked why. Was I ignoring it? Had I closed my mind to obvious facts? Let me say most emphatically that I had not ignored the argument, I had analyzed and studied it to the best of my ability. The result? The more I thought about it, the more illogical it seemed. How was it possible, I asked, for the Church to fail when the divine Lord had guaranteed that she would not fail? But then there were the evil deeds of the Church leaders. What about them? They could not he erased from the record. They were there for all to see and contemplate. Were they not conclusive? They seemed to be conclusive for others; why not for me?

Perhaps these facts were conclusive for me; but, if so, it was in the other direction. If they proved anything, it was that the Catholic Church is indestructible. She must be solid indeed, I reasoned, not to have been destroyed. The Church had lived through enough calamities to annihilate a mere human institution. The salient fact is that She had lived through them, a feat of survival which becomes more extraordinary the more the historical mistakes are played up. The sad experiences of the Church, to which my attention had been called, only demonstrated her divine nature. Far from frightening me away from Her, they helped open the door for me"); *The Continuity of the Catholic Church* (1959) (written to counter Mormon claims that there was an apostasy in the early centuries of the Church and a loss of Divine authority) ("The sources from which I draw material are the sacred Scriptures and history. In these it is clearly demonstrated that the person known as our Lord and Savior, Jesus Christ, established the Christian religion; for this fact, no proof need be offered here. What is necessary to note is that Christianity is both visible and invisible, both physical and spiritual, both body and soul. Man himself, for whom Christianity was ordained, is a composite of body and soul; most reasonably, therefore, the religion which he needs must be a composite of body and soul.

Here is another illustration of what I mentioned a moment ago, and I digress to call attention to it. There are Christians, how many I do not know, who deny that our Lord established a visible church. They believe that what he gave the world was a spiritual gospel only, along with his exemplary way of life. According to them, the organization is merely a human creation and is subject, therefore, to human changes from time to time. In my judgment this opinion does not deserve an explicit refutation; it will be sufficiently dealt with in the data which I present relative to other subjects.

My thesis is stated very simply: The Church which our Lord established is continuous from him to the present day and will be continuous until the end of the world. This means, first of all, that the body of the Church, the organization, has lived every day during the past nineteen centuries and will continue to live every day until the end of the world. It means, furthermore, that the soul of the Church, her doctrines, her ideals, her means of grace, and her supernatural protection, have remained constant, that they have not changed and never will change").

Hunt, Gaillard – historian, editor and civil servant; b. 8 September 1862, New Orleans, Louisiana; d. 20 March 1924; son of William Henry Hunt, Secretary of the Navy under President James Garfield; in 1901 he married Mary Goodfellow Hunt (1871-1934), the grandniece of Bishop John Carroll (1735-1815); converted to his wife's Catholicism; distinguished historian; expert on the American Revolution and the relationship between Catholicism and the formation of the American nation; served in the Department of State 1887-1909 and 1917-1924 in various capacities; chief of the Division of Manuscripts at the Library of Congress 1909-1917; historian-general of the American Historical Association; president of the American Catholic Historical Association; his son, Gaillard Hunt, Jr. (1903-1949), a novelist; buried with his wife in St. John the Evangelist Catholic Church Cemetery, Forest Glen, Montgomery County, Maryland; see *The Life of James Madison* (1902); *The Department of State of the United States: Its History and Functions* (1914); "The Virginia Declaration of Rights and Cardinal Bellarmine," *Catholic Historical Review*, October 1917, p.276 ("The American idea went far beyond Magna Carta, for that declared that certain rights and liberties could not be taken away save by the law of the land. America proclaimed that there were certain rights and liberties which could *never* be taken away, even by law. It set these rights above the law. Never before had a people voluntarily subscribed to certain definite principles of right which they bound themselves to regard"); ."The American Idea," *Catholic World*, June 1919, p.293; Patrick Allitt, *Catholic Converts: British and American Intellectuals Turn to Rome* (1997), pp.137; 245-247 ("The historians Gaillard Hunt, Ross Hoffman [see above], and Carlton Hayes [see above], for example, all argued that the U.S. Constitution embodied the wisdom of the 'great tradition' of natural law political philosophy which traced its roots back through the pagan-Christian synthesis in Aquinas to the principles of Augustine's *City of God.* All denied that its intellectual origins could be traced to John Locke...

Gaillard Hunt...traced some of Thomas Jefferson's ideas on liberty to Catholic scholars such as Cardinal Robert Bellarmine and argued that the Constitution belonged to the Catholic tradition of natural law and limited government").

Hunter, Ian – lawyer and biographer; b. 1945; c. 2 July 2006 (his brother Graeme was received in 2007 and his mother, Margaret Elizabeth Hunter, was received later that year, at the age of ninety-five); educated at the University of Toronto (degrees in Political Science (BA) and Law (LLB and JD)); Professor of Law at Western University, London, Ontario, Canada, 1974-1996 (later Emeritus Professor); also taught at other Canadian and English universities; Visiting Scholar at Wolfson College, Cambridge University; author of several biographies; regular columnist in Canada in the *Globe and Mail* and the *National Post* in which he strongly defended orthodox Catholic teaching; Anglicanism was the religion of his adulthood, but he became disillusioned with it; see (ed), Things Past / Malcolm Muggeridge (1978); Nothing to Repent: The Life of Hesketh Pearson (1987); Malcolm Muggeridge: A Life (2003); (ed), The Very Best of Malcolm Muggeridge (2003); "Hilaire Belloc and Being Principled in Politics," catholicregister.org, 25 March 2010; "Religion vs. Agnostic Know-Nothings," catholicregister.org, 30 September 2010 ("[T]he proposition that agnosticism is the only honest religious position, while useful to provoke discussion, [suffers] three basic flaws: it is an oxymoron; it is contrary to human experience and therefore likely to be false; and it is a placebo for the spiritually timid.

The Oxford English Dictionary defines agnosticism as the belief that nothing beyond material phenomena can possibly be known. Given that definition the proposition is an oxymoron. It refutes itself. If nothing about religion can reliably be known, then it cannot be known whether anything about religion can reliably be known. If it is impossible to decide the truth or falsity of religious claims, then it is impossible to decide whether agnosticism is a preferable religious claim to even the narrowest or most fanatical religious prejudice.

Like all deconstructionist propositions, it deconstructs itself. It is a variation on the old 'All men are liars' conundrum; if true, it must be false. If false – if indeed all men are not liars – then the person making the assertion cannot be believed for he is himself a liar. An oxymoron does not advance understanding. It serves only to inveigle one into self-contradiction.

Second, if indeed agnosticism is the only honest religious position, this is contrary to human experience in other fields of human endeavor, and therefore unlikely to be true. If it were impossible to decide truth or falsity in other areas, human advancement would be impossible. Take science and medicine, for example; these disciplines would be stillborn. But, you say, these are 'hard' sciences. True enough, but agnosticism would also render music, art, invention and philosophy impossible.

Philosophy's rules of logic are as inexorable as the rules of mathematics; indeed they are often corollaries to the rules of mathematics. Logic stipulates that propositions can be tested for truth and falsity. But the proposition as framed denies the possibility of truth or falsity in respect of one particular area of human inquiry, religion. At very least, a proponent of a proposition so contrary to human experience bears a heavy onus to prove why and how religion is so unusual, so idiosyncratic, that it is the one area in which deeper, truer understanding is, by definition, impossible.

Finally, the proposition appeals to the spiritually timid. Its attraction is that it gives the illusion of a safe harbor in a rolling sea. In fact, it offers no harbor, only spiritual seasickness. It leaves the voyager without a compass, guide, destination and hope...

Aimless in a churning sea, the timid agnostic frets that he might put ashore in the wrong harbor. Admittedly, that is a possibility. But perhaps even a false harbor is better than no harbor at all...

The psalmist of the Old Testament wrote: 'The fool has said in his heart: "There is no God."' More honest, more commendable, is the atheist fool, for he is more likely to be right than the agnostic know-nothing"); That Time of Year: The Best of Ian Hunter (2011) (account of his conversion story; this extract is also available at *catholiceducation.org* under the title "My Path to Rome" and in *Canadian Converts: Roads to Rome* (2009)) ("It is difficult to write objectively about something as intensely personal as conversion; I recognize also that my own conversion is but one case among many, but since it is the one I know best, it is what I shall try here to explain.

Let me dare to begin with a question that perhaps should best come last: What is the alternative to conversion? Except what G. K. Chesterton, writing of his own conversion, called a sorry surrender to '…the awful actualities of our time?' I came to believe that there is no answer, except Rome, to that question.

Still it is legitimate to ask why someone, in the sixth decade of his life, with more of life behind than ahead of him, would abandon his denomination and the liturgies and traditions with which he is familiar, for the remote, somewhat intimidating vastness of Rome. In short, why become a Roman Catholic?

Well, all such stories are long ones, and just as aspects of one's human birth remain mysterious, so also aspects of one's spiritual rebirth, perhaps opaque beyond human explanation. But here is what I know. My conversion story is, in part, the story of four men, only two of whom were Catholics…

[T]he first of four men responsible for my becoming a Catholic, by name Karol Wojtyla, a relatively obscure Polish Cardinal who astonished the world when on October 16, 1978 he stepped out on the balcony at St. Peter's, announced his new identity as Pope John Paul II, and declared in a dozen or more languages: 'Be not afraid... Open the doors to Jesus Christ!'

In that sense I suppose that I am what might be called 'a JP II Catholic'; if so, I am honored to be called after a man I so much admire. Without the papacy of John Paul II, I doubt I would have been drawn so inexorably to the Roman Catholic Church…

With growing admiration, I watched John Paul II discharge the duties of his office, including his worldwide pilgrimages – especially the triumphant homecoming to Poland. Wherever he went, I noticed how he confounded the ecumenists and pluralists. He appeared always cheerful; he listened attentively, he exuded warmth and compassion. But his words were blunt and uncompromising, so much so that they startled even those like me who had longed to hear such things said: 'Do not be afraid of the truth.' 'Human life is forever,' he said. On the ordination of women? No. On abortion: No. On marriage: Indissoluble. On celibacy: Yes. On priestly vows: Forever. This was a man who clearly knew his faith and his mind and was not afraid to speak unequivocally about either.

The main reason why Pope John Paul II was so significant in my conversion is that without his pontificate I doubt that I would have wrestled with the ecclesiological claims that the Roman Catholic Church makes. Ecclesiology might seem an arcane subject, but for me it was pivotal. Yet nothing in my family background or upbringing would have prompted me to reflect on it. Just the opposite, in fact.

This brings me to the second influential man in my story, my father. My father, James Hogg Hunter, was born in 1890 in Maybole, Scotland - in the Covenanting district of Scotland where men and women died as martyrs to the Protestant faith. Two of my father's novels (*How Sleep the Brave* (1955) and *The Hammer of God* (1965)) are about the persecution of Scottish Covenanters. My father was a Presbyterian and among his bedrock beliefs was the conviction that Rome was the enemy of the Christian faith. It is difficult to communicate today the depth and sincerity of his conviction.

My father immigrated to Canada in the early part of the twentieth century, and he spent the next six decades engaged in Christian journalism, primarily as editor of a monthly magazine called *The Evangelical Christian*. In its pages he denounced '...Popery in all its forms' and, as he put it '...sought to expose the shams and deceits of this "Mystery of Iniquity", the Roman Catholic Church.'

The zenith of my father's anti-Catholic polemics was his 1945 book, *The Great Deception*, a book that would be banned today as hate literature...Yet, when I consider who played a part in my decision, my father is near the top of the list, and I'll tell you why: *he took religion seriously.* In fact, his faith was the most important thing in his life. For him Christianity was not a convenience but a life creed; attending church was not a social outing but an opportunity to worship in the presence of Almighty God; religion was not a subject for social chatter, but a life-changing commitment...

Because he took his faith seriously, because it was the defining feature and center of my father's life, I wonder sometimes what - had he lived to survey the ruins of Protestantism, where mainline Churches like the Anglican and United Church compete in bringing ridicule upon the faith he cherished - he would have done; given this sorry spectacle, might he not have made a similar pilgrimage to Rome? I wonder, but can never know.

The third influence was a man who did not himself become a Roman Catholic, C. S. Lewis. All my Christian life I have been reading and learning from C. S. Lewis' books; particularly to pick three - *Mere Christianity, Surprised by Joy*, and *The Great Divorce.*

The distinguished American novelist, Walker Percy, once remarked on the countless converts who had come to Catholicism through the writings of C. S. Lewis: Walker Percy wrote: '...[In stories told by Catholic converts] writers one might expect, from Aquinas to Merton, turn up. But guess who turns up most often? C. S. Lewis.'

Yet Lewis himself never converted; he lived, and died (in November 1963) a lifelong Anglican...[I]n the nineteen forties, fifties and early sixties, when Lewis lived and his influence was at its height, it was still possible to regard the Church of England (particularly in its Anglo-Catholic manifestations) as part of that '…one holy, catholic, and apostolic Church' that all Christians, when they recite the Nicene Creed, profess to believe in.

Today, such a belief requires self-deception, or at least willful blindness. In his time, Lewis was spared the spectacle of what the Anglican Church has become, with Bishop Michael Ingham devising rites for same-sex unions, while New Hampshire Bishop Vicki Gene Robinson abandons his wife and children to take up with a homosexual lover. In short, in C. S. Lewis' time, the Anglican Church was not yet the self-parody it has become.

Walter Hooper, Lewis' confidante, editor and biographer, sometime Anglican priest, and most assiduous keeper of the Lewis flame, in 1988 converted to Catholicism. He believes, and has said publicly, that Lewis would do likewise were he alive today. And Lewis' longtime friend, Christopher Derrick, said in 1996: 'It's difficult to imagine what Lewis would make of today's Church of England. The Church of England is such a pathetic ghost nowadays ...You can't agree with it or disagree with it. There's just nothing there.'

If C. S. Lewis were alive today, he would almost certainly be a Roman Catholic. That is the short answer - and, I believe, the most convincing answer - to the Lewis paradox. When I discovered that I believed that, then my last feeble justification for remaining an Anglican – 'If it was good enough for C. S. Lewis, then it's good enough for me' - was gone. I believe now that anyone who reads and understands Lewis is on the path to Rome.

And so I come to the last, and perhaps most important influence, Malcolm Muggeridge. In 1966, when I was a law student at U. of T. law school and should have been spending my time immersed in statutes, regulations and cases in the law library, I was more often ensconced in the periodical stacks at Central Library reading Malcolm Muggeridge's prolific journalism.

I had stumbled across Muggeridge quite by chance and was at first struck by his eloquent, wry, effortlessly readable prose, so clear, pungent, and often devastating. His skeptical mind and loathing for cant were a welcome purgative to the academic conversations going on all around me…

I first met Malcolm in the autumn of 1968, when he came to Toronto to give a lecture at the St. Lawrence Centre. On this occasion, I asked him about a short story he had written in India in the early twenties. At first, he barely remembered it, then he said: 'Nobody has mentioned that story to me in 50 years! Now we really must talk.' He went on to tell me how he had sent such early stories to Mahatma

Gandhi who had published them in his newspaper, *Young India*. Thereupon, Malcolm and I fell into real conversation, and then correspondence, which continued, pretty much uninterrupted, until his death in 1990.

The same year we met, Muggeridge published *Jesus Rediscovered*, which became an immediate, unlikely bestseller; all of his books from then on dealt with religious themes, including *Something Beautiful for God*, the book that brought Mother Teresa to worldwide attention.

In 1978–79, Muggeridge and I swapped houses, and that year I lived in his house in Sussex where I wrote the first biography of Muggeridge. Central to the book was charting his religious pilgrimage, from a Fabian socialist upbringing to his reception, at age 80, into the Roman Catholic Church. 'Rome, sweet Rome, be you never so sinful, there's no place like Rome.' So, mockingly, Muggeridge had written in the mid-seventies. Yet on 27 November 1982, Muggeridge knelt at the altar of a little chapel in the Sussex village of Hurst Green and was received into the Catholic Church. When I asked him why, he replied: 'The day will come, dear boy, when you must decide whether to die within the Church or outside the Church. I have decided to die within the Church.'

From the day that Malcolm Muggeridge became a Catholic, I thought more seriously of conversion. I remembered how difficult Malcolm's struggle had been and how Mother Teresa had written telling him to submerge his hesitations in Christ's unbounded love. I especially remembered one of her letters to him; let me quote it: You are to me like Nicodemus '...unless you become as a little child'...I am sure that you will understand beautifully everything if you would only become a little child in God's hands. The small difficulty you have regarding the Church is finite. Overcome the finite with the infinite...

Looking back now, I see that three considerations became of paramount importance to me: Rome's authority, historicity, and universality. But more even than these considerations, I came to believe not just that truth is to be found within Rome but - something quite different - that in a unique way, the truth *is* Rome. Incidentally, from within Rome's embrace I did not expect modernity to appear any more comely, but perhaps more bearable. And so it has proved.

Unlike much of Protestantism, Rome is innately suspicious of feelings and enthusiasms; still, the predominant feeling on the day of my reception was of a homecoming, of responding to a bell that I had long heard toll, of taking my place at a table that had long been set, of finding spiritual companionship among those unashamed to profess the faith of the fathers...

I have noticed that Rome does

not alter its message to suit shifting fashions, nor tailor its doctrine, however persistent or clamorous the public outcry against it may be.

I discovered too that I had grown to believe that only Rome can trace a direct line to the Church's rock, St. Peter. It was to St. Peter, after all, and to his descendants, that our Lord promised that the gates of hell would not prevail. Against most Churches, the gates of Hell seem to be prevailing very well. Only the Roman Catholic Church, the repository of teaching and traditions that date to our Lord's first disciples, '...the unmoved spectator of the thousand phases and fashions that have passed over our restless world' (to use Ronald Knox's elegant phrase), has the history, the guts, the inner wherewithal, to survive a postmodern age. Rome's claim to speak with authority in matters of faith and morals is the last refuge, or so I now believe, against the all-corrosive acid of postmodernism.

Let me state the position I was in as simply as possible: I came to believe that there is no source of authority outside the Roman Catholic Church. I could abandon the Christian faith, which had nourished me since childhood, or I could submit to and seek membership in the Church which, as St. Paul expresses it '...has the mind of Christ.' But there was, for me, no longer any middle ground left.

That doughty old warrior, Hilaire Belloc, once wrote to a friend that the Catholic Church was like a landfall at sea, at first glimpsed hazily and only through the mist: '... but the nearer it is seen, the more it is real, the less imaginary: the more direct and external its voice, the more indisputable its representative character...The metaphor is not that men fall in love with it: the metaphor is that they discover home. "This was what I long sought," they say. "This was my need."'

I owe also a special debt to Catholics, many unknown to me, whom I have since discovered had been praying for my reception, some for a long time. Such prayers flood the universe with light...

[A]bove all, first, last, and always, [my conversion] is the same old story that it always is – a story of God's grace and forgiveness and love. *Deo gratias*"); "The Catholic Church is Always Awaiting You," catholicregister.org, 29 November 2011.

Hunter-Gault, Charlayne – journalist and broadcaster; b. 27 February 1942, Due West, South Carolina; c. 1957; daughter of Charles S. H. Hunter, a U.S. Army colonel and regimental chaplain, and Althea Brown; brought up as a Methodist; parents separated in 1955; in 1961 she and Hamilton Hunter became the first two Afriocan-American students to enroll in the University of Georgia (met with taunts and racial epithets); she graduated in Journalism in 1963; shortly beforehand she married a white classmate, Walter L. Stovall (one daughter of the marriage), which caused much publicity (divorced in 1971); editorial assistant at the *New Yorker* magazine; joined the news team at WRC-TV, Washington D.C. in 1967; worked for *The New York Times*; in 1971 she married Ronald T. Gault, an African-American businessman; (one son of the marriage); national correspondent for *The Newshour* 1983-1997; National Public Radio's chief correspondent in Africa 1997-1999; CNN's Johannesburg bureau chief and correspondent 1999-2005; winner of several awards for journalism and broadcasting; see *In My Place* (1992) (memoir of her childhood and years at university); Calvin Trillin, *An Education in Georgia: Charlayne Hunter, Hamilton Holmes, and the Integration of the University of Georgia* (1964); Robert A. Pratt, *We Shall Not Be Moved: The Desegregation of the University of Georgia* (2002).

Huntington, Christopher – Catholic priest; b. 27 February 1911; c. 6 May 1937; d. 10 March 2000; brought up in a devout Low-Church Episcopalian family; all of his grandparents were also strong Episcopalians, one of them being William Reed Huntington (1838-1909), who originally put forward the four-point plan for church unity, known as the Quadrilateral, adopted by the Lambeth Conference of 1889; educated at Harvard University (graduated in 1932) and while there came to believe that the basis of religious principles was uncertain, if not illusory; worked in a publishing house in Germany 1932-1935; impressed by the sermons of a priest at Cologne cathedral and in particular, by the sermon *Light and Darkness*, by Cardinal Faulhaber, Archbishop of Munich, who not only defended what the Nazis were attacking, but attacking what they stood for; in this he saw the Catholic Church the abiding instrument of the mission of Christ ("I brought back with me to America the discovery that, as far as Germany was concerned, Rome was doing the job of the Church Gradually I began to find out what a tremendous reality Cardinal Faulhaber and the preacher in Cologne Cathedral had uncovered for me: the concrete presence of the Church of Christ, a living entity with relevance to every possible phase of life"); did graduate work at Harvard 1935-1936; also influenced in his conversion by the public statements of Pope Pius XI and by the writings of St. Thomas Aquinas, Cardinal Newman, Christopher Dawson, Karl Adam and Mgr. Robert Hugh Benson; became assistant dean of Freshmen at Harvard; co-founder with Catherine Clark, later one of the founders of the Slaves of the Immaculate Heart of Mary, and Avery Dulles (see above), then a law student at Harvard, of the St. Benedict Center as a religious and social meeting place for Catholics from Harvard, Ratcliffe, and neighbouring colleges (Fr. Leonard Feeney, SJ, became chaplain in 1943 and the center was later engaged in controversy with the Church over his interpretation of "Extra Ecclesiam nulla salus"); he did not support Fr. Feeney; ordained to the priesthood 7 June 1952; worked as a priest on Long Island, New York; buried in Most Holy Trinity Catholic Cemetery, East Hampton, Suffolk County, New York; see "The Voice of Authority," in John A. O'Brien (ed), *The Road to Damascus, Volume III: The Way to Emmaus* (1953) ("As everyone knows, there is one institution on earth, the Papacy, which claims that the Church of which it is the head is precisely that *whole* Church, One, Holy, Catholic, and Apostolic. And among the countless denominations on earth which reject this claim, there are very many members of at least one, the Anglican, who regard the Roman concept as limited and - unworthy. Their judgment, I am convinced, is as mistaken as it could possibly be. But I know that their view in this matter is not one which of itself leads to the view which I now hold, although there are more experiences than mine to show that it may well precede it…

Close upon the reappearance of active religion in my life had come the first real notice I had ever taken of the Roman Catholic Church at all, as seen in the persons of Cardinal Faulhaber and the preacher in Cologne Cathedral. The beginning, therefore, was an awareness, however imperfect, of the present reality of the Church as a sure witness to the reality of Christ. The next stage (June 1936) was a totally new awareness of the awful magnitude of the Church's claim. The all but final stage now to be described was the realization that the true Church, if she did exist, could not claim less.

At length the day came when I sought out the chaplain [of St. Paul's Catholic Chapel], Father (now Bishop) John B. Grellinger… He was sitting in his study reading his breviary…[I]n a few calm, recollected, and strangely secure sentences, he told me that in attempting to understand anything Catholic, I must always remember the three foundations: belief in God, belief that Christ was the Son of God, and belief that Christ, as Son of God, had founded the Church. He then put into my hand a copy of the Baltimore Catechism and a pamphlet called Father Smith instructs Jackson, suggesting that I read both of them all the way through at any speed I liked and bring back any questions if I cared to. As I was leaving the room, I noticed that he resumed his breviary.

If ever there was absence of pressure, it was here! There had been no attempt to convince me of anything, just quiet and courteous replies to my questions, and a statement of what Catholic thinking rested on - the three foundations of Cardinal Faulhaber's sermon - and the same unruffled, timeless assurance as that shown by the eloquent preacher in Cologne... And as far as anything personal was concerned, the distance in thc study was as great as that in Cologne Cathedral - no eagerness to argue, no curiosity to interfere. How was it that such aloofness could be so to the point, such indifference so concerned? I sensed then what I now know to be back of this attitude, truly neither aloof nor indifferent: faith (in the Catholic sense, that is, belief in revealed truth), love, and prayer.

It is one of the earmarks of a high order of love, and therefore, above all, of the divine virtue of charity, that it grants its object perfect freedom. Jesus, looking on the young man, 'loved him' (Mark 10.21); and He let him go. The Church is the true disciple of her Master: she knows what a man must do to inherit eternal life, and she declares it; but she does not force him to do it. She has solicitude for all the children of God, but no constricting anxiety; for she knows that their heavenly Father wants their love freely given, and that to this end He has given them their freedom. In her capacity, then, as the chosen instrument for bringing men to God and God to men, she offers herself, as also her Master, in constant sacrificial prayer; and she takes care that it is God who does the bringing. 'And I, if I be lifted up from the earth, will draw all things to myself' (John 12. 32).

Of this I understood little at the time. All I knew was that I felt perfectly free to visit the chapel rectory or not to bother with it, and I found that whenever I sought out the chaplain, though he explained much, he never argued. Years later someone pointed out to me the plain fact that Our Lord never argued, either. He taught.

This same gentle at-homeness in the Church, somehow likewise firm and apostolic, characterized all three of the other priests with whom I talked during these eleven months, one of whom, Father Joseph McSorley of the Paulists in New York, gave me four rules for the investigating process. First, purify your motive until you are sure that it is nothing less than truth itself. If you are simply grinding some axe or building yourself some refuge, your motive is not pure. Second, collect all the facts you can. Third, think about them. Fourth, pray. Pray constantly, pray for purity of motive, pray for guidance to all you need to know, pray for proper understanding of it, and – pray.

What, then, was the struggle? Was there anything in this program which a Protestant would not likewise have recommended? Not a thing. Nor was there, from the Protestant side, any lack of the same basic restraint of interference, the same personal freedom, which, as I have said, only a high order of love can grant. Nor was the struggle even a matter of lining up historical data pro and con - pro and con the promise of Our Lord to Peter (Matthew 16.18), pro and con the papalism of the primitive Church (as witnessed to by Ss. Clement, lrenaeus, and Cyprian, for instance), or pro and con the English 'settlements' of religion under Henry VIII and Elizabeth I.

Everybody I read had something to say about all these things, and I was doing my best to come to some conclusion about them - was, in fact, of the opinion that the conclusions set forth in Monsignor Robert Hugh Benson's *Religion of the Plain Man* rang the most true. But the struggle had to do with the present, the argument from 'fruits'. 'By their fruits you shall know them' (Matthew vii. 16). How could the present reality of the Catholic Church, as I had come to see it, be discarded as a fruit, not of Christ, but of more human devising, or worse? This was the judgment of earnest Protestants whose background and training and cultural environment I shared,

The Protestant charge, as put to me by a prominent minister in New York, had two parts: first, that the verdict of history (not the evidence of historical research, but the tangible verdict of present-day conditions) was against Rome; and second, that the religion of Rome, however spiritually helpful it might prove to be to some states of mind, was an unworthy thing, unworthy of Christ, and unworthy of the human soul.

First, the verdict of history. In all countries where Catholicism had been untempered by the opposition of a strong Protestantism - notably in France, Italy, and Spain - modern civilization was at its lowest and anti-Christian movements were at their most violent. In Protestant countries, on the other hand, there was moderation, and the human spirit breathed in comparative freedom. So ran the charge.

I was not prepared to admit that this was the final verdict. There was strong evidence, then as now, that it was an evil day for Europe when Catholic Vienna began to decline and Protestant Berlin began to rise. Of this day we have not yet seen the end. And the man who understood this was Chesterton, a Catholic.

Nor was I prepared to accept as an unquestioned good the whole post-Reformation development of the capitalism in which we now live (plausibly linked by Max Weber with Calvinism). The man who understood this, and whose tremendous stature I had just discovered, was Leo XIII, a Pope.

In England, considered as a whole, materialism had all but frozen out the warmth of her Christian heritage; and in our own country the cult of respectability and the pursuit of license were combining to stifle the one necessary 'fruit' - personal sanctity.

As to the violence of anti-Christianity in Spain, there were two possible considerations: one, that maybe the violence was against an abuse of Catholicism; and two, that the Devil might well take the fiercest action where he saw his Enemy the strongest.

But admittedly I could not be sure of these things. There was a strong pull to the ideal of nobility of character (a clearer concept to the Protestant mind than sanctity), and the argument left me in a quandary

The second charge - that of unworthiness - had been put most succinctly in these words: 'Catholicism is more a religion about Christ than a religion of Christ.' It is clear what is meant: The Church is more concentrated upon the matter of Who and What Christ is than upon the matter of following Him. To this I could only say that I saw no way of getting along without both. My reason for wanting to follow Christ is not my approval of what He commands, but rather my acceptance of the authority of Him who commands it. 'I am WHO AM' (Exodus 3.14). 'Before Abraham was, I AM' (John 8.58). And 'You have heard that it was said…But I say unto you (Matthew 5.21-22 *ff*).

The nature of things as they are - the nature of God, the nature of Christ, the nature of man - this objective reality *behind* precept and obedience was just what had been drawing me. I could not refute the charge, because I did not see that it was a charge at all. But again, I could not overlook the humility of the man who was making it - an eloquent testimony to his own religion *of* Christ. So here, too, a quandary.

But speculatively the quandary did not last long. I made what Newman calls a notional assent, but no real assent. I told Father McSorley that I thought the claim of the Church to be verified - but what of it? In some uncanny way it seemed to have nothing to do with me whatever. I might just as well have been looking at a picture. 'Perhaps,' said Father McSorley, 'you have been forgetting the fourth step. Pray'…I withdrew into silence, and did my best to pray.

One morning about a month later, waking up at the usual time, I sat bolt upright in bed, filled to overflowing with but one thought: 'There is the Church of Christ on earth, and I am outside it. Isn't that appalling? I must do something about it.'

The experience was so simple that it is impossible to describe. I was not more certain; I was just certain. But even that does not accurately describe the thought, because there was nothing introspective about it: I was aware, not so much of my own certainty as of the Church – the Church of Christ, with its center over there in Rome. And here was I, sitting up in bed, not of it").

Huntington, Joshua – Catholic apologist; b. 1812, New England; d. 1900; raised as a Protestant Congregationalist; as a child he found religion "stern and repulsive"; had a "religious awakening" at the age of ten, but superficial and external only; educated at

Yale College, when varied from indifference to practicing religion; went on to the theological seminar at Princeton; found it hard to accept Protestant doctrines; lost all faith in the Christian religion and stopped his theological studies; came to believe his religion to embody bigotry, narrowness, superstition and revivalism; his criticism of Protestant theology was that it gave no certain or exact criterion of doctrine and no sufficient rule of action; remained a believer in God and gradually came back to belief in Christianity; returned to his studies for the Protestant ministry but eventually became a Catholic; see *Gropings After Truth: A Life Journey From New England Congregationalism to the One, Catholic and Apostolic Church* (1870) (a very detailed account of his journey from Puritanism to the Catholic Church) ("I will mention one other objection to the claims of the Catholic Church which has always had more weight in my mind than any other, and which was one of the last to yield its place. It is this: The doctrine of the Church is that her clergy have peculiar authority and peculiar powers conferred upon them by the Sacrament of Holy Orders. They are regarded as the immediate representatives of the Lord himself, and as chosen by him for this office. It seems, therefore, a fair presumption that they would all be holy men. Yet several of them in past times, as is admitted by every one, have been very bad men. How can this notorious fact be reconciled with the doctrine that they were his chosen ministers, through whose hands the gifts of sanctifying grace were to be conferred upon the people? The presumption against such a supposition would be almost unanswerable, were it not offset by one fact stated in Scripture itself, which shows it to be ill-founded. I refer to the apostleship of Judas Iscariot. It is very likely that you will, at first, fail to see the bearing of his case upon this point, in consequence of your having never thought of him as an apostle, but only as a bad man, tolerated for a time by the rest of the twelve, and admitted among them merely because it was necessary that Jesus should be betrayed by one of his pretended friends. It was thus that I had always regarded him, until it suddenly occurred to me that there is nothing in the gospel narrative to justify such an idea. When our Lord sent out the twelve, he gave them, in proof of their ministry, miraculous powers to heal the sick and cast out devils in his name; these powers were evidently conferred upon Judas just as upon the others. St. Mark says he sent them by two and two, so that there is no possibility of supposing Judas was omitted. Equally impossible is it to suppose there was any apparent difference between his mission and that of the rest, for this would have made him a marked man among them, which he evidently was not. So far was this from being the case, that no one seems to have suspected him even at the last supper, when their Master announced to them that one of their number was about to betray him. He even held a sort of official position among them, having charge of the money which was possessed by them in. common. Yet it appears from the words of St. John, that he was a bad man, a hypocrite, and an unbeliever, throughout his whole ministry, though no one knew it except the Lord himself. Here, then, was a man chosen by him 'Have I not chosen you twelve?' commissioned directly by himself to preach his Gospel, gifted with miraculous powers, in evidence of his mission, and treated by him precisely as he treated those whom he knew to be faithful to him, and yet who never had any love for him, or faith in him as the Messiah, and who finally betrayed him to a cruel death. Now, as everything which our Lord did was designed for the instruction of his disciples in all ages, is it not likely that he meant by this to teach us that, even among his own chosen apostles, we might always expect to find more or less traitors and hypocrites ? Does it not afford, at least, a possible explanation of the fact, that there have been wicked priests and bishops and popes, who have, nevertheless, received authority from him to preach his Gospel and dispense his sacraments?"); *Catholic Persuasion: The Individual Desire to Find the Truth in Religion* (nd; revised and enhanced edition 2013).

Hutton, Betty (born Elizabeth June Thornburg) – actress and singer; b. 26 February 1921, Battle Creek, Michigan; d. 12 March 2007, Palm Springs, California; her father, Percy Thornburg, a railroad brakeman, abandoned the family for another woman when she was two years old, and in 1939 he committed suicide; her mother Mabel Lum (1901-1967) took the surname Hutton and ran a speakeasy out of their flat; brought up Lutheran; a singer in several bands in her youth; appeared in a supporting role on Broadway and in several short films; vivacious blonde who was once described as "the noisiest girl in Hollywood"; signed to featured roles at Paramount Pictures from 1942 (*The Fleet's In* (1942); *The Miracle of Morgan's Creek* (1944)); co-star with Bob Hope in *Let's Face It* (1943) (Hope said that if the Allies put a propeller on Hutton and sent her to Germany, "the war would be over by Christmas"); became a major star (Paramount's number one female), appearing in such films as *Incendiary Blonde* (1945), *The Perils of Pauline* (1947), and *Let's Dance* (1950); biggest screen success was in *Annie Get Your Gun* (1950); later in *The Greatest Show on Earth* (1952); had several recording contracts as a singer; some success in radio, nightclubs and television; married four times, but all ended in divorce; her mother died in a house fire; her mother's death and the failure of her last marriage led to depression and alcohol and prescription drug addiction; declared bamkruptcy; had two nervous breakdowns and after losing her voice in 1970 attempted suicide; went to a clinic and benefited from the help of a Catholic priest, Fr. Peter Maguire, who was instrumental in bringing her into the Catholic faith; after her conversion she worked as a cook and housekeeper in a Catholic rectory in Portsmouth, Rhode Island; developed a great devotion to Our Lady; returned to some television and theater performances and appeared in *Annie* on Broadway; studied for a Master's Degree in Psychology from Salve Regina University, Newport, Rhode Island; taught acting; after the death of Fr. Maguire she moved to live in California in 1999; buried at Desert Memorial Park, Cathedral City, California; see *Backstage You Can Have: My Own Story* (2009); Gene Arceri, *Rocking Horse, a Personal Biography of Betty Hutton* (2009); *ANB.*

Ingraham, Laura Anne – radio host, author and political commentator; b. 19 June 1964, Glastonbury, Connecticut; father a conservative Protestant who stopped attending church during her childhood; her mother was raised Catholic, but had left the Church; educated at Dartmouth College and the University of Virginia School of Law; in the late 1980s worked as a speechwriter in President Reagan's administration; served as a law clerk for Supreme Court Justice Clarence Thomas (see below); then worked as an attorney for a New York law firm; CBS commentator in the late 1990s; employed by *Fox News Channel* in 2008; launched a nationally syndicated talk show, *The Laura Ingraham Show* in 2001 (one of the most-listened-to talk radio programs); writer of several best-selling political commentaries, some satirical, from a conservative perspective; has attacked "liberal elites" in several fields and "liberal feminism"; in 2005 she announced that she had undergone breast cancer surgery; adopted three children; see *Shut Up and Sing: How Elites from Hollywood, Politics, and the U.N. are Subverting America* (2003); *The Hillary Trap: Looking for Power in All the Wrong Places* (2005); *Power to the People* (2007) ("Listeners who have heard me mention my conversion to the Catholic faith often ask – 'what made you do it?' I usually say something funny like, 'I'm half-Polish, so it was a John-Paul II thing!' But the only real answer I have (at least thus far in my spiritual journey) is the Holy Spirit came to me. My conversion began with heartfelt conversations I had with Pat Cipollone, an old friend who would eventually become my godfather. I did what most curious God-seekers do – I read the Bible, reflected on the Gospels, and really focused on praying. I found myself praying all the time

– while brushing my teeth, on the treadmill, on the drive to the studio.

I remember when I walked into the rectory of St. Patrick's Church in Washington to meet with Monsignor Peter Vaghi for the first time. Pat had suggested I chat with him. On the outside I was a cool cat. On the inside, I was freaking out. But after our first half-hour meeting, I felt like I had known him for years. I was totally comfortable opening up to him, and by the time I walked out the door I realized that something profound was happening to me.

Monsignor Vaghi and I would continue to meet each week at St. Patrick's and during those sessions I slowly learned to forgive myself and others. Mother Angelica, the spunky media mogul, once said: 'forgiveness means, "to give." It means to give before your neighbor does.' I learned that with forgiveness, it's always better if we make the first move.

At the Easter Vigil in 2003, I was baptized by Monsignor Vaghi (I had no baptismal record), was confirmed, and received my first Holy Communion…I was walking on air that night. For the first time, for as long as I could remember, I felt like I was finally 'home.' It was the strangest thing – this faith thing. How could this have happened to me? The person who used to make catholic jokes in junior high school! The person who walked into her first meeting with a priest and said, 'Great to meet you, but there is no way in hell that I'm going to become a Catholic!' God has a sense of humor, doesn't He?"); *The Obama Diaries* (2010); *Of Thee I Zing: America's Cultural Decline from Muffin Tops to Body Shots* (2011) (with Raymond Arroyo).

Ives, Levi Silliman – theologian; b. 16 September 1797, Meriden, Connecticut; c. 25 December 1852 (received in Rome by Pope Pius IX; his wife, Rebecca, a daughter of the Protestant Bishop of New York, John Henry Hobart, Jr., and a godchild of Elizabeth Seton (see below) was received some months later); d. 13 October 1867, Manhattanville, New York; eldest of ten children in a Presbyterian family; while he was still at school the war with England broke out in 1812 and he served in the army for a year; his father committed suicide in 1815; further education at Hamilton College, Clinton, New York; converted to Episcopalianism in 1819; in 1823 ordained a minister of the Episcopal Church; elected first Episcopal Bishop of North Carolina and served from 1831 to 1852; worked for the education and religious training of black people; very interested in the Oxford Movement and became leader of the High Church party in his area; he founded at Valle Crucis in North Carolina a religious community, called the Brotherhood of the Holy Cross, composed of persons bound by a vow of celibacy, poverty and obedience; his advocacy of Tractarian ideas led to proceedings being taken against him by the Episcopal Church; in 1852 he went to Rome and made his submission to the Pope; he became the first Protestant bishop since the Reformation to convert to Catholicism; he and his wife stayed two years in Rome; spent the rest of his life as a Catholic layman; after his conversion he was appointed Professor of Rhetoric at St. John's College (now Fordham University); also lectured at Joseph's Seminary, Dunwoodie, New York, and the convents of the Sacred Heart and Sisters of Charity; lost both of his young children to illness and his wife was frequently ill herself; did much charity work; joined and became New York leader of the Society of Saint Vincent de Paul; founder and first president of the Society for the Protection of Destitute Roman Catholic Children in the City of New York, which most called the Catholic Protectory (sheltered about 100,000 Irish Catholic boys); buried in the grounds of the Catholic Protectory, Westchester; see *Humility, A Ministerial Qualification* (1840); *The Apostles' Doctrine and Fellowship* (1844); *The Obedience of Faith* (1849); *The Trials of a Mind in its Progress to Catholicism: A Letter to His Old Friends* (1854) ("But the circumstance which at this period shook my confidence most of all, was the absence, in my view, of any instituted method among Protestants for the, remission of post-baptismal sin. Sins before baptism were expressly forgiven in that sacrament. But for the remission of those committed after, however deadly, I could see in Protestantism no provision. That Christ left power in His Church to remit these I had no doubt. And for a time, after my mind had become alive to the importance of the exercise of this power, I believed that it existed and might be lawfully exercised in the communion of which I was a bishop. But upon stricter examination and more mature thought, I became convinced that if the existence of such power was not actually denied, its exercise, except in a very modified sense and within very restricted limits, was virtually prohibited. The discovery filled me with dread, which daily observation increased, till finally it passed into absolute consternation. No one, who has not been in my state, can fully appreciate my sensations, when I opened my eyes to the fact that multitudes around me entrusted to my care, were goaded by a conviction of mortal sin and demanding relief, and I was not allowed by my Church to administer that relief in the only way which seemed to me to be directed by God's word as understood by His early Church. The question now forced itself upon me, Can that be an institution of God which thus locks up the gifts (supposing it to have received them) which He commands His priesthood to dispense to the needy and perishing souls for whom Christ died?"); John O'Grady, *Levi Silliman Ives* (1933); Katherine Burton, *In No Strange Land: Some American Catholic Converts* (1942), p.1 ("He spoke over and over again of the one thing that moved him most to leave his own loved communion, the fact that Our Lord had so deep a love and compassion for the poor – 'Go to the poor,' He had said - and that the Protestant Church was doing very little in the way of charity. He felt the 'utter incompatibility of the system in which I act compared with Christ's mission to the poor'"); William J. Stern, "Once We Knew How to Rescue Poor Kids," *City Journal*, Autumn 1998 ("The key to re-socializing the children, Ives believed, lay in giving them a faith-based system of values. 'Every child committed to this institution,' he proclaimed, 'will be thoroughly trained in the faith and morality of the Gospel as revealed and entrusted to the Catholic Church.' On first sight, this might look like boilerplate, without much meaning except to believers. But recall that religion has a centuries-old experience in effectively teaching people the difference between right and wrong, and that some of the most up-to-date social thinkers have rediscovered inner-city ministries as one of the most effective agencies for redeeming underclass kids today. It's easy enough to understand what these ministers are doing, and why Ives was successful, in modern, purely psychological terms. The Protectory provided the clearest possible statement of right and wrong, confidently asserted that these values were absolute and backed up by divine authority, provided a discipline of practice and reflection that reinforced these values, held out complete forgiveness for past wrongdoing, and offered membership in a community organized around this code. Speaking more broadly still, Ives understood that at the center of the underclass condition is a moral and social void, and he knew how to fill it.

Respect was an essential component of the Protectory's moral lesson - respect for oneself, for parents, for other children, for teachers, and for God. Ives wanted to introduce the children to a world of obligations and make them aware that they weren't the sole arbiters of what they should and shouldn't do. He cultivated in them a host of ethical responsibilities where formerly there had been only caprice and impulse. Among other things, he made the Protectory children responsible for one another. '[I]t has occurred several times that a couple of our boys, having been sent on an errand to the city, have there fallen in with one who absconded, and have brought him back in triumph to the Protectory,' Ives proudly observed.

One of the most effective disciplines the Protectory used to turn impulsive, often criminally inclined, children into personally responsible individuals was the sacrament of confession. Confession meant that each week the children had to examine their behavior, decide if it conformed to the ethical code they'd been taught, and take responsibility for it by confessing to a priest. Thus, they learned to reflect habitually on themselves and on morality, to lead an examined and responsible life.

The Protectory's Catholic teaching gave more than a stern set of dos and don'ts to these emotionally shipwrecked children. It offered them love and a sense of their own worthiness. If you keep the commandments, Ives's teachers told the children, God would be father and friend, offering an infinite and unshakable love. For children who had never known a parent's tender care, this was strong solace. The sacrament of the Eucharist had an equally positive psychological resonance for Protectory dependents, dramatizing to them that an all-powerful God had been willing to sacrifice his own son for their sake - that's how much they were worth. This teaching conveyed a powerful message of self-esteem, to use today's debased term.

Ives aimed to give the Protectory's children the means of making a living. He 'resolved to cause these children . . . to be trained in some industrial occupation or mechanic art while they are instructed in all the essential branches of an English education.' Vocational training also had a moral purpose, Ives believed, for it 'diverts young minds from the evil suggestions of the tempter.'

Ives believed that classical and sacred music were crucial to a complete education. He launched a full brass band and a string orchestra at the Protectory. Playing in a band or orchestra taught kids how to play their parts exactly in a disciplined communal activity to which they were essential. Beyond that, the message of serious music is order, harmony, and transcendence, all in tune with the Protectory's teachings.

The inner and outer worlds of abandoned children are chaotic - to them, frighteningly so - and Ives understood those kids' special need for rigid structure, to provide them with a sense that the world is secure and predictable and to bring some order to their emotional lives.

In sum, Ives sought a total inner transformation of the Protectory's wards. He wanted to educate them, give them useful skills, and, most of all, change their values and worldview"); Michael T. Malone, "Levi Silliman Ives: Priest, Bishop, Tractarian, and Roman Catholic" (PhD dissertation, Duke University, 1970). *Catholic Encyclopedia*; *ANB*.

Jacobson, Joseph R. – priest; b. 1940, Milwaukee; c. 22 April 2000 (Easter Vigil; received with his wife Carolyn; his two children were received later); father a Lutheran clergyman; studied at

St. Olaf College, Minnesota (BA); then University of Strasbourg, France (Bachelor of Divinity); graduated from Northwestern Lutheran Theological Seminary in Minneapolis in 1965; ordained a Lutheran minister; fluent in French, German, and Spanish, which led him to serve in western Canada, where there were many first generation immigrants; served for ten years as bishop of the Alberta Synod of the Evangelical Lutheran Church in Canada; served as co-chairman of the Lutheran-Catholic theological dialogue for Canada for almost eight years; spent much time wrestling with the issue of authority and after a long period of prayer and reflection he became a Catholic; in 2006 ordained to the Catholic priesthood for the Grouard-McLennan Archdiocese, Alberta, Canada; married with two children; see *A Gift of Love: The Joys and Treasures of a New Catholic* (2001), *archgm.ca* (his conversion story) ("I read an article recently which pointed out that one of the distinguishing marks of the Catholic Church is that it views all of life from a supernatural perspective. This most assuredly does distinguish the Catholic Church from what typical Protestantism has become. It explains why the average Catholic is more at home in the world view of a Bach Church Cantata than is the typical Lutheran these days.

Perhaps this Catholic perspective comes from being so steeped in Scripture and so rooted in the long Tradition of the Church, perhaps from having continual access to so many ways of maintaining a vital link to the realm of the spirit and to the Church Suffering and Triumphant …

The whole world gets some exposure on a regular basis to the Church's supernatural view of all things through the eyes of Christ whose mystical extension in time and space she knows herself to be. Every time people like the Holy Father, Mother Teresa, Jean Vanier, Archbishop Oscar Romero, Bishop Bilo and their like make public utterances, the world is exposed to a striking alternative view of reality. It is a view that is hard to ignore, even though it defies the logic of the age, because it is uttered by people whose relationship to our age has been so wholesome and admirable. They are a real puzzle for many. It is clear to all that the Reality out of which they and the Church are living extends way beyond this world, and yet that Reality seems to be the very reason why their lives touch this world in such an extraordinarily effective way.

This jars the sensibilities of the largely secularized public which has been taught to write off those who 'are so heavenly minded they are of no earthly good.' What's going on here with these heavenly-minded Catholics?...

The source of the Church's resilience and indomitable hope in this world is precisely her life in God, her connection to the supernatural. What are the first signs of the supernatural that strike a new Catholic on entering the Church?

First, there is the reverence for the Holy. Many Catholics lament the erosion of this reverence in North America and Europe over the past several decades. But to a former Protestant, what remains of it is manna to the soul: The holy water that marks you as you enter and leave the church, the genuflecting before the eucharistic Jesus in the Tabernacle, the kneeling, the sign of the cross, the votive candles, the silence before worship, the mystery of the Mass, even the prayers of the faithful for priests who before all else are holy men.

Then there is the vivid communal awareness of God (and the angels and saints!) that you have been used to finding only around the edges of modern Protestantism, in populist renewal movements or elitist liturgical societies. Here it is, at the very heart of the Church and in every part of it, offered to all in the same integrated and "natural" way that Jesus embodied and offered it to all.

You see it immediately also in the fearless way in which moral and ethical issues are assessed from a consistently supernatural vantage point. Accountability to God takes precedence over all lesser considerations in the knowledge that only thus are the best interests of people truly served. And so a Mother Teresa can say to a President Clinton at a White House sponsored Prayer Breakfast, 'It is a very great poverty to decide that a child must die so that you may live as you wish.' When almost no one else is willing or perhaps able to tackle issues like abortion, euthanasia, marriage, suffering, sexual morality, birth control, and family life in any way that challenges individuals to consider the good of others ahead of their own, the Catholic Church keeps pressing the prior claim of God on us for our own greater good and the greater good of all.

And the Pope keeps canonizing new saints! He keeps telling the Church and the world that there are people like us who are now closer to God than we are and who are eager to help and guide us on our way to God. He tells us how they have demonstrated their ability to do this through a rigorous screening process which involves, among other thing, verifiable miracles of intervention. There are thousands of them, and Catholics turn to them as naturally as a Protestant might turn to a trusted neighbour for help. Talk about a supernatural perspective!...

'You are Peter (Rock), and on this rock I will build My Church,' Jesus said to Simon Bar-Jona. (Matthew 16:17). And Jesus said to Simon Peter, 'Feed My lambs… Tend My Sheep.' (John 21:15ff.)… [We celebrate] what it means to this former Lutheran to belong now to the Church that sees herself as the flock whose Chief Undershepherd has for nearly 2000 years heard these words of Jesus as directed specifically to him.

The contrast is stark. These days most Protestant leaders have trouble speaking publicly about Jesus, and none would presume to speak for Him in public. But this is exactly what the Holy Father does. And he does it so unassumingly and so authentically that non-Catholics who would never endorse the Petrine office are often heard to say that he speaks for them, not noticing that he can speak that way only by virtue of the Petrine office.

Because of the Petrine office, the Holy Father is placed under the strictest faithfulness to Jesus and he lives this out in a humble and natural way. He does this not because he is overreaching himself but because he accepts that this is Jesus' will for the Church. It is his duty to do it, and to do it right, even though this means that his way on earth is one long Way of the Cross. The office he exercises, created by Jesus as a service to the Church in its life and mission on earth, requires this of him. It comes supplied by Jesus with the graces needed to achieve His purposes in the varying conditions of each succeeding generation, precisely through weak human beings like Peter, Giovanni Roncalli and Karol Wojtyla. (cf. Matthew 16:19, 23; John 21:18-19; Pope John Paul II"s appeal in *Ut Unum Sint* etc.)...

I will not here try to make excuses for the more infamous holders of the Petrine office or for its sometimes chequered history. It is sufficient to indicate that an office is not destroyed by an unworthy office-holder. Judas betrayed but did not destroy his office. It was still there for the Lord to fill with a Matthias (Acts 2:15-26). Likewise, the Borgias and the Medicis may have disgraced but they could not destroy the Petrine office. Rather, we celebrate the incalculable blessings that have accrued both to the world and to the Church every time a faithful and humble successor to Peter has accepted his role as Jesus' Chief spokesman for his time and courageously upheld the Kingdom of God and confronted evil...

[A]s the Holy Father and the College of Bishops guide the storm-tossed ship of the Church over the wild seas of our time, with a sure sense of Jesus' presence and help, who can fail to note the contrast [with Protestantism]? The ship he is steering is still on course despite the mutiny of some of its crew. This is in no small measure due to the fact that the sailors have not taken control of the rudder.

If the Protestants are to board that ship and join its crew with the intent of trusting its captain, a thorough change of mind-set is required. Such a change must be compelled by more than the desperation born of fleeing their own sinking ship for one that is still afloat. There has to be some sense that this ship is floating and will stay afloat for the very good reason that Jesus is on board (cf. Mark 4:35-41) and that it is on course only because its captain is the very one Jesus Himself has picked for the job (cf. Matthew 14:28-33).

The change in mind-set can be facilitated by imagining yourself to be the Pope. Try it once. Your mandate at all times is the ministry which Jesus entrusted to Peter. You are as personally responsible to Jesus today as Peter was in his day for the role within the Church which He spells out so clearly in Matthew 16, Luke 22, and John 21, as we have noted already.

It can also help to put yourself mentally into the place of a Catholic bishop. Your mandate at all times is now the ministry Jesus entrusted to the Twelve in Matthew 18, Matthew 28, John 13, John 20, etc.

Mentally putting ourselves into the position in which the Pope and the bishops actually find themselves before Jesus can help us understand why authority continues to work in the Catholic Church even in our unruly times. Not perfectly, but better than it works anywhere else. It works because it is being exercised by those whom Jesus has invested with it. They know it and the whole Church knows it. Even to a large extent the gainsayers know it. Jesus is calling the Pope and the bishops to be His foremost martyrs in our culture of self-worship, pleasure, and death, and they know that, too. Their accountability to Jesus and to one another for this martyrdom is their paramount preoccupation. If you think this is an exaggeration, you do not know very many of them either singly or as a college, and you are probably operating out of pre-conceptions dating from a much different era.

The joy in this for a new Catholic is not in some romantic notion of a Church isolated from the trials and turmoil of our age. The joy lies rather in the fact that in the Catholic Church the center is capable of holding against all assaults from within and from without, the rock remains solid against all the blows that could crush it. For that center and that rock is Jesus Christ Himself operating through His chosen apostles and Peter"); Ramon Gonzales, "Ex-Lutheran Bishop to be Ordained Catholic Priest," *Catholic Online, catholic.org*, 2006 ("'There was a long process leading up to it and a long process that followed after it. But the key moment was in Ireland in 1997 when I realized that the teaching authority of the Church is something Jesus gave to Peter and the bishops and no other church really can duplicate what Jesus gave,' he explained in a recent interview...'You can't substitute for it. You can't find something better. You can't do without it. 'The Church needs a rock and the rock is the one Jesus gave us and it's the holy father with the bishops and without that there is no rock. Any church that tries to live without that is subject to the shifting sands. Most churches function by a majority vote of members and that means they are very vulnerable to the popular culture. In fact they are exposed to all kinds of extremes with the result that there is no safeguard that we are going to stay on the rock, stay on the foundation of Christ.'

That realization hit him like a ton of bricks while sitting on a rock in Ireland looking at the Atlantic Ocean. 'I said, "Oh, good Lord. I have been trying to reinvent something Jesus made right the first time."

'Once the causes of the Reformation were reckoned with, many Lutherans believed that union with Rome would be the way the church would go. But it became apparent about 1990 to many of us that this was not about to happen within any Protestant church at this point in history. And so whereas I was always on a homecoming journey, back into the Catholic Church for my entire ministry, all of a sudden I realized that the church that I was part of was not'")

Jindal, Bobby (legal name Piyush Jindal) – politician; b. 10 June 1971, Baton Rouge, Louisiana; c. 1989; parents were immigrants from Punjab, India; brought up in a nominally Hindu household (stated that he was raised "in a monotheistic home with a firm belief in a God with traditional values - the same sort of values you find in the Ten Commandments and other mainstream religions"); converted to Christianity in high school; the nickname "Bobby" comes from that of a character in the sitcom *The Brady Bunch*; educated at Brown University; studied at New College, Oxford, as a Rhodes Scholar and received an M Litt degree in Political Science; conversion to the Catholic faith influenced by several writers, notably C. S. Lewis; appointed Secretary of the Louisiana Department of Health and Hospitals in 1996; member of the Republican Party; nominated by President George W. Bush as Assistant Secretary of Health and Human Services for Planning and Evaluation in 2001 (unanimously confirmed by the Senate); narrowly lost the 2003 election for Louisiana Governor; in 2004 elected as member of the United States House of Representatives; in 2007 elected as 55th Governor of Louisiana (the first Indian American governor in the United States); mentioned as a possible Presidential running mate for Senator John McCain in 2008; re-elected Governor in 2011; opposes all abortions; opposes expanding public funding of embryonic stem cell research; opposes the legalization of same sex marriage; has opposed efforts to restrict gun rights; caused controversy in 2012 by agreeing with the recent pronouncement of the American College of Obstetricians and Gynecologists that birth control pills should be available without a prescription and bought over the counter; author of several scientific and law review articles; married to Supriya, *née* Jolly (three children of the marriage); see "Perspectives of an Indian Convert," *America*, 31

July 1993 ("The motivation behind my conversion, however, was my belief in one, objectively true faith. If Christianity is merely one of many equally valid religions, then the sacrifices I made, including the loss of my family's peace, were senseless. I was comfortable in my Hindu faith and enjoyed an active prayer life; I only gradually felt a void and stubbornly resisted God's call from within the Church. It was Truth and Love that finally forced me to accept Christ as Lord. 'Jesus said to him, "I am the way and the truth and the life: No one comes to the Father except through me"' (Jn. 14:6). Christ's redemptive sacrifice proved that God loved me and was lifting me up to Him"); "Physical Dimensions of Spiritual Warfare," *New Oxford Review*, December 1994; "How to Witness to Your Faith," *New Oxford Review*, October 1995; "How Catholicism Is Different," *New Oxford Review*, December 1996 ("Just as C. S. Lewis removed any room for comfortable opposition to Jesus by identifying Him as either 'Lord, liar, or lunatic,' so the Catholic Church leaves little room for complacent opposition to her doctrines. Without inflating the issues that separate Catholics from Protestants, for we do worship the same Trinitarian God who died for our sins, I want to refute the notion that Catholicism is merely another denomination with no more merit than any other.

The Reformers who left the Catholic Church rejected, to varying degrees, five beliefs which continue to be upheld by the Catholic Church. The Church claims that these points are found in Scripture, and they have been consistently and clearly taught throughout the Church's history. I will support the Church's claims here.

(1) *Scripture and Tradition*: Is *sola scriptura* (the Bible alone) a sufficient basis for the modern Christian to understand God's will?

The Bible does not contain either the claim that it is comprehensive or a listing of its contents, but does describe how it should be used. Scripture and Tradition, not the Bible alone, transmit God's revelation. Tradition is reflected in the Church's authority to interpret Scripture.

(2) *Apostolic Succession*: Does apostolic succession insure that the Catholic Church is continuous with the Church founded by Christ through the apostles?

Christ founded the Church and vested her with unique authority. The apostles, the very men who wrote much of the New Testament, were the Church's first bishops, and they appointed successors. The hierarchy of the Catholic Church traces its lineage directly to the apostles, and, thus, the Church claims to be the one Jesus founded.

(3) *Papacy*: Is the Pope the successor of St. Peter and thus recipient of special authority?

Christ established the office of the papacy, installed Peter as the first Pope, and gave to him certain privileges and responsibilities, which belong today to John Paul II.

(4) *Sacraments*: Do the sacraments actually transmit Christ's grace?

Christ instituted seven sacraments as recorded in Scripture. The sacraments are more than mere symbols and actually transmit grace; subjective faith is required to receive the objective grace (Mt. 9:20-22; Mk. 5:28-34), just as Christ's sacrifice becomes efficacious for our salvation after we accept Him. This concept of a physical sign presenting, not representing, God's grace is paralleled in many biblical incidents (2 Kings 13:20-21; Mk. 5:27-34; Mt. 8:3, 9:29-30, 14:36, 15:36, 20:34; Mk. 5:23, 6:56, 7:33-35, 8:22-25; Lk. 4:40-41, 5:12-13, 8:43-46; Jn. 4:48, 9:6-7, 9:10-11, 11:41-42, 13:8; Acts 5:15, 19:11-12).

(5) *Salvation*: Is *sola fide* (faith alone) all that is required for eternal life? Do Catholics ignore Christ's sacrifice and try to 'earn' their way into heaven?

Salvation requires living faith expressed in a changed life - i.e., in good works. The process of obtaining eternal life involves ongoing submission to the Lord, allowing His grace to work within and gradually sanctify us.

[T]he Catholic Church deserves a careful examination by non-Catholics. It is not intellectually honest to ignore an institution with such a long and distinguished history and with such an impressively global reach. I am not asking non-Catholics to investigate the claims of my neighborhood minister, but rather am presenting a 2,000-year-old tradition, encompassing giants like Aquinas and Newman, with almost a billion living members, including modern prophets like Mother Teresa and Pope John Paul II"); "Reflections of a Seven-Year-Old Catholic," *New Oxford Review*, February 1998 ("I spent much time learning particular Catholic teachings from both Scripture and history, and eventually I distilled the wide array of issues down to the one central teaching on Church authority. I discovered that the Catholic Church has thoughtful and scriptural justifications for each of her beliefs, which are at least defensible if not always overwhelmingly convincing. The Church's teachings, considered one at a time, appeared to me to be credible but not especially inspiring, but, when considered together, quite substantial. So the most decisive and efficient way to discern whether Rome was an incredible fraud or Christ's Church was to examine the foundational principle upon which her other teachings depend. For if the Church is right in claiming a divine mandate to interpret Scripture and to articulate infallible doctrines, then even the most outrageous assertion becomes binding.

I surprised many of my Catholic friends with the weight and gravity I accorded to their Church's teachings, but, despite my suspicions, I respected the institution enough to take it seriously. I was not tempted by the expedient path of ignoring difficult teachings, and there was no reason to swallow Rome's demanding morality if her authority were less than divinely inspired. After all, if I wanted the aesthetics without the inconvenient morality I could become Episcopalian. I fully expected that my vigorous examination of the pivotal issue of authority would find Rome wanting.

Months of studying history, theology, and (surprisingly) Scripture led me to one simple and inescapable conclusion. The papacy was right, and I was wrong. The same submission to authority commanded by Christ and then Peter and Paul was, unbeknownst to me and many other American Christians, also accepted and continued by the earliest Christians and their successors, who now constitute the dreaded Catholic Church. Despite my best efforts, I could find no justification in the Bible or the early Church for any individual to establish his own church apart from the one established by Christ. A Protestant might find it ironic that I was driven to Rome by my love for Scripture and my desire to learn how Christ and His Church intended for me to understand Scripture"); *Leadership and Crisis* (2010) (semi-autobiographical).

Johnson, Abby – pro-life activist; b. c.1980, Texas; c. 4 December 2011; brought up in a conservatice pro-life family; raised Southern Baptist; educated at Texas A&M University (BS in Psychology) and Sam Houston State University (MA in Counseling); was introduced to Planned Parenthood while at college and in 2001 volunteered to work for them, progressing to the position of community services director; she worked in their clinic at Bryan, Texas, for eight years, eventually becoming director of the clinic; described death threats to herself and her family from anti-abortion activists; in 2009, as a result of a personnel shortage, she was called in to assist in an ultrasound-guided abortion of a thirteen week old baby; she saw that the ultrasound image looked like her own daughter and that it tried to avoid the vacuum tube; also claimed her bosses pressured her to increase profits; she resigned from Planned Parenthood; soon afterwards she joined Coalition for Life; she has also worked with other pro-life organizations, 40 Days For Life, Live Action (research director), and Americans United for Life (senior policy advisor); Planned Parenthood sought a court order that would have prevented her from discussing her past work, but their lawsuit failed; she has revealed that she had two abortions before the birth of her daughter; left the Southern Baptists because they objected to her work at Planned Parenthood; she and her husband Doug (raised a Lutheran) stopped attending church, but later joined the Episcopal Church; after her public announcement on abortion she felt unwelcome in the Episcopal Church and was received into the Catholic Church; married with one daughter; see *Unplanned* (2011) ("For the briefest moment, the baby looked as if it were being wrung like a dishcloth, twirled and squeezed. And then it crumpled and began disappearing into the cannula before my eyes. The last thing I saw was the tiny, perfectly formed backbone sucked into the tube, and then it was gone"); Benjamin Mann, "Abby Johnson Reveals Details of Pro-life Turnaround and Catholic Conversion," *Catholic News Agency*, 13 January 2011 ("She said that one of the final obstacles, in the course of her Catholic conversion, had been the Church's teaching on the immorality of all artificial methods of birth control.

Planned Parenthood's mentality toward contraception, as she explained, stuck with her for a period of time even after she rejected abortion. Even as she became interested in the Catholic Church, she clung to the notion that artificial birth control was an advance for women and society. But she kept an open mind, studying Pope John Paul II's 'Theology of the Body' and other sources of Church teaching.

Abby Johnson's final decision to reject contraception, like her change of mind on abortion, occurred suddenly, and because of something she saw. This time, however, the sight that changed her mind was not a child's death within the clinic walls, but quite the opposite. An experience in a Catholic church, she said, finally made her understand the fullness of the Church's teaching on sexuality.

This time, the vision of a child was not shocking, but profounbdly life-affirming. 'One day we were sitting in Mass…I was sitting behind this woman who I don't know, and this little infant. Gazing at that child, she finally understood the Church's insistence on marriages remaining open to new life. 'It was just clear to me, like a switch had gone off, that we had to stop contracepting'").

Johnston, Ben (Benjamin Burwell Johnston, Jr.) – composer; b. 15 March 1926, Macon, Georgia; c. 31 May 1970 (Feast of Corpus Christi); educated at William and Mary College, the Cincinnati Conservatory of Music and Mills College; taught composition and theory at the University of Illinois at Urbana-Champaign 1951-1983; then retired to North Carolina; in the 1950s he was a neo-classical composer influenced by his teacher Darius Milhaud (1892-1974); in the 1960s he explored serial techniques and then indeterminacy; was in contact with several avant-garde figures, notably John Cage (1912-1992); worked with the composer Harry Partch (1901-1974), another teacher and friend; he extended Partch's experiments in just intonation (or pure intonation), as opposed to equal temperament, to traditional instruments through his own system of microtonal notation; has used many processes and forms; his aim is to return to a kind of musical beauty he believes is diminished in Western music since the adoption of equal temperament; major works: *Knocking Piece*; *String Quartet No. 4* ("Amazing Grace") (being perhaps his best known composition and one of ten string quartets in total); *Duo for Flute and String Bass*; *Quintet for Groups*; *Sonnets of Desolation*; *Camilla* (an opera); *Sonata for Microtonal Piano*; *Suite for Microtonal Piano*; *Trio for Clarinet, Violin, and Cello*; *Ponder Nothing* (the work's basis is the French hymn *Let All Mortal Flesh Keep Silence*; the title comes from a line in the hymn: "Ponder nothing earthly minded"); recipient of many honors; on the spiritual side he was interested in and eventually disillusioned by the teachings of the philosopher G. I. Gurdjieff (1872-1949), who was greatly influenced by "Eastern" philosophies; after his conversion to the Catholic faith he subsequently became the organist at a local Catholic church; see *"Maximum Clarity" and Other Writings on Music* (2006); Heidi Von Gunden, *The Music of Ben Johnston* (1986) ("I am trying very hard to let every work be a religious intention, not simply an 'expression' of my ego. It means taking on quite a lot and not writing large numbers of works"); William Duckworth, *Talking Music: Conversations with John Cage, Philip Glass, Laurie Anderson, and Five Generations of American Experimental Composers* (1995).

Johnston, John Warfield- lawyer and politician; b. 9 September 1818, "Panicello", near Abingdon, Virginia; d. 27 February 1889, Richmond, Virginia; born in the house of his paternal grandfather, Peter Johnston, a judge; only child of Dr. John Warfield Johnston and Louisa Smith Bowen; educated at Abingdon Academy, South Carolina College at Columbia, then at the Law Department of the University of Virginia at Charlottesville; admitted to the bar in 1839 and then practiced law; in 1841 he married Nicketti Buchanan Floyd (1819-1908), the daughter of Governor John Floyd (see above) and Letitia Preston Floyd (see above); his wife was Catholic, having converted when young; he himself converted after the marriage; he and his wife had twelve children; served in the Virginia Senate; little known about his activities during the Civil War, but sided with the Confederacy; judge of the Circuit Superior Court of Law and Chancery of Virginia; elected as a representative for Virginia for the United States Senate 1870-1883; he had been ineligible to serve in Congress because of the Fourteenth Amendment, which forbade anyone from holding public office who had sworn allegiance to the United States and subsequently sided with the Confederacy during the Civil War; but his restrictions were removed when he aided a sick and dying former slave after the War; he was the first person who had sided with the Confederacy to serve in the United States Senate; became a Conservative Democrat; later resumed his legal practice; buried in St. Mary's Cemetery, Wytheville; see *Reminiscences of Thirteen Years in the Senate* (n.d.)

Johnston, Richard Malcolm - educator and writer; b. 8 March 1822, near Powelton, in Hancock County, Georgia; c. 1875 ("accepting the truth after long hesitation" (*Catholic Encyclopedia*); his wife was received six months earlier); d. 23 September 1898, Baltimore, Maryland; son of a planter and Baptist minister; raised a Baptist, but later became an Episcopalian; graduated from Mercer University in 1841; admitted to the Georgia bar in 1843; worked as both teacher and lawyer; in 1844 he married Mary Frances Mansfield (d. 1897) (twelve children of the marriage); professorship of belles lettres and oratory at the University of Georgia 1857-1861; wrote a textbook on English, plus humorous short fiction; in 1861 started on his farm in Hancock County a select boarding school for boys, Rockby, which gained a high reputation; organized the state militia during the Civil War; ran another school, Pen Lucy, in Baltimore 1876-1883; his conversion to the Catholic Church reduced school revenues, since his patronage came mainly from Baptists; so he devoted himself entirely to writing; this proved very successful nationally; his son Lucien became a priest; see (selective list) *The English Classics* (1860); *Georgia Sketches* (1864); *Dukesborough Tales* (1871, 1874 and 1883); *Mr. Absalom Billingslea and Other Georgia Folk* (1888); *The Primes and Their Neighbors* (1891); *Dukesborough Tales: The Chronicles of Mr. Bill Williams* (1892); *Mr. Billy Downs and His Likes* (1892); *Mr. Fortner's Marital Claims and Other Stories* (1892); *Little Ike Templin and Other Stories* (1894); *Lectures on Literature* (1897); *Old Times in Middle Georgia* (1897); *Autobiography of Colonel Richard Malcolm Johnston* (1900); Walter Lecky, *Down at Caxton's* (1895), p.7; Bert Hitchcock, *Richard Malcolm Johnston* (1978); *Catholic Encyclopedia* ("He relates that he was thirty years old when he first saw a priest, and that his first investigations into the Faith were during the "Know-Nothing" campaign of 1855, when he read some of Bishop England's and Newman's works to confute a political opponent"); *ANB* ("Seen by family and friends as the charming embodiment of the Old South plantation gentleman, he is viewed by literary historians as a revealing transitional figure between earlier realistic 'Old Southwest humor' and the more romantic, local-color humorous fiction of the late nineteenth century. Although his range was limited and he sometimes wrote over-fondly about the past, Johnston was able through his characters to re-create a culture and way of life that readers may still find informative, entertaining, and sometimes moving").

Jones, Casey (real name John Luther Jones)–railroad engineer; b. 14 March 1863, Southern Missouri; c. 11 November 1886 (received at St, Bridget's Church, Whistler, Alabama); d. 30 April 1900, Vaughan, Mississippi; son of Frank Jones, a school teacher; fascinated by trains from a young age; family moved to Cayce, Kentucky, in 1876 (when he was asked later where he was from by some railroad men, they branded him "Casey" after his hometown); his first job at the age of fifteen was with the Mobile and Ohio Railroad as a telegrapher and later as brakeman and fireman; company transferred him to Jackson, Tennessee; he fell in love with the daughter of the boarding house owner, Mary Joanna ("Janie") Brady (1866-1958), and proposed marriage; since she was a Catholic he decided to be baptized to please her; they were married in 1886 (three children of the marriage); in 1888 he moved to the Illinois Central Railroad, firing a freight locomotive; in 1891 he was promoted engineer; he was famed for his timing and punctuality; also famous for the unusual sound of his train whistle, which became his trade mark; in 1895 he heroically rescued a little girl from the track at Michigan City, Mississippi; he eventually transferred to the more lucrative passenger trains; fatally injured in a crash when his train traveling in dark, rainy and foggy conditions from Memphis, Tennessee, to Canton, Mississippi, crashed into part of a freight train that (due to locked brakes) was on the main track, the other portion being on a sidetrack; he told the fireman (Simeon T. Webb (1874-1957)) to jump (which he did and survived), and blew his whistle to warn anyone still in the freight train; because he stayed on board to slow the train, he no doubt saved the passengers from serious injury and death (Jones himself was the only fatality of the collision); the press reports raised the incident and his heroism to legendary status; his wife wore black nearly every day for the rest of her life and never remarried; buried in Mount Calvary Cemetery, Jackson; the official report of the accident stated that "Engineer Jones was solely responsible having disregarded the signals given by Flagman [John M.] Newberry," but some railroad historians have disputed the official account over the years; the traditional ballad, *The Ballad of Casey Jones*, and other songs and media representations have increased its fame; see Fred Lee, *Casey Jones* (1940); Bruce Gurner, *Casey Jones and the Wreck at Vaughan* (1973); Eleonore Villarubia, "Casey Jones: Legendary Railroad Engineer and

Catholic," *catholicism.org* ("His company soon transferred him to the important railroad town of Jackson, Tennessee. This was the move that was to be the cause of his conversion to Catholicism, for he boarded at the home of one Mrs. Brady, whose abode was a boarding house for the traveling railroad workers. The Brady family were practicing Catholics and they must have had a good influence on Casey. Smitten by Mrs. Brady's daughter, Janie, Casey decided to become a Catholic").

Jones, E. Michael ((Eugene) Michael Jones) – writer and editor; b. 4 May 1948, Philadelphia, Pennsylvania; c. summer 1973 (revert; his wife Ruth, previously an Episcopalian, converted in the same year); raised in the Catholic Church, but lapsed from it in the late 1960s; taught English at a school in Germany; returned to the Catholic faith there; earned his PhD in American Literature from Temple University, Philadelphia; taught at Saint Mary's College of Notre Dame, Indiana; his opposition to abortion at this Catholic college led to his contract not being renewed after a year; author of several books and many articles; editor of *Culture Wars* magazine (earlier *Fidelity* magazine); much work on the relationship between the Catholic Church and secular culture, especially in relation to the sexual revolution; later writing on the relationship between the Catholic Church and the Jews ("Jesus Christ, who is God, became man. At this point the Jews, who were God's chosen people, had to make a choice. They had to either accept Jesus Christ as the long-promised Messiah or not. Those who accepted him became known as Christians; those who rejected him became known as Jews"); argues that the rejection of Christ led historically to a revolutionary spirit and opposition to the Church; he has been accused of anti-semitism, but he denies this and states that any form of racism is against the Catholic faith; he emphasizes that the Church imputes to *Christians* "the gravest responsibility for the torments inflicted upon Jesus, a responsibility with which they have all too often burdened the Jews alone," but that "we fall into...grave error by claiming that Jews were not primarily responsible at the time and place for bringing about the actual event in history that is known as the crucifixion"; father of five children; see (selected list) *Is Notre Dame Still Catholic?* (1989; revised edition 2009); *The Angel and the Machine: The Rational Psychology of Nathaniel Hawthorne* (1991); *Degenerate Moderns: Modernity as Rationalized Sexual Misbehavior* (1993) ("There are ultimately only two alternatives in the intellectual life: either one conforms desire to the truth or one conforms truth to desire. These two positions represent opposite poles between which a continuum of almost infinite gradation exists. So, to give two extremes first, we might have St. Thomas Aquinas or, more dramatically, St. Augustine, representing the former position – desire subject to the truth – and Sigmund Freud or Martin Luther representing the latter – truth subject to desire...

The intellectual life is a function of the moral life of the thinker. In order to apprehend truth, which is the goal of the intellectual life, one must live a moral life. One can produce an intellectual product, but to the extent that one prescinds from living the moral life, the product will be more a function of internal desire – wish fulfillment, if you will – than external reality. This is true of any intellectual field and any deeply held desire. In the intellectual life, one either conforms desire to truth or truth to desire...

Lust is a common enough vice, especially in this age. The crucial intellectual event occurs, however, when vices are transmuted into theories, when the 'intellectual' sets up shop in rebellion against the moral law and, therefore, in rebellion against the truth. All the modern 'isms' follow as a direct result of this rebellion. All of them entail rationalization. All of them can be best understood in light of the moral disorder of their founders, proponents, and adherents.

So the antithesis of...modernity's dualism is summed up in the following passage from *The Silence of St. Thomas* by Joseph Pieper: 'Since we nowadays think that all a man needs for acquisition of truth is to exert his brain more or less vigorously, and since we consider an ascetic approach to knowledge hardly sensible, we have lost the awareness of the close bond that links the knowledge of truth to the condition of purity. Thomas says that unchastity's first-born daughter is blindness of the spirit. Only he who wants nothing for himself, who is not subjectively 'interested', can know the truth. On the other hand, an impure selfishly corrupted will to pleasure destroys both resoluteness of spirit and the ability of the psyche to listen in silent attention to the language of reality.'

It is the curse of this age to have to prove on its own pulse and in the degrading minutiae of the biographies of its *prominenti* the lessons that the Catholic Church in her wisdom (which was once the collective wisdom of the West) knew all things...

Modernity was rationalized sexual misbehavior. All the intellectual and cultural breakthroughs of modernity were in some way or other linked to the sexual desires their progenitors knew to be illicit but which they chose nonetheless. Their theories were ultimately rationalizations of the choices they knew to be wrong. The lives of the moderns are, then, an uncanny substantiation of the power and scope of the moral law. 'All who desert you,' St. Augustine says in his *Confessions*, 'and set themselves up against you merely copy you in a perverse way.' St. Augustine is talking about God here and those who rejected him in his age; however, his words apply equally well to the moral law and those who reject it in ours."); *Dionysos Rising: The Birth of Cultural Revolution Out of the Spirit of Music* (1994); *Living Machines: Bauhaus Architecture As Sexual Ideology* (1995); *John Cardinal Krol and the Cultural Revolution* (1995) ("It must have been difficult for Leo Pfeffer to suppress a smile of satisfaction as he stepped to the podium to deliver his talk to the Society for the Scientific Study of Religion at the end of October in 1976. The title of the talk gives some indication that Pfeffer had come to Philadelphia to gloat. It was called 'Issues that Divide: The Triumph of Secular Humanism' and it provided a catalogue of the revolutionary changes that had transformed American culture during the fifteen years prior to Pfeffer's talk. During the period in question, America had quite simply revised its culture. lf America were a computer, one could say that the default settings had been changed. At the beginning of the seventh decade of the twentieth century, the culture of the country was based on a pan-Protestant reading of Christianity whose assumptions favored, in imperfect form albeit, a rough approximation of the moral law. By the end of the decade, the default settings had been changed in favor of a culture that was individualistic, rationalistic, and hedonistic, especially in matters sexual. It was not just that people's behavior had changed; those changes had been inscribed in the culture, in the constitution, or at least how it was interpreted, in the rules that governed people's lives, and Leo Pfeffer was one of the main agents of that change...

If Pfeffer had come to talk about the 'triumph of secular humanism,' he was well-qualified. He had been intimately involved in virtually all of the battles that had brought about that triumph. Beginning with the *Schempp v. Abington* in the early '60s and ending with the *Lemon v. Kurtzman* decision in 1970, Pfeffer was the architect of the legal strategy which removed the last vestiges of Protestant culture from the public schools and denied government funding to Catholic schools...

Pfeffer tells us all who exactly the enemy was in the, from his perspective at least, successfully concluded cultural wars in the United States...For Pfeffer the enemy was quite simply the Catholic Church...

One major difference between the Catholic Church and all other churches and synagogues, according to Pfeffer, was its unity; another was its authority. No other denomination was as threatening to the view of the world Pfeffer held because no other denomination made the same magnitude of belief claims on its adherents...

If the Catholic Church had been

willing to declare fornication and abortion the eighth and ninth sacraments respectively, it seems doubtful that the liberals would have been upset by her authoritarianism. The fact remains, however, that she wasn't and therein lies the real reason for the animus of the liberals and the *casus belli* in our *Kulturkampf.* During the entire post-World War II period in the United States, the Catholic Church opposed the main article of faith of secular humanism, namely, sexual liberation. Beginning with the creation of the Legion of Decency in 1933 and culminating in the opposition to *Roe v Wade* forty years later, the Catholic Church consistently picked up the banner of sexual morality which the mainstream Protestant denominations had let fall. The one great thaw in the liberal animus toward the Church came in the early '60s during the Second Vatican Council when it looked as if the Church might reach a *modus vivendi* with modernity by legitimatizing the use of contraceptives. That dream was laid to rest in 1968 when Pope Paul VI slammed the door shut on the *conditio sine qua non* of cooperation with the liberal regime. When *Humanae Vitae* hit the streets, the liberals broke off relations and turned instead to a combination of open hostility and fomenting rebellion within the ranks. The lull in the fighting in the liberals' ongoing *Kulturkampf* with the Catholic Church ended abruptly in 1968. Thereafter, the hostilities were out in the open again...

What we witnessed during those years was a struggle for the control of the instruments of culture which was remarkably similar to the struggle in Germany ninety years before. What we witnessed in the 60s in the United States was America's *Kulturkampf*...Both the German and the American *Kulturkampf* involved a conflict between the Enlightenment and the Catholic Church...

Both the German *Kulturkampf* of the 1870s and the American one of the 1960s were spawned by an ecumenical council. The reactions were, however, initially quite different. The German liberals were quite simply outraged by Pius IX's *Syllabus of Errors* and the doctrine of infallibility and turned that outrage on their German Catholic compatriots. If someone could believe such things, his patriotism was in question. His status as a German was in doubt. He was quite simply under the suspicion of subverting the regime. The effect of Vatican I on German Catholics was, however, quite the opposite. After languishing as cultural second-class citizens, German Catholics were suddenly reinfused with a new sense of identity and purpose that was bound to make itself felt in the newly unified country, a country whose unification was to take place under the unspoken aegis of German philosophy, German science, and Prussian Protestantism.

The *Kulturkampf* which took place in the United States during the 1960s followed on the heels of a council as well, in this case Vatican II. But its trajectory was different. Unlike the *Syllabus of Errors*, Vatican II sought to be as irenic as possible in its approach to modernity. So irenic was the council, in fact, that a large segment of the Catholic population felt that its mission was to convert the Church to the categories of modernity. When it became obvious that the Church was not going to modernize to the satisfaction of the liberals, the American *Kulturkampf* began in earnest. *Humanae Vitae* was the opening shot, *Roe v Wade* the liberals' major counter-offensive. The irenic approach of Vatican II to the modern world gave the liberals within the Catholic Church their major opening, and it also provided the secular humanists with a major foothold in weakening the Church's opposition to its agenda.

Which brings us to one of the major differences between the *Kulturkampf* in 1870 and the one in 1960. In Prussia, Bismarck tried to divide the Church, but in vain. In America, the secular humanists were much more successful in finding a fifth column within the Church to do their bidding. Bismarck's attack on the Catholic Church in Ermland was a frontal assault...As a result of Catholic unity in face of frontal assault, the *Kulturkampf* of 1870 was a much more violent fever which, as a result, passed much more quickly.

In America, the assault was much subtler. The carrot of government funding, publishing contracts, foundation money, and *pro bono* legal services was proffered more readily than the stick of government regulation. As a result, the cultural revolutionaries in America in the 1960s found a fifth column within the Church willing to aid and abet their plans...The story of the cultural revolution in America in the 1960s is the story of the Catholic Church at war on two fronts. There was the enemy outside the gates, people like Pfeffer, and there were the collaborators within, who were often taking the money of the cultural revolutionaries to undermine the Church's position...

Which brings us to the various theaters of combat in the cultural war. Pfeffer delineates three major areas of contestation. First, as in the *Kulturkampf* in Germany beginning in 1870, there was the battle over the schools...

The second area of contestation he mentions is obscenity in general and film in particular...

The final area of cultural revolution delineated by Pfeffer had to do with whose idea of the family would dominate in the culture. The major issue in the '60s was contraception, but that was soon replaced by abortion in the '70s"); *The Medjugorje Deception: Queen of Peace, Ethnic Cleansing, Ruined Lives* (1998); *Libido Dominandi: Sexual Liberation & Political*

Control (1999) ("Pornography is now and has always been a form of control, financial control. Pornography is a way of getting people to give you money which, because of the compulsive nature of the transaction, is not unlike trafficking in drugs…Just as the history of pornography is one of progress (technological, not moral progress, of course), so the exploitation of compulsion has been explored in more and more explicit form during the past two hundred years of this revolutionary age. What began as the bondage of sin eventually became financial control and what became accepted as a financial transaction has been forged into a form of political control. Sexual revolution is contemporaneous with political revolution of the sort that began in France in 1789. This means we are not talking about sexual vice when we use the term *sexual revolution*, as much as the rationalization of sexual vice, followed by the financial exploitation of sexual vice, followed by the political mobilization of the same thing as a form of control. Since sexual 'liberation' has social chaos as one of its inevitable sequelae, sexual liberation begets almost from the moment of its inception the need for social control...

It is no secret now that lust is also a form of addiction. My point here is that the current regime knows this and exploits this situation to its own advantage. In other words, sexual 'freedom' is really a form of social control. What we are really talking about is a Gnostic system of two truths. The exoteric truth, the one propagated by the regime through advertising, sex education, Hollywood films, and the university system - the truth, in other words for general consumption - is that sexual liberation is freedom. The esoteric truth, the one that informs the operations manual of the regime - in other words the people who benefit from 'liberty' - is the exact opposite, namely, that sexual liberation is a form of control, a way of maintaining the regime in power by exploiting the passions of the naive, who identify with their passions as if they were their own and identify with the regime which ostensibly enables them to gratify these passions. People who succumb to their disordered passions are then given rationalizations of the sort that clog web pages on the Internet and are thereby molded into a powerful political force by those who are most expert in manipulating the flow of imagery and rationalization.

Like laissez-faire economics, the first tentative ideas of how to exploit sex as a form of social control arose during the Enlightenment as well. If the universe was a machine whose prime force was gravity, society was a machine as well whose prime force was self-interest, and man, likewise, no longer sacred, was a machine whose engine ran on passion. From there it was not much of a stretch to understand that the man who controlled passion controlled man...

The idea that sexual liberation could be used as a form of control is not a new idea. It lies at the heart of the story of Samson and Delilah. The idea that sin was a form of slavery was central to the writings of St. Paul. St. Augustine in his *magnum opus* in defense of Christianity against the accusations of the pagans that it contributed to the fall of Rome, divided the world into two cities, The City of God, which loves God to the extinction of self, and the City of Man, which loves self to the extinction of God. Augustine describes the City of Man as 'lusting to dominate the world' but at the same time 'itself dominated by its passion for dominion.' *Libido Dominandi*, passion for dominion, then, is a paradoxical project, practiced invariably by people who are themselves in thrall to the same passions they incite in others to dominate them.

The dichotomy Augustine describes is eternal. It will exist at least as long as man exists, The revolutionaries of the Enlightenment created no new world nor did they create a new man to populate their brave new world. What they did was adopt the worldview of Augustine and then reverse its values. 'The state of the moral man is one of tranquility and peace, the state of an immoral man is one of perpetual unrest.' The author of that statement was not St. Augustine (although he would have wholeheartedly agreed with it); it was the Marquis de Sade. I mention this to show that both Augustine and the Marquis de Sade shared the same anthropology and the same rational psychology, if you will. Where they differed was the values they attributed to the truths of those sciences. For Augustine, motion was bad; for de Sade, the revolutionary, the perpetual motion caused by unruly passions was good because it perpetuates 'the necessary insurrection in which the republican must always keep the government of which he is a member.'

The same could be said of freedom. What the one called freedom the other called bondage. But the dichotomy of the two cities - one abasing the self because of its love of God, the other abasing God because of its love of the self and its desires - is something that both could agree upon.

What follows is the history of a project born out of the Enlightenment's inversion of Christian truths. 'Even those who set themselves up against you,' Augustine writes, addressing the Almighty in the *Confessions*, 'do but copy you in a perverse way.' The same could be said of the Enlightenment, which began as a movement to liberate man and almost overnight turned into a project to control him. This book is the story of that transformation. It can be construed as a history of the sexual revolution or a history of modern psychology or a history of psychological warfare. What all of these histories have in common is a transgenerational project that would come by way of trial and error and with an intention perverted by passion to the same conclusions that Augustine reached at the end of the Roman Empire. A man has as many masters as he has vices. By promoting vice, the regime promotes slavery, which can be fashioned into a form of political control. The only question which remained was whether that slavery can be harnessed for financial and political gain and, if it could, how to do it. The best way to control man is to do so without his awareness that he is being controlled, and the best way to do that is through the systematic manipulation of the passions, because man tends to identify his passions as his own. In defending them he defends his 'freedom,' which he usually sees as the unfettered ability to fulfill his desires, without, for the most part, understanding how easy it is to manipulate those passions from without. It took the evil genius of this age to perfect a system of financial and political exploitation based on the insight that St. Paul and St. Augustine had into what they termed the 'slavery of sin.' This book describes the systematic construction of a worldview based on that insight. It explains how sexual liberation became a form of political control"); *Monsters From the Id: The Rise of Horror in Fiction and Film* (2000); "What Happened to America in the 60s?" *Saint Austin Review*, January/ February 2003; *The Slaughter of Cities: Urban Renewal as Ethnic Cleansing* (2005); *The Jewish Revolutionary Spirit and Its Impact on World History* (2008) ("The real topic of Pope Benedict XVI's Regensburg speech was Logos [which is the Greek word for the rational order of the universe] and the central role it plays in both Europe and the Church.

Unlike Christianity, Islam is not docile to Logos, nor for that matter is Islam's God; God's will is arbitrary, inscrutable.

Christianity is different from Islam in this regard: the Christian God acts with Logos. In using the term Logos, the Pope situates Christianity and, by extension, the European culture which grew up under its influence, in the tradition of Greek philosophy. Greek philosophy is part of God's plan for humanity...'In the beginning was the logos, and the logos is God,' says the Evangelist...This means that Logos, far from being some cultural accretion, is part of the nature of God and, therefore, part of creation. [We] are born into a world that is radically reasonable, radically logical, because that world mirrors the mind of God, who behaves in ways that sometimes go beyond what human reason can comprehend but never in ways that contradict that reason.

So far so good...We can see without too much effort that Islam has a radically different attitude toward the relationship between faith and reason. Europe has dealt with the threat for centuries, but from an historical perspective, the Islamic threat to Europe is only half the story. At this point we come to the attack on Logos which is not mentioned in the Pope's speech, the Jewish attack on Logos, which manifests itself not by the threat of invasion from without, as is the case with Islam, which has sought to spread its faith by military conquest, but by the threat of subversion from within, otherwise known as revolution. If Muslims are alogos,...then Jews are anti-logos, in the sense that they reject Christ altogether. Islam did not reject Christ; Islam failed to understand Christ, as manifested in its rejection of both the Trinity and the Incarnation, and ended up trying to mask that misunderstanding by honoring Jesus as a prophet.

The situation with Jews is completely different. The Jews were God's chosen people. When Jesus arrived on earth as their long-awaited Messiah, the Jews, who, like all men, were given free will by their God, had to make a decision. They had to either accept or reject the Christ, who was, so Christians believe, the physical embodiment of Logos. ...[T]he Jews began by wanting to have the Messiah save them on their terms, which were suffused with racial pride. When the Jews tell Jesus in John 8 that they are the 'seed of Abraham,' in Greek 'sperma Abraam,' He changes the terms of the argument by replying 'If you were Abraham's children, you would do as Abraham did,' which is to say follow God's will and accept Jesus as the son of God and Messiah. Since the Jews, or those to whom Jesus is speaking, reject Jesus, they reject their father Abraham as well, and show that 'the devil is [their] father.'

Once Jesus arrives in Jerusalem, the term Jew in the Gospel of St. John is no longer a purely racial term. Jew has come to mean a rejecter of Christ. Race is no longer the focus. The Jews who accept Jesus will henceforth be known as Christians. The Jews who reject him are known henceforth as 'Jews.' As St. John reports in the Apocalypse, 'those who call themselves Jews' are really liars and members of the 'synagogue of Satan' (Rev 2.9, 3.9)...

The Jews rejected Christ because he was crucified. They wanted a powerful leader, not a suffering servant. Annas and Caiaphas mockingly told Christ that if he came down from the cross, they would accept him as the Messiah. When the Jews rejected Christ, they rejected Logos, which includes within itself the principles of social order, they became revolutionaries.

Jews may have become revolutionaries at the foot of the cross, but the full implications of their decision didn't become apparent until thirty years later, when the Jews rebelled against Rome, and Rome retaliated by destroying the Temple. At this point, the Jews had no temple, no priesthood, and no sacrifice, and as a result they had no way of fulfilling their covenant. Seeing which way the battle for Jerusalem was going, a rabbi and deputy head of the Sanhedrin, by the name of Jochanan ben Zakkai had himself smuggled out of Jerusalem in a shroud, and, after being recognized by Roman authorities as a friend of Rome, was granted the privilege of founding a rabbinical school at Jabneh.

It is at this moment, some thirty years after the founding of the Church, that modern Judaism, Judaism as we know it, was born as essentially a debating society, because in the absence of a Temple, that was all that Jews could do. the results of these interminable debates became known as the Talmud, which got written down over the next six centuries. The debating did nothing to eradicate the spirit of revolution from the Jewish mind, but in many ways intensified it by teaching the Jews to look for a military Messiah.

The Jews got their military Messiah roughly sixty years after the destruction of the Temple, when Simon bar Kokhba rose up against Rome in 131. The rabbis in Jerusalem, with a few exceptions, recognized bar Kokhba as the Messiah, and so as if to prove that racial Judaism had become incoherent, the Christian Jews were expelled for not recognizing him as the Messiah. It didn't matter whether your mother was Jewish; the ultimate determinant of Jewishness had become rejection of Christ, and that rejection led inexorably to revolution. Such enmity to Logos as represented in the person of Jesus Christ is present in the Talmud. Princeton Jewish scholar Peter Schaefer notes that Talmudic stories mock claims of Jesus's birth from the Virgin Mary, challenge His claim to be the Messiah, and state that He was rightly executed for blasphemy and idolatry, and that He resides in Hell, where His followers will go...

While the Talmud refers to the justice of Christ's execution, the Christian must believe that Christ died for our sins. According to the Catholic Church: 'sinners were the authors and ministers of all the sufferings that the divine redeemer endured. Taking into account the fact that our sins affect Christ himself, the Church does not hesitate to impute to Christians the gravest responsibility for the torments inflicted upon Jesus, a responsibility with which they have all too often burdened the Jews alone.' Moreover, the Catholic Catechism goes on to quote from an earlier Catechism: 'We, however, profess to know him. And when we deny him by our deeds, we in some way seem to lay violent hands on him.'

It is all too easy to minimize

this profound teaching, but in maximizing it we fall into another grave error by claiming that Jews were not primarily responsible at the time and place for bringing about the actual event in history that is known as the crucifixion. Such a position directly contradicts the Gospel accounts and makes any understanding of the nature of the Jewish split impossible. After all, that famous Jewish convert St. Peter (Acts 3.14-15) refers directly to those who killed Christ in addressing and appealing to the very people he saw as having done this. This rejection of Logos, rooted in an historical event, continues to play a part in what it means to be a Jew...

Rabbi Louis Israel Newman points out how Jews have consistently supported revolutionary movements throughout history. Jews joined forces with heretics during the Albigensian crisis, the Hussite revolution, the reformation, and at the birth of modern England. They joined forces with revolutionaries during The Enlightenment, the Russian Revolution and the Civil Rights movement. We also see the conflict between the Church and Judaism working itself out at the birth of the Spanish Inquisition, the spread of the Polish empire and the Chmielnicki rebellion that began the break up of that empire. Finally, we see a Jewish presence in the rise of the American Empire...

The Catholic response to the revolutionary Jewish rejection of Logos came to be known as '*Sicut Iudeis non...*,' a doctrine codified by Pope Gregory the Great and reiterated by virtually every pope after him. According to '*Sicut Iudeis non...*,' no one has the right to harm Jews or disrupt their worship services, but the Jews have, likewise, no right to corrupt the faith or morals of Christians or subvert Christian societies...

The Church was consistent in its opposition to revolution on the one hand, and in defending the Jews against genuine persecution on the other. Both parts of this teaching are necessary. If either one is ignored, trouble follows"); *Ballet Parking: Performing The Nutcracker as a Counter-Revolutionary Act* (2009); "History Lesson," *Culture Wars*, September 2012, p.20 ((1) "Both St. Augustine and I came to the Catholic Faith by reading a book. *The Seven Storey Mountain* had been a surprise bestseller in 1948, the year when I was born. It was part of the Catholic revival in America which followed World War II. I don't remember any specific argument from the book... *The Seven Storey Mountain* I thought was first-rate writing and if a man with this much literary talent could believe in God, well belief in God was good enough for me too. And so I gave up on everything else and decided to put my life in God's hands, especially since it wasn't going any place special when I thought that I was totally in control of it. If I had to characterize my life as a young apostate, I could not characterize it as anything other than the gradual evaporation of being. When a seminarian picked me up one day when I was hitchhiking to graduate school, I described my life to him as a scene from a novel by Samuel Beckett which entailed the gradual loss of mobility. So I gave up all of my illusions and put my faith back where my baptismal sponsors had put it in 1948 in God." (2) "Whether you accept Jesus Christ or not is very important. In fact, your eternal destiny depends upon it. It is so important that his arrival on this earth is universally acknowledged as the turning point in history. Even the most flaming atheist, if asked would have to affirm when he writes a check or sends a birthday card that that check was written 2012 years after the birth of Christ.

And what happened back then? Jesus Christ, who is God, became man. At this point the Jews, who were God's chosen people, had to make a choice. They had to either accept Jesus Christ as the long-promised Messiah or not. Those who accepted him became known as Christians; those who rejected him became known as Jews. In America we're taught to be polite to members of other religions, and this is a good thing, but it's a bad thing if it leads us to believe that there is no difference between accepting Jesus Christ as our Lord and savior and rejecting him and calling for his crucifixion.

When the Jews rejected Christ, they rejected Logos, which is the Greek term for the order of the universe flowing from the mind of God. Logos is mentioned in the first sentence of the Gospel of St. John, when the Evangelist tells us, 'εν άρχη ήν ό λόγός – *en arche een ho logos*,' 'In the beginning was the word (Logos) and the Word (Logos) was with God and the Word (Logos) was God.' When the Jews rejected Logos, they rejected the moral and political order which God intended for the world as well. As a result, the Jews who rejected Christ became revolutionaries, which means that they continue to seek a messiah who sets out to set the world aright (*Tikkun olam* is their way of saying this) but always fails, whether it's the new economics of Karl Marx or the new science of psychiatry as propagated by Sigmund Freud or the counter-culture of sex, drugs and rock and roll brought to us by Alan Freed, Leonard Chess and Bob Dylan, among others. None of these things or people have saved the world. There is only one savior - Jesus Christ. The world we live in is imperfect but it can only be ordered properly through Jesus Christ, the Logos; it can't be ordered or saved by people who are in rebellion against that order.

That means that it can't be saved by 'white guys' or 'conservatives' or 'Southerners' or believers in 'Western Civilization,' either. Jews may constitute a permanent *avant garde* for revolution, but they are not the only revolutionaries. In fact, the history of the last 500 years bespeaks the carnage which follows when nominal Christians decided to act like Jews and become revolutionaries"); *culturewars.com.*

Jones, Jason Simon – film producer; b. 1974, Chicago, Illinois; c. 6 August 2003; last in class at school; never went to church and became an atheist; at age sixteen he found that his girl friend was pregnant; they decided to have the child, disguising the fact of the pregnancy; he joined the army at seventeen; his girl friend's father forced her to have an abortion; got involved with working for pro-life groups, including thirteen years when he was still an atheist (influenced by the writings of Ayn Rand); studied at University of Hawaii; co-executive producer of the pro-life film, *Bella* (2006), winner of the 2006 Toronto International Film Festival People's Choice Award; producer of several documentaries; much experience in running political campaigns and has worked for the Republican National Committee; worked for a time for Sam Brownback (see above); founded a website called "Movie to Movement," designed to help audiences find and support positive faith-based films that speak to their values; founder of the Human Rights Education and Relief Organization (HERO), which comprises "Movie to Movement," "Whole Life America" (a non-profit organization that promotes the dignity of the human person, regardless of ability, age, status, race, or geography) and "The Great Campaign for Human Dignity"; producer of *Christiada (For Greater Glory)* (2012), the true story of the war between the Catholic Church and the Communists in Mexico in 1926; influenced also by Pope John Paul's *Memory and Identity* (2005), and by the writings of Hadley Arkes (see above); see "John W. Kennedy, Interview with Jason Jones," *beliefnet.com*, October 2011 ("I was an Ayn Rand objectivist from about the seventh grade on…I never went to church a day in my life. The dominant religion (influence) in my family was my grandfather who was a Scientologist but, by about the seventh grade, I discovered Ayn Rand (*Atlas Shrugged*) and sort of became an atheist objectivist. And, in graduate school, there was a line from the French existentialist Jean-Paul Sartre that said something like if we're going to deny God's existence, we have to deny human dignity. What was actually said was much more poetic than that and was very persuasive. In reading that line, I became a theist. The intrinsic beauty of value of the individual person was always self-evident to me. It's what animated me and I think that's why I found Ayn Rand so attractive but she would always fall back on human dignity as axiomatic…which, of course, it is but after reading Sartre I needed more than saying it's axiomatic");

"From a Clear Blue Sky," *Crisis*, 24 October 2011; "Life Lessons from Joseph Stalin," *Crisis*, 1 November 2011; "A Nation with the Soul of a Church," *Crisis*, 14 November 2011; "We Proud Sons of Onan," *Crisis*, 23 November 2011 ("Where did the West go wrong? The tragic flaw we share with our cousins over in Europe is not so much political or economic as cultural. You see, Marx was wrong: Economic reality is not the DNA that forms the social organism, dictating which poems will be written and which constitutions amended. Marx's vulgar materialism, predicated on an *a priori* rejection of God, refuted itself over seven blood-soaked decades from Königsberg to Cambodia, as the world re-learned this truth: *It is culture that drives politics,* and the dance between the two that produces the kind of economy which emerges from a country. Leave aside 'black swan' events like the Potato Famine or the Black Death, and you can trace a people's economic fortunes to the social values that motivate them, and the institutions these values have built. The hyperinflation that ravished Germany in the 20s and paved the way for Hitler was caused by the debt and reparations incurred during World War I - which the Germans launched after some ninety years of post-Napoleonic romantic nationalism and militarism. The stagnation and instability that pervades the Islamic world can be traced straight to their credal rejection of reason and even causality in understanding nature. (A rock falls not because of gravity, but because God happens to will it - and it's perfectly possible that any given rock might hang in mid-air forever, should He wish it.) I could multiply instances all day - but like you, I've got some turkey sitting here that's not going to eat itself.

We live now for ourselves, and for pleasures in present or future. Our culture, and hence our economy and politics, now stand for absolutely nothing else. To cite the old *Seinfeld* line, we are now a 'civilization about nothing.'

Our forefathers may have lapsed from time to time into foolish, self-destructive acts of hedonism, but the culture in which they lived and the faith they followed called things what they were: They knew sin as sin, and knew the need for repentance and reparation. These people knew that we live not only for ourselves, but at the very least for the sake of our children. Italians planted olive trees which their children would some day profit from; now they have ceased even to plant the children, attaining one of the lowest birth rates now on earth. (They compete with the Spaniards and the Quebecois for that honor.)

Since the Sexual Revolution and its ugly stepsister, feminism, overturned our assumptions about what sex means and what it's for, we have almost forgotten how to form families, or what they are. Divorce laws have made the contract of marriage laughably easy to escape from, even as we have tightened up bankruptcy laws and canonized student loans as sacramental covenants. Voters - not just judges, real live American voters - have redefined marriage in several states to include homosexual unions. Single people can adopt children, and couples can cook them up in petri dishes, discarding the 'surplus' embryos or sending them up to Harvard to be cannibalized for parts. What agenda is served by all these bizarre acts of rebellion against the plain nature of things and the immemorial structure of human society? Nothing so elevated or insane as Marxist-Leninism. Nothing so cool and mathematical as capitalism. The philosophy underpinning our current crisis, which explains our Keynesian politics and addiction to credit card debt, Europe's falling and our own flat birth rates, our willingness to tax our children (via deficits) instead of ourselves, is a simple creed known to every teenager: *'We want the world and we want it now,'* in the words of Dionysian rock-god Jim Morrison, who died a bloated shell of a man at age 28, leaving behind no acknowledged children, but at least 20 paternity suits filed by women he had abandoned"); "Of Human Dignity and Shoes," *Crisis*, 22 January 2012 ("The age we mark as modernity began with grand, exhilarating gestures: discourses on method that would set us free from the dead hand of tradition (Descartes); declarations of the rights of man (the French Revolutionary Assembly); manifestos rejecting the tyranny of mere economic laws over the lives and labor of men (Karl Marx). The grand progression of the movement Henri de Lubac dubbed 'heroic humanism' was full of such golden moments, which moved through the dark night of history like torches leading us forward, ever forward, to a glittering future that would make life at long last *worthy of man*. At the end of all the struggles, after the next (surely final!) conflict, or the next, we were promised without any irony a brave new world, an earthly paradise. Descartes had no doubt that science would end disease and aging, so men could live forever. Robespierre offered public safety and a reign of absolute virtue. Marx fought to eliminate war, inequality, and even boring jobs: in the stateless, classless Communist endpoint of history, no one would even have to specialize in anything. We could move from one career to another from day to day, and have ample time in the evening to philosophize or write poetry. As Thomas Paine said, 'We have it in our power to begin the world over again.'

And we did. That's what we spent the 19th and 20th centuries doing, energetically. We broke up historic empires into nation-states, where men forgot their loyalty to tiny village or global Church, and learned to think as members of ethnic tribes or aggrieved social classes. After these collectives had done their work, and proved themselves too dangerous (in 1945, and 1989, respectively) we set about smashing them, too. We broke down the ramshackle, inefficient structure of the old extended family to its minimal, nuclear core - and then when that didn't prove as economically useful, we split that into atoms. When we learned that families have no economic use or political import, we redefined them at last as consensual, temporary alliances of adults - to whom the State contracts the duty of caring for children overnight, in the hours when schools and daycare facilities aren't open. We have very thoroughly accomplished the job modernity's founders set us: *liquidating every barrier to the assertion of the Self, short of the laws of physics.* We have killed all the fathers. We are free to make of ourselves exactly what we will, no less and no more...

The road we took to get here should be clear: In the high-minded, ruthless war of liberation we fought against the past, against authority, against every duty or imperative that each of us as individuals *had not freely signed on to as consenting adults*, we had to destroy the village in order to save it. That village was the vision of human life our superstitious ancestors clung to, in which a human being was something radical and unique, an amalgam of spirit and flesh whose destiny may have begun inside the uterus, but which stretched on forward into eternity. You would meddle with such a mystery at your peril, remembering that the penalties could haunt your own eternity. So the peasants used to mutter at the soldiers and the secret policemen, who laughed as they carted them off. They weren't afraid of judgment, and had no hopes of pie in the sky when they died.

The only support, it turned out, for having a high opinion of *other people's lives* (our own are sacred by definition) lay not in the shiny new laboratories or libraries we were building, but in the drafty, candlelit houses of worship we had to bulldoze to make room. The old sacred books that old men quoted to thwart the free play of our desires, which we piled in bonfires or smirked at as curiosities, were more important than we realized. They held crucial information, the shibboleths needed to make men treat each other a certain way - a way we had come to take for granted. That way of treating people - respecting the weak, sacrificing for the young, venerating the old - emerged in human history as the side-effects of specific assertions about the world. We didn't want to believe this. We were sure we could have the milk without the smelly cow or the raging bull"); Stephen Herreid, "Never Respectable: An Interview With Jason Jones," *Crisis*, 1 June 2012 ("We can disagree on many things. We can disagree on how best to provide education, on how to take care of the poor, on foreign policy, et cetera. But we must have agreement on the founding principles of this country. We must have agreement that all men are endowed by God with inalienable rights. We must have agreement that marriage is a fundamental institution for the well being of the person. We must take these issues off the table. We must settle the abortion issue and the marriage issue soon in favor of life and of family if our republic is to survive…

Our abortion laws are still more permissive than those of *France* and *Sweden*. So what kind of success have we really had? And our lack of success is due to the fact that, while we were fighting in Washington, the radical Left was fighting from Hollywood. They have the songs of our nation.

And these Jacobins have divorced themselves from the sources of beauty. God, family, culture, tradition - the radical Left has absolutely divorced itself from these sources of beauty. So all they can communicate is vulgar pornography - just a rapid succession of sound, images, sex and violence. That's their formula, because they cannot really share beauty.

But I believe that Christians grounded in their culture, their tradition, their faith in God - *we* will be able to communicate Beauty in the entertainment industry. And we must do that. We have a responsibility to do that…

The irony is that the 'right' to abortion is a 'freedom' that denies a human person all freedoms. Freedom rightly understood would seek to defend the dignity of the child in the womb as a person. Freedom *misunderstood* - this Ron-Paul-Libertarian idea of freedom that has the same birthplace as the radical Left, which is the French Revolution - is alien to the Western Tradition. This misunderstanding of freedom is a cancer in the Western Tradition. But if we *rightly* understand freedom, we will want to celebrate the dignity and freedom of the human person; we will want to protect life. There is no freedom without life…

Everyone who has ever had an abortion or been close to someone who has had an abortion knows how devastating abortion is to women. Everyone! The only people who may not get that are those 'respectable' folks we were talking about earlier, who have never personally known someone who's had an abortion, but I know several people who have had abortions; friends and family members. And some of them still claim to be pro-abortion. But when they talk about their own abortion they talk about it as the most devastating event in their life").

Jones, Robert Tyre ("Bobby") – amateur golfer and lawyer; b. 17 March 1902, Atlanta, Georgia; c. 15 December 1971 (deathbed; received by Mgr. John D. Stapleton, rector of the Cathedral of Christ the King, Atlanta); d. 18 December 1971, Atlanta, Georgia; born into a well-to-do family; educated at Georgia Institute of Technology (BSc in Mechanical Engineering in 1922); BA in English Literature from Harvard College in 1924; entered Emory University School of Law in 1926; passed the Georgia bar exam and joined his father's law firm in Atlanta; child prodigy at golf and reached the third round of the U.S. Amateur Championship at the age of fourteen in 1916; qualified for his first U.S. Open Championship in 1920; at first somewhat hot-tempered; later the most successful amateur golfer ever, competing successfully against the world's best professionals; played in thirty-one major championships (as they were classified at the time), winning thirteen and finishing in the top ten twenty-seven times; in 1926 he was the first to win the U.S. And British Open Championships in the same year; in 1930 he won the then "Grand Slam" of all four major championships (U.S. Open and Amateur, British Open and Amateur) in the same year; won U.S. Open 1923, 1926, 1929, 1930; British Open 1926, 1927, 1930; U.S. Amateur 1924, 1925, 1927, 1928, 1930; British Amateur 1930; represented the United States in the Walker Cup five times (won nine of his ten matches); playing captain in 1928 and 1930); had a great reputation for sportsmanship and fair play, arising out of two incidents in U.S. Opens when he called a penalty against himself after the ball moved when addressed (when Jones was praised for his honesty, the amateur golfer replied, "You'd as well praise me for not breaking into banks. There is only one way to play this game"); formed a unique relationship with the town of St. Andrews, Scotland, the home of golf (on his first appearance at the famous Old Course there in the British Open of 1921 he tore up his card, withdrew from the championship and criticized the course; but he came to love the course and the place, and was named a Freeman of the City of St. Andrews in 1958; retired from golf in 1930 and concentrated on his law practice; made many golf instructional films and advised on golf club design; co-designed (with Alistair MacKenzie the Augusta National golf course in Georgia and founded the U.S. Masters tournament in 1934, which became one of the four modern major championships; officer in the U.S. Army Air Forces in World War II, reaching the rank of lieutenant-colonel; in 1948 he began to have regular neck and shoulder pain; had several operations, but in 1956 he was diagnosed with syringomyelia, a chronic and progressive disease of the spinal cord; led to paralysis and eventual restriction to a wheelchair; married Mary Rice Malone in 1924 (three children of the marriage); Mgr. Stapleton credited the fine example of Mrs. Jones, a life-long

Catholic, as being a key factor in her husband's conversion; one of his favorite axioms was: "First come my wife and children. Next comes my profession - the law. Finally, and never as a life in itself, comes golf"; buried in Oakland Cemetery, Atlanta; see *Down the Fairway* (1927) (with Oscar Bane ("O.B.") Keeler); *The Rights and Wrongs of Golf* (1933); *Golf Is My Game* (1959); O. B. Keeler, *The Boys' Life of Bobby Jones* (1931); Grantland Rice (ed), *The Bobby Jones Story: From the Writings of O. B. Keeler* (1955); Stephen Lowe, "Demarbleizing Bobby Jones," *Digital commons. olivet.edu*, 1 January 1999.

Jones, Walter B, Jr. – politician; b. 10 February 1943, Farmville, North Carolina; c. 1974; his father, Walter B. Jones, Sr., was a Democrat and a member of the House of Representatives 1966-1992; brought up as a Southern Baptist; attended Hargrave Military Academy in Chatham, Virginia (graduated in 1966 with a BA); served in the North Carolina National Guard 1967-1971; worked as a wine salesman; elected as a Democrat to the North Carolina House of Representatives in 1982; served there until 1992; in 1992 ran for the U.S. House of Representatives and his father's old seat, but was defeated; in 1994 he switched to the Republican Party and ran for the House in another North Carolina seat, winning; re-elected ever since; changed from being a strong supporter of the war in Iraq to strong opposition; leader of the move to have french fries renamed "freedom fries" in the House cafeteria; but one of the first to call for a withdrawal of U.S. forces; argued for limits to be placed on the President's power to order military action; a lifelong resident of Farmville; see Robert Dreyfuss, "The Three Conversions of Walter B. Jones," *Mother Jones*, January-February 2006 ("One day on the Hargrave campus, Jones glanced through an open door and spied a fellow cadet on his knees, saying the rosary. 'I was impressed by his devoutness,' he says. Jones began thinking and reading about Catholicism. 'I didn't so much get into the history of the church as I got into the ritual,' he recalls. When he was thirty-one, he formally converted").

"Joseph, Brother" – see under Dutton, Ira Barnes.

Karr, Mary – poet; b. 16 January 1955, Groves, Texas; father, J. P. Karr, worked in an oil refinery; mother, Marie, business woman and amateur artist (married seven times); both parents agnostic; very troubled childhood; interested in literature from an early age; after high school she traveled to California and became a hippie; involved in drugs and later alcoholism; became involved in the anti-apartheid movement, through which she met the poet Etheridge

Knight, an important influence on her poetry; did graduate studies in creative writing at Goddard College, Vermont; one of her teachers there was Tobias Wolff (b. 1945), whose book *This Boy's Life* influenced her own writing; also studied with the poets Robert Bly (b. 1926) and Robert Hass (b. 1941); worked in the computer and telecommunications industries while writing and publishing poetry; assistant professor at several colleges and universities until obtaining a post in 1991 in the English Department at Syracuse University, New York (became Peck Professor of English Literature there); Guggenheim Fellow in Poetry in 2005; has argued for content over style in poetry; argues that poetry and prayer arise from the same sources within us; has written three volumes of memoirs, the first volume, *The Liars' Club*, being a bestseller; in 1983 she married poet Michael Milburn, with whom she had a son, but the couple divorced in 1991; eventually she was attracted to the Catholic Church ("I think what struck me really wasn't the grandeur of the Mass. It was the simple faith of the people. For me this whole journey was a journey into awe. I would just get these moments of quiet where there wasn't anything. My head would just shut up, and I knew that was a good thing. And also the carnality of the church: there was a body on the cross"); her conversion helped to conquer her drink problem; see (poetry) *Abacus* (1987); *The Devil's Tour* (1983); *Viper Rum* (2001); Sinners Welcome (2006); (memoirs) *The Liars' Club* (1995) (about her childhood); *Cherry: A Memoir* (2000) (about her late adolescence and early womanhood); *Lit: A Memoir* (2009) ("concerns my journey from blackbelt sinner and lifelong agnostic to unlikely Catholic (maybe not the Pope's favorite, but still an on-my-knees spouter of praise and beggar for favors")); (selected essays) "Facing Altars: Poetry and Prayer," *Poetry*, November 2005 ("The faithless contenders for prayer's relief who sometimes ask me for help praying (still a comic notion) often say it seems hypocritical to turn to God only now during whatever crisis is forcing them toward it - kid with leukemia, say, husband lost in the World Trade Center. But no one 1 know has ever turned to God any other way. As the adage says, there are no atheists in foxholes (poet Stanley Moss says he was the exception). Maybe saints turn to God to exalt him. The rest of us tend to show up holding out a tin cup. Put the penny of your prayer in this slot and pull the handle - that's how I thought of it at first, and I think that's typical. The Catholic church I attended in Syracuse, New York (St. Lucy's) said it best on the banner stretched across its front: Sinners Welcome.

That's how I came to prayer nearly fifteen years back, through what James Laughlin (via *Pilgrim's Progress*) used to call the 'Slough of Despond,' and over the years prayer led me to God, and God led me to church - a journey fueled by gradually accruing comforts and some massively freakish coincidences...

But the Church's carnality, which seemed crude at the outset - people lighting candles and talking to dolls - worked its voodoo on me, The very word *incarnation* derives from the Latin *in carne* in meat. There is a *body* on the cross in my church. (Which made me think at first that the people worshipped the suffering, till my teenage son told me one day at Mass: 'What else would get everybody's attention but something really grisly? It's like *Pulp Fiction*.' In other words, we wouldn't have it any other way.)")

Kendall, Willmoore – political philosopher and journalist; b. 5 March 1909, Konawa, Oklahoma; d. 30 June 1967; his father was a blind Methodist minister; precocious child (learned to read at age of two); reared a Methodist, he then became a skeptic; educated at University of Oklahoma (graduated with a BA in Romance Languages in 1927); MA degree in Romance Languages from Northwetern University in 1928; Rhodes Scholar at Oxford University 1932-1935; became a Communist there and went to Spain in 1936 to fight for the Republic; his experience in the Spanish Civil War led him to renounce his Communist beliefs; obtained a PhD in Political Philosophy from the University of Illinois with a thesis on John Locke; served in the Office of Strategic Services (OSS) in World War II; stayed with the organization after the war when it became the CIA; taught at Yale University 1947-1961, when he left after many disagreements; one of his students was William F. Buckley, Jr., with whom he founded the *National Review*; as a senior editor he had many arguments with the other editors; taught at the University of Dallas until his death, founding the political program there; admirer of the work of Leo Strauss (1899-1973), the political theorist; married three times, the first two being annulled by the Church (no children); see *Baseball: How to Play It and How to Watch It* (1927) (under the name of Alan Monk); *Democracy and the American Party System* (1956) (with Austin Ranney); *John Locke and the Doctrine of Majority-Rule* (1959); *The Conservative Affirmation* (1963); *The Basic Symbols of the American Political Tradition* (1970) (with George W. Carey); Nellie Kendall (ed), *Willmoore Kendall Contra Mundum* (1971) (his collected essays); George W. Carey, "How to Read Willmoore Kendall," *Intercollegiate Review*, Winter-Spring 1972 ("[Willmoore Kendall] was a conservative populist of sorts. One will detect a shift of thinking on his part over the years. His early writings, and even those not published here which appeared in the middle 1950s, illustrate this. 'Majority Principle and the Scientific Elite' and 'On Preservation of *Democracy in America*'... indicate his early liberal bent of mind...

What brought about the obvious change in his thinking and in what ways did he change?...[I] n his early writing he accepted all the fundamental premises of liberalism. All opinions were deemed equal, which in very short order led him to the proposition that all values are equal, and, then, into the swamps of relativism. In sum, by a tortuous route well known to Western man, he accepted the fact-value dichotomy. By the late 1950s, certainly after his conversion to Catholicism, we can discern a distinct shift in his writings with respect to the fact-value dichotomy and the liberal interpretation of majority rule. This is brilliantly manifest in his seldom-read article, 'The People Versus Socrates Revisited.' And he hammers away at this thesis in 'How to Read Milton's Areopagitica.' He nails all of this to the door with his 'Fallacies of the Open Society'...

I do not mean to imply that Willmoore's conversion to Catholicism produced the change in his thinking to which I have referred. It was, so far as I can determine, the other way around. In his earliest writings such as those I have cited, one will, if he reads closely enough, detect a tension, points and issues involving liberal premises with which Kendall did not quite feel at home...Over the years he came to realize that there is a hierarchy of values, that there are transcendent Truths which, however clumsily we might try, we should seek to explore with our 'heart' *and* intellect. The tensions produced by this realization led him to join the Catholic Church. But this was simply the result of reading carefully the works of Voegelin and Strauss, along with a very careful re-reading of *The Federalist.* In retrospect we can see that his early writings manifested the latent potential for a major shift in his thinking"); George W. Carey, "Willmoore Kendall: Conservative Iconoclast," *Modern Age* (1975), p.127; Yvonna Kendall Mason (ed), *Oxford Years: Letters of Willmoore Kendall to His Father* (1993); Jeffrey Hart, "The Deliberate Sense of Willmoore Kendall," *The New Criterion*, March 2002; John Alvis and John Murley (ed), *Willmoore Kendall: Maverick of American Conservatives* (2003); *The Willmoore Kendall site*; his papers are at the University of Dallas Library, Irving, Texas; *ANB*.

Kent, Michael – see under Brown, Beatrice Bradshaw.

Keyes, Erasmus Darwin – soldier, businessman and banker; b. 29 May 1810, Brimfield, Massachusetts; c. 1866 (received in San Francisco); d. 14 October 1895, Nice, France (remains brought back to New York); came from Puritan stock; his father, Justus Keyes, a renowned doctor and surgeon; educated at West Point Military Academy (graduated in 1832); commissioned a lieutenant in the Third Artillery; served in the South during the Nullification troubles 1832-1833; military aide to General Scott, with the rank of captain 1837-1841 when he was on duty connected with the Indian conflicts; instructor of calvary and artillery tactics at West Point 1844-1848; member of the Academy's Board of Visitors; served on the Pacific frontier 1854-1860; while there he was influenced towards his later conversion to the Catholic faith by conversations with Fr. (John) Joseph Augustine Joset, SJ (27 August 1810-19 June 1900) of the Sacred Heart Mission to the Coeur d'Alene indians at Coeur d' Alene, Idaho, in 1858; commissioned as major in 1858; served as General Scott's military secretary 1860-1861; on the outbreak of the Civil War promoted to colonel of the 11th U.S. Infantry in 1861; took part in the first battle of Bull Run; promoted to rank of brigadier general of volunteers (the third-ranking brigadier general in the Army); given command of IV Corps in the Union Army of the Potomac 1862-1863; for gallantry at the battle of Fair Oaks, he received the brevet of brigadier-general in the regular army; promoted to major general U.S. Volunteers; resigned from the army in 1864 and went to San Francisco; worked in mining and other businesses; buried in West Point Cemetery; see *Fifty Years' Observation of Men and Events, Civil and Military* (1884) ("The next day I visited the mission, which was established in 1846. The church was built of logs, spacious, but unfinished. Everything within and around had a rustic appearance. Father Joset, Father Minitree, and two lay brothers were there. In this savage, out-of-the-way place they were obligesd to live and labor with the Indians. In the evening I supped with the fathers. They had plenty of excellent beef, vegetables, and milk, but the table and its service were as plain as possible.

In Father Joset I found a cultivated gentleman in the prime of life, fit to adorn the most polished society in the world. I was unable to restrain my expressions of astonishment when he informed me that he had passed the last fourteen years in the wilderness with the savages. I asked him if he had no longings for a better life and society. 'No,' said he, 'I am content and happy where I am. In your profession an outward obedience to orders is all that is required of you, but in the society to which I belong obedience must be internal, and cheerful, and ready. I am happy, and have no desire to exchange situations with any person.'

Twice every day while I remained at the mission I had conversations with Father Joset, which increased my admiration for his character and my estimation of his self-denial. He instructed me how his Church had preserved the traditions and dogmas of Christianity, and sustained the purity of the faith, and it was primarily due to his influence that I enrolled myself, at a subsequent date, in the Roman Catholic Church. By his explanations and revelations Father Joset revealed to my mind vistas through which the light from calvary shone more pure and brilliant than ever before"); *From West Point to California* (1950); *Catholic Encyclopedia.*

Keyes, Frances Parkinson (*née* Wheeler) (Keyes rhymes with eyes) – author; b. 21 July 1885, Charlottesville, Virginia (in James Monroe's house); c. 1939 (received into the Church by Bishop Picaud of Bayeux and Lisieux in the Chapel of the Benedictines, where St. Thérèse made her first communion); d. 3 July 1970, Beauregard House, New Orleans, Louisiana; brought up with strong religious beliefs in a Congregationalist family, but confirmed in the Episcopal Church; father Professor of Greek at the University of Virginia; educated mainly privately; traveled widely in Europe with her mother at the age of nine; married Henry Wilder Keyes (1863-1938) in 1904 (three children of the marriage); her husband became Governor of New Hampshire in 1917 and later a Republican Senator; prominent political and social life, mainly as a Washington hostess; travelled widely; prolific writer of biographies, memoirs, popular and best selling novels and magazine articles, many of which contain Catholic beliefs and themes; several of her books tell of life in the southern United States; strong belief in the virtue of chastity and the traditional morality of courtship and marriage; in her account of her conversion she referred to it as of the "blinding flash" variety; edited 1937-1939 the *Daughters of the American Revolution Magazine*, which she renamed the *National Historical Magazine*; see (fiction; selective list) *Senator Marlowe's Daughter* (1935); *Honor Bright* (1936); *Dinner at Antoine's* (1948); *Joy Street* (1950); *Steamboat Gothic* (1952); *Blue Camellia* (1957); *The Chess Players* (1960); *Madame Castel's Lodger* (1962); (non-fiction) *Written in Heaven: The Life on Earth of the Little Flower of Lisieux* (1937); *The Sublime Shepherdess: St. Bernadette Soubirous* (1940); *Along a Little Way: The Story of a Conversion* (1948) ("[F]inally, on one snowy silent afternoon in mid-winter I went to the shrine of St. Anne de Beaupré, in Canada. It was not a time of pilgrimage. There was not a soul in the church besides the friend who was with me, and myself. I dipped my fingers in holy water as I entered, knelt down, and crossed myself; in the same way that I had done hundreds of times before, first merely because it seemed courteous to follow prevalent custom in the house of God, as one would in the house of a friend, and later: because this had become instinctive. Then I raised my eyes to the lighted altar, and in one blinding flash, my whole life was transformed.

I never had to say 'Lord, I believe. Help Thou my unbelief!' There is no room for reservations in a miracle. I was not even troubled because, since I was totally unprepared for what had occurred, and totally unguided, that is in a technical sense, I did not know exactly what to do next. As a matter of fact, the first thing I did when I returned to my hotel room, was to sit down and write a sonnet addressed to St. Anne, or rather to permit my fingers to form the words of one that flowed without effort from my mind"); "An Invitation Heeded," in John A. O'Brien (ed), *The Road to Damascus* (1949) ("The more I traveled about, the more it was borne home to me that no Catholic with whom I came in contact seemed to consider that any reasonable pleasure was in itself an evil thing. It could be converted into evil, of course. But that was entirely different. Enjoyment of life, in all its normal phases, was regarded as natural and desirable...

At the same time that I was absorbing the essential joyousness of Catholicism as contrasted with the essential austerity of Puritanism, I was also observing the unswerving policy of the Catholic Church in regard to what, for lack of a better expression, might be called basic decency. With this, so I discovered, it never compromised. In the midst of a confused and chaotic world it remained steadfast in its attitude not only towards the famous Seven Deadly Sins, but towards degeneracy and depravity in any form. It declined to countenance lewd literature or debased dramatics. It stood unswervingly for the permanence and sanctity of family life. It encouraged and upheld its children's groping efforts to achieve and maintain a state of grace, guiding and forgiving, but never condoning...

It was the attitude of the Catholic Church, with which by this time I had become thoroughly familiar, that made me realize, more than any other one thing, that the old standards were not all gone, that they did still matter, that they were vital and essential, and that they always would be...

As I continued to go, with increasing frequency, into Catholic churches, I did this with a mounting sense of naturalness and of joy. In the beginning I had gone primarily to pray, when I could find no other churches open; in due course of time I went also for correlative reasons, because, in remote places where I was, there was actually no other church of any kind and because churchgoing is as essential to me as breathing. I learned, not as a precept but as a practice, the universality of the Catholic Church; I knew that in this respect at least it met one of my most overwhelming needs. I learned that while it was the open door of the church which gave the first sense of welcome it was the Real Presence which transfigured and sublimated this. Previously I had often wondered when I entered a church which had once been Catholic but had been shorn of its altar during the Reformation, why it seemed so sterile to me. Now I thought I knew"); *The Grace of Guadalupe* (1951); *Bernadette of Lourdes: Shepherdess, Sister and Saint* (1953); *St. Anne: Grandmother of Our Savior* (1955); *The Land of Stones and Saints* (1958); *Mother Cabrini* (1959); *Roses in December* (1960); *Thérèse: Saint of the Little Way* (1960); *The Rose and the Lily: The Story of Two South American Saints* (1961); *Tongues of Fire: The Story of Christian Missionaries from St. Paul to the Present* (1966); Walter Romig, *The Book of Catholic Authors* (1952) (reprinted in *catholicauthors.com*); *ANB*.

Keyerslingk, Robert Wendelin – journalist; b. 1905, St. Petersburg, Russia; c. 20 April 1946 (Holy Saturday; received with his wife Sigrid and his five children); d. 1990; born into a Lutheran family; his father was a naval officer of the Imperial Russian Navy who came out of retirement to serve in World War I; in 1917 the family fled from the Russian Revolution to Japan; went to boarding schools in Japan and later China; he went to Canada and worked as a logger and fisherman; enrolled at the University of British Columbia in Vancouver and graduated in 1929; had a career as a journalist, first as a correspondent for the United Press in Berlin, then in Zurich; general manager of British United Press in 1936 and managing director in 1942; he became an Anglican; returned to Canada in 1938; after his conversion he founded (with Murray Ballantyne) Canada's national Catholic weekly, the *Ensign*, in 1947 (first issue in 1948), but it closed down in 1956; see *Unfinished History* (1948); "By What Authority," in John A. O'Brien, *The Road to Damascus, Vol. IV: Roads to Rome* (1955), p.215 ("[A Catholic acquaintance] could see that I had a very Protestant approach to the priesthood. In a few very simple but clear words he explained the sacramental powers of a priest, which are strictly apart from the individuality of the man, and that it would have been impossible for the Church to survive merely on the human attributes of its ministers. To my surprise he spoke of certain popes and other ecclesiastics, drawing a sharp line of distinction between their office and functions in the Church and their often regrettable but nevertheless human attributes.

Suddenly, that clarified certain points in history which I always wondered how Catholics could ignore. He was not ignoring anything but he was placing things in their true context, with illustrations from history which I had always believed no Catholic was allowed to know. I was sure that a Catholic could only know them at the peril of his religion. It gave me the first inkling of the Church not being, what I had always assumed, a sort of congregation of men, but a divine institution for men, but not made or dependent on men…

A fellow Balt and distant family connection who was a friend of mine and also a newspaperman, startled me one day with the statement that he was contemplating becoming a Catholic…He reminded me that after all our ancestors had left their Westphalian homelands some six hundred years ago to move into the Baltics on a mission for the Pope and that the Duchy of Courland, which they founded, was once known as Marienland (Maryland). After all, he contended, he was not leaving the old but merely returning to the faith of the fathers. That was not a theological argument…but I had never had our own Catholic tradition, the Catholic tradition of all Protestant and Christian people, impressed upon me before. It is so obvious and still it was the cleavage, not the common background, which I had always had underlined for me…

It was in Anglicanism that I found the most impelling reasons for repeating and repeating to myself the question: By what authority? As I would sit through lengthy discussions at synod meetings and observe how the most varying and contradictory beliefs on fundamental points of dogma would be reconciled merely by evading the answers. I began to feel an increasing desire to probe deeper into the questions.

Here was a particular Anglican church which reserved the sacraments, which would have confessionals and high liturgy, and there would be within the same communion churches where such 'popishness' would be derided and the sacrament interpreted as almost optional. I came across ministers of the Anglican Church whose 'modernism left doubts about the divinity of Christ and the virgin birth, without it seemingly being considered heretical. I listened to sermons expounding rigid dogmatism and to others equally insistent on most contradictory and undogmatic approaches to the divine.

For some reason I had always been led to believe that the Bible at least was a direct and uninterrupted testament which had nothing to do with Rome. Catholics, I was told, shunned the Bible like the Devil shuns holy water. It gave me a jolt when I discovered that even that was not true. Instead I could check for myself that for several early centuries the Bible was not the possession of Christendom. That the authority of the Bible rests on the authority of the Church, which chose and set down from amongst many written records the books which were to be accepted as divinely inspired, was an important discovery. There seemed to be a strange irony that in recognizing the authority of the Bible there must be an implicit and very definite recognition of the teaching authority of the Church.

One day the thought struck me that, apart from the differences of appraisal of the positions saints hold in the divine economy of redemption, they are all either venerated or at least respected as saints within all Christian communities. The Dutch Calvinist will celebrate St. Nicholas Day in the same way that All Saints' Day is observed by Lutheran and Anglican alike. There are universal saints and there are local saints in Protestant as well as Catholic countries. Whose authority is being recognized by all in the designation of these saints? Who has elevated them to the altar? But only canonizations up to the Reformation seemed universally valid.

Suddenly it became clearer to me that one fundamental distinction between the Catholic and the Protestant belief is that one is pulsating with the continuing life of inspired revelation through the Holy Spirit, whereas the other accepts this up to a certain date only. Then the Reformation figuratively closed the chapter of growth and replaced it with the commemorative exploitation of what has happened through God's revelations through His Church.

It seemed almost as though God lived with men through His presence in the Church up to the Reformation and then, if one accepts the general Protestant view, God withdrew His living presence amongst men and retired to Heaven. From there He watches how man can manage his salvation from memory for the balance of time allotted until Judgment Day.

The deposit of Faith entrusted to the Church could be dispensed by the teaching Church, clarified and enunciated in dogma up to a certain, comparatively recent date and then, after Martin Luther, the heavens were locked and the deposit of Faith no longer drawn upon for further knowledge. Humanity then is restricted for its guidance merely to the dead past, instead of moving spiritually in a living present").

Kilmer, (Alfred) Joyce – poet and literary critic; b. 6 December 1886, New Brunswick, New Jersey; c. 5 November 1913 (received with his wife); d. 30 July 1918, Seringes-et-Nesle, France; his father was Dr. Frederick Barnett Kilmer (1851-1934), a chemist and the inventor of Johnson's baby powder; his mother, Annie Ellen Kilburn (1849-1932), was a minor writer and composer; brought up as an Episcopalian; educated at Rutgers College 1904-1906, then at Columbia College of Columbia University, graduating BA in 1908; married a fellow poet, Aline Murray (1888-1941) (see below) in 1908 (five children of the marriage); taught Latin for a while; established himself as a published poet; one of his daughters, Rose

(1912-1917), was stricken with poliomyelitis (deeply moved by this, he believed it influenced his conversion to the Catholic faith); also influenced by Coventry Patmore, Francis Thompson, and Alice Meynell; with the publication of the much imitated poem *Trees* (opening lines: "I think that I shall never see/ A poem lovely as a tree") in the magazine *Poetry* he became very popular as a poet across the United States; wrote for several literary journals, including essays, literary criticism and book reviews, and gave lectures; when the United States entered World War I in 1917 he at once enlisted in the army rising to the rank of sergeant and refusing the opportunity of a commission as an officer; mainly served in the 69th New York Regiment ("The Fighting Irish"); admired by the troops for his bravery; killed at the Second Battle of the Marne; posthumously awarded the Croix de Guerre by the French Republic; buried in the Oise-Aisne American Cemetery and Memorial, near Fere-en-Tardenois, Aisne, Picardy, France; his work has been neglected and criticized for being simple, sentimental and traditional; one of his daughters, Deborah (1914-1999) became a Benedictine nun; see *Summer of Love* (1911); *Trees and Other Poems* (1914); *The Circus and Other Essays* (1916); *Main Street and Other Poems* (1917); (ed), *Dreams and Images: An Anthology of Catholic Poets* (1917); *Literature in the Making by Some of its Makers* (1917); Robert Cortes Holliday (ed), *Poems, Essays and Letters in Two Volumes* (*Volume One: Memoir and Poems*, *Volume Two: Prose Works*) (1918) (Letter from Joyce Kilmer to Father James J. Daly: "I need some stricter discipline, I think, and it's hard to get it. I enjoyed Father Cullen's direction very much, he is a fine Irishman with no nonsense about him…And I wish I had some medieval confessor - the sort of person one reads about in anti-Catholic books - who would inflict real penance. The saying of Hail Marys and Our Fathers is no penance, it's a delight"); Katherine Brégy, "Joyce Kilmer, Poet and Patriot," *The Outlook*, 23 July 1919, p.467 ("[H]e entered, with all of a convert's zeal but none of a convert's crudity, that old, old Catholic Church - so mystical at once and so practical! - to which he ever after gave a young and proud allegiance. 'If what I write nowadays is considered poetry,' he declared in one of his last letters written from France, 'then I became a poet in November 1913.' That is to say, he became then the greatest American representative of that little band of 'modern medievalists' which on the other side of the Atlantic included the Chestertons, Hilaire Belloc, and a group of younger singers - all sworn to recapture something of the robust faith, the fine fervor, and heroic folly of Merrie England"); *The Circus and Other Essays and Fugitive Pieces* (1921); Annie

Kilburn Kilmer, *Memories of My Son, Sergeant Joyce Kilmer* (1920); James J. Daly, *A Cheerful Ascetic and Other Essays* (1931) (Letter from Joyce Kilmer to Father James J. Daly: "Of course you understand my conversion. I am beginning to understand it. I believed in the Catholic position, the Catholic view of ethics and aesthetics, for a long time. But I wanted something not intellectual, some conviction not mental - in fact I wanted Faith. Just off Broadway, on the way from the Hudson Tube Station to the Times Building, there is a Church, called the Church of the Holy Innocents. Since it is in the heart of the Tenderloin, this name is strangely appropriate - for there surely is need of youth and innocence. Well, every morning for months I stopped on my way to the office and prayed in this Church for faith. When faith did come, it came, I think, by way of my little paralyzed daughter. Her lifeless hands led me; I think her tiny feet still know beautiful paths. You understand this and it gives me a selfish pleasure to write it down"); Pearl H. Campbell, "Kilmer, Late Laureate of the Catholic Church," *Magnificat*, June 1939, p.78; Helen Connolly, "Kilmer the Essayist," *Magnificat*, July 1945, p.128; Norah Smaridge, *Pen and Bayonet: The Story of Joyce Kilmer* (1962); Harry J. Cargas, *I Lay Down My Life: A Biography of Joyce Kilmer* (1964) ("A somewhat antagonistic non-Catholic once remarked to Kilmer that the Catholic priesthood in this country was, to a rather large extent, recruited from the sons of Irish policemen and scrub-women, to the detriment of the ecclesiastical state. Kilmer flushed an angry red, and rebuked the person in great indignation, saying: 'I do not for an instant admit that you are right. And even if you were right - which you most certainly are not - then I should consider it to be the greatest glory of the Catholic Church in this country that its clergy are (as you falsely state) largely recruited from the sons of Irish policemen and scrub-women; and I should have the greatest pride and happiness in telling you or any one else that I feel it the highest privilege to receive the Sacrament of the Catholic Church at the hands of such priests"); Kenton Kilmer, *Memories of My Father, Joyce* Kilmer (1993); John E. Covell, *Joyce Kilmer: A Literary Biography* (2000); *ANB.*

Kilmer, Aline – see under Murray, Aline.

Kinsman, Frederick Joseph – church historian; b. 27 September 1868, Warren, Ohio; c. 24 November 1919; d. 18 June 1944, Lewiston, Maine; his family was Episcopalian, but descended from New England Puritans and then Congregationalists; received a High Church education at St. Paul's School, Concord, New Hampshire, then at Keble College, Oxford (BA in Theology); influenced by the Oxford Movement, especially by the writings of Keble and Pusey; believed in the Real Presence and Eucharistic Adoration; later schoolmaster and Episcopalian clergyman (in the United States); Professor of Church History, Berkeley Divinity School, Connecticut 1900-1903; Professor of Ecclesiastical History, General Theological Seminary, New York 1903-1908; elected Episcopal Bishop of Delaware in 1908; started to have doubts about Anglicanism in 1911; resigned his post in 1919 and was; subsequently received into the Catholic Church; appointed Professor of Modern Church History at The Catholic University of Ameica; lived in a nursing home 1933-1944; see *Principles of Anglicanism* (1910); *Catholic and Protestant* (1913); *Prayers for the Dead* (1915); *Issues Before the Church* (1915); *Outlines of the History of the Church* (1916); *Salve Mater* (1920) (his conversion story) ("Dr. Gairdner described the first stage of [the English Reformation] as merely 'the old religion with the Pope left out.' I should now wish to teach 'the old religion with the Pope put back'...

As I came eventually to feel that in the English Reformation there had been real breaches in the continuity of what was essential to the Catholicity of the Church, I considered chiefly: (1) changes involved in the recognition of Royal Supremacy, (2) changes in the Ordinal, (3) changes in the Mass, and incidentally (4) the obscuration of Penance, and (5) change in what constituted 'the mind of the Church.' My first concern with these was not to relate them to Roman claims, but to ancient principles as they would now be interpreted by the Eastern Church. I came to recognize that the burden of responsibility for the Anglican schism must be placed on Cranmer, Henry VIII, and Elizabeth...

I wished to see the spirit of the English Reformation especially embodied in Erasmus(!), but ultimately had to admit that there is no getting away from Anne Boleyn. The brutality of her husband and caprices of her daughter forced revolutionary change on the English Church. I should now admit the accuracy of Cobbett's violent statement that 'the Reformation was engendered in lust, brought forth in hypocrisy and perfidy, and cherished and fed by plunder, devastation, and by rivers of innocent English and Irish blood.'

Schism is the voluntary isolation of superior persons, and hence was an easy sin for those endowed with insular complacence. There was plenty of this in the sixteenth century. As the Venetian ambassador wrote home: 'The English are great lovers of themselves and of everything belonging to them; they think that there are no other men but themselves and no other world but England, and whenever they see a handsome foreigner they say, "he looks like an Englishman," or that "it is a great pity he should not be an

Englishman." When they partake of any delicacy with a foreigner they ask him "whether such a thing is made in his country" (quoted in Gasquet, *England under the Old Religion*, p.19). Henry VIII forced the Church of England to separate itself from Catholic Christendom because he wanted to marry Anne Boleyn; the Privy Council persisted in separation because they wanted excuses for plunder; Elizabeth made the breach final to ensure her own possession of the throne: eventually the English people accepted the religion, adopted from royal policy and enforced by parliamentary forms, as their own and believed in it on the assumption of the superiority of everything English. It is impossible not to concede that insular complacence is the genius of Anglicanism.

In spite of all temptations, that belong to other nations, He remains an Englishman:/ And by magnifying smirches, that attach to other churches, He persists an Anglican...

The authority exercised by the Pope in England, as elsewhere in the West, consisted chiefly of two things: the Pope instituted all Bishops, and the Pope was supreme Ecclesiastical Judge. If, in repudiating papal supremacy, effort had been made to recognize that ultimate authority for doctrine and jurisdiction rested with the episcopate as a whole, there would have been approximate agreement with the Eastern assumption of the ultimate authority of a General Council. This was not done. Elizabeth had her Parliament pass an Act depriving the Pope of these powers in England; and she annexed them to the Crown. She made herself supreme judge in ecclesiastical matters...

When did the Catholic Church of England cease to exist and a Protestant Church take its place? There is no moment when in theory this happened. The legal fiction that one Church of England passed through all the changes of the Tudor reigns was always maintained. Yet continuity of spiritual things cannot be determined by forms of parliamentary law. The Church of England as a legal entity did not cease to exist. Its character as a provincial extension of the Holy Catholic Church did. The moment is determined by three things: (1) the abandonment of Catholic doctrine of sacraments by adoption of a Prayer Book which partly denies and almost wholly obscures it; (2) the acceptance of the royal supremacy in a form which overthrows the ancient government of the Church, episcopal as well as papal; and (3) a matter not yet considered, radical change in the Ordinal. When actually did these things happen? Not later than 1559...

My opinions in regard to Roman Catholicism passed through four stages: it is not so bad after all; it is really quite good; it is the best thing I know; it is the Church. Only when the last was reached was there genuine conversion...

My attitude for a long time was that of an approving critic: I knew that, if conversion came, it must become that of a penitent sinner.

The change came eventually with recognition of the principle of primacy as integral and essential to the Church, that is, of the papal claim...For some time it has seemed to me that the only possible alternatives are Roman Catholicism or Agnosticism. To my surprise I have been feeling the force of agnostic arguments. Never for a moment have I believed it possible that I should end in Agnosticism; but I have been seeing plainly the plausibility of much that can be said in its behalf. Divided Christendom repels and paralyzes. So I have wished to wait a little, on my own account, as well as, for various reasons, on account of others. The conviction has become stronger and clearer day by day. All sorts of things, before confused, have dropped into obviously right places. There has come a new semblance of order in the world as one looks out upon it. The efforts of private judgment to appraise, understand, and pronounce upon everything have come to seem ridiculous. Many old opinions appear useless and foolish, though often having new value as gaining a place in relation to things as a whole. So far as I am personally concerned, the only feeling is one of content. I have not been seeking personal happiness, or peace, or usefulness. I have wished to be identified with the Catholic Church to which my life has been pledged. In having found what I believe to be the true Ark of Salvation, every personal wish is satisfied by reception into it. Presumably my active life ends; but that makes no difference. It is certainly a great relief to exchange the task of trying to reform the Church - the necessary effort for all who hold my former point of view - for the simpler one of letting the Church try to reform me! That seems a more reasonable way to view things.

One satisfaction in making this decision, if that word can be applied to recognition of an obvious duty and necessity, is that it is the choice of the leaden casket. 'Who chooseth me, must give and hazard all he hath.' There can be no other condition for gaining anything really worth while. 'What many men desire' and 'As much as he deserves' obviously correspond to inferior motives and inferior attainments. In Delaware I had what many men desire and much more than I deserved. To begin with, it was so identified with all I was bound to value most highly, that from every point of view I could give and hazard everything for what it stood for. It was impossible to wish for anything else. But with a changed point of view, so that for me it no longer stood for the things of supreme value, I could not keep it. That would have been an injury to all concerned. What now possesses chief value for me is elsewhere. The

Kingdom of Heaven is 'treasure hid in a field' and a 'pearl of great price.' Possession, not cost, is the thing to consider. And this even when part of the price must be paid by other people. The end can only bring good and happiness to all concerned. The only thing worth while is doing duty as we see it; the only things worth having are those for which we most care. I for one have had things I set great store by; and I have them now"); *Trent: Four Lectures on Practical Aspects of the Council of Trent* (1921); *The Failure of Anglicanism* (1922) (Letter of 1 July 1919 to the Presiding Bishop of the Protestant Episcopal Church of America in order to explain why he could no longer continue to hold Episcopal office in that Church: "The view of the Church's position which I have held, certainly the prevailing view in the House of Bishops, is simply that the Episcopal Church, strong in its 'appeal to antiquity,' stands firmly for the doctrine of the Incarnation as contained in the Scriptures and the Creeds, and, by emphasis on its sacramental character, perpetuates the life of the Catholic Church. But I have ceased to believe and here I part company with the Bishops, and contradict my convictions and teaching in past years - that the actual facts bear out this contention. In spite of the greatest unwillingness, I have come to feel that the interpretation of the Anglican position which connects it chiefly with the Protestant Reformation is the one more consistent with its history viewed as a whole ; and that its dominant tendencies are increasingly identified with those currents of thought and development which are making away from the definiteness of the ancient Faith towards Unitarian vagueness. This would seem to me to be due not merely to local or temporary conditions but to certain informing principles always more or less apparent in Anglican history. To preserve balance and proportion of the truth, the Episcopal Churches have aimed at comprehension by compromise. I have come to believe that this habit of compromise involves increasing surrenders of truth, in spite of religious revivals aiming at stronger insistence on the ancient Faith.

The chief causes of difficulty for me have been three: (i) tolerance of denials of the Faith, seeming to indicate failure to defend the Church's doctrine; (2) tolerance of imperfect views of sacraments, seeming to result in failure rightly to use them; (3) a theory of Orders which seems to nullify them...

'Is the Creed worth defending?' 'Are the sacraments Divine mysteries? 'Is Holy Orders a Sacrament?' I believe the only answer the Church should make to all of these questions to be a prompt and emphatic 'Yes'; yet I have come to feel that our communion by its non-committal attitude virtually answers 'No.' Hence I have no choice but to resign my place and to declare my withdrawal from the ministry: the Bishops have no choice but to accept the resignation and proceed to my deposition, since resignation for these reasons involves renunciation at least of the Discipline and Orders of the Protestant Episcopal Church"); *Americanism and Catholicism* (1924); *Reveries of a Hermit* (1936).

Kirk, Russell – political theorist, literary critic and author; b. 19 October 1918, Plymouth, Michigan; c. mid-1964; d. 29 April 1994, Piety Hill, Mecosta, Michigan; his ancestors were the spiritual descendants of Emmanuel Swedenborg; his parents were hard working people largely indifferent to religion and did not have him baptized; educated at Michigan State College, majoring in History; obtained a masters degree in History at Duke University; served in the army in World War II, when he did much reading on the great Stoic authors, Marcus Aurelius and Epictetus; after the war he taught Western Civilization at Michigan State College; studied for Doctor of Letters degree at St. Andrews University, Scotland, his dissertation being published as *The Conservative Mind* and being very successful; he saw the term *conservative* as a framework for analyzing all issues, regardless of the culture or era in which they arose, the framework applying to all cultures and eras because it is built around mores or norms that transcend the world's cultures; said that Christianity and Western Civilization are "unimaginable apart from one another"; also said that that "all culture arises out of religion. When religious faith decays, culture must decline, though often seeming to flourish for a space after the religion which has nourished it has sunk into disbelief"; in economics he favored distributism; early on influenced by Mark Twain ("More than any other writer, Twain set me to thinking early on about ultimate questions. For me, Twain demolished the notions of Progress and Perfectibility"); later influenced by Cardinal Newman, Orestes Brownson (see above), Edmund Burke, T. S. Eliot, George Scott-Moncrieff, Flannery O'Connor, Roy Campbell, Hew Lorimer; also influenced by the writing of Fr. Martin D'Arcy, SJ; final influence on his conversion was his wife, Annette Courtemanche, a cradle Catholic and devout student of St. Thomas Aquinas, who answered his questions about Catholic doctrine (four daughters of the marriage); retained a Stoic-influenced mindset; his house, Piety Hill, in Mecosta, Michigan, provided help for displaced persons; eventually reacted against neo-conservatism and in favor of paleo-conservatism; author of thirty-two books and approximately eight hundred articles; founded two quarterly publications, *Modern Age* and *The University Bookman*; wrote fiction, notably numerous ghost stories and three novels; declined posts in the Nixon and Reagan administrations; loved the saints and had a great reverence for the Shroud of Turin; close relationship and lengthy correspondence with Ross Hoffman (see above); see (selective list) *The Conservative Mind: From Burke to Eliot* (1953; 7th revised edition in 2001); *Prospects for Conservatives* (1954); *Academic Freedom: An Essay in Definition* (1955); *Beyond the Dreams of Avarice: Essays of a Social Critic* (1956); *The American Cause* (1957); *Confessions of a Bohemian Tory* (1963); *Edmund Burke: A Genius Reconsidered* (1967); *Enemies of the Permanent Things: Observation of Abnormality in Literature and Politics* (1969); *Eliot and His Age: T. S. Eliot's Moral Imagination in the Twentieth Century* (1972), *The Roots of American Order* (1974), (ed), *The Portable Conservative Reader* (1982); *The Wise Men Know What Wicked Things Are Written on the Sky* (1987); *Economics: Work and Prosperity* (1988); *America's British Culture* (1993); *The Politics of Prudence* (1993); "Civilization Without Religion?" *Touchstone*, Winter 1993; *Sword of the Imagination: Memoirs of a Half-Century of Literary Conflict* (1995) (autobiography, written in the third person) ("For his part, Kirk had commenced to move, very languidly, beyond Stoicism to something more...Something made Kirk inquire within himself by what authority he presumed to doubt - although he had not yet read Newman's observation that it is better to believe all things than to doubt all things. Upon authority all revealed religion rests, and the authority that lies behind Christian doctrine is massive. By what alternative authority did Kirk question it?...So, by slow degrees, mind and heart are moved. In the Great Salt Lake Desert he began to perceive that pure reason has its frontiers and that to deny the existence of realms beyond those borders - why, that's puerility"); *Redeeming the Time* (1996); *Rights and Duties: Reflections on Our Conservative Constitution* (1997); William F. Buckley, *Nearer My God: An Autobiography of Faith* (1997) (letter from Russell Kirk to the author: "What I found in the Church was Authority. Catholicism is governed by Authority; Protestants, by private judgment. I had become painfully aware of the insufficiency of Private Judgment in the twentieth century - every man creating his own morals. In my search, over the years, for a sound apprehension of the human condition, I came at last to recognize in the Roman Church the elements of Truth, as sustained by two thousand years of continuity; by the wealth of wisdom in the Church's pronouncements; by the lives and words of Saint Augustine of Hippo and Saint Gregory the Great, particularly, among the Church Fathers; by Acton's observation, if you will, that no institution purely human could have survived, over the centuries, so many blunders. I was not 'converted' to the Church, but made my way into it through what Newman calls 'illation' – fragments of truth collecting in my mind through personal experience, conversations, knowledge of exemplars, and much reading and meditating"); *The Essential Russell Kirk* (2007); "Moral Imagination," *Crisis*, 22 March 2012; James E. Person, Jr., *Russell Kirk: A Critical Biography of a Conservative Mind* (1999); James E. Person, Jr. "The Holy Fool as Bohemian Tory: The Wise Faith of Russell Kirk," *Touchstone*, June 2003 ("On 4 May 1956, exactly three years after the publication of *The Conservative Mind*, [Peter J. Stanlis presented Kirk with a copy of the book *Catholic Approaches to Modern Dilemmas and Eternal Truths*, a collection of essays by ten contributors and edited by Elizabeth Pakenham. Of these essays, Kirk's attention must have been drawn especially to the first in the collection, a study called 'The Mystery of Evil,' by Martin D'Arcy, with whose work Kirk was familiar…

D'Arcy, a thoughtful old-school Jesuit, whose Christian-Humanist mindset and rigorous thought processes predated more politically focused left/liberal Jesuits of the succeeding generations, used his essay…to present to the reading public a God of Chestertonian paradoxes, one whose words and actions seem foolishness to the world, who achieves victory through surrender, who defeats human suffering through suffering. At the center of D'Arcy's essay is the Son of God, who is beloved of God but made a despised sin-bearer for mankind. Of the Crucifixion, D'Arcy writes: 'The Son of God is not only repulsed; he is made an enemy and put to death - and it is as if all evil erupted and canalized itself in the hatred and brutality of the murder. But by a complete reversal of the expected, this evil unresisted and in full flood is dammed and transformed into life-giving love.' Further: 'The evil that man does is not defeated by force, but in the silence of God dead and hidden away from the sight of man. In this story then, God does the opposite of what we expect; he does not quell evil; he loses his life in a more bitter way of suffering than is the lot of most other men, and yet he prevails. Moreover we have here the supreme manifestation of what God is like; so far from indifferent he makes the worst abuse of liberty a form of love and marriage. It is not surprising, therefore, if suffering is often the lot of the good and is recognized by the saints as the covenanted way of true happiness. God has more than justified himself; he has mysteriously made naught of death and sin.'

Philosophically, this is a logical step beyond Stoicism - and entirely in line with Kirk's own growing understanding of

Christian doctrine, especially that of Kirk's friend T. S. Eliot, who had written much poetry and drama that presented the essence of the Christian experience as a pilgrimage of faith along the Way of Suffering. D'Arcy's conclusion to his discourse on suffering and the ways of God must have rung true to the Stoical Kirk: 'It is only, I think, in the light of the suffering of the Son of God that we can look without dismay at the wounded man in his "private world of pain"...The world in which "all things are hard: man cannot explain them by word," where "all is vanity and vexation of spirit, and the perverse are hard to be corrected, and the number of fools is infinite"; this same world in which hopes are stillborn and good causes are brought to nothing, so full of wastelands and crosses, is, if the Christian revelation be true, a cross on which God has stretched his arms, making of it a tree of life'"); Eric Scheske, "The Conservative Convert: The Life and Faith of Russell Kirk," *Touchstone*, June 2003; The Russell Kirk Center for Cultural Renewal, *kirkcenter.org*.

Kite, Elizabeth Sarah – historian and social scientist; b. 1864, Philadelphia, Pennsylvania; c. 1906 (received in England; in the following decades she persuaded fifteen members of her extended family to convert also); d. 6 January 1954, Wilmington, Delaware; brought up in a strict Quaker household; her mother, brother and sister all died when she was in her early twenties (other relatives died later leaving her responsible for five nephews and nieces); took a vow of chastity after finding out that the man she loved was already married; studied for six years in England, France, Germany and Switzerland; converted to the Catholic faith after a series of religious experiences in England; returned to the United States and worked as a teacher in private schools; participated in psychological research on intelligence and mental disability 1909-1918; the influence of Emil Reich (1854-1910), a Hungarian Jewish professor, with whom she studied at London University, caused her to see Catholicism as a great *historical* religion; she began to research the history of France's role in the American Revolutionary War and argued that without the aid of France and its pious king, Louis XVI, the United States would never have become independent; placed photostats of documents of the French Revolution in the Library of Congress and for this was awarded the Cross of Chevalier de la Légion d'Honneur; archivist for the American Catholic Historical Society of Philadelphia; first laywoman to receive the degree of doctor of literature at Villanova; Third Order Franciscan; after her conversion she did continue her earlier research into eugenics despite the Church's opposition to this; unmarried; buried at the Friends Burial Ground, Philadelphia; see

Beaumarchais and the War of American Independence (1917); *L'Enfant and Washington* (1929); *Correspondence of General Washington and Compte de Grasse* (1931); *Lebegre Duportail, Comdt. of Engineers, 1777–1783* (1933); Lafayette and His Companions in the Victorie (1934); *The Catholic Part in the Making of America* (1936) (deals with the policy of Louis XVI and his foreign minister in aiding America's fight for independence); Joan N. Burstyn (ed), *Past and Promise: Lives of New Jersey Women* (1997), pp.160-161 ("While living in London Kite was aware of a growing 'spiritual hunger,' and her experiences in Catholic France and in Algiers during a trip with friends led to her conversion to Roman Catholicism in 1906. She was a devout Catholic for the rest of her life"); Patrick Allitt, *Catholic Converts: British and American Intellectuals Turn to Rome* (1997), pp.134-141 ("Feeling intellectually and spiritually dissatisfied after flirting with socialism, Hinduism, and theosophy around the turn of the century, she attended a sermon in Westminster Abbey, only to find the preacher dispensing the cold comfort of the historical-critical method: 'I was a starving soul begging imploringly for the bread of life, but all the minister had to offer were stones, stones, stones, or rather baked clay tablets from old Babylon, with which he frittered away the whole Gospel narrative as an absurd myth… It seemed to me that Almighty God had permitted me to hear the very worst this evidently popular speaker could do in the way of giving a so-called higher criticism interpretation of the Christian religion, so that never again would I turn to the Church of England when in search of spiritual food.'

After that she began to visit a Catholic church. She found herself there on Holy Thursday, 1906, joining a procession to kiss the feet of the crucified Jesus. As she did so she experienced an intense psychological or spiritual sensation: 'As I rose the corpus as it were came alive and as I gazed, a glance from under the partly closed lids struck to the inmost center of my being cleaving me in twain. For I, from above the feet, distinctly saw myself, even to the dress I wore that day, with head bowed and downcast eyes, join the retreating line of worshippers. At the time I did not understand, but I now see that what had happened was the miracle of *Belief* – a pure gift from the divine heart of Jesus.

Within a few weeks she had taken instruction and was confirmed in the Catholic faith…

[Emil Reich's] lecture on the confrontation of Emperor Henry IV and Pope Gregory VII in the snowy Alps had an effect on Kite almost as profound as had her religious conversion…Reich's description of a moment when the pope enjoyed a great victory over the temporal power showed

Kite Catholicism in a new light, as a great *historical* religion, the 'miracle of the ages,' which combined 'perfect democracy with perfect authority.' History became for her a quasi-religious vocation… Coming from a venerable American Protestant family, Kite made it her mission to force honest patriots to admit that the nation – antipopery prejudice notwithstanding – owed its genesis to the selfless work of *Catholics*. Other convert scholars in the early twentieth century worked along similar lines. The historians Gaillard Hunt, Ross Hoffman and Carlton Hayes [see above for all of these], for example, all argued that the U.S. Constitution embodied the wisdom of the 'great tradition' of natural law politicial philosophy which traced its roots back through the pagan Christian synthesis in Aquinas to the principles of Augustine's City of God. All denied that its intellectual origins could be traced to John Locke. Kite's work on Franco-American relations contributed a new dimension to this wide-ranging effort to 'Catholicize' American history"); the Elizabeth S. Kite Collection is at Rutgers University, New Jersey and contains *A Conversion Story from Quakerism to the Catholic Church* (typescript) and her unpublished autobiography *The Beggar Maid and the King*.

Klein, Leonard R. - priest; b. 1946, Easton, Pennsylvania; c. Summer 2003; raised in the Lutheran Church Missouri Synod; studied at Yale University from 1963 (BA in Religious Studies); Master of Divinity from Yale Divinity School; Master of Sacred Theology from the Missouri Synod seminary in St. Louis; ordained to the Lutheran ministry in 1972; editor of the *Lutheran Forum* and the *Forum Letter*; understanding of Lutheranism as deeply Catholic in substance; also had a deeply sacramental understanding of the Church; attacked the Evangelical Lutheran Church of America for its policy of paying for abortions in its health plan, saying that "real churches don't kill babies"; after his conversion he studied for the Catholic priesthood at St. Mary's Seminary and University, Baltimore, Maryland; ordained to the priesthood 1 April 2006; in 2010 appointed director of pro-life activities in the diocese of Wilmington; married with three children; see *EWTN Audio Library, The Journey Home* (29 January 2007) ("In many ways my understanding of Lutheranism had to tilt me towards the Catholic Church. It had to make the Catholic Church a friendly looking place to me, not a hostile one. When people say to me, 'When did you first start thinking about the Catholic Church'...the answer is in seminary. As I confronted particularly the work of Thomas Aquinas and of Karl Rahner, the modern and the medieval theologian, I saw issues being raised there that I didn't think Lutheranism was able to raise, was able to deal with, that there was a breadth there, and over my years as a Lutheran pastor I tended more and more to feel that the sharp division of law from gospel, the very negative view of law that Lutheran theology took, was not only wrong and unhelpful but downright unbiblical. So, there was always that inclination.

But what finally opened my heart?...I think it really was John Paul II , the man himself, the incredibly powerful witness, and of course the rejuvenation of the Church and the rescue of Vatican II as represented by John Paul II. Like many a serious and theologically conservative Protestant I watched those early years after Vatican II with considerable dismay. I wanted to say, ''Fellows, we've been here already. Let us tell you, you don't want to go in the direction of a kind of radical subjectivity, rejection of authority. This is a dead end.' And in the words of a famous Southern Baptist, I forget who it was, 'All of a sudden we had a pope who knew how to pope.' And that made me say to myself, 'OK, why am I outside?' My heart and my head are inclining me to full communion, towards the fullness of the Catholic Church, the richness of tradition, the incredible richness of material which you have to work with, the people and the sacraments, the lives of the saints, the devotions, the traditions. These things I identified with; I identified with strongly. And I think finally that witness said to me that I needed to do what I'd been tending toward for an awfully long time...

Every time the Protestant minister picks up the Bible and says, 'The Bible says...' he is granting credibility and authority to the bishops of the early Church, who after all were the ones who determined what books would be in it. Apart from the witness of the Church and of Israel from which the Scriptures come, and the decision of those two communities what these books would be, we couldn't use the term 'Scripture' at all. We'd be referring to merely generic ancient writings. The fact that there is a Bible at all is itself a witness to the authority of the Church...

In many ways Luther was his own magisterium while he lived. Once he was gone, holding the Lutheran movement together and holding together even some of the genius of his insights, to say nothing of holding together his continuity with the Catholic Church, became much more difficult, and finally I think in the end was an impossible undertaking").

Kluge, John Werner (pronounced Kloog-ee) – entrepreneur and philanthropist; b. 21 September 1914, Chemnitz, Germany; d. 7 September 2010, Charlottesville, Albemarle County, Virginia; son of an engineer who died in World War I; his mother re-married and the family emigrated to the United States in 1922, settling in Detroit;

worked for a time on a Ford assembly line; educated at Columbia University (BA in Economics from Columbia in 1937) (financed his study partly by his skill at poker); served as a captain with U.S. Army intelligence during World War II; perceiving that television was the medium of the future, he bought into several broadcasting companies; in the 1950s he bought stock in the Metropolitan Broadcasting Corporation; gained control of the company in 1959; expanded the company further into radio, television and advertising; later changed the company's name to Metromedia (the nation's first major independent broadcasting entity); Metromedia subsidiaries included a franchise of over 800 restaurants; in 1967 he acquired the Harlem Globetrotters basketball team; in 1986 he sold the Metromedia television stations to the 20th Century Fox film studio for a reported $4 billion; in 1987 *Forbes Magazine* placed him top of its list as the richest man in America; bought many Palm Beach, Florida, estate properties; bought a library of major films and syndication rights to many television programs; in 1997 he sold off most of the film library to Metro-Goldwyn-Mayer; art collector; gave many millions of dollars to charity; in 2000, on the 200th anniversary of the Library of Congress, he donated $60 million to create the John W. Kluge Center at the library; he also established a $1 million prize to be given in recognition of a lifetime of achievement in the human sciences; he gave over $500 million to Columbia University; in 2001 he donated his large estate in Albemarle County, Virginia, to the University of Virginia; he paid for life saving surgery for British cancer patient Craig Shergold after being asked to send a greeting or business card to the young patient (he decided that the child needed medical treatment instead of a Guinness world record for most cards); married four times (three children, two of whom were adopted); he converted to the Catholic Church from Lutheranism when he married his third wife in 1981; buried in Monticello Memorial Park, Charlottesville (headstone reads "In the sands of time, individuals make very little difference, no matter who they are, but what little difference you can make you should try to make").

Klyber, Arthur Bernard, CSSR – priest; b. 1900, Delancey Street, New York; c. 8 February 1920; d. 10 October 1999; brought up in a strictly orthodox Jewish family, which emigrated from Russia; on the death of his parents from tuberculosis, he was committed to a Jewish orphanage at the age of six and stayed there until twelve, but was never taught about prayer, God, or sin ("I had been given a convenient push toward the dark abyss of rationalism which has benighted the souls of thousands of Jews today, especially in the

United States"); lived with various families before going to live with his mother's sister (a genuinely pious and orthodox Jew) at the age of sixteen; paid lip-service only to Judaism; served in the United States Navy 1917-1921; in 1919 a Catholic navy friend introduced him to his family who impressed him by their thoroughly Catholic lifestyle and good example; presence with this family at a Solemn High Mass made a great impression; conversion also influenced by Gibbons, *Faith of Our Fathers*, Conway's *Question Box* (both supplied by his friend's mother whose deceased husband had used them when preparing to leave the Episcopal Church to become a Catholic), and the catechism; all his relatives were opposed to his conversion, but softened later; joined the Redemptorist Order; ordained Catholic priest on 29 June 1932; founder and director of the Remnant of Israel; see *To Be or Not To Be a Jew* (1942); *Jews and You* (1944); *Queen of the Jews* (1956); *This Jew: A Book for Christians about the Crucifixion of Jesus* (1969); *He's a Jew* (1973); *Once a Jew* (1973); "The Power of Good Example," in Rosalie Marie Levy, *Why Jews Become Catholics* (1924), p.53; "God Had Other Plans," in John A. O'Brien (ed), *The Road to Damascus: Vol. III: The Way to Emmaus* (1953) ("When we entered the church, I knelt down with the rest because I had too much human respect to sit! Vaguely I noticed the devotion of the worshippers; I did not pray because, I suppose, I did not know how. The service itself was very impressive. I am sure that Jesus spoke to my heart from his Altar Throne that memorable morning...

To worldly hearts the supernatural is only the fiction of a fevered imagination, a sort of self-hypnotism into a dreamy existence, in which the whole of life is painted in unnatural or fancy colors. It seems to me that in this total ignorance or unwillingness to admit the reality of the supernatural and the actuality of its influence on the minds of men, lies hidden the basic cause of misunderstanding between non-Christians and Christians. The supernatural, considered as an influence which lifts men to the dignity of 'partakers of the nature of God,' must of necessity come from God Himself.

As a consequence of all this, the *necessity of prayer* stands out in vivid light: prayer by Catholics that this marvelous light, divine grace, may pierce the blindness of souls. Natural effort is futile without earnest prayer...In the affairs of your daily life you often subordinate spiritual values to worldly pleasures: they all pass away with time, leaving behind them, as a rule, a sense of unsatisfied desire, even dissatisfaction. What if there should be, after all, a supernatural life, a life which leads to the eternal, consummate fulfillment of your desires? Is it not worth the effort of a tiny prayer?"); "Jewish

Knight of Columbus," in Ronda Chervin (ed), *The Ingrafting: The Conversion Stories of Ten Hebrew-Catholics* (1987); "Jewish Knight of Columbus," in Roy H. Schoeman, *Honey From the Rock* (2007) (slightly revised version of the essay in *The Ingrafting* (see above)).

Koons, Robert C. - philosopher, theologian and Christian apologist; b. 1957, St. Paul, Minnesota; c. 25 May 2007 (Vigil of Pentecost); brought up in a good Christian home owing to the faith of his parents, who were Missouri Synod Lutherans; exposed to philosophy at high school; studied at Michigan State University, then at Oriel College, Oxford University (first class honors in Philosophy and Theology 1981); then graduate work at UCLA; saw Newman as the essential background to his conversion to the Catholic Church, on the ground that Newman showed that the supremacy of the pope and other contemporary distinctively Catholic doctrines were not innovations; always saw the doctrine of justification as the key issue between Catholics and Lutherans; also influenced by the Church Fathers; Professor of Philosophy at the University of Texas; involved in debates over the question of academic freedom and has proposed a concentration in colleges on Western Civilization and American institutions (specifically promotion of study of the "Great Books" of the Western tradition); involved in the intelligent design movement and a fellow of the Center for the Renewal of Science and Culture at the Discovery Institute; married with three children; see *Paradoxes of Belief and Strategic Rationality* (1992); *Realism Regained: An Exact Theory of Causation, Teleology, and the Mind* (2000); "The Check is in the Mail," in William Dembski (ed), *Uncommon Dissent: Intellectuals Who Find Darwinism Unconvincing* (2004), p.3; *Introduction to Logic* (2005); "A Lutheran's Case for Roman Catholicism," *web.archive.org*, 13 July 2006 (a detailed analysis of his thesis that the doctrine of justification is the crux of the Lutheran/Catholic controversy); *EWTN Audio Library, The Journey Home* (31 March 2008) ("As a Lutheran I assumed that Lutheranism was restoring Christianity as it had existed, not just at the time of the Apostles, but throughout history until very recently before the Reformation, when Aristotle had corrupted theology and Luther corrected it. So, we didn't think as Lutherans that Christianity died out when the Apostles died out, and that Luther re-created it again a thousand years later. We didn't think that at all. Athanasius, Augustine, those were our guys you know. we didn't think of them as evil Catholics, because they were part of the Christian tradition and they were saints. And so I expected when I opened up all those Church fathers that they would sound Lutheran, basically they would be sort of proto-Lutheran, and I was very surprised to find they sounded much more Roman Catholic than we did. They talked about the Church, the episcopacy, the bishops, the historical succession, the apostolic succession, and all of that. And that was disturbing to me. It made me think things through again.

But the thing that held me back was the doctrine of justification. It's basically the doctrine of what you have to do to be saved, what you have to do to have eternal life. And the Lutheran Church understood that to mean that you're justified by faith alone, by grace alone, God's unmerited love for us. And we appropriate it by faith alone, not faith plus love, not faith plus works, or anything like that. And there are passages in Paul's Letters, to the Romans and Galatians, that certainly seem to teach that, and as a Lutheran I had read them that way.

Then I read the Council of Trent, which was responding to Luther's ideas shortly after Luther's death, and the Sessions V and VI. To Lutheran ears they sound pretty shocking. They sounded like basically the Fathers were saying, 'Oh, Paul's just wrong. We're justified by works and not by grace, not by faith.' So, in my own mind I thought, well, you know, because I was impressed by what I'd read from the Fathers, ideally we should all be Catholics, but unfortunately the Church had got it wrong on justification, and so there's kind of an emergency situation where we Lutherans can justify ourselves and can say we're to be there to be a witness to this doctrine of justification until the Church comes around on it and then we can rejoin it. that was my justification for a long time to remain Lutheran. So the final straw then had to be rethink that doctrine, and that started happening about five years ago...

A number of things started raising this issue of justification again in my mind. One was this joint declaration where the Catholic Church and the Lutheran Church had stated that the differences on justification weren't that significant. I don't in the end agree with what they said. There are deeper differences than the joint declaration let on. But it did raise the issue again for me. It made me think, 'Well, I'd better look at this again, because it's not quite as simple as I thought it was.' Not as black and white, you know, faith alone versus works...It made me go back and read and examine things again. So now, of course, I looked at Scriptures, looked again at Paul... So, first thing I looked back at the texts again carefully to see what exactly is Paul getting at, what's the point, what's the argument?

I also started looking at the Church Fathers on justification, and I think of all of them the one that's most important was Augustine, because again Lutherans think of themselves as Augustinian. Luther was an Augustinian monk. We thought that Lutheranism was just pure Augustine again, eliminating some of the errors like those of Pelagius. What I found when I read Augustine himself again was he didn't sound Lutheran. When you read the actual text he sounded very close to what the Council of Trent said. He said that you are justified by grace, that is infused into us, that enables us to love God.

So, it is grace, hundred per cent grace, not anything that we can do through our own natural human ability. But it's not faith alone that appropriates that grace. Faith is a beginning, as the Council of Trent said. It's the foundation for justification, but it's not the whole story. Faith working in love, faith that expresses itself in love, and in a life of obedience.

So, again this was disturbing, especially when I went back to the Lutheran Confessions and read Melanchthon, his *Apology*, who was one of the authors of the Augsburg Confession, where he says, 'Oh, yes, we're agreeing with Augustine' and he quotes from Augustine's book on the Letter and Spirit. And so I went back to the *Letter and Spirit*, to Augustine's actual text. What I found was that Melanchthon was taking stuff out of context and he was really misrepresenting, I think, what Augustine was saying. That was really disturbing to me, because Melanchthon had been one of my heroes. I thought he was a straight shooter and I found out that I couldn't really trust him at that point any more.

So, then I looked at the Council of Trent again and this time I had a little more background to make sense of that. I knew a little bit more of medieval philosophy. I knew a little bit more about the history, and I could read everything a bit more sensitively, a bit more charitably, and I realized that actually the Fathers were correcting some of the errors that Luther had reacted to. In fact, I think Luther in his early protest was right. There were distortions of the Gospel that had crept in through Ockham, and Scotus, and other philosophers, that had over-emphasized what humans could do with our own natural power, and that really did create some insecurity by teaching people that you had to do your absolute best or God wouldn't save you.

So, Luther was legitimately reacting to some of those problems, but unfortunately Luther did not know Aquinas well. He hadn't been trained in Thomistic philosophy, and of course he didn't know the Council of Trent, because it was after he died. The point is that after he died the Church did correct, I think, some of the errors that Luther had reacted to. And, unfortunately, at that point the two sides were so far apart that the Lutherans didn't feel they could participate and didn't really take the Council seriously as they should...

I found some Lutheran theologians who admitted that the Lutheran doctrine of justification wasn't found in the early Fathers at all... That's a pretty awful confession. That admits that Lutherans really did introduce an innovation with their doctrine of justification. And once I saw that, then at least in my mind the burden of proof shifts here. I mean if it's an innovation and it divides the Church, the Church doesn't accept it, then you better have pretty solid proof from the Scriptures. So, again, going back to the Scriptures, I found that, no, taking the Scriptures as a whole into account, they really favored the Roman position rather than the Lutheran position.

And so in the end of the day I had to say, 'Well, you know, I was wrong about the justification issue. At the very best it's a draw and the burden of proof is on us, so it looks as if the Catholics have won this one. And that was my only thing that was keeping me from being a Catholic at that point"); (ed), *The Waning of Materialism: New Essays in the Philosophy of Mind* (2010) (co-editor with George Bealer).

Koontz, Dean Ray - author; b. 9 July 1945, Everett, Pennsylvania; born into the United Church of Christ; brought up in a dysfunctional family; suffered from beatings and abuse by his father, though sheltered by his mother; educated at Shippensburg University of Pennsylvania (graduated in 1967), where he won a fiction competition sponsored by *Atlantic Monthly* magazine; worked as an English teacher and on a federal initiative designed to help poor children; author of over one hundred and fifty novels and short stories; many science fiction novels; also suspense and horror fiction, several books written under different pseudonyms; has written a number of screenplays; several books have been adapted as films; very highly paid author; books have been published in many languages; there are a number of novels, articles and letters from the 1960s and 1970s attributed to him, which he has stated he did not write; has contributed funds to Conservative Republican candidates and causes; became a Catholic after marrying his wife Gerda, a Catholic, while at college; influenced in his conversion by the example of his wife's family; also influenced by such writers as St. Thomas Aquinas and G. K. Chesterton; came to appreciate that faith and science are not enemies ("The birth of science comes out of the Catholic Church. People always say, 'No, no, Galileo.' They don't really know the history; they just know talking points. The reality is through various times in the Catholic Church, various sciences were founded and encouraged"); see (selective list) *Star Quest* (1968); *Beastchild* (1970); *Legacy of Terror* (1971) (as Deanna Dwyer); *Chase* (1972) (as K. R. Dwyer); *The Face of Fear* (1977) (as Brian Coffey); *Whispers* (1980); *Watchers* (1987); *Mr. Murder* (1993); *Fear Nothing*

(1998); *The Book of Counted Sorrows* (2003); *Odd Thomas* (2004); *In Odd We Trust* (2008); Katherine M. Ramsland, *Dean Koontz: A Writer's Biography* (1997); Tim Drake, "Chatting With Koontz About Faith," *National Catholic Register*, 6 March 2007 ("Catholicism permits a view of life that sees mystery and wonder in all things, which Protestantism does not easily allow. As a Catholic, I saw the world as being more mysterious, more organic and less mechanical than it had seemed to me previously, and I had a more direct connection with God.

I feel about Catholicism as G. K. Chesterton did - that it encourages an exuberance, a joy about the gift of life. I think my conversion was a natural growth. Even in the darkest hours of my childhood, I was an irrepressible optimist, always able to find something to fill me with amazement, wonder and delight. When I came to the Catholic faith, it explained to me why I always had - and always should have - felt exuberant and full of hope.

If you remain alert to the lessons of life and aware of the mystery of the world, it is difficult to deny the existence of design in all things. I can walk in the rose garden, watch the joyful capering of my dog and see the indisputable work of God. The key is beauty. If the world is merely a complex and efficient machine, beauty is not required. Beauty is in fact superfluous. Therefore beauty is a gift to us. If we were soulless machines of meat, the survival instinct would be all we needed to motivate us. The pleasures of the senses - such as taste and smell - are superfluous to machines in a godless world. Therefore, they are gifts to us, and evidence of divine grace. The older I've gotten, the more beauty, wonder and mystery I see in the world, which is why there are ever more of those three things in my books"); Dena Ross, "Dean Koontz: Angels, Demons, and Our Mysterious World," *beliefnet*, October 2008 ("What's your favorite thing about being a Catholic? It gives me a sense that the world has shape and form and function and meaning. I suppose that's my favorite thing about it, because I don't wander aimlessly seeking for some meaning in things. I have a sense of what those meanings are. It opened my eyes to a deeper, more complex world, and that leaves you a lifetime of exploring to follow.

What's your least favorite thing about being a Catholic? How Vatican II threw away so much tradition. It's only beginning to come back. The Latin Mass and all of that was a great loss, something that is embraced and promoted for hundreds upon hundreds of years and then disappears overnight in an attempt to satisfy an urge toward trendiness. It was a great loss to the church, and I think it still is"); Maryellen O'Brien, "Interview with Dean Koontz," *examiner.com*, 17 November 2009

("The most humorless people I've ever known are ardent atheists. Many Catholic writers have been howlingly funny, not least of all Evelyn Waugh, Graham Greene in books like *Travels With My Aunt*, Dorothy Sayers [sic], certainly the singular G. K. Chesterton. We once had a party, about sixty people, and half a dozen were friends who were monks. There was also an avowed atheist present. The evening was marked by much laughter and high good spirits. Near the end, the atheist said to me, in astonishment, 'The monks are very funny. You must be playing a joke on us. They can't really be monks.' When I assured him that monks - they were all priests as well - are usually highly accomplished, deeply educated, and nearly always amusing, he looked at me as if I were insane. He said, 'But they're Catholics.' At other functions, he had met and liked numerous other friends of ours, but he had no idea that many of them were Catholics - or that I was. When I noted this, his eyes widened even further. The Catholic view of the human condition is fundamentally tragic, but that does not mean that we are required to be glum. Indeed, quite the opposite. The human condition may be tragic, but we have been given a beautiful world to enjoy and the promise of eternity, and if we are open to the grace of God, we must be happy because faith and hope and happiness are the proper reaction to what we've been given"); *deankoontz.com.*

Kreeft, Peter John – author and Catholic apologist; b. 1937; c. 1960 (received at Yale University); brought up in the Dutch Reformed Calvinist Church; studied Philosophy at Calvin College, Michigan, and Fordham University (PhD); did postgraduate study at Yale University; taught at Villanova University 1962-1965; Professor of Philosophy at Boston College, Massachusetts (from 1965), and The King's College, New York; notable speaker and writer on Catholic apologetics and critic of liberalism ("To be a Catholic is to take the whole deal"); author of numerous books; conversion to the Catholic faith influenced most by the writings of St. John of the Cross, G. K. Chesterton, C. S. Lewis, and Ronald Knox ("The book that more than any other decided it for me was Ronald Knox's *The Belief of Catholics*"); see (selective list) C. S. Lewis: A Critical Essay (1969); Love Is Stronger Than Death (1979); Heaven, The Heart's Deepest Longing (1980); Everything You Ever Wanted to Know about Heaven (1982); Between Heaven and Hell (1981); The Unaborted Socrates (1982); The Best Things in Life (1983); Philosophical Questions (1984); *Yes or No? Straight Answers to Tough Questions About Christianity* (1984); *Prayer: The Great Conversation* (1985); *Making Sense Out Of Suffering* (1986); *Socrates Meets Jesus* (1987);

A Turn of the Clock: A Book of Modern Proverbs (1987); "Hauled Aboard the Ark," in Robert Baram (ed), Spiritual Journeys (revised edition, 1988), p.165 (reproduced in *The Coming Home Network International*, *Conversion Stories*, *chnetwork.org*, 31 October 2011) ("The first independent idea about religion I ever remember thinking was a question I asked my father, an elder in the church, a good and wise and holy man. I was amazed that he couldn't answer it. 'Why do we Calvinists have the whole truth and no one else? We're so few. How could God leave the rest of the world in error? Especially the rest of the Christian churches?' Since no good answer seemed forthcoming, I then came to the explosive conclusion that the truth about God was more mysterious - more wonderfully and uncomfortably mysterious - than anything any of us could ever fully comprehend…

[In] college I quickly fell in love with English, and then Philosophy, and thus twice changed my major. Both subjects were widening my appreciation of the history of Western civilization and therefore of things Catholic. The first serious doubt about my anti-Catholic beliefs was planted in my mind by my roommate, who was becoming an Anglican: 'Why don't Protestants pray to saints? There's nothing wrong in you asking me to pray for you, is there? Why not ask the dead, then, if we believe they're alive with God in Heaven, part of the "great cloud of witnesses" that surrounds us (Hebrews 12)?' It was the first serious question I had absolutely no answer to, and that bothered me…

I developed a strong intellectual and aesthetic love for things medieval: Gregorian chant, Gothic architecture, Thomistic philosophy, illuminated manuscripts, etc. I felt vaguely guilty about it, for that was the Catholic era. I thought I could separate these legitimate cultural forms from the 'dangerous' Catholic essence, as the modern Church separated the essence from these discarded forms. Yet I saw a natural connection.

Then one summer, on the beach at Ocean Grove, New Jersey, I read St. John of the Cross. I did not understand much of it, but I knew, with undeniable certainty, that here was reality, something as massive and positive as a mountain range. I felt as if I had just come out of a small, comfortable cave, in which I had lived all my life, and found that there was an unsuspected world outside of incredible dimensions. Above all, the dimensions were those of holiness, goodness, purity of heart, obedience to the first and greatest commandment, willing God's will, the one absolute I had discovered, at the age of eight. I was very far from saintly, but that did not prevent me from fascinated admiration from afar; the valley dweller appreciates the height of the mountain more than the dweller on the foothills. I read other Catholic saints and mystics, and discovered the same reality there, however different the style (even St. Thérèse 'The Little Flower'!) I felt sure it was the same reality I had learned to love from my parents and teachers, only a far deeper version of it. It did not seem alien and other. It was not another religion but the adult version of my own.

Then in a church history class at Calvin a professor gave me a way to investigate the claims of the Catholic Church on my own. The essential claim is historical: that Christ founded the Catholic Church, that there is historical continuity. If that were true, I would have to be a Catholic out of obedience to my one absolute, the will of my Lord. The teacher explained the Protestant belief. He said that Catholics accuse we who are Protestants of going back only to Luther and Calvin; but this is not true; we go back to Christ. Christ had never intended a Catholic-style Church, but a Protestant-style one. The Catholic additions to the simple, Protestant-style New Testament church had grown up gradually in the Middle Ages like barnacles on the hull of a ship, and the Protestant Reformers had merely scraped off the barnacles, the alien, pagan accretions. The Catholics, on the other hand, believed that Christ established the Church Catholic from the start, and that the doctrines and practices that Protestants saw as barnacles were, in fact, the very living and inseparable parts of the planks and beams of the ship.

I thought this made the Catholic claim empirically testable, and I wanted to test it because I was worried by this time about my dangerous interest in things Catholic. Half of me wanted to discover it was the true Church (that was the more adventurous half); the other half wanted to prove it false (that was the comfortable half). My adventurous half rejoiced when I discovered in the early Church such Catholic elements as the centrality of the Eucharist, the Real Presence, prayers to saints, devotion to Mary, an insistence on visible unity, and apostolic succession. Furthermore, the Church Fathers just 'smelled' more Catholic than Protestant, especially St. Augustine, my personal favorite and a hero to most Protestants too. It seemed very obvious that if Augustine or Jerome or Ignatius of Antioch or Anthony of the Desert, or Justin Martyr, or Clement of Alexandria, or Athanasius were alive today they would be Catholics, not Protestants.

The issue of the Church's historical roots was crucial to me, for the thing I had found in the Catholic Church and in no Protestant church was simply this: the massive historical fact that there she is, majestic and unsinkable. It was the same old seaworthy ship, the Noah's ark that Jesus had commissioned. It was like discovering not an accurate picture of the ark, or even a real relic of its wood, but the whole ark itself, still sailing unscathed on the seas of history! It was like a fairy tale come true, like a 'myth become fact;' to use C. S. Lewis' formula for the Incarnation.

The parallel between Christ and Church, Incarnation and Church history, goes still further. I thought, just as Jesus made a claim about His identity that forces us into one of only two camps, His enemies or His worshippers, those who call Him liar and those who call Him Lord; so the Catholic Church's claim to be the one true Church, the Church Christ founded, forces us to say either that this is the most arrogant, blasphemous and wicked claim imaginable, if it is not true, or else that she is just what she claims to be. Just as Jesus stood out as the absolute exception to all other human teachers in claiming to be more than human and more than a teacher, so the Catholic Church stood out above all other denominations in claiming to be not merely a denomination, but the Body of Christ incarnate, infallible, one, and holy, presenting the really present Christ in her Eucharist. I could never rest in a comfortable, respectable ecumenical halfway house of measured admiration from a distance. I had to shout either 'Crucify her!' or 'Hosanna!' If I could not love and believe her, honesty forced me to despise and fight her.

But I could not despise her. The beauty and sanctity and wisdom of her, like that of Christ, prevented me from calling her liar or lunatic, just as it prevented me from calling Christ that. But simple logic offered then one and only one other option: this must be the Church my Lord provided for me - my Lord, for me. So she had better become my Church if He is my Lord...

There were many strands in the rope that hauled me aboard the ark, though this one - the Church's claim to be the one Church historically founded by Christ - was the central and deciding one...

But if Catholic dogma contradicted Scripture or itself at any point, I could not believe it. I explored all the cases of claimed contradiction and found each to be a Protestant misunderstanding. No matter how morally bad the Church had gotten in the Renaissance, it never taught heresy. I was impressed with its very hypocrisy: even when it didn't raise its practice to its preaching, it never lowered its preaching to its practice. Hypocrisy, someone said, is the tribute vice pays to virtue.

I was impressed by the argument that 'the Church wrote the Bible.' Christianity was preached by the Church before the New Testament was written - that is simply a historical fact. It is also a fact that the apostles wrote the New Testament and the Church canonized it, deciding which books were divinely inspired. I knew, from logic and common sense, that a cause can never be less than its effect. You can't give what you don't have. If the Church has no divine inspiration and no infallibility, no divine authority, then neither can the New Testament. Protestantism logically entails Modernism. I had to be either a Catholic or a Modernist. That decided it; that was like saying I had to be either a patriot or a traitor...

One crucial issue remained to be resolved: Justification by Faith, the central bone of contention of the Reformation. Luther was obviously right here: the doctrine is dearly taught in *Romans* and *Galatians.* If the Catholic Church teaches 'another gospel' of salvation by works, then it teaches fundamental heresy. I found here however another case of misunderstanding. I read Aquinas' *Summa* on grace, and the decrees of the Council of Trent, and found them just as strong on grace as Luther or Calvin. I was overjoyed to find that the Catholic Church had read the Bible too!

At Heaven's gate our entrance ticket, according to Scripture and Church dogma, is not our good works or our sincerity, but our faith, which glues us to Jesus. He saves us; we do not save ourselves. But I find, incredibly, that nine out of ten Catholics do not know this, the absolutely central, core, essential dogma of Christianity. Protestants are right: most Catholics do in fact believe a whole other religion. Well over 90% of students I have polled who have had twelve years of catechism classes, even Catholic high schools, say they expect to go to Heaven because they tried, or did their best, or had compassionate feelings to everyone, or were sincere. They hardly ever mention Jesus. Asked why they hope to be saved, they mention almost anything except the Savior. Who taught them? Who wrote their textbooks? These teachers have stolen from our precious children the most valuable thing in the world, the 'pearl of great price,' their faith. Jesus had some rather terrifying warnings about such things - something about millstones.

Catholicism taught that we are saved by faith, by grace, by Christ, however few Catholics understood this. And Protestants taught that true faith necessarily produces good works. The fundamental issue of the Reformation is an argument between the roots and the blossoms on the same flower.

But though Luther did not neglect good works, he connected them to faith by only a thin and unreliable thread: human gratitude. In response to God's great gift of salvation, which we accept by faith, we do good works out of gratitude, he taught. But gratitude is only a feeling, and dependent on the self. The Catholic connection between faith and works is a far stronger and more reliable one. I found it in C. S. Lewis' *Mere Christianity*, the best introduction to Christianity I have ever read. It is the ontological reality of *zoë*, supernatural life, sanctifying grace, God's own life in the soul, which is received by faith and then itself produces good works. God comes in one end and out the other: the very same thing that comes in by faith (the life of God) goes out as works, through our free cooperation.

I was also dissatisfied with Luther's teaching that justification was a legal fiction on God's part rather than a real event in us; that God looks on the Christian in Christ, sees only Christ's righteousness, and legally counts or *imputes* Christ's righteousness as ours. I thought it had to be as Catholicism says, that God actually *imparts* Christ to us, in baptism and through faith (these two are usually together in the New Testament). Here I found the fundamentalists, especially the Baptists, more philosophically sound than the Calvinists and Lutherans. For me, their language, however sloganish and satirizable, is more accurate when they speak of 'Receiving Christ as your personal savior'...

I have been happy as a Catholic for twenty-six years now. The honeymoon faded, of course, but the marriage has deepened. Like all converts I ever have heard of, I was hauled aboard not by those Catholics who try to 'sell' the church by conforming it to the spirit of the times by saying Catholics are just like everyone else, but by those who joyfully held out the ancient and orthodox faith in all its fullness and prophetic challenge to the world. The minimalists, who reduce miracles to myths, dogmas to opinions, laws to values, and the Body of Christ to a psycho-social club, have always elicited wrath, pity, or boredom from me. So has political partisanship masquerading as religion. I am happy as a child to follow Christ's vicar on earth everywhere he leads. What he loves, I love; what he leaves, I leave; where he leads, I follow. For the Lord we both adore said to Peter his predecessor, 'Who hears you, hears Me.' That is why I am a Catholic: because I am a Christian"); *The God Who Loves You* (1988); *Fundamentals of the Faith* (1988); *Advent: Meditations for the Season* (1988); *Two Arguments from the Heart for Immortality* (1989); *Letters to Jesus: Answered* (1989); *Three Philosophies of Life* (1989); *Everything You Ever Wanted to Know About Heaven – But Never Dreamed of Asking* (1990); *Making Choices: Practical Wisdom for Everyday Moral Decisions* (1990); *You Can Understand the Old Testament* (1990); *Reading and Praying the New Testament* (1991); *Summa of the Summa* (1991); *Back To Virtue: Traditional Moral Wisdom for Modern Moral Confusion* (1992); *A Shorter Summa* (1993); *Christianity for Modern Pagans* (1993); *The Snakebite Letters* (1993); *Handbook of Christian Apologetics* (1993; revised edition 2009) (with Ronald K. Tacelli); *Your Questions. God's Answers* (1994); *Shadowlands of C. S. Lewis* (1994); *Women and the Priesthood* (1994) (with Alice von Hildebrand) ("The most egregious error of all is a demand to be priestesses for empowerment. I can think of no term that more perfectly proves the speaker's utter incomprehension of what she says than that. It is like wanting to manage the Chicago Cubs because of a thirst for success. Priests are not power-brokers or managers. They are sewers. Like Christ, they drain off the world's sins. They are spiritual garbage men. Like Christ, they clean up our spiritual garbage. They wash feet; dirty, smelly souls - ours. The Pope, priest of priests, is servant of the servants of God. this is not a clever Public Relations slogan, this is his real job description"); *The Angel and the Ants: Bringing Heaven Closer to Your Daily Life* (1994); *C. S. Lewis for the Third Millennium* (1994); *Angels and Demons: What Do We Really Know About Them?* (1995); *Ecumenical Jihad: Ecumenism and the Culture War* (1995); *The Journey: A Spiritual Roadmap for Modern Pilgrims* (1996); *A Refutation of Moral Relativism: Interviews With an Absolutist* (1999); *Prayer for Beginners* (2000); *Catholic Christianity* (2001); *Socratic Logic* (2001); *How to Win the Culture War* (2001); *Philosophy 101 by Socrates: An Introduction to Philosophy Via Plato's Apology* (2002); *Three Approaches to Abortion* (2002); "The Problem of Suffering Reconsidered," *This Rock*, March 2002; "Are Apologetics and Evangelization at Odds?" *This Rock*, January 2003; *Socrates Meets Machiavelli* (2003); *Socrates Meets Marx* (2003); *The God Who Loves You; Love Divine, All Loves Excelling* (2004); Paul Camacho, "A Conversation With Peter Kreeft," *Boston College Observer*, 22 April 2004 (reprinted in Catholic Education Resource Center, catholiceducation.org) ("'You used to be a Reformed Protestant. When and why did you decide to become a Catholic?' 'I became a Catholic for the only honest reason anyone should: because it's true. I read my way into the Church in the same way Newman did: I tried to prove to myself that the Church Christ established was Protestant and then went wrong, that is Catholic, later. I found the opposite. For instance, not one Christian in the world for the first 1000 years ever denied the Real Presence in the Eucharist'"); *Socrates Meets Sartre* (2005); *The Philosophy of Tolkien* (2005); *You Can Understand the Bible* (2005); *The Sea Within: Waves and the Meaning of All Things* (2006); *Before I Go: Letters to Our Children About What Really Matters* (2007); *A Pocket Guide to the Meaning of Life* (2007); *The Philosophy of Jesus* (2007); *Socrates Meets Descartes* (2007); "My Conversation With Solzhenitsyn" (Parts I and II), *Saint Austin Review*, July/August 2007, p.13 and September/October 2007, p.25; *Because God Is Real: Sixteen Questions, One Answer* (2008); *Jesus Shock* (2008); *I Surf, Therefore I Am: A Philosophy of Surfing* (2008); Interview with Peter Kreeft, *Envoy Magazine*, 2008 ("You entered the Catholic Church as a young adult, having been raised in a Reformed/ Calvinist home. What initially attracted you to the Catholic Faith and what was at the heart of your decision to become Catholic?

Kreeft: What initially attracted me to the Catholic Church was, first, stepping inside St. Patrick's Cathedral in New York at about age twelve, feeling like I was in heaven (I had never been in a cathedral before), and wondering why, if Catholics got everything else wrong, as I had been taught, they got beauty so right. How could falsehood and evil be so beautiful?

Secondly, a few years later, it was reading St. John of the Cross's *Ascent of Mount Carmel,* out of curiosity, not understanding him, but knowing that here was a mountain, something so massively real it had to be true.

Then, at Calvin College, reading Catholic stuff and trying to exorcise the temptation to like it more than I was supposed to by taking a course in Church history to prove to myself how Protestant the early Church was. I knew one thing for sure: whether I was going to stay Protestant or become Catholic had to be decided not by me but by Christ, so I had to know what kind of Church He left us. If you read John Henry Newman's *The Development of Christian Doctrine,* you know the rest of the story. The doctrine that bowled me over was the Eucharist: not a single Christian doubted the real presence - as most Protestants did - for a thousand years (until Berengar of Tours, I think")); *If Einstein Had Been a Surfer* (2009); *Socrates Meets Kant* (2009); *Between Allah and Jesus: What Christians Can Learn From Muslims* (2010); *Socrates Meets Hume* (2010); *An Ocean Full of Angels: The Autobiography of Isa Ben Adam* (2011) (novel).

Kreisler, Fritz (born Friedrich Kreisler) – violinist and composer; b. 2 February 1875, Vienna, Austria; c. late 1950s (received by Bishop Fulton Sheen; his wife Harriet also converted; both were reverts, having lapsed into secularism); d. 29 January 1962, New York City; one of the greatest violinists who ever lived; his father, who was Jewish, was a doctor and enthusiastic amateur violinist; baptized at the age of twelve; studied at the Vienna Conservatory (youngest student ever to enter (age seven then)) and in Paris; his teachers included Anton Bruckner, Léo Delibes, and Jules Massenet; made his American debut at the age of thirteen in New York in 1888-1889; then performed in Austria; left music to study medicine; returned to the violin in 1899 and had great success; in 1910 he gave the premiere of Elgar's Violin Concerto (written for him by the composer) with Elgar conducting at the Queen's Hall, London; at the outbreak of World War I he joined the Austrian Army; medically discharged in November 1914 after being wounded; moved to the United States (his wife's native country); returned to Europe and lived in Berlin 1924-1934, then in France; at the outbreak of World War II he settled again in the United States; involved in a serious traffic accident in 1941 when crossing the road, impairing his hearing and eyesight; became a naturalized American citizen in 1943 and lived there for the rest of his life; returned to his career; effortless ability (he practiced very little); sweet tone and emotionally expressive mode of playing; recorded the main works for violin; wrote a number of pieces for the violin, operettas, a string quartet and cadenzas; Bishop Fulton Sheen delivered the eulogy at his funeral (also that of his wife); interred in a private mausoleum in Woodlawn Cemetery, Bronx, New York; see *Four Weeks in the Trenches: The War Story of a Violinist* (1915; 3rd revised edition, 1981); Louis P. Lochner, *Fritz Kreisler* (1950); Fulton J. Sheen, *Treasure in Clay* (1982), pp. 258-260; Amy Biancolli, *Fritz Kreisler: Love's Sorrow, Love's Joy* (1998); Boris Schwarz, *Great Masters of the Violin* (1983); Henry Roth, *Great Violinists in Performance* (1987); Margaret Campbell, *The Great Violinists* (2004); Fr. Charles P. Connor, *Classic Catholic Converts* (2001); his papers are in Library of Congress Music Division; *ANB*.

Kresta, Al – broadcaster, journalist and author; b. 1951, New Haven, Connecticut; c. 16 April 1992 (Holy Thursday; revert; his wife, Sally, and their four children were received 18 April 1992); oldest of five children in a solid Catholic family; adolescent doubt led from high level school performance to a conviction for possession of heroin; stopped taking drugs and experimented with many different religious cults, including the New Age movement 1969-1974; enrolled in Michigan State University in 1973 and graduated in 1976; eventually accepted the Bible as his authority; started to appreciate the Church Fathers and the development of doctrine; impressed by Cardinal Newman's writings and those of C. S. Lewis; suffered from clinical depression 1982-1985; made a retreat at the Trappist Abbey of Gethsemani ("The quiet liturgical rhythm of the place was like balm to my soul"); despite his uncertainty with Protestantism he became the pastor of an independent charismatic church in 1985; managed Christian bookstores and also a radio evangelist; in 1990 he became convinced of the truth of the Catholic faith and resigned his pastorate; after further study he re-entered the Catholic Church; after his conversion he was recruited by Tom Monaghan to launch the media apostolate, Ave Maria Communications; president of Ave Maria Radio; host of the radio program, *Kresta in the Afternoon*; in 2003 he lost his left leg to necrotizing fasciitis; see "All Detours Lead to Rome," in Patrick Madrid (ed),

Surprised by Truth (1994), p.253 ("In reviewing the beliefs of the primitive Church, I noticed that the Church Fathers didn't hesitate to invoke biblical authority, but they never tried to prove their case by the Bible alone. They also appealed to an authoritative Church tradition handed down through a succession of bishops that could be traced all the way back to the apostles themselves…I wondered how it could be that there were Catholic, not Protestant, doctrines *everywhere* in the writings of the early Church Fathers. Were they perhaps what the apostles themselves had taught, or had they been cunningly introduced just after the apostles died?

I also saw how doctrine developed in the early Church. The Trinity and the divinity of Christ were doctrines that were clearly rooted in Scripture but were not as self-evident as I had been led to believe. The full form of these doctrines, as we know them today, were not derived straight from Scripture, but are the result of centuries of deep reflection on Scripture and the oral tradition of interpreting Scripture that had been handed on to the Church by the apostles. The nineteenth century convert, John Henry Newman, became a Catholic largely because he grasped this point…

After much prayer and study, I could no longer accept the Protestant doctrine of Scripture alone on any other than purely pragmatic grounds. The Catholic Church's authoritative role in the formation of the canon of Scripture, coupled with the lack of biblical evidence for *sola scriptura*, were the weak links in the Protestant chain that could no longer tether me. I continued somewhat half-heartedly as an Evangelical, but I was grappling with the question, 'Can I follow Christ and remain a Protestant?'…

Without the teaching guidance of the Church, all sorts of fanciful and erroneous interpretations of Scripture can spring up (2 Pet. 3:15). That's why Paul admonished the early Christians to always hold fast to the unity of doctrine: 'I appeal to you, brothers, in the name of our Lord Jesus Christ, that all of you agree with one another so that there may be no divisions among you and that you may be perfectly united in mind and thought' (1 Cor. 1:10).

The Evangelical vision of the Church as the invisible union of all who genuinely trust in Christ seemed spectral in comparison; even a subtle form of Docetism. Docetists believed that the Word did not truly take flesh but only appeared to, the invisibilists similarly denied the materiality of Christ's Body, the Church. By refusing to accept the visible Church Protestantism denied the extension of the Incarnation…

The New Testament records conflict between believers; sharp disputes over circumcision, dining on meat sacrificed to idols, the person of Christ. And yes, the New Testament describes the sin and corruption of various Church members. But nowhere are the believers given the option of hiving off into independent splinter groups; in fact one of the few offenses that give us reason to expel a brother is the offense of causing disunity: 'I urge you brothers, to watch out for those who cause divisions. Keep away from them' (Rom. 16:17). Without a visibly united Church, excommunication can't achieve its purpose: the repentance and restoration of the offender (Matt. 18:15-20, 1 Cor. 5:1-13; 2 Cor. 2:1-11). I wondered how Protestantism, which has splintered into over 20,000 denominations worldwide, could be what Jesus had in mind in John 17:21, when he said that the world will know that the Father sent the Son by the unity of his disciples. 'Where is the visible expression of unity and universality in Protestantism?' I asked...

I also asked how it could be that Jesus would command visible unity but leave his Church without the necessary infallible means of settling doctrinal disputes in order to maintain that unity? Would he command the impossible? And if Jesus had not given that sort of infallible teaching authority to the ministers of his Church, is it not presumptuous for a minister or a body of ministers to insist upon this or that form of church government, this or that form of baptism, or some other doctrine? That, after all, was Jesus' complaint against the Pharisees. They imposed practices, traditions of men (cf. Mark 7:6-13), for which there was no divine warrant"); *Why Do Catholics Genuflect?: And Answers to Other Puzzling Things About the Catholic Church* (2001); *EWTN Audio Library, The Journey Home* (9 September 2002) ("As I worked through the New Testament it began as a sort of a drumbeat. Every page I was seeing the assumption, the presupposition, of visible unity. In John 17:21 Jesus prays for the unity of the people. In fact, something I learned from Francis Schaeffer many years before was that in that passage Jesus gives the world the right to judge whether the Father sent the Son by the degree of observable love and unity they witnessed on the part of his people. Now, if it's observable, it can't purely be spiritual. It has to be something which can be witnessed, it has to take shape, it has to take form. It has to exist in space and time. So, that was eating away at me. I began to take a look at how you do church discipline if you don't have visible unity. And again the questions compounded and just grew stronger and stronger...

If you don't have a high theology of the Church, if you don't have a sense of visible unity, then I think membership becomes like membership in a club. It is something that you want to tally up. You want to check your census and see what kind of resources are there, so you can get on with the next building project...

Along with my emphasis on visible unity I began to see that authority in the New Testament had been given to Peter, that there was something called apostolic succession, and that this was given in order to serve the unity of the body. So you see it in Acts, chapter 15, for instance in the Jerusalem Council where it looks as though there's going to be this spinning off of different groups, because they're fighting over the basic proclamation of the gospel and the validity of Paul and Barnabas's ministry. Then what happens is that the Council is called and that the Council issues written decrees, and those decrees are expected to be adhered to by all those who claim the name Christian. I thought that that was pretty important, that you had the use of authority there in order to serve the interests of unity.

And then another thing came up. I began to get attracted to the idea of eucharist and the centrality of the Lord's table, and that was the sacrament of the Eucharist...

'Catholic' is not the name of a denomination. It is a mark of Christ's Church universal. Well, so is 'one.' So is 'holy.' So is 'apostolic.' And that oneness that we refer to is the oneness of the sacraments. It's the one body, the one bread, the one cup.

So, all of the things dovetailed for me into this hunger. I had to see visible unity...

When you do not have a visible, united body, church discipline becomes virtually impossible"); *EWTN Audio Library, The Journey Home* (6 December 2004); *Why Are Catholics So Concerned About Sin?: More Answers to Puzzling Questions About the Catholic Church* (2005); *Moments of Grace: Inspiring Stories From Well-Known Catholics* (2008); *Catholicism's 21st Century Opponents* (2012).

Kudlow, Lawrence ("Kuddles") – economist; b. 20 August 1947, New Jersey; c. November 1997 (received by Fr. C. John McCloskey III); born into a Jewish family; degree in History from the University of Rochester, New York, in 1969; as a Democrat he was involved in left-wing and anti-Vietnam politics; in 1971 he studied Politics and Economics at Princeton University; Staff Economist at the Federal Reserve Bank of New York; during the first term of the Reagan administration, 1981-1985, he worked as Associate Director for Economics and Planning in the Office of Management and Budget; worked for some years as a private economist; had addictions to cocaine and alcohol, but took the twelve step program; Economics Editor at *National Review Online* in 2001; hosted several television programs before becoming host of CNBC's *The Kudlow Report*; columnist for many U.S. newspapers and magazines; free-market economist; supporter of George W. Bush's policies on economic growth and jobs; introduced to the Catholic Church by Jeffrey Bell, political consultant; influenced in his conversion by Fr. C. John McCloskey III; married three times; see *American Abundance: The New Economic and Moral Prosperity* (1997).

Kurek, Michael – composer; b. 1955, Nashville, Tennessee; raised in Nashville; one of four children in a Catholic family; his mother was a commercial artist; left the Catholic Church while in high school and later became an Evangelical Protestant; majored in Music Theory at the University of Tennessee in Knoxville (BM); in 1978 enrolled at the University of Michigan at Ann Arbor (MM 1981; AMusD 1985); won a Charles Ives Scholarship from the American Academy of Arts and Letters in 1983; studied as a composition fellow with Hans Werner Henze at Tanglewood; music influenced by Ravel, Debussy and Barber; his music has evolved "from academic modernism to a lush tonal melodicism"; many awards, including the Academy Award in Music from the American Academy of Arts and Letters (the Academy's top lifetime achievement award); influenced to return to the Church by, inter alia, *Evangelical Is Not Enough* by Thomas Howard (see above) and by the writings of Scott Hahn (see above); professor of music composition at the Blair School of Music at Vanderbilt University; see Catherine Deavel, "An Interview With Michael Kurek," *Saint Austin Review*, July/ August 2009, p.36 ("I think there is still a great Catholic sensibility towards beauty in the arts, due to our role in the development of Western art and music. As a composer I want to uphold the tradition of valuing beauty...

The single biggest technical factor for me personally in composing as a Christian is narrative form. By that I mean that the music has a teleology or motion toward a goal that seems purposeful rather than random. This directedness symbolizes for me a purpose to life, the story of redemption. By contrast, what makes much contemporary music sound 'modern' is not, as many suppose, simply a matter of dissonance. Rather, it is the loss of perceptible narrative and dramatic direction, as this music floats in what the vast majority of people perceive as atonal randomness or a post-modern collage of sounds that seem to come and go without purpose. These kinds of music seem to be an apt representation of our age's relativism. We can redeem the culture of the arts, in part, by restoring to them symbolic representations of purposefulness"); "What is Music?" *Saint Austin Review*, November/December 2009. p.32; *michaelkurek.com.*

Lambert, Rollins E. – priest; b. 3 March 1922, Chicago; c. 24 December 1941; d. 25 January 2009, Palos Heights, Illinois; African-American and Cherokee; his mother followed a mixture of the teachings of Christian Science and the Unity School of Christianity; he attended a Christian Science Sunday school (the only negro child enrolled); joined the Christian Science church at the age of twelve or thirteen; studied at the University of Chicago; stopped attending church; a friend invited him to the solemn pontifical Easter Mass at Holy Name Cathedral, Chicago and he was impressed by the the beauty of the liturgy, the music (Gregorian chant) and the use of the Latin language; began attending Mass and obtained a daily missal; after his conversion he studied for the priesthood at St. Mary of the Lake Seminary as a student for the Archdiocese of Chicago; ordained to the priesthood 7 May 1949 (first African-American ordained for the Archdiocese of Chicago); worked for many years in the archdiocese; chairman of the Black Catholic Clergy Caucus in the late 1960s; advised the U.S. bishops on African affairs 1975-1987; buried in Holy Cross Cemetery, Calumet City; see "The Keys of the Kingdom," in John A. O'Brien (ed), *The Road to Damascus, Volume III: The Way to Emmaus* (1953) ("In following this missal closely for a year there came before my eyes the whole panorama of Christian doctrine. All the dogmas of the Church were demonstrated in the feasts of Christ and the Blessed Virgin; the moral teachings were embodied in the examples of the saints. Not only were these doctrines shown to me in the missal, but, by God's grace, they seeped into my mind and were accepted...By this time, not only the Latin and the music drew me to the altar, but the Sacrifice of the Mass itself, the renewal of Christ's redeeming death, had taken on meaning for me...

On one of the Feasts of St. Peter's Chair, the celebrant of the Mass I attended chanted the famous passage of the Gospel of St. Matthew in the sixteenth chapter: 'I say to thee, thou art Peter, and upon this rock I will build my church, and the gates of hell shall not prevail against it. And I will give thee the keys of the kingdom of heaven; and whatever thou shalt bind on earth shall be bound in heaven, and whatever thou shalt loose on earth shall be loosed in heaven.'

These words were already familiar to me and had made me think seriously about the Catholic Church's claim to be the original Church of Christ and the Pope's claim to be the successor of Peter. On this day the words struck me with new force; they were like a personal revelation, a personal message from Jesus Christ to me. Instantly there was no longer the slightest doubt in my mind about the truth of the Church's claims. An image filled my mind, a picture of the succession of Popes, ruling over a Church which moved through history triumphantly and serenely, surrounded now by friends, now by enemies, but always confident in the promise, 'The gates of hell shall not prevail.'

Someone may wonder why I unhesitatingly applied these words of Christ to the Roman Catholic Church and did not merely take them in a general way, as they are interpreted by some Protestants. This is easily answered: I knew too much history. My previous interest, the Christian Science Church, was founded in the nineteenth century; the oldest of Protestant churches dates back not even five hundred years. It was too much for me to believe that Christ's magnificent promise to Peter had been deferred for a thousand years or more before being realized.

No, the Church had existed continuously since Peter received the 'keys' from Jesus; this was the Church, the Catholic Church, which I had studied in high-school history as the civilizer of barbarians, the preserver of culture in the Dark Ages, the all-powerful organization which interdicted nations, brought kings and emperors to their knees when they transgressed, inspired artists and architects to their most splendid achievements. It was the Catholic Church and no other which could lay claim to these historical deeds...

God made conversion easy for me, as far as the intellectual side of it was concerned. Once I had accepted the Church I had to accept everything the Church teaches. Here again there was no alternative, infallibility and indefectibility, the two jawbreaker words used to describe the teaching authority of the Church, were no problem at all. Almost everything the Church teaches is backed up by the words of the Bible; I had found this out by reading my missal, because the Church gathers together in its Mass texts all the dogmatic passages of Scripture which bear on a feast being celebrated").

Landsteiner, Karl - biologist and physician; b. 14 June 1868, Baden bei Wien, near Vienna, Austria; c. 1889 (received with his mother); d. 26 June 1943, New York City; his father Leopold (1818-1875), a celebrated Viennese journalist, died when he was only six; close relationship with his mother Fanny (*née* Hess) (1837-1908) (he kept her death mask all his life in his bedroom); studied Medicine at the University of Vienna (PhD in 1891); studied chemistry in Würzburg, Munich and Zürich; returned to Vienna where he published many papers; he discovered the infectious character of poliomyelitis and isolated the polio virus; he identified the blood groups of human blood; he made major discoveries about blood transfusions, allowing blood types of donors and recipients to be matched before transfusion and making transfusion a routine medical procedure; after World War I he did research work in Holland and for the Rockefeller Institute in the United States; much work on the problems of immunity and allergy;

became a United States citizen in 1929; in 1930 he was awarded the Nobel Price in Physiology or Medicine in recognition of the achievements relating to transfusions; in 1940 he discovered the rhesus (Rh) factor in blood; he was known as the "melancholy genius" because he was so sad and intense; he wrote 346 papers during his career; considered the father of hematology, immunology, polio research and allergy research; married Leopoldine Helene Wlasto (1880 - 25 December 1943) in 1916; their only son, Ernst Karl (b. 1917) became a surgeon; see *The Specificity of Serological Reactions* (1936); G. R. Simms, *The Scientific Works of Karl Landsteiner* (1963); Michael Heidelberger, "Karl Landsteiner (1868-1943): A Biographical Memoir," *National Academy of Sciences*, 1969; P. Speiser and F. Smekal, *Karl Landsteiner* (1975); P. Mazumdar, *Karl Landsteiner and the Problem of Species* (1976); Hans Peter Schwarz and Friedrich Dorner, "Historical Review: Karl Landsteiner and His Major Contributions to Haematology," *British Journal of Haematology*, 2003, p.556; *ANB*.

Lane, Joseph ("Joe") – politician and soldier; b. 14 December 1801, Buncombe County, North Carolina; c. 1867 (received by Archbishop Blanchet of Oregon); d. 19 April 1881, near Roseburg, Oregon; his father, John Lane, was a veteran of the American Revolutionary War; grew up in Kentucky; married Polly Hart and moved to Indiana in 1820 (ten children of the marriage); mainly self-educated; successful freight transport business on the Ohio River; his fine public speaking helped him to win election to the Indiana House of Representatives in 1822; later moved to the Indiana State Senate; when the Mexican-American War broke out in 1846 he was elected colonel (soon appointed brigadier-general) of the Indiana Volunteers; fought with distinction in Mexico and was promoted to major-general; governor of Oregon Territory 1848-1850; elected Oregon Territory's Delegate in Congress as a Democrat (served 1851-1859); when Oregon became a state in 1859 he was elected one of its first two U.S. Senators; vice-presidential nomination for the pro-slavery Southern wing of the Democratic Party in 1860, but defeated; pro-secessionist; purchased a ranch and did not fight in the Civil War; after some years of study and investigation of Catholic doctrine he became a Catholic; buried in the Roseburg Memorial Gardens; his son John fought in the Civil War for the Confederacy; his son Lafayette a U.S. Representative 1875-1877; see Sr. M. Margaret Jean Kelly, *The Career of Joseph Lane, Frontier Politician* (1942); James E. Hendrickson, *Joe Lane of Oregon: Machine Politics and the Sectional Crisis, 1849-1861* (1967); *ANB*.

Lathrop, George Parsons – poet and novelist; b. 25 August 1851, near Honolulu, Oahu, Hawaii; c. March 1891 (received with his wife at the Church of St. Paul the Apostle, New York); d. 19 April 1898, New York City; he came of Puritan stock; father a doctor and U.S. consul in the Hawaiian Islands; educated in New York and Dresden, Germany, before returning to New York; husband of Rose Hawthorne Lathrop (see below), daughter of Nathaniel Hawthorne (1804-1864), the novelist; associate editor of the *Atlantic Monthly* 1875-1877; worked on newspapers in Boston and New York; in 1883 he founded the American Copyright League, which secured international copyright law; one of the founders of the Catholic Summer School of America; in 1883 he edited a complete and the standard edition of Nathaniel Hawthorne's works; ill with a severe gastric disorder in his last years (some say he was an alcoholic, but no evidence of this); his marriage failed; see (poetry) *Rose and Rose-Tree* (1875); *Dreams and Days* (1892); (novels) *Afterglow* (1876); *Newport* (1884); (other works) *A Study of Hawthorne* (1876); *Spanish Vistas* (1883); *A Story of Courage: Annals of the Georgetown Convent of the Visitation* (1894) (with his wife) (centenary history of the Georgetown University, D.C.); adapted Nathaniel Hawthorne's *The Scarlet Letter* for Walter Damrosch's opera of that name; Walter Lecky, *Down at Caxton's* (1895), p.94 ("Humanly speaking, I entered into Catholicity as a result of long thought and meditation upon religion, continuing through a number of years. But there must have been a deeper force at work, that of the Holy Spirit, by means of what we call grace, for a longer time than I suspected. Certainly I was not attracted by 'the fascinations of Rome,' that are so glibly talked about, but which no one has ever been able to define to me. Perhaps those that use the phrase refer to the outward symbols of ritual, that are simply the expressive adornment of the inner meaning - the flower of it. I, at any rate, never went to Mass but once with any comprehension of it, before my conversion, and had seldom even witnessed Catholic services anywhere; although now, with knowledge and experience, I recognize the Mass - which even that arch, unorthodox author, Thomas Carlyle, called 'the only genuine thing of our times' - as the greatest action in the world. Many Catholics had been known to me, of varying merit; and some of them were valued friends. But none of these ever urged or advised or even hinted that I should come into the Church. The best of them had (as large numbers of my fellow-Catholics have to-day) that same modesty and reverence toward the sacred mysteries that caused the early Christians also to be slow in leading catechumens - or those not yet fully prepared for belief - into the great truths of faith. My observations of life, however, increasingly convinced me that a vital, central, unchanging principle in religion was necessary, together with one great association of Christians in place of endless divisions - if the promise made to men was to be fulfilled, or really had been fulfilled. When I began to ask questions, I found Catholics quite ready to answer everything with entire straightforwardness, gentle good-will, yet firmness. Neither they nor the Church evaded anything. They presented and defended the teaching of Christ in its entirety, unexaggerated and undiminished; the complete faith, without haggling or qualification or that queer, loose assent to every sort of individual exception and denial that is allowed in other organizations. I may say here, too, that the Church, instead of being narrow or pitiless toward those not of her communion, as she is often mistakenly said to be, is the most comprehensive of all in her interpretation of God's mercy as well as of his justice. And, instead of slighting the Bible, she uses it more incessantly than any of the Protestant bodies; at the same time shedding upon it a clear, deep light that is the only one that ever enabled me to see its full meaning and coherence. The fact is, those outside of the Church nowadays are engaged in talking so noisily and at such a rate, on their own hook, that they seldom pause to hear what the Church really says, or to understand what she is. Once convinced of the true faith, intellectually and spiritually, I could not let anything stand in the way of affirming my loyalty to it"); Josephine J. Fay (Sister Francis Michael), *George Parsons Lathrop: A Nineteenth Century Critic* (MA thesis, St. John's University, (1945)); Marie Harte Stafford, *The Literary Theories and Practice of George Parsons Lathrop* (MA thesis, George Washington University, 1958); Rose Valenti, *To Myself a Stranger: A Biography of Rose Hawthorne Lathrop* (1991); *Catholic Encyclopedia*; *ANB*.

Lathrop, Rose Hawthorne (name in religion Mother Mary Alphonsa, OP) ("Rosebud" to her father) – nun and founder of a religious order; Servant of God; b. 20 May 1851, Lenox, Massachusetts; c. March 1891 (received with her husband, George Parsons Lathrop (1851-1898), the author (see above) at the Church of St. Paul the Apostle, New York); d. 9 July 1926, Hawthorne, New York; second daughter and youngest child of the author Nathaniel Hawthorne (1804-1864); her mother was Sophia Peabody Hawthorne (1809-1871), a painter and sculptor; raised as an Episcopalian; family moved often during her childhood and youth; most of her childhood was spent in England, where her father had been appointed as consul to Liverpool in 1853; close relationship with her father; educated in London, Paris, Rome and Florence; wrote short stories and poetry; married her husband in 1871 in Chelsea, England; they had a son, Francis, who died of diphtheria in 1881 at the age of five; they separated permanently in 1895 and she moved to New York; trained as a nurse in order to aid cancer victims; she opened a refuge for cancer victims on the Lower East Side of New York, and a year later moved to a larger house, St. Rose's Free Home for Incurable Cancer; joined in her work by Alice Huber (d. 1942); after her husband's death she became a nun, joining the Dominican Order, Alice Huber also joining as Sister Mary Rose (later, as Mother Mary Rose, her successor as Superior General of the Order); they founded the Dominican Congregation of St. Rose of Lima, later called the Servants of Relief for Incurable Cancer (now known as the Hawthorne Dominican Sisters); in 1901 she opened Rosary Hill Home in Hawthorne, New York (now the mother home of the Order); the cause for her canonization opened in 2003; see *A Story of Courage: Annals of the Georgetown Convent of the Visitation* (1894) (with her husband) (centenary history of the Georgetown University, D.C.); *Memories of Hawthorne* (1897); Letter from Samuel L. Clemens (Mark Twain) to Rose Hawthorne Lathrop, 19 October 1901 ("And certainly if there is an unassailably good cause in the world, it is this one undertaken by the Dominican Sisters, of housing, nourishing, and nursing the most pathetically unfortunate of all the afflicted among us - men and women sentenced to a painful and lingering death by incurable disease. I have seen this lofty work of yours rise from seedling to tree with no endowment but the voluntary aid which your patient labor and faith have drawn from the purses of grateful and compassionate men; and I am glad…to know that this prosperity will continue and be permanent…It cannot fail until pity fails in the hearts of men, and that will never be"); James J. Walsh, *Mother Alphonsa: Rose Hawthorne Lathrop* (1930); Katherine Burton, *Sorrow Built a Bridge: A Daughter of Hawthorne* (1937); Katherine Burton, *In No Strange Land: Some American Catholic Converts* (1942), p.173 ("There is one difference between [Rose Hawthorne Lathrop and her father]. She held the unclean and the hideously deformed and did not let them go again – at least not until God took them from the safety of her arms to the safety of His own. Her father had done the philosophizing about it. He had laid the groundwork for her later life, by his love for his own family and his sympathy and his understanding of the pain of the world. His great contribution was to help in words; his books were a plea for pity and for understanding of the human soul. Her contribution, having, as he had not, the power of the Catholic faith to sustain her, was to transmute her inheritance into deeds, to offer her human sorrow and love and the broken bodies that came to her for helping – to offer them all to God, to unite small human pity to the Everlasting Mercy"); Theodore Maynard, *A Fire Was Lighted* (1948), Marguerite Vance, *On the Wings of Fire: the Story of Nathaniel Hawthorne's Daughter, Rose* (1955); Theodore Maynard, *Great Catholics in American History* (1957), p.223; Sister M. Josepha, *Out of Many Hearts: Mother Alphonsa Lathrop and Her Work* (1965); Patricia Dunlavy Valenti, *To Myself a Stranger: A Biography of Rose Hawthorne Lathrop* (1991); Diana Culberson, *Rose Hawthorne Lathrop: Selected Writings* (1993); Lucille M. Pimenta, *Nathaniel Hawthorne's Daughter: Rose Hawthorne Lathrop* (2004); Charles P. Connor, *Classic Catholic Converts* (2001), p.45; *ANB.*

Lax, Robert – poet; b. 1915, Olean, New York; c. 19 December 1943; d. 26 September 2000, Olean, New York; born a Jew; attended Columbia University, New York, studying under Mark van Doren; met Thomas Merton (see below) at Columbia and worked with him on the college humor magazine; he and Merton became close lifelong friends; graduated in 1938; also a close friend of Adolph ("Ad") Reinhardt (1913-1967), the abstract painter; worked for several magazines; left in order to live a simpler life and wandered around, working in a circus as a juggler for part of the time; eventually settled in the Greek islands in 1962, living there hermit-like for the next thirty-five years (latterly on Patmos) almost until his death; returned to his home town in 2000; wrote many books and poems, but relatively unrecognized; his poems became more and more minimalist; worked on the editorial staff of *The New Yorker* in 1941; taught at the University of North Carolina in 1943; worked at *Time* magazine in 1945; wrote screenplays in Hollywood in 1946; helped to start *Jubilee*, a lay Catholic magazine founded by Edward Rice (also a friend at Columbia) in 1953; close friend of Jack Kerouac (1922-1969), the writer; buried in the cemetery of St. Bonaventure University, New York; see *Selections* (1978); *Circus of the Sun* (1960) (his most famous book, a meditation on creation); *A Catch of Anti-Letters* (1994) (with Thomas Merton); *Circus Days and Nights* (2009); Thomas Merton, *The Seven Storey Mountain* (1948); David Miller and Nicholas Zurbrugg (ed), *The ABCs of Robert Lax* (1999); Arthur W. Biddle, *When Prophecy Still Had a Voice: The Letters of Thomas Merton and Robert Lax* (2001); Steve T. Georgiou, *The Way of the Dreamcatcher: Spirit Lessons With Robert Lax, Poet, Peacemaker, Sage* (2002); James J. Harford, *Merton and Friends: A Joint Biography of Thomas Merton, Robert Lax,* *and Edward Rice* (2006); Sigrid Hauff: *A Line in Three Circles: The Inner Biography of Robert Lax & A Comprehensive Catalog of His Works* (2007); John Dear, SJ., "The Wisdom of Robert Lax: 'Cultivate, Exercise Compassion,'" *National Catholic Reporter*, 22 February 2011 ("'Lax was born with the deepest sense of who God was,' Thomas Merton wrote. 'He was much wiser than I, and he had clearer vision, and was, in fact, corresponding much more truly to the grace of God than I. He had seen what was the one important thing.'

In a memorable scene in Merton's book *The Seven Storey Mountain*, Lax and Merton are walking down Fifth Avenue one day when Lax asks: 'What do you want to be anyway?' Merton hesitates, and says, 'I guess I want to be a good Catholic.' 'What you should say,' Lax declares, 'is that you want to be a saint.' 'How do you expect me to be a saint?' Merton asks. 'By wanting to,' Lax answers. 'All that is necessary to be a saint is to want to be one. All you have to do is desire it.'

That conversation set Merton's heart and mind on a long search that took him to Gethsemani. Lax, on the other hand, seems to have achieved a palpable holiness at an early age. Merton really admired Lax. That comes through in the recently published collection of their zany letters, called *If Prophecy Still Had a Voice*"); Robert Lax Archives, St. Bonaventure University, near Olean, New York.

Lee, Dixie (born Wilma Winifred Wyatt) - actress, dancer and singer; b. 4 November 1911, Harriman, Tennessee; c. 31 October 1952 (deathbed conversion); d. 1 November 1952, Holmby Hills, Los Angeles, California; her original professional name was "Dixie Carroll", but was changed to Dixie Lee; married Bing Crosby at the age of eighteen; four sons of the marriage, two of whom, Lindsay and Dennis, committed suicide as adults; short film career (most notable film *Love in Bloom* (1935)); shy and private person, but problem with alcoholism; died early from ovarian cancer; buried at Holy Cross Cemetery, Culver City, California; see Garry Giddins, *Bing Crosby: A Pocketful of Dreams - The Early Years, 1913-1940* (2001); Richard Grudens, *Bing Crosby - Crooner of the Century* (2002).

Lee, Thomas Sim - planter and statesman; b. 29 October 1745, Upper Marlboro, Maryland; c. 1771; d. 19 November 1819, Needwood, Frederick County, Maryland; from a branch of the Lee family of Virginia; raised as an Anglican; educated in private schools; in 1771 he married Mary Digges (1745-1805); his wife's family were prominent Catholic landowners in Maryland; he had to give an assurance that he would convert and that all their children would be raised Catholic; they had eight children; he backed the patriot cause in the Revolutionary War and was colonel of a local militia; member of Maryland Legislature 1777-1779; governor 1779-1782 (he signed the Act ratifying the Articles of Confederation and Perpetual Union); member of the State convention that ratified the U.S. Constitution in 1788; again governor of Maryland 1792-1794; declined a seat in the U.S. Senate; worked closely with many of the Founding Fathers; buried in Mt. Carmel Catholic Cemetery, near Upper Marlboro, Maryland; see Maura Jane Farrelly, *Papist Patriots: The Making of an American Catholic Identity* (2012) ("In order to get permission from Mary's father, Thomas Sim Lee had to convert to Catholicism and promise to raise the couple's children as Catholics. He also had to promise that any slaves Mary brought to the union with her would be allowed to practice their Catholic faith. It was not a small requirement. When he agreed to it in 1771 Thomas Sim Lee was essentially giving up what promised to be a very powerful political career. At the time, Maryland was still a proprietary colony, and Catholics were still barred under the laws passed by the General Assembly from voting or holding office.

In just five years time, however, all of that would change. In 1776, Lee joined his fellow Catholics Ignatius Fenwick, John Dent, Thomas Semmes, and Charles Carroll of Carrollton in drafting a written constitution for the newly independent state of Maryland that disestablished the Anglican Church, guaranteeing religious freedom for all Christians, and nullified the legislation that three generations of Catholics had insisted was 'odious' to Maryland's unwritten, historical constitution").

Lehrman, Lewis E. ("Lew") – investment banker, historian, philanthropist and conservative activist; b. 15 August 1938, Harrisburg, Pennsylvania; c. 7 April 1985; brought up in a Jewish family; educated at Yale University (BA 1960); Carnegie Teaching Fellow at Yale; Woodrow Wilson Fellow at Harvard University (MA); in 1972 he founded the Lehrman Institute, a public policy think tank; co-founder of the Gilder-Lehrman Institute of American History; also co-founded with Richard Gilder the Lincoln and Soldiers Institute (for the study of President Lincoln and the Civil War period) and the Gilder Lehrman Center for the Study of Slavery, Resistance and Abolition; involved with several investment companies; in 1981 he was narrowly defeated for the governorship of New York, running on Republican and Conservative Party lines; active in several conservative causes; member of the U.S. Gold Commission in 1981; in 2005 awarded the National Humanities Medal for his scholarly contributions; written for many major newspapers and other publications; many awards and honorary degrees; see *The Case for Gold* (1982); *Lincoln at Peoria: The Turning Point* (2008); "Slavery and Abortion," *Crisis*, 14 October 2010; *The True Gold Standard* (2nd edition, 2012).

Levertov, Denise – poet; b. 24 October 1923, Ilford, Essex, England; c. 1989; d. 20 December 1997, Seattle, Washington; mother Welsh, father a Russian Jew who became an Anglican minister; educated at home; a civilian nurse in London in World War II; moved to the United States in 1947; became a naturalized American in 1955; supporter of feminist and left wing politics; anti-war themes and opposition to the Vietnam War reflected in her poetry; taught at several universities before becoming full-time professor at Stanford University 1982-1993; religion a major theme in her work, especially the notion of a spiritual journey towards deeper understanding; became a Christian in 1984 and converted to the Catholic Church in 1989 ("Why, when the very fact of life itself, of the existence of anything at all, is so astounding, why - I asked myself - should I withhold my belief in God or in the claims of Christianity until I am able to explain to myself the discrepancy between the suffering of the innocent, on the one hand, and the assertions that God is just and merciful on the other?"); buried at Lake View Cemetery, Seattle, Washington; see *The Stream and the Sapphire: Selected Poems on Religious Themes* (1997) (collection of poems from earlier volumes intended to trace her slow development from agnosticism to Christian faith); Linda W. Wagner, *Denise Levertov* (1967); William Slaughter, *The Imagination's Tongue: Denise Levertov's Poetics* (1981); Harry Marten, *Understanding Denise Levertov* (1988); Linda W. Wagner-Martin (ed), *Critical Essays on Denise Levertov* (1990); Albert Gelpi (ed), *Denise Levertov: Selected Criticism* (1993); Audrey T. Rodgers, *Denise Levertov: The Poetry of Engagement* (1993); *ANB*.

Lewis, Letitia Floyd – philanthropist; b. 1814; c. about 1832; d. 16 February 1887; eldest daughter of John Floyd (see above) and Letitia Preston Floyd (see above); taken by her mother to hear the sermons of Fr. Shriver in Richmond and later Fr. O'Brien, she became very interested in the Catholic faith and she applied for books and instruction from Fr. O'Brien; in 1837 she married a widower Colonel William Lymm Lewis; the first fruits of her conversion were the conversion of her two sisters, Lavalette and Nicketti; within a year of their marriage her husband also entered the Catholic Church; some years later her mother and three of her brothers took the same step; her influence also led to the conversion of John P. Matthews, the esteemed clerk of the County Court of Wythe County, that of his wife, and twelve out of thirteen children (one of their daughters became a Sister of St. Joseph, and was made superior of the convent); the daughters of Colonel Harold Smyth also entered the Church by the same influence, and one of them became a nun; after her father's death she became mistress of his Sweet Springs estate; gave much of her life to charity and good works; built a chapel for local Catholics; see *Catholic Encyclopedia* ("The conversion to the Faith about 1832 of Mrs. Letitia Floyd Lewis, daughter of Governor John Floyd, which, owing to her prominence, caused a sensation throughout the state, was followed by that of her two sisters, Mrs. Lavalette Floyd Holmes, wife of the erudite Professor George F. Holmes of the University of Virginia; Mrs. Nicketti Floyd Johnston, wife of Senator John W. Johnston [see below], and of three of her brothers, Hon. Benjamin Rush Floyd (a formidable opponent of Knownothingism), Dr. William Preston Floyd, and Colonel George Rogers Floyd. Then followed the conversion of her father, John Floyd, when ex-governor, and of her mother, Mrs. Letitia Preston Floyd...The conversion of the Floyd and Johnston families led into the Catholic Church other members of the most distinguished families of the South").

Lewis, (Mary) Edmonia – sculptor; b. 4 July 1844, probably at Greenbush, New York; c. 1868 (probably received in Rome at that time, but some writers claim that she was converted at the age of fourteen before being sent to school in Ohio); d. 17 September 1907, Hammersmith Borough Infirmary, London; father was Haitian of African descent; mother was of Mississauga Ojibwe and African descent; her Indian name was Wildfire; both parents died when she was young; she went to live with her mother's sisters; her education was funded by her brother, a successful prospector during the California gold rush; she was enrolled in 1856 at New York Central College, a Baptist school; she studied at Oberlin College, Cleveland, Ohio; she was falsely accused of poisoning two female white students and was beaten savagely; left before completing her degree; moved to Boston in 1863 and studied under Edward Augustus Brackett (1818-1908); opened her studio to the public in 1864 and had much success; the first African-American, and Native American, female sculptor; in 1865 she went to Rome to study; joined a circle of expatriate artists; spent most of her career in Rome; inspired by classical Rome and worked in a neo-classical style; her work sold for large sums of money and she had many successful exhibitions; Pope Pius IX visited her studio; great success with a huge sculpture, *The Death of Cleopatra*, for the 1876 Centennial Exposition in Philadelphia (the statue was lost and only found again in the 1980s, then donated to the Smithsonian American Art Museum in 1994 and restored); her style became unfashionable in the late 1880s; she moved into creating altarpieces and other works for Catholic customers; nothing known of her later years, but she moved eventually to Hammersmith, London; unmarried; see Rinna Evelyn Wolfe, *Edmonia Lewis: Wildfire in Marble* (1998); Kirstan Buick, *Child of the Fire: Mary Edmonia Lewis and the Problem of Art History's Black and Indian Subject* (2010); Harry Henderson and Albert Henderson, *The Indomitable Spirit of Edmonia Lewis: A Narrative Biography* (2012); *edmonialewis.com*; *ANB*.

Lewis, Theophilus – writer; b. 4 March 1891, Baltimore, Maryland; c. 23 August 1939 (received at the Mission of St. Benedict the Moor, Jamaica, Long Island, New York); d. 1974; brought up in the Protestant faith by an aunt as his parents (who were Baptists) died when he was a child; after graduating from grammar school he worked at various occupations (for example, steamboat waiter, bell hop, store porter, and laborer in the automobile industry); fought in World War I; moved to New York and became agnostic; self-taught drama critic of the Harlem Renaissance era; freelance columnist for Catholic papers and magazines (including *Catholic World, Commonweal* and *America*) and others; co-editor of the *Interracial Review* (official organ of the Catholic Interracial Council); also worked as a postal worker until his retirement; advocated the development of a national African American theater; most significant writing was theater reviews and commentary, but also wrote a satirical column, general commentary, poetry, and a few short stories; conversion influenced in part by Catholic teaching on the race question and, paradoxically, by Zola and Renan; see "It's Safer Inside," in John A. O'Brien (ed), *The Road to Damascus, Vol. V: Where Dwellest Thou* (1956) ("It is hardly likely…that a missionary priest would recommend Zola and Renan as appropriate conversion reading. Still, it was those unbelievers who first made me aware of the magnitude of the Church in history and society, while providing me with an inoculation against the cynicism I was later to encounter in Anatole France and the materialism of Marx…

Somehow or other one of Zola's novels fell into my hands, and the book happened to be Lourdes. While Zola was an atheist, and a Hollywood glamour girl with four divorces in her docket would frown on his personal morals, he was essentially an artist. Lourdes was intended to discredit the miracles of the shrine, but he was too sincere an artist to permit his intellectual bias to paint a false picture. His leading characters are Pierre, a young priest, and Marie, a crippled girl he is taking to the shrine for the cure. Here was a type of character I had never before encountered in fiction – people whose decisions were not pre-determined or colored by their desire for personal happiness. Pierre and Marie were the first Catholics I had ever met who made me at least partly understand what religious faith can mean in the lives of people, and for years they were the only Catholics I knew…

Renan's contribution to my conversion was his sympathetic portrait of the human side of the Savior in his life of Jesus…I never had a vivid impression of the human personality of our Lord until I discovered Renan. His portrayal of Jesus as a virile and magnetic character – not as the Savior, of course; but as a man who was wise, compassionate and the paragon of human excellence – had the immediate effect of reviving my interest in the Gospels").

Likoudis, James – writer and speaker on Catholic issues; b. 1928, Lackawanna, New York; c. 1952 (his wife Ruth was received earlier); brought up in a Greek immigrant family, his parents coming to the United States after World War I; parents were Greek Orthodox (memories of "the majestic and solemn ceremonies of the magnificent Liturgy of St. John Chrysostom which transfixed my soul with a sense of the awesomeness of God and the splendor of His heavenly court"); impressed by Catholic schools and Catholic children; studied History and Philosophy at the University of Buffalo; his conversion resulted from a detailed study of the origins of the schism between the Catholic Church and Eastern Orthodoxy; also influenced by the writings of Cardinals Newman and Manning, St. Thomas Aquinas, Ronald Knox, Father Faber, Hilaire Belloc, G. K. Chesterton, and Fr. Owen Dudley; also the remarkable saints produced by the Church; served in the Korean War; college instructor in history and government for twenty years; several books and many articles; president-emeritus of Catholics United for the Faith; see (selective list) *The Pope, the Council, and the Mass* (1981; revised edition, 2006) (with Kenneth D. Whitehead); "To Be Truly Orthodox Is to Be in Communion with Peter's See," in Robert Baram (ed), *Spiritual Journeys* (revised edition, 1988) ("I think it true from my earliest days that I have never really doubted the existence of God, the Divinity of Christ, or the fact that Our Divine Lord had established a visible Church – graces that I attribute to the supernatural virtue of faith received in baptism…

I read everything I could find on the origins of the Schism between the Catholic and Eastern Orthodox churches, the history and doctrine of the Papacy, and on the

Ecumenical Councils of the first eight centuries. One of the books I found, *The Eastern Churches and the Papacy* by the Anglican scholar S. H. Scott, was especially helpful to me, as were the remarkable books on the Primacy of Peter by that great Anglican convert and friend of Cardinal Newman, Thomas William Allies [see above], who spent his life in scholarly defense of the Papacy. Allies confirmed for me once and for all the patristic support for the Primacy of Peter in the early Church…

The great Catholic Czech scholar Fr. Francis Dvornik had shown by his researches that the famous Patriarch Photius (often presented as the fervent opponent of Papal Supremacy over the entire Church) had actually died in communion with Rome. The latter had never repudiated the teaching of the Popes of his time (Nicholas I, Hadrian II, John VIII) concerning their succession to the Primacy of Peter whom Our Lord had established as head and center of the Universal Church.

By the Orthodox polemicists' own fatal admission that 'prior to 1054 the Roman Catholic Church was fully joined to the Orthodox Church' it was evident that the Eastern patriarchates had been in communion with Popes who were unequivocal in declaring their universal jurisdiction over the Church in both East and West. The statement made by dissident writers to our own day that 'the Bishop of Rome was *never* at any time accorded any rights or powers over the entire Church' was simply false to the history of the Byzantine Church before 1054 and even into the middle of the 12th century when the first denials of Papal Supremacy began to be made. Pro-Unionist Byzantines continued to defend the Petrine Primacy of the Popes before and after that great Reunion Council of Florence (1439) which at first appeared to have ended three centuries of rupture, discord, estrangement, and formal schism. In his classic work *Russia and the Universal Church* the 'Russian Newman,' Vladimir Soloviev, had written powerfully of the Papacy as 'that miraculous ikon of universal Christianity' demonstrating that the Roman Primacy was of the *essence* of the Church as a visible institution in the world. Since the Orthodox agreed with Catholics in professing that 'the Holy Spirit unfailingly preserves the form of government established by Christ the Lord in the Church' (see Vatican II's *Lumen Gentium*, No. 27), then the testimony of the early pre-Schism Popes regarding their own role in the Church could not be rejected…

The witness of the pre-Schism Popes, Fathers, and Councils (whatever the historical and theological difficulties encountered) was overwhelming in their cumulative impact as supporting the dogma of Papal Primacy as defined in the decrees of Vatican I. The utterly supernatural nature of the Apostolic Primacy of the 'first of Bishops;' the Roman Pontiff, was profoundly grasped by the great 19th century German theologian Matthias Joseph Scheeben. His especially rich theological exposition was of particular value to me in dissipating the misconceptions of Orthodox polemicists...

The great heretical and schismatical movements combated by the first seven Ecumenical councils had involved sometimes hundreds of Bishops engaged in rebellion against the See of Peter and the Bishops in communion with him. When Patriarchs and Bishops disagreed with one another over the most complex and intricate questions of dogma, how could a simple believer (much less scholars) possibly resolve the question as to which group of Bishops had preserved the orthodox and apostolic faith? The 'Eastern Orthodox' had no answer to this burning question. Catholics, however had a *visible criterion* easily applied by any believer to determine where the true Church was - which group of Bishops had embraced schism and/or heresy and which group was in continuity with Catholic Tradition. St. Ambrose had put it as succinctly as possible: 'Where Peter is, there is the Church.' The visible criterion of Catholicity had always been visible communion with the See of Peter. The true Church of Jesus Christ is always identifiable by its communion with the infallible Chair of Peter. Since the 'cursed schism' with Rome, the autocephalous Eastern Orthodox churches lacked that supreme authority with which Christ had endowed his Church to assure its remaining always One, Holy, Catholic, and Apostolic. In the 13th century, as Byzantine polemics against the Apostolic Primacy increased, the Angelic Doctor St. Thomas Aquinas pointed out the disastrous consequences of negating the *Petro-centric structure of the Hierarchical Church*: 'And while they deny that there is one (visible) head of the Church, that is to say, the Holy Roman Church, they manifestly deny the unity of the Mystical Body, for there cannot be one body if there is not one head, nor one congregation of the faithful where there is not one rector. Hence, "there shall be one flock and one shepherd"' (*Contra Errores Graecorum*, Part II)...

[B]y my last year of University study I had become convinced that to be true to itself as well as to the simplest facts of Church history, Eastern Orthodox ecclesiology logically demanded belief in the Catholic dogmas of Papal Primacy and Infallibility. Belief in One Visible Church constituted by Christ as 'a People made one with the unity of the Father, the Son, and the Holy Spirit' made historical and theological sense only in the context of a Primacy of supreme authority bonding in unity the entire collegial-episcopal structure of the Church. 'Thou knowest that I love Thee,' thrice replied the Prince of the Apostles to the Risen Lord before receiving the chief authority in the Church (Jn. 21:14-18). This Apostolic Primacy of Peter and his successors, the Roman Pontiffs, was also a Primacy of Love. This Primacy of fatherly love in the Church established by Jesus Christ, the 'Lover of Mankind,' to endure perpetually in Peter and his successors had its fitting exemplar in the effusion of love that characterized the Procession of the Holy Spirit from the Father and the Son"); *Ending the Byzantine Greek Schism* (1992); *St. Thérèse of Lisieux: Doctor of the Church* (1992); *EWTN Audio Library, The Journey Home* (19 March 1999); *The Divine Primacy of the Bishop of Rome and Modern Eastern Orthodoxy: Letters to a Greek Orthodox on the Unity of the Church* (2002) (with Wilhelm Emmanuel Freiherr von Ketteler); *Eastern Orthodoxy and the See of Peter* (2006); *credo.stormloader.com.*

Lippert, Rudolph M. – lecturer and astronomer; b. Illinois; c. 17 November 1947; born into a Protestant family, which belonged to a strict pietistic sect; one of nine children; father was a minister for fifty years and many other ministers in the family; when a little boy he moved to St. Gall in Switzerland, the home of his mother's parents, where he attended the public schools; his grandmother was his only Catholic relative and her gentleness, kindness and sympathy won his heart; his father was very anti-Catholic and caused him to be prejudiced against the Catholic Church; became a Protestant pastor of a small church in Los Angeles and held other similar posts later; found much disagreement and doctrinal strife within Protestant denominations as opposed to the unity which Christ had declared would always be the mark of His Church; resigned his pastorate and turned to the science of astronomy ("I discovered that science can fascinate the mind but it can't satisfy a hungry heart. There is in man, I came to learn, a 'God-ache' which no science can ease and a spiritual hunger which no secular erudition can appease"); see "United with Christ," in John A. O'Brien (ed), *The Road to Damascus, Volume III: The Way to Emmaus* (1953) ("I remember [my Catholic grandmother] taking me at Easter to the beautiful cathedral. The lights, flowers, music, statues, and paintings were in pleasing contrast to the plain, unadorned hall in which my father held forth from the pulpit. In her hands she clasped her beloved rosary, which was a great source of joy and consolation, especially in her hours of trial. It was made in the Holy Land of olive wood and mother-of-pearl and was her chief prayer book. Little did Grandmother ever dream that her beloved grandson

(I was her favorite) would one day clasp her precious rosary as he turned to God for light to lead him out of the darkness of agnosticism and despair...

My father was pronouncedly anti-Catholic and instilled into me much of his hatred and prejudice against the Church. One day he took me into Germany to visit the old city of Constance. Pointing to a monument, he remarked: 'Here is where the Catholics put John Huss to death for translating the Bible into German.' From that moment I hated Catholics, particularly priests. It was many years later that I was to discover that Huss was executed for heresy, which at the time was a capital offence.

Father said nothing, however, about his great leader John Calvin instigating the execution of Servetus for the same offence of heresy. Silent, too, was he about the origin of the great universities, the majestic cathedrals, the immortal paintings, and the masterpieces of sculpture which crowned with diadems of fadeless beauty the culture of Europe and drew admiring visitors from far and near. Only years later did I come to realize that they owed their very existence to the Church, the Fertile Mother of European civilization at whose bosom poet, painter, philosopher, musician, and sculptor found their inspiration...

[A]s I began to understand what the Catholic Church really believes and teaches, I found that what I had been fighting was not the teachings of the Church but grotesque caricatures of them. The labels which my father and I had pinned on her doctrines turned out to be chiefly libels. Out of the material supplied us by the defamers of the Church we had unwittingly built scarecrows to frighten people from her threshold. We had built a wall of paper around the Catholic Church, and on that wall we had written what we wanted outsiders to believe about her.

This truth did not break upon me at once. Deep-rooted fears, prejudices, and hatreds do not vanish like shadows before the light: like icebergs they thaw out slowly under the fickle and intermittent sun and freeze again when it disappears behind a cloud. But this I can say: As my understanding of the Catholic Faith increased, I found some of my inveterate hostility beginning to yield grudgingly to respect and even incipient appreciation. As I look back now, I can see that what I needed desperately to do at that time was to get down on my knees, as Newman did, and pray to God to send me His kindly light to lead me out of the darkness. This I failed to do; in consequence the light was slow in coming, and like the Israelites I was to journey for years in the wilderness before reaching the Promised Land...

One evening I was walking down Market Street in San Francisco when I saw throngs of people entering St. Boniface Church. I entered and saw it filled with people from all walks of life. There was a singing of hymns, some prayers, and then a priest preached a fine, sensible sermon on the love of God and our neighbor and the duty to translate such love into appropriate action in our daily life. Prayers, in which the congregation joined, were offered for the sick and for special intentions.

The service closed with Benediction, during which the priest raised aloft the monstrance containing the Holy Eucharist and, with it, made the sign of the cross in blessing over the people. The silent reverence and the deep devotion of the great congregation made a lasting impression upon me. They were not in a meeting-house but in the temple of God, where He dwelt in the tabernacle upon the altar. It was this *Real Presence*, I discovered, which explained their profound reverence and brought them, even more than the sermon, to the services. Here was a nice perception of the difference between the human and the divine – a perception which lies at the very heart of the Catholic Faith").

Lipscomb, John - priest; b. 1950; c. December 2007 (received with his wife Marcie); father a Baptist preacher; grew up in the Baptist faith; in 1967 he became an Episcopalian (influenced in his decision by his wife); served as the Episcopalian Bishop of Southwest Florida 1997-2007; married with two children; after his retirement he converted to the Catholic faith; ordained catholic priest in 2009; see *vocatum.co.uk*, 8 May 2008 ("I attended a gathering of Catholics in the DFW area a few weeks ago to hear former Episcopalian bishop John Lipscomb share the story of his conversion to the Catholic Church in December 2007... Hearing his story was like a breath of fresh air. So, here are some of his major points, from my notes...

1. The Episcopalian experience was primarily one of inward-looking mediation and reconciliation attempts from day one, and all along Lipscomb was less and less able to be at peace about what he was doing. First, ECUSA continually took positions which refuted sound moral theology. Secondly, the 'gifts' of catholicity that Lipscomb had hoped to infuse into ECUSA were simply not wanted. And, he was just so tired of the jargon which carefully differentiated 'Anglicanism' from ECUSA, and shopped for bishops; to have such a misguided sense of boundaries in the Church is not 'catholic' at all.

2. The unity which John 17 calls for is a unity for the purpose of a united mission. This had become impossible in ECUSA. And, ECUSA's brand of ecumenism apart from truth could never produce any sense of unity at all; added to that is the fact that the English Reformation was about rebellion from the outset, the quest for unity becomes futile. In other words, the Anglican crisis is 500 years old.

3. For those who bristle about the idea of submitting to Catholic authority in the See of Peter, the heart of the issue is that for those who walk in the Spirit, freedom and law are not contradictions; rather than being a burden, the service of Christ in the places of His authority is not a burden, but perfect freedom.

(Lipscomb suggested that this idea would be most difficult for those who had already submitted to ECUSA's dogma of postmodern relativisim, and had agreed to be a community that would merely accomodate the public, or, that would equate Church order with friendly small talk) The straw that ultimately broke the camel's back, he said, was the American Primate explaining that Jesus is actually not the Way, the Truth, and the Life.

4. Regarding the hope for prophetic action through local options in the world, Lipscomb pointed out that Biblically, prophecy calls God's people to repent and to return to the place they came from. Furthermore, he urged that it is impossible to think that ecclesial communities that are totally opposed in confession and practices from ecclesial communities in other parts of the world (as is the case for the Anglican Communion) will not inevitably contravene each other's mission; they will...

5. To other clergy, Lipscomb said that when told that he had 'sold out' on the Episcopalian vision, his rejoinder is that he is proud to have sold out to the truth, and that he is eager to bring to the fullness of the Church the fullness of who he is, without compromise.

My favorite point went to a notion that has become popular in the thought of Episcopalian clergy like Ephraim Radner, who has urged his brothers that the thing to do is to 'live in the wounded church' as a way of living the Christian life most fully. The idea is that the wounded church, in her divisions, best reflects the wounded body of her Lord.

I've always thought that there are some serious problems with this idea. First, it's the *world* that is wounded- and certainly not on account of sharing in the wounds of Christ, but because of sin. It's not a problem to become content with, but a disaster for the Church to fix.

The Church, on the other hand, is the body of those people who are healed by the wounds of Christ- not in order to remain weak and wounded - but so that we may get about the business of healing a broken world. And, we *worship* the wounds of Christ. To equate the Church with His redemptive wounds seems terribly presumptive. In as much as the Church is the Father's good and perfect gift to the Son, the damages and divisions inflicted and suffered in schismatic communities are antithetical to the Church's very nature.

Yes, the Church is Christ's body in the world, but as a creature she is also qualitatively different from the divine and humanly wounded body of her Lord. What's more, she is a nuptial body, formed in hope and beauty to be Christ's flourishing lover and the mother of His children so that the world may believe... not His ailing convalescent so that the world might empathize").

Longenecker, Dwight – priest and writer; b. Pennsylvania; c. February 1995 (received in the crypt of the Abbey Church at Quarr, Isle of Wight, England, with his wife Alison and their two young children); descended from Mennonites in Switzerland in the eighteenth century on his father's side and from Swedish reformed Christians on his mother's side; brought up in Pennsylvania in a Bible church, which was part of a loose-knit confederation of churches called the Independent Fundamental Churches of America; graduate from Bob Jones University, Greenville, South Carolina, with a degree in Interpretative Speech and English; introduced to the Episcopalian Church and was baptized; influenced by C. S. Lewis and the Book of Common Prayer; studied for the Anglican ministry at Oxford; drawn to the Catholic spiritual tradition in the Church of England; served as Anglican chaplain at King's College, Cambridge and as a country vicar; after his conversion to the Catholic Church he worked for seven years as a regional organizer for the St. Barnabas Society; freelance writer and broadcaster in both Britain and America; author of several books and many articles; he and his family moved back to the United States in 2006; he was ordained in December 2006 to the Catholic priesthood for the diocese of Charleston, South Carolina under the special pastoral provision for married former Anglican clergy; see (selective list) "Home Away From Home," *This Rock*, November 1995 ("There is a deep inconsistency at the heart of Anglicanism. For all its beauty and claim to comprehensiveness it is a divided church. There is no real agreement between Evangelicals, Anglo-Catholics, and liberals in the church. They believe radically different things and are held together only by their being English. For Anglicans theological language is only 'a way of speaking.' The modern Anglican doesn't believe in any objective theology. When an Anglo-Catholic talks of the Real Presence or apostolic succession, he is merely using a form of poetic language he happens to like that is no more valid or true than the words Evangelicals or liberals happen to use.

The Anglican Church is the ultimate Protestant body because you can stay within it and believe whatever happens to appeal to you, and nobody will say 'Boo!' They can't insist on orthodoxy or appeal to shared beliefs because there aren't any such things for Anglicans.

On the other hand Catholics use language as a connecting point to real, solid truths. The language is almost as concrete as the thing it represents. The contrast is shown by the comment of a Catholic bishop. He said with all modesty, 'I am not a successor of an apostle, I am an apostle.' An Anglican bishop would never dream of such a claim…

In November 1992 the Church of England voted to ordain women to the priesthood. I knew it was coming, but thought the measure would be defeated. The vote immediately focused my mind on some real issues. The division in the Anglican Church was suddenly clear. This was not really an issue of whether women could be priests. The real question was whether the Church of England was a Protestant church which could make women ministers or a Catholic church which could not ordain women as priests.

After the vote I went to an Anglo-Catholic support group. It became clear that the Church of England had declared its colors. It was definitely a Protestant church. The Anglo-Catholics were coming up with all sorts of intellectual ways around the decision, but they were all far-fetched and improbable. I realized that to be a good Catholic in the Church of England you had to be a good Protestant. All you could do was defend your own corner and your own type of beliefs against all comers. This is essentially a Protestant mentality.

I went to see the Catholic bishop. As I poured out my frustration I said, 'But the Anglican clergy and bishops don't seem to understand what the apostolic succession is all about.' 'Of course not,' he replied gently, 'otherwise they would become Catholics.'

So Ali and I began instruction with Fr. Joe, a young Canadian monk at Quarr. We began by reading *Dei Verbum*. Joe, a former Evangelical, stressed how Catholics give equal weight to Scripture and the teaching of the Church. Catholic Christianity believes in revelation passing through the divine institution of the Church.

This was the heart of our debate within Anglicanism. People now had to take sides. It was all very simple - either you believe in a relative religion or a revealed religion. If the first, you can happily choose what you want to believe and remain a Protestant. If the second, your only consistent move is to become a Catholic"); "Affirming All Things," in Marcus Grodi (ed), *Journeys Home* (1997) (revised edition 2011) ("The next few years were a terrible time of indecision. By now I was married and we had two young children. I hadn't trained for any other career and if we left the Anglican church there seemed nothing but an uncertain future. Then one Sunday evening I went to Quarr Abbey for Vespers and Benediction. As the monks chanted I agonized over the decision to leave the Church of England. 'But I only wanted to serve you in the ancient church in England!' I cried out to the Lord. As the incense wafted heavenward and the monstrance was lifted, the still small voice replied, 'But THIS is the ancient church in England.' Then the struggles ended. My mind was made up"); "The House of Mirrors," in Dwight Longenecker (ed), *The Path to Rome* (1999) ("[W]hen the General Synod of the Church of England voted to ordain women as priests all the doubts and disenchantment which had remained vague started to crystallize. How could the Anglican church, which claimed to be part of the Catholic and Apostolic church, take such a decision unilaterally? The desperate and well-meaning attempts to keep Anglo-Catholics on board that followed looked like the principle of Anglican 'comprehensiveness' was really the only thing that mattered. The bishops had maintained a formal unity, but without doctrinal unity what kind of foundation was the house built on? In contrast, the other Protestant groups seemed to have doctrinal agreement, but had split up into sectarian denominations and had so lost the structural unity which the Anglicans retained. Why couldn't a church maintain unity in both form and doctrine?

It was then that I read Newman's *Essay on the Development of Christian Doctrine* and something he said hit me between the eyes. Newman wrote: 'If Christianity is both social and dogmatic, and intended for all ages, it must, humanly speaking, have an infallible expounder, else you will secure unity of form at the loss of unity of doctrine, or unity of doctrine at the loss of unity of form; you will have to choose between a comprehension of opinions and a resolution into parties; between latitudinarian and sectarian error... You must accept the whole or reject the whole...it is trifling to receive all but something which is as integral as any other portion. Thus it would be trifling indeed to accept everything Catholic except the head of the body of Christ on earth.'

There wasn't any way around it. In Newman's terms Anglicanism was social. It was latitudinarian. It was comprehensive of opinion. But to retain these strengths it had to sacrifice unity of doctrine. On the other hand the other Protestant groups were dogmatic. They were sectarian, they had resolved into parties. They had kept doctrinal agreement but sacrificed structural unity. The only way to retain unity of form and unity of doctrine was to have an agreed, visible, infallible authority. Such an authority would faithfully interpret the Scriptures to ensure unity of doctrine while providing the structure which would ensure unity of form...

At the same time I was reading Eamon Duffy's monumental work, *The Stripping of the Altars*. All the Protestant propaganda about the corrupt and moribund pre-Reformation church began to fall away in the face of Duffy's relentless accumulation of facts and documentation. To make matters worse I began to read the apostolic fathers - works that I had never been encouraged to read in my Evangelical training. I was astounded to find them Catholic through and through. As Newman had discovered, any trace of Anglican or distinctively Evangelical thought was completely absent...

Within Anglicanism I found a sense of history and continuity, but within Catholicism I found a history and continuity which went back not five hundred years, but two thousand"), *Listen My Son: St. Benedict for Fathers* (2000); *EWTN Audio Library, The Journey Home* (18 September 2000) ("One of the things I was taught about the Catholic Church was that they invented certain things much later in the day, which were completely unscriptural, things like the infallibility of the Pope, or the Marian doctrines and so forth; and of course in understanding the Catholic development of doctrine, the Catholic Church teaches firmly that nothing that the Catholic Church teaches is contrary to Scripture.

Instead, on the other hand, there are certain things and certain truths from Scripture which will be given over time. Remember when Jesus said to his disciples that he is sending the Holy Spirit and the Holy Spirit will teach you all things, and he said later that you're not ready for all things right now. And so the implication is that things will be unfolded in time, and sure enough in the early centuries of the Church doctrines like the Incarnation and the Trinity were developed and understood by the Church, sometimes through great controversy, but eventually the Church came together and decided the truth and decided the right interpretation of the truth, and that doctrine developed.

Other doctrines developed later, and the understanding is that the doctrines are developed when they need to be developed, because the Church is facing some sort of heresy or some sort of problem and then it comes to define those things.

I also like to think of it like the acorn and the oak. You look at an acorn and it doesn't look anything like an oak tree, but of course the oak tree comes from the acorn. And the development of doctrine is a bit like that, so that as the acorn is planted and grows into an oak tree, so that seed doctrine, that kernel of doctrine is there, and sometimes takes centuries for the Church to come to a full understanding of that doctrine...

When history is important we can see that doctrine has developed, and some people want to say that they're happy with the development up to a certain point like, maybe, the development of the Incarnation doctrines and the Trinity doctrines. But they don't want some other developments, like the papacy and the Marian doctrines, which were developed"); *Adventures in Orthodoxy* (2002); *Challenging Catholics: A Catholic Evangelical Dialogue* (2002) (with

John Martin); *More Christianity: Finding the Fullness of Faith* (2002; expanded revised edition 2010); *St. Benedict and St. Thérèse: The Little Rule and the Little Way* (2002); "An Anglican Priest Discovers 'More Christianity,'" in Patrick Madrid (ed), *Surprised by Truth 3* (2002) ("When I began to express my own increasing convictions about the claims of the Catholic Church, people were shocked and upset. Some had listened closely to my preaching and had seen the crisis coming. Others were angry and accusatory. I was being disloyal to my own Church, or even worse, I was calling their Christian life into question by leaving. Still others were confused and frustrated. Their feelings were summed up by a good Methodist woman who came to our church with her Anglican husband: 'Surely the only thing that matters is how much we love Jesus!'

Her statement is difficult to answer, not because there is no answer, but because there are too many answers. In a letter to an inquirer, Cardinal Newman said, 'Catholicism is a matter; it cannot be taken in a teacup.' He meant that Catholicism was so vast, and the reasons for conversion so overwhelming and complex, that it is impossible to sum up the whole thing in a neat and pithy formula.

In one sense, the good Methodist woman was right. It could be said that the only thing that matters *is* how much we love Jesus. Hers is the right answer, but it is also the right question. How much do we love Jesus, and how can we be sure that we love Jesus and not just our idea of Jesus?

I had seen so many Jesuses amongst different Christians, and each one was strangely like that particular Christian. Charismatics saw a Spirit-filled prophet of God. People concerned with justice and peace saw a radical revolutionary who spoke for the poor. Intellectuals saw a Jesus who was cleverer than anybody else and suffered for it. Tasteful Christians at Cambridge saw a Jesus who was a kind of persecuted agnostic poet. Snobs saw a lofty Jesus who was head and shoulders above everyone else, and working class people saw Jesus the humble carpenter. I began to see that my Jesus was also a reflection of myself. I'm inclined to be intellectual, contemplative, and intuitive. I followed a Jesus who pondered problems, went out to the wilderness to pray, and found crowds of people difficult. My Jesus walked a lonely path to a distant Cross because that's how I was walking through life myself.

But to follow Christ should mean to lose yourself, not to worship yourself. I wanted an objective Jesus - one who was not my own reflection. I wanted a Christ who was cosmic, not a Christ who was comfy. Where was this Jesus to be found? In the Incarnation. In His body. Where was His Body to be found? The Scriptures were clear: the Body of Christ was the

Church. Saint Paul was inspired to use this image for the Church.

I had been taught that the Church was the Body of Christ in a symbolic way, that all of us in a particular congregation should work together like members of a body. But the emphasis in that teaching was on only one half of the image: it stressed *body* - not *Christ*. When I put the two together and saw the Church as the Body of Christ, a window opened. As an Evangelical I was taught that the different churches were man-made organizations that were useful, but essentially unnecessary. Now I saw the Church as the Mystical Body of Christ - a living, dynamic organism empowered by the Holy Spirit to continue the work of the risen Lord in the world.

The Church was suddenly a sacrament of Christ. In my brothers and sisters, I could find Jesus. In my service to the Church, I could find Jesus. In our worship, I could find Jesus. In obedience to the teaching of the church, I could find Jesus. By immersing myself in the Church, I immersed myself in Jesus and transcended the limitations of my personal walk with the Lord.

But if my church was only a gathering of people like me, and Jesus was only a reflection of us, then we were serving ourselves, not Him"); "God-Bearer," *This Rock*, April 2002; *Adventures in Orthodoxy* (2003); *Is Anybody There?: The Question of God* (2003); *The God Man: Finding the Real Jesus* (2003); *The Fire of Life: Who is the Holy Spirit?* (2003); *The Great Battle: Living by Faith* (2003); *Welcome Home: Belonging to the Church* (2003); *Mary: A Catholic-Evangelical Debate* (2003) (with David Gustafson); *How to Be an Ordinary Hero; The Magic Key for Taking Charge of Change and Reaching Your Heroic Potential* (2005); *Why Do You Believe That?: A Protestant-Catholic Conversation* (2005) (with John Schwartz); "How Do We Know It's the True Church," *This Rock*, May-June 2007; *Praying the Rosary for Inner Healing* (2008); *EWTN Audio Library, The Journey Home* (3 November 2008) ("[During the discussion and debate on the question of women's ordination] I began to ask the question how do you make up your mind? Do you just put it to the vote? And this then caused me to look again at the question of authority in the Catholic Church, and saying, well, where is the historic, scriptural, universal voice of Christ's authority in the world today? And there was only one source, or one church, which made that claim and that made me look from England a little bit further East to Rome"); *The Gargoyle Code* (2009); *A Sudden Certainty: Priest Poems* (2009); "Peter's Authority," *This Rock*, May 2010; *dwightlongenecker.com*.

Longstreet, James ("Pete") – soldier; b. 8 January 1821, Edgefield, South Carolina; c. 7 March 1877 (received in New Orleans); d. 2 January 1904, Gainesville, Georgia; brought up an Episcopalian; his family moved to Alabama in 1831; educated at U.S. Military Academy at West Point and graduated in 1842; commissioned captain; on the outbreak of the Civil War he resigned his commission and entered the Confederate service; received at once the rank of brigadier general; took part with distinction in the first battle of Bull Run (21 July 1861); appoinred a major-general in 1862; commanded the right wing of Lee's army at Antietam (17 September 1862); at the head of a corps at Gettysburg (2-3 July 1863); severely wounded in the battle of the Wilderness (6 May 1864); resumed his command during the siege of Petersburg; Lee referred to him as his "Old War Horse"; at the end of the war he became a member of the Republican party and appointed by President Grant surveyor of customs at New Orleans (these things resulted in his memory being blackened in the South for many years); supervisor of internal revenue and postmaster; in 1874 he became adjutant general of the Louisiana militia; his conversion was brought about by Father Abram J. Ryan, known as the "Poet Priest" of the Confederacy; U.S. Minister to Turkey 1880-1881; appointed U.S. railway commissioner in 1898; in 1897, eight years after the death of his first wife he married Helen Dortch Longstreet (d. 1962), a Catholic (he was seventy-six and she was thirty-four); she defended his memory and his record in the Civil War; she was also the first female Assistant State Librarian of Georgia; she authored "The Dortch Bill" passed by the Georgia Legislature in 1896 to allow a woman to serve as State Librarian; she was known as "The Fighting Lady"; his funeral Mass was said by Bishop Benjamin J. Keiley of Savannah, Georgia, who had served in the Army of Northern Virginia during the Civil War; see *From Manasses to Appomattox* (1904); H. J. Eckenrode and Bryan Conrad, *James Longstreet: Lee's War Horse* (1936); Donald Bridgman Sanger and Thomas Robson Hay, *James Longstreet: Soldier, Politician, Officeholder, and Writer* (1952); Wilbur Thomas, *General James "Pete" Longstreet: Lee's "Old War Horse," Scapegoat for Gettysburg* (1979); William Garrett Piston, *Lee's Tarnished Lieutenant: James Longstreet and His Place in Southern History* (1987); Jeffrey D. Wert, *General James Longstreet: The Confederacy's Most Controversial Soldier* (1993); *Catholic Encyclopedia* ("He...attained the distinction of being one of [the Confederate's] greatest fighters and of winning the unbounded confidence and affection of his soldiers").

Longworth, Paulina (married name Sturm) – charity worker; b. 14 February 1925; c. 1953; d.

27 January 1957; only daughter of Alice Roosevelt (1884-1980), who was the oldest child of President Theodore Roosevelt (1858-1919); her legal father was her mother's husband, Nicholas Longworth (1869-1931), Speaker of the House, but her biological father was Senator William Borah (1865-1940); Nicholas Longworth died when she was six; difficult relationship with her mother, who stifled her; as a child often invited to the White House to play with her cousins, and later to attend dinner parties; attended Vassar College briefly; very shy with a bad stammer; in 1944 married Alexander McCormick Sturm ("Sandy") (1923-1951), an artist (one child of the marriage, Joanna Sturm (see below)); already depressive, this, plus drug dependency, increased after the early death of her husband; she sought spiritual solace and converted to the Catholic faith; worked as a volunteer at several Washington hospitals; joined the Chrystie Street hospitality house of Dorothy Day (see above); died of an overdose of sleeping pills (autopsy said accidental death; some thought suicide, which she had earlier attempted; the Church allowed a Catholic burial); buried in Rock Street Cemetery, Washington; see Carol Felsenthal, *Princess Alice: The Life and Times of Alice Roosevelt Longworth* (1988); Betty Boyd Caroli, *The Roosevelt Women* (1998).

Lorimer, William ("The Blond Boss") - politician; b. 27 April 1861, Manchester, England; c. 1914; d. 13 September 1934, Chicago, Illinois; son of a Scottish Presbyterian minister; the family emigrated to the United States in 1865, moving to Chicago in 1870; self-educated; many laboring jobs; joined the Republican Party in a traditionally Democrat area and used friendship patronage and favors to gain influence; in 1884 he married Susan K. Mooney, an Irish Catholic (eight children of the marriage; devoted to his family); elected to the U.S. House of Representatives 1895-1901 and 1903-1909; used his power for personal as well as political gain; the Illinois General Assembly elected him to the U.S. Senate (prior to the 17th amendment to the Constitution, ratified in 1913, selection of U.S. Senators rested with state legislatures, rather than popular vote); after three enquiries the full Senate adopted a resolution declaring "that corrupt methods and practices were employed in his election, and that the election, therefore, was invalid"; he never regained his former power; indicted on charges of misappropriation of funds and conspiracy to defraud relating to banks which he owned or had interests in, but he was acquitted; whether he was truly corrupt remains an open question; went back to banking and went into the lumber business; buried in Calvary Catholic Cemetery, Evanston, Illinois; see Joel A. Tarr,

A Study in Boss Politics: William Lorimer of Chicago (1971); *ANB.*

Lowell, Robert Trail Spence IV ("Cal") – poet; b. 1 March 1917, Boston, Massachusetts; c. 29 March 1941 (received in Christ the King Chapel, Louisiana State University, by Fr. Maurice Schexnayder, the Catholic chaplain; his wife, Jean Stafford (1915-1979), the novelist, was received a few years earlier, but soon lapsed); d. 12 September 1977, New York City; member of a Boston Brahmin family, which included two other poets, Amy Lowell (1874-1925) and James Russell Lowell (1819-1891); his father was an engineer in the U.S. Army; his mother was a descendant of Jonathan Edwards (1703-1758), the Calvinist theologian; brought up as an Episcopalian; educated at Harvard University for two years before transferring to Kenyon College in Gambier, Ohio; studied there under John Crowe Ransom (1888-1974), the poet and critic, and Allen Tate (see below); conversion to Catholicism was partly in rebellion against his parents; main literary influences on his conversion were Etienne Gilson, Cardinal Newman, Jacques Maritain, Gerard Manley Hopkins, Christopher Dawson, and E. I. Watkin; the Catholic faith influenced his first two books, *Land of Unlikeness* (1944) and *Lord Weary's Castle* (1946); conscientious objector during World War II and served periods of imprisonment; Poet Laureate Consultant in Poetry to the Library of Congress 1947-1948; totally serious about his conversion, but left the Church in 1946, though returned in February 1949; fluctuated in his belief (the only act of faith he could make any more was a creed which stated, "I don't know what I don't know"), until he formally rejoined the Episcopalian Church in November 1955; friend of George Santayana (1863-1952), the philosopher, poet, essayist and novelist, and adopted his position ("feeling the Church's historic and moral authority, and yet seeing that its doctrine is not true"); one of the major literary figures of his generation; won the Pulitzer Prize in both 1947 and 1974; won the National Book Award in 1960; some of his best poetry (e.g., *The Quaker Graveyard in Nantucket*) came out of that early period, his "fire-breathing Catholic C.O." period as he called it years later; during the 1960s he was active in the civil rights movement and opposed the United States involvement in Vietnam; his later poetry was more personal and political; suffered from manic depression; in 1948 he divorced Jean Stafford (no children of the marriage) and married essayist and novelist Elizabeth Hardwick in 1949 (one child of this marriage; divorce 1972); married Caroline Blackwood later in 1972 (one son of this marriage); in 1977 returned to Elizabeth Hardwick; buried in Stark Cemetery, Dunbarton, New Hampshire; see Robert Giroux (ed),

Collected Prose (1987); *Collected Poems* (2003); Steven Gould Axelrod, *Robert Lowell: Life and Art* (1978); Ian Hamilton, *Robert Lowell: A Biography* (1982) ("For Lowell, Catholicism had three prongs: reason, faith and practice. Since he was a good Thomist, the first two presented him with no difficulties: 'Reason permeates faith...The Incarnation is only a probability, under examination it becomes more probable, after a while you believe...the point is the religious coincidences are all in favor of the Incarnation. Science, medical practice, psychology etc. These are ultimately irrelevant.' Thus, faith stands to reason.

As to practice, Lowell concedes in this same letter that the Church's social achievements have been far from satisfactory: 'Incompetence, stupidity, cruelty, conservatism, compromise and dogmatism all abound.' In personal terms, though, he believes that every Catholic should 'work for a corporate state, guild systems etc.'"); Vereen Bell, *Robert Lowell: Nihilist as Hero* (1983); Steven Gould Axelrod, "Robert Lowell and Hopkins," *Twentieth Century Literature*, Spring 1985, p.55; Jeffrey Meyers, *Manic Power: Robert Lowell and his Circle* (1987); Jeffrey Meyers (ed), *Robert Lowell: Interviews and Memoirs* (1988); Terry Witek, *Robert Lowell and "Life Studies": Revising the Self* (1993); Paul Mariani, *Lost Puritan; A Life of Robert Lowell* (1994) ("The descendant of Puritan and Unitarian and Episcopalian clergy, the descendant of Jonathan Edwards, the man who had once told [Peter] Taylor that Catholicism was the religion of Irish servant girls, was about to become a Catholic himself...

'I've just been to *Tenebrae* at the [National] Cathedral,' he wrote [Carley Dawson] in the middle of Holy Week. He'd listened to a choir of Franciscans in their brown habits, 'awkward, gangling young men, looking like minor employees at the Library,' chanting the Psalms and Lamentations so effectively that he'd wondered why anyone who wanted to believe should have much trouble doing so. But then the long-winded 'grim pomposity' of the Irish Catholic priest's sermon had jolted him back into reality. The sentiments had come right out of Joyce's *Portrait of the Artist as a Young Man.* Ah, 'what a benign, cultured old world country this would be,' he thought, if only the Irish clergy could all be made 'literary mutes.' So it had all come full circle; in spite of that other Dawson – Christopher – and Maritain, and Dante and Hopkins, and even [J. F.] Powers, Catholicism had once again become for Cal a religion fit only for Irish serving girls"); Henry Hart, *Robert Lowell and the Sublime* (1995); Richard Tillinghast, *Robert Lowell's Life and Work: Damaged Grandeur* (1995); *ANB.*

Luce, Clare Boothe (born Ann Clare Boothe) – journalist, playwright, politician and socialite; b. 10 April 1903, New York City; c. 16 February 1946 (received at St. Patrick's Cathedral, New York, by Mgr. Fulton Sheen); d. 9 October 1987, Watergate complex, Washington D.C.; second illegitimate daughter of Anna Clara Schneider and William Boothe; her father was a professional concert violinist and businessman who was the son of a Baptist minister; her mother was a born Catholic, but she fell away from the Church when she met her father, who was divorced; childhood spent in a number of cities (she described it as "unusually unhappy and bitter"); she had little religion when she grew up; her parents never married and separated in 1912; her original ambition was to become an actress; after graduation she went temporarily to a theater school in New York City; her stepfather, whom her mother married in 1919 was Dr. Albert E. Austin (1877-1942), a politician; went to a High Episcopalian boarding school and was confirmed in the Anglican communion; became interested in the women's suffrage movement; in 1923 married George Tuttle Brockaw (1879-1935), heir to a New York clothing fortune (one child of the marriage), but the marriage ended in divorce in 1929; in 1935 she married Henry Robinson Luce (1898-1967), Presbyterian and Republican, wealthy publisher of *Time*, *Fortune*, and *Life*; successful writer for stage, film and magazines; associate editor of *Vanity Fair*, for which she wrote satirical pieces about New York society; reputation as cold and calculating; in 1940 traveled to Europe as a journalist for *Life* and reported on the war; later reported from Africa, India and the Far East; in 1942 she won a Republican seat in the U.S. House of Representatives representing Fairfield County, Connecticut (formerly held by her late stepfather); fine public speaker; warned against the threat of international Communism; in January 1944 her daughter, Anne, by her first husband, was killed in a car accident, giving her a nervous breakdown; her mother and brother died within a few years also; she became disenchanted with liberalism, Freudianism, Marxism and scientific materialism; her conversion to the Catholic Church was greatly influenced by Mgr. Fulton Sheen; she wrote a brilliant account of her conversion in *McCall's Magazine* (see extracts below); collected and edited a series of essays on various saints (*Saints for Now*); many former critics noticed that her previous self-centeredness was replaced by unselfishness and compassion; in 1953 appointed ambassador to Italy by President Eisenhower (served until 1956); nominated and confirmed for post of ambassador to Brazil, but resigned; maintained her association with the conservative wing of the Republican party; supported Senator Barry Goldwater in 1964, then retired from public life; in 1981 President Reagan appointed her to the President's Foreign Intelligence Advisory Board, where she served until 1983; President Reagan awarded her the Presidential Medal of Freedom in 1983; since 1989 the Clare Booth Luce foundation has provided grants for women in science, mathematics and engineering; in 1993 the Clare Booth Luce Policy Institute was founded to advance American women through conservative ideas; the Clare Booth Luce Heritage Foundation gives the Clare Boothe Luce Award (its highest award), established in 1991, for distinguished contributions to the conservative movement; gave the Luce home in South Carolina to the Trappist Order (it is now Mepkin Abbey and she and her husband are buried there); see (plays) *Abide With Me* (1935); *The Women* (1936); *Kiss the Boys Goodbye* (1938); *Margin for Error* (1939); *Child of the Morning* (1951); *Slam the Door Softly* (1970); (screenplay) *Come to the Stable* (1949); (books and articles) *Stuffed Shirts* (1933); *Europe in the Spring* (1940); "The 'Real' Reason, Part One," *McCall's Magazine*, February 1947 ("[L]iberal thought gave us an enormous amount of personal freedom. Plainly if there were no Judge in Heaven, sitting over society, there was no judge sitting over us. If mankind was God then each individual ego shared in the Godhead equally. Liberalism allowed us, indeed required us, to be the sole judges of the morality of our own actions. Indeed, as liberalism had destroyed with God, the concept of Absolute Good, or Absolute Morality, nothing could be judged to be finally moral or immoral. You followed, if you cared to, or if it were expedient, current fashions in morals. These were developed, or destroyed in a liberal world, by the pain-pleasure method. What gave pleasure to you or your neighbors was moral. What gave pain to you or your neighbors was immoral. Unhappily, the whole thing often got rather confusing for you, your neighbor *and* society. One person's, or group's, or even nation's pleasure, and therefore morality often proved to be the very thing that gave pain to the neighbor, and was immoral. Moreover, your own pleasure (good) of today often revealed itself as your pain (evil) the next day. Society – and the individuals within it – were therefore in constant need of saving themselves from the immoral consequences of their own infallible and godlike moral judgments"); "The 'Real' Reason, Part Two," *McCall's Magazine*, March 1947 ("The cancer of the soul is selfishness. And yet the supremacy or final authority of the self was one of the 'Liberal's' most cherished tenets. Indeed, it was the inevitable reduction of his philosophy...

The great poets and artists and

benefactors of the human race were motivated, I felt sure, by a richer and sweeter, a more *ineffable* purpose than a sublimated infantile sexuality. The thought that they were not suddenly turned the world into a pageant of monstrous obscenity…

[H]ow could the classless society guarantee that there would be love without hate, generosity without greed, truth without lies, justice without injustice, tenderness without cruelty? Wouldn't the children still pull the wings off butterflies? And how would you stop them in a classless society if you couldn't tell them that God made even the insects for our pleasure and didn't want us to be cruel to anything, if there were no God and no such thing as 'cruelty'?...

If so much as *one* honorable man lived to suffer unjustly in the Communist commonwealth of the world, would not that *one* innocent man's sufferings rob all life in the Communist commonwealth of its meaning?...

Ah, where does one find priests who have the light of faith burning so clear in their minds that will cry: 'God is Love and Jesus is our Savior,' and to *this* proposition it makes no difference whether the universe expands or contracts, whether the atom has been split or not. The uses to which man will put atomic energy will entirely depend on whether or not he worships the God of Love. I am here to tell you about the Trinity, not atomic fission"); "The 'Real' Reason, Part Three," *McCall's Magazine*, April 1947 ((1) "[T]he essential problem remained what it had always been for me, a modern 'Liberal': Can the existence of God be proved?

There is a pragmatic but wholly negative way to know whether the name of 'God' may mean something. That is to try to think and behave as though it meant nothing. This is what I had done for years. This is what millions of people have been doing throughout human history, though never in such great numbers as now. When this way results in personal misery or ineptitude and in worldwide catastrophe, commonsense suggests that 'God' may mean something. What, then?

There are two positive ways to decide whether the name 'God' stands for a Real Being. The first is to use the intellect to analyze the nature of man and the world, to discover what proof they offer of His existence. The second is to consult the testimony of human history and human experience (one's own included) to discover if they offer real awareness of a Supreme Being and, if so, when, how and under what conditions. That is the scientific approach. Catholic teaching develops both of these affirmative approaches with relentless logic…" (2) "The climax of Catholic Instructions concerns the Doctrine of the Divinity of Jesus Christ. The historical and intellectual proofs of that doctrine are many, and curiously compelling. They are so compelling indeed that for 1900 years even those who refused to believe them were at all times under the fiercest of inner compulsions to rationalize their disbeliefs. Never have so many men, and men often with superior minds, spent so much time and effort to disprove an 'error.' That circumstance alone is suspicious. Errors have an extraordinarily simple way of disproving themselves. Today, freedom from worship prevails everywhere. There is no condign punishment and no social ostracism attached to atheism, and often much prestige. And still one can seldom find a book by a well-known scientist, philosopher, sociologist, historian or psychoanalyst which does not devote pages to lengthy explanations of why the author cannot accept the Divinity of Jesus. Paradoxically enough, in most books by Western authors we are cautioned to hold on to Christian 'virtues' and 'principles,' but to do away with the belief in the Christ. This is much as though the authors should advocate that we keep our streets and houses well lighted, but do away with power plants.

The fact remains, never in all the history of the world has an error persisted so long, nor inspired so many hearts to noble thoughts and noble actions. Surely if the Man-God be error, then all the sacrifice, selflessness, tenderness, piety, sanctity, holiness and love, not to mention the great art, music and literature inspired by that error are error too? Can an effect exceed its cause? And would not the Father Himself be in error if the error of the Divinity of our Lord Jesus be proved on Him? Then surely what would also be proved is that God did not and does not love his most loving creatures very much. For 2000 years, the best, the purest and the noblest have lived and died – sometimes hideous deaths – in the name of that error.

A second strange fact bearing on the kinship of Father and Son remains for dispassionate consideration. No man ever brought up to believe in the Son has ever been able later to reject Him without a severe loss of faith in the Father, a loss which generally results in the rejection of God as a personal Deity.

'You know neither me, nor my Father: If you had known me, you should have known my Father also...If God were your Father, you would love me: for I proceeded forth and came from God; neither came I of myself but He sent me...Before Abraham was I am...I and my Father are one...'

I have come to think that even in our own day, very few people would reject the Son completely if they knew about Him. And by that, I mean knowing of His own word. How many of our moderns have ever sat down and read the New Testament, with the 36,450 words spoken by our Savior, as carefully as they would read a 100,000 word report of a business enterprise in which their fortunes were mildly involved? How many atheists reading this paragraph can honestly say, '*I* have!' I couldn't have said it, two years ago, that is certain. I see now that I rejected the Son, not as I knew Him, but as I thought I knew Him, through the distortions my mind accepted of the distortions of other minds.

My pre-Catholic concept derived by rumor and distortion of the Christian God was, possibly, revolting enough to drive anyone to atheism. The Father was an absolute tyrant, living in lush felicity while his children suffered unbearable agonies. And the Son was an effeminate, saccharine, mournful and naïve character, with a martyr-complex. This was certainly the kind of God I could get along without – and did for twenty years. The kind of God I could not get along without was the kind I found in the New Testament when Father Sheen finally put me to reading it. (I read it, with the same attention I was giving, at that very time, to the atomic legislation before the House of Congress. And then it was plain, for the first time, that the only hope mankind had of controlling the bomb lay not in the legislation we were passing, but in the law of our Lord, to love one another as he loved us.)

It was just about at this time that a number of friends wrote to me, inquiring the real reason why I was becoming a Catholic. I wrote to each a letter, in which I enclosed a slim compendium of those 36,450 words of our Blessed Lord, culled from the Four Gospels. I said, if they would read these words we would both be in better shape, when we next met, to discuss the matter.

For, I said, *Jesus Christ Himself was the Real Reason!* And I added I was eager to discuss that real reason, providing we both knew thoroughly the text that must be the foundation of our discussion."

(3) "It finally took two world wars, the overthrow of several dozen thrones and governments, the Russian revolution, the swift collapse, in our own time, of hundreds of thought-systems, a small number of which collapsed on me, the death of millions, as well as the death of my daughter, before I was willing to take a look at this extraordinary institution, the Catholic Church. So much and more – God's Grace – was needed to fasten my mind on the fact that this One Church has survived towering o'er the wrecks of time. And to make me see that while it has been accused during these many million days of committing some crimes and sheltering some knaves and hypocrites and of having a somewhat overdeveloped taste for theological hairsplitting it has never been accused of cheating, watering, deserting, canceling, or shilly-shallying about its basic beliefs, nor of any break in its historic continuity.

I too was once so bigoted that rather than admit that it has bred in its bosom a glorious and spectacular crew of poets and philosophers, saints and martyrs, I ignored them"); (Undated letter to Fulton Sheen, ca.1948: "Father, the poor in America know that almost none can become and stay rich and famous, and really be pure in heart, or full of that hidden sanctity you spoke of. That is why they hate the rich so… So, the poor know that to all the other sins of envy, greed, lust, pride and ruthlessness, they committed on the road up, they add the sin of indifference, forgetfulness – betrayal of those they left behind…

Forgive me, father but I fear that too many of His priests have not understood that the poor are right, not right because they are poor, but right about how wrong the rich are. That's why they can't make converts in any numbers…

Oh, do not think I do not understand how it is with the Church in America. How sweet it is to be at long last on the right side of the tracks…and to be in the religious field, as one of my Catholic friends put it, a real-up-and-comer!...Oh could it be that the Church itself is beginning to be just a little like the rich young man…? Men I say should not spend all their novenas and so much of their life of prayer in her contemplation - not in times like these, that call for eagles, and lions and tigers of the Lord!... Ravage the world with the Truths of Christ crucified…This is a lush land of glittering corruption…No King but saints"); "Under the Fig Tree," in John A. O'Brien (ed), *The Road to Damascus* (1949) ("If happiness was the background of conversion, as it sometimes is - especially with the young and the innocent - that happiness in retrospect seems a wonderfully mysterious and lovely act of Grace. These might be called the Palm Sunday converts. They sing their hosannas *before* His triumphal entry. The blithe and innocent converts recall the words of a fourteenth-century English mystic writing about some young cloistered nuns: 'The true anchoresses are birds of heaven that fly aloft and sit on the green boughs singing merrily. A bird sometimes alights on earth to seek food, but never feels secure there, and often turns herself about.' The happy convert feels that his former happiness was a song sung in the instinctive certainty that his soul's joyous flight to God was imminent.

Most converts are Good Friday converts. They have entered His Kingdom through the gates of pain. After their conversion they view their old misfortunes and afflictions, the hardships and handicaps, in an entirely new light. They seem no longer the vicious visitations of a blind fate. The bludgeonings of chance that once left the convert's head bloody - and generally bowed - are God's harrowing, the ploughing up of his hard heart…"); (ed), *Saints For Now* (1952); Alden Hatch, *Clare Boothe Luce: Ambassador Extraordinary* (1956) ("Monsignor Sheen telephoned Clare in Washington and invited her to have dinner with him…That first night Clare, supercharged with theological excitement, began to talk about it as they sat down to dinner. With his engaging grin Monsignor Sheen said, 'Let us not talk religion at the dinner table.'

After the meal they went to the monsignor's library-office, and there he took firm direction of the proceedings. 'We cannot cover the whole subject of religion in an evening,' he said. 'Therefore, in order that our discussion may be decorous and orderly, let us talk about one subject tonight - we can talk about the others next time we meet. 'First we will consider the existence of God. I should like to talk for five minutes without interruption. After that you may say anything you please, and ask as many questions as you like, for two or three hours, or all night if you wish.'

When Bishop Sheen described this interview, he smiled and said, 'Of course I was a fool to think I could talk to Clare for five minutes without being interrupted.'

The priest began by pointing out the philosophical necessity of finding a First Cause for the universe. It could not have leaped out of nothing by accident, he said; and since the universe is finite, and therefore has been created, we must look for an infinite, a transcendent Power as its Creator. 'Since existence does not belong to things by their own nature, the reason for existence must be sought extrinsically and transcendently to the things themselves...They are caused by one First Being, Who possesses being most perfectly. This Being is called God.'

But Monsignor Sheen said that God is also immanent in this world. 'God is in the universe but not shut up in it; God is outside the universe but not excluded from it.' In other words He did not create the universe and then wash His hands of it. Rather, He is immanent in the world by His wisdom, by His goodness, and by His power.

Monsignor Sheen talked first of the divine order of things. God is present in things as the Wisdom which planned them, and His Wisdom participating in things explains our own intelligibility. 'God made things intelligently. We know, not because we invent, but because we discover - discover the Wisdom of God hidden in the things which He made.'

God is also immanent in the universe because of His Goodness, Monsignor Sheen explained. He has placed in all beings a desire to strive for their own perfection and thus to share in some way His own perfect Goodness and Love. 'We are attracted to God by the immanent gravitational pull of Goodness and Love.'

It was at this point that Clare erupted. She jumped up and shook her finger under Monsignor Sheen's nose. 'If God is good,' she cried, 'why did he take my Ann?'

Very gently the priest answered her, 'Perhaps it was in order that you might become a believer. Maybe your daughter is buying your faith with her life.'

Bishop Sheen believes that 'This was the turning point'"); Stephen C. Shadegg, *Clare Boothe Luce: A Biography* (1973); Wilfred Sheed, *Clare Boothe Luce* (1982); Fulton J. Sheen, *Treasure in Clay* (1982), pp.264-265; Ralph G. Martin, *Henry and Clare: An Intimate Portrait of the Luces* (1991); Sylvia Jukes Morris, *Rage For Fame: The Ascent of Clare Boothe Luce* (1997); Thomas C. Reeves, *America's Bishop: The Life and Times of Fulton J. Sheen* (2001), *passim*; Lorene Hanley Duquin, *A Century of Catholic Converts* (2003), p.147; her papers are housed in the Manuscript Division of the Library of Congress; *ANB*.

Lyman, Dwight Edward – priest; b. 3 December 1818, Mount Pleasant, New York; c. 27 August 1853 (received at St. Joseph's Church, Baltimore); d. 29 December 1893, Govanstown, Maryland; his father was an Episcopalian bishop; brought up in the Episcopalian Church; educated at Columbia College, New York; ordained to the Episcopal ministry; influenced by the Tractarian Movement; entered St. Mary's Seminary, Baltimore, in 1853; ordained to the priesthood 29 June 1856 at Baltimore Cathedral; pastor of St. Mary's, Govanstown, for thirty-three years; over three hundred conversions were due to his work there.

McCorvey, Norma Leah (*née* Nelson) ("Jane Roe") – pro-life activist; b. 22 September 1947, Simmesport, Avoyelles Parish, Louisiana; c. 17 August 1998 (received in Dallas by Fr. Frank Pavone, international director of *Priests for Life*); of Cajun and Cherokee ancestry; her mother tried to abort her, but was told it was too late; her father left the family when she was thirteen and her parents later divorced; brought up in Houston, Texas as a Jehovah's Witness, the religion of her stepfather; her mother was a Catholic, but a violent alcoholic; very difficult childhood; convicted of theft at ten and later sent to reform school; on release she was sexually abused by a relative; she dropped out of high school at the age of fourteen; married at sixteen, but abused by her husband and returned to live with her mother; had children in 1965 and 1966; in 1969 at the age of twenty-one she became pregnant again; the father was a married man; she attempted to obtain an illegal abortion, but the clinics in question had been closed down by the authorities; eventually two lawyers, Sarah Weddington and Linda Coffee, took on her case; they were looking for a case with which to challenge the anti-abortion laws in Texas; in order to strengthen her case she alleged falsely that she had been raped; after three years of trials the case reached the Supreme Court under the name of *Roe v Wade* (1973) (meanwhile, she had given birth to the baby who was eventually adopted); the Supreme Court overturned individual states' laws against abortion by ruling them unconstitutional; in the following years she worked at a local abortion clinic; she remained a strong supporter of abortion rights until 1994; later her opinion on abortion changed radically after conversations with volunteers of Operation Rescue, which campaigned to make abortion illegal; she became an Evangelical Christian in 1994; she joined Operation Rescue; she spoke to many pro-life groups; in 1998 she finally became a Catholic (she said, "I listened to [Fr. Pavone] and came to realize that what God was actually saying to me was to 'come all the way home to Him' in His Church - the Church Jesus Christ Himself founded, the Mother Church"); she had lived for a time as a lesbian, but now stated that she was no longer a lesbian; in 2005 she petitioned the Supreme Court to overturn the 1973 decision in *Roe v Wade*, arguing that the case should be reheard on the grounds that it harms women; her petition was denied; continued to be active in pro-life demonstrations; see *I Am Roe* (1994) (autobiography); *Won By Love* (1998) (account of her change of position on abortion) ("I was sitting in Operation Rescue's offices when I noticed a fetal development poster. The progression was so obvious, the eyes were so sweet. It hurt my heart, just looking at them. I ran outside and finally, it dawned on me. 'Norma', I said to myself, 'They're right.' I had worked with pregnant women for years. I had been through three pregnancies and deliveries myself. I should have known. Yet something in that poster made me lose my breath. I kept seeing the picture of that tiny, ten-week-old embryo, and I said to myself, that's a baby! It's as if blinders just fell off my eyes and I suddenly understood the truth - that's a baby!

I felt crushed under the truth of this realization. I had to face up to the awful reality. Abortion wasn't about 'products of conception.' It wasn't about 'missed periods.' It was about children being killed in their mother's wombs. All those years I was wrong. Signing that affidavit, I was wrong. Working in an abortion clinic, I was wrong. No more of this first trimester, second trimester, third trimester stuff. Abortion - at any point - was wrong. It was so clear. Painfully clear"); Lorene Hanley Duquin, *A Century of Catholic Converts* (2003), p.222 ("But it was a seven-year-old girl who had the greatest impact on her. Norma had always avoided children. 'It was part of my denial,' she admitted. 'When you know what is happening to the children behind closed doors, it's difficult to become attached to them outside.'

Seven-year-old Emily never noticed any of Norma's negativity. When she came to the demonstrations with her mother she would run over to hug Norma. Emily's unconditional love eventually broke down Norma's barriers. One day, Norma saw a bumper sticker that read: 'Abortion Stops a Beating Heart.' In that instant, she realized that 'her law' made it legal to stop the life of an unborn child, a child that would never grow up to be like Emily").

McGarvey, Mgr. William I. – priest; b. 1861; c. 1907; d. 1924; became a minister in the Episcopal Church; in 1896 he became the leader of a group known as the Companions of the Holy Savior, linked with St. Elizabeth's Episcopal parish in Philadelphia; a disagreement arose with other ritualist Episcopal groups over an "open pulpit" resolution, allowing anyone who called himself a Christian to preach from the pulpits of the Episcopal Church; as a result he and many other like-minded persons joined the Catholic Church; this led to a reaction against ritualism by the Epicopal Church; see *The Purpose of the Catholic Movement in the Episcopal Church* (1908); E. Hawks, *William McGarvey and the Open Pulpit* (1935) ("For [McGarvey] the Open Pulpit legislation was something more than an unfortunate and easily remedied mistake. The extent of its acceptance was not, for him, its real importance. That many bishops treated it as a dead letter, and that few Protestant ministers cared to accept its privileges, had little or nothing to do with his arguments. For him it was a revelation of the fundamental inconsistency of Anglicanism. It was something pivotal in an inevitable development. He analyzed its nature and foretold its eventual results. He ventured to prophesy what has since been abundantly fulfilled. He did not assert that Anglicanism was departing from its moorings, but rather that it was demonstrating its lack of moorings. He did say, however, that it was departing from its denominational traditions, and in doing so showed its lack of fundamental principles…

The prophecy made by McGarvey in the Tracts that he published at the time of his leaving the Episcopal Church has been remarkably fulfilled. He did not, of course, suppose that the new legislation would lessen the liberty of those Anglicans who held Catholic views. On the contrary, he knew that it would give them greater freedom than they yet enjoyed. What it would do, would be to make impossible the exclusive claim of the Anglo-Catholics to represent true Anglicanism. The most that they could now expect was toleration (greatly extended) for themselves which they would now be compelled to give to others. Toleration was not the object that William McGarvey sought. What he and his associates strove for was the complete victory of what they considered to be the truth. Unless their Anglo-Catholicism was the true expression of Anglicanism, it was useless. It was their purpose to drive out of the Episcopal Church by constitutional means the errors that Lutheranism and Calvinism had brought in. The Open Pulpit legislation tolled the knell to such hopes. It was the outcome of a growing philosophy of Comprehensiveness. It was subversive of any standard of orthodoxy. It rejected authority in favor of empirical subjectivism. It was not without cogency that the year 1907 saw the condemnation of Modernism by the Pope. The General Convention of the same year intended that the new legislation should be a challenge to Christendom.

Since 1907, Comprehensiveness, as a theory of arriving at unity, has grown to be a dogma with Protestants generally, and with most Anglicans, including many who have adopted some of the beliefs and practices of the Catholic Church. Anglican clergymen have cleared the way for comprehensive reunion by denying the Divinity of Christ, His Virgin Birth, and His bodily Resurrection. In doing so they have aroused less objection than did the Open Pulpit amendment itself. The Anglican Church as a whole, and the Anglo-Catholic Party as a powerful factor in it, have increasingly subscribed to a policy of live and let live. With the least struggle offered by any of the Protestant denominations they have yielded to the entrance of Liberalism, now called Modernism"); George E. DeMille, *The Catholic Movement in the American Episcopal Church* (1941).

McKay, Claude (born Festus Claudius McKay) – writer and poet; b. 15 September 1890, Nairne Castle, near James Hill, Clarendon, Jamaica; c. 11 October 1944; d. 22 May 1948, Chicago, Illinois; parents were well-to-do peasant farmers; youngest of eleven children; read widely as a young boy; published his first book of poems, *Songs of Jamaica*, in 1912; went to the United States in 1912 and lived in South Carolina, where he was shocked by the racism; studied at Kansas State University; moved to New York in 1915; married his childhood sweetheart, Eulalie Imelda Lewars, but they separated after a year (one child of the marriage); brief period of homosexuality; became one of the best poets of the Harlem Renaissance of the 1920s; his poetry exhibited a hatred for Western civilization, and rage against Christianity; spent time in London, rest of Europe, North Africa and Soviet Russia; he was at this time a Communist (recruited by John Reed (1887-1920), the American journalist) and atheist; became disillusioned with Communism; very anti-Communist after the Hitler-Stalin pact; returned to the United States and became an American citizen in 1940; came to believe in God, studied Islam, but finally became a Catholic; conversion influenced by the treatment he received for stress through his friend Ellen Tarry (see below), at the Catholic-run Friendship House in Harlem, which enabled him to see the social aspects of Catholicism, including its opposition to Communism; even before his conversion he moved to Chicago and began working as Bishop Sheil's advisor on black affairs and on Soviet Communism; see (poetry) *Songs of Jamaica* (1912); *Harlem Shadows* (1922); *Selected Poems* (1953) (his collected poems were published posthumously); (fiction) *Home to Harlem* (1928); *Banjo* (1929); *Gingertown* (1932); *Banana Bottom* (1933); (autobiographical) *A Long Way From Home* (1937); *Harlem: Negro Metropolis* (1940); *My Green Hills of Jamaica* (1979); Addison Gayle, *Claude McKay: The Black Poet at War* (1972); Wayne F. Cooper (ed), *The Passion of Claude McKay* (1973); James R. Giles, *Claude McKay* (1976); Wayne F. Cooper, *Claude McKay: Rebel Sojourner in the Harlem Renaissance, A Biography* (1987); Tyrone Tillary, *Claude McKay: A Black Poet's Struggle for Identity* (1992); David Goldweber, "Home at Last: The Pilgrimage of Claude McKay – Black Poet Converted to Christianity," *Commonweal*, 15 September 1999 ("The seeds of McKay's attraction to Christianity began in the late 1920s after he became aware of the beauty of the great European cathedrals, especially the Catholic ones in Spain. At this same time he found himself disappointed with Communism, which he increasingly found to be close-minded, partisan, and cold. In 1925, McKay extolled not Lenin's tomb in Moscow but Saint Isaac's Church in Petrograd. 'What jeweled glory fills my spirit's eye,' he wrote, 'What golden grandeur moves the depths of me! ...Bow down in worship, humble and alone,/ Bow lowly down before the sacred sight/ Of man's divinity alive in stone.' He could not shake the sense of something transcendent working in and through human life...

In the March 1946 issue of *Ebony*, McKay published a one-page explanation, 'Why I Became a Catholic,' which associates Protestantism with bigotry, slavery, and greed; Catholicism with tolerance and compassion. He warns black Americans to beware 'the materialistic Protestant god of progress' and declares, 'In joining the Roman Catholic church, I feel proud of belonging to that vast universal body of Christians, which is the greatest stabilizing force in the world today - standing as a bulwark against all the wild and purely materialistic 'isms' that are sweeping the world'"); Lorene Hanley Duquin, *A Century of Catholic Converts* (2003), p.132 ("He wrote to a friend that he was 'doing a lot of reading and research, especially on Catholic work among Negroes, and I am also researching myself to discover how I can be a Catholic. Because if and when I take the step I want to be intellectually honest and sincere about it. From the social angle I am quite clear and determined. I know the Catholic Church is the one great organization which can check the Communists and probably lick them. But there is also the religious angle.'

One of his socialist friends tried to change his mind by encouraging him to die with intellectual freedom, McKay insisted, however that life is a mystery. and most people relate to that mystery through their belief in God.

'I no longer think it is smart or enlightened to be a rationalist or an agnostic,' he explained. 'I don't believe in Communism or National Socialism or Democracy as a solution to man's problems here on earth. The Catholic Church does not pretend to have any solution either, but it does provide an outlet for my mystical feelings, and I do believe in the mystery of the symbol of the Mystical Body of Jesus Christ, through which all humanity may be united in brotherly love'"); *ANB*.

Mackintosh, Hugh Fraser – editor and writer; b. 11 May 1862, Hamilton, Ontario, Canada; c. 23 October 1883 (received by Archbishop Lynch); d. September 1928; his parents were descended from Scottish Jacobites, but were rigid Presbyterians (his father was a ruling elder); as a child he was well drilled in the theology of Calvinism; he wondered "how a chivalrous and imaginative people like the Highland Celts could have fallen under the sway of so cheerless and so unlovely a creed as Calvinism"; after reading the romances of Sir Walter Scott dealing with the heroic ages of Scottish history, "it was borne in upon me that in breaking with her past Scotland had committed national suicide and given the lie to all that was most inspiring in her history"; impressed when once in a Catholic church by Benediction of the Blessed Sacrament ("All that I then discerned was its beauty and solemnity, so unlike the empty forms to which I was accustomed"); his conversion to the Catholic Church was first prompted by an article on Cardinal Newman written by C. Kegan Paul; this directed him to Newman's *Apologia Pro Vita Sua*; after becoming a Catholic he became a collector of books and articles associated with Newman; worked as an accountant and commission merchant; he became a writer concentrating on the history of the Church, first in Scotland, then in Canada; in 1889 co-founder. first secretary, and later president of the Canadian Catholic Truth Society; was an editor of the *Catholic Weekly Review*; assistant editor of the *Catholic Record* of London, for which he wrote his "Notes and Comments" 1910-1928; in 1890 married Maria Josephine Hazelton (d. 1893) (two children of the marriage, Newman and Marie); in 1898 he married Ellen Mary Harris (d. 1916) (one child of the marriage,

Eleanor); see *Life of Father Louis dell Vagua (Capuchin)* (1888); *Life of Bishop Macdonell, First Bishop of Kingston* (1892); *Life of Bishop Power, First Bishop of Toronto* (1892); "History of the Catholic Church under Bishop Macdonell and from 1819 to 1849," in Fr. Teefy (ed), *Jubilee History of the Diocese of Toronto* (1892); essay in Georgina Pell Curtis (ed), *Some Roads to Rome in America* (1909), p.300 ("The Catholic party stood for the national life of Scotland, while the Reformers played into the hands of Elizabeth and Cecil. So far then as Scotland was concerned the Reformation was her undoing. With Queen Mary, Cardinal Beaton and those other heroic souls upon whose destruction the success of the new order depended, I had always had the deepest sympathy, and the more I pondered upon the infamous slanders that have been heaped upon them the greater became my contempt for their miserable traducers, and the more remote any possibility of my own permanent identification with the cause which the Calvinists represented. On the one hand I contrasted the known purity of Mary's early years, her courageous adherence to her faith in troublous times, her absolute selflessness in her relations with her friends and dependents, and, crowning all, her heroic death. On the other hand was the seething mass of corruption in which her lot was cast in the Calvinistic Scotland of the sixteenth century. Was ever a helpless and defenseless woman encompassed by so cruel, so cunning, so unprincipled a set of knaves? There is, apart from Mary's own personality and the unselfish devotion of her humbler retainers, scarcely a bright spot to relieve the dark background of the picture. And towering over all is the grim figure of John Knox, than whom history records few more despicable characters. Coward, bully, traitor, apostate - applauding the murder of the patriot Cardinal and, without doubt privy to the deed; browbeating a gentle and refined woman whom the trend of events had placed at his mercy, and fleeing to Geneva to save his own precious skin when danger threatened in his native country - this is the man whom unthinking Presbyterians delight to honor. It has not been my good fortune to meet with one who could satisfactorily justify this man's dominance in the Scottish history of the period, far less his elevation to a species of patron-saintship, except that a hero a cause must have, and in the stress of poverty one is sometimes manufactured out of very questionable material. In the selection of John Knox, I concluded, the very worst elements in the great upheaval found their most signal triumph...

In the midst of such thoughts as these the subject of Church authority was brought before me...As I read the scriptural narrative, authority to teach unerringly was clearly committed to a body of men by our Lord Himself and power to bind and to loose was conferred upon them with the same definiteness as He had derived it from His Father. I found nothing to correspond with this in the Presbyterian standards, and the result was a state of perplexity of mind which gave me much concern and might have issued in total unbelief had not Providence opened to me the way to the Catholic Church.

Lastly, I was confronted in the years of which I speak with the majestic idea of the Real Presence...[W]hen later I met with the idea of the Real Presence as the natural and proper meaning of our Lord's words it furnished a key to ecclesiastical history which, without the light of that great truth, was hard and inexplicable. And this seems the proper place to say that, as I progressed, I was impressed by the fact that the Catholic interpretation of Scripture was invariably in keeping with the natural and obvious meaning of the text, while, in inverse ratio, the Protestant interpretation was forced and strained. I found, too, that the late Bishop Brownlow's maxim that when scripture is quoted against the Church the most effective retort is usually to ask the disputant to read the next verse, is a sound one. I had myself been struck with the incongruity of our Lord in instituting this sacrament not meaning apparently what He said, and when gradually it dawned upon me that the great Catholic Church, existing from the beginning and alone teaching with the voice of authority, proclaimed that Christ really gave us His own Flesh and Blood, a definiteness and consistency was given to the sacred narrative which bore in upon me with irresistible force. I have read much on this subject both before and after I became a Catholic, and have come to consider the argument for the Catholic interpretation of the words of institution, apart altogether from the Divine character of her teaching, as simply irresistible. It was Cardinal Newman, however, who first brought me face to face with this sublime truth, and while as I have said I did not at once grasp the full import of it, a train of thought was opened to me which 'ere long subdued me completely and brought me to realize that the Catholic Church was my true home.

When then in the *Apologia*, the fair form of the everlasting Church burst upon my vision these thoughts of many years had produced in me a receptive mind and a temper to reverence and admire...

We hear much in these days of a reunion of various forms of Protestantism, but any such reunion must be built upon the sacrifice of the cherished, if mistaken, convictions of former generations. This is indeed the one prevailing characteristic of all the sects: that what formerly were cherished as divine truths have now ceased to have any force or vitality and must not so much as be named among them. The dogma of a state of future retribution is a case in point. This elementary truth is no doubt held by a considerable number in private but is rarely heard of in public, and, like many other traditional beliefs, has gone down before the all-corroding intellect of man. Even belief in the Divinity of Christ is not immune from this overmastering tendency and no extraordinary qualities of penetration are necessary to discern in the near future, religion outside of the Catholic Church transformed into pure humanitarianism bent solely upon making the most of this world. Things have already advanced far in this direction and no human power can stem the torrent. But, as God has not deserted his people, out of this evil may come good, and as the years pass an increasing number of the more serious minded, appalled by the impending destruction of all faith in the supernatural, find their way into the one Church whose builder and maker is God"); essay in Georgina Pell Curtis, *Beyond the Road to Rome* (1914), p.272 ("I say nothing of the riches of devotion which I have found in the Church; of their adaptability to every condition of human life; or of the kinship with the ages which is the common heritage of her children. These are but the accidents, though withal adding beyond measure to the wealth of their heritage. I have in mind the answer given by a Bishop of my acquaintance to a Protestant minister who had ventured the statement that he had prayed for the Bishop's 'conversion.' 'I can assure you,' was the reply, 'that I am not flattered to hear you say so. You give small credit to my reason and common sense to presume for an instant to think that I could leave the old historic Church of Christendom, to put it on no higher ground, for a miserable little petty sect of yesterday'"); *The Catholic Truth Society: Its History and Objects* (1919); "History of the Catholic Church in Toronto," in J. E. Middleton (ed), *The Municipality of Toronto* (1923); James E. Day, KC, "Hugh Fraser Mackintosh," *Canadian Catholic Historical Association Report*, 1942-1943, p.97 ("[T]he distinguishing feature of his 'Notes and Comments' column was the skilful way in which he used the news of the day as a peg on which to hang either answers to attacks on the Church, or sparkling reminders of what Canadian history owed to it, and for that matter of the many debts which civilization, culture, and all that was good in life owed to the Church").

McLoughlin, John (baptized Jean-Baptiste McLoughlin) – doctor and pioneer; b. 19 October 1784, La Rivière du Loup, Quebec, Canada; c. 1842; d. 3 September 1857, Oregon City, Oregon; Irish, Scottish, and French-Canadian descent; of Catholic parentage and was baptized, but brought up as an

Anglican; his father died when he was young and he was brought up in the home of a maternal relative; educated in Canada and Scotland; qualified as a doctor and practiced for a short time, but then became a trader; became a partner of the North-West Company on Lake Superior, which joined with the Hudson Bay Company in 1821; ruled for twenty-two years as the "absolute but kindly autocrat" of the Oregon Country; founded and named Oregon City; he was the great hero of Oregon's pioneer period and is known as the "Father of Oregon"; in the late 1840s his general store was the last stop on the Oregon Trail; he became a U.S. citizen in 1849; buried in the churchyard of St. John's Catholic church in Oregon City; see Eloise McLoughlin and Daniel Harvey, *Life of John McLoughlin, Governor of the Hudson's Bay Company Possessions on the Pacific Slope, at Fort Vancouver* (1878); Eva Emery Dye, *McLoughlin and Old Oregon: A Chronicle* (1900); Richard Gill Montgomery, *The White-Headed Eagle, John McLoughlin, Builder of an Empire* (1934); Alberta Brooks Fogdhall, *Royal Family of the Columbia: Dr. John McLoughlin and His Family* (1978); Dorothy Morrison, *The Eagle and the Fort: The Story of John McLoughlin* (1979); *Catholic Encyclopedia* ("He had no military force, but by his own personality and the aid of his officers and employees, he established order and maintained peace so that persons unaccompanied by escort could travel over the country without danger from formerly hostile Indians. There were no Indian wars in the Oregon Country until after he resigned from the Hudson Bay Company. The Methodist, Presbyterian, and Catholic missionaries he aided and protected, although at that time he was an Anglican. In 1842 he joined the Catholic Church, and became a devoted Catholic, being created a Knight of St. Gregory in 1846. In 1843 the first of the Oregon home-building immigrants arrived in Oregon. Dr. McLouglin fed and clothed them and cared for the sick; he supplied them with seed and farming implements, and loaned them domestic animals. He gave similar assistance to the immigrants of 1844 and 1845. As he furnished most of this aid on credit and did not discourage the settlement of Oregon by citizens of the United States, he was forced to resign by the Hudson Bay Company in 1846"); *ANB*; *DCB.*

McLuhan, (Herbert) Marshall – educator and philosopher; b. 21 July 1911, Edmonton, Alberta, Canada; c. 24 March 1937 (his wife was received in 1946); d. 31 December 1980, Toronto, Ontario, Canada; his father, Herbert Ernest McLuhan, owned a real estate firm (which failed in World War I) and was a Methodist; his mother, Elsie Naomi, *née* Hall, a Baptist, was a schoolteacher and later actress; grew up in Winnipeg, Manitoba; raised in the Baptist Church; studied at the University of Manitoba from 1928 (BA in 1933, MA in 1934); at this stage an agnostic; entered Trinity Hall College, Cambridge University in 1934 (BA in 1936, MA in 1940); studied under F. R. Leavis and I. A. Richards; at this time he moved towards converting to the Catholic faith; conversion influenced by his reading of G. K. Chesterton, whom he met in 1935 ("[H]ad I not encountered Chesterton, I would have remained agnostic for many years at least"); devout throughout the rest of his life, but kept religion a private matter; after his conversion taught only at Catholic colleges; taught English at Saint Louis University 1937-1944; Cambridge PhD on the history of the verbal arts (grammar, logic and rhetoric) from Cicero to Thomas Nashe (suffered from benign brain tumor while there) 1967-1968, then back to the University of Toronto for the rest of his career; his later career concentrated on the study of the influence of communication media independent of their content (his famous aphorism, "the medium is the message," draws attention to this); also coined the expression "the global village"; became a world famous media figure; predicted the Internet nearly thirty years before it was invented, and the rise of social media; appreciated how counter-cultural the Catholic faith is ("The modern media are engaged in a Luciferian conspiracy against the truth" (letter written 1972 to Fr. John Mole)); married to Corinne, *née* Lewis (six children of the marriage); suffered a stroke in 1979; see *The Mechanical Bride: Folklore of Industrial Man* (1951); *The Gutenberg Galaxy: The Making of Typographic Man* (1962); *Understanding Media: The Extensions of Man* (1964); *The Medium is the Massage: The Inventory of the Effects* (1967); *War and Peace in the Global Village* (1968); *From Cliché to Archetype* (1970); D. J. Dooley, "Marshall McLuhan's Faith," *The Tablet*, 24 January 1981, p.80; Matie Molinaro, Corinne McLuhan, and William Toye (ed), *Letters of Marshall McLuhan* (1987) (Letter to his mother, 1935: "Catholic culture produced Chaucer and his merry story-telling Canterbury pilgrims. Licentious enthusiasm produced the lonely despair of Christian in *Pilgrim's Progress* — what a different sort of pilgrim! Catholic culture produced Don Quixote and St Francis and Rabelais. What I wish to emphasize about them is their vanous and rich-hearted humanity. I need scarcely indicate that everything that is especially hateful and devilish and inhuman about the conditions and strains of modern industrial society is not only Protestant in origin, but it is their boast(!) to have originated it. You see my 'religion hunting' began with a rather priggish culture hunting'. I simply couldn't believe that men had to live in the mean and mechanical joyless rootless fashion that I saw in Winnipeg. And when I began to read English Literature I knew that it was quite unnecessary for them so to live… It was a long time before I finally perceived that the character of every society, its food, clothing, arts, and amusements are ultimately determined by its religion…"); Philip Marchand, *Marshall McLuhan: The Medium and the Messenger* (1989; revised edition 1998) ("("The book [Chesterton's *What's Wrong With the World*] was a magnificent defense of certain notions that McLuhan was already predisposed to champion: personal liberties, the sanctities of the family, the traditions of Christian Europe that were opposed to both socialism and rampant capitalism…

Chesterton also pointed McLuhan in the direction of Roman Catholicism. Chesterton's writings constantly reaffirmed the Catholic belief that the world, although very complex and not easily explained, was real and ultimately reasonable: it was not a tangle of deceptive appearances and it was not to be reduced to any intellectual or mathematical formulas. Also, the world was good, since it was created by God.

In its goodness can be seen all sorts of reflections of God. The medievals, for example, saw the faithfulness of the dog guarding the sheepfold as a reflection of the faithfulness of the priest guiding his flock, which in turn was a reflection of the faithfulness of Christ to his people. But the dog, claimed Chesterton, was not just a 'symbol' of faithfulness. The dog *was* faithful - faithful according to its being, as the priest was faithful according to his being, that is, his human being; and both were related by analogy to the faithfulness of Christ. who was Being itself. The dog and the priest were real, and they were distinct; and yet they participated in the one Being of God.

Such was the analogical reasoning of St. Thomas Aquinas, which was replaced in later Western thought by the logic of Descartes and the dialectics of Hegel. There never was any doubt about which kind of reasoning Marshall McLuhan preferred. Analogical thinking shaped his view of life in the way that laws of probability color existence for mathematicians. It was a mode of thinking that became as ingrained and unremarked for McLuhan as his accent…

McLuhan never lost sight of what Chesterton taught him - that all things were real and lovable and ultimately coherent because God had created them. So profound was the impression made on him by this simple truth that McLuhan in his later years maintained that the real heresy of the twentieth century was not materialism but gnosticism - the denial of the reality, reasonableness, and goodness of God's creation in favor of some intellectual construct or of the One, an esoteric and hidden reality denied to human senses…

For McLuhan, the life of a believer, fortified by the teachings of the Church, was the supreme human adventure…

Throughout his career, he remained circumspect about his religion in public; in private, however, he was as Catholic as only a convert from Protestantism can be. He said the rosary, went to Mass almost every day, prayed to Saint Jude (patron saint of lost causes) in exceptionally trying circumstances, and was particularly devoted to Mary, the Mother of God…

He also avoided theology in his religion, at least after his decision to convert. Making the decision itself settled all theological questions for him; they no longer had to be reasoned out or defended in his mind. After his conversion, in fact, he seems to have adopted the time-honored Catholic habit of leaving theology to the professionals, as if investigation into matters of divinity was dangerous to the rank and file.

For McLuhan, prayer and the seven sacraments were all that a good Catholic need cling to - the supreme sacrament being the Eucharist, the Body of Christ consecrated in the Mass and partaken by the faithful. McLuhan maintained that daily reception of this sacrament was as necessary to him as his daily bread. It was the most efficacious channel of divine grace for a Catholic; and intellectually the sacrament was a keystone in McLuhan's thought. The fact that real bread and real wine were transformed, through the actions of the priest, into the real Body and the real Blood of Christ was the ultimate refutation of both materialism and gnosticism, the denial of the supernatural world and the denial of the natural world. It also meant that Christ blessed the very senses of the human body, giving humans an advantage even over the angels.

McLuhan described prayer as ideally consisting of 'a constant, nonstop dialogue with the Creator.' He was emphatic that life without this dialogue was unthinkable. Part of the urgency of prayer for McLuhan was his recognition of the consequences of the loss of God's friendship. He believed that hell existed, and he was rather puzzled that the Church did not play this supernatural trump card, as it were, more often. He frequently noted that, just as one needed bad news ('real' news) to sell the good news (advertising) in newspapers and journals, so one needed bad news (hell) to sell the good news (the Gospel) in religion. It was the job of the Church, he said, 'to shake up our present population. To do that you'd have to preach nothing but hellfire. In my lifetime, I have never heard one such sermon from a Catholic pulpit.'

Heaven and hell were as real to McLuhan as the planet earth, and he did not exempt himself from the possibility of eternal misery. In the 1970s he told a friend that he was worried about his own fate after death. But if his religion increased anxiety about the hereafter, it decreased anxiety for the world. Catholics could, McLuhan believed, see the world more clearly than those who lived in and for the world - just as strangers can often see a place more clearly and visibly than those who have lived in it all their lives. One could simply enjoy and explore this created universe, confident of its ultimate coherence and intelligibility, unconcerned that it fell short of perfection…"; (2) "McLuhan…recognized that much of the traditional theology of the Church, based on Christianized reworkings of Plato and Aristotle, was derived from the Greco-Roman world now finally dissolving in the electronic world. Such theology was obviously in danger of becoming useless. But that was no excuse, according to McLuhan, for the Protestantization of the Catholic Church that occurred after Vatican II. This process - marked by the abandonment of Latin in the Mass, the de-emphasis of such Catholic doctrines as purgatory, the invocation of the saints, and so on - thoroughly disgusted him.

The devastation of the Mass wrought by post-Vatican II changes was particularly painful. He did not like the fact that the priest now looked at the congregation, 'with his face hanging out,' as McLuhan put it, and a microphone around his neck. That microphone, according to McLuhan, automatically eliminated Latin from the Mass, since the Latin was not really intended to be the focus for participants at the Mass but rather a kind of audio backdrop. The mumbled Latin was almost a subliminal element, playing off against the vernacular in such a way as to provide a rich and almost magical multilayered expressiveness. In addition, this backdrop freed participants to meditate or pray during the Mass. Not so the vernacular, amplified through the wretched microphone - a 'hot' medium killing off the 'cool' medium of the nearly inaudible Latin. The new Mass, it is true, did afford McLuhan the chance to belt out old, familiar Protestant hymns (he wondered why no one else in the pew joined him), but even that did not compensate for the loss of Latin or the new, folksy attitude of the priest trying to 'communicate' with the congregation. The Mass, he noted in May 1972, was getting 'longer, limper, lumpier'"); Eric McLuhan and Frank Zingrone (ed), *The Essential McLuhan* (1996); W. Terrence Gordon, *Marshall McLuhan: Escape Into Understanding: A Biography* (1997); Janine Marchessault, *Marshall McLuhan: Cosmic Media* (2005); Douglas Coupland, *Marshall McLuhan: You Know Nothing of My Work!* (2011); Fr. Raymond J. de Souza, "Marshall McLuhan and the Divine Message," *National Post*, 19 July 2011 (reprinted in *catholiceducation.org*) ("'What do you think Marshall McLuhan ought to do if he wants to be taken more seriously in the world today?' asked a television interviewer of the man himself. 'Marshall McLuhan is taken far too seriously,' he replied.

The centenary of his birth is 21 July, and we take him seriously still. In the Internet age, his ideas appear more relevant than ever. The mark of a great idea is that it is obvious once stated. That how we think and act is shaped by the mode of communication itself is now obvious to all.

'Printing, radio, movies, TV - they actually alter our organs of perception without our knowing,' McLuhan wrote, observing and also anticipating how patterns of thought, friendships and philosophies would change in the electronic age. When McLuhan was raising his six children, being sent to one's bedroom was a punishment of deprivation; today, parents try to get their kids out of their bedrooms, away from the laptop, video games and mobile phones.

McLuhan is rightly celebrated as a scholar of communications and mass culture, but his ideas about communication and religion, which is at the heart of culture, are generally neglected. As a devout convert to Catholicism, a man who went to Mass daily, prayed the rosary with family every night, and rose early to read the scriptures, McLuhan's religious thinking is essential to understanding his entire work.

'Above all, he believed that because God made the world, it must, in the end be comprehensible, and that a sense of the divine could lead to an understanding of the mundane,' writes Douglas Coupland in his quirky biography of McLuhan, published as part of Penguin's 'Extraordinary Canadians' series. 'He came to feel that his religion was indeed a sense, a sensory perception that colored his life as much as, if not more so than, sight, taste, touch, hearing, smell or gravity. He'd found his key to eternity.'

Yet that same biography by the perceptive Coupland does not examine in depth McLuhan's Catholicism. 'In Jesus Christ, there is no distance or separation between the medium and the message,' McLuhan would write. 'It's the one case where we can say that the medium and the message are fully one and the same.'

McLuhan's famous dictum noted how something that is communicated - the medium - has its own effect on the message, independent of what is communicated. A text message may contain words of lapidary import, but the medium empties them of the significance they would assume if they were literally lapidary, carved in stone.

In the person of Jesus Christ, a divine person with a human nature, McLuhan saw that God reveals that He is personal, and that He freely implicates Himself in the full breadth and depth of the human experience. The incarnate God chose a medium - our human nature - that contains its own message, namely that God loves His creation, enters it, suffers for it and redeems it.

Coupland is right that McLuhan considered his faith like another sense. McLuhan knew that faith is a means of knowing reality, even as we use our senses to tell us about reality. The Christian faith added something deeper though for McLuhan. God came into this world of time and space in Jesus Christ; therefore, this world of time and space was infused with indications, intuitions and icons of the divine.

'It seems incongruent that the man could be ahead of the world in some ways and yet be retrograde in others,' writes Coupland, who considers Catholicism rather retro. 'And I don't think it's even about being ahead of the times or behind the times. Marshall didn't really believe in time. He believed in eternity. Being alive on earth was but one phase of a larger process.'

That larger process is what Christians call sanctification, becoming holy. McLuhan's Catholic faith is that God makes us holy through the sacraments - baptism and holy communion above all. The Catholic sacramental imagination, the conviction that God uses the tangible things of this world - water, oil, bread, wine - as means of grace, is arguably the key to McLuhan's broader analysis of communication and culture.

Sacraments communicate the presence of an intangible person - God - through tangible things. In the same way, our body makes presence an intangible reality greater than our body, namely our full personhood. The encounter of persons seeking not only communication but true communion - that deeper friendship rooted in a shared identity and mission - requires at some level an encounter of bodies, whether it is a smile, a handshake, a conversation or an embrace.

But our bodies are limited, and to overcome the distance that separates us we move to other forms of communication, each less corporeal than its predecessor - books, letters, phone calls, emails. 'When you are on the phone or on the air, you have no body,' McLuhan said, speaking about modern communications creating 'discarnate bodies.'

The electronic age is thus fundamentally anti-sacramental. It does not make the intangible present through tangible matter, but rather takes tangible bodies and discarnates them, converting a person to a series of digital impulses that are present everywhere and nowhere all at once.

Here we glimpse McLuhan's importance as a religious thinker for the 21st century. The human spirit is uneasy with ever more powerful communications that leave the desire for communion unfulfilled. That is an opportunity for a renewed proclamation of the incarnate, personal God. Yet at the same time the means of making present that incarnate God - the sacraments - are radically undermined by very same media culture.

Addressing this phenomenon is

to take up McLuhan's ideas thirty years after his death. He died in his sleep. The evening before a priest offered Mass in his home. McLuhan received Holy Communion, and then enjoyed a glass of champagne and a cigar. All three were media with a message: God is here, present in the good things He gives us, the greatest of which is communion with God Himself in Jesus Christ"); Bill Baker and Evan Leatherwood, "The Catholic Who Foresaw Facebook," *Catholic Herald*, 22 July 2011 (reprinted under the title of "Marshall McLuhan's Unmediated Faith," in *thirteen.org*, 12 September 2011) ("Though he was Canadian, McLuhan's conversion is best understood as belonging to the tradition of intellectual Anglo-Catholics like Evelyn Waugh, who were attracted to Catholicism in sharp contrast with the Church of England, and from the noisy disenchanted world that had grown up around it and, in many ways, because of it.

Protestantism was fundamentally linked in McLuhan's mind with the excesses of capitalism, and the disorienting world of advertising and mass media that it had spawned. Catholicism, in contrast, was staunchly on the side of art and intellect. When he converted in 1937 McLuhan came into the Catholic Church as a grateful refugee from a fearful world.

But in the end it was not ideas that brought McLuhan into the Church, but first-hand experience. Open-minded in all things, the young McLuhan decided to approach the Church on its own ground. He saw that, above all else, that ground was prayer. Though not yet a man of faith, McLuhan prayed fervently and persistently to be shown proof that Catholic doctrine is true. 'The evidence,' he says, 'came unexpectedly and from many quarters and unmistakably.' He never stopped praying during the five decades from his conversion to his death. Prayer for McLuhan was a 'constant appeal for daily nourishment.'

Though a man of profoundly complex ideas in his professional and public life, McLuhan felt no need to immerse himself in the subtleties of theology and dogma. For him, the Church was a living, sacred presence which entered his life on a level deeper than conscious thought. Faith, for McLuhan, was a matter of the human heart in resonance with the divine word.

The open-mindedness that served him so well in the world of scholarship was what brought him to the certainty of faith. And it was from the security of his faith that McLuhan could look out at a world in turmoil and, without sentimentality, bear honest witness to how it was changing"); Lorene Hanley Duquin, *A Century of Catholic Converts* (2003), p.99 ("He [said] that he believed the Catholic faith 'is the only religion – all sects are derivative.' He pointed out that the Catholic culture produced art, philosophy, poetry, music, mirth, fellowship, and a varied collection of saints. 'I find the fruits and theory of our sects very bitter,' he added…

In January 1939 he wrote Corinne [his future wife] a long letter explaining what Catholics really believe about the Mass, saints, and other devotions and practices.

'More important than any other single difference between Catholic attitudes and others is perhaps that the Catholic does not fear God, but has every reason to love him,' he explained. 'The first thought which a Catholic has of God is that which a man has for a real friend. It is only his second thought which may suggest to him how little he deserves such a friendship. Taking this fact, together with the social nature of the Church, it is easy to see why Catholics speak so freely and naturally of their prayers and devotions'"); *mcluhan.utoronto.ca.*

McMaster, James Alphonsus – editor; b. 1 April 1820, Duanesburg, New York; c. 1845; d. 29 December 1886, Brooklyn, New York; father a prominent strict covenant Presbyterian minister; studied at Union College, Schenectady, New York, in preparation for the ministry; left before graduating; in 1840 began studies for the Episcopal ministry at New York City's General Theological Seminary (influenced by Tractarianism and was dismissed in 1844); under the guidance of the Redemptorist Gabriel Rumpler and Bishop John McCloskey he became a Catholic; after his conversion, believing himself to have a vocation to the priesthood, he entered the Redemptorist Order and was sent to Belgium; soon found he was not suited to the religious life and returned to the United States; became a journalist and his abilities enabled him to write in several papers and periodicals; also contributed to the *The New York Freeman's Journal*, then owned by Bishop John Hughes, and one of the important Catholic American newspapers of the time; he bought the paper from Bishop Hughes in 1848, borrowing the money from George V. Hecker, brother of Isaac Hecker (see above); had an independence at some time averse to Episcopal supervision; tendency to quarrel; politically he was an Anti-Abolitionist and a States Rights Democrat; his editorial attacks on President Lincoln and his administration led to his being arrested in 1861 and confined for eleven months in Fort Lafayette as a disloyal citizen; he modeled his paper politically on Louis Veuillot and his *Univers*; after the events of 1870 he championed the rights of the Holy See; opposed the attendance of Catholic children at the public schools; as an old man his eccentricities adversely affected the paper and its circulation was much reduced; married Gertrude Fetterman in 1856 (seven children of the marriage, four of whom survived to adulthood; the three daughters joined religious orders); see Maurice F. Egan, "A Slight Appreciation of James Alphonsus McMaster," *U.S. Catholic Historical Society, Historical Records and Studies* (1921); Katherine Burton, *In No Strange Land: Some American Catholic Converts* (1942), p.77 ("The other novice was James McMaster, a country lad who by his appearance had excited the amusement of his more sophisticated colleagues at the Seminary when he first appeared there. He was over six feet tall, with a thin face, big nose, eagle eyes, and country ways. But the amusement soon passed as his colleagues had learned that he had an excellent brain and great ability to argue and know what he was arguing about. Though he proved to have no vocation and went home, he was later to become a prominent Catholic editor"); Sr. Mary Augustine Kwitchen, *James Alphonsus McMaster: A Study in American Thought* (2006); *ANB* ("For nearly forty years McMaster's newspaper served as a national organ for militant Catholicism as well as a northern voice defending the Democratic party's pro-southern platform. McMaster feared no opponent, from the U.S. president to the local archbishop, and he employed incendiary language as often as he thought necessary...

Catholics, lay and clergy, also became the butt of McMaster's vituperative rhetoric. He found especially distasteful any Catholic whom he judged to be willing to compromise the faith in favor of modernity").

MacNab, Sir Allan Napier, first Baronet - political leader; b. 19 February 1798, Newark (Niagara-on-the-Lake), Ontario, Upper Canada; c. 7 August 1862 (deathbed conversion); d. 8 August 1862, Dundurn Castle, Hamilton, Canada West; father was Lieutenant Allan MacNab, an incurable spendthrift and often in gaol for debt, who had come from Scotland to Canada as an officer in the Queen's Rangers; mother was Anne Napier, daughter of Captain William Napier, Commissioner of the Port of Quebec; baptized as an Anglican in 1799; family moved to York, Toronto; at the age of fourteen he fought in the War of 1812, taking part with his father in defense of York when it was attacked by an American army; articled as a law student in the office of the attorney-general; after graduating in law he moved to Hamilton and set up a successful law office; called to the bar in 1826 and became the first QC ever appointed in the province; in 1830 elected Tory member of the Legislative Assembly of Upper Canada for Hamilton (held this position for twenty-six years); he opposed the reform movement in Upper Canada and was part of the British militia that defeated the Upper Canada Rebellion in 1837; knighted for his actions in suppressing the rebellion (the Duke of Wellington referred to him as "the right arm of British power in North America"); initiated into Freemasonry in 1841 and became Provincial Grand Master of Canada; served in the Legislative Assembly of the Province of Canada; Prime Minister of the Province of Canada 1854-1856; after being forced to resign he went to England to recover and was created a baronet in 1858; settled again in Canada and was elected to the Legislative Council in 1860; was speaker at the time of his rather sudden death; one of the people responsible for the construction of the Great Western Railway (Ontario); thirteenth chief of clan MacNab; generous and sociable, with abounding confidence ("the gallant Knight of Hamilton," to his friends and admirers, and, to his enemies and his political opponents, "a bluff old Scotch bully"); married first to Elizabeth Brooke (d. 1826) (two children of the marriage); married secondly to Mary Stuart (d. 1846), a devout Catholic (two daughters, Sophia Mary and Minnie, both raised as Catholics; although their mother died when the daughters were very young; he never interfered with them in any way regarding the practice of their religion); Sophia Mary married William Coutts Keppel, Viscount Bury, later seventh Earl of Albemarle (d. 1894) (who was received into the Catholic Church 13 April 1879) and became Countess of Albemarle (mother of Arnold Allan Cecil Keppel, eighth Earl of Albemarle, and of nine other children); six months before his death he told Bishop Farrell that he intended to die a member of the Catholic Church; his deathbed conversion came as a sudden shock to his many Protestant friends and political associates; attacks were made upon Bishop Farrell by George Brown, the bigoted and fanatical editor of the *Toronto Globe*; doubts were expressed about it, but the bishop was called by a written invitation from Sir Allan to his dying bedside for "spiritual purposes"; his Catholic baptism is recorded at St. Mary's Cathedral, Hamilton, at the hands of John Farrell, Bishop of Hamilton; when his Protestant friends arrived for the funeral and were told of his conversion they all withdrew; buried in an unmarked grave in the Hamilton Catholic cemetery (Holy Sepulchre); see Rev. Brother Alfred Dooner, FSC, LLD, "The Conversion of Sir Allan MacNab, Baronet (1798-1862)," *Canadian Catholic Historical Association* (1942-1943), p.47 ("[George] Brown seemed to forget that the 'clan MacNab' was of Catholic birth, and that it had remained Catholic for hundreds of years, until the ancient faith was torn from it by violence and persecution. The clan MacNab had inherited, with the other Highlanders, the Catholic faith of Iona which Columba, in 563, had brought from Ireland to 'Abyn Hills.' If, therefore, Sir Allan did become a Catholic before his death, it was simply the return of a child to the paternal roof tree, the ancient Catholic Church of Scotland...

By a strange irony of fate, George Brown's own daughter became a Catholic after her father's death in 1917"); Donald R. Beer, *Sir Allan Napier MacNab* (1984) (contains an account on pp.395-398 of the conversion controversy); *DCB*.

Magaret, Helene – author of historical works; b. 18 May 1906, Omaha, Nebraska; c. December 1940; d. 1 February 1998 (Omaha, Nebraska); brought up as a Methodist; later attended also Congregationalist and Episcopalian churches, and Unitarianism (saw religion as a matter of subjectivist feeling); attended Grinnell College, Iowa, the Municipal University of Omaha, and took her BA degree at Barnard College, New York City; worked for several years as a Spanish translator and a secretary; then obtained MA and PhD degrees from the State University of Iowa; wrote a biography of Father Pierre-Jean De Smet, the great Jesuit missionary; worked as a Professor of English at several colleges, finally moving to Tarrytown, New York; see *Father DeSmet, Pioneer Priest of the Rockies* (1940); *Gailhac of Béziers* (1946); *Giant in the Wilderness: A Biography of Father Charles Nerinckx* (1952); "Prayer Was My Undoing," in John A. O'Brien, *The Road to Damascus, Vol. IV: Roads to Rome* (1955), p.137 ("Now I read Plato and Aristotle and learned the difference between that truth which is ascertainable by an accumulation of facts and that truth which can be known only through reason. I saw for the first time that humanitarianism is a doctrine grounded upon plumbing and the belly; that scientism, which promises to find a God or a no-God behind the atom, is repudiated by science itself.

Finally I learned that if a man throws faith out of the window, he must relinquish not only his faith in religion, but also his faith in science, in authority, in reason – even his faith in unfaith and in himself. Henceforth he dare not accept the diagnosis of his physician or eat the soup which his wife has prepared. At the same time it became clear that those scholars who so fervently advocated justification not by faith but by verification had rejected Christianity by any arbitrary act of faith in its falsehood. Most of them were woefully ignorant of both its doctrines and its history...

All of western culture is the fruit of Hellenism and Catholic Christianity and that Protestantism, being a branch cut from the parent tree, has borne no fruit"); *The Head on London Bridge: Life of St. Thomas More* (1956); *A Kingdom and a Cross: St. Alphonsus Liguori* (1958); *Felipe: Being the Little Known History of the Only Canonized Saint Born in North America* (1962).

Marianne of Jesus, Mother – see under Gurney, Marion Frances.

Marshall, Bruce D. – theologian; studied at Northwestern University (BA 1977); Yale Divinity School (MA in Religion); Yale University (PhD 1985); Lehman Professor of Christian Doctrine and Director, Graduate Program in Religious Studies, SMU Perkins School of Theology; Dallas, Texas; specialist in a wide range of theological topics in systematic theology and philosophy of religion; convert from Lutheranism to the Catholic Church; see (selective list) *Christology in Conflict* (1987); (ed), *Theology and Dialogue: Essays in Conversation With George Lindbeck* (1990); (ed), *Trinity and Truth* (2000) (with Daniel W. Hardy); "The Dereliction of Christ and the Impassibility of God," in Thomas Joseph White (ed), *Divine Impassibility and the Mystery of Human Suffering* (2009); "Renewing Dogmatic Theology," *First Things*, May 2012; Richard J. Neuhaus, "Bashing Darwin, Becoming Catholic," *First Things, On The Square*, 30 March 2007 ("Bruce Marshall of Southern Methodist University and a former Lutheran, protests the suggestion that he had an idea of catholicity and then looked around for a church that most closely approximated that idea. He writes: 'There have no doubt been converts who approached the matter in this way. But as for myself, I wasn't drawn to the Catholic Church because I had a catholic vision; I had a catholic vision because I was drawn to the Catholic Church. A catholic vision of things is the work of the Catholic Church, built up and borne by it over time in aid of its own witness and self-understanding. This is a product of the Catholic Church 'scrutinizing her own mystery,' as Vatican II says in another connection. Such a vision depends upon the reality of the Catholic Church, without which it would not be attractive or credible").

Marshner, William Henry – theologian and philosopher; b. 1943, Baltimore, Maryland; c. 1967; raised in the Lutheran Church; studied at Gettysburg College, Pennsylvania, as a pre-ministerial student (majored in Greek); postponed entry into the Lutheran seminary to study Semitic languages at Yale Graduate School out of an interest in Old Testament exegesis; member (and for a term chairman) of POR (Party of the Right)) at Yale; his conversion to the Catholic faith was influenced by apostolic tradition and the writings of the early Church Fathers; when he converted he became a Latin rite Catholic, but later joined a Melkite parish for reasons of spirituality and the beauty of the liturgy there; began writing for *Triumph* magazine (assistant editor 1971-1973) and for *The Wanderer* newspaper (Washington D.C. editor 1972-1975); MA from the University of Dallas in 1975; later gained the licentiate and doctoral degrees in sacred theology from the Lateran University,

Rome; teacher of Theology at Christendom College, Front Royal, Virginia, since 1977 (chairman of the Theology Department and a founding professor); theologian of the Thomistic school and specialist on ethics; author of many works and translator of Aquinas; see "Membership in the Church: Fundamental Questions," *Faith and Reason* (1976), p.54; *Annulment or Divorce?* (1978); "Early Christological Faith: An Ignatian Formula," *Faith and Reason* (1979), p.3; "Redemption and Preservation," *Faith and Reason* (1981), p.109; *Reasons for Hope: Apologetics* (1982) (with Warren H. Carroll, Kristin Popik, and Jeffrey A. Mirus); "Dignitatis Humanae and Traditional Teaching on Church and State," Faith and Reason (1983), p.222; "Is There a Natural Law?" in Ernest van den Haag (ed), *Smashing Liberal Icons: A Collection of Debates* (1984); *Cultural Conservatism: Towards a New National Agenda* (1987) (with William S. Lind); "The Structure of Platonism and the Dogma of the Trinity," *Faith and Reason* (1987), p.2; "Tale of Two Beatitudes," *Faith and Reason* (1991), p.218; "Concept, Judgment, and Dogmatic Relativism," in R. A. Herrera, James Lehrberger, O.Cist., and M. E. Bradford (ed), *Saints Sovereigns, and Scholars: Studies in Honor of Frederick D. Wilhelmsen* (1993), p.231; "Aquinas on the Evaluation of Human Actions," *The Thomist* (1995), p.355; "Can a Couple Practicing NFP Be Practicing Contraception?" *Gregorianum* (1996), p.677; *EWTN Audio Library, The Journey Home* (20 February 1998) ("I began to see that I could not hold fast to the historical-critical method [of biblical exegesis] and at the same time agree with what the Apostles were saying in the New Testament was the meaning of the Old Testament texts. Things that St. Paul was interpreting as a prophecy I was being taught not to interpet as prophecy. And things that Matthew had seized upon as a prophecy I was being taught not to take as a prophecy. I realized that something was wrong and I had to find my way to a more solid biblical exegesis that was in line with apostolic practice.

And so I said to myself, 'Look, I know that what's written in the New Testament is written under the inspiration of the Holy Spirit. This is telling me the meaning of the Scripture. But, now, what are these Apostles doing to find these meanings? How are they reading the Old Testament? What are their methods?'

Well, there's only one way to begin to get a clue to their methods, and that's to read the rest of Christian exegesis that comes from that age. So, I turned to the Epistle of Barnabas, which may have been written by the Barnabas who's mentioned in the Bible, but anyway it was written shortly after the ink was dry on the rest of the New Testament; and the Epistles of St. Ignatius of Antioch. There you see what that method of exegesis was. Also in the *Apologies* of Justin Martyr. And so I began to realize there was an apostolic tradition, and these works were showing me what it was, and it was the guide to the reading of the Scriptures.

Now, this was a great light to me. I realized that there was more to the technique of reading Scripture than I was being told in the theology I had grown up with. What we were told was *sola sciptura*, just what's in the book. Well, look, we all knew that the Epistle to the Romans was more important and more central than Second Chronicles. But the Bible doesn't say that. It was our own denominational tradition that made Romans central. Just as John's writings might be center for another ecclesial tradition.

And so I began to realize that there was a tradition that had shaped my approach to the Scriptures from the beginning, and now the thing to do was to get hold of God's tradition with a capital G, the apostolic tradition. And when I picked up the Apostolic Fathers it didn't take long before I realized what the early Church had been like…Once I realized that the early Church had been like the Catholic Church, and not like a Protestant one, I still thought maybe the Reformation had been justified, because maybe somewhere along the way the truth about how we are saved had been lost. And so I had to study that whole justification issue. Well, within a year I was satisfied that Luther had been wrong and the Council of Trent had it right"); *EWTN Audio Library, The Journey Home* (2 July 1999) ("It became clear to me that the prevalent methods of interpretation as you would find in a big Protestant divinity school like Yale Divinity School were producing a conflict between the Old Testament and the New. The critics were giving to the Old Testament a meaning in opposition to what the Fathers of the Church, indeed the Apostles, had said it meant. I was being taught to use tools that could not justify the way St. Paul interpreted the Old Testament, and couldn't justify what the Gospels said the prophecies meant. And so I knew something was wrong. And that was the first inkling that there was an apostolic way of reading the Bible. They learned it from Our Lord Himself, who applied Scriptures to himself and said, 'This is fulfilled today in your hearing.' And from that source they learn how to interpret the Scriptures, and that apostolic tradition had come down in the Church, and I realized I didn't know anything about it. And it became clear that I had to rethink *sola scriptura*. And then I started reading in the early Church Fathers, discovered Ignatius of Antioch, discovered the priesthood, the Episcopate, the Eucharist, that whole portrait of the early Catholic Church that emerges right there in the year 107AD, and it was so powerful and so compelling that I said to myself, 'Look, there's only one conceivable reason that I shouldn't be a Catholic, and that would be if somehow over the course of time the Church had lost its way on this cruciial business of how we are justified before God.

So, I took up the study of the doctrine of justification...A couple of very interesting things happened in that period. I was blessed to be able to read the works of St. Robert Bellarmine, who was the great Catholic apologist in the period right after the Council of Trent. And...I had lunch with a very famous Lutheran theologian... and I said, 'Well, the only reason that I can really think of why the Reformation might be justified is if there's a problem about the Catholic understanding of justification'... And this fellow said, 'Oh, that's not where the problem is.' I practically fainted. I said, 'That's not where it is?!' 'No, no, no, we're past all that. We basically agree about that. The real problem is about the nature and structure of the Church.' And I said, 'Well, if that's the problem, then Ignatius of Antioch is my answer, and bye-bye!'

So, then it was just a matter of overcoming, you know, my sins. Because, you know, I knew that the Catholic Church was the place to be for a whole year before I got there. It was just the lethargy of the flesh and the inertia, and all of these things that come into your mind, 'Oh my mother won't like it, and so-and-so won't like it, and so,' but in the end, with the help of God's grace, I finally did the right thing"); "Does Practical Reason Start with 'Good' or with 'Complete Good'?" *Faith and Reason* (2001), p. 339.

Mary Alphonsa, OP, Mother – see under Lathrop, Rose Hawthorne.

Mary Augustine, Sister - see under Barber, Jerusha (*née* Booth).

Mary Veronica, Mother - see under Starr, Mary Dannat.

Mayo, Virginia (born Virginia Clara Jones) – film actress; b. 30 November 1920, St. Louis, Missouri; c. early 1950s; d. 17 January 2005, Los Angeles, California; her aunt provided her with dancing instructors, after which she was recruited to appear in vaudeville; on Broadway in 1941; continued to work as a dancer, then signed with Samuel Goldwyn and went to Hollywood; appeared in several comedies; then appeared as the iconic voluptuous Hollywood beauty (it was said that she looked like a "pin-up painting come to life"; and reputedly the Sultan of Morocco declared that her beauty was tangible proof of the existence of God!); her major films were *The Best Years of Our Life* (1946) and *White Heat* (1949) (opposite James Cagney); many supporting roles; in 1947 she married the actor Michael O'Shea (1906-1973) (one child of the marriage); she and her husband co-starred in several stage productions and she did so on her own in others; one of Bishop Fulton Sheen's converts; a lifelong Republican in politics; see *Virginia Mayo, The Best Years of My Life* (2002); *ANB.*

Merrill, William Stetson - librarian, editor and author; b. 16 January 1866, Newton, Massachusetts; c. 24 December 1892; brought up in the sect of the Swedenborgians, but doubted it by the age of fifteen; claimed descent on his mother's side from one of the Mayflower pilgrims, Stephen Hopkins; educated at Harvard University (graduated in 1888); sometimes attended Episcopalian services; worked at the Harvard College Library 1884-1888 and the Newberry Library 1889-1931; did original work on the principles governing the consistent placing of books in a system of classification; editor of several journals on Catholic issues, librarianship, history, archaeology and literature; author of many articles; married Mary Hancock Allen, author of several stories for children; see essay in Georgina Pell Curtis, *Some Roads to Rome in America* (1909), p.333 ("There was...in the conception of a church that is one, holy, catholic, and apostolic something that appealed to my imagination as none of the sects had done; and that idea also conformed to my ideal of what a church should be. I readily admitted...that a church that is divinely established to guide men to eternal salvation must be an infallible interpreter of revelation. The American Constitution, although it was expressed in the clearest possible terms and subjected to the scrutiny of the finest legal minds of the time when it was promulgated, yet has required a judiciary culminating in the Supreme Court to interpret its meaning and to determine its application; and even these safeguards have proved insufficient to save the Union without an appeal to arms. How much more does the Bible, which is the constitution, as it were, by which man must direct his life in the Christian commonwealth, need an interpreter if Christian unity is to be maintained and the laws of the spiritual life wholesomely observed! A divine revelation must reveal truth to man. If it is liable to more than one interpretation, or is open to contradictory meanings upon vital points of belief - and there would be no need of revelation if no truths were vital or essential to salvation - then revelation is incomplete. The Catholic Church claims to be an infallible interpreter of the teachings of Christ as recorded in Scripture or handed down by tradition. Theologians may discuss, sometimes for centuries, questions of interpretation or of speculative theology; yet in the fullness of time, when the welfare of the faithful demands that a definition be made, the Church, acting under the divine guidance, is competent to make it. Revelation thus becomes a living truth and is not left, as Protestants make it to be, a dead letter.

The charge of intolerance, so often brought against the Church, was...my most serious difficulty. My intellectual sympathies were wide. I rejoiced in the progress of science and archaeology, and in the application of critical and historical methods to various branches of knowledge. Does not the Church oppose or at least discourage such inquiries, I asked [a] correspondent. The Catholic Church, he replied, encourages and fosters every movement by which the bounds of human knowledge are enlarged; but she tests results by the criterion of revealed truth. The scientific sphere along its periphery touches upon truths essential to man's spiritual welfare and to the conservation of these truths the Church cannot be indifferent. Her problem is, so to speak, how to be faithful to the divine 'deposit' of revelation and yet yield to reason its legitimate fruits. Her policy may change from age to age as to the means by which this end is to be attained, just as the policy of administration in the civil State changes with the times; but the obligation laid upon her by the divine commission remains constant. Scientists and critics are never so far-seeing as the Church; they look only along the line of their own researches. The Church, like a city set on a hill, sees in all directions. True catholicity is not an easy-going acceptance of opinions as all more or less true, but it is a critical incorporation of truth wherever found into the unity of one self-consistent whole. This catholicity is found in the philosophy as well as in the theology of the Church. The system of St. Thomas is founded upon the most comprehensive thinker of antiquity - Aristotle - who in turn utilized the best thought of his predecessors. The activity of Catholic scholars, of the so-called Neo-scholastic Movement, in interpreting and criticising the theories of modern psychologists and metaphysicians in the light of scholastic principles, bears testimony to the vitality and adaptability of the method. In Biblical studies too, the late Pope Leo, while urging Catholic students to keep abreast of the progress of criticism, pointed out the mode in which the language of the sacred writers should be interpreted in the face of seemingly contradictory evidence from science or archaeology.

I had reached a point in my search after religious truth where I was satisfied that the Catholic Church is the true fold; I need be a wanderer no longer...The Catholic is not bound to prove his faith, although when properly instructed he is fully capable of doing so. It is enough for him that the Catholic Church has an unbroken continuity with Christ and St. Peter, the leader of the Apostles. The Catholic Church is in possession, and possession is nine points of the law. It is for others to disprove, if they can, her claim to be the one fold of Christ; and to show that the promises of Christ do not apply to her. Such is the attitude in which I think the convert should place himself; standing thus upon the Rock of Peter, he is impregnable"); essay in Georgina Pell Curtis, *Beyond the Road to Rome* (1914), p.286 ("Two features of the Church have always interested and attracted me: one is her consistency, the other is her catholicity. The perfect accord of Catholic practice with Catholic belief is in itself a mark of stability and truth. This is notably the case with the doctrine of the Incarnation. Catholics alone, of all Christians - save perhaps the Greek Church - seem to realize the full significance of the phrase He 'was incarnate by the Holy Ghost of the Virgin Mary and was made man.' Devotion to the Blessed Virgin is the natural and fitting outcome of belief in this stupendous fact. Non-Catholics may say with their lips that Christ was God and was born of Mary; but they will not say 'Mary, the Mother of God,' thereby betraying their lack of real faith in the Incarnation. They may talk of the communion of saints, but they have no real communion with the saints. A few Anglicans pray to the saints in times of danger or of sorrow; but even the Anglicans ridicule prayers to St. Anthony for petty temporal favors: as if the doctrine implied that the saints were aristocrats, too high and mighty to concern themselves about minor matters.

Catholics take the words of our Lord in their literal sense when the context shows plainly that He intended them to be so understood. Non-Catholics are less concerned to ascertain what our Lord meant than what He ought to have meant to bring His words into harmony with the spirit of this age. The argument for the Real Presence, simply and forcibly put by Cardinal Gibbons in his *Faith of Our Fathers*, has always seemed to me unanswerable by anyone who concedes the authenticity of the Gospels. After Christ had said 'Unless ye eat the flesh of the Son of Man and drink his blood, ye shall not have life in you,' we are told that some 'murmured and walked no more with Him,' evidently because they took His words literally. Christ not only said nothing to correct such an interpretation of His words but even reiterated them to His disciples and then asked: 'Will ye go likewise?'

The doctrine of the Holy Eucharist pervades Catholic theology as the theory of gravitation enters into the natural sciences. Our worship is meaningless without it; with it, every act, every symbol is fraught with meaning. We believe that Christ is present on the altar and we bow the knee before Him; in passing a church a man lifts his hat and a woman crosses herself. By Holy Communion we 'become partakers of His Godhead who vouchsafed to become partaker of our manhood, as the Ordinary of the Mass so wonderfully expresses it. Consistency is characteristic of Catholicity as inconsistency is characteristic of Protestantism. Catholicity affirms, embraces; Protestantism denies, criticises.

Catholicity is to me the most stately of the notes of the Church. It is like a cathedral in its grandeur; lofty and solemn like the Gothic aisle, elevating like the spires pointing heavenward; resonant and stirring like the chimes in the belfry. Besides connoting the universal mission of the Church to all men, catholicity suggests to my mind the comprehensiveness and finality of the Catholic Church. She not only teaches to mankind the truths necessary to salvation but she embraces within the unity of her system all truths attained by human wisdom, genius and inquiry. Painted by the hand of Raphael upon the walls of the Camera della Segnatura of the Vatican, at the command of Pope Julius II, are four frescoes representing respectively Theology, Philosophy, Poesy and Jurisprudence - 'the four grand centers around which intellectual life revolves,' as Miss Starr calls them in her monumental work upon the subject. Nothing could teach more plainly the catholicity of the Church and the place which all knowledge and achievement hold in her estimation than these symbolical works of art adorning the Capitol of the Catholic world.

Theology, philosophy, canon law, painting, sculpture, education, all point to the universality of the Church. The most precious literary and artistic monuments of the ancient world have been preserved to us by the Church. The most valuable codex of the Bible is in the Vatican Library; her museum contains the masterpieces of Greek art; historical scholars from all over the world flock to Rome to use the Vatican Archives.. The theological system of the Church has been built up by intellectual giants from St. Augustine to St. Thomas. The official philosophy taught in her seminaries is the work of the keen intellects of the middle ages, based upon Aristotle, 'the Master of those who know,' as Dante calls him. The work of St. Thomas is a marvel of patient and critical examination of all human learning, so far as known to him at the time; an impartial synthesis of whatever commended itself to his comprehensive mind, and could be brought into agreement with the teachings of divine revelation. The revival of the philosophical principles of Scholasticism by Pope Leo XIII and the enthusiastic application of these principles, by the New Scholastics, to the solution of social and metaphysical questions of to-day, have shown how enduring are these fundamental teachings of the Schoolmen...

But why, we may ask, has the Church, if she is truly so Catholic in her spirit, opposed science at times and hindered the course of free inquiry? The answer is two-fold: (1) The Church does not oppose science or research of any kind as such, but only conclusions of science that contradict the truths of divine revelation; (2) the Church has a duty and a right to maintain the truths of revelation just as science has a duty and a right to seek truth in the natural order. Between these two orders of truth there can be no fundamental and final contradiction; but adjustment of apparently diverging conclusions presents a difficulty. The history of what has been called the 'conflict of science and religion' is really the history of efforts to solve a series of grave problems. The difficulty has been to discern the line between revealed truths and merely human opinion or tradition. If the Church has at times, in her praiseworthy zeal to maintain revealed truths, displayed a lack of consideration for scientific theories, so scientists, in asserting the rights of reason, have manifested indifference toward revelation. The error in viewing the situation has been to overlook the rights of revelation altogether and to judge the matter entirely from the point of view of science"); *Code for Classifiers* (1914, 1928, and 1939); *Catholic Authorship in the American Colonies* (1917); "Types of Philosophy," *The New Scholasticism*, July 1930, p.307; Anita S. Coleman, "William Stetson Merrill and Bricolage for Information Studies," *Journal of Documentation*, 2006, p. 462.

Merton, Thomas, OCSO (known in religion as Father Louis) – monk and writer; b. 31 January 1915, Prades, Pyrénées-Orientale, France; c. 16 November 1938 (received at Corpus Christi Church, Morningside Heights, New York; his only brother, John Paul (1918-1943), was received 6 July 1942); d. 10 December 1968, Bangkok, Thailand; both parents were artists, his father, Owen Merton (d. 1931), a New Zealander, a landscape painter, and an Anglican, his mother, Ruth, *née* Jenkins (d. 1921), an American and Quaker; baptized into the Church of England; family moved to the United States in 1916; brought up originally in New York; visits with his father to France (interest in Catholicism awakened by its Catholic culture), where he went to school for two years; moved to a school in England in 1928 and was for a while Anglican in religion; agnostic after the death of his father; spent a summer in Rome, which rekindled religious feelings; in 1933 he spent a year at Clare College, Cambridge, studying Modern Languages; rather wild youth and adolescence; in 1935 enrolled at Columbia University; graduated in English Literature in 1938; met Robert Lax (see above) at Columbia and they became close, lifelong friends; flirted briefly with Communism; discovered *The Spirit of Medieval Philosophy* by Etienne Gilson, which opened his mind to Catholicism; conversion influenced in particular by Jacques

Maritain, Thomas Aquinas, Gerard Manley Hopkins, Richard Crashaw and William Blake; taught at Columbia and wrote book reviews; taught English Literature at St. Bonaventure College, Olean, New York 1940-1941; made a retreat at the Trappist monastery of Our Lady of Gethsemani in Kentucky and on 10 December 1941 entered the monastery there; ordained priest 26 May 1949; many works in both poetry and prose (his autobiography, *The Seven Storey Mountain* was an international best-seller); suffered a vocational crisis in the 1950s arising out of the consequences of the conflict between his religious vocation and his conviction that he was meant to be a creative writer; consulted Gregory Zilboorg (see below), the Catholic psychiatrist, who was severely critical of his self-absorption and his tendency to intellectualize, rather than address, his own problems and their damaging effects on his vocation ("You want a hermitage in Times Square with a large sign over it saying *Hermit*"); worked for dialogue with other religions; took a non-violent stance in the 1960s over the race riots and the Vietnam War; became very interested in Eastern religions, especially Zen Buddhism; in 1966 he had an affair wuth a student nurse; in 1968 while attending a meeting of Asian Benedictines and Cistercians in Thailand, he stepped out of his bath, reached out to adjust an electric fan, apparently touched an exposed wire, and was fatally electrocuted; buried at Gethsemani Abbey; see (selective list) *The Seven Storey Mountain* (1948) (published in Great Britain under the title of *Elected Silence*) ("And the one big concept which I got out of [Etienne Gilson's *The Spirit of Medieval Philosophy*] was something that was to revolutionize my whole life. It is all contained in one of those dry, outlandish technical compounds that the scholastic philosophers were so prone to use: the word *aseitas*. In this one word, which can be applied to God alone, and which expresses His most characteristic attribute, I discovered an entirely new concept of God – a concept which showed me at once that the belief of Catholics was by no means the vague and rather superstitious hangover from an unscientific age that I had believed it to be. On the contrary, here was a notion of God that was at the same time deep, precise, simple and accurate and, what is more, charged with implications which I could not even begin to appreciate, but which I could at least dimly estimate, even with my own lack of philosophical training.

Aseitas – the English equivalent of a transliteration: aseity – simply means the power of a being to exist absolutely in virtue of itself, not as caused by itself, but as requiring no cause, no other justification for its existence except that its very nature is to exist. There can be only one such Being: that is God. And to say that God exists *a se*, of and by and by reason of Himself, is merely to say that God is Being Itself. *Ego sum qui sum.* And this means that God must enjoy 'complete independence not only as regard everything outside but also as regards everything within Himself'...

When St. Jerome says that God is His own origin and the cause of His own substance, he does not mean, as Descartes does, that God in a certain way posits Himself in being by His almighty power as by a cause, but simply that we must not look outside of God for a cause of the existence of God...

...I had never had an adequate notion of what Christians meant by God. I had simply taken it for granted that the God in Whom religious people believed, and to Whom they attributed the creation and government of all things, was a noisy and dramatic and passionate character, a vague, jealous, hidden being, the objectification of all their own desires and strivings and subjective ideals. The truth is that the concept of God which I had always entertained, and which I had accused Christians of teaching to the world, was a concept of a being who was simply impossible. He was infinite and yet finite; perfect and imperfect; eternal and yet changing – subject to all the variations of emotion, love, sorrow, hate, revenge, that men are prey to. How could this fatuous, emotional thing be without beginning and without end, the creator of all?...

I think one cause of my profound satisfaction with what I now read was that God had been vindicated in my own mind. There is in every intellect a natural exigency for a true concept of God: we are born with the thirst to know and to see Him, and therefore it cannot be otherwise.

I know that many people are, or call themselves, 'atheists' simply because they are repelled and offended by statements about God made in imaginary and metaphorical terms which they are not able to interpret and comprehend. They refuse these concepts of God, not because they despise God, but perhaps because they demand a notion of him more perfect than they generally find: and because ordinary, figurative concepts of God could not satisfy them, they turn away and think that there are no other: or, worse still, they refuse to listen to philosophy, on the ground that it is nothing but a web of meaningless words spun together for the justification of the same old hopeless falsehoods.

What a relief it was for me, now, to discover not only that no idea of ours, let alone any sensible image, could delimit the being of God, but also that we *should not* allow ourselves to be satisfied with any such knowledge of Him"); *Seeds of Contemplation* (1949); *The Waters of Siloe* (1949); *What is Contemplation* (1950); "The White Pebble," in John A. O'Brien (ed), *The Road to Damascus, Vol. II* (1950) ("The intellectual basis of my conversion was simply this: I found that God existed, and that He was the source of all reality; was, in fact, Reality, Truth, Life itself. He was pure actuality. On the other hand, I found that I had an intellect made to apprehend the highest and most perfect Truth in a supernatural intuition born of love, and that I had a free will that was capable of turning all the powers of my being either toward that Truth or away from it. Finally, since I could not attain this consummation by my own unaided natural powers, I would have to enter into the economy of means and helps called 'graces' won for me by Christ. Therefore I was baptized and became a Christian at least in name"); *The Ascent to Truth* (1951); *The Sign of Jonas* (1953); *Bread in the Wilderness* (1953); *No Man is an Island* (1955); *The Living Bread* (1956); *Praying the Psalms* (1956); *Silence in Heaven* (1956); *Thoughts in Solitude* (1958); *The Secular Journal of Thomas Merton* (1959); *Disputed Questions* (1960); *Spiritual Direction and Meditation* (1960); *The New Man* (1961); *New Seeds of Conteplation* (1962); *Life and Holiness* (1963); *Seasons of Celbration* (1965); *Conjectures of a Guilty Bystander* (1966); *Gethsemane: A Life of Praise* (1966); *Raids on the Unspeakable* (1966); *Contemplative Prayer* (1969); *Contemplation in a World of Action* (1971); *The Asian Journal of Thomas Merton* (1973); *He Is Risen* (1973); *The Collected Poems* (1977), *Day of a Stranger* (1981); *The Literary Essays* (1981); *A Vow of Conversation: Journals 1964-1965* (1988); John Howard Griffin, *A Hidden Wholeness: The Visual World of Thomas Merton* (1970); Monica Furlong, *Merton: A Biography* (1980); John Howard Griffin, *The Hermitage Journals: A Diary Kept While Working on the Biography of Thomas Merton* (1983); John Howard Griffin, *Follow the Ecstasy: Thomas Merton's Hermitage Years, 1965-1968* (1983); Michael Mott, *The Seven Mountains of Thomas Merton* (1984) ("Merton had made his decisions a few weeks earlier, when he had reached a point where his reading and his life came quietly and surely together. The book Merton was reading early in the afternoon that October day in 1938 was G. F. Lahey's life of Gerard Manley Hopkins, but all the books he had read that summer and much else were to be focused in a few minutes. It was raining hard outside the windows of the room on the top floor of 548 West 114th Street, and there was a certain pressure on Merton's time. He had spent the morning in the library. At four, he had to give a tutorial in Latin to one of the private students Miss Wegener had found for him to supplement his income. The student was ill in bed and lived in Central Park West.

In the Lahey biography, Merton had arrived at the passage where Hopkins broke through his own indecision during his conversion crisis. Hopkins had written to Newman asking for Newman's help. Merton asked no one's help. He closed the book and walked through the rain to the rectory of Corpus Christi. Father Ford was out. As Merton stood outside the door the maid had closed, uncertain what to do, he saw Father Ford approaching. They went together into the small parlor just off the entrance hall, which must have looked then very much as it does today. There, Merton told Father Ford he wanted to become a Catholic"); William H. Shannon, *Silent Lamp: The Thomas Merton Story* (1992); M. Basil Pennington, *Brother Monk, The Quest for True Freedom* (1997); Robert Royal, "The Several Storied Merton," *First Things*, February 1997; Lawrence Cunningham, *Thomas Merton and the Monastic Vision* (1999); Robert Waldron, *Walking with Thomas Merton* (2002); Fred Herron, *No Abiding Place: Thomas Merton and the Search for God* (2005); William H. Shannon, Christine M. Bochen and Patrick F. O'Connell, *The Thomas Merton Encyclopedia* (2006); Michael Baker, "The Tragedy of Thomas Merton," *superflumina.org*, 19 March 2007 ("On the morning of 29 July, before Mass, Merton spent an hour and a half with Dr Zilboorg who told him, bluntly - 'You are a gadfly to your superiors. You are very stubborn - you keep coming back until you get what you want. You are afraid to be an ordinary monk in the community. You and [another monk in the community] can very easily become a pair of semi-psychotic quacks. [When you were] talking to Dr Rome (about Zen) you thought only of yourself using him as a source of information and self-aggrandizement. You thought nothing at all of your priesthood, the apostolate, the church, his soul. You [would] like to be famous; you want to be a big shot; you keep pushing your way out - to publicity. Megalomania and narcissism are your big trends. Your hermit trend is pathological. You are a promoter. If you were not in a monastery, you are the type that would clean up on Wall Street one day and lose it all on the horses the next. It is not intelligence you lack, but affectivity. It will do you no good to be forbidden to write - you need silence and isolation, but it needs to be prohibited in your heart. If it is merely forbidden, it will not seem prohibited to you'...

In fairness to him, Merton reports this trenchant criticism in detail in his diary: 'While he said all this I thought "How much he looks like Stalin" but in reality I am tremendously relieved and grateful - and when I sung Mass with the monks I was praying hard to know what to do about it'"); Patricia Burton, *More Than Silence: A Bibliography of Thomas Merton* (2008); Jim Forest, *Living with Wisdom: A Life of Thomas Merton* (2008); Anthony E. Clark,

"Can You Trust Thomas Merton?" *This Rock*, May-June 2008; Lorene Hanley Duquin, *A Century of Catholic Converts* (2003), p.104; Ralph McInerny, *Some Catholic Writers* (2007); *The Thomas Merton Annual*; *The Thomas Merton Seasonal*; *thomasmertonsociety.org*; *ANB* ("Merton's writings from the 1940s into the late 1950s focused on his convictions about the need for prayer, penance, an ascetic approach to life, and the value of contemplative silence. These sentiments touched a deep nerve in American Catholicism, whose beau ideal had been the gregarious priest exemplified by Bing Crosby in the film *Going My Way* (1944) or the popular preacher Archbishop Fulton Sheen. Merton not only found millions of lay readers, but many men, inspired by his example, came to the monastery to try their vocation.

In the late 1950s Merton refocused his energies outward from the monk's interior life to the needs of the world. He wrote on issues of peace and racial harmony. His interest deepened in the religions of the East, especially Zen Buddhism. He wrote widely on literature. He also carried on a wide-ranging correspondence with religious leaders, literary figures, activists, and old friends").

Metcalfe, Ralph Harold – athlete and politician; b. 30 May 1910, Atlanta, Georgia; c. 1933 (his mother was received earlier; she had become interested in the Church because she had friends of her own, both white and black, who were of the Faith; she was impressed by their sincerity of purpose, their zealousness, their calmness in difficulties because of their religion); d. 10 October 1978, Chicago, Illinois; studied at Marquette University; silver medal in the 100 meters at the 1932 Olympic Games (bronze in the 200 meters); known as the world's fastest human 1932-1934; jointly held the world record of 10.3 seconds for the 100 meters (equaled it on a number of occasions as well as equaling the 200 meter record of 20.6 seconds); silver medal (behind Jesse Owens) in the 100 meters at the 1936 Olympic Games (gold medal in the 4x100 meter relay); completed a masters degree at the University of Southern California; joined the armed forces and served in World War II; coached track at Xavier University, Louisiana; became a successful businessman in Chicago; went into politics and served in the United States Congress, representing Illinois in the House of Representatives 1971-1978; in 1975 inducted into the United States Track and Field Hall of Fame; buried at Holy Sepulchre Cemetery, Alsip, Illinois; see "A Race Well Run," in Severin and Stephen Lamping, OFM (ed), *Through Hundred Gates* (1939) ("[N]one of the glories and honors that have come my way because I happen to have had some success in running, can compare with the pleasurable thrill that was sincerely mine when I realized, for the first time, that I was a Catholic. I have found new happiness in my religion, an undreamed-of consolation in my prayers. My conversion, very likely, was the most important single act in my whole life and I surely have no regrets. It may seem odd or unusual to many readers to hear of a Negro convert to the True Church, particularly in the United States. My race, however, is a rich field for domestic missionaries, cultivated more and more, and with increasing success. There has been some splendid work accomplished among my people in the cause of Catholicity. Schools and churches for colored parishioners testify to that fact"); Michael Cornfield, *Ralph H. Metcalfe: Democratic Representative from Illinois* (1972); William J. Baker, *Jesse Owens: An American Life* (1986); Arthur Ashe, Jr., *A Hard Road to Glory* (1993); *ANB.*

Meyer, Frank Straus – philosopher and political activist; b. 1909, Newark, New Jersey; c. 1972 (deathbed conversion); d. 1972; educated at Princeton University for one year, but then transferred to Balliol College, Oxford University; later studied at the London School of Economics (president of student union, but then expelled and deported in 1933 for Communist activism); member of the Communist Party of America, but then, partly under the influence of Friedrich Hayek (1899-1992), he converted to political conservatism in 1945; joined the staff of *National Review* magazine in 1955 (book review editor and author of a regular column, "Principles and Heresies"); close advisor to and confidant of the editor William F. Buckley, Jr.; founded the American Conservative Union; influenced by the political philosopher Eric Voegelin (1901-1985); developed a modern American conservative political philosophy under the name of fusionism, which aimed at uniting elements of libertarianism and traditionalism into a synthesis; his philosophy influenced President Ronald Reagan; see *The Moulding of Communists: The Training of the Communist Cadre* (1961); *In Defense of Freedom: A Conservative Credo* (1962); *The Conservative Mainstream* (1969); R. J. Stove, "From Marx to Maciel: What An Ex-Communist Can Teach Us About False Catholics," *Crisismagazine.com*, 5 June 2012.

Mielziner, Joseph ("Jo") – scenic and lighting designer for the theater; b. 19 March 1901, Paris, France; c. 1936 (his wife, Jeanne also a convert); d. 15 March 1976, New York City; from an artistic family; his grandfather, Rabbi Moses Mielziner, was one of the founders of Reformed Judaism; his father, Leo Mielziner, an artist, was a practising Jew though not orthodox; mother, Ella (*née* Friend) was a writer and an agnostic; his mother's brother was the actor-director, Kenneth MacKenna (1899-1962); moved to New York early on; studied at the Art Students League and the Pennsylvania Academy of the Fine Arts; after his education he spent a year in Europe studying the revolution in traditional stage design; in 1923 he worked for the Theatre Guild in New York as an assistant stage manager and bit actor; made his Broadway debut as a designer in 1927; worked on both stage plays and musicals; one of the most influential theatre designers of the 20th century, designing the scenery and often the lighting for more than two hundred productions, many of which became American classics; won an Academy Award for Best Color Art Direction; won five Tony awards and nominated for another seven; his conversion was influenced by G. K. Chesterton's *Orthodoxy*; attended a Mass at which the then Fr. Fulton Sheen preached and arranged to be instructed by him; designed the set for Fulton Sheen's television program *Life Is Worth Living*; see Milton Lomask, "Jo Mielziner's Story," in John A. O'Brien (ed), *The Road to Damascus, Vol. V: Where Dwellest Thou* (1956) ("[I]n the ensuing six months of instruction, priest and catechumen encountered only one serious obstacle. That had to do with the fact that Mother Church asks her children to observe certain restrictions consistent with a love of God and a belief in the dignity of His creatures. It was not that Mielziner wanted to do or think evil, for he had been brought up by people faithful to the reason and morality of their own religions. But as an artist, the disciplinary requirements of the Church struck him at first glance as abridging intellectual freedom itself.

Father Sheen did not argue with his pupil. He merely asked him, 'And are there no limitations which you find it necessary to observe in your own work?' Mielziner thought that over. He saw that there were limitations indeed. There was the limitation of space. It is commonplace for the scene designer to be asked to create an impression of something close to infinity on what is after all only a telephone booth of a platform some forty feet wide at most and some twenty-six feet or less deep. There are limitations imposed by the author of the play or musical… Finally, there are the limitations of art itself. There are after all only so many colors, and only so many tools, each capable of being made to do only so many things.

It came to Mielziner that in this respect art is a reflection of life itself. The limitations inherent in the nature and purpose of the human being are not restrictions on his freedom but merely the conditions under which it exists. Every man makes his choice. He observes these inherent limitations and so freely works out his destiny within them. Or he flouts them and runs the risk of losing the freedom they make possible"); Mary C. Henderson, *Mielziner: Master of Modern Stage Design* (2001); his papers are at the New York Public Library for the Performing Arts, Lincoln Center; *ANB.*

Miller, Ann (born Johnnie Lucille Ann Collier) – actress and dancer; b. 12 April 1923, Chireno, Texas; d. 22 January 2004, Los Angeles; father a criminal attorney who defended Bonnie Parker and Clyde Barrow, and George "Baby Face" Nelson; suffered from rickets as a young child, and was given ballet lessons to strengthen her legs; a natural dancer; her mother separated from her father and took her to Hollywood in 1933; earned money with a tap routine in clubs; had small roles in films; the RKO studio signed her to a contract in 1937 (she produced a fake birth certificate giving her birth year as 1919); the studio renamed her Ann Miller; her break through was in *You Can't Take It With You* (1938); successful in a revue on Broadway in 1939; starred in several musicals for Columbia, becoming somewhat typecast as a dancer; co-starred for MGM in several major films, *Easter Parade* (1948), with Fred Astaire and Judy Garland, in *On The Town* (1949), with Gene Kelly, in *Kiss Me Kate* (1953), and several others in the 1950s; tall and slim, her legs were insured for $1 million; famed for her speed in tap-dancing; in 1955 she started a course of instruction with a view to being received into the Catholic Church, but did not convert; went back to clubs and Broadway, and then on to television; at one time had an interest in spirituality and reincarnation; married three times, each briefly (divorce in the first two; the third was annulled); received into the Catholic Church on her deathbed; buried in Holy Cross Cemetery, Culver City; see *Miller's High Life* (1972) (with Norma Lee Browning) (memoir); Jim Connor, *Ann Miller, Tops in Taps: An Authorized Pictorial History* (1981); *ANB.*

Miller, Walter Michael Jr. – science fiction writer; b. 23 January 1923, New Smyrna Beach, Florida; c. 1947; d. 9 January 1996, Daytona Beach, Florida; at school he called himself an atheist; studied at the University of Tennessee, Knoxville; in World War II he served in the Army Air Corps as a radioman and tail gunner; he flew fifty-three bombing missions over the Balkans and Italy, including the bombing of the Benedictine Abbey at Monte Cassino, which proved a traumatic experience for him; married Anna Louise Becker (d. 1995) in 1945 (four children of the marriage), but lived with another science fiction writer, Judith Merril (1923-1997), in 1953; between 1951 and 1957 he wrote many short stories (winning a Hugo Award in 1955) and television scripts; he and his family moved to Florida in the mid-1950s; had a great success with the novel *A Canticle* *for Leibowitz*, a post-apocalyptic novel based on three earlier novellas, and revolving around the canonization of a character named Saint Leibowitz; the book won the 1961 Hugo Award for Best Novel and was praised highly by Walker Percy (see below); the book sees the Catholic faith as a force for stability during the dark periods of history; he published nothing more during his lifetime; in his later years he became a recluse (avoided contact with family members and never allowed his literary agent for forty years to meet him) and suffered from severe depression; he completed a six hundred page manuscript for a sequel to *Canticle*; shortly after his wife's death he shot and killed himself (despite the fact that the third section of *Canticle* is a polemic against suicide); the sequel, under the title (given by Miller himself) of *Saint Leibowitz and the Wild Horse Woman*, was completed by the science fiction writer Terry Bisson (b. 1942) and published in 1997; see *A Canticle for Leibowitz* (1959); *The Science Fiction Stories of Walter M. Miller, Jr.* (1977); *The Best of Walter M. Miller, Jr.* (1980); *Saint Leibowitz and the Wild Horse Woman* (1997); W. H. Roberson and R. L. Battenfield, *Walter M. Miller, Jr.: A Bio-Bibliography* (1992); Rose Secrest, *Glorificemus: A Study of the Fiction of Walter M. Miller, Jr.* (2002); W. H. Roberson, *Walter M. Miller, Jr.: A Reference Guide to His Fiction and His Life* (2011); Terry Bisson, "A Canticle For Miller; or, How I Met Saint Leibowitz and the Wild Horse Woman but not Walter M. Miller, Jr.," terrybisson.com ("*Canticle* is one of the few science fiction books not only known but read outside the field (unlike, say, *Dune* or *Stranger in a Strange Land*, which render up their pleasures only to those already attuned to the genre). A novel of nuclear anxiety written in the 1950s, it tells the story of an order of monks in the Southwest and their efforts to keep scientific knowledge alive in the new Dark Age after the 'Flame Deluge' or nuclear war. Leibowitz Abbey, and the neighboring village of Sanly Bowitz, are both named after a Los Alamos scientist who became a monk, was martyred by a mob and is - just maybe - a saint. Leibowitz was Jewish, the joke of the title.

The first major post-holocaust SF novel, *Canticle* is a 'fix-up' of three related novellas, which cover some two thousand years, during which science is reborn and destroys civilization once again. 'It was a good year for the buzzards' is Miller's persistent refrain. He didn't, to put it mildly, believe in Progress...

Miller's history is cyclical (nothing gets better) and his heroes are holy fools. He expects little from people, yet loves and forgives them, over and over - which is what Christianity is all about. I guess").

Mills, David – editor and writer; b. 1957; c. 2001 (Easter Vigil; received with his wife and four children); raised in New England in a nominally Christian way; then came under the influence of a saintly Baptist deacon; early on influenced by J. R.. R. Tolkien's *The Lord of the Rings*, appreciating its Christian vision; became a conservative Episcopalian; in that position he was a member of the board of the Evangelical and Catholic Mission and of its successors, the Episcopal Synod of America and Forward in Faith; editor of the groups' theological journal *The Evangelical Catholic* 1986-1998; influenced by Graham Greene's novels and by Flannery O'Connor's letters; editor of *Touchstone Magazine* 2003-2008; executive editor of the journal *First Things*; columnist for *Lay Witness* magazine and the *Inside Catholic* website; contributor to *The National Catholic Register*, *The New Oxford Review*, *First Things*, and *Our Sunday Visitor*; has won many awards as an editor and writer; see (selective list) *The Pilgrim's Guide: C. S. Lewis and the Art of Witness* (1998); *Knowing the Real Jesus* (2001); "It Came from the Roman Church…," *This Rock*, April 2002; "The Church Domestic," *This Rock*, October 2002; *EWTN Audio Library, The Journey Home* (9 December 2002); "Sharing the Church," *This Rock*, January 2004; "Contraception and Conversion," *Crisis Magazine*, December 2008 ("Sometimes a 'progressive' Catholic asks me why my family and I became Catholics…I will often say, in as cheery, boosterish, and cheerleading a voice as I can manage, 'My wife and I discovered the truth of the Church's teaching on contraception, and after a while we just had to join the one body in the world that was telling the truth about it.' That usually shuts down the conversation.

The Church's teaching on contraception was not the only thing that drew us to the Church, of course, but it ranked high, not least because the teaching so thoroughly contradicted everything we had been taught that it had to be either the truth held with supernatural aid or a delusion held for any number of foolish or corrupt reasons.

Everyone I knew, well into my early thirties, assumed that sexual activity without the 'risk' of children was perfectly natural and that the number and spacing of your children was something for you to decide. Even among Christians, no one would have blinked at a married couple who said that they were not going to have children, as long as they in some way (perfunctorily was okay) invoked God's will…

I first began to wonder about contraception as a pro-life activist, when I noted (after reading Joseph Sobran [see below] in the *Human Life Review*) its emotional association with abortion: Contraception sometimes fails, and some people find this failure to be unfair, denying them the child-free sex to which they feel entitled, and thus are inclined to abortion to correct the 'injustice' of having a child they didn't intend. They assume that if children were to be chosen and scheduled, the untimely, unchosen child could be rejected. Aborting him might be 'tragic,' but it was 'a tragic necessity.'

At first I thought the claim absurd, but then I heard some Evangelical Episcopalian friends - mainstream conservatives - say this very thing. They assumed that, for a married couple at least, sexual intercourse whenever desired was mandatory, but that having the baby that resulted was not. This didn't change my mind, but it worried me. Contraception kept bad company.

A few years later, involved in the debate over homosexuality within the Episcopal Church, I was disturbed by the difference between the conservatives' approval of non-procreative sex for married people and their loud opposition to non-procreative sex for homosexual people. They never got beyond the Bible verses against homosexuality, which seemed arbitrary without some idea what sexuality is for - and as a result, the homosexualists who *did* have some idea what sexuality is for seemed to have the better arguments (though they were wrong).

I began to wonder about the end for which sexuality is given us, and to see that sexual activity couldn't be reduced to an emotional connection unrelated to the physical purposes of the organs involved. God had a reason for forbidding people to use their sexual organs with members of their own sex, but this reason implied that he intended them to be used only in certain ways even with a member of the other sex to whom they are married.

My assumptions about sexuality were further disturbed by the unanimity of the Church's witness. Anglicans, having no Magisterium, look to the Christian tradition for guidance, and traditional Anglicans have always weighted it very heavily. And here - though 'traditionalist' Anglicans were almost always in favor of contraception, and even used their opposition as an argument against Catholicism - was a teaching about as universal as could be asked for.

These hints led me to read up on a subject to which I would have given no attention at all before. Gradually I, and my wife too (and on her own), began to understand and then to accept, and finally to appropriate for ourselves, the Church's teaching, which just a few years before had seemed to us utterly bizarre.

When we took it up as a practice, it changed our marriage as the articles had promised. Obedience led to the gift of our two youngest children, born after we accepted the teaching but before we became Catholics, and that addition radically changed our lives for the better. We couldn't imagine life without them, not just for themselves but for the kind of family their addition created.

We naturally noticed, as we grew closer to the Church, that only she proclaimed this truth that, to us, was increasingly self-evident and objectively life-changing. And she did so with a complex and extensive and subtle understanding of man, sexuality, and society, also found in its fullness nowhere else.

To us, the Church's insight and her courage in proclaiming it to a society that thought the whole idea daft was a sign - one of many, but one of the very biggest - that we were not yet where we ought to be. Gratitude for the life the Church had brought us, even when we remained outside her borders, drew us in"); *Discovering Mary: Answers to Questions About the Mother of God* (2009); "From Debate to Discovery: Anatomy of a Conversion," *New Oxford Review*, April 2010 ("People find themselves drawn to the Catholic Church because something in her attracts them, like the order of the liturgy or the depth of the theology. When the romance begins to feel as if it might develop into commitment, they begin to ask questions and pose objections. If they persevere, they come to love the Church, and the way they ask the questions, and the questions they ask, change. They move from debating the Church to discovering the Church.

This description may be of some value to those given the chance to respond to people drawn to the Church. Catholics, and even some converts themselves, do not always understand this movement. They respond as if conversion were a matter of intellectual conviction, and emphasize the superiority of the Catholic case to the Protestant or the secular. The Church does have the better case, but they would often do better to emphasize The Thing itself, rather than what it is not.

When I moved from debate to discovery, I would sometimes ask Catholic friends about the Church and Catholic life, wanting them to explain what it felt like from the inside. They would almost always give me an answer from the apologetic books, which I had already learned. I wanted something like 'In confession, I've really had to face…' or 'Let me tell you about the time I turned to the Blessed Mother…' or 'I love to pray before the Blessed Sacrament because…' I tried to ask more penetrating questions, and was usually answered with a quizzical look and a repetition of the apologetic answer.

I did not find the directly argumentative works very helpful, except at two stages. When I first found myself attracted to the Catholic Church - and 'found' is exactly the right word - they helped explain some Catholic beliefs that baffled or bothered me, and helped me justify pursuing the attraction. When I began to turn to the Church, and my affections were changing faster than my convictions, they provided the kind of point-scoring I found reassuring and confirming. 'Point-scoring' is not meant dismissively, because there were points to be scored, and value to me in seeing them scored.

As I grew closer to the Church, I began to lose interest in having my questions answered in that way, and, I think, looking back after nine years as a Catholic, that this movement in my thinking was right. Judging the Church by her score would have been like listing my girlfriend's virtues and vices (as I saw them then) and deciding whether to call her again based on the final score. I would have missed the deeper realities, the ones apologetics doesn't touch.

When first attracted to the Church, one naturally notices the areas where she says 'no' to one's assumptions and beliefs, the same way the immigrant to a foreign country first notices all the differences and especially the differences that make his time there harder - different ways of queuing up in shops or different relations to time and schedules, for example, or different attitudes toward private property. But the experience ought to lead one to a deeper vision of the whole, in which the questions cease to be so pressing because the beauty and coherence of the whole become more obvious. The immigrant adapts to the differences, and begins to understand and enjoy the culture they express, and eventually to think and feel the way the natives do.

Although, and this is something converts should remember, he will never think and feel exactly as they do because he did not grow up there. What for them is instinct will always be for him to some extent analysis followed by choice. Many practices will always feel awkward and many ideas dubious because he does not know everything they know, even if they don't know all they know. The Thing he loves will always be a mystery.

The particular arguments and answers were important to me, but increasingly so as confirmation of the whole. I was moving from the point where I could think the Church is right about this but wrong about that, so that the decision to join was prudential and comparative - Where can I serve God best? How does it look next to the alternatives? - to the point where I could only believe that the Church was right about everything or reject her, the point where the decision to commit or not had to be total and final"); "Catching Roman Fever", *The Coming Home Network International*, *Conversion Stories*, *chnetwork.org*, 12 January 2011 (extended version of the article that appeared in *This Rock*, January 2002; also in Patrick Madrid (ed), *Surprised by Truth 3* (2002), p.23) ("Roman Fever was, at least for me, much like malaria. It comes and goes unexpectedly and without warning. When you have it you feel it is going to take you off, but when you get better you can easily forget it. When you do not have it, you will tend to think of it as a chronic illness to be suffered until it goes away and you can get back to doing what you think you are supposed to be doing.

I would get the fever most often when reading Catholic writers, though it sometimes came apparently unprovoked. J. R. R. Tolkien's *The Lord of the Rings*, and Evelyn Waugh's later novels, and Flannery O'Connor's letters, and Graham Greene's 'Catholic novels,' and almost any of G. K. Chesterton's books could set it off. Sigrid Undset's *Kristin Lavransdatter* could bring it on, as could Walker Percy's essays and Ronald Knox's apologetics. I loved John Henry Newman - he is my hero - but I knew that if I read him I would feel this painful aching desire to do what he had done.

I could get the fever from reading writers who did not believe in Catholicism, and even from writers who hated it. I had read Albert Camus' books from early adolescence, and they had sometimes led me to look wistfully at the Catholic Church long before I had the slightest interest in joining her, perhaps because the faith he did not believe in was the Catholic faith. Several of the most honest and acute analysts of the modern world had the same effect. George Orwell hated the Catholic Church, but almost everything he wrote showed me that she alone was the answer to the questions he (and I) asked.

At times, I carefully avoided anything that might bring on Roman Fever. I would leave Chesterton's books on the shelf and busy myself with something else. I did not want to feel so strongly an urge to do what I did not want to do, and I am not sure, now, if I was not sinning against the light. Like malaria, it kept coming anyway, till one day I realized that if I kept refusing the invitation it might not come again….

In the end, two insights brought me over the line I had been unwilling to cross. The first was the simple realization that I had to fish or cut bait, lest (to mix metaphors) I harden my heart one too many times and never get Roman Fever again. I became a Catholic in part because one day I realized that God might stop giving me such times when my heart and mind were so well allied that I could more easily overcome the inertia that kept me where I was. This insight was, as far as I can tell, the work of the Spirit.

If the first insight pulled me into the church, the second insight pushed me in. About a year before we began instruction, I sat for several days in a conversation about divorce and remarriage with twelve Evangelicals, all learned, all biblically conservative, all holding more or less the same hermeneutic, who came to (I think) nine different and to some extent deeply opposed positions.

The decision they came to was a now familiar appeal to a shared ideal (lifelong marriage) with a range of views on the acceptable ways to fail to reach the ideal. Most of them would have said the Bible is on the question of divorce not clear or can be read in different ways, at which point one has to ask quite what use is it, if it fails to teach clearly on this matter?

This diversity bothered me, but what bothered me more was that no one but me found it a problem. Here were learned and godly men who read the Bible the same way, who could not agree on what it said about a matter crucial to the Church's life and to human happiness, but thought God had left the issue open, the sole evidence of which was that they did not agree with each other.

I thought that God could not have meant us to live in such confusion and with such an effectively minimalistic doctrine — which had already grown and would grow ever more minimal as the self-identified Evangelical party broadened in theology. But this minimalism, I suddenly realized, was one of the principles of the church to which I belonged, as held by its finest servants. This, I realized, was not the Catholic Church. I had known this for years, but only with the earnest discussion of my friends, showing that those with the highest view of the authority of Scripture could not tell you authoritatively what it said, did the insight become a reason to move.

The Deeper Reason: I do not want to give the wrong impression in explaining the seductions of Roman Fever. If it kept me from becoming a Catholic when I should have done, then I had it in the first place because I began to love the Catholic Church. I began to love her saints, and great men like John Paul II and Cardinal Ratzinger; and saw that she alone fought for the things I was fighting for, like the lives of the unborn; and found in her leading minds a commitment to reason found nowhere else; and found in her also a pastoral wisdom which understood human frailty without giving up the call to sanctity; and so on, and so on.

But in the end, I began to love the Catholic Church for the Mass, because in her my Lord and God came to me. My Roman Fever finally broke when I could no longer stay outside the place where God could be touched and tasted").

Minoka-Hill, Lillie Rosa – physician; b. 30 August 1876, St. Regis Mohawk Indian Reservation in northern New York; d. 18 March 1952, Fond du Lac, Wisconsin; daughter of Joshua G. Allen, a Quaker physician, and a Mohawk Indian woman of unknown name, who died following childbirth; her father sent her to live with maternal relatives on the reservation; she then went to a Quaker boarding school; after graduation she went to live in a convent in Quebec, where she rejected her Quakerism and became a Catholic; entered the Woman's Medical College of Pennsylvania in 1896 (graduated in 1899); after an internship there she ran a successful medical practice with another woman graduate, Frances Tyson; married Charles Abram Hill, an Oneida Indian, in 1905; gave up her medical practice, farmed with her husband and brought up six children; she became the informal doctor for this Indian area (lack of a license restricted her services); after her husband's death in 1916, she struggled on and extended her medical practice to non-Indian areas also; she obtained her license in 1934; despite a heart attack in 1946, she continued her practice into the 1950s; awarded many honors, including being adopted by the Oneida tribe of Wisconsin; see *ANB*.

Minton, Sherman ("Shay") – politician and judge; b. 20 October 1890, Georgetown, Floyd County, Indiana; c. 1961; d. 9 April 1965, New Albany, Indiana; his father, a day laborer for the railway, became disabled by heatstroke and could not work; the family had to subsist on their small farm; his mother died during an operation for breast cancer carried out by a traveling doctor (he blamed God for her death and refused to go to church); his father took him to political rallies; often in trouble as a youth, but changed his outlook and wanted to become a lawyer; worked in a meat packing plant and saved enough money to go to school; studied at Indiana University 1911-1913 (graduated top of his class); went to Benjamin Harrison School of Law, Indiana (graduated in 1915, again top of his class); won a one year post-graduate scholarship to Yale University; opened a law practice in Albany in 1916; when the United States entered World War I he enlisted in the army; commissioned as a captain and served in France and Belgium; after the war he studied law for several months at the Sorbonne in Paris; at home he entered politics as a Democrat; unsuccessful in two attempts to get into Congress; elected to the Senate in 1934 as a supporter of the New Deal; he was fiercely partisan in his views, supporting President Roosevelt's unsuccessful court packing plans; lost his Senate seat in 1940; in 1941 appointed as a judge of the Seventh Circuit Court of Appeals; in contrast with his liberalism as a Senator, he took a conservative position as a judge, being always an advocate of judicial restraint; forged a high reputation; a close friend of President Truman, he was nominated by him to the Supreme Court, and appointed in 1949 (served until 1956); generally ruled in favor of order over freedom; voted to uphold anti-communist legislation; against racial segregation and voted to strike down the school segregation practices at issue in *Brown v Board of Education* (1954); he was a late convert who had shunned Christianity most of his life; buried in Holy Trinity Cemetery, New Albany; married Gertrude Gurtz, a Catholic, in 1917 (three children of the marriage); his eldest son Sherman Anthony Minton Jr. (1919-1999) was an eminent herpetologist and toxicologist; see William Franklin Radcliff, *Sherman*

Minton: Indiana's Supreme Court Justice (1996); Linda Gugin and James E. St. Clair, *Sherman Minton: New Deal Senator, Cold War Justice* (1997); *ANB.*

Mises, Richard Marten Edler von – scientist and mathematician; b. 19 April 1883, Lemberg, Austria-Hungary (now Lviv, Ukraine); d. 14 July 1953, Boston, Massachusetts; born into a Jewish family; his brother was Ludwig von Mises (1881-1971), the economist; educated at the Vienna University of Technology (graduated in mechanical engineering); PhD awarded in 1908; appointed Professor of Applied Mathematics in Strasbourg in 1909-1918; several posts in Germany, but on the rise to power of Hitler he went to the University of Istanbul and then on to the United States to Harvard University where he stayed until his retirement in 1953; chiefly known for his work on the foundations of probability and statistics; introduced the famous "birthday problem," which asked how many people must be gathered before the probability of two people sharing a birthday exceeds 50 percent (the surprising answer: 23); published 142 papers; converted to Catholicism shortly before World War I but became an agnostic later; authority on the poetry of the Austrian poet Rainer Maria Rilke !875-1926) and of the Austrian novelist, Robert Musil (1880-1942); married Hilda Geiringer (1893-1973) in 1943 (no children of the marriage); see Philipp Frank and Garrett Birkhoffis (ed), *Von Mises's Selected Papers* (2 vols, 1963-1964); his papers are in the archives of Harvard University; *ANB* ("He was 'an elegant, rich, intellectual young gentleman,' who discovered a lifelong interest in Catholicism and in the works of the Austrian poet Rainer Marie Rilke at this time. His mathematical interests also flourished").

Monroe, James – soldier; b. 10 September 1799, Albemarle County, Virginia; d. 7 September 1870, Orange, New Jersey; his father, Andrew Monroe, was a brother of President James Monroe (1758-1831); he greatly resembled his uncle; educated at the U.S. Military Academy at West Point (graduated in 1815); commissioned a lieutenant of artillery; wounded in the war with the Algerian pirates in 1815; served in the army until resigning in 1832; moved to New York and entered public life; elected to Congress 1839-1841; member of the New York legislature 1850-1852, then retired from public life on the death of his wife; before the Civil War he sought to prevent the secession of his native state of Virginia; strong upholder of the Union during the war; his brother Andrew F. Monroe (1824-1872), also a graduate of the U.S. Naval Academy, converted in China in 1853, joined the Society of Jesus in 1854, and was ordained priest in

1860; his uncle's eldest daughter, Eliza, often served as the official White House hostess during her father's presidency due to her mother's ill health; after her father and husband died, Eliza moved to Paris and became a Catholic, living out her remaining days in a convent; see *Catholic Encyclopedia.*

Moody, John – financial analyst and investor; b. 1868, Jersey City, New Jersey; d. 16 February 1958, Los Angeles, California; brought up "a Low Church Protestant Episcopalian, then a Broad Church Episcopalian"; developed the rating of bonds; founder of the credit rating agency Moody's Investors Services, which still issues Moody's Manuals; appointed by Pope Pius XI Knight Commander of the Order of the Holy Sepulchre of Jerusalem; inspired by Peter Maurin, co-founder with Dorothy Day (see above) of the Catholic Worker Movement; married to Anna Mulford Addison (1877-1965); his children included Ernest Addison Moody (1903-1975), philosopher and medievalist; see *The Masters of Capital: A Chronicle of Wall Street* (1919); *The Railroad Builders* (1919); *The Long Road Home* (1933) (autobiography); "As A Little Child," in Severin and Stephen Lamping, OFM (ed), *Through Hundred Gates* (1939) ("I am asked…'Why, in leaving your agnosticism behind, did you jump over Protestantism and choose the Catholic Church, rather than one of the other Christian bodies of the orthodox type?'

The answer to that is easy. Many of these critics freely admit that their own partly self-constituted beliefs are 'wobbly and jittery,' uncertain and shaky, just as were mine in the old days. Now, after almost a lifetime of holding 'wobbly and jittery' notions of truth, I had at last made the discovery that what I was starving for, were not more wish-fancies, as formulated from the views of Tom, Dick, and Harry. What I wanted was some dependable authority to guide me to all truth, and correctly interpret it for me. But could such an authority be found? Then I ran across a statement of G. K. Chesterton, in his *Orthodoxy*, published thirty years ago. He said, 'Christianity came into the world firstly in order to assert with violence that a man had not only to look inwards, but to look outwards, to behold with astonishment and enthusiasm a Divine Company and a Divine Captain.'

From that hour I began to 'look outwards.' I gave up relying on my inner consciousness; I ceased depending wholly on private judgment. Instead I turned to the storehouse of truth. I had discovered that Truth is One, and is objective, not subjective; and that trying to find it by the 'inner light' alone would forever lead to frustration.

To explain more concretely. My whole investigation of the Catholic point of view had been inconclusive and futile until I had definitely begun to seek for the proof of the infallible authority of the Catholic Church. This at once led me, of course, to an examination of the Catholic Papal question - the Church's claim that she speaks with the infallible authority of Christ. And with what result? Why, of course, I discovered 'with astonishment and enthusiasm a Divine Company and a Divine Captain.'

Objective facts have always appealed to my more practical side; all my business life has been spent in a place where one's exclusive urge is to secure the facts and get results from them. I have sometimes said it was my Wall Street training that led me into the Catholic Church! And so now, in my accustomed fact-finding way, I dug deeply into the history of the Church; and when I had finished I had discovered the meaning of Catholic Unity, the Oneness of Catholic Truth; the need and the reality of the infallible authority of the Catholic Church.

'I might not be able to believe the Gospel, did not the authority of the Catholic Church move me,' said St. Augustine in the fifth century; and a long line of thinkers have been saying the same ever since. At first blush this had looked to me like a "hard saying' - but not so any more. For it is the key to the whole Catholic structure. Without a clear apprehension of the authoritative voice by which the Catholic Church speaks, neither you nor I can really be a Catholic"); *Fast By The Road* (1942) (autobiography); *John Henry Newman* (1946); Charles Rich, *Autobiography* (1990) ("I heard of a story told of John Moody, the founder of the *Wall Street Journal.* He and his wife with their twenty-one year old son, were vacationing in Italy. While there, their son died. After the body had been lowered in the grave, the grief-stricken father said these words to the Episcopalian minister who was presiding at the grave: 'Is that all there is to it?' The answer he received was expressed in these words: '1 don't know.' Mr. Moody left the cemetery with this determination. He wanted an answer which was yes or no. He found the answer was yes, there is another life and as the result of this answer be became a Catholic").

Moore, Grace (born Mary Willie Grace Moore) (known as "The Tennessee Nightingale") – opera singer and actress; b. 5 December 1898, Slabtown, Cocke County, Tennessee; c. 1947 (under instruction from Mgr. Fulton Sheen at the time of her death; as a catechumen she would have had an association with the Church in the equivalent of the ancient Church and now the modern Church); d. 26 January 1947, Copenhagen, Denmark; brought up in Tennessee; baptized in the local Baptist church; studied music in Washington D.C. and New York; got a job singing at the Black Cat Cafe in Greenwich Village; first appeared on Broadway in the early 1920s; trained for opera in France; made her operatic debut at the Metropolitan Opera in New York City in 1928 (played the role of Mimi in Puccini's *La Bohème*); then played the same role in Paris; performed with the Metropolitan Opera for sixteen seasons; in 1931 she married Valentin Parera, a Spanish film actor (no children of the marriage); in the 1930s and 1940s gave many concerts in United States and Europe; entertained American troops abroad in World War II; first screen role in 1930, but returned to films in 1934; nomination for the Academy Award for Best Actress in 1935 for *One Night of Love*; criticized for curtseying to the Duchess of Windsor in Cannes in 1937; killed in a plane crash at Copenhagen; buried in Forest Hills Cemetery, Chattanooga, Tennessee; her life story was made into a film, *So This Is Love* (1953); her papers are housed at the University of Tennessee at Knoxville; see (book) *You're Only Human Once* (1944; republished in 1947 after her death) (autobiography) ("For the Catholics I had a warm and atavistic sympathy – a feeling that lurked in my Irish ancestry. One of the great prides of Jellico was being able to take visitors to one side of the town and say 'Look, put one foot there, another here – see, now you're half in Tennessee and half in Kentucky.' Right over the line in Kentucky was a tiny Catholic church. Rather shabby, ugly, and ramshackle on the outside, it held the mystery of a strange other world within. I would come into it in awe; then, falling solemnly to my knees, would say a quick little prayer and run away, back to the Baptist solidity of Tennessee. Today I am married to a Catholic, and that kinship for the warm, passionate pageantry of the Church still holds"); (films) *A Lady's Morals* (1930) (aka *Jenny Lind*); *New Moon* (1930); *One Night of Love* (1934); *Love Me Forever* (1935); *The King Steps Out* (1936); *When You're in Love* (1937); *I'll Take Romance* (1937); *Louise* (1939); Rowena Rutherford Farrar, *Grace Moore and Her Many Worlds* (1982); Thomas C. Reeves, *America's Bishop: The Life and Times of Fulton J. Sheen* (2001) ("In 1946 she contacted Sheen and expressed her desire to enter the Church. Her schedule was such that Sheen gave her instruction in three days but he refused to baptize [receive?] her until she had taken several months more to consider the step she was taking. In early 1947 the forty-eight-year-old singer was killed in an airplane crash in Copenhagen. Sheen sadly noted that she was to have been inducted into the Church upon her return to the United States"); *GraceMoore.net.*

Morley, Sylvanus Griswold ("Vay") – archaeologist; b. 7 June 1883, Chester, Pennsylvania; c. 1948; d. 2 September 1948 Santa Fe, New Mexico; eldest of six children; his father Colonel Benjamin F. Morley was vice-president of Pennsylvania Military

College (PMC); the family moved to Colorado in 1893; developed an interest in archaeology; graduated in Civil Engineering at PMC in 1904, but went on to study Archaeology at Harvard University, focusing on the pre-Columbian Maya (graduated in American Research in 1907); worked for several years for the School of American Archaeology traveling through Central America and Mexico, visiting and exploring several Maya sites; also conducted espionage in Mexico on behalf of the United States during World War I, seeking evidence for pro-German and anti-American agitation and looking for secret German submarine bases (which turned out to be non-existent!); there is some speculation that he may have provided some of the inspiration for the character of Indiana Jones in the Spielberg films; particularly noted for the extensive excavations of the Maya site of Chichen Itza that he directed on behalf of the Carnegie Institution for many years, but also explored other Maya sites; remains an important figure in Maya scholarship, though some of his views have now been superseded by later scholarship; published several treatises on Maya hieroglyphics; supported the career of several Maya scholars; also wrote popular accounts of the Maya for a general audience; did field research on modern Yucatec Maya communities; acted almost as the spokesman for the Maya in several matters; always suffered from fragile health; in 1946 he was appointed director of the School of American Research and the Museum of New Mexico; married twice; buried in a plot in Santa Fe's Fairview Cemetery; see *An Introduction to the Study of the Maya Hieroglyphs* (1915); *The Inscriptions of Copán* (1920); *The Inscriptions of Petéen* (5 Vols.) (1938); *The Ancient Maya* (1946); J. Eric S. Thompson, "Sylvanus Griswold Morley, 1883–1948," *American Anthropologist*, April-June 1949 ("Shortly before his death Vay left the desert of agnosticism, in which he had wandered for many years, and was received into the Roman Catholic Church"); Alfred V. Kidder, "Sylvanus Griswold Morley, 1883–1948," in Arthur J. O. Anderson (ed), *Morleyana: A Collection of Writings in Memoriam, Sylvanus Griswold Morley 1883-1948* (1950); Robert L. Brunhouse, *Sylvanus G. Morley and the World of the Ancient Mayas* (1971); Charles H. Harris and Louis R. Sadler, *Was a Spy: Sylvanus G. Morley and the Office of Naval Intelligence. Albuquerque* (2003); *ANB.*

Mosher, Steven Westley – social scientist and writer; b. 9 May 1948; c. 31 March 1991 (Easter Sunday); mother a member of the Nazarene church; at fifteen he started attending a Lutheran church; studied Biology and Oceanography at the University of Washington; MA in Cultural Anthropology from Stanford University 1977; MA in East Asian Studies from Stanford University 1979; an authority on China and population issues; in 1979 he was invited to China by the Chinese government; he was the first American social scientist to visit mainland China; he witnessed women being forced to have abortions under the new "one-child policy"; returned to Stanford University and wrote up what he had witnessed in China for a PhD; Stanford expelled him rather than grant him the PhD; allegations that this was done because of pressure from the Chinese government; filed suit against the university; although a pro-choice atheist at the time of the China visit, this experience led him to revise his position; since China he has fought against coercive population control programs; he received no support from feminist groups; eventually he became a practicing pro-life Catholic; he was profoundly affected by the Gospels in his conversion, and also by Fr. John Hardon's *Catholic Catechism*; he has appeared before Congress as an expert in world population, China, and human rights abuses; he argues that overpopulation is a myth and that great human rights abuses have resulted from the efforts of population controllers to reduce human numbers; many appearances on television and radio; articles in many publications; director of the Claremont Institute, Asian Studies Center 1986-1995; since 1996 president of the non-profit making Population Research Institute (founded in 1989 by Fr. Paul Marx, OSB, to investigate population-related issues); married to Vera Mosher (nine children of the marriage); see *Broken Earth: The Rural Chinese* (1984); *Journey to the Forbidden China* (1985); *Korea in the 1990s: Prospects for Unification* (1992); *China Misperceived: American Illusions and Chinese Realities* (1992); *Mother's Ordeal: One Woman's Fight Against China's One-Child Policy* (1993); *Hegemon: China's Plan to Dominate Asia and the World* (2000); *China Attacks* (2000) (with Chuck DeVore) (novel); *Population Control: Real Costs, Illusory Benefits* (2008); "Finding God in China," in Donna Steichen (ed), *Chosen: How Christ Sent Twenty-Three Surprised Converts to Replant His Vineyard* (2009) ("It was around this time that I stumbled upon the work of Saint Thomas Aquinas, which for me personally was something akin to finding the Dead Sea Scrolls. For just as the scrolls demonstrated the authenticity of the Scriptures, so did the *Summa* of Saint Thomas Aquinas teach me the validity of reasoning one's way to the Truth, which is God. Or, as Pope John Paul II was later to write in his 1998 encyclical *Fides et Ratio*, 'Faith and reason are like two wings on which the human spirit rises to the contemplation of truth; and God has placed in the human heart a desire to know the truth - in a word, to know himself - so that, by knowing and loving God, men and women may also come to the fullness of truth about themselves'...

The secular humanists at Stanford, by rejecting God, had sheared away the two wings referred to by the Holy Father. This is easy to see in the case of faith, which they openly and scornfully rejected as myth and superstition. But reason, which they claimed to honor, actually fared little better, for they hedged it with such conditions as to render it largely impotent. I had been expected to believe that man's capacity for objective knowledge was limited, that the search for ultimate truth was futile, and that the question of whether a Supreme Being exists had long been answered in the negative. Other dogmas that were beyond reproach included materialistic evolution and socialism. With the large questions - What is man? What is God? What is the state? - foreclosed or predetermined, we were left, in the Department of Anthropology, to think in a minor key. Our theories were mostly inconsequential efforts to explain trivial phenomena in mostly moribund cultures. Most of the time we busied ourselves recording the exotic minutiae of such cultures, many of which will almost certainly cease to exist within a few generations. A dead-end occupation if there ever was one.

Reading Saint Thomas Aquinas, these scales fell from my eyes. For here was a philosophical edifice that not only encompassed all of creation but also reached up to the very heavens, including proofs for the very existence of God. Perhaps it was just intellectual snobbery on my part, but I was tremendously relieved not to have to make a blind leap of faith of the kind popularized by that apostate monk Martin Luther and his *sola fide*, I doubted that my still wobbly legs of faith were strong enough to carry me over the vast chasm between me and God. On the other hand, if I could construct a bridge to Heaven out of solid blocks of reason, then perhaps, just perhaps, I stood a chance of making it to the top. And it was Saint Thomas Aquinas of blessed memory who revealed this possibility to me, teaching me from across the centuries that God spoke to man through his reason, as well as through his faith, and that one could therefore read, think, and study one's way into the Catholic Church. This I proceeded to do...

As I learned more about the Catholic faith, no doctrine touched me more deeply than the communion of saints. The idea that we wayfarers should be aided in our pilgrimage by those who have gone before us links our world to the next in a marvelous and positive symmetry. Once I recognized this truth, it seemed especially applicable to my own circumstances, in which the great cloud of witnesses that Saint Paul speaks of in Hebrews (12:2) bore mostly the visages of Chinese babies. I had spoken out on behalf of these millions of innocent victims of China's inhuman one-child policy in books, articles, and interviews, in congressional testimony and at pro-life conferences, in season and out of season. Not to be outdone in generosity, this vast multitude of heavenly intercessors had implored the Father on my behalf for a decade, or so I came to believe. I had interceded for them in a weak human way, while they had interceded for me in a powerful supernatural way, an arrangement much to my benefit").

Moss, David (born David Moskovitz) – engineer and lay Catholic; b. 1941, Brooklyn, New York; c. February 1979; of Russian and Hungarian Jewish immigrant parents; elder brother of Rosalind Moss (see below); grew up in a conservative Jewish family (going later to a Reform position) in largely Catholic areas and grew to love Christmas carols and saw Schubert's *Ave Maria* as the most beautiful music he had ever heard; lost his faith between ages of fourteen and fifteen and became rebellious and idealistic; came to believe that the whole idea of "God" was invented by men; went through the left wing and liberal camp; qualified as an engineer and worked for IBM; in 1964 married a Protestant in a civil ceremony; moved to a pro-life and a conservative position; started attending a Southern Baptist church and had Catholic friends also; after many setbacks finally converted to the Catholic faith; later became full-time President of the Association of Hebrew Catholics; he has rejected the idea that the Church replaced the people of Israel and identified the latter idea as an "erroneous theology" taught for two thousand years by the Catholic Church; this is contrary to the infallible teaching of the Council of Florence, the Catechism of the Council of Trent ("the people, aware of the abrogation of the Mosaic Law…"), and the statement of the United States Conference of Catholic Bishops in 2008, and would mean that the Church has taught error in its official teaching; he has also called for a Hebrew branch of Catholicism that would re-introduce the distinguishing marks of ancient Judaism (e.g., the liturgical practices), but the Church teaches (e.g., the Council of Florence; Pius XII in *Mystici Corporis*; and St. Thomas Aquinas (see (*Summa Theologiae*, I, II, Q. 103, Art. 3 & 4)) that the rituals and observances of the Mosaic law have been abolished; after an annulment, he married Kathleen, who had converted from Judaism in 1979; see *EWTN Audio Library, The Journey Home* (14 January 2000); *EWTN Audio Library, The Journey Home* (7 March 2005); "Called to Fulfillment," in Roy H. Schoeman, *Honey from the Rock* (2007) ("My studies had provided reasonable answers to a lot of questions, but not to those I was obsessed with. There were three questions...Somehow I came to think that I would find the meaning of life bound up in the answers to these questions. The questions were: 1. How does one explain the fact of existence? Not only that something *exists*, but that there is a reality that is *existence*? 2. How does one explain sacrificial love? I was thinking of the soldier, who against every instinct for survival, throws himself on a grenade to save his buddies. I also thought of the mothers I knew growing up in Brooklyn who took care of their children and husbands and homes all day and then went out on a second or third shift to clean offices on their knees. The money they earned was put in the cookie jar for their children's education. How did one explain such self-donation? 3. How does one explain the sense of *ought*? This was not a virtue that one could learn Nor did it have to do with the keeping or breaking of a commandment. It was rather like a little internal nudge directing one to a good deed, a good deed that might well go unrecognized. I thought of a man who missed an important business appointment by taking the time to pick up a wallet and return it to the old man who had dropped it. Where did this sense that he ought to return the wallet come from?

As I sat back in my chair and stared at these questions, having exhausted every avenue I could think of to study and find answers, a feeling of dread and the ultimate blackness of a meaningless life settled upon me. As I found myself slipping into a despair that I feared I would not recover from, I remembered my youth and I cried out, 'God, if You really exist, I need to know now.'

I cannot adequately describe what took place next. I can only say what it seemed like and what I can remember. My office at IBM vanished, and I appeared to be in the sky, in clouds. They parted, the sun shone on me, and they came back together. I was back in my office at IBM.

And I was no longer the same. The feelings of despair and blackness disappeared, and all the baggage of meaninglessness and absurdity I had carried all those years was gone. I now knew there was a God. And I now knew that my life had meaning and purpose. I knew the answers to those questions. And I knew the answer to a question I had never asked: I knew that Jesus was the Messiah and the Divine Son of God"); Robert A. Sungenis, "Judaizers in the Catholic Church; An Analysis of the Ministries of David Moss and Roy Schoeman," *Culture Wars*, November 2005, p.28 ("The early Church Fathers, as well as numerous official Church declarations, regarded Rabbinic Judaism as an obsolete and false religion. The Fathers, to a man, condemned the rabbis for both their refusal to accept Christ as sent from God, and equally condemned their obstinate insistence on adherence to Mosaic rituals. At no time did the Church ever consider rabbinic Judaism as some sort of way-station to determine the sincerity of Jews toward God or as a preliminary stage of enlightenment. Rabbinic Judaism was, pure and simple, a rejection of Jesus Christ and the New Covenant, not 'an earlier stage of covenant development'...

[A]ccording to Moss, the last two millennia of Jewish unbelief is not due, as St. Paul says, to the obstinate heart of the Jew, but because the Church has insisted that Jewish ceremonies and identity markers are forbidden. The main reason for Jewish unbelief is the Catholic Church's insensitivity to 'Post-biblical Rabbinic Judaism.' This complaint, of course, was the same thing the Judaizers of St. Paul's day were asserting. They complained that the Church was insensitive to the law of Moses (Acts 15:5), but the Church insisted that if they continued to practice the rituals of the Mosaic law, they would be condemned (Acts 15:10-12; Gal 3:10-12; 5:1-4). The Council of Florence reiterated this very teaching, quite forcefully, 1400 years later when Judaizers were again preaching to the Christian community ("That the matter pertaining to the law of the Old Testament, of the Mosaic law...after our Lord's coming had been signified by them, ceased and the sacraments of the New Testament began")...

When St. Paul converted to Christianity he resolutely left his Judaism behind. He certainly wasn't calling for a Hebrew Association of Christians, for at every opportunity he sought to break down those artificial and prideful barriers. One means of doing so was to put his Judaism in proper perspective as an obsolete religion that was now an obstacle to knowing Christ. In Philippians 3:2-8 he makes it quite clear.

The Council of Florence was not the only magisterial decree against Judaizing. Pius XII reiterated the same truth [in *Mystici Corporis*]" ("The New Testament took the place of the Old Law which had been abolished...Jesus made void the Law with its decrees and fastened the handwriting of the Old Testament to the Cross"); Raymond A. Kevane, "An Open Letter to the Hebrew-Catholic Conference," *Culture Wars*, February 2006, p.8 ("In a public statement on EWTN, Dave Moss rejected the idea that the Church replaced the people of Israel. He clearly identified the latter idea as an 'erroneous theology' that was taught for 2000 years by the Catholic Church. He further stated that the Church no longer teaches that the people of Israel are superseded. They are an eternal people with an irrevocable calling. How can any *individual* declare that the Catholic Church ('...Whatever you bind on earth it will he bound in heaven...') has taught erroneous theology for 2000 years? Surely, intended that way or not, this has to be the height of arrogance. Both statements are heretical. The most important 'irrevocable calling' the Jews have is the same as it is for the rest of us - to save their eternal souls. In one stroke Dave Moss denied the Scriptures as inspired by God, the infallibility of the Pope and Ecumenical Councils, and the fact of Tradition (the office of the Magisterium of the Catholic Church).

Nowhere in *Nostra Aetate* (the section in Vatican Council II which deals with the relationship with non-Christian religions), is there even a hint that the teaching of the Church has changed. It deals simply with the need to treat non-Christian religions with respect"); Robert A. Sungenis, "The Old Covenant is Revoked: The USCC Removes Heretical Sentence from Its Catechism," *Culture Wars*, October 2008, p.12.

Moss, Rosalind (later Mother Miriam of the Lamb of God, OSB) – nun and Catholic apologist; b. 1943, Brooklyn, New York; c. 15 April 1995 (Easter Vigil; received at St. Joseph's Church, Millbrook, New York); Jewish parents of Russian and Hungarian descent; younger sister of David Moss (see above); brought up in a fairly Conservative Jewish family going later to a Reform position; as a child enjoyed all the Jewish High Holy Days and feasts and saw them as uniting in a community every generation of Jews; in her twenties she moved towards an agnostic position; fifteen year business career as an executive with corporations in New York and California; in 1975 she met groups of Jewish people ("Jews for Jesus") in California, who believed that Jesus Christ was the Jewish Messiah and that he was God, and took her through the Old Testament prophecies, especially those of Isaiah, and the sacrificial system; she then became a Protestant Evangelical in 1976; earned a masters degree in ministry from Talbot Theological Seminary; later converted to the Catholic Church (important influences were the magazine *This Rock*, and hearing in Summer 1990 Scott Hahn (see above), which led to a four year search for the truth); also greatly influenced by St. Francis de Sales' *Introduction to the Devout Life*; worked 1999-2005 on the staff of *Catholic Answers*, a non-profit apostolate promoting the Catholic faith; broadcaster on EWTN; in 2008 founded a new religious order called the Daughters of Mary, Mother of Israel's Hope, in the Archdiocese of St. Louis, Missouri, moving in 2011 to Tulsa, Oklahoma; prioress of the Priory of Our Lady of Guadalupe in northeast Tulsa; see *EWTN Audio Library, The Journey Home* (17 October 1997); "A Journey Home," in Marcus Grodi (ed), *Journeys Home* (1997; revised edition 2011) (reproduced in *The Coming Home Network International*, *Conversion Stories*, *chnetwork.org*, 16 May 2011); "O Jerusalem, Jerusalem," *This Rock*, October 2002; "From Promise to

Fulfilment," in Rosalind Moss (ed), *Home at Last: Eleven Who Found Their Way to the Catholic Church* (2001) (with Michael J. Sheehan), p.137 (reproduced in Jennifer Ferrara and Patricia Sodano Ireland (ed), *The Catholic Mystique: Women Converts Tell Their Stories* (2004), p.43); "All This and Heaven, Too," in Roy H. Schoeman, *Honey from the Rock* (2007) ("They took me through the sacrificial system of the Old Testament, which I never knew through all my years in synagogue. They explained that we come into the world separated from God… They explained 'original sin,' the sin of our first parents that plunged the entire world into sin. They told me that the Scriptures state that the wages of sin is death. The wages – our 'salary,' what we've earned, what is *due* us! – is death. And they explained that 'death' means 'separation'…They explained that God is a holy God who must punish sin…But God, they quickly added, is also a *loving* God who created us for a relationship with Him. And then they unfolded the most incredible story the world would ever hear, which, at the age of thirty-two, I was hearing for the first time. They told me…how God, in His love, without compromising His holiness, provided the way for us – fallen children of Adam and Eve - to be restored to a relationship with Him…

The Israelites, according to the law given Moses on the mountain, would bring lambs to the altar as a sin offering for their own sins and for the sins of the nation…

They told me that the blood of thousands – no millions – of lambs slain over 1,500 years of that Mosaic sacrificial system could never take away sin. They were a *kippur*, a covering, for sin…*[B]ut every sacrifice and all of them together were a sign* that would point to the One who would come and take upon Himself, not the sin of one person for a time, but the sin of all men, of everyone who had ever lived and who ever would be born, for all time.

And with that, they took me, for the first time, to a scene in the New Testament. It was the appearance of Jesus as he came to be baptized by John the Baptist in the Jordan River. Recognizing immediately who it was that was walking toward him, John proclaimed to the Jewish crowd who had come to be baptized by him: 'Behold, the Lamb of God, who takes away the sin of the world!' (Jn 1:29). The *Lamb*? The Lamb? The Lamb to which every Old Testament sacrifice pointed?

I was shattered. I could hardly believe what I had just heard. I thought silently to myself…, 'If one little four-legged lamb, under the Old Testament sacrificial system could take upon itself the sin of a single individual, temporarily, for a time, what then could the blood of *God's Son* do on that Cross, the Altar of altars? If *He* is the Lamb of God, His would be the only perfect and acceptable sacrifice, not just for Israel's sins, but for the sins of the *entire world*...I knew it was true. My hang-up all this time was that a *man* cannot be God. I realized that night that, indeed, a man *cannot* be God. But *if God is*, if He exists, *God* can become a man! He can do anything He wants to do and I'm not about to tell Him how to be God!"); *Reason For Our Hope* (2007); Trent Beattie, "Rosalind Moss's Unexpected Journey," *National Catholic Register*, 8 December 2011 ("Actually, my calling, unknown to me at the time, started many years before becoming Catholic. I was twenty years old when I read a story in the newspaper about nuns receiving permission to shorten their habits. It was at the beginning of the mini-skirt era of the 1960s. I believed that these religious women were in the world to affect the world for God, but, alas, I thought at the time, the world had affected them.

Something physical ripped through me. What I assumed had nothing to do with me became my deep and immediate loss. I had lost something that wasn't mine. Or so I thought. I did not imagine that years later I would find myself fully given to restoring those hemlines and longing to fill the world with religious in habits as the glorious sign to God that they are.

We're a contemplative-active teaching and evangelistic community. A religious community must be rooted in prayer, and we are as well. Our active apostolate, however, has two main goals: The first is to walk the streets in habits, reaching out to all we meet with the love of God and the truths of his glorious Church. The second goal is to help restore the stewardship of the home by helping parents to know and live their faith and impart it to their children.

The No. 1 thing that attracted me to the Diocese of Tulsa was Bishop Edward Slattery's decision to offer the *Novus Ordo* Mass *ad orientem*, that is, facing east, liturgically speaking. It is the posture of the shepherd leading the people to Christ and has been the case for centuries").

Murdick, Mgr. Olin John – priest; b. 29 April 1917; c. 6 November 1940; d. 6 January 2004, Cuyahoga County, Ohio; brought up in an actively religious Methodist family; family and individual religious practice gradually ceased; but another Methodist family impressed him with their religious dignity; became involved in Methodist youth work ("Prompted by certain leads in the Methodist youth program itself, I became imbued with socialistic and pacifistic ideas, which I sought constantly to justify in the teachings of Christ"); became interested in philosophical questions ("Now I was convinced that the most important question which one could ask ['Why do we exist?'] could be answered only in that mysterious world of ideas known as philosophy. From now on I had a certain skepticism about or a sense of the limitation of other disciplines"); studied at the University of Michigan where he adopted secularism and "progressive education"; then his progressive views were effectively attacked; he desired to acquire a personal religion, but after reading widely (and even accepting a position as a student minister for the Congregationalist Church) he took instruction from a Catholic priest and then became a Catholic; entered the seminary of the Sulpician Fathers at Washington, D.C.; ordained to the priesthood on 22 May 1948; O'Neil D'Amour Award 1977 for Catholic education; see "My Happiest Day," in John A. O'Brien (ed), *The Road to Damascus, Volume III: The Way to Emmaus* (1953) ("People, I believed, were just full of good. It had to come out. Progressive schools and progressive society would encourage the good within men to assert itself. So the thing to do was to jump on the band-wagon of progress and start rolling.

It was not until the summer of 1938 that my 'progressive' ideals were challenged. As a graduate student I was taking a course in social psychology at the University of Michigan…One afternoon the instructor, Marshall Levy, a Jew, made the statement that history showed that one factor which had been successful in the past in promoting a healthy, integrated society was the moral law. This was an interesting social psychological fact worthy of mention, he thought. I jumped to my feet. Common sense had not left me altogether. I was still capable of logical thinking.

'If the moral law was such a good thing in the past,' I said, 'why isn't it a good thing now, or in the future? Isn't it deserving of more than a historical mention? What can take the place of moral law as a principle of social organization?'…

After class one of the students, whom I had hardly noticed before, approached me. His name was Bill Bujak, the camp naturalist, a senior in the biology department. The conversation which he began with me then was undoubtedly the most important one I ever had with anyone.

First he commended me on the questions which I had raised during the class. This, of course, was the right way to begin. Next, he induced me to examine the questions more thoroughly until I saw some of their implications.

Moral law meant fixed standards. It meant moral responsibility and the ability to make moral choices. And did I know that these ideas were identical with teachings of the Catholic Church?...

It took me another full year to come to the realization that organized religion was the only institution capable of true, abiding moral influence…

Even before I had gone to Chicago Theological Seminary I had become well disposed toward the Catholic religion. One author especially had done much to make me appreciate the wisdom and beauty of Catholic piety. That was a non-Catholic writer, Hermann von Keyserling [1880-1946]. I can't even remember now the titles of his books. But I read them all. One of them, I think, was called *The Travel Diary of a Philosopher*. And all of them represented the thoughts of a cosmopolitan man who was constantly comparing Western and Eastern cultures. The writer seemed always to have great esteem for the mystery and profundity of the East and an inevitable word of praise for Catholicism, in so far as it preserved in the West those qualities which he so much admired elsewhere.

At Chicago Theological Seminary I discovered for the first time *The Imitation of Christ*, a book which I studied assiduously....In the spring of 1940 I made up my mind. I had never talked with a Catholic priest. I had attended Mass only once. But I was convinced that only the Catholic religion was worthy of belief. It was the only religion that could hold itself together. It was the only religion that appeared to be competent to teach men to pray, individually and collectively. Whatever shortcomings might appear from further study and experience, the positive qualities of wisdom and stability which history could not conceal put it in a class by itself.

The sacramental system and sacrificial worship of the Catholic Church seemed to me to be the perfect answer to man's religious needs. Without the Holy Eucharist, conceived strictly in the Catholic sense, there could be no real corporate worship. And without corporate worship there could be no Christianity. It all went together.

Still there were difficulties. The chief one was papal infallibility. But gradually I saw it through. If there were no infallible Pope, I reasoned, then no one could be sure of anything. From a purely natural point of view the Pope was a much better authority on matters of faith and morals than I was or than any person I had ever met. Certainly no one at Chicago Theological Seminary could rightly claim to be a dependable theological authority. Without the Pope I was forced back into the futile position of spending my life searching for a true religion which I could never get around to practicing.

Of course this purely negative reasoning wasn't enough. Eventually I had to see that no Pope, regardless of his natural competence as a religious authority, could possibly do the job demanded of him without the help of the Holy Ghost...

The thing that finally decided me was a conversation I had with two other Protestant seminarians with whom I was associated while at a youth camp on Lake Coeur d'Alene in Idaho. It was an August afternoon. We were having a typical college bull session on religion. Finally I made the simple but startling statement: 'I believe that the Catholic Church is the true Church.'

Silence followed. Then the lad from

Yale Divinity said thoughtfully: 'Olie, if you really mean that, then you'll have to become a Catholic if you want to save your soul.'

I had prided myself on being logical. But it took the logic of this Protestant divinity student to convince me"); *Journey Into Truth: The Autobiography of a Catholic Convert* (1958); *The Parish School Board* (1967); "Religious Freedom: Some New Perceptions in Light of Vatican II," *Religious Education*, 1976, p.416.

Murray, Aline (also known under her married name of Aline Kilmer) – poet and author; b. 1 August 1888, Norfolk, Virginia; c. 5 November 1913 (received with her husband); d. 1 October 1941, Stillwater, New Jersey; daughter of Ada Foster Murray, poet; step-father was Henry Mills Alden (1836-1919), editor of *Harpers Magazine* for fifty years; educated at Rutgers College Grammar School, New Brunswick, New Jersey, and at Vail-Deane School, Elizabeth, New Jersey; in 1908 married Joyce Kilmer the poet (see above) (five children of the marriage); buried in the Catholic cemetery in Newton, New Jersey; author of poetry, essays, and children's books; see *Candles That Burn* (1919); *Vigils* (1921); *Hunting a Hair Shirt and Other Spiritual Adventures* (1923); *The Poor King's Daughter and Other Verse* (1925); *Emmy, Nicky and Greg* (1927); *A Buttonwood Summer* (1929); *Selected Poems* (1929); Francis X. Talbot, "A Tribute to Aline Kilmer," *America*, 18 October 1941, p.46; see also the reading under the entry for her husband.

Murray, Jef (born Jeffrey Patrick Murray) – fantasy artist and illustrator; b. 1960; c. 2 April 1994 (Easter Vigil); was a student of his later-to-be wife, Lorraine V. Murray (see below), at Georgia Tech; he at first believed in a higher being, but had no attachment to any particular religion, although fascinated by Eastern thought; worked as an engineer, then at Georgia Tech Research Institute; gradually became more open to Christianity and Catholicism and began going to Mass; undertook instruction in the faith and was finally received into the Church; went back to his childhood love of drawing and painting; best known for his illustrations of works by J. R. R. Tolkien; artist-in-residence for the *St. Austin Review*; see *How Shall We Celebrate: Embracing Jesus in Every Season* (2005) (with Lorraine V. Murray); *Divining Divinity* (2008) (with Joseph Pearce); *Black & White Ogre Country: The Lost Tales of Hilary Tolkien* (2009) (with Hilary Tolkien and Angela Gardner); *The Magic Ring: Deluxe Illustrated Edition* (2010) (with Baron de la Motte Fouque and Amy H. Sturgis); Lorraine V. Murray, *Confessions of an Ex-Feminist* (2008).

Murray, Lorraine Viscardi – author and columnist; b. 29 August 1947, New York; c. 15 December 1993 (revert; her husband Jef Murray (see above) was received later); family originally from Italy; father a taxi-cab driver; brought up as a Catholic; grew up in Miami; educated at the University of Florida (BA in English in 1968; PhD in Philosophy in 1982); lost her faith at university when influenced by atheism and radical feminism, which positions she adopted for twenty years; taught philosophy at college level for many years, in which she attacked religion and Christianity; discovering she was pregnant she had an abortion, which resulted in an emotional trauma, and began the process of re-assessing her feminism; after marriage she began writing as a freelance journalist; conversion influenced by Thomas Merton's *Seven Storey Mountain*, St. Augustine, G. K. Chesterton, C. S. Lewis, Mother Teresa and the Missionaries of Charity; "I began to experience a mysterious sense of someone reaching into my life and tugging at me"; after returning to the Church she at first continued to dissent on certain life issues, e.g., contraception and pro-choice on abortion (although working to help women in post-abortion crisis); "But once I understood the theological and historical underpinnings of Church declarations and recognized that teachings about life form a seamless web, I realized that I could not, in good faith, remain a 'cafeteria' Catholic"; through Fr. Richard Lopez she met Elizabeth Fox-Genovese (see above) and the movement of Feminists for Life; she was diagnosed with breast cancer in 2000 and wrote a book about her spiritual journey with cancer; free-lance columnist for the *Atlanta Journal Constitution*, *The Georgia Bulletin*, the *National Catholic Register*, and *America*; see *Grace Notes: Embracing the Joy of Christ in a Broken World* (2002); *Why Me? Why Now?: Finding Hope When You Have Breast Cancer* (2003); *Confessions of an Ex-Feminist* (2008) (her conversion story) ("With Father Lopez's help, I began to glimpse the mysterious connection between human freedom and suffering. I discovered that, according to traditional Catholic theology, God did not create human beings as robots that would always make the right choices but instead as creatures with free will. Thus, much of the world's suffering results from crime and war, a result of terrible choices that human beings freely make. Other suffering comes from the flawed fabric of our fallen natural world, into which earthquakes, tsunamis, and diseases are interwoven.

I realized that even a question like 'Why did God cause me to get cancer?' was ridiculous. Yes, it is true that God had allowed the illness to occur, because he is in charge of the world, and nothing happens that he does not know about. But to say that God causes a particular person's cancer is absurd. Perhaps a better description of causes might be my own past choices, made in ignorance, such as my decision to use birth control pills and then hormone replacement therapy at various times in my life.

When I confessed my shame over my wild and sinful past, Father Lopez asked a simple question: 'What is greater in your life - your past or the power of God to work through your past?' He assured me, time and again, that God's grace can transform any situation. He also told me that depression can be a cross for many people and advised me, whenever I was having a melancholy day, to offer my suffering to God.

At first I just didn't get it. What did 'offer it up' really mean? I had heard that expression when I was a child but never could make sense of it. Gradually, through my sessions with Father Lopez, I began to see that Christianity, among all religions, has a unique answer for what traditionally is called the 'problem of evil' and that 'offering it up' plays a role in it.

Christ's death on the Cross shows that God can take any suffering and any evil and turn it around. That was the ultimate meaning of the Crucifixion: An innocent man had experienced an agonizing and terrible death, which had given way to new life in the Resurrection. Christ himself had offered up his suffering on the Cross. He had given his life out of love for mankind.

According to traditional Catholic theology, those who love Christ will not be spared from suffering, but he will help them bear it. In the end, Christianity offers the only satisfying solution to the problem that I grappled with when I was teaching philosophy: Why do good people suffer? During the Crucifixion, God himself experienced the absolute depths of human suffering. But the final chapter of that story was not the tomb but the transformation that occurred through the Resurrection. As Alice von Hildebrand so eloquently stated it, 'From a supernatural point of view; there is nothing, absolutely nothing, which cannot be turned to God's glory. *Every defeat can become a victory*'"); *Death in the Choir* (2009) (novel); *The Abbess of Andalusia: Flannery O'Connor's Spiritual Journey* (2009); *Death of a Liturgist* (2010) (novel); Carl E. Olson, "From Catholicism to Feminism and Back: An Interview With Lorraine V. Murray," *Ignatiusinsight.com*, April 2008.

Nathanson, Bernard N. – doctor; b. 31 July 1926, New York; c. 8 December 1996 (baptized by Cardinal John O'Connor in St. Patrick's Cathedral, New York); d. 21 February 2011; brought up as a militant atheist; graduated in medicine; very impressed by Karl Stern (1906-1975), the neurologist and psychiatrist, one of his teachers at McGill University, Canada; specialized in obstetrics and gynecology; one of the founders in 1968 of the National Association for the Repeal of the Abortion Laws in the United States; coined the phrases "pro-choice" and "a woman's right to choose"; director of America's largest abortion clinic in the 1970s, where he oversaw seventy-five thousand abortions and personally performed five thousand; became known as the "abortion king"; author of *Aborting America* (1979); greatly influenced by the development of ultrasound technology, which enabled him to see images of unborn babies, and in the late 1970s became a pro-life activist; produced the films *The Silent Scream* (1984), which shows graphic footage of an abortion, and *Eclipse of Reason* (1987); conversion greatly influenced by coming across in 1974 a copy of Karl Stern's *The Pillar of Fire* ("Karl Stern and I encountered each other twice, with twenty-five years between the encounters; the second encounter launched my search for spiritual truth. Only the Hand of God could have engineered such a ratifying experience as this"); also influenced by Opus Dei priest, Fr. C. John McCloskey III; see *Aborting America* (1979) (with Richard N. Ostling); *The Hand of God: A Journey from Death to Life by the Abortion Doctor Who Changed His Mind* (1996) ("A few years ago I was asked to review a book by an internist, Dr. Larry Dossey, who claimed to have adduced scientific proof that intercessory prayer works. I remained unconvinced by his data, but nevertheless one of the stories, that of Dossey's visit to a patient dying of cancer, has stuck with me. The man was constantly praying. When Dossey asked what he was praying for, the man said he wasn't praying for anything. 'Well,' said Dossey, 'if prayer isn't asking, then what is it for?' 'It isn't for anything,' the patient replied. 'It mainly reminds me that we are not alone.' I am no longer alone. It has been my fate to wander the globe in search of the One without Whom I am doomed, but now I seize the hem of His robe in desperation, in terror, in celestial access to the purest need I have ever known. My thoughts return to the hero of my medical school years, Karl Stern, who was undergoing a spiritual metamorphosis at the very time he was instructing me in the arts of the mind, its orders, and its sources, and the words he wrote in a letter to his brother: 'And there was no doubt about it,' Stern wrote, 'toward Him we had been running, or from Him we had been running away, but all the time He had been in the center of things'"); Julia Duin, "Bernard Nathanson's Conversion," *Crisis*, June 1996 ("One cold January morning in 1989, Bernard Nathanson, famous Jewish abortionist-turned atheistic-pro-lifer, began to entertain seriously the notion of God. Seven years later, thanks to a persistent

Opus Dei priest, the sixty-nine-year-old doctor, author of *Aborting America* and *The Abortion Papers*, is becoming a Roman Catholic.

Even though pro-lifers have had him on their prayer lists for some time, Nathanson is still considered quite a big fish to reel in. Unique in the medical profession for having made a public turnabout on the abortion issue in the 1970s, he had been aware of being a spiritual target for nearly a decade.

'I was not unmoved as time wore on,' he now says. But back then, he was not letting on that he was gripped by despair, waking up mornings at 4 or 5 a.m., staring into the darkness or reading from St. Augustine's *Confessions* along with heavy-duty fare from other intellectuals: Dostoyevsky, Tillich, Kierkegaard, Niebuhr, Lewis Mumford, and Waldo Frank; what he termed the 'literature of sin.' As he read and pondered, the doctor realized his despondency had to do with just that, a worthy consideration in that, in his time, he had presided over 75,000 abortions and had helped sculpt the landscape from whence emerged *Roe v Wade* in 1973. Sixteen years later, there was no escaping the interior dialogue that haunted and accused, then pointed out Albert Camus's central question of the twentieth century: Whether or not to commit suicide. A grandfather and sister had gone that route; his father had attempted to.

Along came the fateful January morning at a Planned Parenthood Clinic on Manhattan's Lower East Side, where he witnessed 1,200 Operation Rescue demonstrators wrapping their arms around each other, singing hymns, smiling at the police and the media. Nathanson, who was already well known for founding the National Abortion Rights Action League in 1968 and overseeing the world's largest abortion clinic before the advent of ultrasound in the 1970s changed his mind forever on the subject, was writing a magazine article on the morality of clinic blockades. He circled about the demonstrators, doing interviews, taking notes, observing the faces.

'It was only then,' he writes in his new book, *The Hand of God*, "that I apprehended the exaltation, the pure love on the faces of that shivering mass of people, surrounded as they were by hundreds of New York City policemen.' He listened as they prayed for the unborn, the women seeking abortions, the doctors and nurses in the clinic, the police, and reporters covering the event.

'They prayed for each other but never for themselves,' he writes. 'And I wondered: How can these people give of themselves for a constituency that is (and always will be) mute, invisible and unable to thank them?'

'It was only then,' he adds, 'that I began seriously to question what indescribable Force generated them to this activity. Why, too, was I there? What had led me to this time and place? Was it the same Force that allowed them to sit serene and unafraid at the epicenter of legal, physical, ethical and moral chaos?'

Prodded by an intellectual compulsion to find out more, Nathanson changed his reading material. His conversion was by now not 'if'; it was 'when'. He plunged into Malcolm Muggeridge, Walker Percy, Graham Greene, Karl Stern, C. S. Lewis, Simone Weil, Richard Gilman, Blaise Pascal, and Cardinal Newman, all of whom had taken the path he was considering.

By then he had already gotten to know John McCloskey, an Opus Dei priest based in Princeton with a doctorate in theology and a reputation for helping intellectual seekers. 'He'd heard I was prowling around the edges of Catholicism,' the doctor says. 'He contacted me and we began to have weekly talks. He'd come to my house and give me reading materials. He guided me down the path to where I am now. I owe him more than anyone else.'

Other than McCloskey, the biggest influence on Nathanson's decision was Karl Stern, a world-renowned psychoanalyst who was one of his professors in the 1940s at McGill University Medical College in Montreal. Stern had converted from Orthodox Judaism to Catholicism in 1943 and later chronicled his spiritual journey in *Pillar of Fire*. Nathanson never knew of this until 1974, when he discovered a tattered copy of Stern's book. Nathanson would return to this book again and again, fascinated with how Stern could use his brilliant mind to embrace faith and adopt as his heroine Teresa of Avila, a doctor of the Church. Nathanson found Stern's demeanor exquisitely sensitive to the doubts and questions of intellectuals who struggled with how much to allow for reason, how much to turn over to faith.

By then, Nathanson had been involved in abortion for nearly thirty years, beginning in 1945 when he persuaded a pregnant girlfriend to abort their child, which, he says, 'served as excursion into the satanic world of abortion.' Years later, he impregnated another woman and aborted that child himself. He was directing the country's largest abortion clinic in New York.

'What is it like to terminate the life of your own child?' he writes in the book. 'I have aborted the unborn children of my friends, my colleagues, casual acquaintances, even my teachers. There was never a shred of self-doubt, never a wavering of the supreme self-confidence that I was doing a major service to those who sought me out.'

Still, his confidence was wavering by the early 1970s. Ultrasound, a new technology, was making it clear that what was in the womb could suck its thumb and do other human-like things, and thus Nathanson began distancing himself first from the clinic, then from abortions altogether. In 1984, he premiered a movie, *The Silent Scream*, that showed an ultrasound of a child being aborted. The spectacle of such film backed by a cofounder of NARAL lent it credibility and created a sensation. Pro-lifers scrambled to watch it; pro-choicers repudiated their former ally.

But Nathanson was no angel of light. He had already broken the Hippocratic Oath, which forbids abortions; he was failing at the upbringing of his one son, Joseph, now thirty, and he was plowing through his second and third marriages with a vengeance. His divorce from his third wife, Adele, is final this spring.

For a while, he tried therapy, self-help books, counseling, and spiritualities ranging from theosophy to Swedenborgianism while finding his Judaism inadequate at best. Except for his first marriage in a Jewish ceremony and getting his son bar mitzvahed, he had hardly functioned as a Jew after his mid-teens. Still he went to speak with two rabbis, one Orthodox and the other Conservative, about his doubts.

'I was looking for a way to wash away my sins,' he says. 'There's no such formal mechanism for doing that in Judaism. One can atone for sins, as in Yom Kippur, but that doesn't absolve you. That's not to condemn the religion but I just didn't find in it what I needed.'

Another Orthodox rabbi, David Lapin, founder of the Mercer Island, Washington-based *Toward Tradition*, wonders if Nathanson ever understood his Jewish faith. 'Atonement is the action that leads to absolution,' he says, 'and absolution is only granted during the Day of Atonement. Then there are steps taken throughout the year that include rejecting the wrong and resolving not to repeat it again.'

There may be a deeper reason to Nathanson's disenchantment, the rabbi guesses, which has to do with the high level of Jews involved in the abortion business. Nathanson has written of the high percentage of Jewish abortionists. The new national leader of Planned Parenthood, who comes on board in June, is Gloria Feldt, a Jew. 'I believe that Bernard Nathanson's conversion to Catholicism is spurred not by theological deficiencies in a Judaism I don't believe he knew but by a deep compelling desire to distance himself from a faith whose secular wing has embraced abortion with a fervor,' Lapin says.

And there's no question about it. *Boston Herald* columnist Don Feder points out nearly half of the religious organizations endorsing abortion are Jewish in spite of Jews being 2.3 percent of the U.S. population, not 50 percent. The Jewish community is disproportionately represented in the pro-abortion movement. 'This taking up the cudgels for abortion is not by any means an expression of Judaism. It is a rejection of God and a rejection of the religious core of Judaism, and in those terms I understand why Bernard Nathanson had to seek another faith.'

Nathanson also felt he had

to seek something that had the theological construct he needed to face his sin. Life's twilight was approaching and inexorable judgment looming, and the doctor was entranced by the idea of going round and round in one of Dante's seven circles of hell [*sic*] 'I felt the burden of sin growing heavier and more insistent,' he writes. 'I have such heavy moral baggage to drag into the next world that failing to believe would condemn me to an eternity perhaps more terrifying than anything Dante envisioned in his celebration of the redemptive fall and rise of Easter. I am afraid.'

He began casting about for a system that provided space for guilt and could assure him 'that someone died for my sins and my evil two millennia ago.' 'The New Testament God was a loving, forgiving, incomparably cossetting figure in whom I would seek, and ultimately find, the forgiveness I have pursued so hopelessly, for so long.'

McCloskey, now 42, was half Nathanson's age when he met the doctor nine years ago and was all too glad to help along the way. The well-read priest was Nathanson's intellectual equal, able to discuss everything from medieval [*sic*] Jewish philosophers like Spinoza to Etienne Gilson, a twentieth century French philosopher as Nathanson wrestled with his questions. 'He's receptive, he's a listener, and he speaks the language of reason and erudition,' Nathanson says of his instructor. 'He's simpatico with someone like myself who's seeking faith but still wants reason - a difficult language to speak simultaneously.'

'I needed faith but I needed reason to prop me up. Reason was a safety net for the leap of faith,' he said, borrowing the term from Kierkegaard. 'You can remove the net, but only after you've made the leap.'

Nathanson was likewise fascinated with Luke the evangelist, who besides being a physician was also a credible first-century historian. Reading Luke and Acts was essential to Nathanson's slow switch to Christianity as he grasped Luke's point that the unbelievable events such as a physical resurrection of the dead were possible and had actually happened.

'It requires true courage to admit not only you're wrong but you're awfully wrong,' McCloskey says. 'He is a man of goodwill and a man interested in pursuing the truth no matter what the cost. I think he's been doing enormous penance for the pro-life cause since the late '70s when he changed his mind. In a human sense, he's been making reparation. The cross of Jesus Christ and the sacrament of baptism washes away any guilt and temporal punishment for his sins. Once he's baptized, he's a different man. That's the whole essence of Christianity.'

Nathanson has since taken off a year to take courses at the Kennedy Institute of Ethics at Georgetown University. He then wrote the book, floating through which are occasional references to his new love: Jesus Christ, as opposed to his old love: himself. He is considering changing careers and taking up a teaching position at a hospital, possibly a Catholic one. There are several offers. He attends a parish in Manhattan's Chelsea district where soon he will stand before the baptismal font and renounce forever the world, the flesh, and the devil. 'I will be free from sin,' he says. 'For the first time in my life, I will feel the shelter and warmth of faith'"); Lorene Hanley Duquin, *A Century of Catholic Converts* (2003), p.218.

Neal, Patricia (born Patsy Louise Neal) – actress; b. 20 January 1926, Packard, Whitley County, Kentucky; c. 30 March 2010; d. 8 August 2010, Edgartown, Martha's Vineyard, Massachusetts; grew up in Knoxville, Tennessee; studied drama at Northwestern University; moved to New York and worked in the theatre there, winning the 1947 Tony Award for Best Featured Actress in a Play (Lillian Hellman's *Another Part of the Forest*); became successful as a Hollywood film actress, featuring in such films as *Bright Leaf* (1950); *The Breaking Point* (1950); *Operation Pacific* (1951); *The Day the Earth Stood Still* (1951); *A Face in the Crowd* (1957); *The Miracle Worker* (1959) and *Breakfast at Tiffany's* (1961); during and after her starring role in *The Fountainhead* (1949) she had a five year affair with her co-star Gary Cooper (see above) during this time; she was persuaded to have an abortion by Cooper in 1950 ("For over thirty years, alone, in the night, I cried. For years and years I cried over that baby...If I had only one thing to do over in my life, I would have that baby"); returned to Broadway as well as doing films; in 1963 she won the Academy Award for Best Actress in *Hud*; later films were *In Harm's Way* (1965) and *The Subject Was Roses* (1968) (nominated for an Academy Award for the latter); won a Golden Globe for her performance in the television movie *The Homecoming: A Christmas Story* (1971); received three Emmy nominations; famous for her husky voice; married the British writer Roald Dahl (1916-1990) in 1953; they had five children, but suffered the following tragedies: in 1960 their son Theo, four months old, suffered brain damage when his baby carriage was struck by a taxicab in New York City; in 1962 their daughter, Olivia, died at age 7 from measles encephalitis; in 1965 she suffered three strokes while pregnant, was in a coma for three weeks, and had to learn again to walk and talk; her husband left her for a younger woman and her marriage ended in divorce in 1983; in 1981 a television movie of her life, *The Patricia Neal Story*, was produced; she did much work for the pro-life cause and for paralysis victims; she was a narrator in *The Face: Jesus in Art*, a 2001 documentary series that traced the dramatically different ways Christ has been represented in art throughout seventeen centuries; became reconciled with Gary Cooper's wife and daughter, who influenced her towards the Catholic faith by encouraging her to visit the former film star, Mother Dolores Hart (see above), in her monastery; buried in that monastery, the Abbey of Regina Laudis, Bethlehem, Litchfield County, Connecticut; see *As I Am* (1988) (autobiography) ("The abbess suggested that I spend the month of December at the nunnery. Not merely as a guest, she said; if I accepted, I would live in the monastery like a pre-postulant...

I did not live the exact life of a postulant, but I did my best. I followed a strict schedule of work and prayer. I kept silent at meals, was on time for church. I helped bake bread. And I weeded in the greenhouse. I did a lot of that. There were times during that month I felt I never wanted to return to the outside world.

But still, I could not get the thought of Felicity Crossland [the woman for whom her husband left her] out of my mind. Like a venom it poisoned the times I should have been concentrating on other things.

Time after time, I raged to the sister that that bitch - and I used the word to shock and hurt - now had thirty years of my life. That *bitch* had everything *I* had conceived. I had gone through labor for nothing.

She would ask if I really thought it was possible to go through life all for nothing. Sure as hell looked that way, I told her. She told me I could not lose what I had honestly given my body to bring into being.

The stroke was the key. She said I would never have come to the abbey or into a reflective dimension of an enclosure except for the stroke... 'Everyone has to face the stroke of the Cross,' she said, 'Yours had to be more dramatic because you are an actress and the Lord is a very faithful husband to you.'
'I built my husband up all over the world and he is a shit now.'
'You are not a mother if you build someone else up and then resent him for it.'
'I have lost everything, don't you understand? She has taken it away from me.'
'You haven't lost yourself.'

I was so tired of hearing that. 'I have had a *f***ing* stroke! I am a *f***ing* cripple! 1 am so scared that I can't make it on my own, that I'll end up a *f***ing bag lady*! Can't you see? That's why I hurt'
'To bear suffcring always has meaning.'
'And I'm tired of that *f***ing shit.*'

Suddenly she was on her feet. Those eyes were blazing. And I am tired of *your* f***ing, f***ing, f***ing nonsense! I am so tired that nothing else matters to you. A *great* woman is *whole*. She is *for* others and, yes, Patricia, 'one hundred percent honest.' She is pure because she is penetrable. There is a part of you that has to call a spade a spade, but also a part that has to find some fertility in the rot. You want your femaleness but you don't want your Woman. I thought if I let you vomit long enough you would get it out of your system and begin asking for something. You are not asking for anything here, so you will get nothing here. Now will you get out!'

She turned and left. I could not believe she had treated me that way. It took me a long, long time before I could cry, and then I wept my heart out. But I could not leave.

That night at supper she came into the dining room, and when I saw her I began to weep again. I was so desperately sorry. She spoke quietly. 'You are a great mother, Patricia. You can give life forever - if you will stop trying to keep score'"); Stephen Michael Shearer, *Patricia Neal: An Unquiet Life* (2006); *creativeminorityreport.com* ("Mgr. Lisante said this of Patricia Neal who was receiving a pro-life award in 2003: 'I met Patricia Neal over 20 years ago, and we have become good friends ever since. One time when she was on my television show, I said to her, 'Pat, in so many ways you are a female Job.' She had, as you know, several strokes which put her in a coma for a month. She had a daughter who died of the measles at the age of seven. She had a son who was hit when he was an infant by a car in New York City, and he remains alive but brain-damaged and will be forever. Another daughter who suffered from drug and alcohol addiction; a husband who was great to her once she had the strokes, but he ultimately left her for a younger woman.

And I said, 'In your life, Pat, if there was one thing you could change, what would it be?' And Patricia Neal said, 'Father, none of the things you just mentioned.' But she said, 'Forty years ago I became involved with the actor Gary Cooper, and by him I became pregnant. As he was a married man and I was young in Hollywood and not wanting to ruin my career, we chose to have the baby aborted.' She said, 'Father, alone in the night for over forty years, I have cried for my child. And if there is one thing I wish I had the courage to do over in my life, I wish I had the courage to have that baby.'

Patricia Neal has put herself on the line in saying to many, many women who have experienced abortion or thought about abortion, 'Don't make my mistake. Let your baby live.' What's particularly painful, but poignant in this story is that some years later, Patricia became good friends with Maria Cooper, the only child of Gary Cooper and his wife. And Maria Cooper said, 'You know, I know you had the affair with my father and I have long ago forgiven that. But one thing I find it hard to accept is that as an only child, I so wish that you'd had my brother or my sister. Because in so many ways, I wish that you had chosen life'").

Neuhaus, Richard John – priest; b. 14 May 1936, Pembroke, Ontario, Canada; c. 8 September 1990 (received by John Cardinal O'Connor); d. 8 January 2009, New York; one of eight children of a Lutheran minister; parents both U.S. citizens; brought up as a Missouri Synod Lutheran; at age of fourteen moved to Nebraska; dropped out of high school at age of sixteen; educated at Concordia University, Austin, Texas; entered Concordia Lutheran Seminary, in St. Louis, Missouri; ordained a Lutheran minister in 1960; involved in Lutheran-Catholic dialogue; worked on civil rights and social justice issues; spoke out against the Victnam War; at that time a liberal in politics; his whole perspective he claimed was altered by the decision in *Roe v Wade* (1973) legalizing abortion ("I said then, and I've been saying all these years, that the most decisive and most tragic thing that has happened in American life is that the liberal flag got planted on the wrong side of the abortion debate"); he became a neo-conservative and advocated "democratic capitalism"; helped to found the Institute on Religion and Democracy in 1981; established as part of the Rockford Institute (publishers of *Chronicles* magazine) the Center for Religion and Society and its journal, *First Things*, which he edited to publicize the neo-conservative cause; he and the center were "forcibly evicted" from the Institute in 1989 under disputed circumstances (some say for exceeding the budget; others see it as a sign of the divisons between paleo-conservatives and neo-conservatives); became a Catholic in 1990; ordained to the priesthood in 1991 by Cardinal John O'Connor of New York; regular broadcaster for the Catholic television network *EWTN*; he was a vigorous advocate for denying communion to Catholic politicians who supported abortion and voted against the church's teaching on life issues; important adviser to President George W. Bush on a series of religious and ethical matters, e.g., abortion, cloning; stem-cell research, and the defense of marriage amendment; became a naturalized United States citizen; see *Unsecular America* (1986); *The Naked Public Square: Religion and Democracy in America* (1986); *Jews in Unsecular America* (1987); *The Catholic Moment: The Paradox of the Church in the Postmodern World* (1987); *Believing Today: Jew and Christian in Conversation* (1989) (with Leon Kliniki); (ed), *Guaranteeing the Good Life: Medicine and the Return of Eugenics* (1990); Mary Arnold, "Richard John Neuhaus Interviewed," *AD 2000*, June 1991 ("I think the Lutheran Reformation was intended to be a movement of reform within and for the Catholic Church in full communion with Rome. That was Luther's intention. And, more important than Luther himself, was the *Augsburg Confession* of 1530 in which the intention quite clearly was not to break away and start a Lutheran Church. However, after 1530, for political, social and theological reasons, the divide became so unbridgeable that the 'reformers' believed they had no alternative but to break from Rome and start their own Church"); *Doing Well & Doing Good: The Challenge to the Christian Capitalist* (1992); *America Against Itself: Moral Vision and the Public Order* (1992); *Freedom for Ministry: A Guide for the Perplexed Who Are Called to Serve* (1992); *To Empower People: From State to Civil Society* (1996) (with Peter Berger); *The Best of the Public Square* (1997); *Appointment in Rome: The Church in America Awakening* (1999); (ed), *The Eternal Pity: Reflections on Dying* (2000); *A Free Society Reader: Principles for the New Millennium* (2000); (ed), *There We Stood, Here We Stand: Eleven Lutherans Rediscover Their Catholic Roots* (2001) (with Timothy Drake); (ed), *The Second One Thousand Years: Ten People Who Defined a Millennium* (2001); *The Best of the Public Square: Book 2* (2001); *Death on a Friday Afternoon: Meditations on the Last Words of Jesus from the Cross* (2001); *As I Lay Dying: Meditations Upon Returning* (2002); (ed), *The Chosen People in an Almost Chosen Nation: Jews and Judaism in America* (2002); (ed), *Your Word Is Truth: A Project of Evangelicals and Catholics Together* (2002) (with Charles Colson); "How I Became the Catholic I Was," *First Things*, April 2002 (reprinted in *Canadian Converts: The Path to Rome* (2009)) ("[T]he Lutheran chapter in the history of the Church did occasion schism, and for that unhappy fact there was blame enough to share all around. In my judgment, the division was tragic but not necessary. There was and is no truth that requires division from the pillar and bulwark of truth. The Catholic Church, as Chesterton observed, is ever so much larger from the inside than from the outside. And especially is that the case, I would add, for those whose identity as Protestants depends upon their being outside. And so it was that for thirty years as a Lutheran pastor, thinker, and writer…, I worked for what I incessantly called 'the healing of the breach of the sixteenth century between Rome and the Reformation.' For a long time there seemed to be believable, albeit painfully slow, movement toward that goal…These hopeful signs, however, were not to last.

The last several decades have not been kind to Lutheranism. By the end of the 1980s it seemed evident to me that real, existent Lutheranism - as distinct from Lutheranism as an idea or school of thought - had, willy-nilly but decisively, turned against the fulfillment of its destiny as a reforming movement within the one Church of Christ. Lutheranism in all its parts, both in this country and elsewhere, had settled for being a permanently separated Protestant denomination; or, as the case may be, several Protestant denominations…

Mine was a decision mandated by conscience. I have never found it in his writings, but a St. Louis professor who had been his student told me that the great confessional Lutheran theologian Peter Brunner regularly said that a Lutheran who does not daily ask himself why he is not a Roman Catholic cannot know why he is a Lutheran. That impressed me very deeply. I was thirty years a Lutheran pastor, and after thirty years of asking myself why I was not a Roman Catholic I finally ran out of answers that were convincing either to me or to others. And so I discovered not so much that I had made the decision as that the decision was made, and I have never looked back, except to trace the marks of grace, of *sola gratia*, each step of the way.

My reception occasioned some little comment, including the observation that I and others who make this decision have a 'felt need for authority.' This is usually said in a condescending manner by people who believe that they are able to live with ambiguities and tensions that some of us cannot handle. Do I have a felt need for authority, for obedience, for submission? But of course. Obedience is the rightly ordered disposition toward truth, and submission is subordination of the self to that by which the self is claimed. Truth commands, and authority has to do with the authorship, the origins, of commanding truth. By what authority? By whose authority? There are no more important questions for the right ordering of our lives and ministries. Otherwise, in our preaching, teaching, and entire ministry we are just making it up as we go along, and, by acting in God's name, taking His name in vain.

It was sadly amusing to read that a Lutheran denomination in this country is undertaking a major study with a view toward revising its teaching on sexual morality, with particular reference to homosexuality. Especially striking was the assurance that the study would be conducted 'without any prior assumptions.' Imagine that. The entire course of Christian fidelity is obedience to the received truth of God's self-revelation in Jesus Christ, and the Spirit's guiding of the Church's reflection on that truth. At some point this Lutheran body will arrive at its new teaching. Through a complicated process of bureaucratic planning, interest group agitation, and a legitimating majority vote, it will eventually arrive at the point of saying 'this we believe, teach, and confess.' Undoubtedly Scripture will be cited, but, as Luther said, biblical texts, like wax noses, can be twisted to fit. If, as seems probable, this body adopts a new teaching and one asks by what authority it teaches this new doctrine, the only honest answer will be, 'Because we will it to be so.' 'It is what was decided by the procedures adopted by our religious society,' they might say. 'Ours is, after all, a voluntary association, so nobody else has any right to complain.' By the rules of that denomination, the Church through time and the contemporary Church universal, to which Christ promised the Spirit's guidance, does not get a vote.

From my boyhood intuitions as an ecclesial Christian, it seemed self-evident that, if God intended to reveal any definite truths for the benefit of humankind, and if Jesus intended a continuing community of discipleship, then some reliable means would be provided for the preservation and transmission of such truths through the centuries. Catholics believe that God did provide such reliable means by giving the apostles and their successors, the bishops, authority to teach in His name and by promising to be with them forever. The teaching of the apostles and of the apostolic churches, securely grounded in the biblical Word of God, continues to this day, and will continue to the end of time. Catholics believe that, under certain carefully prescribed circumstances, the pope and the whole body of bishops are able to teach with infallibility. That is a word that frightens many, but I don't think it should. It means that the Church is indefectible, that we have God's promise that He will never allow the Church to definitively defect from the truth, to fall into apostasy. Infallibility, Avery Cardinal Dulles [see above] writes, 'is simply another way of saying that the Holy Spirit will preserve the Church against using its full authority to require its members to assent to what is false.' Without that assurance, he adds, 'the truth of revelation would not be preserved in recognizable form.' And, I would add, to obey the truth we must be able to recognize the truth.

The question of authority, the question of Who says so?, has been with the Church from the beginning. In Corinth some invoked Peter, some Paul, some Apollos, and some Christ. And so it was later with the Montanists, the Arians, the Nestorians, the Valentinians, the Donatists, and on and on. A sure mark of a heretical and schismatic community, said St. Augustine, is that it names itself by a man or an idea rather than by the simple title 'Catholic.' Also centuries later, for example in the sixteenth century, those who had sense enough to know that the Church did not begin with their new theological insight tried to reconstruct Christian history to fit their views. Thus the Lutheran Matthias Illyricus Flacius compiled the *Magdeburg Centuries*; thus followers of John Knox claimed to have reestablished the polity of the New Testament Church; thus the 'Landmarkist' historiography of American Baptists who trace the lineage of the one true Church through

Cathari, Waldensians, Lollards, Albigenses, and all the way back to Jesus himself. All such efforts attempt to answer the question of authority. Some are less ludicrous than others, but none is plausible. As St. Augustine and all Catholic teachers have known, the teaching of the Church is lived forward, not reconstructed backward.

St. Augustine appealed to the *securus judicat orbis terrarum* - the secure judgment of the whole world, by which he meant the Catholic Church. Yes, but what do you do when that judgment is unclear or in heated dispute? Augustine's answer is that you wait, in firm communion with the Catholic Church and in firm confidence that the Holy Spirit will, as promised, clarify the matter in due course. The point is that apostolic doctrine cannot be maintained over time without apostolic ministry, meaning ministry that is both apostolic in its origins and apostolic in its governing authority. This argument is brilliantly advanced in his polemic against the Donatists, who appealed to St. Cyprian as precedent for refusing to recognize the sacraments of the *traditores*, those who had lapsed in time of persecution. Yes, answered Augustine, the holy Cyprian was confused, and admitted as much; but he awaited clarification by the *securus judicat orbis terrarum*. The one thing he would not do, unlike the Donatists, was to break communion with the Catholic Church.

The Church is holy in practice and correct in doctrine, said the schismatic Donatists, and therefore it cannot exist in communion with the unholy and erring. It follows that the Donatists are the true Church. To which Augustine replied: 'If, therefore, by such communion with the wicked the just cannot but perish, the Church had already perished in the time of Cyprian. Whence then sprang the origin of Donatus? Where was he taught, where was he baptized, where was he ordained, since [you claim that] the Church had been already destroyed by the contagion of communion with the wicked? But if the Church still existed, the wicked could do no harm to the good in one communion with them. Wherefore did you separate yourselves?'

'Wherefore did you separate yourselves?' Augustine's question echoes down through the centuries, directed at all who have separated themselves from communion with the Catholic Church. Today the criticism is heard that the Catholic Church, for all its magisterial authority, will permit almost anything in teaching or practice so long as one does not formally break communion with the Church. There is truth in that, although I think it not a criticism but a compliment. While what Lutherans call the *publica doctrina*, the public teaching, of the Catholic Church is lucidly clear, it is true that the Church bends every effort, puts the best construction on every deviant opinion, in order to avoid what Augustine calls 'the heinous and damnable sin of schism.' For instance, in the twenty-three years of the supposedly authoritarian pontificate of John Paul II, the number of theologians publicly censured can probably be counted on the fingers of one hand, and the only schism has been that of the integralist Lefebvrists of France. Disagreement, confusion, and false teaching can do great evil, but the remedy for such evil is always to be found in communion with that body that is gifted with the charism of providing *securus judicat orbis terrarum.*

Councils can err, said the Reformers. No, says the Catholic Church, but the Church's teaching lives forward, and no definition, including that of councils, is entirely adequate to the whole of the truth. The Catholic Church has always taught with St. Paul that now, as he says in 1 Corinthians 13, we see in a mirror dimly, but then face to face. Now we know in part; then we shall understand fully, even as we have been fully understood. Along the way to that eschatological fullness - which is a frequently jagged, confusing, and conflicted way - it is promised to the Church that she will not, she will not irretrievably, lose the way. It is not everything that we might want, but it is enough; it is more than enough.

The Church's teaching lives forward; it is not reconstructed backward—whether from the fifth century or the sixteenth or the nineteenth or the twenty-first. But through all the changes of living forward, how do we know what is corruption and what is authentic development? Recall Cardinal Newman's reflection on the development of doctrine, a reflection that has been incorporated by magisterial teaching. He suggested seven marks of authentic development: authentic development preserves the Church's apostolic form; it reflects continuity of principles in testing the unknown by the known; it demonstrates the power to assimilate what is true, even in what is posited against it; it follows a logical sequence; it anticipates future developments; it conserves past developments; and, throughout, it claims and demonstrates the vigor of teaching authority. And thus it is, said St. Vincent of Lerins in the fifth century, that in authentic development of doctrine nothing presents itself in the Church's old age that was not latent in her youth. Such was the truth discovered by Augustine, a truth 'ever ancient, ever new.'

And so it is that this ecclesial Christian, this son of St. John's Lutheran Church in Pembroke, this former Lutheran pastor of St. John the Evangelist in Brooklyn, was led to 8 September 1990, to be received into full communion by John Cardinal O'Connor in his residence chapel of St. John the Evangelist, my patron saint. In every way, including my awareness of the intercession of St. John, the continuities are ever so much more striking than the discontinuities. In the words of the Second Vatican Council, my Protestant brothers and sisters are, by virtue of baptism and faith in Christ, truly but imperfectly in communion with the Catholic Church. Which means also, of course, that I am truly but imperfectly in communion with them. Moreover, and according to the same Council, all the saving and sanctifying grace to be found outside the boundaries of the Catholic Church gravitates toward the perfection of that imperfect communion. Some view the Catholic Church as claiming to be self-sufficient, but that is not true. Her ecclesiology is such that, of all Christian communions, she knows herself to be most in need. Nowhere are the words *Ut unum sint*, 'that they may all be one,' prayed so fervently; nowhere is the wound of our broken communion felt so keenly; nowhere is the commitment to reconciliation so relentless or irrevocable.

It would take another essay to survey the current prospect for such reconciliation. Suffice it to say that, whether with respect to the Orthodox Church of the East or the separated communions of the West, these are hard times for ecumenism, hard times for the hope for Christian unity. But the Church has known many times that were harder, much harder; she has learned that the better part of fidelity is sometimes simply persistent waiting upon the movement of the Holy Spirit toward possibilities that she can neither anticipate nor control, but for which we must together pray.

As for now, I end where I began - as in my life's course I began where I have ended - by saying again: 'To those of you with whom I have traveled in the past, know that we travel together still. In the mystery of Christ and his Church nothing is lost, and the broken will be mended. If, as I am persuaded, my communion with Christ's Church is now the fuller, then it follows that my unity with all who are in Christ is now the stronger. We travel together still'"); *EWTN Audio Library, The Journey Home* (26 May 2003) ("In *Lumen Gentium* in the Second Vatican Council, the great Constitution on the Church, it says that anyone who believes that the Catholic Church is what she claims to be is then in conscience bound to enter into and remain in communion with the Catholic Church. Well, long before I entered into full communion…, I had been led to the conclusion that, yes, the Catholic Church is what she claims to be. Therefore, according to that rule of *Lumen Gentium*…, obviously I should enter into full communion. That decision had already been made you see. The question was *how* do you enter into full communion? Working with a lot of other Lutheran theologians and pastors and writers and so forth, I hoped that we would come into communion together through a process of ecclesial reconciliation. Gradually it became apparent to me by the mid-1980s that Lutheranism was not moving towards ecclesial reconciliation; indeed that the dominant part of Lutheranism, the ELCA Lutherans in this country, were moving away from the very evangelical Catholic direction that so many of us had invested so much of our lives...

And so at that point, then, the decision having been made that *Lumen Gentium* talks about, namely is the Catholic Church what she claims to be, that decision having been answered positively. Then it just became a question of my having to act personally rather than in the collective reconciliation that I hoped for...

Much more important than trying to get straight the history and the theology of Luther and Reformation intent is that within the American ethos is a very widespread gnostic, radically individualistic, kind of spirituality. Ralph Waldo Emerson is perhaps the grand-daddy of it all – that finally the self is the divine spark, and it is God or the transcendent and myself, and this has nothing to do with tradition. Tradition is a bad word. It transcends history. History is a burden; history is bunk; history is yesterday. 'Don't talk to me about authority, goodness knows, whether apostolic, or divine, or anything. I am my authority. It works for me. It is the truth for me, you see.'

And this, call it gnostic, call it Emersonian, call it transcendentalist, whatever one wants to call it. 'Gnostic' I think is the best term. This is pervasive throughout American culture... Running through almost everything that calls itself spirituality, whether with a new age label or not, is this gnostic notion that somehow true spirituality, authentic spiritual fulfilment, means the transcendence of institutions, authority, history, tradition.

Whereas Christianity, of any sort that is recognizably Christian, says 'No, it all begins with the transcendence, with God, the absolute, entering into history, creation, tradition, arguments, the human condition in short, you see, including the Church. So that for Christians, if Christ is Lord, then there can only be one Lord, one Christ, and therefore there can only be one Body of Christ, the Church.

So that a couple of years ago the Congregation for the Doctrine of the Faith, Cardinal Ratzinger's office, put out a statement, as you may remember, called *Dominus Jesus*, which caused an enormous ecumenical ruckus, in which he simply said what I think all Christians surely have to agree to, that ultimately because there's one Christ, there can only be one head and one body and therefore one Church. And therefore it's not adequate, it is not accurate, it is not finally faithful to our biblical faith, to speak about many churches, except in the sense of local churches of the one Church. The one Church is the Body of Christ. Now, what does the Catholic Church say? The Catholic Church says that this one Church of Jesus Christ subsists in the Catholic Church in a way that cannot be said of any other Christian community...

Of course, we know what it means to be a Catholic. To be a Catholic is to be in communion with the bishop who is in communion with the Bishop of Rome, who is in succession to the apostles and to our Lord Jesus Christ. So that's a simple enough definition of what it means to be a Catholic. What, then, does the Catholic Church claim? The Catholic Church claims that this is the Church of Jesus Christ most fully and rightly ordered through time. To be obedient to Christ, to want to be a disciple of Jesus, has built into it an ecclesial or churchly dynamic. It is to want to be part of the community of disciples through time, as that community of disciples, namely the Church, is most fully and rightly ordered, which is the Catholic Church"); *The Best of the Public Square: Book 3* (2007); *Catholic Matters: Confusion, Controversy, and the Splendor of Truth* (2007); *American Babylon: Notes of a Christian Exile* (2009); *First Things*, In Memoriam Issue, April 2009; George William Rutler, *Cloud of Witnesses: Dead People I Knew When They Were Alive* (2010); Lorene Hanley Duquin, *A Century of Catholic Converts* (2003), p.206; Neuhaus online archive.

Neumann, John Louis von ("Johnny") (Hungarian name Neumann János Lajos) – mathematician, physicist and economist; b. 28 December 1903, Budapest, Hungary; c. 1930; d. 8 February 1957, Washington, D.C.; eldest of three brothers in a wealthy Jewish family; his father Max Neumann was a banker; child prodigy in mathematics (had mastered calculus by the age of eight), memorization and language; attended a German-speaking Lutheran high school, but received private tuition in mathematics; studied chemistry and mathematics at the University of Berlin 1921-1923; by the age of nineteen he had published two major papers; PhD in Mathematics from the University of Budapest by the age of twenty-two; taught at the University of Berlin 1926-1930; accepted an invitation to Princeton University in 1930; one of the first four people selected for the faculty of the Institute for Advanced Study at Princeton (two of the others being Albert Einstein and Kurt Gödel); Mathematics Professor at the Institute until his death; became a naturalized citizen of the United States in 1937; married Mariette Kövesi in 1930 (one daughter of the marriage; they divorced in 1937), then married Klára Dán in 1938; regarded as one of the greatest ever mathematicians; made major contributions to many areas of mathematics, notably set theory, quantum mechanics, game theory, functional analysis, ergodic theory and operator theory; he was also a principal member of the Manhattan Project; developed the equilibrium strategy of mutually assured destruction ("MAD"); a founding figure in computer science; advisor on U.S. scientific and military policy; wrote 150 published papers; staunch anti-communist; he partly inspired the character of Dr. Strangelove in the film of that name; won many honors; baptized Catholic on his first marriage, but did not practice his religion after the divorce and had a reputation as an agnostic; while in hospital suffering from cancer, from which he died, he invited a Catholic priest, Father Anselm Strittmatter, OSB, to visit him for consultation and the priest administered the last sacraments to him; buried at Princeton Cemetery in Princeton, Mercer County, New Jersey; his only daughter, Marina (by his first wife) a professor of International Trade and Public Policy at the University of Michigan; see A. H. Taub (ed), *Collected Works of John von Neumann* (1963); P. R. Halmos, "The Legend of von Neumann," *The American Mathematical Monthly*, April 1973, p.382 ("The speed with which von Neumann could think was awe-inspiring. G. Pólya admitted that 'Johnny was the only student I was ever afraid of. If in the course of a lecture I stated an unsolved problem, the chances were he'd come to me as soon as the lecture was over, with the complete solution in a few scribbles on a slip of paper.' Abstract proofs or numerical calculations - he was equally quick with both, but he was especially pleased with and proud of his facility with numbers. When his electronic computer was ready for its first preliminary test, someone suggested a relatively simple problem involving powers of 2. (It was something of this kind: what is the smallest power of 2 with the property that its decimal digit fourth from the right is 7? This is a completely trivial problem for a present-day computer: it takes only a fraction of a second of machine time). The machine and Johnny started at the same time, and Johnny finished first") (this article also deals with his conversion on the occasion of his first marriage); Norman Macrae, *John von Neumann* (1992); *ANB* ("A common reaction to him is expressed by Herbert F. York's observation that smart people found him the smartest person they had ever met").

Nevada, Emma (born Emma Wixom) - opera singer; b. 7 February 1859, Alpha, California; c. 1884; d. 20 June 1940, near Liverpool, England; her father, William Wallace Wixom, was the physician for gold and silver mine camps; spent her childhood in nearby Nevada City (from which she took her stage name); showed musical talent from an early age; studied music and many languages at Mills College, Oakland, California; studied singing for three years in Vienna with Matilde Marchesi, the famous voice teacher; made her stage debut at Her Majesty's theatre, London, as Amina in Bellini's *La Sonnambula* in 1880; debuts La Scala, Milan (performance engaged by Verdi) in 1881 and in Paris in 1883; toured the United States with great success in 1884, but then continued her career in Europe; her conversion to the Catholic faith around then probably influenced by her godmother Mrs. John Mackay, wife of the "Bonanza King" who made a fortune in Virginia City mining silver; concert tours of the United States in 1885-1886, 1899 and 1901-1902; one of the finest coloratura sopranos of her generation; most notable for her performances in operas by Bellini, Donizetti, Gounod and Delibes; in 1885 she married Raymond Palmer, a physician, who became her manager; they settled in Paris; hosted salons and musical gatherings; her last performance was in *Lakmé* in Berlin in 1910; her medallion is one of three (along with those of Malibran and Pasta) that adorns Bellini's monument in Naples; she taught singing in England in her retirement; her daughter, Mignon (1886-1971), became a celebrated opera singer under the name of Mignon Nevada; buried St. Peter and St. Paul Churchyard, Crosby, Merseyside, England; see web site on her life and career, *msu.edu/~graye/emma.*

Newton, John - soldier and engineer; b. 24 August 1822, Norfolk, Virginia; d. 1 May 1895, New York City; son of General Thomas Newton and Margaret Jordan; enrolled in the U.S. Military Academy in 1838; graduated second in a class that included James Longstreet (see above), John Pope and William Rosencrans (see below); commissioned second lieutenant of engineers; assistant professor of engineering at West Point; commissioned first lieutenant in 1852, and promoted colonel in 1856; commissioned major in August 1861 and brigadier-general of volunteers in September 1861; worked on construction of the defenses of Washington and commanded a brigade in defense of the city; distinguished himself in many actions, including the battle of Antietam; for his gallantry he was brevetted lieutenant-colonel of regulars; he led a division at Fredericksburg in the storming of Marye Heights and was then made major-general of volunteers; brevetted colonel of regulars for gallant service at Gettysburg; he fought in all the major actions during the pursuit of the Confederate forces and for his gallantry was brevetted major-general of volunteers and brigadier-general and major-general of regulars; after the Civil War he became chief of the engineers in the regular service; he became famous for his improvement of the defenses of New York and of the river system; married to Anna M. Starr; see *Catholic Encyclopedia* ("In his early manhood he became, and until his death remained, an earnest and devout member of the Catholic Church"); *ANB*.

Northrop, Lucius Bellinger – army officer and physician; b. 8 September 1811, Charleston, South Carolina; d. 9 February 1894, Pikesville, Maryland; father was Amos Bird Northrop, a lawyer who was a legislator and attorney-general of South Carolina; he was only a baby when his father died; mother was Claudia Margaret Bellinger from a notable Charleston family; became a Catholic when a young man (along with his mother and sisters and his brother, Claudian, father of the Catholic Bishop of Charleston); attended West Point Military Academy (graduated in 1831), where he became a close friend of Jefferson Davis; suffered much illness and was kept on the sick list recuperating at home; studied medicine, which he then practiced; married Maria Euphenia Joanna de Bernabeu, one quarter French and three quarters English; at the start of the Civil War he joined the Confederacy; President Davis made him colonel in charge of the Commissary Department (responsible for foodstuffs), in which post he faced great problems for reasons beyond his control; given continual support by Jefferson Davis; at the end of the war he was taken prisoner in North Carolina; farmed sporadically until 1890; buried in the New Cathedral Cemetery, Baltimore, Maryland; see his papers located at the New York Public Library; *ANB*.

Novak, Robert David Sanders ("Bob") – journalist, author and political commentator; b. 26 February 1931, Joliet, Illinois; c. 20 May 1998 ("My conversion to the Catholic faith has put in perspective any petty personal difficulties"; received on the Vigil of the Ascension at St. Patrick's Church, Washington; his wife Geraldine converted a little earlier and his son Alexander was received before that); d. 18 August 2009, Washington, D.C.; his paternal grandparents were from the Ukraine; mother's family from Lithuania; parents had Jewish background, but rarely practiced their religion; as a high school student he wrote for a local newspaper; educated at the University of Illinois at Urbana-Champaign 1948-1952; wrote for the student newspaper; left university without a degree to work as a full-time journalist; served in the U.S. Army as a lieutenant during the Korean War; worked for the Associated Press as a political correspondent 1954-1958; worked for the Wall Street Journal 1958-1963; in 1963 created with Rowland Evans (1921-2001) the *Inside Report* (also known as *Inside*

Washington), a newspaper column published four times a week, which ran until 2008, the longest running syndicated political column in American history; gradually moved to a Conservative position; he was a "persistent shoe leather" investigative reporter; he obtained some legendary scoops; broadcaster for *CNN* 1980-2005 (co-host of the political talk show *Crossfire*); worked later for *Fox News*; given the nickname "Prince of Darkness" by his friend, reporter John Lindsay, because Lindsay "thought for a young man I took a very dim view of the prospects for our civilization"; wrote for numerous publications; referred to by Brent Bozell (see above) as a "gladiator" of American Conservatism ("I like to cause trouble and stir up strife. In the Dark Ages, there was a French nobleman named Bertrand de Born who really stirred up strife. He raided other people's castles, killed, and caused tumult. In *The Inferno*, Dante places Bertrand de Born at the door to Purgatory, with his severed head in his hand, where he is condemned to stand for all eternity because in life he was a stirrer-up of strife. Bertrand de Born has been my idol ever since I read about him as an English-literature major in college" [Note: Bertrand de Born appears in the *Inferno*, which is Hell, not Purgatory. He is a "Sower of Discord" in circle 8. If he were in Purgatory, he would not be there for "all eternity." It is Cato the virtuous Pagan who is "at the door to Purgatory"]); married twice; agnostic for several years; political and religious views influenced by the anti-communism and moral absolutism of Whittaker Chambers' book *Witness* ("The book really convinced me that to reject God was a huge mistake and was folly. So I was a believer. But I was unchurched. I wasn't a Christian"); supported the Korean and Vietnam wars, but was opposed to the Iraq war, and expressed doubts about the invasion of Afghanistan; when interviewed in 2007 he said, "I do believe the American people are really up to making the best of their politicians...When I am given a chance to address college students, I always tell them, 'Always love your country but never trust your government.' I believe that"; wrote in support of the Palestinian cause and critical of Israel's policies; lived as an agnostic for seventy years; in the early 1980s he nearly died from spinal meningitis; at that time he was given some books on the Catholic faith by his friend Jeffrey Bell (b. c.1943), a political consultant; in the early 1990s he started to go to Mass regularly and decided to become a Catholic a few years later; influenced by Fr. C. John McCloskey III of Opus Dei and by Mgr. Peter Vaghi, a former lawyer and also a former source for the Evans and Novak column (he believed the Holy Spirit was behind coincidences such as his former source becoming a priest. "I consider this the only one true faith, so I believe the Holy Spirit led me to it"); instructed by Mgr. Vaghi ("The semipublic nature of RCIA was not for me, and Monsignor Vaghi agreed to give me private instruction"); always pro-life (it was his wife's pro-life convictions that first drew his attention to matters of faith); against divorce, abortion, and the ordination of women; also against innovations in the liturgy ("Once my wife and I were in Palm Beach and we went to Mass there...It was horrible - all that rock music, singing, and swaying. I said at the time that if this had been my introduction to Catholicism, I would have never converted. Of course the Holy Spirit probably would have made sure it wasn't my first exposure"); had prostate cancer in 1991 and lung cancer in 1994 and died from a brain tumor; see *The Agony of the G.O.P.* (1964); *Lyndon B. Johnson: The Exercise of Power* (1966) (with Rowland Evans); *Nixon in the White House: The Frustration of Power* (1971) (with Rowland Evans); *The Reagan Revolution* (1991) (with Rowland Evans); *Completing the Revolution: A Vision for Victory in 2000* (2000); *The Prince of Darkness: 50 Years Reporting in Washington* (2007) (his memoirs) ("On 22 October 1996, I came to Syracuse to deliver the annual Flowers Lecture, partially financed by the Conservative Young America Foundation and sponsored by the College Republicans. Standard procedure for college lectures is a prespeech dinner for the speaker, hosted by the sponsoring student committee. There was one woman on the College Republicans committee, seated across the table from me. She was striking looking, wearing a gold cross on her neck.

What happened next may be distorted in my memory and shaped by the religious mysteries that I see entwined in this episode. Without mentioning the cross, I was impelled to ask the woman a question that normally I would not consider posing. Was she a Catholic? I thought she answered yes and then asked me whether I was one. 'No,' I replied, 'but my wife and I have been going to mass every Sunday for about four years.' 'Do you plan to join the Church?" she asked. I answered: 'No, not at the present time.'

Then the young woman looked at me and said evenly: 'Mr. Novak, life is short, but eternity is for ever.' I was so shaken by what she said that I could barely get through the rest of the dinner and my speech that night. Sometime during the short night before rising to catch a seven a.m. flight back to Washington, I became convinced that the Holy Spirit was speaking through this Syracuse student"); Barbara Matuswo, "The Conversion of Bob Novak," *The Washingtonian*, 1 June 2003; Barbara Matusow, "Pray For Me" *The Washingtonian*, November 2008 (Interview: Q: "You've said your Catholicism was helping you deal with your illness."

A: "Well, nobody wants to die. I certainly don't. But all Christian faiths, and certainly Catholicism, hold that there's an afterlife, that we are not just dust to dust. And that's comforting, particularly now that I have an illness and there's very little chance I will recover. A priest who visited me told me I've been given a chance to prepare myself. So I began to think about my life and what I've done right and not done right and to prepare myself for the last days. I've found that reassuring").

Nutting, Willis Dwight – historian and philosopher; b. 1900, Iowa City, Iowa; c. July 1930; d. 1975; raised in a Presbyterian family; father a distinguished zoologist; educated at University of Iowa; in late teens joined the Episcopal Church; won a Rhodes Scholarship to Keble College, Oxford in 1921; at Oxford he came into contact with Anglo-Catholicism and studied for the Anglican ministry for which he was ordained in 1924; returned to the United States; began to feel that when he said that the Church taught thus and so, he simply meant that that was what *he* believed: "*L'Eglise, c'est moi*"; that his religion was "just private judgment with some historical and ceremonial trimmings"; his character was one of constant questioning, which led him to the Catholic Church ("A person acts and thinks as he does because he has certain convictions. A principle duty of every thinking man is to make a thorough examination of his convictions to see how they are proved true. The holding of unexamined opinions is the mark of an ignorant man"); conversion influenced by Newman's *Essay on the Development of Doctrine*; studied for the priesthood in Rome but discerned that this was not his vocation; in 1933 he obtained a PhD in Philosophy from the University of Iowa; moved to the History Department of the University of Notre Dame; ran a very successful adult education program "Seminar on the Great Human Problems"; great interest in liturgy; advocate of the back-to-the-land movement; married Eileen Barry in 1934 (three children of the marriage); see *How Firm a Foundation?* (1939) (criticism of aspects of modern thought as deriving from errors made by Descartes) ((1) "The old proofs of the supernatural were rejected by the application of the second principle of the Cartesian method. They were subjected to a test of certainty which could be met only by mathematical demonstrations, and naturally, not being concerned with mathematics, they did not meet the test. Therefore they were considered to be no proofs at all, and the whole of mankind's knowledge of the supernatural was rejected as unproved and therefore false.

But this rejection itself cannot pass the test of reasonableness. Since the satisfying certainty of mathematics comes purely from the nature of mathematics itself, it is entirely unreasonable to demand it anywhere else.

If the modern philosopher were to see a complicated piece of machinery in operation, and were to be informed, upon asking for a designer, that it had no designer but that it simply came together by accident, he would consider his informant crazy. Even though he could not prove with mathematical certainty (that is, with no possibility of opposition) that the machinery must have a designer, he would still recognize his demand for a designer to be reasonable. Yet he rejects the argument for a designer of the universe because the argument cannot be shown to have mathematical certainty

And if this same philosopher, having witnessed an explosion, should be told that it did not have a cause, but just happened, he would certainly not be satisfied. He would realize that there must have been a cause, although he would not be able to give an apodeictic, i.e., clear demonstration of this 'must" which would silence all objectors. And yet he rejects the argument for a first cause of the universe because the argument does not have apodeictic certainty.

If, as even a philosopher will recognize, it is unreasonable to demand mathematical certainty when arguing from a structure to its designer and from an event to its cause in every-day experience, it is likewise unreasonable to demand such certainty when arguing from the visible world to its cause and designer.

Such being the case we can rightly maintain that, since the proofs of the supernatural have been rejected for having failed to meet an essentially unreasonable test, their rejection has itself been unreasonable, and that therefore the modern claim that none of mankind's knowledge of the supernatural has been proved, is an unjustified claim. The question of the validity of these proofs has not been honestly met. They were dismissed without fair consideration, simply because they could not meet an impossible test. The proofs have not been overthrown by the application of the Cartesian principle, for that principle can rationally be applied only in an entirely different sphere of knowledge, that is, in mathematics."

(2) "When a certain event in New Testament history is being studied, it is often found, on comparing the Gospels one with another, that some of them omit the event in question altogether. Moreover, it very frequently happens that when an event is mentioned in more than one Gospel, it is described in quite different ways in the different accounts. Sometimes the divergence in description is so great as to have the appearance of a contradiction.

When this kind of situation occurs, the '[Higher] Critics' have a way of handling it which is the distinguishing mark of their historical method.

The divergence in the testimony of the two or more accounts is held to cast doubt upon the reliability of all of them; for since we know that when one witness contradicts another, only one of them can be right, and since in this case we have no way of deciding which one it is that is right, we are naturally rather suspicious of both of them.

The reliability of the witnesses being thus put under suspicion, the critics feel under no obligation to accept the testimony of any of them in regard to the event which is being studied. But they are not satisfied merely with denying that the event took place as any of the witnesses record it. They must have something positive to say, for they are writing 'history.' Therefore, disregarding the witness of all the Gospels (and often, too, the corroborative testimony of some of the Epistles) they proceed to reconstruct the event according to their opinion of what probably happened - and this reconstruction becomes one of the 'assured results of modern scholarship.'

Take, for instance, the Virgin Birth of Jesus. There is record of this in two of the Gospels, but the accounts are quite different. Therefore it is claimed that there were two divergent traditions in the early Christian community. Moreover, since two of the Gospels do not mention the Virgin Birth explicitly, and since Joseph is referred to as the father of Jesus at least once, it is claimed that in the first days of Christianity there was also another tradition, according to which there was nothing extraordinary about the birth of Jesus. This last 'tradition' is naturally favored by the critics, who brand the other 'two' as unreliable. Thus the Virgin Birth, which is recorded definitely in two Gospels and not contradicted by the other two, is 'reconstructed' into an ordinary birth from two human parents, Mary and Joseph - a fact not affirmed by any Gospel and expressly denied by two!

Or take the Resurrection of Jesus. This is mentioned in detail in all the Gospels and in many of the Epistles. The details differ considerably, and the critics think that they detect contradictions which show all the accounts to be unreliable. Therefore they reconstruct what really happened. There is not much agreement as to this, except that they all are sure that what happened was something quite natural, and nothing miraculous. Thus an account of a miraculous rising from the dead, recorded in all the documents, is 'reconstructed' into one story or another of mistake or deception, of which there is no record in any of the documents!

As a result of a whole series of such reconstructions we are presented with a 'history' which is quite different from any of our records. A very important fact about this reconstructed New Testament story is that every trace of the supernatural has been rigorously eliminated. That Life which all the documentary evidence clearly describes as supernatural, has in the process of criticism become a life of entirely human 'sweet reasonableness'...

The concept of statistical probability is sometimes invoked to support the Higher Critics' reconstruction of early Christian history, in which the miraculous element is rather forcibly thrown out. A miracle, it is said, is so highly improbable as to be impossible.

But the answer is easy. If a modern thinker denies the resurrection of Jesus on the grounds that it is very highly improbable, the reply is, 'That is true. It is so highly improbable that of all the billions of persons who have died, only one has risen from the dead.' To say that preternatural events are improbable in the statistical sense is quite in line with Christian belief, for, according to this belief, these events are so rare that they call for an extraordinary explanation. It is only when we confuse the concept of statistical probability with the popular use of the term 'improbable' (signifying unbelievable) that we think that the statistical improbability of miracles means that they do not happen"); *Reclamation of Independence* (1947); "What I Gained," in John A. O'Brien (ed), *The Road to Damascus* (1949) ("What did I mean when I said I believed in One Holy Catholic and Apostolic Church? If the Church must be visibly one, then either the Anglican Church must be the One Church or I was not in the One Church. But if I were content with an invisible unity (whatever that may mean), then how did my position differ from the Protestant conception of the 'Church Invisible'? The idea that there is a unity among various conflicting religious bodies simply because they all possess the historic episcopate and valid sacraments now began to seem preposterous. Almost all the early heretical bodies possessed bishops and valid sacraments, and yet I had always regarded Arianism as outside the unity of the Church. If an Arian with his bishops and sacraments was outside the Church, how could an Anglican, even if he had the same equipment, consider himself inside?

As I turned these questions over in my mind it became evident that there was no rationally and historically justifiable conception of the visible Church which could include the religious body that I belonged to. Either the gates of hell had prevailed against the Church, or there was the True Church somewhere and I was not in it...

The Anglican Church having turned out to be but an overnight hostel, I had now to set about finding a real home. It was natural that the Roman Church should come under consideration, for one cannot be looking for the One Holy Catholic Apostolic Church without seriously reviewing Rome's claims to be that Church...

Leo XIII's pronouncement

on Anglican orders seemed to me, once I had ceased to regard Anglicanism with loyalty, to be eminently sensible. Newman's *Essay on the Development of Christian Doctrine* perhaps helped me the most, by showing that it is the Roman Church that possesses a continuity with apostolic times through a legitimate development of theology and practice, and that such a continuity is real, whereas the attempt to return to the 'primitive Church' was a break in continuity...

If I were to name the greatest gain that comes from entering into the Church from outside, I would say that it is depth...With this depth comes a broader charity and an understanding of those who differ from us...The Ark of the Lord will remain firm without my having to steady it. I know it is not going to fall, and I do not have to jump in to counter-attack everyone who disagrees. With this depth also comes freedom. The Faith is so much more than any professor of it that one is liberated from the domination of colorful personalities; one worries no more about public opinion; and one no longer feels under pressure to join the scramble for worldly success. But most important, there is a depth of understanding of the meaning of the worship of God, and a depth of participation in that worship which could not exist elsewhere. And with this deeper participation in the worship of God comes also a deeper knowledge of God"); *Schools and the Means of Education* (1959); *The Catechetical Crisis* (1966); *The Free City* (1967); Matthew Hoehn, OSB (ed), *Catholic Authors* (1952).

O'Brien, Kevin – actor; c. 30 July 2000 (received with his wife Karen); was an only child; parents nominally Christian; went to a Lutheran grade school; at age of nine or ten he saw Madeline Murray O'Hair, the famous atheist, on television, and became convinced she was right; he was a vocal atheist and remained one through most of his teenage years; performed in theater at school; came to an experience of something beyond him, a creative spirit, needed to create a good dramatic performance; read Carl Jung and loved his spiritualism, reacting against Freud's theory that we are nothing more than our base desires; but reacted against Jung's new ageism and Gnosticism; later greatly influenced by reading C. S. Lewis's *God in the Dock* and G. K. Chesterton's *What's Wrong With the World* and *The Everlasting Man*; then also Hilaire Belloc; he and his wife started going to a Lutheran church as his wife had been Lutheran originally; then became Episcopalian, but although he loved its liturgy, music and art, horrified that it supported abortion; read the Catholic catechism and concluded that the logical next step was to become a Catholic; he and his wife were instructed by Fr. John Jay Hughes (see above); founder and artistic director of the *Theater* *of the Word Incorporated*, which travels the country, evangelizing through comedy and drama; host of the television series *The Theater of the Word* on EWTN; appeared in episodes of EWTN's *The Apostle of Common Sense* and *The Quest for Shakespeare*; contributor to several Catholic magazines; see *EWTN Audio Library, The Journey Home* (15 December 2008) ("I had been reading for several months these two authors [C. S. Lewis and G. K. Chesterton] and I was thinking, 'If this stuff is true, as they both claim it is, I can't keep it on the shelf, it's not like Shakespeare, which you maybe take off the shelf and then perform and put back on the shelf. If this is true, I have to live with this and I have to give my whole life to it'…

Having been through the whole circuit: atheist, fundamentalist, Episcopalian, and Catholic, I can tell you that the confirmation for the authority of the magisterium of the Catholic Church comes in thousands of different ways. For example, after I became Catholic my journey didn't end. I struggled with the Church's teaching on some of the sex issues, and it wasn't until after I began praying the rosary and trying to follow the Church's teaching seriously that whole new worlds of grace opened up to me. For example, if you take the Church's position on contraception, it seems outmoded. How can this be an infallible teaching? And yet when you look at what's happened since the pill; when you look at what Paul VI said would happen; when you look at how the Church's teaching is of one cloth, so that if you pull out a thread the whole thing comes apart. And sexuality, from everything the Church teaches about it, abortion, contraception, masturbation, pornography, all of this is unified. It's philosophically unified and it's unified in the heart. That's one of the confirmations that what the Church teaches infallibly is true. If I didn't have these confirmations in a thousand different ways, I would probably still be much more skeptical about it. Yes, my authority is fallible, but I see evidence, and speaking as a true skeptic I see evidence, that the Church's magisterium is in fact infallible"); *theateroftheword.*

Olson, Carl E. – Catholic apologist; b. 17 April 1969, Hot Springs, Montana; c. 29 March 1997 (Easter Vigil; received with his wife Heather); brought up in Plains, Montana in a fundamentalist Protestant home (parents became born again Christians just before he was born); raised to believe that Catholics were not really Christians; studied graphic design and fine art at Phoenix Institute of Technology and Northwest Nazarene College, Idaho; then studied at Briercrest Bible College, Saskatchewan, Canada 1989–1991; between 1992 and 1995 he and his wife-to-be went through the questions evangelicals ask about the Catholic Church, e.g., Mary, the

Pope, authority, the Bible, tradition, the liturgy, the Eucharist; began to be bothered by all the splinterings and break-ups within evangelical and fundamentalist Protestantism; also never received any answers to his questions about such as John. 6 and Christ's shocking words about eating his flesh and drinking his blood; he and his wife's studies were influenced by T. S. Eliot and C. S. Lewis and later by Chesterton, Newman, the Roman Catechism, Russell Kirk, and Karl Keating's *Catholicism and Fundamentalism*; worked as a graphic designer and illustrator; eventually converted to the Catholic Church; in 2000 graduated from the University of Dallas (MA in Theology); was editor of *Envoy* magazine; editor of *Catholic World Report* and of *Ignatius Insight*, the on-line magazine of *Ignatius Press*; contributing editor to *This Rock* magazine; regular contributor to a variety of newspapers and periodicals; married with three children; see (selective list) "Turn About," *This Rock,* June 1998; "Lessons Learned from Great Apologists," *This Rock,* November/December 1999; "Dogma Is Not a Dirty Word," *This Rock*, October 2000; "Dorothy Sayers," *CatholicExchange.com,* 22 May 2001; "Blaise Pascal," *CatholicExchange.com,* 5 June 2001; "Walker Percy: Diagnostician of the Modern Malaise," *CatholicExchange.com,* 19 June 2001; "I Was Almost Left Behind," in Patrick Madrid (ed), *Surprised by Truth 3* (2002), p.57 ("Chesterton's *Orthodoxy* was even more thought-provoking. This dazzling apologetic for Christianity against the errors of modern philosophies showed me how central 'paradox' is to the Christian Faith. True Christianity is a radical balance of 'both/and' instead of just 'either/or'. Jesus Christ is both God *and* man; God is both one *and* three; the Church is both holy *and* made up of sinners. Of course, Protestants agree with at least the first two propositions. But many, especially Fundamentalists, insist on adhering to the Bible only – not Scripture and Tradition. Likewise, they believe they are saved by faith alone, not by faith *and* works performed by God's grace. These distinctions helped me better to understand core Catholic teachings and further appreciate the mystery of the Incarnation.

Then I read *The Everlasting Man*, Chesterton's study of the Incarnation and its effect on human history, which showed me how large, how breathtaking, how incarnational the Catholic view of reality is, compared with the often pitiful perspectives I held. I was getting glimpses into the larger world of Catholic thought, a world so large that it was frightening and so intimate that it was comforting. As I considered the reality of the Incarnation, I recognized the logic and beauty of a sacramental faith in which God works through physical matter, not just through spiritual impulse"); *EWTN Audio Library, The Journey Home* (17 June 2002) ("I was doing a lot of artwork and I was reading a lot about art and politics and literature. And what I began to find was that it was the Catholic authors who said the most compelling, deep, and rich things about the arts, about literature and politics, about how we are to be in the temporal order, how we are to act as Christians in the political realm…

For me, as a Fundamentalist and Evangelical, the heart of my faith was of course in Jesus Christ and, as a Catholic, it still is Jesus Christ. But now, because of my understanding more and more of Catholic theology, Catholic teaching, and seeing it in this covenantal framework, seeing how all Scripture ties together, seeing how the fact that God would become man points to a sacramental reality. God entered into the material realm, showing us that God would use material things, water, wine, bread, oil, to convey spiritual grace, supernatural life. And so these things – it's not an issue of whether they're magic, it's an issue of God taking material things and using them by his grace and goodness for our good.

That was a big part of it. Then, of course, seeing that the Church was not just an invisible reality. Just as Christ is fully human, He is fully divine, the Church is fully human. It's also fully divine. It's holy and yet it consists of sinners. This is one of the great paradoxes, but it is a great truth of the Catholic faith.

In Fundamentalism…there is an either/or mentality. Either the Church is holy or it's rotten. Either it's this or that. It's human or divine, it can't be both. Well, the Incarnation shows us that it is both. And you get that same paradox in the Trinity. God is one and yet He is three persons. Well, how is that? It's a mystery that we can't ever understand, though we can learn and appreciate it more and more. I found within the Catholic faith the ability to do that. There are many means, intellectually, spiritually, even in a mystical, contemplative level…

As you know, one of the great differences between Protestantism, especially classical Protestantism, and Catholicism, are the differing understandings of grace. And for me the real mind blowing, eye-opening was to see that grace was not just the external favor of God. It was more than that. It was the actual divine supernatural life of God by which he makes us partakers of the divine nature, as Peter writes in 2 Peter 1:4. And so it's not just this external reality, but it is an internal reality and that then leads us to a completely different understanding of the Church. It's not just that we're bound together by external force, but by sharing in God's own life we become his actual sons and daughters, his actual children"); *Will Catholics Be "Left Behind"? A Catholic Critique of the Rapture and Today's Prophecy Preachers* (2003); *The Da Vinci Hoax: Exposing the Errors in The Da*

Vinci Code (2004) (with Sandra Meisel); "Be A Catholic Apologist Without Apology," *Ignatiusinsight.com*, October 2004; "Traveling in a Strange Land With Walker Percy," *Saint Austin Review*, March/April 2005, p.6; "Love and the Skeptic," *This Rock*, May 2007; "Why Believe?: An Apologetic of Faith," *This Rock*, December 2007; "Are the Gospels Myth?" *This Rock*, March 2008; *EWTN Audio Library, The Journey Home* (3 March 2008) ("I had read [John 6] many times as a Fundamentalist and as an Evangelical. What was interesting was that I never heard any sermons about it, especially the latter part of that chapter. I never really had any of my classes in my two year Bible study college that addressed what Jesus meant when he said 'Eat my flesh, drink my blood.' Now, certainly it has been addressed and I went to and I found eventually various fundamentalist evangelical works that dealt with it. But what I found was that they really didn't seem to me to be answering with satisfaction the shocking nature of Jesus's words there. So John 6 for me became this passage that did not fit into the world that I knew, into the Christian theological vision that I was raised with, where we tried to explain it away as symbolical language or metaphorical language, that Jesus was trying to just use metaphor as when he says, you know, 'I am the vine' or 'I am the door.'

And as I began to read more and more about it and began to read early Church Fathers and began to read what the Catholic Church but also the Eastern Orthodox churches believe about the Eucharist, I began to realize that belief, that Jesus was talking about actually eating his true flesh, blood, soul, and divinity, that made sense to me, especially looking at history; and then looking at other passages of Scripture, I Cor. 10 and 11, the Last Supper narratives and so forth. So I think that John, chapter 6 as a whole chapter was a kind of wake up call for me"); "True Happiness and the Consolation of Philosophy," *This Rock*, July 2010.

O'Neill, Cherry Boone – songwriter and author; c. 19 April 1981 (Easter Sunday; received with her husband); oldest of the four daughters of the entertainer Pat Boone (b. 1934); brought up with Christian values and influences in a Protestant denomination; in 1968 her parents made a spiritual renewal in their lives through a Protestant charismatic movement; this was condemned by their present denomination; the family became members of a small Four Square church (called the Church on the Way) in the San Fernando Valley, Southern California, a charismatic assembly; in 1974 she met Dan O'Neill (see below) who was on his way towards Catholicism; found they had a similar approach to the issue of Catholicism; she became ill with anorexia nervosa, the severe eating illness; they married in October 1975, but she had a very serious relapse and ended up in hospital weighing eighty pounds; struggled for survival through 1976 and 1977; after her recovery they lived in Hawaii 1977-1979, doing volunteer work in a Christian community; in 1979 they founded Mercy Corps International to aid humanitarian work in the Cambodian refugee crisis; assisted in her conversion by the then Bishop Bernard Law (later Cardinal Law); wrote a best-selling book, *Starving for Attention*, on her recovery from anorexia and bulimia; twice nominated for a Grammy Award for her songwriting; see *Starving for Attention* (1982); *Dear Cherry: Questions and Answers on Eating Disorders* (1985); "The Family Reunion," in Dan O'Neill (ed*), The New Catholics: Contemporary Converts Tell Their Stories* (1987), p.181 ("The Bible was our ultimate authority in all matters. Although I had certain questions, such as who could claim to interpret the Scriptures and how this authority of interpretation was passed down from generation to generation, I generally accepted the legalistic bearing the church had on our lives. I also wondered why we were never taught the history of Christianity from the time of the Apostles. It seemed there had been a great historical leap - we were simply to take our current denominational status on faith. I knew there had to be more to the story - a bigger picture of Jesus as seen through His people...

As a songwriter, my artistic sensibilities had enabled me to experience God through symbols, images, and analogies - like the parables of the Bible. As I discovered the wealth of the sacraments and the liturgy of Catholicism, my spirit eagerly embraced an expression of Christianity that spoke in the language of my heart, while simultaneously satisfying the needs of an expanding intellect...

The more I learned of Catholicism the more I was able to readily accept and adapt it to my own belief system. It was not so much a matter of discarding the old in favor of something new as it was a feeling of coming home. It felt right. It was where I knew I belonged. My Protestant upbringing had been like that of a child reared by a kind and loving stepmother, but upon entering the Catholic Church, I felt I had discovered my true mother - the Mother Church - at long last. I found a richness of history, tradition, and symbolism in the liturgy, along with the realities of the sacraments and apostolic authority that I had never before known. To deny myself access to this storehouse of treasures would have been to deny my own nature, my own mode of spiritual expression, my own growth process"); Lorene Hanley Duquin, *A Century of Catholic Converts* (2003), p.188.

O'Neill, Dan – author and publisher; b. 1948, Olympia, Washington; c. 19 April 1981 (Easter Sunday; received with his wife); born into an Assemblies of God family; the family then moved home and attended a conservative Baptist church; in high school he attended a non-denominational Bible church with his family; later went to a Free Methodist university; in 1967 he became an Episcopalian in Seattle and was involved in charismatic renewal; he became disappointed with all of this ("I had no foundation on which to stand. When my emotional exhilaration inevitably cooled, there was no consistent, authentic church teaching to undergird my spiritual convictions and I became easy prey for well-informed critics"); was a skeptic, even an agnostic, 1968-1971; stopped attending church and was involved in drugs and self-indulgence ("If there was no God, there could be no absolute moral values – a very liberating thought at first, until the consequent despair of self-destructive nihilism became apparent: spiritual, and occasionally, physical death"); began a search for the truth; experienced an intense repentance of sin; inspired yet sobered by Jesus's parable of the pearl of great price in Matthew 13; about to graduate from the University of Washington in 1972 with a degree in Visual Communications, but began to question his professional ambitions; joined Youth with a Mission, volunteering for an assignment in Africa, traveled and lived in Africa, being confronted with terrible poverty, famine and disease; then in Europe and the Middle East, studying Christianity and Judaism (influenced there by Professor Ed Durst); also influenced in his conversion by the then Bishop Bernard Law (later Cardinal Law); eventually yielded and was received into the Church; married to Cherry Boone (see above under the entry for Cherry Boone O'Neill), daughter of the entertainer Pat Boone; co-founder in 1979 of Mercy Corps International, a relief and development agency assisting the world's poor; president of Messenger Communications; author of many books; see *Marrying for Life* (1982) (with Raymond E. Vath, MD); *Mother Angelica: Her Life Story* (1986); "The Pearl of Great Price: My Search for the Church," in Dan O'Neill (ed), *New Catholics: Contemporary Converts Tell Their Stories* (1987), p.173 ("Each one of hundreds of Protestant denominations claim a right to interpret the Bible. It was, they all agreed, their 'final authority?'...But there was no consensus on its interpretation. It seemed a bit like handing a technical 747 flight manual to a roomful of schoolteachers and expecting agreement on how to fly the jumbo jet. Without the authors present to interpret the data, a plane flight would be out of the question. This competing jumble of voices, which claimed as their ultimate authority a book that commanded Christian unity, seemed to me a scandal of divisiveness...

I found the historical, liturgical churches to be the most intriguing and I grew ever more uneasy about historically recent and diverse Western Christian spinoffs. When viewed from the perspective of two millennia, most American Protestant churches are mere blips on the time line of history and quite alien to the theological development of the ancient Christian faith. Troubling indeed...

I studied in a mild panic to discern the issues at stake in Luther's rebellion and the subsequent schism that rent Christianity. A most startling realization for me was the fact that it was the Catholic Church, through its councils and canonical process that authenticated and compiled the Scriptures. The Bible, that supreme authority for Protestants, is essentially a Judeo-Catholic document.

I found that the objects of typical Protestant challenges to Catholicism - the role of Mary (Protestants frequently state that Catholics *worship* Mary), the pope, the sacraments, and prayers to the saints, among others - were easily understood when studied from Catholic teachings instead of secondhand Protestant propaganda. I came to see that I was terribly uninformed about what the Catholic Church actually teaches, as, unfortunately, are a significant number of Catholics...

If the Jews continued to be the people of God before the advent of Christ in spite of their many human failings, the Roman Catholic Church could be the people of God today even though the sin and failure of its members may be quite apparent.

Slowly, but very surely, I was becoming convinced that the Catholic Church was indeed that Christian entity with authentic, apostolic credentials. The teaching authority of the Church, I discovered, interpreted the Scriptures in much the same way as Jewish written and oral traditions ratified each other. At last - an objective Church authority to teach and interpret a consistent, integrated, and enduring theology!

As I attempted to lay my Protestant prejudices aside, I came to see at first a vague image of the Church, emerging like a gradually developing photographic image, increasing in clarity and detail. When asked what attracted me most to Catholicism, I cannot say, for it wasn't *something*: it was *everything*. The art, the architecture, its antiquity, the beauty of the liturgy (which had come to make perfect sense to me), the social conscience of the Church, its prophetic role in our modern world, the lives of the saints, the mystery, the presence of Christ, the sheer universality - I was falling in love - and perfect love casts out fear, if not all apprehension.

When pressed to share a single thing that attracted me more than others, I will point to the sacrament of the Eucharist. In all the churches I had encountered in my life, Communion was a monthly (at most) appendage, hurriedly tacked on at the end of a service. Grape juice (never, God forbid, real wine) and crackers represented *symbolically* Christ's presence. In Catholicism, Communion was central, Christ's presence real - a sacrifice and a celebration. In the same way ancient Jewish sacrifices were real sacrifices that atoned for sin and looked toward Christ's sacrificial death as the unblemished lamb, the sacrifice of the Eucharist was a real sacrifice, looking back at, and celebrating, Christ's atoning death. In the same way humankind fell from grace through eating the forbidden fruit, we are redeemed through eating in the Eucharist. I longed to enter in.

My Protestant heritage, emphasizing literal scriptural interpretation, suddenly and unexplainably became symbolic and weak in the face of John 6, a most significant Eucharistic teaching of Christ: 'I am the living bread that came down out of heaven; if anyone eats this bread he shall live forever…truly I say to you, unless you eat the flesh of the Son of Man and drink his blood, you have no life in yourselves. He who eats my flesh and drinks my blood has eternal life; and I will raise him up on the last day. For my flesh is true food and my blood is true drink. He who eats my flesh and drinks my blood abides in me, and I in him.'

Now, how much more literal can a passage of Scripture be? Jesus forcefully states and restates his case with unambiguous, shattering clarity, yet Communion was dispatched as symbolic or parabolic in Protestant teaching. Not that this passage of Scripture was frequently the subject of discussion in Protestant churches. In fact, I cannot recall ever hearing a Protestant sermon preached on these particular verses.

I was hungry for Jesus; I was in a desert and he was the manna, the Bread of Life! I was beginning to find the pearl of great price - in the Catholic Church. As I continued to study, pray, and converse with friends, priests, and other faithful Catholics, my objections, while fewer in number, became more strenuous in nature. I was resisting - grasping for any excuse to slow my plunge into the waters of Catholic baptism. I searched for a fatal flaw. G. K. Chesterton pinned me to the wall, saying in his book *The Catholic Church and Conversion*, 'For the convert's sake, it should also be remembered that one foolish word from inside does more harm than a hundred thousand foolish words from outside' Only the words of a Catholic could now keep me from Catholicism.

My search seemed to undergo three phases. At first, in learning more about Catholicism, I began out of fairness to defend it as a legitimate expression of Christian faith (I'm O.K., you're O.K.). This quickly led, however, to further exploration and a process of discovery rather like, as Chesterton says, 'discovering a new continent full of strange flowers and fantastic animals, which is at once wild and hospitable.' Finally, the most terrible phase was that of trying not to be converted. I had come to hear the truth, as Chesterton points out, and truth is a magnet with the powers of attraction and repulsion. The moment I ceased pulling against it, I was drawn into it.

Like a drowning man whose desperate struggle gives way to exhausted acceptance of the inevitable, I yielded to, and embraced, the Catholic Church"); *Signatures: The Story Of John Michael Talbot* (2004); Lorene Hanley Duquin, *A Century of Catholic Converts* (2003), p.188.

Oursler, (Charles) Fulton – author, playwright, editor and lecturer; b. 22 January 1893, Baltimore, Maryland; c. 1943 (his son, Will, a noted writer, was received in 1944 and his wife in 1945; his daughter, April, converted in 1948); d. 24 May 1952, New York City; from a poor family; parents devout Baptists and he was raised in the Protestant tradition and baptized at the age of ten; at age fifteen he declared himself to be agnostic and remained in that state for several years (but "at no time, I thank God, did I ever lose the sense of the wonder and mystery of life"); as a teenager he got a job as a reporter on the *Baltimore American* paper; first marriage ended in divorce; moved to New York where he worked as a freelance on a variety of papers and magazines; wrote fiction (mainly detective stories) under the pseudonym Anthony Abbot; in 1925 he married Grace Perkins (1900-1955), author and former actress, who had been raised Catholic but left the Church in her teens; they did not practice any religion and did not raise their children in any faith; in 1935 he toured the Holy Land with his family and then wrote a book, *A Skeptic in the Holy Land*, which brought him closer to conversion; drawn to Christian morality by the growing threat of Communism and Nazism; after his conversion, amazed at the ignorance of people about Christ, he wrote a biography of him, trying "to make it as interesting as a serial story in a popular magazine", under the title of *The Greatest Story Ever Told* (a radio presentation took place in advance of publication, and it was adapted into a film of the same name in 1965); later wrote further books on religion; also wrote several plays; was senior editor of the *Reader's Digest*; buried with his wife in Gate of Heaven Cemetery, Hawthorne, Westchester County, New York; see *A Skeptic in the Holy Land* (1936); *The Precious Secret: A Prescription for Happiness* (1947); *Father Flanagan of Boys Town* (1949) (with Will Oursler); *The*

Greatest Story Ever Told: A Tale of the Greatest Life Ever Lived (1949); "The Greatest Thing in My Life," in John A. O'Brien (ed), *The Road to Damascus* (1949) ("In the year 1935 I had come to agree with Goethe when he said: 'I see that nothing can be known.' It was at this point in my life that I made a vacation trip to the Middle East and spent a week in Palestine. And almost literally on the road to Damascus I began to turn back to Christ...

It began on the S.S. Roma one warm night when we were cruising from ancient Athens to the port of Haifa at the foot of Mount Carmel...[W] e were to drive to Nazareth where Our Lord had lived with Mary and Joseph and then we would go on to the ancient city of Tiberias on the edge of the Sea of Galilee...

I think there is no travel experience comparable to a Christian's first visit to these hallowed places, even to one who felt he had put aside all religion, as had I. There was evocation wherever the eye would light. As the days passed, I was astonished to find how much of the four Gospels had remained in my memory and how many of the texts I could quote. The carpenter shop, the home of the Holy Family, touched my spirit with forgotten power. On the stony beach of the Galilean lake I looked around me, peopling the shore with Peter and James and John. By the ruins of the Synagogue at Capharnaum I stood wondering how the voice of the Master had sounded when it rang out here, commanding evil spirits to depart from a bedeviled young man, writhing on this very pavement. How could I guess that even then the devils of doubt and indifference which were in me were also being commanded?

From the stable in Bethlehem to the hill of Calvary I went with a strange awareness of deepening concern, a heartache like the throbbing of an old wound that had never healed. While I was still not a believer upon departing from Judea, I had reached a point where I was wishing that the story was true. On our homeward voyage I started work on a new book which I called *A Skeptic in the Holy Land.*

Looking back on it now, I see it as an ignorant and impious work. Yet in some of its anguished phrases there stirred the grief and loneliness and heartbreak that lie buried deep in every man whose faith has been lost, The last chapter of that book was far less skeptical than the first. Indeed, to read that book today is to discern between the lines the pale image of reviving faith coming through dark corridors of my thoughts like dawn creeping silently through the streets just before sunrise.

After the book was published I expected to forget the whole matter. But something had hold of me, would not let me go. I began to believe that the ethical statements of Christianity needed to be re-emphasized in a world that became less and less attractive as

Nazism offered its hand, wined with the blood of the Jews, and received the clasp of Communistic Russia. No man with eyes to see and ears to hear could mistake the fact that one great and simple moral issue must sooner or later confront the world. Within our generation the people must make a choice between principle and expediency, between good and evil.

Every man, I felt, must contribute what he could to that struggle, and I began to consider one job that I could do which might help. That was to restate the ethics of Christianity in the simplest possible terms. More and more I was astonished to find a great illiteracy all around about the life and teachings of Christ.

One day I said to myself: 'I will write an elevator boy's life of Jesus and try to make it as interesting as a serial story in a popular magazine. I will call it *The Greatest Story Ever Told*.'

At this time I had not the slightest idea that I was already on the road to conversion. I began to read the New Testament and then various familiar biographies of Our Lord - Renan, Papini, even one by Charles Dickens. For two years I pursued this reading, making copious notes, until I began to feel that soon I might be ready to do the book. Then suddenly I found myself once more overwhelmed with doubt...

Wasn't I just a sentimental fellow who had been under some kind of poetic spell in Palestine? If I went back there again, wouldn't I look at it much more objectively? There was only one way to find out. That night I decided to make a second journey to the Holy Land.

The end of this second voyage was in Beirut, Syria [*sic*], and that afternoon my wife and I rode through steep and snowy defiles of the Lebanon Mountains, actually and literally on the road to Damascus! And we slept that night in the city where St. Paul had been blinded by an access of the light. I like to think that night's dreams of strange and wonderful peace in the heart were a promise from my guardian angel.

This time I entered into the land of Our Lord through the northern frontier. I saw the snow on Hermon Hill, and how my heart pounded when across the shepherds' fields I beheld once again the waters of the Lake of Galilee. This time there was an immense difference in me. Since my last visit here I had read so much and meditated so much that the very air was rich with historic meaning, as if I breathed in the teachings of a blessed life. He had walked here and talked yonder, healing the sick, feeding the hungry, forgiving the sinners, and offering salvation freely and for all. I sat in an automobile but my soul was on its knees.

When at last I came home again I knew my job was cut out for me. I was not ready to write; my ignorance was vast, my eagerness so intense, that years of more study lay before me. The more I read, the more I thought, the easier it was for me to pray. The day came when I knew that I had come home"); *Why I Know There is a God* (1950); *The Greatest Book Ever Written: The Old Testament Story* (1951); *Modern Parables* (1951); *The Greatest Faith Ever Known: The Story of the Men Who First Spread the Religion of Jesus and of the Momentous Times in Which They Lived* (1953) (completed by his daughter April Oursler Armstrong); *Lights Along the Shore* (1955); *The Happy Grotto: A Journalist's Account of Lourdes* (1957); *A String of Blue Beads* (1957); *Behold This Dreamer! An Autobiography* (1964); Charles P. Connor, *Classic Catholic Converts* (2001), p.202; Lorene Hanley Duquin, *A Century of Catholic Converts* (2003), p.129 ("Oursler later said that he was in front of the shrine of St. Bernadette at St. Francis of Assisi Church on Thirty-first Street in New York when he received the gift of faith. Any doubts or reservations he had about becoming a Catholic evaporated").

Owen, Hugh - Catholic apologist; c. 1972; Welsh father and American mother; his father was Sir David Owen (d. 1971), General Secretary of International Planned Parenthood; very secular upbringing; educated at New York University (BA in History) and at the Bank Street College of Education (MSc in educational supervision and administration); worked for twenty years as a teacher and school administrator; his conversion to the Catholic faith (while studying at Princeton University) was influenced by having witnessed his father's drift into anti-life secular humanism ("Became convinced that faith in macro-evolution, including theistic evolution, lay at the root of the spiritual and moral decline of modern times. He was equally convinced that a restoration of the traditional teaching of the Church on creation would help to bring about a moral and spiritual reformation"); later a writer and editor for various Catholic organizations; on 8 December 2000 he founded the Kolbe Center for the Study of Creation (encouraged by Fr. Robert Ruskamp), based in Mount Jackson, Virginia; the purpose of the center was to provide a forum for Catholic theologians, philosophers and natural scientists who reject the evolutionary hypothesis and who defend the traditional Catholic interpretation of Genesis 1-11; the center hosted the first international Catholic conference on creation; involved in prison ministry and evangelization with the Legion of Mary; attends a Melkite Greek Catholic church; he and his wife Maria have fourteen children; both are members of the Third Order of St. Augustine; see *Thy Kingdom Come: The Life and Mission of Luisa Piccarreta* (1997); "Darwin Revisited: The Negative Impact of the Evolutionary Hypothesis on Scientific Research," *Saint Austin Review*, January/February 2011, p.11.

Palmer, Gretta (*née* Brooker) – journalist and editor; b. 1905, St. Louis, Missouri; c. December 1946 (instructed and received by Mgr. Fulton Sheen); mother a Presbyterian and father a lapsed Catholic; baptized a Catholic, but had virtually no religious instruction and considered herself an atheist; dabbled in Freud; graduated from Vassar College in 1925; worked as journalist in New York; later a prolific and eloquent freelance journalist and reporter; served as a war correspondent in Europe in 1944 and Indo-China in 1945; conversion influenced by meeting Mgr. Fulton Sheen after being assigned to write an article on Sheen and his converts; also greatly influenced by St. Thomas Aquinas and G. K. Chesterton; wrote and lectured about her conversion; in collaboration with Father George [Stjepan Tomislav Poglajen (1906-1990)], she wrote *God's Underground* (1949), an account of this Croatian priest's fight against the Nazis in Dalmatia and later incognito work with Catholics in the Soviet Union; see "Escaping From an Atheist's Cell," in John A. O'Brien (ed), *The Road to Damascus* (1949) (originally published in *The Sign*, November-December 1947) ("My most painful sacrifice, intellectually and emotionally, was the surrender of the belief in man's perfectibility. I did want to think that an extension of goodwill and a development of knowledge would enable all of us, here and now, to become happy and whole for ever. It is the ideal of our century – the belief in unaided achievement of the Brotherhood of Man without a Father. It is the dearest fallacy of our times...

[I]f you once open your mind to the *possibility* of a divine Man, you are out of the woods. Christ *could* have been a madman when He claimed to be God, but it is a curiously catching madness in which the world has believed for two thousand years. He *could* have been a cruel liar making gulls of the disciples by promising redemption. If so, it is odd that such a lie told to a group of fishermen in an obscure village of a backward colony, a kind of ancient Puerto Rico, should have toppled Empires and led generations of men to martyrdom and monasteries and scholarly concentration on this lie. The only possible alternative answer is the truth of what He said: that He was truly God, and truly come to save the world. The 'good man' theory, which would turn Christ into a Jewish Confucius, will not wash, good men do not delude friends into persecution with promises they cannot fulfil. And if Christ is truly God, then everything else must follow...

I said 'Could one reason for the Incarnation be the fact that it is easier for us to love a human being than any other form a God could take?' I had surprised myself by the question; but as soon as I had stated it, I knew I believed in the divinity of Jesus Christ. And that, I think, is the watershed of belief. Once a convert has embraced that truth, everything else is apt to follow...[I]f you believe that Christ was truly God and that the Gospels are true accounts of what He said, then you must take His sayings seriously. And His sayings – written down when the Church had already spread to many lands – have implicit in them everything a modern Catholic believes. The knowledge has only been deepened and developed by new insights and by increased scholarship in the centuries since then"); *God's Underground* (1949); "4 Years Later," *The Sign*, September 1951 (story of her first four years in the Church); *God's Underground in Asia* (1952); Thomas C. Reeves, *America's Bishop: The Life and Times of Fulton J. Sheen* (2001), pp.178-181 ("Palmer was first jolted from what she called the 'atheist's cell' by the world war: this was mankind regressing, not progressing, and physical and social scientists seemed to have no clue how to solve the problem of human hostility. She was appalled to hear a priest, in answer to her questions about changing the hearts of men, refer to original sin. Wartime travels, however, added to her perplexity about human nature and ultimate values as she observed the pain and heroism of combat troops. After the war Palmer fell into despair...

Sheen agreed to talk with her about returning to the Church if she would not use anything he said for publication...Sheen urged her not to reject reason in her pursuit of truth. 'That's the mistake the followers of Hitler made. That's the kind of thing that makes people believe that some man in Moscow, Idaho, is God, because he claims to be. Let me tell you what we Catholics believe, and if your reason rejects it, go away with my blessing. But I beg you, as a friend, don't throw in the sponge on using your intellect.

Sheen's encouraging words drove Palmer to Chesterton, and then to a vast assortment of books both for and against Catholicism. The atheist's cell began to crumble, as she later wrote: 'I found that there is no fact or hypothesis of modern physics or astronomy which cannot be comfortably accommodated inside the ample arms of the Church. I discovered that, historically speaking, people seem to leave the Church because they want forbidden things, never because they want a deeper truth. I found that people enter the Church because they want the fulfillment of either heart or brain or soul. Many men have abandoned Rome because they wished to worship at the altar of man's self-sufficient intellect; nobody ever left the Church because the best in him could not find fulfillmemt there'"); Matthew Hoehn, OSB (ed), *Catholic Authors* (1952).

Pancake, Breece D'J (born Breece Dexter Pancake) - writer; b. 29 June 1952, South Charleston, West Virginia; c. 1977; d. 8 April 1979, the Farmington Estate, Charlottesville, Virginia; brought up in Milton, West Virginia as a Methodist; as a young man he did much traveling in the western United States and Mexico; several manual jobs; attended West Virginia Wesleyan College in Buckhannon in 1970, then transferred in 1971 to Marshall University in Huntington, West Virginia (BA in English in 1974); worked as an English teacher; badly affected by the death of his father and of a close friend in 1975; studied creative writing at the University of Virginia; always loved the outdoors; became a Catholic in his mid-twenties; wrote several short stories, mainly about working class characters; only a few of his stories were published in his lifetime; but they were very well received by readers, acclaimed by critics (comparing his work to Ernest Hemingway and Flannery O'Connor) and nominated for a Pulitzer prize; the unusual middle name derived from a magazine's misprint for D.J. (for Dexter John) in the galley proofs of the first of his stories (he took the name John on his conversion); unmarried; died in the yard of his rented Charlottesville cottage on Blue Ridge Lane from a self-inflicted shotgun wound to the head; buried in Milton Cemetery, Milton, Cabell County, West Virginia; see *The Stories of Breece D'J Pancake* (1983; revised edition 2002); Ellesa Clay High, "A Lost Generation: The Appalachia of Breece D'J Pancake," *Appalachian Journal* (1985); Galt Harpham, "Short Stack: The Stories of Breece D'J Pancake," *Studies in Short Fiction* (1986); Albert E. Wilhelm, "Poverty of Spirit in Breece Pancake's Short Fiction," *Critique: Studies in Modern Fiction* (1986); Cynthia Kadohata, "Breece D'J Pancake," *Mississippi Review* (1989); Thomas E. Douglass, "The Story of Breece D'J Pancake," *Appalachian Journal* (1990); Cynthia Kadohata, "Breece D'J Pancake," *flipmagazine.net*, 1996; Thomas E. Douglass, *Room Forever: The Life, Work, and Letters of Breece D'J Pancake* (1998); Grace Toney Edwards, "Breece D'J Pancake: A Life Too Short," *Appalachian Heritage*, Summer 2012 ("[H]e had converted to Catholicism, a faith that seemed to offer the structure that he craved in his life"); John Casey, "Afterword to The Stories of D'J Pancake," *johndcasey.com* (n.d.) ("Not long before Breece and I got to be friends, his father and his best friend both died. Sometime after that Breece decided to become a Roman Catholic and began taking instruction. I'm as uncertain finally about his conversion as I am about his suicide. I've thought about both a lot, and I can imagine a lot, but there is nothing certain I would dare say. Except that it was (and still is) startling to have had that much fierce passion so near, sometimes so close.

Breece asked me to be his godfather. I told him I was a weak reed, but that I would be honored. This godfather arrangement soon turned upside down. Breece started getting after me about going to mass, going to confession, instructing my daughters. It wasn't so much out of righteousness as out of gratitude and affection, but he could be blistering. And then penitent.

As with his other knowledge and art, he took in his faith with intensity, almost as if he had a different, deeper measure of time. He was soon an older Catholic than I was. I began to feel that not only did he learn things fast, absorb them fast, but he aged them fast. His sense of things fed not only on his own life but on others' lives too. He had an authentic sense, even memory, of ways of being he couldn't have known firsthand. It seemed he'd taken in an older generation's experience along with (not in place of) his own…

[L]ater a friend of his showed me a letter from Breece in which he'd written, 'If I weren't a good Catholic, I'd consider getting a divorce from life.' No one close to him guessed. Even that sentence about getting a divorce from life is only clear in retrospect. And from other signs and letters it's hard to say how intentional, how accidental his state of mind was when he killed himself.

One of Breece's favorite quotations was from the Bible - Revelation 3:15-16. I know thy works, that thou art neither cold nor hot: I would thou wert cold or hot. So then because thou art lukewarm, and neither cold nor hot, I will spew thee out of my mouth.

This is a dangerous pair of verses. Untempered by other messages, by the gentler tones of voice of the Spirit, they can be a scourge. It may have been simply a bad accident that Breece didn't allow himself the balms that were available to him after his self-scourgings"); his papers are at West Virginia University Library; *ANB*.

Parker, James – priest; c. 12 June 1981 (received (with his wife) by the then Bishop of Springfield-Cape Girardeau, the Most Rev. Bernard F. Law); ordained an Episcopal minister; provincial vicar of an Anglican-wide secular institute for clergy; became concerned at the liberal moves in world-wide Anglicanism; resigned his Episcopal ministry in 1981 and was received into the Catholic Church; ordained to the priesthood on 29 June 1982 (he was the first married Latin rite priest in the United States under the guidelines of a pastoral provision requested by the American bishops and granted by the Holy See); Bishop Law was appointed ecclesiastical delegate to implement the provision; served as assistant in this work to the then Cardinal Law, Archbishop of Boston; this continued, although he moved to Charleston, South Carolina, and served as diocesan director of Catholic charities; see "A Married Catholic Priest," in Dan O'Neill (ed), *The New Catholics: Contemporary Converts Tell Their Stories*(1987),p.169("Fourcenturies ago political causes brought about a schismatic division between the Roman Catholic Church and the Church in England. For dynastic reasons Henry VIII took advantage of the influences of the continental Protestant Reformation to renounce allegiance to Peter's successor and to place himself in administrative leadership of the Church of England. Mind you, he tolerated no Protestant novelties, but he cut the tie to the magisterium. This *Ecclesia Anglicana* considered itself the inheritor of the past glories of English Catholicism and continuous with the Church of Saint Augustine of Canterbury, the VenerableSaintBede,SaintAnselm, Saint Richard of Chichester and Saint Hugh of Lincoln. But Henry himself martyred John Fisher and Thomas More, whose perseverance in faith was formed by the same ancient Church in the British Isles.

The reigns of Edward VI and Elizabeth I, the Puritan movement, and other less grave influences brought to the Church of England a kind of national spirit that introduced a need for survival based on a spirit of compromise. Its state connection molded Anglicanism into a national religion intended to encompass every Englishman's private search for God. The schism from Rome set the Church of England adrift from the gospel's magisterial truth and opened her to the prevailing attitudes of many who had tasted the flavor of the Reformation of Calvin and Luther.

The Oxford movement of the early nineteenth century revived a sense of the English church's Catholic heritage. With great courage the Oxford fathers began to teach anew the faith that they saw as England's true heritage, and with this great revival came a deeper understanding that the separation from Rome was no boast but the real tragedy of the Anglican Church. Far from freeing English churchmen from spiritual bonds, it had, in fact, wrenched them from the guarantor of the Catholic truth the Church was heir to. There had always been a faithful remnant who held that the Church of England had no faith but Catholic faith and no guide but Rome. The Oxford movement at its very core took up that cause and taught a need for corporate reunion with the See of Peter. The argument held that the Church of England was not a Protestant denomination sprung anew from the Reformation like the Lutheran and Presbyterian bodies, she was a schism from the rest of the Catholic Church that needed to be brought back to communion with Rome, where she would again be loyal to the universal pastor of Christ's flock. The so-called Anglo-papalists who held and taught this faith found in the Book of Common Prayer only Catholic religion and

Catholic sacraments, believing that the faith of an Anglican was Roman Catholic. They earnestly and devoutly prayed and worked toward a day when Canterbury and Rome would join in full communion, a day not to be expected in the twentieth century any more than the nineteenth but a goal that seemed real to them. As long as the *official* teachings of Anglicanism were compatible with a Catholic understanding, the Anglo-papalist felt justified in remaining outside full communion because he saw himself as a means toward union.

In recent years, actually since the 1970s, the Canadian Church, the Episcopal Church in the United States, and a few other Anglican bodies began to deal with theological matters as though they were sociological issues. For the first time in Anglican history many of us began to feel that the integrity of Catholic faith in the Episcopal Church was being formally violated. Certain decisions were taken that led us to believe that the corporate union so deeply desired was no longer a viable goal. We were no longer morally justified in being out of communion with the successor of Peter").

Parsons, Louella (born Louella Rose Oettinger) – journalist and screenwriter; b. 6 August 1881, Freeport, Illinois; d. 9 December 1972, Santa Monica, California; parents both of German Jewish descent but they and she had attended an Episcopal church; her father died when she was eight; the Freeport *Journal-Standard* published a story of hers while she was still in high school; after high school she enrolled on a teachers' course, but while in college she worked part-time on a local newspaper; in 1914 she began writing the first gossip column in the country for the *Chicago Record Herald*; then wrote a movie column for the *New York Morning Telegraph* and came to the attention of William Randolph Hearst (1863-1951) who gave her a contract on one of his newspapers (possibly because she had praised Hearst's mistress, Marion Davies (1897-1961)); became a syndicated Hollywood columnist for Hearst; her columns appeared in the *Los Angeles Examiner* 1926-1965 and hundreds of newspapers worldwide; had a reputation for getting the "big scoop", which was consolidated when she was the first to report on the break up of Douglas Fairbanks, Jr. and Mary Pickford; also hosted radio programs interviewing film stars; she was the unchallenged queen of Hollywood until Hedda Hopper (1885-1966), ex-actress, was hired by a rival newspaper; she and Hopper had a vicious rivalry for years; she wrote her final column in 1964; married three times, the first two ending in divorce; her last marriage in 1930 to Dr. Henry Watson Martin, as a result of which she converted to Catholicism, was a happy one and lasted until his death in 1951; she had one child only, her daughter Harriet from her first marriage; buried in Holy Cross Cemetery, Culver City, California; see *The Gay Illiterate* (1944) (memoirs); *Tell It To Louella* (1961) (further memoirs); George Eells, *Hedda and Louella* (1972); Samantha Barbas, *The First Lady of Hollywood: A Biography of Louella Parsons* (2005); *ANB* ("She was a devout adherent to her adopted faith, and it brought her much solace both during her years of influence in Hollywood and her later years of illness").

Patterson, Floyd – professional boxer; b. 4 January 1935, Waco, North Carolina; c. 31 March 1956 (received by Mgr. Archibald McLees); d. 11 May 2006, New Paltz, New York; third of eleven children from a poor family (father an odd-jobman, mother a domestic servant); the family moved to Brooklyn, New York; difficult childhood with criminality and truancy; sent to an approved school from age ten to twelve ("they taught me to read and write and how to live with myself and others"); began boxing at age fourteen; spotted by the trainer Cus D'Amato, who acted like a father to him; won the national Golden Gloves amateur championship in 1951 and the Amateur Athletic Union championship in 1952; won the middleweight gold medal at the Helsinki Olympic Games in 1952 within twenty seconds of the first round; as an amateur he won forty fights (thirty-seven knockouts) and lost four; turned professional at first as a light heavyweight; conversion to the Catholic faith influenced by the peace and tranquility he found in the church in contrast to the turmoil and trouble of the streets; in November 1956 he won the World Heavyweight Championship by knocking out Archie Moore in the fifth round; at that time he was the youngest world champion in history, and the first Olympic gold medalist to win a professional heavyweight title; lost the title in 1959 to Ingemar Johannson; in the rematch in 1960 he knocked out Johansson in the fifth round (the then first man in history to regain the undisputed world heavyweight title); in 1961 he knocked out Johansson in the sixth round of their third fight; defended the title until losing it to Sonny Liston in 1962 by a first round knockout; again knocked out in the first round by Liston in 1963; re-established his career until beaten in twelve rounds by the then champion Muhammad Ali in 1965; won several more fights until losing to Ali in seven rounds, his last fight; as a professional he had fifty-five wins (forty knockouts), eight losses and one draw; nicknamed "The Gentleman of Boxing"; he trained for part of his boxing career his adopted son, Tracey Harris Patterson, who won two world championship titles; organized safety measures for boxing and counseled troubled children; suffered from Alzheimer's disease; buried at New Paltz Rural Cemetery in New Paltz, Ulster County, New York; see *Victory Over Myself* (1962) (with Milton Gross); *Inside Boxing* (1974) (with Bert Randolph Sugar); Jack Newcombe, *Floyd Patterson, Heavyweight King* (1961); Alan Howard Levy, *Floyd Patterson: A Boxer and a Gentleman* (2008); W. K. Stratton, *The Black White Hope: The Life and Burdens of Floyd Patterson* (2011); *ANB.*

Percy, Walker – author; b. 28 May 1916, Birmingham, Alabama; c. 13 December 1947 (his wife, Mary Bernice Townsend (known as "Bunt") converted at the same time; also her close friend, Jidge Minyard); d. 10 May 1990, Covington, Louisiana; born into a distinguished and prosperous Southern Protestant family; grandfather (in 1917) and father (in 1929) both committed suicide; family moved to Georgia; in 1931 his mother died in a car crash when she drove off a bridge (probably accidental death, but he always wondered whether this too may have been suicide); he and his two brothers were then adopted by his bachelor uncle, William Alexander Percy ("Uncle Will") (1885-1942), lawyer and poet, and moved to live with him in Greenville, Mississippi; brought up agnostic, though nominally liberal Presbyterian; met there the future historian Shelby Foote (1916-2005), his life-long best friend; educated at University of North Carolina at Chapel Hill; trained as a medical doctor at University of Columbia; contracted tuberculosis when serving as an intern in a pathology lab; spent recovery time reading literature and philosophy; influenced particularly by Dostoevsky and Kierkegaard; but also by St. Augustine and St. Thomas Aquinas (debates with a Catholic patient, Arthur Fortugno led to this reading); decided that Christianity offered the most realistic assessment of human nature; in 1945 he said to a friend: "If you take the claims of Christianity seriously, then it seems to me that Catholicism is where you have to end up", but he was not ready to take that step; other influences on his conversion were his friend Caroline Gordon (see above) and Mgr. Fulton Sheen's broadcasts; began his literary career writing philosophical essays; then wrote philosophical novels; his first novel, *The Moviegoer*, won the National Book Award for Fiction in 1962; also wrote works on semiotics; chief concern as a novelist is with "the dislocation of man in the modern age," with the sense of ennui and meaninglessness that has shadowed so many lives; questioned the ability of science to explain the basic mysteries of human existence ("[T]he burden of my non-fiction is a demonstration that man is different from other creatures. That he has this extraordinary capacity to know things, a certain freedom, and he can find himself in a predicament. You can't explain these things by deterministic biology"); co-founder in 1987 of the Fellowship of Southern Writers; awarded the 1989 *Laetare* Medal by the University of Notre Dame; buried in the grounds of St. Joseph Benedictine Abbey in Benedict, Louisiana; see (selective list) *The Moviegoer* (1961); *The Last Gentleman* (1966); *Love in the Ruins: The Adventures of a Bad Catholic at a Time Near the End of the World* (1971); John C. Carr, "An Interview With Walker Percy," *Georgia Review*, Fall 1971, p.317 (reprinted in Lewis A. Lawson and Victor A. Kramer (ed), *Conversations with Walker Percy* (1985)) ("I remember at North Carolina that classical behaviorism in the psychology department was running very strong. And at Columbia, it was the idea of the mechanism of disease, which is very valuable, the idea that disease is a mechanism of response in the body to the disease agent. So I began to be interested in a view of man as such, man as man. And I saw one day…maybe it was something of a breakthrough, something of a turning of a corner, that science can say so much about things, objects or people, but by its very method, by its own definition, by its own self-imposed limitation, the scientific method can only utter a statement about a single object, a glass or a frog or a dogfish – or a man – only insofar as it resembles other things of its kind. If you want to make general statements – which scientists recognize, that's the nature of science insofar as one dogfish resembles another dogfish – that is what science is interested in, making general statements about certain kinds of things and certain kinds of responses and reactions and changes. Well, I suddenly realized that when you apply this to man, you stop short at the very point where it matters to man. Science can say everything about a man except what he is in himself…

I think my writings reflect a certain basic orientation toward, although they're not really controlled by, Catholic dogma. As I say, it's a view of man, that man is neither an organism controlled by his environment, nor a creature controlled by the forces of history, as the Marxists would say, nor is he a detached, wholly objective, angelic being who views the world in a God-like way and makes pronouncements only to himself or to an elite group of people. No, he's somewhere between the angels and the beasts. He's a strange creature whom both Thomas Aquinas and Marcel called *homo viator*, man the wayfarer, man the wanderer"); *The Message in the Bottle: How Queer Man Is, How Queer Language Is, and What One Has to Do with the Other* (1975); Marcus Smith, "Talking about Talking: An Interview with Walker Percy," *New Orleans Review* (1976), p.13 (reprinted in Lewis

A. Lawson and Victor A. Kramer (ed), *Conversations with Walker Percy* (1985)) ("In the first chapter of *The Message in the Bottle* I talk about the hypothetical Martian who's been reading books by physiologists and behaviorists and biologists explaining man. When he lands on earth he's astonished to find everybody's talking all the time, either talking or engaging in symbolic transactions. And he asks 'How do you explain that?' The scientist and his companions give him the standard textbooks and keep reassuring him that man is not really qualitatively different from the animals, that both respond to stimuli. And the Martian keeps saying, 'Yeah, but you're still talking!' To the Martian the scientist must seem like Kilroy - he is there, and he is always talking or writing, whether it is nonsense or whatever. He never quits. This is a peculiar phenomenon when you come to think of it. Any other creature would find it peculiar except man himself. He is too busy talking"); *Lancelot* (1977); "*Questions They Never Asked Me* So He Asked Them Himself," *Esquire*, December 1977 ("Q: But aren't you a Catholic? A: Yes. Q: Do you regard yourself as a Catholic novelist? A: Since I am a Catholic and a novelist, it would seem to follow that I am a Catholic novelist. Q: What kind of Catholic are you? A: Bad. Q: No. I mean are you liberal or conservative? A: I no longer know what those words mean. Q: Are you a dogmatic Catholic or an open-minded Catholic? A: I don't know what that means, either. Do you mean do I believe the dogma that the Catholic Church proposes for belief? Q: Yes. A: Yes. Q: How is such a belief possible in such an age? A: What else is there? Q: What do you mean, what else is there? There is humanism, atheism, agnosticism, Marxism, behaviorism, materialism, Buddhism, Muhammadism, Sufism, astrology, occultism, theosophy. A: That's what I mean. Q: To say nothing of Judaism and Protestantism. A: Well, I would include them along with the Catholic Church in the whole peculiar Jewish-Christian thing. Q: I don't understand. Would you exclude, for example, scientific humanism as a rational and honorable alternative? A: Yes. Q: Why? A: It's not good enough. Q: Why not? A: This life is much too much trouble, far too strange, to arrive at the end of it and then to be asked what you make of it and have to answer 'Scientific humanism.' That won't do. A poor show. Life is a mystery, love is a delight. Therefore I take it as axiomatic that one should settle for nothing less than the infinite mystery and the infinite delight, i.e., God. In fact I demand it. I refuse to settle for anything less… Q: But isn't the Catholic Church in a mess these days, badly split, its liturgy barbarized, vocations declining? A: Sure. That's a sign of its divine origins, that it survives these periodic disasters… Q: How do you account for your belief? A: I can only account for it as a gift from God. Q: Why would God make you such a gift when there are others who seem more deserving, that is, serve their fellowman? A: I don't know. God does strange things. For example, he picked as one of his saints a fellow in northern Syria, a local nut, who stood on top of a pole for thirty-seven years. Q: We are not talking about saints. A: That's true. Q: We are talking about what you call a gift. A: You want me to explain it? How would I know? The only answer I can give is that I asked for it, in fact demanded it. I took it as an intolerable state of affairs to have found myself in this life and in this age, which is a disaster by any calculation, without demanding a gift commensurate with the offense. So I demanded it. No doubt other people feel differently. Q: But shouldn't faith bear some relation to the truth, facts? A: Yes. That's what attracted me, Christianity's rather insolent claim to be true, with the implication that other religions are more or less false. Q: You believe that? A: Of course"); *The Second Coming* (1980); "A View of Abortion With Something To Offend Everybody," *The New York Times*, 8 June 1981, A-15; *Lost in the Cosmos: The Last Self-Help Book* (1983); "A 'Cranky Novelist' Reflects on the Church," *The Quarterly*, Summer 1983, p.1 ("We Catholics have a way of taking things for granted, the very sort of things which other people find extraordinary. I'll give you one example. The other day I happened to read a short review of a book in a magazine. The book was a new edition of the Rule of St. Benedict, published to celebrate the sesquimillenium of the saint's birth. Do you know what a sesquimillenium is? I had to look it up. It is 1,500 years. Now, that is remarkable. What struck me as even more remarkable is that no one seemed to find this remarkable. Yet every day we hear about this or that anniversary celebration: five hundred years since Luther's birth, two hundred years since Goethe's birth, seventy-five years since the Wright brothers' flight, a stamp commemorating James Audubon or Joe Louis. This is all very well. But here is a man who was born 1,500 years ago, who lived in a critical, disorderly time with certain resemblances to our own, who devised a rule for living in a community, a practical, moderate, yet holy rule which apparently is quite as useful now as it was 1,500 years ago. 1,500 years. I call that remarkable. Yet very few people seem to find it remarkable - very few Catholics. Maybe the Benedictines do, but they don't say much about it, and the Jesuits practically nothing"); *How to Be an American Novelist in Spite of Being Southern and Catholic* (1984); *Diagnosing the Modern Malaise* (1985); *Novel-Writing in an Apocalyptic Time* (1986); The

Thanatos Syndrome (1987); "If I Had Five Minutes With the Pope," *America*, September 12, 1987, p.127; *State of the Novel: Dying Art or New Science* (1988); Foreword to Dan O'Neill (ed), *The New Catholics: Contemporary Converts Tell Their Story* (1989), p.xiii ("How to write about conversion if it is true that faith is an unmerited gift from God? How to describe, let alone explain it, if this is the case? When it comes to grace, I get writer's block. How to write about other people's conversions when one hardly understands one's own? What one does, of course, is write about the causes other than God's grace, the 'proximate,' the 'material,' the 'psychological' causes. One can write about conversion two ways. One way is to put the best possible face on it, recount a respectable intellectual odyssey. Such as: Well, my tradition was scientific. I thought science explained the cosmos – until one day I read what Kierkegaard said about Hegelianism, the science of his day: that Hegel explained everything in the universe except what it is to be an individual, to be born, to live, and to die. And for me this 'explanation' would be true enough, I suppose. But then there is this. When I was in college, I lived in the attic of a fraternity house with four other guys. God, religion, was the furthest thing from our minds and talk – from mine, at least. Except for one of us, a fellow who got up every morning at the crack of dawn and went to Mass. He said nothing about it and seemed otherwise normal.

Does anyone suppose that one had nothing to do with the other? That is, thinking about Kierkegaard's dilemma and remembering my roommate's strange behavior – this among a thousand other things one notices or remembers, which, if they don't 'cause' it, at least enter into it, at least make room for this most mysterious turning in one's life..

[I]t is not merely the exotic provenances of these pilgrims that dazzle the reader, but the inkling that it is the very catholicity of the Thing, the old-new Jewish-Christian Thing, the one holy Catholic apostolic and Roman Thing that, come at from so many directions, looks so different at the beginning and finally so much the same. Sure enough, all roads seem to lead to and so forth. Here they certainly do. She is the object of the pilgrimage and there She is, blemishes and all. Or as one convert puts it here: what else do you expect anything this enormous and this old to be than, at times, something of a horror show?"); "The Fateful Rift: The San Andreas Fault in the Modern Mind" (18th Annual Jefferson Lecture in the Humanities), 3 May 1989, *C-Span Video Library*; "Why Are You a Catholic?" in Clifton Fadiman (ed), *Living Philosophies* (1990) ("The great paradox of the Western world is that even though it was in the Judeo-Christian West that modern science arose and flourished, it is .Judeo-Christianity which the present - day scientific set of mind finds the most offensive among the world's religions.

Judaism is offensive because it claims that God entered into a covenant with a single tribe, with it and no other. Christianity is doubly offensive because it claims not only this but also that God became one man, He and no other.

One cannot imagine any statement more offensive to the present-day scientific set of mind. Accordingly, Hinduism and Buddhism, which have no scientific tradition but whose claims are limited to the self, its existence or nonexistence, which are far less offensive to the present-day scientific set of mind, are in fact quite compatible.

The paradox can be resolved in only two ways. One is that both the Jewish and the Christian claims are untrue, are in fact nonsense, and that the scientific mind-set is correct. The other is that the scientific method is correct as far as it goes, but the theoretical mind-set, which assigns significance to single things and events only insofar as they are exemplars of theory or items for consumption, is in fact an inflation of a method of knowing and is unwarranted"); *Signposts in a Strange Land* (1991) (contains most of Walker Percy's major non-fiction writings) ("While no serious novelist knows for sure where his writing comes from, I have the strongest feeling that, whatever else the benefits of the Catholic faith, it is of a particularly felicitous use to the novelist. Indeed, if one had to design a religion for novelists, I can think of no better. What distinguishes Judeo-Christianity in general from other world religions is its emphasis on the value of the individual person, its view of man as a creature in trouble, seeking to get out of it, and accordingly on the move. Add to this anthropology the special marks of the Catholic Church: the sacraments, especially the Eucharist, which, whatever else they do, confer the highest significance upon the ordinary things of this world, bread, wine, water, touch, breath, words, talking, listening – and what do you have? You have a man in a predicament and on the move in a real world of real things, a world which is a sacrament and a mystery; a pilgrim whose life is a searching and a finding.

Such a view of man as wayfarer is, I submit, nothing else than a recipe for the best novel-writing from Dante to Dostoevsky. Even an excellent atheist novelist like Sartre borrows from this traditional anthropology for the upside-down pilgrimage of his characters into absurdity.

It is no accident, I think, that the great religions of the East, especially Hinduism and Buddhism, with their devaluation of the individual and of reality itself, are not notable for the novels of their devotees.

Only recently, in so-called post-modern fiction, has the novelist abandoned this anthropology in favor of absorption with self or with the text, not the meaning, of words. The results are predictable"); Martin Luschei, *The Sovereign Wayfarer: Walker Percy's Diagnosis of the Malaise* (1972); Robert Coles, *Walker Percy: An American Search* (1979); Ralph C. Wood, "Walker Percy as Satirist: Christian and Humanist Still in Conflict," *Christian Century*, 19 November 1980, p.1122; Peter S. Hawkins, *The Language of Grace: Flannery O'Connor, Walker Percy, and Iris Murdoch* (1983), Ch. 3; Robert H. Brinkmeyer Jr., *Three Catholic Writers of the Modern South* (1985) ("Percy has written very little about his decision to become a Catholic. According to his close friend Robert Coles, Percy experienced a very intense religious crisis during 1946 and 1947, which led him eventually to the Church. Coles says that Percy experienced no dramatic moment of conversion; rather, in Coles's words, 'a deeply introspective and somewhat withdrawn man gradually began to make commitments, and affiliation to a particular faith was one of them.'

Certainly Percy must have found the Catholic view of man compatible with the existential dilemma he saw facing modern man. In an interview he characterized the Catholic view as being 'that man is neither an organism controlled by his environment, nor a creature controlled by the forces of history as the Marxists would say, nor is he a detached, wholly objective, angelic being who views the world in a godlike way and makes pronouncements only to himself or to an elite group of people. No, he's somewhere between the angels and the beasts. He's a strange creature whom both Thomas Aquinas and Marcel called *homo viator*, man the wayfarer, man the wanderer.' Certainly, too, Percy must have been attracted to the great historical authority of the Catholic Church, the original bride of Christ, the Church of Peter and John and the Apostle Paul…'If I had to single out one piece of writing which was more responsible than anything else for my becoming a Catholic,' Percy has said, 'it would be that essay of Kierkegaard's ["Of the Difference between a Genius and an Apostle"]. Percy was fascinated by the dichotomy Kierkegaard drew between what he called the genius and the apostle. A genius, says Kierkegaard, is a man who discovers truth; he uses the example of a scientist who works in the realm of the immanent; he can discover truth anywhere, anytime, anyplace. The apostle, however, bears news, his realm is the transcendent, and he speaks with divine authority. Those who hear the apostles are faced with a choice, as Kierkegaard describes, using the example of an apostle's message: 'These words were spoken by Him to whom, according to His own statement, is given all power in heaven and on earth. You who hear me must consider within yourselves whether you will bow before this authority or not, accept and believe the words or not.' Walker Percy heard the message of the modern apostles, whom he saw as present-day Catholic priests, and he believed"); William Rodney Allen, *Walker Percy: A Southern Wayfarer* (1986); Harold Bloom, *Walker Percy* (1986); John Edward Hardy, *The Fiction of Walker Percy* (1987); Linda Whitney Hobson, *Walker Percy: A Comprehensive Descriptive Bibliography* (1988); Lewis A. Lawson, *Whose Following Percy: Essays on Walker Percy's Work* (1988); Gary M. Ciuba, *Walker Percy: Books of Revelations* (1991); Jay Tolson, *Pilgrim in the Ruins: A Life of Walker Percy* (1992) ("Percy's intellectual journey [to Rome] took him by way of science and scientism and involved a dialectical movement away from everything he once believed toward its apparent antithesis – but only apparent. As Percy would insist, science properly understood was not a contradiction of faith. Percy's labors in science had brought him to the firm conclusion that the only thing science could say about man were those generalizations that held for the entire species. But while science could generalize about the human creature, it could not put its finger on that creature's unique endowment, his individuality. Claiming that science could explain everything was not only scientific hubris but the root of much mischief and confusion in the modern world. And the supreme instance of that mischief, Percy came to believe, was its attempt to relegate that which it could not speak about, the individual's existence (much less his soul), to insignificance, and thereby to demote mankind to its generalizable qualities. Man thus conceived was no more than a beast.

If science could say nothing about the most important facet of the human creature - the joyous, suffering, and perverse self - what or who could? If man was free, and not simply an overdetermined animal, he was free to make choices. That created a problem, of course. For on what basis would one determine the right or wrong course of action, in the smallest matters as well as the largest? By what principles should one live a life? The perils of moral relativism were evident to Percy in his own disabling drift and lassitude, and the assorted postreligious solutions - the Kantian categorical imperative, utilitarian notions of the greatest good for the greatest number, and even the Nietzschean will to power - seemed to him inadequate. The first two led back to a dependence on the methods of science (ethics as decision science) and the third, potentially, to barbarism...

The one nonreligious alternative to moral relativism that was closest to Percy was the Stoicism that had been so nobly represented by Uncle Will. But as beautiful and noble as this ethic was, Percy felt that it would never work for him - and wouldn't for the simple yet decisive reason that he lacked the strength of character, the *virtu*, that was necessary for the upholding of such an ethic. Percy's great feelings of self-disgust and unworthiness made the Stoic option seem beyond his reach. Percy came to Christianity precisely out of this powerful sense of his own unworthiness. Indeed, it seemed to him the principal brilliance of the Christian 'anthropology' (a word that he liked to use in its radical, nonacademic sense) was that it put human corruption and inadequacy at the center of its picture of man, and furthermore, that it taught that recognition of this inadequacy was the first step in hearing the Christian message"); Lewis A. Lawson and Victor A. Kramer (ed), *More Conversations with Walker Percy* (1993); Marion Montgomery, "Walker Percy and the Christian Scandal," *First Things*, April 1993; Joseph J. Feeney, "Walker Percy: The Novelist as Prophet," *The Month*, June 1994, p.240; Peter Kreeft, *C. S. Lewis for the Third Millennium* (1994), Ch. 5: "Walker Percy's *Lost in the Cosmos*: *The Abolition of Man* in Late-Night Comedy Format"; Robert Lauder, *Walker Percy: Prophetic, Existentialist, Catholic Storyteller* (1996); Jay Tolson (ed), *The Correspondence of Shelby Foote and Walker Percy* (1996); John F. Desmond, *At The Crossroads: Ethical and Religious Themes in the Writings of Walker Percy* (1997); Kieran Quinlan, *Walker Percy: The Last Catholic Novelist* (1998); Patrick Samway, *Walker Percy: A Life* (1999); Michael Kobre, *Walker Percy's Voices* (2000); Carl Olson, "Walker Percy: Diagnostician of the Modern Malaise," *catholicexchange.com*, 19 June 2001); Gerald O'Collins, *Incarnation* (2002) ("During the Mass he attended at Christmas 1986, the American novelist Walker Percy was deeply surprised by a powerful religious experience. He wrote about it at once to Robert Coles, a psychiatrist friend at Harvard University: 'Dear Bob, The Mass was going on, the homily standard – that is "true" but customary. A not-so-good choir of young rock musicians got going on "Joy to the World," the vocals not so good but enthusiastic. Then it hit me: What if it should be the case that the entire cosmos had a Creator, and what if he decided for reasons of his own to show up as a tiny baby, conceived and born under suspicious circumstances?'

'Well, Bob,' Walker Percy continued, 'you can lay it on Alzheimer's or hang-over or whatever, but – it hit me. I had to pretend I had an allergy attack so that I could take out my handkerchief.'

Walker Percy was always an intellectual, tightly controlled man, who had never had anything close to a mystical experience or even a twinge of Pentecostal enthusiasm. The experience he wrote about came late in his life, that sense of stunned amazement at the divine Word becoming flesh and living among us. Despite his Southern reserve, Percy was profoundly astonished and wept at the sheer loving simplicity of what God had done at the first Christmas"); Farrell O'Gorman, *Flannery O'Connor, Walker Percy, and Catholic Vision in Post-War Southern Fiction* (2004); Carl E. Olson, "Traveling in a Strange Land WQith Walker Percy," *Saint Austin Review*, March/April 2005, p.6; David Horace Harwell, *Walker Percy Remembered: A Portrait in the Words of Those Who Knew Him* (2006); Rhea Scott Rasnic, *Walker Percy and the Catholic Sacraments* (2007); Marion Montgomery, *With Walker Percy at the Tupperware Party* (2008); Victoria Nelson, "Walker Percy's *Love in the Ruins*: Moving Beyond Paradise to the New Jerusalem," *Saint Austin Review*, May/June 2008, p.16; *Walker Percy: A Documentary Film* (2011); *The Walker Percy Project, An Internet Literary Center*, *ibiblio.org/wpercy*; Lorene Hanley Duquin, *A Century of Catholic Converts* (2003), p.151; Ralph McInerny, *Some Catholic Writers* (2007); *ANB* ("In each book [after *The Moviegoer*] Percy takes his protagonist through an emotional encounter with his tragic past and brings him to a choice between suicide and Christian faith. Secular society, either in its guise as empty hedonism or misguided social engineering, is a constant satiric target in these novels").

Peter, Sarah Anne Worthington King (Worthington was her maiden name; King her first married name) – philanthropist and penal reformer; b. 10 May 1800, Chillicothe, Ohio; c. March 1855, Rome; d. 6 February 1877, Cincinnati, Ohio; her father, Thomas Worthington, who was descended from an ancient Lancashire, England, Catholic family, was a wealthy landowner, U.S. senator and later governor of Ohio 1814-1818; her family were devout Methodists; educated at private schools; in 1816, she married Edward King, member of the Ohio senate (he was a devout Episcopalian and she joined his religion), who died in 1836; five children of the marriage, three of whom died early; did much charitable work for the poor; in 1844, she married William Peter, a widower and British consul at Philadelphia, with whom she did much traveling in Europe and the Middle East until his death in 1853 (no children of the marriage); in 1850 she founded the School of Design for Women in Philadelphia; after her husband's death she returned to Cincinnati and spent most of the rest of her life as a patron of art, and in works of philanthropy and charity; her conversion was influenced by conversations with American bishops and visits to Rome; many religious orders (e.g., the Order of the Good Shepherd, the Little Sisters of the Poor, the

Sisters of Mercy, and the Sisters of St. Francis) owed much to her generosity; worked as a nurse during the Civil War; close friend of Pope Pius IX; member of the Third Order of St. Francis; see Margaret Rives King, *Memoirs of the Life of Mrs. Sarah Peter* (1889); Anna Shannon Macallister, *In Winter We Flourish: Life and Letters of Sarah Worthington King Peter, 1800-1877* (1939); Katherine Burton, *In No Strange Land: Some American Catholic Converts* (1942), p.13 ("The thing that finally brought Mrs. Peter into the Catholic Church was a visit to the catacombs. There she saw in concreteness and reality the continuity of worship and dogma of the Christian Church. When she told Archbishop Hughes of her intention, he arranged a retreat for her at the Convent of the Triniti dei Monti.

She wrote reassuringly to her son of her change of faith, telling him that he knew she was steady and considered in other things and was in this too, 'Now as I come nearer to the clear light of truth I marvel that I should always have been so near and yet never discovered it.' But it was for her really only 'a return to old ways,' she insisted"); Alma Power Waters, *Sarah Peter: The Dream and the Harvest* (1965); *Catholic Encyclopedia*; *ANB*.

Poindexter, John Marlan – naval officer and Department of Defense official; b. 12 August 1936, Washington, Indiana; c. 14 August 2001 (his wife Linda Poindexter (see below) converted in 1999); raised as a Methodist; graduated from the United States Naval Academy in 1958 (first in his class); married in 1958 and converted to the Episcopal Church afterwards, finding the liturgy of the *Book of Common Prayer* very satisfying; graduate student 1961-1964 (PhD in Nuclear Physics in 1964 from the California Institute of Technology); Commander of a destroyer squadron in the Pacific Ocean and Indian Ocean; Deputy Commander of the Naval Education and Training Command; twenty-nine years active duty in the navy, rising to rank of Vice-Admiral; served in President Reagan's administration as Military Assistant 1981-1983, as Deputy National Security Advisor 1983-1985, and as National Security Advisor 1985-1986; played a significant role, *inter alia*, in the Strategic Defense Initiative, the Achille Lauro incident, and the Reykjavik Incident; convicted in 1990 of several felonies as a result of his actions in the Iran-Contra affair, but his convictions were reversed on appeal in 1991; worked as a defense contractor 1988-2002; recalled to public service 2002-2003 as the director of the DARPA Information Awareness Office for the administration of President George W. Bush; father of five children, including Alan G. Poindexter, a NASA astronaut and Space Shuttle pilot; converted to the Catholic Church from Episcopalianism; see Foreword to the tenth anniversary edition of Dwight Longenecker and Cyprian Blamires (ed), *The Path to Rome* (2010) ("I often say that one of the strongest elements in my own Christian faith is the endurance for two thousand years of the faith and the witness of people from all over the broad spectrum of human society...

After sixty years as a Protestant, I found that the only way to be true to Christ was to 'come home' to his Church...At first I had hoped we could remain within the Episcopal Church, as it seemed like home and it had undeniably beautiful liturgy. However, I found that I could not accept changes within the Church that were driven by secular society and not by the guidance of the Holy Spirit. Worse, those changes often occasioned denial of the great statements of our faith found in the Creeds. Once human beings begin to see themselves as arbiters of truth, truth itself becomes as changeable as the weather and subject to human manipulation.

My Christian faith and specifically my Catholic faith is not something that has been reinvented with each generation. I find grerat support from the countless talented and gifted individuals down through the ages who have been guided by the Holy Spirit and led their lives accordinglyintheCatholicChurch")

Poindexter, Linda (*née* Goodwin) – b. 1938, Indianapolis, Indiana; c. 3 April 1999 (Easter Vigil; her husband, John Poindexter (see above) converted in 2001); raised in the Disciples of Christ Church, a very Protestant group; attended University of Vermont, University of Maryland, and graduated from University of Southern California in 1960; married in 1958 and converted to the Episcopal Church afterwards (influenced very much by the beauty of the liturgy); started at an Episcopal seminary in 1983; in 1986 ordained to the Episcopal ministry and served in that capacity for thirteen years; mother of five children, including Alan G. Poindexter, a NASA astronaut and Space Shuttle pilot; see *EWTN Audio Library, The Journey Home* (17 September 2001); "A Matter of Conscience," in Jennifer Ferrara and Patricia Sodano Ireland (ed), *The Catholic Mystique; Women Converts Tell Their Stories* (2004), p.85 ("In high school, I dated a very nice boy from the local Catholic boys' high school. I was too young and inexperienced to recognize the training in purity and respect for young women he had been given. (I only wish young people today had the benefit of the education in purity and decency that was part of Catholic education in the past.)...

The Episcopal Church is completely preoccupied with the human sexuality issues with which the whole world has been dealing. Over time, I became disheartened by many of the clergy who were coming to believe that homosexual unions were something that could be blessed by the church and that sexually active homosexuals could be ordained. I know they were trying to be compassionate and just; but instead, they were leading people astray, encouraging that which is not from God. Those of us who disagreed - and there were many - were told that we were unchristian and unloving. No longer was it acceptable to love the sinner but hate the sin…

I decided to do some further study of Catholic belief and doctrine. I bought the Catechism of the Catholic Church and eventually began to read it. Cradle Catholics often do not realize the great gift of having the beliefs of the Church so clearly presented. According to many Episcopalians, God is essentially mysterious; therefore, the truth, as much as we can know of it, lies in the questions and not the answers. I started to really wonder about this kind of thinking. Does God want us to wander in the dark? Is He not a God who has chosen to reveal Himself to us? I began to have a new appreciation and respect for the teaching authority of the Church, that is, the Magisterium. Previously, I had been appreciative of definitive Church teachings only when they coincided with my own thinking. Now, I felt myself drawn to that most famous of Anglican converts, John Henry Cardinal Newman. In Newman's *Apologia Pro Vita Sua,* I came across this powerful argument for the Magisterium: 'I am brought to speak of the Church's infallibility, as a provision, adapted by the mercy of the Creator to preserve religion in the world, and to restrain that freedom of thought which is one of the greatest of our natural gifts, and to rescue it from its own suicidal excesses'…

Although I have always intuitively felt the Protestant and Catholic understanding of ordination was profoundly different, I did not have the words to explain the difference. I am indebted to George Weigel for his excellent exposition of the difference in *The Truth of Catholicism.* He identifies the Protestant view of ordained ministry as a functional one; the pastor is the one who does certain things. By contrast, in the Catholic sacramental imagination, the priest is an icon. He represents Christ the High Priest. Since Christ's relationship to the Church is spousal, the priest, acting as an icon of Christ, makes Christ's loving gift of Himself present in the consecration of the bread and the wine. In order for the priest to truly represent Christ, the priest must be male"); "Women Clergy Take the Path to Rome: From (American) Anglicanism," in Dwight Longenecker and Cyprian Blamires (ed), *The Path to Rome* (2010) ("The first hint of any problem came when I became convinced that the outcome of the celebrated *Roe v Wade* case had not been liberating but tragic. Until this conviction was borne home to me,

I had happily chanted the illogical slogan that I was 'antiabortion but pro-choice' In many ways this was the simplified version of the official Episcopal Church position as adopted in General Convention (the ruling body of the national church that met every three years). The strangeness of having such issues decided by a body of elected delegates and bishops in a very political type of setting had not yet entered my consciousness. Thanks to the unwavering witness of the Roman Catholic Church, the loving witness of many friends in the Episcopal Church and the position taken by notable public figures, especially President Reagan, I became convinced of the absolute right to life of the unborn child at any stage of development...

The next hurdle...was the developing issue of the ordination of homosexuals and - to a lesser extent at the time - the blessing of homosexual unions. I could understand the compassion and urge to love and welcome all people that drove these issues but I believed that it was a false compassion, encouraging such persons to engage in practices which were extremely unhealthy spiritually, morally, and physically...

The final blow to my contentment was the work of one of our bishops who, in successive books, denied most of what we say in the Creeds. I could not understand why few voices were raised in protest, but charging someone with heresy and removing them was not ever thought of...

The simple fact forced itself little by little into my consciousness that there was no real authority to speak for the truth in the Communion in which I worshipped and worked...I sought refuge in prayer at the Catholic church nearby. I walked into that church and was immediately at peace. I said to myself almost at once, 'Can I become a Catholic? Is this what God wants of me?' And I really wanted to hear 'Yes'. It took me almost five years of study and thought and prayer...

Reading the words of *Lumen Gentium* 14 was eye-opening. I am indebted to my friend Jennifer Ferrara [see above] for bringing it to my attention in an article in *First Things* magazine. The passage states that 'Those could not he saved who refuse either to enter the church, or to remain in it, while knowing that it was founded by God through Christ as required for salvation.' This gave me the answer I was seeking. My path was to enter the Church and thereby witness to its truth...

I had absorbed a good bit of propaganda that the Roman Catholic Church was a man's domain and that it disrespected women in most ways. I found instead that women were exalted in it, and that their traditional role as wife and mother was honored, not least because having a large family and staying at home to raise them was considered praiseworthy and blessed...It was not the Roman Catholic Church, but society in general, that disapproved of women being womanly!...

It has been in the years since I converted that I have come to appreciate the theological thinking and reasoning behind a male-only priesthood...

The problem arises from applying the Enlightenment terms of natural and rational rights to the supernatural understanding of creation and rights. Our true rights are derived from our place in Creation. God made us all equal in his eyes but this does not imply that everything in life is to be equal. God did not make all the peoples of the world equal as his special and chosen people – rather he picked the Jews as those who would know him first and bring him to the world...

God created human beings; he could have created them without sex, exactly alike in all respects, but he did not. He created us male and female in his image. He did not choose to make us exactly alike – we have different qualities: different appearance, different bodies, which do rather drastically different things. Male and female are two different and wondrous ways of being human, of being in the image of God.

In the Apostolic Letter *On the Dignity and Vocation of Women*, John Paul II speaks of the beauty of the creation of man and woman...Human beings do not exist in isolation. They are created male and female for community. From the very beginning we have nuptial imagery. Human beings are created for life in communion and to be fruitful and multiply...

There is no denying that women historically have been abused, dominated and ill-used. But in the ultimate deformity, radical feminism seeks to remedy that historical abuse by denigrating all the beauty that God created in femininity and turning women into imitation men. Existing for the other becomes existing for the self, existing for the fulfillment of the self. Thus, anything that is particular to males should be open to females. The Church and God himself are seen as dishonoring women and closing the door on their advancement or even on their ability to serve Christ, to love and honor him...

Why has the Church said, infallibly (*Ordinatio Sacerdotalis* of 1994 and the response of the Congregation for the Doctrine of the Faith in 1995) that only men will be ordained?

First in my thinking is that the priesthood is a sacrament. The priest represents Christ and is *in persona Christi*. The priest is a symbol of Christ within that sacrament and symbols are not arbitrary and interchangeable. Even in pagan religions, priestesses did not serve and represent male gods but rather goddesses. The old (and new) pagans understand the power of symbols.

While God created all of humanity equal in his eyes with equal dignity and worth, he did not give to all the same gifts, the same calling. He did not call all peoples initially to be his chosen, to show him forth to the world, but only the people Israel. Again the nuptial imagery. Israel is the bride of the Lord, frequently the unfaithful bride. Israel is the spouse - called to live in that relation to God.

God does not choose to come into human life as an angel, without sex, but the Word becomes fully human and fully divine as a male person born of a female person. This is not insignificant or accidental but God's plan of salvation.

Continuing the imagery and language of the nuptial relationship present since Creation, Jesus speaks of himself as the bridegroom. He calls forth and establishes his bride the Church built upon the rock of a man, Peter.

Jesus chooses the Apostles, those who will be his representatives and they are all men. Some will tell you that Jesus was choosing men because of the culture of his time and the lowly place of women. Do these people accuse Jesus of sexism or political correctness? Jesus interacted with women all of his earthly life in a way that was counter to the prevailing customs of that time. He gave them great honor, so the argument that only the culture prevented the calling of women to be apostles does not hold water. Consider a few instances of the 'firsts' that women hold in the Scriptures:
1. The first to learn of the coming birth of the Messiah (Luke 1: 26-38).
2. The first to recognize that Mary was carrying the Divine and human child was Elizabeth (although one could make the case that it was John in her womb - Luke 1: 39-45).
3. The first miracle came at the behest and instigation of Mary (John 2: 1-10).
4. The first to view the Empty Tomb (Luke 23: 24, 8; Matt 28: 1-8; Mark 16: 1-8).
5. The first to see the Risen Lord was Mary Magdalene (Matt 28: 9-10; Mark 16: 9-11). And, perhaps, the first to be told by Jesus that he is the Messiah is the Samaritan woman who has no standing at all - she is female, not Jewish and a 'sinner' (John 4: 5-30). Then there is the conversation with Martha; one of the most important in the Gospel. Jesus tells her 'I am the Resurrection and the Life' (John 11: 17-27). There is the presence of many women who were followers of Jesus on Calvary as he was crucified (a sensational contrast with the notorious cowardice of Peter, who denied three times that he knew Jesus) (Mark 15: 40-41). Jesus never belittles the ways of women; their caring and loving. Rather he uses occasions such as the woman anointing his feet and the woman who pours the anointing oils on his head prior to the Passion, as teaching moments, showing the men around how they should be (John 12: 1-8).

If God had chosen to be incarnate as a woman, the message of servanthood and humility and taking the lower seat would hardly have been surprising, since this is what women did and how they lived anyway. It is almost as if he were trying to teach the men how to learn to behave as the women did without losing their manliness. He was teaching them to become the servants, not the rulers and the masters...

[W]hat do we say to women who love Jesus with all their hearts and want to serve him in their lives? Some of those women feel that they are called to be priests; to be the one who says the words that make Christ's true Body and Blood present for the faithful. I can understand their longing to be close to Christ; to be close to the Body and the Blood in the Eucharist. It is, I believe, what I too was seeking in ordination.

First, we have to say that those who wish to be closest to Christ must do the very tough job of living within him, of offering themselves not for what they want to do but for what God calls them to do. It is hard to be open to a call in one direction when we yearn to go in another. But that way of humility and self-offering is the way of Christ and the way of ultimate fulfillment.

Then I think it is time to meditate on and honor the particular gifts of women. It is difficult to speak of some of these gifts without seeming to be sexist - that is to deny those gifts in men, which is not my intention. It is a commonplace however to recognize the particular piety and devotion of women; somehow they seem to be the ones who keep society on an even keel with their relationship to the sacred. By nature, by creation, women are more receptive and, says Alice von Hildebrand, receptivity is the key to Holiness. Edith Stein said that all women need to accept their maternal nature if they are to accept their vocation specifically as women. All women, married or celibate, are mothers all the time. The same can he said of men and fatherhood. John Paul reminds us that celibacy is not a rejection of marriage but a different form of marriage. It is a 'nuptial giving of one's self for the purpose of reciprocating in a particular way the nuptial love of the Redeemer'").

Ponnuru, Ramesh – columnist and editor; b. 16 August 1974, Prairie Village, Kansas; of Asian-Indian descent; father Hindu, mother Lutheran; brought up in Kansas; raised with not much religious instruction; liberal in politics in high school, but conservative before he became an adult; educated at Princeton University (BA in History); columnist and senior editor for *National Review* magazine; has written for many newspapers and journals; writes from a conservative perspective; has launched several attacks on the Democratic Party over its approach to life and death issues; married to April Ponnuru, a policy adviser to the Majority Whip in the House of Representatives; see "Catholic and Conservative: A Conversation with

Ramesh Ponnuru," *ignatiusinsight.com*, October 2004 ("The process by which the Church drew me to her was long. It would be presumptuous for me to say that I myself entirely understood how the Holy Spirit worked here. To summarize the intellectual aspect of the process: I first came to see that many of the virtues the Church inculcates were good for people, and then to see that they were good for people because this was the way we were meant to live - and so forth until I saw that I now believed the Church's claims for itself to be true"); *The Party of Death: The Democrats, the Media, the Courts, and the Disregard for Human Life* (2006); "The Zeal of a Convert," *catholicity.com*, 20 September 2007 ("In our time, what would have struck our predecessors as the merest common sense is now held to be fundamentally religious. Even when I was not a Christian, I believed that there was such a thing as truth, including moral truth, and that reason could apprehend at least some of these truths. I thought everybody implicitly accepted these postulates. In the response to my book, I have come to find out that these views make me a raging fundamentalist. I feel a bit like the character in Molière who discovers that all his life, without knowing it, he has been speaking prose.

I can't help it; it is not a choice. We don't choose what is true. And while I continue to insist that revelation is unnecessary to show that unborn human beings have a right to be protected from violence, I do not shy away from saying that Christianity is relevant here. Christians have special obligations: to orient themselves toward truth, to seek justice and mercy").

Pope, Clarence Cullum – churchman; b. 26 October 1929, Lafayette, Louisiana; c. 1 February 1995 (received in Arlington, Texas, together with his wife, Dr. Martha Pope, by Bernard Cardinal Law); d. 8 January 2012, Baton Rouge, Louisiana; educated at Centenary College of Louisiana (BA 1950) and the University of the South, Sewanee, Tennessee (BD 1954); ordained as an Episcopalian clergyman in 1955; a leader of the traditionalist wing of Anglicanism in North America; appointed Anglican Bishop of Fort Worth in 1985; president of the Episcopal Synod of America 1989-1993 (now Forward in Faith/North America); long-time advocate for corporate reunification with the Catholic Church; retired on 31 December 1994; then converted to the Catholic Church; he applied for re-ordination in the Catholic Diocese of Baton Rouge; the bishop gave his conditional approval, subject to the agreement of his diocesan priests' council, but the council refused his request; he returned to the Episcopal Church in the United States of America in August 1995; on 6 August 2007 he resigned from the Episcopal Church and was again received into the Catholic

Church; he explained his return to the Episcopal Church as due to depression brought on through advanced cancer, and his "tepid" reception by the Catholic Church; see George Conger, "Fort Worth Bishop Clarence Pope Dead," *Anglican Ink*, 8 January 2012 ("At the time of his return to Rome, Bishop Pope explained that he believed the Catholic movement in Anglicanism had died. 'We are left with lots of Catholic vestments worn in areas of the Episcopal Church where low church used to be the order of the day; but no Catholic faith order. 'Without the stable center provided by the Holy See of Peter,' he said, 'the Anglo-Catholic movement within the church will 'ultimately die away'").

Porter, Katherine Anne (born Callie Russell Porter) - journalist, writer and political activist; b. 15 May 1890, Indian Creek, Texas; c. 1906; d. 18 September 1980, Silver Spring, Maryland; fourth of five children of a farming family; her mother died when she was two years old; little formal education; left home at the age of sixteen and married John Henry Koontz, a Catholic, and converted to his religion; physically abused by her husband; they divorced in 1915 and she changed her name; began writing for newspapers; almost died in the 1918 flu pandemic; moved to Greenwich Village, New York; became a political radical and moved between New York and Mexico; acquainted with Diego Rivera but became disillusioned with the revolutionaries; also critical of religion for most of rest of her life, but dealt with religious issues ("I have a great deal of religious symbolism in my stories because I have a very deep sense of religion"); her short stories won critical acclaim; married several times and had several miscarriages; no children born to her; taught at several universities; her only full-length novel, *Ship of Fools*, about a troubled world on the brink of World War II, was a best seller; close friend of Caroline Gordon (see above) and Allen Tate (see below) and their houseguest for a time; in 1966 she was awarded the Pulitzer Prize and the National Book Award for *The Collected Stories of Katherine Anne Porter*; returned to the Catholic Church in the last decade of her life; often dealt with themes of death in her writing; her ashes were buried next to her mother in Indian Creek Cemetery, Texas; see *Flowering Judas and Other Stories* (1930); *The Leaning Tower and Other Stories* (1934); *Noon Wine* (1937); *Old Mortality* (1937); *Pale Horse, Pale Rider* (1939); The *Days Before* (1952); *The Old Order: Stories of the South* (1955); *The Ship of Fools* (1962); *Collected Stories* (1965); *A Christmas Story* (1967); *Collected Essays and Occasional Writings* (1970); *The Never Ending Wrong* (1977) (account of the Sacco and Vanzetti case and of her political activism); *Letters of Katherine Anne Porter* (1994); Jane Krause DeMouy, *Katherine Anne Porter's Women: The Eye of Her Fiction* (1983); Darlene Harbour Unrue, *Truth and Vision in Katherine Anne Porter's Fiction* (1985); Joan Givner, *Katherine Anne Porter: A Life* (1991) ("There were many aspects of Catholicism which appealed to Porter. In the first place, it provided the security of her childhood faith without recalling any of the disagreeable memories associated with it. There was none of her grandmother's repressive morality; no long list of prohibitions against dancing, drinking, card playing, or other activities that she enjoyed; there were no wild scenes of unleashed emotion such as she witnessed at revival meetings.

On the other hand. there was a great deal that appealed to her aesthetic sense. She loved the dramatic qualities of the Mass, the beauty of the liturgy, the sound of the church music and the Latin words. She liked the atmosphere of the churches, with their ornate windows, high altars, intricate vestments, and she was moved by the symbolism inherent in word and gesture. It is possible that Father Hennessy's instruction not only prepared her for entry into the Church but also laid the basis of her future literary techniques.

She was particularly interested in the saints and began reading saints' lives. Later she collected every version she could find of the lives of her favorite saints, Joan, Ursula, and Teresa of Avila, and of her own patron saints, Anne and Catherine of Siena. Her indispensable bedside text, replaced numerous times during her life, was *The Confessions of St. Augustine…*

Even when she wavered in her ability to believe in God, she never wavered in her preference for Catholicism over every other religious creed. She usually kept a rosary beside her bed, and on the many occasions when she hovered near death she received the last rites of the Catholic Church. Catholicism was the faith of her fictional family and she indicated that it was the religion of her actual family until assiduous researchers established that Porter's parents and grandparents were Methodists and Presbyterians. She never regretted her decision to convert to Catholicism and said at the end of her life that no other religion had ever attracted her"); Thomas F. Walsh, *Katherine Anne Porter and Mexico: The Illusion of Eden* (1992); Janis P. Stout, *Katherine Anne Porter: A Sense of the Times* (1995); Darlene Harbour Unrue, *Critical Essays on Katherine Anne Porter* (1997); Mary Titus, *The Ambivalent Art of Katherine Anne Porter* (2005); Darlene Harbour Unrue, *Katherine Anne Porter: The Life of an Artist* (2005); Darlene Harbour Unrue, *Truth and Vision in Katherine Anne Porter's Fiction* (2008); Darlene Harbour Unrue, *Katherine Anne Porter Remembered* (2010);

her papers are housed primarily at the McKeldin Library of the University of Maryland; *ANB*.

Preston, Mgr. Thomas Scott – priest and founder of a religious order; b. 23 July 1824, Hartford, Connecticut; c. 14 November 1849 (received with his brother William and Dr. John Murray Forbes, rector at his church, by Fr. James Roosevelt Bayley (see above)); d. 4 November 1891, New York City; father was of Puritan stock; brought up as an Episcopalian; religious minded from his youth; studied in the Episcopalian general seminary in New York (leader of the American version of the Oxford Movement there); ordained to the Anglican ministry in 1848; after his conversion to the Catholic faith he was ordained to the priesthood on 16 November 1850; in 1853 appointed secretary to Archbishop John J. Hughes of New York; and chancellor of the diocese 1855-1891; vicar-general 1873-1891; fine apologist for the Catholic Church; he founded and directed until his death the Sisters of the Divine Compassion (co-founder Mother Mary Veronica Starr (see below)); buried in the chapel of the mother house of the order; see *Ark of the Covenant* (1860); *Lectures on Reason and Revelation* (1868); *Christ and the Church* (1870); *Lectures Upon the Devotion to the Most Sacred Heart of Jesus Christ* (1874); *Vicar of Christ* (1878); *The Divine Paraclete* (1879); *The Protestant Reformation* (1879); *The Sacred Year: Sermons* (1880); *Christian Unity* (1881); *Protestantism and the Church* (1882); *God and Reason* (1884); *The Sacred Year* (1885); *The Watch on Calvary* (1885); *The Divine Sanctuary* (1887); *Gethsemani: Meditations on the last Day on Earth of Our Blessed Redeemer* (1887); *Protestantism and the Bible* (1888); William Preston, *Remembrances of My Brother Thomas* (n.d.); Henry Brann, *The Rt. Rev. Thomas S. Preston* (1893); Sister Mary Teresa, RDC, *The Fruits of His Compassion: The Life of Mother Mary Veronica* (1962); *National Cyclopedia of American Biography* ("In a magazine article, written a few years ago, he said, 'All human influences around me would have kept me where were all my earthly ties, but I felt that the voice of my conscience was more to me than any earthly attraction. If there was one church founded by the Lord I must seek and find it. There were some worldly sacrifices, but, although they sombered my face a little, they did not drive the sunshine from my heart. At last I was in my Father's house, and never from that moment have I had one doubt of the truth of the Catholic religion'"); *Catholic Encyclopedia* ("He was a deep student of the early history of the Church and of the Fathers, and thus gradually began to feel the branch theory untenable. He was convinced of the truth of Catholicity, as well as of his obligation to embrace it, before he had ever read a professedly Catholic book, or spoken to a priest… He was a man of exquisite refinement, of tender piety, and of intense loyalty"); *ANB*.

Price, James Harry – lecturer; b. 1902, Baltimore, Maryland; c. 16 May 1953 (Washington D.C.; received by Fr. Ferdinand Schoberg, SJ); brought up an Episcopalian; educated at Tufts College, Maryland; studied at the Episcopal Theological School, Cambridge, Massachusetts; ordained a minister of the Episcopal Church in 1928; expert in the culture of the American Indian; taught Great Books courses and began to appreciate that the vast majority of the "Great Writers" of Western Civilization were Catholic writers; later lecturer in the History of Western Civilization at Iona College, New York; contributor to many journals; see "My Prayer Was Answered," in John A. O'Brien, *The Road to Damascus, Vol. IV: Roads to Rome* (1955), p.181 ("In the old-line, accepted, conventional Protestant groups [the] principle of private judgment has a strangely logical way of eventuating in its becoming almost a duty to refuse 'to be told what to believe or do.' To an outsider it may look as though this or that Church is flourishing and orderly, and indeed it may be for immediate and practical purposes. Yet there is that ever-present basic principle which makes it a matter of conscience to disagree with whatever displeases…

All during this period there was one dogma to which I subscribed…I held a firm conviction that there are no absolutes and that there was no such thing as absolute truth. Now, I hope my logician friends will not take me to task at this point and ask, 'Well, didn't you believe that absolutely?' The answer would be 'yes,' but I had not read the Categories and, besides, this dogma was mighty convenient for justifying novelty, experiment and a change of emphasis in my religious, political and social thinking…

Then 'the thing' happened…I lunched with an apostate Unitarian. The conversation turned to absolutes…He said, 'Yes, a lot of these modern thinkers scoff at absolutes, but you know they can't get round a thing like: 'The whole is greater than the part,' or 'Things equal to the same thing are equal to each other'…

There was a Principle of Order observable that was consistent with the Order of Nature and of Natural Law. I saw that no other religious group even claimed to be identified with that order except the Catholic Church. I was not certain, at this point, whether Natural Order produced the Church or whether the Church set up its own order. But order I could see, and there was no mistaking it and the necessity of it. In Catholicism ever so much was settled and agreed upon. It was accepted and adhered to both officially and in practice. It was unified and ordered in a manner simply unknown in Protestant Christianity, where the fundamental principle was disorderly on an *a priori* basis").

Price, Vincent Leonard, Jr.–actor; b. 27 May 1911, St. Louis, Missouri; c. 1974 (his wife converted several years previously); d. 25 October 1993, Los Angeles, California; his father was president of the National Candy Company; raised as an Episcopalian; traveled through Europe at the age of seventeen; studied at Yale University (graduated in Art History and Fine Art in 1933); teaching apprentice in a school briefly; studied at the Courtauld Institute in London (wrote his master's thesis on "Dürer and the School of the Danube"); attracted to the theater; became an actor in London and moved on to Broadway, making his screen debut in 1938; played many minor roles; began to appear in low budget horror movies, notably *House of Wax* (1953); first major success *The Fall of the House of Usher* (1960); starred in a series of well received Gothic horror movies, such as *The Pit and the Pendulum* (1961) and *The Abominable Dr. Phibes* (1971); gave up films in the 1970s and presented cooking programs on television; returned to films with roles in *The Whales of August* (1987) and *Edward Scissorhands* (1990); appeared in over one hundred films in all; numerous play and television appearances; recorded many Gothic horror short stories; had a love of fine art of which he acquired much; married three times; he and his second wife Mary Grant Price donated hundreds of works of art and a large sum of money to East Los Angeles College in the early 1960s in order to endow the Vincent and Mary Price Gallery there; he converted to the Catholic faith on marrying his third wife, the actress Coral Browne (1913-1991); wrote many books on art and cooking; cremated and his ashes scattered off Point Dume in Malibu, California; see *Vincent Price Collects Drawings* (1957); *I Like What I Know – A Visual Autobiography* (1959); *The Book of Joe: About a Dog and His Man* (1961); *A Treasury of Great Recipes* (1965); *The Vincent Price Treasury of American Art* (1972); Robert Parish, *Vincent Price Unmasked: A Biography* (1974); John Brosman, *The Horror People* (1976); Iain McAsh, *The Films of Vincent Price* (1978); Lucy Chase Williams, *The Complete Films of Vincent Price* (1995); Victoria Price, *Vincent Price: A Daughter's Biography* (1999); his papers are at the Library of Congress, Washington, D.C.; *ANB*.

Prince, Erik Dean – private military company executive; b. 6 June 1969, Holland, Michigan; youngest of four children from a very wealthy family; his parents share a Dutch heritage; his father, Edgar D. Prince (d. 1995), ran the Prince Corporation; raised in the Calvinist

Christian Reformed Church in North America; toured the world with his father; entered the United States Naval Academy, but left after three semesters; BA in Economics from Hillsdale College, Michigan, 1992; also trained as an emergency medical technician; internship for California Congressman Dana Rohrabacher; commissioned as an officer in the United States Navy via Officer Candidate School in 1992; went on to become a Navy SEAL; left the navy in 1995; sold the family company in 1996; in 1997 he financed the formation of Blackwater Worldwide, which became the world's largest private military company; served as CEO until 2009 and later as chairman until Blackwater was sold in 2010 to a group of investors; in recent years Blackwater came under much criticism; became a Catholic; has provided funding for Catholic organizations; married to Joan Nicole Prince (d. 2003) (four children of the marriage); then married to Joanna Ruth Prince (*née* Houck) 2004-2012 (three children of the marriage); brother of Betsy DeVos, Republican politician and school choice activist; see Robert Young Pelton, *Licensed to Kill: Hired Guns in the War on Terror* (2006); Jeremy Scahill, *Blackwater: The Rise of the World's Most Powerful Mercenary Army* (2007); Suzanne Simons, *Master of Water: Blackwater USA's Erik Prince and the Business of War* (2009).

Prophet, (Nancy) Elizabeth – sculptor; b. 19 March 1890, Warwick, Rhode Island; c. 1951; d. 8 December 1960, Providence, Rhode Island; of both African-American and Narragansett Indian descent; from a modest family, she paid for her education by working as a housekeeper; studied drawing and painting at the Rhode Island School of Design 1914-1918; married Francis Ford (ten years older than her), but left her husband in 1922 and went to France where she lived until 1934; much poverty and malnutrition while trying to work on her sculpture; concentrated on heads and figures; little success at first; exhibited in both France and the United States, but few sales and helped from destitution by friends; helped by the actress Louise Brooks (see above); returned to the United States in 1929-1930 and 1932-1933, where she received some support, but made little profit; in France much debt, but obtained a teaching post in the United States; became a Catholic, believing the Church offered the last hope for sculpture; died in poverty; still a significant figure in African-American art history; many of her sculptures were destroyed or are in private hands; see Theresa Leininger-Miller, "African-American Artists in Paris, 1922-1934" (PhD dissertation, Yale University, 1995); *ANB*.

Pugh, George Ellis - politician and lawyer; b. 28 November 1822, Cincinnati, Ohio; c. 1868; d. 19 July

1876, Cincinnati, Ohio; his father was a banker and merchant; of Quaker stock, but became a Baptist in his youth; educated at Miami University, Oxford, Ohio (graduated 1840); admitted to the bar of the Supreme Court of Ohio in 1843; celebrated legal practice; served in the Mexican War 1847-1848 when commended for bravery; member of the Democratic Party; member of Ohio House of Representatives 1848-1849; attorney-general State of Ohio 1851-1854; elected to the United States Senate from Ohio 1855-1861 (first native of Ohio to sit), but then defeated; defeated for Lieutenant-Governor for Ohio in 1863; ran for the United States House of Representatives in 1864, but lost; married Theresa Chalfant (d. 1868) in 1855 (three children of the marriage); after his wife's death he finally yielded to her wishes and became a Catholic; see *Catholic Encyclopedia*; *ANB* ("A renowned lawyer, gifted with a remarkable memory, a powerful and commanding voice, acute logic, and a combative temperament, Pugh prepared his cases with 'admirable method and precision,' in the words of the obituary that appeared in the *Cincinnati Daily Gazette* on the day after his death. He gave himself to each case and became as 'fully absorbed in each as if it were the sole work of his life'").

Purtill, Richard Lawrence - philosopher and writer; b. 13 March 1931, Chicago, Illinois; conversion to the Catholic faith in his teens in high school largely due to reading C. S. Lewis' *The Screwtape Letters and many works by G. K. Chesterton; spent some time in the army stationed in England, where he met Maisie Ward and Frank Sheed, the famous Catholic writers and publishers; this led him to writing and philosophy; received his PhD from the University of Chicago;* Professor of Philosophy, Western Washington University in Bellingham, Washington (later Emeritus Professor); author of several books and articles; also author of science fiction and fantasy novels; see (non-fiction) "Chesterton, the Wards, the Sheeds, and the Catholic Revival," in James E. Barcus (ed), *G. K. Chesterton and C. S. Lewis: The Riddle of Joy* (1989) (reprinted in *Reason to Believe: Why Faith Makes Sense* (2009) ("In the early 1950s I was coming out of Foyle's bookstore on Charing Cross in London when I saw a rather surprising sight. In a blind alley between two parts of Foyle's was a small folding platform, rather like a stepstool with a tall railing on one side. On the railing was a crucifix and a rectangular sign on which was painted in rather faded gold letters, 'Catholic Evidence Guild.' Standing on the platform, leaning on the railing, was a young man who was speaking with an Australian accent about the Catholic faith. He was surrounded by a small crowd whose members frequently interrupted him with questions and objections. As I walked over to the platform, the young man was arguing about free will with an older man in the crowd. In light of later knowledge, I imagine that they had gotten onto the topic by way of the problem of evil and the argument that a good deal of the evil in the world is due to human misuses of free will. The man in the crowd was defending determinism, denying that we have free will, and I was not entirely satisfied with the young man's reply. I do not remember if I intervened in the argument, but after the young man had finished speaking and come down from the platform, I buttonholed him and said something like this: 'Why didn't you refute what he was saying by telling him that if determinism were true, he was determined by causes beyond his control to believe in determinism and you were determined by causes beyond your control not to believe in it, so there would be no use arguing?'

I think my thought was something along the lines of C. S. Lewis' argument against naturalism in *Miracles*: since the man did think there was some use in arguing, this in itself was an argument against determinism"); *Logic For Philosophers* (1971); *Lord of the Elves and Eldils: Fantasy and Philosophy in C. S. Lewis and J. R. R. Tolkien* (1974); *Reason to Believe* (1974); *Philosophically Speaking* (1975); *Thinking About Ethics* (1976); *Thinking About Religion: A Philosophical Introduction to Religion* (1978); *Logic: Argument, Refutation, and Proof* (1979); *C. S. Lewis' Case for the Christian Faith* (1981, revised edition 2004); *J. R.. R. Tolkien: Myth, Morality and Religion* (1984); *Philosophical Questions: An Introductory Anthology* (1984) (with Peter J. Kreeft and Michael H. MacDonald); *Moral Dilemmas* (1985); *A Logical Introduction to Philosophy* (1988); "Did C. S. Lewis Lose His Faith?" in A. Walker and J. Patrick (ed), *A Christian for All Christians: Essays in Honor of C. S. Lewis* (1990); *Logical Thinking* (1992); *Lord of the Elves and Eldils: Fantasy and Philosophy in C. S. Lewis and J. R. R. Tolkien* (2006); *Reason to Believe: Why Faith Makes Sense* (2009) (revised and expanded version of the 1974 original); (fiction) *The Kaphtu Trilogy* (1979, 1980 and 1983); *Murdercon* (1982); *The Parallel Man* (1984); *Enchantment at Delphi* (1986); *Lost Tales of Kaphtu* (2005, 2006 and 2008); plus many short stories; *alivingdog.com.*

Ranney, William (Tylee) - painter; b. 9 May 1813, Middletown, Connecticut; d. 18 November 1857, West Hoboken, New Jersey; son of a ship's captain who was lost at sea in 1829; adopted by an uncle in North Carolina and lived there; went to New York to study painting and drawing, but basically self-taught; fought in the Texas Army in 1836 in the Texas

War of Independence; stayed on to make sketches of the trappers, pioneers, wild horses and prairies, which became his subject-matter in later paintings; in 1848 he married Margaret Agnes O'Sullivan two children of the marriage); worked in various areas before settling in the artist community of West Hoboken, New Jersey; noted for his images of western frontier life; also painted sporting scenes and historical paintings drawn from the American Revolution; his paintings were popular and sold well; became unfashionable after the Civil War, but now recognized as one of the most important pre-Civil War American painters whose art is still highly valued today; one of the founders of the New York cricket club; converted from Protestantism to the Catholic faith during his last days; buried in Bergen cemetery; see Francis Grubar, *William Ranney: Painter of the Early West* (1962); Linda Ayres, "William Ranney," in Ron Tyler et al. (ed), *American Frontier Life: Early Western Painting and Prints*, (1987); Mark Thistlethwaite, *William Tylee Ranney East of the Mississippi* (1991).; Ranney Moran (his great-grandson), *Forging an American Identity: The Art of William Ranney* (2006); *ANB.*

Ratner, Herbert Spencer Albert – doctor and writer; b. 23 May 1907, New York City; c. 1938; d. 6 December 1997, Cleveland, Ohio; youngest of seven children of Russian-Jewish immigrants; named after the English philosopher Herbert Spencer; his father, Leo, was a doctor who was a socialist and had no religion; his mother, Sophia ("Sonia"), was a professional singer in her youth and the sister of Lorin Maazel (b. 1930) the violinist, conductor, and composer; his father died when he was fourteen; educated in the University of Michigan in Ann Arbor (BA 1929); studied Medicine there and received MD degree in 1935; married Dorothy Lillian Smith (1907-1996), another medical student, and after graduating they became research assistants; he took courses in philosophy from Herbert Schwartz (see below); in 1937 he went to the University of Chicago where he was appointed by Robert Maynard Hutchins (1899-1977), the President of the University, to be a senior member of the Committee of Liberal Arts (he worked there until 1939); worked with Mortimer Adler (see above); many of his friends, in particular his classmate, Raphael Simon (see below), were becoming attracted to the Catholic Church; he felt this same attraction and converted (he remained a committed Catholic until his death); great love for the writings of St. Thomas Aquinas; scientific consultant to Hutchins 1939-1940; worked in general practice 1941-1949; did much work in relation to medical organizations and publications; made an association of increased deaths with use of the contraceptive pill and pioneered the use of informed consent; much work on preventive family mental health based on natural norms; Pope John Paul II appointed him as consultant to the Pontifical Council on the Family in 1982; three daughters of his marriage; buried with his wife in Marygrove Cemetery, Richfield Township, Lucas County, Ohio; his papers are in the John Paul II Library at Franciscan University, Steubenville, Ohio; see Letter to Dr. C. Everett Koop, 27 February 1981 ("[T]he basic issue that confronts America is the survival and preservation of the traditional family - one of the most enduring and resilient realities of human history. Aberrations and deviations, innovations of one sort or another come and go, but never thrive or survive. Because the traditional family is based on nature, it has a habit of burying its own undertakers.

[M]ost of our social problems are symptomatic of the insecurities engendered in early childhood by virtue of the dysfunctioning family, a dysfunction brought about by a seduction of parents from their nurturing roles and the lack of moral support of the family by society's institutions. These problems run the gamut from alcoholism to suicide to sexual escapism which has now descended down through adolescence into pre-adolescence.

[G]iven the failure of current solutions (the more the establishment spends and the more it propagandizes the worse the state of affairs) a new fresh approach to the problem is imperative, an approach based on the realities of human nature and not on the infirm hypotheses of tunnel visioned experts. As Aristotle (quoted by Sir Francis Bacon in his attack on specialists) once said 'Those who contemplate few things have no difficulty deciding.' The momentous problems that are facing our country are simply too important to be left in the hands of public health specialists. We desperately need at the helm an experienced and broadly knowledgeable physician dedicated to lifc and to the enduring values of the traditional family, a physician who has the character and the stamina to be independent of the pressures from voluntary agencies and those social engineers who ignore common sense and the lessons of history...

Children are the hope: of the future. With our birth rate plummeting below replacement levels and with 75% of couples now infertile by virtue of venereal disease, the Pill, the IUD, abortion and voluntary and involuntary sterilization, children are more precious than ever and more needed than ever by our country"); Mary Tim Baggott (ed), *Nature, the Physician, and the Family* (second edition, 2007) (a selection of his writings edited by his daughter); Dorothy Vining, "What Does Christian Love Look Like?: A Tribute to Herbert Ratner, MD," *musingsat85.com*, 2008 ("Dr. Ratner was a Jewish convert to

Catholicism partly because of the Church's stand on marriage and birth control. As a member of the Catholic Physicians Guild he spoke often about the 'gift of a child' and the sanctity of life. 'Without science we all know that the pregnant woman is a woman "with child." This is what pregnancy is about: two human beings, two lives, the life of the mother and the life of the child, both patients of the physician.' For twenty-five years as editor of *Child and Family* magazine he showed how the revelations from Scripture and from the Book of Nature do not contradict each other.

I look at those old issues of *Child and Family* and my heart swells. It is all so clear there - the value of the child, the value of the family, the value of nature's norms, the value of breast milk to the infant and (even!) the value of semen to the wife. Didn't anyone listen?

He knew the cure for AIDS, too. It is so obvious. '[Nature] has apparently thrown down the gauntlet with AIDS. It is as if Nature is saying, "You have misbehaved long enough, get back to abstinence and monogamy or perish." The sooner we live up to this fact of life, the sooner will man's destiny be secured and the sooner will man reap the benefits of the natural institution of the family, the cornerstone of society'").

Ray, Stephen Kim ("Steve") – Catholic apologist; b. 29 December 1954, Detroit, Michigan; c. 22 May 1994 (received with his wife Janet and their four children); brought up in a strong fundamentalist Baptist family; father was a deacon and Bible teacher ("The Bible was our creed"); lapsed from Christianity as a teenager, but then joined a small non-denominational church, the New Testament Fellowship ("The Catholic Church was not even on the radar screen at that time... We figured that the pope was the anti-Christ, that the Church was the 'whore of Babylon' mentioned in Revelation, that she had done everything to pervert and twist the Gospel...The Catholic Church was the enemy"); influenced in his conversion to the Catholic Church by the way Protestantism had displaced the Eucharist for a sermon and by the many different denominations in Protestantism; influenced by the book *Evangelical Is Not Enough* by Thomas Howard (see above) (given to him by his friend Al Kresta (see above)); began and ran very successfully his own cleaning businesssee, which he later sold in 2007 in order to develop other interests; much writing, radio and television work on the faith; see (selective list) *Crossing the Tiber: Evangelical Protestants Discover the Historical Church* (1997) ("Where does Scripture tell us that 'God's word' can and must be only in written form, typed on paper or parchment? Jesus Christ himself never wrote anything down (other than unknown words on the ground), and it was not recorded that he ever commissioned his followers to write everything down. Had it been as important to him as it was to me as an Evangelical, shouldn't he have made it clear for all time that only what was written down could be considered God's word? But Jesus never promised us an authoritative book, nor did his apostles; rather, he promised us an authoritative Church. Jesus' 'word' was orally transmitted to the twelve apostles. We know from the Old Covenant that oral tradition was established side-by-side with the Torah. Jesus was Jewish, and his teachings and his Church were built upon the Old Testament and the Jewish experience – traditions he laid out during his three years of traversing Israel. He passed this word and teaching on to the Twelve in the form of oral tradition. He promised that when the Holy Spirit came he would teach them all things and bring to their remembrance 'all that I said to you' (Jn 14:26). The Apostle John tells us that if everything Jesus accomplished were written down, all the world could not contain the books. Since Jesus spent three intimate years with his disciples, we know for a fact that the content of the Gospels is only a small fraction of what Jesus taught them. Few realize that Jesus spent forty days after the Resurrection instructing the twelve apostles through the Holy Spirit, giving them special commands concerning the Kingdom of God and the Church. The early Church depended upon the apostolic tradition. The Apostle Paul referred to the Church, not the Bible, as the pillar and foundation of the truth. This...was clearly understood and taught for fifteen centuries and is still faithfully held within the sacred tradition of the Catholic Church.

Did Jesus ever promise to give us an authoritative book? No...Did the apostles promise or hand us an authoritative book? Again, the answer is No. Did Jesus promise us an authoritative Church? Yes. He instituted a Church, his Body, that would pass on the truth, always carefully preserving the tradition entrusted to her...The Church was viewed as the bank into which Christ and the apostles deposited the fullness of the faith... The truth had been delivered from Christ to the apostles, and the apostles deposited the truth into the Church"); *EWTN Audio Library, The Journey Home* (28 September 1997) ("A lot of questions began to arise for us. For my wife the question was 'What is worship?' we would go to church and hear a sermon and the Protestant churches had displaced the Eucharist, which had always been the center of worship. We had displaced the Eucharist for a sermon. And my wife got to the point where she would be asking me, 'How can I go for an hour and listen to a sermon and call that worship?' She said, 'There's something not right'...

For myself I loved the Scriptures and I loved to study the Bible.

So, as I did…I realized that there were contradictory ideas, and even though I liked to believe that we had a core essence of basic structured ideas, I found that as time went on that was becoming less and less. Some Evangelicals believed in infant baptism, others didn't. There was a whole range of ideas. And then I found out there were thirty thousand different Protestant denominations. And then you read in the Gospel that Jesus wanted his Church to be one. He wanted it to be a visible minority, and that started to bother me. How could I, who said I had the Holy Spirit leading me as I read and studied the Scriptures, be in conflict with you who also said you had the Holy Spirit leading you, and yet you came up with contradictory ideas.

Either something was wrong in the methodology of coming to the truth, or else the Holy Spirit was mixed up. I knew *that* wasn't the case, so I had to look at the Church aspect, where we were coming from, why there were all these divisions…

We began to look at why the Church was so fragmented and realized that the Catholic Church had so many signs of its visible unity. At least on the surface there was this unity. And we read in the Fathers that for the first thousand years there wasn't the divisions of the Church like there is today. There was one Church and if you were a Christian you were in the Catholic Church. There wasn't the divisions. And in reading the passages that I had one time interpreted a different way by my own fundamentalist position on Peter, for example Peter being the rock and being the shepherd of the sheep; reading those passages again in the light of some of the things I was beginning to think about the Catholic Church, made that not only attractive but very simple…

From a fundamentalist position, a Baptist position, I could not accept the fact that Peter was the rock, because to do that put me in a very uncomfortable position. I was beginning to accept Catholic thinking. This is why so few Baptist churches will preach on this, because you're kind of getting too close to the line…

There are two parts to this passage here. One says 'you are Peter and on this rock I will build my Church.' One of the unfortunate things in English is that we lose the impact of that verse, because when Jesus first said it, it would have sounded like this: 'Peter, you are rock, and on this rock I will build my Church.' There was no ambiguity there in the Aramaic. In the Greek it lost a little, because it went from *petra* to *petros*. And in English it really lost it, because now we get Peter and rock, it's totally divorced. But originally it was 'Peter, you are rock and on this rock I will build my Church.' OK, there's no question about that.

'And the gates of hell will not prevail against it'…Three weeks ago I was in Caesarea Philippi. We made the trip up north of

Galilee up to Caesarea Philippi where Jesus made that statement in Matthew 16…He went up there in order to make that pronouncement to Peter because of that unique environment…When you go to Caesarea Philippi there's a huge rock, it's about five hundred feet long and two hundred feet high, and it kind of overhangs you. And right in the left there's a huge cave which at the time of Jesus they could never find a bottom to it. They would roll ropes down, but they could never find the bottom. And that was considered to be the jaws of death. That's where the gates of hell, the gates of the nether world, were there. And they turned that into a center of pagan worship.

Now, in regards to the rock, one of the interesting things is: on the rock was a temple to the divine Caesar Augustus…Herod had built it there for Caesar in appreciation for some favors. As Jesus sits at this rock, a false rock with a false temple to a false God, he says 'Peter, we're going to do something different now. You are the true rock and on this rock I will build the true temple, the true Church. The gates of hell here will not prevail against it.'

They used to throw the pagans as sacrifices into this cave and there was a spring, and as the water would rush out underneath, that was the source of the Jordan river. It came right out of this cave. If you think of that implication of Peter as well, that out of this rock came the water that watered all of Israel. All of God's people were watered from the spring that came out of that rock. So, Peter now being the rock, the false temple has gone, the true Church has been built on Peter and the water that comes from the Church waters God's people. It sustains them. And these gates of hell now will not prevail.

When these pagans saw the sacrifices that were thrown into the cave, if the blood came out of the stream it meant that God had rejected the sacrifice. But in Christianity it's the opposite. When the sacrifice of Jesus was made it was when the blood was flowing that God did accept the sacrifice. So here we've got this great scenario. It's very sad that most commentators do not bring out this issue. They don't bring out the background of Caesarea Philippi…

The Jews understood these things. The Jews in Israel understood not only all the implications of the temple and the sacrifices, but they understood Caesarea Philippi. Right there now is a plaque put there by the Israeli government, which says that this site, with the mountain and the cave there, was a singular site in all the Greco-Roman world. For Jesus went there for that specific purpose.

At the same time Jesus then shifts to the second point, for he is now telling Peter that he is giving him the keys to the kingdom of heaven. What does that mean? Is it just a clever little saying? All the Jewish listeners would have understood what he meant, and when you go back in the Jewish Old Testament there are passages about the royal steward of the kingdom who carried the keys for the king. Whatever he opened would stay open and whatever he locked would stay locked. He had access to the treasury, to the city gates. He could exclude people from the city. He could include people into the kingdom. He had power delegated to him by the king. So, when Jesus says this to Peter there's a lot going on at that point. He is delegating Peter to a position of the steward of the kingdom.

Remember, back in David's time, the Davidic kingdom, and it was promised that it would be external, and for all the kings after David there was an office of royal steward and those royal stewards carried the keys of the kingdom. But around 700BC the kingdom came to an end when Babylon took the Jews away to Babylon and the Davidic kingdom ceased. It ended.

But what did Gabriel say to Mary in the Gospel of Luke? He said, 'Your offspring will inherit the throne of David. And his kingdom will be an eternal kingdom.' So what does Jesus do? He re-establishes the kingdom of David. And as the new king of Israel, the eternal kingdom, what does he do? He appoints his new steward over his kingdom, and delegates him the keys of the kingdom with the power to bind and to loose, and to control the everyday judicial and legislative areas of his kingdom.

Now one more tie-in analogy. In that rock, carved into that two hundred foot high rock are niches, and in those niches were the god Pan. It was the pagan center for the worship of the god Pan. Pan is the god of sheep and shepherds. So here is Jesus appointing his new shepherd right under the rock which has been the place where pagans came to worship the false god of shepherds for many years and here he is appointing his new shepherd to lead his people...

We really had a crisis on our hands, because we had to make a decision. We all of a sudden realized that Jesus had appointed a shepherd over his sheep. John 21 tells us that too: 'Do you love me, Peter? Then feed my sheep. Shepherd my sheep. Tend my lambs.' He gave Peter that responsibility as one of God's sheep. Then I had the responsibility to obey the shepherd. When Jesus commands the shepherd to take care of the sheep, that's really two commands in one. The command of the shepherd is to care for the sheep. But there's another implicit command also to the sheep: that you've got to follow my shepherd. So, we had to make a decision to do the unthinkable, that we become Catholics...

I always assumed that the early Church was Protestant and they later got all this Catholic nonsense and became corrupted and became the Catholic Church...When I started to read the early fathers of the first centuries it shook the foundation right out from under me. I could not find my favorite Protestant writings in those documents. In fact, they were so distinctly Catholic…

My question at that point became: Who should I listen to? My pastor today, two thousand years removed from the Apostles, or Clement and Ignatius who knew the Apostles and were no innovators. They were trying very hard to maintain the purity of the doctrine taught by the Apostles…The early Fathers are genuine transmitters of the ancient tradition of what the Apostles taught. I had to listen to them. I could no longer ignore their voice"); *Upon This Rock* (1999); *The Papacy Learning Guide* (2000) (with R. Dennis Walters); *Saint John's Gospel: A Bible Study and Commentary* (2002); *EWTN Audio Library, The Journey Home* (4 November 2002); *EWTN Audio Library, The Journey Home* (7 June 2004); "What Does Catholic Mean?" *This Rock*, January 2005; *The Footprints of God*, DVD series; "Why I'm Catholic," *catholic-convert.com.*

Regnery, Alfred S. – lawyer, author and publisher; b. 21 November 1942, Chicago; father was Henry Regnery (1912-1996), founder in 1947 of Regnery Publishing; educated at Beloit College, Wisconsin (BA 1965), then University of Wisconsin Law School (JD 1971); practiced general business law 1971-1978; served in President Reagan's administration in the U.S. Justice Department as deputy assistant attorney general, Land and Natural Resources Division 1981-1983 and as administrator of the Office of Juvenile Justice and Delinquency Prevention 1983-1986; from 1986 president and publisher of Regnery Publishing, a Washington D.C. book publishing firm; founded and worked in a law firm 1986-2003; publisher of *The American Spectator* 2003-2012; managing director of the Paul Revere Project from 2012; articles in many magazines and periodicals; converted to the Catholic faith under the guidance of Fr. C. John McCloskey; attracted by the Church's "commitment to principle, institutional vastness and forgiving attitude"; four children; see *Upstream: The Ascendance of American Conservatism* (2007).

Reid, Christian – see under Tiernan, Frances (Christine) (*née* Fisher).

Reiner, Fritz (born Frederick Martin Reiner) – conductor; b. 19 December 1888, Budapest, Hungary; c. 10 November 1908 (his mother Vilma converted at the same time and remained an ardent communicant for the rest of her life); d. 5 November 1963, New York City; brought up in a music-loving secular Jewish family; studied law at the University of Budapest under the pressure of his father, Ignácx (d. 1904), but his ambition was to become a conductor; abandoned his legal studies in 1905 and studied music (one of his teachers was Béla Bartók); graduated from the Academy of Music in Budapest in 1909; conducted at several places before becoming a leading conductor at the Dresden Semper Opera House; in 1911 he had married Angela (Elça) Jelaçin (two children of the marriage), but divorce in 1916; married Berta Gerster-Gardini in 1921 (no children) (divorce 1930); in 1930 he married Carlotta Irwin (no children); from 1922 his career was mainly in the United States; music director of the Cincinnati Symphony Orchestra 1922-1931; became an American citizen in 1928; music director of the Pittsburgh Symphony Orchestra 1938-1948; a leading conductor at the Metropolitan Opera 1949-1953; music director of the Chicago Symphony Orchestra 1953-1963 (the pinnacle of his career); he rebuilt all these three orchestras; conductor of great stature; wide repertoire; precise and economical technique; autocratic manner; one of his pupils was Leonard Bernstein; see Philip Hart, *Fritz Reiner: A Biography* (1994); Kenneth Morgan, *Fritz Reiner: Maestro & Martinet* (2005) ("Both Reiner and his mother relinquished their Jewish faith in 1908 and converted to Roman Catholicism. The reasons for this dual conversion are not entirely clear. Reiner's daughter Eva was convinced that her father and grandmother acted with foresight by reacting to the extensive anti-Semitism then common in Budapest. Becoming a Catholic meant greater assimilation into Central European society...Despite this conversion, deep religioous convictions never played a major part in his subsequent career"); *Podium: Magazine of the Fritz Reiner Society* (1976-1988); his papers are in the Deering Music Library at Northwestern University; *ANB*.

Reno, Russell Ronald III (R.R. Reno) ("Rusty") – theologian and editor; b. 1959, Baltimore, Maryland; c. 18 September 2004 (received in the Martyrs' Chapel of St. John's Church on the Creighton University campus); grew up in Towson, Maryland; brought up in the Episcopal Church; BA from Haverford College, Pennsylvania in 1983; began graduate study at Yale University in the Department of Religious Studies in 1984 (PhD 1990); worked at Creighton University 1990-2010 (Professor of Theology); main areas of expertise systematic and moral theology and biblical interpretation; many contributions to *First Things* magazine and editor from 2011; very actively involved in the Episcopal Church as an adult; became disillusioned at liberal developments there, but argued in *In the Ruins of the Church* that one should "stay put and endure the diminishments of Christianity in our time"; conversion to the Catholic Church especially influenced by St. Augustine and Newman ("as an Episcopalian I needed a theory to stay put, and I came to realize that a theory is a thin thread easily broken. The Catholic Church needs no theories"); married to a Jewish wife, Juliana, with two children; see (selective list) *The Ordinary Transformed: Karl Rahner and the Christian Vision of Transcendence* (1995); *Heroism and the Christian Life: Reclaiming Excellence* (2000) (with Brian S. Hook); *Redemptive Change: Atonement and the Christian Cure of the Soul* (2002); *In the Ruins of the Church: Sustaining Faith in an Age of Diminished Christianity* (2002); *Sanctified Vision: An Introduction to Early Christian Interpretation of the Bible* (2005) (with John J. O'Keefe); "Out of the Ruins," *First Things*, February 2005 ("John Henry Newman has long been one of my favorite writers. His ability to combine syllogism with sentiment is remarkable, and I have always been romanced by the long, cloistral, silver-veined sentences that give my students fits when I assign him…

Newman was to me an accelerant. His observation (drawn from his study of the Arian controversy) that 'the truth lay, not with the *Via Media*, but with what was called the extreme party' struck me as a bracing correction to the sensible liberalism of my childhood and education. He endorsed the principle of dogma. 'Religion as mere sentiment,' he wrote with denunciatory directness, 'is to me a dream and a mockery.' He had no patience for vague fantasies of spiritual fellowship. Like Augustine, he saw no hope in seeking. The basis of the Christian life is not our longing; it is the 'visible Church, with sacraments and rites which are channels of invisible grace.' We cannot move through the spiritual life the way we drift through the marketplace. Dogma and the sacramental system must define and circumscribe our belief…

Newman is excruciatingly detailed in his account of his own thinking, but for my purposes, I can simply report his conclusion: he came to think that the basic rationale for Anglicanism lacked validity. Even more strongly, he came to think that Anglicanism was a midwife for a liberalism that led to atheism. I still do not think Newman correct in the way he sets up Anglicanism, liberalism, and atheism as falling dominos, but I have come to think that the Episcopal Church is disastrously disordered and disarrayed. Here my own reasons and analysis are of no more moment than Newman's. What matters is the way one responds to the judgment that Anglicanism is in ruins.

As he looks back in his *Apologia*, Newman reports that the realization that his prior confidence in Anglicanism was mistaken did not produce an immediate conviction that he must leave. He developed a figural interpretation of his circumstances that justified staying put. 'I am content,' he wrote to a friend at the time, 'to be with Moses in the desert, or with Elijah excommunicated from the Temple.' When I wrote *In the Ruins of the Church*, I also adopted a figural strategy to make sense of my situation. I clearly saw that the apostolic inheritance bequeathed to the Episcopal Church - a liturgy more medieval than reformed, a veneration of the ancient creeds, a love of the Church Fathers, a scriptural piety that did not confuse being learned with being critical - was being dismantled by a revisionist ideology that knew no limits. But I did not see myself as a prophet who hectored at a distance. I appealed to the scriptural figure of Nehemiah's return to the ruins of Jerusalem. The gates of the Temple had been thrown down, but rather than leave in despair, we should follow Nehemiah's pattern and live in the ruins of the Church with redoubled loyalty…

As Newman looks back on his own figural interpretation, he uses one of his most potent swear words. He calls it 'a theory' that fed a 'methodistic self-contemplation.' Moses in the Sinai desert may be clearly depicted within the biblical text, and it may have a powerful reality in the lives of countless Christians…But in retrospect, Newman sees that his own use of the figure had lacked reality. It was a theory, an idea, a theological construct designed to fit his circumstances. He used the figures of Moses and Elijah to comfort himself, but they did not structure his sentiments and habits. He had not been, in fact, content to remain in the desert. He could not live in excommunication.

At various points after the election and consecration of Gene Robinson (a man who divorced his wife to live with his male lover) as bishop of New Hampshire, I found that my real ability to be loyal to the Episcopal Church slowly evaporated. The indifference to apostolic tradition and constraint overwhelmed me. I may have wanted to return to the ruins of the Church with Nehemiah's devotion, but in reality I was thinking bitter thoughts as I sat in my pew...

The whole point of my figural interpretation of loyalty to the fallen stones of Jerusalem was to follow Christ, who so loved our destroyed world that he died for us on the cross. He did not kick the dust off his feet and leave the earthly city that rejected him. When I wrote *In the Ruins of the Church*, that figure seemed to have a real existence for me. 'Yes,' I said to myself, 'I must follow the way of the cross and stay put.' Perhaps I was only deceiving myself then. I am not entirely sure, but I am sure that in 2003 the figure had lost its hold on my sentiments and habits. It had become, to use Newman's epithet, a theory. Nehemiah, who goes with Christ-like love to a ruined Jerusalem, may have lived on in my mind, but my spirit was overtaken by a waspish bitterness that contradicted in my life what

I had tried to argue in my book.

Modern Christianity is modern precisely in its great desire to compensate for what it imagines to be the superannuation, impotence, and failures of apostolic Christianity with a new and improved idea, theory, or theology. The disaster is not the improving impulse. I certainly wish that all Christians would expect more from their teachers and leaders. The problem is the source of the desired improvement. For Newman, 'theory' is a swear word because it connotes the ephemera of mental life, ephemera easily manipulated according to fantasy and convenience. Yet in my increasing disgruntlement, there I was, more loyal to my theory of staying put than to the actual place that demanded my loyalty. It was an artifact of my mind that compelled me to stay put. Unable to love the ruins of the Episcopal Church, I was forced to love my *idea* of loving the ruins. With this idea I tried to improve myself, after the fashion of a modern theologian.

Modern theology is profoundly corruptive. The light of Christ must come from outside, through the concrete reality of the Scriptures as embodied in the life of the Church. The whole point of staying put is to resist the temptation to wander in the invented world of our spiritual imaginings. St. Augustine wandered thus, and, as he reports, the motion was circular and futile. Now my real loyalty to the flesh and blood of an actual, existing church was disappearing, and I was in danger of trying to navigate by my own ideas...

I cannot say whether mainline Protestantism's ongoing dalliance with apostasy prevents any particular man or woman from living in substantial loyalty to the primary instruments of divine love from within a mainline church. I have friends whose commitment to staying put is real and not theoretical. They are an inspiration to me. The faithful Episcopalian or Lutheran or Methodist who can be still and stay put out of love for the fragments of the apostolic tradition that continue to be radiant with divine love are exhibiting, I think, an enviable spiritual discipline. Moreover, the support they provide to mainline Protestantism is of incalculable value - not only to their particular communities but also to the strange and vulnerable ecosystem of American Christianity.

I had hoped to provide my friends with the support of companionship in loyalty to a ruined church, but my errand became spiritually foolish. I turned staying put into a spectral idea that took the place of a living reality. I turned it into a theory of self-appointed spiritual heroism that was neither spiritual (since it was laced with bitter anger) nor heroic (since it was notional rather than real)...

In the end, my decision to leave the Episcopal Church did not happen because I had changed my mind about any particular point of theology or ecclesiology. Nor did it represent a sudden realization that the arguments for staying put are specious. What changed was the way in which I had come to hold my ideas and use my arguments. In order to escape the insanity of my slide into self-guidance, I put myself up for reception into the Catholic Church as one might put oneself up for adoption. A man can no more guide his spiritual life by his own ideas than a child can raise himself on the strength of his native potential…

The Catholic Church did not deliver me from apostasy and false teaching. I teach at a Jesuit University, so I am not naïve about just how insouciant about orthodoxy priests can be. Nor did Catholicism provide me with a neat, efficient, and trouble-free church. I do read newspapers. What my reception into the Catholic Church provided was deliverance from the temptation to navigate by the compass of a theory. The Catholic Church has countless failures, but of this I am certain: Catholic Christianity does not need to be underwritten by an idea…

A Pentecostal friend came to the Mass of reception at the Jesuit Martyrs' Chapel. He is a close friend and a man whose faith I admire. After the Mass we talked for a while. He asked me, 'So, what did it feel like to become a Catholic?' I told him, 'It felt like being submerged into the ocean.' He reacted with a look of thinly disguised horror. That look reminded me that, while I sometimes suffer from an attraction to Emersonian fantasies of self-reliance and disdain for hierarchy, I have never wanted to be alone with God. It has always seemed to me that such a desire too easily turns into a longing to be alone with one's idea of God, and that is the same as being alone with oneself.

The ocean needs no justification. It needs no theory to support the movement of its tides. In the end, as an Episcopalian I needed a theory to stay put, and I came to realize that a theory is a thin thread easily broken. The Catholic Church needs no theories. She is the mother of theologies; she does not need to be propped up by theologies. As Newman put it in one of his Anglican essays, 'the Church of Rome preoccupies the ground.' She is a given, a primary substance within the economy of denominationalism. One could rightly say that I became a Catholic by default, and that possibility is the simple gift I received from the Catholic Church. *Mater ecclesia*, she needed neither reasons, nor theories, nor ideas from me"); "The Return of the Fathers," *First Things*, November 2006; "Nietzsche's Deeper Truth," *First Things*, January 2008; *Genesis (Brazos Theological Commentary on the Bible)* (2010); "A Richer Bible," *First Things*, August/September 2010; *Fighting the Noonday Devil:*

And Other Essays Personal and Theological (2011); "He is Risen," *First Things, On the Square*, 2 May 2011; Richard J. Neuhaus, "Bashing Darwin, Becoming Catholic," *First Things, On The Square*, 30 March 2007 ("Rusty Reno of Creighton University, a former Anglican, says that the weighing of ecclesiastical options was irrelevant to his becoming Catholic. He writes 'I didn't so much choose to become Catholic as collapse into Catholicism out of a spiritual exhaustion that was as much a result of my own sinfulness and intellectualized perversity of heart as any defect or failure of the Episcopal Church. The sheer fact of the Catholic Church, its place as the prime substance of Christianity in the West, did not attract me. It was simply there, and it stopped me from falling into unbelief - or worse, into a loveless simulacrum of belief that derives its life and energy from imagined roles of crusader-for-orthodoxy and defender-of-faith - something my own acknowledged attraction to Newman's polemical passages indicates was a real danger. I grant that one can theorize and theologize about the givenness of the Catholic Church and its role as source of Western Christianity (just as one can theologize about its betrayals of that role). But at least for me, the fact of the church worked upon me rather than any ideas or theories I might have had about "catholicity"').

Rescher, Nicholas – philosopher; b. 15 July 1928, Hagen, Westphalia, Germany; c. March 1981; came from a line of solid middle class professional people; father a lawyer; parents belonged nominally to the Lutheran-Evangelical Church; came to the United States in 1938; educated at Princeton University (PhD in Philosophy (on Leibniz) in 1951); served in the U.S. Marine Corps 1952-1954; mother drawn to Quakerism in mid-1950s; spent some years flirting with Quakerism; taught at Princeton in 1960; worked at the University of Pittsburgh from 1961; chair of the Department of Philosophy and later co-chair of the Center for Philosophy of Science with the status of Distinguished University Professor of Philosophy; has written some hundred books and many articles in many areas of philosophy (e.g., epistemology, ethics, logic, metaphysics, the philosophy of science); seen as a pragmatist; has taught at many universities; editor of *American Philosophy Quarterly* and of *History of Philosophy Quarterly*; has won many awards, including the American Catholic Philosophical Society's Aquinas medal in 2007; elected to the American Academy of Arts and Sciences in 2009; married to Dorothy Henle (three children); see (selective list) *The Riddle of Existence: An Essay in Idealistic Metaphysics* (1984); *Pascal's Wager* (1985); *Moral Absolutes* (1989); *Human Interests: Reflections on Philosophical Anthropology* (1990);

Ethical Idealism: An Inquiry into the Nature and Function of Ideals (1992); "In Matters of Religion," in Kelly James Clark (ed), *Philosophers Who Believe* (1993) ("Perhaps, ideally, the conversion of an intellectual to a form of religious commitment ought itself to be an intellectual product – a matter of secured conviction in theses and principles. But it was certainly not so in my case. Here it was primarily a matter of sentiment, loyalties and feelings of allegiance and kinship. Perhaps Pascal was right. If you would be a believer, he said, just go and do the things that believers do: 'You desire to attain faith, but you do not know the way. You would like to cure yourself of unbelief, and you ask for remedies. Learn from those who were once bound and gagged like you, and who now stake all that they possess. They are men who know the road that you desire to follow, and have been cured of a sickness of which you desire to be cured. Follow the way by which they set out, acting as if they already believed, taking holy water, having masses said, etc. All this will naturally cause you to believe' (*Pensées*, sec. 233)"); *The Limits of Science* (1999); *Luck: The Brilliant Randomness of Everyday Life* (2001); *Enlightened Journey: The Autobiography of an American Scholar* (2002) ("There is no doubt that two intersecting factors were instrumental in introducing me to make a Christian commitment: a sense of intellectual and personal solidarity with those whom I could accept as role models among believers and a sense of estrangement from those whom I deemed naively cocksure in their rejection of belief. For while I have lived almost my whole life as an academic among academics, I have always felt alienated from the easy certainties with which they generally view the world about them – confident that 'they have all the answers.' It has always seemed to me that the more we learn, the fewer answers we actually have, because the more questions open up. This aspect of things, which a religious outlook does or should encompass, seems to me to be something of deep and significant truth.

Religious belief alters our evaluative frame of reference, enabling us to view our own lives with a clearer and more enlightened sense of priorities. Its commitment to the larger, 'spiritual' values helps us to realize the extent to which various issues that many people see as supremely important are actually trivia. This sort of view, at any rate, gradually became the substance of my religious outlook. As a philosopher, I had to decide upon my spiritual kindred in life. Did I want to align myself with the religious-disdaining Lucretiuses, Voltaires, Humes, Nietzsches, and Bertrand Russells of the world, or with its theistically committed Platos and Plotinuses, its Anselms and Aquinases, its Leibnizes and Hegels? I was free to choose those who were to be my spiritual kinfolk, and I felt myself drawn towards those who saw humanity as subject to transcendent aspirations and obligations – and for whom forms of worship and religious styles of thought really mattered...

How do I reconcile my religion with my dedication to science and the scientific point of view? Basically by a division of labor... Science addresses the factual issue of how things work in the world.; religion addresses ideological issues of values, principles, and choices. Science describes how the pieces move on the chessboard of the world. Religion is a matter of learning about what sorts of moves to make. And learning how the pieces move is a good deal simpler than knowing how to play a good game.

For everything depends on the nature of the questions. Those questions about how things work in nature belong to science, and here it reigns supreme. But not all of our questions are of this sort, and when the questions do not figure in the natural agenda of science, science enjoys no special advantage in relation to them. With questions that relate not to how things are but how they should be, that address matters not of how to proceed if we must achieve certain goals, but rather ask what those goals ought to be – questions of meaning and value, in short – then we enter a domain of deliberation where science enjoys no special prerogatives.

Some of our beliefs are such that we can and should expect to get evidence for them. Matters of human evolution are in this category. Other beliefs lie outside the possibility of accessible evidence. Issues of our human mission on Earth and of the duties we have in relation to our opportunities for action are in this second category. Issues of the former sort we can and should consider in point of their probable truth or falsehood. But issues of the latter sort have to be considered differently. Here the question is whether they are life-enhancing or life-constricting. It is a matter of their tendency in relation not to being better knowers but to being better persons. And as a philosopher I have always attached particular importance to the latter range of issues, attached less in relation to action than in relation to that understanding which is, after all, a crucial component of the mission of philosophy. Being a philosopher may well not make one a better person; but it should by rights help one to achieve a fuller understanding of what it is that being a better person involves.

Of the many forms of human failings, the failure of imagination is one of the saddest. And one of the gravest failures of imagination is that of the person who cannot manage to project the concepts of a God worthy of ardent desire – a God whose nonbeing would be the occasion for genuine grief. Compared with this, an inability to imagine a friend worth having or a spouse worth loving is a pale shadow – though all alike betoken a regrettable impoverishment of personality of the same general sort. Sensible people would clearly prefer to number among their friends someone who was willing to invest hope and trust in himself, his fellow and his world. To refrain, in the absence of preponderating reasons to the contrary, from letting hope influence belief – even merely to the extent of that sort of tentative belief at issue in a working assumption made for practical purposes – betokens a crabbed failure of confidence that has nothing admirable about it.

In the final analysis, then, I have become and continued to remain a committed Catholic because this represents a position that, as I see it, is intellectually sensible, evaluatively appropriate, and personally congenial. Accordingly, the answer to the question of why I am a Catholic is perhaps simply this: Because that is where I feel at home. It is in substantial measure a matter of affinity and concinnity – of being in communion with people whose ideas, allegiances, and values are in substantial measure congenial to my own.

In any case it was not dogmas and doctrines that drew me to Catholicism but an inner need of a sort that is difficult to describe. It was not a need for relief from a sense of sin, nor yet a need of relief from the intimations of mortality. Rather, it was a need for relief from a sense of isolation – the desire to feel oneself part of a wider community of spirits who are in some degree kindred, who share with oneself a sense of values and priorities geared to the spiritual dimension of our species and to a sense of human insignificance in the awesome face of the mysteries of our existence"); *Metaphysics: The Key Issues from a Realistic Perspective* (2006); *Issues in the Philosophy of Religion* (2007); *Philosophical Inquiries: An Introduction to Problems of Philosophy* (2010); *Productive Evolution: On Reconciling Evolution With Intelligent Design* (2012); Dale Jacquette (ed), *Reason, Method and Value: A Reader on the Philosophy of Nicholas Rescher* (2009).

Revere, Joseph Warren - general; b. 17 May 1812, Boston, Massachusetts; c. 19 October 1862 (his son Paul was received some years afterwards); d. 20 April 1880, Hoboker, Pennsylvania; descended from a French Huguenot family; a grandson of Paul Revere (1734-1818); joined the United States Navy in 1828; traveled the world in the service and became a lieutenant; commended for bravery in the Mexican-American War; resigned from the navy in 1850; joined the Mexican Army with the rank of colonel and was knighted in the Order of Isabella the Catholic in 1851; retired in 1852 and went to live in New Jersey; toured Europe in 1857-1858 and then went on to India; awarded a British medal for service in the Indian Mutiny Campaign of 1857-1858; was also present at the Battle of Solferino during the Italian Campaigns of 1858-1859; when the Civil War started he enlisted in the Union Army (no officer posts in the navy); commended for bravery at the Second Battle of Bull Run (badly injured); appointed a brigadier-general in 1862; General Hooker pronounced him the best disciplinarian in the army; controversial "regrouping effort" at the Battle of Chancellorsville led to his being censured; reinstated by Abraham Lincoln, but his resignation was accepted; voted Brevet Major-General by the United States Congress in 1866; traveled the world writing books, even though his health had been affected by his Civil War service; see *A Tour of Duty in California, Including a Description of the Gold Region* (1849); *Keel and Saddle: A Retrospect of 40 years of Military and Naval Service* (1873) (autobiography); Rev. Joseph M. Flynn, *The Catholic Church in New Jersey* (1904) ("It was after the Peninsular campaign that one day, in Washington, brooding over the severe losses his regiment suffered from the terrific struggle, he was led almost unconsciously to a Catholic church. On the moment he felt the impulse, or rather inspiration, to become a Catholic.

For years he had carefully studied religious matters, and consequently, when he presented himself to the priest and asked to be baptized, he was found thoroughly instructed in the principles of the Catholic Church").

Reynolds, Bede, OSB (born Kenyon Llewellyn Reynolds) – monk, oilman, teacher and writer; b. 26 January 1892, East Lansing, Michigan; c. 30 June 1933 (an older brother Graham (1888-1929) was received on 22 May 1912 and ordained a Catholic priest in 1917); d. 17 December 1989, Westminster Abbey, Mission, British Columbia, Canada; ancestors originally from England and Wales; his father Henry Graham Reynolds (1851-1918) was a farmer, then taught at an agricultural college; his mother Francis, *née* Llewellyn (1850-1899), was from Kentucky; youngest of seven children; raised as a Protestant Low-Church Episcopalian in southern California; worked as a mining assayer's helper before going to university; entered Cornell University in 1910 to study mechanical engineering; transferred to University of California at Berkeley and civil engineering; originally heavily prejudiced against the Catholic Church, he fell in love with Patricia Pfitzer, a Catholic girl, and married her in 1915 (no children of the marriage); he became a civil engineer and was vice-president and a partner in a little company, Pacific Gasoline, based in Pasadena; in 1920 he used his skill to build one of the first gasoline cracking plants to extract gasoline from natural gas; in 1926 Standard Oil of California handed over $20 million to buy the partners out, making him a millionaire; he retired that year and he and his wife traveled around the world and bought a summer home at McKenzie Bridge, Oregon; during this time he was received into the Catholic Church, his wife playing a major role in his conversion; he returned to the oil business to serve as the U.S. Government's West Coast petroleum coordinator during World War II; after his wife died of cancer in 1945 he donated much of his wealth to the Catholic Church (including the summer home, which became a retreat center) and joined the Benedictine Order; he was ordained to the priesthood in 1951; he taught Theology and English at Westminster Abbey, near Mission, B.C., and wrote several books; buried in Westminster Abbey Cemetery; his wife's remains were exhumed and re-buried in the Basement Crypt beneath the bell tower at Westminster Abbey; see *A Rebel From Riches: The Autobiography of an Unpremeditated Monk* (1970) ("Patty simply asked how any Church beside the Catholic Church could be the one founded by Christ, since it was the only one that had been in existence since the time of Christ. My answer that the corrupt hierarchy of the sixteenth century had betrayed the people, did not seem very convincing in the face of Christ's promise that that was exactly what would not happen. It occurred to me that if it *had* happened, the 'Gates of Hell' had certainly 'prevailed'. And how could that he reconciled with the belief that Christ is God?...

It was not long before I heard myself framing an answer to somebody's question something like this: 'When you come right down to brass tacks, the rewards which the Catholic Church claims to offer and the promises of Christ which she claims to interpret, are so prodigious compared any and all material values, that a person is really stupid if he does not learn what it takes to qualify *just on the chance that it is all true!*'...

[A fallen-away priest whom I know] said: 'From what you tell me I think you must believe that Christ is God and that the Gospel proves that He founded a visible Church. If that is what you believe, there is no place for you except in the Catholic Church.'

When I reported this piece of information to Father O'Shea, he amplified it in a way that I shall never forget. Quoting Saint Augustine, he said: 'The Church of God came into being when God took human nature in the womb of the Virgin Mary. It was perfect then and embraced all humanity of all time. Christ, in His lifetime, provided all its visible and physical attributes and tools. It functions now by His Spirit and will continue for all time.

'The Church today is a continuation

of Christ Himself made possible in a way that only God could devise and provide. It consists of two principal elements, equally necessary. First, the prolongation of His words by means of a continuing body of ordinary men supernaturally and divinely equipped with all the truth which God wished to have taught to the rest of men. He made certain of the protection of this truth by choosing one man to be the Vicar of His very Self, supernaturally empowered to govern and direct those chosen with him to carry forward the word. All of these men would be like other men in human frailty. They would be protected supernaturally only as necessary to keep the Church free from error.

'The second principal element provided by Christ was a marvelous union of the divine and supernatural with the visible and tangible. It was the gift of Sacrament and Sacrifice to bring His saving power to all future generations. There were seven Sacraments to give supernatural provision for all the needs of men. Then Christ crowned all this at the Last Supper with His Apostles by an all-but-unbelievable gift. His redeeming Sacrifice and His own Body and Blood were to be made present for all men for all time'"); *How Come My Faith* (1974); *Let's Mend the Mess* (1975); *Project Sainthood: Your Business* (1975); *Help Us, Oh God* (1980); *Draw Your Strength from the Lord* (1982).

Rich, Charles (often known as Charlie) – lay contemplative; b. 1899, Hungary; c. 18 March 1933 ("I became a Catholic because I was given the grace to do so by Almighty God"); d. 1998; brought up in a strictly orthodox environment in a Chasidic community; contemplative even as a child, but lost his faith in Judaism at age fourteen when he and his family moved to New York; concentrated then on culture and education ("By the age of thirty-three I had read every important literary work held famous in the eyes of men"), but found this unfulfilling spiritually; then studied other religions; was for a time inspired by Spinoza's pantheism, but found it unsatisfying; fell into despair and attempted suicide three times; an experience of a painting of Christ on the wall of a Catholic church speaking to him directly in his heart led to a belief in the divinity of Christ; influenced by reading the great Catholic writers (especially devoted to Dante's *Divine Comedy*; became a lay contemplative in a Jesuit house; St. John of the Cross became the indispensable mainstay of his spiritual life; see *Embrace of the Soul: Meditations on the Song of Songs* (1984); *Reflections* (1986) ("I read the New Testament and tried to fathom the full meaning of Our Lord's sayings. I felt that there was something about these utterances with which I was deeply in sympathy and which was different from anything ever spoken by a human being, different in tone from the utterances of the great poets I admired so much. There was a note of hope in them, of confidence and trust which became medicinal to a mind tormented and distracted by anxiety and doubt. But in spite of the healing influence which the reading of the Gospel writings had upon me, there was yet, I felt, something vitally lacking. I was still searching. Christ had not yet become God to me. I regarded Him as but a man, a supereminently and august man, this and no more. I was still under the influence of the view which Renan and the rationalist school represented…

If I could only believe that the words in the Gospel are really true, that Christ really existed, and that these words are exactly those that came from His own mouth, were uttered from His own human lips, and that they are literally true. Oh if this were only a fact, if I could only believe that this were a fact, how glorious and wonderful that would be, how consoled, happy, and comforted I would be, to know and to believe that Christ was really Divine, that He was God's own Son come down from another world to this earth to save us all! Could it be possible, I felt, that that which seemed too wonderful to be true actually was true, that it was no deception, no fraud, no lie? All of a sudden something flashed through my mind and I heard these words spoken in it. 'Of course it is true, Christ is God, is God come down to make Himself visible in the flesh. The words in the Gospels are true, literally true'…[F]rom that day on, the name of Our Lord Jesus Christ took on a significance which it never before had. There was an ineffable fragrance about the words Jesus Christ, a sweetness with which nothing can be compared. The sound of these words to this day fills me with a strange inexpressible joy, a joy which I feel does not come from this world…

The thought of entering the Catholic Church seriously entered my mind. I was spiritually homeless, and what better thing could I do than to ally myself with a people with a whole viewpoint with which I already had so much in common? I could accept Christ, then why not Catholicism also? After hearing you [his spiritual director] say that the Catholic Church was 'Jesus Christ diffused and communicated,' I was convinced that the next logical step was to embrace Catholicism"); *Autobiography* (1990) (mainly about his spiritual and intellectual life) ((1) "Anyway, I one day passed a Catholic Church - it was a hot summer day, and I felt weary and exhausted. So I thought if I went inside I could cool off. But I was afraid that not being a Catholic, I would he unwelcomed, and this as I was shabbily dressed and unkempt. But overcoming my fears. I went inside and found myself completely alone…

From now on, the story of my life will take on a delicacy which can hardly be expressed in words of earth, for it has to do with a remarkable experience that took place in my whole spiritual and intellectual make-up during the few moments I kept kneeling in thanksgiving for a favor from heaven I never thought would ever be granted me in the present life, the favor from heaven which enabled me to believe in the divinity of Christ, and with that belief put an end to the misery I went through for a period of so many years - it was as if God Himself came to my rescue that day, and that He Himself spoke to me with His own voice saying to me that Christ is God, fulfilling the prophecy made by my agnostic friend so many years ago when he said to me these words: 'You have such a strong desire to believe that you won't be able to do so until God Himself will talk to you,' and talk to me He did, during the few minutes that brought such a profound change in me spiritually and intellectually that I have since that time been unable to recognize the self I had been prior to that experience, an experience the full nature of which will only be able to be made known after this life is over, and this on account of the extraordinary nature of that experience, an experience which I felt had to be confirmed by the Church before it could be accepted as coming from God. And it was confirmed by an incident which took place in the following manner: It was my custom to stop in the branch library near my house before going home. So a few minutes after what took place in the church, I found myself in the vestibule of this library looking at a green card posted on the billboard and on it were these words: 'The Mystical Christ and the Modern World,' a series of lectures to be given by Ignatius W. Cox, SJ, at the Fordham University Chapel on Sunday at 4:00 PM. I was shabbily dressed, so dreaded going to the Chapel to hear this talk. But overcoming my diffidence, I found myself seated and saw a priest mount the pulpit. As soon as I heard his voice, I said to myself that he would be the kind of person to whom I would want to relate what took place in the church…I went home and wrote Fr. Cox a ten page letter beginning with my life as a young boy in Hungary and ending up with this experience in the church. In this letter I asked Fr. Cox if he had time to talk to me about this experience and if he himself did not have time could he let me know if there was another priest I could talk to about this matter - I felt that everything depended on what a Catholic priest would have to say about such an experience and that without confirmation by him such an experience could not be taken seriously and the whole thing could have been an illusion and deception. Anyway, two days passed and when I looked at my mailbox, I saw the words 'Fordham University' on the side of the envelope. I immediately opened the letter and read these words: 'Dear Charles, how can I fail to find time to have talks with one to whom Christ Himself has spoken.'

It would be almost impossible to express in words what took place in my heart after reading these words, since I felt a weight had been lifted from my soul that I carried about me for so many agonized years, the weight in the form of my inability to believe that Christ was God and that he came on earth to save my soul." (2) "Someone said these words: 'What happiness to be a Catholic even were it for this life alone,' and now after having the grace to be one for the past fifty-two years, I can more than confirm the truth of the above words - one day, waiting for the elevator, someone said these words to me: 'How's things, Charlie?' The surprising answer made to this question was framed in these words: 'I am a Catholic; I can't complain.' I said these words surprised me by their stark simplicity and yet they were as profoundly true as if a whole treatise of theology were given as an answer to the question asked. And though it is true, that St. Augustine says 'we are Christians only on account of our belief in the Resurrection,' it's belief in the Resurrection which is the source of such intense delight all the time we stay in this life thus rendering true what was said of the happiness there is in being a Catholic were it for this life only, thus bringing it the realization what joys they miss who have not received the grace to become the members of the only true faith, since had they received such a grace, they would feel themselves compensated by it for everything else they did not have, since having the true faith, they, with the having of that faith, possess everything worthwhile this side of heaven"); "A Chasid in the Heart of the Church," in Ronda Chervin (ed), *The Ingrafting: The Conversion Stories of Ten Hebrew-Catholics* (1987) (reprint of the account of his conversion in the introduction to *Reflections*, above); Ronda Chervin (ed), *The Holy Dybbuk: Letters of Charles Rich, Contemplative* (1988); Ronda Chervin (ed), *Letters For Eternity: Collected from the Correspondence of Charles Rich with Ronda Chervin, 1985-1993*, (1994); Ronda Chervin, *Hungry for Heaven: The Story of Charles Rich, Contemplative* (1993); Roy H. Schoeman, *Salvation is from the Jews: The Role of Judaism in Salvation History* (2003); "Taste and See the Sweetness of the Lord," in Roy H. Schoeman, *Honey from the Rock* (2007) (excerpts from *Reflections* and *Autobiography*, above); Friends of Charles Rich website.

Richards, Jay Wesley – philosopher; b. Texas; brought up as a mainline Presbyterian; later long term Evangelical Protestant; BA in Political Science and Religion; MAs in Divinity and

Theology; PhD from Princeton Theological Seminary; taught apologetics at Biola University, California; Director of Research at Discovery Institute's Center for Science and Culture; author of many articles; emphasis on neo-conservatism; advocate of intelligent design since 1996; has expressed skepticism about global warming; see *Unapologetic Apologetics: Meeting the Challenges of Theological Studies* (2001) (with William A. Dembski); *The Untamed God: A Philosophical Exploration of Divine Perfection, Immutability and Simplicity* (2003); *The Privileged Planet: How Our Place in the Cosmos is Designed for Discovery* (2004) (with Guillermo Gonzales); *Money, Greed, and God* (2009); (ed), *God and Evolution* (2010) ("From the time of Darwin, who first proposed it, to the present, Darwinists have contrasted their idea with the claim that biological forms are designed. Here's how the late Darwinist Ernst Mayr put it: 'The real core of Darwinism, however, is the theory of natural selection. This theory is so important for the Darwinian because it permits the explanation of adaptation, the 'design' of the naturaltheologian,bynaturalmeans, instead of by divine intervention.

Notice that he says 'instead of.' Darwinists almost always insist that their theory serves as a designer substitute, That's the whole point of the theory. This makes it different from other scientific theories, like Newton's law of gravity. Newton didn't formulate the law to get God out of the planet business (in fact, for Newton, God was involved in every aspect of the business). And theories that invoke ordinary physical laws are determinate: they allow the scientist to make specific predictions about what will happen, all things being equal.

Darwin's theory isn't like that. It simply says that whatever has happened, and whatever will happen, the adaptive complexity we see in organisms is (primarily) the result of natural selection and random variation, not design. From the very beginning, the theory was intended to rule out teleological (purposive) explanations. As William Dembski once said: 'The appeal of Darwinism was never, That's the way God did it. The appeal was always, That's the way nature did it without God.' That's why, even if nor all agree with Richard Dawkins that Darwin 'made it possible to be an intellectually fulfilled atheist,' the vast majority of Darwinists claim that Darwin's mechanism makes God superfluous. It's their theory, so presumably they have a right to tell us what it means. Theists, in contrast to Darwinists, claim that the world, including the biological world, exists for a purpose, that it is, in some sense, designed"); "Opposing the Culture of Contraception," *patheos.com*, 20 May 2011 ("I'm now Catholic. Years before I became

Catholic, however, I realized that my indifference to contraception was a big mistake. I was awoken from my dogmatic slumber when I learned that the 'Catholic' view of artificial contraception was, for centuries, the *Christian* view: Catholic, Orthodox, and Protestant. The early Church and Church Fathers were of one mind on the matter. Luther, Calvin, and Wesley all condemned contraception. Calvin called it 'monstrous.' And all Protestants agreed with that consensus until the Anglican Lambeth Conference in 1930...

Of course, once I realized that Protestants, too, opposed artificial contraception until the middle of the twentieth century, I had to confront a dilemma: Who's right? Did the Anglican bishops discern the Spirit in 1930 while all other Christians had been misguided for 1,900 years? Or, did the entire Church until 1930 know something that many of us have forgotten? I confess that I never took comfort in the company of those Anglican bishops.

Why was there such unanimity of opinion among Christians until the last century? Historically all Christians believed that God's commandment and blessing to be fruitful and multiply disclosed something about the proper end of our sexuality, namely, childbearing (even if that end is not always fulfilled). That is its *purpose*, though not, of course, its only purpose. Christians believed that God intended for not just sex and marriage, but sex and childbearing to go together. To intentionally sever the link between the two, then, was to rend asunder what God had joined together. So opposition to contraception need have nothing to do with being anti-sex, and everything to do with thinking through the divine design of our sexuality.

Did God send a new revelation in 1930 telling the Anglican bishops that this was all a mistake? Did someone discover that 'be fruitful and multiply' meant something different from what all Christians thought it meant for the previous 1,900 years? Did we suddenly come to understand human sexuality better than our spiritual ancestors? Or, perhaps, did we pick up an idea from a culture that is increasingly hostile to fertility and chastity? Did we take a wrong turn?

One way to tell if you've taken a wrong turn is to look at the consequences of the turn. After all, if there is and ought to be, by God's design, an intrinsic link between sex and childbearing, then separating them would probably mess things up. And so it has. Contraception separates sex from procreation, and also weakens the consequences of extra-marital sex. As a result, many scholars see the widespread acceptance of contraception as a logical and cultural precursor to both legal abortion and the demise of marriage.

In his encyclical *Humanae Vitae*, Pope Paul VI warned of the effects of cultural effects of contraception: 'Responsible men can become more deeply convinced of the truth of the doctrine laid down by the Church on this issue if they reflect on the consequences of methods and plans for artificial birth control. Let them first consider how easily this course of action could open wide the way for marital infidelity and a general lowering of moral standards. Not much experience is needed to be fully aware of human weakness and to understand that human beings - and especially the young, who are so exposed to temptation - need incentives to keep the moral law, and it is an evil thing to make it easy for them to break that law. Another effect that gives cause for alarm is that a man who grows accustomed to the use of contraceptive methods may forget the reverence due to a woman, and, disregarding her physical and emotional equilibrium, reduce her to being a mere instrument for the satisfaction of his own desires, no longer considering her as his partner whom he should surround with care and affection.' Paul VI wrote those words in 1968, at the height of the sexual revolution and five years before the *Roe v Wade* decision.

Of course, abortion and contraception are not the same thing. You could coherently oppose one and not the other. Moreover, it makes sense that abortion is a legislative priority but contraception, for the most part, is not. Abortion involves killing a human being. A simple ultrasound image is enough to expose its evil. Not so with most forms of contraception. Contraception severs the link between sex and conception, thus preventing a new human being from forming in the first place. Its moral problem is more subtle. It tends to reveal its character only at the end of a longer chain of inferences…[J]ust because abortion and contraception are different doesn't mean they are unrelated. All Christians should consider the possibility that we will never fully restore a culture of life until we have extracted ourselves from the culture of contraception"); *Indivisible: Restoring Faith, Family, and Freedom Before It's Too Late* (2012) (with James Robison); Celeste Behe, "Discovery Institute Fellow is Dedicated to Christian Unity," *National Catholic Register*, 24 October 2012, ("The coherence of *sola scriptura* (Bible alone) had worried me for years, since it seemed that the most thoughtful evangelicals had a sort of de facto magisterium that they relied on. For instance, no passage of Scripture says what books are supposed to be in the New Testament, so there's an implicit trust in the judgment of the early Church. There's also an implicit trust in the judgment of the early councils that established the Trinity and the two natures of Christ, and so on. Moreover, the fact that the New Testament wasn't even canonized until the end of the fourth century meant that there must have been some deposit of faith given to the Church that it preserved for centuries without a fully established canon.

This led to the question of the Protestant justification for not recognizing the Deuterocanonical books in the Old Testament (Judith, Tobit, 1 and 2 Maccabees, Wisdom, Baruch and Ecclesiasticus). These had been treated as authoritative until the Reformation, but Luther demoted/removed them. (He also wanted to remove James, Hebrews and Revelation, but the other Reformers disagreed).

So I read the best Protestant and Catholic articles on the subject and concluded (to my dismay at the time) that the Protestant arguments didn't hold up. Essentially, Luther demoted the books that contained kernels of doctrines that he disagreed with - which is not an especially promising procedure.

I recall one argument by a prominent Protestant theologian whom I respect. His presumably knock-down-drag-out argument against these books was that they contained unbiblical doctrines. But since the question was: 'What books should be in the Bible?' his reasoning was obviously circular…

The Real Presence was a huge deal. Even a cursory glance at the early Christian writings establishes that everyone understood that, in some mysterious way, the bread and wine, while remaining under the appearance of bread and wine, really become the body and blood of the glorified Jesus.

As early as 110, Ignatius of Antioch taught this, and it was treated as one of the touchstones of orthodoxy until 1517. I also studied the central biblical texts at issue, such as the Last Supper narratives and John 6. Although I had seminary degrees, I had never really done that. I found that the typical Protestant ways of explaining these texts away didn't hold up to scrutiny").

Ripley, Sophia Willard (*née* Dana) – philanthropist; b. 6 July 1803, Cambridge, Massachusetts; c. sometime between September 1847 and March 1848 (Sarah Steam, her niece, also converted); d. 4 February 1861; her parents were from two distinguished New England families, Dana and Willard; her great grandfather had been a signer of the Declaration of Independence; excellent education in the classics and in modern languages; she and her sisters established a school for advanced studies for girls at what is now Radcliffe College; in 1827 she married George Ripley (1802-1880), the social reformer, Unitarian minister, and journalist associated with Transcendentalism; in the 1840s she co-founded with her husband an experimental Utopian community called Brook Farm; her conversion to the Catholic faith was influenced by Orestes Brownson (see above) and by Fr. Isaac Hecker (see above) (her husband never converted); Fr. Hecker served as her father confessor from 1851 until her death; she did much charitable work in hospitals and prisons; much suffering in later life when she had cancer; see Katherine Burton, *In No Strange Land: Some American Catholic Converts* (1942), p.31 ("One day she heard Theodore Parker quote St. Augustine: 'O God, Thou has made us for Thyself and our hearts are restless until they rest in thee.' Suddenly it came to her that that was what Dante had meant in those beautiful passages she had loved for so long but thought of only as literature, not as the exponent of a living faith. Dante meant that once you had a real belief in God, you would never ignore it again. She remembered one especially cherished phrase: 'One who has looked upon the light cannot turn to other objects willingly'...

She turned to other authors and began studying the early Fathers in the original Greek. One evening she said excitedly to George, 'You should really read some of this and see how continuous it is, and how it is all the same now as it was then as far back as the second century'... She read and read books primitive, medieval, renaissance, modern, until she could say to her husband with conviction, 'George, I am fully persuaded. Here is a Church that is immortal. She has withstood the treason of her own children and the pride of her unworthy servants, and her strength comes from the great love given her by the Saints and the sinners too'...

When Isaac Hecker came back to the United States, a Redemptorist priest, she smiled at him at their first meeting. 'I am without doubt the only convert you and Dante have made between you,' she told him"); Jenny Franchot, *Roads to Rome: The Antebellum Protestant Encounter with Catholicism* (1994), Ch. 15, "Sophia Ripley: Rewriting the Stony Heart"; *ANB* ("Deciding that her existence at Brook Farm had been 'childish, empty, and sad,' before 1847 Sophia decisively converted to the Roman Catholic Church, a religious antithesis to the uncluttered and ethereal tenets of Unitarian and Transcendental thought...Her life thereafter was one in which virtually all waking hours were spent in prayer, contemplation, and charitable work, the translation of religious tracts, and visits to hospitals, prisons, and insane asylums").

Robins, Julia Gorham – author and lecturer; b. 1846, Boston, Massachusetts; c. May 1899; d. 1918; descended from Colonel Thomas Crafts (1740-1799), who read the Declaration of Independence from the balcony of the Massachusetts State House; brought up in Unitarianism of the Conservative type (sometimes spoken of as Channing Unitarianism); later became a Liberal or Radical Unitarian; educated in the private schools of Boston; her conversion came from a mental process of breaking down former doctrinal prejudices against the Catholic faith; contributor to the *Sacred Heart Review*, *America*, and the *Catholic Encyclopedia*; traveled extensively in Europe; see *A New England Conversion* (1903) (reprinted in Georgina Pell Curtis (ed), *Some Roads to Rome in America* (1909), p.344) ("Without premeditation, I took a step which eventually led me into the Catholic Church. I questioned a Catholic as to his belief...

In trying to recall what one new point of view was so forcibly put before me that afternoon as to rouse me out of my old-time lethargy, I am sure that it was the explanation given to me of the grounds on which the Catholic Church bases her belief in the Real Presence of our Lord in the Blessed Sacrament of the Altar; that belief cherished by her as so unspeakably precious, as the very centre of her life. I was the farthest away possible from any understanding as to why the Catholic Church held this belief, and thus had a repugnance towards the doctrine, and that scorn which is often most tenaciously clung to when it springs from ignorance. I did, however, try to rid my mind of all prejudice as I listened; and to my amazement I saw at once the strong logic in the reasoning brought forward in support of the Catholic doctrine, which declares that our Saviour meant His words to be taken literally, while the Protestant looks upon them as used in a figurative sense.

In order to be perfectly fair in the matter, what ought one to do first, to get at the proper interpretation of Christ's words? Simply by going back in imagination to the time when they were spoken and joining the multitude, to discover there on the spot what He meant His words to convey, and how His hearers there present understood them.

Is it to be supposed that Christ meant to speak figuratively when He told His hearers of the fearful penalty attached for non-compliance with His commands? – 'Except ye eat the flesh of the Son of Man, and drink His blood, ye have no life in you.' The command has equal force with that when, in teaching the necessity of the Sacrament of Baptism, He said, 'He that believeth and is baptized shall be saved; but he that believeth not shall be damned' (Mark xvi, 16).

What was the effect of our Lord's words on the multitude? Did the people believe that He had taken back His words, or that He had spoken figuratively? What became of those who had so angrily muttered against this strange idea of eating His flesh? Did they accept it? Quite the reverse. They turned away in disgust, and 'walked no more with him.' Did Christ even then call them back, seeing the effect of His words? No. He let them go; then turning to His twelve Apostles, asked sadly, 'Will ye also go away?' and Simon Peter, the spokesman instantly replied, 'Lord, to whom shall we go? Thou hast the words of eternal life, and we believe and are sure that thou art that Christ, the Son of the living God.'

This explanation made a most powerful impression upon me; yet it was a long time before I was able to accept it, for my brain was so obscured by a tangle of misconceptions of Catholic truth that it was impossible to clear them all away at once. There is no doubt, however, that my conversion to the faith dates from first hearing this explanation of the belief in the Real Presence. I could find no argument whatever against it, and the logic of it held such sway over me that it urged me on to further investigation of Catholic doctrine. The memorable scene of the Last Supper was a solemn reiteration of the same truth, when our Lord, taking a morsel of bread in His Hand, said, 'This is my body'…

I was shaken out of my old-time security. This mighty Catholic Church was confronting me with her claim of being the very Church that Christ had planted on earth, and given into the charge of St. Peter. Was it so? I would at least find out what the Holy Scriptures had to tell me on the subject. I would read Christ's words afresh, as if I had never read them before, trying to forget all preconceived notions. I would do my best to get acquainted with St. Peter, St. John, and St. Paul, as living personalities, and see what they had to say about it. In this study of the Bible, alone and unaided, but read in this spirit, as if it were a new book, light began to stream in upon me. I soon saw that my old way of reading the Bible had been with distinct ideas beforehand as to what I should find there. The puzzling texts and apparent contradictions I had always forced to fit in with my conception of what God must be, as my ideal of perfect goodness. Truly such a standard by which to test divine truth is much like making God in man's image.

Merely studying the Bible from this fresh point of view made it come home to me with the force of a new revelation. The claims that Christ advanced definitely for Himself and that His disciples made for Him, had little in common with the old Unitarian basis of belief. He claimed to be God. His words come crowding to my mind. It is hard to decide which among the many to choose. How vivid that wonderful scene when Christ had told His followers that they had 'seen the Father.' Philip asks his Master 'Lord show us the Father, and it sufficeth us.' Could such an extraordinary request have been made to a merely human creature? And the answer, instead of a rebuke to his effrontery, is a gentle reproach that he could have ever doubted; for with a tone of disappointment, our Lord answered, and those glorious words ring out as clearly now as they did 1900 years ago: 'Have I been so long time with you, and yet hast thou not known me, Philip? He that hath seen me hath seen the Father; and how sayest thou then, "Show us the Father.'"

After trying to become acquainted with those who had actually sat at our Lord's feet - and with St. Paul, so close to that time - my next interest was to learn about the early Church, to find out if at the beginning the Christian Church and the Catholic Church were identical. What do we learn from Polycarp, who studied with St. John? And what does St. Irenaeus, his pupil, tell us, who reports from his teacher's lips the words which he had 'heard John and the others say'? Everything that I could glean of this early Church proved to me that it was the Catholic Church from the beginning. This is not only a matter of history but is written in stone throughout the Catacombs.

When once I grasped this idea that our Lord had founded a Church, and that He had promised to be with it to the end of the world, the victory was largely won. Every inquiry that I made went to prove that in the Catholic Church alone was His divine promise fulfilled"); Paula M. Kane, *Separatism and Subculture: Boston Catholic 1900-1920* (1994) ("[H]er conversion filled her with zeal to correct popular prejudices about Catholics. Accordingly, she always carried a 'huge telescope suit-case fairly crammed with Catholic reading matter' to distribute at any opportunity. The experience of a convent retreat during Passion Week in 1899 convinced her that she 'did not wish to run the chance of dying outside the Catholic Church'").

Robinson, Felix Griffon – freelance writer and historian; b. 24 July 1898, Oakland, Maryland; c. 1952 (his eldest daughter Muriel converted first, then he and the rest of the family); d. 11 September 1967, Oakland, Maryland; brought up as the eldest of seven children in a devout Lutheran family; from an early age he became aware of very serious difficulties within his church ("At the very center of its life was doctrinal confusion together with an absence of effective authority"); BA at Gettysburg College 1920; studied at the Lutheran theological seminary at Gettysburg, Pennsylvania (BD 1925); married to Lucille Henry (four children of the marriage); ordained a Lutheran minister and worked in New York, then West Virginia ("Finally I was called to a church of all creeds and of no creeds, the Arthurdale Community Church, Arthurdale, West Virginia"); cultivated Christian musical heritage by running choir festivals; attracted by the beauty of the Catholic Church's liturgy; conversion also influenced by the ineffective Protestant pulpit due to a presumptuous laity; his conversion caused great financial hardship to his family, as his source of income as a pastor disappeared; he wrote on local history, but had to supplement his income by working as a sales agent; buried in Oakland Cemetery; see "A Priceless Blessing," in John

A. O'Brien (ed), *The Road to Damascus, Vol. III: The Way to Emmaus* (1953) ("I realized, with the help of God's grace and the unerring religious instinct of my dear wife and children, that the true Church must have the mark of true unity in all its majesty and fullness.

Since Christ and His Church are the same yesterday, today, and forever, we have the materials at hand, not fashioned by man or nature, but offered by God to create in us a clean heart and renew a right spirit within us...

The realization that Christ is the head of His Mystical Body, the Church, is but a fulfillment of what was the very kernel of the faith we received from our parents. I did not forsake the simple, sweet, strong faith of my parents. Rather I, together with my wife and five children, found the fulfillment of that faith in the Catholic Church.

The conversion of our family was a long and painful apprenticeship in the school of experience. Our family could not have survived in a sectarian culture. The reasons should be obvious to any family: (1) the Catholic Church alone interprets and administers marriage as a sacrament. This makes marriage primarily a spiritual vocation. (2) The Catholic Church's concept of the individual is freedom through obedience, beginning in the home where children are willingly born, not accidentally. (3) It is the only Church which provides a sound religious life integrated with the cultural, holding the home, school, and Church in unbreakable relationship. This is the very essence of the kind of unity our modern world so desperately needs.

The account of our family's conversion, coming into the Church as a unit, should illustrate and dramatize the struggle against the non-sacramental concept of marriage, against the commercialized distractions that have invaded the home, and against a kind of institutionalism that has resulted in the breakdown of family morale through the encouragement of proxy management and rearing of children.

We were convinced that the spiritual and cultural survival of our family depended on being rescued by the one Ark of Salvation, Mother Church"); *The Story of Dr. Felix G. Robinson* (1960); his papers are at Georgetown University.

Rockne, Knute Kenneth (born Knut Larsen Rokne) – American football coach and player; b. 4 March 1888, Voss, Norway; c. 1923; d. 31 March 1931, Bazaar, Kansas; emigrated with his parents to Chicago when five years old and grew up there; brought up as a Lutheran; educated at the University of Notre Dame; in 1913 captain of Notre Dame's football team, which went undefeated for the third consecutive season; graduated in Chemistry and Pharmacology in 1914; married Bonnie Gwendoline Skiles (1891-1956), a Catholic, in

1914 (four children of the marriage); remained at Notre Dame as a chemistry instructor and assistant football coach; head coach 1918-1930; one of the greatest coaches in American football history; coached Notre Dame to 105 victories, twelve losses, five ties, and five national championships, including five undefeated seasons without a tie; helped popularize the forward pass nationally; reason for converting: tired of being the "lone Norwegian Protestant among the Catholic Hibernians"; dedicated family man with four children; killed in a plane crash while en route to participate in the production of the film *The Spirit of Notre Dame*; found with his rosary in his hands; inducted into the College Football Hall of Fame in 1951; buried in Highland Cemetery, South Bend, Indiana; see *The Autobiography of Knut Rockne* (1931); "Crossing the Goal Line," in Severin and Stephen Lamping, OFM (ed), *Through Hundred Gates* (1939) ("I used to be impressed by the sight of my players receiving Holy Communion every morning, and finally I made it a point to go to Mass with them on the morning of the game. I realized that it appeared more or less incongruous when we arrived in town for a game, for the general public to see my boys rushing off to church as soon as they got off the train, while their coach rode to the hotel and took his ease. So for the sake of appearance, if nothing else, I made it a point to go to church with the boys on the morning of the game.

One night before a big game in the East, I was nervous and worried about the outcome of the game the next day and was unable to sleep. I tossed and rolled about the bed and finally decided that I'd get up and dress, then go down to the lobby and sit in a chair alone with my thoughts. It must have been two or three o'clock in the morning when I arrived in the deserted lobby, so I took a chair and tried to get that football game off my mind by engaging some bellboys in conversation.

Along about five or six o'clock in the morning, I started pacing the lobby of the hotel, when suddenly I ran into two of my own players hurrying out. I asked one of them where they were going at such an hour, although I had a good idea. Then I retired to a chair in the lobby where I couldn't be seen, but where I could see everyone who went in or out of the door. Within the next few minutes, my players kept hurrying out of the door in pairs or groups, and finally, when they were about all gone, I got near the door so I could question the next player who came along.

In a minute or two, the last of the squad hurried out of the elevator and made for the door. I stopped them and asked them if they, too, were going to Mass, and they replied that they were. I decided to go along with them. Although they probably did not realize it, these youngsters were making a powerful impression on me with their piety and devotion, and when I saw all of them walking to the Communion rail to receive, and realized the several hours of sleep they had sacrificed in order to do this, I understood for the first time what a powerful ally their religion was to those boys in their work on the football field. Then it was that I really began to see the light; to know what was missing in my life, and later on I had the great pleasure of joining my boys at the Communion rail"); Harry Stuhldreher, *Knute Rockne, Man-Builder* (1931); Robert Harron, *Rockne, Idol of American Football* (1931); John W. Cavanaugh, "Rockne's Greatest Victory," in John A. O'Brien, *Paths to Christ* (1952); Ken Rappaport, *Wake Up the Echoes: Notre Dame Football* (1975); Jerry Brondfield, *Rockne: The Coach, the Man, the Legend* (1976); Michael R. Steele, *Knute Rockne, a Bio-Bibliography* (1983); Gene Schoor, *100 Years of Notre Dame Football* (1987); Murray Sperber, *Shake Down the Thunder: The Creation of Notre Dame Football* (1994); Ray Robinson, *Rockne of Notre Dame: The Making of a Football Legend* (1999); his papers are at the University of Notre Dame; *ANB*.

Rose, Lila Grace – pro-life activist; b. 27 July 1988, San Jose, California; c. 2009; third of eight children; at nine years old she saw an image of an aborted baby in a book at her home and asked, "How could anybody do this to a baby?"; at the age of fifteen she founded the pro-life group Live Action; she studied history at the University of California, Los Angeles, and continued with pro-life work there (founded the student magazine *The Advocate*); subject of several awards for her pro-life work; several high profile campaigns involving visits to clinics wearing secret video cameras, and acting various parts; has targeted in particular Planned Parenthood, the largest provider of abortions in the United States, exposing corruption and illegal activity there, involving the cover up of sexual abuse, willingness to assist sex trafficking and medical misinformation; has focused also on the high abortion rate in the African-American community; see Kathryn Jean Lopez, "Lila Rose Among Deadly Thorns," *National Review Online*, 18 February 2011; Justin Bell, "How Lila Rose Became Pro-Life… and Catholic," *National Catholic Register*, 3 February 2012 ("You said you converted to Catholicism not that long ago. Can you walk me through that process a little bit? 'I was received into the Church two and a half years ago. Best day of my life, although every day after that has been pretty good, too. I was raised as a Protestant, and my parents were very faithful people; and they taught us to read the Bible and love and respect life. I learned about Jesus Christ as a Protestant.

But in my upbringing, my dad

was on his own spiritual journey, reading the Church Fathers and doctors. So we had these books in the home: a lot of *Ignatius Press* books, for example. And so, I was reading these as a young teen. I read *Joan of Arc* by Mark Twain when I was 12. I was reading Mother Teresa's writings at 12, 13…like *Total Surrender, Loving Jesus*. Then I was reading St. Thomas Aquinas, and I was actually translating him in and out of Latin. That was part of the education experience that I was given by my parents because we're home-schooled. They really pursued classical education for us. That was really neat, too; that's another side of the story, but…

I was becoming formed by some of the best thinkers and saints of our Church, doctors of our Church, as a teen. I was very much drawn to the Church. I was drawn to Our Lady. I admired her so much, although the Protestant community doesn't really talk about her very much… My family talked about our faith, and, of course, about theology and different aspects of the Catholic tradition and everything. But we were still Protestant.

So then, when I got to UCLA, I fell in with - literally, one day I was looking for a church to go to - I had been experimenting with different Protestant churches, and I couldn't find one that I clicked with, as they say, because the Eucharist wasn't there and the theology was not sound. And I knew it, but I hadn't really gotten to the place in my head that: *Oh, I need to be Catholic; that just makes sense.* I had been intellectually convinced over a period of years, but I really didn't have Catholic friends, you know, strong Catholic friendships or anything like that, so it didn't really occur to me that I could convert.'

'You didn't see a way to convert then?' 'I didn't see a way to that. And my family, I thought, well, maybe one day if they do [convert], then I could with them, but they were not doing it at the time.

So I was looking for churches and [said] "I'll go to Mass." I had been to Mass a few times before…so I called up my friend Jen, and she was going to a Mass at this women's Catholic center, which turned out to be a women's Opus Dei center…I didn't realize there were all women in the little chapel; I was kind of clueless.

I went, prayed through the Mass, and then I was sitting with a woman in the back of the Mass; and I turned to her afterwards, and I said, "You know, is there someone here that can mentor me, or something like that?" She was a numerary [a type of member of Opus Dei who, according to the institution's website is 'completely available to attend to the apostolic undertakings and the formation of the other faithful of" Opus Dei], and she's like, "Yes, I'll see you tomorrow."

She ended up becoming my sponsor; a year and a half later, I was received into the Church. I got formation there. I started meeting with a priest on a weekly basis, my spiritual director. I was all of a sudden awash with desire, awakened with desire to be part of the Church and to get to receive the Eucharist. And all these things that I knew intellectually were suddenly becoming very real in my heart. And so, it was only a matter of time'").

Rosencrans, Sylvester Harden – bishop; b. 5 February 1827, Homer, Ohio; c. 1845; d. 21 October 1878, Columbus, Ohio; brother of William Rosencrans (see below); his family came originally from Holland; his mother was a daughter of Samuel Hopkins, a soldier of the Revolution; brought up as an Episcopalian; sent to Kenyon College, the leading Episcopalian institution in Ohio; so impressed by his brother's conversion that he also sought instruction and became a Catholic; studied at St. John's College, Fordham, New York, graduating in 1846; decided to study for the priesthood and was sent by the Bishop of Cincinnati as a student to the College of Propaganda, Rome; gained doctorate in Theology; ordained priest in Rome in 1852; returned to Cincinnati and was a professor in the diocesan seminary; in 1862 he was consecrated titular Bishop of Pompeiopolis and Auxiliary of Cincinnati; in 1868 appointed first Bishop of the Diocese of Columbus; he had lived a life of austerity and on his death he left two silver half-dollars and a watch; buried in the crypt of St. Joseph's Cathedral, Columbus; see *Catholic Encyclopedia.*

Rosencrans William Starke ("Old Rosy") – soldier; b. 6 September 1819, Kingston, Ohio; c. 1845; d. 11 March 1898, Rancho Sausal Redondo, Redondo Beach, California; brother of Sylvester Rosencrans (see above); his family came originally from Holland; his mother was a daughter of Samuel Hopkins, a soldier of the Revolution; baptized by the Methodist circuit rider, but brought up as an Episcopalian; as an undergraduate he was impressed by the Transcendentalists like Emerson and Thoreau; graduated from the U.S. Military Academy, West Point, in 1842 (fine student there); served briefly in the engineer corps; in 1843 he married Ann Eliza Hegman (d. 1883) (eight children of the marriage, three dying early); in 1844 an Irish book peddler told him about the Catholic Church and got him to read John Milner's *The End of Religious Controversy*; as a result he converted to the Catholic Church (in 1845 he wrote to his brother and suggested he read the same book); served at West Point as a professor until 1847; resigned from the army in 1854; worked as an architect and consulting engineer; became an inventor in the chemical and engineering field; on the outbreak of the Civil War he was made a colonel of volunteers; in 1861 appointed a brigadier-general of regulars; held several important commands (he was a fearless officer) until defeated by General Bragg at the battle of Chickamauga in September 1863; relieved of command; resigned from the army at the end of the war; served as U.S. Minister to Mexico; involved in railroad and industrial businesses 1869-1881; elected to Congress as a Democrat in 1880 and in 1882; registrar of the U.S. Treasury 1885-1893; buried in Arlington National Cemetery; one son, Adrian Louis (1849-1876), became a priest of the Paulist Order; one of his daughters, Mary Louise (1851-1877), joined the Ursuline Order of nuns as Sr. St. Charles; another, Anna Dolores (1857-1903), also became an Ursuline nun, but left the order because of ill-health; see *Catholic Encyclopedia.*

Rosenthal, Joseph John ("Joe") - photojournalist; b. 9 October 1911, Washington D.C.; d. 20 August 2006, Novato, California; parents Jewish immigrants from Russia; converted to Catholicism when a young man; experimented with photography at an early age; after high school began working as an office boy with the Newspaper Enterprise Association, where he gained experience in photojournalism; became a photographer for the *San Francisco News* and later for the San Francisco bureau of the Associated Press; rejected by the U.S. Army as a photographer because of poor eyesight; in World War II he was an official war photographer for the Associated Press and was sent out to the Pacific theater; on 23 February 1945 he took the famous *Raising the Flag on Iwo Jima* photograph that made his name; won a Pulitzer Prize for the photograph in 1945; there was some controversy about whether the image was staged (the photo was the second of two similar incidents, but was not posed); married Dorothy Lee Walch in 1947 (two children of the marriage, but divorced later); continued to work as a photographer until retiring in 1981; posthumously awarded the Distinguished Public Service Medal by the U.S. Marine Corps; see Tedd Thomey, *Immortal Images: A Personal History of Two Photographers and the Flag Raising on Iwo Jima* (1996); James Bradley's, *Flags of Our Fathers* (2000); Hal Buell, *Uncommon Valor, Common Virtue: Iwo Jima and the Photograph that Captured America* (2006); Steve O'Brien, "A Shot at the Summit: The Forgotten Mass on Iwo Jima," *remnantnewspaper.com, archive*, 2006 (the story of the Mass said under the flag); *ANB.*

Roth, Lillian (born Lillian Rutstein) – theatre and film actress; b. 13 December 1910, Boston, Massachusetts; c. 14 August 1948; d. 12 May 1980, New York City; brought up within Judaism; began as a child star; then on to Broadway revues; then a career in Hollywood, gaining fame and fortune in her teens; then a decline caused by alcoholism;

a radio sermon about Our Lady of Fatima moved her towards the Catholic Church ("I think that Catholicism is a fulfillment of Judaism as far as the acceptance of the Messiah"); triumphant return to Broadway in 1971; married five times, though the first four, entered into before she was a Catholic were not recognized by the Church (allowing her to marry finally Burt McGuire); buried in Mount Pleasant Cemetery, Hawthorne, Westchester County, New York; see *I'll Cry Tomorrow* (1954) (best-selling autobiography, later made into a successful Hollywood film in 1955); "Over Many Hurdles," in John A. O'Brien (ed), *The Road to Damascus, Vol. V: Where Dwellest Thou* (1956) ("She ends her book by quoting Francois Mauriac to the effect that we are constantly being remade by the people who love us"); *Beyond My Worth* (1958).

Rubin, Jeffrey – writer; c. 1984; father came from a Reform Jewish family; mother was nominally Episcopalian, but converted later to Reform Judaism; brought up with only a sense of a Jewish identity in a very Jewish area of New York; became atheist early; influenced by his father's promotion of Freud; educated at Harvard University where he majored in Art History; part of the radical movement; won acceptance to the Juilliard Theatre Center and toured as an actor; influenced by the life and work of Wilhelm Reich; influenced later by the Shroud of Turin and by Fr. Vincent Micelli, SJ's refutation of atheism in *The Gods of Atheism*; baptized into a Protestant sect; finally came to believe in the claims of the Catholic Church; editor of *The Latin Mass* magazine; see "Crooked Lines," in Robert Baram (ed), Spiritual Journeys (revised edition, 1988), p.315 ("It seems that the one thing that all Jews, however defined, can agree on (excepting, of course, converts like myself) is that one can't be Jewish and believe in Christ...

[I] decided to major in Art History. Wholly unaware of it at the time, painting and sculpture functioned for me in those years as they had for the Christian people throughout their great periods of ascendancy in art: as instruction in the Gospel. When I later came to consciously consider Christian doctrine, I was surprised at how much I had already learned of it through the medium of pictures...

G. K. Chesterton writes in *Orthodoxy* that 'a man is not really convinced of a philosophic theory when he finds that something proves it. He is only really convinced when he finds that everything proves it. And the more converging reasons he finds pointing to this conviction, the more bewildered he is if asked suddenly to sum them up. Accordingly, I can only sketch how, in this final phase before my Confirmation, even the 'stumbling blocks' I had encountered in my journey toward the Church became the very 'rocks' of my growing faith. Wasn't the Successor of St. Peter, I reasoned, rather than some earthly barrier to Christian knowledge and unity, nothing less than the sole guarantee of coherent, consistent doctrine and worship, the visible sign of the One Shepherd and the One Faith? And didn't the example of our present pope (who bestrode the world, it seemed to me, like a moral Colossus – battling Satan, teaching and exhorting with all the humility and courage of Christ Himself) prove the matchless potential of his great office for world spiritual leadership?

And what of the charges – and the promises – of 'enlightened' secularism, of the believers in a society 'liberated' by unbelief? Hadn't those regimes where atheism had ruled – Nazi Germany and the Communist nations – killed more people, in a single century, than all the religious wars since Christ? And what could they offer to compare with the many charities, hospitals, orphanages, the great art, music, literature and accumulated wisdom that were the legacy of the Catholic Church? – nothing but lies, terror and despair. And in our own decadent West, what had we to show for our rejection of the Church's 'hard teachings' on sexual ethics, contraception, abortion, divorce and remarriage? – nothing but broken families, fatherless children, and what Paul VI, in *Humanae Vitae*, had long since predicted: a mountain of slaughtered innocents. The Church had stood firm against all this insanity with the fury of a prophet – and prophecy, it seemed to me, was a mark of Holiness...

'God writes straight with crooked lines,' my mother-in-law is fond of saying, and mine has certainly been a twisted path"); Ronda Chervin (ed), *Bread From Heaven* (1994).

Rubio, Marco - politician; b. 28 May 1971, Miami, Florida; c. 1984 (revert); parents Cubans who came to the United States in 1956 and naturalized as U.S. citizens in 1975; his parents were Catholics, but they became Mormons when the family moved to live in Las Vegas when he was eight; as a youth he told his family he wanted to return to the Catholic faith, after watching a papal Mass broadcast on television during the Easter season; also influenced in his conversion by reading books by Scott Hahn (see above); moved back to Miami in 1985 with his family; graduated from University of Florida in 1993 with a BA degree; JD from University of Miami School of Law in 1996; elected to the Florida House of Representatives in 2000 and served until 2009; Speaker of the Florida House 2007-2009; member of the Republican Party; elected to the U.S. Senate from Florida in 2010; co-sponsored the Blunt Amendment in the Senate, a failed attempt to restore the right to religious freedom for employees in the wake of the HHS mandate issued by the Obama administration;

also member of the Congressional Hispanic Conference; he has been called the "crown prince" of the Tea Party movement; mentioned as a potential choice for the Republican vice-presidential nomination in 2012; married to Jeanette Dousdebes (of Colombian descent) with four children; attends Mass every Sunday with his family and raising his children as Catholics, but criticised for also attending services with his family at Christ Fellowship, a Southern Baptist church, to which his wife is drawn; confirmed and married in the Catholic Church; see *100 Innovative Ideas for Florida's Future* (2006); *An American Son: A Memoir* (2012); Manuel Roig-Franzia, *The Rise of Marco Rubio* (2012); Charlie Spiering, "Marco Rubio: America's Favorite New Catholic," *Crisis*, 2 July 2012.

Rush, William R – priest; b. 7 April 1904; c. 6 March 1939 (his sister later also became a Catholic); brought up in the Episcopalian Church; graduated from Carleton College, Northfield, Minnesota; attended Seabury Divinity School, Faribault, and General Theological Seminary in New York City; ordained to the Episcopal ministry in 1929; spent ten years in the Episcopalian ministry, adopting a High Church stance; developed many doubts regarding the Episcopal Church and sought instruction in the Catholic faith; after conversion he decided to train for the priesthood; entered St. Paul Seminary, Minnesota in September 1940; ordained to the priesthood 28 October 1945; see "Home at Last!" in John A. O'Brien (ed), *The Road to Damascus, Volume III: The Way to Emmaus* (1953) ("My first admiration for Rome was based on the fact that Roman Catholics did agree on the Real Presence of Christ in the Eucharist. They had a doctrine that I did not understand, but at least they all agreed on it…

Would I have stayed in the Episcopal Church if it had been proved that I had valid orders? The answer is 'No!' I wanted truth and conclusiveness, not chaos and confusion. Rome has valid orders; but more than that she has congruity and conclusiveness.

It is strange that since I have become a Catholic I have discovered something that I was not sure of before about the doctrines and discipline of the Catholic Church. I have discovered that the truths proclaimed by the Roman Catholic Church are based not upon caprice but upon sure proof. In fact the Catholic Church is 'truth-conscious'. Rome says, 'Stick to the facts! If you can't prove it, don't say it with finality. Whatever you say may be a fine, workable theory or hypothesis, but stick to the facts and prove your case.' My opinion now is that too many scholars outside of the Catholic Church do not take time enough to examine carefully the claims and proofs of the Church. Also, they are too uncritical of their own authorities.

[B]eing dissatisfied with things as they appeared to me in my own church did not, in my opinion, constitute a sufficient reason for my leaving it for Rome unless it could be proved that the Roman Catholic Church really was the *only* true Church...

Now I wanted...to find out, if possible, what was the truth without fear of being contradicted by someone in the same Church which I professed as my own. I wanted *freedom* to put into practice what I believed. I wanted cogent proof for my belief. I wanted assurance that the *whole* Church approved of my belief and practice. Actually what I really wanted (although I did not think of it that way at that time) was to have the *Church* give *me* the Faith which she wanted me to profess...

At the time of the instructions I was like so many other converts or inquirers: I feared that information would be held back from me and would come up later when it was too late to turn back. I feared that only the attractive things would be presented to me just to get me into the Church and that I would be left to find out the other things later...

I really did find out many things that were not given to me in the instructions. After all these years I must concede that there is much concealed information in the Catholic Church. Let me hasten to add, however, that it is certainly not secret or hidden or forbidden. It is concealed from me only because of my limited faculties in discovering it all at once. Each day I discover something new and exciting. All the truth and all the information in the Catholic Church is *all* mine just as soon as I am able to possess it all. I grow impatient at my lack of ability to grasp it all at once. The best way I know how to express it is this: The Catholic Church is a treasure-house full of many rich things, but it seems to grow and grow with each bit that is taken out of it.

Another thing which did not come out during the instructions but which I found later is that, even though there may be some bad Catholics, I can be unaffected by them in my spirituality and righteousness. I can be perfect if I care to be – or at least I can approach as close to perfection as my limited capacity will permit – and all this in spite of anybody else in the Church...

In retrospect, I further believe that one reason why the Episcopal Church seemed so empty to me is that it was a household devoid of a Mother. Because of its many divisions, the Blessed Virgin is not enthroned properly in the Episcopal Church. The devotion to Mary is not consistent. She is not present there; and on those parishes where she is venerated to some extent, the situation seems much like giving respect to an adopted Mother or to someone else's Mother. Today, I am not only in the household of the Faith, but I am at home because our Mother Mary is here").

Rutler, George William – priest; b. 23 March 1945; c. 28 September 1979 (received at St. Patrick's Cathedral, New York City by Terence Cardinal Cooke; his parents, Adolphe and Dorothy, were received into the Church in 1982); brought up in a pious Episcopalian family in New Jersey and New York; his father saw duty in World War II as a Merchant Marine officer on convoys to Russia; precocious intelligence with a love for the Classics; unfamiliar with Catholics (whom he associated with certain ethnic and cultural groups) and their practices (memory of once entering a Catholic church as a small boy, seeing the multitude of candles, and thinking that the church was on fire!; also that the Catholic Church was vast, and at the time seemed to him rather "unfriendly"); educated at Dartmouth 1961-1965; moved to a High Anglican position; pursued graduate studies at the Johns Hopkins University, receiving an MA in Theology in 1966; entered the General Theological Seminary, Manhattan (graduated first in his class in 1969); was an Episcopalian clergyman for nine years; was the youngest Episcopalian rector in the United States; witnessed the Episcopalian Church coming to an agreement with the new social perspective; the Anglican Communion's ordination of women and the local Episcopal church's support for abortion led to his decision to pursue union with Rome; his conversion was also influenced by Newman's *Apologia Pro Vita Sua* ("When I read Newman's *Apologia* it seemed to me that - just change the names and places, and it was rather what I was seeing around me"); became uneasy with the authenticity of the Anglican primacy; after his conversion to the Catholic Church he went as a seminary student to the North American College in Rome; ordained to the priesthood in 1981 (by Cardinal Cooke); was a university chaplain for the Archdiocese of New York; many posts including chaplain of the New York Guild of Catholic Lawyers; holds several degrees from the Gregorian and Angelicum Universities in Rome, including the Pontifical Doctorate in Sacred Theology; studied at the Institut Catholique in Paris; in 1988 Oxford University awarded him the degree of Master of Studies; since 1988 he has broadcast a weekly television program on EWTN; honored by the city of New York for his help at the World Trade Center on 11 September 2001 (He saw firefighters and police officers headed into the towering infernos in a desperate attempt to save as many people as they could, and he responded to their requests for general absolution); has given many lectures and retreats; has published many books; belief that there should be few options in the liturgy and no attempt to be creative; musician, painter, and art historian, with an extensive collection; see (selective list) *Impatience of Job* (1981); *The Four Last Things* (1986); *Christ and Reason: Introduction to Ideas from Kant to Tyrrell* (1990); *The Seven Ages of Man: Meditations on the Last Words of Christ* (1991); *This Is Our Faith* (1997); *Today with Father Rutler* (1997); *Brightest and Best: Stories of Hymns* (1998); *Beyond Modernity* (1999); *Curé D'Ars Today* (1999); *Seven Wonders of the World* (1999); *Coincidentally* (2007); *A Crisis of Saints: The Call to Heroic Faith in an Unheroic World* (2009); *Cloud of Witnesses: Dead People I Knew When They Were Alive* (2010); "The Liturgical Experts' Long Tassels," *First Things, On the Square*, 27 August 2010 ("Under the avalanche of commentary on the new translation of the Ordinary Form of the Mass, just approved by the Vatican, I poke my head above the erudite criticisms, to speak as a man whose entire priesthood has been in parishes…

Liturgy should be chantable, reverent, and expressive of the highest culture we know, without self-consciousness. *Ars est celare artem.* In tandem with Ovid, for whom it is art to conceal art, Evelyn Waugh said that Anthony Eden was not a gentleman because he dressed too well. It is typical of some schismatic sects that the more they lapse into heresy, the more ritualistic they become. So one will see pictures of a woman claiming to be a bishop, vested like Pius X on his jubilee.

A genius of the Latin rite has been its virile precision, even bluntness. Contrast this with the unsettled grammar of 'alternative opening prayers' in the original books from ICEL (the International Commission on English in the Liturgy), whose poesie sounds like Teilhard on steroids.

They were much wordier than the Latin collects or their English equivalents, and gave the impression of having been composed by fragile personalities who had not had a happy early home life. So too, the Prayers of the Faithful cloyingly pursued 'themes' usually inspired by an undisciplined concern for air pollution and third world debt.

I think there should be few options in the liturgy, and no attempt to be 'creative,' for that is God's particular talent. As Vatican II taught in *Sacrosanctum Concilium*, '[T]here must be no innovations unless the good of the Church genuinely and certainly requires them; and care must be taken that any new forms adopted should in some way grow organically from forms already existing'…

While I am glad for the new and more accurate translation of the Mass, which is not perfection but closer to it than one deserves in an imperfect world, a far more important reform would be the return of the *ad orientem* position of the celebrant as normative. It is the antidote to the tendency of clerisy to impose itself on the people. When a celebrant at Mass stops and says, 'This is not about me,' you may be sure he thinks it may be about him. It would be harder for him to harbor that suspicion were he leading the people humbly to the east and the dawn of salvation.

John Henry Newman was the greatest master of English letters in his century of brilliant English, but he gave no countenance to his vernacular replacing the sacral tongue. That is another matter for another day. But he knew the meaning of *cupio dissolvi*, and he taught that without such self-abnegation the gift of personality reduces the Passion to pantomime. It was because his priestcraft was also soulcraft, that he solemnly invoked the Sacred Heart at the altar in order to speak 'heart to heart' with the people in the street: 'Clad in his sacerdotal vestments, [the priest] sinks what is individual in himself altogether, and is but the representative of Him from whom he derives his commission. His words, his tones, his actions, his presence, lose their personality; one bishop, one priest, is like another; they all chant the same notes, and observe the same genuflections, as they give one peace and one blessing, as they offer one and the same sacrifice. The Mass must not be said without a Missal under the priest's eye; nor in any language but that in which it has come down to us from the early hierarchs of the Western Church. But, when it is over, and the celebrant has resigned the vestments proper to it, then he resumes himself, and comes to us in the gifts and associations which attach to his person. He knows his sheep, and they know him; and it is this direct bearing of the teacher on the taught, of his mind upon their minds, and the mutual sympathy which exists between them, which is his strength and influence when he addresses them. They hang upon his lips as they cannot hang upon the pages of his book'"); "The Tragic Heroism of Pope Pius XII," *Crisis*, 22 October 2012; "Glorious Janitor: The Life of Brother Joseph," *Crisis*, 14 November 2012; John Janaro, *Fishers of Men* (1985), Ch. 7: "Fr. George Rutler" ("In 1976 the Anglican Communion voted to permit the ordination of women. He found himself confronted with a harsh reality: 'Via Media,' or 'Middle Road' of Anglicanism was dying. As he watched the sand being washed away from under the edifice of the Episcopal Church, his eyes turned toward the Church of Rome, and the Rock upon which it is built. 'Simon, son of John, do you love me' (Jn. 21:17)? On a pilgrimage to the Holy Land, he spent a night by the Sea of Galilee thinking of those words. Objections to the primacy of the See of Peter seemed to fade in the light of the glowing witness that Peter had given, and was still giving to the integrity of the Gospel, an integrity his own Church had abandoned. 'If it were wrong to have a Pope,' he thought to himself, 'it had to be very wrong that he should be so right'").

Ryan, Thomas Fortune – tobacco and transport magnate, philanthropist; b. 17 October 1851, near Lovingston, Nelson County, Virginia; d. 23 November 1928, New York City; descended from Anglo-Irish Protestant settlers in the seventeenth century; father a tailor and hotel manager; mother, Lucinda Fortune Ryan, died when he was five; father re-married and moved away; brought up by his mother's Protestant family; educated at home by local Baptist ministers; in 1868 he moved to Baltimore to seek work; after long discussions with a conductor on the train he converted to the Catholic faith; worked for John S. Barry, a dry goods merchant; in 1872 Barry obtained for him a position as a brokerage assistant on Wall Street; tutored by William Collins Whitney (1841-1904), the financier, who said around 1890, "If Ryan lives long enough, he'll have all the money in the world"; in 1873 he opened a brokerage firm, Lee, Ryan & Warren; in 1873 he married Ida Mary Barry (1854-1917), whose family were devout Catholics; in 1874 his firm purchased him a seat on the New York Stock Exchange (he was the youngest ever member); became active in politics, especially in Tammany Hall; worked in public transit, founding the New York Cable Railroad and the Metropolitan Traction company; by 1900 controlled most of the city streetcar operations; went into the tobacco industry eventually forming the American Tobacco Company and the British American Tobacco Company; in 1905 he purchased the Equitable Life Assurance Society, but sold it in 1911; made further fortunes with banks, coal mines, public utilities, railroads and guns; his wife made large benefactions; they both funded churches, convents and hospitals; they funded the construction of the Cathedral of the Sacred Heart in Richmond, Virginia; in all they gave $20 million dollars to Catholic charities in the United States; also funded cultural and historical interests, the fine arts and exploration; father of seven children, the eldest being the financier and writer John Barry Ryan (1874-1942); in 1912 moved back to Virginia; Virginia delegate to the Democratic National Convention; twelve days after his wife died in 1917 he married Mary Townsend Lord Cuyler (1860-1937), a widow; buried with his second wife in the Ryan Mausoleum adjacent to Oak Ridge Estate Cemetery, Arrington, Nelson County, Virginia; reputed to have been the wealthiest man in the South and the tenth wealthiest in the country; highly private person; see Edwin Slipek, Jr., "The Tycoon: The Story of Thomas Fortune Ryan, and His Legacy in Richmond," *Style Weekly*, 10 January 2005; *ANB*.

Ryland, Raymond ("Ray") – priest; b. in Oklahoma; c. 1963 (Pentecost; received with his wife Ruth and their five children);

brought up in a Protestant sect, the Disciples of Christ; impressed by the nuns at a local convent ("I saw a serenity, a calmness that strangely contrasted with what I saw in the faces of determined, hurrying shoppers"); earned his bachelor's degree from Phillips University, Oklahoma, in 1942; enrolled in the Harvard Divinity School to train as a church minister, but then moved to Union Theological Seminary, New York; he and his wife then joined the Episcopalian Church and he became a clergyman there; he and his wife saw themselves as Anglo-Catholics; they became disillusioned by the Episcopal Church and rejected other forms of Protestantism and the Orthodox Church; saw the question of authority as the key issue and this led to their conversion to the Catholic Church; also influenced by Karl Adam's *The Spirit of Catholicism*; received a doctorate in Religious Studies from Marquette University; then worked for the diocesan department of education in Oklahoma; joined the theology faculty of the University of San Diego where he was Professor of Theology for more than twenty years; ordained a permanent deacon; took advantage of the Pastoral Provision for the United States under which married Catholic laymen who had formerly been Episcopal clergy were allowed to apply through their bishops for a dispensation from the rule of celibacy and for ordination to the Catholic priesthood; his application was the first one sent from the United States to Rome; in early 1983 ordained to the Catholic priesthood; adjunct Professor of Theology at Franciscan University of Steubenville; chaplain of the *Coming Home Network* and of *Catholics United for the Faith*; contributing editor of *This Rock* magazine; see "Will the Real St. Cyprian Please Stand?" *This Rock*, April 1997, p.28; *EWTN Audio Library, The Journey Home* (10 October 1997); "On Whose Authority," in Marcus Grodi (ed), *Journeys Home* (1997) (revised edition 2011) (reproduced in *The Coming Home Network International*, *Conversion Stories*, *chnetwork.org*, 13 May 2011 (originally published in *This Rock*, January 1995); "Wonderful Leo," *This Rock*, February 1999; "Apologetics Is Where the Action Is: But Ecumenism is Equally Important," *This Rock*, March 2000; "Meeting Christ on His Terms, Not Ours," in Patrick Madrid (ed), *Surprised by Truth 2* (2000), p.61 ("Authority is the basic issue that divides Christians into thousands of competing sectarian traditions. In the midst of all these vying claims, how can we know with certainty what God has revealed about Himself (faith) and what He expects of us (morals)? Surely He foresaw the emergence of these thousands of competing churches. Has He left us in the lurch, so to speak, with regard to finding the truth among them? If He has, then the life, death, and Resurrection of Jesus Christ - indeed, the whole of salvation history - were all in vain.

Each of the thousands of denominations today claims to have its own solution for this problem. The honest seeker has to ask, 'Do any of them, in fact, solve the problem?' After much study, prayer, and examination of Scripture and Church history, my wife and I discovered that none do. At the outset of our seeking-become-pilgrimage, neither of us clearly saw authority as the fundamental issue. Only through a years-long process did the Spirit gradually lead us clearly to see that. Not only is authority the rock-bottom issue in all Christian divisions; it is the key to understanding the Roman Catholic Church...

I spent the summer between Harvard and Union Theological Seminary studying the first four centuries of the Church's history. I focused on the early Christological controversies and their resolution... During that summer of intensive study, repeatedly the thought came to me that all these struggles with heresy directly impinge on my life and belief as a Christian and must not he ignored. I began to yearn somehow to be part of that institution which fought so valiantly for its life in those early centuries...

The longer we lived within the Episcopal Church and the more we studied its history, the more we saw its theological and moral fragmentation. (We deeply regret that in recent decades that fragmentation has greatly accelerated.) Initially, at Union, we were attracted by the Anglican claim of 'comprehensiveness,' which means embracing many different approaches to theology. Now we began to see the term as a euphemism for chaos.

We gradually realized that Anglo-Catholicism, like Anglicanism itself, is essentially, inescapably Protestant. Its appeal to the Faith of the original 'Catholic' Church, like the appeal to the Tradition of the early centuries, is flawed. There is no one in the Anglican system to say authoritatively what that Faith is, or what that Tradition is, or what that Tradition says about Scripture. Each Anglo-Catholic decides for himself what is 'catholic' - or chooses a clergyman to decide for him - and proceeds accordingly.

Before he entered the Catholic Church, John Henry Newman was the most distinguished of all Anglo-Catholics and the author of the Anglo-Catholic manifesto the *Via Media* (the 'Middle Way'). Anglo-Catholics have claimed that in that work, Newman definitively set forth the true nature of the Church of England. Only after I became Catholic did I study the introduction to *Via Media* closely enough to learn that Newman plainly stated he was setting forth a *theory* only: what he hoped the Church of England might *become*. A dozen years later, he recognized the futility of his hope and entered the Catholic Church. There is no visible entity to which the Anglo-Catholic can point and say, '*That* is the "Catholic Church" to which I belong.' That 'Catholic Church' is only an abstraction.

We thought we had found historical continuity in the Episcopal Church, but it was not there. We now knew that continuity and Tradition go hand in hand; that Scripture has to be interpreted in the light of Tradition. But we had failed to find a structure or an office to fulfill the interpretive function. Now where to turn?...

Anglo-Catholics have always looked on Eastern Orthodoxy with awe. At the same time, because of their prejudice, Anglo-Catholics consider Rome simply unacceptable, so Eastern Orthodoxy becomes 'the last, best hope'...

So we began to wonder, 'Is Orthodoxy the answer to our seeking?' Perhaps the Eastern Churches that separated from Rome have the proper grasp of Tradition...

Our reading of history showed us that Orthodox Churches have been insular for a millennium or more. Apart from some Russian Orthodox missionary activity in Alaska and on the West Coast in the nineteenth century, no Orthodox Church has evangelized any significant part of the world since Russia was evangelized a thousand years ago. (The spread of Orthodox Churches to this country and elsewhere has occurred by the immigration of Orthodox people from their various homelands. Not one of these ethnic Churches has demonstrated universal appeal.)...

More serious difficulties in Eastern Orthodoxy gave us further pause. One is the lack of unity among the Orthodox Churches. The terms *Eastern Orthodoxy* and *Orthodoxy* commonly designate the Orthodox Churches as a whole, but the terms are abstractions. There's no institution to which one can point and say, 'There is Orthodoxy.' The Churches hold basically the same Faith, but, jurisdictionally, they're very divided...

In harmony with Catholic teaching, the Eastern Churches generally hold that Scripture has to be interpreted in the light of Tradition. Eastern Orthodox theologians often practically identify Tradition with the teachings of the Fathers, whose era came to an end in the eighth century. But which of the Fathers should we follow? Which traditions should we embrace?

When Ruth and I asked ourselves this, we had taken the final step in facing the key issue: authority. Look carefully - as we began to do - at Eastern Orthodox logic. Scripture must be interpreted in the light of Tradition. What Tradition or which traditions? How can we know which are authentic? Eastern Orthodoxy responds: They must be tested in the light of Scripture. In other words, Scripture interprets Tradition, which interprets Scripture. But Scripture and Tradition can't be mutually validating criteria for each other either simultaneously or sequentially. This is circular reasoning. It can't solve the problem of authority...Orthodoxy did not have the answer. Where should we look next?...

At Harvard I had questioned the enterprise of restorationism. It is impossible to go back in time and re-create or re-establish an institution or even a situation of the past. ('The moving finger writes, and having writ, moves on...' (Edward Fitzgerald, *The Rubaiyat of Omar Khayyam*)). This fact is obvious, and yet non-Catholic Christians ignore it.

Now I realize that all non-Catholic traditions are essentially restorationist. Every one of the thousands of denominations was founded by someone who claimed simply to be restoring the 'primitive Church' (of the first century).

Sola scriptura ('Scripture alone') is a form of restorationism. It's the key slogan of Protestantism: every Christian belief must be clearly proved from Scripture. Ironically, the belief itself - that all must be proved from Scripture - can't be proved from Scripture. Scripture nowhere asserts it...

Protestants claim they restore the 'primitive Church'; Anglicans, the Church of the first five centuries; Eastern Orthodox Churches, the Church of the first eight centuries. They are all restorationist, differing only with regard to how much they claim to have 'restored'.

So where should we turn? Almost before we dared ask the question one more time, we knew the answer: Rome. There was no other alternative...

Frequently during my study, the question came to my mind: If St. Augustine were to come to D.C. today, where would he go to church? I never had to work to find the answer; it came immediately. I knew with certainty that St. Augustine would not go to one of our Episcopal churches; he would go to one of his churches, a Catholic Church. Had I taken that signal as seriously as I should have, my journey to Rome might well have been shorter...

The problem of authority must he solved. God has entered history, revealing Himself in the redemption of mankind through our Lord Jesus Christ. Has He left no means in His Church to ensure man's true grasp of that revelation? Jesus Christ promised to lead the Church into all truth through the Holy Spirit. Has He broken His promise by failing to establish criteria and means of expression for that truth? Our Blessed Lord has prayed that all members of His Mystical Body would be one. Has He given His Church no earthly center of unity by which this prayer can be answered?...

Our conscience as well as our reason demanded an answer to these questions and others like them. We were forced to examine Rome's claims with great care. Rome answers these questions in the teaching office of the Holy

See, established by Jesus Christ in His charge to St. Peter. For years, this was the great stumbling block in Roman Catholicism for us. But accept it, and the whole design of Christian truth becomes clear"); "No Salvation Outside the Church," *This Rock*, December 2005; *Catholic Answers to Catholic Questions* (2010) (with Paul Thigpen and Francis Hoffman); *Jesus Gives Himself to Us: Transubstantiation* (2010); *Drawn from Shadows into Truth : A Memoir* (2013); Ruth Ryland, "I Never Dreamed I'd be Married to a Catholic Priest," in Marcus Grodi (ed), *Journeys Home* (1997) (revised edition 2011) (reproduced in *The Coming Home Network International*, *Conversion Stories*, *chnetwork.org*, 13 May 2011).

Sanderson, Sibyl - opera singer; b. 7 December 1864, Sacramento, California; c. 1 December 1897; d. 16 May 1903, Paris; eldest of four daughters of Silas Sanderson (1824-1886) who was a politician and lawyer, and served as Chief Justice of the Supreme Court of California; was engaged to the newspaper publisher William Randolph Hearst (1863-1951), but the engagement was broken off; after her father's death she and her mother moved to Paris and she studied at the Paris Conservatory; very gifted and popular singer with a unique voice (had a three octave range) and great acting skills; she was the favorite soprano of the composer Jules Massenet (1842-1912), who created for her the title roles in *Thais* and *Esclarmonde* (Massenet included in *Esclarmonde* what she called her Eiffel Tower cadenza, which climbed to the highest note ever asked of a singer on score paper: G above high C); she was also a famous interpreter of Massenet's opera *Manon*; Camille Saint-Saëns (1835-1921) wrote the title role in *Phryné* for her; she was considered a great beauty and lived the life of a socialite; dubbed by the Parisian newspapers as "the California nightingale" and "the American linnet"; in 1897 she married Antonio E. Terry (d. 1899), a flamboyant Cuban millionaire; became a Catholic two days before the wedding; had one daughter who died soon after birth; suffered from depression, and the effects of alcoholism in her last years; she helped the career of another famous soprano, Mary Garden (1874-1967); see Jack Winsor Hansen, *The Sibyl Sanderson Story: Requiem For A Diva* (2004).

Sands, Benjamin Franklin – rear-admiral; b. 11 February 1812, Baltimore, Maryland; c. 1850 (his daughter-in-law, Elizabeth Mary, *née* Meade, the wife of his son James Hoban Sands, also converted); d. 30 June 1883, Washington, D.C.; appointed a midshipman in the navy in 1828; passed through the successive grades of promotion until he received the rank of rear-admiral in 1871; held several important commands during the Civil War; superintendent of the Naval Observatory at Washington 1867-1874; retired 1874; converted, having married a Catholic, Henrietta M. French (1817-1883), sister of Major-General William H. French; member of the Catholic Indian bureau in Washington for many years; his son James Hoban (1845-1911) was also a rear-admiral and his example as a Catholic was a strong influence in the navy in developing a spirit of tolerance towards Catholics in the service, and in making religious practices of whatever creed more respected; two other sons, William Franklin (1838-1861), and Francis Preston Blair (1842-1928), also served in the navy; another son, George Henry (1856-1920), graduated at West Point and served in the U. S. Army with the rank of colonel; a daughter, Rosa Virginia (1847-1930 became a Visitation nun; buried in Arlington National Cemetery, Arlington County, Virginia, with his wife; see *From Reefer to Rear Admiral: Reminiscences and Journal Jottings of Nearly Half a Century of Naval Life* (1899) (compiled by his son F. B. Sands from notes left behind); *Catholic Encyclopedia*; *ANB*.

Sargent, Daniel – poet, historian and biographer; b. 1890, Wareham, Massachusetts; c. 13 April 1919 (Palm Sunday; his wife, Louise, also brought up as a Unitarian, whom he married in 1920, became a Catholic in Orvieto, Italy, in 1915); d. 24 January 1987, Natick, Massachusetts; both parents were Unitarians; educated at Harvard University; profoundly influenced there by taking a course in Dante, which awakened an interest in the Catholic Church ("I discovered at last what Catholics thought the Church was. I saw, for instance, that there could not be more than one Church. There had to be only one Church, or no Church. God, with his perfection of love, had to establish a Church, because His son had come to earth, to join men to Him by means of a Church. There could not be two Churches coming from Calvary. The picture of a one Church had been hideous to me; now it became beautiful"); studied and taught in Europe before World War I; in 1916 he joined the ambulance corps of the French army (narrowly escaping death when his ship was torpedoed in the Channel) ("My motive in so doing was partly restlessness, but also an antagonism to German philosophy, particularly that of Nietzsche, against which it seemed the French were fighting. I wished to help the French"); on the entry of the United States into the war, he served in the U.S. artillery; his conversion was influenced by his wartime experiences and by two books: *Le Voyage du Centurion* by Ernest Psichari and *Morceaux Choisis: Poesie* by Charles Péguy; reading the Greek classics taught him that human nature was not changing ("There had been only one event that had changed human nature, and that was the Incarnation, the birth of Our Lord at Bethlehem, of the Blessed Virgin. By that, the clumsiest private soldier in any army could become divinized to a glory which far outshone that of endless ambrosial laughter on Mount Olympus. The Greeks had looked forward to the Incarnation, and we looked back to it. Otherwise we were the same"); after the war he taught History and Literature at Harvard University 1920-1934, then left to devote himself full time to writing (from 1946 he turned to writing poetry exclusively); co-president of the American Catholic Historical Society 1936; president of the Catholic Poetry Society of America 1936-1937; see *My Account of the Flood. By Noah's Brother-in-Law* (1930); *Thomas More* (1934); *Four Independents: Studies of Charles Péguy, Paul Claudel, Gerard Manley Hopkins, Orestes Augustus Brownson* (1935); *God's Ambuscade: A Book of Poems* (1935); *Catherine Tekakwitha* (1936); *Our Land and Our Lady* (1939); *All the Day Long: James Anthony Walsh, Co-founder of Maryknoll* (1941); *Christopher Columbus* (1941); *Our Land and Our Lady* (1941); *Mitri; or The Story of Prince Demetrius Augustine Gallitzin, 1770-1840* (1945); "The Pearl of Great Price," in John A. O'Brien (ed), *The Road to Damascus, Vol. II* (1950) ("There was a war going on, and after several months in a quiet sector I became acquainted with the full fury of it at Verdun in June 1916, where the battle which caused more carnage than any other in history was at its height. We in our ambulances would glide through the demolished city of Verdun after dark and cross the Meuse up to an obliterated village, Bras, where we would find the wounded. The road there, simply by its stench, made the circles of Dante's Inferno seem salubrious. The detonations around it were like the end of the world. On this road, I remembered Dante well enough to recite the prayer *Vergine Madre*. There was no dear earth left. There was only Heaven.

It was at Bras that I had my first glimpse of French Catholic chaplains under fire. I remember one in particular - bearded, beskirted in a cassock, with a V-shaped fatigue cap on his head - who used to help us load the stretchers into the Fords and who was singularly efficacious and unperturbed.

Years later, after my conversion, people said to me, as if ferreting out why I had become a Catholic: 'So you found the Catholic chaplains better than the Protestant ones?'

Better! I had never thought of it in terms of better or worse. The Catholic chaplains were different. They went about their work more unselfconsciously, bringing with them not their virtues but God's sacraments. They were never in the way. They did not stand with their own personalities between the dying men and God. I had caught sight of the divinity of the Church, not in a book, but in a drama of which I was a part.

From then on the Catholic Church became vivid and living about me. I could scarcely see anything else, whether I was driving along the roads, or unloading the wounded in a hospital, or buying cigarettes in a village, or reading a newspaper. I saw France as a building which had been constructed by the Church. Part of the building was in ruins, but even the ruins spoke of the Church.

And not only did I everywhere see the Church, but I everywhere admired it. Everything that was admirable in France showed the touch of the Church.

While my eyes were open this way I enjoyed several periods of leave in Paris. They were somewhat hilariously spent, for Paris was a resplendent city and it was joy to be alive there, yet in my hilarity I did not fail to see the Church. Tourists can go to Paris and see Notre Dame, and yet not see the Church at all. I did not often enter Notre Dame, yet I passed it often, and, in passing it, I did not regard it merely as a beautiful monument: it seemed what it had been to the men of old, a 'sermon in stone.' In its portals I saw, sculptured, Christ enthroned, Our Lady crowned, the elect going to heaven and the damned to hell. Once upon a time I had stared at such things as an outmoded myth. Now there was nothing truer. All other knowledge seemed comparatively unimportant. The Church had become to me the perennial and ever-patient teacher...

In December 1916 we were stationed at Monastir. On Christmas Eve a Frenchman said to me: 'Come to the Midnight Mass at the Chapel of the Sisters of Charity.' I had never in my life attended a Mass, although I had stared in detachment at Masses going on. I accepted the invitation and, in the still darkness - for the enemy for once had let up their bombardment - I walked to the chapel. It was very small, and there were not fifty of us in it. There were some Sisters of Charity present in their blue robes, with their white cornucopia hats. A French priest before our eyes took off his soldier's jacket and put on his vestments with simple dignity. And the altar candles were lighted, and the Mass began.

I have read of how St. Patrick converted pagans in old Ireland simply by celebrating Mass, in all its splendor, before them in a grove, and I have asked myself can such a conversion be a real conversion, It can, especially where the pagans have already, as is common to all men save disinherited Christians, a sense of offering sacrifice. I was a disinherited Christian, yet the sight of the Mass sent its light all through me. I discovered there and then what a sacrifice was, and recognized this sacrifice as no invention of man, but as God's own act - Christ offering himself to God, the Father.

Several Frenchmen whom I knew kneeled to confession openly on this occasion and then received Holy Communion. They were not among the 'naturally pious.' That is what impressed me most about their action. Here was a Church not for those who felt good, but for those who knew they were not.

By the time the snow was melting on the hills about Monastir, I had gained through more than a year of war a soldier's acquaintance with the Catholic Church. It was certainly not that of a theologian, but it served to convince me that the Catholic Church was of divine origin. First and last, it was not a church which bore any resemblance to other so-called churches. Its excellence did not depend on the merits of its clergy or its laity, although I found them admirable. It had the confidence of a body which derived its authority from outside itself; and all its actions, even its defects, bore witness to that. It was calmly not emotionally, confident...

I had not come to the Church by first learning that Christ was God. I had begun by finding the Church to be divine, and inferred that its founder must be divine"); Brother André Marie, "Black Robes and Flat Heads and French, Oh My!" *catholicism.org*, 8 May 2008.

Scammon, Ellakim Parker – army officer; b. 27 December 1816, Whitefield, Maine; c. 1846; d. 7 December 1894, New York City; graduated 5th in the class of 52 of 1837 from the United States Military Academy at West Point; stayed at West Point as Assistant Professor of Mathematics 1837-1838 (among his pupils were the future Generals Grant, Rosecrans, Newton, and other famous army officers); served in the Seminole Wars and the Mexican-American War (1846-1847); from 1847 to 1854 he was attached to the topographical corps surveying the Upper Lakes; made captain in 1853, but left the service in 1858; moved to Ohio and appointed Professor of Mathematics at Mount Saint Mary's College; President and Professor of Mathematics, Polytechnic College of the Catholic Institute in Cincinnati; on the outbreak of the Civil War he volunteered for service and was appointed Colonel of the 23rd Ohio Infantry (commanded two future Presidents of the United States, Rutherford B. Hayes and William McKinley); assigned to the IX Corps in the Army of the Potomac; then commanded the 1st Brigade, Kanawha Division; fought well at the Battle of Antietam; appointed brigadier general of volunteers in 1862; captured twice in 1864, but was exchanged each time and returned to duty; placed in command of a brigade in the Department of Florida; after the War he was United States Consul to Prince Edward Island 1866-1871; Professor of Mathematics at Seton Hall College, South Orange, New Jersey 1875-1882; buried in the Calvary Cemetery in Long Island City, New York; his brother, Jonathan Young Scammon, became one of the wealthiest men in America as a Chicago attorney, newspaper owner, philanthropist and businessman; see *Catholic Encyclopedia.*

Schenck, Paul Chaim Benedicta - priest and pro-life activist; b. 1958, Glen Ridge, New Jersey; c. 10 March 2004 (received by Fr. Frank Pavone); raised in a Jewish home; his mother was born Catholic, converted to Judaism on her marriage, but later returned to the Catholic Church; at college near Rochester, New York; baptized at the age of sixteen; married his wife Becky in 1977 (eight children of the marriage); founded the New Covenant Tabernacle Church in New York in 1982; joined the Reformed Episcopal Church in 1994 and became a minister in 1995; executive vice president of the American Center for Law and Justice 1994-1997; ordained a Catholic priest on 12 June 2010, under the Pastoral Provision allowing married former clergy of the Anglican tradition to be ordained without the requirement for celibacy; his twin brother, Robert, is a minister of the Methodist Episcopal Church; he and his brother were involved in the founding of Operation Rescue; they organized blockades of abortion clinics (Robert was arrested for showing Bill Clinton an aborted fetus during the 1992 Democratic National Convention); he was arrested for peacefully distributing pro-life literature outside an abortion clinic; won his case, *Schenck v Pro-Choice Escorts*, in the United States Supreme court relating to pro-life speech and the First Amendment to the Constitution, and restraining orders for protesters around abortion clinics; after his conversion to the Catholic Church he pursued further graduate and post-graduate qualifications at Catholic universities; served as a Pastoral Associate in Priests for Life 2004–2007; National Representative of Catholics United for Life; founder and chairman of the National Pro-Life Action Center (NPLAC) on Capitol Hill in Washington, D.C.; see Robert Schenck, *Ten Words That Will Change a Nation* (2002).

Schoeman, Roy H. – author; b. early 1950s; c. early 1992; parents were conservative Jewish refugees born in Germany; grew up in a suburb of New York City; from early on being Jewish was the basis of his identity; went to ordinary secular school and to Hebrew school at the synagogue; naturally devout nature; aware of the Christian presence, especially the Christ child; studied Judaism under some leading conservative rabbis; saw Christianity then as a "watered-down, mongrelized version of Judaism," yet felt drawn to Jesus; studied in Jerusalem under a Hasidic rabbi, but found a coldness there; returned to the United States and studied at M.I.T., adopting the counter-culture, falling away from Jewish religious practice, and becoming a hedonistic agnostic; worked as a computer engineer; MBA. at Harvard University before teaching there; felt then that his life had no meaning; on one occasion in 1987 he had a consciousness of the presence of God, and a year later a dream of the Blessed Virgin Mary, whom he began to revere; at first went to various Protestant churches (found there a denigration of the Blessed Virgin); but started attending Mass and visited many Marian shrines and developed a desire for the Blessed Sacrament; particularly influenced by Fatima and La Salette; sought instruction and became a Catholic; he has written that supersessionism (that the Old Covenant has been superseded by the New Covenant) is an error, yet supersessionism was taught infallibly by the Council of Florence ("That the matter pertaining to the law of the Old Testament, of the Mosaic law… after our Lord's coming had been signified by them, ceased and the sacraments of the New Testament began"); the Council also stating that anyone who observed the Mosaic rituals is "alien to the Christian faith and not in the least fit to participate in eternal salvation"; nothing in Vatican II or statements of recent popes alters this; also the traditional teaching was reiterated by the United States Conference of Catholic Bishops in 2008; he has also been criticized for interpreting certain Old Testament prophecies of the first coming of Christ as being prophecies of political Zionism; he has claimed that Jewish converts should be allowed to resurrect Jewish festivals, but this is expressly forbidden by the Church; see *Salvation Is From the Jews: The Role of Judaism in Salvation History* (2003) ("It might seem odd to refer to the entry of Jews into the Catholic Church as 'the return of the Jew.' It is, however, the natural image for one who sees the Catholic Church as simply the continuation (and filfilment) of Judaism after the first coming of Jesus, the Jewish Messiah. In such a case, it is the Jews who accepted Him and became the first Christians who stayed within the core of Judaism, while those who rejected Him left the mainstream, the fullness of truth of the religion...

Almost every Jew who enters the Catholic Church feels deeply the sense of 'return' that St. Paul captures in his image of the olive branch being grafted back on to its original, natural root - that they are in no way leaving Judaism but rather coming into its fullness. As Rosalind Moss [see above], a well-known contemporary Jewish-Catholic evangelist put it, becoming Catholic is 'the most Jewish thing a person can do'"); *EWTN Audio Library, The Journey Home* (10 January 2005) ("Obviously, in some fundamental way Judaism and Christianity are actually the same religion separated by a point of fact, which is 'Who was Jesus?'

And if Jesus really was the Jewish Messiah, then Christianity is actually in some sense the correct form of Judaism, the continuation of Judaism after the coming of the Messiah. And if Jesus wasn't the Messiah, then Christianity is a sort of apostasy off of Judaism. So they are not unrelated religions at all...

There's no question that in general one is crippled by not being Catholic. Excuse me but if the Eucharist really is the body, blood, soul, and divinity of the God-man, then obviously one's at a great disadvantage not participating in that, and it's a double tragedy in the case of the Jews, because essentially the Gentile Catholics are part of that relationship through adoption, but the Jew comes into that relationship as a son in a way, as opposed to the adopted child... There's something particularly poignant about a Jew not coming into his own inheritance in that way...

What at the time of Jesus was the sect of the Pharisees...has become Judaism. Essentially with the destruction of Jerusalem and of the final dispersal of the Jews from the Holy Land, the strain of Judaism which survives is the strain of the Pharisees. They were the dominant force in developing what's called rabbinical Judaism. And obviously the Judaism in the Old Testament can no longer be followed once the temple was destroyed. The temple was at the center of Jewish historical life and it was actually required for the removal of sin, for the atonement of sin, the temple sacrifices. So Judaism to some extent had to be re-invented in the absence of the temple, and the rabbis who kind of re-invented it, re-defined it, determined how we should go on from here, were the tradition coming from the Pharisees"); *Honey From the Rock* (2007) ("There [at a Carthusian monastery] I became aware of how the Catholic Church was itself an outgrowth of Judaism. It was unavoidably obvious, given how the monks spent many hours a day chanting the Old Testament psalms, with their continual references to Israel, Zion, Jerusalem, the Jewish Patriarchs, and the Jewish people, visibly identifying with the Israel, and the Jews, of the psalms"); *Judaism from a Catholic Perspective* (2008); E. Michael Jones, "Salvation and the Jews," *Culture Wars*, February 2004, p.38 ("Since the Catholic Church is now Israel, Jews can only find their completion as Jews by becoming Catholics. This much is in Schoeman's book [*Salvation Is From the Jews*]. The converse of that statement, however, does not get expressed. The Jews who reject Christ now prepare the way for the coming of the anti-Christ every bit as much as the faithful Jews prepared the way for the coming of the real Christ"); Robert A. Sungenis, "Judaizers in the Catholic Church; An Analysis of the Ministries of David Moss and Roy Schoeman," *Culture Wars*, November 2005, p.28 ("Schoeman makes the claim that supersessionism 'has… recently been definitively rejected by the Church.' Strong words, indeed. In canonical circles, 'definitively' usually carries the connotation of defined dogma. Seemingly unbothered by the inherent contradiction he has created in Church protocol by pitting 'two-thousand years' of Church teaching as something that is now 'recently…rejected,' Schoeman proceeds to give us his proof texts in a tersely worded footnote. One would think that, for such a 'definitive' rejection of two-millennia of Church teaching Schoeman would have an arsenal of dogmatic statements to prove his case. In fact he has none, and the few non-dogmatic sources he cites do not say what Schoeman wishes they would say. He cites 'Vatican II's *Nostra Aetate*' as his first source for the 'definitive rejection' of supersessionism, but fails to cite any statements from the document supporting his contention. For those who know *Nostra Aetate*, the reason why becomes readily apparent: *Nostra Aetate* does nor contain any statements that deny the two-thousand year old teaching of supersessionism, let alone do so 'definitively'… Schoeman also cites three speeches of John Paul II…There is absolutely nothing saying that supersessionism has been rejected by the Church, and nor would we expect to see any, for it is a defined dogma of the Church"); Raymond A. Kevane, "An Open Letter to the Hebrew-Catholic Conference," *Culture Wars*, February 2006, p.8; Robert A. Sungenis, "The Old Covenant: Revoked or Not Revoked?: 'Jews and Christians: A Journey of Faith,'" *Culture Wars*, January 2008, p.12; Robert A. Sungenis, "The Old Covenant is Revoked: The USCC Removes Heretical Sentence from Its Catechism," *Culture Wars*, October 2008, p.12; Robert A. Sungenis, "Is the SSPX Anti-Semitic?" *Culture Wars*, July/August 2009 ("Vatican II, although perhaps more emphatically than in the past, merely reiterated the same teaching that Catholic tradition maintained, namely 'neither all Jews indiscriminately at that time, nor Jews today can be charged with the crimes committed during [Christ's] passion' (*Nostra Aetate* 4), for in no official teaching, past or present, have the Jews ever been declared a 'deicide people' or blamed, as a race, for the death of Christ. The Catholic Church has consistently taught that it is not the Jews of today who are responsible for the death of Christ, but the Jewish leaders and their followers in 33 AD who instigated his murder. In fact, the New Testament implies that a majority of the Jews were involved in that instigation, even though it is said that they did so in 'ignorance' (Acts 3:17…)").

Schultz, Dutch (born Arthur Simon Flegenheimer) – mobster; b. 6 August 1901, The Bronx, New York City; c. 24 October 1935 (deathbed); d. 24 October 1935, Newark, New Jersey; born to German-Jewish immigrants, Herman and Emma Flegenheimer; when he was fourteen his father abandoned the family (throughout his life he was in denial about his father's action); left school to find work and at first did legitimate jobs; moved into crime and was sent to prison for burglary; got involved with mobsters and took on the name "Dutch Schultz"; during the Prohibition period he brought liquor and beer from Canada into New York City and became a wealthy man; worked in a speakeasy and gained a reputation for violence; became a partner in the firm and opened more operations with the profits; involved in conflict with rival gangs; other mobsters were murdered by him or on his orders; gained overall control; acquitted of tax evasion; after the end of Prohibition he found new sources of income from the numbers racket, and from extorting restaurant owners and workers; acquitted again of tax evasion charges; said to have had only one rule: "I don't make money off women or narcotics"; said by some to have converted to Catholicism at this time in order to better relations with Charlie "Lucky" Luciano (1897-1962), a rival mobster, but this is almost certainly untrue; he asked the Mafia Commission for permission to kill his enemy, U.S. Attorney Thomas Dewey (1902-1971), who had been appointed to break up the rackets; the Commission refused and decided to kill him (Schultz) instead; he and his main associates were shot by hitmen at the Palace Chophouse, Newark on 23 October 1935; taken to hospital where he was registered as a Jew; before surgery he was baptized and given the last rites at his request by a priest (Fr. Cornelius McInerney); died later the same day; his deathbed ramblings inspired works by a number of writers, notably *The Last Words of Dutch Schultz* (1970) by the Beat Generation author William S. Burroughs (1914-1997); buried in Gate of Heaven Cemetery, Westchester County, New York (at the request of his Orthodox Jewish mother, his coffin was draped with a talit, a traditional Jewish prayer shawl); outrage followed that such a notorious person had been permitted burial in sacred ground; he was estimated to be worth $7 million when he died, but no trace of the money was ever found (it was supposedly in a safe, buried by him in upstate New York, but has never been recovered, despite the annual meeting of treasure hunters in the Catskills!); see John A. Toomey, SJ, "The Death and Burial of Dutch Schultz," *America*, November 1935, p.128; Paul Sann, *Kill the Dutchman!: The Story of Dutch Schultz* (1970) ("The controversy surrounding Schultz hardly ended with his burial, of course. The funeral was barely over when the great debate began: what right did that man have to be laid to rest with the rites of the Catholic Church? John A. Toomey, S.J., took up the problem in the Catholic weekly, *America,* noting at the outset that there were thousands of people saying that 'if a guy like that can go to heaven there won't be anybody in hell.' But the article went on:

'To these thousands, glaring contradictions appeared to be involved. Here was the Catholic Church, which always had impressed on her children a horror of even the slightest sin; which had ceaselessly warned them concerning the danger of presuming on the chances of a death-bed conversion, which had ever inculcated high ideals in asceticism, in selflessness, in heroic virtue; here was the Catholic Church beckoning into her fold a man who through his entire life had represented everything which the Church abhorred and condemned.

Dutch Schultz with the angels! Dutch Schultz whose beer-trucks once rumbled over the Bronx, whose gorillas blustered through the sidewalks! Dutch Schultz associating with the holy saints in Heaven! He to get the same reward as valiant souls who have clung to the Faith through a ceaseless hurricane of trial and temptation. It seemed more than unjust. It seemed ridiculous, preposterous, almost laughable.

But it may not be so laughable after all. There were a number of things not taken into account by the... judges. One little thing they missed completely was the fact that there is just One in the entire universe Who is capable of accurately judging the complex skein of a man's life. The influence of bad example, of environment in general: of heredity; the lack of religious training; the exact strength of temptations... That One is God Almighty. No one else can even begin to do the job.

Another element that appeared to be fumbled was the interesting truth that the time of mercy for sinners does not expire until the moment of death; that there is no crime and no series of crime...which God will not forgive, this side of eternity, to the truly contrite of heart.

The dynamic power of Divine Grace to move the most obdurate heart to repentance was also omitted from the consideration. Indeed, the intimate and essential connection of grace with final salvation is widely overlooked... Other important bits of evidence were neglected as the clamorous verdict was reached: for example, the fact that nothing happens in this world without the permission of God. The reason Schultz was not killed instantly was because it was God's will that he be not killed instantly, and so he was conscious the morning after, and able to receive the grace of conversion, a grace that comes from God.

If Schultz's conversion was sincere, it means that God gave

him a last chance to save his soul, and that Dutch took advantage of the offer. It does not mean that God, or His Church, condoned the evil life of Schultz but that...God judged he should be given another opportunity to save his soul...

After all, Heaven belongs to God. If He wants Dutch Schultz to be there, it is difficult to see what we can do about it. Perhaps, instead of worrying about Schultz a somewhat more profitable occupation for us would be to do a little more worrying about our own salvation - to make sure we get there ourselves. We may not be given the opportunity for a death-bed repentance. Relatively few are given that chance.

And whether we meet Schultz in Heaven or not, there is one individual we are certain to encounter there; a gentleman who was in more or less the same line as Schultz - the Thief who, as he was dying on Calvary, asked the Man on the next Cross for forgiveness and who heard that Man say: 'This day thou shalt be with Me in Paradise.'

The penitent thief and the Man on the Cross at Calvary also were called to mind by the Right Reverend Monsignor John L. Belford, pastor of the Roman Catholic Church of the Nativity in Brooklyn, in a defense of Father McInerney's ministrations to Schultz. In an article for *The Monitor*, a church publication, Monsignor Belford decried 'the cries of shame...from Catholics and non-Catholics...who thought it a crime to administer the sacraments of the church to a man who had been all his life not only a stranger to religion but a particularly vile and violent criminal,' and he went on: 'Was Dutch Schultz worse than the penitent thief? He was a criminal. He seemed unworthy of the least consideration. Perhaps he was. But who will close the gates of mercy? The fact that he received the sacraments is no guarantee that he received God's forgiveness.

If he was not really penitent, the priest's absolution had no effect. Yet that priest did right when he baptized or absolved him. The dying man said he was sorry he had offended God; he declared he would do all in his power to avoid sin in the future and to repair the harm he had done. If he meant this, God ratified the action of the minister.

But, remember, the sinner contracts two debts; the debt of guilt and the debt of pain. God can forgive the former and insist on payment of the latter. He could forgive Schultz and yet keep him in purgatory until the end of time to atone, so far as man can atone, for his wickedness"); Victor R. Claveau, MJ, "Stealing Heaven," *Lay Witness Archive*, March/April 2007 (also at *cuf.org*) Above all, these critics forgot one story from the Bible: the story of the good thief. To that dying criminal on Calvary, the Son of God Himself promised paradise. Christ's Church continues to do what Christ did. Sacred Scripture tells us that two criminals were crucified together with Christ, one on His right, the other on His left. Both were evildoers. Both had committed serious crimes. Both were guilty of death. Even while hanging on the cross, onc of them, the criminal to the left, joined the Jews in jeering at Jesus. He shouted: 'Are you not the Christ? Save yourself and us!' The 'good thief' to the right rebuked him: 'Do you not fear God, since you are under the same sentence of condemnation? And we indeed justly, for we are receiving the due reward of our deeds; but this man has done nothing wrong.' Then, turning to Jesus, he said: 'Jesus, remember me when you come into your kingly power.' And Jesus said to him: 'Truly, I say to you, today you will be with me in Paradise' (see Lk. 23:39–43).

To the good thief on His right, Jesus promised the kingdom of heaven. He promised He would, this day, lead this condemned man into paradise, and to heaven when He ascended forty days later (Eph. 4:8). In the twinkling of an eye, salvation - the goal and prize of life - was given to this criminal. As someone has said, he was a robber to the last; he even stole heaven…

Our Lord saw the contrite heart of the thief who defended Him publicly as they hung side-by-side on Golgotha. He invited that penitent criminal into His own home in heaven, even in a moment of pain and agony as he was being reviled and blasphemed. This is the God of whom we read: 'God so loved the world that he gave his only-begotten Son, that those who believe in him may not perish, but may have life everlasting. For God did not send his Son into the world in order to judge the world, but that the world might be saved through him' (Jn. 3:16).

The good thief, traditionally called Dismas, received Christ's precious promise because he cooperated with the great grace that God gave him. In a moment, a truly great sinner became a saint. In the face of this fact, how can any sinner despair? To every one of us, God gives His bountiful grace. We must follow the good thief's model of repentance and his cooperation with grace. And then, in cooperation with that grace, we must strive to live a life of faith, to follow Christ").

Schwartz, Herbert Thomas – philosopher; b. 4 December 1903, New York; d. 1980; Jewish, but from a non-religious background; his mother ordered all her children, "You must be geniuses!"; equally at home in mathematics, literary criticism, poetry and science, while gaining distinction in music and in philosophy; dropped out of medical school to gain a PhD in Philosophy at Columbia University; Professor of Music at University of Chicago (since the Philosophy Department would not take him); worked with Mortimer Adler (see above) and Robert Maynard Hutchins; later at Laval University, Canada (developed there his view that the underlying reason for modern secularism was the failure of modern fatherhood to provide loving, forgiving, and wise governance, hence the remedy was spiritual direction by a true Father); sometime Professor of Philosophy at Xavier University, Cincinnati; disciple of the work of St. Thomas Aquinas whose influence led to his conversion to the Catholic faith (his second wife Charleen, a Protestant, also converted); friend of the then Kenneth Simon (see below under Rev. M. Raphael Simon) and of Herbert Ratner (see above); direct source of the conversion of some twenty non-religious Jewish students; member of the Dominican Third Order; see "God's Love Breaks Through," in John A. O'Brien (ed), *The Road to Damascus, Vol. V: Where Dwellest Thou* (1956) ("If there is a God, there is no rational reason why He could not have established a Church. In fact, that is the only possible definition of a true Church. If there is a true Church at all, *it is the Church that God established.* And if He did establish it, how in the world could it work to carry out God's will without divine guidance? Thus, viewed rationally, no Church could possibly be the true Church unless it claimed divine guidance…

The true God, because He is true, demands subjection. He demands subjection, not to lord it over His creature, but because He wills the perfection of His creature; and the perfection of a creature is to be subject to his Creator just as the perfection of an instrument, say an automobile, is to be subject to the will and impulse of the driver…So the true God gives Himself to you only on condition that you give yourself to Him.

The false god whispers words of flattery, lying to you that 'you shall be as gods.' The true God tells you deep within your heart that you are acceptable to Him because He made you to His own image and likeness and died for you, but that everything you have done without Him is sin and corruption, that it will have to change, that the old man must die. 'He that hateth his life in this world, keepeth it unto life eternal.' He doesn't tell this to you in words you can hear or imagine; He tells it to you by giving you the grace to see it in yourself.

If you want to see this knowledge of your own corruption operating, ask yourself why you are so concerned with what people think about you; why you are so upset when you are not appreciated or perhaps slighted; why are you so exalted when things go your way, depressed when they don't. Has God changed in any way? Does He love you the less because you have failed for all your efforts? There is an old Jewish proverb which my mother used to quote from time to time: 'We try to convince the world of what we are not; of what we are, the world is already long convinced.' What I am trying to say is that you come to God when you realize that 'it is hard to kick against the goad.' It is an awful strain trying to convince yourself, and everyone else, that you are perfect. It is much easier (at bottom it is always easier to do things the right way) to admit the awful truth…

The workings of grace were brought home to me in a startling and dramatic manner long after I had entered the Church. There was a certain woman pianist, who had come to symbolize everything that I admired in pianistic art... She represented everything I wanted to accomplish in the art, which I secretly despaired of ever accomplishing…Well, after I had come into the Church and many years after I had given up the idea of a musical career I happened to meet another young pianist, Jewish and a personal friend of the woman pianist I so admired. He was not Catholic, but she was, as I vaguely knew. Then he told me something about her which I shall never forget: this woman spent a whole hour before an altar of the Blessed Mother before each recital and after the recital she rushed back to that same altar to bring Mary all her flowers. I cannot tell you the impact this made on me. It was as if Mary herself had told me, through her child, that it was she I was pursuing all the time. More accurately I should say it was Mary's way of making plain to me that *she* was pursuing *me* [the pianist was the legendary Brazilian, Guiomar Novaes (1895-1979)]…

It is natural to think that one comes into the Church through elaborate proofs for the existence of God, the historicity of Christ, and other proofs of that character. But if my experience is at all typical, that is not the way it works. Actually I had never had any difficulty in accepting God. In fact, I do not remember a time when I disbelieved in God. My problem was not one of accepting God: rather the problem was of God accepting me – or, more accurately, my realizing how much God accepted me. And I don't really think I am at all peculiar in this…[T]he effect of sin is to cause us not to want to know God because the very hardness caused by sin hardens us to the knowledge of the divine mercy. The problem then in our relation to God, since sin is so universal ('He who says he is without sin is a liar,' St. John tells us), is not so much one of knowing God as it is of being convinced that God can love us knowing just what *we* are. That is why it always seems a little comical the way some young Catholic students will get all worked up about proving God exists to an unhappy pagan who is running away from God as fast as he can because he is so scared. The problem is not to accept God, but to realize that He accepts us. Without communicating the loving mercy of God, proving his existence is tantamount to sending the unfortunate fugitive to hell").

Searle, George Mary, CSP – priest and astronomer; b. 27 June 1839, London; c. 15 August 1862; d. 7 July 1918, New York; father an American Unitarian; mother English and an Anglican; baptized by a clergyman of the Established Church; family moved to Boston, Massachusetts, in 1840; soon orphaned; raised as a Unitarian by a wealthy uncle; educated at Harvard University (BA 1857; MA 1860); worked as astronomy "computer" at several observatories; in 1858 he discovered the asteroid 55 Pandora; assistant professor of mathematics, at the Naval School in Newport, Rhode Island, 1862-1864; assistant at the Harvard University Observatory; spent time in Rome and entered the Paulist Order 1868; ordained to the priesthood 25 March 1871; Professor of Theology and Science at the Paulist seminaries in both New York and Washington, D.C., designed the ceiling of St. Paul the Apostle church in New York (the Paulist mother church) with its depiction of the stars and planets as they were positioned on 25 January 1885, the night of the church's dedication; Professor of Mathematics and Astronomy at the Catholic University of America, Washington, D.C.; founded the school's observatory and was awarded the University's first doctorate in 1896; fourth Superior General, Paulist Fathers, 1904-1909, succeeding George Deshon (see above); at University of California, Berkeley, 1910-1911; his computation of the orbit and reappearance of Halley's comet in 1910 was considered definitive by American astronomers; author of seven books; wrote many scientific and apologetic articles; buried at St. Paul the Apostle Church, Manhattan, New York (church basement); see *Elements of Geometry* (1877); *Plain Facts for Fair Minds* (1895) (a best-selling work on Catholic apologetics) ("There [is] no conflict between *science* and religion; but I do not mean by 'science' all the crude or half-baked theories which scientific men may put forwards. I do not blame them for putting them forward; theories, or what are called working hypotheses, are necessary means for the advancement of science. But no genuine scientific man claims that his hypotheses, put forward and intended to be used as a means of directing his own observation or experiments, and those of others, is the final truth. It is put up with the expectation that it will be to a great extent demolished, or even perhaps so battered out of shape that it will in the end be hardly recognizable...

[T]he Church has no quarrel with genuine science, with that which is legitimately directed by truly scientific methods to the attainment of truth. She cannot have such a quarrel; for she believes in the truth of what she preaches, and she knows, what all having the use of reason must know, that truth cannot contradict truth. But she has a quarrel with those of whom I have spoken, who announce as certain truth what they ought to know well has not been proved to be so. Nor does she prohibit any Catholics who are competent to undertake scientific investigation from doing so. She places absolutely no obstacle in the way of their penetrating into all the facts of nature as it stands, or of their considering the probable indications as to its past history, or of their weighing actual historical testimony.

She does indeed caution them against being swept away from their moorings to the known truths of religion by the temporary appearances of a science as yet incomplete…

Also she warns those weak in faith, or intellectually incompetent, against venturing on what to them personally might be dangerous ground. And she may also, at certain stages of scientific inquiry prohibit the general and indiscriminate reading of scientific works in some particular department, on account of the practical impossibility of discernment at the moment between the false and the true, the doubtful and the certain, the theory and the fact. Scientific men themselves, on purely scientific grounds, may often be of the same mind. It is well, sometimes, for those not competent to judge thoroughly of a subject, to abstain from meddling with it; it may do them more harm than good; give them more false and confused ideas than true and clear ones. Sometimes the words of the poet are specially applicable: 'A little learning is a dangerous thing; drink deep, or taste not the Pierian spring.'

The difficulty [in this matter of the so-called conflict between religion and science] has been much magnified by some of our scientific friends who want to force an issue. In point of fact, there are not by any means so many even apparent divergencies between science and the Catholic religion as they, in their ignorance of the latter, suppose. Evolution, for instance, in quite an extended sense, is not condemned by Catholic dogma; when you assert that man was developed, soul as well as body, out of a monkey, that is quite another thing. Again, the Church is not committed to believe that the universe, or even this planet, was made in six days of twenty-four hours; nor that Adam lived just exactly so many years ago. If you say the world grew of itself, or that matter existed from all eternity, or that man has been here millions of years; that again is something quite different. But you notice that these things which the Church cannot accept are nothing more than mere hypotheses or private opinions, not scientific results…

[N]o Catholic scientist well instructed in his religion finds anything in religion or science which tempts him to give up either. And there are great numbers of Catholic scientific men, and have been in all ages; *How to Become a Catholic* (1905); "A Possible

Calendar," *Catholic World*, 1 November 1905; essay in Georgina Pell Curtis (ed), *Some Roads to Rome in America* (1909), p.363 ("I made up my mind to get this book [the *Catechism of the Council of Trent*] and see what the Roman Church had to say for itself…I read the book at night, after everybody else had gone to bed. It may seem strange to say it, but what surprised me was its 'Evangelical' tone. I had a general idea that the Roman Church placed the means of salvation in works and outward observances; but here I found the Blood of Christ and His merits put forward as the one price of our redemption, as forcibly as in any book, I had ever read or any sermon I had ever heard. What added much to its weight was that I felt sure this was really Catholic teaching. Controversial books might be traps to catch Protestants, in which the genuine Roman doctrine was manipulated or partly concealed; but here was a real official book, meant for Catholics themselves.

However, I got controversial books, plenty of them, and read them in the same way…[A]t last my convictions became so strong, at least of the falsity of Protestantism, that I could not continue to teach in Sunday-school…This was a critical time; for the alternative now presented was between the Catholic Church and the abandonment of Christianity as a revelation altogether. I had followed the historical road, as it may be called, and had seen plainly enough by this time that Christianity, if it was anything more than mere human speculation, was Catholicity. All this time I had never spoken to a single Catholic on the subject of religion, and hardly knew one to whom I could speak. It never occurred to me to go to a priest till after sixteen months from my first start, when my mind was made up as far as it could be; by which I mean that, though I did not believe, I saw no reason for not believing. The argument was as complete, as mere argument could be, to prove the divine construction of the wonderful edifice at the door of which I sat waiting; but practically I was not quite convinced or ready to enter. The grace of God was what I needed; and it came through reading some of the 'Annals of the Propagation of the Faith,' I think. It moved me to act, to go to a priest and ask to be received. The veil was still between my eyes and the truth as Catholics see it; what might be behind that veil I could not tell; there was no way of telling but by trying; it was, as Cardinal Newman says, 'a leap in the dark,' but one that reason, conscience, and the voice of God required. It must come in this way, I think, to all converts who have the common Protestant traditions.

I rang the priest's door-bell; he himself came to the door. 'I want,' I said, 'to be a Catholic.' I thought that was all; that he would do what was needed to make me one without delay. But of course he put me under instruction; gave me books, which I already was pretty well filled up with; but his instructions, his answers to my questions, did more good than all the books he could have furnished. But still the old practical obstacle remained till the very end: 'What if the priest himself be insincere? How do I know but that some things are being kept from me which will come out when it is too late?' Modern miracles made a special difficulty, not one that was going to turn me back now, for my mind was made up to go behind that veil and see. But did Catholics really believe in them? I was almost afraid to ask. The miracle of St. Januarius was a thing I had to bring up, and I half-expected to hear that, at least, dismissed, as a superstition. And then did Father - himself really abstain from meat on Friday, or was this only something palmed off on the people? Strange to say, even after I was received, though very strict about the matter, I was shame faced about it, and did not know whether Catholics were really expected to be so"); *Talks for the Times: Indifferentism, Revelation, the Catholic Church and Science, the Friend of True Progress, the Purpose of Life* (1912); *Why the Catholic Church Cannot Accept Socialism* (1913); *The Truth About Christian Science* (1916); *New Catholic Encyclopedia.*

Seattle, Chief – Duwamish chief; b. ca.1780-1786, on or near Blake Island, Washington; c. 1848 (Olympia, Washington; given the baptismal name Noah); d. 7 June 1866, Suquamish reservation, Port Madison, Washington; his mother Sholeetsa was Duwamish, his father Schweabe was chief of the Suquamish tribe; at a young age became renowned as a leader and warrior; married first to La-Dalia, who died after bearing a daughter, Angeline (1820-1896); he married secondly Oiahl (d. 1852) (two sons and three daughters from this marriage); it was after one of his sons died that he took comfort in Catholicism; he and his family were baptized and religion became a large part of his life; when the white people arrived and his people were driven from their grounds, he negotiated an accommodation with them through Dr. David S. Maynard, thought of as the founding father of Seattle; the city of Seattle was named after him; his funeral was attended by hundreds of white people; buried according to the rites of the Catholic Church with Indian customs added; his daughter Angeline (known as Kikisabku and as Princess Angeline) became famous (she was a devout Catholic, frequently seated on the sidewalk reciting her beads); see Clarence B. Bagley, "Chief Seattle and Angeline," *Washington Historical Quarterly*, October 1931 ("Through the efforts of the French missionaries Seattle became a Catholic and inaugurated regular morning and evening prayers in his tribe, which were continued by his people after his death"); Eva G. Anderson, *Chief Seattle* (1944); Warren Jefferson, *The World of Chief Seattle, How Can One Sell the Air* (2001); *ANB*.

Seawell, Molly Elliot (born Mary Elliot Seawell) (*pseud.* Foxcroft Davis; Vera Sapoukhin) – novelist, short story writer and historian; b. 12 October 1860, Gloucester County, Virginia; c. 1878; d. 15 November 1916; her father John Tyler Seawell (d. 1880) was a lawyer and nephew of President John Tyler (1790-1862); brought up as an Episcopalian at the family's secluded plantation home; mainly educated at home on history, encyclopedias, Shakespeare and the Romantic poets; not permitted to read a novel until the age of seventeen; made many journeys to Europe, including Russia; finally settled in Washington, D.C.; entertained artists and writers there; popular and widely read writer in her time; wrote forty books; many essays and political columns for newspapers; her historical romances draw on her Catholic faith and are notable for their characterization; in 1891 she wrote an article in the *New York Critic*, in which she put forward the theory "That in the nobler part of human nature - the emotions and the affections - women are superior to men. In the inferior part of human nature - the mere intellect - men are superior to women" (this provoked much discussion); she opposed the woman suffrage movement; in poor health for a number of years; unmarried; buried in Greenmount Cemetery, Baltimore; see *Maid Marian* (1886); *Hale-Weston* (1889); *Little Jarvis* (1890); *Throckmorton; A Novel* (1890); *Midshipman Paulding* (1891); "On the Absence of the Creative Faculty in Women," *New York Critic*, 29 November 1891; *Paul Jones* (1892); *Children of Destiny* (1893) (shows familiarity with St. Thomas Aquinas); *Decatur and Somers* (1893); *The Berkeleys and their Neighbors* (1894); *A Strange, Sad Comedy* (1895); *The Sprightly Romance of Marsac* (1896); *The History of Lady Betty Stair* (1897); *Twelve Naval Captains* (1897); *A Virginian Cavalier* (1898); *The Rock of the Line* (1898); *The Loves of the Lady Arabella* (1899); *The House of Egremont: A Novel* (1900) (includes a Jesuit priest-martyr); *The Fortunes of Fifi* (1903); *The Whirl* (1909); essay in Georgina Pell Curtis (ed), *Some Roads to Rome in America* (1909), p.376 ("In the old country house, the Shelter, in Gloucester County, Virginia, where I grew up, there was a typical eighteenth century library. It had been partly selected for my great-grandfather by Thomas Jefferson, when he was minister to France. The eighteenth century philosophers were all well represented in it, and also much English history, of the period when history was merely the expression of individual prejudices.

Everything in this library was strongly anti-Catholic. Contrary to this, however, my father and mother had much respect for the Catholic Church, my mother being especially inclined that way. I was allowed great liberty in reading, and from a very early age I read these books, which, of course, I only half understood. I soon noticed, however, that the Catholics were always represented as being in the wrong, in every religious and political collision. This seemed to my childish mind to be unjust, and I began to have a kind of sympathy with the Catholics.

When I was about fourteen, with a very precocious mind, I came across Macaulay's *Essays*, which I devoured. Macaulay's denunciation of the Anglican Church made a deep impression upon me, as my family were all nominally Episcopalians, and my associations were solely with that communion. The two essays - one on Von Ranke's *History of the Popes*, and the other on Henry Hallam's *Constitutional History* - suddenly gave me a new view of religious questions. I began to see that the Church which Macaulay said would be in full vigor 'when the traveller from New Zealand, shall, in the midst of a vast solitude, sit on a broken arch of London Bridge to sketch the ruins of St. Paul's,' was an enormous and living fact. I also began to appreciate dimly that in my own country the steady advance in education and enlightenment was closely followed by a corresponding advance in Catholicism.

Then, after Macaulay, I made acquaintance with Thackeray, whose leanings toward Catholicism in his later life were so marked as to give rise to the report that he died a Catholic. Certain it is, he had an extraordinary knowledge of Catholic ritual and language, which could only have been acquired by often attending Catholic worship; indeed, he is said to have habitually frequented Catholic Churches when he was on the Continent. It will be remarked that Thackeray seemed to have a grudge against the Anglican Church, and like Anthony Trollope, he commonly made the Anglican clergy in his books appear as being the most ridiculous, if not the most odious, of men. Witness the Reverend Charles Honeyman, in *The Newcomes*, etc. His favorite characters, if his art permitted, were likely to turn up in Catholic Cathedrals, or even to be Catholics, while Father Holt, the Jesuit, is a most sympathetic portrait.

After having readily imbibed from Thackeray, as from Macaulay, his admiration and sympathy for Catholicism, I read Thackeray's noble tribute to the Catholic Church - 'the stately structure of eighteen centuries, the mighty and beautiful Roman Catholic Church.' The effect upon a young mind of these splendid tributes, from two great masters of English literature, may be imagined. I began to make inquiries about the Church and to read all I could find on the subject, from my fifteenth to my eighteenth year. I asked Protestants many puzzling questions, to which they could give me no answer, such as the meaning of Christmas - 'Christ's Mass' - which dated back into the shadow and traditions of the first Century after Christ. None of these Protestant friends could explain to me why they celebrated Christ's Mass without a Mass, and why the same prayer book which contained a special service for Christmas, also contained a declaration that the Mass was blasphemous and idolatrous.

These questions, from Catholic books and teachings, received a prompt and logical answer. Thus I found myself a Catholic, by the operations of my own mind, under God; and when I announced my intention, at the age of eighteen, of joining the Catholic Church, I had never even conversed with a priest. I now put myself for a few weeks, under ecclesiastical instruction, and was then received into the Church.

The spirit of inquiry which made me a Catholic has never left me, and from that day to this I have been a constant reader of Speculative Philosophy and the history of religion. In the course of this reading, I have grown stronger in the Catholic faith. It has proved, according to my lights, to be the one practical system of philosophy which gives men mental peace, and which has, from the beginning, fed and clothed the poor, succored the orphan, taught the ignorant, and reformed the sinner. I have great respect for all Christian bodies; but, in their practical aspect, the Catholic Church as compared with the other Christian religions of the world, is like a regular army, ready for service anywhere, to a local militia"); *The Ladies Battle* (1911) (brings out her opposition to feminism and woman suffrage; she dedicated the book to "those of my countrywomen who think for themselves." She maintained that granting women the right to vote would result in a "general revolution" and an "overturning of the social order"); essay in Georgina Pell Curtis, *Beyond the Road to Rome* (1914), p.347; *Diary of Molly Elliot Seawell 1900-1916* (1990); Thomas L. Long, "A Profile of Virginia's Molly Elliot Seawell," *community.tncc.edu* ("In 1891 Seawell published an essay 'On the Absence of the Creative Faculty in Women' that created a debate in the pages of *The Critic* for several months. Through articles and in a book, *The Ladies' Battle* (1911), she argued against women's right to vote. Sally Mitchell observes that Seawell 'attacked suffragists as women "born with socialistic and communistic rather than domestic tendencies" who 'have an antagonism to men.' While these sentiments may surprise us, they might not shock us when we remember that similar claims have been made in the last twenty years about the National Organization for Women, the Equal Rights Amendment, and the feminist movement generally.

Molly Elliot Seawell's essay in *The Critic* begins, 'It may be stated, as a general proposition, that no woman has ever done anything in the intellectual world, which has had the germ of immortality. This is equivalent to saying that the power to create is entirely lacking in women.' Clearly she is arguing from a particular definition of 'creative,' which she relates to 'genius' and the contributions of men, as distinct from mere 'talent.' In addition, she argues her case from the traditional canon of 'works of genius' of the Western world, whose constructors we might call today 'dead European males.' While she admits the talent of Sappho, George Eliot, George Sand, and Mme. de Stael, their renown was temporary: 'It is a singular fact, that all women whose claims to genius have been seriously considered, have had an enormous contemporary reputation - and it is strikingly true that posterity has not in a single instance endorsed this contemporary verdict.' Even Jane Austen, who comes closer than any woman to threatening the male artistic hegemony, lacks the 'universality which is the mark of genius,' a universality evident in Shakespeare, for instance. The woman artist, therefore, cannot create; 'she can only describe, and hence her work must always lack the catholicity of genius.' She acknowledges the claim that women may simply have lacked the opportunity for creative action. But she asserts that women have been putting pen to paper as long as men and that civilizations first give women the leisure that creative action requires. Miss Seawell goes on to dismiss women's contributions to music, painting, technology: 'For thousands of years women did all the baking and washing and sewing done on this planet - and yet every contrivance to lighten their labor has been put into their hands by men...women left to themselves would have remained in utter barbarism'"); *ANB.*

Senior, John – teacher and Catholic thinker; b. 1923; c. 14 April 1960 (Holy Thursday; received along with his family); d. 8 April 1999; grew up in rural Long Island; sight of social injustice as a youth led him to Marxism; educated at Columbia University (studied under Mark Van Doren), where he saw the importance of religion in literature; in the late 1950s he found the realist philosophy of being of St. Thomas Aquinas, which greatly influenced his conversion from Episcopalianism to the Catholic Church; taught at Bard and Hofstra Colleges, and Cornell University; then at University of Wyoming 1961-1967; moved to the University of Kansas in 1967, where he became renowned as a teacher of Humanities and Latin; with two other professors, Dr. Dennis Quinn and Dr. Frank Nelick (both converts), he launched the Pearson Integrated Humanities Program in 1970 (motto: *Nascantur in admiratione*, Let them be born in wonder); this had a great impact on students through teaching the Great Books of Western Civilization; he understood that Christian culture is the seedbed of the Faith; some 150 students entered the Catholic Church under his guidance (included Bishop James Conley (see above)); encouraged others to visit the Benedictine monastery of Fontgombault in France, and a number entered the noviciate; seven persevered in the monastic life and were among the thirteen founders of Our Lady of the Annunciation Monastery, Clear Creek, Oklahoma; retired in 1983 because of a severe heart condition; see *The Way Down and Out* (1959); *The Death of Christian Culture* (1978) (reissued by his son, Andrew Senior, in 2008) ((1) "The best of us are prone to sophistry when an obvious truth contradicts a strong desire. Recent ecumenical commissions from various churches have tried to create approaches to unity by reconstructing their articles of faith so as to make room for contradictory articles of faith held by others. Protestants and Catholics can both keep and give up their identities at the same time. Jacques Maritain, for example, speaking of a declaration of the Council of Florence notoriously obnoxious to any convergence of doctrine, says:

'What matters here is the declaration itself, not the manner in which one understood it in that epoch...according to the mentality of the epoch, without having been conscious of the ambiguity...It is with the time that the ambiguity in question appeared - and at the same stroke the true sense in which the declaration must he taken. There has therefore been a mutation, not with regard to the declaration itself, but with regard to the manner in which those who formulated it understood it. The declaration is infallibly true (provided it is rightly understood).'

Surely no Protestant in his right mind will accept an argument like this as the price of peace, because the whole Christian revelation, church authority, all authority, the noble mind of Maritain, and reason itself are here overthrown. 'Words,' said the Mad Hatter to Alice, 'mean exactly whatever I say they mean.' Go back to start! Begin again. We are here at the first of the first principles. A definition that includes its contradictory is not a definition at all. And any agreed statement by theologians who think this way is a trap. You will be signing a contract with a huckster who tomorrow will not be held to the bargain he struck according to the mentality of today. Peace at the price of one's reason can only be that 'evil peace' St. Augustine speaks of as the violent enforcement of injustice. No. It is very much in the interest of everyone that clear distinctions be kept. The current defection of Catholic theologians from their own explicit doctrines is the worst setback for Protestants since they took up the puerilities of the Higher Criticism. If we are to love one another as ourselves, it is one another we must love, not ourselves pretending to be others, all the while pretending others to be ourselves. It is easy for men of good will (and bad will) to come together if they affirm contradictions. 'The declaration is infallibly true (provided it is rightly understood).' That is either a truism - anything must be rightly understood—or what used to be called 'Jesuitical.' Understood by whom? Gospels, Epistles, the Law and the Prophets, creeds, confessions - all these are infallibly true if 'rightly understood' according to the ideals of the French Revolution and the mind of Maritain...

Infallible? Such music hath a dying *fall.* The only rational way for Protestants and Catholics to get along together is to practice the difficult virtue of tolerance - not to falsifytheirclaimsbyambiguities..." (2) And for the whole of Christian evidence...we must finally ask which is more likely, that, for example, there really is life after death or that Jesus lied. We have all memorized this answer long since. It is contained in the Act of Faith: 'We believe these truths because Thou hast revealed them Who canst neither deceive nor be deceived.' If anyone else revealed them, Hume would he right. But who is being reasonable? Which is more likely? Let us above all be reasonable and choose the likelier course. Which is more likely? That a man could be God or that Jesus - when at His trial He expressly made that claim and went on to suffer and die on the Cross for it - that Jesus told the truth and nothing but the truth? As Chesterton summed the case up in a phrase, a non-Christian has got to believe that Christ - author of the Sermon on the Mount, this man Whom we come to know so well in the course of His history in the New Testament and in the figures of the Old - that this man was at the same time either a liar or a lunatic. Now let us appeal to experience, as Hume would have us do. What is our experience of liars and lunatics? Do they speak sermons on the mount? There are men who claim to be God - they are for the most part in asylums. Are they anything like Him? And if, on the basis of a totally irrational prejudice that no miracle can possibly be true despite your experience, you pick the New Testament apart, ascribing this to truth and that to someone else's lies or lunacy, you will discover in the end that the more you tear it down the more it will cohere and that the Christ of the trial is the same as the Christ of the sermons, that the Christ of the beautiful maxims cannot be torn from the Christ of the miracles, and that the maxims you cannot deny as being beautiful and good and sane are of a piece with the harsher maledictions that repel you because to avoid them you would have to change your life. You cannot evade [the] case by higher criticism. The Apostles, though they knew Him directly and personally, had a time as hard as you believing the ultimate Christian fact, and with them, and with Doubting Thomas touching His wounds, you have to say, like the consequences or not, 'My Lord and my God'"); *The Restoration of Christian Culture* (1983) (re-issued by Andrew Senior in 2008) ("Whatever we do in the political or social order, the indispensable foundation is prayer, the heart of which is the Holy Sacrifice of the Mass, the perfect prayer of Christ Himself, Priest and Victim, recreating in an unbloody manner the bloody, selfsame Sacrifice of Calvary. What is Christian culture? It is essentially the Mass. That is not my or anyone's opinion or theory or wish but the central fact of 2,000 years of history. Christendom, what secularists call Western Civilization, is the Mass and the paraphernalia which protect and facilitate it. All architecture, art, political and social forms, economics, the way people live and feel and think, music, literature —all these things when they are right are ways of fostering and protecting the Holy Sacrifice of the Mass. To enact a sacrifice, there must be an altar, an altar has to have a roof over it in case it rains; to reserve the Blessed Sacrament, we build a little House of Gold and over it a Tower of Ivory with a bell and a garden round it with the roses and lilies of purity, emblems of the Virgin Mary - *Rosa Mystica, Turris Davidica, Turris Eburnea, Domus Aurea,* who carried His Body and His Blood in her womb, Body of her body, Blood of her blood. And around the church and garden, where we bury the faithful dead, the caretakers live, the priests and religious whose work is prayer, who keep the Mystery of Faith in its tabernacle of music and words in the Office of the Church; and around them, the faithful who gather to worship and divide the other work that must be done in order to make the perpetuation of the Sacrifice possible – to raise the food and make the clothes and build and keep the peace so that generations to come may live for Him, so that the Sacrifice goes on even until the consummation of the world"); *Pale Horse, Easy Rider* (1992); *The Idea of a School* (1994); *The Remnants: The Final Essays of John Senior* (2013) Robert Wyer, "Magister Johannes: A Tribute to Dr. John Senior," *Edocere: A Resource for Catholic Education, edocere.org* ("Dr. Senior believed that the Catholic Faith represents the highest expression of truth. When he was led to the Church later in life, he embraced it with Pauline zeal and sought to steep himself in her wisdom and traditions. He loved the Latin language because it was her language; he loved St. Benedict as the patron of Europe and his monastic rule as the plow of Christendom; he loved the Fathers and St. Thomas Aquinas. He prayed the ancient Divine Office and preached the merits of the traditional Roman liturgy. He loved the Blessed Virgin Mary and all of her angels. He loved the Holy Sacrifice of the Mass because there he found Christ Himself. He led students to the baptismal font, to the altar as priests, to the bonds of good and fruitful marriages, and to the choirs of monasteries"); Dana Lorelle, "Where Wonder Cultivated Catholicity: Remmbering Kansas' Late, Great Integrated Humanities Program," *National Catholic Register*, 7 March 2005 ("Three decades ago, three professors at the University of Kansas sat in the front of a lecture hall and talked about books. Students weren't allowed to take notes, although the professors didn't mind if they knitted. They taught students the state song of Kansas, took them star gazing, spoke Latin out loud and introduced the freshmen and sophomores to classic literature and poetry.

The core of this program was its motto: *Nascantur in admiratione* (Let them be born in wonder). In the midst of this cultivation of wonder, through a diverse and often spontaneous curriculum, many of the students found their way to the Catholic Church.

Although the program has been gone for twenty-six years, its nine-year lifespan is worth considering in light of the challenges and opportunities facing Catholic higher education today.

The University of Kansas in the 1970s was, like many larger universities, a fine place to be an anonymous underclassman. That began to change when the Pearson Integrated Humanities Program, funded by a federal grant, set out to bring together freshmen and sophomores through bi-weekly gatherings to help them form a community. University administrators tapped Professor Dennis Quinn, known for his classes on Shakespeare, to direct the program. They gave him free rein over the curriculum and the selection of professors.

Quinn chose two close associates, professors John Senior and Frank Nelick of the university's classics department. Quinn and Nelick were converts to the Catholic faith; Senior, an Episcopalian, would later convert as well. 'We very quickly decided what we wanted to do,' Quinn recalls. 'We wanted to teach the Great Books, the classics, from the Greeks up through the Romans and through the Middle Ages and the Renaissance into the modern times.'

The first 100 students entered the program in 1970. The program was structured as a voluntary semester-long class open to all freshmen and sophomores. Each semester's itinerary was unique and each class was unpredictable. 'We didn't plan lectures,' Quinn says. 'We (the professors) had lunch together before the class started and on the way over to class I'd say, "Well, what are we going to talk about?" and they'd say, "I don't know. What book are we reading?"'

Often the curriculum diverged onto unexpected tangents. The professors, noticing that the students had no skill in formal ballroom dancing, organized an annual waltz. They took students to Ireland and Greece. They told stories, required the students to memorize poems and spoke of callings rather than careers. But the basis of the program was literature - and, beyond that, truth. Few students, the professors learned early on, professed any sort of belief in objective, absolute truth. To this Quinn would reply: 'Do you believe it's true that there's no truth?' They read Plato, Herodotus, the *Iliad* and the *Odyssey*, as well as classic books that touched on the Catholic faith without overtly promoting it. So why, Quinn wonders to this day, do so many former students name the Integrated Humanities Program - which only lasted from 1970 to 1979 - as the defining educational experience of their religious and professional lives?

Bishop Paul Coakley of the Diocese of Salina, Kansas, praised the ground-breaking program in the brief biography released upon his installation last December. 'It was an extraordinary experience, it was an extraordinary time and it was unquestionably the most significant educational experience of my life,' he said. 'Our professors taught as if they believed there was a truth and that that truth was knowable.'

Bishop Coakley was raised Catholic, but the Integrated Humanities Program, he says, played a role in securing his decision to enter the priesthood. 'In a certain sense, the focus was on educating the person, forming the person, not so much on training for a career,' he points out. 'It was a very good foundation for life, whether one entered a trade or a career or a religious vocation. Many people found their life's vocation as a result of that program.'

Some of these religious vocations were discerned at the Abbey of Notre Dame de Fontgombault in France, a popular student destination. While most enjoyed a sojourn at the Benedictine monastery's guesthouse before returning to Kansas, six stayed behind and took vows. In 1999, those six graduates returned to their homeland to establish a new Benedictine monastery, Annunciation Priory of Clear Creek in Oklahoma.

Among other Integrated Humanities Program alumni are farmers, vintners, calligraphers, educators, lawyers, magazine editors and many religious. Some, like David Whalen, associate provost of Hillsdale College in Michigan, call the program 'absolutely determinative' for their path in life. Specifically, says Whalen, the professors' focus on the three transcendentals - the true, the good and the beautiful - made an impact on his view on life. 'I give credit to that experience,' he adds, 'for opening my eyes to permanent truth.'

Besides the faith of the professors, the only Catholic connection was within the context of literature like St. Augustine's *Confessions* or the writings of Cardinal John Henry Newman. Those led to discussions of the faith, but, as Bishop Coakley points out, "How could you study *The Canterbury Tales* without a discussion of the Catholic Church or the Christian imagination?"

'The class was not a place where proselytizing occurred,' says Whalen, who re-embraced his Catholic faith while in college. 'People were not pressured to adopt a particular religion. The professors did not hide what they thought, but they didn't browbeat people about the Catholic religion.'

Still, students converted - by some accounts more than 100 - and, according to Quinn, not all the parents were happy about it. Of the professors' possible influence on the conversions, Quinn says, 'You teach what you are. Well, we were Catholic, and it came out without us talking about it at all.' Then again, Quinn reasons, perhaps the program created a community of close relationships where the Catholic faith could blossom. Bishop Coakley proposes a different rationale. 'You put people in touch with the true, the beautiful and the good and let the Holy Spirit work,' he says.

When the program underwent what Quinn has called a 'discreet and slow euthanasia' at the hands of university officials as the '70s drew to a close, Quinn returned to the English department. Nelick and Senior have since died. The question 'Why?' prompts several possible answers. Perhaps, as Quinn believes, 'It was a victim of its own success.' That success could have been the program's popularity and the jealousy it engendered in other departments. Or it could have been the disproportionate number of converts to the Catholic faith. But perhaps, like the ancient civilizations that produced the literature of the program, its time simply ran out.

Both Quinn and Whalen say no colleges today are doing what the Integrated Humanities Program did. While some Catholic grade schools and home-school curriculums have tried to incorporate facets of the program, often intermingling the educational philosophy with the Great Books approach, none, they believe, has recreated the program's atmosphere of wonder that proved so fertile for uncovering truth.

Whether any schools could emulate the Integrated Humanities Program with the same results today remains a question for the future. But Bishop Coakley believes that any such initiative must involve one component outside of man's control. 'It was the working of grace,' he says of the program's success. 'The years of the program were a special time of grace'"); Patrick Martin, "A Tribute to John Senior," *The Catholic Thing*, 9 April 2009 ("John Senior, like Socrates, had the uncanny ability to get young people to think, to wonder, and to change course in midstream. How he did this owed a great deal to his own sense of wonder and appreciation of God's presence in our lives"); Philippe Maxence, "John Senior: In Piam Memoriam," *Crisis*, 5 April 2012 ("'The restoration of reason presupposes that of love,' insists John Senior once more. There is, in truth, no other path. Caritas in Veritate!").

Seton, Saint Elizabeth Ann (*née* Bayley) – nun and founder of a religious order; b. 28 August 1774, New York City; c. 14 March 1805 (Ash Wednesday; received by Fr. Matthew O'Brien at St. Peter's Church, Barclay Street, Lower Manhattan, New York; her sister-in-law, Cecilia Seton (d. 1810) was received in 1806 and Cecilia's sister, Harriet (d. 1809) in 1809); d. 4 January 1821, The White House, Saint Joseph's Valley, near Emmitsburg, Maryland; from a wealthy society family; her father, Dr. Richard Bayley (1744-1801), a prominent surgeon, was the first Professor of Anatomy at Columbia College, New York; her mother, Catherine Charlton, the daughter of an Episcopal minister, died when Elizabeth was three years old; her father married again and one of her step brothers was the father of James Roosevelt Bayley (see above), who became Archbishop of Baltimore; she had great affection for her stepmother who was a devout Anglican; brought up in the Episcopal Church; educated mainly by her father; read widely and was very religious; married in 1794 to William Magee Seton (1768-1803), a wealthy businessman (five children of the marriage); went for her husband's health (he was dying of consumption) to Livorno, or Leghorn, Italy, with him to stay with their business friends, the Filicchi family; her husband died in Pisa; her conversion was influenced by her visit to Italy and her stay with the devout Filicchis who guided her in her Catholic instructions (the major influence being Antonio Filicchi, also a generous benefactor to her family); she was drawn to the tabernacle in their private chapel; in one of Signora Filicchi's prayer books she came upon the text of St. Bernard's *Memorare* and found in the Virgin Mary the tenderness and the pity of a mother ("I assure you my becoming a Catholic was a very simple consequence of going to a Catholic country, where it was impossible for any one, interested in any religion, not to see the wide difference between the first established faith, given and founded by our Lord and His Apostles, and the various forms it has since taken...Certainly though, it was the knowledge of the Protestant doctrine with regard to the faith that made me a Catholic, for as soon as on inquiring I found that Episcopalians did not think everybody right, I was convinced my safe plan was to unite with the Church in which, at all events, they admitted that I would find salvation, and where also I would be secure of the Apostolic Succession, as well as of the many consolations which no other religion but the Catholic can afford. The whole is, that, with the convictions of my conscience, my salvation depended on embracing the Catholic faith"); guided also by Bishop John Carroll and two future bishops, John Cheverus and Louis William DuBourg; went through a period of spiritual searching in which her favorite prayer was "If I am right Thy grace impart still in the right to stay. If I am wrong Oh, teach my heart to find the better way"; much family illness and death at this time; on her conversion she was ostracized by her family; moved with her five children (two sons and three daughters) to Baltimore where she opened a school for girls; took vows privately before Archbishop Carroll before forming a new community with other postulants at Emmitsburg to take charge of a new institution for teaching poor children; the rule for the new community, based on that of the Sisters of Charity of St. Vincent de Paul, with some modifications, was approved in 1812; she was elected superior and became known as Mother Seton; she and the other sisters made their vows in 1813 (the first congregation of religious sisters to be founded in the United States); the school was the first free Catholic school in the United States; the school and the sisters' work among the poor prospered; her eldest daughter, Anna Maria (d. 1812), who had accompanied her parents to Italy in 1803, became afflicted with tuberculosis, and made her vows as a Sister of Charity on her deathbed; her youngest daughter Rebecca ("Bec") (d. 1816) died of a very painful spinal disease; another daughter Catherine Charlton (1800-1891) entered the Sisters of Mercy in New York City in 1846 and, as Mother Mary Catherine, she devoted herself for more than forty years to prison ministry in New York; one grandchild was Robert Seton (1839-1927), Archbishop of Heliopolis; another was William Seton III (1835-1905), author, novelist and popular science writer; another was Sr. Mary Catherine (1879-1906), a New York Sister of Mercy; the many diaries and correspondence show her spiritual depth; "Be children of the Church!" she told her Sisters and daughter as she lay dying; buried in the basilica that bears her name, the Basilica of the National Shrine of Saint Ann Elizabeth Seton; her cause for canonization was opened in 1911; declared Venerable in 1959; beatified in 1963; canonized on 14 September 1975 (first native born citizen of the United States to be canonized); her feast day is

4 January; seen as a patron saint of Catholic schools; the Shrine of St. Elizabeth Ann Seton in Our Lady of the Holy Rosary's Church, New York, was built on the site of her home in Manhattan; see *The Italian Journal* (1804) (recounts the intimate details of her inner struggle and conversion to the Catholic faith); *Spiritual Journal* (1807); Ellin M. Kelly and Annabelle M. Melville, (ed), *Elizabeth Seton: Selected Writings* (1987); Regina M. Bechtle and Judith Metz, *Elizabeth Bayley Seton: Collected Writings* (2002); Charles Ignatius White, *Life of Mrs. Eliza Seton* (1853); Robert Seton (ed), *Memoir, Letters and Journal of Elizabeth Seton*, 2 Vols. (1869); Katherine Burton, *His Dear Persuasion: The Life of Elizabeth Ann Seton* (1940); Annabelle M. Melville, *Elizabeth Bayley Seton, 1774-1821* (1951); Theodore Maynard, *Great Catholics in American History* (1957), p.99; Joseph I. Dirvin, *Mrs. Seton: Foundress of the American Sisters of Charity* (1962); Bernard Basset, SJ, *Saint Elizabeth Seton* (1975); Jane F. Hindman, *Elizabeth Ann Seton, Mother, Teacher, Saint for Our Time* (1976); Sr. Marie Celeste, *Elizabeth Ann Seton: A Self-Portrait (1774-1821), A Study of Her Spirituality in Her Own Words* (1986); Ann Ball, *Modern Saints: Book Two* (1990) ("Elizabeth's desire for the Bread of Life was to be a strong force leading her to the Catholic Church. To her dear sister-in-law Rebecca, her 'Soul's Sister,' she wrote, 'How happy would we be, if we believed what these dear souls believe: that they *possess* God in the Sacrament, and that He remains in their churches and is carried to them when they are sick!...The other day, in a moment of excessive distress, I fell on my knees without thinking when the Blessed Sacrament passed by, and cried in an agony to God *to bless me*, if He was *there* – that my whole soul desired only Him.'

Having lost her mother at an early age, Elizabeth felt great comfort in the idea that the Blessed Virgin was truly her mother. She asked the Blessed Virgin to guide her to the True Faith. Elizabeth was also attracted to the Catholic teaching that suffering can expiate sins. In the Anglican church the prayerbook's Ash Wednesday reference to 'fasting, weeping and mourning' had been explained as being simply an old custom; but Elizabeth noted that the Catholic Mrs. Filicchi did not eat until 3 p.m. during Lent, offering the sacrifice for her sins in union with the Savior's sufferings. Elizabeth was deeply impressed.

Elizabeth also noticed the difference between Catholic and non-Catholic deathbeds. She wrote to Mrs. Filicchi that in assisting at non-Catholic deaths, I go through an agony never to be described,' while a Catholic dying person is consoled and strengthened by every help of religion, and the priest, 'the one you call *Father* of your soul, attends and watches it in the weakness and trials of parting nature with the same care you and I watch our little infant's body in its first struggles… on its entrance into life'…

Finally, after much interior anguish, Elizabeth decided, 'I will go peaceably and firmly to the Catholic Church: for if faith is so important to our salvation, I will seek it where true Faith first began, seek it among those who received it from *God Himself*'"); Joseph I Dirvin, *The Soul of Elizabeth Seton* (1990); Jenny Franchot, *Roads to Rome: The Antebellum Protestant Encounter with Catholicism* (1994), Ch. 14, "Elizabeth Seton: The Sacred Workings of Contagion"; Sr. Marie Celeste, SC, *The Intimate Friendships of Elizabeth Ann Bayley Seton* (2000); Julie Walters, *Elizabeth Ann Seton: Saint for a New Nation* (2002); Mary Hilaire Tavenner, *My Friendship with Saint Elizabeth Ann Seton* (2008); Charles P. Connor, *Classic Catholic Converts* (2001), p.17; *Catholic Encyclopedia* ("While with these Catholic families and in the churches of Italy Mrs. Seton first began to see the beauty of the Catholic Faith"); *ANB*.

Sewell, (Margaret) Elizabeth – writer; b. 1919, India; c. 1948; d. 12 January 2001, Greensboro, North Carolina; both parents English; began to write verse from a very early age; educated at Newnham College, Cambridge (First Class Honours in Modern Languages); in the civil service, the Ministry of Education, in London 1942-1945; obtained a PhD in French at Cambridge; received into the Catholic Church as a result of this research ("an odd but good way in which to arrive"); author of poetry, novels and short stories, plus literary criticism; commuted between Britain and the United States for many years; became American citizen in 1973; much work to attempt to reunite the disciplines of poetry and science; friend and colleague of Michael Polanyi; see (criticism) *The Structure of Poetry* (1951); *Paul Valéry: The Mind in the Mirror* (1952); *The Field of Nonsense* (1952); *The Orphic Voice: Poetry and Natural History* (1960); *The Human Metaphor* (1964); (novels) *The Dividing of Time* (1952); *The Singular Hope* (1955); *Now Bless Thyself* (1962); *The Unlooked-For* (1995); (poetry) *Poems, 1947-1961* (1962); *Signs and Cities* (1968); *Acquist* (1984); (essays) *To Be a True Poem* (1979); (memoir) *An Idea* (1983); David Schenck and Phil Mullins, "On Reuniting Poetry and Science: A Memoir of Elizabeth Sewell, 1919-2001," *missouriwestern.edu/org*; Matthew Hoehn OSB (ed), *Catholic Authors: Contemporary Biographical Sketches* (1952)

Shea, Mark - writer and blogger; b. 1959; c. December 1987; raised with no particular religious belief, though he did always believe there was something supernatural about the world; studied at the University of Washington in the late 1970s; impressed by the writing of C. S. Lewis; became in 1979 a non-denominational Evangelical and Charismatic Christian (introduced to a group of Evangelicals at university and formed a "church" with them); later had a growing sense that all was not well and eventually came to appreciate the role of sacred tradition, and became a Catholic; author of several books and articles; he has claimed that the Old Covenant remains in force for unbaptized Jews, but this is contrary to the Council of Florence ("That the matter pertaining to the law of the Old Testament, of the Mosaic law…after our Lord's coming had been signified by them, ceased and the sacraments of the New Testament began"), the Catechism of the Council of Trent ("the people, aware of the abrogation of the Mosaic Law…"), and the statement of the United States Conference of Catholic Bishops in 2008; married to Jan Shea, a cradle Catholic (four sons of the marriage); website under the name of *Catholic and Enjoying It!*; see (selective list) *This is My Body: An Evangelical Discovers the Real Presence* (1993); *By What Authority?: An Evangelical Discovers Catholic Tradition* (1996); *EWTN Audio Library, The Journey Home* (19 December 1997) ("I began to look at what Catholics actually mean when they are talking about sacred tradition. We read for example books on great revivals of the Church and the books took us back to the Reformation. And then there was this huge gap, and then there was St. Paul, and I just started wondering, 'There must have been something going on in the Church for fifteen centuries, you know. Surely it can't have been all that bad. And part of the reason I got curious about that was because of my interest in evangelization and apologetics. I ran into many non-Christians who spoke as though all of Christian history was just a sort of meaningless blank where all Christians were fools. But I knew they weren't right. So was it really wise of me to be speaking as though all Catholics were fools? Especially since of those Catholics were people like St. Thomas and St. Augustine. I thought they don't seem terribly dumb to me, perhaps I'm missing something?

And when I began to look at the way in which the Church actually regards tradition, I was particularly struck by Chesterton's comment that tradition is the democracy of the dead; that it was in fact a way of giving voice to other Christians who had had a valid experience of Christ, just as I had, and the only reason we didn't listen to them was that they happened to be dead. And I started thinking, 'Maybe it's worth listening to the voices of my great great grandfathers and hearing what they learned.' Mark Twain mentions that when he was fifteen he thought that his father was the stupidest man alive, and he was amazed at how much the old man learned in ten years. And I had the same sort of experience. I started to think, 'Perhaps people who lived before me knew a thing or two'...

One of the things I began to do was to take a good look at the Fathers of the Church and, gee, they don't look very Evangelical. And these are people, some of them, some of the very early Fathers of the Church, were people who heard the Apostle with their very own ears; and they had the distinct impression that the Eucharist was the body and blood of Christ, for example; and they spoke about apostolic succession; and they had a sacramental world view. So all of this was percolating then. I read a very important book, *Evangelical Is Not Enough* by Tom Howard, which is a magnificent book, and this really opened up the whole sacramental, liturgical way to me. It made me realize a couple of things, speaking of tradition. We thought as charismatics that we were not a liturgical church, but what I discovered was that we were a liturgical church...and there were rubrics...We tended to gravitate towards re-creating something that at least approximated to what is done in Catholic circles.

So, I thought we didn't believe in sacred tradition, for example,... but as I began to look at the way we lived as Evangelicals, the fact was, of course, we believed in sacred tradition.

The difference was not that Catholics believed in sacred tradition and we Evangelicals didn't. The real difference was that Catholics believed in sacred tradition and knew they did, and we Evangelicals believed in sacred tradition and didn't know we did.

And so, for example, how do we know what books belong to the Bible? The table of contents is not inspired. So how do we know? We know because we've accepted this piece of sacred tradition that's percolated down to us through the Reformation.

What does the Catholic Church mean by tradition? The Catechism is pretty straightforward. Sacred tradition means 'the common life, common worship and common teaching of the Church.' That means not only what is written in Scripture, but also the whole life and worship of the Church; the way the Church reads Scripture, for example; the way in which it understands the revelation; the way in which it lives out the revelation and certainly the very structure of the Church, is tradition. All of these things are the way in which the spirit of Christ works through his people. So, we call it living tradition.

Does that mean it's always changing, always evolving? Not evolving, but growing, yes. Jesus very aptly describes the kingdom of God as a mustard seed. The one thing the mustard seed doesn't do is stay the same. But, on the other hand, when you plant a mustard seed, you don't get a rhinoceros, or something else. you get something that's even more mustardy than it was originally, and this is one of the things that convinced John Henry Newman who wrote the great *Essay on the Development of Christian Doctrine*. He said what would the early Church look like if you planted it and let it grow for eighteen centuries? And he concluded it would look like the Catholic Church.

What is the connection, then, between what we call tradition and, let's say, the apostolic deposit of faith? Well, the apostolic deposit of faith is the revelation that is given to us. There is the acorn. The acorn is planted in the soil of the earth and it begins to grow, and it begins to do unexpected things almost immediately.

So, for example, as an Evangelical I would have said, 'The assumption of Mary, where is that in Scripture. Show me this in Scripture.' Well, it's not explicit in Scripture, but Scripture read in the light of tradition, it's there…

If you look, for example, at the book of Acts at the great circumcision controversy in the early Church, should Gentiles be circumcised in order to become Christians? Well, if you were to go on the basis of Scripture alone at that time, let's see. God commands Abraham to be circumcised and to circumcise all his offspring of the everlasting covenant. Moses is circumcised, all of the prophets are circumcised. Jesus is circumcised, the Apostles are all circumcised. Everybody at the Council of Jerusalem is a circumcised Jew. Could anything be clearer from Scripture than that circumcision is required by God for ever and ever. And yet the Council says, 'No, we don't need to do this anymore.' Because they read the Scriptures in the light of the Apostolic tradition; and the Church has continued to do that to this day"); "The Witness of Isaiah 7:14," *This Rock*, July/August 1998; *Making Senses Out of Scripture: Reading the Bible as the First Christians Did* (1999); *The Da Vinci Deception* (2006) (with Edward Sri); *Mary, Mother of the Son* (3 Vols.) (2009); *The Work of Mercy: Being the Hands and Heart of Christ* (2012); *The Heart of Catholic Prayer: Rediscovering the Our Father and the Hail Mary* (2012); on the issue of the Old Covenant see Robert A. Sungenis, "The Old Covenant is Revoked: The USCC Removes Heretical Sentence from Its Catechism," *Culture Wars*, October 2008, p.12; *markshea.com*.

Sheen, Martin (born Ramón Antonio Gerardo Estévez) – film actor; b. 3 August 1940, Dayton, Ohio; father Francisco Estévez Martinez (1898-1974) a factory worker and machinery inspector, immigrant from Spain; mother Mary Anne, *née* Phelan (1903-1951), immigrant from Ireland; seventh of ten children (nine boys and a girl) in a poor family; raised Catholic by parents who were devout Catholics; drawn to acting and moved to New York; met

Dorothy Day and worked with her Catholic Worker Movement (later, in 1996, he played Peter Maurin, co-founder of the Catholic Worker Movement, in an independent film, *Entertaining Angels: The Dorothy Day Story*); took his stage name in part from Bishop Fulton Sheen, but never changed his name officially; after working in a theater company he developed a very successful career in films and television; acclaimed Broadway performance in *The Subject Was Roses* (1964); gained wide recognition for his starring role in *Apocalypse Now* (1979); other notable films include *Catch-22* (1970), *Badlands* (1973), *Catholics* (1973), *Gandhi* (1981), *Wall Street* (1987), *The Departed* (2006), *The Way* (2011) and *The Amazing Spider-Man* (2012); his major television role was as the fictitious President Josiah Bartlet in *The West Wing* (1999-2006); broke with the Church and went through a period of heavy drinking and drug taking in the 1970s culminating in a minor heart attack; this led to a four year spiritual journey that resulted in his return to the Catholic faith; winner of many nominations and awards, but never nominated for an Academy Award; director of one film; known for his support of mainly leftist political causes (arrested many times for protests), including asylum policies, Central America, nuclear test sites, immigration reform legislation, and Israeli abuses in the Occupied Territories; opponent of abortion and capital punishment; anti-war campaigner; in 2003 opposed the invasion of Iraq; critic of assisted suicide; in 2004 campaigned for Presidential nominee John Kerry and in 2008 Barack Obama; has called himself a "radical Catholic" ("That is someone who follows the teachings of the nonviolent Jesus and takes the gospel personally, and then pays the price. I fall into that category"); married Janet, *née* Templeton, artist, in 1961; four children of his marriage, three sons (Emilio (b. 1962), Ramón (b. 1963) and Carlos (b. 1965)), and one daughter (Renée (b. 1967)), all of whom are actors; all the children kept the name Estévez, except Carlos, known as Charlie Sheen; in 2003 awarded the degree of LLD by Marquette University for his work on social and Catholic issues; in 2008 awarded the *Laetare* Medal by the University of Notre Dame; with his son Ramon he created Estevez Sheen Productions, a company affiliated to *Warner Bros*; the company made *The Way*, directed by his son Emilio, a drama set around the pilgrimage to Santiago de Compostela; played a parish priest in the Irish film *Stella Days* (2011); criticized for his continuous support for Democratic pro-choice politicians; in 2012 he stated that he supports same-sex "marriage"; see David Kupfer, "Martin Sheen Interview," *The Progressive*, July 2003 ("Q: Who have been your spiritual influences? Sheen: Terrence Malick (director of the film *Badlands*) is a deeply spiritual, bright, articulate man who had a profound influence on me at a critical time. Twenty years ago, I left India and went to Paris to do a film which I was not wild to be doing because I was not feeling focused at the time. I had just experienced India for the first time, and it had a very profound impact on me. I went to Paris and ran into Terry, who'd been living there for a couple of years, and we got reacquainted and got very close, and he became a mentor in a lot of ways for me. He was able to see where I needed to focus and was able to guide me to a little clearer place. He would give me material, books to read. Finally, the last book he gave me was *The Brothers Karamazov*, and that book had a very profound effect on my spiritual life, and that was like the final door that I had to go through. I finished reading that, and it was May Day, and I went into what turned out to be the only English-speaking Catholic church in all of France. I had not gone to church in years. I came across an Irish priest. I told him I'd stayed away from the faith for a long time, and I'd like to make a confession. He said you come to see me Saturday afternoon at the appointed hour, and I did. That was for me the journey home. Terrence was key to my awakening. Also, many of my beliefs were influenced by Dan and Phil Berrigan and the Jesuit community they helped run in New York").

Sherlock, Richard – philosopher; b. 1947; c. 7 April 2012 (Easter Vigil; "All true roads do lead to Rome"); grew up in a Mormon household, but his mother was semi-active and his father was not a member until late in life; graduated from the University of Utah in 1970; studied Moral Theology and Ethics at Harvard Divinity School; drawn all along to Catholic teachings on social issues, and opposed abortion, euthanasia, and artificial birth control; Professor of Moral Theology at Fordham University in the mid 1980s; then Professor of Philosophy, Utah State University; for many years he had doubts regarding the Mormon view of the so-called "Great Apostasy", i.e., that the pure gospel was lost to the world after the New Testament apostles and disciples died, and that Christ's truth languished during centuries of the Catholic Church, and needed to be "restored" by Mormon founder Joseph Smith; he came to believe that this story was intellectually unsustainable; he did not believe that God withdrew from the emerging Church or that the Church Fathers abandoned Christ's teaching ("They used reason to explore, develop and make reasonable sense of biblical convictions. If you believe in the apostasy, you have to believe it was wrong to do what they did. Without the Catholic Church we wouldn't have the Bible or great thinkers like Augustine and Aquinas"); remained a Mormon for many years for social reasons, but eventually converted to the Catholic faith; married with two children; see "Converting to Catholicism: My Journey," *catholic.org*, 12 May 2011 ("One should never leave the religion in which one was born or raised for anything but the most serious of reasons. Warm feelings, family, friends, a social ethos, should never be the reason for joining or leaving a religion. The fact that you do not like the priest, pastor or parishioners should never be a reason for staying or leaving…

Conversion must be a matter of both the head and the heart, both the intellect and the spirit. But it must be a whole reorientation of one's life, a whole that transcends just the sum of the parts. Two further points I must make. First, conversion in the Catholic faith is never a completed event. It is always a process. Even devout 'cradle Catholics' are still on a journey to become closer to God. Second, conversion as an adult Catholic cannot be begun and completed in a short period of time…

Conversion is a matter of both the heart and the head. Mormonism is all about feeling and almost never about a conversion of the head. But conversion must be more than just feeling. The experience of the Holy Spirit often, but not always, involves feeling to be sure; The Holy Spirit, however, is a profound sense of the presence of God, not merely emotion. It is hearing a music that is transcendent. But if it is truly the presence of God it will lead to wisdom and intellectual curiosity, not away. Reason is a precious Divine gift. We should use it. If the beliefs to which you become emotionally attached are intellectually wrong, emotional attachment won't magically make them right.

In a truly moving opening passage in his seminal encyclical *Fides et Ratio* Pope John Paul II expresses this marriage of faith and reason: 'Faith and reason are like two wings on which the human spirit rises to the contemplation of truth; and God has placed in the human heart a desire to know the truth - in a word, to know Himself - so that by knowing and loving God, men and women may come to the fullness of truth about themselves'…

I was a 'head convert' much longer than I have been a heart convert. It began really at Harvard. Even a non-specialist study of patristic literature convinced me that the story I had grown up with about the 'great apostasy' in patristic period was wrong. Of course the Nicene Creed is not found literally in the New Testament. But it is an essential development out of the teaching of scripture. I am not even in the same intellectual universe as Cardinal John Henry Newman. But my journey, like his, was begun by realizing that there is a development of Christian doctrine, not a sharp break.

A passage from a book chapter written by one of the most

distinguished Mormon thinkers of the last fifty years tells a story so much like mine that I must quote it. It is from Edwin Firmage, a truly distinguished law professor at the University of Utah and grandson of the beloved Mormon leader Hugh B. Brown. Ed writes this after he has left Mormonism: 'As I consciously look back, it began for me probably in the mission field because I smuggled into my digs in England and Scotland the writings of the early fathers - Origen, Tertullian, Clement of Rome, Clement of Alexandria…As I read these writers of the second, third, fourth, fifth, sixth, and seventh centuries I felt that they had been touched by God…I was laying some mines that would be detonated later, because the idea of preaching an apostasy and restoration was wrong…The idea that God was sort of snoozing until 1820 now seems to me absurd'"); *EWTN Audio Library, The Journey Home* (8 April 2013).

Sickles, Daniel Edgar ("Yankee King of Spain") - politician, soldier and diplomat; b. 20 Oct. 1819, New York City; d. 3 May 1914, New York City; son of a lawyer and politician; educated at the University of the City of New York; admitted to the bar in 1843; member of the Democratic Party; elected to the New York State Assembly in 1847; became secretary of the American legation in London; elected to the U.S. House of Representatives 1857-1861; married sixteen-year-old Teresa Bagioli (1836-1867) in 1852 (one child); her grandfather was Lorenzo Da Ponte (1749-1838), Mozart's librettist; he was widely known for infidelity; when his wife had an affair with Philip Barton Key he shot Key dead; was tried for murder, but acquitted on the ground of temporary insanity (the first use of that defense in U.S. legal history); he publicly forgave his wife; on the outbreak of the Civil War he was appointed brigadier-general of volunteers; promoted to major general of volunteers in 1862; fought at Chancellorsville and Gettysburg (he caused controversy by disobeying an order there; also his right leg was smashed and had to be amputated); commanded military districts during the Reconstruction period; became a Republican and worked for Ulysses S. Grant's presidential bid; minister to Spain 1869-1874; married Caroline Martinez Guerrera de Creagh in 1871 (two children of the marriage); acquired his nickname in part from his romantic involvement in Paris with Spain's deposed Queen Isabella II; returned to his law practice in the United States, leaving his family in Europe; U.S. Congressman 1893-1895; his contemporaries either loved or hated him; buried in Arlington National Cemetery; see Edgcumb Pinchon, *Dan Sickles: Hero of Gettysburg and "Yankee King of Spain"* (1945); W. A. Swanberg, *Sickles the Incredible* (1956); Nat Brandt, *The*

Congressman Who Got Away With Murder (1991); Thomas Keneally, *American Scoundrel: The Life of the Notorious Civil War General Dan Sickles (2002);* James A. Hessler, *Sickles at Gettysburg* (2009);

Simon, M. Raphael OCSO (formerly Dr. Alwyn Kenneth Simon) – Cistercian monk of the Strict Observance (Trappist); b. 6 August 1909, New York; c. 6 November 1936; d. 12 November 2006; brought up by Reformed Jewish parents; drifted into agnosticism; qualified in medicine, then specialized in psychiatry in Berlin, finding there in philosophy 'the possibility of the unity of knowledge'; studied philosophy under Robert Maynard Hutchins, Mortimer Adler, Richard McKeon (and Simon's friends Herbert Schwartz (see above) and William Gorman) at the University of Chicago, which led him to the writings of Aristotle and St. Thomas Aquinas (supported in this by his friend, Herbert Schwartz (see above); after his conversion he practised psychiatric medicine; on 8 December 1940 he entered the Trappist Cistercian Order, making his solemn profession on 6 November 1946; ordained Catholic priest on 30 or 31 May 1947; see *The Glory of Thy People: The Story of a Conversion* (revised edition, 1986) ((1) From the preface by Archbishop Fulton Sheen: "Here is a man who went the whole way, who was content with no half-drawn swords, divided loyalties and compromising surrenders. Pascal once said in defense of the Evangelists' writing the truth in their Gospels: 'I will believe any man who leaves what Dr. Simon left to become a Monk of the Order of the Cistercians of the Strict Observance, and to live the rest of his days in the shades and shadows of the Cross where Saints are made."

(2) From the text: "At this time I realized that the Catholic Church alone laid claim to possessing the whole religious truth, that it alone claimed an infallible teaching authority. When Dr. [Mortimer] Adler, himself said, in comparing the different religious faiths, that the Catholic Faith was the most complete, I understood what he meant; I also understood the so-called dogmatism of the Catholic religion. Knowing that, in the natural order, eternal, changeless truth existed, and that in attaining to it, one must reject as erroneous all that was contradictory to it, I readily understood that if in the natural order religious truth existed, the authority to which it was entrusted would be obliged to deny all contradictory opinions as erroneous. That is, a religious society which has Divine truth, must claim that everything which contradicts its doctrine is erroneous, and that every other faith which omits part of its teaching is incomplete. Otherwise it does not really believe that it has the truth, and that all parts of its doctrine are

equally true. Likewise, I had come to realize that the word 'catholic' means 'universal.' The Church held its Faith to be objectively true and therefore true for all. The Protestants were divided into hundreds of disagreeing sects, the Jewish religion laid no claim to be other than a religion for Jews, while the Catholic Church proposed its religion as *the* single Divine religion and it invited all equally to accept it"); "To Church and Cloister," in John A. O'Brien (ed), *The Road to Damascus* (1949) ("I was deeply impressed by the words and actions ascribed to Jesus. Their wisdom, beauty, dignity, exceeded anything literature, philosophy, or history presented. A special quality inhered in them, so transcendent that my intelligence asked in amazement: Who is this? Such was the question in the minds of the men of Palestine. This question allowed of no middle course. It was to be answered either by the answer of the scribes and Pharisees or by that of those selfless seekers of the truth who left all to follow Jesus. For myself, I soon determined to put aside all doubts and questions...

I was prepared by recent experience and reflection to see that the acceptance of the divinity of Jesus Christ and the revelation of divine things which He came upon earth to teach required the acceptance of the Catholic Church. If He had not appointed Simon Peter to be the Rock upon which His Church was founded, then His doctrine would not have had the safeguard which Peter's undisputed authority gave it...

And if Peter's authority to confirm his brethren in the Faith had perished with him, the foundation laid by Christ would not have been for all generations. But with an unbroken succession of popes, Christ's doctrine is preserved and taught to all generations of men.

A convincing proof of the wisdom of Christ's building is the witness of Protestantism. Within four centuries, in the United States, statistics show that it has disintegrated into over four hundred different sects.

My Jewish origin was not an obstacle but an incentive to accept the Catholic Church as the true Church of God. Was not its founder, Jesus Christ, a Jew? His mother? His Apostles? The first Church, the Church of Jerusalem, was it not composed of Jews? Had He not said, I have come not to destroy the Law and the Prophets, but to fulfil them; was not Catholicism, then, the religion for the Jew? That, unlike Judaism, it held out its arms to receive all men, only confirmed its divine origin in my estimation, for surely God must desire all men to be members of that Church which He founded for mankind... In the Church I found that which had been lacking in modern Judaism. God was dwelling in the midst of His people, the spiritual Semites, in the phrase of the late Pope Pius XI. In assisting at Holy

Mass I felt the reverence which the Hebrews of old had experienced in the temple of Jerusalem, and as the Sanctus told of the entrance to the Canon of the Mass. I realized that solemn moment had arrived which in olden days came but once a year, when the high priest entered into the Holy of Holies, open to him alone, to offer the blood of the lamb for the sins of all the people. Here indeed upon the altar was that blessed Victim, the true Lamb of God, the crucified Jesus prefigured by the divinely appointed sacrifice of the Old Testament. Truly He is a Propitiation for the sins of all men, Who on Calvary offered for all His sacrifice, an abundant satisfaction for the sins of all men, including his enemies and executioners: 'Forgive them, Father, for they know not what they do'"); *Hammer and Fire: Way to Contemplative Happiness, Fruitful Ministry and Mental Health* (revised edition, 1987); Matthew Hoehn OSB (ed), *Catholic Authors: Contemporary Biographical Sketches* (1952) ("I came to appreciate more and more the unity of the Catholic faith. The same faith, the same doctrine taught by Christ and then by His Apostles is taught in every Catholic parish by every Catholic priest throughout the entire world"); "Discovering the Father," in Ronda Chervin (ed), *The Ingrafting: The Conversion Stories of Ten Hebrew-Catholics* (1987) ("What Aristotle's philosophy, perfected by Thomas, offered was a philosophy based on common sense and empirically known reality. All knowledge, for them, starts with the senses. But it does not stop there. Truth depends on the truth of the premises and the correctness of the reasoning from these premises. Reason, starting from what is observed and known through the senses, can draw conclusions which lead to insight into even non-material reality, such as God, the first cause of all material being (*Physics*, ch. 8; *Metaphysics*, ch. 10)…Philosophy provided a check for examining the unconscious philosophic assumptions of scientists, who stepped outside the field of their competence in making philosophic statements as if they were scientific truths…

At this juncture I read the Gospel…In reading it, a comment of [Robert] Hutchins proved meaningful. He said that if one wanted *to make sense* of the Bible, one should read it as if it were true. He did not say that it *was* true, but that reading it as if it were true would help to understand it. Perhaps this was in my mind when, in order to give the Gospel a fair reading, I bracketed for later reflection those elements in it which touched on my sensibilities and prejudices – for example, the miracles. This permitted a more critical reading than if I had allowed my antagonistic emotions to interfere with an intelligent perusal of the text.

What I found was a narrative told unimpassionedly, a drama unfolding among characters whom

I could identify with those in my current experience. Jesus, with his flaying, cutting rejoinders to his enemies, did not fit my ideal of the wise, balanced man who 'followed in all things the golden mean.' But much less could I identify with his enemies. As the story unfolded, I became aware of the beauty of the personality of Jesus and its power and authority. Where did such authority, such brilliance, come from? I could not attribute it to the editors of the Gospels or the milieu from which they came. I could not account for it as being purely human. I realized that in this drama, so true to life in a way that defied human artistry or ingenuity alone to explain, I was forced to take sides and not remain a mere spectator").

Smith, Ada Beatrice Queen Victoria Louise Virginia ("Bricktop") – entertainer and nightclub owner; b. 14 August 1894, Alderson, West Virginia; c. 5 December 1943; d. 1 February 1984, Manhattan, New York City; youngest of four children; her father was a barber and her mother a seamstress; after her father's death the family moved to Chicago; her nickname "Bricktop" resulted from her flaming red hair and freckles; performed in theatre from age four or five; then began singing and dancing in vaudeville; her performance tours brought her to New York at the age of twenty; was performing in Paris by 1924, where she was the entertainer at many of Cole Porter's parties; opened her own nightclubs in Paris, notably "Chez Bricktop", which became the chic place to go; famous for the big black cigars she smoked; during World War II she closed the club and moved to the United States, then to Mexico City where in 1944 she opened a new nightclub; she became interested in the Catholic Church through a convert friend; then listening to Fulton Sheen's radio addresses on the *Catholic Hour* confirmed her desire to become a Catholic, and she was received into the Church; after her conversion she remained a devout Catholic for the rest of her life; in 1949 she returned to Europe; in 1951 she moved to Rome and started a club there; active in charities for Italian orphans; she closed her club and retired in 1961, returning to the United States; as the doyenne of café society she attracted many celebrities to her clubs, notably the Duke and Duchess of Windsor, Cole Porter, F. Scott Fitzgerald, John Steinbeck, Ernest Hemingway, the Aga Khan, and Tallulah Bankhead; T. S. Eliot wrote a poem for her; she furthered the careers of such as Duke Ellington (1899-1974), Josephine Baker (1906-1975), Mabel Mercer (1900-1984) and Langston Hughes (1902-1967); Cole Porter's song "Miss Otis Regrets" was written especially for her to perform; worked in cabaret well into her eighties; married Peter Ducongé, a saxophonist, in 1929 (no children);

buried in Woodlawn Cemetery in the Bronx; see *Bricktop by Bricktop* (1983); Thomas C. Reeves, *America's Bishop: The Life and Times of Fulton J. Sheen* (2001) ("A few years later, Bricktop eagerly seized the opportunity to meet Sheen, an encounter she would describe as 'beautiful.' Some time later, in Rome, the two met again. Bricktop said she was broke and needed money. 'He went and got a checkbook. "What, do you need? Five hundred dollars, five thousand, what?" She accepted five hundred. Fulton was astonished when Bricktop eventually appeared at his office to return the $500. It was the first time in his long lending career that anyone had repaid him. One of the entertainer's most cherished gifts was a Sheen book inscribed by the author to 'My child in Christ, Bricktop, who proves every walk of life can be spiritualized?'"); *ANB* ("To the end she was a lady of the dawn who drank only champagne and expected a rose from every male visitor").

Smith, Kate (born Kathryn Elizabeth Smith) - singer and radio and television presenter, b. 1 May 1907, Greenville, Virginia; d. 17 June 1986, Raleigh, North Carolina; brought up as a Presbyterian; as a young girl she won many singing and dancing contests; graduated from Business High School in Washington in 1923; began training in nursing, but decided to be an entertainer; physically large with a powerful contralto voice; appeared on Broadway in musicals from 1926; very successful on a series of radio programs (notably "Kate Smith Sings," which was soon expanded to six shows a week, and the "Kate Smith Hour," a leading variety show); she also toured in several reviews; always highly popular with the public; recorded 580 songs over forty-seven years; she became a symbol of patriotism when Irving Berlin composed the patriotic anthem "God Bless America" for her radio program, and she sang it throughout World War II (in the film *This Is the Army* (1943) she had a cameo role recreating the radio introduction of the song); all proceeds from her performances of this song went to the Boy Scouts and Girl Scouts of America; she was at the height of her popularity during World War II; no-one was able to match her ability to sell war bonds; known as "The Songbird of the South" and "The First Lady of Radio"; her most notable songs were "Dream a Little Dream of Me" (1931); "River, Stay Way From My Door" (1931); "The Woodpecker Song"; (1940); "The White Cliffs of Dover" (1941); "Rose O'Day" (1941); "Last Time I Saw Paris" (1942); "I Don't Want to Walk Without You" (1942); "There Goes That Song Again" (1944); "Seems Like Old Times" (1946); "Now Is the Hour" (1947); her noontime news and comment radio program "Kate Smith Speaks" ran from 1938 to 1951 and ranked first among daytime listeners for several years; on television she hosted the "Kate Smith Hour" daily weekday program and the "Kate Smith Evening Hour", plus several others; converted from Presbyterianism to Catholicism; a tradition arose of playing "God Bless America" before Philadelphia Flyers ice hockey games, and on several occasions she performed this in person (remarkable success for the team resulted when it was played or sung in person!); in 1987 the team erected a statue of her outside their arena in her memory; did much charitable work; she received many awards, including the Medal of Freedom in 1982; unmarried; interred at Saint Agnes Cemetery, Lake Placid, New York, in an above-ground sarcophagus-style tomb; see *Living in a Great Big Way* (1938) (autobiography); *Stories of Annabelle* (1951) (children's book); *Upon My Lips a Song* (1960) (autobiography); Richard K. Hayes, *Kate Smith: When the Moon Came Over the Mountain* (1995); *ANB*.

Smith, Lucy Eaton (name in religion Mother Catherine de Ricci of the Sacred Heart of Christ) – nun, b. 1845, New York City; c. 1865 (her sisters, Isabella and Lillie both became Catholics subsequently; her mother was received in 1890 and her brother John in 1891; her grandmother was received at the age of ninety-four); d. 1894; father, William Smith, a well known engineer and nominally a Presbyterian; mother a Deist; the family was wealthy; brought up as an Episcopalian by her grandmother; grew interested in the Catholic faith through hearing the Mass and church music in a neighboring Catholic church; a friend introduced her to a Paulist priest, Fr. Alfred Young (1831-1900), who taught her about the faith; her family deeply perturbed at this, except her father, who was very friendly for the faith, but died shortly afterwards; used her poor health as an excuse to go on a vacation to Europe; spent three years in Europe visiting convents and shrines and put herself under the spiritual guidance of Fr. Aquilanti, OP; became a secular Dominican tertiary while in Rome; started a foundation among orphans in New York with two convert sisters who were also Dominican tertiaries; her name in religion was that of a Dominican mystic and stigmatist of whom she had read much while she was in Europe, and who especially appealed to her because of her devotion to the Blessed Sacrament; her initiative failed, so she went home again and spent the next two years mainly in studying the life of the Ursuline and Visitation orders; then with the two others took over a school; set up a formal novitiate and ran retreats for lay women; established foundations at Albany and Saratoga Springs; in 1883 her sister Isabella, now a widow, entered the community; in 1888 her other sister Lillie entered; see

Katherine Burton, *In No Strange Land: Some American Catholic Converts* (1942), p.159 ("The Catholic Faith draws its chosen in many and varied ways. For Lucy the path led at first through music…

Her own room was on the side of the house that faced the French Church of Saint Vincent de Paul. On Sundays she used to sit close to her window and listen to the singing of High Mass next door. After a while she decided she wanted to see as well as to hear, and one Sunday she slipped in with the crowds and spent a wonderful hour listening to the chanting and feasting her eyes on candles and blue clouds of incense and soft colored vestments…

Sunday after Sunday she went there, understanding nothing of the ceremonies at all, but loving it and feeling content just to be a part of it. When, on a week day as she was starting out for school unusually early, she saw people going into the church, she followed them and was surprised to find the Sunday ceremonies were being repeated. Only the music was missing on a week day.

When the service was over she had forgotten all about school she went shyly up to the altar for the first time, and knelt for long minutes at the rail, not praying, not even thinking, just loving it all, looking at it all.

One of her playmates who was a Catholic saw her as she came out of the church. 'Are you a Catholic ?' she asked in surprise. Lucy shook her head. 'Oh, no.' 'Then why are you kneeling in our church and adoring the Blessed Sacrament?' demanded the other girl. Lucy stared at her, 'Adore the Blessed Sacrament?' she replied. 'But I don't even know what is. I never heard of it. I just went there and knelt because I wanted to and because I really couldn't help myself.'

Interested in such religious zeal, her friend took her one day to see Father Alfred Young of the Paulist Fathers, to whom she had told the strange story of the little girl who knelt in a Catholic church and didn't know why. Gradually, Lucy Smith learned why she was kneeling at that altar. And gradually she learned about the Faith from Father Young who had seldom had a more interested pupil or one who so quickly saw the essentials of the Faith. She was not quite twenty-one when she was conditionally baptized in the church of Saint Paul the Apostle. As she knelt before him, her innocent face lifted, her eyes shining, Father Young thought that the snow falling outside the church seemed an emblem of the purity of this girl").

Smith, Thomas Kilby – soldier, lawyer, and politician; b. 23 September 1820, Boston, Massachusetts; d. 14 December 1887, New York City; all his forefathers were prominent in the public life of New England; brought up in Cincinnati; educated in military school; studied law in the office of Chief Justice Salmon

P. Chase; in 1848 he married Elizabeth Budd McCullough, who had been brought up Catholic by her convert mother (five sons and three daughters of the marriage); joined the Union Army in 1861 as lieutenant-colonel; fought conspicuously at the Battle of Shiloh in 1862; carried out duties with Sherman and Grant; brigadier-general of volunteers from 1863; distinguished service during the Red River Expedition in 1864; brevetted major-general for gallant and meritorious service; after the war he moved to Philadelphia and in his last years worked as a journalist in New York; buried in Saint Dominic Church Cemetery, Torresdale, Philadelphia; see Walter George Smith, *Life and Letters of Thomas Kilby Smith* (1897); *Catholic Encyclopedia* ("[His wife] was a gifted and devout woman, and through her influence and that of the venerable Archbishop Purcell he became a Catholic some years before his death. He was remarkable for his facility of expression, distinguished personal appearance, and courtly bearing").

Snow, Robert Anthony ("Tony") – journalist and political commentator; b. 1 June 1955, Berea, Kentucky; d. 12 July 2008, Georgetown, Washington, D.C.; brought up in Cincinnati, Ohio; educated at Davidson College, North Carolina (graduated in Philosophy in 1977); converted to the Catholic faith while in college; attended graduate programs in Philosophy and Economics at the University of Chicago 1978-1979; worked for several newspapers 1979-2000; became a nationally syndicated columnist; appeared on several television and radio programs; in 1991 he was appointed to work in the White House for President George H. W. Bush, first as chief speechwriter (Deputy Assistant to the President for Communications and Director of Speechwriting) and later (1992-1993) as Deputy Assistant to the President for Media Affairs; from 1996 to 2003 he served as the first host of *Fox News Sunday*, and worked on other Fox programs; served as the primary guest host of Rush Limbaugh's program from the mid-1990s; also a frequent commentator on National Public Radio; presented the *Tony Snow Show* on Fox News Radio 2003-2006; in 2005 diagnosed with colon cancer; White House Press Secretary in President George W. Bush's administration 2006-2007; subsequently CNN commentator; politically conservative; very popular for his integrity and admired for his fight against cancer; he married Jill Walker, an Evangelical, in her church in the mid-1980s; he continued to worship with her in her church, although considering himself still a Catholic; influenced by Fr. C. John McCloskey III, he read voraciously books on philosophy, theology and apologetics; finally got his marriage regularized and returned to the regular practice of his Catholic faith; see "Reason, Faith, Vocation," 118th Annual Commencement Address, Catholic University of America, 12 May 2007 ("When it comes to faith, I've taken my own journey. You will have to take your own. But here's what I know. Faith is as natural as the air we breathe. Religion is not an opiate, just the opposite. It is the introduction to the ultimate extreme sport. There is nothing that you can imagine that God cannot trump. As Paul said 'Faith is the substance of things hoped for, the evidence of things not seen.' And once you realize that there is something greater than you out there, then you have to decide, 'Do I acknowledge it and do I act upon it?' You have to at some point surrender yourself. And there is nothing worthwhile in your life that will not at some point require an act of submission. It's true of faith and friendship"); "Cancer's Unexpected Blessings," *Christianity Today*, 20 July 2007 ("Blessings arrive in unexpected packages - in my case, cancer. Those of us with potentially fatal diseases - and there are millions in America today - find ourselves in the odd position of coping with our mortality while trying to fathom God's will. Although it would be the height of presumption to declare with confidence What It All Means, Scripture provides powerful hints and consolations.

The first is that we shouldn't spend too much time trying to answer the why questions: *Why me? Why must people suffer? Why can't someone else get sick?* We can't answer such things, and the questions themselves often are designed more to express our anguish than to solicit an answer.

I don't know why I have cancer, and I don't much care. It is what it is - a plain and indisputable fact. Yet even while staring into a mirror darkly, great and stunning truths begin to take shape. Our maladies define a central feature of our existence: We are fallen. We are imperfect. Our bodies give out.

But despite this - because of it - God offers the possibility of salvation and grace. We don't know how the narrative of our lives will end, but we get to choose how to use the interval between now and the moment we meet our Creator face-to-face.

Second, we need to get past the anxiety. The mere thought of dying can send adrenaline flooding through your system. A dizzy, unfocused panic seizes you. Your heart thumps; your head swims. You think of nothingness and swoon. You fear partings; you worry about the impact on family and friends. You fidget and get nowhere.

To regain footing, remember that we were born not into death, but into life - and that the journey continues after we have finished our days on this earth. We accept this on faith, but that faith is nourished by a conviction that stirs even within many non-believing hearts - an intuition that the gift of life, once given, cannot be taken away. Those who have been stricken enjoy the special privilege of being able to fight with their might, main, and faith to live - fully, richly, exuberantly - no matter how their days may be numbered.

Third, we can open our eyes and hearts. God relishes surprise. We want lives of simple, predictable ease - smooth, even trails as far as the eye can see - but God likes to go off-road. He provokes us with twists and turns. He places us in predicaments that seem to defy our endurance and comprehension - and yet don't. By his love and grace, we persevere. The challenges that make our hearts leap and stomachs churn invariably strengthen our faith and grant measures of wisdom and joy we would not experience otherwise.

Picture yourself in a hospital bed. The fog of anesthesia has begun to wear away. A doctor stands at your feet; a loved one holds your hand at the side. 'It's cancer,' the healer announces.

The natural reaction is to turn to God and ask him to serve as a cosmic Santa. 'Dear God, make it all go away. Make everything simpler.' But another voice whispers: 'You have been called.' Your quandary has drawn you closer to God, closer to those you love, closer to the issues that matter - and has dragged into insignificance the banal concerns that occupy our 'normal time.'

There's another kind of response, although usually short-lived - an inexplicable shudder of excitement, as if a clarifying moment of calamity has swept away everything trivial and tinny, and placed before us the challenge of important questions.

The moment you enter the Valley of the Shadow of Death, things change. You discover that Christianity is not something doughy, passive, pious, and soft. Faith may be the substance of things hoped for, the evidence of things not seen. But it also draws you into a world shorn of fearful caution. The life of belief teems with thrills, boldness, danger, shocks, reversals, triumphs, and epiphanies. Think of Paul, traipsing though the known world and contemplating trips to what must have seemed the antipodes (Spain), shaking the dust from his sandals, worrying not about the morrow, but only about the moment.

There's nothing wilder than a life of humble virtue - for it is through selflessness and service that God wrings from our bodies and spirits the most we ever could give, the most we ever could offer, and the most we ever could do.

Finally, we can let love change everything. When Jesus was faced with the prospect of crucifixion, he grieved not for himself, but for us. He cried for Jerusalem before entering the holy city. From the Cross, he took on the cumulative burden of human sin and weakness, and begged for forgiveness on our behalf.

We get repeated chances to learn that life is not about us - that we acquire purpose and satisfaction by sharing in God's love for others. Sickness gets us partway there. It reminds us of our limitations and dependence. But it also gives us a chance to serve the healthy. A minister friend of mine observes that people suffering grave afflictions often acquire the faith of two people, while loved ones accept the burden of two people's worries and fears.

Most of us have watched friends as they drifted toward God's arms not with resignation, but with peace and hope. In so doing, they have taught us not how to die, but how to live. They have emulated Christ by transmitting the power and authority of love.

I sat by my best friend's bedside a few years ago as a wasting cancer took him away. He kept at his table a worn Bible and a 1928 edition of the Book of Common Prayer. A shattering grief disabled his family, many of his old friends, and at least one priest. Here was a humble and very good guy, someone who apologized when he winced with pain because he thought it made his guest uncomfortable. He retained his equanimity and good humor literally until his last conscious moment. 'I'm going to try to beat [this cancer],' he told me several months before he died. 'But if I don't, I'll see you on the other side.'

His gift was to remind everyone around him that even though God doesn't promise us tomorrow, he does promise us eternity - filled with life and love we cannot comprehend - and that one can in the throes of sickness point the rest of us toward timeless truths that will help us weather future storms.

Through such trials, God bids us to choose: Do we believe, or do we not? Will we be bold enough to love, daring enough to serve, humble enough to submit, and strong enough to acknowledge our limitations? Can we surrender our concern in things that don't matter so that we might devote our remaining days to things that do?

When our faith flags, he throws reminders in our way. Think of the prayer warriors in our midst. They change things, and those of us who have been on the receiving end of their petitions and intercessions know it.

It is hard to describe, but there are times when suddenly the hairs on the back of your neck stand up, and you feel a surge of the Spirit. Somehow you just know: Others have chosen, when talking to the Author of all creation, to lift us up - to speak of us!

This is love of a very special order. But so is the ability to sit back and appreciate the wonder of every created thing. The mere thought of death somehow makes every blessing vivid, every happiness more luminous and intense. We may not know how our contest with sickness will end, but we have felt the ineluctable touch of God.

What is man that Thou art mindful of him? We don't know much, but we know this: No matter where we are, no matter what we do, no matter how bleak or frightening our prospects, each and every one of us, each and every day, lies in the same safe and impregnable place - in the hollow of God's hand").

Sobran, (Michael) Joseph, Jr. – journalist and writer; b. 23 February 1946, Ypsilanti, Washtenaw County, Michigan; c. 1961; d. 30 September 2010, Fairfax, Virginia; raised by lapsed Catholic parents who divorced when he was seven or eight; his parents gave him no instruction, never took him to the sacraments, and never sent him to a Catholic school; he started to read about the faith and when fourteen years old, decided he wanted to be a Catholic; his public high school teacher attempted to talk him out of it, but he persisted and made his first communion as a teenager; graduated from East Michigan University in English; after graduation did Shakespearean studies; lectured on a fellowship at the university in Shakespeare and English; worked at the *National Review* 1972-1993 (18 years as senior editor); practiced the faith irregularly during the late 1970s and the 1980s, but returned to the Church during the papacy of John Paul II; removed from the *National Review* in controversial circumstances in 1993, over articles alleged by the editor William F. Buckley to be anti-semitic; commentator on the CBS Radio "Spectrum" program series for twenty-one years; syndicated columnist with the *Los Angeles Times*, then with the *Universal Press Syndicate*; published his own newsletter, *Sobran's*, 1994-2007; columnist under the by-line "Washington Watch" for the Catholic newspaper, *The Wanderer* 1986-2007; wrote a monthly column for *Catholic Family News* and many articles for *Human Life Review*; wrote the "Bare Bodkin" column for *Chronicles*; for most of his career identified as a paleo-conservative; argued that Edward de Vere, the 17th Earl of Oxford, was the true author of the plays usually attributed to William Shakespeare of Stratford-on-Avon; twice married and divorced; had four children; see (selective list) *The Church Today: Less Catholic Than the Pope?* (1979); *Single Issues: Essays on the Crucial Social Questions* (1983); "Pensées: Notes for the Reactionary of Tomorrow," *National Review*, 31 December 1985; "Sins of Organized Irreligion," *Center Journal*, Spring 1985; "AIDS and Social Progress," *Human Life Review*, Fall 1987, p.9; *Alias Shakespeare: Solving the Greatest Literary Mystery of All Time* (1997) (on the authorship of Shakespeare's plays); *Power and Betrayal* (1998); "The Optional Jesus," *Sobran's*, July 1998 ("After 2,000 years, the most unlikely people still want to claim Jesus for their side, even when they aren't Christians - and often, it seems, when they hate Christianity. They usually say that the churches have twisted the simple original message of love, superimposing layers of dogma, theology, and repressive morality. Jesus was great, but ever since St. Paul it's been downhill, what with St. Augustine, Cotton Mather, and all those popes. For the last two centuries a curious breed of demi-Christian has tried to disengage 'the historical Jesus' from all that dogma and stuff. What did Jesus 'really' say and do?

The trouble is that nearly everything we know about Jesus stems from the four Gospels, all of which were written by believers in the Resurrection, the central dogma. In a sense, all classic Christian theology is the working out of the implications of the Resurrection, considered as the fact the first Christians insisted, even under torture, it was. St. Paul himself said bluntly that without the Resurrection, Christianity was pointless.

That hasn't stopped the hunt for the 'historical' Jesus, the presumably real figure behind the Gospels. Since the only documents we have attest a life of miraculous deeds, supernatural orientation, and eschatological purpose, the belief that a stripped-down 'natural' life of Jesus can be reconstructed is totally at odds with the records"); "The Church and Jewish Ideology," *Sobran's*, May 1999; "Christianity and History," *Sobran's*, November 1999; "Hitler's Pope," *Sobran's*, November 1999; "The Man They Still Hate," *Sobran's*, December 1999 ("The world has long since forgiven Julius Caesar. Nobody today finds Socrates or Cicero irritating. Few of us resent Alexander the Great or his tutor, Aristotle. No, only one man in the ancient world is still hated after two millennia: Jesus Christ. This does not in itself prove the divinity of Christ, but it does show that his words and example haven't dated. They still have an amazing power to provoke hatred as well as adoration. Of course the hatred of Christ usually pretends to be directed at side targets: St. Paul, the 'institutional' Church, or, more vaguely, 'organized religion' (as if religion would be all right if only it were a solitary activity). The cliché of the Christ-haters, including many 'liberal' theologians, is that he was a 'great moral teacher' who 'never claimed divinity,' but that his 'simple message of love' was 'corrupted' by his followers. But why would anyone want a man crucified for preaching an innocuous message of benevolence? Jesus was accused of blasphemy for equating himself with the Father: 'I and the Father are one.' 'No man comes to the Father but by me.' And if his claim were untrue, the charge of blasphemy would be fully justified.

People not only saw him after the Resurrection, many of them died under torture to bear witness to him. The martyrs were the principal human 'media' of Christianity in its infancy, deeply impressing and finally converting others. Christ was 'revealed' to the ancient world in the courageous love of his best disciples. Other 'media' included the four Gospels of Matthew, Mark, Luke, and John, as well as the epistles of Paul and other apostles. Each Gospel views Jesus from a slightly different angle, but all four of them (along with the epistles) portray the same recognizable man. As Thomas Cahill notes in his book *Desire of the Everlasting Hills: The World Before and After Jesus*, this 'makes Jesus a unique figure in world literature: never have so many writers managed to convey the same impression of the same human being over and over again.' Moreover, these writers weren't polished professionals or literary geniuses. Yet they achieved something beyond the powers of such titans as Homer, Dante, Shakespeare, and Milton: they depicted a character who exudes holiness.

Cahill goes on: 'What especially makes the Gospels - from a literary point of view - work like no others is that they are about a good human being. As every writer knows, such a creature is all but impossible to capture on the page, and there are exceedingly few figures in all of literature who are both good and memorable.' The Gospel writers thus 'succeeded where almost all others failed. To a writer's eyes, this feat is a miracle just a little short of raising the dead.' Amen! In the epic poems *Paradise Lost* and *Paradise Regained,* for example, Milton notoriously made Satan more vivid than God and Christ. This led the poet William Blake to remark that Milton 'was of the Devil's party without knowing it.' Be that as it may, world literature boasts many convincing villains but few convincing saints. And no literary saint has ever spoken words with the lasting impact of Jesus' teachings.

To a writer's eyes, as Cahill might say, the sheer power of Jesus' sayings (which the poet Tennyson called 'his greatest miracle') are almost enough to prove his claim. Physical miracles might be feigned, but not these verbal miracles. Yet he apparently never wrote them down; he spoke them, often off the cuff, trusting them to 'carry' by their inherent power. Most writers are flattered if their words are remembered at all. But the spiritually demanding words of Jesus - which condemn even looking at a woman with lust - are still carried in the hearts of millions after 2000 years, even though we know them only in translations from translations. (Jesus spoke Aramaic, but the Gospels are written in Greek.) Even conveyed to us so indirectly, those words have 'carried' like no others in all history, because so many people have found them true and compelling. The durability of those words is all the more striking when you consider that they are always out of fashion, as the secular world goes through its successive fads and crazes. Jesus is Lord!"); *Hustler: The Clinton Legacy* (2000); "The Papal 'Apology,'" *Sobran's* May 2000; "Smearing a Pope," *Sobran's*, May 2000; "The Critics of Christ," *Sobran's*, June 2000 ; "The Words and Deeds of Christ," *Sobran's*, November 2000; *Anything Called a "Program" is Unconstitutional: Confessions of a Reactionary Utopian* (2001); "Christ the Culprit," *Sobran's*, February 2001; "Belloc's Prophecy," *Sobran's*, December 2001; "The Cross and the Swastika," *Sobran's*, March 2002; "The Catholic Position," *Sobran's*, May 2002 ("A few weeks ago I tried, in my feeble way, to express why I fell in love with the Catholic Church. I received many gracious and grateful responses from others who felt the same way, some of them converts like me.

Inevitably, there were also a few jeers, directed not so much against me as against the Church. Some dredged up old scandals of wicked popes, or supposedly shocking utterances of Catholic saints, or mere clichés of traditional anti-Catholic polemics. Most of these were meant to embarrass, not to persuade; the usual ahistorical nuggets.

What is startling is the perpetual passion of anti-Catholicism. You'd think that by now people who reject Catholicism would calmly ignore its teachings as old and irrelevant superstitions. After all, the Church has none of her old political power, adherence is now totally voluntary, and she has enough trouble getting her own children to listen to her.

But Catholicism still has a strange moral authority, and many people are unable to achieve a calm and assured disbelief. They are still driven to discredit the Church - perhaps for the same reason so many of us believe in her.

Catholicism offers a complete and comprehensive morality, one which most of us still recognize as the faith of our fathers. Bit by bit, the world, including other churches, has abandoned much of this morality; the Church continues to teach it, even when some of her own priests scandalously violate it.

A few generations ago, nearly all Christians shared the same sexual morality. They abhorred artificial birth control, for example. Many state laws banning the sale of contraceptive devices in this country were passed by Protestant majorities while Catholics were politically weak.

Gradually, however, Protestants ceased to oppose contraception, and Catholicism almost alone continued to condemn it. What had long been a consensus became censured as a 'Catholic position.' We now see the same process well under way with abortion and homosexuality.

If cannibalism ever becomes popular, and the rest of the world, led by its progressive-minded intellectuals, decides that anthropophagy is a basic constitutional right, opposing cannibalism will become a 'Catholic position' too. Catholics will once more be accused of wanting to 'impose' their 'views' on everyone else (even when they are far too weak to do so), and the reformers will cry, 'Let's keep government out of the kitchen!'

I don't defend the Church's morality because I am a Catholic. I became and remain a Catholic because the Church maintains a consistent morality - while the rest of the world keeps veering off into moral fads. My conviction that she is right is only strengthened by the world's strident demand that she change along with it, as if it were a sort of moral duty to change one's principles, like underwear, with reasonable frequency.

'The world' includes many nominal Catholics who side with the secular world against their own Church. These are the Catholics you are most likely to see in the major media. They deny the Church's authority to keep teaching what she has always taught, yet they can't rest until she approves their pet vices - contraception, sodomy, same-sex marriage, and all the rest.

Notice that the proposed reforms usually have to do with sex. When the Church refuses to change, she is accused of being 'obsessed' with sex, when it's really her critics who are obsessed with it. Catholic morality recognizes seven deadly sins, of which lust is only one; but this happens to be the one the modern world can't stop thinking about. Nobody demands that the Church 'change its outdated teachings against sloth.'

At any rate, the Church can't change. She can no more change her teaching about lust than her equally emphatic teachings about pride, gluttony, and sloth, because God has made the world as it is and no human will can repeal its moral order. These aren't the Pope's personal opinions; they are objective truths.

Powerless, hardly able to keep her own flock in line, and betrayed by many of her shepherds, the Church is still treated as a threat. All she really threatens is the false comfort of the dormant conscience; but this is enough to make bitter enemies.

After all, her Founder warned her not to expect gratitude from men for trying to save their souls. She is the mother of Western civilization, and to this day, all too often, she is blamed for everything and thanked for nothing"); "The Catholic Ogre," *Sobran's*, June 2002; "Can God Speak to Us," *Sobran's*, January 2005; "Resisting Jesus," *Sobran's* January 2005; "The End of a Papacy," *Sobran's*, May 2005; *Regime Change Begins at Home: Confessions of a Reactionary Utopian* (2006); "St. Paul and the Liberal Agenda," *Sobran's*, July 2006; "Jesus' Government," *Sobran's*, April-May 2006; "Science, Religion, and Hate," *Sobran's*, January 2007; "Happy Easter!," *Sobran's*, April 2007 ("It's nearly Easter, and the atheists, God bless them, are writing bestselling books to prove the good Lord's non-existence. Truly, they have their reward. One of the most famous of them, a British professor named Richard Dawkins, says atheists are generally smarter than Christians. I wouldn't doubt it. After all, St. Paul says God has chosen the foolish people of this world to confound the wise. I don't know how many times some simple soul has put me to shame when I thought I was being clever. Oops! Maybe polished professors never have this experience. Of course atheists are clever! People who spend a lot of time justifying themselves generally are. If you devote your waking hours to seeking reasons not to believe, you'll find plenty of them. Darwin sold a lot of books to clever people like that. Then there is the argument from comparative religion. Religions are a lot alike, they can't all be true, so isn't it probable that they are all false? By that kind of reasoning, you can prove not only that we don't know who wrote *Hamlet,* but that it was never written at all.

Jesus was just like a lot of other religious leaders? Such as? Do other religions have prayers like the Our Father? Did the ancient Greeks ask Zeus to 'forgive us as we forgive others?' Did the Aztecs pray like that? How many other religions command their votaries to rejoice, be of good cheer, have no fear? ('Trust in Poseidon?') And many other religious figures, we are told, have performed miracles every bit as impressive as those attributed to Jesus. Really? Did they cure blind men and cripples while assuring them that their sins were forgiven? And did they, even after they had died (and risen again, it goes without saying), make converts who would die for what they had taught? Did any of them ever give a speech like the Sermon on the Mount? If so, where can I find a copy?

For that matter, did any of these impressive religious teachers, who seem to have been very numerous, match Jesus in what has been called his 'command of the moment,' making memorable retorts, still quoted centuries later, to enemies trying to trap them with trick questions? Have any of their reported ad libs endured as permanent moral teachings, like 'Whoever among you is without sin, let him cast the first stone?' Come to think of it, the atheists could strengthen their case somewhat by producing the prayers of other religions to show how much they resemble, or even surpass, Christian prayers. Why don't they? Just asking. But I have my suspicions. Just as President Bush says Islam is a 'religion of peace' because he assumes that all religions are pretty much alike (and like Christianity) by definition, so the atheists seem to assume that all religions share the features of Christianity they detest. I wish they would go all out and really press the analogies - honestly, not selectively.

When you point to the rather horrid regimes run by atheists in the twentieth century, you can count on the atheists to disown them, on the pretext that men like Stalin were the 'wrong' sort of atheists because they were just as 'dogmatic' as Christians. With people who argue this way, you'd better cut the deck before letting them deal the cards. They're saying that empirical evidence is inadmissible - except when they want to use it. If Hitler and Stalin believed in Darwinism, that doesn't count against Darwinism, because they 'abused' it. You get the impression that Darwinism can be safely applied only by people who practice Christian morality - but of course that such people are mostly atheists. In other words, atheists make better Christians than Christians do. Well, at least they are smarter.

How can God be both good and omnipotent, when there is so much evil in the world? I can't answer this one, and it has tormented believers so deeply that the Scriptures themselves ask it many times. It's known as the Problem of Evil. I can say only that it's trumped by the real mystery, the Problem of Good"); "The Sanctimony of the Atheists," *Sobran's*, 8 May 2007; "Cruel Doctrines," *Sobran's*, 8 June 2007; "Behind the Times," *Sobran's*, 12 July 2007; ("Pope Benedict keeps reminding me why I am a Catholic. If I hadn't converted as a boy, I would now. In the space of a few days he has moved to correct the very things that once helped me (along with my own sins) to lose my faith.

First, he took steps to restore the ancient Tridentine Rite, commonly known as the Latin Mass. This beautiful liturgy connects today's Church with its ancestors all the way back to the days of persecution in ancient Rome, and its use has given worshippers the sense not only of antiquity, but eternity. I still love the responses I learned as a youth: Domine, non sum dignus…

I never understood why anything so gravely beautiful and venerable should be abandoned for jejune modern vernaculars; what was gained by the supposed 'reform'? The Novus Ordo liturgy has always made me feel as if I'd dropped in on a slangy Unitarian ceremony.

The liturgical 'reform', moreover, backfired miserably on its own terms. It impaired belief itself; and Mass attendance, Catholic education, frequent confession, and big families decreased sharply along with belief. These were the opposite of the happy results the liberal reformers confidently predicted, and the Church lost both its authority with Catholics and the wider respect and influence it had enjoyed among Protestants and even in the secular world.

The entire world has suffered from the misguided changes wrought by the Second Vatican Council. Try to imagine the solar system if the sun dimmed and lost its attraction for the planets, and you have the idea. If the Council had never occurred, would the U.S. Supreme Court have dared to strike down laws against feticide? Would the Episcopal Church be ordaining sexual perverts today? Such questions answer themselves. The world has never seen so consequential an abdication of authority. It has been like the effect on a family of a father's suicide.

The Pope has also reaffirmed the supremacy of the Catholic Church, a doctrine never denied, but certainly soft-pedaled since the disastrous Council. For some reason this has irritated many Protestants, who seem to think their sects can thrive without the strong presence of Catholicism. Incredibly, one Protestant editor has referred to Catholicism as a 'denomination,' rather like Mormonism. Does he know what the word means? He might as well speak of the sun and moon as 'planets'.

Like its Founder, the Catholic Church has an unending power to inspire hatred in those who reject it. The world's hate is one of the proofs of its divine origin and authority. After 2,000 years, it is still persecuted, still treated as a threat. But no worldly persecution could have damaged it as much as Vatican II.

And yet the Church never compromised the essentials of faith and morals. Amid the hysteria of a 'population explosion' in the Sixties, even the weak Pope Paul VI, against tremendous pressure, refused to relax the Church's condemnation of contraception. Now look. White Europe is depopulated and overrun with aliens; its very survival is in doubt.

But the last thing man gives up, even in the face of death and damnation, is his pride, and very few Europeans, even in formerly Catholic countries, can bring themselves to admit, 'We were wrong. The sexual revolution has been a calamity for our civilization. The Church was exactly right.' Europe could finally see that Communism was a dreadful failure, but it still can't bear to repent. Even as the end draws near, the syphilitic Prodigal Son is still whoring away. God wants to save us so much more than we want to be saved!

As G. K. Chesterton, one of the greatest and most joyously funny writers in the English language, wrote seventy years ago, 'The Church is always in advance of the world. That is why it is said to be behind the times.' 'Only the Catholic Church,' he also observed, 'can save a man from the degraded slavery of being a child of his age.'

It's ennobling to belong to a church centuries behind the times, as they say, and indifferent to the fashions of the day; but it's supremely undignified to belong to a church five minutes behind the times while always huffing and puffing to catch up. Benedict's papacy is already a glorious one"); "A Prophecy Fulfilled: The Wisdom of *Humanae Vitae*," *The Reactionary Utopian*, 21 August 2008; "Jesus' Simple Message," *Chronicles*, January 2008 ("The loveliest argument I know against unbelief was made by a woman whose name I have forgotten, quoted by the theologian John Baillie in *Our Knowledge of God* [Note: the woman referred to was the writer Katherine Mansfield]; it boils down to this: 'If there is no God, whom do we thank?'

The force of this hit me on a mild November evening when I was oppressed by woes; I prayed for a little relief and tried counting my blessings instead of my grievances. I've long known that a great secret of happiness is gratitude, but that didn't prepare me for what happened next.

It wasn't a mystical experience, just a simple mental one (speaking of simple messages). I began by comparing my lot with that of countless others, many of whom are starving or dying of horrible diseases. Then, I reflected that the modern world teaches us to be ingrates. What else is political life for? Democracy is obsessed with supposed rights, injuries, and entitlements.

Within a few minutes, as I munched a cheeseburger, my mind told me how unlikely my own existence was: My parents' meeting (remarkably improbable, too, just in mathematical terms), the love they gave me, my living in the Christian Era, my later Baptism (I became a Catholic at age fifteen), the priests who taught me, my dear stepfather and his holy parents, my friends, my children, and on and on - in spite of all my own sins. I could hardly think of anything in my life that couldn't be seen as a gift from God. Now I was over sixty-one, still showered with blessings every day, despite all my attempts to make myself unhappy by brooding on my petty dissatisfactions.

As one of the characters in *Lear* tells his father 'Thy life's a miracle.' Of whom is that not true?

The more we reflect on the sheer oddity of our very existence and, in addition, of our eligibility for salvation, the deeper our gratitude must be. Amazing grace indeed! To call it astounding is to express the matter feebly. Why me? How on earth could I ever have deserved this, the promise of eternal joy?

And given all this, in comparison. with which winning the greatest lottery in the world is just a minor fluke, how can I dare to sin again, or to be anything less than a saint for the rest of my life?

Yet I know that my own horrible spiritual habits will keep drawing me downward every hour. Like most men, or maybe more than most, I am my own worst enemy, constantly tempted to repay my Savior with my self-centered ingratitude. When I think of my sins, the debt of thanksgiving itself seems far too heavy to pay. No wonder He commands us to rejoice. It's by no means the easiest of our duties"); "Eccentric Catholicism," *The Reactionary Utopian*, 29 May 2009; "The Incomparable One," *The Reactionary Utopian*, 4 June 2009 ("Jesus was far from being an old man when his earthly life ended. He was probably well under 40, roughly the age of Mozart, who died at 35, as his genius was still approaching its unimaginable peak.

By contrast, nobody thinks of Jesus as having died prematurely, as if he had been killed before his teaching had been fully developed, and as if it might have ripened into something more profound and interesting had his life span been longer. There is about his life a sense of completeness; he had done what he had come to achieve. At the very end, he said, 'It is consummated.' He had foretold his own death and resurrection.

The Jesus Seminar, a liberal group that includes theologians as well as the director of *Robocop*, has tried to distinguish between authentic and inauthentic sayings of Jesus in the four Gospels; but nobody has ventured to suggest what he might have said if only he had survived another ten years or so. Those Gospels do seem to indicate the fulfillment of a mission, don't they?

It is, of course, impossible for anyone to invent a single saying worthy of Jesus. Much easier to coin a phrase worthy of a human genius like Shakespeare! 'Heaven and earth shall pass away,' Jesus said, 'but my words shall not pass away.' Once we have heard those words, they become part of us. They seem so familiar that we may think they are trite, but they are not. They are eternally new, even when we have heard them all our lives, and they always reward meditation on them.

Some day when you have nothing better to do, try improving on the Lord's Prayer. 'Forgive us our trespasses, as we forgive those who trespass against us.' Don't all religions agree on that? No. In most religions - see the *Iliad,* the *Koran,* and the *Psalms,* for example - it is normal to pray for revenge. Forgiving and praying for one's enemies are among the hardest duties of a Christian. Being 'nice' is far from the same thing as being a Christian; after all, Jesus was not tortured to death for urging good manners on his disciples.

But he did recommend good manners. As G. K. Chesterton wrote, the assertion that the meek shall inherit the earth is not at all a meek statement. 'Meek' does not mean cowardly or timid; it means polite and unassuming.

If you want to contend that the Gospels are packs of lies and that Jesus never said all those things or performed all those wonders, you should at least admit that Christianity is the most brilliant hoax of all time. Everything fits so well. How could a few unlearned and provincial Jews invent such a supremely memorable character, endow him with the ability to speak immortal words on all occasions, then make virtually all the details of his story cohere so well, tallying even with Old Testament prophecy?

A cliché of literary criticism tells us that evil characters are more interesting than good ones. If so, why is this best of all characters - indeed, he is sinless - so fascinating? And how could four unpracticed amateur writers create the most vividly virtuous personality in all literature? And why does he sound like the same utterly unique man in all of their accounts of him? In Jesus, goodness is not at all bland; it normally inspires, but it can also be disturbing, challenging, even frightening. He is incomparable; he never reminds us of anyone else. He spiritually dwarfs even the charismatic John the Baptist.

It has been said (again, by Chesterton) that whereas the death of Socrates seems to come as a rather arbitrary interruption of a conversation that might have gone on forever, Jesus' death is the center of his story. Even during his infancy, his mother received intimations of his agonizing destiny. And he knew when his fatal hour had come.

Unbelievers have made it their never-ending task to explain Jesus away. Some have even suggested that he never existed at all! That degree of unbelief is itself unbelievable. Such daft doubts remind us that atheism is the extreme form of wishful thinking. But there will be no wishful thinking in hell, where all comforting fantasies end forever"); "Thank God for Atheists," *The Reactionary Utopian*, 24 March 2010; Shakespeare Explained series (*Hamlet* (2008); *Julius Caesar* (2009); *A Midsummer Night's Dream* (2009), *Henry IV, Part I* (2009-2010); *Twelfth Night* (2009-2010)); Fran Griffin (ed), *Joseph Sobran, The National Review Years: Articles From 1974-1991* (2012).

Sothern, Ann (born Harriet Arlene Lake) – actress; b. 22 January 1909, Valley City, North Dakota (in old age she claimed it was 1919 and Minneapolis, Minnesota); c. 1952; d. 15 March 2001, Ketchum, Idaho; raised in Minneapolis; trained by her mother as a classical singer, but more suited to musical comedy; went to Hollywood in 1933; appeared as a chorus girl and an extra in films and on Broadway; contracts with several Hollywood production companies; first major success in the title role ("a scatter-brained, accident prone, but resourceful blonde") in *Maisie* (1939), followed by several comedy sequels on film and for five years on radio; celebrated performance in the Academy Award winning film *A Letter to Three Wives* in 1949; in the 1950s she mainly appeared in television shows, including her own show 1958-1961; she became a Catholic under the influence of Richard Egan (1921-1987), the actor; on her conversion she took the name Anna Maria Sothern; suffered a serious back injury on stage in 1974 when a piece of scenery fell on her; occasional television appearances until the mid-1980s and made her last film in 1987, *The Whales of August* (nomination for Best Supporting Actress Academy Award; married

Roger Prior (1901-1974), actor, in 1936 (divorced in 1943); married Robert Sterling (1917-2006), actor in 1943 (one daughter of the marriage, the actress Tisha Sterling (b. 1944)), but divorced in 1949; see Colin Briggs, *Cordially Yours, Ann Sothern* (2006).

Spearman, Frank Hamilton – author; b. 6 September 1859; d. 29 December 1937; his parents were originally from Delaware and of Methodist stock, but moved west and joined the Congregational Church; brought up with simple Evangelical Christianity; after the death of his parents he too joined Congregationalism at the age of sixteen; lapsed into indifference; became a freemason; president of a bank in McCook, Nebraska; influenced in his conversion to the Catholic Church by his Catholic wife; wrote Western fiction and both fiction and non-fiction works on railroads; politically held libertarian views; both his religious and political beliefs were reflected in his novels; his most celebrated Western novel was *Whispering Smith*, based on two real life Union Pacific railroad detectives; it was made into a film on eight occasions, and into a twenty episode television series in 1961 featuring Audie Murphy and Guy Mitchell; see *The Nerve of Foley* (1900); *Held for Orders* (1901); *Doctor Bryson* (1902); *The Daughter of a Magnate* (1903); *The Close of the Day* (1904); *The Strategy of Great Railroads* (1904); *Whispering Smith* (1906); essay in Georgina Pell Curtis (ed), *Some Roads to Rome in America* (1909), p.409 ("When I say, then, that I came into the Church clinging to the hand of a woman it will readily be understood that I married a Catholic wife. Yet to dismiss the story with this mere statement, as I am aware might be done, would be to lose some of its significance. Conversions of this sort are not, I believe, uncommon; but if this were all, the results in all of these cases should be pretty much the same; whereas, they are markedly, even distressingly, different. What is easily lost sight of in such a matter is that as a means of grace a Catholic wife - actual or prospective - can serve only to bring an enquirer to the door, so to say, of the Catholic Church. There is still the vital matter of working out an understanding of a faith that must seem very new and strange: and upon the character of this working out everything depends...

What stands most clearly out of the new body of confused impressions that came to me at that time is the influence of one personality, that of John Henry Newman. It was, it seems to me, Newman - kindly, serious, patient, and consoling as the great Church itself - who most smoothed the way for me to understand. I read his *Apologia*. It is the story of a road to Rome as far removed as possible from that which I could expect or hope to travel - the story of the intimate working of the mind of a great and learned divine. No doubt much of it I failed to grasp: possibly pages and pages of it were not written for me, but there were, I am sure, things of importance in it that I did grasp. For example, from Newman's story I got my first glimpse of the heart of a boy entirely innocent; and I was able to compare it with the heart of another boy that I knew. Here, curiously enough, was a starting point for thought. Here was an innocence to which I had grown, if I had not always been, a stranger. And I believed Newman: he convinced me. Rousseau never did this: the *Confessions*, to me, bore the stamp of insincerity. During the earlier period in which I had read them I simply did not believe the professions of Jean Jacques. If, indeed, he did tell everything he is entitled to the crown which he industriously spent his life in hammering out for himself. But I never could satisfy myself that Rousseau made what Catholics term a good confession.

As to Newman, I was disposed on the very strength of this novel and innocent candor to listen to the grave man. Disposed to listen! How much that means. How much depends on what confidence we put in the teacher. Others, very many others, than Newman could have led me, for the Mother of Saints is never without instruments to guide enquirers: it was Newman chiefly, I think, who did. He softened my suspicions and disarmed my distrust: and... brought my ignorances home to me, so graciously, so delicately, that they became, as it were, ashamed and slipped away unperceived. Then he left me to myself.

On the subject of miracles I found that my difficulties were based, as nearly as enquirers' difficulties are, on mere misapprehension of Catholic doctrine. I learned that the only miracles that were 'of faith' were those miracles recorded in the Bible or necessarily deduced from the deposit of faith. To anyone who believes that Christ is God there is obviously no difficulty in receiving the record of His miraculous power. Upon the Divinity of Christ I had always hung the first link in the chain of my faith. It has never been other than a matter of instant recognition and acceptance to me that this Man was different, not in degree but in kind from all other men. Toward later miracles, then, my attitude when I entered the Church was naturally one of suspicious skepticism. It is needless, almost, to say that many years and the Catholic viewpoint have greatly softened this. I was asked on becoming a Catholic to accede on this point to only one proposition: that in the life of the Church, miracles always had been and always would be possible: but that the authenticity of any particular miracle is a matter of evidence...And as to the matter of miracles in the life of the Church itself, its history so abounds in them and they are in so numberless cases thoroughly attested that I could only look upon myself as utterly crass if I still shook my head at them.

Devotion to the Blessed Virgin was, of course, with me a sore, not to say offensive, point in the Catholic practice. And the unfortunate Saints! God will surely recompense them in some way for the lively suspicion with which they are regarded by non-Catholics. Fancy the feelings of St. Alphonsus Liguori at the indictments that have been drawn sternly against him! And it would seem that the distance to which the sects have variously wandered from the teachings of real Christianity may accurately be measured by their attitude towards devotion to the Blessed Virgin, or 'Mary' as she is familiarly known not by her friends. To invoke the most favored servants of God that they may join us in asking for the petitions we lay before Him - how odious hatred has made the beautiful custom wherever it has had a chance to blind the human heart to Catholic truth! The white prayers of the just - living and dead - how consoling the thought that we can enlist them to plead with ourselves for our unworthiness!...

When I came to discriminate - as even a slight consideration must force me to do - between the sins of unworthy Catholics and the doctrines of the Catholic Church itself I saw that upon the charge of cruelty [hitherto his major objection to the Catholic Church], at all events, the ground was slipping from under me. I was reminded very kindly that Christ had never promised perfection to human nature, nor that scandals should not arise among his followers. The question left for me to thrash out was, to what were these cruelties, real and alleged, due: to the doctrines of the Catholic Church or to human nature still unregenerate ? There could be, there can be, but one issue here and but one answer. The Church of Christ has never been, I was to learn, other than all merciful. It is not alone that its spirit has been that of mercy, but that its teachings become, the more deeply they are studied, most wonderful of all in the depths of their mercy. To take one passing instance out of many that might suggest themselves, who was there to tell me, before I began to study, that it is of Catholic doctrine that we are not permitted to say that a soul is lost? That no matter how depraved the life may have been, no matter how abhorrent the transgressions of human and divine law it is still of the Catholic belief that a merciful possibility remains: and that in the very last moment of such a life, even during a flash of consciousness in a death of repulsive delirium, there still may come, unseen by the closest observer, an instant of perfect contrition to save that soul from eternal damnation. I offer but this instance of what has so struck me in this regard. As to cruelty, men there have been, no doubt, within the Catholic Church sufficiently infamous; but if kings, rulers, prelates or priests have disgraced their profession of its faith by enacting or countenancing savagery they are simply answerable where we shall all one day be answerable - not for the sins of others but for our own.

It is really curious that because Catholics have committed murder we should charge murder upon the teachings of the Catholic Church. We do not follow these accusations against it, as we logically should, through the decalogue. No one asserts, because a Catholic may steal, that the Catholic Church conducts a novitiate for pickpockets. The Christian religion - and here I use the term as identical with the Catholic Church because experience teaches that none of the sects exercise over their followers anything approaching the control exercised by the Catholic Church over its followers - the Christian religion, I say, has to do with a human nature possessing a propensity almost incredible for wrongdoing. Though, indeed, there is a limit it would seem that it must often have been passed by Christians. But to admit that Christianity has not always made saints of men is in no way to disparage its truths. And thus it is, I repeat, that the whole miserable subject of religious persecution has nothing proper to do with religious truth. The causes of the former lie deep in the least tolerable qualities of human nature itself. Those things most inhuman are paradoxically most human. In the matter of religious zeal - if we consider that alone - it always has been and always will be easier to smite off the ear of the servant of the high priest than to watch for one hour in the garden of Gethsemane; but the rewards are sure to be something radically different. In matter of fact the more deeply one goes into the inquiry of religious persecution, insofar as it affects the claims of the Catholic Church, the more will he come to realize that it is a scarecrow dressed up for his disedification. The sum of the matter has been outrageously exaggerated; the lying about it has been as relentless and implacable as its pictured ferocities; and in the end it will be found that the Church itself has when possible alleviated its horrors and when impossible protested against them. It is a bogey which at its worst should deceive no one: has nothing relevantly to do with the case: and puts on the enquirer's shoulders nothing to apologize for but the sins of individual Catholics. For that matter, if he begin to apologize for sin at all, he will find, with even indifferent industry, quite enough outside the question of Catholic claims and religious persecutions to busy him very comfortably.

In speaking with frankness as I have done in this matter I do not for a moment lose sight of that maxim containing so much of human as well as of divine wisdom, 'By their fruits ye shall know them.' The Church of Christ may well on the last day bring its fruits before its Master to prove its identity. Who, indeed, shall speak in the presence of those legions of Catholic Christians who from the greatest to the least of earth have given themselves as missionaries, martyrs, virgins and confessors to its work? The honor roll of the Roman Catholic Church! What a silence its august centuries impose upon the detractor"); *Robert Kimberly* (1911); *The Mountain Divide* (1912); *Merrilie Dawes* (1913); *Nan of Music Mountain* (1916); *Laramie Holds the Range* (1921); *The Marriage Verdict* (1923); *Selwood of Sleepy Cat* (1924); *Your Son's Education* (1925); *Flambeau Jim* (1927); *Spanish Lover* (1930); *Hell's Desert* (1932); *Gunlock Ranch* (1935).

Springer, Reuben Runyan - businessman and philanthropist; b. 16 November 1800, Frankfort, Kentucky; d. 11 December 1884, Cincinnati; father a farmer and postmaster; educated in local schools up to the age of thirteen; helped his father in the post office; became postmaster after his father's death in 1816; became a clerk on several steamboats; in 1830 he married Jane Kilgour (d. 1868), the daughter of a partner in one of the firms and a Catholic (no children of the marriage); he himself became a partner in the firm; in 1840 the partners retired and the firm was dissolved; he then invested some of his earned wealth in banking, railroads, and real estate, making a high profit; collector of art from France and Germany; after accompanying his wife to Mass he too became a Catholic; gave very generously to Catholic institutions and charities; gave very considerable sums in order to build up the cultural life of Cincinnati; while alive he refused to allow his name to be attached to buildings associated with these initiatives; quiet, methodical and modest; see *ANB* ("Although reared without strong religious beliefs, he found his wife's Roman Catholicism a source of strength").

Squanto (also known as Tisquantum) – b. c.1580s (many say 1 January 1580); d. November 1622, Chatham, Massachusetts; member of the Patuxet tribe; kidnapped in 1614 by Thomas Hunt, an Englishman (a lieutenant of Captain John Smith (1580-1631), the explorer rescued by Pocahontas); Hunt attempted to sell him and others into slavery in Malaga, Spain; some local priests discovered this and took custody of them; he was instructed by them in the Catholic faith and baptized; he persuaded the friars to let him try to get home, and he managed to get to London, where for a few years he lived and worked with John Slany, a shipbuilder, learning some English; in 1619 he returned to his homeland, but his tribe had been wiped out by a devastating plague;

the Mayflower Pilgrims arrived in 1620 and he settled with them at the site of his former village, which the Pilgrims had called Plymouth; he assisted them in recovering from their first hard winter; taught them to fish and to cultivate maize by the native method; worked as assistant to the colony, translating and negotiating between the colony and tribal leaders; died of fever; buried in an unmarked grave, possibly in Plymouth's cemetery, Burial Hill; see N. Salisbury, "Squanto: Last of the Patuxets," in David G. Sweet and Gary B. Nash (ed), *Struggle and Survival in Colonial America* (1989), p.228.

Staples, Tim – Catholic apologist; c. 1988 (his father, mother, and his brothers were also received later, one, Terry, becoming a priest); brought up a Southern Baptist; drifted away from religion in his early teens, but came back at eighteen through the Assemblies of God; spent four years as part of the Marine Corps; also became a youth pastor at an Assemblies of God church; during his final year in the Marines he met a marine who was a well-informed Catholic, Sergeant Matthew Dula; this encounter led him to search for the truth over two years and finally convert to the Catholic faith; after his conversion he studied for the priesthood for six years, earning a degree in Philosophy from St. Charles Borromeo Seminary in Overbrook, Pennsylvania; then studied Theology on a graduate level at Mount St. Mary's Seminary in Emmitsburg, Maryland, for two years; realizing that his calling was not to the priesthood, he left the seminary in 1994; then worked in Catholic apologetics and evangelization; became Director of Apologetics and Evangelization at *Catholic Answers*; see "The Bible Made Me Do It," in Patrick Madrid (ed), *Surprised by Truth* (1994), p.211 ("One day Matt asked, 'Tim, why do you believe in the inspiration of Scripture?' My response was, 'Because the Bible says it's inspired. 2 Timothy 3:16 says "All Scripture is given by inspiration of God."' Then Matt showed me the fallacy of circular reasoning that flawed my response. I was right, of course; Scripture is inspired, but I hadn't proved it by citing 2 Timothy 3:16. The mere fact that the Bible claims to be inspired doesn't prove that it is. Plenty of other 'holy books' claim to be inspired: the Qur'an, the Book of Mormon, the Hindu Vedas, just to name three.

Matt explained that Catholics and Protestants alike have received the testimony of the Church that Scripture is inspired. The Church did not make the books of the Bible inspired, of course, but it is the trustworthy witness God uses to attest to Scripture's authenticity and inspiration…

Matt often told me how much authentic Christian truth I was missing out on because I denied the Church's tradition which could so enrich Scripture for me. He said my views would remain incomplete without this gift of God. As a Fundamentalist, tradition had always carried a negative connotation for me. I connected 'tradition' with Jesus' stern condemnation of 'traditions of men' which nullify the Word of God (Matt. 15:9).

Until Matt and I began to hammer away at *sola scriptura* I hadn't noticed the Bible's positive discussion of traditions. For example, Paul commanded the first Christians to 'stand firm and hold fast to the traditions that you were taught, either by an oral statement or by a letter of ours' (2 Thess. 2:15). Here Paul says that divine revelation comes to us in both written and oral form, and both are equally binding. I noticed too that this text says that the written Word is a subset of the overarching category of Tradition.

Other passages dealing with tradition helped me gain an appreciation of the biblical role of divine revelation preserved in the Church's oral Tradition. For example, Paul said, 'I praise you because you remember me in everything and hold fast to the traditions just as I handed them on to you' (1 Cor. 11:2; see also Luke 10:16; 1 Thess. 2:13; 2 Tim. 2:1-2)… The writings of the Church Fathers clearly show that the early Church was Catholic long before the time of the Emperor Constantine. St. Ignatius, bishop of Antioch who knew St. John and who wrote in A.D. 110, speaks of the Church of Rome having primacy. He said the Roman Church has 'the presidency of love.' A shiver went up my spine when I read these words from Ignatius: 'Let no man do aught of things pertaining to the Church apart from the bishop. Let that be held a valid Eucharist which is under the bishop or one to whom he shall have committed it. Wheresoever the bishop shall appear, there let the people be; even as where Jesus may be, there is the Catholic Church'"); *EWTN Audio Library, The Journey Home* (14 August 1998) ("I met a Catholic who was not like the Catholics I had met before...When I began to share what I believed was the fullness of the truth with him, and when I began to share my normal anti-Catholic arguments with him, for the first time in my life I had a Catholic response. And not only did he respond, he responded rapid fire and with Scripture. I'll give you a couple of quick examples... One of the first ones I always use: Why do you call priests 'father'? You know it well, Matthew 23:9: 'Call no man on the earth father, you have one father and he is in heaven.' 'Man, how can you be a Christian and directly contradict what the Christ said?' Of course, I sat back and said, 'OK, you can't answer that.' But, again for the first time in my life, Matthew responded and he said, 'Tim, you have considered Luke 16:24?' And I was, like, 'Wait a second. Catholics aren't supposed to do that.' And of course in Luke 16:24 Jesus tells the story of Abraham and he refers to Abraham as father Abraham...

And he didn't stop there. He goes to Romans 4:1-18 and we see St. Paul calls Abraham father seven times; 1 John 2:13: John refers to the elders as fathers; Acts 7:1-2: Stephen calls him father; 1 Cor 4:14-15: St. Paul calls himself father and in front of the Christians. And on and on. There are many more. In fact, he ended up saying this to me, and I remember he kind of ticked me off a little bit. He said, 'Tim, the question is not why we call a priest father. Why don't you call your ministers father? Everybody does in the Bible...

So that was a real experience... He showed me in context it's clear that Jesus was saying we don't refer to anyone's father in the sense that we refer to God as father. A father, whether he's a physical father or a spiritual father, is only a father inasmuch as he participates in that fatherhood...

It was doctrine after doctrine. You know, we covered a lot of smaller, less significant, doctrines. I came back and said, 'Well, what about vain repetition in Matthew 6:7?' and he responded quickly on that one and blew me out of the water once again. It got to the point where I was afraid to bring up any more doctrines, and then we started getting to the heavy ones and I found that Matthew had responses to justification by faith alone of course. He showed me the only place in the Bible where the words 'faith alone' are found. The words 'not by' are right in front of them in James 2:24. And of course I knew that. But, most importantly, and I think it's important for our Catholic listeners to understand, is here I experienced a Catholic who had a living relationship with Jesus Christ and he was presenting these truths. He was presenting these things - look, not new Scripture. I had read the New Testament through thirty times, had probably a good portion, half of it, memorized. But, he presented it to me by the power of the Holy Spirit, and the Holy Spirit began to work on me.

So, we started to move to the more important doctrines: the authority of the Church, the papacy (Matthew 16), and on and on, until finally it was Mary. Mary was the last straw. I can remember thinking in my mind. 'OK. man, this guy is rocking my world here. But I'm going to hold on.' In my mind I was thinking the one thing that is going to keep me Protestant is Mary. Boy, was I in for a surprise! Because all the time Mary, of course, was interceding for me to God that I may be brought to the fullness of the faith. And that would really be the final straw for me, Mary...I can remember when he shared with me the first verse that he used and I can remember the context. I was saying to him, 'Well, Matt, there is no way you are going to show me Mary without sin in

Scripture and I quoted 1 John 1:8 and Romans 3:23...He fired back. There are two main contexts...The one was Luke 1:28. He showed me when the angel Gabriel first comes down to the Blessed Virgin Mary; and the angel says, 'Hail, full of grace' (χαίρε κεχαριτωμένη in Greek). He pointed out to me that that word there, κεχαριτωμένη, is power-packed inasmuch as it means literally 'she who has been perfected in grace.' And I went to my Protestant sources and such and argued, 'Well, that's not what it means.' He brought back such scholars as St. Jerome. You know, one of the greatest Scripture scholars who ever walked the planet, who translates it in Latin, 'gratia plena', full of grace.. 'Hail, she has been full of grace.' Now, if Mary is full of grace, then you and I are still working on it. St. Paul himself (Philippians 3:12) said, 'I am not yet perfected, but I press on towards perfection.' Now, according to the angel in Luke 1, Mary is already perfected in grace, which means she is without sin.

And I remember when he shared this with me, he showed me the context of Luke 1, you know, where you have an angel doing obeisance to Mary. I mean there's something strange going on here when the angel comes down and says 'χαίρε'. That's the first Greek word there, that we translate 'hail'. 'Hail, she who has been perfected in grace.' Now, that's kind of strange. You have an angel showing deference to Mary. Because in every other situation where an angel appears, there's no doubt who the big guy is and who the little guy is. But here the angel seems to be telling us something. He uses a term, χαίρε, that is used for royalty, like we see in John 19:3: 'Hail, King of the Jews.' It's used in the context of a 'hail Caesar', that sort of thing. It's not the common greeting, but it's 'χαίρε', a term of royalty.

Well, he's showing me all this in context and I'm thinking, 'Oh my goodness.' But then I said, 'OK, it's one thing to say Mary was perfected in grace, but how do you know she was immaculately conceived? That it went all the way back to the time of her conception? What do you do for that?' And he pulls out this concept that I'd never heard of, Mary as the new Eve. Mary as the new Eve is a concept which really blew my mind for several reasons. One, if you go to John 2, the wedding feast at Cana…They are running out of wine and, of course, Mary comes to Jesus and says that they have no wine. And Jesus says this in Greek, 'τί ἐμοὶ καὶ σοί, γυναί' or literally 'What to me and to you, woman? 'Now, that word 'woman', you know, is loaded, and I didn't know this. I had no clue, but he pointed out to me that, though on the surface it looks problematic, Jesus calling his mother 'woman'… It seems as though, and you can almost understand how some of our Protestant brothers would say, 'Jesus is here putting Mary down'…

But of course not. Jesus can't do that. I mean, that would be breaking the Fourth Commandment and we know that Jesus, as the perfect God-man…could never dishonor his mother. In fact, that would be, according to Deuteronomy 21, punishable by death, and I don't think Jesus is going to fall into that.

But he pointed out to me that that word 'woman' is so significant, not only in Scripture, but in the tradition. For two thousand years it's been taught this is the fulfillment of Genesis 3:15. Right after the fall of Adam and Eve, Eve was first called 'woman', which in the Greek Septuagint, remember… the word 'γυναί' was applied to Eve seven times in Genesis 3. But, there's an eighth time there, where it refers prophetically to the woman who was to come, the mother of the redeemer who, together with her son, would crush the head of Lucifer, of the Devil. This is the fulfillment in John 2. When Jesus referred to his mother as 'woman', he is referring to her as the new Eve of Genesis 3. And, boy, when I heard that, I didn't want to hear any more…

He challenged me to get into reading the Church Fathers about this, and especially about the new Eve. I found it in scripture in John 19, Revelation 12, key passages of Scripture"); *EWTN Audio Library, The Journey Home* (7 May 2001) ("[Matthew] challenged me and I'll never forget the day he said, 'Tim, you're reading Jimmy Swaggart's book; you're reading Dr. Walter Martin's book; you're reading Dr. R. C. Sproul. Why don't you read Catholics. If you want to write about Catholicism, why don't you read Catholics and, in particular, the Church Fathers and the actual canons and decrees of Councils? And so I took him up on that, thinking I was going to just destroy this misguided Catholicism; and that is where I saw the beauty of Catholicism!"); *Apologetics for the New Evangelization* (1999); *Beyond a Reasonable Doubt (Matters of Truth)* (1999); *Nuts and Bolts: A Practical How-To Guide for Explaining and Defending the Catholic Faith* (1999) (with Patrick Madrid); *Islam Exposed: The Crescent in the Light of the Cross* (2001); *All Things Catholic* (2005) (with Scott Hahn); *EWTN Audio Library, The Journey Home* (1 March 2010).

Starr, Eliza Allen – art historian, artist and teacher; b. 29 August 1824, Deerfield, Massachusetts; c. 23 December 1854, Boston; d. 8 September 1901, Durand, Illinois; forebears, who came from England, settled at Cambridge, Massachusetts in 1633; brought up as a Protestant; studied in Boston; several private and boarding school teaching posts; in 1846 a Unitarian preacher destroyed her religious faith; after years of struggle she converted to the Catholic faith; main influence in her conversion was Rt. Rev. Francis Patrick Kenrick, later Archbishop of Baltimore, and her cousin George Allen, Professor of Classics at University of Pennsylvania, and himself a convert; applied for admission to a convent, but was discouraged because of her poor health; member of the Third Order of St. Dominic; daily mass goer and living life of mortification and self-denial; from 1856 wrote and lectured on art and literature; became well known throughout the United States for her works on Catholic art; in 1865 she became the first woman to receive the *Laetare* Medal from University of Notre Dame; co-founder of the Catholic Women's League; aunt of Ellen Gates Starr (see below), whom she greatly influenced; unmarried; see *Poems* (1867); *Patron Saints* (1869); *Pilgrims and Shrines* (1883); *Songs of a Life-time* (1887); *Isabella of Castille* (1889); *Christian Art in Our Own Age* (1891); *Christmas-tide* (1891); *What We See* (1891); *The Virgin Mother of Jesus* (1892); *Three Keys to the Camera della Segnatura of the Vatican* (1896); *The Seven Dolors of the Blessed Virgin Mary* (1898); *The Three Archangels and the Guardian Angels in Art* (1899); James J. McGovern (ed), *The Life and Letters of Eliza Allen Starr* (1905); Eliza Allen Starr Papers, University of Notre Dame; Patrick Allitt, *Catholic Converts: British and American Intellectuals Turn to Rome* (1997), pp.131-133 ("She had a 'majestic theory' that 'the Catholic Church will give a crowning grace to the art and literature of America'... To her, as to her English counterpart Augustus Pugin, it seemed 'monstrous' to find most American Catholics totally indifferent to their religion's rich artistic, musical, and literary heritage. She noted that the revival of Gregorian chant, exquisite ancient Catholic music, was taking place in Episcopalian churches, 'while Catholic congregations grumbled over its reintroduction to our choirs. They are not satisfied unless they can have a polka to come out of church by'"); *Catholic Encyclopedia*.

Starr, Ellen Gates – social reformer; b. 19 March 1859, near Laona, Illinois; c. 1920 (St. Joseph's Benedictine Abbey, Louisiana; she believed ultimately that she had been "a Catholic at heart" for a good while); d. 10 February 1940, Suffern, New York; father a farmer and businessman; came from a Unitarian background; no religion in her early upbringing, but she spent much of her life in search of religious truth; joined the Episcopalian Church in 1884; taught for several years in Chicago; in 1888 toured Europe with her long-standing friend Jane Addams (1860-1935), the social and political activist; in London they were impressed by the English settlement movement; on return to Chicago they founded Hull House in 1889 as a social settlement; they worked together in the west-side slums of Chicago for many years; member of the Women's Trade Union League and fought to improve working conditions, assisting on picket lines; joined the Socialist party in 1916; interested in the Catholic faith for many years, but her conversion to the faith in 1920 was influenced by the Church's social teaching; greatly influenced by her aunt Eliza Allen Starr (see above); after her conversion she spent much of her time writing and speaking about Catholic art and worship and her own conversion experience; their differing religious views caused a rift between her and Addams (her confidant for many years, Charles Wager, a mathematics professor, filled that void); due to serious illness she retired in 1930 to a convent of the sisters of the Holy Child Jesus in Suffern, New York; became an oblate of the Third Order of St. Benedict in 1939; unmarried; buried at the convent; see "A By-Path Into the Great Roadway," *Catholic World*, May and June 1924; "A Few Trials of a Happy Convert," *Abbey Chronicle*, March 1929, p.33; Eleanor Grace Clark, "Ellen Gates Starr, OSB, 1859-1940: Life of the Co-Founder of Hull House," *Commonweal*, March 1940, p.444; Patrick Allitt, *Catholic Converts: British and American Intellectuals Turn to Rome* (1997), pp.147-148; Ellen Gates Starr Papers, Smith College, Northampton, Massachusetts; Ellen Gates Starr Papers, University of Chicago, Illinois; *ANB* ("Influenced by John Ruskin, William Morris, and the arts and crafts movement, Starr began to see the disconnected relationship between industrialism and craftsmanship. She believed that handicrafts, such as bookbinding, should be taught to laborers to give them a renewed sense of purpose and pride in craftsmanship as well as a greater understanding of the industrial process").

Starr, Mary Caroline Dannat (name in religion Mother Mary Veronica) - nun and founder of a religious order; b. 27 April 1838, New York City; c. 11 April 1868; d. August 1904; oldest of six children; in 1849 her eight-year-old brother died, her parents sought consolation in religion, and the family started to attend the Baptist church; became inclined towards piety, but of a sweet disposition; married in 1857 Walter S. Starr; they moved to Brooklyn and she joined the Pilgrim Church, a branch of Congregationalism; influenced by her father, she moved to the Swedenborgian exposition of Christianity and then to a rationalistic view of Christianity; impressed by the solidity of the Catholic Church; instructed and received into the church by Fr. Thomas Scott Preston (see above), who remained her spiritual guide; influenced by such Scripture texts as "Blessed are the poor in spirit," her desire was to bring help to the poor; in 1868 she opened with the help of several friends a sewing school for children; large numbers attended and the Association for

Befriending Children and Young Girls, with her presidency, grew out of this; a fund was collected and in 1870 the House of the Holy Family was opened as a residential school for the reformation and education of abused and delinquent girls; this provision was expanded in time; her husband died; with the help of Fr. Preston she founded in 1886 the Sisterhood of the Divine Compassion; she was the Mother Superior General from the start until her death; gave her own inherited money to the development of the order; she expressed the gravity of the order's vocation: "Sisters of the Divine Compassion must be deep-hearted, true-souled, strong, generous, earnest women, - not butterflies"; she opened "The Catholic Girls' Club of the House of Our Lady" for former children of the Association and for all Catholic working girls to foster two aims: (a) zeal for their religion and resistance to attacks upon it, and (b) self-improvement; persevered through several serious illnesses; see Rev. Herman Joseph Heuser, *Mother Mary Veronica: A Biography* (1915) ("Something...told her that the old Church must have claims which even the abuses of them suggested, and that the deductions which religious animosity prompted were not always just or logical...[W]e find her one day... in serious conversation with her father on the subject of which a record is preserved in her notes.

'Ah, well,' I said, 'we stand on shifting grounds. I cannot live in this way. We must have something to rest upon. In reading history I see no institution that has withstood the shock of time and change but the Catholic Church. I think I will go there.'

And to a Catholic church she went that same afternoon...Step by step she informed herself of the doctrine here taught, until she gained the assurance of its reasonableness and sincerity. Then she applied to the priest for direction in order that she might be received into the fold"); P. J. Kenedy, *Mother Mary Veronica, Foundress of the Sisterhood of the Divine Compassion: A Biography* (1915); Sister Mary Teresa, RDC, *The Fruit of His Compassion: The Life of Mother Mary Veronica* (1962).

Starr, Mgr. William Edmund – priest; b. 1840, Baltimore, Maryland; c. 1861; d. 26 October 1921, Baltimore, Maryland; brought up a Presbyterian; educated at City College, Baltimore; after becoming a Catholic he went to seminary; ordained to the priesthood in 1869; Prelate of the Papal Household; see essay in Georgina Pell Curtis, *Some Roads to Rome in America* (1909), p.436 ("I found my way into the Church, after a period of utter disgust with the divisions of Protestantism, for which I could see no earthly reason. I was brought up a Presbyterian, but early learned that my elders could give me no rational account of their position over others, who, equally with themselves, undertook to form their religion out of the Bible. I was so utterly disheartened, that I had reached the conclusion, very reluctantly indeed, that if God wanted me to know what I must know and do to please Him, He has taken great pains to make the discovery impossible. The principle of authority, I had heard flouted from earliest childhood, and it was only when I grew to see that it was that or nothing, that I looked about me to find if there was in the world anywhere an authority that was of divine origin. The result was inevitable for a mind both logical and religious"); Georgina Pell Curtis, *Beyond the Road to Rome* (1914), p.353 ("Of a reverential spirit, but by no means devout, I had no misgivings concerning the foundations of religion until about my eighteenth year, when I discovered that my elders, my natural guides and teachers, had themselves no firm grasp of the subject. In fact, I very soon perceived that they were annoyed by my questions which they put down to the conceit of a youthful prig, not to be taken seriously. Any explanation vouchsafed at all was driven home and clinched by an injunction against being too wise. I had grown up loving the Bible and was disconcerted to find that there were so many and such irreconcilable views of its character and content. Christianity, as it was presented to me, was a hopeless mixture of discordant sects. The account it gave of itself I found distasteful, perplexing and illogical, a palpable compromise under which each sect claimed to live by letting all the others live. Upon one thing they were all passionately agreed, that God had given no infallible expositor of His Word, and that any claim of the sort was to be sternly reprobated.

Upon one occasion it was suggested to me to seek an interview with the pastor of the church which I attended, the Presbyterian, and lay before him my difficulties and my heartburnings. That course seemed to promise well. The minister was a scholarly man and an interesting preacher, with a large and influential following. Before venturing upon the interview, I hazarded a question as to its outcome. I was anxious to know if he would guarantee the results of his Bible study as so indisputably true that no other clergyman of equal gifts with himself had ever drawn different and even opposite conclusions. I can recall my disgust upon being told that he would be a very arrogant and presumptuous man, if he did. The ridiculous impasse never seemed to strike my friends. When I remarked that it was hardly worth while to bother about it, I was told that I was an infidel, a skeptic, an atheist, and a lot of other reprehensible characters. If agnostics had existed in those days, I should doubtless have been pilloried with them, if hopeless ignorance be agnosticism.

This was the more pitiable, as I had a reverent mind for God and all holy things. I knew good, devout people in plenty; but they could afford me no help. It was no longer a question of personal worth and piety. The foundation itself of all reverence was at stake and there was no one to help me lay it.

But the climax of my troubles was reached when a man failed me to whom I was devotedly attached, a man of serene intelligence, and unblemished integrity, the factor of the most of my opinions, upon whose faith I confidently leaned. Upon my putting a question to him concerning one of the fundamentals of the Christian religion, which called for a clear and straightforward answer, he shuffled for a moment or two and then declined to answer me, saying that he feared his views on the subject would not be considered orthodox. There were then, and still are, I fear, numbers of men in a like cruel dilemma. They are ill at ease, and would be most unhappy were they to undertake the study of their religious position. They dread becoming unbelievers, and the Roman Catholic Church is an impossible alternative not to be for an instant considered. For relief from their perplexities they throw themselves heart and soul into benevolent and philanthropic activities. The problems of the soul are covered up and put out of sight, smothered under a multitude of projects for the uplift of the submerged masses. All this may seem quite aside from the purpose of this book, which seeks to know how we converts have fared since we crossed the great divide. And yet in my case the prospect of the old confusion of mind, and spiritual disquiet, gives the reply to the question. God in His own good time brought me face to face with His Holy Church and by His grace 'I was not disobedient to the heavenly vision.'

Not only have I never had the slightest temptation, much less inclination, to examine the Protestant position as to the rationale of Faith, but the passion of my life is to teach and to defend, to the utmost of my poor faculty, God's Holy Catholic Church. That is my one enthusiasm. Her teachings completely satisfy my mind, her precepts are all I need to guide my life; and the type of holiness which she displays has no exemplar among the most devout souls whom I have ever known outside her fold").

Stebbins, H. Lyman – stockbroker and prominent Catholic layman; b. 3 September 1911, Manhattan, New York City; c. 28 May 1946 (received at the Jesuit's Farm Street Church in London); d. 19 February 1989, New Rochelle, New York; his father Rowland Stebbins worked on Wall Street, but left in 1929 to become a successful theatrical producer on Broadway; his great-grandfather, Henry George Stebbins, was president of the New York Stock

Exchange and one of the founders of the Metropolitan Museum of Art; brought up Episcopalian in a nominal way; educated at Yale University (graduated in 1933) where he had no particular religious identity; worked on Wall Street and was a member of the New York Stock Exchange; very successful career, but became aware of the emptiness of this way of life and that life must mean something more; became ill with tuberculosis in 1938 and had to take leave of absence from work for two years; during this time read deeply; this and the grace of suffering, together with later reading, led him to God and the Church; returned to work in 1940; in 1951 he founded Mount Savior Benedictine Monastery in Elmira, New York; in the 1950s and early 1960s he led a life of semi-retirement and solitude as a Benedictine oblate and devoted himself to Catholic lay activities; became friend and editor to the Catholic scholars Dietrich von Hildebrand and Baldwin Schwartz; after the promulgation by Pope Paul VI of his encyclical Humanae Vitae in 1968 he and a group of other laymen founded Catholics United for the Faith to support, defend, and advance the efforts of the Teaching Church in accord with the teachings of the Second Vatican Council, and support the doctrinal teachings of the Pope (to counter the rise of dissent to papal teaching); Cardinal Newman's writings were a great influence; he saw "the cult of obsessive contemporaneity," Christopher Derrick's aphorism for the age as the crucial problem facing the Church; in 1987 awarded a knighthood of the Order of St. Gregory by Pope John Paul II; married to Madeleine (three children of the marriage); see The Priesthood of the Laity in the Domestic Church (1978); "Praying the Rosary," Parts One, Two and Three, Lay Witness, March, April and May 1982; James A. Sullivan, "Catholics United for the Faith: Dissent and the Laity," in Mary J. Weaver and R. Scott Appleby (ed), Being Right: Conservative Catholics in America (1995), p.107 ("In 1942 while seeking a volume by C. S. Lewis, Stebbins happened into a Sheed and Ward bookstore in Manhattan. From this point forward, he began a reading romance which led him into the Catholic Church. One of the first volumes which captured his attention was The Things Which Are Not Caesar's by the French Thomist Jacques Maritain. The Maritain volume was crucial in enlarging Stebbins's view of the papacy. The book's disclaimer, that the author 'withdraws in advance anything which would contradict the teaching of the Church,' convinced Stebbins that intellectual excellence and submission to religious authority were not mutually exclusive"); "The Boldness of a Stranger: Correspondence Between C. S. Lewis and H. Lyman Stebbins, Lay Witness, November 1998; cuf.org.

Steenson, Mgr. Jeffrey Neil – priest; b. 1 April 1952, Fort Rucker, Alabama; c. 1 December 2007 (received in the Basilica of Santa Maria Maggiore, Rome; his wife was received also); raised on a farm in Hillsboro, North Dakota; grew up in a devout Christian home in the Evangelical Free Church; educated at Trinity International University, Deerfield, Illinois (graduated BA in 1974); Trinity Evangelical Divinity School (MA in Church History in 1976); Master of Divinity from Harvard Divinity School 1978; PhD from Christ Church College, Oxford 1983 on Basil of Ancyra and the course of Nicene Orthodoxy); trained amateur pilot and aircraft builder; always appreciated the witness of the Church Fathers and of Newman; minister in the Episcopalian Church for twenty-eight years, but always wondering about the draw to the Catholic Church; Episcopal Bishop of the Rio Grande 2005-2007, when he resigned; after his conversion to the Catholic faith he studied for the priesthood at the Pontifical Irish College in Rome; ordained a priest for the Archdiocese of Santa Fe 21 February 2009; teacher at the University of St. Thomas and at St. Mary's Seminary, both in Houston; in 2012 he was named the first ordinary of the Personal Ordinariate of the Chair of Saint Peter established as a result of Pope Benedict XVI's constitution *Anglicanorum coetibus* in 2009; at the same time the Pope named him a protonotary apostolic, which carries the title monsignor; married to Debra Jane Steenson (three adult children); see *Installation Homily*, 12 February 2012 ("So much ink has been spilled over the interpretation of these words of our Gospel, which Jesus spoke to Peter in Caesarea Philippi – 'You are Peter, and on this rock I will build my Church' (Mt. 16:18). Of course, for Catholics, the authoritative interpretation was provided at the First Vatican Council. But we must honestly acknowledge that Christians have read this text in different ways. Even amongst the church fathers there was not unanimity over what 'On this Rock' means precisely.

The great Augustine himself said that the reader must choose - Does this Rock signify Christ or Peter? (*Retract.* 1.20). But Augustine quite properly would not have thought this a matter of either/or. For Peter brings everything to Christ. The trajectory is clear. We are Christ's and Christ is God's (I Cor. 3:23).

I am grateful that, over the course of my ministry, the teachings of Pope John Paul II and Pope Benedict XVI have been so clear on this point - the Church exists to bring souls to Christ. But, as our text plainly affirms, Jesus has invested Peter with a ministry of fundamental importance. And he does so by employing three verbs in the future tense - I will build my church. The gates of hell will not prevail against it. I will give you the keys of the kingdom of heaven.

When Jesus speaks in the future tense, he draws all things to himself; we know then that this commission does not end with the historical Peter. The whole life of the Church on earth until the end of time is anticipated in this moment.

In this context, listen to St. Anselm, the 37th Archbishop of Canterbury, perhaps the greatest theologian ever to grace England's green and pleasant land: 'This power was committed specially to Peter, that we might therefore be invited to unity. Christ therefore appointed him the head of the Apostles, that the Church might have one principal Vicar of Christ, to whom the different members of the Church should have recourse, if ever they should have dissentions among them. But if there were many heads in the Church, the bond of unity would be broken' (*Cat. Aur. Mt.* 16:19)"); Elizabeth Ela, "Former Episcopal Bishop Describes the 'Joy' of Being Catholic," *headlinebistro.com*, 11 April 2008 ("The Anglican Communion recently has tried to find the means to order the lives of its member churches, so that the Episcopal Church would not, for instance, promote some teaching or practice that is radically at variance with what is held and believed elsewhere in the Communion. But, when they responded last year, my former colleagues in the Episcopal House of Bishops insisted that the Episcopal Church is first and foremost an organization of Christians democratically constituted and owes its allegiance to no one. I simply could not accept this approach as being Catholic in any sense of the word...

[O]nce you are resolved to be a Catholic and determined to step out in faith, it just won't do anymore to argue with yourself, 'I would become a Catholic if only...'

Certainly the greatest joy is to be in communion with the one with whom our Lord left the keys! That is such an incredible experience, to know the significance of the ministry our Holy Father exercises and to be a part of it. Sometimes I pinch myself just to be sure that it really has happened, that I am a member of this family of faith, not only by desire and intention, but in truth. I want to emphasize the 'in truth' part. The air in the Catholic Church seems denser, more real. There is a rich theological tradition to explain this, but one can also sense it. It drives Anglicans crazy when they hear it said, but the Eucharist in the Catholic Church has a different texture and depth. Then there is the joy of belonging to a really, really big family...

In the Anglican Church there is a calendar of the saints, and the lives of many great men and women of the faith are celebrated. But I always wondered, if St. Basil or St. Athanasius or St. Augustine were to come back today, would they worship in my church? I have absolutely no doubt that they would be in communion with the Church of Rome, and I want to be with them, not only by intention, but truly in the same family...

I doubt that there is any realistic hope for meaningful progress on the ecumenical front now, from a corporate point of view. Anglicanism itself is hopelessly divided, and therefore I don't think it has the capacity to reach an accord with those churches who understand themselves as bound to sacred Tradition. I admire the resolve of the Catholic Church to keep the dialogue going. Perhaps someday things will be different, but modern Anglicanism would first have to undergo a profound change of heart for this to happen. And there is no evidence that such a change is on the horizon...

This past month of September we have been in Assisi, trying to learn some Italian, and our classmates have been the new seminarians from Ireland. What truly amazing young men they are! They are so keen to bring people to Christ! Who can doubt that they will become the young priests God will use to renew the Church in Ireland? This is the great thing about the Catholic Church. She has her ups and downs, and there are times when one might think that death approaches and there is no chance for recovery. But this capacity to be renewed and resurrected, to come back stronger and more confident and reconnected to the apostolic foundations, this is the great thing. I'm not sure that this is possible for Anglicanism in its modern forms. Something essential has been lost, and I don't see how it can be recovered, once the Tradition has been lost"); Nancy Frazier O'Brien, "Former Episcopal Bishop to Head U.S. Ordinariate for Ex-Anglicans," *Catholic News Service*, 1 January 2012 ("The time came, he said, in 2007 when he felt the bishops of the Episcopal Church had decided to give priority to their autonomy rather than to unity with the larger Anglican Communion.

Father Steenson said that for him, gay people were not the issue. 'It was the way the decisions were made and the way they were defended,' placing the local church and modern cultural sensitivities ahead of the universal church and fidelity to tradition, he said.

The priest said that while the Episcopal Church spoke of the importance of Christian unity, it continued to approve practices - ordaining women priests and bishops, ordaining homosexuals and blessing same-sex unions - that everyone knew would be an obstacle to Christian unity.

'The frustration with being a Protestant is that every morning you get up and have to reinvent the church all over again,' Father Steenson said"); *EWTN Audio Library, The Journey Home* (25 February 2013) ("I think there was a kind of hermeneutical revolution that happened [in Anglicanism] and scripture and tradition were asked to share center stage with experience and over and over again when I served in the Episcopal Church I heard this argument that we need to listen to the experience of people, especially on the same-sex questions. I don't care if you're Anglican, Baptist, Presbyterian, even American Roman Catholic. If you let local people make decisions based on experience, they are going to all come out pretty much where the culture is. The big difference, of course, is the Catholic Church has Peter and has an ability to look objectively at the direction that a particular culture is taking and to speak prophetically to it. I'm not sure that [the Catholic Church] would be so different from any of the other liberal denominations, except for the fact that there is Peter. That's the heart of the matter...

[If] you take that hermeneutic [of experience] and you go back and you say, 'Now, let's use that and let's isolate the writers of the New Testament, let's lock them into the context of the day, so they're not speaking to us eternal truths. They are speaking to us that this is a snapshot of their understanding of where they were in the spiritual life at that time in their circumstances; and I think that destroys the idea of Revelation itself").

Stern, Karl – psychiatrist, philosopher and writer; b. 8 April 1906, Bavaria, Germany; c. 20 December 1943 (his wife, Liselotte (*née* von Baeyer), who was brought up as a Lutheran, but then fell away from religion, plus two older children of their three, were received on Whit Sunday 1941); d. 7 November 1975, Montreal, Canada; brought up in a family of Jewish shopkeepers; family orthodox in some respects, but not in others (he was sent to a Catholic kindergarten as it was the only class in the town); influenced by the simple piety of Kati Huber and Babette Klebl, two Catholic maids ("Obviously the Babettes and Katis have their own shortcomings and secret passions. But their approach towards life transcends ours. While we were engaged in a continuous flight from ultimate reality...there existed all the time among us people who lived unknown lives of humility and charity. And they did, believe me, with a mystical fervor"); in his teens he went through a period of adopting orthodox practices and again in college; studied Medicine at the universities of Munich, Berlin and Frankfurt, graduating in 1930; accepted dialectical materialism, which he later rejected, along with Communism and Nazism; specialized in psychiatry and worked at the German Institute for Psychiatry in Munich; influenced in 1933 (when persecution of the Jews was increasing) by a lecture of Cardinal Faulhaber, who simply clarified the birth certificate of Christ, a Jew in the flesh, and reasserted the oneness, the complete organic unity of the

God of the Church and the God of the Patriarchs and Kings of Israel; in 1936 he moved to London as a research scholar at the National Hospital for Nervous Diseases; in 1940 he emigrated to Montreal, Canada, working at McGill University, where he was the dominant figure and a great teacher, then head of the Department of Psychiatry at University of Ottawa; further influenced by Joseph Pieper's book on St. Thomas Aquinas' concept of hope; also influenced by Jacques Maritain (who told him to stop trying to psychoanalyze what was happening to him and move with God's grace to a deeper level of spirituality) and by Dorothy Day's inner peace; taught at University of Montreal 1955-1975; became a naturalized citizen of Canada; see *Pillar of Fire* (1951) (autobiographical account of his conversion) ("Someone once remarked that you should try experimentally to live for one day as if the Gospel were true, even if you do not believe it. In the same way I invite you to think of the nature of Man as if Christ had been God-Man and died for your and my salvation. The whole of anthropology as conceived by philosophers and psychologists is at once deepened in a very peculiar way. It is as if a great, but albeit two-dimensional, picture received a third dimension and came to life...I used to sit on a bench on Primrose Hill and look over all the City of London. If it were true, I used to think, that God had become man, and that His life and death had a personal meaning to every single person among all those millions of existences spent in the stench of slums, in a horizonless world, in thc suffocating anguish of enmities, sickness and dying – if that were true, it would be something tremendously worth living for. To think that someone knocked at all those millions of dark doors, beckoning and promising to each in an altogether unique way. Christ challenged not only the apparent chaos of history, but the meaninglessness of personal existence...

One evening I began to talk to [Reha Freier] about Christ, about the significance of His life and death, about Christians...At this time I was already so certain that I must have sounded very convincing. Like all of us, she had what you might call a cold admiration for the human person of Jesus. 'I do admit,' she said, 'that there is some strange mystery by which His suffering and death have drawn millions of people to Him for two thousand years.' I had kept all my thoughts back for a long time. Then it poured out of me under much pressure. The darkness, bewilderment and discord of the Christian epoch in Jewish history dissolved the moment you saw that one thing. The Christians who hit Jews were hitting Christ their brother. The Jews who rejected Christ rejected their own God, their own supernatural essence. As long as Christ crawled like a wounded man in the no-man's-land between those two fronts, no political measures would ever solve the 'Jewish problem.' Reha became pensive and said: 'All this sounds as if it must become very important to us Jews sometime'...Later in the evening she said: 'It would all come so natural to us Jews, wouldn't it? There is something about that story of Mary the Virgin Mother as if it were specially written for us, and I could just see how we all would go for it'"); "Letter to My Brother," (a superb account of Stern's discovery of Christian faith, reprinted as chapter 30 of *The Pillar of Fire*) ((1) "I have in my life experienced the most incomprehensible abyss of Evil, and of suffering, as far as it affected those closest to me... People were thrown into those trains like potato bags...Many of them did not arrive alive. But those who lived saw scenes of which we could not dream in our worst nightmares. Babies were killed by being smashed against trees in front of their mothers. Finally the people were shaven, stripped naked and killed.

I knew them. They were just as good as you and I, and in some respects they were better than many of us. Now here is something that might strike you as strange. The more I meditate on them, on those nightmarish last years, months and hours of their lives, the more I come to believe in Jesus Christ, the Son of the living God. Let me make this clearer. Confronted with this horrifying picture of innocent suffering there remain only a few ways in which I can react. One is despair, moral nihilism and suicide...There is a second possibility. I might have reacted as I originally did, with an increased Jewish national fervor...I might have tried a third possibility, dialectic materialism... There is a fourth solution. This is a rationalist pragmatism which is becoming more and more prevalent in the Western countries...

Thus we see four possible answers to the riddle of the abysmal suffering, which we have witnessed in our time. Not one of these answers is adequate. Each one of them misses the point. Despair is no solution; even if we wished to despair we cannot because we believe. Resentment is no solution; our dead ones themselves seem to warn us against such a spirit and it would so easily lead us to commit the same cruelties on others which were committed on us. Statism is no solution. Scientism is no solution.

There is only one way: Jesus Christ. If we are concerned with the suffering of those innocent ones, we have first to look at Him. If we are concerned with the Evil which has brought it about, we have first to look at ourselves. Everything else is deception. If I want to renew the world I have to begin right in the depths of my own soul. This is the only true and permanent revolution which I am able to achieve...

There is something extraordinary in the suffering of Christ. It seems to include all human suffering, and yet it can be 'completed' by the suffering of individual persons...

No matter to what degree suffering individuals may resemble one another, there always remains, somewhere in the depth, a nucleus which is unique...

There is only One Who unites all these secrets in His suffering, and that is Jesus Christ. The more you dwell on it, the more it becomes clear that in His agony He anticipated the hidden agonies of innumerable individuals. For centuries the church has meditated on the Five Sorrowful Mysteries of the Rosary or on the Fourteen Stations of the Cross. And the more people did so, the more the Agony of Our Lord became revealed. It has innumerable facets. It anticipates, it contains your and my life in a singular way. Newman once expressed this idea of the Church in an unforgettable sermon on the Night of Gethsemani in which he unrolled before our eyes with poetic genius the universality and infinite multiplicity of the suffering of our Lord...

[W]e must realize that it is Christ Himself who is present in all this suffering...It is He who is present in the agony of millions of deaths and secret humiliation. This is neither sentiment nor melodrama – it is just a basic fact. I am almost tempted to use the word 'scientific' in this connection because it has nothing to do with emotions. It is an axiom. Our Lord Himself indicated it, and the Church has upheld it throughout the centuries. It is with this axiom in mind that Pascal said that Jesus is still suffering on the cross"). (2) "The Incarnation was not only an event acted out in historical time. It left its indelible mark on the world. It was perpetuated in the life of men. I believe Bergson once said towards the end of his life that everything good that happened in the world since Christ has happened through Him. The Incarnation was perpetuated in a very specific way in. the Holy Sacraments, particularly in the sacrament of the Holy Eucharist, in the Communion of Saints and in the visible physical unity of the Church. There are many saintly Christians in the world today who do not believe that faith in Christ necessitates faith in those other things. They believe that matter has been transformed once, as it were, at the actual time when God took human flesh, and that the subject was exhausted at that single historical event. That disbelief in the sacramental life of the Church has two roots. It is firstly based on an ancient and profound disrespect for Matter, and secondly on the development of what the philosophers call Positivism which arose with modem science. It is possible that both these roots are two expressions of the same thing, and I believe that this disbelief corresponds

only to an historical phase...
The Church mirrors the facets of History. The Gospel is always the same. But the life of the Gospel in the turmoil of the fourth century is seen in Saint Augustine. The life of the Gospel at the height of the Middle Ages (some people would say the early dawn of the Renaissance) is perceived in Saint Thomas. In the nineteenth century, the century in which the human mind began to rule systematically the material forces of the universe, the Church began to extol the Little Way, the mystic life in hidden 'little people.' This is the only logical answer to the threat of a coming managerial age. Christ always has the appropriate answer, and He gives it in His saints...
Saint Thérèse of Lisieux lived that obscure life which represents the lesson for our present age. By that is not meant our practical philanthropy, the do-goodism of everyday life, which is important too, but is only a beginner's exercise. The true thing is an intense, all-out transformation of our lives in the life and passion of Christ"); "St. Thérèse of Lisieux," in Clare Booth Luce (ed), *Saints for Today* (1952); "A Psychiatrist Finds the Way," in John A. O'Brien (ed), *The Road to Damascus, Vol. V: Where Dwellest Thou* (1956) ("That one simple question, whether Jesus of Nazareth was God incarnate, becomes increasingly decisive between people, as history moves forward. Dostoevsky once said that it is the one question on which everything in the world depends. The answer to this question cuts into human ties and seems to reflect even on the nature of inanimate things. What if all that is folly in the eyes of the Greeks, and scandal in the eyes of the Jews, is Truth?...
There was no use denying it. A tiny people at the periphery of the Roman Empire, submerged within an ocean of a thousand creeds, had jealously guarded the precious treasure of Revelation within the walls of its City. Here, two millenniums later, those who did belong to Israel in the flesh defended the God of Abraham, Isaac and Jacob, Moses, Isaias, and Job as if their lives were at stake... Let there be no mistake. Jewish religion is based on the axiom that Revelation is a national affair and that the Messiah to the nations has not been here yet. Our liturgy proved that this was so. Jewish religion was racial exclusiveness, if in its noblest, most elevated form. It was exactly opposed to that of the Nazis, but it was racism just the same. It had the highest justification, as long as its basic premise was correct, namely that the anointed One was still to be expected.
Secondly, Jesus had not come as the 'founder of Christianity,' the 'daughter religion.' He had come to Jews with the claim of being the Messiah, the Son of the living God. The question whether he was what He claimed to be must be answered with a clear Yes or No.

If the divinity of Christ was an error or a lie the force which radiated from this idea was impossible to explain. In a paradoxical sense Tolstoy was right. For without the divinity of the Messiah the simple piety and heroic sanctity of some peasant maids were somehow unthinkable, but so were Chartres and Grunewald, Bach and Mozart. My experience of the 'historical argument' was very intense and, it seemed, quite personal. I discovered much later that Pascal wanted to make it the foundation stone of Christian apologetics. The scientist Pascal was astonished at an obvious fact; just as the Prophets had predicted, the fruit of Israel had burst at a definite historical moment, the seeds had been flung to the far corners of the earth, and had brought forth plants a thousandfold. Pascal wanted to forestall the flood of modern positivism which was to drown the western world...Only in Judaeo-Christianity do time and eternity meet in history. It was their meeting which overwhelmed Pascal"); *The Flight from Woman* (1965); Ronda Chervin (ed), *Bread From Heaven* (1994); Bernard N. Nathanson, *The Hand of God: A Journey from Death to Life by the Abortion Doctor Who Changed His Mind* (1996) ("The reader may wonder why I dwell on [Karl] Stern. There was something indefinably serene and certain about him...In the last section of his book...he explained to his brother, an observing Jew who had survived the Holocaust, why he had converted to Catholicism, and how science and religion coexist: 'The Church is immutable in her teaching. There is only one supernatural truth, as there is only one scientific truth. What in the mastering of matter constitutes the law of Progress, in things of the spirit is the law of Preservation'...

In this extraordinary document, he asks the question that has dogged me for too many years. He puts the question to his brother this way: 'Now perhaps you will say: "How can you, as an educated person...?" or "How can you, as a man with scientific training...?" or "How can you with knowledge of psychoanalysis...?" There seem to be a great number of How Can You questions. In all sincerity I do not even understand why these questions are asked.'

He goes on to answer these pointless conundra in a manner as simple as a child's, as sophisticated as a world-renowned psychiatrist, as humble as the most faithful Servant of God. But the answer that captivated me was the one I had been searching for, the one that answers the How-Can-You-as-a-Scientist question; he says: 'The question about science is even harder to understand. I have never experienced any conflict of that sort. Some time ago I read in a German history of philosophy that Pascal's early death was caused by the inner tortures he endured resulting from the conflict between Science and Religion. It is quite possible that Pascal suffered inner conflicts but there is no indication that this was one of them. I presume that de Broglie is a Christian and that Planck was a Christian. Pascal and Newton were Christians. It is possible that they were Christians *besides* being Scientists or *on account of* being Scientists, but why should they have been Christians *in spite of* being Scientists?'"); Matthew Hoehn, OSB (ed), *Catholic Authors: Contemporary Biographical Sketches* (1952); Lorene Hanley Duquin, *A Century of Catholic Converts* (2003), p.125; Stanley L. Jaki, "Jewish Psychiatrist Turns Catholic," in *A Late Awakening and Other Essays* (2006), p.171 ("In *The Pillar of Fire* Truth is stated time and again with aphoristic force. First, some aphorisms of his that relate to the rapport of Judaism with Christianity and vice versa: 'Heresies are based on denials. In this respect Christianity was no heresy from Judaism; it rejected nothing essential but made a new positive claim.' Again, 'The misdeeds of one member are more broadcast than the sanctity of a hundred of others.' On the charge that Jews as a whole are responsible for Jesus' crucifixion, there is his reminder: 'For centuries every Catholic man, woman and child prayed: 'I have crucified my loving savior Jesus Christ,' a reminder also appropriate about the steady reduction, in the 'new' theology, of sin to a purely psychological wound administered by the self to the self. Jews who harp on the Church's shortcomings may ponder Karl Stern's reminder: 'Do not forget a lesson which we know so well from the history of Judaism, that is the fact that Evil has more publicity than Good.' Psychologists in particular should ponder such dicta of his: 'Suffering cannot be quantified'; 'Psychoanalysis gives us an embryology of love'; and 'Either the psychological method is not valid to decide whether Christianity is true or not, or there are no truths which transcend the material plane of God's existence.' Karl Stern portrays the protagonists of modern, secularized culture in grippingly graphic terms: 'With faith gone, they are in the same position as that shipwrecked man stranded on an island with crates full of canned food but with no can-opener'...As to the deception of what can be seen from ivory towers he offers a great one-liner: 'Philosophers and mathematicians feel at ease only in the abstract'").

Stevens, Cora–nun; c. 17 December 1927; parents were devout members of the Methodist Episcopalian Church; on the sudden death of her father, she found that her religious upbringing did not provide her with the vital faith which could have tided her over in a crisis ("I had been taught the doctrine of the resurrection in the Apostles' Creed, but believing it as a reality was quite another thing"); studied History at University of Illinois from 1920, graduating in 1924; attending Mass at the invitation of a Catholic friend had a great effect upon her ("Mass, whatever it was, had something intensely serious and absorbing about it. The peaceful, reverent silence in that church, filled to capacity with devout worshippers, impressed me profoundly. I marveled at the way everyone was attending strictly to his own personal business between himself and God, Who seemed to be actually present somewhere. [W]hat impressed me most that day…was the awareness of the presence of God. The very attitude of the worshippers was one of unquestioned belief"); also impressed by the writing on Church history by Catholic priests (e.g., Dr. John A. Ryan of the Catholic University of America and by Fr. John A. O'Brien, editor of *The Road to Damascus* series of books on converts); in 1927 she attended a series of instructions on the Catholic Faith given by Fr. O'Brien; conversion also influenced by Cardinal Gibbons' *The Faith of Our Fathers*; after her conversion she joined the Congregation of the Sisters of St. Joseph of Carondelet, being admitted to St. Mary's Novitiate in Los Angeles in 1931; pronounced first vows in 1933; see "Lovely Are Thy Tabernacles," in John A. O'Brien (ed), *The Road to Damascus, Vol. III: The Way to Emmaus* (1953) ("The time came when I began thinking my own thoughts about religion. One day my grandmother, in a checking-up mood, commanded me to recite the Apostles' creed – which I did to her evident satisfaction. Then I asked, 'What is the Catholic Church, and why do we say we believe in the Holy Catholic Church, when we don't?' 'That,' she replied, with a show of certainty, 'means the invisible church.' 'But, Grandma,' I objected,' what is an invisible church like, and how can we belong to it; and why don't we?' 'Oh, hush, child; wait until you are a little older [I was sixteen], and then you'll understand,' she answered…

[W]hen I started work in my major history, I was jolted into the knowledge that the Catholic Church, nearly two thousand years old, was founded by Jesus Christ and was the most powerful institution and the greatest force for good that the world had ever seen. She had seen nations rise and fall, had withstood bloody persecutions, had spread her doctrines all over the world, and had given the best in every field of human endeavor to civilization…

I held to the opinion that joining the Catholic Church was optional, that I could go on attending Mass without taking any further step - that is, until, in a closing chapter of one of the books, I was stunned to read that as long as a non-Catholic believes his particular denomination is the right one and lives up to what he thinks is the will of God, he has a good chance of salvation; but once he doubts seriously the validity of his Church, he is obliged to seek the true Church, to investigate her truths, or suffer the danger of losing his soul.

That was food for serious thought and more prayer, and soon I came to see that there was no choice in the matter but to submit to God's Church. Of course! If Christ founded a Church, He certainly intended that Christians belong to it. Now there was no longer any doubt in my mind that He founded the Catholic Church...Holy Scripture relates that He founded a *Church*, not *churches*; and that He promised to be with that Church until the end of time. (No wonder the Church has withstood nearly two thousand years of intermittent persecution, as history shows!) Furthermore, the best writers, Christian and pagan, of the early centuries referred to that one Church as universal, or Catholic.

It was not the proof of Scripture or the writers, however, which most appealed to me, but rather the common sense of it all. It was this more than anything else which convinced me that there could be but one Church; for how could God, Eternal Wisdom, found hundreds of different churches, resulting in confusion, conflicting ideas, misunderstanding, and even hatred? As to the interpretation of the Bible and the exercise of private judgment to which Protestants hold tenaciously, would Christ teach certain definite things and at the same time permit each individual to read into those doctrines another meaning, to accept or reject at will any of His teachings? To affirm that He did so is to make Him responsible for all the confusion, contradiction, and chaos among the hundreds of Christian denominations.

My problem regarding the Real Presence of Christ in the Eucharist was answered clearly and convincingly by the instructing priest and a study of the sixth chapter of St. John. In this chapter I noted a striking proof that Christ was speaking literally when He taught His hearers that they must eat His flesh and drink His blood if they wished to attain eternal life. When he reiterated His statement, many complained that His teaching was 'hard' and, turning their backs upon their Savior, 'walked no more with Him.' At this juncture I was quite impressed with the fact that Christ did not call them back. Not at all! He let them depart rather than deny the truth of His sacred words.

I believed without further question that Jesus is really present, soul, body, and divinity, in the Sacrament of the Altar; moreover, I was most happy and grateful for the grace to believe this most consoling of all the beautiful truths of the Catholic Church. At last I was able to see why Catholics gaze lovingly at the tabernacle. The Hidden God is truly there, 'How lovely are Thy tabernacles, O Lord of Hosts. My soul longeth and fainteth after the courts of the Lord'").

Stevens, Wallace James - poet; b. 2 October 1879, Reading, Pennsylvania; d. 2 August 1955, Hartford, Connecticut; father was a lawyer who wrote occasional poems; born to Pennsylvanian Dutch Puritan parents; family had been farmers for several generations; brought up as a Presbyterian; at a school with a Lutheran church attached; educated at Harvard University; while there he was a close friend of George Santayana (1863-1952), the philosopher, poet, essayist and novelist, who influenced him; then at New York Law School, graduating in 1903; when at university he moved away from Christianity, and his reading focused on Coleridge, Nietzsche and Bergson; worked as a lawyer in New York until 1916; spent most of the rest of his life in Hartford where he worked as a lawyer for the Hartford Accident and Indemnity Company; made many visits to Key West, Florida, which influenced his poetry; politically a conservative; he was a major modernist poet; most of his best poetry was written late in his life; won the Pulitzer Prize for Poetry in 1955; won the National Book Award in 1951 and 1955; he said to Anthony Sigmans, who worked under him, that he belonged to no church, but if he ever joined a church it would be the Catholic Church; there is evidence that during his final days, when he was in St. Francis Hospital, Hartford, suffering from stomach cancer, he was baptized and received into the Catholic Church by Fr. Arthur Hanley, chaplain of the hospital; this purported deathbed conversion was disputed, particularly by his daughter Holly, and there is no record of his baptism, but there was testimony in favor by Dr. Edward Sennett, the head radiologist, and by the sisters at the hospital; buried in Cedar Hill Cemetery, Hartford; see *Collected Poems* (1954); *Collected Poetry and Prose* (1997); Lucy Beckett, *Wallace Stevens* (1974); Letter from Father Arthur Hanley to Professor Janet McCann, dated 24 July 1977 ("Dear Janet: The first time he came to the hospital, he expressed a certain emptiness in his life. His stay then was two weeks. Two weeks later, he was in, and he asked the sister to send for me. We sat and talked a long time. During his visit this time, I saw him 9 or 10 times. He was fascinated by the life of Pope Pius X. He spoke about a poem for this pope whose family name was Sartori (meaning tailor) at least three times, he talked about getting into the fold - meaning the Catholic Church. The doctrine of hell was an objection which we later got thru that alright. He often remarked about the peace and tranquility that he experienced in going into a Catholic Church and spending some time. He spoke about St. Patrick's Cathedral in N.Y. I can't give you the date of his baptism. I think it might be recorded at the hospital. He said he had never been baptized. He was baptized absolutely. Wallace and his wife had not been on speaking terms for several years. So we thought it better not to tell her. She might cause a scene in the hospital. Archbishop at the time told me not to make his (Wallace's) conversion public, but the sister and the nurses on the floor were all aware of it and were praying for him. At the time I did get a copy of his poems and also a record that he did of some of his poems. We talked about some of the poems. I quoted some of the lines of one of them and he was pleased. He said if he got well, we would talk a lot more and if not - he would see me in heaven. That's about all I can give you now. [Signed] God's Blessing, Father Hanley"); Peter Brazeau, *Parts of a World: Wallace Stevens Remembered* (1983); (Statement by Father Arthur Hanley: "He really wanted to talk. There was something bothering him all the time. He believed strongly in God. When he went to New York, he told me, he used to spend at least a couple of hours at St. Patrick's Cathedral, meditating. He said he got so much peace and enjoyment that he always, when he went to New York, went to St. Patrick's Cathedral. I think he had such a marvelous idea of what God was. The absolute idea of God. 'Everything,' he said, 'has been created. There is only one uncreated.' And that was God.

He was unusual in this respect. He said, 'I think I ought to be in the fold, but there's one thing that bothers me. That is that I don't see how a just God could construct a place like hell, because I do think that a merciful God, knowing the weakness of mankind, would not fashion a place like that to punish anyone - not even a dog.' So we went through all that business about whereas God is merciful, He is also just. And in His justice, He must recognize that some people, no matter what grace is given them, will repudiate Him. I said, 'As far as we know, we don't know that there's anyone specifically in hell except the devil and his cohorts.'

I think he was a bit upset by the mysteriousness of the world. That was one thing that bothered him, the evil in the world. And he was always coming back to the goodness of God: how could a good God allow all this evil in the world? So we went into free will and all that business. But he was more of a poet than a Scholastic philosopher.

He gave me the impression he knew quite a bit about the Church. The impression he gave me was there were just a few little things that kept him from being a Catholic, and that was this hell business. I told him hell was mentioned fifty-seven times in the Bible and that our Lord said there was a hell, so we believe what our Lord said. 'Well,' he said, 'that sounds logical.'

So we talked along that line quite a bit, and he was thinking and thinking and thinking. One day he had a bit of a spell. He called for me, and he said, 'I'd better get in the fold now.' And then I baptized him, and the next day I brought him Communion"); Joan Richardson, *Wallace Stevens: The Early Years, 1879-1923* (1986); Joseph Carroll, *Wallace Stevens' Supreme Fiction: A New Romanticism* (1987); Joan Richardson, *Wallace Stevens: The Later Years, 1923-1955* (1988); D. Z. Phillips, *From Fantasy to Faith: The Philosophy of Religion and Twentieth-Century Literature* (1991), pp.21-29; Maria J. Cirurgião, "Last Farewell and First Fruits: The Story of a Modern Poet," *Lay Witness*, June 2000 ("Poetically speaking, he kept a vacillating foothold on each side of the abyss between Christianity and the paganization of the Christian conscience - modernism. Stevens's poetic voice is a voice of ambivalence. In the ambivalence, though, he made room for grace, and his poetry can truly be said to be a poetry of conversion...

A more intimate glimpse at Stevens's early preoccupation with the crisis of faith is provided by his diaries, long since published. One entry, dated 1 August 1899, is most peculiar for a young man not quite 20-years-old and raised with a mixture of Calvinist and Lutheran teachings. It reads: 'I would sacrifice a great deal to be a St. Augustine.' It was no passing fancy, but the beginning of a lifelong companionship of the mind and heart. Not only are Augustinian writings and teachings echoed throughout Stevens's *Collected Poems*, but the acute reader cannot miss the importance of the great Church Father as the moral compass by which the poet measured the integrity of his verse...

It is worthy of note that from the time he left Harvard and moved to New York City, where he attended law school and was admitted to the Bar in 1904, this meditative poet chose to meditate in St. Patrick's Cathedral. 'I go [there] now and then in my more lonely moods,' he wrote in his diary in 1902... [He] never outgrew his need for St. Patrick's. The quiet hours in the pews left a stamp on his poetry that is hard to miss, in verses such as: 'Now both heaven and hell / Are one, and here, O terra infidel'... Likely, these verses give us all the insight we shall ever have into why it was St. Patrick's Cathedral that beckoned irresistibly to Wallace Stevens; why he made St. Augustine the companion of his meditative hours; and why he chose St. Francis Hospital when terminally ill"); Tony Sharpe, *Wallace Stevens: A Literary Life* (2000); Catherine Wood, "Imagination and Incarnation: Wallace Stevens' Poetry in Light of His Alleged Deathbed Conversion to Catholicism," *Saint Austin Review*, March/April 2005, p.24; Lucy Beckett, *In the Light of Christ: Writings in the Western Tradition* (2006), pp.432-474 ("[George Santayana] gave to the young Wallace Stevens...not only the certainty that to believe Christianity is true was no longer possible, and the certainty that the vocation of the poet was the highest possible calling in a world that had lost religious conviction, but also a sense of the substance and value of the Catholic faith as a 'real religion' that remained in the back of Stevens's mind for the rest of his life...

Stevens in his years alone in New York haunted Saint Patrick's Cathedral, occasionally attended Mass and spent hours 'in the dark transept where I go now and then in my more lonely moods'...[H]e identified in his journal another division in himself, contrasting the God he encountered in the cathedral with the divine presence he sensed, walking in the country, behind the beauty of the earth. 'The priest in me worshipped one God at one shrine; the poet another God at another shrine. The priest worshipped Mercy and Love; the poet, Beauty and Might...As I went tramping through the fields and woods I beheld every leaf and blade of grass revealing or rather betokening the Invisible.' He had no one to connect the two for him, as they had been connected, for example, for [Gerard Manley] Hopkins"); John N. Serio (ed), *The Cambridge Companion to Wallace Stevens* (2007); Eleanor Cook, *A Reader's Guide to Wallace Stevens* (2009); Thomas Francis Lombardi, "Wallace Stevens and the Celestial Possible, " *Saint Austin Review*, May/June 2011, p.16;

Stillman Chauncey Devereux – philanthropist; b. 14 December 1907; d. 24 January 1989; his great-grandfather Charles left colonial roots in Connecticut to establish a fortune in Mexican cotton, real estate and silver mines, and by the end of the Civil War was one of the richest men in America; grandson of James Stillman president of what became the Citigroup bank; his father Charles Chauncey Stillman and his father's brother married two of the daughters of William Avery Rockefeller Jr. (1841-1922), the younger brother of John Davidson Rockefeller (1839-1937); graduate from Harvard University; also degree in Architecture from Columbia University; director of Freeport-McMoRan, the copper and gold producer, from 1931; squadron air combat intelligence officer during World War II on the USS Enterprise; later served as a staff officer with the National Security Council; supported many schools and charities; endowed the Chair of Roman Catholic Studies at the Harvard Divinity School, of which the first holder was Christopher Dawson from 1958 to 1962; chief benefactor of Thomas More College of Liberal Arts, Merrimack, New Hampshire; developed his 1,200 acre Wethersfield estate, promoting formal Italian gardens and the revival of classical design; very fine art collection; president of the Wethersfield Institute, which he set up to promote Catholic culture;

commodore of the New York Yacht Club in the 1960s; his sister Elizabeth Goodrich Stillman (d. 1956) married Langbourne Meade Williams Jr. (1903-1994), the businessman; see George William Rutlcr, *Cloud of Witnesses: Dead People I Knew When They Were Alive* (2010) ("Aesthetics did not throttle ascetics, and when he was dying of lung cancer I occasionally met him praying the rosary in a hideously modern Manhattan basement chapel. The last Mass he heard was in his Madison Avenue apartment, and his whispered request of me was that the sign of peace be omitted 'because the butler finds it awkward'").

Stockum, Hilda Gerarda van – author, illustrator, translator and painter; b. 9 February 1908, Rotterdam, Netherlands; c. 1938 (her mother was received a year later); d. 1 November 2006, Berkhamsted, England; of Dutch-Irish parentage; her father Abraham (Bram) van Stockum was a naval officer and an inventor; her mother Olga was the daughter of a Dutch newspaper editor Charles Boissevain; her brother Willem Jacob (1910-1944) was a mathematician who contributed work on general relativity, and was killed on an RAF mission; her parents were atheists; taught by her father for the first years of her life; the family moved to Dublin, Ireland, when she was sixteen; studied art for two years at the Dublin Metropolitan School of Art, Ireland, then at Rijksacademie van Beeldende Kunsten, Amsterdam; became an Anglican, as did her friend the artist Evie Hone (1894-1955) (later to become a Catholic also); married Ervin Ross ("Spike") Marlin (1909-1994), an American civil servant, in 1932 (six children of the marriage); moved to the United States in 1933; became an American citizen in the 1930s; after a long search for religious truth she became a Catholic there; several things influenced her conversion to the Catholic faith, including the writers of the Oxford movement, St. Teresa of Avila, St. Thomas Aquinas, G. K. Chesterton, Fulton Sheen, Ronald Knox, but her journey came to an end when she closed the book by Arnold Lunn *Now I See* (1933); her husband never became a Catholic and did not continue in the Anglican Church; lived in Canada 1945-1951; lived in England from about 1973; she changed her nationality to British after her husband's death, because three of her four daughters were living there and she figured she would stay there till she died; her books for children, frequently autobiographical, are noted for their vivid portraits of family life; served as president of the Children's Book Guild for two consecutive terms; her paintings and drawings consist mainly of still life, landscapes and portraits; see *A Day on Skates* (1934); *The Cottage at Bantry Bay* (1938);

Francie on the Run (1939); *Kersti and St. Nicholas* (1940); *Pegeen* (1941); *Andries* (1942); *Gerrit and the Organ* (1943); *The Mitchells* (1945); *Canadian Summer* (1948); *The Angels' Alphabet* (1950); *Patsy and the Pup* (1950); *King Oberon's Forest* (1957); *Friendly Gables* (1958); *Little Old Bear* (1962); *The Winged Watchman* (1962) (her most famous book, a novel about the Dutch resistance in World War II) ("In the camp we saw our own people kill each other over a crust of bread. In the old days I used to think that religion did not matter much, that people could be good without it. That was not true in the camps. If you had no hope or faith to keep you human, you sank to the lowest depths. I'll practice my religion more faithfully now"); *Jeremy Bear* (1963); *Bennie and the New Baby* (1964); *New Baby is Lost* (1964); *Mogo's Flute* (1966); *Penengro* (1972); *Rufus Round and Round* (1973); *The Borrowed House* (1975); Christine Marlin, "Catholic Formation Through Children's Literature: The Novels of Hilda van Stockum," *The Notre Dame Centre for Ethics and Culture (nd.edu)*, 20 November 2004; Randal Marlin, "Hilda van Stockum: Artist-Philosopher," *hildavanstockum.com* ("Mom did however have a very philosophical mind and in retrospect I marvel at how she was able to deal with difficult philosophical questions very simply but so penetratingly that I still come back to her answers for enlightenment, because she got to the nub of a problem and seized on the key point or image from which a solution was forthcoming.

On the matter of the problem of evil, her answer was that a good novel couldn't do without evil somewhere, and a good painting couldn't do without darkness to contrast with the light. So the Creator of the world could not produce moral goodness without giving us free will and the means to avoid evil, without forcing us as if we were automatons. In that set-up evil becomes a necessary part of a whole better than one where we do not have free will. I express this in ponderous language, but Mom could put it in simpler language without missing anything that the more technical language conveys…

Much later, Mom was still a good source of philosophical gems. I pass on to students today the insight of Hans Urs von Balthasar that Truth, Goodness, and Beauty are jealous sisters, and you can't raise one above the other two without them pulling it down. In other words, start deceiving in the name of some good to be achieved and the truth will take its revenge. Ignore beauty, and ugliness will have its effect on truth and goodness"); Christine (Marlin) Schintgen, "Hilda van Stockum: An Appreciation," *Saint Austin Review*, March/April 2007, p.38; Olga Marlin, "Mother's Religious Life and Thought," *hildavanstockum.com* ("It is not possible to think of Mother without thinking of God. Her faith was the driving force of her life and she transmitted it to her children...

When Mother was five, she accompanied her mother to a clinic in Switzerland where she needed treatment. Mother was looked after by one of the nurses, and one evening when she was being put to bed, she noticed a crucifix on the wall. "Who's that funny man?" she asked. The nurse looked startled: "You don't know Jesus?", and picking Mother up, she plonked her on the bed and kneeling down in front of her, told her the whole story. Her manner was rough and brusque, so Mother always said that it was surprising that the story made such a deep impression on her, despite the manner in which it was told...

It was Arnold Lunn's *Now I See* that finally brought Mother to the Catholic Church. She always said that when she closed the book it suddenly hit her: 'I'm not thinking about being a Catholic, I AM a Catholic!' With that she went out into the street and asked the first passer-by 'Where is the nearest Catholic Church?' She went up to the rectory door, knocked, and said to the priest who opened it: 'I'm a Catholic and I want to be baptized!' After a few enquiries he said: 'You're a case for Fr X.' It turned out that this was an elderly priest, a bit confused, but eager to make converts. After talking to Daddy, Mother went through the classes and the time came for her to be received into the Catholic Church. 'What about the children?' she asked. And Daddy said 'You better look after them.' So we were all baptized together. The priest was a bit harassed with three children and Mother to baptize, and in the end he asked anxiously: 'Have I done them all, or have I done one twice?'...

Mother lived the liturgical year and vibrated with the life of the Church. Every January she would get a Church calendar, with the story of each saint on it, and then tell it to us when the day came... She made the two great seasons of the year - Christmas and Easter - into great celebrations, after taking us through the penitential seasons of Advent and Lent...

Mother moved in the world of God and related everything to Him. She loved His Creation and she painted, reflecting the glory of God. 'There is beauty even in a garbage bin!' she said, and in fact she painted one. It was like a challenge - to find God in unexpected places. She had the heart of a child and her relations with God were simple and transparent. She sometimes commented that she felt before God 'like a doggie wagging its tail!'").

Stoddard, Charles Warren – author, editor and educator; b. 7 August 1843, Rochester, New York; c. 1867; d. 23 April 1909, Monterey, California; ancestors came from England; in his youth he lived in both New York and San Francisco; quit school and dedicated himself to a literary career; he wrote early poetry, which was very successful; missed a college education because of poor health; visited the South Sea Islands several times and wrote books about them; he visited Molokai several times and became well acquainted with Father Damien, the apostle to the lepers, and wrote a book about this, which brought Father Damien to true esteem; lived with the painter Frank Millet in the 1870s in Venice; made a roving commission for the *San Francisco Chronicle* to Europe and the Middle East 1873-1878; chair of English Literature at the University of Notre Dame in 1885, but ill health forced his resignation in 1886; held a corresponding position in the Catholic University, Washington D.C. 1889-1902, but resigned through ill health; his writing was not fully appreciated by the American public; witty and amiable; had enduring relationships with Ambrose Bierce, Bret Harte, and Mark Twain; close friend of Robert Louis Stevenson; returned to California in 1905; was homosexual; great traveler, yet mystic and recluse; see *Poems* (1867); *South-Sea Idyls* (1873) (published in England in 1881 as *Summer Cruising in the South Seas*); *Mashallah! A Flight into Egypt* (1881); *Diary of a Visit to Molokai* (1884; published in 1933); *A Trip to Hawaii* (1885); *The Lepers of Molokai* (1885); *A Troubled Heart and How It Was Comforted At Last* (1885) (the story of his conversion: "Here you have my inner life all laid bare") ("I was groping in the dark when a little light threw a ray across my path, suddenly, unexpectedly, as if a star had fallen. One day, on the mantel-piece in our dining-room, - shall I ever forget that mantel, or the corner of it on which the wee book in its brown paper cover was lying! - I found a copy of 'The Poor Man's Catechism.' I had never before seen a Catholic catechism, nor any Catholic book whatever; but we had stores of anti-Catholic works, and the discovery of this little Spy in the camp somewhat startled me. I at once took it away to my chamber and began to read it.

I was on my guard when I turned the first pages of that homely little pamphlet; it was a poor and ragged thing, by no means calculated to prepossess any one in its favor. I was even inclined to be antagonistic when I began to read; but the simplicity and truth that shone from every page disarmed me; the plain, direct questions and the plain, direct answers were just such as I had been longing to ask and to receive. Here they were in my own hands, to be asked as often as I chose, and answered immediately and always. I became profoundly interested; I could not lay down the little oracle till I had gone through it two or three times over. I read it first with curious interest; and afterward reread it, to make sure that I had read it aright; then read again, to clear some obscure point or to get the full meaning of certain passages. What a reading was that when, finally, I read it slowly and earnestly, asking myself after each separate answer, 'Can you believe this?' 'Do you believe it?" After each and all of those answers I answered, and I answered triumphantly, 'I can and I do!' I resolved to become a Catholic at once"); *In the Footprints of the Padres* (1892); *Hawaiian Life: Being Lazy Letters from Low Latitudes* (1894); *Saint Anthony, The Wonder-Worker of Padua* (1896); *A Cruise Under the Crescent: From Suez to San Marco* (1898); *Over the Rocky Mountains to Alaska* (1899); *Father Damien: The Martyr of Molokai* (1901); *Exits and Entrances: A Book of Essays and Sketches* (1903); *Father Damien, a Sketch* (1903); *For the Pleasure of His Company* (1903) (his only novel; autobiographical); *The Island of Tranquil Delights: A South Sea Idyll, and Others* (1904); *With Staff and Scrip* (1904); *Hither and Yon; The Confessions of a Reformed Poet* (1907); *The Dream Lady* (1907); essay in Georgina Pell Curtis (ed), *Some Roads to Rome in America* (1909), p.437 (shorter account of his conversion taken from *A Troubled Heart and How It Was Comforted At Last* (see above)); Walter Lecky, *Down at Caxton's* (1895), p.39; Carl G. Stroven, "A Life of Charles Warren Stoddard" (PhD dissertation, Duke University, 1939); Robert L. Gale, *Charles Warren Stoddard* (1977); *Catholic Encyclopedia*; *ANB* ("*A Troubled Heart and How It Was Comforted at Last* (1885) is his tender, touching *Apologia Pro Vita Sua*. In it, Stoddard never intellectualizes but chooses instead to dramatize the incffable comfort he found in his church").

Stoddard, John Lawson – writer and lecturer; b. 24 April 1850, Brookline, Massachusetts; c. 1922 (his wife was also received, but his son Lothrop remained agnostic); d. 1931; brought up a Protestant; graduated from Williams College in 1871; studied Theology for two years at Yale Divinity School; taught Latin and French at Boston Latin School; traveled around the world; for many years he gave a series of lectures based on his travels and published these in book form (very popular); agnostic for over thirty years before his conversion to the Catholic faith; later published books on religion; proponent of the restoration of the Jews to Israel; see *Red-Letter Days Abroad* (1884); *John L. Stoddard's Lectures* (ten volumes and five supplements) (1897-1898); *Rebuilding a Lost Faith* (1924) ("In what way, then, did the Incarnate Son of God, before departing from this earth, provide for the continuance and advancement of His kingdom. One thing is certain: He did not write a book, nor did He order one to be written. Instead of doing that, He founded a Church, against which He declared the gates of hell should not prevail, and with which He promised to be present while the world should last. This being so, it is evident that every faithful follower of Jesus should become a member of that Church.

But which of all the Churches that profess to be Christian is the one which Christ established? Unquestionably the Roman Catholic Church, *for this alone goes back to the Savior's lifetime.* This was the Church which naturally succeeded Judaism; this was the Church whose early history is chronicled in the Acts of the Apostles, and this is still the only Church which, since the days of Christ, has maintained an uninterrupted life of nearly two millennia. Her documents, history and traditions all go back to the age of the Apostles. From her all other forms of Christianity have been derived. The authors of the Gospels, Acts and Epistles were members of the original Catholic Church, and she it was that finally selected, from the manuscripts which had been written hy her sons, the books of the New Testament, and was for centuries their sole custodian. But since the Church existed sixty years at least before the writing of those Scriptures was completed, and more than three hundred years before the Canon of the New Testament was definitely fixed, there must have been during all that time, some other guide and guardian of the Church besides the Bible. What was this?

Evidently Tradition, - that mighty link between the past and present, consisting of the oral instructions, interpretations and ecclesiastical observances, handed down in the Church from generation to generation from the very days of the Apostles. Thus St. Paul wrote to the Church of Corinth: 'Keep the traditions, as I delivered them to you' (1 Cor. 11:2). To Timothy also he wrote: 'The things that thou hast heard of me among many witnesses, the same commit thou to faithful men, *who shall be able to teach others also.*' Those 'faithful men' undoubtedly did teach others, and these taught others still. Origen, the great representative of the Church at Alexandria, said: 'Let the ecclesiastical teaching, handed down by order of succession from the Apostles, be observed. That only is to be believed to be the truth, which in no way differs from ecclesiastical and Apostolic tradition'...

Those were the years when the Church was struggling upward from the catacombs to the conquest of the world, when she was preaching the Gospel to the heathen, converting Europe, sacrificing her martyrs, producing her Saints, and forming that magnificent liturgy, whose words are still pronounced at every Catholic altar in the world. During those centuries not only countless individuals, but also entire nations, learned and accepted Christianity, not by a book, but solely *by the teaching of the Catholic Church.* In fact, when, in the sixteenth century, the Bible (interpreted by private judgment) was proclaimed to be man's *only* and sufficient guide, the Scriptures instantly became the source of strife and schism.

Accordingly, having now resolved to join some Christian Church, I had no difficulty in deciding which one. In this respect I shared the sentiments of the Unitarian preacher Dr. James Martineau, who, in his *Seats of Authority in Religion* (p. 169), says of the Roman Catholic Church: 'Her plea is that she has been there all through; that there has been no suspension of her life, no break in her history, no term of silence in her teaching; and that, having been always in possession, she is the vehicle of every claim and must be presumed, until conclusive evidence of forfeiture is produced, to be the rightful holder of what has rested in her custody. If you would trace a divine legacy from the age of the Caesars, would you set out to meet it on the Protestant tracks, which soon lose themselves in the forests of Germany or on the Alps of Switzerland, or on the great Roman road of history, which runs through all the centuries and sets you down in Greece and Asia Minor at the very doors of the churches to which the Apostles wrote?'

Of all the Protestant sects, from which a selection could be made, I saw none which I wished to enter. A space of 1500 years lay between even the oldest of them and the origin of Christianity, and experience had already taught me to expect in them no ecclesiastical unity, no real authority, and no doctrinal agreement. Moreover, even since my youthful days their number had decidedly increased…

[W]e recognize the incontrovertible fact, that *Christ Himself founded one Church, and only one, and laid upon it certain commands and sacraments…*

But surely a Church, which was established by the Son of God, and which is still controlled and guided by the Holy Spirit, ought to deliver the same message, with authority, everywhere. Does any Protestant sect do that? Certainly not. Year after year the Protestant schismatic spirit continues its erosive work…

Neither of the many sects of Protestantism is either large enough, old enough, or strong enough to be likened seriously to the universal, ancient Apostolic Church of Rome, and even a collection of such sects forms only an incoherent group of mutually repellent particles. On the one hand, therefore, stands *discordant Protestantism*, - wanting in discipline, lacking doctrinal unity, repudiating most of the original sacraments of .Mother Church, and tending fatally to dissolve either into continually augmenting sub-divisions or into ever-increasing Rationalism. On the other hand stands *united Catholicism*, - immovable amid the ebb and flow of human innovations, impregnable to the attacks of heresies, indifferent to the rise and fall of empires, surviving spoliation, superior to schism, steadfast in persecution, and calmly watching the disintegration of its enemies! Thus does the changeless Church of Rome endure, and thus she WILL endure, till Christ who founded it shall come again.

Wonderful Body of the Living Christ! In faith, in sacraments, in doctrine, in ceremonial, in language, in discipline, in its identical catechism, and in its one obedience to a single Head; - in chapel, cathedral, in hamlet, in metropolis, in Europe, Asia, Africa, America and on the islands of all seas, - everywhere and at all times *it is the same*! Surely if the testimony of 1900 years does not effectually prove the Church of Rome to be the Institution founded by our Savior on the Rock of Peter, then has the world no Church of Christ at all"); *Twelve Years in the Catholic Church* (1930) ("[S] ince intellectual conviction of the truth is not *conversion*, something more is needed, and that is *faith*, without which, St. Paul tells us, it is impossible to please God. And what is this faith? It is something more than trust or confidence, or even a religious inclination of the heart. It is a *voluntary* devout and unquestioning acceptance of the Revelation of Christ's divinity, His precepts and the authoritative and unchanging teachings of the Church He founded.

When once we are convinced that Jesus Christ was the son of the Living God, and that His Revelation and precepts have been faithfully reported to us, it is not our business to quibble or dispute about them, but to give to them the full consent of our intellect. We have then to do three things only: accept, obey, and adore"); D. Crane Taylor, *John L. Stoddard* (1935).

Stone, James Kent (name in religion Fr. Fidelis of the Cross) – priest; b. 1840; c. 8 December 1869; d. 15 October 1921, San Mateo, California (in the arms of his daughter Frances during a visit to her home); came from a well-known Boston Protestant family, renowned for its Episcopalian and Presbyterian clerics; his grandfather, also James Kent, was an eminent lawyer; his father, Dr. John Seely Stone, was a minister of the Evangelical branch of the Episcopalian Church in Boston, who established a school of theology at Harvard University to combat Unitarianism; very well versed in Latin as a child; educated at Harvard 1855-1861; close friend of the jurist Oliver Wendell Holmes (1841-1935); fought in the Civil War as a private, refusing a commission; ordained to the Episcopalian ministry; became president of Kenyon College, Gambier, Ohio; influenced by the Tractarian movement in England; a famous preacher, but controversy arose about the High Church nature of his sermons, and he was almost forced to resign; appointed president of Hobart College, Geneva, New York, which was High Church; his young wife, Cornelia, *née* Fay, died suddenly in 1869 and he was left with three young daughters; he began to feel uneasy about Episcopalianism; suddenly came the thought, "What if the old Roman Church is right after all?"; he resigned his post and sent his children to his grandparents while he considered his position alone; supported throughout by his parents; wrote a most powerful apologia for the Catholic Faith, *An Invitation Heeded*; because of his style and reasoning he was sometimes called "the American Newman"; after his conversion he had his daughters baptized Catholic and established them in a convent of the Sisters of Mercy (one died there of pneumonia); ordained a Paulist priest in 1872; he gave his children up for adoption to a wealthy Catholic family in California, but this tortured him for years afterwards; in 1877 he joined the Passionists, taking the name Fr. Fidelis of the Cross; became one of their best preachers; sent as a missionary to Argentina in 1881; he also started foundations in Chile, Brazil, Panama, Spain and the United States; Passionist provincial in the United States and later South America; finally reunited with his family in 1921 and ended his days in their company, celebrating daily Mass at his daughter Frances' home; see *An Invitation Heeded: Reasons for a Return to Catholic Unity* (1870) (his apologia) ("The Catholic Church is the great incubus which is perpetually haunting and troubling the dreams of the world. Men try to ignore it; but it obtrudes itself upon their unwilling notice. They would fain remand it to a place among the effete superstitions of the past; but when they think the spectre is laid, it returns unbidden, and casts its vast shadow over the present. In that shadow the world lies uneasily; and, consciously or unconsciously, it betrays its dissatisfaction. In every great political and social movement, in the literature of the day, nay, in every magazine and newspaper which drops from the teeming press, the influence may be more or less distinctly discerned of the mysterious presence of this great spiritual organization. The world has always been puzzled to account for this influence. Protestantism it can understand perfectly; there is nothing unearthly or mysterious about that; but in the life and progress of the Catholic Church there is something which defies every attempt at rational and systematic explanation.

What is there behind the policy? What puts life into the machinery, and guides the great engine in its noiseless, frictionless activity? Will 'discipline' explain the devotion of the Catholic Priesthood? Men do not turn hypocrites in order to spend their years in prayer and fasting; neither do they voluntarily elect to become the passive tools of a sordid despotism, to be rewarded only by a life of sacrifice and toil.

One of the best things ever said

by that acute thinker, the Count de Maistre, was that 'no test is so infallible as the instinct of infidelity' (*Du Pape*, liv. iv. ch. xi. 14). Certainly in examining the claims of rival Christian bodies it will be the part of prudence to watch narrowly the tactics of the opponents of all Christianity. And here at once we come upon something definite; for the application of this criterion gives us results which no sincere lover of truth can disregard. Infidelity does not stop to make war upon Protestantism; it is too cunning by far to quarrel with those who are ignorantly doing its own work; it greets them with a covert sneer, or an insolent nod of recognition, and goes on to do battle with its ancient and inveterate foe.

The Catholic Church makes no truce, holds no parley, with the world, the flesh, nor the devil. Her enemies can neither frighten her into silence nor cajole her into compromise. At every point they find her guarded, vigilant, and unrelenting; and, driven from her citadel, they are forced to stand forth in open warfare and rail at her in furious defiance. In France and Spain and Italy a man is either a Catholic or an infidel. But in Protestant countries unbelief salutes Christianity; it puts on the livery of the saints, and builds its chapels, and pays its preachers; and in the course of a generation or two it has made Protestantism as godless as itself.

If all the cruel things which in a single day are written and spoken throughout the world against the Roman Catholic Church could be brought together, they would make a volume which few would have the stomach to read. Every hour calumnies are uttered against that Church which in their essence are but repetitions of the dreary tales, refuted by Tertullian and St. Justin seventeen centuries ago. Surely this undying hate of the world is a sign which cannot be misunderstood. To be hated of the world is a note of the Church. 'If the world hate you, know ye that it hated me before you. If you had been of the world, the world would love its own: but because you are not of the world, but I have chosen you out of the world, therefore the world hateth you. Remember my word that I said to you: The servant is not greater than his lord. If they have persecuted me, they will also persecute you: if they have kept my word, they will keep yours also. But all these things they will do to you for my name's sake, because they know not him that sent me…

Why is it that the Roman Catholic Church is so perpetually disappointing the prophecies of mankind? The standing prediction of its approaching dissolution is good evidence that the Papacy does not contain in itself any apparent principle of life and growth, and yet it continues to put forth the signs of immortal youth after empires have fallen and passed away.

It would be entertaining, if we had

the time, to get together some of the theories which have been proposed for the solution of this enigma, and to test their satisfactoriness. There is Hobbes's famous saying, for instance, that the Papacy is 'the ghost of the deceased Roman Empire, sitting crowned upon the grave thereof.' It is very witty, one of the most brilliant *jeu d'esprit* I know of, but nothing more…

Let me close this topic, then,… with a passage from one who did believe, with all his soul, in the Roman Catholic explanation. It is from a sermon preached in Notre Dame by the great Dominican, le Père Lacordaire: 'Assuredly the desire has not been wanting to lay hold of us, or put us to fault against immutability; for what a weighty privilege to all those who do not possess it; a doctrine immutable when everything upon earth changes! A doctrine which men hold in their hands, which poor old men in a place called the Vatican guard under the key of this cabinet, and which without any other defence resists the course of time, the dreams of sages, the designs of kings, the fall of empires always one, constant, identical with itself! What a prodigy to deny! What an accusation to silence! Therefore, all ages, jealous of a glory which disdained their own, have tried their strength against it. They have come, one after the other, to the doors of the Vatican; they have knocked there with buskin and boot, and the doctrine has appeared under the frail and wasted form of some old man of threescore years and ten. It has said; 'What do you desire of me?' 'Change.' 'I never change.' 'But everything is changed in this world. Astronomy has changed, chemistry has changed, philosophy has changed, the empire has changed. Why are you always the same?' 'Because I come from God, and because God is always the same.' 'But know that we are the masters; we have a million of men under arms; we shall draw the sword; the sword which breaks down thrones is well able to cut off the head of an old man and tear up the leaves of a book.' 'Do so; blood is the aroma in which I recover my youthful vigor.' 'Well, then, here is half my scepter; make a sacrifice to peace, and let us share it together.' 'Keep thy purple, O Caesar! To-morrow they will bury thee in it; and we will chant over thee the Alleluia and the De Profundis, which never change'"); essay in Georgina Pell Curtis (ed), *Some Roads to Rome in America* (1909), p.448 (Prefatory Chapter from *An Invitation Heeded*); *An Awakening: And What Happened* (1920) ("If there be a Church of God upon earth, that Church, as we have seen, must be supernaturally protected against error. If the Church has ever gone astray, if it can *possibly* depart from the truth, it does not cease to be divine - which is an absurdity - but it never was divine. Those who assert the fallibility of the Church must end by denying the facts of the Incarnation and the Descent of the Holy Ghost. Sooner or later all Protestants must come to look upon these primary truths of the Church merely as beautiful myths in the great poem of Christianity. On the other hand, those who admit the existence of a Church founded and sustained by Almighty power, must, if they would escape inconsistency, acknowledge that it can never lose or be in doubt about the truth which it has always possessed. But there can be only one infallible Church, and there is only one Church which claims infallibility.

The assertion of such a claim puts instantly an infinite distance between the Church which makes it and all other institutions whatsoever. A society which admits its fallibility confesses itself human; an organization which assumes its own inerrancy claims to be divine. 'Claims,' did I say? The very fact of such a claim becomes a proof of its validity. No human society would dare to put forth such a pretension. No human voice could sustain such a tone without faltering. But look at the Catholic Church. Her attitude is the most astounding thing in history. Has she ever flinched or been irresolute? Has she ever forgotten herself? Never for an instant. There has been no tremor in her voice; through the long centuries it has sounded like a ceaseless roll of thunder. She came forth from God, and her supernatural consciousness has never failed her. She has carried herself with the lofty instinct of divinity. *Vera incessu patuit dea!*

It is passing strange to me that I did not sooner see that infallibility is of the very essence of the Church, and how those who attempt to get rid of it, and to conceive of a fallible divine Church, are inevitably involved in hopeless contradictions.

Let us go back to the beginning of the sixteenth century. Either there was a Church of God then in the world, or there was not. If there was not, then the Reformers certainly could not create such a Church. If there was, they as certainly had neither the right to abandon it nor the power to remodel it. The Reformers admitted the existence of such a Church; in the Apostolic Symbol, they daily made an act of faith in the Holy Ghost and the Holy Catholic Church. And yet they proclaimed that the Church which they professed to believe, instead of being by the Holy Ghost preserved from error, had become foul with falsehood and deadly contagion. Their action belied their profession. They did not really believe either in the Holy Ghost or the Holy Catholic Church.

Well, as they could not have their way with the Old Church, they went out and founded a new one - a hundred new and improved Churches. And having set up their Churches, they furnished them each with well-digested and elaborate confessions of faith. The new Churches and articles were based upon the assumed failure and corruption of the old. But the fact of such a failure would have rendered all Churches henceforth impossible, and all creeds forever worthless. Of what value to me is the teaching of a Church which approaches me with words such as these; 'My child, I admit frankly that I may be mistaken. God forbid that I should arrogate to myself what it would be impious madness for a human institution to assert. The Church of Rome has erred. All churches have erred. To err is human. Nevertheless, I represent to you in some way the visible Church. And, somehow or other, I have authority in controversies of faith. Here are my Articles of Religion. You may interpret them, I am happy to say, in any way you please; for they are rather articles of peace than articles of faith; I do not oblige you to believe them, but only not to contradict them. They are supposed to be in accordance with God's Word written, which is also supposed to contain all necessary truth although I can give no reason for supposing so. If, however, you should be convinced of a discrepancy, you are not only at liberty, but it will be your bounden duty, utterly to repudiate them. In which event, nevertheless, it will be my painful duty theoretically, at least to eject you from my communion.' This is rather mournful than amusing. When, however, a Church which confesses itself fallible undertakes to arraign one which claims infallibility, the case becomes purely ludicrous. The Church of Rome says: 'I come from God, and God is ever with me; therefore I speak with authority.' The Church of England answers: " I make no such preposterous pretension. I have nowhere been so indiscreet as to give the slightest intimation that I either came from God or that God is with me. I am fallible. And I stake my reputation for fallibility on the assertion that the Church of Rome has erred'...

It has been proved that a Church which is divinely commissioned to teach must be divinely protected against error in its teaching. The Church is infallible. Therefore the Head of the Church is infallible; for, as St. Thomas demonstrates, the faith of the Church must be fixed by the decisions of its Head. An infallible Church with a fallible Head would be an absurdity.

The infallibility of the Head of the Church is, then, a logical inference from the infallibility of the Church. The argument is one from effect to condition...From the infallibility of the Church we infer the infallibility of its Head, inasmuch as the latter is an essential condition of the former.

It is time to sum up. Either there is a divine revelation or there is not. If there is a revelation, it must rest upon authority; but there is no authority outside of the Catholic Church. If men give up the Catholic Church, they must go back slowly, it may be, and reluctantly, but inevitably to paganism"); essay in Georgina Pell Curtis, *Beyond the Road to Rome*

(1914), p.373; Walter George Smith, *Fidelis of the Cross: James Kent Stone* (1928); Katherine Burton, *In No Strange Land: Some American Catholic Converts* (1942), p.109 ("When [*The Invitation Heeded* was] published it was hailed as a masterly presentation of the papal position... It was in the main the story of a man who had found Protestantism an inadmissible compromise between rationalism and Catholicism, and who at the last found himself in agreement with Cardinal Newman that there was no medium in true philosophy between atheism and Catholicism. 'If,' he wrote, 'this Holy, Roman, Catholic, and Apostolic Church be not the Church then Christianity adds another load to the burden of Mysteries'"); Katherine Burton, *No Shadow of Turning: The Life of James Kent Stone* (1944); James Likoudis, "James Kent Stone/ Fr. Fidelis of the Cross, CP: The Newman of New England," *Social Justice Review*, January-February 2009 ("In his survey of the history of the Church concerning the Papacy, the 'American Newman' was to conclude: 'The Primacy of the See of Peter is the most prominent fact in the history of Christianity. And it is a fact which is inseparably associated with a distinct prophecy. Moreover, the Primacy is not only professedly grounded upon the prophecy in question, but is actually so grounded. I mean that the words of Christ [in the famous Petrine texts of Scripture] are so substantially the foundation of the Papal power that the latter could never have existed without the former. No intelligent student will think of denying this. Indeed, without looking into the past at all, it is perfectly plain that, if it were not for the divine sentences so often quoted, the Pontifical claims would be wholly without sanction, and the Papacy would fall to pieces in an hour... *Thou art a Rock; and upon this Rock I will build My Church; and the Gates of Hell shall not prevail against it.* Stupendous prophecy! Where among all the words of God shall its mate be found?'").

Storck, Thomas – writer; b. 1951, Brooklyn, New York; c. 12 February 1978 (received with his wife); brought up in Ohio; his father was a skeptic in religion, but valued the social aspects of church attendance; the family was Protestant, then Unitarian, and finally Episcopalian; read himself into becoming a theist; then in 1968 began to accept the Incarnation after reading C. S. Lewis on the idea of a playwright writing himself a part in his own drama; came to see from high-church literature the nature of the Church ("I got a sense of the Church of Jesus Christ as a visible, corporate, and institutional Body, with a liturgy and sacraments and a faith handed down from our Lord and the Apostles"); he graduated in English Literature from Kenyon College, Gambier, Ohio; MA from

St. John's College, Santa Fe, New Mexico; further graduate studies in history and economics; writer on Catholic issues (notably Catholic social teaching) and philosophy; has described himself as a Catholic creationist; contributing editor for *Caelum et Terra* 1991-1996 and the *New Oxford Review* 1996-2006; member of the editorial board of the *Chesterton Review* from 1998; married with four children; see (selective list) *The Catholic Milieu* (1987); "How We Understand the Bible," *Homiletic and Pastoral Review*, October 1989; "Why Are People So Bad, and So Good?" *Catholic Twin Circle*, 15 April 1990; "The Christian House," *Homiletic and Pastoral Review*, May 1991; "What is Western Culture?" *Faith and Reason*, Spring 1994; "New Testament: Witness to the Catholic Faith," *Homiletic and Pastoral Review*, June 1995; "The Catholic Intellectual Revival," *Homiletic and Pastoral Review*, July 1995; "The Beauty of the Truth," *Caelum et Terra*, Fall 1995 ("When I converted to the Catholic faith early in 1978 at the age of twenty-seven I was motivated by only one thing: my conviction that Catholicism was true, that Catholicism's account of reality was in fact the way things really are. But long before that date, when I did not yet believe that the Catholic religion was true, I found myself increasingly attracted by the beauty of the Faith. And though I would never urge anyone to become a Catholic simply because of the beauty of the Faith or of Catholic life, nevertheless I am still convinced that not only is the Faith true but that it is compellingly attractive and beautiful, even exciting. Moreover, I think that the beauties of the Faith are not merely accidents, but are close to the heart of what God has done for us.

Though I had little contact with Catholics or Catholic things while I was a boy, my father's library did contain a few important Catholic books. These included part of Aquinas's *Summa Contra Gentiles*, Chesterton's *The Everlasting Man*, Ronald Knox's *The Belief of Catholics*, and the *Baltimore Catechism*. As I was growing up I read some of these books and parts of the others. And two things about the Catholic Church gradually impressed themselves on my mind. The first was the fondness of Catholicism for clear thinking. Distinctions were distinctions, if A was A, then, dammit, A was not B. If something was proved true, then it was true, whatever we felt about it. In contrast I found most of the other religious ideas I encountered, either in people or in other books, mushy and vague (I exempt C. S. Lewis from this charge). But though it is easy to see how I became aware of the tight logic and clear distinctions of the Catholic mind, I am less clear on the second thing. Indeed, I am not sure I can even define or name it very well. But I must try, for I think it is one of the most salient features about

Catholicism, and something that ought to be attractive, especially to those of my generation.

What is this second thing? it is simply that at some point in my adolescence and early manhood I began to find the Faith attractive, exciting, beautiful. Catholicism gradually became to me a vision of things at once more vibrant and full of life than the culturally Protestant world in which I had always lived. I say here deliberately 'Catholicism' rather than 'the Catholic Church,' not because I felt any coldness toward the Church itself, but because my vision was broader. In the center of it indeed stood the Church, but around that Church stood Catholic civilization, Catholic life. The latter obviously came from the former, but the latter also made manifest what was often hidden and latent in the former: the beauty and vibrancy of Catholicism.

Now, as I say, I do not remember how this conception arose in my mind. As an undergraduate I read some more in various Catholic authors, especially Chesterton and Belloc, and I am sure that they helped strengthen this image of the Faith. I remember at the time reading some of Chesterton's *The Catholic Church and Conversion* and accepting without demur his words about Catholicism being the new religion, one of the 'enthusiasms that carry young people off their feet and leave older people bewildered or annoyed,' the very reverse of an old, feeble or stodgy affair. As he writes here, 'It is perhaps no longer the custom to regard conversion as a form of dissipation; but it is still common to regard conversion as a form of revolt. And as regards the established convention of much of the modem world, it is a revolt. The worthy merchant of the middle class, the worthy farmer of the Middle West, when he sends his son to college, does now feel a faint alarm lest the boy should fall among thieves, in the sense of Communists; but he has the same sort of fear lest he should fall among Catholics.'

For a time as an undergraduate I was also part of a folk choir that sang regularly at a Saturday night Mass. It was certainly not the music nor even the liturgy (by 1970 already Englished) that especially reinforced my attraction to the Faith, but rather parts of Catholic life that I was now beginning to experience. Although it is a caricature that Episcopalians are all crusty, rich and stuck-up, nevertheless it is true that among Catholics I saw a popular and familiar side to religion that I did not see among Episcopalians or other Protestants. This Catholic atmosphere is touched on by Ronald Knox in *The Belief of Catholics*: 'There is among Catholic saints a familiarity which seems to raise this world to the level of eternity. There is among Catholic sinners a familiarity which seems (to non-Catholic eyes) to degrade eternity to the level of this world. The point is most clearly demonstrated in connection with that attitude toward religious things which we call 'reverence.' For good or for evil, the ordinary, easy-going Catholic pays far less tribute to this sentiment than a Protestant, or even an agnostic brought up in the atmosphere of Protestantism. No traveler fails to be struck, and perhaps shocked, by the 'irreverence' or 'naturalness' (call it what you will) that marks the behavior of Catholic children wandering about in church. Even grown-up Catholics will usually talk in church if anything needs to be said, while Protestants will usually whisper.

The essence of this Catholic atmosphere, at least as it attracted me, was this easy intermingling of the sacred and the secular. In our conventionally Protestant culture piety is associated with an overtly 'religious' sort of behavior. And when one is not being religious one is being entirely secular. The twain do not meet. But among Catholics I was seeing that the twain do indeed meet, in fact, that the twain are intertwined. Religion is not something apart from our everyday lives, requiring a special and sanctified kind of comportment. I saw this same thing during a visit to a popular pilgrimage site, the Shrine of Our Lady of Consolation in Carey, Ohio, on Assumption Day in 1974. Here were crowds of pilgrims of many ethnic groups, Chaldean rite Catholics (originally from Iraq) prominent among them. Now the pilgrims at Carey are by no means all pious in the conventional understanding of that term. That is, they do not walk around with long faces and folded hands; they mill around talking with friends, teenagers parade around the streets, little children dart about playing. People come to Carey for a pilgrimage to a shrine of the Mother of God and yet this act is not cut off from the rest of their lives by some kind of wall, a wall which sharply demarcates the sacred from the secular. As it was for Chaucer's pilgrims, journeying to a shrine unites much of what some might seek on a vacation with what would clearly be accounted works of piety...

[T]here is something objective that was always at the root of my attraction toward the Church and toward Catholic life. This is the Incarnation. '*And the Word was made flesh and dwelt among us.*' From the doctrine and fact of the incarnation, the taking of a human nature by the Eternal Logos, come, I think, those aspects of the Faith that so attracted and excited me, and still do. In the first place, the Incarnation was surely the most wonderful and startling intermingling of the divine and human that is possible. Here was the almighty Creator of the universe living among us. Here he was a suckling at his Mother's breast, eating his first solid food, playing, assisting Joseph, eating, sleeping.

Although hardly able to put it into words, I discerned a difference between Catholics and Protestants, including cultural Protestants, in their approach to the sacred. Catholics had a familiarity with God and the things of God that others did not seem to have, a familiarity that, as I said, seems to me to be rooted in a wholehearted acceptance of the Incarnation and its implications and which, when translated into actual living acts and material objects, has created a culture of great beauty and liveliness.

There is another and related aspect of Catholic life that is likewise, I think, rooted in the Incarnation. This is the concreteness of Catholicism. After our Lord assumed flesh he was always in a particular place. Though, of course, he was also at the same time everywhere (since he is God), you could still find him in one particular place doing one particular thing. He might be preaching or eating or healing or sleeping or walking. As if two men who were arguing could say, 'Well, let's go over and ask God what he thinks about this. He's staying in the third house from the corner.' And the means of grace and sanctification that God instituted in his Church are concrete and use concrete things: water and oil and bread and wine. Each is uniquely itself and uniquely different…

Moreover, the vibrancy that I perceived underlying this colorful concreteness was the vibrancy of the Logos, the force that upholds all creation in the veins and bones of the God-man. If the divine life could pulsate within human flesh, as it were, then something of that divine strength could also lie behind Catholic life. It is certainly the principle on which our sacramental theology is based and in the Eucharist we have it in its most complete form. Indeed, there it is almost a second Incarnation, for again Almighty God comes down to dwell within the things of earth and to inhabit what is made by the hands of man.

So it was chiefly these two things, the daring juxtaposition of the sacred and the secular and the bold concreteness of Catholic life, both rooted in the Incarnation, that attracted me to the Faith, that made Catholicism seem exciting, especially in contrast to the cultural Protestantism of my childhood and of our surrounding society. And the Incarnation is also the reason why, I think, that the events of Christmas, and in fact all that concerns Our Lady, have such compelling charm for us. Mary has no meaning for us apart from the Incarnation, and whenever we turn to her we are at least implicitly recognizing the Incarnation, And the Word becoming flesh is a fact astonishing, and attractive because it is astonishing, so that we never tire of repeating the stories of Bethlehem, of the stable and the shepherds, of the beasts and the angels"); "The Old Testament Messianic Hope," *The Catholic Faith*, November/December 1996; "Catholics and Religious Liberty:

What Can We Believe?" *Homiletic and Pastoral Review*, January 1997; "Is Opposition to Homosexual Activity Irrational?" *New Oxford Review*, May 1997; "To Renew the Catholic Mind," *Homiletic and Pastoral Review*, June 1997; *Foundations of a Catholic Political Order* (1998); "Into Peter's Barque," *New Oxford Review*, March 1998 (reproduced under the title "Into Peter's Ark" in *The Coming Home Network International*, *Conversion Stories*, *chnetwork.org*, 12 September 2011) ("I wrote a long paper for an English history class on the question of the continuity of the Church of England with the pre-Reformation Catholic Church. I remember being shocked when I discovered that those who had assisted King Henry VIII in setting up the Church of England regarded ultra-Protestants such as Calvin as their friends and co-religionists. So much for the Branch Theory in the 1540s! However my Episcopal professor suggested that instead of looking at the intentions of the Anglican founders, I should look for how much of Catholicism (as he and I understood it) had managed to survive the Protestant Revolt, despite what Cranmer and his colleagues may have desired. This satisfied me and helped to keep me in the Episcopal Church for another few years…

The crisis…came after the General Convention's authorizing of the ordination of women in 1976. I knew that this was entirely against the Catholic tradition in any sense, and indeed a flat repudiation of the Branch Theory, which held that none of the three branches should act unilaterally…

I knew that for me the key to the entire question was the attitude of the early Church toward the papacy. I actually had read very little of the Fathers, except for Augustine's *Confessions*. So, among other things, I did some reading in the Fathers and other early writers. I was shocked to find passages such as the following: 'This church [Rome] has a position of leadership and authority; and therefore every church…must needs agree with the church at Rome; for in her the apostolic tradition has ever been preserved...' (St. Irenaeus, *Adversus Haereses*, iii, I)…

[These passages], under the inspiration of the Holy Spirit completed the change in me, and at that point I accepted the fundamental principle of the Faith and thus the entire corpus of Catholic belief. I did more reading after that but the question was essentially settled. Since I now recognized that the true Christian Church was gathered in communion with the successor of Peter, I did not need to debate separately such articles of faith as the Infallibility of the Pope or Our Lady's Immaculate Conception and Assumption. It was enough to know that those Christians who were grouped in the true Church had authoritatively defined those dogmas…

In looking back from my standpoint as a Catholic, I now see that the 'Anglo-Catholic' Branch Theory of the Church is profoundly contrary not just to the Fathers, but to the New Testament itself. The kind of unity that St. Paul continually appeals to and, in fact, practices, as he travels among the various small congregations of Catholics in Asia Minor and Greece, has nothing in common with the 'unity' supposed in the Branch Theory (e.g., see 1 Cor. 1:10-15). Moreover, of the three supposed branches of the Church, both the Roman and the Eastern Orthodox emphatically reject the Branch Theory, while among Anglicans, most are indifferent to it, with only a small group of 'Anglo-Catholics' accepting it!

One other point I will mention. Sometimes when people, either Catholics or non-Catholics, ask me what I was before becoming a Catholic, and I tell them, they say something like 'Oh, an Episcopalian, well, that's not very different.' Yes and no. As an Anglican I did believe most of Catholic doctrine. But there was one thing that was very different. All Protestants, including Anglo-Catholics, basically make up their own religion. That is, those Protestants who profess to believe only the Bible can decide for themselves just what the Bible means and how to interpret difficult passages. And if they choose to follow a particular pastor or evangelist on some disputed point, still they themselves choose which pastor or evangelist to follow, The decision is in their own hands.

This is true also for high-church Anglicans, so-called Anglo-Catholics. Although as an Episcopalian I professed to follow the Fathers of the undivided Church and the traditions common to Rome, Canterbury, and Constantinople, still I decided exactly which traditions were 'really' universal and thus binding on all Christians. I decided when the testimony of the Fathers was sufficiently unanimous. Even if I followed an author I thought was sound, it was my decision which author to trust. I essentially made up my own religion. The ultimate decision was always mine. This was the biggest difference I noticed after becoming a Catholic: finding the locus of authority truly outside myself. It was like having cold water thrown over me on a hot day - a bit of a shock but very refreshing.

The refreshment I felt at no longer having to make up my own religion was the refreshment that comes from beginning to learn a bit of humility, as well as from leaving off a job that was never meant to be mine in the first place. Of course, this does not mean that I denigrate reason. The Catholic tradition of reasoning, and Catholic esteem for human intellect, are well known. True and genuine authority is in no way contrary to reason, but rather its friend and ally"); "Three Obstacles to Evangelization," *Homiletic and Pastoral Review,*

June 1998; "Survivals and New Arrivals," *Homiletic and Pastoral Review*, October 1998; "How to Form a Catholic Mind," *New Oxford Review*, February 1999; "A Glimpse of Catholic Culture," *New Oxford Review*, April 1999; "Catholicism: The Perfection of Religion," *Homiletic and Pastoral Review*, August/September 1999; "A Course for Catholic Inculturation," *The Catholic Faith*, September/October 1999; "Catholicism and the Natural World," *The Catholic Faith*, November/December 1999, p.6; "Hating the Body," *New Oxford Review*, December 1999; "Liberalism's Three Assaults," *Homiletic and Pastoral Review*, January 2000; *Christendom and the West* (2000); "A Dialogue of a Freethinker and a Catholic" (2 Parts), *Catholic Way* (2000); "Sola Scriptura: An Impossible Theory," *New Oxford Review*, December 2000; "The New Testament: *In Medio Ecclesiae*," *The Catholic Faith*, January/February 2001; "What is the Magisterium?" *The Catholic Faith*, May/June 2001; "Is There Such a Thing as 'Mere Christianity'?" *New Oxford Review*, July/August 2001; "The Universal Import of God's Revelation in the Old Testament," *The Catholic Faith*, January/February 2002; "Manichaeanism: The Heresy That Hates Creation," *Homiletic and Pastoral Review*, February 2002; "Christendom: God's Beachhead in a Rebellious World," *Homiletic and Pastoral Review*, June 2002; "C. S. Lewis: Reason vs Easy Assumptions," *New Oxford Review*, November 2002; "The Shrinking of Sacred Time," *New Oxford Review*, Janauary 2003; "Is the Bible Protestant," *Homiletic and Pastoral Review*, July 2003; "Reflections of a Catholic Creationist," *Homiletic and Pastoral Review*, January 2004 ("Microevolution is simply the changes that occur in living things, plants or animals, but changes that are strictly limited… [W]hen God created an original plant or animal there was a certain genetic variability within it, as we can see in the many different types of dogs, for example. But a dog cannot become an elephant nor a fish a bird. When Darwin saw fourteen different types of finches in the Galapagos islands in 1835 he tightly concluded that they were modifications of finches whose ancestors had come from the South American continent, But finches are finches. We cannot reasonably conclude from the fact that since finches can change a bit, thus, as one author put it, from Darwin's insight about the finches 'man received a first intimation that he might once have been an ape [i.e., macroevolution]'"); "Democracy and God," *Chronicles*, November 2004; "A Preface to Apologetics," *Homiletic and Pastoral Review*, November 2004; "The Apostasy of the Gentiles," *Homiletic and Pastoral Review*, July 2005; "Where Have All the Protestants Gone," *New Oxford Review*, January 2006;

"The Liturgy: Mother of Cultures," *Homiletic and Pastoral Review*, October 2007; "What is rhe Church of Jesus Christ," *Homiletic and Pastoral Review*, March 2008; "Orthodoxy as Personal Statement or Cultural Blueprint," *Chesterton Review*, Fall/Winter 2008; "What Is Faith?" *Homiletic and Pastoral Review*, November 2008; "St. Thomas and Chesterton on Law, Human and Divine," *Homiletic and Pastoral Review*, February 2010; "Four Sins That Cry to Heaven," *New Oxford Review*, July/August 2010; "Catholicism as Cult and Culture," *Saint Austin Review*, September/October 2011, p.9; "The Catholic Faith Is Not a Noble Lie," *Homiletic and Pastoral Review*, January 2012; "Pesch v. Chesterton," *Culture Wars*, May 2012, p.14; *thomasstorck.org*.

Storer, Bellamy – diplomat; b. 28 August 1847, Cincinnati, Ohio; c. 1896 (his wife and daughter Margaret were received in 1892); d. 1922, Paris, France; son of Bellamy Storer (1796-1875), diplomat and U.S. Representative from Ohio; educated at Harvard University (graduated in 1867); graduated from the law school of Cincinnati College in 1869; admitted to the bar in 1869 and practiced in Cincinnati; married Maria Longworth Nichols Storer (see below) in 1886; elected as a Republican to the House of Representatives from Ohio, and served from 1891 to 1895; Assistant Secretary of State in 1897; supported William McKinley (1843-1901) in his campaigns for Governor of Ohio and President of the United States; McKinley appointed him Ambassador to Belgium (served 1897-1899), then to same post in Spain (served 1899-1902); President Theodore Roosevelt appointed him to Austria-Hungary (served 1902-1906); he and his wife lobbied for Archbishop Ireland to be made a cardinal, embarrassing President Roosevelt by giving the false impression that he supported their approach (became known as the "Dear Maria Controversy"); as a result he was dismissed from his post; resumed the practice of law; buried in Le Cimetière Neuf, Marvejols; France.

Storer, Horatio Robinson - gynecologist and anti-abortion activist; b. 27 February 1830, Boston. Massachusetts; c. 1879; d. 18 September 1922, Newport, Rhode Island; born into a Unitarian family; son of David Humphreys Storer (1804-1891), a prominent naturalist and medical professor at Harvard Medical School; studied natural history at Harvard College (graduated in 1850); studied medicine at Harvard Medical School, in part under his father (MD in 1853); worked in Europe and brought back the anesthetic technique of the use of chloroform in childbirth and surgery; set up in Boston one of the first specialty practices in obstetrics and gynecological surgery in the

United States; one of the founders of gynecology as a separate medical field; he married Emily Elvira Gilmore, a Catholic, in 1853 (four children of the marriage); partly inspired by his father's efforts in the same field, he began in 1857 the "physicians' crusade against abortion"; he and other doctors proved that induced abortion was common among married Protestant women at that time (the public often had the false perception that early abortion was not a crime); the "physicians' crusade" led to the passage of laws in almost every state that protected the fetus from conception by banning abortion at any point in gestation; this taught people that the fetus was alive prior to "quickening" and the deleterious effect of abortion on women's health; he campaigned for specific statutes banning abortion at any point in gestation (unless performed to save the life of the mother) and covering other actions, such as assisting in abortion and advertising abortifacient drugs; he wrote both specialist and popular texts on the subject; the "physicians' crusade" led to a drop in induced abortions; these laws continued until (at least) 1973 when all state laws were overturned by *Roe v Wade*; he converted to Episcopalianism in 1869; after his wife's death in 1872, he married in the same year her sister, Augusta Caroline Gilmore; Augusta died in 1874; in 1876 he married Frances S. Mackenzie; with this marriage he became a fervent Catholic; serious illness in 1872 led him to Italy to seek a cure before returning to Newport in 1877; he continued his work; he also built up the Catholic infrastructure of Newport and left part of his estate to various Catholic agencies there; he became Harvard's oldest living graduate; see *On Criminal Abortion in America* (1860); *Why Not? A Book for Every Woman* (1866) ("If we have proved the existence of fetal life before quickening has taken place or can take place and all by analogy, and a close and conclusive process of induction, its commencement at the very beginning, at conception itself, we are compelled to believe unjustifiable abortion always a crime.

And now words fail. Of the mother, by consent or by her own hand, imbrued with her infant's blood; of the equally guilty father, who counsels or allows the crime; of the wretches who by their wholesale murders far out-Herod Burke and Hare; of the public sentiment which palliates, pardons, and would even praise this so common violation of all law, human and divine, of all instinct, of all reason, all pity, all mercy, all love, - we leave those to speak who can"); *Is It I? A Book for Every Man* (1867); *Criminal Abortion: Its Nature, Its Evidence, and Its Law* (1868) (with Franklin Fiske Heard); Joseph M. Toner, *A Sketch of the Life of Horatio R. Storer, M.D.* (1878); Herbert Thoms, *Chapters in American Obstetrics* (1933); James C. Mohr,

Abortion in America: The Origins and Evolution of National Policy, 1800-1900 (1978); Frederick N. Dyer, "Horatio Robinson Storer, MD and the Physicians' Crusade Against Abortion," *Life and Learning* (1999) ("Dr. James Joseph Walsh, Dean of the Fordham Medical School, was a close friend of Horatio and provided at least three sketches of Horatio. In the last year of his life, Horatio provided a number of autobiographical letters to assist Walsh in his biographical efforts, noting in one of these that 'one does not like to have part in his own obituary.'

Horatio was aware...that he and the American Medical Association initiated a crusade that saved many thousands from an unnecessary uterine death. In an earlier letter to Walsh Horatio also had discussed his own and the American Medical Association's effective roles in opposing abortion which 'produced a very general change in belief and practice,' and had instructed Dr. Walsh, 'Think this over seriously, and then appreciate with me the character and universal extent of the change.' This strongly suggests that Horatio recognized the ramifications of 'the change' on the offspring of these survivors, and the offspring of offspring for the three generations he monitored from 1857 to 1922. He may have also appreciated the expanding ramifications on every succeeding generation as long as human beings survive on the planet.

It is not farfetched to indicate that the reader can thank his or her existence to this man, since the effects of even a small increase in surviving pregnancies exponentially increase on succeeding generations, and there is evidence that this increase in surviving pregnancies was not small (If only one generation showed an increase in surviving pregnancies amounting to 3% of children, this would provide a parent (or two) for 5.9% of the next generation, for 11.5% of the second generation, for 21.6% of the third generation, *etc.*). Even if each ancestor of the reader would have been in place without Horatio, some key teachers, coaches, mentors, friends, would not have been around to make their contribution to that existence. Is Dr. Horatio Robinson Storer thus the most important figure in America in the 19th century? Only decades of reluctance to discuss the taboo topic of criminal abortion may have prevented recognition of this long ago"); Frederick N. Dyer, *Champion of Women and the Unborn: Horatio Robinson Storer, MD* (1999); Frederick N. Dyer, "The Physicians' Crusade For the Unborn," *The Human Life Review*, Winter 2003 ("Not the least factor in keeping the rate of unnecessary abortions from being even higher was the Catholic clergy. Catholic readers can thank their grandmothers', great grandmothers', and great great-grandmothers' priests for their own existence. Storer noted the rarity of abortion among Catholic women in 1859 and reported that there had been no change when he wrote in 1868. He gave credit for this fact to the Catholic confessional, as did numerous other physicians, including Alfred A. Andrews, of Windsor, Ontario. In a paper published in the *Canada Lancet* in June 1875, Andrews noted the similarities between the Catholic confessional and the doctor's private office: 'I had for many years noted and wondered at the fact that, of the married women who sought my cooperation, nearly all were Protestants. Being myself a Protestant of the broadest Orange stripe, and not ready to acknowledge any marked moral inferiority in my co-religionists, I was for a long season puzzled, but I think the solution is this. The Pulpit is debarred, but the Roman Catholic priesthood have in their confessional an opportunity of instructing and warning their flock. Protestant women do not go there, but we, and we only, have the private confidential ear of the whole sex, and it is, I conceive, our duty to lose no opportunity of diffusing the information we possess in this regard. Let us purify the moral atmosphere. Let us make the whole sex know that it is murder, when the embryo is but four weeks old, as completely as if the nine months of fetal life had been reached or passed. We have a duty to perform, and we have countless opportunities of doing it"); Frederick N. Dyer, *The Physicians' Crusade Against the Unborn* (2005); Frederick N. Dyer, "The Physicians' Crusade Against the Unborn," *New Oxford Review*, November 2006; Frederick N. Dyer, "Are You Alive Because of the Laws Against Abortion," *jillstanek.com*, 15 March 2007; Frederick N. Dyer, "How Abortion Became Illegal in the United States," *patheos.com*, 25 May 2011; John F. Quinn, "The Good Doctor: Horatio Robinson Storer," *Crisis*, 10 December 2012 ("[H]e had converted to Catholicism, probably in part because of the influence of his devoutly Catholic wife, Frances. Storer surely had other reasons to convert as well. He had long admired the Catholic Church for its clear teaching on abortion and had been associated with the Franciscan Hospital for Women in Boston in the 1860s. He also was friendly with Bishop John Fitzpatrick of Boston and corresponded often with Bishop Francis Chatard of Indianapolis, who had trained to be a doctor before studying for the priesthood"); his papers are in the Countway Library, Harvard Medical School; *horatiostorer.net*; *ANB*.

Storer, Maria Longworth Nichols - artist, patroness and writer; b. 20 March 1849, Cincinnati, Ohio; c. 26 June 1892 (her daughter Margaret was received in April 1892 and her second husband in 1896); d. 11 April 1932, Paris, France; born to a very wealthy family;

parents both communicants of the Protestant Episcopal Church; brought up as a High-Church Episcopalian; very interested in fine art from her youth; married Colonel George Ward Nichols (d. 1885), a Civil War veteran and art aficionado, in 1868; founder of the Cincinnati May Festival held in 1873; began painting china, eventually incorporating Japanese art into her work; founded the Rookwood Pottery, now famous, in 1880; friend of her fellow painter Mary Louise McLaughlin (1847-1939), her chief competitor; married Bellamy Storer (1847-1922), the diplomat (see above) in 1886; influenced in her conversion to the Catholic faith by Archbishop John Ireland; also impressed by the encyclicals of Pope Leo XIII; several awards for her art work; friend of Presidents McKinley, Taft, and Roosevelt; she and her husband lobbied for Archbishop Ireland to be made a cardinal, embarrassing President Roosevelt by giving the false impression that he supported their approach (became known as the "Dear Maria Controversy"); as a result her husband was dismissed from his post; she did much charitable work; spent her last ten years in Paris; see *The Story of a Miracle at Lourdes, August 1907* (1908); essay in Georgina Pell Curtis, *Some Roads to Rome in America* (1909), p.460; *The War Against Religion in France* (1910); essay in Georgina Pell Curtis, *Beyond the Road to Rome* (1914), p.376 ("When I became a Catholic, twenty-one years ago, some of my non-Catholic friends accounted for the vagary in a way quite satisfactory to themselves; they said that I was lured into the Church by the beauty of her temples and by her impressive ceremonies. It is quite true that the Catholic Church appeals to the senses and satisfies them. The eye revels in the wonders of Catholic architecture; the master-works of Catholic art as seen in the sculpture of tombs and altars, the coloring and splendor of pictures and of vestments. The ear is enraptured by Catholic music - the grandeur of masses and anthems and the dignity of Gregorian chants; even the sense of smell is delighted by the soft breath of incense, or the odor of roses and lilies before Our Lady's altar. The beauty of the Catholic Church is undeniable to the senses; but it has a deeper meaning to the soul, as the Shrine of God! If Protestant demonstrations of prayer or praise seem meagre and plain in comparison, one must remember that the 'reformers' would have it so. They were eager to hack in pieces the statues and to shatter the stained glass windows; to simplify the Church of England and to divest her ministers of their 'trinkets' and 'muniments of superstition.' In all this they were quite logical. Having driven the King from His tabernacle, there surely was no longer any reason for preserving His Royal splendor; nor the beauty of the House where

His Glory dwelt, after that Glory had departed. In every Protestant church, therefore, the minister is the central figure: his sermon the important event. If he talks well and is amusing (above all, in these modern times, if he be intelligently heterodox) he draws delighted crowds; if he be a pious and dull man, he has only a small congregation of strict 'church-goers' and they complain about his preaching !

For us Catholics, on the contrary, the sermon - if there be one - is a mere episode - the Divine sacrifice is everything; for the Old Testament prophecy is fulfilled in every Catholic Church throughout the world: 'They shall make me a Sanctuary, and I will dwell in the midst of them.' At every celebration of the Mass Christ's promise is kept; ''I will not leave you orphans: I will come to you.' 'The Bread that I will give is my Flesh for the life of the world. If any man eat of this bread, he shall live forever.' Here is the source and center of Christ's Church, whence Divine Light goes forth like rays from the sun; here is the beating heart of all Christendom, the magnet that draws souls to the Sacred Tabernacle. Take that away and the whole fabric would fall to pieces. This Divine Life is in the Catholic Church, and nowhere outside; for the Reformation deliberately banished the Real Presence, suppressed the sacrifice of the Mass, and even substituted tables for the altars of God"); *The Borodino Mystery* (1916); *The Villa Rossignol; or, The Advance of Islam* (1918); *The Beginning of the Rookwood Pottery* (1919); *Theodore Roosevelt the Child* (1921); *In Memoriam Bellamy Storer* (1923); Marvin R. O'Connell, *John Ireland and the American Catholic Church* (1988); Rose Angela Boehle, *Maria: A Biography of Maria Longworth* (1990).

Strong, Carlton – architect; b. 1862; d. 1931; brought up in a Darwinized type of Zwinglian Anglicanism; through the instrumentality of a High-Church clergyman he was eventually led to accept Christianity as "reasonable and true"; practiced architecture in Buffalo, then in New York City, and finally in Pittsburgh; first known as a designer of apartment buildings, but in Pittsburgh concentrated on ecclesiastical buildings for Catholic parishes and institutions; wrote under the pen name of Thomas L'Estrange; see Georgina Pell Curtis, *Beyond the Road to Rome* (1914), p.382 ("In spite of her captivity to political and other evils, Anglicanism was pictured as the normal center of religious unity for the English-speaking race, and especially was it the duty of those whom God had placed in her fold to labor for the restoration of her past glories in freedom of faith, Catholic practice and good works.

But this position will lead one in time to become more or less acquainted with the 'arrogant'' claims of another 'great

Communion' and while we were rather strenuous in our effort to make her past glories our own, we were inclined not only to exaggerate her faults, but to insist that they were too great to be curable without the example and influence of a purified Anglicanism to guide her back to the Primitive model.

When one has at last made all these, and many more points of view to the same purpose, his own, it is very disturbing to be confronted, against one's will, with a growing conviction that Anglicanism owes its separate existence as an institution to motives and deeds which were not such as a well meaning man can entirely commend. In fact, he comes to see that the separation was accomplished by fraud and violence and for mixed purposes that were, for the most part, essentially evil.

The questions then quite naturally arise: 'Were these men with these purposes right and the body of the old believers consequently wrong?' 'Did the property of infallibility, which they admit resides in the Church, leave the old body headed by Rome and attach itself to them and to their work?'

These questions are not merely disturbing, but they lead one to take up a very disagreeable and unwelcome line of investigation. In the end, such an investigation, - unless grace intervenes to save the trouble, - finally narrows down to the question of Orders. One is afraid in his conscience to deny the validity of sacramental forms given and received in good faith, and with comfort at the time, without the clearest and most certain conviction; at least not until he has properly grasped the old principle of a living final authority.

The period of experimentation was never more tersely summarized than by a recent lecturer (Rev. Vincent McNabb, OP) at the Waldorf-Astoria, New York, when he said: 'The Established Church, as such, is the child of Elizabeth. The last convocation of the *Ecclesia Anglicana* in 1559 declared its belief in the Supremacy of the Successors of St. Peter. But the politicians…drew up an oath deliberately repudiating the doctrine. With one exception the entire hierarchy of England refused the oath *and was deposed* and, with two or three exceptions, suffered the martyrdom of life imprisonment. With that act the… *new hierarchy* and its followers severed their communion with

(a) the *Ecclesia Anglicana* of the convocation;

(b) with the Patriarch of the West (the pope of Rome);

(c) with the *Ecclesia Catholica.* This was the moment of deliberate separation from Rome.'

Elizabeth's choice for first Primate of the new line fell upon Matthew Parker, whom she knew as one who had willingly served as chaplain to her mother, Anne Boleyn, Her mandate to several bishops in good standing with the old church to consecrate Parker as Archbishop of Canterbury was refused by all of them.

After much scurrying about, four persons, - Barlow, Hodgkins, Scory and Coverdale, - were found willing to 'consecrate' Parker on Royal authority and impart to him, as far as they could, the 'Apostolic Succession' and the mission and jurisdiction of an episcopate of which they had never themselves been members. Scory and Coverdale were creatures of the Edwardine rite and therefore not Catholics at all. Coverdale did not believe in the episcopal office and never, save at this time to please the Queen, would he consent to act as a bishop. Hodgkins was a *suffragan* and consequently never held the title or jurisdiction of an English See on any authority.

The claim for continuity between the old and the State Church of England must therefore rest entirely upon Barlow, 'sometime bishop of Bath and Wells,' who is referred to as the 'chief consecrator' of Parker. Although no record or proof of Barlow's consecration has ever been discovered, he is the only one of the four who is *claimed* to have been consecrated to, and to have held the title of, an English See under the old Pontifical.

But by who's authority? Barlow, it seems, was a monk who, under Henry VIII, acquiesced in the confiscation of his own religious house and in the betrayal of his brethren, in consideration of his being made a 'bishop' by Royal authority. And this at a time when the King, being short of friends, was willing to reward those who supported him in his struggle with the Church on a plain moral issue! Against the Church and his brethren. Barlow stood with the King 'with a zeal born of favors yet to come.'

But did Barlow thereby become a bishop of *Ecclesia Anglicana*? Let the Primitive church, to which the reformers appealed, speak for itself. If one can suppose the bishops under Henry VIII, after the separation, to have been in good standing with the old Church, and that they actually did consecrate Barlow under the old Pontifical by Royal authority, - a better status than history warrants, - we have something like a parallel to some primitive cases.

Canon XXX, of the Apostolical Canons, says: 'If any bishop obtain possession of a church by the aid of *temporal power*, let him be deposed and excommunicated, and all who communicate with him.'

The Second Ecumenical Council, - I Constantinople, - A.D. 381, says: Canon IV. 'Concerning Maximus the Cynic and the disorder which has happened in Constantinople on his account, it is decreed that Maximus *never was* and *is not now a Bishop*; that those *who have been ordained by him are in no order whatever* of the clergy; since all which has been done concerning him or by him, is declared to be invalid (*Ibid.*).

Maximus, surnamed the Cynic, was a scamp who betrayed his

friends and who fooled and won the backing of many Churchmen, including the Patriarch of Alexandria. He sought his ends by fraud and violence and, about A.D. 379, was intruded in the See of Constantinople after a private consecration by legitimate bishops whom he had won over to his cause with the aid of supporters imported from abroad. He affected zeal for the Nicene Faith, though he mixed this with cynic philosophy. He posed, of course, as an uncompromising reformer, and questioned the regularity of the friend whose place he plotted to obtain.

These canons appear to establish the principle that Episcopal Orders cannot be validly conveyed on *temporal* authority, nor even by real bishops when acting for themselves or for a party against the normal and public authority of the Church.

The case of Maximus was referred to Pope Damasus, who condemned the proposal 'to consecrate a restless man, an alien from the Christian profession' to such an office. Even the most zealous Anglican students ought to be satisfied when both the Pope and an undisputed General Council are agreed on a general principle…

Now as touching necessary faith, Cyril, in his Epistle to Nestorius, about 431, says: 'But it would not be *sufficient* for your reverence to confess with us only the symbol of the faith...for you have *not held and interpreted it rightly*, but rather perversely; even though you confess with your voice the form of words' (*Ibid.*).

The first canon cited was reaffirmed by the Seventh General Council, II Nicea, A.D. 787. The ancient Epitome of Canon III says: 'Every election made by a secular magistrate (prince) is null' (*Ibid.*).

Can anyone hesitate between a Primitive General Council and the opinions of the Elizabethan court circle? (This statement may lead to some controversy; it may be thought I do not distinguish between what is *invalid* and what is *illicit*. But it involves *intention*; a person conferring orders must intend to do what Christ intended. It is debatable whether the men who consecrated Barlow or Parker had the requisite intention ; the Holy See has said they had not. I think the General Council that condemned Maximus felt that the 'Consecrators' lacked the necessary intention when they acted for a party, and not for the Body of Christ - the Church. The claim of Maximus was stronger than that of either Barlow or Parker, and the early Church said he was no Bishop. I have pointed out the parallel, and let the Council speak for itself. It is clear that the conclusion the Council arrived at expressed the *mind* of the Church).

Is there any room for the suspicion that the Spirit of Truth may have left the old Church and followed a clique of political and religious experimenters who, for the most part, are pictured as scamps by reputable historians?");

Carlton Strong Collection, Architecture Archives, Pittsburgh.

Sturm, Joanna Mercedes Alessandra – philanthropist and historian; b. 9 July 1946; c. 1953 (received with her mother); daughter of Alexander McCormick Sturm and Paulina Longworth (see above); great-granddaughter of President Theodore Roosevelt (1858-1919); granddaughter of Alice Roosevelt Longworth (1884-1980); father died when she was five; mother died when she was ten; brought up by her grandmother to whom she was very close; received a Catholic education; did graduate study at Georgetown University; major source of historical information on the Roosevelt family and, in particular, on her grandmother; great contributor to charitable organizations, especially in relation to conservation; active member of the Democratic Party.

Summerfield, Charles - see under Arrington, Alfred W.

Sungenis, Robert A. ("Bob") – Catholic apologist; b. 1955, Philadelphia; c. 1992 (revert; his wife Brigitte also became a Catholic); father a physician; raised as a Catholic in a nominally Catholic home in southern New Jersey; studied at George Washington University, where he fell away from the Church; in 1974 he had an intense spiritual experience after reading the Bible and "decided to surrender my life to Christ and decided to devote my life to studying Scripture"; became persuaded by Protestants that the Catholic Church had strayed far from the Bible; developed a hatred for Catholicism; spent seventeen years as a staunch Evangelical Protestant; found great divisions between each Protestant denomination and left one after another due to disagreements in doctrine; returned to George Washington University and graduated BA in Religion in 1979; pursued graduate studies at Westminster Theological Seminary in Philadelphia and obtained MA in Theology in 1982; worked for two years at Family Radio, Oakland, California, where he had his own call-in radio program, but disagreements with the station on doctrine led to his dismissal; became a Presbyterian, then joined the Boston Crossroads Movement of the Church of Christ, then an independent Bible church, but doctrinal problems arose in each case; finally converted to the Catholic Church; has debated many Protestant apologists; obtained a Ph.D. in 2006 from the Calamus International University; author of several books on theology and the Bible, in particular in relation to apologetics and critiquing Protestant doctrines; later became an advocate of geocentrism; founder of Catholic Apologetics International, renamed the Bellarmine Theological Forum in 2007 and later called The Bellarmine Report; has been criticized for his views on the Jews, but maintained that he is against Zionism but not anti-semitic; see (selective list) "From Controversy to Consolation," in Patrick Madrid (ed), *Surprised by Truth* (1994), p.101 ("As I studied the Catholic case against *sola scriptura* I knew instinctively that the whole debate between Catholicism and Protestantism could be boiled down to authority. Every doctrine one believes is based on the authority one accepts. I decided to test this pet theory of the Reformers by asking numerous Protestant scholars and pastors to help me find *sola scriptura* in the Bible. By this point, I wasn't too surprised to find that none was able to provide a convincing answer… If *sola scriptura* – the idea that the Bible is formally sufficient for Christians – is not taught in the Bible, *sola scriptura* is a false and self-refuting proposition…

The more I thought about it the more I began to see that the theory of *sola scriptura* had done untold damage to Christendom. The most obvious evidence of this damage was Protestantism itself: a huge mass of conflicting, bickering denominations, causing, by its very nature of 'protest' and 'defiance', an endless proliferation of chaos and controversy…

As a Protestant I greatly admired Martin Luther and John Calvin for their boldness to interpret the Bible for themselves. Now I was faced with the probability that these heroes of mine were very intelligent but also very prideful and rebellious men. After I had read a few scholarly biographies of these two reformers I realized that much about their personal lives was never told to us in seminary. These insights caused me to take an even more skeptical look at the reformers and the Reformation as a whole.

I realize that there are problems within the Catholic Church. In every age, the Church has had to endure the blight of worldly, sinful, and heretical members. At present, the Church is fighting the destructive forces of liberalism which have influenced a portion of the Church, especially in the United States. But one must realize that aberrations among its members does not negate the Catholic Church's authenticity as Christ's true Church. One must distinguish between what is done in the name of Catholicism from what is officially taught by the Catholic Church. Rebellious members should not surprise us. The Bible warns that many in the Church will sin and become corrupt, although maintaining the appearance of spirituality. As Jesus said himself, the wheat will grow up with the tares until he comes back to judge the world.

Many Protestants are amazed that despite these grave challenges, the Catholic Church has an uncanny ability to weather the storms of controversy, heresy, and schism. There have been countless predictions of Rome's imminent demise, but it still stands. As I studied Church history I saw that of all the churches (dioceses) mentioned in the New Testament, with the exception of Jerusalem, only the church at Rome still exists. Besides the major sees of Corinth, Ephesus, Philippi, Thessalonica, Colossae, and the region of Galatia, the New Testament reminds us of less prominent churches which today are extinct (cf. Rev. 2 and 3). The longevity and universality of the Catholic Church is indicative of its divine origin.

There is no purely natural explanation for the fact that the Catholic Church still exists after all these centuries - but there is a supernatural explanation. Jesus promised he would lead his Church into all truth and would protect it from all forces aimed at its destruction, without or within, including even the gates of hell. In light of Jesus' clear promises of the doctrinal integrity and temporal perpetuity of the Church (cf. Matt. 7:24-25; 16:18-19; 18:18; 28:20; Luke 10:16; John 14:16-18; 14:26; 16:13), the Protestant claim that for fifteen hundred years the Church was corrupt and did not know the way of salvation, is absurd and unbiblical.

Sensing the logic of these Catholic arguments, some Protestants try to get around Jesus' statements by claiming that the church he protects is a 'spiritual,' invisible church, not a particular visible church. This notion is refuted by Jesus' teaching that the Church is a 'city set on a mountain [that] cannot be hidden' (Matt. 5:14). This is an example of the error of 'spiritualizing' biblical passages that don't fit with one's pre-fabricated theology. The word 'church' (Greek: ekklesia) appears over one hundred times in the New Testament, not once with the meaning of a 'spiritual' church. The thought of a merely spiritual and invisible church composed of some sort of amorphous collection of 'true believers' from every denomination, as many Protestants conceive of it, is completely unbiblical. Jesus established only one Church, not a group of squabbling rival denominations...

The Catholic Church rests secure in Jesus' promise that he would send the Holy Spirit to lead his Church into all truth (John 16:12), that he would bind and loose in heaven whatever is bound and loosed on earth (Matt. 18:18), and that he would protect it from destruction (Matt. 16:18).

Jesus established a Church through which he intended to make himself known to the world (Matt. 5:14-15, 28:18-20, Eph. 3:10). Through the authoritative Scripture, oral preaching, and infallible decisions that came from Jesus through his Church (Luke 10:16, Acts 15), the Lord began the slow but steady process of working through the instrumentality of his Body the Church (cf. Rom. 12:1-5; 1 Cor. 12:12-27; Eph. 3:4-6; 5:21-23; Cot. 1:18) to bring all things captive in obedience to himself (2 Cor. 10:5).

In order to accomplish this mission of God's mercy, the Church must be able to teach the truth all the time. If the Church is not protected from teaching error, God's people would have absolutely no trustworthy foundation upon which to build their faith. Protestants disagree, claiming that their doctrinal certitude is based on Scripture alone. But Scripture nowhere claims to be sufficient for this task. It warns that it can be misinterpreted (2 Pet. 1:20, 3:15-16)...

The decision as to which books should be included in the Bible and which books should not, was made by the Catholic Church in the councils of Hippo (AD 393), and Carthage (AD 397 and 419). These decisions were later ratified and solemnly defined by the ecumenical councils of Second Nicea (797), Florence (1440), and Trent (1525-1546)...

The truth is, Protestants are living off the borrowed capital of the Catholic Church, for it was the Catholic Church that infallibly recognized, under the divine guidance of the Holy Spirit, the canon of Scripture. Each time Protestants quote from the Bible they unwittingly acknowledge their trust in the infallible divine guidance given to the Catholic Church by Christ...

I realized that if the Holy Spirit did inspire the Church to write infallible Scripture, preach infallible doctrine, and infallibly determine the biblical canon, there was absolutely no rational basis to claim that the Church was not infallibly guided down through the ages until the present day. Jesus promised to guide his Church into all truth (John 16:13) and to be with it till the end of the world (Matt. 28:19-20)...

Another compelling factor that convinced me of the truth of the Catholic Church was the realization that since Christ had given the Church the mission to teach the truth (Matt. 28:18-20), mere men could not take away either the mission or the authority to carry it out. The Protestant Reformers claimed that the Catholic Church had become hopelessly corrupted and lost its identity as Christ's true Church. To reinforce this claim they called the Catholic Church the 'Whore of Babylon' and pointed to certain scandalously sinful popes as 'antichrists.'

Many Protestants claim that the Church of the first three centuries was a 'pure' church, and only after the legalization of the Christian faith by the Roman emperor Constantine (in AD 312) did the church become 'Catholic' and corrupt. But upon studying this issue I found that the doctrines of post-Constantine Catholicism are the same doctrines, some in more primitive form, that were held by Christians for the preceding three centuries.

My study of the writings of the Church Fathers revealed that the early Church believed in the Real Presence of Christ in the Eucharist, confession of sins to a priest, baptismal regeneration, salvation by faith and good works done through grace, that one could reject God's grace and forfeit salvation, that the bishop of Rome is the head of the Church, that Mary is the Mother of God and was perpetually a virgin, that intercessory prayer can be made to the saints in heaven, that purgatory is a state of temporary purification which some Christians undergo before entering heaven. Except for the perpetual virginity and divine motherhood of Mary, all of these doctrines were repudiated by the Protestant Reformers, If the Catholic Church is in error to hold these beliefs, then it was in error long before Constantine legalized Christianity. This would mean that the Church apostatized before the end of the first century, when the apostles were still alive! An absurd theory which even the most anti-Catholic of Protestants can't quite bring themselves to accept.

What I discovered by reading the Church Fathers was that present day Catholic interpretations of Scripture were held by the earliest Christians. They were passed down by Sacred Tradition and preserved and disseminated just as carefully as the Scripture was preserved and copied. Verses I had read hundreds of times concerning 'tradition' now took on a whole new meaning. I finally understood the value and necessity of Sacred Tradition. Tradition did not contradict the Bible, rather, it supported it and made it clearer…

After so many wrong turns and blind alleys, I now see and love the Catholic Church for what it is: the ancient, indestructible Church that Jesus established 2000 years ago"); *Not By Faith Alone: The Biblical Evidence for the Catholic Doctrine of Justification* (1996); *Not By Scripture Alone: A Catholic Critique of the Protestant Doctrine of Sola Scriptura* (1997); *How Can I Get to Heaven? The Bible's Teaching on Salvation Made Easy to Understand* (1997); *Not By Bread Alone: The Biblical and Historical Evidence for the Eucharistic Sacrifice* (2000); *The Gospel of St. Matthew* (2004); *The Apocalypse of St. John* (2007); "The Old Covenant: Revoked or Not Revoked?" *Culture Wars*, January 2008, p.12; "The Old Covenant is Revoked: The USCC Removes Heretical Sentence from Its Catechism," *Culture Wars*, October 2008, p.12; *Galileo Was Wrong: The Church Was Right: The Scientific Evidence for Geocentrism* (2009); "Is the SSPX Anti-Semitic?" *Culture Wars*, July/August 2009, p.30; *Speaking in Tongues: Sign of Blessing: Sign of Judgment: A Critical Analysis of the Pentecostal and Charismatic Movements* (2010); *Catholic/Jewish Dialogue: Controversies and Corrections* (2010); "The Wax Nose of Catholic/Jewish Dialogue," *Culture Wars*, July/August 2011, p.10; *catholicintl.com*.

Swenson, Julie – Catholic layperson; c. 1 November 1992 (received with her husband Bob and their four children); "born into a fundamental baptistic family and grew to adulthood utterly content with the Evangelical piety and theology of my upbringing"; always had deep love for Christ and for the Bible; as an adult became a Dutch Reformed Calvinist; conversion to the Catholic faith influenced by the music of the Catholic singer John Michael Talbot (see below); also influenced by the contrast between the worship taking place around the throne of God, and the nature of Protestant services; attracted by High Anglican liturgy, but sensed that Anglicanism lacked the fullness of faith; came to realize the earliness of the belief in the Real Presence of Christ in the Eucharist; also influenced by St. John of the Cross, Thomas Merton (see above) and Fr. John Hardon, SJ; see "This I Seek: To Dwell in the House of the Lord," in Patrick Madrid (ed), *Surprised by Truth* (1994), p.135 ("I began to sense that Anglicanism, although filled with beautiful liturgical traditions and 'Catholic' doctrines, was not the destination of my pilgrimage. However close to Catholicism it came in outward form, it isn't actually Catholic. I knew that although the Anglican church was a pleasant and instructive rest stop, it wasn't home...

If my Protestant presuppositions were correct, the gates of hell had prevailed against the Church shortly after the apostolic era, and the Holy Spirit abandoned the Church. Either Christ let us down and deceived us by teaching us that there would be one Spirit, one faith, one baptism and one Church which would endure until the end of the world (cf. Matt. 28:20), or my anti-Catholic bias and interpretation of Scripture and Church history was unrealistic and unscriptural.

John Henry Newman, the famous Evangelical Protestant convert to Catholicism, once said, 'Knowledge of Church history is the death of Protestantism.' He was right. My study of the early Church showed clearly that it was Catholic in its beliefs and practices - in fact, it had begun calling itself 'Catholic' at least as early as the end of the first century...

I began to question why we as Anglo-Catholics were not part of the Catholic Church. As we questioned their 'branch' and 'via media' theories (the former being the Anglican concept that the "Catholic Church' is validly expressed in three branches, Roman Catholic, Anglican, and Orthodox; the second being that the Anglican Church was a viable 'middle way' between Protestantism and the Catholic Church), we saw that though Anglicans were outwardly 'Catholic,' they were inwardly Protestant - they were living in a de facto state of 'protest' against the Church of Rome by not submitting entirely to its doctrines and to its authority. The essential question was, 'did Christ leave behind a fallible Church, capable of teaching error?' If so, we were left as orphans, insecure and fighting among ourselves without protection. But that option contradicts Jesus' express promise when he said, 'I will not leave you orphans' (John 14:18). Increasingly, I wanted to be identified with 'Holy Mother Church' as She is affectionately called by her children. I yearned to 'go home' and claim the marvelous spiritual heritage and doctrinal certitude - the fullness of the Christian faith that had been mine all along...

One statement in the excellent three-volume apologetics work, *Radio Replies* (1979), where the authors respond to a question on church unity, particularly struck me: 'If you believe that the Church of England ought to be in communion with Rome, and is not, how can you justify yourselves in remaining where you ought not to be, in refusing to take that step personally which the corporate Anglican Church cannot and will not take?'").

Swetland, Mgr. Stuart W. – priest; b. 15 May 1959, Pittsburgh, Pennsylvania; c. 21 April 1984 (Easter Vigil; received in the Newman Center, Oxford University); youngest of three children of devout Lutheran parents; at age three moved to rural northeast Pennsylvania, where there wasn't always a Lutheran church close by, so attended Methodist and Baptist churches as well - each Evangelical; great appreciation of Christ in early teens; went to the United States Naval Academy; found the Lutheran church nearby was very different and stopped practising as a Christian; graduated in Physics from the Naval Academy in 1981 (first in class); studied at Oxford University as a Rhodes Scholar 1981-1984 (BA and MA in Politics, Philosophy and Economics); converted to the Catholic faith while studying at Oxford; saw active service in the navy; studied for the priesthood; ordained on 25 May 1991 a priest for the Diocese of Peoria, Illinois; MDiv and MA from Mount St. Mary's Seminary, Emmitsburg, Maryland; STL and STD from the Pontifical Lateran University; served as Theological Advisor to the Catholic Conference of Illinois; Director of Homiletics and Pre-Theology (for 2006) at Mount St. Mary's University, Emmitsburg, Maryland; served as vice-president for Catholic Identity and Mission 2008-2009; in 2009 appointed The Most Reverend Harry J. Flynn Professor of Christian Ethics at Mount St. Mary's University (succeeding Germain Grisez); host of *Catholicism on Campus* on EWTN; many articles in Catholic and secular newspapers and magazines; see "A Twentieth-Century Centurion Swears Allegiance to Christ," in Marcus Grodi (ed), *Journeys Home* (1997) (reprinted in Patrick Madrid (ed), *Surprised by Truth 3* (2002), p.3) (revised edition reproduced in *Coming Home Network*

International, *Conversion Stories*, *chnetwork.org*, 18 January 2011) ("Often when someone asks me why I became a Catholic, I answer with a clever line stolen from some famous convert. A favorite is G. K. Chesterton's quip, 'To get my sins forgiven.' Another favorite is the short affirmation: 'Because it's true.'

Sometimes it's more an accusation than a question. If the person asks, 'Why did you become a *Catholic*?' with the emphasis on *Catholic*, he has a problem with the Church. If the emphasis is on *you*, he's usually an intellectual elitist who believes that no educated person would become (or remain) Catholic. If the emphasis is on *become*, the questioner finds it possible that a person raised in the Church would remain in it, but inconceivable that someone with my background would choose to *become* Catholic.

I love to challenge such prejudices, because I too once held them. When I 'went up' to Oxford, as the English say (the expression assumes that everyone is coming from London, thus going 'up,' north, to Oxford), my religion could have best been described as lapsed Protestant with strong anti-Catholic biases. In many ways, I was a functioning pagan steeped in all the fashionable ideas of modern American ideology. Politically and economically, I was a conservative with a libertarian tendency. I was a pretty typical product of my background...

Having begun to ask myself (and others) to justify all beliefs - moral, intellectual, and religious - I soon found myself face to face with the basic claims of Christianity. I could no longer simply bracket them.

There God's grace worked in me, especially through certain Christians He placed in my life. As I began my studies at New College in Oxford, a group of young men and women, several of them believing Catholics, befriended me. During our next three years together, their influence, their patience, and especially the witness of their lives helped lead me into the Church.

Having inherited all the anti-Catholic prejudice of a typical Evangelical Protestant, I resisted what was becoming plain to me: that there is a wisdom in the teaching of the Catholic Church that is explainable only by its greater-than-human inspiration. As I searched for answers to the questions my tutors asked me, I kept finding that the best responses - the most reasonable, well articulated, and convincing - came from the Catholic tradition. The writings of the saints (especially St. Augustine and St. Thomas Aquinas and those influenced by them, such as Blessed John Henry Newman, Elizabeth Anscombe, and John Finnis) were superior to those proposed by other sources.

It seemed to me that Catholic thought about social questions - for example, the issues for war and peace (especially the just-war tradition) - was clearer and better thought-out than other arguments that I was studying. At first, I thought this was a coincidence. But as time went on, I could not deny that something different was behind the writings of these men and women.

On my own, I began to examine the basic assumptions of the Christian faith. First, did Jesus exist? Yes, this is well documented. Next, is He who He says He is? I had to admit that I agreed with C. S. Lewis's ideas that He was either 'liar, lunatic, or Lord.' But how could I judge the authority of His claims?

After much thought and study (and just a little prayer; to this stage I wasn't yet seriously praying), I decided that the central claim of Christianity is the claim of Jesus' bodily resurrection. The truth of the biblical witness seemed to me to hinge on this claim. So how should one judge the authenticity of the Resurrection?

I tried to approach the biblical texts as I did other ancient texts. At this time, I was also reading Julius Caesar and Thucydides for their insights into military strategy and tactics. Most thinkers accepted these texts fairly straightforwardly. Was Scripture less trustworthy?

The text I first found most compelling was 1 Corinthians chapter 15. Here St. Paul tells of all those who had seen and experienced the risen Lord: more than five hundred witnesses, many of whom were still alive when Paul wrote the letter (about twenty years after the events). This letter seems to be an authentic testimony to the truth of the bodily resurrection of Jesus. The hundreds of witnesses lend credibility to Paul's own experience of the risen Lord. If these others had not really experienced the convincing proofs of Jesus' resurrection, Paul would quickly have been seen as a fraud.

As I studied more, I was startled by the overwhelming evidence for the Resurrection, especially in the life of the early Church. Almost to a person, those first believers went to a martyr's death for their firm and certain belief in the Resurrection. No other explanation made sense of the data.

Could it be that Jesus really had not died? No, the medical evidence in John's Gospel of 'blood and water rushing from His side' shows that He really died. And even a cursory reading of Roman history shows that no Roman soldier would so botch a crucifixion as to allow a condemned man to survive.

No, for anyone 'with eyes to see and ears to hear,' the accounts of the Resurrection and the lives of the men and women who had witnessed the life, death, and resurrection of Jesus were convincing evidence of the authenticity of that startling event.

In addition, there were existential, subjective reasons for me to believe. Throughout my sojourn away from practicing the Christian faith, I had never been comfortable in denying what I had experienced in prayer and worship as a child. On some level of my being, I knew that I had encountered the living God in my life... As I studied and prayed more, I kept encountering the issues that divided Catholics and Evangelical Protestants. I read of how Jesus commissioned His Apostles to forgive sin in John 20:22–23. But where and how was this power exercised today in the community? Scripture talked about anointing the sick in James 5:14–15. Yet only Catholics seemed to take this text seriously. What Jesus said about Holy Communion seemed very straightforward to me, especially in John 6. Yet Evangelicals speak of the Lord's Supper as only symbolic.

The Scriptures talked about the transformative power of God's grace, so that one can speak like St. Paul of total transformation of oneself to become like Christ (see 2 Cor 3:18). But most Evangelicals believe that Christ's righteousness merely covers our sinful nature instead of transforming it.

Sacred Scripture speaks of the intercession of the heavenly host on behalf of God's people on earth (see Rev 8:2–4). But only Catholics prayed to the saints and angels as intercessors and friends.

Then there were the moral teachings of the Church, which seemed to make more sense to me each day. As I examined the alternatives, secular and religious, no other ethical system had the same internal consistency and tight argumentation that I found in the Catholic moral tradition of natural law.

In addition, the Catholic moral tradition answered the question of *how* to decide moral issues - by appealing to the teaching authority given to the Apostles and to their successors (the Magisterium of the Church). This teaching authority made sense of God's love and desire to lead His children into all truth.

Still another influence was the example of the Catholics I knew as friends, who lived their faith with a peace and joy about them that I didn't find elsewhere in the world. In fact, it was a peace and joy that "surpassed all understanding" (see Phil 4:7). I knew that I needed and desired that same peace and joy...

By this time, my friends knew I was examining questions of the Faith. I was trying to see whether I could accept every aspect of the Church's teaching. But my friend Dermot Quinn pointed out to me the futility of this approach.

Even if I could study every detail of every teaching, he observed, and come to say honestly that I agreed with the Church, this would not make my faith truly Catholic. What made a person Catholic, Dermot insisted, was not just belief that the Church taught the truth in matters of faith and morals, but the belief that the Church is a 'truth-teaching thing.'

In other words, the most important question I had to answer was this: Is the Catholic Church who she says she is? Is she the Church founded by Jesus Christ, containing all that Christ's believers need for their instruction and sanctification?

If I believed this, I should be (had to be!) Catholic. If I did not, it really didn't matter whether I happened to agree with particular Church teachings. The choice before me was clear. I had come to believe that the Church was who she claimed to be. The fact that I still had difficulties with some of her teachings didn't really matter. As Newman said, 'A thousand difficulties do not make for one doubt.' I didn't doubt that the Church was the Mystical Body of Christ extended through space and time. I was confident that the Church's teachings in faith and morals were true even if I didn't fully understand why they were true, because I believed that God had endowed His Church with a special charism of the Holy Spirit that ensured that her authentic teachings in matters of faith and morals are, at least, not false. So I was ready to be received into full communion"); *EWTN Audio Library, The Journey Home* (14 June 2004) ("I found as I was studying philosophy that there were wonderful answers to the questions that my professors had set me to answer in Catholic philosophy, in Catholic thinkers, in Catholic writers…I read people like Thomas Aquinas and St. Augustine and some of the more modern followers of those traditions. The 150th anniversary of the Oxford Movement happened while I was at Oxford. So there was a lot of discussion of that movement and of course John Henry Newman being a big part of that. As I began reading these texts I said there's a wisdom here, there's an insight here and also they have an answer to the question, 'How do you make sure that the text in its proper interpretation is given to every age. That the whole word of God, the whole witness to Christ is handed on to every age, faithful, and interpreted correctly for that day and age. It seems to me that if God loves us, he has to have a way for that to happen, because he has to give his word to every generation. It's the question of one truth. How are we going to answer that? Well, the Catholic Church believes that the Holy Spirit has been given to the Church in a particular way, to guard it and guide it in answering the questions of faith (what we are to believe) and morals (how we are to live) in every age. And there you have the charism, through the official teaching of the Church's magisterium, to ensure that those things taught to us are the word of God and are faithful to the decisions of the magisterium").

Tabb, John Banister (often incorrectly spelt as Bannister) – priest, poet and educator; b. 22 March 1845, "The Forest," Amelia County, Virginia; c. 8 September 1872; d. 19 November 1909, Ellicott City, Maryland; descended from an old and wealthy Virginian family, which emigrated from England in the seventeenth century; educated privately; his poor eyesight at the age of fourteen meant he had to give up his books ; became very proficient as a pianist; served in the Confederate navy in the Civil War (taken captive and imprisoned in 1864 at which time he formed a life long friendship with Sidney Lanier (1842-1881), the poet); after the war ended he obtained a teaching position in Baltimore; planned to enter the Episcopal ministry, but came under the influence of Rev. Alfred Curtis (see above), an Episcopal clergyman, later Catholic Bishop of Wilmington, who in 1872 converted from Episcopalianism to the Catholic Church (received by Newman); followed Curtis into the Church, being also influenced by Newman; his family and relatives were amazed by his conversion and some were horrified; entered St. Charles College, Ellicott City, Maryland, to prepare for the priesthood; after completing his classical studies, he taught English at the college, thus delaying the completion of his theological studies; finally ordained priest 20 December 1884; continued to teach English grammar at St. Charles until shortly before his death; his sight failed completely about a year before his death; being a devoted teacher, he wrote his poetry when and where he could; a fine lyric poet, published in both popular and prestigious magazines; buried in Hollywood Cemetery, Richmond; the Tabb Monument in Amelia County, Virginia, is dedicated to his memory; see *Poems* (1882); *An Octave to Mary* (1893); *Poems* (1894); *Bone Rules; or, Skeleton of English Grammar* (1897); *Lyrics* (1897); *Child Verse* (1899); *Two Lyrics* (1900); *Later Lyrics* (1902); *The Rosary in Rhyme* (1904); *Quips and Quiddits* (1907); *Later Poems* (1910); Walter Lecky, *Down at Caxton's* (1895), p.68 ("All his verse-gems are redolent of his faith. They are religious in the sense that they are begotten by faith and breathe the air of the sanctuary. To read them is to leave the hum and pain of life behind and enter the cloister where all is silent and peaceful, where dwelleth the spirit of God"); Alice Meynell (ed), *A Selection From the Verses of John B. Tabb* (1906); Alice Meynell, "Father Tabb," *Catholic World* (1910), p.577; Sister Mary Paulina Finn, *John Bannister Tabb: The Priest-Poet* (1915); John B. Kelly, "The Poetry of a Priest," *Catholic World* (1916), p.228; Jennie Masters Tabb, *Father Tabb, His Life and Work: A Memorial* (1921); Katherine Brégy, "Of Father Tabb," *Catholic World* (1921), p.308; Francis A. Litz, *Father Tabb: A Study of His Life and Works* (1923); Francis A. Litz, *The Poetry of Father Tabb* (1928) (*Mary* (1893): "Maid-Mother of humanity divine,/ Alone thou art in thy supremacy,/ Since God Himself did reverence to thee/ And built of flesh a temple one with thine,/ Wherein, through all eternity, to shrine/ His inexpressive glory. Blessed be/ The miracle of thy maternity,/ Of grace the sole immaculate design!"; *The Immaculate Conception* (1894): "A dew drop of the darkness born,/ Wherein no shadow lies;/ The blossom of a barren thorn,/ Whereof no petal dies;/ A rainbow beauty passion-free,/ Wherewith was veiled Divinity"); George N. Schuster, "Father Tabb and the Romantic Tradition," *The Month*, December 1924, p.516; Gordon Blair, *Father Tabb: Poet-Priest-Soldier-Wit* (1940); Katherine Burton, *In No Strange Land: Some American Catholic Converts* (1942), p.143 ("The first confession Father Curtis heard as a priest was that of John Tabb, and through the years Tabb and Father Curtis – later Bishop Curtis of Delaware – remained close to each other"); William McDevitt, *My Father, Father Tabb, at Home and at College* (1945); Francis A. Litz (ed), *Letters - Grave and Gay and Other Prose of John Banister Tabb* (1950); Brother C. S. C. Roberto, *The Rambling Rebel: A Story of Father John Banister Tabb* (1961); E. L. Core (ed), *Poetry by John B. Tabb: A Centenary Selection* (2009); *poetry.elcore.net*; *Catholic Encyclopedia*; *ANB* ("Tabb set his later works, by and large, in the timeless realm between heaven and earth. His faith was sometimes explicitly and often implicitly the subject of his verse. One quatrain, 'Tenebrae,' literally suggests darkness, but the word specifically refers to a Catholic rite during Holy Week in which candles lighted at the beginning of the ceremony are extinguished one by one after each psalm is read to commemorate the darkness during the crucifixion. Tabb, whose gradual blindness became complete during the last years of his life, could have made the quatrain his motto: 'Whate'er my darkness be,/ 'Tis not, O Lord, of Thee./ The light is Thine alone;/ The shadows, all my own'").

Tabor, Horace Austin Warner ("Haw") ("The Bonanza King of Leadville") – prospector, businessman and politician; b. 26 November 1830, Holland, Vermont; one of five children born to Cornelius Tabor and Sarah Ferrin; d. 10 April 1899, Denver, Colorado; trained as a stonemason and worked in the quarries of Maine and Massachusetts; farmed in Kansas; married Augusta Pierce in 1857 (one son of the marriage); they ran a store in Colorado; he sought gold until 1877; they settled in Leadville, Colorado, where he continued to prospect, but also they ran the general store and postal system; served as mayor in 1878; made great wealth in silver mining (mainly through the profitable "Matchless Mine"); he established a bank, newspapers and two opera houses; in 1878 he was elected Lieutenant Governor of Colorado, serving until 1883; served as a U.S. Senator in 1883; divorced Augusta and legalized his long-standing relationship with Elizabeth "Baby Doe" McCourt (1854-1935) (two daughters of the marriage); ran for Colorado governor in 1884, 1886, and 1888, but without success; in 1893 he lost his entire fortune due to the repeal of the Sherman Silver Purchase Act; Baby Doe lost control of the Matchless Mine (she lived in poverty in the toolshed there for thirty years and died there); her story inspired Douglas Moore's opera *The Ballad of Baby Doe* (1956); he converted to the Catholic faith a few days before he died; huge crowds attended his funeral; body finally reinterred at Mt. Olivet Cemetery in Jefferson County, Colorado, where it now rests beside that of Baby Doe; see David Karsner, *Silver Dollar: The Story of the Tabors* (1932); Duane A. Smith, *Horace Tabor: His Life and Legend* (1989); Glenda Riley and Richard W. Etulain (ed), *Wild Women of the Old West* (2003), Ch. 1 "Baby Doe Tabor, The Culture of Beauty"; Judy Nolte Temple, *Baby Doe Tabor: The Madwoman in the Cabin* (2007).

Talbot, John Michael – Franciscan brother and singer-songwriter; b. 8 May 1954, Oklahoma City, Oklahoma; c. 8 February 1978 (Ash Wednesday; a short time later his mother was received; in 1979 his father became a Catholic, and a few years later his sister converted); born into a secure Methodist family; learned to play musical instruments at an early age; fell away from religious belief for a time in the 1960s; dropped out of school at fifteen; formed several folk and then country rock bands with his older brother, Terry; recorded a number of albums, but saw the unhappiness of this lifestyle; returned to religion, going through several varieties before having a visionary experience of Christ and eventually becoming a Protestant fundamentalist, but this led into a legalistic 'bibliolatry' and despair; the gift to him by a friend of a book about St. Francis of Assis changed his life; he retreated into prayer at the Franciscan Retreat Center of Alverna in Indianapolis; he subsequently became a Catholic and joined the secular Franciscan order in 1978; founded his own monastic community, the Brothers and Sisters of Charity at Little Portion Hermitage, Eureka Springs, Arkansas; community was composed of celibate brothers and sisters, singles, and families; in 1989, with the permission of the Catholic Church, he married Viola Pratka, a former Incarnate Word Sister, who had come to the community in 1986 (his first marriage ended in divorce and was later annulled by the Church); a fire in 2008 caused great damage to the hermitage's chapel, library and other areas; in 2010 Bishop Anthony Taylor dedicated the new buildings, and the new monastery church and centre were subsequently opened; he has continued to release many religious recordings and give performances of his music; he has written numerous books of a spiritual nature; very active in Mercy Corps International and founder of Franciscan Mercy Corps, both of which help the hungry and the homeless; see "On Becoming a Radical for Christ," in Dan O'Neill (ed), *The New Catholics: Contemporary Converts Tell Their Story* (1987), p.77 ("It was at this point of despair that a friend gave me a copy of a book about Saint Francis of Assisi alled *The Journey and the Dream*, by Murray Bodo. In the pages of this short book I read about a man who lived some eight hundred years ago; yet his story inflamed my soul with God's love. He had what I had lost and sought to regain. God used this poverello, this little poor man from Assisi, to transform and renew the Western Christian world with the original fire and fervor of the Holy Spirit.

He was a radical Christian, but he was not a fanatic. A radical is one who is rooted firmly and deeply in the gospel. A fanatic is hung up on mere externals, emphasizing one or the other points of the gospel to undue extremes...In Saint Francis of Assisi I saw a way back to my first love. Like a prodigal son, I wanted to come back home.

There was just one small problem: Saint Francis of Assisi was a Catholic! His home was 'mother Church'. He was a radical reformer, but he always carried out renewal with a humility that kept him ardently submissive to the authority of the Church. Francis was a 'papist' through and through...

Then I came face to face with another dilemma: the obvious disunity of the professing faith communities of Jesus Christ... All claimed the Scriptures as their primary source of knowledge about Jesus and the church...Yet, try as they might, they could not agree among themselves. They could not bring unity. This disagreement was not about some irrelevant, speculative theological issue. It was about the basics of the faith. Who is Jesus? What did He say and do? Who does He want us to be?

We could not find agreement about the one thing Jesus commanded us to do when we assembled together in His name - the Lord's Supper. Obviously, if we could not agree on the meaning of Communion, sharing it would destroy its credibility. It would be like consummating the union between lovers before they agreed on the real meaning of marriage. It is something Jesus commanded us to do, but we cannot do it. How sad, yet how fitting that this great sacramental sign of unity is prohibited precisely because we are still divided.

What, then, is the answer? There had to be an additional God-given dimension to discerning the truth of the gospel as a united people.

It was here that I stumbled upon universal truth: if the Scriptures came forth from God through the Church, they can only be properly interpreted through the Church. Failure to recognize the God-given authority of the Church destroys the authority of the Scriptures themselves. So, if there is a debatable passage of Scripture that divides Christian communities today (and there are many) it only makes sense to go back to the early Church from which the Scriptures came to see how they interpreted that same passage. If a substantial agreement can be found among them, then application can be made to the modern world in a developed way.

I tried it. But to my chagrin, I found out that the Fathers of the early Church were Catholic! The primitive seeds of all modern Catholic doctrines were firmly planted in the soil of the Church of the first centuries. The doctrines about Mary, prayer to the saints, purgatory, the role of the pope - all were clearly visible and accepted in the early Church, at least in their primitive form. Most especially, the place of Eucharist, or the Lord's Supper, as both a symbol and the real presence of the Body and Blood of Christ, was central to the common worship and prayer of the assembled Christian Church. Furthermore, all these beliefs and practices were centered squarely on the Jesus all Christians hold dear. Every doctrine, every sacrament, and every structure began with Jesus, were centered on Jesus, and led to Jesus. They existed for no other reason. There was no other conclusion for me to reach: the early Christian Church was Catholic! For me, the conclusion was clear. Fundamentalism leads to Catholicism because if you zealously fight to guard the authority of Scripture, you must fight for, respect, and even submit to the authority of the Church. Otherwise you deny the very authority of the Scripture upon which you base and guide your Christian faith. Ironically, the true fundamentalist must become a Catholic and, as a Catholic, can no longer be a fundamentalist...

[W]hat about the Anglicans and the Orthodox? What about the Lutherans? Don't they all consider themselves 'Catholic' too? What about the phenomenon of the small new sects trying to return to the catholicity of the Church Fathers by an awareness of liturgy, sacraments, and Apostolic Succession in their church structures of bishop, presbyter, and deacon?

I would answer these questions by a simple appeal to the reality of the pope. All of these catholic-oriented expressions claim to have the Apostolic Succession and structure that Jesus ordained to insure unity in the Church. Yet none of these expressions can accomplish that hoped-for unity. They might even have valid bishops, with a continued succession of apostolic antiquity or history (such as the Patriarchs of Constantinople, Jerusalem, Antioch or Alexandria). But none of these bishops who succeed even the greatest and best known apostles have been able to bring unity without a leader who can claim the objective authority of both

Scripture and apostolic tradition.

The Orthodox are still divided among themselves. The Archbishop of Canterbury cannot exert the needed authority to unite the Anglicans. The Lutheran approach to things 'catholic' is still only hesitantly accepted among this church's members.

Only the Bishop of Rome can claim the full authority of both Scripture and Tradition to unite the Church. Only Peter was universally understood in the Early Church to stand in Christ's place as the leader of the Apostles, ordained by Jesus Himself. Only the Bishop of Rome was seen as Saint Peter's legitimate successor. Common sense and experience deemed that someone had to take the place of leader. Otherwise, even the best college of apostles and succeeding bishops could be deadlocked in controversy and debate. That 'someone' was the Bishop of Rome, the successor of Saint Peter, the pope. Only he could claim an authority based on both Scripture and apostolic tradition that, objectively and historically, link and unite the Church of Jesus Christ with the authority of Jesus Christ.

The mere existence of the Roman Catholic Church argues in favor of this position. There is no larger unified group of professing Christians on the face of the earth. Yet the people would not be united without the pope and the pope would not carry such weight in proclaiming the gospel to the world, without the people. Think of it: no other Christian leader has such impact in preaching the gospel of Jesus Christ...

Today we are at a turning point. Never before has the world possessed the potential for bringing God's blessings to so many, yet never before have so many faced poverty, war, and ultimate destruction. The issues that face us are awesome and vast. Widespread sexual immorality breaks down the human family. Abortion, global poverty, and the ever-present threat of nuclear war are problems set deeply within our modern society. They require a radical Christian response. I believe it is the Roman Catholic Church that lifts up its voice most radically for Jesus Christ as it meets the challenges of our modern world. No other institution has spoken out so loud and clear since the beginning of the atomic age, that the nuclear arms race is an immoral option for the just defense of the nations of this world. No other institution on the face of the earth has spoken out so consistently for a preferential option for the poor, speaking out prophetically against both atheistic Marxism and the immorality of the materialism of the West. No other institution can match the Catholic stand against the devastation and devaluation of human life through abortion.

Ironically, it is that much-debated document of Pope Paul VI, *Humanae Vitae* (Human Life), that is proving to be most prophetic. Standing in uncompromising reverence of God's creation of human life, it calls forth a sophisticated and consistent moral theology of life to the Church and the world. It is also proving to be fundamental in all areas concerning basic human rights and reverence of all life. I believe this document will prove to be one of the most prophetic works of this era. Once again, it is an encyclical of a pope"); Dan O'Neill, *Signatures: The Story Of John Michael Talbot* (2004); Lorene Hanley Duquin, *A Century of Catholic Converts* (2003), p.173.

Tarry, Ellen – author; b. 26 September 1906, Birmingham, Alabama; c. 8 December 1922; d. 23 September 2008, New York; father a barber and a Congregationalist, mother a seamstress; brought up in the Methodist Church of her mother; in 1918 she joined the Congregational Church, where her father was a deacon; shortly after her father's early death she went to a Catholic boarding school, St. Francis de Sales Institute, in Rock Castle, Virginia (run by the White Sisters of the Blessed Sacrament) and while there was received into the Catholic Church; educated at Alabama State Normal School (later Alabama State University); teacher in Birmingham; wrote a column on racial injustice for a local African-American paper; in 1929 moved to New York intent on becoming a writer; associated with several Harlem Renaissance literary figures; published several African-American picture books; author of literature for children and young adults; her children's literature defied racial stereotypes and depicted interracial friendship; co-founder, along with Catherine Doherty (see above), of Harlem's Friendship House, a Catholic outreach center promoting interracial friendship; friendship with Claude McKay, the writer (see above); see *The Third Door: The Autobiography of an American Negro Woman* (1955) ("I was only half-awake that first morning when a Sister walked through the dormitory and started the day with a prayer. I barely had time to wash before Anna came, fully dressed, and handed me a white veil. 'What's this for?' I asked. 'To wear, on your head,' she answered. 'I don't want to wear a veil,' I objected. 'I want to wear my hat.' 'We all wear veils to Mass,' she said. 'We'll both be late if you don't hurry.'

A Sister walked down the aisle ringing a bell and the girls began forming a line at the door. Anna and I were last.

As we filed into the chapel I thought the gray marble altar must be the most beautiful one in the world. The floors of the chapel looked like a wide taffy-colored river. I had once gone to Mass with Lena, but the priest prayed so fast I did not even recognize the 'Our Father.' The first morning at St. Francis de Sales the priest spoke more slowly and Anna shared a prayer book with me. One side of the page was printed in Latin and the other in English, with a picture now and then which explained what the priest was doing. The girls sang, bells rang, incense burned, and the sun shone through the stained-glass windows in brilliant rays. Only my sleepiness and hunger detracted from the beauty of the scene...

In spite of my convictions daily Mass was comforting and inspiring. My spirit soared each morning when the priest stood at the foot of the altar and said in Latin;

'I will go unto the altar of God, at which the God-man is both the High-Priest and the victim of the Sacrifice. I come to Thee, dearest Lord, confessing that I have sinned exceedingly; humbled and ashamed, yet confident in Thy fatherly pity. Create a clean heart in me, O my God, and take not Thy Holy Spirit from me. O Blessed Mother, who didst stand at the foot of the Cross, when Jesus was suffering for us, be with me now that He is being offered up in sacrifice.'

In the gospels I recognized familiar passages and during the Credo I repeated the Apostles' Creed as it had been taught to me back home in Sunday school. When the priest offered the bread, then proceeded to mix the wine and the water in preparation for the coming of Our Lord, I was filled with awe by the beauty of the act. With the ringing of a bell my heart echoed the words of the Sanctus: 'Holy, Holy, Holy, Lord God of Hosts. The heavens and earth are full of Thy Glory. Hosanna in the highest. Blessed is He who cometh in the name of the Lord. Hosanna in the highest...'

With the next tinkling of the bell the priest extended his hands over the bread and wine, recalling the Last Supper, and I bowed my head in the presence of 'My Lord and my God! My God and my All!'

The proper meaning of transubstantiation was to come to me later. During those first troubled months it was enough for me to know that Christ broke the bread and drank the wine with His disciples at the Last Supper and said: 'This is my Body – This is my Blood...' Because the disciples had believed, and because I believed what they had passed on to me, each morning a miracle took place in front of my eyes and Jesus was present upon the altar before which I knelt.

When the Catholic girls went to the communion rail, I begged God to enter my unworthy heart and felt no less loved than they. With the words: 'The Lord be with you – *Ite, missa est* – Go, it is ended,' I felt He was with me wherever I went that day...

Sister Inez gave me a little book for my first retreat. When she placed The Prisoner of Love, by Reverend F. X. Lasance, in my hand, I had no intention of reading it. Thumbing through the foreword I came to a quotation from St. Augustine which said: 'Do not, O reader, condemn a book until thou hast finished the perusal thereof; for it may be that having done this, thy blame will be less severe!' The little book became my constant companion and its simple words gave new and precious meaning to many of the practices I had questioned. Through the miracle which I had come to believe took place during Mass at the solemn moment of Consecration, whereby the bread and wine was changed into the body and blood of Our Lord, the same Christ who died for me came down and remained on all the altars of the world – a prisoner of the love He bore for all mankind. Before, I had believed 'the Word was made flesh' to be only a phrase whose purpose was to fill out the sermon of the minister telling me that I should be good and do no evil. Fr. Lasance's little book told me that it meant Jesus was in the Tabernacle waiting for me to adore him, waiting to comfort me and quiet my doubts and my fears...

Suddenly God seemed closer than ever. Instead of being a God I worshiped on Sunday, He had become a God I wanted to worship every minute of every day. He was my prisoner of love – always waiting. I longed to march up to the communion rail and whisper, 'Here I am. Please make my poor heart your abode'"); *Katherine Drexel: Friend of the Neglected* (1958); *Martin de Porres, Saint of the New World* (1963); *The Other Toussaint: A Post-Revolutionary Black* (1970); *Pierre Toussaint: Apostle of Old New York* (1998); Stephanie Brown, "Bourgeois Blackness and Autobiographical Authenticity in Ellen Tarry's *The Third Door*," *African-American Review*, Fall 2007, p.557; Lorene Hanley Duquin, *A Century of Catholic Converts* (2003), p.63.

Tarski, Alfred (born Alfred Teitelbaum) – mathematician and logician; b. 14 January 1901, Warsaw, Poland; c. 1924; d. 27 October 1983, Berkeley, California; parents were Polish Jews; entered the University of Warsaw in 1918 to study Biology, but changed to Mathematics (he became the youngest person ever to complete a doctorate there); in 1923 he and his brother, Waclaw, changed their surname to Tarski; he (and also his brother) converted to Catholicism, despite the fact that he was an atheist, since he was a Polish nationalist who wanted to be fully accepted as Polish; taught at the university; wrote several textbooks and many original articles; in 1929 married Maria Witkowska, a Polish Catholic (two children of the marriage); left Poland for the United States in August 1939; taught at several universities before moving to the University of California, Berkeley, in 1942, where he spent the rest of his career (Professor 1946-1968; Emeritus Professor from 1968); he became an American citizen in 1945; he was a brilliant and demanding teacher; many visiting lectureships and honors; most of his collected papers were on mathematics, but along with Kurt

Gödel he revolutionized the study of logic; also major contributions to semantics and the philosophy of language; see Stephen R. Givant and Ralph N. McKenzie (ed), *The Collected Papers of Alfred Tarski*, 4 Vols (1986); Anita Burdman Feferman and Solomon Feferman, *Alfred Tarski: Life and Logic* (2004); his archives are in the Bancroft Library, University of California, Berkeley; *ANB.*

Tate, (John Orley) Allen – poet, essayist and social commentator; b. 19 November 1899, Winchester, Kentucky; c. 22 December 1950 (his godparents were Jacques and Raïssa Maritain); d. 9 February 1979, Nashville, Tennessee; mother with Presbyterian background, father Episcopalian, but later a freethinker; brought up in the traditions of Old South decorum; educated at Vanderbilt University; close friend of Robert Penn Warren (1905-1989), the poet, novelist and literary critic, with whom he came under the influence of John Crowe Ransom (1888-1974), the poet and critic, and joined the group of southern poets known as the Fugitive Poets and later as the Southern Agrarians; immersed in Modernism; interested in Catholicism from an early stage; almost converted in 1929 ("I am more and more heading towards Catholicism. We have reached a condition of the spirit where no further compromise is possible. That is the lesson taught us by the Victorians who failed to unite naturalism and the religious spirit; we've got to do away with the one or the other; and I can never capitulate to naturalism"); in 1924 he moved to New York where he lived a bohemian existence; friend of Hart Crane (1899-1932), the poet; in 1925 he met and married Caroline Gordon (see above); in 1928 he wrote his most famous poem, *Ode to the Confederate Dead*; in his poetry he increasingly portrayed the modern world in dark terms; in the 1930s he wrote biographies and southern conservative social commentary; very influential on *The American Review*; explored the relationship between religion and naturalism, seeing the Catholic Church as a bulwark against the latter; recognized the fallen state of man and nature; in 1938 he wrote his only novel, *The Fathers*; poet in residence at Princeton University; influential, together with his friend, Andrew Lytle (1902-1995), the novelist, in raising the profile of *The Sewanee Review*; poetry consultant to the Library of Congress in 1943; conversion mainly influenced by Jacques Maritain, St. Augustine and Dante; Professor at University of Minnesota in Minneapolis 1951-1968; other friends and associates were Dorothy Day (see above), Robert Lowell (see above), and Julien Green (1900-1998), the writer (see above); his personal life during his last years did not always adhere to Catholic teaching (married Isabella Gardner, the poet, but they divorced in 1945, followed by a 1946 remarriage and an ultimate divorce in 1959, though they continued to correspond and remained friends; then married Helen Heinz, an ex-nun, one of his students); see *Collected Poems* (1970); *Stonewall Jackson: The Good Soldier* (1928); *Jefferson Davis: His Rise and Fall* (1929); *Robert E. Lee* (1932); *Reactionary Essays on Poetry and Ideas* (1936); *The House of Fiction: An Anthology of the Short Story* (1950) (with Caroline Gordon); *The Man of Letters in the Modern World* (1955); *Collected Essays* (1959); *Essays of Four Decades* (1969) ("The Catholic faith has not changed since Dante's time. But the Catholic sensibility, as we see it in modern Catholic poetry, from Thompson to Lowell, has become angelic, and is not distinguishable (doctrinal differences aside) from poetry by Anglicans, Methodists, Presbyterians, and atheists. I take it that more than doctrine, even if the doctrine be true, is necessary for a great poetry of action. Catholic poets have lost, along with their heretical friends, the power to start with the 'common thing': they have lost the gift for concrete experience. The abstraction of the modern mind has obscured their way into the natural order. Nature offers to the symbolic poet clearly denotable objects in depth and in the round, which yield the analogies to the higher syntheses. 'The modern poet rejects the higher synthesis, or tosses it in a vacuum of abstraction.' If he looks at nature he spreads the clear visual image in a complex of metaphor, from one katachresis to another through Aristotle's permutations of genus and species. He cannot sustain the prolonged analogy, the second and superior kind of figure that Aristotle doubtless had in mind when he spoke of metaphor as the key to the resemblances of things, and the mark of genius.

That the gift of analogy was not Dante's alone every medievalist knows. The most striking proof of its diffusion and the most useful example for my purpose that I know, is the letter of St. Catherine of Siena to Brother Raimondo of Capua. A young Sienese, Niccolo Tuldo, had been unjustly convicted of treason and condemned to death. Catherine became his angel of mercy, giving him daily solace - the meaning of the Cross, the healing powers of the Blood; and so reconciled him to the faith that he accepted his last end. Now I have difficulty believing people who say that they live in the Blood of Christ, for I take them to mean that they have the faith and hope some day to live in it. The evidence of the Blood is one's power to produce it, the power to show it as a 'common thing' and to make it real, literally, in action. For the report of the Blood is very different from its reality. St. Catherine does not report it; she recreates it, so that its analogical meaning is confirmed again in blood that she has seen. This is how she does it: 'Then [the condemned man] came, like a gentle lamb; and seeing me he began to smile, and wanted me to make the sign of the Cross. When he had received the sign, I said, "Down! To the bridal, my sweetest brother. For soon shalt thou be in the enduring life." He prostrated himself with great gentleness, and I stretched out his neck; and bowed me down, and recalled to him the Blood of the Lamb. His lips said naught save Jesus! and Catherine! And so saying, I received his head in my hands, closing my eyes in the divine goodness and saying, "I will." When he was at rest my soul rested in peace and quiet, and in so great fragrance of blood that I could not bear to remove the blood which had fallen on me from him.'

It is deeply shocking, as all proximate incarnations of the Word are shocking, whether in Christ and the Saints, or in Dostoevsky, James Joyce, or Henry James. I believe it was T. S. Eliot who made accessible again to an ignorant generation a common, Christian insight, when he said that people cannot bear very much reality. I take this to mean that only persons of extraordinary courage, and perhaps even genius, can face the spiritual truth in its physical body. Flaubert said that the artist, the soldier, and the priest face death every day; so do we all; yet it is perhaps nearer to them than to other men; it is their particular responsibility. When St. Catherine 'rests in so great fragrance of blood,' it is no doubt the Blood of the Offertory which the celebrant offers to God *cum odore suavitatis*, but with the literal odor of the species of wine, not of blood. St. Catherine had the courage of genius which permitted her to *smell* the Blood of Christ in Niccolo Tuldo's blood clotted on her dress: she smelled the two bloods *not alternately but at one instant*, in a single act compounded of spiritual insight and physical perception.

Chekhov said that a gun hanging on the wall at the beginning of a story has got to be fired off before the story ends: everything in potency awaits its completed purpose in act. If this is a metaphysical principle, it is also the prime necessity of the creative imagination. Is not St. Catherine telling us that the Blood of Christ must be perpetually recreated as a brute fact? If the gun has got to be fired, the Blood has got to be shed, if only because that is the first condition of its appearance; it must move towards the condition of human action, where we may smell it, touch it, and taste it again.

When ecclesiastical censorship of this deep insight in the laity exceeds a just critical prudence, the result is not merely obscurantism in the arts; it is perhaps a covert rejection of the daily renewal of the religious life. Twenty-five years ago the late W. B. Yeats had a controversy with the Irish bishops about the famous medieval 'Cherry Tree Carol,' which the hierarchy wished to suppress as blasphemous. The Blessed Virgin is resting under a cherry tree, too tired to reach up and pluck a cherry. Since Christ lives from the foundations of the world, He is omnipotent in the womb, and He commands the tree to lower a bough for His Mother's convenience; which it obligingly does, since it cannot do otherwise. Here again the gun is fired and the Blood is shed. If the modern Church has lost the historic experience of this kind of symbolism, which is more tolerable, I believe, in the Latin countries than with us, it is at least partial evidence that the Church has lost the great culture that it created, and that at intervals has created the life of the Church"); *Memoirs and Opinions, 1926-1974* (1975); Derek Stanford, "Tradition and Mr. Allen Tate, " *The Month*, July 1959, p.39; Robert H. Brinkmeyer, Jr., *Three Catholic Writers of the Modern South* (1985) ("Particularly influential was Maritain's *The Dream of Descartes* (1944), in which he argued that the split in the consciousness of modern man derives from Descartes' quest to formulate a cosmos merely through introspective reasoning without regard to the sensible world. Descartes' efforts, in essence, separated the realm of sense from the intellect – hence the Cartesian split in consciousness... Tate himself wrote...: 'My debt to Mr. Maritain is so great that I hardly know how to acknowledge it...

Paving the way for Tate's conversion to Catholicism was an important realization that he reached through Maritain: that it was not, as he had once feared, a belief in Catholicism that separated one from the world, but rather man's angelism, resulting from his split consciousness. In other words, being a Catholic did not necessarily mean being cut off from the natural world.

Remaining in the here and now while at the same time exploring the mysterious realms of faith was a lesson he learned also from another mentor, Saint Augustine. Both philosophically and artistically, Augustine emphasized the importance of the earthly realm, his 'City of Man,' in attaining the heavenly realm, the 'City of God.' Rather than counseling a total immersion into one of these realms at the expense of the other. Augustine urged man to seek a balance between them...

Dante was Tate's most important guide in bringing together faith and art. Tate's deep study of *The Divine Comedy*, probably more than anything else, helped him to allay his fears that Catholicism would destroy him as an artist. Using Dante's example, Tate formulated a way to resolve artistically the split between his own naturalism and angelism"); John M. Dunaway (ed), *Exiles & Fugitives: The Letters of Jacques & Raïssa Maritain, Allen Tate & Caroline Gordon* (1993); Anne Barbeau Gardiner, "The Catholic Sensibility of Allen Tate," *New Oxford Review*, March 2000 ("For Tate, then, the remedy for the fragmented Western mind is the renewal of faith in God. He warns that 'a society which has once been religious cannot, without risk of spiritual death, preceded by the usual agonies, secularize itself'...

One sign of Tate's Catholic sensibility is that he is not afraid to use the word dogma in a positive sense. He asserts (as early as 1936) that 'dogma in criticism is a permanent necessity: the value of the dogma will be determined by the quality of the mind engaged in constructing it. For dogma is coherent thought in pursuit of principles.' He is careful to distinguish dogma from preconception or 'prejudice,' and he illustrates the distinction with this witty remark, which is still true sixty-four years later: 'If prejudice were dogma, the *New York Times Book Review* would be a first rate critical organ.' Another proof of his Catholic sensibility is that Tate values the virtue of humility. He urges the literary critic to cultivate humility, 'in order to fulfill his main task unfolding thc knowledge of life contained in the work of art.' A critic needs 'the self-abnegation of the saint' to do his work well"); *ANB* ("For Tate...'the end of social man is communion in time through love, which is beyond time'").

Tekakwitha, Saint Kateri (pronounced as "Te-kak-wee-da") (also known as Catherine Tegakwitha or Takwita; "The Lily of the Mohawks") – religious lay woman; b. 1656, Ossernenon, on the Mohawk river, Iroquois Confederacy (New France, until 1763), near present-day Auriesville, New York; c. 18 April 1676 (Easter Sunday; near what is now Fonda, New York; baptized by Fr. Jacques de Lamberville, SJ); d. 17 April 1680 (Wednesday of Holy Week), Kahnawake, near Montreal, Quebec, Canada; daughter of Kenneronkwa, a Mohawk chief, and Tagaskouita, a Catholic Algonquin; her mother was baptized and educated by French missionaries in Trois-Rivières, Quebec, Canada, then captured by the Iroquiois and taken to the Mohawk homeland; at age four Kateri contracted smallpox (which killed her parents and her brother) and was left with poor eyesight and scars on her face; adopted by her uncle, also a chief; resisted the pressure of the tribe on her to marry; given a rosary by her mother (which was taken away by her uncle); impressed by the piety and kindness of the French Jesuits who came to preach, she became interested in the Catholic faith and converted; at her baptism, she took the name Kateri, a Mohawk pronunciation of the French name Catherine, after Catherine of Siena; Tekakwitha means, "one who puts things in order"; exercised physical mortification of the flesh as a route to sanctity; shunned and attacked by the members of her family and community; fled to join a group of Christian Mohawks who had migrated to the French mission of St. Francis Xavier, at Sault

St. Louis on the south shore of the St. Lawrence River, opposite Montreal, Quebec (the Indians called the site Caughnawaga, but it is often referred to as Kahnawake); there she lived a life dedicated to prayer, penance, and care for the sick and aged; took a vow of chastity (from which the title Lily Flower is obtained) on the Feast of the Annunciation, 25 March 1679; other terms used to refer to her are the Mohawk Maiden, the Flower of the Algonquins, the Pure and Tender Lily, the Flower among True Men, the Lily of Purity, the Genevieve of New France, and The New Star of the New World; her last words are said to have been "Jesus, I love You!"; according to Fr. Pierre Cholenec, who was present, her smallpox scars vanished fifteen minutes after her death; her gravestone reads "Ownkeonweke Katsitsiio Teonsitsianekaron" (The fairest flower that ever bloomed among red men); many miraculous events are said to have occurred after her death (claims that many pilgrims at her funeral were healed; and that she appeared to two persons shortly afterwards); declared Venerable in 1943; beatified in 1980; canonized on 21 October 2012 by Pope Benedict XVI who referred to her as the "protectress of Canada and the first Native American saint"; see Ellen Hardin Walworth, *The Life and Times of Kateri Tekakwitha the Lily of the Mohawks, 1656-1680* (1891) ("A young Indian suddenly rushed in upon her, his features distorted with rage, his eyes flashing fire, his tomahawk raised above his head as if to strike her dead at the least opposition. Tekakwitha did not cry out, or make an appeal for mercy, or promise to abandon the course she was taking in the midst of this ever increasing torrent of threats and abuse. With perfect composure, without the tremor or twitch of a muscle, she simply bowed her head…as immovable as a rock. Words were not needed on either side. With all the eloquent silence of the Indian sign language, her gesture and attitude spoke to the youth and said: 'I am here, I am ready. My life you can take; my faith is my own in life or in death. I fear you not!' The rage in the Indian's eye died out, and gave place to wonder, then awe. He gazed as if spellbound. The uplifted tomahawk dropped to his side. Her firmness unnerved him. Admiration, then a strange fear, overmastered the young brave, whose brain perhaps had been somewhat clouded with liquor when he thus undertook to rid the old chief's niece of her Christian whims…Cowed and abashed, he slunk away, as if from a superior being; or rather, he turned and fled with as much precipitation as if pursued by a band of warriors"); Daniel Sargent, *Catherine Tekakwitha* (1936); Theodore Maynard, *Great Catholics in American History* (1957), p.41 ("The ideal of virginity was for Kateri the key to her whole life, and was the basis of the spirituality she attained. From the outset the priests at Caughnawaga recognized that Kateri was a girl who, while only recently a pagan, was already far advanced in divine things, rudimentary as may have been her knowledge of many of the elements of faith"); Margaret Bunson, *Kateri Tekakwitha: Mystic of the Wilderness* (1992); Lillian M. Fisher, *Kateri Tekakwitha: The Lily of the Mohawks* (1995); Allan Greer, *Mohawk Saint: Catherine Tekakwitha and the Jesuits* (2004); Darren Bonaparte, *A Lily Among Thorns: The Mohawk Repatriation of Kateri Tekakwitha* (2009); Ellen Hardin Walworth, The Life and Times of Kateri Tekakwitha: The Lily of the Mohawks (2009); Giovanna Paponetti, Kateri, Native American Saint: The Life and Miracles of Kateri Tekakwitha (2010); Francis MacDonald and Charles L. Dougherty, *Star of the Mohawk: Kateri Tekakwitha* (2011); Matthew Bunson and Margaret Bunson, St. Kateri: Lily of the Mohawks (2012) ("Having converted and received the sacraments after so many years of searching and waiting, Kateri was filled with an exaltation that altered her vision of everything around her…[T]hese reactions are experienced by most converts to Catholicism…[T]he reception of baptism means the expunging of the past, the rapture of having discovered truth amid so many lies, and the joy of becoming part of a universal family, both on earth and in heaven. It is a plunge into the depths of love and the spirit, so far removed from the halfway measures of many human lives"); Catholic Encyclopedia; ANB ("At the mission, Tekakwitha went to church daily at 4 a.m. to attend the dawn mass. During the day she occasionally left work to pray in church, and she returned in the evening to pray late into the night. When her sister tried to convince her to marry, she told the priest, 'Ah, Father, I am not any longer my own. I have given myself entirely to Jesus Christ, and it is not possible to change masters'… By the beginning of winter, she had decided never again to return to her own village. She lived gladly in poverty, dressed in rags, and subsisted only on Indian corn. The Christian Indian community at Caughnawaga reinforced her tendencies, fasting constantly and inflicting on themselves punishments such as wearing belts lined with points of iron.

During conflict between the French and the Iroquois in the late 1670s, the Iroquois invited their kin at the mission to return, promising them the freedom to practice their religion. Most refused, and the Iroquois declared them enemies. They captured some and tortured them mercilessly. Such sufferings only served to spur the surviving Christianized Indians on to greater fervor; the women at the Sault became so zealous

even the priests tried to moderate their behavior. Tekakwitha was foremost among these...
She continued to punish her body in search of spiritual enlightenment; walking with friends in the forests during the winter, for instance, she took off her shoes and walked with naked feet over ice and snow. Another time she slept for three nights on a bed of thorns she had placed on her mat. Her body proved unable to withstand such treatment for long, and she died in the spring at Caughnawaga").

Tenney, William Jewett – author and editor; b. 1814, Newport, Rhode Island; d. 20 September 1883, Newark, New Jersey; studied Medicine at Yale University, but abandoned it for Law and was admitted to the bar; opened a law office in New York; tried journalism, working for the *Journal of Commerce* and the *Evening Post* between 1841 and 1848; in 1853 became an editor for a firm of publishers; did much literary and critical work; compiled the *Annual Cyclopedia* from 1861 until his death; indexed T. H. Benton's *Abridgment of the Debates of Congress* and produced a further volume for the series; holder of several public offices in New Jersey; became a convert to the Catholic Church and married, as his second wife, Sarah (1839-1876), writer and daughter of Orestes Brownson (see above); see *Military and Naval History of the Rebellion in the U.S.* (1865); *Grammatical Analysis* (1866); *Catholic Encyclopedia.*

Terry, Randall Almira – pro-life activist; b. 1959; c. 2006; founded the pro-life organization Operation Rescue, which he led until 1991; arrested on numerous occasions; involved in several high profile cases, including that of Terri Schiavo; in 2003 he founded the Society for Truth and Justice; in 1998 he ran as a Republican for Congress in upstate New York and in 2006 for the Florida Senate, but lost both times in the primary; in 2009 arrested on the campus of University of Notre Dame when he protested against the invitation to President Obama to speak at the Commencement; criticized by some for his very forceful statements on the abortion issue; challenged President Obama in the Democratic Party primaries for the presidential election of 2012; unsuccessful independent candidate for Congress in Florida in 2012; married twice with several children, some fostered and adopted; member of several Protestant denominations before becoming a Catholic; see *Accessory To Murder: The Enemies, Allies, and Accomplices To The Death of Our Culture* (1990); *Why Does A Nice Guy Like Me...Keep Getting Thrown In Jail?: How Theological Escapism and Cultural Retreatism in the Church Have Led to America's Demise* (1993); *The Sword: The Blessing Of Righteous*

Government and the Overthrow Of Tyrants (1995); *A Humble Plea: To Bishops, Clergy, Laymen: Ending the Abortion Holocaust* (2008).

Thayer, John – priest and missionary; b. 1755, Boston, Massachusetts; c. 25 May 1783; d. 5 February 1815, Limerick, Ireland; his family were among the early Puritan settlers of New England; educated at Yale University and became a Congregationalist minister; during the Revolutionary War served as chaplain to a company organized for the defense of Boston; after the war he wandered over Europe and was in Rome when the beggar-saint Benedict Joseph Labre (1748-1783) died; his attempt to dispute some of the miracles wrought through Benedict Joseph Labre's intercession resulted in his own conversion to the faith; for the purpose of converting his own fellow countrymen he took a theological course under the Sulpicians in Paris; ordained to the priesthood in 1787 (first native of New England ordained priest); worked for three years among the poor in the Southwark district of London, where he converted "thirty-six heretics" to the Faith; returned to America in December 1789; put in charge of the newly organized Catholic congregation in Boston; increased the size and level of activity of the Catholic community, but his combativeness let him down and he was not always tactful; he went to Kentucky as a missionary for four years, where he was a Catholic voice against slavery; left for Europe again and visited London, La Trappe (France), and Dublin; in 1811 he settled down in Limerick, Ireland; he died there with a reputation for piety and asceticism; see *An* Account *of the Conversion of the Reverend John Thayer* (1787); Brother André Marie, "The First Yankee Priest, Father John Thayer," *catholicism.org*, 4 June 2008 ("In order to broaden his horizons and learn something of the languages and culture of the Old World, he traveled to Europe. In 1781, he found himself in France, where he became seriously ill. As he says it, his 'first concern was to forbid, that any Catholic Priest should be suffered to come near me, such was my attachment to my own sect.' In Italy, he became acquainted with a Jesuit who was able to undo many of his prejudices. For the first time, he began to see an admirable cohesion to the ancient religion, something in stark relief to the sectarian divisions spawned by the Reformation.

While he was in Rome, an important thing happened: a beggar dropped dead of exhaustion. This was not just any beggar, though, but Saint Joseph Benedict Labre, the French holy man who moved to the Eternal City to live as a poor, penitential pilgrim. His death was 16 April 1783. From that date until 6 July 1783, no less than 136 miraculous cures were certified and credited to the recently-deceased.

Some of these, at least, resulted from the relics of the beggar's clothing. Reverend Thayer scoffed at the superstition of it all. Setting out to investigate, he found himself convinced by the evidence. This was providential, for, in his words, 'of all my prejudices against Catholics, the deepest rooted was a formal disbelief of the miraculous facts which are said to have happened among them…' On 25 May of that same year, John Thayer renounced his heresies and embraced the Catholic religion, in the very seat of 'Popery' itself: Rome…

While in the seminary he wrote a booklet, *An Account of the Conversion of Reverend John Thayer*. What did this *Account* have to say on the all-important question of salvation? In one passage, the convert cites a prayer to the Holy Ghost from a book that had come into his hands shortly before he embraced the Faith. The book was in Italian and gave the account of another Protestant's conversion to Catholicism. Thayer prayed this prayer and attributed to it no small part in his conversion. Here is a section of that prayer:

'I am sure that as there is but one true God; so there can be but one faith, one religion, one way of salvation, and that every other way which is opposite to this, can only lead to endless misery. It is this faith, Oh my God, which I earnestly desire to embrace, in order to save my soul'

Elsewhere the same subject comes up as the polemicist inveighs against the Reformation. This time, the words are Father Thayer's:

'All those, who *knowingly* and *willingly* follow those pretended [Protestant] Reformers are in evident danger of eternal ruin. Those persons can never give a satisfactory answer to the following argument: In Luther and Calvin's time, either the Catholic church was Christ's true spouse, or some other society was so; or else, Christ's true church had ceased. If the Catholic society was at that time Christ's church, no one could separate from it without risking his salvation, since there is no salvation for those that are separated from Christ: If any other society was then Christ's true church, they were obliged to join it under pain of damnation: If they say that Christ's church had ceased, they make Christ a liar, who has promised its perpetual duration in spite of the combined rage of earth and hell'"); *Catholic Encyclopedia* ("His own account of this conversion, one of the first of prominent New England Protestants, was printed in 1787 and reissued in several editions in the United States in London, and in Ireland. It was also translated into French and Spanish, and created a great controversial sensation at the time").

Thigpen, Paul – writer; c. 1993 (received with his wife Leisa, son and daughter); brought up in the Presbyterian Church in the

South; as a young man attracted to a crucifix ("I asked my father to get me one. But he shook his head and said, 'That's just for Catholics.' There was no malice in his words; he simply spoke matter-of-factly"); encouraged at school to read Voltaire, who convinced him that all religion was delusion; experimented with occultism; convinced that humanity could perfect itself through education; reading C. S. Lewis acted as an antidote to Voltaire; impressed by the figure of Christ; had an experience interpreted as a baptism of the Holy Spirit; majored in religious studies at Yale University; took a graduate school program in religion; served as a missionary evangelist in Europe; associate pastor of a charismatic congregation; writer and editor for several Christian publications; moved between several Protestant denominations, but a Methodist for the longest period; sometimes felt a longing for Catholic things; entered a PhD program in Historical Theology at Emory University, Atlanta; was influenced in his conversion by such as St. Augustine, Newman, Chesterton, and Thomas Merton (see above); after his conversion he founded a Catholic apostolate, the Stella Maris Center for Faith and Culture, and became editor of *The Catholic Answer*, a bi-monthly magazine about the Catholic faith; assistant professor of Religious Studies at South West Missouri State University; set up an association, The Friends of the Georgia Martyrs; see "His Open Arms Welcomed Me," in Patrick Madrid (ed), *Surprised by Truth* (1994) (reproduced in *The Coming Home Network International*, *Conversion Stories*, *chnetwork.org*, 13 January 2011) ("Once you grant the existence of supernature, you can't rule out God; and if there's a God, what's there to stop him from invading nature? If there's a God, I knew, then the rest of the story, however shocking – Virgin Birth, miracles, the Resurrection – surely becomes possible…

[I]n quiet moments, I sometimes felt a longing sweep over me. It washed across my heart whenever I heard a recording of tranquil Gregorian chant or Schubert's aching 'Ave Maria.' It erupted inside me when I visited the great cathedrals of Europe – humbled by the grandeur of their architecture and the sweaty devotion of all the forgotten saints who had labored to raise those stones to the sky.

I felt it when I read St. Augustine's *Confessions*, St. Catherine's *Dialogue*, and St. John's *Dark Night of the Soul*. These were more than books - they were doorways into a communion with the saints who had written them. I felt their presence as I read; I even found myself talking to them, though my theological training told me that such conversations weren't permitted.

Most of all, I ached when I knelt quietly in the sanctuaries of Catholic churches. I felt drawn to the tabernacle and the altar... But my mind rebelled against the attraction. Those matter-of-fact words from so long ago always returned to dampen my desire: 'That's just for Catholics'...

Some puzzles were solved, not by the writings of great Christian teachers or a new approach to Scripture, but by the outcome of great Christian dramas of the past. Church history, I found, was theology teaching by example.

For some, the study of Christian behavior over the centuries, with all its horrors, has led to doubt, cynicism, even atheism. They see church councils bickering over petty jealousies, popes amassing wealth, bishops fathering children, monks living in dissipation; and at that dismaying sight, they lose faith. For me, however, Church history became one long confirmation of two realities: the universality of sin and the sovereignty of grace...

[T]he scandal was overcome when I finally admitted that no Christian community has ever even come close to being perfect. In fact, I saw the Catholic Church's problems repeated in the history of all the groups that repudiated her, that vowed they would never be like her. They reminded me of the adolescent daughter who swears she'll never be like the mother she resents - yet ends up becoming just like her in spite of her vow...

In taking the long view, I also came to marvel at the sovereign grace of God. Those same bickering councils that Protestants have disparaged nevertheless demonstrated the most astonishing wisdom in crafting creeds that would stand the test of time. Those avaricious popes gave their blessing to men and women of blessed poverty whose explosive holiness shamed their lax brothers and sisters and turned the Church upside down...

[T]hrough all the confusion, I came to see, Rome remains the solid theological standard for those who have separated from her. As even the oldest denominations have succumbed to the spirit of the age on one critical issue after another, the Catholic Church has remained firm - on the sanctity of life, on the nature of sexuality, on the supernatural foundations of faith, on the essence of God and the identity of Christ. Today as yesterday, *Veritatis Splendor* - the splendor of truth, as the Holy Father has so aptly called it, blazes forth from Rome. 'The light shines in the darkness, and the darkness has not overcome it.'

Perhaps most importantly, my reading of Erasmus and Newman and my study of the history of liturgy helped me to see that the primitivist assumption underlying Protestant views of the Church was seriously mistaken in at least two ways. First, Erasmus and Newman taught me that the Church is a maturing organism whose life span stretches across the centuries - not an archaeological expedition always searching for fossils to help it reconstruct a primitive campsite. They challenged me to defend the Protestant notion that we should desire the embryo over the mature organism; and having studied Church history, I found such a defense impossible.

Second, when I studied the history of Jewish and Christian liturgy, I found that even if we could return to the 'primitive' Christian experience, that experience would not resemble most of the Protestant, especially the charismatic, churches of today. The congregations I'd been part of were for the most part assuming that they had recovered a 'New Testament' model of strictly spontaneous worship, local government, and 'Bible-only' teaching. But the early Church, I found, was in reality liturgical in worship; translocal and hierarchical in government; and dependent on a body of sacred Tradition that included the Scripture, yet stretched far beyond it as well"); *Jesus We Adore You: Prayers Before the Blessed Sacrament* (2001); *The Rapture Trap: A Catholic Response to "End Times" Fever* (2001) (with Marcus Grodi); "Did Christ Have to Suffer?" *This Rock*, February 2004; *The New Catholic Bible* (2005) (with Dave Armstrong); *The Questions Catholics Are Asked* (2007); *EWTN Audio Library, The Journey Home* (28 May 2007) ("I began to read the Church Fathers especially, and to see that all my notions of what the early Church was all about were very contrary to the case. That when I read people like St. Ignatius of Antioch and St. Clement and others that had received their faith from the Apostles, many things that were not part of my tradition were right there in the Catholic faith, like the Eucharist and the Real Presence. The Eucharist really was the body and blood. The hierarchy already existed. That kind of thing; and other very important things; that those were present from the very beginning.

I fell in love with St. Augustine. In particular in his work I remember reading the *Confessions* and feeling like it was a heart cry as an echo many centuries later of his. And I'll never forget the day I was reading St. Augustine's essay against the Donatists, who were a group starting out in northern Africa in the early centuries, who broke away from the Catholic Church because they felt the Church wasn't pure enough, and set themselves up as a schismatic group, in many ways like an early Protestant forerunner in that way; and he began to say all the reasons why they should come back to the Church. I was saying, 'Yes, yes, that's right. You tell them, St. Augustine, you tell them.' And all of a sudden I put the book down and I said, 'Oh my goodness, I am a Donatist. He's talking to me.' And I realized that he was responding to all my reasons for being Protestant.

So, that and a number of other situations, hunger for the Eucharist, but especially Church history, then drove me into the Church and to embrace it as the fullness of

Catholic truth that it is"); *Praying the Rosary with St. Paul* (2008); *EWTN Audio Library, The Journey Home* (11 October 2010) ("Once I started reading history, as we all know, 'To be deep in history,' to quote Blessed John Henry Cardinal Newman, 'is to cease to be a Protestant.' And as I began to read the Church Fathers in particular the call to come to the Catholic Church began to become very clear, very explicit. So, seventeen years ago, a long process there of course of all kinds of things, learning what the Church Fathers had to say, learning about Church history since that time, learning what the Catholic Church really teaches rather than what many people think it teaches, and practices, I came to a point where, as a matter of conscience, I had to come in. I believed it was the Church of truth and I couldn't stay out any longer"); *Catholic Answers to Catholic Questions* (2010) (with Ray Rylands and Paul Hoffman); *The Burden* (2013); *paulthigpen.com.*

Thomas, Clarence – Associate Justice of the Supreme Court; b. 23 June 1948, Pin Point, Georgia; c. 1996 (revert); born to a Baptist family; father a farm worker, mother a domestic worker; father left the family when he was two years old; brought up as a Catholic (mainly raised by his maternal grandfather, a Catholic convert); at the age of sixteen he considered training for the priesthood; attended minor seminary in Savannah and also briefly a seminary in Missouri, but left later; left the Catholic Church in 1968; educated at the College of the Holy Cross in Worcester, Massachusetts (graduated in English Literature in 1971); entered Yale Law School and graduated Juris Doctor in 1974; assistant attorney general of Missouri 1974-1977; then practiced law privately; a legislative assistant in Washington 1979-1981; joined President Reagan's administration in 1981; Assistant Secretary of Education for the Office for Civil Rights in the U.S. Department of Education 1981-1982; Chairman of the US Equal Employment Opportunity Commission 1982-1990; judge on the United States Court of Appeals for the District of Columbia Circuit 1990-1991; nominated for the Supreme Court in 1991; during the bitterly fought confirmation hearings Anita Hill, an attorney who had worked with him, made allegations of sexual harrassment by him; he denied the allegations; confirmed by the Senate by 52 votes to 48; the second African-American to serve on the court, succeeding Thurgood Marshall, the first; seen as an originalist and conservative judge; views the court's role as an interpreter of law rather than as a maker of law; regarding abortion he contends that the constitution does not address the issue, and dissented when the court in Planned Parenthood v Casey (1992) re-affirmed *Roe v Wade*; married twice; attended

Episcopalian Church with his first wife, Kathy Ambush; second wife, Virginia Lamp, founder of a conservative lobbying firm; see *My Grandfather's Son: A Memoir* (2007); Phillip E. Johnson, "Nihilism and the End of Law," *First Things*, March 1993; Ken Foskett, *Judging Thomas: The Life and Times of Clarence Thomas* (2004).

Thompson, Sir John Sparrow David – jurist and politician; b. 10 November 1844 or 5 December 1844, Halifax, Nova Scotia, Canada; c. 1871; d. 12 December 1894, Windsor Castle, England; son of John Sparrow Thompson, born in Ireland, queen's printer and superintendent of the money order system; his mother Catherine Pottinger was of Scottish descent; both parents were rigid Methodists; studied Law and was admitted to the bar in 1865; in 1870 he married Annie E. Affleck (1842-1913), a strong character and his great supporter, and shortly afterwards became a Catholic; two of their children died at birth, two others died very young and two sons and three daughters survived childhood; went into public life and progressed rapidly; member of the Conservative party; alderman in Halifax in 1871; became a member of the House of Assembly in 1877; Attorney-General 1878-1882; in 1882 became Premier of Nova Scotia and judge of the Supreme Court; co-founder of Dalhousie Law School in 1883 and a professor there; Minister of Justice of Canada 1885-1894; his dealing with the 1885 North-West Rebellion increased his popularity; he was primarily a judge (with a passion for justice) and a rcluctant politician, but was a brilliant parliamentarian; introduced the first Criminal Code of Canada; knighted by Queen Victoria for his work as legal adviser to the British government in connection with the Fisheries Commission; Prime Minister of Canada (the fourth to hold this office and the first Catholic to do so) 1892-1894; one of his concerns was the possibility of the annexation of Canada by the United States ("These Yankee politicians are the lowest race of thieves in existence"); he was one of the judges on the international tribunal to settle the Canada-U.S. dispute over the seal harvest in the Bering Sea; the tribunal sided with Canada, ruling that there was no justification for the U.S. to claim that the Bering Sea was reserved for American seal hunters; in recognition of his work on this he was appointed one of the members of the Privy Council of Great Britain; an hour or so later he died suddenly of a heart attack; buried in Holy Cross Cemetery, Halifax, Nova Scotia; see J. Castell Hopkins, *Life and Work of the Rt. Hon. Sir John Thompson* (1895); Peter B. Waite, *The Man from Halifax: Sir John Thompson* (1985) ("Thompson was probably never attracted to the emotional manifestations of Methodism: the steamy confessions of sin, the passionate abjuring of evil, the golden catharsis that promised everything. These had not been what held his father either. Old J .S. Thompson liked Methodism's leveling, republican honesty, its absence of class, its instinct to measure a man by what he was rather than by what he appeared to be. It was to J. S. Thompson a plain-clothes religion, affirming the fundamental truth that all men were equal in the sight of God.

But for John David the Methodist faith may have been unsatisfying metaphysically. The religious upheavals of the 1840s and 1850s within the Church of England about the church and its doctrines, the revival of Roman Catholicism in Britain and in British North America, stirred his search for some towering theology, some better articulated eschatology than the simplicities that Methodism provided. About the time of his father's death John David began to attend the Church of England and the Roman Catholic Church, to listen to sermons, to read religion, to search actively for the true faith. In this search he met the sophisticated, intelligent, courageous Roman Catholic archbishop of Halifax, Thomas Connolly...

In 1867 and 1868 Archbishop Connolly preached a series of sermons in St Mary's Cathedral on the foundations and doctrines of the Church. These sermons and the man himself strongly influenced young Thompson. He was not yet a Roman Catholic, but, like so much else he did, he was carefully surveying the ground. Thompson was not the only one influenced by Connolly's high courage and strong mind. Connolly made a signal impression at the Vatican Council in Rome in 1869-70, where he spoke out strongly against the proposed doctrine of papal infallibility. It was this sort of courage that attracted Thompson, and he was undeniably drawn to Connolly and the Roman Catholic faith over the more obvious, socially easier, claims of the Church of England. Nor was Thompson's conversion sudden. The manner of it was characteristic: 'I had been attending the Church of England and Roman Catholic services exclusively for upwards of four years, and reading all of the controversy I could get my hands on, and finally yielded only when to believe and not to profess appeared to be wretched cowardice.'

Thompson's favorite character in history was Sir Thomas More. It suggests the bent of his mind: he was not seeking a church but the church"); Peter B. Waite, "Canada's Little Known Fourth Prime Minister," *CBC Digital Archives*, 29 April 1985; *Catholic Encyclopedia*" ("He became a Catholic not because his wife was a Catholic. He deliberately left changing over until nine months after their marriage, when Annie was pregnant with their first child, deliberately to say, 'I changed because I believe, not because my wife was a Catholic'"); *DCB.*

Thompson, (Terry) Dunstan – poet; b. 30 August 1918, New London, Connecticut; c. 1952 (revert); d. 19 January 1975, Cley-next-the-sea, Norfolk; only son of Terry Brewster Thompson, a naval officer, and Virginia Leita Thompson, *née* Montgomery; the Thompson family came originally from Protestant New England stock; both his paternal grandparents converted; his parents were both devout Catholics who brought him up in the Catholic faith; grew up in Washington, D.C., and Annapolis, Maryland; studied English Literature at Harvard University from 1936; at some time between his final year at a Catholic prep-school and his first year at Harvard he lost his Catholic faith, left the practice of his religion, and adopted what was eventually to be a highly promiscuous homosexual lifestyle; while at Harvard he explored his vocation as a writer, especially as a poet; left the university without graduating; had independent means and lived mainly in New York; co-edited a literary magazine, *Vice Versa* 1940-1942; drafted into the army in 1942; the poems from this period are passionate, their themes including war, violence, death and homo-eroticism; posted to England in 1943; served in the Office of War Information in London; met the leading literary figures in London, including T.S. Eliot, the Sitwells, Cyril Connolly, Stephen Spender, Conrad Aiken, and John Lehmann; in the mid and late 1940s seen as a major poet; after World War II he settled in England in a village, Cley-next-the-sea, Norfolk with Philip Trower, a fellow writer; gradually drew closer to the faith of his childhood and returned to the Catholic Church ("His conversion involved both a rejection of his homosexual lifestyle and a withdrawal from the world of literary ambition" (Gregory Wolfe)); after his return to the Church he remained as a faithful practicing Catholic and lived a platonic life of friendship with Philip Trower; the subject and style of his work changed as far back as 1945; he now wrote fine religious verse, but his poetry stopped being accepted for publication, and he was forgotten; continued to write and lived a quiet and retired life; he gave instructions that his early poetry was not to be reprinted; buried in the cemetery at Cley-next-the-Sea; see *Poems* (1943); *Lament for the Sleepwalker* (1947); *The Phoenix in the Desert* (1951) (travel book); Letter to George Rock, 13 June 1953 ("I began to read the Gospels - all four. I used the translation by Monsignor Ronald Knox, because it was in understandable English and wasn't printed in two columns and with every sentence made into a separate paragraph. As I read, it became perfectly clear to me that Jesus Christ had said that He was

God, had acted as only God could act, had been put to death by the Jews for saying that He was God, and had been accepted by his disciples as God. It also became clear to me that He spoke with an authority which one would expect God made man to speak with. His personality, his whole character, were unique. One could find no one comparable. I was convinced that He was God.

When I realized that, I realized that what He said was vital. He was extremely clear about a great many things. He said that He had come to call sinners, not the just, that there was more joy in heaven over one sinner who repented than over ninety-nine just men; He told the parable of the prodigal son. He said that of His own free will He was giving His life for us. He said that He would rise from the dead. He said that He was founding a church to last to the end of time and that He chose one of his followers to be the rock on which that church would be built. He told him to 'feed my sheep', to confirm his brethren. This same follower denied him three times. After dying and rising from the dead, He three times asked that follower if he loved Him. It was impossible to overlook the preeminent position which that follower, Saint Peter, occupied in the Gospels, just as it is impossible to overlook the pre-eminent position which the Church, which he was the first bishop of in Rome, occupies in history and occupies today.

I read the history of the Church. That there were bad popes was not surprising; the first one had denied Our Lord three times. That there were bad people in the Church - sometimes in high positions - was not surprising; after all, there is the parable of the wheat and cockle. What was surprising, and humanly speaking incomprehensible, was the extraordinary life of the Church. Again and again persecuted and left for dead, still flourishing all over the world. And the quality of that life; at every moment from the beginning, men and women leading lives of such remarkable goodness and heroism, willing, happy even, to suffer and die for their faith. And these people of every sort and condition; simple and brilliant, rich and poor. It was the lives of the saints which helped to open my eyes to what was going on all around me - priests, nuns, lay people, all spending themselves for others and for God in circumstances and conditions which the world dreads. And then the tone of voice with which the Church spoke today as always, it was the same tone of loving authority which Our Lord used for His followers.

I also read books of philosophy and theology. I made a try at reading the *Summa*, but my lazy mind boggled at the form it is written in, and I took the easier way of a four volume As I read a four volume *Companion to the Summa* by Fr. Walter Farrell, an American Dominican, who uses modern examples to demonstrate St Thomas's teaching. As I read, the feeling grew that this was just plain common sense; black is different from white, events have causes, men are not animals...

The three ways, then, were praying, reading the Gospels, and reading everything I could get hold of on the history and teaching of the Church, with special attention to the lives of the Saints.

So far so good. Reason told me that God exists, that Jesus Christ was God, that He founded a Church, that the Catholic Church is His Church. Well, what was I waiting for?

I believed everything - and yet I didn't believe that God meant what He said. Or rather I didn't believe that He meant it for me. He said: 'If you love Me keep my commandments,' and He meant all ten. But how could I keep them? And yet God who gave those commandments also made me; there are no special cases; the commandments had every man ever to exist in view. Comb the Gospels as I might, there was no out. Just as Our Lord didn't say: 'I am founding several churches, and any one of them will do,' so He didn't say: 'There are exceptional people who can love Me without keeping My commandments.'

For a long time I had prayed that I might meet a good priest, someone like St Philip Neri, the apostle of Rome (in the 16th century). By 'chance' one afternoon in London I dropped into a church; there was a sermon, and I stayed to listen. The priest was old, rocked back and forth in the pulpit, talked about the love of God, mentioned St Bernard. As I listened and watched, I thought 'He seems to be a good man.' When I went out, I looked for his name on the notice board.

I had been saying the rosary every day for some months. As I was doing so one evening, I realized that the next day was the feast of All Saints and I decided to go to mass - as it was a holy day of obligation.' On the way back from mass. I thought; 'Every Sunday is a day of obligation too,' and all at once I knew that I must trust God, go to Confession, and lead a Catholic life.

I telephoned the priest I had listened to in the church three or four months before. He said he would see me and I went to London. I encouraged myself on the train by thinking that even the boldest men would not fancy having to confess their sins for the past seventeen years and that it wasn't surprising that I didn't like the idea one bit. I had a good lunch, went into the church and prayed, and then called at the presbytery.

God had answered my prayers and sent me to a very holy priest. I talked to him for a moment about meaningless things, and then said that I wanted to go to Confession. I did so, and when he gave me absolution, it was the happiest moment in my life. When I left, he told me to trust God and not to be afraid"); *The Dove With the Bough of Olive* (1954) (novel); *Poems* 1950-1974 (1984); Philip Trower, *Dunstan*

Thompson: A Memoir (2009) ("Of his parents Dunstan used to say that they would both have died for their faith 'but would have mounted the scaffold from different sides,' which was an observation about their differences of temperament rather than about their religion. The father was a good, intelligent and necessarily well disciplined man, while his mother was highly strung, nervous and emotional...

Because of his father's upbringing and Washington connections, from the time he was a small boy he was used not only to a somewhat cosmopolitan family atmosphere where French was often spoken (though he himself never became a fluent French speaker) but to meeting the higher clergy of the Washington-Baltimore area, kissing the rings of cardinals and archbishops, serving their masses, hearing higher ecclesiastical chitchat, and taking part in frequent religious services. Before he was twelve he had been three times to Europe, including Rome, where he was present at the canonizations of St Joan of Arc and St. Thérèse of Lisieux and met the reigning Pope, Pius XI...

The recovery of his faith and return to Catholic practice took place in 1952. After discussing with me what it involved, he went up to London to see a Jesuit priest [Fr. William Peers Smith] at the Church of the Immaculate Conception in Farm St, made his confession and was reconciled...

Perhaps I should add that with 'lapsed Catholics' there is usually a difference between those who have given up the practice of their faith for intellectual reasons and those with whom it is mainly a matter of morals. The former really do no longer believe. It all seems unreal and untrue. With the latter belief may have been damaged but will not necessarily have gone altogether. There will often be an underlying intention to return 'eventually' or 'if and when it becomes possible'. Dunstan belonged to the latter category.

Although his decision initially took me by surprise, looking back I can now see signs which, had I been more familiar with the way Catholics think, would have indicated to me the direction in which his mind and heart were moving. But ever since I first knew him his conversation had always been full of references to things Catholic if only because they had been so much part of his boyhood and youth. His talking about them a lot, or being interested in them, did not necessarily indicate any notable change of mind.

Among the things he used to mention about the time when he was a GI in London during the war was going into Farm St. Church to have masses said for his father after his father's death.

Then there was our trip to Rome in 1950. 1950 was a Jubilee Year and he had read that on 1st November Pius XII was going to proclaim the Assumption of Our

Lady a dogma of the Church. This, I later realised, had been his main reason for wanting to make the trip.

Back home I missed a still bigger clue to what lay ahead. From the time we moved to Norfolk in 1948 he had taken an increasing interest in the little town of Walsingham nine miles from where we were living.

Down to the end of the middle ages, Walsingham had been the site of one of the greatest shrines in Europe in honor of the Blessed Virgin. Destroyed by Henry VIII and his agents in the 16th century, the devotion had been revived in the 1920s both among Catholics and high Anglicans. The ruins of the original shrine are now in the grounds of a large country house. But the Anglicans have a modern shrine in the village, and the Catholics a medieval chapel, known as the Slipper Chapel, a mile outside. After his return to the Church, we were often at Walsingham either for Mass or to help with pilgrimages in some way"); Gregory Wolfe, "Dunstan Thompson: Underground Poet," *Hillside Review*, Fall 1986; Philip Trower, "A Phoenix in a Desert: Dunstan Thompson," *Saint Austin Review*, May/June 2008, p.4 (reprinted in the set of essays edited by Powell and Prufer, see below) ("The years after Harvard were the years of his public success as a poet and writer. But by 1948, throwing off the Faith was proving not to be the intoxicating access to freedom and happiness which it had seemed to promise at first"); D. A. Powell and Kevin Prufer (ed), *Dunstan Thompson: On the Life and Work of a Lost American Master* (2010); Gregory Wolfe, "The Poetry of Exile," *Image*, Summer 2011 (also available at *dustinthompson.co.uk*) ("Both sets of poems, early and later, are the work of the same man, but a man in different circumstances and a different frame of mind. In the first it is a bit as though we were hearing the voice of a man running around in a forest fire, while in the second it is the voice of the same man after he has reached safety and has had time to reflect on his experience and the surrounding world in relative tranquillity.

Or exaggerating a bit and using another image it is not unlike moving from listening to Stravinsky's *Rite of Spring* to Bach's *48 Preludes and Fugues*.

To quote Eliot, having found 'the still centre of the turning world', it is from this point that Thompson is now able to celebrate its mysteries, sing of its wonders, lament its tragedies or launch darts and javelins at any follies and misdeeds of the inhabitants that attract his attention").

Tiernan, Frances (Christine) (*née* Fisher) (*pseud.* Christian Reid) – novelist ; b. 5 July 1846, Salisbury, North Carolina; c. 1868 (received with her sister; her brother was received earlier); d. 24 March 1920, Salisbury, North Carolina; member of an aristocratic

Southern family; father, Charles Frederic Fisher, president of the Western North Carolina Railroad, was a Confederate officer killed at the Battle of Bull Run; her mother, Elizabeth Ruth Caldwell Fisher, died early; she was brought up by an aunt Christine Fisher, a recluse and an occasional writer who in the 1850s converted to Catholicism from the Episcopal faith; educated primarily at home; "aristocratic and aloof in manner"; supported herself by writing rather formalized "polite literature"; wrote a series of five "plantation novels", romances about the South before the Civil War; in 1879 traveled for a year in Europe; in 1887 married James Marquis Tiernan (d. 1898), a widowed land speculator; they moved to Mexico; spent time in the West Indies and the Dominican Republic; all of her traveling was reflected in the themes of her novels; after her husband's death she returned to North Carolina; active with the Daughters of the Confederacy; raised funds for the Jefferson Davis monument in Richmond, Virginia, and a monument to the Confederate dead; believing that reading was a means of moral enlightenment, she established two Catholic women's reading circles; in 1909 she was awarded the *Laetare* Medal by the University of Notre Dame; forty-six published works, most of them novels and short stories; see (selective list) *Valerie Aylmer* (1870); *Morton House* (1871); *Mable Lee* (1872), *Nina's Atonement and Other Stories* (1873) (conversion theme); *A Daughter of Bohemia* (1874); *Hearts and Hands* (1875); *A Question of Honor* (1875); *"The Land and the Sky"; or, Adventures on Mountain By-ways* (1876) (travel sketch of the back country of western North Carolina); *After Many Days* (1877); *Bonny Kate* (1878); *Hearts of Steel* (1883); *Armine* (1884); *Carmela* (1891); *A Comedy of Elopement* (1893); *The Land of the Sun* (1894); *A Woman of Fortune* (1896); *The Picture of Las Cruces* (1896; *Lady of Las Cruces* (1896); *The Man of the Family* (1897); *The Chase of an Heiress* (1898); *Weighed in the Balance* (1900); *Under the Southern Cross* (1900) (her only play); *A Daughter of the Sierra* (1903); *The Chase of an Heiress* (1898) *Princess Nadine* (1908); *A Coin of Sacrifice* (1909) (a religious short story); *The Light of Vision* (1911); Kate Harbes Becker, *Biography of Christian Reid* (1941); Patrick Allitt, *Catholic Converts: British and American Intellectuals Turn to Rome* (1997), pp.129-132; *novelguide.com*; *ANB* ("Guided by a firm sense of morality, Tiernan typically wrote of the refined, cultured class, creating gentle, unaffected, modest women and intelligent, highly respected men. A romantic, she depicted not necessarily what life was but what it might be. Her descriptive power was probably her greatest strength as a writer, followed by her ability to create a tale filled with dramatic incident. Her novels, although initially quite popular, are generally admired today as period pieces, and several of her later works, including *Carmela, A Woman of Fortune*, and *A Daughter of the Sierra*, according to critic Archibald Henderson, are marred by 'religious propagandizing'").

Tillotson, Robert Beverley, CSP – priest; b. 23 October 1825, New York City; c. 1848 (received by Newman); d. 31 August 1868, New York City; his father, Robert Tillotson, was "a gentleman of fortune"; brought up as an Episcopalian; studied at Saint Paul's College, Flushing, Long Island; entered the Episcopal General Theological Seminary, lower Manhattan, became a Tractarian, being especially attracted to Newman's writings, and left the General; went on to Oxford and became a Catholic; lived on his father's estate on the Hudson 1848-1851, unsure of what to do with his life; in 1851 he returned to England and joined Newman's Oratory; ordained to the priesthood on 21 September 1856; granted a leave of absence in 1859 and returned to New York, never returning; he met the newly formed Paulists and informed the Oratorians that he wished to join the Paulists, doing so formally in 1860; much parish work; fine preacher, confessor and convert-maker; had chronic ill health and died of tuberculosis; buried in the "Cathedral vault" at Old Saint Patrick's Church, Manhattan, New York; see *Paulist Archives* ("[Father Deshon] told us of [Tillotson's] preaching, how after Father Baker, it was the favorite of the people of the parish. He told us of his beautiful qualities as a confessor, how patient, sympathetic, wise and understanding he was. He spoke of his care for the sick, being himself never a well man. He also described his convert-making, his private interviews with enquirers, his wisdom, prudence and persistent zeal").

Tincker, Mary Agnes ("M.A.T.") – novelist; b. 18 July 1833, Ellsworth, Maine; c. 1855; d. 4 December 1907, Dorchester, Massachusetts; father, a descendant of Thomas Tincker of the Mayflower, was deputy sheriff, then high sheriff, of Hancock County, and warden of the Maine state prison; brought up a Congregationalist; at the age of thirteen she began teaching in the public schools; at fifteen her first literary work was printed in anonymous newspaper and magazine fiction; she was so shocked by an incident in which a Catholic priest was tarred-and-feathered by a mob of Know-Nothing agitators, that the incident became central to her conversion to Catholicism; worked as a volunteer nurse during the Civil War until she fell ill; on recovering she went to live in Boston and concentrated on journalistic and literary work; she wrote short stories for *The Catholic World* and her earliest novels at this time; in 1873 went to Europe, visiting France, England and Spain, and lived in Italy (in Rome) for many years; became a celebrated novelist during this period; in 1887 returned to the United States; frequently dealt with the themes of death and criminality; unmarried; see The *House of Yorke* (1872); *A Winged World and Other Sketches and Stories* (1873); *Grapes and Thorns, Or, A Priest's Sacrifice* (1874); *Six Sunny Months* (1878); *Signor Monaldini's Niece* (1879); *By the Tiber* (1881); *The Jewel in the Lotus* (1884); *Aurora* (1885); *The Two Coronets* (1887); *San Salvador* (1889); *Autumn Leaves* (1898); Patrick Allitt, *Catholic Converts: British and American Intellectuals Turn to Rome* (1997), pp.133-134; *Catholic Encyclopedia* ("A lapse from the practice of her religion cast its shadow perhaps over a few of her novels written at that time [late 1880s]. She returned to her religious duties many years before her death"); *novelguide.com.*

Tisquantum – see under Squanto.

Toklas, Alice B. (born Alice Babette Toklas) – literary figure; b. 30 April 1877, San Francisco, California; d. 7 March 1967, Paris, France; born into a middle-class Jewish family; descended from Polish immigrants; first child and only daughter of her parents, Ferdinand and Emma (Levinsky) Toklas; after private schools she studied piano for a short time at the University of Washington; went to Paris, meeting Gertrude Stein (1874-1946), the writer, poet and art collector, on the day she arrived, 8 September 1907; they lived together and hosted one of the liveliest literary and artistic salons in Paris from 1907 until Stein's death; it attracted avant-garde painters (e.g., Picasso, Matisse and Braque) and expatriate Americans (e.g., Ernest Hemingway (see above), F. Scott Fitzgerald and Thornton Wilder); scores of other artists, writers and musicians attended; she wrote personal books, plus articles for newspapers and magazines; later on had poor health and financial problems (died in poverty); became a Catholic in her old age; buried next to Gertrude Stein in Père Lachaise Cemetery, Paris, France (there is no gravestone on her bare plot, but her name appears on the back of Stein's marker); see *The Alice B. Toklas Cookbook* (1954) (reminiscences and recipes, including the famous recipe for hashish fudge); *Aromas and Flavors of Past and Present* (1958); *What Is Remembered* (1963) (autobiography); Gertrude Stein, *The Autobiography of Alice B. Toklas* (1933) (Stein's memoirs written in the style of Toklas); Edward Burns (ed), *Staying On Alone: Letters of Alice B. Toklas* (1973); Samuel M. Steward (ed), *Dear Sammy: Letters from Gertrude Stein and Alice B. Toklas* (1977); Harriet Levy, *920 O'Farrell Street* (1947); Linda Simon, *The Biography of Alice B. Toklas* (1977);

Anna Linzie, *The True Story of Alice B. Toklas: A Study of Three Autobiographies* (2006); Janet Malcolm, *Two Lives: Gertrude and Alice* (2008); her papers are at the Harry Ransom Humanities Research Center, University of Texas, Austin, and the Beinecke Library, Yale University; *ANB*.

Troide, Lars Eleon - Professor of English; b. 15 June 1942, Stamford, Connecticut; c. 22 March 2008 (Easter Vigil; received by Bishop Paul-André Durocher); d. 10 September 2013, Cornwall, Ontario, Canada; both parents born in Sweden and raised as Lutherans, emigrating separately to the United States; given a strong moral education by his mother and confirmed in the Lutheran faith; slowly drifted away from religious practice; graduated in English Literature from Yale University in 1964 (by this time a confirmed agnostic); completed an MA at Columbia University in 1967; editor of the correspondence of Horace Walpole (1717-1797) at Yale University 1968-1973; became a Unitarian; received his PhD from Yale University in 1976; appointment at McGill University, Montreal, from 1976, culminating in Professorship in English Literature; editor of the correspondence of Fanny Burney (1752-1840) at McGill; two U.S. National Endowment for the Humanities Research Fellowships (1980 and 1998); became disturbed by a strongly anti-Christian element in the Unitarian Church and joined the United Church, the most liberal of the Protestant Christian denominations in Canada, though never felt really complete there; the death of his wife Teresa ("Tess"), *née* Marganska (1949-2005), plunged him into despair and he looked again at the ultimate questions in life; Catholic memories from childhood, relatives and Polish Catholic parents-in-law came back to him ("I remembered being intrigued by, and at some level probably mildly jealous of, the ritual aspects of Catholicism I had seen, in or out of church: the sign of the cross, the incense, the rosary beads, the Hail Mary, the bells, the Latin, etc."); also affected by the kindness of Catholics at times of crisis in his life; "a highly personal reason was that I had lost my wife, Tess, of thirty-seven years, and the faith assured me that I could pray for her soul (and vice versa); in 2010 married Mercy (Mercedes) San Agustin; see "My Winding Road to Rome," in *Canadian Converts: The Path to Rome* (2009) ("Finally my intellectual questions began to resolve themselves into a few basic choices: either the universe is random, or it is meaningful. Either there is a Creator, or there is not. If there is a Creator, the Creator is either impersonal, or personal. I gradually began to see that the scientific skepticism that had burdened me for so many decades was just as much a matter of belief as any of the faiths so scorned by Richard Dawkins and his fellow neo-atheists. I began to see that in fact belief in a Creator was far more *reasonable* than belief in a random, impersonal universe that had somehow miraculously sprung out of nothing (the Big Bang), ordered itself and then produced personality, self-awareness, conscience, *love.* I began to believe in a personal, loving God that I had pushed away for so many years but who had pursued me down the decades, 'the Hound of Heaven'...In short, I rediscovered the God of Love, the Christian God, the Revealed Holy Trinity of God the Father, God the Son, and God the Holy Spirit...

Of course there were problems I had to deal with before my conversion, such as the priestly abuse scandal that had exploded in 2002. But I came to realize that such things (like the Spanish Inquisition, also tossed at me by knee-jerk anti-Catholics) are the result of human sinfulness, and not caused by any of the intrinsic doctrines of the Church. The Catholic world-view in fact holds together beautifully, unlike the multiple and conflicting views of the 20,000 (and counting) Protestant denominations. As for multiplicity, a United Church minister, writing recently in the *Ottawa Citizen*, has even opined that 'there are as many Christianities as there are Christians.' In *my* opinion such radically subjective 'theology' is madness, and little different from New Age cafeteria-style spirituality, where the individual in effect cherry-picks those beliefs which are 'comfortable.' For example: God is all-loving and all-merciful, so there is no hell and we are all saved, no matter what (but where is the God of Justice?). *Sola Fides*, 'once saved, always saved'; therefore it doesn't matter what we do once we believe in Jesus (but what happens, then, to the necessity for good works so often underscored in the Scriptures?).

Besides *Sola Fides*, I began to understand the problems with Luther's other reforms, such as the concept of *Sola Scriptura.* Luther in effect ignored or tried to explain away the fact that the New Testament scriptures arose out of the sacred oral tradition, which therefore in its later written form cannot be ignored for purposes of interpretation. As for the Old Testament, because certain of the 'deuterocanonical' books did not agree with his 'personal revelation,' he simply subtracted them from the canon. When I finally came to the Catholic Church, I discovered all seven of the sacraments instituted by Christ Himself; as a Lutheran I had known only two. As for the Catholic liturgy, suddenly I understood that everything, *everything*, in it made sense. Those mysterious bells, that incense, the vestments, the genuflections, the Gregorian chants: these were not superstitious mumbo-jumbo, as I once had been taught to think, but were all beautifully designed to elevate the soul to God. In sum, I had found 'the fullness of the faith,' the *original*, *true* faith, a faith that was practiced daily, and everywhere, and that was indeed 'catholic,' that is, universal.

Of course, many of these revelations would only come *after* my conversion. But the clincher, the single argument that motivated me most to make my move, was the defense [by a Polish friend] of the concept of Purgatory, 'subtracted' by Luther when he jettisoned the Deuterocanonical Books. It makes such sense that almost no one at death is pure enough to be in the presence of God, and that a spiritual purification is necessary. I thought of Tess, who had left the One True Church and had not yet found her way back into it at her death. I had felt such helplessness, such impotence as a husband as she lay dying. I now know that her awful suffering was her purgatory on earth, and that I now can pray for her departed soul and by my own faithfulness hasten her into the Beatific Vision, wherever she may be now. Such empowerment! Such joy!

In general, perhaps what persuades me most of the truth of the Holy Roman Catholic Church is the magisterial authority of its readings of the Scriptures. As I suggest above, the Protestant emphasis on the individual's interpreting the Scriptures by himself has led to an endless wasteland of error. No one person, however intelligent and learned (like Luther), is capable of understanding by his own lights the Scriptures' incredible riches and subtleties. Only the magisterium of the Church, informed by the early Church Fathers right down to the latest encyclicals of the Pope, can make proper sense of the Divine Word of God. And, most important, a proper reading of the Scriptures affirms the astounding truth of the Real Presence of Christ in the Eucharist, and the profound truth of the apostolic succession, whereby only a Catholic priest or bishop can enable this transubstantiation"); Letter to John Beaumont, ("When I came to the Catholic Faith I felt that I had found at last the Rock of Peter, and hoped that I had left behind forever the shifting sands of my Protestant origins. But I soon discovered how mistaken I was. Especially in the wake of Vatican II, I found a too broad diversity of opinion in the Church – doctrinally disputatious bishops, revisionist or 'progressive' or heretical theologians (Hans Kung and Teilhard de Chardin spring to mind), renegade 'feminist' nuns, lapsed cradle Catholic laity who no longer practiced their faith at all, and so on. Encountering 'Catholics' who are 'pro-choice' (a euphemism if ever there was one), I thought to myself, 'Why do such people even consider themselves still to be Catholics, especially when they could join any number of Protestant denominations that favor such things: abortion, contraception, women priests, married priests, gay "marriage," etc., etc.?' I realized that, for some, conversion to another faith was unthinkable: 'Once a Catholic, always a Catholic.' But, at a deeper level, I believe that, beyond a certain point, attempting to reform the Church from within, without full acknowledgment of the authority of the Pope and the magisterium, is a form of pride or *hubris*. Our Church is blessed with a teaching magisterium that has grown over two millennia, and with popes such as John Paul II and Benedict XVI who are truly wise and holy men. Radical opposition to pope and magisterium is, in my opinion, grave error or sin...

Indeed, while acknowledging the need for some *non-doctrinal* accommodations to the modern world, I find myself more and more drawn to certain pre-Vatican II practices. What I missed in the Protestant world was the vertical dimension. So many Protestant congregations and denominations have become exclusively this-worldly, addressing social rather than spiritual issues. With regard to pre-Vatican II practices, I would prefer, for example, that the priest face the Blessed Sacrament, rather than *me*. And I love the Latin rite, while recognizing that mass goers should be instructed as to what the Latin words *mean* (perhaps by way of bilingual lectionaries). I don't like priests going about in 'civilian clothes' outside the Church. They (and nuns) should always witness the Faith by their dress. And so on.

To conclude: I did not convert to the Catholic Church simply to find it becoming just another Protestant denomination. Fidelity to scripture and the oral tradition is not negotiable. The Pope, not Hans Kung or Teilhard de Chardin, is God's vicar. So be it")'

Tyler, Julia Gardiner – United States First Lady; b. 4 May 1820, Gardiner's Island, off Long Island, New York; c. 1872 (her daughter Pearl Tyler-Ellis (1860-1947), then twelve years old, converted with her mother); d. 10 July 1889, Richmond, Virginia; from a wealthy family; her father was David Gardiner, a lawyer and New York State Senator 1824-1828; received the best education; second wife of John Tyler (1790-1862), tenth President of the United States, thirty years older than her; introduced to John Tyler in early 1842; Tyler's first wife, Letitia Christian Tyler, died 10 September 1842; she began seeing Tyler in January 1843; her father was killed by the explosion of a naval gun and Tyler comforted her in her grief; she agreed to a secret engagement; they were married on 26 June 1844; she was First Lady of the United States until 4 March 1845; they had seven children, including Lyon Gardiner Tyler (1853-1935), the educator and historian; her husband had eight children from his first marriage, making him the most prolific President; they managed a large plantation; she publicly defended slavery in an essay in 1853; she espoused the principles of the South in the Civil War; the Panic of 1873 depleted her fortunes; after her conversion she remained a devout Catholic for the rest of her life; buried next to her husband at Hollywood Cemetery, Richmond, Virginia; Robert Seager II, *And Tyler Too: A Biography of John and Julia Gardiner Tyler* (1963); Theodore C. DeLaney, "Julia Gardiner Tyler: A Nineteenth-century Southern Woman" (PhD dissertation, College of William and Mary, 1995); *ANB* ("Like other southerners, Tyler clearly believed that black slaves were better off than white wage laborers of Europe and the northern United States. She admonished English ladies to direct their benevolence to peasants in their own land. Tyler's defense of slavery was also noteworthy for its affirmation of southern womanhood. She asserted that English ladies had stepped outside of their proper sphere, something that southern women would never do…

Tyler remained loyal to the southern cause but was ready to see the wounds of the nation healed by 1870…Her reconciliatory attitude resulted from a profound religious conversion. In 1872, amid much publicity, she joined the Roman Catholic Church after being influenced by Jesuit priest Patrick Healy, later president of Georgetown University…She remained faithful to the Catholic Church until the day of her death").

Tyler, William – bishop; b. 5 June 1806, Derby, Vermont; c. 1821 or 1822; d. 18 June 1849, Providence, Rhode Island; father was a farmer; mother was the daughter of Daniel Barber (see above) and sister of Virgil Horace Barber (see above); grew up in New Hampshire; studied theology in Boston, Massachusetts, in the household of Bishop Fenwick; ordained to the priesthood 3 June 1829; in November 1843 appointed the first Bishop of the new diocese of Hartford, Connecticut (which covered the whole of Connecticut and Rhode Island) by Pope Gregory XVI; moved his residence to Providence, Rhode Island, which had more Catholics; suffered from poor health and died early; Richard Henry Clarke, "Right Rev. William Tyler, DD" in *Lives of the Deceased Bishops of the Catholic Church in the United States* (1888), p.272.

Vanauken, Sheldon (born Sheldon Frank Van Auken) ("Van") – author; b. 4 August 1914, Auburn, Indiana; c. 15 August 1981, Portsmouth Abbey, Rhode Island (received by Dom Julian Stead, OSB); d. 28 October 1996; son of a wealthy lawyer and state senator; attended several military academies; took his undergraduate degree from Wabash College in 1938; while there he met Jean "Davy" Palmer Davis (25 July 1914-28 January 1955), who had had a child at the age of fourteen, whom she named Marion and gave up for adoption; they fell in love and married secretly; he studied at Yale University and received a masters degree in 1948; they were agnostics then; they moved to England so that he could study at Oxford University; awarded BLitt degree in 1967; they became friends with a group of young Christians and with C. S. Lewis; both became Anglicans, he with some reluctance; she contracted a virus and died; his acclaimed book, *A Severe Mercy* (winner of seven awards), recounts his struggle after the death of his wife, his correspondence and friendship with Lewis, and his increasing Christian faith; eventually looked for and in 1988 met the daughter his wife had given for adoption; spent most of his career teaching English and History at Lynchburg College, Virginia; critic of the Vietnam war; supporter of the feminist movement, but abandoned it, believing that it had become too extreme ("My insight… experimentally proved again and again, that the presence of even one woman in a male group – and the confirmation by women that the presence of even one man in a female group – alters the character of that group whatever its raison d'être established for me the falsity of the feminist insistence that men and women are, apart from a few physical irregularities, identical"); drawn to the High Church, but came to believe that Anglicanism was not part of the Catholic Church and converted to Rome; after his conversion he was a contributing editor to *New Oxford Review*; writer of numerous articles and poems; sympathetic to the Confederacy in the Civil War; he was also a great Anglophile; after his death his ashes were scattered in the churchyard of St. Stephen's Episcopal Church in Forest, Virginia (where his wife's had been scattered on her death); see (selective list) *A Severe Mercy* (1977); *Gateway to Heaven* (1980) (novel); "The English Channel," *New Oxford Review*, March 1981, p.9 (written while still an Anglican) ("The spires of Oxford, long ago, directed my thoughts successively to two great questions. Although nominally an Anglican, a 'highchair Anglican' (as one says 'Cradle Catholic'), I was, in fact, a vaguely theistic agnostic. It had never occurred to me, not since childhood, to *believe* in fairies at the bottom of the garden or all that old stuff about Jesus's being the Son of God. But now I suddenly saw that the towers and spires of Oxford had been raised in heart-lifting beauty by men who *had* believed: and I perceived that the question - the Question of Jesus - that I had never asked had got to be answered: Was Jesus, in fact, God? God incarnate crying forsaken upon the Cross? I saw that the world might hinge upon this Question. Thus I became 'an Anglican with leanings towards Christianity' by setting myself, as I have told in my book, *A Severe Mercy*, to finding the answer. Here

I need say only that, after much writhing about, I finally answered: Yea, my Lord and my God.

Not long after this life-&-death affirmation, being now astonishingly a Christian, I realized that if the towers and spires of Oxford spoke in stone of deep Christian faith, it was the *Catholic* faith they spoke of. And I perceived that logically a further question followed the Question of Jesus, followed it so logically indeed that I marvel that all converts to the Faith do not at once ask it: If Jesus is God the Son, a fact that very naturally (or very supernaturally) casts a new light upon His words, then what of His words about His Church, founded so clearly upon the Rock that was Peter? What of the mere existence of the Catholic - the Universal - Church, twice as large as all the splinters of Protestantism put together? Twice as large, too, as the faithful Eastern Orthodox, which for centuries had accepted the primacy of the successors of Peter in Rome before the unhappy separation. Rome was the centre of the ancient unity, the centre of Christendom. Logically (and C. S. Lewis had taught me to be logical) the claims of Rome came first, that is, before I as a new Christian could decide whether Anglicanism's *Via Media* or any other separated church was a legitimate offspring and a valid way, I had to decide whether the *Mother* Church - as unmistakably the Mother Church as England is the mother country of English-speaking North America - was exclusively what she has always, whilst empires rose and fell, claimed to be: the *visible* One, Holy, Catholic, & Apostolic Church that Christ founded. Logically that was where one *began*. First things first. I was already an Anglican, loving the Book of Common Prayer; if *any* separated church was legitimate, then I would remain an Anglican. But first, logically, there was the Question of Rome…

I looked at the glorious spire of St. Mary the Virgin there in Oxford, conscious of the missing spire of Osney Abbey, destroyed by the reformers; and I looked at the melancholy ruins of Godstow Nunnery and Tintern Abbey and Great Glastonbury with thoughts about the less-than-inspiring origin of the semi-detached Church of England (hereafter: C of E). I knew of course that we - we Anglicans - asserted daily in the creeds that we believed in (and, hence, were in) that One, Holy, Catholic, & Apostolic Church; and we handsomely admitted that Rome was, too. And we asserted that our church - the 'Bridge Church' or the *Via Media* - had valid apostolic orders and the Catholic Faith, even though we had cleverly seen through the pretensions of the Papacy, which previously, for a thousand years, we had accepted; and we cut off the heads of Sir Thomas More and Bishop Fisher and others who were willing to die for the ancient loyalty. But the fact that our moment of keen insight into the governance of the Catholic Church had come about through a pope's refusing the self-willed Henry VIII, not perhaps a *good* man, a divorce to marry his doxy (a not-uncommon cause of others leaving Christ's Church ever since) didn't suggest a *holy* insight. And I was not persuaded by those who claimed, pointing to Wycliffe and the Sarum Rite, that the C of E had 'really' had an earlier, nobler origin. Not only Sir Thomas More, Saint, but the Pilgrimage of Grace argued against it...

One might suppose from the foregoing that I was near to answering Yea to the Mother Church also. Perhaps I was, but *near* is not *there*. Both Newman's *Apologia* and *Brideshead Revisited* (which one read at Oxford) haunted my mind; and my wise mentor, C. S. Lewis, had instilled in me an essentially Catholic vision of the Church, incidentally making that 'Romish Doctrine concerning Purgatory' (Article XXII of the Thirty-Nine Articles) not only believable in *Great Divorce* but necessary. But, at the same time, Lewis, who had, I presumed, thought deeply on the Question of Rome, remained C of E. And I myself wished the Question of Rome would go away. I loved the C of E: it was at once beautiful and homely: and there was holiness in it. Besides, I was having enough trouble just *being* a Christian without venturing into 'foreign' RC (Roman Catholic) country. I continued, therefore, to follow the beloved Anglican way with one eye upon C. S. Lewis and with occasional bouts of uneasiness.

So the years passed - I was caught up in various kinds of crisis that made deep thought on the matter impossible - but the Question of Rome did not go away. In reading of theological and ecclesiastical disputes I found myself invariably on the Catholic side. The real question for me (as for Newman) was not whether Catholicism was right but whether I as an Anglican *was* a Catholic...

I saw no doctrinal obstacle to becoming Catholic, least of all, as I've said, the Magisterium or the infallibility of the pope in his rare *ex cathedra* pronouncements. It was altogether clear that, just as Christianity itself stood or fell upon whether Jesus was all God as well as all man, so the Catholic Church - defined as the Successor of Peter and all those in communion with him - stood or fell upon whether it was *The* Church, the visible Church that Christ founded. The Question of Rome. What did Christ, doing the will of the Father, *mean* by 'Church' when He said, 'I will build my Church'? Did He mean the Church in the singular or in the ten-thousand-sect plural? He *spoke* of His Church in the singular (and those who believe in an inerrant Bible may well contemplate that singular).

Protestants, to be sure, have an answer: The Church, they say, is the invisible church of the faithful: this is appealing (though it may be confusing the Church and the Kingdom), but the fact that the invisible church was never heard of until after the Protestants broke away, fifteen hundred years after Christ, does rather suggest rationalizing after the fact. I, at all events, could not escape the impression that He did not intend the incredible splintering of Protestantism. Moreover, that very splintering showed the inadequacy of the major Protestant doctrine of *Sola Scriptura* and the necessity of the teaching authority - the Magisterium - of the Church Catholic. Even a relatively simple document like the U.S. Constitution requires a 'Teaching authority', the Supreme Court, to interpret it: How infinitely more does the Bible and the Tradition need it! How *obviously* necessary, if we, many of us, were not blinded by old hostilities! Just as the Apostles under Peter - long before there was a New Testament - interpreted Christ's truth, so their successors, the Bishops under the Successor of Peter, have ever since interpreted that truth. Protestantism (probably the first known instance of throwing out the *mother* with the bath water) has no 'Supreme Court' - hence the continual splintering. The Catholic Church has the Magisterium.

Moreover, although Protestants will not squarely face the fact, we must, if we are to rely upon the New Testament, accept that the Church, which guided by the Holy Spirit defined (chose the canon of) the New Testament, was then infallible. The question, therefore, is not whether the Church can be infallibly guided by the Spirit in matters of Faith (as she has always claimed to be) but, rather, when did the Spirit leave off the infallible guidance - if it did? When men, when popes, became sinful? But when were they not, even Peter? Their fallenness is, precisely why the guidance is needed.

Three arguments in particular convince me that the Holy Spirit did not leave off His guidance of the Church of Peter in matters of the Faith. The first of these concerns that very period that Protestants rightly point to as having the most corrupt of popes: the hardly-Spirit-filled popes of the Avignon 'Captivity' and the Great Schism as well as the not-noticeably-religious popes of the Renaissance who triggered the Protestant revolt. Lots of sin. No question about that - the sin - but the Protestant critics fail to notice the really significant fact: not one of those wicked popes altered doctrine. To this historically-minded sheep, that fact is quite the most remarkable proof that the Holy Spirit was on the job, guiding His Church away from error. In the very year that Henry VIII's obedient Parliament named him head of the English church, Pope Paul III went through the streets of Rome in sackcloth and ashes for the sins of his predecessors -

but not for their errors in doctrine. That is the significant fact: not what the good popes did, but what the bad ones *didn't* do.

The second argument for the continued guidance of the Holy Spirit is the timing of the pronouncement of the long-believed-in doctrine of papal infallibility (the infallible Church saying infallibly that the pope is infallible). Springing from the Tradition, it was formally defined as dogma by Pope and Council a little over a century ago. Newman, though not disagreeing with it, thought the definition 'premature'. That it was not. It was just *before* the unforeseeable inroads of Secularizing Modernism. Imagine the howls from the likes of Hans Küng if it were defined today! As it is the Catholic faithful (and all the faithful everywhere) know that, if need be, out of the depths of Parnassus the oracle will return, into the world: the *ex cathedra* utterance of the Magisterium. The Church has the bomb.

The third indication to me of a Spirit-led Church guided beyond the vision of men is the series of events that made possible the pontificate of John Paul II, the pope we need at this moment of history, the white knight of Christendom. First, following the beloved John, a reserved, seemingly timid and cold pope, Paul VI. Then the cardinals met, determined, it is reported, to choose an elderly pope who wouldn't live too long but would project an image of warmth. Cardinal Wojtyla had no chance—too young and vigorous, as well as non-Italian. The cardinals had their way. John Paul I: warmth indeed, captivating the world; and dead in a month. Now the weary cardinals re-assembling wanted a younger man, and now perhaps a non-Italian. So John Paul II strode forth from behind the Iron Curtain, where, like the early Christians, he had dwelt under the shadow of martyrdom (which wonderfully concentrates the mind upon the Faith), to become the intellectually powerful Defender of the Faith. No mortal - no cardinal - could have foreseen this chain of events that alone could have led to John Paul II: but the Holy Spirit could"); "Crossing the Channel," *Communio*, Spring 1982 ("In the May of 1981, a couple of months after the 'Channel' was published, I went up to Portsmouth Abbey on Rhode Island, a monastery of the English Congregation of the Benedictines, to see my old friend and Confessor, Dom Julian...At the Abbey in late May, Dom Julian and I had been visited by Peter Kreeft [see above]...and Tom Howard [see above]. We were all four writers, two Catholics and Tom and me, Anglicans...In the course of the discussion Peter suddenly said; 'I have a question for Tom and Van. If you knew you were going to die tomorrow, what would you do about the Church?' Tom hesitated; but I said instantly: 'I should ask Julian to. receive me into the

Catholic Church.' I was faintly surprised at my own certainty, but then I added: 'Because, you know, if I were going to die, I should be leaving St Stephen's anyway.'

Now at home that question and my reply came back to me. I hadn't thought much about it at the time, but now it occurred to me that I had, in fact, suggested to God a way to bring me to decision: perhaps I had best decide on my own first. 'Not to decide *is* to decide.' To decide by drift. Then it came to me that perhaps I could go on drifting, but, if I faced up to decision, I could not *reject* Holy Mother Church – just as, long years before, I had realized that I could not reject Jesus. But if I cannot reject the Church, that means that only one way is now possible, for I couldn't finally choose Anglicanism without rejecting the Catholic Church. (I, at least, cannot go on drifting unless I can persuade myself that either way is possible.) Therefore, if I *cannot* reject the Church – if only one way is possible – I *have* decided, haven't I?"); "The Knight's Move," *Fidelity Magazine*, 1983 ("Eventually I wrote an essay, 'The English Channel'...showing that intellectually, for me, the road led to Rome: that, despite all counter-arguments, Holy Mother Church was the Church founded by Christ upon the Rock that was Peter. But for an Anglican (C of E or Episcopal), unlike other Protestants, there is another question: is he *already* a Catholic? is he *in* the Church? After all, when England broke with Rome back in the troubled 16th century, it retained and still retains in unbroken succession its bishops and archbishops: is it, as some insist, still Catholic? That is the peculiar Anglican difficulty - the 'English Channel' of my title. But I came to see that it is the Chair of Peter that is the mark of the Catholic Church, the essence of Catholicity: where *it* is, is the Catholic Church. To break with it is to cease to be Catholic. Moreover, I saw that, just as the U.S. Constitution, short as it is, needs a Supreme Court to interpret it, so the enormous complexities of Scripture and Tradition desperately need a supreme court to preserve the true Faith against what Newman called 'the energy of human skepticism,' which has led to the incredible splintering of Protestantism into thousands of sects. But the Catholic Church *has* that 'supreme court': the Magisterium. So, despite pain at leaving my homely and dear Anglicanism, I was received into Holy Church...My Channel essay was graced with another chapter, 'Crossing the Channel'"); *The Glittering Illusion: English Sympathy for the Southern Confederacy* (1985); *Under the Mercy* (1985) (an account of the three decades following the death of his wife and including the text of several of his most important articles) ("Before he submitted to Rome, John Henry Newman, leader of the Oxford Movement, published in 1841 his 'Tract 90,' demonstrating that the 39 Articles of the Church of England are quite consonant with Catholic belief. The ensuing storm was the prelude to his becoming a Catholic. So, since 'The English Channel' (the first part, now called 'The White Cliffs') was written a year before I even knew that I would submit to Rome and was published in an Anglican journal, causing a certain amount of shock and controversy of its own, I can't help but think of it as *my* 'Tract 90'.

The English Channel of my title is not only that body of water – the Narrow Seas – that separates England physically and spiritually from Europe, it is, figuratively, what separates Anglicans (whether Church of England or Episcopalian) from the Catholic Church under the successor to Peter. Or, more succinctly, what separates Canterbury from Rome. It is the *English* Channel"); "Encounter With Light," in Robert Baram (ed), Spiritual Journeys (revised edition, 1988), p.331; "The English Channel: Between Canterbury and Rome," in Dan O'Neill (ed), *The New Catholics: Contemporary Catholics Tell their Stories* (1987), p.122 (a revised version of "The English Channel" and "Crossing the Channel"); *Mercies: Collected Poems* (1988); "Choosing a Church," *New Oxford Review*, April 1993 ("In my account of becoming Catholic…in my *Under the Mercy*, I said, almost as an aside since it seemed obvious: 'Choosing a church is not like choosing a suit or a house, a matter of taste and comfort. A little matter of truth.'

But it wasn't obvious, even with the remark about truth. A number of readers wrote to me, asking innocently and plaintively, 'Why isn't it like choosing a house to live in?' What they were saying or implying was something like this: 'If we all believe in the Risen Christ, what difference does it make whether we are Baptists or Episcopalians, Presbyterians or Catholics? Isn't it just a matter of taste and comfort if we're all Christians hoping for Heaven?' What was implicit in all the questions was the idea that the Catholic Church is just one of the multitude of 'churches' or, more accurately, sects.

But a sect, the dictionary says, is 'in religion: a party dissenting from an established or parent church.' The Catholic Church is the original Mother Church - not a sect. Not 'a church,' but *the* Church. Christ (Mt. 16) spoke of His *Church* - not churches. The creeds spoke of one holy catholic Church (*catholic* means *universal*). But if there is one holy universal Church, there can be no other churches.

So it was for a thousand years, and then - basically because of a question of authority, not doctrine - the Orthodox eastern wing of the Church, where bishops and patriarchs were under the direct control of the Byzantine emperor, drew apart from the West - but still, men in East and West believed in one visible Church and said so in the creeds. (Even today the Pope refers to the Orthodox as 'the other lung' of the one Church.)

Five hundred years later - 1,500 years after Christ - came the Protestant Revolt. Luther, Calvin, Henry VIII, backed by nobles hungry for Church lands, broke away from the universal Church. They left the Church, really. But (understandably) they were reluctant to admit that they were no longer in the one Church of the creeds. They therefore called their broken-off fragments 'churches,' as the Lutheran churches or the Church of England. At the same time they indulged in a masterpiece of rationalizing: The Church in the singular that Christ spoke of, the one catholic Church of the creeds, was *not* the 1,500-year-old visible Catholic Church that they had left - no, no; the Church was an *invisible* church of all the faithful. This idea was and is extremely comforting to the Protestants who today accept it as gospel. The only trouble with it is that it was never heard of until after the fact of breaking away, and there was already a term for all the faithful: the Kingdom of God. But the makers of the creeds had no such idea; they meant the perfectly visible one holy catholic and apostolic Church on earth. And there is not a particle of evidence that Christ, in saying that He would build his Church upon the Rock that was Peter, meant an invisible Church - or churches.

In choosing a church one must take the meaning of 'Church' into consideration. The broken-off fragments were sects. I say this, not to give offense, but to be precise. And the three major sects that splintered off from the Catholic Church continued to splinter - sects of sects - as, for instance, the Methodists broke off from the Anglicans. And the further splintering has gone on so briskly in the four or five centuries since the Protestant Revolt that there are now, according to the *Oxford Encyclopedia of World Christianity* (1982), more than 28,000 sects of varying degrees of Christianity, some like the Mormons hardly Christian at all. But does that mean that the Catholic Church has been reduced to nothing more than a small sect herself? Not at all. The Mother Church is twice as big as all the 28,000 sects put together.

The questioners I began with who asked if we were not all on the road to Heaven if we believed in the Risen Christ, God Incarnate, were right so to ask. The faithful members of the sects may indeed reach Heaven without being Catholics. It isn't their fault they were brought up Protestant (whether Luther and company sinned or not). Still, the question of the meaning of 'Church' may be significant in whether they remain Protestant. And there are other significant considerations.

G. K. Chesterton, who converted from orthodox Anglicanism to the Catholic Church, compares the Church to a great Gothic Cathedral, like the beautiful cathedrals she raised all over Europe. Round the Cathedral are the innumerable meeting houses or tents of the countless sects. But, he says, the one thing, the *only* thing, that gives life and vitality to the sects is what they took with them when they left the Cathedral. They took with them the Faith in the Risen Lord that the Church had spelled out. Some of them took the creeds. And they all took the Bible - what would they be without the New Testament? But not only had the early Church written it, but the Church had selected what was to go into the Testament and what was excluded. That, above all, the Protestants took when they left. And some took her actual churches or copied her architecture and stained glass. Moreover, they took theological ideas that especially appealed to them, sometimes stressing them in an unbalanced way, that is, without the balance of other truths - for instance, long before Calvin, the Church had contemplated the sovereignty of God, but she balanced it with free will. In the 'Cathedral' of the Catholic Church, the truth-seeker is more likely to find balance.

There is, though, a further consideration. When our Lord (Mt. 16) said to Peter, 'You are Peter, the Rock; and on this rock I will build my Church…,' He also said: 'I will give you the keys of the Kingdom of Heaven, and what you forbid on earth shall be forbidden in Heaven…' So it was for Peter, the first head of the Church, and so for the successors of Peter (popes). Catholic and Protestant alike believe Christ to be God Incarnate who rose bodily from the dead, but the Catholic, to be truly Catholic, must then believe one thing more: that the universal Church under the Successor to Peter will be infallibly guided *as a church*, on matters of faith and morals - and what she forbids is forbidden in Heaven. Sinful popes there were, but none attempted to alter faith and morals.

Nevertheless, it is because the break-away Protestants did take so much from the Mother Church that she calls them separated brethren, really Catholics without knowing it - but also without knowing the *fullness* of the Faith. The Catholic Church is not 'just another church' - she is, simply, the Church"); *The Little Lost Marion and Other Mercies* (1996); Jonathan Poletti, "Paths Trod by Sheldon Vanauken," *New Oxford Review*, January-February 1997; Jack Taylor, "Sheldon Vanauken, RIP," *This Rock*, February 1997; David Hartman, "Remembering Van," *New Oxford Review*, October 1997; Chene Richard Heady, "Sheldon Vanauken Remembered," *New Oxford Review*, October 2011 ("He understood, as C. S. Lewis emphatically did not, that in an age in which all truths are subjective, the best apologetic is autobiography, the story of oneself as a human subject. In a real sense, Vanauken's most powerful case for the faith is Vanauken himself... Throughout his work, he is both symptom and diagnostician of the illness of his times, as he narrates how his own widely varied life coheres only when centered around an eternal Faith. This is his basic apologetic, the underlying story even of *A Severe Mercy*...

Faith saves us from both our own follies and the follies of the age. In a nihilist era, it offers a poetic vision of the universe as a work of art - beautiful, measured, and true. Vanauken anathematizes liberal religion because he sees it as (often unconsciously) reversing this process, vandalizing the ancient poetry of faith so that it mimics a world seemingly devoid of beauty, order, or truth. Liberalizing (or 'neo-Modernist') Churches thus leave the formation of their members to the spirit of the age, and leave the world as a whole unredeemed. This is why the Anglican Prayer Book controversy of the 1970s played such a large role in making Vanauken a Catholic. The contrast between the church that imposed 'The Book of Varietal Prayer' on its faithful and the one that, around the same time, selected John Paul II as her pontiff, grew to be more than he could bear. This is also why he had so little patience with Catholic liberals, whom he caustically depicts as failing even in their misguided attempt to embody the spirit of the age, always remaining one step behind the times, 'just arriving with "with-it" yelps' after everyone else has already moved on to something new").

Vitz, Paul Clayton – psychologist; b. 27 August 1935, Toledo, Ohio; c. June 1979 (St. Thomas More Church, Manhattan, New York; received with his wife); ancestors were ministers in the German Evangelical and Reform Church; parents went to the Presbyterian Church, though tended to neglect religion (and father was rather a skeptic and agnostic); studied Psychology at the University of Michigan (graduated in 1957); awarded PhD in Psychology by Stanford University in 1962; atheist and careerist at university; taught at New York University from 1965; revolted by the sixties counter culture, his secular world view collapsed; in 1973 became an Episcopalian; conversion to the Catholic faith influenced, *inter alia*, by C. S. Lewis, G. K. Chesterton, and French churches and cathedrals; Professor of Psychology at NYU 1985-2003 (Emeritus Professor from 2003); Adjunct Professor, John Paul II Institute for Marriage and Family, Washington, D.C., 1990-2000; married to (Evelyn) Timmie Vitz, *née* Birge (six children of the marriage); in his writings on psychology he argues that there is a link between fatherlessness (in the sense of weak, unloving, or absent fathers) and atheism; see *Psychology as Religion: The Cult of Self-Worship* (1977; second edition, 1994); *Modern Art and Modern*

Science: The Parallel Analysis of Vision (1984) (with Arnold B. Glimcher); *Censorship: Evidence of Bias in Our Children's Textbooks* (1986); *Sigmund Freud's Christian Unconscious* (1988); *The Course of True Love: Marriage in High School Textbooks* (1998); *Defending the Family: A Sourcebook* (1998) (with Stephen M. Krason); *Faith of the Fatherless: The Psychology of Atheism* (1999); *The Self: Beyond the Postmodern Crisis* (2006); "A Christian Odyssey," in Robert Baram (ed), *Spiritual Journeys* (revised edition, 1988, p.375) ("I have always credited an atheist former friend of ours with being partially responsible for my conversion (he would be much surprised to hear this): once, in the course of a conversation, he exclaimed happily: 'Oh, isn't it wonderful to live in an age of decadence!' That remark alone moved me along several steps toward Christianity...

During this time certain books were critically important, especially the writings of C. S. Lewis and G. K. Chesterton. It was an enormous surprise and relief to me to discover that Christianity was intellectually not only defensible but really very powerful! Indeed, I soon found that its intellectual variety and riches were so much deeper and more sophisticated than any secular framework that there was simply no comparison. As a consequence, my mind - my intellectual understanding - soon went through a really momentous conversion. I began to grasp the essential character of Christian thought and to see clearly the weaknesses of modern secular positions...

Meanwhile, as my understanding of Christian theology deepened, I quickly came into conflict with liberal Christian theology, most of which was Protestant in origin. It was obvious to me that liberal theology was at best a compromise with anti-Christian modernist thought, and at worst a thinly disguised denial of Christ. No doubt in the past the primary challenge to the Faith has been rigid pharasaical theology, but today the moral danger is modernist self-indulgent mush: liberal theology. Having been intellectually formed in the heart of the modernist and secular world view - that is, in contemporary social science - it was easy for me to recognize these assumptions and ideas when I saw them creeping into Christianity.

Unfortunately the Episcopal Church was dominated by liberal thought, indeed so dominated by it that many couldn't even see it...

In becoming a Catholic, I further deepened my connection to Western culture and to the general heritage of Christendom both in the West and in the East...Even more, one of the great liberations in becoming a Catholic was to be part of the universal character of the Church. Catholics are all over the world, and in becoming a Catholic I sensed a new kinship with people in countries as diverse as Argentina,

Poland and Zanzibar. This is one of the reasons why becoming a Catholic was an experience of freedom and expansion. I was linked to millions of people of all nations, races and cultures, It was exhilarating. A particular form of this freedom was the realization that Catholics cover the complete social spectrum: a Catholic may be a king or a truck driver, a millionaire or a peasant. To be a Catholic is not to be part of a particular social class"); Evelyn Birge Vitz, "My Path to Rome," in Robert Baram (ed), *Spiritual Journeys* (1988, revised edition), p.363; *EWTN Audio Library, The Journey Home* (19 August 2002); *paulvitz.com.*

Vree, Dale – editor and author; b. 25 February 1944; c. September 1983 (his wife, Elena, and family were also received); raised as an evangelical Protestant (referred to himself as Dutch Reformed and Presbyterian, i.e., Dutch Calvinist); all his family were Protestant immigrants from the Netherlands; he became worried by the lack of concern for social justice in his particular Protestant affiliation; became an Episcopalian because of its social witness (and since it elicited his sense of worship), but found that social action went hand in hand with doctrinal skepticism and modernism; studied at the University of California at Berkeley; participated in the civil rights and peace movements; abandoned Christ and became a Marxist-Leninist and moved to East Germany; while there he converted suddenly to Christ in 1966 on hearing a sermon in a Protestant church proclaiming the physical Resurrection of Christ; on his return to Berkeley he found an Anglo-Catholic parish, which taught him most importantly that the corporate Church – through her tradition – possesses teaching authority; by 1976 it was obvious to him that the Episcopal Church had broken with the apostolic, Catholic faith by approving the ordination of women to the priesthood and by adopting a permissive position on abortion; he saw that if the Church is authorized to teach, the Church must also have an intact teaching authority, a magisterium; helped found the *New Oxford Review* as an Anglo-Catholic publication, which also became Catholic in 1983; see *On Synthesizing Marxism and Christianity* (1976); *From Berkeley to East Berlin and Back* (1985) ("Modernism is a very slippery slope. Once you begin reinterpreting, rationalizing, and demythologizing the faith, no objective criterion exists by which you can distinguish what in Christianity is mythic or symbolic from what is actually true. The only criterion is subjective - what you as the self-appointed spokesperson for modern man find palatable and believable. Whatever fails to pass your private tests, from the Virgin Birth to the deity of Christ, can be considered mythic and reinterpreted in secular terms. This approach is a very convenient one.

Once you have hacked away at those doctrines, nothing prevents your being consistently modern and demythologizing God Himself. The Death-of-God theologians, by being consistent and thoroughly honest about their procedures, did exactly that. They continued to esteem the *man* Jesus and thus called themselves 'Christian atheists;' but they were regular atheists in every sense of the word.

The more I reflected, the more I recognized that the theological modernism I had imbibed was in fact a shrouded atheism. Modernism's assumptions were atheistic: man need only believe what he finds believable, and nothing miraculous or paradoxical is included. The logical conclusion of modernism is atheism"); "A Less Traveled Road to Rome," in Dan O'Neill (ed), *The New Catholics: Contemporary Converts Tell Their Story* (1987), p.49 (also published in Robert Baram (ed), *Spiritual Journeys* (revised edition, 1988), p.395) ("When I converted to Christ in 1966, I did so on *His* terms. No longer would I set myself up as the arbiter of religious truth…If I had converted to Christ on His terms, how could I find out what His terms really were? In Protestantism, the individual is thrown back upon himself and his fallible and highly subjective judgments - or upon the ersatz (and, from a strictly *Sola Scriptura* point of view, illegitimate) traditions of Calvin, Luther, Wesley, and a multitude of others, or worse, upon the ersatz and elusive authority of the modernist theology professors and their shifting opinions. In seeking the living faith of Christ's Church, I was compelled to consider seriously the Roman Catholic magisterium.

Now, there were a few things Rome taught that didn't much appeal to me. But ironically, my qualms about Rome made Rome attractive in a way that seemed fitting. That is, it seemed that if Rome were the authority I thought her to be, I should have some qualms. For it would be awfully arrogant of me to think that my own natural preferences would be in perfect harmony with the will of Christ. If the quest for Christian truth had driven me to submit to Christ and the revealed Word of God in East Berlin, then it might also drive me to submit to the magisterium. Christ asks us to believe and do things we might not really want to believe or do, and so it seemed symmetrical that Christ's teaching authority in the Church would do so too. A Bible-believing Christian doesn't 'pick and choose' from the Bible what he wants to accept - no, he is under authority. The same applies to the magisterium. If in accepting Christ in 1966, it was necessary for me to accept even Christ's hard sayings, then if the necessity of the magisterium became apparent to me, I would have to accept even its hard teachings.

So, the very difficulty of 'submitting to Rome' made such a submission seem appropriate — as well as consistent with my original decision for Christ in 1966.

What attracted me to Christ was, in part, the selfless witness of Christians. Is persistent hardship therefore indispensable to authentic Christian living? I hope not, but I don't know for sure. Be that as it may, my experience in East Berlin gave me a profound appreciation for Christian suffering and mortification - themes I saw more powerfully represented in the Roman Catholic Church than in any other Western church. The Protestantism I had been exposed to as a youth stressed the 'blessings' (often quite self- centered, even materialistic) that follow from accepting Christ.

What was lost sight of was the potentially greater blessings that follow from adversity and suffering. Seldom in Protestant churches did I hear about these inconvenient words of our Lord: 'Blessed are ye, when men shall revile you, and persecute you… for my sake" (Matt. 5:11, KJV).

When I accepted Christ in East Berlin, I did not surrender my 'proletarian consciousness' or my concern about 'the least of these my brethren'…For decades I would search in vain for a way of combining theological orthodoxy and populistic political views. But the more I studied the Roman Catholic magisterium, the more I realized that it was offering what I had been looking for all along, that essentially it taught the unusual mix of convictions - socially Left, theological Right - I had carried with me since boyhood. And it did so with authority. As a Roman Catholic, my theological and social views would not seem idiosyncratic - peculiar to me,

So, in Roman Catholicism I found a church in which I could emphatically affirm both the rights of labor and the ancient creeds, reject both abortion and the use of nuclear weapons, affirm both lifelong marriage and the dignity of the poor, reject both laissez faire capitalism and do-your-own-thing morals, and stand apart from both the philosophical materialism of the East and the practical materialism (consumerism) of the West - and do so in full harmony with the teachings of my church.

Finally, I have always felt that if I were a Christian, my loyalty to Christ would have to transcend my temporal loyalties - whether to nation, ethnic group, or social class. Most non-Roman Catholic churches have identities forged by nationalist preoccupations or affected by national conditioning. Only Rome has been able to stand above nation rivalries and relativities. Moreover, of all the churches, the Roman Catholic is least affected by class and ethnic provincialisms. The Roman Catholic Church is the most 'catholic' - that is, the most universalistic, most international, most all-embracing - of all churches"; Elena M. Vree, "Home at Last," in Dan O'Neill (ed), *The New Catholics: Contemporary Converts Tell Their Story* (1987), p.63.

Wadhams, Edgar Philip Prindle – bishop; b. 17 May 1817, Lewis, Essex County, New York; c. 1846; d. 5 December 1891; sixth and youngest child of General Luman Wadhams and his wife Lucy; his mother was a woman of great piety; raised a Presbyterian; became attracted towards Anglicanism, which he mistook for something Catholic and joined the Episcopal Church; attracted by the Tractarian Movement; became a deacon, but later converted to the Catholic Church; ordained to the priesthood on 15 January 1850; vicar-general of Albany and rector of the cathedral; in 1872 he was consecrated as the first bishop of the new Catholic diocese of Ogdensburg, in Northern New York; he increased the number of priests and parishes, and introduced several religious communities; he founded Catholic schools and built an orphan asylum, a hospital, and an old people's home; friend for many years of Clarence Augustus Walworth (see below); his remains are buried in the crypt of St. Mary's Cathedral; see Clarence Augustus Walworth, *Early Ritualism in America: Reminiscences of Edgar P. Wadham* (1893); *Catholic Encyclopedia* ("At his death the churches and chapels had increased from 65 to 125; priests from 42 to 81; nuns from 23 to 129 and Catholic schools from 7 to 20; the Catholic population had risen from 50,000 to 65,000").

Wagner, Robert F. (born Robert Ferdinand Wagner – politician; b. 8 June 1877, Nastätten, then in the Province Hesse-Nassau, Kingdom of Prussia, German Empire (now in Rhein-Lahn-Kreis, Rhineland-Palatinate, Federal Republic of Germany); c. 24 January 1946 (received by Mgr. Robert F. Keegan); d. 4 May 1953, New York City; came to the United State with his parents in 1886; family settled in New York; parents returned to Europe in 1896, but he remained; brought up in the Lutheran faith by a religious family; during college days attended the Methodist church; later adhered to no sect, but attended most convenient Protestant church; graduated from New York Law School in 1898; admitted to the bar in 1900; married in 1908 Margaret Marie, *née* McTague, a devout Catholic (she died in 1919 and he raised their only child); member of New York State Assembly 1905-1908; member of New York Senate 1909-1918; justice of the New York Supreme Court 1919-1926; Democratic U.S. Senator from New York 1927-1949; involved in labor issues in the thirties, fighting for legal protection and rights for workers; greatly influenced by the social teaching of Leo XIII and Pius XI; close friend of Al Smith, New York Governor and U.S. Presidential candidate; supported

Roosevelt's New Deal policy; his son, Robert F. Wagner, Jr. (1910-1991), was Mayor of New York City 1954-1965; buried in Calvary Cemetery, Queens, New York; see "Growing Into Catholicism," in John A. O'Brien (ed), *The Road to Damascus* (1949) ("The house in which I lived as a boy had a number of Catholic families and because my father was the janitor we got to know most of the families quite intimately. I remember my father one night as he lit his perennial corncob, remark to my mother that the Catholics treated us just as well as, and sometimes better, than our own folks. It was probably the first time I ever gave a thought to Catholicism, or for that matter to a difference in one's religion. It was a fleeting thought, to be sure, but all my life the validity of my father's observation was brought home to me.

I guess my first wish to be a Catholic came from desire to be an altar boy and wear a cassock and surplice like my little Irish pal Timmy. I remember how proud he used to be to wear that shiny cassock. It covered his tattered clothes, and how wonderful he looked to me. I remember also the fact that he sat right up with the priest and was regarded as the equal of the other more fortunate boys whose folks had money. It was the first inkling of what I later came to know as the Church's real democracy.

I many times remarked when discussing the Catholic Church how I always observed that whenever I went into a Catholic Church I would see rich and poor alike sitting next to each other. I never saw a Catholic Church that seemed to be meant just for the rich. It was open to all. Later, too, as I became acquainted and friendly with members of the clergy and the hierarchy, I was impressed with the fact that almost without exception they were from poor families.

As I observed the Church in action through the years I was struck by that same spirit of democracy that was manifest in the complete and total concern of the Church for each individual soul – no matter how poor or rich, or what color or age, or how bad he might be. I always thought it was significant that not even the Pope could dissolve the marriage of the poorest beggar or the most powerful king...

My wife personified to me what I had noticed and admired in so many of my Catholic friends. She enjoyed life to the fullest and was so terrifically human, yet she was strictly and devoutly religious. When staying out late of a Saturday night, fasting after midnight and getting up early for Mass and Communion seemed so natural and easy for her. Religion was part of her and her personality blended into all that she did. But it seemed natural for a great many others too, and later on in life when I began to think more deeply about Catholicism it was the naturalness of the Catholic religion that so strongly appealed to me...

It is during time of sickness and

death that the power and adequacy of our faith becomes most apparent. It seems to offer one such great consolation. My wife was ill for some time before she died, yet right to the end she managed to get to St. Ignatius Loyola every Sunday morning. The pew where she knelt, incidentally, is still there, in her memory, and it always will be. She knew she would not recover, but her faith made her content and she remained happy to the end. Death for Catholics is something holy - it is an expression of God's will. Somehow a Catholic funeral lacked the awful bleakness that I frequently experienced at the funerals of my non-Catholic friends. Yes, you just had to be moved by it all, and I was"); J. Joseph Hutmacher, *Senator Robert F. Wagner and the Rise of Urban Liberalism* (1968); his papers are in the Lauinger Library at Georgetown University; *ANB.*

Waldman, Milton (Sylvester) - writer and publisher; b. 4 October 1895, Cleveland, Ohio; c. mid-1940s; d. 6 March 1976, London; son of a tailor; parents were Jewish immigrants from the Austro-Hungarian Empire; sent to Reform Sunday school; admitted to Yale College in 1913 (BA in English 1917); worked as a journalist for several years; married to Hazel Guggenheim at this time (their two children died in infancy; marriage dissolved); moved to Europe permanently in 1922; graduate studies at the Sorbonne 1922-1923; returned to journalism as assistant editor of the *London Mercury* 1924-1927; wrote several major historical works, although not a professional historian; particular interest in the Renaissance period; literary editor for several publishers, discovering much new talent and working with and advising many notable authors, e.g., J. R. R. Tolkien, Thornton Wilder, Vincent Cronin, and Arthur Bryant; translated several books; married Marguerite "Peggy" David in 1934 (two daughters, from her previous marriage, and a son); much of his time was spent in Italy, but when his wife died in 1969 he returned to London; see *Americana: The Literature of American History* (1925); *Sir Walter Raleigh* (1928); *The Disinherited* (1929) (novel); *King, Queen, Jack: Philip of Spain Courts Elizabeth* (1931); *The Omnibus Book of Travelers' Tales: Being the History of Exploration Told by the Explorers* (1931); *Elizabeth, Queen of England* (American title, *England's Elizabeth*) (1933); *Joan of Arc* (1935); *Biography of a Family: Catherine de Medici and Her Children* (1936); *Some English Dictators* (1940 (first published in the United States as *Rod of Iron: The Absolute Rulers of England* (1941)), *Sir Walter Raleigh* (1943); *Elizabeth and Leicester* (1944); *Queen Elizabeth* (1952); *The Lady Mary: A Biography of Mary Tudor, 1516-1558* (1972); *ANB* ("A picture of Waldman would be incomplete without any mention of his devout

Catholicism, to which he formally converted in the mid-1940s, partly as a result of his research into the lives of the Medicis and Joan of Arc").

Walworth, Clarence Augustus – priest and lawyer; b. 30 May 1820, Plattsburg, Clinton County, New York; c. 16 May 1845 ("The creed of Pius IV sounded most musically in my ears, and I took pleasure in repeating it very slowly and distinctly"; he subsequently converted many members of the Walworth family, including his stepsister Ellen Hardin Walworth (see below)); d. 19 September 1900, Albany, New York; fourth child and oldest son of Reuben Hyde Walworth (1788-1867), lawyer, politician, and last chancellor of the State of New York; brought up in a Presbyterian family; graduated in 1838 from Union College in Schenectady, New York; studied law and was admitted to the bar in 1841; after a short time he abandoned the law and, having turned away from his family religion, studied for the Episcopal ministry at the General Theological Seminary, New York City; attracted by the Tractarian Movement; conversion to the Catholic faith influenced by Newman, and by Johann Adam Mohler's *Symbolism*; before completing his studies, he decided to become a Catholic priest and entered the Redemptorist Order; ordained to the priesthood in Holland in 1848; worked in England before returning to the United States; gave many missions with his four companions Fathers Baker, Deshon, Hecker, and Hewit (see above and, in particular, the entry for Fr. Hecker); broke with the Redemptorists in 1865 and tried to resume missionary work, but poor health forced him to a less rigorous field, and he left to become a secular priest at St. Mary's Church, Albany, New York; in 1853 he translated from the original German the hymn *Holy God, We Praise Thy Name*; also wrote an English metrical version of the Te Deum; friend for many years and biographer of Bishop Edgar P. Wadhams (see above); blind for the last ten years of his life (after his eyes began to fail he was accustomed to say fifteen decades of the rosary daily, by privilege from Rome secured for him by Bishop Wadhams, instead of reading the office from the breviary); somewhat mercurial character; buried in Greenridge Cemetery, Lincoln Road, Saratoga Springs, New York; see The *Gentile Skeptic, or, Essays and Conversations of a Country Justice on the Authenticity and Truthfulness of the Old Testament Records* (1863); *The Doctrine of Hell* (1873); *Ghosts* (1878); "The Trinity in Simple English," *Catholic World*, December 1885; *Andiatorocté, or, The Eve of Lady Day on Lake George: and Other Poems, Hymns, and Meditations* (1888); *Reminiscences of Edgar P. Wadhams, First Bishop of Ogdensburg* (1893); *The Oxford*

Movement in America (1895); Rev. Walter Elliott, "Father Walworth: A Character Sketch," *Catholic World*, June 1901; Ellen Hardin Walworth, *Life Sketches of Father Walworth, With Notes and Letters* (1907) (Letter to his father, 21 July 1845: "Our Blessed Saviour's cross was not covered with flowers, nor did a crowd of admirers follow Him to Calvary. He was not honorable, nor respectable, nor comfortable; but God appointed to Him poverty, contempt and agony. Did He endure these that his followers might be spared? No! He said the world would hate them as it hated Him, and "except a man take up his cross and follow Me, he cannot be My disciple." We are not privileged to gather to ourselves enjoyments in this life, and plead the sufferings of Christ for enjoyment in the next, but if we would reign with Him then, we must suffer with Him now. It is difficult to believe that many moral, kind and neighborly persons, whose amiable qualities win our affections, who are called Christians, and yet who take care to avoid troubles or ill remark, and enjoy the good opinion of all about them, are really in danger of suffering with the damned; but so the Gospel teaches, and I can not think that salvation is so easily won. Certainly, when the way of duty leads to suffering, there is no safety in any other course. And such is clearly my own path of duty.

I have become a Catholic, because I am persuaded that the Catholic Church is the Christian fold into which Christ gathers his own flock. In these United States, this Church is misunderstood and hated. Not only the spiritual destitution of the whole country so proud in its infidelity, calls for help, but multitudes of Catholics are deprived of the sacraments of the Church and the privilege of public worship and instruction, from want of priests. There is an especial call upon me then who have looked forward so long to the priesthood. And why should I not? My parents and my best friends do not love the Catholic religion and cannot bear that I should become a Catholic priest. Here is then on one hand, the call of God, and on the other the cry of flesh and blood. Which shall I follow? Clearly I must follow God, although my heart should break in the meanwhile, and indeed I think it cannot bear much more. Farewell! then, dear Father, and forgive me all the grief I have ever caused you, and especially this last of all. It is I who give you the wound, but I strike through my own flesh"); Katherine Burton, *In No Strange Land: Some American Catholic Converts* (1942), p.77; Mary E. Dougal, "An American Victorian Family: The Walworths of Saratoga" (MA thesis, State University of New York, Oneonta, 1979); the Walworth Family Papers are at the Saratoga Historical Society, Saratoga, New York; *ANB* ("He had a strong sense of the American need for community and authority in reaction to what he perceived to be the disintegration of American religious, political, and economic life. In the antebellum period he presented Catholicism as the antidote to the disease of individualism. In the postwar period he saw Catholicism as a corrective to the growing threat of historical relativism, atheistic evolutionism, socialism, and secularism").

Walworth, Ellen Hardin – activist and author; b. 20 October 1832, Jacksonville, Illinois; d. 23 June 1915, Washington, D.C.; eldest of four children of John J. Hardin (1810-1847), U.S. Representative from Illinois (killed in the Battle of Buena Vista in 1846), and Sarah Ellen (Smith) Hardin; brought up Presbyterian; educated at Jacksonville Academy and had access to the large family library; family moved to Saratoga Springs, New York, in 1851 when her mother married the much older Reuben Hyde Walworth (1788-1867), lawyer, politican, and the last chancellor of New York State; after moving she became a Catholic despite the strong protest of her mother; influenced in her conversion by her stepbrother Clarence Augustus Walworth (see above); in 1852 she married Mansfield (Manse) Tracy Walworth, lawyer and writer, her stepfather's youngest son; eight children of the marriage (three died in infancy); she was physically abused by her husband and she left him, taking the children with her, finally obtaining a "limited divorce" in 1871; her husband continued to threaten her and in 1873 her eldest son, Frank, shot him dead; Frank was sentenced to life imprisonment; she studied law (gaining a degree at New York University) in order to gain his freedom and succeeded in 1877 on grounds of insanity (pardon also issued); practiced law; published works on history and on science, particularly geology; wrote a book about her travel to Europe in 1873; worked to preserve historical sites; one of the founders of the Daughters of the American Revolution in 1890 and was the first secretary general; played a major role in the founding of the Women's National War Relief Association (she was director-general of the new organization); buried in Green Ridge Cemetery, Saratoga; see *An Old World as Seen Through Young Eyes, or, Travels Around the World* (1877); *Battles of Saratoga* (1891); *The Life and Times of Kateri Tekakwitha the Lily of the Mohawks, 1656-1680* (1891); *Life Sketches of Father Walworth, with Notes and Letters* (1907); Mary E. Dougal, "An American Victorian Family: The Walworths of Saratoga" (MA thesis, State University of New York, Oneonta, 1979); Allison P. Bennett, *Saratoga Sojourn: a Biography of Ellen Hardin Walworth* (2002); the Walworth Family Papers are at the Saratoga Historical Society, Saratoga, New York; *ANB*.

Ward, James Harman - naval officer; b. 25 September 1806, Hartford, Connecticut; d. 27 June 1861, Mathias Point, King George County, Virginia; attended the American Literary Scientific and Military Academy at Norwich, Vermont (graduated in 1823); served as a midshipman in the navy in the Mediterranean 1823-1827; scientific studies at Washington College, Hartford (now Trinity College) in 1828; promoted lieutenant in 1831; served again at sea and also taught courses in ordnance and gunnery; on the opening of the new Naval Academy at Annapolis, Maryland, he was a member of the faculty; served during the war with Mexico 1847-1848; continued to serve in the navy and to write naval textbooks; promoted commander in 1853; on the outbreak of the Civil War he was called to Washington to counsel the navy department, and organized the Potomac flotilla, of which he was given command; took part in the attack on Mathias Point and became the first officer of the Union navy to be killed during the Civil War; buried in Old North Cemetery, Hartford, Connecticut; he was the great-grandfather of the actor Andy Devine; see *An Elementary Course of Instruction in Ordnance and* Gunnery (1845); *A Manual of Naval Tactics* (1859; ran to four editions); *Steam for the Million* (1860) (a popular treatise on steam engineering); *Catholic Encyclopedia.*

Ward, Justine Bayard (*née* Cutting) – musical educator; b. 7 August 1879, Morristown, New Jersey; c. 27 January 1904; d. 27 November 1975, Washington, D.C.; second of four children of an Episcopalian family; daughter of William Bayard Cutting, an enormously wealthy business man and philanthropist; one brother, Bronson, was Republican Senator from New Mexico, another, Bayard, was private secretary to Joseph Choate, the American Ambassador to England; mainly privately educated; skilled at music; in 1901 at the Brompton Oratory, London, she married George Cabot Ward, a lawyer and a Catholic, but the marriage was annulled in 1911; converted to the Catholic faith under the influence of Fr. John B. Young, SJ (1854-1928) (also a musician and teacher) and Fr. William Pardow, SJ of the church of St. Francis Xavier, New York City; using pre-existing ideas (those of the Galin-Paris-Chevé Method of sight-singing, Rev. Thomas Shields' (1862-1921) teaching manuals, and Fr. Young's musical teaching techniques) she developed a system for teaching music to children, which became known as the Ward Method; she strongly believed in the superiority of chant over other music with the latter's dance and secular connotations; in 1916 she founded in New York, at Manhattanville Academy, run by the Sacred Heart nuns, the Pius X Institute of Liturgical Music; worked closely with Mother Georgia Stevens (1870-1946), also a convert (1895); used her great wealth to assist in her mission; in 1920 she organized an International Congress of Gregorian Chant at St. Patrick's Cathedral, New York; also influenced by the Benedictines of Solesmes (in particular, her mentor, Dom André Mocquereau, OSB (1848-1930), the foremost authority on Gregorian chant rhythm, and Dom Augustine Anselm Gatard, OSB); her aim was to further the liturgical and musical reforms of Pope St. Pius X by teaching children vocal music reading skills; studied for a time under Mocquereau, residing at Quarr Abbey on the Isle of Wight where the monks of Solesmes were living in political exile; joined the Benedictine Oblature; the method was very successful and spread throughout the United States, Europe and other parts of the world (at its basic level it did not require music specialists as instructors); trained many thousands of school children ("The little Catholic school child is learning to pray, not only in words, but also in song; not only in the Church's language, Latin, but in her musical language, Chant; and when these children grow up, our choirs will be the whole Catholic world"); also trained many adults to teach the method; the School of Music building of the Catholic University of America was donated by and named for her; several audiences with Pius XI and Pius XII; several splits with the various bodies; see "The Reform of Church Music," *Atlantic Monthly*, April 1906 ("It may be useful... to bring out as clearly as possible the fundamental principle of the art of musical prayer, in order that principle, and not caprice, may be brought to bear to the solution of the problem. It is, then, with principles that I propose to deal...

First, then, we want an adequate test of church music, an explicit standard of artistic value. We have been too long content to make beauty in the music *as music* the Alpha and Omega of such test, a method wholly inadequate in this case. For church music is an art made up of two elements, music and prayer, and it cannot be judged by the value of one of its elements tested as a separate entity. We need a test that applies to the art as a whole, and we find it in the simple formula 'Lex orandi lex cantandi.' Here the crux of the whole matter; the law of prayer must be the law of song, both that our prayer (I use the word *prayer,* not in the sense of a mere petition, but in its wider meaning, a lifting of mind and heart to God) may be good art and that our art may be good prayer. Prayer and music must so combine as to make *one art;* the music must pray, the prayer must sing. Otherwise the prayer is forgotten in the detached beauty of the music, or the music is forgotten in the detached beauty of the prayer. Unless the prayer and song thus rise to heaven as a single 'spiritual groaning,' unless they become one, merged in a true marriage of the spirit, their association is an offense both artistic and devotional. This, then, is the true test of a musical composition for the church: Does it conform to the law of prayer? It is good art. Does it seek independent paths of edification? It is bad art...

[In the Catholic Church] the music is not merely an accessory, but an integral part of the ritual; words and music form together a complete artistic whole. The ritual of the Catholic Church is fixed, because the idea is fixed of which ritual is the outward manifestation. Ritual bears as natural and inevitable a relation to faith as the gesture does to feeling; the material manifestation, it is true, but a necessary one to the normal creature, who - being not yet a pure spirit - possesses no other means of expression. As ritual without faith becomes a lie, so faith without ritual is ineffective, a talent buried in the earth. So long as we remain human beings, the spiritual must take an outward form - of word, of gesture, of action, - that it may be part of our nature. Even God became man that He might be fully apprehensible to His creatures; He translated Himself into terms of the tangible; which is, indeed, the sacramental principle. And so we must have ritual. But this ritual must really express what is behind it; it must bear a very logical relation to faith, even as the gesture does to the thought. We do not express our affection by a blow in the face, nor gesticulate violently when the heart is an icicle. Every ritual-result must be the direct manifestation of a corresponding faith cause. Herein lies the true importance of church music. For it is not enough that it should not hide the faith; it must reveal it, even interpret it, and, through the outward manifestation of faith, raise the heart to an understanding of its inner meaning; it must, by means of the natural, help the weak human heart to rise to the heights of the supernatural.

This is why the Pope attaches such importance to this reform in music; why he insists that these three hundred million people of his, not all artists by any means – the tiller of the soil and the worker in the subway - should listen to a certain type of music, and no other. What is the music whose use the Pope wishes especially to enforce? The Gregorian Chant. To quote from the Encyclical: 'The more closely a composition for the Church approaches in movement, inspiration and savor, the Gregorian form, the more sacred and liturgical it becomes; and the more out of harmony it is with that supreme model, the less worthy it is of the temple.'

Thus, in the Pope's judgment, the standard is fixed. This sounds, on the face of it, somewhat arbitrary, like binding ourselves to an antiquated art-form, and clipping the wings of progress. And so it will be interesting to examine the claims of the Gregorian music, and determine where and why it is superior to any more modern form as a setting of liturgical prayer.

The Gregorian is objected to as an antiquated art-form, a musical archaism. But an art-form does not become antiquated through mere lapse of time: Greek architecture and Greek sculpture, which dates still farther back, remain the standard in plastic art. The Catholic liturgy is, as we have seen, fixed in its general character and scope; the form that best expresses it, then, need not be the latest fluctuation of popular taste; it need not even be the form which is most interesting, judged from a purely musical standpoint. But the highest art will be the form that best fits the liturgical form. Granting, even, that music, as an art, has advanced and developed since the days of St. Gregory, the question remains, which, for us, is the important one: has it advanced and developed along the lines of prayer, or the reverse, in religious or in secular channels? For if it has not advanced along the lines of prayer, then the earlier form will be the best art for our specific purpose.

One can trace a certain definite sequence in the development of every art. First we have the idea which strives to express itself in form. This form, at first crude, gradually perfects itself, until the point arrives when idea and form become synonymous. Then we have the classical period. Any further development of form is at the expense of the idea; it is the beginning of decadence, the lowest ebb of which is reached when art has descended to pure matter without idea. When form has thus submerged the idea, the painter uses color for color's sake, the musician revels in mere sound, in 'tone color,' the orator in 'fine words,' sonorous phrases, tickling sound, dazzling color, *vox et praeterea nihil,* - and art lies dead. Perfection of form is good art, display of form is decadence; and so the psychological moment when idea and form coincide must remain the classical period for all time, the highest expression of that particular idea. A true development in art can only be brought about by the entrance of a new idea. Thus after the vocal idea comes the instrumental; after the melodic idea, the contrapuntal. One succeeds the other, but one does not improve upon the other. Gregorian Chant represents the culmination of the melodic idea, the highest conceivable development of unisonous music, and further development had to take the form of polyphony.

The important question, then, is not whether we ought to go back to antiquity, but whether, by so going, we shall or shall not find the classical period in the art of musical prayer: the moment when the idea – prayer - and the form – music – became identical.

Let us briefly examine the characteristics of liturgical prayer;

for Chant, as an art, stands or falls on the basis of its adaptability to this purpose. If it can be proved that the Gregorian form, and that form only, succeeds in translating the liturgy into music, in fitting that particular idea with form, then its value as an art is proved.

The liturgy of the Catholic Church serves a twofold purpose: to pray and to teach. The latter, her teaching function, is defeated by the use of any but unisonous music, because polyphony makes the words, in a greater or less degree, incomprehensible. In Chant the words are not repeated, twisted, turned upside down, inside out, and hind part before; they are uttered slowly, distinctly, pensively, each syllable lingered over as though with tenderness. It is a 'musing,' a quiet spiritual breathing. We can hear the Word of God and absorb it. Thus the teaching function of the Church demands the use of Chant.

Her prayer function demands it no less. Structurally, her prayers were conceived in a spirit of Chant and not of music, their very length precluding a more elaborate setting. A single illustration will suffice: during Holy Week the history of the Passion is read in all Catholic churches as the gospel of the day, while the congregation stands. Bach has given the Passion a musical setting, - one of the greatest of all pieces of devotional music. Yet it has one fatal objection: its performance takes no less than five hours, - a somewhat severe test upon the bodily strength of the congregation. Thus the musical structure of the period prevented even the great Bach from clothing his great idea with suitable form. Chant merely enunciates the words, music embroiders on them; one is the principle of concentration, the other that of diffusion. Chant is, therefore, the only form in which the whole liturgy can be sung at all.

So much for the merely structural demands of the liturgy. Its aesthetic demands are no less clear. Liturgical prayer is not the expression of individual reaching up to God, as in private devotion; it is the Church praying as a Church, officially, as a corporate whole. Her prayer has a fixed form, the outgrowth of the spiritual evolution of the Church, a survival of the fittest in the realm of religion. This prayer has, first of all, dignity; it is addressed to Almighty God. For this reason our modern rhythm, the outgrowth of the dance movement, is out of place, the form being too trivial to express the idea. I am speaking on purely artistic grounds. Again, prayer must have spontaneity; any insincerity kills prayer as prayer. For as we have seen a form attracting attention to itself detracts from the idea, and the idea in this case is God. Thus a prayer in rhyme would so obtrude its form as materially to detract from the idea. In precisely like manner is a prayer in music inferior to a prayer in Chant. Music, with its fixed measure, its regular strong and weak beats, is a formal garden, cut and trimmed into conventional avenues, adorned with hothouse plants. Chant is nature, the beauty of the fields and the forests. The formal garden has indeed its own place, its proper functions; but prayer trimmed into a formal garden is an anomaly. The spirit bloweth where it listeth. Music moves with the regular rhythm of poetry; Chant with the free rhythm of prose, the cadence of a fine oratorical period. Chant has feet but no measure, and these feet succeed each other naturally, not artificially, so that there is no conflicting form to obstruct Chant in its effort to take the identical shape of the words and phrases of the prayers.

Modern music has two scales, or *Modes* [the major and the minor]. Chant has eight. It is evident that eight modes give greater variety of expression than two…

We do not find in the ancient modes the same violent contrasts of mood as in the modern. They combine a solemnity, a grandeur, with the most tender and fervent devotion. Their minor tendency gives not so much the impression of sadness as of great solemnity and awe; their major tendency, not so much the impression of merriment as of a tender and ardent devotion. Thus we have the combination that makes true prayer: reverence in love, - the prayer that, like David's, rises as incense before the altar.

There is something obvious about the two scales of modern music. Christianity is not obvious. It is a philosophy of seeming contradictions: joy through renunciation: happiness through suffering, triumph through failure, victory through death"); *William Pardow of the Company of Jesus* (1914); essay in Georgina Pell Curtis, *Beyond the Road to Rome* (1914), p.406 ("Before becoming a Catholic, the exterior unity of the Church is what strikes the convert. After a few years of experience as a Catholic the exterior unity becomes valuable - not only in itself - but as a figure of the interior unity which the Catholic Church alone supplies. The whole interior life is ordered and at peace; not with the peace of inactivity and passive acceptance, as is so often supposed by those who judge by the shell, but the peace of ordered activity of mind and heart that springs from a common source and motive power; that allows no deep disquiet to take root in the soul; permitting storms to ruffle the surface but never to penetrate to the interior of the soul.

Becoming a Catholic changes the whole of life. Everything is seen in fresh perspective, with new; and startling relation to oneself and others. This has been my experience. Some things lose their importance, others become the centre of the picture, but the striking sensation is that of finding all things in life taking on a sudden, an intimate connection with everything else; of each thing falling gradually into its place, held together by a spiritual principle of gravitation. The puzzles that agitated the heart before as to the reasons for things, the apparent inequalities and injustices of life, the meaning of sorrow and of physical pain - all these things, with many more, suddenly fall into place.

One becomes conscious of a new motive power: love. Before, the love of Christ was, and in a sense could only be, the cold impersonal admiration, or enthusiasm, that one feels for a historical character, a person known through a book. After coming into close personal contact with Christ, day by day through the Sacraments, He is known and loved as an intimate friend.

A difference which has struck me perhaps more forcibly than any other is the contrast between the Protestant attitude and the Catholic toward sin. In general the Protestant attitude is that a good person will not be tempted to commit serious sins. The Catholic attitude is that all are tempted; therefore watch and pray; if you stand beware lest you fall. If you fall, there is a remedy - so rise up quickly. The Protestant attitude tends to foster hypocrisy; if you commit a sin you must hide it. The Catholic attitude fosters humility; admit the sin and try to do better.

The institution of the Sacrament of Penance is in itself an admission that we are all sinners. It is humiliating. It teaches us to know ourselves as is possible in no other way. It teaches us to have very little faith in our own strength as we watch, week by week, the startling divergence between resolution and accomplishment. We learn that without the life giving power of the Sacraments we could do nothing and less than nothing.

The mere fact of admitting a sin in words makes an impression that no amount of private repentance could do. Moreover, the psychological effect of starting fresh - forgiven - with a clean slate, saves us from despondency and despair. When, to the psychological effect of believing this true, we add the actual effect of its being in fact no delusion, that the sinning soul is actually made clean by the power of Him who healed the lepers, then it will be seen - or rather it cannot be so much as conceived by one who has not experienced the effect, - what a weight is lifted from a crushed soul, what power is infused by contact with this sacrament.

As Catholics, we are not only taught to use these Sacraments to stimulate growth. We are also carefully trained in the religious life, in spiritual understanding. The soul is not left to grow as a weed, but is led, guided, supported, educated, in general through the ordinary activities of the Church in regard to her children, and in particular through retreats and through the confessional. The personality of a soul is recognized and treated as wisely as an able physician of the body deals with the physical characteristics of a patient. Thus a sane and sound mysticism is possible and is not at all an exception; real spiritual experiences are distinguished from false ones and the danger of self deception is minimized.

Perhaps the most striking impression of all is the power of the Catholic religion in the crises of life. Where other religions fail because they offer mere words, the Catholic Church succeeds because it infuses power. Words, even of the highest wisdom may or may not kindle a response or illumine an obscurity. To infuse power is something entirely different. It needs no words, and if words accompany the action it is the action and not the words alone which produce the result, which act when the heart is too sad or the spirit too crushed or the body too weak to grasp the meaning of words, Christ comes and touches with His life-giving personal contact.

I do not think that anywhere else the same emphasis is given to the value of simplicity. It is often very surprising to one who has grasped the Catholic ideal to receive non-Catholic commiseration because this or that priest may not possess all the mental complexities which to their minds is associated with 'culture.' We have realized that a direct and certain grasp of supernatural principles is more apt to live in a mind which is either naturally free or has freed itself forcibly from complexities in its. outlook upon spiritual truth. The great Saints have all been either simple by nature or simple by acquisition; the complex among them having worked around the entire cycle of complexities and found at last the one simple and complete truth: the Word of God. The Mystics were absolutely single. Contact between mind and mind, moreover, does not depend on those things which are often called 'culture,' but on possessing firmly certain fundamental things in common.

When I entered the Church it was not through any feeling of attraction, but through a forcible overcoming of a deep seated aversion. Indeed it was only the conviction that I could no longer be a sincere person and remain outside the Catholic Church which forced me to enter. There has been no Catholic practice that I have not approached with dislike, and later learned to love, as the prejudices which arose from a supernatural knowledge, melted away before a deeper understanding.

The sensation which has grown with the years has been that of having stepped out into the open, and of having found at last LIFE, - nourished, balanced, adjusted, poised in relation to God and therefore poised, as it were, by reflection, in its relation to the world. One felt oneself in focus, for the first time.

For the first time, one felt free. One dared to look as far as the eye could see - unafraid. The whole great organism planned by God for the human race could bear investigation. The old half faced fears lest a gaze too direct into the foundations of faith might show up the whole structure as unsound, had vanished. Moreover, the solidity of the foundation has meant a rapid, free expansion of the superstructure.

To become a Catholic does not mean restriction in any sense. It means, as I have already said, life, 'He led me forth into a Large Place' has been literally true in my case. In the nine years that it has been my privilege to stand in the 'large place' I have never felt the boundaries restrictive. I have never found the Church standing for restriction of sound growth or of true liberty. Where her restraining touch is felt - in the rare cases when it is felt at all - is precisely where growth would entail weakness, a scattering of energy; where exposure would mean disease; where unchecked development of the poisonous weeds of character would eventually choke the normal growth of the whole person. This is not what is commonly meant by restriction, however. It is, I take it, what we mean by education.

In moments like the present, when we are looking at many of the old problems with fresh eyes, when we have the courage to face frankly the rising flood of moral scourges that threatens to engulf our country, when we find ourselves opposing them so often with still more dangerous 'cure-alls' – the patent medicines of our civilization; when unsound catch-words and misdirected enthusiasms fill our eyes with their dust and our ears with their clatter; at such times we turn with unspeakable relief to the scientifically planned little Ark, which, though fiercely assaulted, sails serenely upon the muddy waters. It is comforting to know that our compass is in working order; it gives us confidence to feel, from time to time, the force of the rudder and the jerk of its stout readjusting pull"); *Hymnal* (1930); *Music: First Year* (1933); *Music: Second Year* (1936); *Music: Third Year* (1938); *Thomas Edward Shields, Biologist, Psychologist, Educator, etc* (1947); Dom Pierre Combe, *Justine Ward and Solesmes* (1987); Richard Ramon Bunbury, *Justine Ward and the Genesis of the Ward Method of Music Education* (2001) *Electronic Doctoral Dissertations for UMass Amherst*; Alise Brown, "How the Ward Method Works," *Sacred Music*, Fall 2007, p.12; Francis Brancaleone, "Justine Ward and the Fostering of an American Solesmes Chant Tradition," *Sacred Music*, Fall 2009, p.6 ("I cannot but remark on the strong religious emphasis permeating the concept. The Method was not just about teaching music, it was also preparing little souls for more meaningful participation in Catholic liturgy. Over time, with the changes brought about by the Second Vatican Council, particularly those dealing with the advocacy of the vernacular and the movement away from Latin and Gregorian chant, the Method's influence necessarily began to wane...

[A]fter the changes initiated in the

Catholic liturgy of the 1960s, her indomitable spirit, conviction, and some of her disappointment come through in a letter to Dom Gajard of Solesmes: 'They [referring to some of the theologians interpreting the Second Vatican Council's documents] wanted to lower the prayer of the Church to mud level in order to attract the most ignorant people. My opinion is completely different: I know that souls can be raised to the level of the Liturgy, by elevating the souls. Children have no preconceived ideas; if they are taught to pray in beauty, they are delighted.' It is probably beyond one's power to imagine her bitterness as she surveyed the erosion of her many years of struggle in the service of an impossible ideal, and it is regrettable that she did not live to see the lasting respect and value which greets her Method whenever it is mentioned today...

When the Church adopted the easy popularity of guitars, amplification and charismatic group participation which could be accomplished by a relatively untrained congregation and moved away from the solitary introspection of personal prayer and training in Gregorian singing, the Ward Method came to be viewed as out of touch and therefore not a profitable promotional tool. However, the book on the Ward Method is not yet closed because of its intrinsic musical value (which may have to be redefined), staying power, and as its centenary approaches, who knows, Pope Benedict XVI's recent relaxation of restrictions on celebration of the Latin Mass may yet provide a catalyst for renewed life").

Warren, Leonard (born Leonard Warenoff) – opera singer; b. 21 April 1911, New York; c. 10 June 1950 (received by Fr. Joseph A. Ganley at St. Catherine of Siena Church, Riverside); d. 4 March 1960, New York; parents were Russian Jewish immigrants; in 1935 he joined the chorus at Radio City Music Hall; in 1937 he entered the Metropolitan Opera Auditions of the Air and was immediately given a contract; the Met sent him to Italy to study; made his concert debut at the Metroplitan Opera in 1938 and his opera debut (in *La Traviata*) in 1939; he sang in many countries, but spent most of his career in New York and at the Met, where he was a leading performer for many years (one of the great baritones of the middle of the 20th century); played many roles, but especially celebrated as one of the finest interpreters of the great Verdi baritone roles (above all in the title role in *Rigoletto*) and also of Puccini; sang in the first-ever live telecast from the Metropolitan Opera in the role of Iago in Verdi's *Otello*; extremely private and low key individual; his wife Agatha (*née* Leifflen) was a very devout Catholic and very influential on his conversion; after his conversion from the Jewish faith to Catholicism he was shunned and damned by his lifelong colleagues and friends who were Jews; he made a total, serious commitment to his new religion, but he rarely talked about religion to anyone; including his father; he died of a massive heart attack on stage in a performance of *La Forza Del Destino* with Renata Tebaldi (the only night that a performance "did not go on" one way or another to its conclusion); buried in St. Mary's Cemetery, Greenwich, Fairfield County, Connecticut; see Rudolf Bing, *5000 Nights at the Opera* (1972); Peter G. Davis, *The American Opera Singer* (1997) ("The rich, rounded, mellow quality of [Warren's] voice, fairly bursting with resonant overtones, may not have been to every taste, particularly those preferring a narrower baritonal focus that 'speaks' more quickly on the note. But by any standards it was a deluxe, quintessentially 'Metropolitan Opera sound', one that seemed to take on a special glow and lustrousness as it opened up and spread itself generously around the big auditorium. And of course the easy top was its special glory - when relaxing with friends Warren would often tear into tenor arias like 'Di quella pira' and toss off the high Cs that many tenors lacked. He could have, but never did, overindulge that applause-getting facility"); Mary Jane Phillips-Matz, *Leonard Warren: American Baritone* (2003) ("Warren came to his Roman Catholic faith slowly, having first taken instructions in 1941...He then let nine years pass before making a decision about his religion...In the end, his was a total, serious commitment and a deeply felt choice...Warren said his first serious experience with Catholicism had come when Francis Cardinal Spellman invited him 'and other friends' to sing in St. Patrick's Cathedral for the Christmas Eve rite. Warren said, '1 remember I sang Malotte's *The Lord's Prayer* and Bizet's *Agnus Dei.*' He then began to reflect on the meaning of the words in those pieces and said he was also influenced by a 'famous Mexican actor and singer named José Mojica,' who had given up his profession to become a Franciscan friar. The historic figures of the Catholic faith also meant a great deal to him. He loved statuettes of the saints and was impressed by the huge Christ of the Andes statue in Buenos Aires...[H]e described seeing Julie Harris as Joan of Arc in *The Lark*, saying that he experienced 'one of the...greatest thrills' of his life... Warren also [said]...that he was attracted to Roman Catholic belief because, as he said, 'Catholicism has everything well defined'...

[I]n making his critical personal decision to become a Roman Catholic, Warren was certainly motivated by love for his wife and respect for the Leifflens [his wife's family] and their faith. Both were constant and absolute factors in his life, from the late 1930s until the day of his death.

More particularly, his love for his mother-in-law influenced him…

[A]fter he became a Catholic he placed religious objects such as prayer cards or pictures of Jesus, the Virgin Mary, and the saints, or religious statuettes near his dressing table mirror…

[S]ome singers who watched him backstage came to learn how deeply religious he was. Jerome Hines noticed that he always stepped away by himself to seek some quiet spot in the wings so he could pray before performances. 'He always made the Sign of the Cross, then he went onstage'…

After his baptism, Warren also trusted Blanche Thebom enough to speak to her one day about his decision to become a Catholic. She and the baritone were alone, Thebom recalled. 'Agatha was not there. He told me how totally he loved and respected and admired her, then he added that because she had found everything in Catholicism, he wanted to share that with her. He said that if that religion had made it possible for there to be an Agatha, he wanted that religion for himself.' The religion Warren wanted was tightly structured, requiring regular attendance at Confession and Mass; a presence at the Communion Rail; the recital of many prayers, including the Lord's Prayer, the Marian Prayers, and the Rosary; the observance of dietary and other restrictions during Lent and on Fridays and other religious holidays; and the practice of all tenets of the Church. For him, for a man who had never before practiced a faith, Catholicism filled a need").

Watomika ("Swift Foot") - see under Bouchard, James Chrysostom, SJ).

Wattson, Paul James Francis, SA (original name Lewis Thomas Wattson) – priest and co-founder of a religious order; b. 16 July 1863, Millington, Maryland; c. 30 October 1909 (received with sixteen others, comprising one lay brother of the Society of the Atonement (a convert from Judaism), five sisters, and ten lay associates); d. 8 February 1940, Graymoor, New York; youngest son of the family; his father, Joseph Newton Wattson, a convert from Presbyterianism, became a pronounced "Puseyite" and later was a High Church rector of an Episcopalian church with a tendency towards Ritualism; shortly after his birth the family moved to Kent Island, Maryland; as a child he heard an interior voice saying that he would found a preaching order like the Paulists; ordained as an Episcopalian minister in 1886; wrote articles supporting the Real Presence, confession and the sacrifice of the Mass; he became an advocate of Christian unity in the sense that the Anglican Church should re-establish ties with the Catholic Church; influenced by reading a life of St. Francis; in 1893 he decided to start a preaching order under the name of the Society of the Atonement, interpreting atonement as "at-one-ment"; in 1897 he received a letter from a young woman, Mary Lurana White (see below), who was seeking an Episcopalian religious community for women living according to the Franciscan tradition with a vow of poverty; this led to a correspondence in which they made a spiritual covenant to work together to start the Society of the Atonement as a Franciscan community within the Episcopalian Church; they founded their religious order at Graymoor in Garrison, New York (then a remote place) with separate communities of men and women; there was great opposition to their message of Christian unity, which was that the only way to repair the breach that had occurred in the sixteenth century was for the Anglican Communion to recognize the reigning Pope as head of the Christian Church and for all Anglicans to return to Rome *corporately*; his magazine, *The Lamp*, became the organ of the pro-Roman party; the end came in 1907 when the General Convention of the Episcopal Church passed an amendment to allow the "Open Pulpit" - that is, to allow any "ordained" minister from any Christian congregation to preach in any Episcopal Church; after this both converted to the Catholic Church, together with the entire Society of the Atonement; he was ordained to the priesthood 16 June 1910; when still an Episcopalian he had originated the Church Unity Octave, which was approved as a Catholic devotion by Pope Benedict XV in 1916 (now known as the Week of Prayer for Christian Unity, observed 18-25 January); founded St. Christopher's Inn, at Graymoor, for the care of homeless men, and also the Graymoor Press; buried in the cemetery of the Mount of Atonement, Graymoor; see *The Prince of the Apostles: A Study of St. Peter* (1907) (with Spencer Jones); essay in Georgina Pell Curtis, *Beyond the Road to Rome* (1914), p.202 ("[I]n 1901 we began openly proclaiming our faith in the jurisdiction of the Apostolic See and that we believed all that Rome believed. We did not hesitate to say to our Anglican hearers that Henry VIII and Elizabeth were entirely wrong in having repudiated the Papacy and in separating England from the Holy See. Furthermore: that the sole salvation for Anglicanism was wholesale repentance, retraction of error, and corporate submission to the Successor of St. Peter"); Katherine Burton, *In No Strange Land: Some American Catholic Converts* (1942), p.185 ("He remembered how Saint Francis of Assisi had obtained the original rule of the Friars Minor by opening the Gospels in the name of the Trinity. Perhaps, thought Father Wattson, God might favor him in the same way. So, on Pentecost Sunday of 1893, he knelt before the altar of his church and opened the Bible. There before his eyes lay a verse from Saint Paul's fifth chapter to the [Romans]: 'And not only so, but we also joy in God, through Our Lord Jesus Christ, by whom we have now received the Atonement' Lewis Wattson felt he had the answer. His Society should bear the name of the Atonement...

The first Christmas at Graymoor after the reception into the Catholic Church was one unlimited in its joyous celebration...They had been received as a body of religious living corporately under the Rule of Saint Francis. Now the Brothers and Sisters bound themselves to work in the future for three things: the reconciliation of sinners to God through the Blood of the Atonement; the winning of Anglicans and non-Papal Christians to the obedience of Peter; and the conversion of the heathen...

He was always a true Franciscan; he loved the poor and he was markedly ascetic. Once a priest who planned to join the Society went to Graymoor to try it out. He came away, however, saying he could not attain the asceticism of such a saint - 'I found him sleeping on the floor of the belfry because the others needed the better places.'

Father Paul worked for his Church with his hands, helping in the actual building of Graymoor. And he helped through his sermons, through *The Lamp*, through his radio program with his head and his heart. 'He teaches us' said the Dominican who delivered his funeral sermon, 'that religion can be most attractive when the instincts of a gentleman are supernaturalized'"; David Gannon, *Father Paul of Graymoor* (1959); Titus Cranny, SA, *Father Paul: Apostle of Unity* (1965); Charles Angell, SA, and Charles V. Lafontaine, SA, *Prophet of Reunion: The Life of Paul of Graymoor* (1975); Charles V. Lafontaine, SA, "'Repairer of the Breach' – Mother Lurana White, Co-Founder of the Society of the Atonement," *The Catholic Historical Review*, July 1976, p.434; Lorene Hanley Duquin, *A Century of Catholic Converts* (2003), p.30; Eleonore Villarrubia, "Father Paul of Graymoor: Founder of the Society of the Atonement and Father of the Church Unity Octave," *catholicism.org*, 18 January 2010 ("There was an attempt to "water down" the intention of the Octave by some Christians, including an influential Catholic priest, Abbé Paul Couturier of France. Their adjusted prayer became 'the reunion of Christians in the manner best pleasing to Christ,' rather than 'reunion under the authority of the Successor of Saint Peter.' Many non-Catholic Christians, especially the Orthodox, jumped on this bandwagon. Although the leaders of this prayer octave tried to enlist Father Paul in their support, he remained adamant that reunion had to come under the auspices of the pope").

Wayne, John (born Marion Robert Michael Morrison) ("Duke") – film actor, director and producer; b. 26 May 1907, Winterset, Iowa; c. 9 June 1979 (baptized and received into the Catholic Church on his deathbed); d. 11 June 1979, Los Angeles; his parents were Methodists; star football player at high school; in 1925 he won a football scholarship to the University of Southern California; in 1927 a shoulder injury ended his football career and he lost his scholarship; he decided to try acting and had bit parts as a stuntman or an extra in low-budget films; met John Ford (1894-1973), the film director and a devout Catholic, and they became life-long friends; married Josephine Saenz (1908-2003), a Latin American Catholic, in 1933; their four children were brought up Catholic; his film name was adopted in 1929; in 1939 John Ford cast him as the Ringo Kid in *Stagecoach* (1939) and he became a star; appeared in more than 250 films; other notable roles were in *She Wore a Yellow Ribbon* (1949), *The Quiet Man* (1952), *The Searchers* (1956), *The Man Who Shot Liberty Vallance* (1962) and *True Grit* (1969) (won best actor Oscar for this role); he divorced his wife and married Esperanza Baur, but this ended in divorce in 1954 with no children; soon after he married Pilar Pallete (b. 1928), a Peruvian actress and Catholic with whom he had three children, all brought up Catholic (he and Pilar separated in 1973); politically a campaigner against Communism; supported the Vietnam War; awarded the Congressional Gold Medal in 1979; he considered his own religious beliefs to be Presbyterian ("When things are going good, I'm a Protestant. When things are not going good I'm a Catholic"), although he was not baptized until two days before his death; received into the Catholic Church on his deathbed and given the last rites; great friend of the Archbishop of Panama, Archbishop Tomas Clavel, who was a major influence in his conversion; posthumously awarded the Presidential Medal of Freedom in 1980; a grandson, Matthew Munoz (b. 1965) was ordained a Catholic priest in 2002; see George Carpozi, Jr., *The John Wayne Story* (1972); George Bishop, *John Wayne: The Actor/The Man* (1979); Pilar Wayne, *John Wayne: My Life with the Duke* (1987) (with Alex Thorleifson); Emmanuel Levy, *John Wayne: Prophet of the American Way of Life* (1988); Randy Roberts and James S. Olson, *John Wayne: American* (1997); Garry Wills, *John Wayne's America: The Politics of Celebrity* (1997); Joseph Sobran, "Is John Wayne Dangerous," *Sobran's*, May 1997; Aissa Wayne, *John Wayne, My Father* (1998); Roger M. Crowley, *John Wayne: An American Legend* (1999); Ronald L. Davis, *Duke: The Life and Image of John Wayne* (2001); Lorene Hanley Duquin, *A Century of Catholic Converts* (2003), p.177 ("He considered himself a Presbyterian, probably because of the Scotch Irish ancestry, but jokingly he referred to himself as a "cardiac Catholic," a reference to people who convert to Catholicism on their deathbeds.

When John Wayne was asked whether he believed in God, he replied, 'There must be some higher power or how else does all this stuff work?'").

Weiskel, Peter K. – writer and geologist; b. southern New Hampshire; c. 1978; son of a Congregational minister and raised in New England Protestantism; when he was six the family moved to Newton, Boston; attracted by the suburban gospel of success that God helps those who help themselves; studied Geology at Yale University 1970-1974, where he was a liberal Protestant; loss of brother, Tom, and grand-daughter, Shelburne, who drowned in a half-frozen pond; this destroyed his faith in the suburban gospel of success; a friendly family led him to join the local evangelical church; impressed by a visit to a Catholic church and began to participate in a student parish; discovered the writings of Thomas Merton (see above) and Dorothy Day (see above); attracted by the mystery of the Eucharist; sought instruction and converted to the Catholic faith; editor and administrative assistant to Fr. Henri J. M. Nouwen, the priest and writer; did graduate study and research in groundwater hydrology at Boston University; see *Love in a Fearful Land: A Guatemalan Story* (1984; revised edition in 2006) (with Fr. Henri J. M. Nouwen); "Drawn to the Sacramental Mysteries," in Dan O'Neill (ed), *The New Catholics: Contemporary Converts Tell Their Stories* (1987), p.70 ("That they [Thomas Merton and Dorothy Day] both had converted freely to Catholicism fascinated me. Each, in a unique way, held together the paradoxes that had ripped American Protestantism into liberal and evangelical/sectarian pieces. For example, Merton chose a highly 'sectarian' option – the Trappist order – while passionately denouncing injustice and indiscriminate warfare. Dorothy Day was an activist-journalist in the social gospel tradition who also wrote with mystical fervor about the 'primacy of the spiritual life and never stopped searching for her crucified and risen Lord among the broken ones she served. My experience in liberal Protestantism had been social concern with little spirituality, whereas the evangelicals had a spirituality that didn't seem to address itself to the transformation of unjust social structures. But both spirituality and social concern were present in the Catholic Church, and in a way I'd not seen before.

I encountered in Merton and Day, and in many other Catholics I was coming to know, a certain kind of awareness or spiritual wisdom. Specifically, they knew themselves in all of their weakness, sinfulness, and giftedness; and they knew

God in the depths of his mercy and healing power. I knew precious little of my own sin, even less of my own giftedness, and by then I knew God only by reputation. How could these Catholics probe their own inner recesses so fully, as fully as any Calvinist or Freudian, and yet not succumb to despair? How could they be so optimistic about the eventual redemption of the entire cosmos, and yet be sober about the exact cost involved?

More and more, I found that the answers to these questions had something to do with the mystery of the Eucharist, and the sacramental life as a whole...

[T]he authentic, life-giving paradoxes of Catholicism are many and diverse. For example, the Catholic Church is both a local, even tribal, phenomenon and a transnational institution with a global reach. It is inclusive: every social class, race, and level of ability is represented. 'Catholic' means 'including everybody.' Moreover, Catholicism is both a sanctuary for adoration and contemplation and an animator of political and social reconstruction. We honor those who surrender everything to devote themselves to prayer and penance, and those who labor patiently as husbands, wives, parents, and workers in the secular arena. We are a vast repository of historic wisdom, culture, and tradition, which is also committed to 'reading the signs of the times' and bound by our Lord to look with hope toward the future. We have a clear, coherent, and authoritative body of moral teaching, as well as a long history of pastoral clemency and solicitude toward human failure. We affirm the dignity and goodness of the human body, and indeed of the entire created order, yet we look toward the transfiguration of all things in the kingdom of God.

We must embrace these paradoxes, celebrate them, and bear them in our very flesh and bones. This is our vocation. I pray that God will help us remain faithful to it, for the sake of our own salvation and that of the world").

Welch, Robert Henry Winborne, Jr. - political activist, author, and businessman; b. 1 December 1899, Chowan County, North Carolina; c. 1984 (deathbed); d. 6 January 1985, Winchester, Massachusetts; gifted child; home schooled by his mother until age ten; admitted to University of North Carolina at Chapel Hill at the age of twelve; in his youth he was a fundamentalist Baptist; later became a Unitarian, which he remained for most of the rest of his life; attended the United States Naval Academy and Harvard Law School, but dropped out of both; founded a one-man firm the Oxford Candy Company in Brooklyn, New York; worked later with his brother, James (d. 1985), who then left to run his own candy company; his company went out of business in 1925, but joined his brother's firm and much success (retired a wealthy man in 1956); from his teens an opponent of Communism and believed in an international Communist plot; he joined the Republican Party; in 1950 he lost an election for Lieutenant Governor of Massachusetts; in 1952 he supported Robert Taft's unsuccessful bid for the Republican presidential nomination; a major contributor to Joseph McCarthy's campaign for re-election as Senator for Wisconsin; in December 1958 he founded the conservative group, the John Birch Society; he named the new organization after John Birch, an American Baptist missionary and United States military intelligence officer who had been shot by Communist forces in China in August 1945, shortly after the conclusion of World War II; he claimed that Birch was an unknown but dedicated anti-Communist, and the first American casualty of the Cold War; he believed the United States should adopt a "Fortress America" policy rather than a policy of armed internationalism through alliances; he opposed the war in Vietnam; he wrote several books and edited and published *American Opinion* and *The Review of the News*; in the 1960s he began to see Communism was merely a front for a master conspiracy, originating from the Illuminati; he alleged that President Franklin D. Roosevelt was a Communist sympathizer and knew about the Japanese attack on Pearl Harbor in advance; also alleged that President Truman was used by the Communists with his knowledge and acquiescence; accused President Eisenhower of being a Communist; founded Robert Welch University, Wisconsin; married to Marian Probert Welch (d. 1988) (two sons of the marriage); see *The Road to Salesmanship* (1941); *May God Forgive Us* (1951); *The Life of John Birch* (1954); *The Politician* (1956) (on President Eisenhower); *The New Americanism* (1966) (collection of his essays); G. Edward Griffin, *Life and Words of Robert Welch Founder of the John Birch Society* (1986); Jonathan Schoenwald, *A Time for Choosing: The Rise of Modern American Conservatism* (2002); Sean Wilentz, "Confounding Fathers: The Tea Party's Cold War Roots," *The New Yorker*, 18 October 2010 ("Wherever he looked, Welch saw Communist forces manipulating American economic and foreign policy on behalf of totalitarianism. But within the United States, he believed, the subversion had actually begun years before the Bolshevik Revolution. Conflating modern liberalism and totalitarianism, Welch described government as 'always and inevitably an enemy of individual freedom.' Consequently, he charged, the Progressive era, which expanded the federal government's role in curbing social and economic ills, was a dire period in our history, and Woodrow Wilson 'more than any other one man started this nation on its present road to totalitarianism.'

In the nineteen-sixties, Welch became convinced that even the Communist movement was but 'a tool of the total conspiracy.' This master conspiracy, he said, had forerunners in ancient Sparta, and sprang fully to life in the eighteenth century, in the 'uniformly Satanic creed and program' of the Bavarian Illuminati. Run by those he called 'the Insiders,' the conspiracy resided chiefly in international families of financiers, such as the Rothschilds and the Rockefellers, government agencies like the Federal Reserve System and the Internal Revenue Service, and nongovernmental organizations like the Bilderberg Group, the Council on Foreign Relations, and the Trilateral Commission. Since the early twentieth century, they had done a good deal of their evil work under the guise of humanitarian uplift. 'One broad avenue down which these conspiratorial forces advance was known as progressive legislation,' Welch declared in 1966. 'The very same collectivist theories and demagogic pretenses which had destroyed earlier civilizations were now paraded forth in the disguise of new and modern concepts'").

Whitaker, Daniel Kimball - editor and essayist; b. 13 April 1801, Sharon, Massachusetts; c. 1878; d. 24 March 1881, Houston, Texas; his father, Jonathan Whitaker was a noted Congregationalist minister and scholar; studied at Harvard College (BA in 1820; MA in 1823); later studied theology and was licensed to preach (organized a specific congregation), but turned to journalism; worked as a farmer in South Carolina; in 1828 he married a widow, Mary H. Firth (two sons of the marriage) and ran her cotton and rice plantation; identified himself with the conservative politics of the South; opened a law office successfully in the mid 1830s; in 1835 he began the *Southern Literary Journal and Monthly Magazine* (editor until 1837) and the *Southern Quarterly Review* (editor 1842-1847; his most notable success), which ceased publication with the outbreak of the Civil War; after his wife's death he married Mary Scrimzeour Furman Miller, a writer, also a widow (two daughters of the marriage); he and his wife started *Whitaker's Magazine: The Rights of the South*, in which he argued that the Union had been a failure; continued journalism after the Civil War on the revived *Southern Quarterly Review*; buried in New Orleans; see *Prospectus for the Rights of the South* (1850); *ANB* ("His elegant writing style, his thoughtful analyses of political and social problems, and the wide range of his intellectual interests won him many admirers throughout his long professional career").

Whitcher, Benjamin Williams - Catholic layman; b. 8 December 1811, Rochester, Vermont; c. 1850 (received by Bishop McFarland at

St. John's Church, Utica, New York); d. 17 December 1891, Whitestown, New York; son of Stephen and Esther Emerson Whitcher; ancestors came from England in 1638; in 1847 he married Frances Miriam Berry (1811-1852), the first notable woman prose humorist in the United States, author of *The Widow Bedott Papers* (which were popular and dramatized); in 1853 he married Martha Letetia Ward (d. 1904); graduated from Geneva College, New York, in 1840; completed his theological studies at the General Theological Seminary of the Episcopal Church in New York City; High Church clergyman 1844-1849; influenced by the Oxford Movements and the writings of Newman; see Ellen Hardin Walworth, *Life Sketches of Father Walworth, With Notes and Letters* (1907) ("Some of [Fr. Walworth's] converts became zealous apostles of the faith. Most of them persevered and rejoiced at the sight of him. A few fell away. Several whom he won were married clergymen, who had to face the trying problem of finding a new means of livelihood for their families. In this last class was a fellow student and Tractarian, one of those who wrote to him just as he was starting abroad for the novitiate. His heart prompted this clergyman to visit the friend of by-gone days during the time of a mission at Utica, N.Y. This was his greeting from the convert and missioner: 'Well, Whitcher, don't let us dodge the one great matter of which we are both thinking. Why are you not a Catholic long before this?' 'Sure enough,' was the response, 'that is the great question, and I don't know how to answer it.' 'Ten long years of your life have passed away,' said Father Walworth, 'and still here you are looking one way and rowing the other. How can you do it? How can your conscience bear it?'

A little more urging and this subdued soul, from which much early life and fire had departed, promised to resign his charge of a church at Whitesboro and put himself shortly in the hands of Father McFarland, pastor of St. John's, Utica, for further instruction. This priest, who soon received Mr. Whitcher into the church, became afterwards the Bishop of Hartford, in Connecticut").

White, Lurana Mary – nun and co-founder of a religious order; b. 12 April 1870, East 22nd Street, New York City; c. 30 October 1909 (received with Paul Wattson (see above) and sixteen companions from the Society of the Atonement; her mother, who hated Catholicism and refused to visit her daughter at Graymoor, was received in 1932, shortly before her death); d. 15 April 1935, Graymoor, New York; born into a wealthy family; her father was an Episcopalian; her mother belonged to the Dutch Reformed Church, but became an Episcopalian shortly after their marriage; the greatest influence on her as a young girl was her maternal grandmother, Mary Jean Mills Wheeler ("[S]he was a woman of intense spirituality, and…of continued prayer…She seemed supremely conscious of some great future need of mine. Was it that she had an interior inspiration as to the vocation to which God would call me?"); at the age of ten or eleven she heard a loud voice say, "Someday you will die," which caused her to reflect every day for the rest of her life on the brevity of life and the certainty of death; in her study of history an early hero was St. Thomas à Becket and she disliked the Puritans; at school she developed a love for High Church Anglican liturgy; in 1894 she was received as a postulant into the Anglican Community of the Sisters of the Holy Child in Albany; she was disappointed that the sisters made promises rather than vows, and that there was no mention of poverty at all in the rule; in 1897 she wrote to Paul Francis Wattson (see above) (then known as Lewis Wattson), a High Church clergyman, inquiring if he knew of a group of sisters in the Episcopal Church which took corporate vows of poverty, chastity and obedience, but he knew of no such group; she eventually made private vows of poverty, but this caused her anguish and she left the order; they corresponded about the possibility of founding a new order together; they agreed that they should begin the Society of the Atonement, dedicated to the Franciscan tradition and the goal of promoting Christian unity and mission; they co-founded the Society of the Atonement at Graymoor, Garrison, New York, then a remote place; their special aim was to convince Anglicans that they should unite with the Catholic Church; when in 1907 the General Convention of the Episcopal Church approved a resolution that allowed ministers of other Christian churches to preach from Episcopal pulpits if the local bishop approved, they could not accept this; they decided to leave the Episcopal Church and become Catholics; the corporate reception of the Society of the Atonement into the Catholic Church was the first such occurrence since the Reformation; the two communities (one of friars and one of sisters) continued their apostolate; sent sisters on the mission, both in the United States and abroad, especially to poor children; founded St. Christopher's Inn, at Graymoor, for the care of homeless men, built a novitiate and a retreat house; promoted the Church Unity Octave; see Charles V. Lafontaine, SA, "'Repairer of the Breach' – Mother Lurana White, Co-Founder of the Society of the Atonement," *The Catholic Historical Review*, July 1976, p.434; Lorene Hanley Duquin, *A Century of Catholic Converts* (2003), p.30.

Whitehead, Kenneth D. – writer and speaker on Catholic issues; b. 1931, Idaho; c. 24 May 1958 (received at the Church of Santa Susanna, Rome); sent to Sunday school as a child, but orphaned early and gave up the practice of religion when thirteen or fourteen; fought in the Korean War; his journey to the Catholic faith was a long one, beginning "in my late teens and early twenties, when the aimlessness and meaninglessness of a life without God was forcefully borne in upon me"; majored in French at the University of Utah and the University of Paris; career diplomat in the capacity of Foreign Service Officer who served in Europe, North Africa and the Middle East; chief of the Arabic Service of the Voice of America; conversion influenced particularly by Etienne Gilson on St. Thomas Aquinas, by Georges Bernanos, and by Francois Mauriac; Executive Vice-President of Catholics United for the Faith 1972-1981; in 1988 he was appointed by President Reagan as U.S. Deputy Assistant Secretary of Education for Higher Education Programs; director of the U.S. Department of Education's Center for International Education; noted for his public defense of the Catholic faith; author of several books and many articles; translator of several books into English; see (selective list) *Respectable Killing: The New Abortion Imperative* (1973); *Agenda of the Sexual Revolution: Abortion, Contraception, Sex Education, and Related Evils* (1981); *The Pope, the Council, and the Mass* (1981; revised edition, 2006) (with James Likoudis); Robert Baram (ed), *Spiritual Journeys* (revised edition, 1988), p.416 ("As will become clear, my conversion took place largely through reading and in the realm of ideas rather than through interaction with flesh-and-blood Catholics. I scarcely knew any Catholics...

In this essay [in the volume *The Wisdom of Catholicism*, edited by Anthony Pegis], [Etienne] Gilson pointed out how the threat from Islamic thought that faced Western Europe in the thirteenth century was every bit as great as the threat to Europe from the Moslem armies that Charles Martel had repulsed at the Battle of Poitiers in 732, more than a half millennium earlier. If Charles Martel had not won that battle, historians agree, Europe would have been quite literally Islamicized. If St. Thomas Aquinas had not won his battle, Gilson argued, Europe would have been Islamicized on the intellectual and spiritual planes...

I was tremendously affected by reading this essay of Etienne Gilson's on St. Thomas Aquinas. The point about St. Thomas which it brought home to me with special force was that the values from my own Western tradition that I held most dear - the Western belief in the freedom and dignity of the individual human person within a democratic society based on principles of justice and the common good - were a direct legacy of the Catholic civilization of the Middle Ages. These values had become established in the West not in opposition to the Catholic faith but rather as a direct result of the Catholic faith as it was lived in Europe in the Middle Ages. And it was none other than the greatest of the Catholic philosophers and theologians, the Angelic Doctor himself, who had succeeded in grounding these values solidly in reality and truth, henceforth enabling them to be affirmed by any human mind with conviction and commitment...

[N]ow I had to recognize that what I was enamored of was, in its most impressive manifestations, largely a creation of the Catholic Church. It gradually dawned on me that this was true not only with respect to foundational principles, but also with respect to concrete social institutions such as hospitals, universities, social welfare, rule of law, separation of powers, and other typical Western institutions...

It might be thought strange that someone on the road to the Catholic Church, as it turned out for me, was not more concerned about Christ during all this time. For initiates, of course, it is quite true that the ultimate religious question is and must remain: 'What do you think of Christ? Whose Son is he?' (Mt 22:41) The fact is, though, that my thoughts rarely turned to Christ at this point on my journey. We should never underestimate how verifiably easy it is for so many in this world that dates its calendars from the birth of Christ simply to put Christ out of their minds - this in spite of what we Christians know to have been Christ's unsurpassed and unforgettable passage through this world and His continuing Presence in it. But we should never forget that it is the Church that Christ Himself left behind that continues to bring Him back to the attention of a world too prone to forget Him. For myself, there was the need to discover the Church first; it was the Church that would then bring Christ to me. At this point in my life, I was still engaged in 'reading my way into the Church'...

Two points became fixed in my mind as a result of my reading of [an article on the suppression of the Hungarian Revolution by Francois Mauriac] under the circumstances in which I read it; the two points corresponded to the two parts of the quotation from Pascal: ['Christ will be in his agony until the end of the world' and 'We must not sleep in the meantime'].

'*Christ will be in agony until the end of the world.*' What St. Paul called 'the mystery of iniquity' (II Thess 2:7) will always be with us. Christ by His holy cross has redeemed the world, but we are still obliged to live out the human lives God destined for us when he created the world. Since it is a world into which, even though it has been ultimately redeemed, sin has nevertheless entered in through human free will, we must perforce bear with the consequent pain and suffering - along with Christ, it is necessary to add, for Christ came into the world precisely for the purpose of sharing our pain and suffering - and death - with us.

'*We must not sleep in the meantime.*' As St. Augustine remarked, God created us without our leave. We were not given a choice about whether we were going to come into existence or not. God made the choice for His purposes, and His purposes are the ones which we are in this world to serve. Whoever and whatever we may be, whatever station we may occupy in life, whatever the means we may be given to serve, this 'serving' is what we are in this world to do. There is in fact no way that we can ever escape our condition and our destiny, and what God wants is that we should freely and gladly embrace it, in imitation of His Son. As Newman wrote, 'God has created me to do Him some definite service; He has committed some work to me which He has not committed to another. I have my mission - I may never know it in this life, but I shall be told it in the next. I shall do good. I shall do His work…if I do but keep His commandments'…

However God may lead us to the faith, whether through Catholic writers and the appreciation of the achievements of Catholic civilization, as in my case, or through attraction to the witness and the virtues of committed Catholics, as in the case of so many other converts that I have known, we must never lose sight of what the real center of the faith is and always has to be: Jesus Christ Himself, a divine person possessing both a divine and a human nature, who came into this world, 'suffered under Pontius Pilate, was crucified, died, and was buried; on the third day He rose again from the dead; He ascended into heaven, and from thence He shall come to judge the living and the dead.' It is necessary to believe this before we can go on to affirm also: 'I believe in the holy Catholic Church,' through which Christ principally remains present to us"); "The Church of the Apostles," *This Rock*, March 1995; "Is There a 'Mere Christianity?'" *This Rock*, December 1995; *Flawed Expectations: The Reception of the Catechism of the Catholic Church* (1996) (with Mgr. Michael J. Wrenn); "The Church of the Early Fathers," *This Rock*, June 1996; "The Church of Nicaea and Constantinople," *This Rock*, May 1997; *One, Holy, Catholic, and Apostolic: The Early Church Was the Catholic Church* (2000); *The Catholic Citizen: Debating the Issues of Justice* (2004); *Voices of the New Springtime: The Life and Work of the Catholic Church in the 21st Century* (2004); *The New Ecumenism: How the Catholic Church after Vatican II Took Over the Leadership of the World Ecumenical Movement* (2009);

Mass Misunderstandings: The Mixed Legacy of the Vatican II Liturgical Reforms (2009); *The Renewed Church: The Second Vatican Council's Enduring Teaching about the Church* (2009); *Affirming Religious Freedom: How Vatican Council II Developed the Church's Teaching to Meet Today's Needs* (2010); "The Contraceptive Imperative," *Crisis*, 13 December 2012.

Wiker, Benjamin – writer and lecturer; b. 1960; c. 1987 (received with his wife); brought up as a mainstream Protestant; baptized in the Church of Christ, then went to Methodist churches, latterly only occasionally, until going to college; inspired by studying the Great Books program; degree in Political Philosophy; obtained his PhD in Ethics from Vanderbilt University; taught at several institutions, e.g., Marquette University, Saint Mary's University of Minnesota, Thomas Aquinas College, and the Franciscan University of Steubenville; member of the Discovery Institute; he argues that materialism, because of its incompatibility with the concept of natural law, undermines the ethical foundations of religion; he also exposes the attack on the culture of life in the nineteenth and twentieth century; influenced by Paul Johnson and E. Michael Jones (see above) in showing how the actual lives of notable thinkers led to fundamentally distorted views about human nature and sexuality; see (selective list) "You Have Ten Minutes to Prove the Existence of God to my Husband," *New Oxford Review*, September 2000; *EWTN Audio Library, The Journey Home* (26 February 2001) ("I began to read a church history course...One of the things we read was J. N. D. Kelly's *Early Christian Doctrines*...and I realized, 'Wait a second, these documents didn't just fall from the sky. There was a battle, a five century battle, trying to define these doctrines and keep from distorting the original revelation. That's one thing I saw carefully, just having the original revelation somehow was not enough, because you saw people using religious texts, the Old Testament and whatever New Testament documents they had then, and coming out with wild ideas about the nature of Christ; and all the fights for the first five centuries were about defining the Trinity in some way.

Well, one thing I realized right then and there is that without ecclesiastical authority none of the creeds would be, period. And I realized that all of the Protestants had the creeds, or some part of them. That worried me into saying 'OK, we're talking bishops and councils here, campers; and arguments on the highest level. Where it's impossible to imagine these creeds ever coming into existence without that authority.' It's not authority that 'you believe this because we said so,' but 'this was the revelation we received.'

You can't say that Christ was not a man. You can't say that Christ was not God. You can't say that Christ had three natures or four natures or whatever you're going to do to him. You can't say he didn't have a real soul. And when you can't do these things, why? Because what we received that distorts.

Right, so it works from what we received originally and protects that, and all the creeds came into being to protect that. Well, I mean for heaven's sakes, you know, that put together for me the political philosophy I learned as an undergraduate, and what proved to be necessary historically, just what is true, what happened to bring these creeds into being. You had to have ecclesiastical authority and to be really serious. It wasn't *sola scriptura*...

In reading that the first official canon was issued in 367 by St. Athanasius at Easter, I thought, 'Well, how can you have *sola scriptura*?' You're saying Athanasius, right; and here is the man saying, or showing, historically that the Church is the one giving its revelation that defined what would be canonical. Because I've read the extra-canonical writings and you read them and say 'Boy, am I glad we don't have the gospel of Thomas or Peter or something.' With any of these you're saying, 'Well, that's nice, but unimaginable.'

To me, then, why on earth would you think that the Bible was the source of the Church? I mean, just historically, it's not true. And that kind of harkened back to the experience of trying to use the Bible for a manual which anyone could pick up!"); "Intelligent Design vs. Blind Evolution," *New Oxford Review*, March 2001; *Moral Darwinism: How We Became Hedonists* (2002) (with William A. Dembski); *The Mystery of the Periodic Table* (2003) (with Jeanne Bendick); *Architects of the Culture of Death* (2004) (with Donald DeMarco); *Answering the New Atheism: Dismantling Dawkins' Case Against God* (2006) (with Scott Hahn); *A Meaningful World: How the Arts and Sciences Reveal the Genius of Nature* (2006) (with Jonathan Witt); *10 Books That Screwed Up the World (And 5 Others That Didn't Help)* (2008) ("Thomas Carlyle, the eminent Scottish essayist and sometime philosopher, was once scolded at a dinner party for endlessly chattering about books: 'Ideas, Mr. Carlyle, ideas, nothing but ideas!' To which he replied, 'There once was a man called Rousseau who wrote a book containing nothing but ideas. The second edition was bound in the skins of those who laughed at the first.' Carlyle was right. Jean-Jacques Rousseau wrote a book that inspired the ruthlessness of the French Revolution (and even more destructive things after that)...

If the books we've covered offer an image of insanity, then perhaps by reversing the image and holding it up to a different light we can recover some outline of sanity. Perhaps we are not merely animals as Darwin would have it, hut something more than animals. Perhaps we are not ghosts in machines, as Descartes would have it, but some other strange and glorious creature, something godlike but with two feet on the ground. Yet, being something godlike, we are not, as Nietzsche would have it, gods ourselves, but something far less, a faint but glowing resemblance to Someone else infinitely more resplendent. Perhaps there are dark corridors of our hearts that must be uncovered and exposed to light, as Freud would have it, but the darkness is not as hopelessly dark, and the light comes from another heart illumined by puncture and resurrection. Perhaps we do need a final revolution, as Marx and Lenin would have it, but it is a revolution from within and from above. Perhaps we should, as Mill bid us, seek the greatest happiness of the greatest number, but by filling our souls with unearthly joy rather than merely feeding our earthly pleasures like pigs. Perhaps, as Nietzsche howled, God did indeed die, but rose again, an *übermensch* of a very different kind, one that can save us from the madness of our own making"); *The Darwin Myth: The Life and Lies of Charles Darwin* (2009); "Happy Birthday, Charles Darwin!" *CatholiCity*, 12 February 2009; *10 Books Every Conservative Must Read: Plus Four Not to Miss and One Imposter* (2010); *The Catholic Church and Science: Answering the Questions, Exposing the Myths* (2011); *Politicizing the Bible: The Roots of Historical Criticism and the Secularization of Scripture, 1300-1700* (2012) (with Scott W. Hahn); *Worshipping the State: How Liberalism Became Our State Religion* (2013).

Wilcox, William Bradford ("Brad") – sociologist; c. 1995; studied as an undergraduate at University of Virginia; PhD from Princeton University; held research fellowships at Princeton University, Yale University and the Brookings Institution; Associate Professor of Sociology at the University of Virginia, and a member of the James Madison Society at Princeton University; director of the National Marriage Project at University of Virginia (research on marriage, parenthood, and cohabitation, and on the ways that gender, religion, and children influence the quality and stability of American marriages and family life); was editor-in-chief of *Regeneration Quarterly*; converted to the Catholic Church from Episcopalianism; conversion influenced by Fr. C. John McCloskey III; much writing for many newspapers and journals; see (selective list) "A River Runs to It: A New Exodus of Protestants Streams to Rome." *Crisis*, May, 1999; *Soft Patriarchs, New Men: How Christianity Shapes Fathers and Husbands* (2004); *Why Marriage Matters:*

Twenty-Six Conclusions from the Social Sciences (2005); "Five Myths on Fathers and Families," *National Review Online*, 19 June 2009; "The Evolution of Divorce," *National Affairs*, Fall 2009; *When Marriage Disappears: The Retreat from Marriage in Middle America* (2010); "Daddy Was Only a Donor," The Wall Street Journal, 18 June 2010; When Baby Makes Three: How Parenthood Makes Life Meaningful and How Marriage Makes Parenthood Bearable (2011); "Sex and the Married American," The Washington Post, 22 May 2011; "Why the Ring Matters," The New York Times, 30 June 2011; "Marriages Haves and Have-Nots," The New York Times, 3 July 2011; "A Shaky Foundation for Families," The New York Times, 30 August 2011; Soul Mates: Religion, Sex, Children, & Marriage Among African Americans and Latinos (2013) (with Eric Kaufmann); *Gender and Parenthood: Biological and Social Scientific Perspectives* (2013) (with Kathleen Kovner Kline); *Knot Yet. The Benefits and Costs of Delayed Marriage in America* (2013); "The New Unmarried Moms," *The Wall Street Journal*, 15 March 2013; *wbradfordwilcox.com.*

Wilken, Robert Louis – author and speaker; b. 1936; c. 1994; brought up in New Orleans in a serious Lutheran family (father often president of the congregation); studied for the Lutheran ministry at Concordia Lutheran Seminary in St. Louis; attracted to the sacramental and liturgical side; studied the Church Fathers at the University of Chicago (awarded PhD); became a Lutheran pastor; taught at a Lutheran seminary in Gettysburg, Pennsylvania 1964-1967; appointed to the Theology Department, Fordham University, (first non-Catholic to have a regular appointment in a Catholic theology department); then taught at University of Notre Dame; also taught at the Sulpician seminary in Baltimore in 1967; conversion to the Catholic Church influenced by the Fathers and Medieval figures; also by the intensity of Catholic spirituality and its larger sense than Lutheranism of what the Christian life could be, and by the contemplative side of monasticism; William R. Kenan, Jr. Professor of the History of Christianity at University of Virginia from 1986; Distinguished Fellow of the St. Paul Center for Biblical Theology; has also taught at the Gregorian University, the Patristicum Augustinianum, and the Hebrew University of Jerusalem; specialist in Patristics; see *The Land Called Holy: Palestine in Christian History and Thought* (1992); *Remembering the Christian Past* (1995) ("A Generation ago it was customary in Lutheran circles for pastors to devote two years to teaching young people Luther's Small Catechism. I once heard of a pastor in St. louis, Missouri, whose practice it was to divide the two years of instruction as follows: 'The first year,' he said, 'I have the students memorize the Catechism. The second year I tell them what it means.'

I first learned of this pastor when I was a young man, and like others my age I guffawed. How ridiculous! The whole point of catechism instruction is to help young people understand the meaning of the Lord's Prayer, the Ten Commandments, the Creed. What is the value of having youngsters memorize the words of the Catechism without telling them what they mean? Now years later I realize that this pastor was much wiser than I. He knew that Christian faith was a matter of words, and that what counted most in the Catechism were the words. To be sure, the words signified things and carried meanings, but religious meaning is not univocal. As we mature it grows and deepens, bending and turning as our lives bend and turn"); *EWTN Audio Library, The Journey Home* (26 February 1999) ("The question really became whether one wanted to be in communion with the Church of the Apostles. The point is the Church of the Apostles, the community that traces its history to the Apostles. There are many Christian communities that have apostolic doctrine: the Apostles Creed, the Nicene creed, the basic teachings of orthodox Christianity. But I don't think that's what Catholicism is fundamentally about. It is about that, but it's being part of the community that is continuous through history going back to the Apostles. It's a sacramental thing. We have to remember that Christ comes to us not primarily through ideas, but through things, bread and wine, through persons, things that you can touch and that you can see. And so we don't come to Christ by leaping through the air with our intellects. We come though a community of people who have been themselves in intimate relation with him. And so the Church, the community, is the most significant thing that the Incarnation brought about; that a community came into being that was different. And only the Catholic Church and the Orthodox Church think that way. I mean they think that way, they act that way, they talk that way, they believe that way. There is no interruption. And the way to Christ is not by going through a set of ideas, but it is by becoming part of a community... Becoming a Christian is not simply agreeing to a certain set of ideas. It's taking on a certain way of life and that has to be formed by community.

Now, there are other ways of talking about fullness. Christianity is a religion about coming to know the living God. The living God is a mystery that means that we don't know and then say let's go on to something else. Augustine says, 'We seek what we have found and we find and we continue to seek.' He takes psalm 105, 'Seek his face always,' and he says, 'Why is it that other psalms say "Those who seek the Lord rejoice," not "Those who find the Lord rejoice."' And so the seeking is a finding and the finding then is a seeking. And the fullness, then, comes to us in many different ways, through signs, through persons, through institutions, through ideas, through creation, and these signs, then, are never exhausted. This is like getting to know a human being. The more you get to know someone the more mysterious they become.

And so the fullness needs to be communicated not just in one way, not just through the mind, not just through the heart, not just through the moral life, not just through a certain set of ideas, but through a community's fullness in life...

...I don't think that the Petrine ministry, the ministry of the Bishop of Rome, was a major factor in my becoming Catholic, though the person of this Pope was, but three years ago I went to live in Rome for three months, and I lived at Sant Anselmo, the Benedictine house of studies and seminary there. I think living there I began to get a sense of the catholicity of the Church in relationship to Rome and to realize how much the Church needs the center. It's something that gives people a point of reference, something that can hold together the many diverse parts of the Church. So, I think that this is something that Orthodoxy does not have, and of course no form of Protestantism. And I think that Catholicism, by having a papacy, and now a strong papacy, is able to give people a sense of the Church as not just the historical communion, though the Popes go back for centuries and there's nothing like that institution, but it's also a worldwide communion. You know, the Pope has bishops in from Thailand, or from Nairobi, or from Ireland, or from the South Sea Islands for regular visits. I mean that's an extraordinary feature. And that's only really possible within Catholicism"); *The Christians as the Romans Saw Them* (2nd edition, 2003); *On the Cosmic Mystery of Jesus Christ: Selected Writings from St. Maximus the Confessor* (2003) (with Paul M. Blowers); *John Chrysostom and the Jews: Rhetoric and Reality in the Late 4th Century* (2004); *Judaism and the Early Christian Mind* (2004); *The Spirit of Early Christian Thought: Seeking the Face of God* (2005); "The Church's Way of Speaking," *First Things*, August/September 2005; *Isaiah: Interpreted by Early Christian and Medieval Commentators* (2007); "How to Read the Bible," *First Things*, March 2008; "Christianity Face to Face With Islam," *First Things*, January 2009; *The First Thousand Years: A Global History of Christianity* (2012); Paul M. Blowers, Angela Russell Christman, and David G. Hunter (ed), *In Dominico Eliquio - In Lordly Eloquence: Essays on Patristic Exegesis in*

Honor of Robert L. Wilken (2002).

Williams, Mary Lou (born Mary Elfrieda Scruggs) – jazz pianist, composer and arranger; b. 8 May 1910, Atlanta, Georgia; c. 7 May 1957 (received by Fr. Anthony S. Woods, SJ, at St. Francis Xavier Church, West Village, New York); d. 28 May 1981, Durham, North Carolina; one of eleven children; grew up in Pittsburgh, Pennsylvania; taught herself to play the piano and played to support the family; at fifteen she played with Duke Ellington's early small band and also impressed Louis Armstrong; married saxophonist John Williams in 1926 and joined a band with her husband; recorded several records and became known nationally; also wrote as a freelance for other artists, notably Tommy Dorsey, Benny Goodman, and Earl Hines; divorced her husband in 1942 and married Harold Baker another jazz performer with whom she played; wrote for Duke Ellington; had her own weekly radio show; collaborated with younger musicians, notably Dizzy Gillespie and Thelonius Monk; played in Europe 1952-1954; took time off from performing; began a "street ministry" to musicians affected by alcoholism, drugs, and illness; turned briefly to the Abyssinian Baptist Church in 1955; then Dizzy Gillespie introduced her to Fr. John Crowley, a jazz-loving Catholic priest, who urged her to offer her playing up as a prayer for others; Fr. Anthony S. Woods, SJ, assisted her in reconciling her musical and spiritual lives, and gave her instruction in the Catholic faith during 1956 and 1957; this led to her reception into the Church; she returned to playing music in 1957; in 1960 she formed the Bel Canto Foundation to help musicians in distress; Fr. Peter F. O'Brien, SJ, became her close friend and personal manager in the 1960s when she concentrated on sacred music in the form of masses and hymns, notably *Black Christ of the Andes (Hymn in Honor of St. Martin de Porres)* (1962) (text by Fr. Woods); also very successful in the 1970s with many albums; in total she wrote hundreds of compositions and arrangements, and recorded more than one hundred records; buried in the Catholic Calvary Cemetery, Pittsburgh; see Linda Dahl, *Morning Glory: A Biography of Mary Lou Williams* (2000); Tammy L. Kernodle, *Soul on Soul: The Life and Music of Mary Lou Williams* (2004); Brian Morton, "Soul Player," *The Tablet*, 11 June 2011, p.27; Mary Lou Williams Archive, Rutgers University, Newark, *rutgersedu.*

Williams, Michael – journalist; b. 5 February 1877, Halifax, Canada; c. 1913 (revert); d. 2 October 1950, Hartford, Connecticut; eldest son of Michael Williams, a sea captain who died from yellow fever, leaving his wife with debts, six sons and one daughter; his mother was Anglican, joining the Catholic Church on her marriage to his father, but never really consenting to its claims and giving them up on the death of her husband; he was brought up superficially Catholic, but lapsed in his early teens ("From my fourteenth to my thirtieth year I cannot recall feeling any, even the slightest interest or concern in the Christian religion, or in any other. Art was the only thing that mattered: art and my self"); left school early and worked in a warehouse to help the family; worked as a writer, then as a journalist between bouts of tuberculosis; married Margaret Olmstead in 1900 (two children of the marriage); successful freelance writer of short stories 1907-1913; in 1913 at Carmel, California, he experienced a religious conversion back to the Catholic faith; wrote for *Catholic World*; founded the Catholic journal *Commonweal* in 1924 to review literature, the arts, politics and religion; editor of the journal 1924-1938; he was the major Catholic journalist of his time; resigned as editor, since the new owners disagreed with his support of General Franco; fought with manic-depressive phases; see *The Book of the High Romance: A Spiritual Autobiography* (1918) ("All I can say about my soul is, that I know very well there is something within me which is more than the life of the body and the mind, and which will not die with the dissolution of the body. It is not to be expressed in words, but no words are to be expressed without it. It is that which recognizes Beauty and which knows Love...

I tried to get to the bottom of my confused and wavering mental condition, and, so far as I can express the result of my effort, it might be summarized as follows: First, I am positive in my belief that I exist, a separate, self-conscious, unique individual. I did not create myself. That is beyond all question true. Moreover, it is for me unthinkable that I am the fortuitous result of accidental material forces, chemical or mechanical.

Therefore, I must accept the belief that I was created. A force not in any way dependent upon myself or the world of matter in which I am living, created me, and created the world of matter and all other things. Words like 'Life-Force' or 'Nature' or 'Creative Principle' do not fully express the nature of this Creator. Pre-eminently am I persuaded of the Creator's Eternal Personality. And the name of God opens up for me marvelous and unending vistas of meaning. Hence, I must believe in and acknowledge a God, and that I am His creature.

Now, if God gave me life, He and no other force it is which sustains me in life, and He of course can do what He will with His own. At any moment, then, He may take my life away from me. But this applies only to my life in this world: the life of my body; not the life of my soul; for concerning this I have the same positive belief that I have in the existence and the supreme power of Almighty God. My soul cannot die. I - the true I - am immortal...

[T]he secret of power, I recognized, consisted in personal action. The most beautiful artistic expression of a truth had no such energy as the doing or living of the truth. Therefore, the words of Christ have transcendent and unapproachable power because He was His words; He lived them; His life was in them, and remains in them for ever. ..'I am the Way; the Truth; the Life. He says, not, 'I write a book about the way.' And the words of those who do not live, because they do not Will, what they say, are without real power.

Now, those who actively and consciously will that which is evil are few indeed - although such perverted souls there have been and there are today, especially in the region of the false mysticism - but the harm they do is frightful. They are priests of the Anti-Church, ministers of the Spirit of Denial. And they are served in turn by a host of followers, mystagogues, charlatans and deceivers, many of whom are great artists, and the leaders of intellectual modernity and of Godless science. They are those who would identify themselves with divinity and throw down all final distinctions between good and evil. They are the evangels of the New Paganism.

The soul-hunger of humanity must find food; and if the true food, the Living Bread, is kept from humanity it will turn perforce to the strange foods of idolatry. But the Grace of God - there is no other explanation - preserved me from the dangers amid which I adventured. More and more in my reading I turned from the false lights of fantasy toward the fixed stars and the everlasting Sun. That is, I turned more and more from Blake, and Swedenborg, and Maeterlinck and Yeats, and Whitman, and Nietzsche, and Wells, and William James, and Vedanta, and New Thought, and Spiritualism, and Mystic Masonry, and Mental Science, and the swarming confusion of egotistical and idolatrous voices and cults and movements of the day, and more and more I turned toward poets like Crashaw and Traherne and Herbert and Thompson, and writers - especially these latter - *who had lived the life of devotion*, the Christian Catholic mystics: Saint Teresa, and John of the Cross, and many, many others.

Too many others, in fact. Also too many writers who were not mystics but who wrote about mysticism. I read too much, and prayed too little; though I had indeed at last begun consciously to pray, petitioning (vaguely at first) the Power above all other powers, the One Supreme and Central Light, for help and light and strength. And by and by my prayers became more definite, and (thanks be to Him) at last I turned to Christ in my prayers...

Only the fact that I had formed a habit of prayer, and that my will was turned in part toward its Object, saved me..."); *American Catholics in the War* (1921); *The Little Flower of Carmel* (1925); *Catholicism and the Modern Mind* (1928); *The Shadow of the Pope* (1932); *The Catholic Church in Action* (1934); Robert Brooke Clements, "'The Commonweal,' 1924-1938: The Williams-Shuster Years" (PhD dissertation, University of Notre Dame, 1972); Rodger Van Allen, *The Commonweal and American Catholicism* (1974); *ANB*.

Williams, Tennessee (born Thomas Lanier Williams III) – writer, principally as a playwright; b. 26 March 1911, Columbus, Mississippi; c. 1968 (some claim he converted "only for one day" at a time when he was having severe personal problems; his brother Dakin was also a convert); d. 25 February 1983, New York City; family descended from English, Welsh and Huguenots; father a traveling shoe salesman with a drink problem who was often away from home; his mother was an unstable character with social aspirations; his early childhood was spent in the parsonage of his grandfather who was the local Episcopalian minister and very high church; rather effeminate child with much ill health; grew up in a female dominated environment; from the age of eight brought up in St. Louis, Missouri; wrote short stories from an early age; attended journalism classes at the University of Missouri, in Columbia 1929-1931; worked at the shoe factory where his father worked; wrote many poems, essays, stories, and plays; suffered a nervous breakdown and left the job; in 1938 graduated from the University of Iowa (BA in English); struggled to get his work accepted until his play *The Glass Menagerie* was an enormous hit on Broadway; followed up with *A Streetcar Named Desire*, which was a huge success; both these plays were later made into very successful films; between 1948 and 1959 seven of his plays were performed on Broadway; several other plays were adapted for the screen; Pulitzer Prize for Drama was awarded to *A Streetcar Named Desire* in 1948 and to *Cat on a Hot Tin Roof* in 1955; his plays were intensely personal and passionate; later plays were failures, leading to depression, much drink and drug abuse; in 1956 Cardinal Spellman condemned the film Baby Doll, which had been adapted from one of his short stories, referring to it as "revolting, deplorable, morally repellent, offensive to Christian standards of decency"; had several homosexual relationships; "I wanted to have my goodness back" was the reason he gave for converting to the Catholic faith, but Christianity never really consoled him, although it tempted him with its ideas about salvation and the glory of self-sacrifice; his later plays, though still dealing with grotesque characters, also dealt with salvation; presented with the Presidential Medal of Freedom in 1980; buried in the Calvary Cemetery, St. Louis, Missouri; see (selective list) *The Glass Menagerie* (1944); *A Streetcar Named Desire* (1947); *Summer and Smoke* (1948); *The Roman Spring of Mrs. Stone* (1950) (novel); *The Rose Tattoo* (1951); *Camino Real* (1953); *Cat on a Hot Tin Roof* (1955); *Baby Doll* (1956) (screenplay); *Orpheus Descending* (1957); *Suddenly Last Summer* (1958); *Sweet Bird of Youth* (1959); *The Night of the Iguana* (1961); *Memoirs* (1975); Dotson Radar, Interview: The Art of Theater No. 5, *Paris Review*, Fall 1981 ("[M]y 'conversion' to the Catholic church was rather a joke because it occurred while I was taking Dr. Jacobson's miracle shots. I couldn't learn anything about the tenets of the Roman Catholic Church, which are ridiculous anyway. I just loved the beauty of the ritual in the Mass"); Donald Spoto, *The Kindness of Strangers: The Life of Tennessee Williams* (1997); John A. Coleman, SJ, "Tennessee Williams at 100," *America*, 1 December 2011 ("Williams was never, conventionally, a religious person. Raised early as an Episcopalian, he converted in his dark years, around 1969, to Catholicism, partially under the push of his younger brother, Dakin. Williams did keep an icon of the virgin by his bedside. When he died in 1983, he was buried from Saint Malachy's Catholic Church in New York City and (against his wishes - since Williams wanted his ashes scattered over the sea in homage to his beloved poet, Hart Crane) buried in the Catholic Calvary cemetery in Saint Louis").

Williamson, Mother Mary Paula – nun; b. Cedar Rapids, Iowa; c. 7 May 1927; deciding upon a teaching career she was educated at Iowa State Teachers College, Cedar Falls; taught for several years in schools and universities; in 1916 obtained a BA degree from Columbia University, specializing in School Administration; in 1917 she met the Episcopalian Sisters of the Holy Nativity and in 1919 she entered their Sisterhood; she followed the usual course of novitiate and vows until 1927; then left the Order and was received into the Catholic Church; in November 1927 she began her religious life all over again in the Society of Our Lady of the Retreat in the Cenacle; her Society sent her to England but in 1938 she returned due to ill health and was sent to the Boston Cenacle; began writing for publication; she wrote journal articles, children's books, and translations; see "Anglicanism is not Catholicism," *The Catholic World*, February 1944; *Our Lady Goes A'Maying* (1945); "A Study of the Conversion of John Henry Newman," *The Epistle*, 1945; translation of Igino Giordani, *St. Paul: Apostle and Martyr* (1946) (with Mother Clelia Maranzana); *Little Brother Ben* (1947); "The

Story of Religious Confession," *The Epistle*, 1947; translation of Igino Giordani, *Mary of Nazareth: A True Portrait* (1947) (with Mother Clelia Maranzana); *That All May Be One* (1949); "Suzanne Nedoncelle: Catholic Action in France," *The Epistle*, 1949; translation of Sister Jean Baptiste, *Faith in God's Love* (1950) (with Mary S. Garrity); *Our Lord Jesus* (1952); Matthew Hoehn, OSB (ed), *Catholic Authors* (1952) ("By that time [1927] she had recognized the weakness of the claims for Catholicity in the Protestant Episcopal Church and the weak reflection of them in the Anglican religious life").

Willis, John S. – judge and politician; c. 25 December 1884; BA and MA degrees; served as Attorney-General of Minnesota and in many other public and private capacities; contributor to the *Catholic Encyclopedia*; see essay in Georgina Pell Curtis, *Beyond the Road to Rome* (1914), p.416 ("None of us will stay here long, and then, what? We shall then be fully alive and shall exist forever, but in a new environment...Contemplating an eternal existence and realizing that a Creator who has planned its manifold beauties and advantages must be, in Himself, all that should inspire love and reverence, every true Christian feels irresistibly impelled to conform with the Will and glorious Purpose of the Creator...He has not made two or more revelations, but, simply, one. That revelation, intended as the supreme guide of mankind and womankind, has been made through the work of the seer and prophet, through the work of divinely inspired record-makers and, lastly, by the Creator, Himself, who, descending to this very world of ours, merged Himself into a human form, at the same time assuming the earthly title, Christ, the Anointed. He founded a society to perpetuate His Incarnation and His work. He called that society 'The Church.' Exercising a power and authority which feeble humanity can neither deny nor withstand, He declared that The Church was to be His Body and that He was the Head of that body, that The Church was a living body and that the Church would never fail.

Now, unless we are blasphemous and assert that Christ's word has failed, then we must admit that He has been present with His Church at every moment since the day of His crucifixion and is still present with that great, that incomparable society. The incarnate Creator founded only one Church. He founded only one system of teaching. He founded only one Philosophy.

There is only one institution that existed among the people of our race - the Caucasian - at the commencement of the Christian Era, that still exists. There is no merely human government, no system of human law, no corporation that existed in the days of Caesar Augustus that has not since perished.

Without a break in her continuity, The Church has remained intact from the hour of Christ's Ascension until the present hour. Her course began among the hills and valleys of Palestine. The Apostles - Peter at their head - transferred her central seat of teaching and authority to the City of Rome and there it still remains, august, serene, imperishable. The Church preserved all the learning, all the civilization, and all the art of classic times when barbarism overwhelmed Europe. She converted the barbarians to the Faith of Christ. She founded all the great universities of the Eastern Hemisphere. She covered all the countries of Europe with stately and beautiful structures which are still, and ever shall be, the models for architects and builders. Under her inspiration, Art glorified Europe and the light reflected therefrom sheds its radiance over America.

Maintaining unflinchingly what Holy Scripture calls 'The Faith once delivered to the Saints,' she has survived many and various hostile assaults and her adherents constitute a majority of all professing Christians.

Even though we should have the hardihood to minimize the force of Christ's sayings, 'There shall be One Fold and One Shepherd' and 'Lo', I am with you all days even unto the consummation of the world,' yet we can scarcely assume that the vast majority of Christians are in error or that any one of the different sects among the minority carries the banner and wields the authority of the One True God. The probability is that the majority, especially as its organization has extended, without break, from the days of the Apostles to the present time, is absolutely right. Providence cannot justly be said to have permitted the majority to go astray; and point is lent to this proposition by the inability of the minority - the non-Catholics - to agree among themselves.

The society which has preserved, in marvellous manner, its world-wide organization, amid the wreck and disappearance of all other organizations, which still lives and possesses an ever-increasing vitality, is The Holy Catholic Church, often called The Roman Catholic Church. This latter name has deep significance. Its meaning is that The Church is 'Roman as to the centre and Catholic (universal or all-embracing) as to circumference.'

The Catholic Church may not appeal to all. To some art is meaningless, poetry uninteresting. Some persons are unresponsive to the dramas of Shakespeare, to the poems of Dante and Milton. To many the beauties of nature are never revealed. To quote Wordsworth: 'A primrose by the river's brim/ A yellow primrose was to him/ And it was nothing more.'

I was, once upon a time, outside The One True Fold. I was a non-Catholic. Divine Providence led me to search the Holy Scriptures and in prayer and meditation upon life here and life eternal to seek the Truth. My prayers were answered. I was led out of darkness by the 'Kindly Light.' Now that I stand under the sun-lit dome of Divine Truth, I am conscious of breathing a new and vital air spiritual, conscious of a larger hope, of the coming of everlasting peace").

Wofford, Harris Llewellyn - politician and writer; b. 9 April 1926, New York City; served in United States Army Air Forces during World War II; graduated from University of Chicago in 1948 (BA); enrolled at Howard Law School, Washington D.C. (first white person to do so in many years); transferred to Yale Law School (graduated 1954); attorney for the United States Commission on Civil Rights 1954-1958; became a law professor at University of Notre Dame in 1959; supporter of the Civil Rights movement; friend and advisor to Martin Luther King; member of Democratic Party; advisor to John F. Kennedy's presidential campaign; appointed as a special assistant to President Kennedy on civil rights in 1961; associate director of the Peace Corps 1962-1966; left politics and was president of the State University of New York at Old Westbury 1966-1970; president of Bryn Mawr College, Pennsylvania 1970-1978; then worked in private practice; Secretary of Labor and Industry for Pennsylvania 1987-1991; Senator from Pennsylvania 1991-1995, but lost his bid for re-election; close to the vice-presidential nomination in 1992; advocate of national service and volunteering; married to Clare Wofford (d. 1996); see *It's Up to Us: Federal World Government in Our Time* (1946); Road to the World Republic: Policy and Strategy for Federalists (1948); Lohia and America Meet (1951); India Afire (1951) (with Clare Wofford); A Lawyer's Case for Civil Disobedience (1961); Embers of the World: Conversations with Scott Buchanan (1970); *Of Kennedys and Kings: Making Sense of the Sixties* (1992).

Wolfe, Gene – science fiction and fantasy writer; b. 7 May 1931, Brooklyn, New York City; c. 1956; suffered from polio as a small child; brought up as a nominal Presbyterian; studied at Texas A&M University, but dropped out; fought in the Korean War; degree from the University of Houston; worked as an industrial engineer; edited the journal *Plant Engineering* for many years; retired in order to write full-time; high reputation as a science fiction writer; author of several novels, most famously the multi-volumed *The Book of the New Sun*; many short story collections; was a marriage convert; writing strongly influenced by his Catholic faith; influenced in his faith by G. K. Chesterton (especially *The Everlasting Man*), C. S. Lewis and J. R. R. Tolkien; influential on other writers; difficult style of writing; see *Operation Ares* (1970); *The Fifth Head of Cerberus* (1972); *The Death of Doctor Island* (1974); *Pease* (1975); *The Devil in a Forest* (1976); *The Computer Iterates the Greater Trumps* (1978) (poem); *The Book of the New Sun* (comprising *The Shadow of the Torturer* (1980), *The Claw of the Conciliator* (1981), *The Sword of the Lictor* (1982), and *The Citadel of the Autarch* (1983)); *The Castle of the Otter* (1982) (essays about the writing of *The Book of the New Sun*); *Free Live Free* (1984); *Soldier of the Mist* (1986); *The Urth of the New Sun* (1987); *Soldier of Arete* (1989); *Storeys from the Old Hotel* (1989); *Castleview* (1990); *Pandora, By Holly Hollander* (1990); *Letters Home* (1991) (letters to his mother from the Korean War); *The Book of the Long Sun* (the story of the priest of a small parish, and comprising *Nightside the Long Sun* (1993), *Lake of the Long Sun* (1994), *Caldé of the Long Sun* (1994), and *Exodus from the Long Sun* (1996)); *The Book of the Short Sun* (comprising *On Blue's Waters* (1999), *In Green's Jungles* (2000), and *Return to the Whorl* (2001)); *The Knight* (2004); *The Wizard* (2004); *Golden City Far* (2005); *Soldier of Sidon* (2006); *Pirate Freedom* (2007); *An Evil Guest* (2008); *The Sorcerer's House* (2010); *The Best of Gene Wolfe* (2010); *Home Fires* (2011); Michael Andre-Druissi, *Lexicon Urthus* (1994); Patrick O'Leary, "If Ever a Wiz There Was," in *Other Voices, Other Doors*; Peter Wright, *Attending Daedalus: Gene Wolfe, Artifice, and the Reader* (2003); Robert Borski, *Solar Labyrinth: Exploring Gene Wolfe's Book of the New Sun* (2004); Robert Borski, *The Long and the Short of It: More Essays on the Fiction of Gene Wolfe* (2006); Peter Wright, *Shadows of the New Sun: Wolfe on Writing/Writers on Wolfe* (2007); John Farrell, "The Distant Suns of Gene Wolfe," *First Things*, April 2007; Michael Andre-Driussi, *The Wizard Knight Companion: A Lexicon for Gene Wolfe's The Knight and The Wizard* (2009);

Wolff, George Dering – editor; b. 25 August 1822, Martinsburg, West Virginia; c. 1871 (his wife Sarah, *née* Hill, also converted, as did his brother, Professor Christian Wolff); d. 29 January 1894, Norristown, Pennsylvania; his father, Bernard Crouse Wolff was a prominent divine of the Lutheran Church; in 1835 the family moved to Easton, Pennsylvania, where his father became the English pastor; graduated from Marshall College, Mercersburg, Pennsylvania; studied law for three years at Easton and was admitted to the bar, but never practiced; took a four year course in theology and became a minister of the German Reformed Church; he and his father became followers of John Williamson Nevin (1803-1886), whose system of theology, while strongly opposing Catholicism, held that Christ's Church was a living organism and aimed to restore certain teaching of Christ rejected by the Reformation; he began to see the inconsistency of his religious views and joined the Catholic Church; editor of the *Catholic Mirror* (published in Baltimore) 1872-1873; editor of the *Catholic Standard* of Philadelphia 1873-1894; co-founder with Dr. James J. Corcoran and Fr. James O'Connor of the *American Catholic Quarterly Review*, first issued in Philadelphia in January 1876, and which he co-edited until his death; wrote mainly on apologetics; see "The Mercersburg Movement," *American Catholic Quarterly Review*, 1878; *Catholic Encyclopedia*.

Wood, James Frederick Bryan – archbishop; b. 27 April 1813, Philadelphia, Pennsylvania; c. 7 April 1836 (received by Bishop John Baptist Purcell); d. 20 June 1883, Philadelphia; brought up in a Unitarian family; both of his parents were from England and had moved to the United States in 1809; studied at a school in Gloucester, England, 1821-1826; in 1827 the family moved to Cincinnati, Ohio, where he became a clerk at the Branch Bank of the United States; a friendship with Bishop John Baptist Purcell led him into the Catholic Church; studied for the priesthood in Rome, first at the Pontifical Irish College and then at the College of the Propaganda; ordained to the priesthood 25 March 1844; served in the Diocese of Cincinnati; in 1857 appointed Coadjutor Bishop of Philadelphia; succeeded as fifth Bishop of Philadelphia in 1860; in 1875 he became the first Archbishop of Philadelphia; presided over a great increase in the Catholic life of the area; did much work for the poor, especially orphans; brought many religious orders into the diocese; built a seminary and completed the cathedral; always devoted to the pope; forced to leave the First Vatican Council because of illness, he voted *in absentia* in favor of the doctrine of papal infallibility; buried in the crypt in Saints Peter and Paul Cathedral, Philadelphia; see Francis L. Dennis, O.S.A., "Most Rev. James Frederick Wood (1813-1883), the Fifth Bishop and First Archbishop of Philadelphia" (master's thesis, Catholic University of America, 1932); *ANB*.

Wood, Steve – family life activist; c. 1 July 1990 (received with his wife Karen and his family); born and raised in a Presbyterian family; part of the 1960s rebellion during his time as a student at the University of Florida; dropped out of college and enlisted in the Naval Reserves; began to reflect on the question whether there was a spiritual meaning to his life; studied various Eastern religions; then studied the Bible and came to believe in Christ as the light of the world; repented and prayed for forgiveness for his sins and felt renewed; became a part of the "Jesus Movement"; started to look for Jesus' church and finally joined the Calvary Chapel in California; the chapel's exciting atmosphere and aggressive evangelization resulted in great growth; but there were differences with the pastor's views on doctrine; he returned to Florida and worked with the Jesus Movement there; in 1978 ordained a minister of an inter-denominational charismatic church, but splits occurred again; did further theological studies at Gordon-Conwell Theological Seminary in Massachusetts; started his own church in Florida, later joining with an evangelical Presbyterian denomination; his conversion to the Catholic faith was influenced by studying the Church Fathers in relation to the role of bishops; by coming to a true understanding of salvation by grace, the unity of the Church and the indissolubility of marriage; and by the Catholic witness to the pro-life movement; also influenced by the conversions of Scott Hahn (see above) and Gerry Matatics; resigned his pastorate and became a Catholic; entered a full-time pro-life ministry in Florida; later launched an apostolate, the Family Life Center International, dedicated to supporting traditional family life; see "A Prodigal's Journey," in Patrick Madrid (ed), *Surprised by Truth* (1994), p.77 ("That's when I did something really dangerous. I started reading the early Church Fathers firsthand. I had studied some early Church history, but too much of it was from perspectives limited by Protestant history textbooks. I was shocked to discover in the writings of the first-, second-, and third-century Christians a very high view of the Church and liturgy, very much unlike the views of the typical Evangelical Protestant. The worship and government of the early Church didn't look anything like the things I saw at Calvary Chapel or my own congregation. It looked a lot more, well, Catholic.

Studying the Apostolic Fathers, the earliest of the Church Fathers, terribly upset my Presbyterian convictions. You see the word 'Presbyterian' comes from *presbuteros*, the Greek word meaning elder. The name of the Presbyterian Church reflects the belief that the Church is to be ruled by elders, not by bishops. My studies showed, however, that the early Church was ruled by bishops. Early Church history attested that the apostles had laid hands on men and installed them as bishops. Once I became a Presbyterian minister I thought my search for the Church was over. But now Church history was forcing me on.

[My wife and I] thought we had two options for a more historic and scriptural expression of the Church, the Episcopal Church, or an Evangelical wing of the Orthodox Church. The Roman Catholic Church, although ruled by bishops, was an unthinkable option.

Our anti-Catholicism was still strong enough to rule that choice out entirely. For one thing, Roman Catholicism was abhorrent to my Evangelical spiritual sensitivities. My chief opposition to Catholicism stemmed from my belief that the Catholic Church was leading millions of people to hell because of its teachings on salvation. I thought, as I had been told by countless Protestants from Calvary Chapel to seminary, that the Catholic Church denied that salvation was by grace alone. Since the Bible is clear that salvation is by grace, not by works, and since I thought the Catholic Church taught salvation by works, as far as I was concerned, Catholicism was fatally wrong. What I didn't realize was that the Catholic Church has consistently condemned the idea of salvation by works, teaching that salvation comes solely by God's free gift of grace. Later, when the Catholic position was explained to me, I was amazed at how often it is misrepresented and caricatured by Protestant critics.

But before I investigated the issue of salvation, I first had to answer a more fundamental theological question that had troubled me for a long time. It came to a head in 1986 when I realized I simply couldn't reconcile two pieces in the biblical puzzle.

The first piece of the puzzle was Christ's high priestly prayer recorded in John 17:1-26, specifically the phrase, '1 pray not only for them, but also for those who will believe in me through their word, so that they may be one, as you, Father, are in me and I in you, that they may also be in us,...so that they may be one, as we are one, I in them and you in me, that they may be brought to perfection as one' (v. 20-23). In this prayer, offered to the Father the night before the crucifixion, Jesus prayed for a visible supernatural unity in his Church. I was struck by the Lord's strong emphasis on the unity of his Church, as illustrated by his repetition of the phrase, 'so that they may be one.'

The second piece to the puzzle was in James 5:16, 'The prayer of a righteous man has great power in its effects.' Here was the problem: Jesus is *perfectly* righteous. Why, I asked myself over and over again, was his prayer for the unity of his Church not realized? How could Protestantism be his 'church' when Protestant was nothing but disintegration, splintered, not unified, a frightening proliferation of squabbling, competing denominations, many masquerading under the title 'non-denominational.' The disunity and doctrinal chaos with Protestantism became deeply unsettling to me. I found I couldn't recite the Nicene Creed without the words "I believe in the one, holy, catholic, and apostolic church" raising afresh this troublesome question...

The Catholic Church has bishops who claim apostolic succession, and can back it up biblically and historically; the Catholic Church, unlike Protestantism, possesses visible doctrinal unity; and like the early Church I had read about so wistfully, the Catholic Church had the Eucharist at the center of its worship. These truths intrigued me, but other questions arose. What about Mary? What about salvation by works? What about the Mass and purgatory and praying to the saints? - doctrines which I thought denied the finished work of Christ on the Cross? A huge misunderstanding of these Catholic beliefs still kept me at a distance from Catholicism. Yet there was one aspect of Catholicism that deeply attracted me.

In the midst of this period of searching for the true Church I was intensely involved in the pro-life movement. Anyone immersed in the pro-life movement will find Catholics everywhere! Through my involvement with Operation Rescue I saw exceptional Christian piety in the lives of the Catholics I met and worked with. This impressed me as no doctrinal arguments ever could have. Sharing a prison cell with Catholics helped me to recognize them as my spiritual friends. I knew that we are living through the greatest holocaust of innocent human lives, the bloodiest assault upon the kingdom of God in human history, and Catholics were standing shoulder-to- shoulder with me and other Evangelicals fighting this horror. Catholics, I began to see, were certainly not God's enemies.

By 1986 1 had been fighting the pro-abortion extremists for more than a decade, with not much visible success. I was open for answers that got to the root causes of the abortion holocaust. Catholic pro-life leaders were providing clear and convincing answers. The abortion holocaust, they explained, is the direct result of the sexual revolution.

The sexual revolution was the direct result of the contraceptive revolution. They pointed out to me the tragic 'coincidence' that both the advent of the pill and the sexual revolution came in the sixties.

I was also shocked when they showed me that until 1930, every branch of Protestant Christianity gave a resounding condemnation of artificial birth control. Since then, all Protestant denominations have capitulated and now allow it, and some even promote it. Why, I wondered, was the Catholic Church alone in holding the line in this vital area? Why did the Protestant churches cave in to the Planned Parenthood philosophy?

A few years before joining the Catholic Church, I heard a warning about the abortifacient nature of the pill from a minister friend. The potential for destruction on a vast scale of innocent human life shortly after conception was incomprehensible to me at first. It took a year or so to sink into my mind that the pill causes an incalculable number of *in utero* deaths...

I saw in the Catholic teaching on birth control and contraception the solution for getting at the root of the abortion holocaust and for achieving victory in the abortion battle...

As a pastor, I was witnessing the pain and devastation that the breakdown of marriages was causing couples, and especially their children. After considerable study and reflection, I saw that Scripture taught the indissolubility of the marriage bond.

An examination of history revealed that the teaching of the ancient Church was the same. I saw firsthand that an exception made to Christ's norm on the indissolubility of marriage would grow into a thousand exceptions, resulting in a 'norm' that ultimately vanished...

Protestants are blind to the fact that divorce and remarriage is unlawful because Protestantism itself is an unlawful divorce from the Church... There may have been several areas within the Catholic Church that needed change at the time of the Reformation, yet problems within the Church, like problems within a marriage, do not merit a divorce"); *EWTN Audio Library, The Journey Home* (26 September 1997); *EWTN Audio Library, The Journey Home* (7 July 2003); *familylifecenter.net.*

Woods, Thomas E. ("Tom") – historian and political analyst; b. 1 August 1972, Melrose, Massachusetts; educated at Harvard University (BA in History) and Columbia University (MPhil and PhD in History); convert from Lutheranism; senior fellow at the Ludwig von Mises Institute in Auburn, Alabama; associate scholar of the Abbeville Institute, which promotes the cultural heritage of the American south; against multiculturalism and political correctness; puts himself forward as a libertarian and a proponent of the Austrian school of economics; several academic awards; his critics say that his free market views do not square with Catholic teaching; was associate editor of The Latin Mass Magazine for eleven years; supporter of the Extraordinary Form of the Mass; contributing editor to *The American Conservative* magazine; contributor to many periodicals; see *Ever Ancient, Ever New: Catholic Intellectuals and the Progressive Era* (2000); *The Great Façade: Vatican II and the Regime of Novelty in the Catholic Church* (2002) (with Christopher Ferrara); *The Church Confronts Modernity: Catholic Intellectuals and the Progressive Era* (2004); *The Politically Incorrect Guide to American History* (2004); *The Church and the Market: A Catholic Defense of the Free Economy* (2005); *How the Catholic Church Built Western Civilization* (2005) ("Philip Jenkins, distinguished professor of history and religious studies at Pennsylvania State University, has called anti-Catholicism the one remaining acceptable prejudice in America. His assessment is difficult to dispute. In our media and popular culture, little is off-limits when it comes to ridiculing or parodying the Church. My own students, to the extent that they know anything at all about the Church, are typically familiar only with alleged Church 'corruption,' of which they heard ceaseless tales of varying credibility from their high school teachers. The story of Catholicism, as far as they know, is one of ignorance, repression, and stagnation. That Western civilization stands indebted to the Church for the university system, charitable work, international law, the sciences, important legal principles, and much else besides has not exactly been impressed upon them with terrific zeal. Western civilization owes far more to the Catholic Church than most people - Catholics included - often realize. The Church, in fact, built Western civilization...

No serious Catholic would contend that churchmen were right in every decision they made. While Catholics believe that the Church will maintain the faith in its integrity until the end of time, that spiritual guarantee in no way implies that every action of the popes and the episcopate is beyond reproach. To the contrary, Catholics distinguish between the holiness of the Church as an institution guided by the Holy Spirit and the inevitable sinful nature of men, including the men who serve the Church...

To be sure, most people recognize the influence of the Church in music, art, and architecture. The purpose of this book, however, is to demonstrate that the Church's influence on Western civilization goes well beyond these areas...

[I]t was in 'Dark Age' Europe that the university system, a gift of Western civilization to the world, was developed by the Catholic Church. Historians have marveled at the extent to which intellectual debate in those universities was free and unfettered. The exaltation of human reason and its capabilities, a commitment to rigorous and rational debate, a promotion of intellectual inquiry and scholarly exchange - all sponsored by the Church - provided the framework for the Scientific Revolution, which was unique to Western civilization.

For the last fifty years, virtually all historians of science - including A. C. Crombie, David Lindberg, Edward Grant, Stanley Jaki, Thomas Goldstein, and J. L. Heilbron - have concluded that the Scientific Revolution was indebted to the Church. The Catholic contribution to science went well beyond ideas - including theological ideas - to accomplished practicing scientists, many of whom were priests. For example, Father Nicholas Steno, a. Lutheran convert who became a Catholic priest, is often identified as the father of geology. The father of Egyptology was Father Athanasius Kircher. The first person to measure the rate of acceleration of a freely falling body was yet another priest, Father Giambattista Riccioli. Father Roger Boscovich is often credited as the father of modern atomic theory. Jesuits so dominated the study of earthquakes that seismology became known as 'the Jesuit science.'

And that is far from all. Even though some thirty-five craters on the moon are named for Jesuit scientists and mathematicians, the Church's contributions to astronomy are all but unknown to the average educated American. Yet, as J. L. Heilbron of the University of California at Berkeley points out, 'The Roman Catholic Church gave more financial and social support to the study of astronomy for over six centuries, from the recovery of ancient learning during the late Middle Ages into the Enlightenment, than any other, and, probably, all other institutions' Still, the Church's role in the development of modern science remains one of the best-kept secrets of modern history.

While the importance of the monastic tradition has been recognized to one degree or another in the standard narrative of Western history - everyone knows that the monks preserved the literary inheritance of the ancient world, not to mention literacy itself, in the aftermath of the fall of Rome - in this book, the reader will discover that the monks' contributions were in fact far greater. One can scarcely find a significant endeavor in the advancement of civilization during the early Middle Ages in which the monks did not play a major role. As one study described it, the monks gave 'the whole of Europe...a network of model factories, centers for breeding livestock, centers of scholarship, spiritual fervor, the art of living...readiness for social action - in a word...advanced civilization that emerged from the chaotic waves of surrounding barbarity. Without any doubt, Saint Benedict [the most important architect of Western monasticism] was the Father of Europe. The Benedictines, his children, were the Fathers of European civilization.'

The development of the idea of international law, while at times tenuously associated with the ancient Stoics, is often attributed to the thinkers and rights theorists of the seventeenth and eighteenth centuries. In fact, however, the idea is first found in sixteenth-century Spanish universities, and it was Francisco de Vitoria, a Catholic priest and professor, who earned the title of father of international law. Faced with Spanish mistreatment of the natives of the New World, Vitoria and other Catholic philosophers and theologians began to speculate about human rights and the proper relations that ought to exist between nations. These Catholic thinkers originated the idea of international law as we understand it today.

Western law itself is very largely a gift of the Church. Canon law was the first modern legal system in Europe, proving that a sophisticated, coherent body of law could be assembled from the hodgepodge of frequently contradictory statutes, traditions, local customs, and the like with which both Church and state were faced in the Middle Ages. According to legal scholar Harold Berman, '[I]t was the Church that first taught Western man what a modern legal system is like. The Church first taught that conflicting customs, statutes, cases, and doctrines may be reconciled by analysis and synthesis.'

The idea of formulated 'rights' comes from Western civilization. Specifically, it comes not from John Locke and Thomas Jefferson - as many might assume - but from the canon law of the Catholic Church. Other important legal principles associated with Western civilization can also he traced back to the Church's influence, as churchmen sought to introduce rational trial procedures and sophisticated legal concepts in place of the superstition-based trials by ordeal that had characterized the Germanic legal order.

According to old economic histories, modern economics comes from Adam Smith and other economic theorists of the eighteenth century. More recent studies, however, emphasize the importance of the economic thought of the Late Scholastics, particularly the Spanish Catholic theologians of the fifteenth and sixteenth centuries. Some, like the great twentieth-century economist Joseph Schumpeter, have even gone so far as to call these Catholic thinkers the founders of modern scientific economics.

Most people know about the charitable work of the Catholic Church, but what they often don't know is just how unique the Church's commitment to such work was. The ancient world affords us some examples of liberality toward the poor, but it is a liberality that seeks fame and recognition for the giver, and which tends to be indiscriminate rather than specifically focused on those in need. The poor were all too often treated with contempt, and the very idea of helping the destitute without any thought to reciprocity or personal gain was something foreign. Even W. E. H. Lecky, a nineteenth century historian highly critical of the Church, admitted that the Church's commitment to the poor – both its spirit and its sheer scope – constituted something new in the Western world and represented a dramatic improvement over the standards of classical antiquity

In all these areas the Church made an indelible imprint on the very heart of European civilization and was a profoundly significant force for good"); *33 Questions About American History You're Not Supposed to Ask* (2007); *Sacred Then and Sacred Now: The Return of the Old Latin Mass* (2007); *Who Killed the Constitution?: The Fate of American Liberty from World War I to George W. Bush* (2008) (with Kevin Gutzman); *Beyond*

Distributism (2008); *Exploring American History: From Colonial Times to 1877* (2008); (ed), *We Who Dared to Say No to War: American Antiwar Writing From 1812 to Now* (2008); *Meltdown: A Free-Market Look at Why the Stock Market Collapsed, the Economy Tanked, and Government Bailouts Will Make Things Worse* (2009); *Back on the Road to Serfdom: The Resurgence of Statism* (2010); *Nullification: How to Resist Federal Tyranny in the 21st Century* (2010); *Rollback: Repealing Big Government Before the Coming Fiscal Collapse* (2011); *The Catholic Church: Builder of Civilization*, a thirteen-episode television series on EWTN (2008); *tomwoods.com.*

Woodson, Silas - politician; b. 18 May 1819, near Barbourville, Knox County, Kentucky; c. Summer 1895 (his third wife was received in 1896); d. 9 October 1896, Saint Joseph, Buchanan County, Missouri; lawyer; member of Kentucky State House of Representatives 1842, 1853-1855; delegate to Kentucky state constitutional convention 1849; he advocated a gradual end to slavery; moved to Missouri in 1854; circuit judge in Missouri 1860-1870; elected twenty-first Governor of Missouri 1873-1875 (first Democrat to hold the post since the Civil War); he organized a force to capture Frank and Jesse James (his distant relatives); again circuit judge in Missouri 1881-1896; married in 1842 to Mary Jane McRoberts (1825-1845) (one son, Miller); married in 1846 to Olivia Adams (1828-1856) (no children) and in 1866 to Virginia Juliet Lard (1846-1907) (three children of the marriage); converted late in life from Protestantism to the Catholic Church; much personal tragedy in his life, including the early deaths of his first two wives and the death of his son Miller at the age of twenty-one; buried in Mount Mora Cemetery, Saint Joseph; see Henry Morton Woodson, *The Woodsons and Their Connections* (1915); Lawrence O. Christensen, William E. Foley, Gary R. Kremer, and Kenneth H. Winn, *Dictionary of Missouri Biography* (1999), p.813 ("Nature blessed Silas Woodson with a handsome physique. His sonorous voice, enhanced with cultivated oratory and sharpened by practical debate, was greartly admired by his colleagues. Juries were influenced by his commandsing figure and exceptional presentations of reason, eloquence, and persuasion; colleagues respected him as a formidable courtroom opponent").

Wright, John C. (born John Charles Justin Wright) – author; b. 1961; c. 2008; brought up a Lutheran; educated at St. John's College, Annapolis, Maryland (studied the Great Books Program); interested in science fiction from a very early age; studied at the Marshall-Wythe School of Law at the College of William and Mary,

Virginia (graduated in 1987); admitted to practice law in New York, Maryland and Washington D.C.; became disillusioned with the law; worked as a journalist, then as a technical writer; became a successful author of science fiction and fantasy novels; married to L. Jagi Lamplighter, fantasy writer and author of the *Prospero's Daughter* trilogy (2009-2011) (they have four children); in 2003 he converted from atheism to Christianity and then in 2008 was received into the Catholic Church ("If Vulcans had a Church, they'd be Catholics"); has also written several short stories and novellas; see (selective list) *The Golden Age* (*The Golden Age* (2002), *The Phoenix Exultant* (2003), *The Golden Transcendence* (2003)); *War of the Dreaming* (*Last Guardian of Everness* (2004), *Mists of Everness* (2005)); *Chronicles of Chaos* (*Orphans of Chaos* (2005), *Fugitives of Chaos* (2006), *Titans of Chaos* (2007)); "Total Conversion," *scifiwright.com*, 11 September 2007; "The Pure Church of Imagination Land," *John C. Wright's Journal*, *scifiwright.com*, 3 January 2012 ("Every person who teaches or believes an opinion on matters of Christian faith and morals not in conformity with Church teaching, (technically known as a heretic) claims to be returning to an original Church uncorrupted by Church teachings.

I know of no exceptions, that is, I know of no prophet who claims to be teaching a new doctrine that improves upon the past and is disconnected with it. Even Mohammad, who repudiates nearly all other Christian teachings, claims the books of the Bible were once valid, and are now corrupt, and that his recital is a return to the purer and older faith.

Since the Old Testament and the New alike are replete with warnings against false prophets, lying spirits, false teachers, and since Our Lord himself warns against the leaven of the Pharisees and the substitution of the customs of men for the commandments of the Lord, these claims cannot be dismissed without careful consideration.

One would think the first thing to be considered would be the Patristic Writings. All a man concerned with the return to the uncorrupted beliefs of the Early Church need do is quote the writings of the Early Church, and note what the Fathers anathematized, and show that the modern Catholic or Orthodox Church supports what was once anathematized, and anathematizes what she once supported.

In my admittedly limited experience, I have yet to see this done. I have not come across heretics quoting passages from the Early Fathers to show that their position was once the orthodox belief of the Church, and only later was ignored or suppressed. I have, in contrast, seen anathematized writings quoted to show that the opinions expressed therein were once current (though the claim that they were official is never made) and I have also seen apocryphal writings dismissed as witnesses that the opinions expressed therein were ever current, because the writing was thought unworthy of inclusion in the canon.

But far more often, the authority of the Early Fathers is ignored: as if history consisted of time from the Creation to the writings of the later Prophets, as covered in the Old Testament, then a small gap, then the Advent of Christ and the events in the Acts of the Apostles as covered in the New, and then a long gap where nothing was written and nothing was said worthy noticing, until the rise of the founder of the breakaway Church, whose words are studied with care.

The lack of interest in the Early Church writings, and the scarcity of them, gives the imagination scope for inventing rather than investigating an imaginary Early Church, which, by no coincidence, resembles the heresiarch's fancy rather than historical fact. The earlier the date of this imaginary pure Church, the fewer writings and records need to be explained or explained away. The earlier this imaginary pure Church is pushed, the less and less I find such an argument convincing, because the greater and greater is the claim of insight being made by the heresiarch: he claims to know the minds of men long dead better than their immediate students knew them. In some cases, they claim to know the message of Christ better than those who learned that message at His feet.

The older the date on the claim, the less believable it is. I am more willing to believe an argument that the Church of AD 1400 went astray than that the Church of AD 400 or AD 40, because the earlier the date, the more outrageous the claim, because the greater and more immediate the corruption.

In a game of Russian Telephone, the boy who hears the message first is, statistically speaking, less likely to be suffering from accumulated errors than the tenth or twentieth boy in line. In the case of the heresiarch, a boy not in the game, who does not even know the names of the boys who were third in line from the source, claims to have an uncorrupted version of the message straight from the source.

It is less unbelievable to say the followers of a student of a disciple of an apostle of Christ mistook or corrupted the teaching of Christ than to say that the disciples of the apostles mistook or corrupted it; still less the apostles; still less Christ Himself.

Ironically, this makes the claim of Mohammad or Joseph Smith more feasible than the claim of Luther or Calvin or Sun Myung Moon, since a prophet claims authority directly from God, whereas a mere theologian claims to have deduced the original and uncorrupted teaching of the Church using no other source than official Church teachings, and the reflections of natural reason. Prophets are supposed to be able to confirm their authority with signs and wonders. By that standard, Mary Baker Eddy (whose church to this day makes weekly, if not daily, reports of miracles, which they claim to be confirmed by multiple witnesses or doctor's testimonies) is a more believable prophet than Mohammad, who healed no sick, opened no blind eyes, and raised no dead. Of course, by that standard, the healings of Lourdes, which continue to this day, and to this day have no scientific explanation, confirm with signs following the prophetic authority of the original Church.

There is also a general problem with the theory of the corrupted Church: If the one, true, catholic, and apostolic Church Christ founded is corrupt and heretical, then Christ is forsworn of his word to send a comforter to guide his disciples in to all wisdom, or, to be precise, that the Church disobeyed this spirit.

This problem is not fatal to the claim of the heretic, because, honestly, it may be so. Men disobey God. Indeed, the common reading of the Book of the Apocalypse warns of an abomination within the nave of the temple itself: this is often read to refer to the Church herself becoming Apostate, deceived by the false prophets and the Beast spoken of darkly by the Apocalyptic riddles and figures. But then again, if we are talking about any point before Doomsday, the charge of an Apostate Church is difficult to square with Scripture.

If the Church of Christ lasted less than 300 years, so that Constantine corrupted it even before the Bible was finalized and before the Nicene Creed written, then God is foolishly limited in his powers.

If the Church lasted less than thirty years, so that with the assumption of Saint John, the last Christian departed the world never to be seen again until the Sixteenth or Eighteenth or Nineteenth Century, then God is more foolish.

If the Church failed during Pentecost, so that none of those baptized of the Apostles of Jesus were true Christians, God is a most enormous fool, because His Church, prophesied never to have the gates of Hell prevail against it, did not prevail a space of 50 days.

AND, by the same logic that says God Himself cannot keep His Church uncorrupted past the ascension of Jesus, the descent of the Holy Spirit or the assumption of John. We have no reason not to assume that the newer and shinier prophet, whoever he might be, Mohammad, or Joseph Smith. or Mary Baker Eddy, or Rev. Sun Myung Moon did not found a newer and shinier church with any more staying power than the first.

Anyone who says that the Catholic Church was corrupted within three centuries or one, or in one generation, or one decade, or fifty days after Jesus ascended, by what right can that one next claim that the revived church resisted corruption for a season, a decade, or a century or three, or however old it is now? By the fruits of the spirit, perhaps? Does the allegedly revived Church have the same unchanging and unyielding teachings about matters of faith and morals as it had since the moment of revival, such as believing as strongly in the perpetual virginity of Mary as did Martin Luther, or being as opposed to contraception and abortion as all Christian denominations before 1934 were? Are the Anglicans as enthused and devout to the Thirty Nine Articles as they were in the days of Elizabeth or Henry VIII? Are they are opposed to divorce and remarriage as Christ?"); "The Theist Widow Cannot Regain Her Atheist Virginity," *John C. Wright's Journal*, *scifiwright.com*, 16 January 2012 ("The reason why I stay a Christian is a matter of pure logic: the atheist world view does not explain the facts it attempts to explain, and so I cannot return to it. A theory that neither predicted the current facts nor explains the past facts is not a theory.

That world view is too shallow to explain anything about human nature or our role in the cosmos, or ultimate fate or the purpose of man in life, and is usually too silly. (Yes, silly. I have more patiently explained more often to men suffering the delusion that they are meat robots without free will that if they were meat robots they could not suffer that or any other delusion, since robots by definition have no points of view, nor consciousness, nor reasoning power, than I care to remember.)

But let us not allow the presence of silly or stupid atheists of the Left to obscure the fact that atheists of the right can, unlike their fellows who are atheists for emotional reasons, give a rational account for their stance. Not all atheist accounts of the world are silly. Some are merely inadequate to explain the facts that the theory attempts to explain. Why do I not return to one of these dignified version of my old haunts?

The reason is because atheism rests on an absolute moral imperative to think and believe the truth, no matter how painful and disheartening, merely because it is true. If it so happens that we mortals exist in a universe created by nothing and no one for no purpose, and the intellectual tools given us are insufficient for determining ultimate questions of ultimate importance, then a moral imperative to seek the truth at any cost demands our view of life consist of the admission of that limitation. To say one does not know what one does not know is what truth demands.

However, if the atheist world view cannot account for the existence of an absolute moral imperative to think and believe the truth no matter the cost and no matter the pain to oneself, then it does not rest on the imperative on which it rests. If natural reason tells us no natural reason to be naturally reasonable, why follow reason? The atheist cannot appeal to a mystical reason for the imperative, nor to a reasonable supernatural reason.

I submit that an atheist world view can account for the existence of an absolute moral imperative only if it has an associated moral code which logically flows from its premises. That code must be based on something other than the transcendental and supernatural truths religion claim to base its values on, because atheists hold such supernaturalism to be against reason.

There are any number of atheist world views. Any world view not requiring reference to a god is atheist. But there are not an infinite number of atheist world views that can be logically consistent and yet uphold a moral code. In order to be logically consistent with the conclusion that the answers to any or all of the ultimate questions of the meaning of man's life in the cosmos is forever beyond human reason one must either be a Stoic, or a hedonist, an idolater or a nihilist.

A Stoic says that he can endure the pain of not knowing his purpose and destiny because he must. Moreover, a moral code based on Stoicism will serve for a military hierarchy, but one cannot erect the moral code needed for an enlightened society on such a narrow base.

A Hedonist says there is no purpose and destiny aside from those pleasures a man can devise for himself before he dies, and laughs at the notion that such pleasures will pall and fail with passing time. Moreover, a Hedonist cannot devise a moral code which commends self sacrifice, even the minor self sacrifices needed for the maintenance of civilization. Hedonism is the vanguard of barbarism.

A man can adopt some human cause, some simplistic and simply wrong idea, such as libertarianism or communism or environmentalism, as a substitute for religion, and bring to the idols of this world those selfless impulses and spiritual hungers which otherwise would draw man's heart to the next world. Alas, the main weakness of such idolatry is that it is local. The libertarian sees exactly one problem in life: how to exercise liberty while escaping tyranny and anarchy. The communist sees exactly one problem: how to ensure the success of the historically inevitable proletarian revolution to usher in an era where the laws of economics will be suspended. And the other simplistic answers likewise: any moral question falling outside the model of the one problem is ruled to be not a problem. For a libertarian, drug abuse and pornography are ruled to be non-issues. Theory says they cannot cause problems, or, at least, no problem where the cure of outlawing the practices are not worse than the disease. For the Marxist, theory says that there are laws of history, but no laws of cause and effect or laws of supply and demand. Scarce goods can be made abundant merely by rationing them and adopting policies that discourage their production. The theory says this will not cause a problem.

Examples could be multiplied. The problem with simplistic answers is that simplicity is not ecumenical or catholic, that is, the world view does not apply to the world, only to one's personal or factional but parochial mental landscape.

A nihilist says such questions can have no answer in this or any other universe, because life is meaningless by definition, and the only truth is that there are no truths. Moreover, so called moral relativism is the only moral code that can float on the vacuous foundations of nihilism. It is a total eclipse of the powers of moral reasoning and moral persuasion: the ability to imagine ethics vanishes along with any motive to make or to heed ethical reasoning

Experience shows that each of these four approaches, Stoicism, Hedonism, Idolatry, Nihilism, eventually fails of its object, which is to produce a satisfactory account for life, a moral standard consistent with human dignity, and a motive to uphold civilization.

Of these, only Stoicism, the philosophy of a warrior elite, can maintain a civilization, but not above the level of the Rome of Marcus Aurelius of the China of Confucius. It cannot, if itself, maintain a non-slaveholding state.

If to maintain an enlightened and modern civilization is one's goal, these four stages of the atheist decay are washed out bridges too short to reach that destination. So logic will not allow me to return to the ideas experience has proved inadequate and cramped to explain the wide wonder of the world, and insufficient a foundation to justify a minimal set of civilized moral standards"); "Amateur Theology Hour: On Irenicism and Heresy," *John C. Wright's Journal*, scifiwright.com, 31 March 2012 ("After my conversion, and having no loyalty one way or the other for any particular communion, and, being an American, having a Constitutional right to join whichever I pleased without fear of legal retaliation, I was in the position of an orphan who, having just discovered that his parents are alive after all, rushes to their arms only to find them divorced, and commanding to choose whether he will live with father or mother. He is put in the position of a judge between them, despite not being trained to judge such disputes, nor being inclined by temperament to do so.

I discovered that you Christians, you foolish Christians, had shipwrecked and severed your Church, and the world is scandalized. The mocking atheist points at this as evidence that She is merely a human institution, no more sacred than the local Zoning Commission, and he says, 'Those who preach love and altruism fight over homoousianism and homoiousianism, the difference of an iota! Religion breeds division rather than quells.' Being a local and lawyerly thinker, I looked to the sources of dispute.

That the Protestants find the Real Presence to be scandalous was no concern to me: I did not see why, if almighty God can incarnate Himself as a Jewish Rabbi, He cannot incarnate Himself as a loaf of bread. Is one so much more dignified than the other?

The existence of icons and statutes likewise meant nothing to me. It was clear even to an outsider that these were objects of reverence but not worship, no more idolatrous than singing a hymn.

I had no enmity against St Mary. I was raised Lutheran, and to this day am not sure what the point of the contempt for St Mary is, or why the mother of the savior merits being ignored.

Whether or not man was justified by works of faith or by faith that produced works was of no moment to me, since I intended both to have faith and to do good works, as do all true Christians.

These were all non-issues, not worth writing a paragraph to discuss, much less write a book, much less fight a war. So, to me, the only point in contention worthy of consideration was the doctrine of *Sola Scrip*tura. My reasoning was as follows.

It is a paradox for a Christian to hold the Bible to be the sole authority settling all matters of Christian dispute. There is no paradox to hold it as a final authority, and that any doctrine which contradicts unambiguous scriptural teaching, such as the prohibition on divorce and remarriage, is doctrine of men and condemned.

But those who propose the Bible to be the sole authority, and the traditions of the Church to mean nothing, propose either a seeming impossibility or a real impossibility. If it is a seeming impossibility, he who proposes the paradox must resolve it, and show us a way out of the dilemma. The paradox is this: the Gospels cannot have more authority, cannot be trusted, more than the Church who wrote it, compiled it, protected and transmitted it, interprets it and teaches from it. No water can rise higher than its source.

The usual way out of this paradox is to propose that the Church at one time, the Early Church had the authority to write the Gospel, but since has grown corrupt and untrustworthy, as proof of which there is much the Church teaches, such as prayers for the dead or the perpetual virginity of Mary, not found in the Gospels. But this is making an historical claim: one must select a date after which the increasing corruption removes the authority of the Church.

The earlier one pushes this date, the less believable is the claim. If Polycarp and other Fathers who learned from the feet of the Apostles in the early Second Century got the message wrong, and if the only message we have is the message they preserved and taught, there are no grounds to assume a theologian or visionary in the Sixteenth or Nineteenth Century somehow can get the message right. Gnostics say the Apostles themselves got the message wrong, before any of them took pen to paper.

Unfortunately, an investigation of the earliest surviving Church writings shows a continuity rather than a discontinuity with current teaching. I refer the curious reader to Cardinal Newman's *Essay on The Development of Christian Doctrine.*

The error with the argument about Church corruption is Donatism, namely, that if the Church is somehow held responsible for the existence, say, of the Spanish Inquisition, and is said to lack teaching authority on that ground, then once the Spanish Inquisition is disbanded, why does the authority not return? Why did the authority lapse in any territory beyond Spanish control?

Or to put it another way, if some bad men mislead an overly worldly Church in days of yore, what does that mean to me, if those bad men are centuries gone, and the Church no longer worldly? Was the Real Presence in the Eucharist up until the time of Ferdinand and Isabella, then it fled?

And since there is no uncorrupted denomination to which to turn in contrast, the question is moot. So we are left with two theories: one is that the Church became heretical beyond redemption at a particular point in time, and the other is that the Protestants are heretics no different from any others, with the sole exception that they were more successful in their rebellion against their fathers and teachers…

[T]here are major differences between the various opinions of Christianity, differences vehement enough to provoke wars and persecutions, and an endless flood of letters. Nothing else can be expected: if Christian teaching is correct, it is the only light in the world, and the enemy has no other weapon aside from heresy and division to quench that light.

What I cannot see is why the Protestant ideas are any more authentic and original than those of other break away sects. I agree that they were more successful, but are they obviously so much more reasonable than say – certain Gnostics, who interpreted Jesus as a purely spiritual being; the Ebionites, who interpreted Jesus as being a Jewish rabbi and prophet and nothing more; the Marcionites, who interpreted Jesus are being not Jewish at all, and repudiated the Old Testament; the Montanists, who interpreted the Church as being the province of private revelation of the Holy Spirit; the Donatists, who quite reasonably said that no one who betrayed the Church could ever hold Church office again, nor were any of their sacraments valid; the Arians, who quite reasonably said that if God is One and God is the Father, Jesus was not God, not eternal, but some lesser (but still very dignified) created being; Pelagius, who, quite reasonably said that the sins of Adam did not necessarily contaminate all human nature, since it would be unfair to punish a son for the sins of the father; Nestor, who, quite reasonably said that Jesus must be both God and Man, and that the godhead absorbed the human nature (or maybe that is monophysite - I get them confused); the Monophysites, who, quite reasonably said that Jesus was one being with one nature, and that was a divine one (or maybe that is a Nestorian - I get them confused).

Shall I go on? I am only up to the Fifth Century, and I have not listed the heresies of Menander, Cerenthis, Saturnalius, Basilides, the Nicholites in the First Century; nor Corpocrates, Valentine, Epiphanes, Prodicus, Tatian, Severus, Cerdonius, Marcion, Apelles, the Cataphrigians, Artotirthrites, Peputians, Ascodrogites, Pattalorinchites, Bardesanes, Theodotus the Currier, Artemon, Theodotus Argentarius and Hermogenes in the Second Century; nor have I mentioned the heresies of Praxeas, Sabellius, Paul of Samostata, of Manes, nor Tertullian and Origen (both of whose writings are preserved and respected by the Church nonetheless) nor the heresies of Novatus and Novatian, nor Nepos and the Angelicals in the Third Century; nor the Circumcellionists of the Fourth Century, who were total nutbags, going around trying to get people to martyr them, and beating and robbing them when they wouldn't.

Now, at some point, the mind starts aching at all this river of diverse opinion, and one either says, as an atheist does, that it is all imaginary nonsense and there is no truth whatever to be had in this morass, or one says, as the Orthodox and Catholic Christian does, that there is a malign spirit in the world attempting to stir up controversy and division - because this amount of divergent opinion on these matters, the degree of hair splitting, the degree of hatred, is unusual.

But if one says that each individual man, by himself, armed only with his own natural wits and a copy of the Bible translated by someone, somewhere, whose names only scholars know, can negotiate this mass of refined and excruciating theological and technical arguments, guided only by the Holy Spirit, one also has to say, as many Protestants do, that God does not desire the unity of His Church. However, nothing in the Bible nor the early Church writings indicates that the Lord desires a marketplace of ideas and a flock without a shepherd.

I admit it is possible that God does not desire a unified Church - Allah certainly does not. Not having a clergy is one of the distinguishing marks to draw the Christians of African and Near

Eastern provinces of the Roman Empire into Muslim society. I limit myself to the statement that the scripture and the Patristic writings do not confirm this theory.

I do not see a remarkable difference between Luther and Calvin and any of these other enthusiasms which carried men away from the mainstream Church. The argument in favor of no Real Presence in the Eucharist or in favor of *Sola Scriptura* has even less evidence, in terms of proof texts from scripture or Patristic writings, than the argument for Arianism.

Worse, I do see that each and every heresy I've looked at in detail, with the sole exception of Gnosticism, the first and oldest, was based on political and cultural considerations: Donatism was Romans versus Egyptians, for example, Filioques was Greek-speakers against Latin-speakers, Lutheranism was Germanic Princes on the fringe of civilization against civilization of the Mediterranean, the Holy Roman Empire.

The rebellion of the Anglicans under Henry VIII was not even given the dignity of being hidden behind a theological dispute: it was a naked power grab by the nobles of England, who looted the monasteries that owned most of the land, and the rich dispossessed the poor because no one was strong enough to stop them.

So I firmly pray all the various branches of the tree planted by Christ would gather back together. I doubt it will happen before the end of the world.

The reason for my loyalty to the Roman Catholic Church is merely my human reason telling me that if Christianity means anything at all, it means what the Church teaches; and, given the painfully obvious weakness of men for heresy, the Church must have a legal process for determining what the Church teaches, such as by General Councils.

Following the opinion of a man with a new idea about why the Church should be stricter than she is, is not, and cannot be that process. Following a man with a private revelation, like Joseph Smith, or a radical new theory of healing, like Mary Baker Eddy, cannot be that process.

So, by all means, let us embrace each in only love, as brothers, despite our differences of opinion. Let us also be aware that not just the worldly powers like German princes and English kings want to tear the Church in sunder, otherworldly princes of Hell wish it also, creatures well able to deceive the wise and great. A little bit of love and good will despite our differences annoys the worldly powers more than anything"); "A Universal Apology," John C. Wright's Journal, scifiwright.com, July/August 2013 (seventeen fine articles on his conversion) ("I have several reasons for accepting that the Catholic Church is what she says she is, and not what the various break-away denominations says she is.

The first was an argument I came across way back when I was an atheist. It was a theological argument presented as a dialog between the ghost Thomas Aquinas and the ghost of Martin Luther with an imaginary C.S. Lewis on the authority of Christian tradition…

It had no effect whatsoever on my belief at the time…Nonetheless, such arguments can have a winner and a loser even from the point of view of a skeptical outsider, because if you grant the unreal premises, one man's conclusions will follow and the opposite will not…

In this case, the ghost of Luther argues that Christianity teaches that there is one scripture, one salvation, and one sovereign Lord; and that therefore the claim by the Catholic Church to have a magisterium, a teaching and interpreting authority in effect adds a second scripture to the first; next, that salvation is by faith alone and therefore the claim of the Catholic Church to require good works in effect adds a second means of salvation; and third, that divine grace alone saves man, not man's cooperation in that grace, and therefore the claim of the Catholic Church that man has free will adds a second sovereign to the universe, and impugns the power of God.

On the other side, the ghost of Aquinas argues that sola scriptura, a doctrine not found in scripture, is a contradiction in terms, that it must lead to endless fissiparation not to mention that it undermines the Church authority by whose sole witness anyone knows the Bible to be authoritative; that man is indeed saved by faith alone, but that good works are a necessary outgrowth of that faith, if it be real faith; and that if sovereign God wills man to have free will, it does not impugn that will, no more than the freedom of Homer to pen Odysseus as a character who, in his tale, has free will and freely makes his character choices within that tale (as, for example the heroine in Trilby does not when her will is robbed by the mesmerism of Svengali).

Now, without going into the details of that argument (which frankly I do not recall) this was the first time it was brought to my attention that the Catholic Church and the Protestant denominations are not making the same claims.

It is not like the old television gameshow To Tell The Truth where a man and two imposters all claim to be one and the same celebrity, and the panelists by cunning questions attempt to discover his identity before the master of ceremonies asks the real celebrity please to stand up. It is more like a law case where a mother and a daughter both claim to have the exclusive right to inherit the patrimony of an absent father, the mother basing her claim on widowhood, and the daughter asking the court to divest the mother and turn the property over to her on the grounds that the mother has mismanaged the estate.

The idea is no doubt familiar to religious believers, but this was the first time in my blissful atheist existence, that I came across the idea that the Protestant claim to speak authoritatively and magisterially on Church teachings logically presupposes the magisterial authority of the Church, that is, the Catholic Church, to establish Church teachings, such as the canon of the Bible...

I thought the ghost of Aquinas scored a clear, perhaps even unanswerable, victory in the debate...Now, let me emphasize that the reason why this argument lodged in my memory was due to sheer contrarian perversity. I had not known the Catholics (sad inmates as they were in that airless tower of superstitious darkness called the Church) could make logical arguments, much less make sound ones. But, neither as an atheist with no dog in that brawl, nor as a Catholic vowed to live and die in the faith, to this day, do I see any error in the argument.

In effect, the Lutheran claim is a claim of the right to rebel against the teaching authority of the Church, on the grounds that the Church is apostate. Unfortunately, the sole witness for the apostasy of the Church is an alleged disagreement between Church teachings and the scriptures on which the Church relies for those teachings.

But the sole witness for the validity, canonicity, historicity, and divinity of those selfsame scriptures is the authority of the Church whose members wrote them, gathered, sanctified, protected, promulgated and canonized them.")

Wyman, Henry Harrison, CSP – priest and author; b. 6 March 1849, Westminster, Worcester County, Massachusetts; c. 1871; d. 6 March 1929, Chicago, Cook County, Illinois; parents led exemplary lives, but his father never joined a church and his mother was only baptized (into Orthodox Congregationalism) when he was eleven; at the age of nineteen he professed religion through reading Scripture, became a Congregationalist and was baptized; also influenced by *The Pilgrim's Progress*; graduated from Brown University in 1871; after becoming a Catholic he entered the Paulist novitiate in 1872; ordained to the priesthood on 8 March 1876; served on the missions 1877-1894; co-founder of a new Paulist house in San Francisco in 1894 and remained there until 1914 (superior from 1899); gave great service to the city; in recognition of this he was appointed chaplain to the State Senate, the first Catholic so honored; worked in Chicago 1914-1920, then transferred to New York; finally returned to Chicago in 1924; wrote a book and pamphlets, as well as articles for *The Catholic World*; buried in St. Joseph's Cemetery, Fitchburg, Worcester County, Massachusetts; see *Certainty in Religion* (1905) ("We can know that there is a God because we can see the things He has made. The fact of a creation by an Omnipotent Being is, therefore, taught us by reason, because a chain of finite causes presupposes a self-sustaining and all-controlling Power which has formed it and which keeps it in existence.

What are called secondary or created causes do not of themselves reasonably account for the existence of anything, because they are limited and dependent. In the last analysis, therefore, we find that an Infinite Creator must exist, or there could be no finite existences. Furthermore, the ultimate or final cause precludes the possibility of anything else being eternal ; hence, we conclude that everything else that does exist must have been created or produced out of nothing. A secondary cause plainly cannot produce any thing greater than itself. For this reason Evolution cannot explain the origin of things. Creation is the only complete rational explanation of the origin of the universe...

Now, if Christ were not really what He claimed to be, we are forced to admit one of two dreadful alternatives: either that He erroneously thought Himself to be God, or that He wished to have His disciples believe that He was God, both of which are too shocking to be even considered by any sincere and devout mind. Furthermore, what could be more unreasonable than to believe that One who taught the world more wisdom than it has ever learned from any other source, and all other sources put together, could have been so deluded as to have imagined that He was God, if He was not. And the latter alternative is too awful to be considered for a moment; for even His worst enemies, when He was upon the earth, did not dare when He challenged them to accuse Him of sin"); essay in Georgina Pell Curtis (ed), *Some Roads to Rome in America* (1909), p.516 ("In the course of my private study I found out that in the fifth century the pope was universally recognized in Christendom as the successor of St. Peter; this was the teaching, too, of our professor. Then I asked myself. Can I suppose an error on such a fundamental point was believed by all Christians universally? That cannot be. All Christendom cannot err. They could not so err even humanly speaking; four hundred years after Christ men had as good means of knowing what His Apostles taught as we have of knowing what the first Reformers taught. They were within hand's reach of the primitive Christians and still in the heroic age of the religion of Christ...

Yet I had a struggle; my greatest difficulty was Papal Infallibility. My early surroundings had kept the Papal question so entirely out of my way that the bearings of Scripture on it had not arrested my attention. It was just after the Vatican Council and the air was full of discussion. Although the Catholic doctrine of Infallibility is as plainly in the New Testament as the Trinity is, yet I spent many hard hours of debate with myself and others over it…

During a course of several interviews [with a priest] we settled down to the study of the typical case of Pope Honorius, fully and elaborately going through the whole evidence, and at the end I was completely convinced of the doctrine of infallibility. An article in *The Catholic World*, by Rev. Augustine F. Hewit [see above], on the apostasy of Dr. Dollinger, helped me very much. Rev. J. Kent Stone's [see above] *Invitation Heeded* fell into my hands, and by the time I finished reading it I was as much a Catholic as I am today"); *The Story of My Religious Experiences* (1920) (account of his conversion); The *Scholastic Philosophy Explained* (1927).

Wyman, Jane (born Sarah Jane Mayfield) – actress; b. 5 January 1917, St. Joseph, Missouri; c. 8 December 1954 (received with her children Maureen and Michael); d. 10 September 2007, Rancho Mirage, California; her parents were Manning Mayfield, a laborer, and Gladys Christian, an office worker; they divorced when she was four and her father died suddenly a year later; her mother wanted to pursue her own career and so put her in the care of foster parents (Richard and Emma Fulks); raised with very strict discipline; worked as a radio singer, manicurist and switchboard operator; obtained small parts in films in Hollywood under the name of Sarah Jane Fulks; began using the name Jane Wyman in 1936; long series of B-pictures until *The Lost Weekend* (1945) made her a star; three Academy Award nominations; won the Academy Award for Best Actress for her role as a deaf-mute rape victim in *Johnny Belinda* (1948); appeared in over eighty films; also many television appearances, notably in *The Jane Wyman Show* and in the soap opera *Falcon Crest* (1981-1990); married Myron Futterman (1900-1965) in 1937 (no children; divorced 1938); married Ronald Reagan (1911-2004) in 1940 (two daughters of the marriage, one of whom died shortly after birth; they later adopted a son); they divorced in 1949; married in 1952 Frederick M. Karger (1916-1979), Hollywood music director and composer (divorced in 1955; re-married in 1963; divorced again in 1965); her conversion to the Catholic faith said to have been influenced by her good friend and fellow actress Loretta Young, with whom she attended Mass, and her role in the film *The Blue Veil* (1951) (filmed in and around St. Patrick's Cathedral in New York City); became a devout Catholic and member of the Dominican Third Order; supported several charitable causes related to the Church and the Dominican Order, and the Arthritis Foundation; buried at Forest Lawn Mortuary and Memorial Park, Cathedral City, California; see Joe Morella and Edward Z. Epstein, *Jane Wyman:*

A Biography (1985); Lawrence J. Quirk, *Jane Wyman: The Actress and the Woman: An Illustrated Biography* (1986); Edmund Morris, *Dutch: A Memoir of Ronald Reagan* (1999); John Berkery, "Two Different Converts to Catholicism," *Catholic Life*, May 2011, p.54; *ANB*.

Young, Alfred, CSP – priest; b. 21 January 1831, Bristol, England; c. 1850; d. 1900, New York City; parents settled in the United States after his birth; studied at Princeton University (graduated in 1848); entered the medical department of the University of New York, becoming a Catholic while there (graduated in 1852); began to practice medicine, but gave up in order to study for the priesthood at the Seminary of St. Sulpice, Paris; ordained as a secular priest on 24 August 1856; appointed at once vice-president of Seton Hall College, New Jersey (there for one year); much parish work; joined the new Paulist Order; worked for many years as a missionary preacher and held many offices in the order; great contribution to Catholic church music in the United States; composer of many church hymns; many articles for magazines and newspapers and some poetry; see *The Catholic Hymnal* (1884); *Catholic and Protestant Countries Compared in Civilization, Popular Happiness, General Intelligence* (1894) ("Considering the fact that the Catholic Church, both in her doctrine and spiritual treatment of souls, has equally drawn all these varied classes to her fold, fully satisfying all their intellectual convictions and spiritual aspirations, it seems to me that that fact alone might reasonably be deemed by any reflecting person quite sufficient evidence that the Church is the true Church of God. In one word, that she is the Church of the divine Truth, of the divine Goodness, and of the divine Love.

The proverb, 'All roads lead to Rome,' is true in so far as it includes all the pathways of those who seek the realization of their ideals and the fulfillment of their desires in what is higher, better, and purer, and in what brings them nearer to God. Rome is like the centre of a circle, the point of unity at which all the countless true radii converge from all possible directions. In that singular unparalleled attraction which the Catholic Church exercises in being the end of the journey of so many persons of diverse gifts, tastes, and needs is fulfilled the prophecy of our Lord: that when He should be lifted up (to be seen and known of all) then would He 'draw all men unto Himself.'

If the life-histories of many converts could be known, even of not a few of those whose names are here recorded, we would see fulfilled in a signal manner the prophecy of Isaias concerning the Church: 'The children of them that afflict thee shall come bowing down to thee; and all that slandered thee shall worship the steps of thy feet, and shall call thee the City of the Lord, the Sion of the Holy One of Israel' (Isaias lx. 14)"); *The National Cyclopedia of American Biography (Supplement I)* (1910) ("His name is most prominently identified with the reformation of Catholic church music in the United States, looking especially to the abolition of the hitherto prevailing concert style of singing and of the use of modern musical masses and vespers rendered by mixed choruses of men and women, and urging a return to the ecclesiastical 'choir' or sanctuary chorus of men and boys for singers, and to the use of the authorized liturgical Gregorian chant for all that is ordered to be sung in the Catholic services. The influence of his writings and personal efforts on this subject has been widely felt throughout the United States, as it has also been in securing the general acceptance by the clergy and people of another similar musical reform, viz., congregational singing in Catholic churches, to the introduction of which he has particularly devoted the latter years of his life").

Young, Joshua Maria (original name Josue Moody Young) – bishop; b. 29 October 1808, Shapleigh, Maine; c. October 1828; d. 18 September 1866, Erie, Pennsylvania; one of ten children of a prominent New England family of Protestant ministers; raised as a Congregationalist; became a printer's apprentice for a newspaper; editor of *The Maine Democrat* newspaper; after borrowing Catholic books from a co-worker, he decided to become a Catholic; after his conversion he changed his name to Joshua Maria in honor of the Blessed Virgin Mary; he studied for the priesthood in Cincinnati, Ohio, and later in Emmitsburg, Maryland; ordained to the priesthood 1 April 1838; worked as a missionary in the West before moving to Ohio; consecrated second Bishop of Erie, Pennsylvania in 1854; opponent of slavery during the Civil War; presided over great growth of diocese; *Catholic Encyclopedia.*

Young, Robert V. Jr. – author and critic; b. 1947; c. 13 April 1974 (Holy Saturday; received with his wife, Suzanna); mother "reared Methodist and drifted into vaguely pious indifference"; father "had early lost his faith and become quite irreligious"; although attended Protestant sevices as a child, brought up with almost no religious formation; thought of himself as an agnostic while in high school; studied at Rollins College, Florida (BA in English), where he became interested in T. S. Eliot and C. S. Lewis, and so in Christianity; in 1967 he and his wife-to-be became Episcopalians (considering themselves as Anglo-Catholics) and in 1968 were married in that communion ("The Episcopal liturgy, using the 1926 Book of Common Prayer, seemed dignified, beautiful, and orthodox in our eyes"); MA and PhD from Yale University; taught at North Carolina State University in Raleigh from 1972; became disillusioned with the liberalism of Episcopalianism ("It was troubling that there could be two parishes in the same 'Church' with liturgical differences so pronounced as to amount to doctrinal differences"); he and his wife were soon very active in right-to-life work and met a number of good Catholics; later Professor of Renaissance Literature and Literary Criticism in the English Department; author of many books and articles on literature and education; has also written on moral and religious topics; conversion of him and his wife influenced by the issue of abortion and the reiteration in 1968 of the traditional Catholic teaching on artificial contraception ("For all the talk about *Humanae Vitae* driving Catholics from the Church, it was instrumental in bringing us in: not only because its teaching is true, but because it was so plainly the work of the Holy Spirit guiding the Vicar of Christ. It seemed obvious to us that Pope Paul VI would have rather walked on hot coals and broken glass than issue the encyclical, which brought so much opprobrium upon him; but he could not flinch on a clear matter of doctrine, despite his timid tergiversation on matters of policy and discipline"); co-founder and co-editor (with M. Thomas Hester) of the *John Donne Journal*; president of the John Donne Society 1998-1999; editor of *Modern Age* from 2007; contributing editor of *Touchstone* magazine; translator of Latin; married with five children; see *Richard Crashaw and the Spanish Golden Age* (1982); "The Old New Criticism and its Critics," *First Things*, August/September 1993; "Nature and Grace in the Character of Western Man," in *Christianity and Western Civilization. Christopher Dawson's Insight: Can a Culture Survive the Loss of Its Religious Roots?* Papers PresentedataConferenceSponsored by the Wethersfield Institute New York City, October 15, 1993 (1993) ("It may be that we are witnesses to the disintegration of a culture and a moral order two thousand years and more in the making. It is no less true for being a truism that Western civilization represents the convergence of Athens and Jerusalem, of classical philosophy and Judaeo-Christian revelation, of nature and grace. As the privileged heir to this tradition, Western man has, for several centuries, tended to take it for granted and, more recently, to despise it altogether. We now confront a generation for many of whom the traditional culture of the West is simply incomprehensible. The dynamic character of Western culture, noted by [Christopher] Dawson, lies precisely in the nexus of nature and grace: in the transfiguration of what is naturally human by divine favor. The divine half of the equation was put in question by the Reformation and has been increasingly neglected or denied in the wake of the Enlightenment; in our era even human nature has been rendered problematic. As long as some sense of natural norms or standards persists, then at least the possibility of grace is implicit precisely in the inevitable failure of human beings to attain what seems to be the fulfillment of their natural birthright; but once this sense of nature is lost, then there can be no conception of the grace that transcends it. The current dismantling of Western culture can be witnessed in two quite diverse but equally fundamental areas of human life: sex and language. Both instances provide evidence of the reciprocal deleterious effects of the vicious behavior of individuals on the health of a culture and of the moral decline of a culture upon the character of individuals. Christopher Dawson observes, in 'The Patriarchal Family in History,' that normative sexuality is necessary to the very existence of civilization: 'It is impossible to go back behind the family and find a state of society in which sexual relations are in a pre-social stage, for the regulation of sexual relations is an essential prerequisite of any kind of culture.' In this 1933 essay, Dawson proceeds to express alarm over the prospect of a general acceptance of contraception in the Western world and its effect upon the family: 'Marriage will lose all of its attractions for the young and the pleasure loving and the poor and the ambitious. The energy of youth will be devoted to contraceptive love and only when men and women have become prosperous and middle-aged will they think seriously of settling down to rear a strictly limited family' (John J. Mulloy (ed), *The Dynamics of World History* (1978), pp. 157-158, 165). Dawson also maintains that language is an integral feature of human culture: 'Culture and language are inseparable aspects of the same process, so that it is impossible to regard one of them as existing without the other.' This linguistic element is the decisive factor in man's capacity to perceive reality: 'Thus a culture and its language taken together,' Dawson continues, 'form an autonomous world of meaning and existence which is indeed the only world of which the individual is conscious' (*The Formation of Christendom* (1967), pp. 35-36). Even with his prescience it seems unlikely that Dawson could have foreseen the extent to which his worst fears would be realized by the 1990s"); *Principles of Letter-Writing: A Bilingual Text of Justi Lipsii Epistolica Institutio* (1996); *At War with the Word: Literary Theory and Liberal Education* (1999); *Doctrine & Devotion in Seventeenth-Century Poetry: Studies in Donne, Herbert, Crashaw, and Vaughan* (2000); *A Student's Guide to*

Literature (2000); "The Bard, the Black, the Jew," *First Things*, March 2004; "The Gay Invention: Homosexuality Is a Linguistic as Well as a Moral Error," *Touchstone*, December 2005; "Hope's Eternal Spring: Shallow Optimism, Vain Hopes and God's Absent Presence," *Touchstone*, September 2006; "The Catholic Mind in the Modern World," *Saint Austin Review*, September/October 2006, p.12 ("It is necessary first to dispel the clouds of ignorance hanging over one of the best kept secrets – at least among the popular information media - of our times; namely, that the modern world rests firmly upon medieval foundations. Civic life and the rule of law, which had their beginnings in the city-states of ancient Greece and republican Rome. were preserved in the scriptoria of monasteries and in episcopal chanceries during the Dark Ages. The resurgence of town life and commerce, the development of representative assemblies and systematic legal codes, and growth of schooling were all made possible by the civilizing as well as the evangelizing work of the medieval Church. The hospital and the university, two institutions that embody what we most prize in modern society. are entirely owing to the Church. Even modern science with all its technological and industrial sequelae takes its origins from medieval Christendom. Hence the modern world that so often seems so hostile to the Catholic Church - that is, the secular, consumer society that is now sweeping the globe - was born and nurtured in the bosom of Western Christian civilization...

Catholics lost an historic opportunity in 1968, for example, by not defending *Humanae Vitae*. 'Progressives' scoffed when Paul VI warned that the willful separation of the unitive and procreative aspects of the marital act would lead to 'conjugal infidelity and a general lowering of morality' (*Humanae Vitae* 17). 'To use this divine gift destroying, even if only partially, its meaning and its purpose is' he maintained, 'to contradict the plan of God and His will' (*Humanae Vitae* 13). The doctrine of human sexuality draws a clear line between the Catholic mind and the modern mind: the former acknowledges that we are God's creatures, and our lives and bodies belong to Him. The modern mind characteristically sets itself apart from the divine law and demands absolute autonomy. We insist upon being the gods of our own world with the result that we become instead slaves to our own basest passions and, ultimately, to dehumanizing political and cultural forces.

There is, paradoxically, hope in the manifest moral disintegration of our world. The proliferation of social pathologies in a society of affluence, abundance, and opportunity has put in question the social-engineering projects of modernity. Disillusion has set in over abortion, divorce, and the vileness of the entertainment industry. Now the specter of homosexual 'marriage' has cast a pall of unease over the regime of forcible tolerance that has displaced the civilization of love. This is a propitious moment for Catholics to remind our fellow citizens that the magisterium 0f the Church has been right all along. Nevertheless, there are no grounds for political optimism: the universities, the government bureaucracies, and the media are still in the grip of the Prince of the power of the air. Cultural disintegration can be very rapid; restoration is always slow and problematic. But there are also no grounds for despair. Nations, societies, and civilizations will all perish and, in Shakespeare's words, 'leave not a rack behind.' Men and women, however, are immortal: their souls will live – in unimaginable bliss or unspeakable horror – forever. Each of us must strive to act and speak as a faithful instrument of grace in the hands of Our Lord. If a faithful word, a hopeful gesture, or a charitable act on our part moves a single soul to live eternally in joy, then we have accomplished something more important than any election victory, military triumph, or political appointment. The modern world, in which we all in some measure 'glory', will vanish into nothing, but Christ is 'Alpha and Omega, the beginning and the end,…who is and who was and who is to come, the Almighty' (Rev 1:8)"); "Residual Catholicism in Hamlet," *Saint Austin Review*, January/ February 2007, p.4; "A Conversion Story," unpublished, 11 September 2012 ("It is fair to say that abortion was the critical issue that made us reconsider our membership in the Episcopal Church. The Catholic Church was the only institution solidly on the right side in the most important conflict, as it still seems to us, of the time.

But *Humanae Vitae* nonetheless played an important role. The encyclical was issued in 1968 a month or so after our marriage. We kept up with religious news then (as now) and assumed with almost everyone else that the encyclical would accommodate 'enlightened opinion.' We were surprised at the encyclical and impressed by its argument, but also sickened by the torrent of vitriol unleashed on Pope Paul VI, who, I am sure, if he could have, would have arrived at a different conclusion. Within a few months, we decided that we were not comfortable using artificial contraceptives, and we have stuck with that decision ever since (although it is hardly relevant now!). It cost us a good deal of explaining over the next few years: 'Why is your wife pregnant again? What kind of birth control are you using?' 'We don't believe in that.' 'Oh, you're Catholic, well…' 'No, we're not Catholic…' When we began taking instruction, we were already doing pro-life presentations, in Catholic parishes as well as other venues. Many 'cradle Catholics' were not pleased with the pro-life message, and many asked us why on earth we wanted to become Catholics anyway ('What's the difference? Churches are pretty much the same.') I eventually settled on one of two answers: one frivolous - I am really fond of balloons and banners in worship - and one deadly serious - to save my soul. The second left my interlocutors more dumb-founded than the first.

Hence the importance of *Humanae Vitae*: it of course has a crucial place in the history and destiny of the Church and of humanity, but it was also a special source of grace for a couple of newly-weds, groping their way to the Truth. It became increasingly clear that 'flesh and blood did not teach' Paul VI this doctrine, nor was it his own rather retiring character that furnished the fortitude to proclaim this sign of contradiction to a hostile world. For Suzanna and me it was a guarantee that the Roman Catholic Church really is the Church of Christ, nurtured and protected from error by the Holy Spirit. If the abortion issue opened our eyes to the Church's Wisdom, *Humanae Vitae* revealed Her strength and courage").

Zaleski, Carol – theologian and writer on religion; c. 11 July 1991 (received in the chapel of the twin Benedictine communities of St. Mary's Monastery and St. Scholastica Priory in Petersham. Massachusetts); Jewish heritage, but had a wholly secular upbringing ("Whatever I knew of Judaism and Christianity came to me mainly through reading. The chief influences were Augustine, Anselm and the monastic theologians of the 12th century, in whose writings I caught sight of a country I longed to inhabit but - I know this will seem strange - didn't know where to find"); educated at Wesleyan University (BA) and Harvard University (MA and PhD in the Study of Religion); taught at Harvard; Professor of World Religions at Smith College, Northampton, Massachusetts; celebrated for her writings on the afterlife; originally influenced by William James' *The Varieties of Religious Experience*, but came to see the importance of dogma ("I have altered mainly by swimming upstream against the currents to which James introduced me, from personal religious experience 'immediately and privately felt' to worship objectively offered; from theology as therapy to theology as queen of the sciences"); further influenced by Newman's approach to dogma and, in particular, by *The Development of Doctrine* and *The Idea of a University*; editor-at-large and regular columnist for *The Christian Century*; has written for several leading newspapers and magazines, including the *Washington Post*, *New York Times*, *America*, and *First Things*; one of the earliest writers to explore

Mother Teresa's reported spiritual trials; married to Philip Zaleski, writer on religion and spirituality; see *Otherworld Journeys: Accounts of Near-Death Experience in Medieval and Modern Times* (1988); *The Life of the World to Come* (1996); *The Book of Heaven* (2000) (with Philip Zaleski); "In Defense of Immortality, " *First Things*, August-September 2000; *Prayer: A History* (2005) (with Philip Zaleski); "The Dark Night of Mother Teresa," *First Things*, May 2003 ("[O]nly in the modern period has the dark night of the soul taken the form of radical doubt, doubting not only one's own state of grace, but God's promises and even God's existence. A wise Benedictine, John Chapman of Downside Abbey, made this point in a 1923 letter to a non-monastic friend: '[I]n the seventeenth and eighteenth centuries most pious souls seem to have gone through a period in which they felt sure that God had reprobated them... This doesn't seem to happen nowadays. But the corresponding trial of our contemporaries seems to be the feeling of not having any faith; not temptations against any particular article, but a mere feeling that religion is not true.'

For this annihilating temptation, Chapman wrote, 'the only remedy is to despise the whole thing, and pay no attention to it - except (of course) to assure our Lord that one is ready to suffer from it as long as he wishes.' The 'feeling of not having any faith' is painful because it is an authentic purgation, during which 'faith is really particularly strong all the time,' and one is being brought into closer union with the suffering Christ.

This was exactly the way Mother Teresa learned to deal with her trial of faith: by converting her feeling of abandonment by God into an act of abandonment to God. It would be her Gethsemane, she came to believe, and her participation in the thirst Jesus suffered on the Cross. And it gave her access to the deepest poverty of the modern world: the poverty of meaninglessness and loneliness. To endure this trial of faith would be to bear witness to the fidelity for which the world is starving. 'Keep smiling,' Mother Teresa used to tell her community and guests, and somehow, coming from her, it doesn't seem trite. For when she kept smiling during her night of faith, it was not a cover-up but a manifestation of her loving resolve to be 'an apostle of joy'"); "Case for the Defense: Arguing For God's Existence," *The Christian Century*, June 2007; "Slow Motion Conversion," *The Christian Century* (2010) ("One still hears complaints about the 'institutional church' - the very expression betrays a *parti pris*. But how would we know Christ without the institutional church? Who else would preserve the great secret of the gospel for us through the centuries, keeping it safe in the wilderness of opinions? We live in a world of institutions or in no world at all, and the institutional church is surely the greatest institution the world has ever known. It is the mediating institution between the family we are thrust into and the government that is either forced upon us or chosen by us from a distance. It equips us with every grace, every insight, every support for a decent life and then, like so many parents, is disappointed but not surprised when we turn around and say - we don't need you, we can do this on our own, you are a fossil, an impediment.

Do we have more reason to trust experimental, free-floating forms of religious life? Give me an institution any day, a big sprawling, international one, where authority resides in structures and traditions and is not invested in particular personalities; where my own personality is of little account, and yet I get to keep it. The ship of faith has its anchorage in the world, and I thank Constantine for it"); "The Mass Finds Its Voice," *The Christian Century*, July 2011 ("I first encountered the mass in mid-air. At least, that's how it felt. I was lying on my stomach on the living room carpet in a Manhattan apartment 13 stories above ground, listening to my parents' recording of Bach's *Mass in B Minor.* I had never attended a religious service of any kind, but with the help of liner notes that included the ordinary of the mass in Latin and a literal English translation, I was able to follow along. For several years the 'Qui tollis peccata mundi' haunted my consciousness; in college it became an instrument of my conversion. Later on I learned that Bach had adapted a melody from Cantata 46 ('Schauet doch und sehet' / 'Behold and see') to serve the Latin text common to Lutheran and Catholic worship. It was an inspired act of translation, wedding a universal language of Christian worship to a musical vernacular.

The second time I heard the mass I was stretched out on the same carpet listening to my parents' 1963 Philips monaural recording of *Missa Luba,* an exuberant setting of the mass sung by a Congolese (Luba) boys' choir. A Belgian Franciscan had found a way to unite the call-and-response improvisational singing of the Luba people with the universality of the Latin words. Once again, I could follow along thanks to a faithful English translation. Those liner notes became my missal and catechism.

Much has changed since then - in the year *Missa Luba* was published, the Roman Catholic bishops at the Second Vatican Council approved the *Constitution on the Sacred Liturgy*, calling for a revision of the liturgical books in the light of biblical and apostolic sources, with the aim of deepening awareness of the Eucharist as the central mystery of Christian life. With regard to music, 'pride of place' was reserved for Latin Gregorian chant, with generous scope for polyphony. The document also sanctioned vernacular translation of the Roman missal, on the understanding that the Latin original would provide the norm, the measure and the ballast for the translators' art.

The third time I heard the mass it was in Spanish, in a small Mexican church. It was and is a vernacular liturgy wonderfully transparent to the Latin original. So too, I have discovered, are the French, the German, the Polish and the Maltese. Among a vast company of successful vernacular liturgies, the English-language mass stands out for its divergence, in the name of 'dynamic equivalence,' from the Latin original. Thankfully, a fresh and improved translation of the third revised edition of the Roman missal, already in use in Australia, New Zealand and southern Africa, will gradually be placed in service in the U.S., Ireland and the U.K. beginning in September, to be fully deployed by the first Sunday of Advent.

If reception of this new translation is as generous as it should be, the period of adjustment will be a chance to rediscover the shape of the liturgy and the essentials of Christian belief and hope. The biblical concreteness of the liturgy and its humbling, exultant, awe-inspiring notes, muted in the old translation, are about to be restored. Thus, for example, when the celebrant echoes the angelic and Pauline greeting, 'The Lord be with you,' the congregation responds, 'and with your spirit,' a more vivid and theologically interesting translation of *et cum spiritu tuo* than the functional 'and also with you.' In the Gloria, 'We praise you, we bless you, we adore you, we glorify you, we give you thanks for your great glory,' replaces the tepid abridgment to 'we worship you, we give you thanks, we praise you for your glory,' so that the summons to adoration may come across as clearly as in the biblically based original. Threefold petitions and rhythmic repetitions, once stripped from the English in the interest of simplicity, evoke a sense of mystery that surpasses prosaic speech.

The Credo duly begins 'I believe,' spoken in unison to convey at once the individual and corporate character of faith. In the account of creation, 'all things visible and invisible' maps the material and spiritual cosmos more adequately than 'all that is seen and unseen.' Speaking of Christ as 'consubstantial with the Father' and 'incarnate of the Virgin Mary' plumbs the divine-human nature more deeply than the abstract 'one in Being with the Father' and 'born of the Virgin Mary.' In 'Holy, Holy, Holy Lord God of hosts' the angels return, having been exiled for no fault of their own from the English Sanctus. Just before communion, the centurion's voice rings out again: 'Lord, I am not worthy that you should enter under my roof' - living words that transport the worshiper into the gospel environment. Best of all, we get to reclaim the beautiful and dignified word *soul* from the dustbin to which a passing fad in theological anthropology had consigned it; 'only say the word and my soul shall be healed' universalizes the centurion's petition and intensifies the communicant's prayer.

Change can be unsettling, but in this case the change is right and just. The post-conciliar Catholic mass has found its English voice. The best response I can imagine is a Hebrew word that survives intact in all tongues, the final word of the New Testament – *Amen*").

Zilboorg, Gregory – psychiatrist and psychoanalyst; b. 25 December 1890, Kiev, Ukraine; c. 1954; d. September 1959; born of Orthodox Jewish parents; studied medicine and psychiatry at the psychoneurological Institute of St. Petersburg in 1917; secretary to the Minister of Labor in Alexander Kerensky's short-lived Social Democratic Government; forced to leave Russia in 1919; went to the United States and became an American citizen in 1925; was a secular Jew until becoming a Quaker soon after his arrival in the U.S.; repeated the last two years of his medical education at Columbia University, graduating in 1926; worked at the Bloomingdale Hospital and in 1931 established his own practice in psychiatry and psychoanalysis in New York City; among his patients were a number of quite famous people (e.g., George Gershwin (1898-1937), Lillian Hellman (1905-1984), and Moss Hart (1904-1961)); converted to the Catholic faith without renouncing his commitment to psychoanalysis; authority on the history of psychiatry and wrote several important works on the subject; on Freud he commented that "religion was for Freud a field of which he knew very little and which moreover seems to have been the very centre of his inner conflicts, conflicts that were never resolved"; on Jung he wrote that "that which Jung calls religion is not a religion at all. Even from an empirical point of view it appears to be only a very incidental manifestation"; in 1956 he was consulted by Thomas Merton (see above) who was suffering a vocational crisis; he made trenchant criticisms of Merton, pointing out the inevitable bad consequences of the conflict between Merton's religious vocation and the conviction that he was meant to be a creative writer ("You want a hermitage in Times Square with a large sign over it saying *Hermit*"); in his later years he worked closely with Catholic priests, especially with the Dominican Father Noël Mailloux (1909-1997), who headed a Pontifical institution in Canada ministering to those religious priests, monks and nuns in need of psychiatric care; at the time of his death he was an instructor at the New York Psychoanalytic Institute; consultant in research and psychotherapy, Butler Hospital,

Providence, Rhode Island; assistant professor of clinical psychiatry at the New York Medical College; chairman of the consulting delegation to the United Nations representing the International Criminological Society; see *The Passing of the Old Order in Europe* (1920); *The Medical Man and the Witch in the Renaissance* (1935); *A History of Medical Psychology* (1941); *Sigmund Freud* (1951); *Psychology of the Criminal Act and Punishment* (1954); *Psychoanalysis and Religion* (1962); Gregory Zilboorg Papers, Yale Collection of Manuscript Literature, Beinecke Rare Book and Manuscript Library.

Zuhlsdorf, John Todd (often known as "Fr. Z" (pronounced Zee)) – priest; b. 28 October 1959, Minneapolis, Minnesota; born to Lutheran parents of Jewish extraction; when he was very young his father and mother divorced; raised by his mother; as a child his two main interests were the beauty of classical music and of Shakespearean theater, fostered by his Presbyterian grandmother; had correspondence as a child with Professor J. R. R. Tolkien, which may have made him more receptive to the Catholic faith later on; studied Drama at the University of Minnesota; found the Lutheran mindset in relation to the depravity of the will offputting and although interested in religion, did not have one (but attracted very much to the Latin language he studied in class); then became mesmerized by Gregorian chant and went to St. Agnes church in St. Paul, Minnesota where it was broadcast live; fascinated by the Austrian baroque of the church and by the beauty of the liturgy; after discussions with Mgr. Richard Schuler, the parish priest, he converted to the Catholic faith; trained for the priesthood; ordained priest by Pope John Paul II on 26 May 1991 in Rome; incardinated in the suburbicarian diocese of Velletri-Segni in Italy; worked at the Ecclesia Dei Commission in Rome; served parishes in both Italy and the United States; was a columnist for the Catholic paper, *The Wanderer*; Catholic internet personality, notable for his blog *What Does the Prayer Really Say?* (slogan "Save the Liturgy, Save the World"); supporter of reverence in the liturgy in both forms of the Mass; see *EWTN Audio Library, The Journey Home* (25 August 2000) ("Beauty is the reflection of the truth, and beauty in material creation is this marvelous echo of the truth that is in God's word, and when we have an experience of beauty we are being drawn closer and closer to the beauty and the truth and the goodness that is God. And so the human soul is made for this. Augustine in his *Confessions* talks about how he was seeking God outside of himself: 'I was seeking you outside, but you were within me, and I was seeking for you everywhere else, and then you gleamed and you glowed and you scattered my blindness.' Well, that's what was happening through the beauty of the Roman Catholic liturgy. There was this dazzling thing that allowed me to see further than just the intellective part and all the studies and the books allowed me to see…

Something that I have heard and I truly believe is that the Church for centuries and for most of her long mission has been the great patron for the arts, and the Church has given two things to the world as a common inheritance: art and saints. In the one case, art is God's beauty shining through in inanimate material creation; and in the other case, it's his beauty shining out through living animate people. And so this is the common inheritance of everyone, and there is this whole factor of incorporation. The Church isn't just there to take on what everybody else is. It's also to shape culture and one of the ways it shapes culture is through this beauty; and of course the clergy are a key component in this, because the liturgy and the liturgical actions to a certain extent have been entrusted to them as a sacred trust for the whole Church"); Anna Arco, "Why Everyone Logs on to 'Fr. Z'", *Catholic Herald,* 29 February 2008, p. 7.

Afterword

Winning New Converts

As the Catechism reminds us, winning converts to our Faith should be a constant concern for all Catholics: "The true apostle is on the lookout for occasions of announcing Christ by word, either to unbelievers...or to the faithful" (#905). How should we go about it? People are brought to the Church one by one. God pours out his saving grace in many ways, but He normally requires, and we could even say desires, the willing collaboration of his sons and daughters in this joyful task. Winning converts is your task and there is no more endlessly satisfying and challenging work than that of saving souls. The famous Catholic philosopher (and convert) Dietrich von Hildebrand said that we should look upon all people we encounter as Catholics in re (in fact) or in spe (potentially). I agree.

Admit it. Don't you from time to time think about sharing with your neighbor, your friend, your family member, your colleague the joy that is in your heart in enjoying the fullness of our Faith in the Catholic Church? No apologies here (except in the "Pro Vita Sua" sense), thank you. Perhaps already some of you have had the wonderful experience of being the godparent or sponsor of a friend whom, by God's grace, you have guided into the Church. You know then the joy that fills the heart in being God's instrument. The only comparable joys are marriage, becoming a parent, and performing "in persona Christi" the sacraments of the Church as a priest!

This delight in a friend's baptism or reception into full communion with the Church is always a cause for holy celebration, but it is a particular joy in the present circumstances of our culture and in the present ecclesial moment. We see ourselves surrounded in our "culture of death" by so many persons bereft of any real meaning in their lives. Has there ever been in the Christian era a more joyless, aimless, lonely society than our own, a society that is truly "Clueless," a society that has appeared to have gained the whole world but forgotten the existence of its own soul? On the other hand, we have surely been blessed in the recent successive Roman

Pontiffs at the head of the Church who have so incessantly and hopefully proclaimed the Gospel in all its fullness throughout the world, addressing the fallen yet redeemed world's hopes and anxieties so completely.

The constant growth through the first three centuries of the infant Church up to the Edict of Milan in the early fourth century took place through the witness and personal influence of thousands of Christians and their families. With the passage of more centuries, Christian ideals lived out in the world by persons and families gradually transformed the West into a form of a Christian culture, which we know as the Middle Ages. In our own time, following the gradual dissolution of that particular culture through, in part, such historical events as the Reformation, the Enlightenment and the titanic struggles of ideas and ideologies of the last two centuries (Darwinism, Marxism, Freudianism, and so on), we are called to do the same. The partial success of these various heresies and ideologies on the world stage has been due in part to the fact that a large portion of the Catholic laity have been "missing in action" in the apostolic sense through the last several centuries, ignorantly content to let the clergy and religious do the "heavy lifting."

This afterword aims to give some insights, largely based upon my own experience, into how we can more effectively spread the gift of faith through example and friendship, or what Blessed John Henry Newman referred to as the "apostolate of personal influence." Having now crossed the "threshold of hope" into the third millennium of the Christian era, it is the historical moment to throw off our timidity, our fear, and let our light shine out not only from under the basket but also upon the shining hill. Why do you think it is that at the end of this century our Faith, so abused, attacked and vituperated, has drawn to it well known Jewish atheists, Protestant ministers by the dozens, prominent politicians, etc.? Why did Pope John Paul II in his pastoral visit to the United States in October 1995 virtually conquer the heart of New York, the capital of secularism? Why is it that in the media today when the word "Church" is used, it is always understood to mean the Catholic Church and not pan-Protestantism? Certainly not because membership in the Church is the road to riches, affluence, fame, good health, and a carefree future! It attracts those seeking eternal verities that promise eternal life, "life everlasting."

If now is "the age of the laity," as is incessantly proclaimed, its success will be measured not by the ever-increasing participation of the laity in ecclesiastical "ministries" but rather by the growth and spiritual health of the Church as manifested in an increase both in numbers and in the intensity of laymen's prayer, sacramental participation and apostolic fervor. This, in turn, will lead inevitably to a gradual transformation of culture into one that reflects faithfully Christ's teaching as mediated through the

Church. As Pope John Paul II said in his address to the American Bishops in Los Angeles in 1987:

> Primarily through her laity, the Church is in a position to exercise great influence upon American culture. But how is American culture evolving today? Is the Gospel influencing the evolution? Does it clearly reflect Christian inspiration? Your music, your poetry and art, your drama, your painting and sculpture, the literature that you are producing – are all those things which reflect the soul of a nation being influenced by the spirit of Christ for the perfection of humanity?

To be able to answer in the affirmative may take decades but the effort will start with our own personal conversion, which will result in the conversion of others.

The prophetic message of the Council and the last two pontificates have led to this thinking about the laity. The same Pope believed that, on entering the third millennium, we were crossing the "threshold of hope" into "a new springtime for the Church." His immediate papal successor, Benedict XVI, continued this drive forward, emphasizing the "hermeneutic of continuity" essential to the life and vigor of the Church. There is no reason to suppose that the impetus begun will slacken off in any significant way under our new Holy Father, Pope Francis. But, if there truly is to be the new springtime referred to, this will depend ultimately on the apostolate of millions of persons and families. Pope John Paul II said this in his letter on missionary activity:

> The witness of a Christian life is the first and irreplaceable form of mission. Christ, whose mission we continue, is the "witness" par excellence and the model of all Christian witness. The first form of witness is the very life of the missionary, of the Christian family, and of the ecclesial community.

And here is Benedict XVI emphasizing the importance of mission in *Verbum Domini*:

> We cannot keep to ourselves the words of eternal life given to us in our encounter with Jesus Christ: they are meant for everyone, for every man and woman…It is our responsibility to pass on what, by God's grace, we ourselves have received.

In addition, on the very day of his election to his office Pope Francis urged his cardinals "to find new ways of bringing evangelization to the ends of the earth."

We may refer to this sharing of our faith, then, as evangelization, giving witness, etc. I like especially the word used most often by the Council fathers in this regard, apostolate. The Second Vatican Council, in its Decree on the Apostolate of the Laity, tells us this:

> The individual apostolate, flowing generously from its source in a truly Christian life, is the origin and condition of the whole lay apostolate, even of the organized type, it admits of no substitutes. Regardless of status, all lay persons (including those who have no opportunity or possibility for collaboration in associations) are called to this type of apostolate and obliged to engage in it.

In relation to this vital role of the laity Pope Benedict XVI referred to activities of this kind in 2007 and reiterated their importance:

> One of the promising indications of a renewal in the Church's missionary consciousness in recent decades, has been the growing desire of many lay men and women…to cooperate generously in the "missio ad gentes." As Vatican Council II stressed, the work of evangelization is a fundamental duty incumbent upon the whole People of God."

In an encyclical on the laity by John Paul II, the point could not have been made clearer:

> The entire mission of the Church, then, is concentrated and manifested in evangelization…In fact, the "good news" is directed to stirring a person to a conversion of heart and life and a clinging to Jesus Christ as Lord and Savior; to disposing a person to receive Baptism and the Eucharist and to strengthen a person in the prospect and realization of new life according to the Spirit.

In short, the buck stops with each one of us to evangelize those who surround us. No excuses. "Every disciple is personally called by name; no disciple can withhold making a response: 'Woe to me if I do not preach the gospel' (1 Cor 9:16)."

Perhaps we should firmly establish our right, as well as our duty, to bring our friends to Christ's Church. First, it is His Church, with the successor of St. Peter as the Vicar of Christ. Pope John Paul II pointed this out in the encyclical *On Commitment to Ecumenism* in this way:

> The one Church of Christ subsists in the Catholic Church. The Decree of Ecumenism emphasizes the presence in her of the fullness (plenitudo) of the means of salvation. Full unity will come about when all share in the fullness of the means of salvation entrusted by Christ to his Church...The Catholic Church is conscious that she has preserved the ministry of the Successor of the Apostle Peter, the Bishop of Rome, whom God established as her "perpetual and visible principle and foundation of unity."

If we can put it more succinctly, all who are saved are saved through the Church even if they are not aware of it on earth. Everyone in heaven is a member of the Church. Belloc had it right, I think:

> One thing in the world is different from all other. It has a personality

> and a force. It is recognized and (when recognized) most violently loved or hated. It is the Catholic Church. Within that household the human spirit has roof and hearth. Outside it, is the night.

Second, there is a mistaken notion that is fairly widespread in our society that the Second Vatican Council was about the role of the lay Catholic in the Church. It was not. It was about the role of the lay Catholic in the world. This role can be summed up in the search for holiness that is our baptismal right and duty and consequently in assuming the right and privilege of extending the kingdom of God here on earth through witnessing to our faith through the Christian example of our family and friendships.

A few words of caution: We are not speaking of proselytism (in the pejorative sense). That is to say our sharing, witnessing, speaking, giving, forming, educating and so on has absolutely nothing to do with coercion, or, perish the thought, lack of respect for the "freedom of the children of God," particularly in that which refers to our "separated brethren" Christians. Quite the contrary. I am in total agreement with the landmark ecumenical statement from *Evangelicals and Catholics Together* in 1994, written by Charles Colson and Richard John Neuhaus and co-signed by many other prominent churchmen of both Catholicism and the Evangelical faiths, which says this:

> It is understandable that Christians who bear witness to the Gospel try to persuade others that their communities and traditions are more fully in accord with the Gospel.

We realize that only God's grace can effect a conversion and that pressure, other than our prayer, sacrifice, good example, and friendship, would not only in the long-term certainly be counter productive but would also not respect "the dignity of the human person" so central to the teachings of the Second Vatican Council.

> Christian witness must always be made in a spirit of love and humility. It must not deny but must readily accord to everyone the full freedom to discern and decide what is God's will for his life. Witness that is in service to the truth is in service to such freedom. Any form of coercion, physical, psychological, legal, or economic corrupts Christian witness and is to be unqualifiedly rejected…

No, we are interested only in our personal total "gift of self" which is never more complete than when we act as God's collaborators in communicating the gift of divine life, God's grace. Blessed John Henry Newman, the proto-convert of the last two centuries, made it clear that "to believe is to love" and that grace of the fullness of faith is only given to those who are freely seeking it.

But now on to more practical matters. How do we "make" converts?

First of all, we don't, God does. Having made that abundantly clear, what is our first step in approaching someone to consider becoming a Catholic? Naturally the desire will flow out of our prayer life. To paraphrase the epitaph written on the tomb of the famous London architect Christopher Wren, if you seek converts, circumspice (look around you). We come into contact with dozens, if not hundreds, of people in the course of our daily lives each month. They range from dearest family members and intimate friends to the butcher, baker, and candlestick maker. We look at them and ask ourselves "could this person be open to our Faith?" If the answer is yes, on to the next step. It is said that the most effective way to raise money for a good cause is simply to ask for it. The same may be applied to our situation. The question "Have you ever thought of becoming a Catholic?" addressed to many people over the course of our life will certainly produce not only converts, but also interesting and thought provoking conversations and new personal relationships. You may have to practice this line in front of a mirror a few times just as you did before asking out your first date. You generally will be surprised at how flattered, if somewhat surprised, people are at the question. Naturally it has to be emphasized that we are not approaching perfect strangers. Indeed, if we are not in the process of developing a deep and lasting friendship with the potential new member of the Church, then our question lacks authenticity and will be rightfully judged as impertinent and insincere. The great majority will say that you are the first person who has ever asked them that question, and more than a few will say they have been waiting for someone to ask them that question all their lives! A few will react negatively, but after all, not all "have eyes to see or ears to hear." We "shake the dust off our feet" and go on. We are not looking for success. It is the "love of Christ that compels us." We may also be surprised to see after the passage of time, even many years, people coming back to us looking for answers because we had the courage to offer them at an earlier time our Faith.

What is more, we are not alone. In his exegesis on the Gospel of Luke (10:1-12; 17-20) Pope Francis speaks to us precisely of this: "Jesus is not an isolated missionary, he does not wish to carry out his mission alone, but involves his disciples. And today we see that, besides the 12 disciples, he calls another 72, and he sends them to the villages, 2 by 2, to announce that the Kingdom of God is near. This is so beautiful! Jesus does not want to work alone, he has come to bring God's love into the world and wants to spread it in communion, in fraternity. Because of this he immediately forms a community of disciples, which is a missionary community. Immediately he teaches them to be missionaries, to go out." We are the successors of these people.

We are challenging people to consider making the most significant decision they will ever make in their lives, infinitely more important than the choice of school, profession, or spouse; one that will affect every fiber of their being for the rest of their lives, and have serious consequences in the hereafter. It is essential that you get to know them well, particularly their religious background, if any, so, as is said in the vernacular, you "know where they are coming from." Of use in this regard would be a thorough reading of *Separated Brethren* (*Our Sunday Visitor*), a survey of Protestant, Anglican, Eastern Orthodox, and other denominations in the United States by William J. Whalen. By engaging in conversation on this point you will be inviting your friend, and committing yourself, to go deep below the surface of everyday trivialities into the heart of the matter. Why are we here? What is truth? Is there a right and wrong? Is there a God? An afterlife? Is Jesus Christ God? Did he found a Church during his lifetime? If so, which one? Do we need to belong to it to be saved? Of course, you need to be not only willing to discuss and answer these queries but prepared.

"Be ready always with an answer to everyone who asks a reason for the hope that is in you" (I Peter, 3:15). To be an evangelist in today's world means to be an apologist. This is the work of a lifetime, but that does not excuse us from evangelizing while we learn on the job. Remember, no matter how little we know, our friends know less. And what is more important, we know where to go for the answers. A lot of our catechetical work with our potential convert friends will be, happily, simply to refer them to the best sources. Obviously we should have a good grasp of the New Testament and the *Catechism of the Catholic Church*, our fundamental texts. However we should also slowly but surely read and study the great British and American apologists: Newman, Lewis, Chesterton, Benson, and Knox and the more modern masters, Sheed and Kreeft. Many of their works are in print. It is also useful to be familiar with the magisterial teachings of the Pope for the most current teachings on matters of faith and morals.

Reviewing our own preparation leads directly to the question of recommending reading for friends who express an interest in our faith. An increasing number of people simply don't understand the basic vocabulary of what it means to believe. An excellent brief volume is *Belief and Faith* by the famous German philosopher Josef Pieper. He draws heavily on Cardinal Newman's much more complex *Grammar of Assent*. Many people today need a book to awaken their interest in Christianity or a volume that helps to make Christianity "reasonable" and understandable. Several books come immediately to mind. Both *Orthodoxy* and *The Everlasting Man* of G. K. Chesterton will stimulate the reader. I am thinking also of a basic primer, *A Map of Life* (Ignatius) by Frank Sheed, and the famous *Mere Christianity* of C. S. Lewis. Most fundamental, of course, is the New Testament. An excellent version with ascetical commentary is *The Navarre*

Bible (Scepter Publishers). And we might recommend a good *Life of Christ* (try Goodier, Sheen, Riccioti, Guardini, Grandmaison). Your friends simply must come to know the life of Jesus Christ if they are going to be able to join His Church. Second is a good Catholic catechism so that they may come to know the Church and her teachings. There are many excellent ones in print, by Frs. Trese, Hardon, Lawler, Noll, and the list goes on. Just choose one that you are comfortable with and one that reflects the sound teaching of the Church updated for the Second Vatican Council and the authoritative recent Catechism.

I would recommend that you whet their appetite for conversion by giving them something on stories of conversions and the present book fits admirably into this category. Our friends will be intrigued to read about both the contemporary and earlier conversion stories of so many people drawn to the faith from such varied backgrounds, and are sure to find at least part of their story in one of these histories. Don't forget, either, the classic spiritual autobiographies of St. Augustine, Blessed John Henry Newman, Thomas Merton and Malcolm Muggeridge, and the more recent one of Dr. Bernard Nathanson. They have changed millions of hearts and minds.

You should also familiarize your friends with the richness of the history of the Church. They clearly will see the continuity of the Faith through the apostolic succession and read the dramatic story of evangelization through the centuries with its ups and downs. I would recommend Msgr. Philip Hughes' *Popular History of the Church* for a short synopsis of Church History, and the first three volumes of the magisterial *History of Christendom* by Warren Carroll (Christendom College Press). The latter volumes read like novels, are painstakingly researched, and reveal the Church in all its heights and depths, in its saints and sinners.

An important part of our work of introducing our friends to the Faith will be exposing them to the beauty of the Catholic liturgy and to the art, literature, and music of Catholic inspiration. Accompanying them to the Holy Mass and other liturgical events, such as the celebration of solemn Benediction, a baptism, a wedding, the Easter Vigil, an Episcopal consecration, or the ordination of new priests, or a Rosary-filled pilgrimage to a Shrine of the Virgin, will bring them to a deep appreciation of the incarnate aspect of our Faith and its sacramental nature. To listen to Gregorian Chant, today so strangely popular, or the great classical compositions centered on the Mass, the Psalms, or various events in the life of Christ and our Lady will also draw them closer to the heart of the Church. Listen with them to the great works of Mozart, Beethoven, Bruckner, and to the more contemporary Gorecki and Messiaen for starters. Surely such beauty in music could only be inspired by the Truth.

Introduce them to the great Catholic authors, starting with Dante and continuing on down the centuries to Manzoni and Sienkiewicz in the last century, to the Undsets, Waughs, O'Connors, Bernanos', Mauriacs, and Endos of our own day. They will thus understand that the truth really does make us free and no one so free as the artist who has the standard of a faith-filled metaphysic that gives him full rein of expression in capturing the divine in the human.

Let's be realistic. Not all of your friends, by any means, are going to be receptive to this heavy "intellectual" approach. You may have to be much more selective in what you recommend to your friends: pamphlets rather than books, Catholic hymns rather than symphonies, a more contemporary (although sound) version of the New Testament rather than the Douay-Rheims, the stained glass in your parish church rather than Chartres. Listen to their needs, their questions and try to satisfy them. A time of prayer spent with them or a visit to poor or elderly people may be much more influential in the process of their movement towards the Church than any possible reading you might give them. Remember also the words of Pope Francis that preaching the gospel requires "humility, service, charity and brotherly love." He emphasized that to approach evangelization with an imperialism, or attitude of conquering "doesn't work." Rather, Christians evangelize by their witness.

Oh yes, let's not forget the parish and the priest. After all, our friend will most probably spend the rest of life normally worshipping in a parish setting. If our friend has not been baptized, the Church normally asks that the budding catechumen be enrolled in the R.C.I.A. program (Rite of Christian Initiation of Adults) in his local parish which will take him through a month by month program of initiation in the Church that culminates normally in Baptism during the Easter Vigil (hopefully with you there as his godparent!). If he has been baptized, he will make his first confession and then receive the Sacrament of Confirmation and first Holy Communion within a Mass on Easter or at another time. It is useful and proper to establish a team approach in dealing with your friends. Find a prayerful, zealous (they really are synonymous) priest with whom you can work and triangulate, which is to say both of you working together can offer your insights and wisdom, your prayer and sacrifice to your friend, The priest may be able, perhaps, to enter better into some areas that you cannot on account of his sacramental power. He will also be able to advise you as to the best way and moment for your friend to be incorporated in the Church, taking careful notice of personal circumstances.

What happens if over a reasonable amount of time your friend doesn't react, he just doesn't "get it?" He claims he doesn't see it. His difficulties with Christ and the teachings of the Church still result in doubt.

His family, parents, and spouse present what appear to be insuperable obstacles. Do you throw him overboard in order to sail off for other prizes? You wouldn't think of it! The answer is prayer, persistence, and patience. The violence of your prayer (remember Who is in charge of this operation) will eventually bear him away. Your persistence and constancy in your true friendship will eventually win him over by showing that your love is unconditional. Remember you may be the one person in his life who is interested only in his salvation. No ulterior motives of any sort. By patience we show our realization that conversion takes place at God's pace, not a minute sooner or later. The conversion may not happen until he is on his deathbed, and you may witness it from heaven.

Good, thanks are to God, he finally made it; he is in! What now? Naturally it is on to the next person, or perhaps you are already dealing with several people at the same time. However, don't forget your newborn Catholic friend. He is just a very young child, taking his first tottering steps into a bright new world that will have its storms and shadows. Some who regard Catholicism and his conversion to it in Chesterton's words as "a nuisance and a new and a dangerous thing" will surround him. He needs nurturing, your encouragement, your friendship, and your support. St. Josemaria Escriva says, "Sanctification is the work of a lifetime" and as your friend's godfather, sponsor, or guide, you have to be with him every step of the way. Perhaps you will introduce him to other institutions and spiritualities of the Church that can further his spiritual progress. He will be eternally grateful to you and you in your turn will echo the words of a famous French convert and poet, Paul Claudel, who said, "Tell him his only duty is to be joyful."

Now is the acceptable time to win a large crop of Catholics to our Faith, famous or not. I will finish by leaving you with the words of the most a famous observer of the United States and its people even though he wrote almost two centuries ago. His name was Alexis de Tocqueville and he was a Frenchman. And a Catholic; and he describes our current situation perfectly:

> At the present time, more than in any preceding age, Roman Catholics are seen to lapse into infidelity, and Protestants to be converted to Roman Catholicism. If you consider Catholicism within its own organization, it seems to be losing; if you consider it from outside, it seems to be gaining. Nor is this difficult to explain. The men of our days are naturally little disposed to believe; but as soon as they have any religion, they immediately find in themselves a latent instinct that urges them unconsciously towards Catholicism. Many of the doctrines and practices of the Roman Catholic Church astonish them, but they feel a secret admiration

> for its discipline, and its great unity attracts them. If Catholicism could at length withdraw itself from the political animosities to which it has given rise, I have hardly any doubt but that the same spirit of the age which appears to be so opposed to it would become so favorable as to admit of its great and sudden advancement.

It is up to you, Dear Reader!

Fr. C. John McCloskey III

Fr. C. John McCloskey III is a Church historian and Research Fellow at the Faith and Reason Institute in Washington D.C.

NOTES

NOTES

NOTES

NOTES

NOTES

NOTES

NOTES

NOTES

NOTES

NOTES

NOTES

NOTES